PUBLIC LAW

AUSTRALIA
The Law Book Company
Sydney

CANADA and USA
Carswell
Toronto

HONG KONG
Sweet & Maxwell Asia

NEW ZEALAND
Brookers
Wellington

SINGAPORE and MALAYSIA
Sweet & Maxwell Asia
Singapore and Kuala Lumpur

PUBLIC LAW

Sweet & Maxwell's Textbook Series

John F. McEldowney, LL.B., Ph.D.
Reader in Law at the University of Warwick

LONDON
SWEET & MAXWELL
2002

Published in 2002 by
Sweet & Maxwell Limited of 100 Avenue Road
London NW3 3PF
(http://www.sweetandmaxwell.co.uk)
Typeset by LBJ Typesetting Ltd of Kingsclere
Printed in Great Britain by
Ashford Colour Press, Hants.

First Edition 1994
Reprinted in 1995
Second Edition 1998

A CIP catalogue
record for this book
is available from
The British Library.

ISBN 0–421–780–703

PREFACE

Fundamental constitutional reforms introduced since 1997 have resulted in an unprecedented transformation of the public law of the United Kingdom. This transformation raises many questions about the scope, content and future direction of public law and how the subject is taught. It is hoped that the new edition of this book will provide readers with an explanation and analysis of the public law of the United Kingdom including the impact of the reforms. The scale of reform is probably more far-reaching than at any time in the past. The development of an Administrative Court and the availability of rights under the European Convention on Human Rights under the Human Rights Act 1998 has far-reaching significance. For the first time judges may declare legislation incompatible with the Convention and Parliament is provided with a fast-track procedure to alter legislation to bring the law into compatibility. There is the major innovation of a House of Lords Select Committee on the Constitution to keep under review the operation of the constitution and to consider the constitutional implications of public bills coming before the House.

Since the election of a new Labour Government there are reforms to the House of Lords, the introduction of devolution to Scotland, Wales, Northern Ireland and the introduction of a strategic authority for London with mayoral elections. The Bank of England is constitutionally independent of the Government as part of the development of an independent central bank, a precursor to entry into the Euro. There is a rash of new legislation including the Data Protection Act 1998, the Freedom of Information Act 2000 and the registration of political parties with controls on donations to parties and on national campaign expenditure under the Political Parties, Elections and Referendums Act 2000. There is the establishment of an Electoral Commission to oversee elections and advise on electoral law. There are many changes to the internal workings of local government including the introduction of a cabinet-style system of governance. Under the general scope of "modernising government" there is steady growth in the creation of a plethora of administrative agencies. The use of the Private Finance Initiative arrangements, government contracting and the regulation of the major utilities are also undergoing considerable change. Further substantial changes are planned. Having removed all but 92 of the hereditary peers, future plans about the composition of the House of Lords are being considered as part of a White Paper consultation. The recent review of the tribunal system undertaken by Sir Andrew Legatt is likely to require new legislation and the Bowman review of the application for judicial review is in line with the introduction of changes in the civil justice system under the Woolf reforms. There are also plans to reform a considerable part of the planning law system of inquiries, the source of much administrative law.

The courts are also active in the development of case law, particularly with an enlarged jurisdiction under the Human Rights Act 1998. There are changes in the European Union and ideas about future expansion including, perhaps one day, a Constitution for Europe.

Substantial legislative changes since the last edition of the book include the following areas: police powers under the Crime and Disorder Act 1998, the Criminal Justice and Public Order Act 2001, amendments to the law on race relations under the Race Relations (Amendment) Act 2001, a new Immigration and Asylum Act 1999, the Terrorism Act 2000 and the most recent amendment in response to September 11, the Anti-Terrorism, Crime and Security Act 2001.

It is inevitable that for reasons of space, the main focus of the book is on the public law that is applicable to England. Developments in Scotland, Wales and Northern Ireland under devolution are examined and relevant points of comparison are made. The asymmetrical nature of our constitutional arrangements today gives rise to a developing specialism in each jurisdiction.

The scale of the constitutional and administrative reforms set out above, have resulted in a number of substantial changes and re-writing of major parts of the book. First the format has been altered to accommodate a student focus in learning about public law. There is the addition of a section at the end of each chapter highlighting the key issues and conclusions. The bibliographical section has been supplemented with a list of the various websites relevant to public law to facilitate updating the most recent information and material. At the end of each chapter there is a section on additional reading and issues raised.

There has been some re-organisation of the book necessitated by the new developments explained above. There is a new chapter on human rights and civil liberties, and rewriting of the material in most of the chapters to incorporate reforms. There is an extended treatment of emergency powers and devolution. The latter is Westminster focused as to the impact the new devolved system of government will have on the United Kingdom. The chapter on local government has taken account of recent changes in the governance of local authorities. In the interests of space, a number of the introductory chapters have been substantially revised.

Finally I would like to thank Sweet & Maxwell who provided support in the work of producing the book. I am very grateful to the New Zealand Law Foundation for their support in my time in New Zealand as the New Zealand Law Foundation Distinguished Visiting Fellow 2001. In writing the third edition of this book I was assisted by the publication of my lectures delivered while I was in New Zealand. Jacquelin Mackinnon and Paul Havemann, editors, *Modernizing Britain: Public Law and Challenges to Parliament New Zealand Law Foundation* University of Waikato, 2002. I am also grateful to the University of Warwick for a term of sabbatical leave. I am most grateful to my colleagues for their support and most of all to Sharron and Emma for their advice and understanding.

March 2002

Contents

For Sharron and Emma

Table of Cases

Table of Statutes

TABLE OF STATUTORY INSTRUMENTS

There is a great difficulty in the way of a writer who attempts to sketch a living Constitution—a Constitution that is in actual work and power. The difficulty is that the subject is in constant change. An historical writer does not feel this difficulty: he deals only with the past; he can say definitely, the Constitution worked in such and such a manner in the year at which he begins, and in a manner in such and such respects different in the year at which he ends; he begins with a definitive point of time and ends with one also. But a contemporary writer who tries to paint what is before him is puzzled and perplexed: what he sees is changing daily.

Walter Bagehot, "Introduction to the second edition", *The English Constitution* (London, 1872).

Part I

GENERAL INTRODUCTION

Part I provides a general introduction to public law setting out a definition of the **I–001** subject and the scope of the book. The sources of constitutional and administrative law are examined and explained. This part of the book contains an outline of the subject from the main principles of constitutional law including the powers of Parliament, government and the courts, and briefly examines the development of administrative law and the impact of the Human Rights Act 1998. Consideration is given to the various constitutional reforms introduced since the election of the new Labour Government in 1997.

Chapter 1

The Public Law of the United Kingdom: Definition and Scope

Introduction

It is first necessary to define not only public law, but also, what public law is intended **1–001** to achieve. The term public law may at first appear unusual. Many writers and textbooks[1] prefer to refer to public law in terms of constitutional and administrative law. In the common law tradition, historically the categorisation of constitutional law was distinguished from administrative law. Often the two branches of constitutional and administrative law were seen as distinct and poorly integrated, a reflection of the absence of a codified or written constitution. There may also have been a reluctance to use the term public law as it is a term used in civil law systems and commonly found in continental jurisprudence influenced by Roman Law. Under a civil law system a clear distinction is drawn between public and private law for two reasons: because of a separate system of courts and because of differences in the development of codes and in the conceptual framework of analysis.[2]

The time is ripe now, however, for the importance of public law to be more fully **1–002** recognised, not only as a subject in its own right, but also for the conceptual framework and analysis which it brings to the understanding of all aspects of power[3] and how power is exercised. The English common law has developed significantly since the nineteenth century. Increasingly it is influenced by membership of the European Union. The election of the new Labour Government in 1997 and the introduction of fundamental constitutional reforms intended to modernise the relationship between the citizen and the state have resulted in a new role for the judiciary and a considerable strengthening of administrative powers. The subject of this book has progressed enormously so that today it is more accurate to understand constitutional and administrative law as linked together and as part of the relationship between the judicial, executive and legislative elements of the constitution. Particularly, in the past five years the subject of public law has developed sufficiently to consider how the close integration of constitutional and administrative law provides a distinct set of concepts and principles.

---

[1] See A.W. Bradley and K.D. Ewing, *Constitutional and Administrative Law* (12th ed., Longman, London, 1997).

[2] See, R.C. Van Caenegem, *An Historical Introduction to Western Constitutional Law* (Cambridge University Press, Cambridge, 1995).

[3] Dawn Oliver, "Common Values in Public and Private Law and the Public/Private Divide" [1997] *Public Law* 630.

1–003   Public law has now evolved sufficiently in the United Kingdom to make it desirable to distinguish between public and private law matters when it comes to litigation in the courts. Even so there is no precise divide between public law and private law. The recently introduced Human Rights Act 1998 requires consideration of the nature of a public body as distinct from a private body. Private law mainly concerns the parties in a dispute over tort, contract or property law. A large part of private law is based on the law of tort covering civil liability for wrongfully inflicted injury. It is possible to regard public law as broadly referring to the relationship between the citizen and the state. Public law is a composite of different aspects of the constitutional and administrative system in this country. This gives public law a unique and distinctive conceptual focus. In one part it is focused on institutions such as parliament, the government and the courts. Surrounding the question as to how these institutions perform their constitutional role are public law issues such as: the relationship between aspects of the state and the citizen; the intricacies of systems of accountability and models of participation and electoral representation. Public law, however, is equally concerned with individual rights and how the rules of good administration are applied. It defines how government may exercise powers and how government may be controlled. It defines political and legal powers. The scope and remit of public law is found in the requirements of judicial review in terms of legality, fairness, and rationality. Public law also sets standards for public life and administration. In the absence of a single written documentary form of a constitution, the sources for public law are found in a plethora of conventions, rules and understandings as well as formal statutory and prerogative powers.

1–004   Finally, recent fundamental constitutional reforms will undoubtedly influence the future development of public law as a conceptual subject. Public law offers a homogenous view of constitutional and administrative law. Thus it could be argued that all public powers however exercised and by whoever should be amenable to review and scrutiny.[4] Wade and Forsyth[5] have noted that "in the context of the rule of law, the aim is to subordinate the government to the ordinary law of the land." This has important significance in the form of accountability that is to be used especially if there is an increase in judicial scrutiny and a decrease in parliamentary control and effectiveness. Public law seeks to address not only the administrative rules developed by the judges, but also the relationship between those rules and government accountability. The historical distinction to be drawn between constitutional and administrative law appears to emphasise the evolutionary way the United Kingdom developed its constitutional arrangements. This may not reflect the reality of today. The English common law is likely to maintain its own distinctive qualities but, under the influence of codified systems of law, provide its unique contribution to problem-solving. It may not be possible to assimilate fully civil and common law systems and the difficulties in achieving this may prove counter-productive.[6]

---

[4] There is a discussion among contract lawyers between those in favour of a law of obligations and others who see contract as a distinct area of law built on mutual promises of the parties. A. Burrows, "Contract, Tort and Restitution—A Satisfactory Division or Not? (1983) *Law Quarterly Review*. More generally, see E. McKendrick, *Contract Law* (4th ed., Macmillan, 2000).
[5] H.W.R. Wade and C.F. Forsyth, *Administrative Law* (8th ed., Oxford University Press, Oxford, 2000), p.31.
[6] J.W.F. Allison, *A Continental Distinction in the Common Law* (Oxford University Press, Oxford, 1999).

The Aims and Functions of Public Law

What are the aims of public law? The question is frequently asked of subjects such as   **1–005**
tort, contract, criminal law or environmental law yet this fundamental question as to
the role and function of public law is hardly considered. The answer is to be found in
the assortment of aims and objectives associated with defining how government is
accountable and representative. Controls exercised by Parliament and the courts are
intended to provide citizens with assurances about the way government makes
decisions and transparency is a key element in public confidence. Public law is required
to provide that transparency, both *a priori* and *ex post* through the systems of
accountability that are in place. Public law is intended to ensure that citizens' rights are
protected and that good administration is supported. Internal systems of accountability
need to be distinguished from external systems. The former is concerned with internal
systems of audit, rules and conventions that apply to the exercise of ministerial
discretion.[7] The latter takes the form of external controls through parliament, the
courts, the media and public opinion.

A striking feature of the United Kingdom's present-day constitutional arrangements   **1–006**
is the dependency on executive self-restraint. This is largely due to the overwhelming
presumption in English law, at least until relatively recently, that if the action or
decision is not categorically prohibited it is assumed to be legal. Government authority
and power is assumed on the basis that the executive may do anything unless
prohibited by statute. An equally familiar presumption was that the protection of rights
is intended to protect minorities, while the protection of the majority is afforded by
Parliament. In that way majoritarian democracy assumes that the casting of one vote in
favour of a particular proposition commands the respect of the loser, even if the
margins are so close as to be meaningless. The culture of majority government
provides a superficial gloss that the winner may take all and there is little to prevent
that abuse. Fairness grounded in the analogy of good sportsmanship expects self-
restraint to be offered in the spirit of compromise and to find a way to accommodate
the interests of the loser. In the eighteenth and nineteenth centuries deference to
authority including government and the monarchy provided cohesion. In an age where
deference has diminished, institutions have had to depend on persuasion rather than
their status. The liberty of the nation also depended on assuming good stewardship by
the holder of public office. Today this cannot be taken for granted and in most cases
the public interest requires that the holder of public office exercises powers in an
accountable way. Press and media attention intrude into the private and public lives of
public figures. Increasing demands for transparency and verifiable outputs such as
league tables and standards are an attempt to address public disquiet and mistrust.
Very often such standards are made legally enforceable. There is a discernable trend
expanding public law into new areas and offering new regulatory techniques with the
potential for an expansion in the supervisory role of the courts.

Remedies available to the individual might take care of the exceptional case where   **1–007**
there is a lapse of judgment or an error. The general presumption is that the ordinary
law and self-restraint are sufficient to control arbitrariness. The high dependency on

[7] John F. McEldowney, "The Control of Public Expenditure" in *The Changing Constitution* (J. Jowell and
D. Oliver ed., 4th ed., Oxford University Press, Oxford, 2001), pp.190–228.

executive self-restraint is also part of the history of the nation and the culture of the people. It is clear that the pre-eminent concern in Britain is political convenience to allow the party in power to govern, a reflection of the way the balance between the different elements of the constitution is expected to be struck.

1–008   The pre-eminence afforded to political decision-making creates another dimension to defining public law and that is in setting the limits on economic power. Extensive economic powers through a diaspora of economic instruments such as the system of budgeting, and the borrowing of money are in the hands of the Executive. As Page and Daintith[8] explain, economic powers are effectively under government control:

> "The executive can do this because basic principles of our constitution recognise it as an autonomous body which can manage its own resources save where Parliament ordains otherwise, and give it co-ordinate power with Parliament in the all-important area of public expenditure."

1–009   Public law has developed beyond the understanding of the accretion of political power and defining the limits of power. Having developed a system of remedies from medieval times and ensured the economic liberty of commerce and contractual relationships in the eighteenth and nineteenth centuries, legislation has pushed the frontiers of public law to develop individual rights.

1–010   The Human Rights Act 1998 defines public law in terms of individual rights and their protection through law. Giving legal priority to rights in this way marks a profound shift to the judicial element of the constitution. This triumph of judicial power over the other parts of the constitution vests legal rules, with a higher authority than the political process. In securing the promotion of legal rules, the question facing judges is: how is judicial power in the hands of appointed judges to be made compatible with the democratic process?

The New Public Law

1–011   The public law of the United Kingdom is defined by the prevailing constitutional order, the Government and the various institutions of the State, the rights of the citizen and membership of the European Union. Local Government exists with statutory powers and responsibilities. There are since 1998 devolved powers to the Scottish Parliament, the Welsh Assembly, the Northern Ireland Assembly and since 1999 an elected mayor for London. The public law of the United Kingdom has lately come of age.[9] There are several reasons for this development. Fundamental constitutional reforms have embraced changes to the electoral system, a more independent Bank of England with the responsibility of adjusting interest rates removed from the government of the day, reforms to the House of Lords, and strategies to modernise almost every aspect of government institutions and procedures. There is also a new

---

[8] T. Daintith and A. Page, *The Executive in the Constitution* (Oxford University Press, Oxford, 1999), p.398. See T. Daintith, "Law as a Policy Instrument: Comparative Perspectives" in *Law as an Instrument of Economic Policy: Comparative and Critical Approaches* (T. Daintith ed., W. de Gruyter, Berlin, 1988), pp.3–55.
[9] See K.D. Ewing, "The Unbalanced Constitution" *Sceptical Essays on Human Rights* (T. Campbell, K.D. Ewing and A. Tomkins ed., Oxford University Press, Oxford, 2001), p.103.

Freedom of Information Act 2000. There are changes to the criminal justice system, tribunals and inquiries, and to the management of the courts system. The most celebrated and acclaimed innovation is the Human Rights Act 1998, which came fully into force in October 2000. The 1998 Act is likely to increase the use of judicial review[10] and thus has the potential to shift decision-making in public law matters from elected ministers to the courts under the direction of increased judicial controls.

In conceptual terms, public law has developed its own technical rules and procedures   **1–012** and techniques of analysis. In academic terms, public law has broadly defined terms of reference including the academic discourse from lawyers, economists, historians and political scientists. There is also a judicial contribution. The development of administrative law is largely a product of judicial creativity and self-regulation. Since the 1960s there is a remarkable judicial self-confidence in defining and articulating the role of the courts in public law matters. As Lord Donaldson remarked in 1984[11]:

> "Parliamentary democracy as we know it is based in the rule of law. That requires all citizens to obey the law, unless and until it can be changed by due process. There are no privileged classes to whom it does not apply."

Changes in judicial attitudes, towards developing the common law in the direction of   **1–013** rights defined more broadly, came through a series of landmark cases in the 1960s. Since then, English administrative law has developed incrementally. *Ridge v Baldwin*,[12] *Padfield v Minister of Agriculture, Fisheries and Food*,[13] and the development of *Wednesbury*[14] unreasonableness enabled the courts to adopt a proactive approach. Instead of relying on instances of past failure in order to develop a systematic approach to administrative law, the courts filled in, through their own initiative, gaps left by legislative neglect. The result was clear: a self-confident judiciary that was prepared to fashion new tools for the development of judicial review. In 1977, Order 53 was introduced, streamlining mechanisms and procedures for the application for judicial review. Two landmark decisions showed the extent of judicial self-confidence. In *O'Reilly v Mackman*[15] the House of Lords established that the Divisional Bench of the High Court had exclusive (subject to certain exceptions) jurisdiction over administrative law matters. In the *Council of Civil Service Unions* decision[16], the House of Lords engaged in a form of judicial codification of common law principles. The grounds for judicial review included unreasonableness, irrationality, proportionality, and procedural impropriety. It is noteworthy that the doctrine of unreasonableness may have to be strengthened to bring it into line with the higher standards required under the Human Rights Act 1998.[17]

---

[10] Practice Statement [2002] 1 All E.R. 633. It is noted that from October 2 to December 31, 2001 some 19 per cent of judicial review cases raised an issue of human rights. In numerical terms judicial review receipts for 2001 showed an overall increase of 11 per cent on 2000.

[11] *Francome v Mirror Group Newspapers Ltd* [1984] 2 All E.R. 408 at 412.

[12] [1964] A.C. 40.

[13] [1968] A.C. 997.

[14] [1948] 1 K.B. 233.

[15] [1983] 2 A.C. 237.

[16] *Council of Civil Service Unions (CCSU) v Minister for the Civil Service* [1985] A.C. 374.

[17] *R. v Secretary of State for the Home Department Ex p. Daly* [2001] 2 W.L.R. 1622.

1-014   As a result of both creative judicial activism and legislation, judges have developed a wide discretion as to when to uphold a judicial review. This flexibility, allowing the courts the power to exclude unmeritorious cases at an early stage, saves time and creates a specialised jurisdiction for the administrative courts. Cases must be taken promptly within a three-month period. The standing of the applicant is determined by the substantial merits of the applicant's case. The courts have a discretion whether or not to grant any remedy.

1-015   The role of the courts must also be placed in the context of the development of an extensive jurisdiction by statutory tribunals. Employment tribunals under the Employment Tribunals Act 1996 cover an extensive jurisdiction over employment issues, including race relations under the Race Relations Act 1976, the Race Relations (Amendment) Act 2000, sex discrimination under the Sex Discrimination Act 1975, equal pay under the Equal Pay Act 1970, and disability under the Disability Discrimination Act 1995. The Social Security Appeal Tribunal[18] covers protection under various provisions of the law relating to the payment of social security, and acts as an appeal tribunal against the decision of the adjudication officer. Mental health tribunals, lands tribunals, and rent assessment committees are also important examples of the work of tribunals in specialist areas. Tribunals offer the advantages of speed, low cost, informality, flexibility, expertise, accessibility, and privacy in the adjudication of disputes.

1-016   The extension of the role of the courts is also part of a larger question of how law is increasingly being used to regulate market power and, through regulatory reform, increase accountability over the newly privatised utility industries. The scale of this challenge provides public law with perhaps its most formidable challenge ranging as it does across different economic instruments and policy considerations.

1-017   Added to this is a rights-based analysis of how rights may allow legal challenge and create changes in the law. In substantive and legal terms there is an administrative court with an exclusive jurisdiction to hear applications for judicial review. Judicial review or administrative law requires its own distinct rules and procedures. The Human Rights Act 1998 provides citizens with enforceable rights and enables the judiciary broadly defined powers to interpret and review potentially all public power in what ever way it may be defined. Lord Hoffman in the House of Lords in *Alconbury*[19] explained the role of the courts under the Human Rights Act 1998 as follows:

> "There is no conflict between human rights and the democratic principle. Respect for human rights requires that certain basic rights of individuals should not be capable in any circumstances of being overridden by the majority, even if they think that the public interest so requires. Other rights should be capable of being overridden only in very restricted circumstances. These are rights which belong to individuals simply by virtue of their humanity, independently of any utilitarian calculation. The protection of these basic rights from majority decision requires that independent and impartial tribunals should have the power to decide whether legislation infringes them and either (as in the United States) to declare such legislation invalid or (as in the United Kingdom) to declare that it is incompatible

---

[18] See Social Security Act 1998 and Social Security Administration Act 1992.
[19] *R. (on the application of Alconbury Developments Ltd) v Secretary of State for the Environment, Transport and the Regions* [2001] 2 All E.R. 929 at 980 para.70.

with the governing human rights instrument. But outside these basic rights there are many decisions which have to be made every day . . . in which the only fair method of decision is by some person or body accountable to the electorate."

There remains a marked reluctance to introduce a wholly written constitution. Amid **1–018** the calls for change, respect is given to the continuity of many existing practices and institutions. This is the unique quality of the United Kingdom's constitutional arrangements: its enduring ability to change, survive and re-invent itself. This flexibility is a remarkable feature of constitutional arrangements that may be traced back to early medieval history but are capable of adapting and supporting a modern system of government. There is an equal reluctance to embrace the codification that is the hallmark of a civil law system. For these reasons the problem focus and approach of the common law will retain its enduring qualities and most likely adapt to change incrementally without a "revolution".

There are a number of purposes for seeking to define constitutional arrangements. **1–019** In formal terms it is clear that defining a country's constitutional arrangements helps to explain the relationship between the citizen and the State. A constitution helps determine how the State may exercise its powers and duties, how duties may be enforced and how the citizen may exercise rights. A constitution defines and sets out the relationship between the main organs of government which in the British context means the Crown, Cabinet, Parliament and the courts. A constitution may also influence how government may govern and may provide for accountability over government activities. A country's constitution may reflect the character of its people, their beliefs, "norms", prejudices and preferences. It may also in turn help to shape and inform attitudes to government, law and relations with other countries.

At the outset it is helpful to categorise the United Kingdom's constitutional **1–020** arrangements. There is much benefit to be gained from the perspective of political scientists. Professor Wheare wrote[20] that in defining a constitution, there may exist six points of classification: written and unwritten; rigid and flexible; supreme and subordinate; federal and unitary; separated powers and fused powers; republican and monarchical. Adopting Wheare's classifications it is at once apparent that the United Kingdom has a unitary constitution—though some would say that because of devolution, a union state. It is also clear that the United Kingdom's constitution is a flexible, monarchical constitution whose powers are fused. The term "fused" refers to the absence, strictly speaking, of the formal doctrine of separation of powers. In the United Kingdom while there is some doubt as to the extent to which, within fused powers, the doctrine of separation of powers may apply, it is claimed that in the exercise of legal powers distinctions are made between the different organs of state. The most distinctive feature of the Constitution remains that the United Kingdom, unlike other European countries, does not have in a single document, a written constitution with overriding legal force and authority. It is necessary to explain what a constitution is intended to achieve and how the United Kingdom's constitution may best be defined and explained. Inevitably, given the historical nature of developments it is necessary to explain how the United Kingdom was formed. So much of present-day constitutional thinking and the way our legal culture has evolved is drawn from the

[20] K.C. Wheare, *Modern Constitution* (London, 1966), pp.4–8.

past. So much of the future is dependent on the way public law has developed in terms of setting standards for administrators and addressing the question of how to regulate. Inevitably public law principles may enlarge the jurisdiction of the courts and public law concepts may begin to infiltrate areas of private law.[21]

Constitutional Reform in its Historical Context

1–021   Tinkering with Britain's constitution is a fine art developed through centuries of incremental change. There has always been cultural resistance to changing the role and function of major institutions or the Constitution itself. One simple reason for this is flexibility: elected governments come and go, but once elected, the government of the day is relatively free to govern with ". . . no institutional restraints on a legally sovereign legislature and a politically sovereign electorate".[22] The essence of political power is its legitimacy. The democratic will of the majority, exercised at a general election under the first-past-the-post electoral system, elects governments with a mandate to govern for up to five years largely free from restraints on their political decision-making or their legal powers to execute their policies.

1–022   Another reason for resisting change is that the common law is largely problem-centred. Unlike the civilian tradition concerned with the application of legal or constitutional principles, the common law rarely involves points of constitutional principle. Drawing on a mixture of past experience, case law or past precedent, pragmatic solutions to problems are often invented to fit the circumstances of the time. Much effort is given to making things work and ensuring where appropriate that the necessary repairs are made before any attempt to develop new structures. As McCrudden has observed:

> "A number of the principles which are said to describe, inform, and underpin the British constitution (majoritarian democracy, parliamentary supremacy, and constitutional conventions) may be seen as the embodiment of this tradition, concentrating as they do on "the authority of experience and the continuity of practice" and ensuring the flexibility of the process by which decisions are made. In this tradition, authoritative constitutional structures *evolve*, they are seldom *made*."[23]

1–023   As a result the constitution is sufficiently flexible to accommodate major political differences through changes in the party in power. Political power, its loss and acquisition have led the way in shaping a modern Britain largely free from much judicial or legal restraint. Incremental constitutional change has occurred over centuries in tandem with Britain's economic development and changing role in the world. At the end of the nineteenth century Britain was a major industrial country with a large empire and equipped to legislate for many countries in the world. The grant of

---

[21] See *Hoechst Marion Roussel v Kirin-Amgen Inc.*, unreported, March 21, 2002.
[22] K.D. Ewing, "The Unbalanced Constitution" in *Sceptical Essays on Human Rights*, (T. Campbell, K.D. Ewing and A. Tomkins ed., Oxford University Press, Oxford, 2001), p.104.
[23] C. McCrudden, "Northern Ireland" in *The Changing Constitution*, J. Jowell and D. Oliver ed., 3rd ed., 1994), p.325.

independence to the colonies developed the art of constitutional drafting, as many countries adopted the Westminster model of government in their constitutional arrangements. Gradually, after the Second World War, Britain began coming to terms with its new position in the world, without the British Empire and with the creation of the Commonwealth. The country has come under new influences, particularly since 1972 and its membership of the European Union: perhaps the greatest change is the impact of the European civil law tradition and the European Union on the United Kingdom's constitution.

In the fundamental shift to accommodate Europe, with its civil law tradition, the way **1–024** Britain is governed has changed. At the same time, the new "value for money" focus has brought modest but significant changes in the way government is able to govern. Such changes have been part of the general progression, an "organic change", rather than any revolutionary or radical break with past tradition, but nonetheless with significant effects. One example is the development of various agencies to conduct the work of the Civil Service. Nearly 80 per cent of the Civil Service may be found in such agency arrangements. Yet the doctrine of ministerial responsibility remains virtually unchanged and must meet the demands of the increasingly complex relationship between civil servant and minister.

It may not be unreasonable to ask whether Britain has a constitution. The question **1–025** arises from the notable absence of a formal written constitution and the difficulties of clearly defining the powers of the executive and the roles of the legislature and judiciary. The constitution may be described as unwritten, as opposed to written; flexible, as opposed to rigid; unitary, rather than federal; and institutional and practical, as opposed to theoretical and doctrinal. The contemporary monarchy maintains a largely symbolic role and continuity of tradition. Bagehot aptly described the monarch's formal powers as "the right to be consulted, the right to encourage, the right to warn".[24] The monarch retains the power to grant a dissolution of Parliament on the advice of the government. There is also the power to invite the leader of the political party with the majority of seats (the Prime Minister elect) to form an administration. In the case of a hung parliament this might not be just symbolic but decisive in the choice of the party to form the government.

The absence of a single codified or written constitution leaves the working out of the **1–026** practicalities of the constitution in the system of laws, conventions and customs that are the hallmark of the medieval inheritance. A notable feature is the use of conventions—essential norms of political behaviour, difficult to categorise in any strictly legal or constitutional sense—that comprise the common practices and workings of government and that link the modern with the ancient, medieval constitution. A.V. Dicey's influence[25] since the nineteenth century has led constitutional lawyers to believe that conventions serve the purpose of examining past practices to determine future conduct. Unlike rules or laws such as statute law, conventions are not enforceable by the courts but often help explain the political workings of the constitution.

---

[24] Walter Bagehot, *The English Constitution* (London, 1867, reprinted and edited by G. Phillipson, Sussex Academic Press, Sussex, 1997), p.42.
[25] See R. Cosgrove, *The Rule of Law: Albert Venn Dicey, Victorian Jurist* (Macmillan, London, 1980).

The Essential Characteristics of the United Kingdom's Constitution

1–027   The starting point for the study of public law is that unlike almost every country in the world the United Kingdom is unique in not having a codified or wholly written constitution. The absence of a codified written constitution is the first obstacle to the study of public law. There is no special significance attached to the word constitutional and until quite recently no special pre-eminence was afforded to constitutional or administrative law. What has changed is the bringing into force of the Human Rights Act 1998. Rights are now included as a characteristic of our constitutional arrangements.

1–028   The Human Rights Act 1998 incorporates most of the European Convention on Human Rights (ECHR) into domestic law. The ECHR was drafted in response to the Second World War and was heavily influenced by the English style of legislative drafting. The substance of the rights under the Convention is narrowly confined to legal rights written in the broad language of negative liberty or "freedom from unjustified interference". Rights included are to liberty and security (Article 5), to a fair trial (Article 6) and to no punishment without law (Article 7). There is a right to life (Article 2) and to freedom from torture (Article 3), and a prohibition against slavery and forced labour (Article 4). There are also freedoms associated with the individual in terms of religion, the right to privacy and the freedom of assembly (Articles 8–12). Such rights have been narrowly interpreted without any formal consideration of their potential impact on issues of economic, social or political significance. The 1998 Act came about through sustained pressure from the judiciary and academic writers. Despite the existence of many draft Bills of Rights (most notably those of Lord Lester),[26] the Government delegated the drafting of the Human Rights Bill to the official parliamentary draftsman. Its form was influenced by the requirements of drafting an official government bill, rather than a private member's one. The latter might have resulted in a different formulation from the one favoured by the Government. The 1998 Act is seen as a model of its kind, but distinctive in the approach taken in the incorporation of Treaty obligations when compared to the European Communities Act 1972. Primacy is given to the sovereignty of Parliament, as the 1998 Act falls short of allowing the courts to hold that an Act of Parliament is unconstitutional or illegal. The most the courts may do is rule on incompatibility[27] between the 1998 Act and the legislation under review. Since the Act came into force there have been three declarations of incompatibility.[28] It is then for Parliament, not the courts, to resolve any incompatibility. The courts are not bound by the jurisprudence of the Strasbourg Court of Human Rights but may give effect to those decisions.

1–029   Nevertheless it remains the case that unlike countries where there is a written constitution and the term "unconstitutional" carries with it a legal meaning which may imply enforcement or consideration by some higher authority or by the courts, British

---

[26] Lord Lester (Anthony Lester), a leading human rights lawyer in the UK, has pioneered a number of draft bills into the House of Lords. He was a member of the team who drafted *A Written Constitution for the UK* (Institute for Public Policy Research, London, 1989).

[27] There is no United Kingdom equivalent of the United States Supreme Court decision in *Roe v Wade* 410 US 113 (1973).

[28] See *R. (on the application of Alconbury Developments Ltd) v Secretary of State for the Environment, Transport and the Regions* [2001] 2 W.L.R. 1389; *Wilson v First County Trust Ltd* [2001] 3 All E.R. 229; *R. (on the application of H) v North and East Region Mental Health Review Tribunal* [2001] 3 W.L.R. 512.

lawyers do not strictly speaking define "unconstitutional" in that legal sense. The term "unconstitutional" frequently appears in common usage and may, in a parliamentary sense, imply the breach of a convention or parliamentary process, or failure to comply with the etiquette of the House of Commons. "Unconstitutional" may be contrasted with the term "illegal" which lawyers use to denote a judgment by a court on the lawfulness of a particular activity.

The common law has provided a rich source of law in the United Kingdom. This **1–030** explains how and why the constitution developed in the way it has. The common law is composed of custom and tradition. The common law has many prerogative powers, and the long history of constitutional principles developed from the common law results in a system of public law that is ad hoc in its development. There is also legislation. In the past five years the volume and extent of legislation has continued to increase. Legislative complexity continues to provide a challenge for government and administrators in the interpretation and implementation of the law. There appears to be little respite in this trend.

The best-known examples of legislation are the Bill of Rights 1688 and Magna Carta **1–031** 1215. Modern examples include the Parliament Acts 1911 and 1949, the European Communities Act 1972, the various devolution acts and the Human Rights Act 1998. There is no mechanism or procedure in place to identify and distinguish legislation that carries a special constitutional significance from legislation that does not. This omission is a reflection of there being no written constitution.

Constitutional lawyers approach the question of where the constitution is to be **1–032** found by pointing out that, whereas there is no written constitution in the formal sense, there are a large number of written documents, statutes, cases and unwritten rules and understandings, commonly called conventions, which comprise the Constitution of the United Kingdom. Constitutional lawyers look to an historical explanation of the development of constitutional law in the United Kingdom. This historical explanation of why the United Kingdom has developed its Constitution in the way it has, does not fully address the question of why the United Kingdom uniquely among other European countries, did not enact its own written constitution in the sense explained above. This question becomes a recurring one throughout this textbook. Some reasons for the lack of a written constitution may be advanced; such as historically there was no revolutionary break which necessitated the writing down of a completely new basis for the authority and legitimacy of government and law.[29] A reluctance to codify, a characteristic of the common law approach to legal problems, may be detected in the eighteenth and nineteenth centuries which may have been linked to the question of drafting a written constitution. Constitutional reform may have had little support as a political demand and consequently may not have been much considered. The English common law tradition encouraged a pragmatic approach to legal change and any constitutional amendment may have been accommodated through the Parliamentary process of statutory reform, rather than major constitutional revision. Characteristically as no great discontent or dissatisfaction may have been evidenced over the years, constitution-drafting was a low priority compared to economic, social and political reforms. A preference for tinkering rather than a

---

[29] P.P. Craig, *Public Law and Democracy in the United Kingdom and the USA* (Oxford University Press, Oxford, 1990).

complete rethink favoured leaving the United Kingdom's Constitution to evolve. Finally, in the nineteenth century a sense of complacency mixed with a reverence for what appeared as ancient and historically consistent with medieval beginnings, left a sense of self-satisfaction with the distinctive attributes of the common law system which had progressed without a formal written constitution. At the beginning of the present century parliamentary government was seen as a triumph of democracy over the despotism of absolute power. No single explanation seems satisfactory, however, and the United Kingdom's unwritten constitution remains as a legacy of the past which endures today.

Summary and Conclusions

1–033   The new public law of the United Kingdom arises from the recently-introduced fundamental constitutional reforms. In setting out the subject of study, account must be taken of the common law tradition and current influences from Europe and the European Union. It is important to remember that the influence of the common law is shared with many jurisdictions in the world. It may be found even in countries that have adopted written constitutions after independence. The countries of the Commonwealth have adapted the common law system to their particular needs. Even countries with a civil law tradition of codified law find elements of the common law valuable in their analysis of legal problems and approaches to comparative law. The most important example is to be found in the 1946 Japanese Constitution, drafted after the Second World War and combining a Supreme Court with a parliamentary system of government, Prime Minister and Cabinet.[30]

1–034   Inevitably looking abroad provides a picture of the alternatives. It may be helpful in identifying the areas of study that have arisen from the presence of a written constitution in other countries, and in considering how the United Kingdom is the same or different.

1–035   A recent innovation, in February 2001, is the appointment of a Select Committee of the House of Lords on the Constitution[31] "to examine the constitutional implications of all public bills coming before the House; and to keep under review the operation of the Constitution". Given the difficulties in defining the Constitution, the House of Lords Select Committee on the Constitution proposed the following working definition describing the issues that fall within the Constitution[32]:

> ". . . the set of laws, rules and practices that create the basic institutions of the state, and its component and related parts, and stipulate the powers of those institutions and the relationship between the different institutions and between those institutions and the individual."

1–036   In summary the Committee identified "five basic tenets" of the United Kingdom's Constitution. These include the following which may act as a guide to the principles that require to be addressed in any study of the Constitution:

---

[30] See C. Milhaupt, J. Mark Ramseyer, and Michael K. Young, *Japanese Law in Context* (Harvard University Press, Cambridge, Massachusetts, 2001), pp.2–17.
[31] *Reviewing the Constitution; terms of reference and methods of working*, First Report, Session 2001–02, HL Paper 11.
[32] *ibid.* para.20.

- the sovereignty of the Crown in Parliament

- the Rule of Law, covering the rights of the individual

- the Union State

- representative Government

- membership of the Commonwealth, the European Union and other international organisations.

The changing nature of the United Kingdom's Constitution raises some tantalising questions about the future and requires careful consideration of the tensions and shifts in the balance of power. Fundamental reforms have been introduced in Britain that have the potential to change some of the underlying principles of the constitution. We need to develop a vocabulary for thinking about the constitution, to express what it is and the principles that underlie it. Thinking about the constitution means understanding how government controls and allocates powers and how citizens participate in the state. It also seeks to prioritise different rules and recognise different values that contribute to the diversity of the constitutional history of the United Kingdom. Exploring the balance of power between individual rights and the authority of decision-makers may ultimately lead to the conclusion that a single document defining the different elements of power may be appropriate for understanding the constitution. Equally significant is the development of administrative law and the setting of standards for judicial review through the courts exercising their supervisory jurisdiction over many different types of bodies, agencies, local and central government and other bodies under direct or indirect political control. As Oliver has noted[33]: **1–037**

> "Indeed, whenever a person or body is in a position of power in relation to another, and in particular where a decision may affect the dignity, autonomy, respect, status and security of another, the question will arise whether such duties arise and what their content is."

The way forward is to recognise how public law derives its scope through the complex relationship between law and the social, political and economic context of the problem that the law is seeking to address. It is only possible to achieve a better understanding of the nature of law and the problems it is attempting to solve by recognising the boundaries of public law and the nature of political and legal power. **1–038**

Further Reading

Introductory books include: Anthony King, *Does the United Kingdom still have a Constitution? (D. Oliver and G. Drewry ed., Sweet & Maxwell, London, 2001); The Law and Parliament* (Butterworth, London, 1998); G. Ganz, *Understanding Public Law* (3rd ed., Sweet & Maxwell, London, 2001); Paul Silk and Rhodri Walters, *How Parliament Works* (4th ed., Longman, Essex, 1999).

---

[33] D. Oliver, *op.cit.*, p.645.

Useful textbooks include: de Smith, *Constitutional and Administrative Law* (Rodney Brazier ed., 8th ed., Penguin, London, 1998); E.C.S. Wade and A.W. Bradley, *Constitutional and Administrative Law* (12th ed., Longman, Essex, 1998). For an historical dimension see: W. Cornish, *Law and Society in England and Wales* 1750-1950 (Sweet & Maxwell, London, 1989); A.V. Dicey, *Introduction to the Study of the Law of the Constitution* (Macmillan, 1885); C. Munro, *Studies in Constitutional Law* (2nd ed., Butterworths, 1999), p.3; *The Changing Constitution* (J. Jowell and D. Oliver ed., 4th ed., Oxford University Press, Oxford, 2001).

For a theoretical perspective, see: Martin Loughlin, *Sword and Scales* (Hart Publishing, Oxford, 2000).

A useful political science perspective may be found in: Ian Budge, Ivor Crewe, David McKay and Ken Newton, *The New British Politics* (2nd ed., Longman, Essex, 2001; Bill Jones, Denos Kavangah, Michael Moran and Philip Norton, *Politics UK* (4th ed., Longman, Essex, 2001).

Chapter 2

THE ASYMMETRICAL CONSTITUTION: THE STRUCTURE OF THE UNITED KINGDOM

INTRODUCTION

In this chapter the main principles and sources which define the United Kingdom's **2–001** Constitution are explained. We begin by first considering some of the historical developments which have helped shape our present arrangements in the Union treaties involving England, Scotland, Wales and Ireland to form the United Kingdom of Great Britain and Northern Ireland. Having examined the historical development of the United Kingdom the introduction of devolution is explained and the government of Scotland, Wales, Northern Ireland and London are considered. The impact of legislation creating the Commonwealth is explained in the context of Parliamentary sovereignty. Also relevant to an understanding of sovereignty is membership of the European Union. Accession into the European Community has ultimately challenged some of our traditional ideas about the United Kingdom Constitution. The future of Europe is also important in defining our sources of law and the direction of change.

THE SOURCES OF CONSTITUTIONAL LAW AND THE COMPOSITION OF THE UNITED KINGDOM

The United Kingdom has been previously described as a unitary state. It is striking that **2–002** there is no federal system for a population of almost 60 million, in a country that is one of the most densely populated member states in the European Union. On the contrary the United Kingdom has a highly centralised system of government, a long tradition of local government and a variety of powers shared between each of the regions. The introduction of devolution to Scotland, Wales and Northern Ireland has created a centrifugal force in favour of allocating powers to regional communities. London, currently with a population of seven million, has a strong tradition of elected autonomy since the Metropolis Local Management Act 1855. In addition to the 32 elected London Borough Councils and the Corporation of London, there is a special form of devolution provided through a directly elected Mayor and a 25-member Assembly under the Greater London Authority Act 1999. It is no longer correct to see the United Kingdom as unitary; rather it may be described as a "union" state. The components of the Union may be examined, first in each of their historical contexts, and secondly in the introduction of devolution.

England

2–003   It is possible to point to a number of fundamental statutes which created important legal principles in the early medieval relationship between the Crown, the courts and Parliament, such as the Magna Carta 1215. Previous history records that under William the Conqueror, England was a feudal state; all land was held of the King; the King's subjects owed allegiance; law-making was in the power of the King. Early historical records show that Parliament had its early origin in the National or Great Council, representing advisers to the King. Parliament's growth in importance began in the thirteenth century and evolved slowly. In the late seventeenth and early eighteenth centuries, statutes such as the Bill of Rights 1689 and the Act of Settlement 1700 are recognisable as having created the institutions of government which have modern day significance. We have already mentioned that no revolution occurred in Britain which necessitated a complete severance from the past causing a major rethink of how government should govern. The fact that the Civil War led to the execution of Charles I and the experiment of republican government through Parliament, created change in the position of Parliament *vis-à-vis* the Crown. Continuity prevailed, however, in that the institutions of government survived albeit in a different form.

2–004   The Bill of Rights 1689 laid the foundations of the modern constitution, because in England both the House of Lords and the last vestiges of Charles II's Parliament approved and thereby confirmed Parliament's, that is the House of Commons' authority. The grant of various freedoms contained in the Bill of Rights is accompanied by a sanction, that of "illegality". This term connotes both the statutory authority of the Bill of Rights and the interpretation of that authority when applied by the courts.

2–005   In Scotland, the Scottish Parliament enacted the Claim of Rights in 1689 following the English model with certain variations. In common with the English Bill of Rights, the use of proclamations to exercise powers was "declared illegal."

2–006   Equally important in constitutional history is the Act of Settlement 1700. This complemented the Bill of Rights by enacting that the Church of England was to be established by law, ensuring the independence of the Judiciary and further regulating the King's authority, such as the power to grant pardons. No historical understanding of the development of the British constitution in its present form would be complete without an explanation of the fact that the United Kingdom was formed through a series of legislative enactments. The Acts of Union with Wales, Scotland and Ireland helped to form a single entity. These Acts created the foundation of a legal entity that acknowledged the sovereignty of Parliament along with a cultural reticence to resist any interference in the maintenance of a unitary state. The enduring quality of the various Acts of Union remains a dominant influence today and may be seen in the various legislative competences of the different devolved powers under devolution discussed below. It is important to remember the extent to which local as opposed to central government was a dominant influence in early English legal history. The early office of Justice of the Peace, since Edward III, provided local justice in local courts. Local administration developed on an incremental basis and local justice provided a variety of regulatory and licensing powers. Much of administration and law was delivered at a local level supervised through central powers maintaining the unitary nature of the Constitution and the pre-eminent authority of Parliament.[1] This remains to the present day with only London granted devolved government. For the future it is proposed to introduce some form of devolution in the English regions. In the case of London, Pt I of the Greater London Authority Act 1999 provides for a directly elected Mayor and a 25-member Assembly.[2] Specific statutory powers require the mayor to develop, implement and revise strategies for transport, planning and development control. The Assembly is to review and scrutinise the Mayor's functions. The 1999 Act makes extensive provision for the carrying out of the Mayor's functions and includes detailed obligations in terms of the environment including a municipal waste management strategy, an air quality strategy, a noise strategy and a biodiversity action plan.

Wales

In the case of Wales, absorption with England may be said to owe its origins to the period of Edward I and the English domination of Wales by conquest.[3] One of the earliest statutory enactments was the Statute of Wales 1284 which applied to only part of what is defined today as modern Wales. It did, however, settle the independence of Wales by asserting the possession of the King of England over Llewellyn the Great's Principality of Wales, leaving the feudal territories of the Lords of the Marches unaffected. In 1471 a Council of Wales and the Marches was set up as an agency of the Privy Council and later in 1535 the Laws in Wales Act[4] was passed which stated that the "Lawes and Justice [were] to be ministered in Wales in like fourme as it is in this Realme." The result was an effective integration between England and Wales, with Wales divided into shires and hundreds comparable to the English equivalent. For a time Wales was administered by a separate system of courts with specific representation for Wales in Parliament. However, the Council of Wales, which survived the early changes, had an expanded role to include some English border counties, but it was abolished in 1689. In 1830 Welsh circuits were absorbed into the English Court system and the judicial system of Wales was thereby assimilated into the English system.   **2–007**

Since 1964, there has been a Secretary of State for Wales, a position of responsibility in the Cabinet. The Welsh language is protected under the Welsh Language Act 1993. This Act provides for the appointment of a Board to encourage the use of the Welsh language in government and the courts. The introduction of devolution in 1998 has created a Welsh Assembly. The details are explained below.   **2–008**

Scotland

In the case of Scotland, there was a distinct entity we know today as Scotland, formed out of four kingdoms between the fifth and ninth centuries. Scotland stands apart from Wales and Northern Ireland as maintaining its own distinct independence.   **2–009**

---

[1] J.P. Dawson, *A History of Lay Judges* (Harvard University Press, Cambridge (Mass.), 1960), p.274.
[2] White Paper, *A Mayor and Assembly for London* Cm.3897 (1998).
[3] John Davies, *A History of Wales* (Oxford University Press, Oxford 1993).
[4] 27 Hen. 8 c.26.

2–010   The attempts by Henry VII to stabilise relations between England and Scotland through marriage of his daughter to Scotland's King James IV in 1503, came to little. Conquest was tried and failed by Henry VIII's union in 1544 and 1545, but in 1603 when Elizabeth I died, James VI of Scotland became James I of England signifying a personal, rather than a completely administrative or constitutional union. Administratively Scotland remained under a separate government from England. In 1707 the Treaty and Acts of Union formed the United Kingdom of Great Britain.[5] Turpin explains how this union was unitary rather than federal[6]:

> In terms of these instruments the two Parliaments were superseded by a Parliament of Great Britain—'a new Parliament for a new State' (Scottish Law Commission, Memorandum No.32, 1975, p.16). This was to be a unitary, not a federal state; as K. C. Wheare observes [Federal Government (4th ed. 1963) p.43] there was no model of federal government in existence which might have been urged against the unitary scheme then proposed and adopted. Scottish arguments for retention of the Scottish Parliament did not prevail.

2–011   The significance of these Acts of Parliament may be clearly appreciated in constitutional law and serve to show the scope and extent of legislative intervention. Through the Acts of Union the United Kingdom was created as a legal entity. Similarly, the granting of independence to various colonies illustrates the authority of Parliament to confer independent status on particular countries, while appearing to exercise self-restraint over future legislative enactments. This self-denying aspect of Parliament's powers is an important convention for the intentions of a future Parliament. Strict constitutional theory forbids Parliament from binding its successors in legal terms. In practical terms Parliament may accept the political and economic limitations on its powers, without conceding any limit on its legal powers to legislate.

2–012   Thus, although the Acts of Union created the Parliament of the United Kingdom, English constitutional lawyers do not ascribe any significant status to those Acts, which are treated in the same way as any other Act of Parliament. We shall see that this assumption may be questioned in the context of British membership of the European Community. Turpin has argued that an Act of Parliament is valid even if it may indirectly interfere with or ". . . violate fundamental provisions of the Union Legislation".[7] Some support for this view may be found in the decided cases, but the courts may appear equivocal on the issue. Some support for Turpin's view over the legal status of the Scottish Union may be found in the case of *MacCormick v Lord Advocate*.[8] In that case the Scottish courts were asked to consider the significance of the Act of Union. The Rector of Glasgow University in Scotland challenged the Queen's title as "Elizabeth the Second" on the grounds that this contravened article 1 of the Treaty of Union 1707.

2–013   The Royal Titles Act 1953 authorised the use of the numeral "II" and the challenge made by the Rector brought into issue the constitutional status of an Act of

---

[5] See D.L. Keir, *The Constitutional History of Modern Britain 1485–1937* (London, 1938); S.B. Chrimes, *English Constitutional Ideas in the 15th Century* (Blackwell, 1966).
[6] C. Turpin, *British Government and the Constitution* (2nd ed., 1990), pp.222–223. See A.V. Dicey and R.S. Rait, *Thoughts on the Union between England and Scotland* (1920).
[7] C. Turpin *British Government and the Constitution* (4th ed., Butterworths, London, 1999), p.241.
[8] 1953 S.C.396.

Parliament.[9] At first instance the justiciability of a challenge to the validity of an Act of Parliament was doubted and the challenge dismissed. On appeal to the First Division of the Inner House of Court of Session, Lord Cooper accepted the reasoning adopted in the lower court, but doubted if the 1953 Act had any bearing on the matter, as that Act had been enacted after the proclamation of the Queen as Elizabeth II. His opinion on the status of the Act of Union between Scotland and England is therefore *obiter dictum*, but nevertheless Lord Cooper questioned the English view of unlimited sovereignty of Parliament "which has no counterpart in Scottish Constitutional law".[10] Instead his view was emphatically that the Union Treaty did contain some fundamental and unalterable elements which made their status distinct and separate from any other Act of Parliament. However, in strict English Constitutional theory Lord Cooper's view does not find favour. The English view is that there is no hierarchy of laws. No Scottish court has held a public Act of Parliament to be void since the Act of Union. When considering the Acts of Union Dicey admitted "the possibility of creating an absolutely sovereign Legislature which should yet be bound by unalterable laws"; but this is insufficient to create "unalterable statutes".

We shall return to consider the question of Parliamentary sovereignty in the following chapter, but it will become apparent that however attractive the notion of a fundamental law is in a constitutional sense, this has been resisted by English constitutional lawyers. Lord Cooper's opinion merely confirmed that a Scottish view of the British Constitution differs markedly from that of an English view! Equally it is clear that the creation of many of the constitutional principles especially the doctrine of the sovereignty of Parliament is the result of judicial decisions reached over the centuries. It is not always possible to rely on a consistent line of judicial precedent, but in some notable constitutional decisions Parliament emerged as the pre-eminent authority of sovereign power.[11]   **2–014**

Devolution was granted to Scotland by the setting-up of the Scottish Parliament with devolved powers under the Scotland Act 1998; this is examined in more detail below.   **2–015**

Ireland

In the case of Ireland[12] its early history was rooted in the law of the early Irish chiefs. The Brehon laws, as they were known, represent some of the earliest forms of law, contained in the form of law tracts which are complex in style and language and   **2–016**

---

[9] See Colin Munro, *Studies in Constitutional Law* (2nd ed., Butterworths, London, 1999).
[10] Lord Guthrie in *MacCormick v Lord Advocate* 1953 S.C.396.
[11] Significant constitutional cases worthy of study: *The Case of Monopolies* (1602) 11 Co. Rep. 84b prohibited the King from dispensing with an Act of Parliament in matters of personal gain. Also see Bates case, *Att.-Gen. v Bates* (1606) 2 St. Tr. 371; *The Case of Prohibition del Roy* (1607) 12 Co. Rep. 63; and *The Case of Proclamations* (1610) 12 Co. Rep. 74 where the judges refused the King authority to create new offences by proclamation. In *R. v Hampden* (1637) 3 St. Tr. 825, the courts by a majority upheld the King's power to levy money re the case of Ship Money for funds to pay for ships to defend the realm under prerogative powers. Also useful to examine for constitutional purposes are *Thomas v Sorrell* (1674) Vaugh. 330; *Godden v Hales* (1686) 11 State Tr. 1166; *The Seven Bishops' Case* (1688) 12 St. Tr. 371.
[12] See J. McEldowney and P. O'Higgins, *The Common Law Tradition: Essays in Irish Legal History* (Irish Academic Press, 1990); C. Palley, "The Evolution, Disintegration and Possible Reconstitution of the Northern Ireland Constitution" (1972) *Anglo-Am. Law Journal*, 368; Anson, "The Government of Ireland Bill and the Sovereignty of Parliament" (1886) 2 *Law Quarterly Review* 427; H. Calvert, *Constitutional Law in Northern Ireland: A Study in Regional Government* (Belfast, 1968); N. Mansergh, *The Government of Northern Ireland: A Study in Devolution* (London, 1936).

riddled with different forms of old and middle Irish. The administrations of England and Ireland before the Norman invasions of 1066 and 1171, shared a common characteristic namely that they were both regional. Ireland, unlike England, was relatively free from significant foreign intervention which allowed secular custom and native common law to take hold. England, from the eleventh century developed its own system of local courts, but under the influence of central administration and Royal power. Ireland, however, did not share the centralising effect of a single or unifying kingship. Instead, in Ireland, tribal loyalties formed the predominant influence and from the sixth to the eighth centuries there is documentary evidence of at least eight significant law tracts, the most notable being *Senchas Mar* or Patrick's law. One feature of these early laws was the division of the society into two groups, one free, the other unfree.

2–017   The English invasion of Ireland, carried out by Henry II, established an English administration in the area around Dublin known as the Pale, circa 1171. There had previously been attempts to establish an Irish Lord in Leinster in return for allegiance to Henry II as feudal Lord, but these efforts had limited success. Once conquest had secured influence, Henry II left the Irish Kings to continue to rule, but owing strict allegiance to Henry. The early records show that in 1226 a justiciar called De Mansio was appointed to act as the royal representative in Ireland. The success of the English monarchy in Ireland was such that the English common law was gradually introduced.

2–018   The adoption of the common law in Ireland endured for many centuries to come. Under the English system of land law, tracts of land were granted and subinfeudation was widespread. Dublin was the administrative centre where the major Royal Courts carried out the King's justice under the King's Writ or Breve. Brehon laws, although referred to in records as late as 1558, were gradually superseded by the English common law. The assumption, often offered as an explanation for the continued preservation of Brehon law, is that Norman law was personal rather than territorial. Gradually Brehon law gave way to common law principles enforceable in the courts.

2–019   The common law taking root in Ireland eventually led to profound constitutional changes. Poynings Law 1494 provided that statutes in force in England had legal force in Ireland. The approval of the King in English Council was required for Irish Bills. The existing Lord of Ireland became King of Ireland in 1541. Religious differences ensured that Ireland was governed according to English law but not that English law was accepted in Ireland. The Battle of the Boyne in 1690 assured Protestant ascendancy with the victory of William of Orange over James II.

2–020   The Act of Union[13] between England and Ireland was passed in 1800 and had the unusual characteristic of being enacted by both the English and Irish Parliaments. The latter succumbed to a degree of English influence and persuasion that tainted the propriety of the entire episode. The Act proclaimed that both pre- and post-Union legislation was subject to the "Parliament of the United Kingdom". It simultaneously ended the life of the Irish Parliament, united the Anglican Churches of England and

---

[13] Generally see Christopher Harvie, "Ideology and Home Rule" (1976) *English Historical Review* 91; James Bryce, "A.V. Dicey and Ireland 1880–1887" *English Historical Review* 298–314; A.V. Dicey, "How is the Law to be enforced in Ireland?" (November 1881) 36 *Fortnightly Review* 539–552; J.F. McEldowney, "Dicey in Historical Perspective—A Review Essay" in *Law, Legitimacy and the Constitution* (McAuslan and McEldowney ed., Sweet & Maxwell, London, 1985), pp.39–61.

Ireland and established the Union as "for ever after". Dicey[14] freely admitted that the Union was not "voluntary" and was, therefore, tainted with suspicion from its inception.

At the time of the Union, the majority of the population were Catholic tenants and   **2–021** excluded from the franchise and land ownership. After considerable pressure Catholic emancipation was granted in 1829 but this only served to make the Irish Land question a dominant issue for the remainder of the century. Protestant resistance and Orange Lodges feared the end to Protestant ascendancy and land ownership. The unsettled state of affairs in Ireland led to calls for constitutional reform, most notably Home Rule. Although a number of Home Rule Bills were presented during the 1880s, these failed to find sufficient Parliamentary support. A failed uprising in Dublin in 1916 eventually advanced the cause of independence for Ireland.

In constitutional terms the Union endured until 1921–22 when the Irish Free State   **2–022** was formed. This necessitated a change to the Act of Union under subsequent legislation namely: the Irish Free State (Agreement) Act 1922; the Irish Free State Constitution Act 1922 and the Irish Free State (Consequential Provisions) Act 1922. While the Irish Free State became a dominion Northern Ireland, comprising six counties of the North East of Ireland, remained within the United Kingdom. The Government of Ireland Act 1920 provided for a separate Parliament and Government in Belfast but ultimate sovereignty resided within the competence of the United Kingdom Parliament. This form of devolved government under its terms of grant under the 1920 Act allowed the Northern Ireland Parliament, powers "to make laws for the peace order and good government of Northern Ireland". Northern Ireland became unique within the United Kingdom in having a written Constitution. Effectively the Northern Ireland Parliament was, within its own legislative competence, unrestrained by the sovereign power who had overriding legal powers under s.75 of the 1920 Act to govern Northern Ireland. A constitutional convention became established that the United Kingdom Parliament would not legislate on matters which were within the "transferred" powers of the Northern Ireland Parliament. Representation from Northern Ireland in the United Kingdom Parliament was set at 13 seats until 1948, and thereafter 12, until 1979 when the number was increased; it is currently set at 18 seats.

This experiment in devolved government was overshadowed by the early historical   **2–023** problem of Ireland's post-Union relationship with England. Catholics comprise about 40 per cent of its population and live under a nationalist identity that rejected the Union with England. Civil liberties, although theoretically protected under the 1920 Government of Ireland Act, were often ignored. From 1921–72 Northern Ireland was ruled by a single majority party, the Unionists, who dominated the Government of Northern Ireland. Religious and political differences were endemic and resulted in civil unrest. From 1968–72 attempts at constitutional reform by the Northern Ireland Government were too late to avert a constitutional crisis which resulted, in March 1972, with the arrival of British troops and the prorogation and eventual abolition of the Northern Ireland Parliament. The functions of the Parliament and Government of Northern Ireland were vested in the Secretary of State for Northern Ireland.

[14] A.V. Dicey, "Two Acts of Union—A Contrast" (1881) 30 *The Fortnightly Review* 168–78. Also see his views on the disestablishment of the Church of England: "The Church of England: The Legal Aspects of Disestablishment" (1890) 39 *The Fortnightly Review* 822–40; and see "The Defence of the Union." (1892) 61 *Contemporary Review* 314–331.

2–024   Direct rule was imposed from Westminster. The first period, from 1972–74, resulted in considerable parliamentary time at Westminster being devoted to Northern Ireland's affairs. A new written Constitution for Northern Ireland in 1973 provided for a system of power-sharing, whereby the two communities in Northern Ireland might form a legislative assembly through proportional representation and an executive broadly representative of the community. The attempt to introduce power-sharing failed after a general strike of loyalist workers forced the resignation of a newly-formed power-sharing executive in 1974. "Interim" direct rule was resumed for a period of five years under the Northern Ireland Act 1974. A second attempt in 1982 to achieve a new form of power-sharing under the Northern Ireland Act 1982 failed and resulted in the return to direct rule. Currently Northern Ireland is governed by direct rule. Direct rule provides that the Government of Northern Ireland is the responsibility of a Secretary of State together with a Minister of State and up to four parliamentary Under-Secretaries of State. The bulk of legislation for Northern Ireland is made through Orders in Council under the Northern Ireland Act 1974. Most Orders are subject to affirmative resolution of both Houses of Parliament but are not subject to amendment in debate. These procedures are heavily criticised for not allowing the same degree of debate and scrutiny as an ordinary Bill.

2–025   Northern Ireland's formal written Constitution was created in order to achieve a greater consensus in its Government. Yet the status of its Constitution is formally that of an Act of Parliament. It may be modified, amended or repealed at a later date. Attempts to address the concerns of Unionists over the status of the Union with the United Kingdom may be seen in the various protections built into the constitutional status of Northern Ireland; for example, the Ireland Act 1949 simultaneously recognised the secession of Southern Ireland and its republican status while declaring that Northern Ireland would not cease to remain part of the "United Kingdom without the consent of the Parliament of Northern Ireland". After the abolition of the Northern Ireland Parliament in 1973, this guarantee was replaced by a new form of protection namely that Northern Ireland would not cease to remain part of the United Kingdom without "the consent of the majority of the people of Northern Ireland voting in a poll held for the purposes of this section". It is questionable whether such a "guarantee" constitutes a fundamental protection that would prevent amendment by a subsequent Act of Parliament. It is worthwhile examining this in more detail below as an example of the difficulty of "entrenching" any fundamental rule by Act of Parliament. However, there are special circumstances prevalent in Northern Ireland which must be taken into account. S.1 of the Northern Ireland Act 1998 reiterates the protection set out under the 1973 Act that Northern Ireland will not cease to remain part of the United Kingdom without the consent of the majority. However, the Northern Ireland Act 1998 also repeals the Government of Ireland Act 1920. The implications of the repeal are that devolution under the 1998 Act is a new departure and that it is necessary to have a break with the past. It is open to debate whether the break with the past includes the idea of the entrenchment of the Union.[15]

2–026   The modern form of protecting the status of Northern Ireland owes its origins to article 1 of the Act of Union with England in 1800, which stated that the Kingdoms of Great Britain and Ireland shall "for ever after, be united in one kingdom". In common

---

[15] Brigid Hadfield, "The Belfast Agreement, Sovereignty and the State of the Union" [1998] *Public Law* 599.

with Scottish and Welsh Acts of Union already noted above, might not the Union with Ireland appear to be a constituent treaty of such fundamental importance that its status absolves it from modification or repeal?

English lawyers addressed this issue in 1868 when the Irish Church Bill was debated **2–027** in the House of Commons. The Bill set out to disestablish the Church of Ireland and thereby dissolve its union with the Church of England—a union guaranteed in the Act of Union 1800. An unsuccessful challenge to the validity of the Act was made in *Ex p. Canon Selwyn.*[16] The Irish Church Act 1869 disestablishing the Church of Ireland, was passed. Parliament may not legally bind future Parliaments. We have already seen how subsequent legislation has successfully amended, revised or changed the Act of Union including the devolution legislation under the Northern Ireland Act 1998.

Since August 31, 1994 and a cease-fire by the Irish Republican Army, attempts have **2–028** continued to provide a peace process in Northern Ireland; the initiatives have involved constitutional innovation. The Northern Ireland (Entry to Negotiations, etc.) Act 1996 provided for elections in Northern Ireland to allow all-party negotiations. The decommissioning of arms has been the subject of a report under United States Senator George Mitchell on January 22, 1996 and the Northern Ireland Arms Decommissioning Act 1997 provides a statutory framework for arms decommissioning. The breakthrough came with an Agreement formed from multi-party negotiations. Known as the Belfast Agreement or the Good Friday Agreement,[17] it was signed on April 10, 1998. The Northern Ireland Act 1998 was passed granting devolution to Northern Ireland. Northern Ireland's form of devolution reflects its unique history and the need for consensus-building as part of the peace process. The close interrelationship between the peace agreement and consensus-building through a devolved system of government is the major reason why devolution is important for the future of Northern Ireland. Thus devolution is only likely to succeed as long as the peace agreement holds; equally if a component of devolution fails, the peace process may be in jeopardy. In order to build a consensus, referendums on the Agreement were held in Northern Ireland and the Irish Republic in May 1998. In Northern Ireland there was a turnout of 80.98 per cent and 71.2 per cent approved the Agreement. In the Republic of Ireland, there was a turnout of 55.47 per cent and 94 per cent voted in favour. Elections for the Northern Ireland Assembly were held under the Northern Ireland (Elections) Act 1998 as part of the Northern Ireland Act 1998 and the requisite Order in Council was made to bring the new devolved Assembly into life. However, the new Assembly endured for no more than 10 weeks following disagreement over the arms decommissioning arrangements. The Northern Ireland Act 2000 suspended the 1998 Act but the devolution Assembly was restored after further negotiations. The main details of devolution are more fully discussed below.

DEVOLUTION

The unitary nature of the United Kingdom emphasises the fact that there is no federal **2–029** system. How is devolution to be defined and what is its significance? Devolution is intended to preserve the unitary nature of the United Kingdom's constitutional

[16] (1872) 36 *JP Journal* 54.
[17] *The Agreement reached in multi-party negotiations* Cm.4292 (1998).

arrangements. The term refers to the delegation of various central government powers to the regions, while retaining the sovereignty of the central legislature. Thus sovereignty is not divided between a federal legislature and a regional legislature. The focus of devolution is on the delegation of powers and the relationship between the regional body, and the central legislature and government. Devolution may be defined as a delegation or re-allocation of power from the centre to the regions. Another feature of devolution is the fact that the sovereign legislature is unaltered. Devolution may be suspended, abolished or redrafted at the discretion of the sovereign legislature. In fact there are many different forms of devolution. Before the 1998 devolution Acts for Scotland and Wales, there existed administrative devolution. The main experiment in devolved government comes from the period in Northern Ireland from 1920, under the Government of Ireland Act 1920, until 1973. Northern Ireland is a useful case study of devolved powers and as such provided a learning experience; the benefit of this is to be found in the 1998 devolution Acts.

Administrative Devolution

2–030   Since the 1960s the arrangements for the government of Scotland and Wales evolved through decentralisation of a large range of administrative tasks. Gradually this resulted in "administrative devolution". In the case of Scotland the Secretary of State for Scotland had five main departments with a wide range of statutory responsibilities and duties. The five departments were the Scottish Office; Agriculture, Environment and Fisheries Department; The Scottish Office Education and Industry Department; The Scottish Office Home Department and the Scottish Office Department of Health. There was also the Scottish Courts Administration, the department of the Registrar General for Scotland, the Scottish Record Office and the department of Registers for Scotland. The administration of the government of Scotland allowed the Secretary of State some freedom in the development of matters of particular significance for Scotland. Scotland has a legal system distinct from that of England and Wales. The Lord Advocate and the Solicitor-General for Scotland advise the Government on Scottish questions. Criminal justice, courts and prosecution matters under the Crown Office provide Scotland with its own distinct legal system.

2–031   In Wales the degree of administrative devolution was markedly less than for Scotland. There is a Secretary of State for Wales with sole responsibility in Wales for ministerial functions relating to a whole host of different areas such as health, education, personal social services, the environment, local government, the European Regional Development Fund and with oversight of economic and regional planning responsibilities for Wales.

2–032   In Northern Ireland following the introduction of direct rule in 1972, administrative devolution resulted in a hotchpotch of functions but without any locally elected Northern Ireland Assembly. What was intended as an interim arrangement of direct rule from 1972 became more permanent. The Secretary of State for Northern Ireland is the minister responsible for the government of Northern Ireland, and has a seat in the British Cabinet of the government in London. In addition there are two Ministers of State with shared responsibilities for a number of key Northern Ireland departments such as the Departments of Agriculture, Economic Development, Education, Environment, Finance and Personnel, and Health and Social Services. The Northern Ireland Office became the United Kingdom government Department for Northern Ireland.

Proposals for devolution in the 1970s

The idea of some form of legislative devolution for Scotland and Wales may be traced **2–033** back to the 1960s. The arguments in favour of some form of devolved government rested on a number of trends that had become clear in the 1970s. The over-centralisation of governmental power in the United Kingdom and the growth of nationalism in Scotland and Wales put the issue of "legislative devolution" on the political agenda and the hiving-off of legislative and most likely fiscal powers to separate assemblies in Scotland and Wales. The experience of devolution in Northern Ireland was influential in considering the way forward to address the issues raised by devolution. The Government of Ireland Act 1920 had provided devolution in Northern Ireland from 1920 until 1972. It formed the Constitution of Northern Ireland and established a Parliament for Northern Ireland with extensive legislative powers. There were powers transferred to the Northern Ireland Parliament and matters retained at Westminster. Overall the sovereignty of the United Kingdom Parliament remained intact and the Government of Ireland Act preserved the unity of the United Kingdom. Devolution offered a non-federal solution to the demands for greater local autonomy. The Northern Ireland experience also proved flexible. After events in 1972 culminating in the fall of the Northern Ireland Parliament after widespread civil unrest and street violence, the Northern Ireland Constitution Act 1973 was passed followed by a Northern Ireland Assembly Act 1973. Although the 1973 Act was overtaken by events in Northern Ireland both the 1973 Act and the Government of Ireland Act 1920 helped provide a model for some form of regional government in Scotland and Wales. The strength of the argument in favour of devolution and the rejection of federalism came from the analysis offered by the report of the Royal Commission on the Constitution, known as the Kilbrandon Report,[18] published in 1973. The Kilbrandon report identified dissatisfaction with the centralised Westminster model of govern-ment. The Report was greatly influenced by the Northern Ireland form of devolution introduced under the Government of Ireland Act 1920 which it regarded as having worked well in providing legislation particular to the needs of Northern Ireland. One strength of the system was the opportunity to judge whether United Kingdom Acts of Parliament ought to be applied in Northern Ireland after a period when the legislation was "tested" in England and Wales.

The United Kingdom Government's response to the Kilbrandon Report was to **2–034** attempt to establish assemblies in Scotland and Wales. The Government ruled out devolution for England but undertook consideration of executive devolution to new English regional authorities. The matter of English devolution was finally dropped after the Government found a lack of consensus on the issue. In the case of Scotland and Wales, separate Scotland and Wales Acts passed in 1978 failed to receive the support of 40 per cent of the electorate necessary for the Acts to come into force. While a majority voted in Scotland in support of devolution, this only amounted to 32.9 per cent of the electorate and not the 40 per cent required. In Wales only 20.2 per cent of the vote favoured devolution representing 11.9 per cent of the electorate, well below the 40 per cent required. After the referendum results, devolution lapsed as a

---

[18] *Report of Royal Commission on the Constitution* (Kilbrandon) Cmnd.5460–61 (1973) and *Memorandum of Dissent* Cmnd.5732 (1974).

major issue for some time. It was conceded by some that the vote may have reflected what was on offer rather than a rejection of devolution in principle.

2–035   Pressure for some form of devolved government or outright independence has grown in recent years. Opposition parties unsuccessfully introduced a Devolution Bill in November 1987. The Campaign for a Scottish Assembly lobbied for devolution in the late 1980s. In July 1988, "A Claim of Right for Scotland" was launched and recommended a Constitutional Convention; its first meeting was held in Edinburgh on March 30, 1989. The left-of-centre Institute for Public Policy Research published its draft Constitution in 1991 which included a devolved assembly for Scotland, Wales and the English regions. More recently the Constitution Unit studied the question of devolution and considered a Scottish Parliament with legislative and tax-varying powers. Similar proposals were discussed for Wales. The election of the new Labour Government on May 1, 1997 firmly established constitutional reforms as a central element in the Government's agenda.

The Devolution Acts of 1998 in Outline

2–036   In September 1997 referendums on devolution were held in Scotland and Wales. The result was that in Scotland 75 per cent of the voters were in favour of devolution, on a 60 per cent turnout. In Wales support for devolution was more marginal, and on a turnout of around 50 per cent the majority were in favour but by the narrowest of margins (0.6 per cent). The new Labour Government with a secure Parliamentary majority at Westminster could afford to be radical.

2–037   The Scotland Act 1998 created a new Scottish Parliament, elected for four years, with defined legislative powers to pass Acts (Sch. 5 of the 1998 Act) and a limited tax-raising authority. There is a Scottish First Minister, and an appointment process for ministers nominated by the first Minister from members of the Scottish Parliament but requiring the agreement of that Parliament. The United Kingdom Parliament maintains overall legislative competence over matters relating to foreign affairs, including the European Union, the Crown, defence, and economic and monetary matters. Over the first few years with a devolved Parliament, Scotland has developed a distinctive style and content in governing its own affairs.

2–038   The Government of Wales Act 1998 creates a Welsh Assembly, more limited in powers and scope than the Scottish Parliament. The Assembly is unable to legislate in terms of passing Acts, but may exercise the functions of the Secretary of State for Wales that have been transferred to the Assembly. This power includes subordinate legislative powers under Pt III of the Government of Wales Act 1998. There is a First Minister, and the Assembly operates cabinet-style committees for decision-making. It is possible that under political influence the powers of the Welsh Assembly could be increased beyond the modest powers it already has. Most notably unlike the Scottish Parliament, it does not have power to raise taxes. However, the Secretary of State for Wales may be forced to concede additional powers under pressure from the Welsh Assembly. This may not have been envisaged in the legislation, but, in practical terms, is how the Welsh form of devolution may result in more autonomy for Wales than originally planned. The Assembly, however, does not have powers to adopt primary legislation. As a result as Burrows has pointed out[19]:

[19] N. Burrows, *Devolution* (Sweet & Maxwell, London, 2000) p.186.

"In Wales there is the anomaly that an Assembly deriving its legitimacy from the will of the people demonstrated in elections lacks the power to carry out the functions associated elsewhere within the United Kingdom with such a body."

Finally, in the case of Northern Ireland, devolution is part of an ongoing peace process and as such has a number of unique qualities. There is an Assembly, elected for a four-year term, and a power-sharing executive unlike any other, with a requirement to address divisions between Nationalists and Unionists. There is a First Minister and a Deputy First Minister who must satisfy the requirements of a majority in the Assembly and a majority of both Unionists and Nationalist members of the Assembly. There is then a complex set of powers that may be devolved to the Assembly once it is up and running, with excepted matters listed in the Act as most likely never to be devolved. This leaves reserved matters which might be transferred under an Order in Council, and transferred matters that are devolved. The essence of devolution is that the constitutional order may create, but not impose, a system of government. As mentioned above, under the Northern Ireland Act 2000 devolution was suspended in May 2000 and then later restored, an indication of the fragility of the peace process underpinning devolution. It also underlines that legal sovereignty continues to reside in the Westminster Parliament. **2–039**

Devolution in Scotland, Wales and Northern Ireland

Devolution also fits the Government's modernisation agenda. In essence the aim is to revitalise regional government. While this is a step towards decentralisation, paradoxically it has not brought about any reduction in the centralising tendencies of government. Devolution does not prevent the United Kingdom Parliament from legislating on matters that fall under devolved powers. For example in the 2000 and 2001 period, there were 14 Bills passed by the United Kingdom Parliament on matters that fell within the legislative competence of the Scottish Parliament. Devolution provides mini-written constitutions for Wales and Scotland for the first time in the United Kingdom. There is an elected Mayor and Assembly for London, a limited form of devolution. **2–040**

This leaves England the major region lacking in a written constitution. It is possible that devolution will grow organically beyond the existing framework, but this will depend on political decision-making in London. It is possible to identify some characteristics common to the different forms of devolution on offer. **2–041**

Common Characteristics and Similarities of Devolution

Each of the four systems of devolution for Scotland, Wales, Northern Ireland and London has its own distinctiveness but they all share common principles. Burrows[20] identifies common characteristics such as inclusiveness, diversity, sustainability, equal opportunity, modern working practices, flexibility and responsiveness, openness and accessibility. Devolution is very much a process rather than a single event. The future of devolution is linked to the generation of regional identity and local interest. The **2–042**

---

[20] N. Burrows, *Devolution* (Sweet & Maxwell, London, 2000).

diversity of these influences makes it difficult to draw out common principles, but there are a number of influences that are common in the devolution of each region. The Westminster model of parliamentary government is shared in each form of devolution in Scotland, Wales, Northern Ireland. All three Executives have different powers and cabinet systems that are intended to reflect the differences, both subtle and practical in the way government operates in each of the regions. There are corresponding principles in each of the three devolved bodies for the regulation and registration of members' interests and powers for the attendance of witnesses and documents. There is also devolution in London. This is different because of the decision to have a directly elected Mayor separately elected from the London Assembly, the Greater London Authority.

2–043   Although the formulation of the sovereignty of the United Kingdom Parliament is expressed differently for each region, it is clear that sovereignty rests with the United Kingdom Parliament. In Scotland and Northern Ireland, each with their own law-making powers, sovereignty is retained by the United Kingdom Parliament over all matters including those matters that are devolved.

2–044   Funding arrangements follow a common arrangement that may be traced back to the period before devolution was introduced, and owe much to the arrangements introduced in the 1880s by the then Chancellor of the Exchequer. Building on the experience gathered over the years' expenditure arrangements for Scotland, Wales and Northern Ireland were negotiated and brought within the overall remit of public expenditure controls. In the 1960s and 70s the rules developed further and in 1978 a non-statutory arrangement known as the Barnett formula was introduced for Scotland. The Barnett formula was further refined and developed even though it was intended to be a temporary arrangement. The formula determines the amount of additional changes to the expenditure of Scotland, Northern Ireland and Wales. The bulk of expenditure is outside the arrangement and large payments fall outside its remit. These are determined by block grant on an annual basis. There are also special circumstances that make the formula's application in Northern Ireland work differently.

2–045   The Barnett formula is intended to allow for an adjustment of any additional payments on the basis of an economic formula. The Barnett formula has three elements:

  • the change in planned spending in departments in England;

  • the extent to which there is comparability in the services carried out by each administrative department in the devolved administration when compared to the equivalent English departmental programme;

  • the population that is proportionate in each country.

2–046   It is generally believed that if the formula is applied strictly then increases in expenditure in Scotland, Wales and Northern Ireland might be slower than the English equivalent. The Barnett formula is criticised for not assessing need, which may lead to distortions in its application.

2–047   Uniquely out of the three, the Scottish Parliament has a limited tax-raising power. The Scottish Parliament may increase or decrease income tax set by the United Kingdom Parliament by a maximum of 3 per cent. On the basis of convergence any decrease must be made up and paid to the United Kingdom Treasury.

The electoral arrangements for devolution share common characteristics. In **2–048** Scotland, Wales and Northern Ireland, election is by way of PR (proportional representation). This was chosen to encourage multi-party government. PR may prevent any one group gaining a monopoly of power, and discourages adversarial politics found in the first-past-the-post system. Although PR is used in each region, there are differences:

Wales and Scotland

Voters have two votes. One vote is for a constituency elected by the first-past-the- **2–049** post system. In Scotland there are 73 members of the Scottish Parliament. In Wales there are 40 members of the Welsh Assembly. The second vote is for the regions based on the constituency for the European Parliament. In Scotland there are eight regions with 7 members in each, making 56 members in total. In Wales there are five regions each returning 4 members, making 20 members in total. The system of voting is adopted from the d'Hondt system of PR. Each elector votes for a particular party list.

Northern Ireland

Voters use the single transferable vote system. Voters mark their preferences for **2–050** their choice of candidate. There is a formula establishing the quota required to elect the number of representatives for the constituency. The constituency is based on the 18 constituencies used to vote for Westminster MPs representing Northern Ireland. There are six members returned for each of the 18 constituencies. This makes a total of 108 representatives for the Northern Ireland Assembly.

London

The Greater London Authority Act 1999 provides for different systems of voting **2–051** for the London Mayor and for the 25-member Greater London Authority. The London Mayor is elected under the Supplemental Vote System, a form of proportional representation. The Greater London Authority is elected under two systems. One system is for 14 constituency members elected from special constituencies on the first-past-the-post system. The other is for 11 members elected across London on a constituency list system using the Additional Member System.

Common to devolution in Scotland, Wales and Northern Ireland is the creation of a **2–052** category of devolution issues. This refers to the matters under the relevant Act that fall under the jurisdiction of the Judicial Committee of the Privy Council. In general terms devolution issues such as the legal competence of the devolved body are the type of constitutional question that might arise. The scheme adopted is that the lower courts in each of the three jurisdictions may refer devolution issues to the higher courts and ultimately the Privy Council to be settled through judicial interpretation. The relevant Law Officers must be notified thereby providing an opportunity to make out a legal opinion.

There are wide powers given to the different Law Officers for this purpose. It is **2–053** clear that this power expands considerably the role of the courts to set standards and give attention to the boundaries of the legislative competences of the devolution settlement in each of the three jurisdictions. Examples of where the boundaries may be set include areas reserved for the United Kingdom Parliament, breaches of European Community law or any incompatibility with Convention rights. It would appear in principle that it is possible for a devolution issue to be raised within any of the legal jurisdictions of the United Kingdom. This gives considerable scope for legal challenges beyond the territory of Scotland, Wales or Northern Ireland.[21] The question of what constitutes a devolution issue is also linked to the fact that all three devolved bodies are bound by the Human Rights Act 1998. Failure to apply the 1998 Act is itself a devolution issue. Legislation that is incompatible with the Human Rights Act 1998 is outside the legal competences of the devolved bodies. In Scotland s.29 of the Scotland Act 1998 applies and s.57 prohibits the Executive from making subordinate legislation that is incompatible with Convention rights. In Northern Ireland s.6 of the Northern Ireland Act 1998 is applicable. Section 24 also makes it incompatible for the Executive to make subordinate legislation that is incompatible with Convention rights. In Wales, s.107 makes a similar rule. There is a difference because the Welsh Assembly does not have legislative powers. If secondary legislation is required by the United Kingdom Parliament for Wales that is incompatible with the Convention then the secondary legislation may be permitted even if it is in breach of Convention rights. The reasoning is that because the United Kingdom Parliament is not bound to apply Convention rights in domestic law and it is within its powers to override the Human Rights Act 1998 by primary legislation then it is possible for Wales and England to undertake legal powers that are not permissible in Scotland and Northern Ireland. The United Kingdom Parliament might, however, enact legislation to override ss.6 and 24 of the Northern Ireland Act 1998 and ss.29 and 57 of the Scotland Act 1998.

2–054   There is a further implication in making devolution issues include Convention rights. The jurisdiction of the Judicial Committee over devolution issues is set out in the respective devolution statutes. Common to all three Acts is the binding nature of the Judicial Committee on all courts and legal proceedings. The Judicial Committee becomes the highest court in each of the three jurisdictions on devolution matters. However, in England the House of Lords is the highest court for Convention matters. Thus the House of Lords in terms of Convention rights is superseded in Scotland, Wales and Northern Ireland by the Privy Council as the highest court.

2–055   The significance of devolution in each of its variants is evaluated as follows:

England

2–056   England is unique as the only region that does not have its own devolved institution. This anomaly is unlikely to remain. One idea is to have regional assemblies for England. A step in this direction was taken under the Regional Development Agencies Act 1998 creating eight new Regional Development Agencies from April 1999. Powers granted to the Agencies provide a discretion to further economic development and regeneration, and to promote business employment and the development of skills within the regions. The Agencies are quangos but are provided statutory powers by the relevant Secretary of State to undertake their functions. For the future there is considerable scope for the extension of the Agencies into working partnerships with

---

[21] Aidan O'Neill "Judicial Politics and the Judicial Committee: The Devolution Jurisprudence of the Privy Council" (2001) *Modern Law Review* 603.

local government bodies. In the eight regions there are regional chambers comprising representatives from business, trade unions and the voluntary sector engaged in setting up so called "assemblies" to develop lines of accountability. The ratio is usually 70 per cent local councillors and 30 per cent social and economic partners. In March 2001 a consultation document was published.[22] *Strengthening Regional Accountability* that envisages funding of a total of £5 million per year for three years with additional funds for collective projects. In embryo this is the beginning of a movement to further expand systems of local community accountability. In May 2002 the Government announced its plans to introduce devolution in eight regional areas of the United Kingdom on the basis of a referendum in each region. Proposals from each region would be considered. It is doubtful if there will be devolution in every region, but at least some of the eight regions are likely to vote in favour. What kind of devolution is on offer? The model is broadly similar to the Greater London Authority outlined below. Elected regional assemblies may receive powers to cover the following:

- economic development: overseeing the work of the eight regional development agencies;

- planning: contributing to major and significant developments;

- housing: dealing with the housing market;

- transport: planning long-term proposals to improve public transport;

- health: developing long-term strategic health plans;

- culture and tourism: co-ordinating regional tourism;

- skills and employment: working with learning skills councils;

- waste management: setting targets and developing recycling plans.

It remains to be seen whether regional devolution will come about speedily. London is an exception to the rest of England, in that is has devolution granted under the Greater London Authority Act 1999. This establishes an elected Mayor and a separately elected Greater London Authority. The responsibilities of the Mayor are provided under Pt IX of the Act as follows: **2–057**

- the state of the environment report;

- the London Biodiversity Action Plan;

- the municipal waste management strategy;

- the London air quality strategy;

- the London ambient noise strategy.

The functions of the Greater London Authority include: **2–058**

- promoting economic development and wealth creation;

---

[22] available from Department for Transport, Local Government and the Regions, now Department for Transport and Office of the Deputy Prime Minister.

- promoting social development and promoting the improvement of the environment.

2–059   The Greater London Authority is also required to review and scrutinise the exercise of the Mayor's functions and proposals that are being considered by the Mayor. In turn the Mayor is expected to inform the Authority with periodic reports and any decisions and proposals. An annual report prepared by the Mayor is expected to be made and the Mayor must attend an annual meeting of the Assembly.

2–060   There is a London Development Agency set up by Pt V of the Greater London Authority Act 1999 amending the Regional Development Agency Act 1998. The London Development Agency is part of the Regional Development Agencies established for the eight English regions.

2–061   The gap left by the absence of devolution for England resulted in the setting-up of a plethora of agencies to support the administration of the eight English regions through a number of Government Offices situated in each region. The potential is to build at grass roots elements of regional decision-making, possibly as a precursor to some form of devolution to the English regions.

Wales

2–062   Devolution in Wales is distinctive from the other models of devolution used in Scotland and Northern Ireland. There is an elected National Assembly for Wales with a four-year term. It does not have formal legislative powers. The legislative element is dependent on representations made after due deliberation by the Welsh Assembly to the United Kingdom government. The recommendation power covers proposals for Bills and amendments. There is a Secretary of State for Wales required to carry out consultation with the Assembly and to attend and participate in the proceedings of the Assembly at least once a year. In many ways the participative role of the Secretary of State has the potential for producing a form of devolution that may grow organically. In the plan of devolution adopted for Wales, it is intended that the Assembly might replace the Secretary of State for Wales and to that end there are a raft of powers in the Government of Wales Act 1998 that cover subordinate legislation including circulars and policy statements.

2–063   The legislative scheme contained in the 1998 Act is that the Welsh Assembly has various powers transferred, conferred and imposed upon it. The scheme is activated by an Order in Council set out in Sch.2 and s.22 of the Act.

> - Transferred powers: The Welsh Assembly has powers under statutory instruments to transfer to itself a variety of powers including the functions of the Welsh Health Authorities, and a variety of public bodies contained in Sch.4 of the 1998 Act. These include further education, tourism and the Sports Council for Wales.
>
> - Conferred powers: There is a long list of powers including agriculture, forestry fisheries and food; culture, economic development; education and training; the environment; health and the health service; highways; local government; social services; sport and recreation; tourism; housing; industry; town and country planning; transport; water and flood defences and the Welsh language. There is scope for the transfer of additional powers that may be given by the United Kingdom Parliament.

There are a number of functions associated with the National Assembly, namely the **2–064** promotion of economic growth for Wales and that local government should be sustained and promoted. Voluntary and business organisations are also to be supported and encouraged.

The Executive and Committees

The Welsh Assembly is a body corporate, supported by administrative staff that fall **2–065** under the category of Home Civil Servants. Uniquely the Assembly is required to give equal treatment to the Welsh and English languages. The running of the Welsh Assembly is also distinctive from any other form of devolution. Because the Assembly has no legislative powers, executive committees are required including subject committees, audit committees, and regional committees. There is a subordinate legislation committee. Instead of a cabinet there is an Executive made up of members of the Welsh Assembly. The absence of the formal structure of cabinet government leaves a gap in Wales as there is no equivalent to the traditional constitutional link between cabinet individual and collective responsibility.

The dynamics of devolution in Wales make its future difficult to predict. Wales has **2–066** always been slightly ambivalent to the development of devolution and its introduction. There are issues about accountability and the problem of whether Welsh devolution is likely to develop into a more substantive legislative form. In the first years of working, devolution weaknesses in the structure of accountability have been exposed. The First Secretary Alun Michael failed to resign after a vote of no confidence. After much political controversy the matter was resolved by resignation following a second vote on the motion of no confidence. Welsh devolution is likely to build on the foundations that are established. It is by no means clear whether there will ever be a demand for legislative functions to be devolved to the Welsh Assembly. What is clear is that the Welsh Assembly with access to Westminster legislation through the office of the Secretary of State for Wales may well prove to develop its own identity and surprise us all.

Scotland

There was greatest demand for devolution for Scotland. As a result, the Scotland Act **2–067** 1998 provides powers for both an Executive and a Scottish Parliament. The scheme adopted is broadly similar to a Westminster style of cabinet government with accountability to the Scottish Parliament. The competence of the Scottish Parliament and Executive is set out in the 1998 Act and is broadly defined. S.28 of the 1998 Act provides that the Scottish Parliament has a general power: ". . . to make laws, known as Acts of the Scottish Parliament". The exercise of this general power must fall within the general legislative competence of the Scottish Parliament under s.29 of the 1998 Act. It is therefore outside the competence of the Scottish Parliament to modify various " protected" provisions set out in Sch.4. This includes the Union Acts 1706 and 1707, the European Communities Act 1972, the Human Rights Act 1998 and the Scotland Act 1998 itself. It is required that the Scottish Parliament and Executive must not act in a way that is incompatible with European Convention rights or community law, or act in a way that has an extra-territorial effect. Protection is given to the Lord Advocate who may not be removed as head of the system of criminal prosecution in Scotland.

2–068   The Executive and Parliament are provided with powers to legislate under the following headings:

- health service; local government (and this includes local government finance and expenditure); education and training; housing; transport; sport; the legal system including law and order; farming; fishing; forestry; the arts; and a limited tax-varying power.
- powers to approve the budget, and general powers of debate even if the matters fall outside the legislative competence of the Scottish Parliament and Executive.

2–069   Sch.5 contains a list of reserved matters where the Acts of the Scottish Parliament may not legislate including:

- Sch.5, Pt I. There are general reserved matters: the Constitution, political parties, foreign affairs, public service, defence, and treason.

- Sch.5, Pt II. Matters that are specifically reserved and not within the competence of the Scottish Parliament and Executive: financial and economic matters, home affairs, trade and industry, energy, transport, social security, regulation of the professions, health, medicine, media and culture. A miscellaneous category set out in Sch.5 is also included.

2–070   S.30(2) provides that an Order in Council may increase the powers of the Scottish Parliament and Executive. This provides the opportunity for the further expansion of the role of the devolved Parliament and Executive.

The Scottish Executive

2–071   In general the Westminster model is used for the way the Scottish Executive is devised and organised but there are some important differences. S.44 of the 1998 Act sets out the arrangements for a First Minister and other ministers appointed by Her Majesty on the recommendation of the First Minister. Special attention is given to the Law Officers comprising the Lord Advocate and Solicitor General. The appointment of the First Minister is in the name of Her Majesty but subject to nomination by the Scottish Parliament from its members. The Presiding Officer is to forward the nomination for Her Majesty to make the appointment. The nominations for the Executive are made by the First Minister to Her Majesty and must first be approved by the Scottish Parliament. The normal Westminster style constitutional conventions apply for resignation or removal of a minister. A simple majority in favour or a vote of no confidence in the Executive will result in resignation of the Executive as a whole and a general election may be held if a replacement executive cannot be made.

2–072   The functions of the Executive are related to the devolved competences set out above. Future devolved powers or the sharing of functions between Scottish ministers and the United Kingdom Government may take place. S.57 of the 1998 Act provides that there are shared powers under s.2(2) of the European Communities Act 1972 to implement obligations that fall under Community law. Powers that remain with Westminster may in the future be delegated under any new devolved arrangements for Scotland. Westminster retains controls over the payment of money into the Scottish

Consolidated Fund and there are powers retained to deal with international relations, elections and overall Parliamentary sovereignty.

The Scottish Parliament

The Westminster model of committees is used extensively in the working of the **2–073** Scottish Parliament. Specific individual committees are required by the 1998 Act on Standards, procedures, audit, Europe, subordinate legislation, equal opportunities and public petitions. All committees adopt a common framework. At the discretion of the Parliament, there are in addition committees covering various subject areas. To date eight have been established covering Education; Culture and Sport; Enterprise and Life-long Learning; Health and Community Care; Justice and Home Affairs; Social Inclusion; Transport and Environment. The committees' remit is much broader than the Westminster equivalent and they have powers to scrutinise, conduct inquiries, initiate legislation and scrutinise financial procedures.

The 1998 Act provides procedures for the passage of legislation, its scrutiny and **2–074** debate. Primary legislation is subject to a pre-legislative consultative process. The Bill must include various memoranda on the financial implications, if any, of the proposals; an explanatory note; a policy memorandum setting out objectives of the Bill; and most importantly a certificate of legislative competence signed by the member of the Executive and the Presiding Officer under s.31(1)(2).

Once presented the Bill must complete the three-stage process before being **2–075** presented for the Royal Assent. A novel power under s.33 is that within four weeks of the Bill being passed, the Law Officers may refer a question of legislative competence to the Privy Council for determination. There are procedures for secondary legislation and there is a Subordinate Legislation Committee which must report within 40 days as to whether the instrument is to be approved or not.

In general terms the Scottish Parliament is expected to scrutinise the Executive and **2–076** hold Government to account. A two-thirds majority is required for an election to be called inside the four-year life of the Parliament. If there is a vacancy for the post of First Minister and this is not filled within 28 days then a general election must be called. The death of the First Minister, Donald Dewar, required the filling of the post before the 28-day period. There remains the post of the Secretary of State for Scotland, as a sign that the Scottish Parliament remains a subservient one to Westminster.

Devolution to Scotland has considerable potential to develop and expand. It is most **2–077** likely to create differences in policy and political outlook from Westminster because of the power, albeit limited, granted to the Scottish Parliament to adjust tax. The Scottish Parliament has broad discretion on how to spend the £15 billion budget it is allocated. There is considerable scope for political differences to emerge between Scotland and Westminster over spending priorities. Already this is seen in the activities of the Scottish Parliament. An early example was the decision that Scottish students do not have to pay top-up fees to universities when their English equivalent are required to pay. This decision may result in a change in the position of students in England.

Northern Ireland

Devolution in Northern Ireland is inextricably linked to the ongoing peace agreement. **2–078** There is a Northern Ireland Assembly with legislative powers and an Executive with a complicated procedure for its formation because of the requirements of power-sharing between Unionists and Nationalists.

2–079   The legislative competence of the Northern Ireland Assembly follows a pattern of devolution first attempted under the Government of Ireland Act 1920. There are three categories of powers that fall within the legislative scheme of the 1998 Act. These are transferred matters, excepted matters and reserved matters. In addition the Northern Ireland Executive and Assembly are required to act within their competent powers. This means that the powers they exercise must fall within the category of transferred matters that are not excepted or reserved matters. Even in respect of transferred matters the general principles that must be followed are that the Acts of the Northern Ireland Assembly or decisions of the Executive must never:

- have extra-territorial effect;

- be incompatible with the European Convention on Human Rights or European Community law;

- discriminate against any person on the ground of religious or political opinion;

- modify any protected or entrenched enactment;

- deal with an excepted matter other than in some ancillary way.

2–080   It is therefore important to set out the three categories as follows:

Excepted matters are those which, under Sch.2 of the 1998 Act which will never be transferred to Northern Ireland institutions. They include: Crown matters, UK Parliament matters, international relations, defence, treason, elections, national security, nuclear energy and the Northern Ireland constitution.

Reserved matters are under Sch.3 of the 1998 Act and include: Crown property, the post office and postal services, criminal law, the courts, firearms and explosives, telecommunications, measurements, surrogacy, data protection and consumer safety. The category of reserved matters may eventually fall into part of the legislative competence of the Northern Ireland Assembly if the consent of the Secretary of State for Northern Ireland is given under s.8(b) of the 1998 Act.

Transferred matters. The legislative powers of the Northern Ireland Assembly include: agriculture, environment, education, health, social services, culture and the arts. Also the Northern Ireland civil service, employment and social security fall within the jurisdiction of the Assembly. The Assembly has powers to confer on the Executive responsibility that falls within the legislative competence of the Assembly under s.22 of the 1998 Act.

2–081   The Northern Ireland Executive is established by the Northern Ireland Act 1998. The executive power in Northern Ireland remains with Her Majesty although it may be exercised by a department under a Minister in Northern Ireland (s.23). The creation of the Northern Ireland Executive is at the centre of the controversial idea of power-sharing. The arrangements are complex and intended to build on the peace process. The past experience of failed power-sharing executives has helped to create the current arrangements. They are incremental. This is designed to encourage participation and reward agreement over disagreement. The Assembly elects the First and Deputy First Ministers and both are designated as Chairman of the Northern Ireland Executive

Committee. The latter is in essence a cabinet but with a distinctive role and powers intended to address the cross-community support necessary for any functioning system of government in Northern Ireland. They are intended to act jointly. This includes any exercise of prerogative powers or in nominating ministers to the North–South and British–Irish Councils. In deciding on the functions and the number of ministers the First Minister has no powers. The First Minister has no powers to nominate, appoint or dismiss other ministers who are members of the Northern Ireland Executive Committee. Instead the Executive Committee relies on the Northern Ireland Assembly to whom it is answerable. Consistent with the approach of requiring cross-community support, the decisions of the Assembly are circumscribed by a legal requirement of cross-community support for many of its powers. Calculations are made on the designation of the members of the Assembly as either Unionist or Nationalist, a requirement of registration on all members of the Assembly on signing the electoral roll.

Organising the policy-making of government in Northern Ireland is linked to the **2–082** peace process and the Belfast Agreement. A draft programme of government has been drawn up and is intended to begin building a consensus about government. It is too early to evaluate whether the arrangements will endure. It is important to realise how much the peace process and devolution are inextricably linked.

The Northern Ireland Assembly

A hallmark of the Assembly is the formation of statutory committees intended to **2–083** advise ministers on policy formulation. Election to the committees is linked to cross-community representation. Assembly members must be committed to serving all the people of Northern Ireland on an equal basis and also to non-violence and exclusively peaceful and democratic means. This is intended to build the peace process into the working of the Northern Ireland system of devolution. It is possible for a minister to be excluded on a vote of no confidence based on a failure to observe the requirement of peaceful means. The function and role of the Assembly to ensure that ministers are acting correctly and with the proper standards of accountability is supplemented by a Code of Conduct for Ministers modelled on the English equivalent in 1999. Holding to account is through debate, scrutiny and questions and through the use of committees. The committee structure is intended to familiarise members with the need to work co-operatively and through consensus building.

The traditional role of a select committee in the United Kingdom—to hold the **2–084** executive to account, to scrutinise and revise legislation through the procedures of passage of legislation, and to report—is found in the committees of the Assembly. Legislation passed by the Northern Ireland Assembly for both subordinate and primary legislation follows the same pattern as for Scotland. There is an addition of consultation with the civic forum for Northern Ireland, and the Presiding Officer of the Northern Ireland Assembly has responsibilities to ensure that the Bill is compatible within the Northern Ireland Human Rights arrangements including sending a copy of the Bill to the Northern Ireland Human Rights Commission. Various ways have been used to build into the scrutiny function degrees of preview of legislation. The Presiding Officer must ensure and certify that the Bill is within the competence of the Northern Ireland Assembly. In cases that fall within excepted or reserved matters these must be referred to the Secretary of State for Northern Ireland. The Attorney-General for

Northern Ireland has, within a four-week period of the passage of the Bill, the power to refer to the Privy Council any question regarding the legislative competence of the Assembly.

2–085   Once a Bill is passed by the Assembly it receives the Royal Assent in the normal way. However, the Secretary of State has a discretion not to send a Bill for Royal Assent (s.14).

Co-ordinating Devolution

2–086   The administration and co-ordination of the different forms of devolution in each region require careful consideration. Various agreements and understandings are used to co-ordinate the relationship between the different parts of the devolved administrations and central government agencies. These *Concordats* provide a working relationship based on formal and informal means of decision-making. Nevertheless it is clear that against the direction in devolving more decisions to the regions, there is considerable centralisation and co-ordination. Since devolution was introduced it has operated under a government with a large majority in Westminster. A minority government at Westminster may find it difficult to co-ordinate the diverse political groups and decision-making. In fact one of the issues for the future is the extent to which central government will be able to govern when there is no overall majority. Devolution cannot be seen as a panacea for political inertia or grid-lock when there is no majority government at Westminster.

2–087   There remains the interesting and difficult question that arises from the fact of devolution, namely how representation in the United Kingdom parliament might be adjusted to take account of devolution. In the case of Scotland, s.86 of the Scotland Act 1998 provides that in the future between 2002 and 2006 there will be a reduction in the 72 constituency seats for Scotland in the United Kingdom Parliament. The exact number for the reduction in representation is to be determined by the Boundary Commission. There is no corresponding reduction planned for Wales or Northern Ireland.

2–088   The concern is that there is unfairness. MPs who represent English, Welsh or Northern Ireland constituencies do not have any say in the Scottish Parliament. Should Scottish MPs continue to have a right to participate in the United Kingdom Parliament on legislation applicable, to England and Wales and Northern Ireland? The question was first posed by Tam Dalyell MP in the 1970s and became known as the West Lothian question. The question remains unresolved. It is likely to become relevant if there are major party political differences between the Government of the United Kingdom and the elected government in each of the devolved regions.

The Future of Devolution

2–089   It may be concluded that devolution has an organic quality. Self-reliance and a desire to be distinctive from the history of English influence are potent forces that will pull in the direction of greater independence. Nationalism may claim a stake in drawing together distinct and different groups as elected, subordinate bodies develop in confidence and legitimacy. These are potent forces that have the potential to develop in opposition to the centralising tendencies of the past. Most significant are the features common to all the devolution arrangements: four-year instead of five-year terms; unicameral assemblies or parliaments as distinct from the Westminster bicameral system; forms of proportional representation for elections, rather than the existing first-past-the-post electoral system for Westminster elections; and the continuation of United Kingdom sovereignty, rather than any settlement resolved around federalism. With the exception of Northern Ireland where political instability is an inherent feature of party political differences, devolution is proving to be remarkably stable. This leaves unanswered the question of the future role and functioning of the United Kingdom's Parliament and the possibility of its reform. Indeed, one of the difficulties with devolution at present is how to develop small nation states within a larger community? The population of the devolved areas—Scotland (5 million), Wales (3 million), Northern Ireland (1.5 million) and London (7 million)—may make it difficult to develop along strategic lines. The relationship with Brussels is therefore important for future economic growth. However, Westminster remains as the policy-maker on the distribution of European funds through the regions. Setting up permanent offices in Brussels by each of the devolved regions is one way to try to gain influence at the centre of Europe. Finally, there is the question of whether devolution will be introduced into the English regions. In May 2002 the Government announced its plans to extend devolution to eight English regions. The proposal is dependent on a referendum being held in each region in favour of devolution. The powers are likely to follow the example of the Greater London Authority outlined above.

THE COMMONWEALTH

The Commonwealth is relevant when discussing the United Kingdom's constitutional arrangement. When granting independence to former colonies, Parliament also considered their new constitutional status and relationship with Britain. Thus Parliament's authority and jurisdiction was altered by the Colonial Laws Validity Act 1865 and the Statute of Westminster 1931. In a sense such statutes preserved the theoretical doctrine of sovereignty while providing a new reality as to the practical scope of constitutional power.   **2–090**

The Colonial Laws Validity Act 1865 changed what had once been a vague common law rule that colonial constitutions enacted before 1865 and possessing a legislative assembly could not pass laws repugnant to the law of England. The 1865 Act assumed that colonies were subject to Parliamentary regulation by the "Imperial Parliament" but added the caveat that a colonial legislature was required to observe only those Acts of Parliament which expressly or impliedly applied to the colonies. This marked a gradual shift in the development of constitutional relations between the colonies and the United Kingdom. Colonies such as Canada, Australia and New Zealand enjoyed greater freedoms than other colonies in the actual exercise of their powers. Gradually this gave rise to the creation of a new legal status of dominion. In 1907 the term "dominion status" was first used and after the First World War, it signified a country's greater status and independence from the Imperial power. Various colonial conferences recognised the governance of these countries as having a "dominion status" rather than being in a colonial relationship. In 1926 the famous Balfour Declaration[23]   **2–091**

[23] Cmnd.1768 (1960).

accepted that "status, equality and autonomy" should be given to dominions within the British Empire.

2–092   Many dominion governments still experienced great dissatisfaction with the Colonial Laws Validity Act 1865. This centred on the practical restrictions and limitations experienced by dominion legislatures. In particular: restrictions on passing laws which might have extra-territorial effect; the convention that Bills would be reserved for the views of the United Kingdom Government; and the application of United Kingdom Acts of Parliament expressly or impliedly relevant to the dominion legislation rendering the latter void if inconsistent or repugnant to a United Kingdom Act. These restrictions contributed to a general unease that the United Kingdom's influence remained too powerful. The right of appeal to the Judicial Committee of the Privy Council was also seen as an indication of the lack of independence enjoyed by dominions.

2–093   In 1931 the Statute of Westminster put into legal effect the various resolutions made over the preceding few years. For the first time, the dominions were defined to include Canada, Australia, New Zealand, South Africa, the Irish Free State and Newfoundland. The Colonial Laws Validity Act 1865 ceased to apply to dominions, thus granting a dominion power of parliament to amend or repeal Acts of the United Kingdom Parliament. A dominion parliament was also given power to make laws having extra-territorial operation. Included in the Statute of Westminster was the power for dominion parliaments to abolish the right of appeal to the Judicial Committee of the Privy Council.

2–094   The 1931 Statute of Westminster still left a number of matters unresolved. It was unclear, for example, whether independence statutes such as the British North America Acts 1867-1930, which formed the basis of the Canadian Constitution, required legal authority from the United Kingdom Parliament to be amended. The view which prevailed was that the United Kingdom Parliament had to give assent if the Acts were to be changed and this was duly given by the Canada Act 1982. This Act placed sole responsibility in Canada for the amendment and modification of the Constitution of Canada.

2–095   In the cases of Australia and New Zealand, the effect of the 1931 Statute of Westminster was withheld in respect of the power to alter or amend their Constitution (see ss.8 and 9(1)). This resulted in both countries lacking the power to legislate in ways repugnant to United Kingdom law, to abolish on their own initiative appeals to the Privy Council, or to legislate extra-territorially. Eventually in 1986 the Australia Act abolished such limitations and ended the power of the United Kingdom Parliament to legislate for Australia. New Zealand had received complete constitutional powers under the New Zealand Constitution (Amendment) Act 1947. In 1996 the New Zealand Parliament enacted a Constitution Act including under s.15(1) that the Parliament of New Zealand has full power to make laws and that thereafter no Act of the United Kingdom Parliament will extend to New Zealand. Interestingly from the point of view of United Kingdom sovereignty, s.25 provides that the Statute of Westminster is to cease to have effect as the law of New Zealand. New Zealand has in many respects developed differently from the United Kingdom. The most striking difference is that, well in advance of the United Kingdom, New Zealand has attempted to innovate in the way the public sector is governed. The introduction of a new, mixed member proportional (MMP) electoral system in 1993, following an electoral referendum in October 1992, is one example of this innovation. Other examples include a fundamental experiment[24] in the role of the public sector, the development of strategies to manage the economy, the introduction of a Bill of Rights in 1990,[25] and the development of Maori rights. All these have contributed to the changing shape of the New Zealand legal system and constitutional rights. The New Zealand judiciary has also contributed to the change through a series of landmark decisions.[26]

New Zealand is a good example of the realities of constitutional power that leaves   **2–096** the United Kingdom Parliament with only a cultural identity and the symbols of the monarchy. New Zealand has developed in its own way from the 1840 Treaty of Waitangi, while many of the remnants of the colonial past are retained. Maori identity is strong and contributes to the growing national self-confidence. Continuing to promote Maori culture and a cohesive New Zealand identity provides one of the most exciting challenges for the present century. At the same time, the legal systems of the United States, Australia, and Canada have been influential in the development of New Zealand law. Judges and academics, educated partly in North America, draw on that experience when thinking about the future of legal education and possible directions for New Zealand. As the United Kingdom becomes integrated within the European Union, New Zealand appears to go its own way.

Constitutional supervision of colonial states by the United Kingdom Parliament has   **2–097** led to constitutional difficulties. One example illustrates the problem. In the case of Southern Rhodesia,[27] a colony since 1923 which today is the independent republican State of Zimbabwe, the United Kingdom faced a direct challenge to its constitutional authority. In 1965 an illegal Unilateral Declaration of Independence (UDI) led to the passage of the Southern Rhodesia Act 1965, a United Kingdom Act of Parliament asserting sovereignty over Southern Rhodesia. The 1965 Act declared that Southern Rhodesia remained part of Her Majesty's dominions and the power to make laws by Order in Council was maintained under the Act. The UDI purported to establish independent legislative powers for the Southern Rhodesian legislature, originally set up under the 1961 Constitution with a large measure of self-government granted thereunder by the United Kingdom. The terms of the UDI declared that Southern Rhodesia was to cease to be a colony and conferred full legislative powers on the Southern Rhodesian legislature, including the abolition of appeals to the Judicial Committee of the Privy Council. It also sought to protect the status of independence by removing the jurisdiction of the courts to question its validity.

The constitutional crisis, whereby the government in Southern Rhodesia continued   **2–098** unrecognised in law and enacted rules expressly repugnant to an Act of the United Kingdom Parliament, tested the authority of Parliament against the self-proclaimed independence of a newly formed state. This matter was raised as an issue in

[24] Jane Kelsey, *The New Zealand Experiment*, 1995.
[25] The New Zealand Bill of Rights Act 1990. See M. Taggart, "Tugging on Superman's Cape: Lessons from the Experience with the New Zealand Bill of Rights Act 1990" [1998] *Public Law* 266; Geoffrey Palmer and Matthew Palmer, *Bridled Power* (3rd ed., 1999).
[26] Lord Cooke of Thorndon is particularly influential, especially in developing the work of the New Zealand Court of Appeal. See *Flickinger v Crown Colony of Hong Kong* [1991] 1 N.Z.L.R. 439; *Ministry of Transport v Noort* [1992] 3 N.Z.L.R. 260, *Fraser v State Services Commission* [1984] 1 N.Z.L.R. 116; *Simpson v Attorney-General* [1994] 3 N.Z.L.R. 667. Also see *R v Grayson and Taylor* [1997] 1 N.Z.L.R. 399 for a different approach under Richardson P.
[27] See Cmnd.7758 (1979) and Cmnd.7800 (1980); see also Southern Rhodesia Act 1979; Zimbabwe Act 1979. Particularly useful on the aftermath of the Unilateral Declaration of Independence is C. Palley (1967) 30 *Modern Law Review* 263; [1968] *Public Law* 293.

Madzimbamuto v Lardner-Burke[28] which the Privy Council heard in a special application made by Madzimbamuto who challenged his detention under Southern Rhodesian emergency laws made in 1966. Lord Reid in the Privy Council made some useful
observations as to the extent of the legal powers of the United Kingdom's Parliament,
including the case where even if the United Kingdom Parliament acted "unconstitu-
tionally" it would not render the Act of Parliament invalid. The decision of the Privy
Council declared the UDI illegal and sought to enforce the Rhodesia Act 1965. It also
declared Madzimbamuto's detention illegal. Lord Reid's dicta included the following:

> "It is often said that it would be unconstitutional for the United Kingdom
> Parliament to do certain things, meaning that the moral, political and other
> reasons against doing them are so strong that most people would regard it as
> highly improper if Parliament did these things. But this does not mean that it is
> beyond the power of Parliament to do such things. If Parliament chose to do any
> of them the courts could not hold the Act of Parliament invalid".[29]

2–099   The decision in the Madzimbamuto case, while observed under United Kingdom law,
was not given effect in Southern Rhodesia. Attempts to solve the constitutional
impasse were long and difficult. Economic sanctions were applied by the United
Kingdom Government. After protracted discussions in 1980, following the passage of
the Southern Rhodesia Act 1979, the Zimbabwe Act 1979 and various statutory
instruments under that authority, enabling legislation permitted the setting-up of
Zimbabwe.[30] Zimbabwe became an independent state recognising black majority rule.

2–100   The above examples serve to show how the unwritten United Kingdom Constitution
has coped with a wide variety of diverse changes, stresses and innovations. As we have
seen, this includes: the creating of a union state and its evolution through devolution
into a new relationship between the regions and central government; the definition of
the constitutional status of other countries; the conditions for the granting of
independence to newly formed states; as well as the supervision of legislative changes
brought about by newly independent legislatures. In defining the shape of the political
union which makes up the United Kingdom of Great Britain and Northern Ireland, we
have seen that change has come about through gradual adaptation rather than a
radical reform of the constitution. Flexibility and a certain pragmatism characterise the
ability of the United Kingdom's constitutional arrangements to be reformed and
changed without seeming to alter any fundamental constitutional principle. This
characteristic of evolutionary change is also present when it comes to explaining
political and social developments within the United Kingdom such as the broadening
of the franchise in 1832, 1867 and 1880. This changed the nature of many political
institutions, but did not cause a reform of the constitutional arrangements. The South
Africa Act 1995 marked a significant change to take account of re-admission of South
Africa as a member of the Commonwealth on June 1, 1994.

[28] [1969] 1 A.C. 645.
[29] *ibid.*, p.723.
[30] Zimbabwe Act 1979.

APPEALS TO THE PRIVY COUNCIL

One of the most important implications of the United Kingdom's reputation and **2–101** influence is that the common law provides remedies for injustice. Upholding the rule of law is seen by many as a means to guarantee rights and liberties. The legacy of the common law and its international reputation has in part been built upon by the creation of a Judicial Committee of the Privy Council under the Judicial Committee Act 1833. The extension of the jurisdiction of the Judicial Committee to any appeal to the Privy Council was provided by the Judicial Committee Act 1844 from any court within any British Colony or possession abroad. The composition of the Judicial Committee has changed over time but consists of:

- the Lord Chancellor, the Lords of Appeal in Ordinary and the Lords Justices of Appeal and may include ex Lord Chancellors and retired Lords of Appeal;

- senior judges or ex-judges of Australia, New Zealand and other Commonwealth countries where an appeal lies;

- the Lord President and ex-Lord Presidents of the Council who do not normally sit.

The status of the Privy Council is enhanced by the seniority and experience of the **2–102** judges who sit. The original jurisdiction of the Judicial Committee included appeals from the Channel Islands, the Isle of Man, the colonies and at one time India. Today appeals to the Privy Council have declined. This is a sign of the growing self-confidence of many commonwealth countries and a desire to develop autonomy in judicial decisions. Countries such as Australia and Canada have abolished the right of appeal. Newly independent countries such as India, Pakistan and Cyprus have abolished the right of appeal. In New Zealand consideration is given to abolishing the right of appeal; however, in New Zealand appeals to the Privy Council are available from the Supreme Court and Court of Appeal.

The jurisdiction of the Privy Council includes a limited appellate jurisdiction over **2–103** the ecclesiastical courts of the Church of England, a legacy from the past. In recent times the scope of the work of the Judicial Committee has been expanded, initially through appeals granted by statute for a number of professional bodies and organisations such as under the Medical Act 1983, the Dentists Act 1984, and the Osteopaths Act 1993. The devolution statutes discussed above provide wide powers for the Judicial Committee to advise and rule on the constitutionality of legislation before it is enacted by the devolved Assembly or in the case of Scotland, devolved Parliament. There is also an important power for the Judicial Committee to hear devolution issues that may arise in litigation in the jurisdiction of the devolved powers.[31]

The Judicial Committee appears to be emerging as a constitutional court. In this **2–104** modern guise there is an issue of whether the work of the Judicial Committee should be merged with that of the House of Lords. The case in favour is that there is some overlap in membership so that members of the Judicial Committee hear appeals from

---

[31] D. Oliver, "The Lord Chancellor, the Judicial Committee of the Privy Council and devolution" [1999] *Public Law* 1.

countries that have written constitutions. This provides a breadth of experience in interpreting constitutional matters that is missing from the House of Lords on its own. The case against is that merging the jurisdiction of the two might require a fundamental re-think of the role of the judiciary.

2–105   There is a reserve power under s.4 of the Judicial Committee Act 1844 for the Crown to refer to the Judicial Committee matters for opinion. The future of the Judicial Committee looks secure as it is likely to develop its expertise in constitutional matters.

Europe and the Europeanisation of UK law

2–106   The continental influence on the common law extends from the development of the European Convention on Human Rights to membership of the European Community. Human rights are examined more fully later in the book. The result is recognisable as a hybrid, namely that the English common law system is overlaid with civil law principles and influences while still retaining its main common law characteristics. No one should underestimate the extent of the long-term impact of the United Kingdom's membership of the European Union. The development of the Community into the European Union signalled one of the considerable achievements of the past twenty years' efforts.

2–107   Joining the European Community in 1972 brought the United Kingdom into legal relations with a community legal order which already possessed an independent legal personality and its own institutions. The Community is the creation of three Treaty agreements: the Treaty of Paris 1951 setting up the European Coal and Steel Community; and two Treaties of Rome 1957 setting up the European Economic Community (EEC) and the European Atomic Energy Community. Only six countries formed the original membership which presently stands at 15. Five institutions carry out the objectives and exercise the powers of the Community, namely the Commission, the Council, the European Parliament, the Court of Justice and the Court of Auditors. A fourth Treaty, the Treaty on European Union, was signed at Maastricht and ratified in 1993 under the European Communities (Amendment) Act 1993. The creation of citizenship of the European Union is seen as a progression towards enjoying rights conferred by the Treaties as well as duties under them. Maastricht established the structures of the European Union, described in terms of the "three pillars" of the Union. The first and central pillar consists of the three European Communities each with their own legal status and functions. The two other pillars (detailed later) consist of intergovernmental agreements entered into by all 15 Members States of the Community. These agreements are implemented by joint action or agreement, but the European Court of Justice does not have jurisdiction over such agreements. The second pillar is the Common Foreign and Security Policy and the third pillar was first described as the Co-operation in Justice and Home Affairs, but it is now described as Title VI of Provisions on Police and Judicial Co-operation in Criminal Matters which covers immigration policy and police co-operation. Significantly the third pillar has been considerably extended to cover corruption, fraud, and preventing and combating crime including terrorism.

2–108   Since Maastricht, the European Union has developed considerably. The Treaty of Amsterdam which came into effect in 1999 and the Treaty of Nice signed on February

26, 2001 amends the Treaties further in terms of a *tranche* of amendments to the EC Treaty that will be incorporated after ratification. There are around 90 amendments and the aim is twofold: first to prepare the enlargement of the EU to around 27 members; and secondly, to make changes to the decision-making system in the EU especially in terms of Qualified Majority Voting. A further development is the Laeken Declaration and the Convention on the Future of Europe. The European Council in Laeken on December 14–15, 2001 concluded a Declaration on the Future of Europe and a timetable for implementation. The Convention's remit under the former French President Valery Giscard d'Estaing is "to consider the key issues arising from the Union's future development and try to identify the various possible responses". The findings of the Convention are intended to form the basis of an Intergovernmental Council in 2004. Progress within the European Union is largely dependent on the increase in its size and in its economic prosperity. Our starting point is to consider the five institutions of the Community in outline as follows.

The Commission

Under Articles 211–219 (Articles 155–163 as amended), the Commission consists of 20 members, made up of two each from the four largest member states and Spain and one from each of the other states. The Commission has primary responsibility for guarding the Treaties. The role of the Commissioners is settled in Article 10(2) of the Merger Treaty which requires that Commissioners refrain from "any action incompatible with their duties" and requires that they must not take instructions from their own governments. Article 213 stipulates that the Commissioners must be independent. As guardian of the Treaty, the Commission oversees Treaty obligations to be carried out by Member States. Powers to ensure compliance are contained in Article 226(169) of the EEC Treaty. The Commission has a five-year term and this is renewable. It is headed by a President who is appointed by common agreement among the Commissioners and by common accord of the Member States. **2–109**

The Commission has a triple obligation. First, it has the power to initiate Community action and relay to the Council proposals for consideration that fall within the remit of the Treaties. There is a new power granted to the Parliament under Article 192 to submit policies to the Commission and make proposals. The Council also may request the Commission to undertake studies. The Commission's second obligation is to formulate policy and, under a general power (Art. 308), to set the framework for the debate in the various institutions. This includes the main drafts of proposals and the legislative timetable for the year ahead. The third role is to act as the watchdog of the Community. Article 10 provides extensive powers to investigate and bring to an end any infringement of the Community rules. Particularly important is EC competition law. The implementation role of the Commission is probably its most complex. Implementation is undertaken through consultation with a wide range of regulatory committees and advisory bodies. The process is known as comitology and is one of the areas that has come under criticism for its complexity and lack of progress. The Commission may impose sanctions and penalties on individuals or companies that breach community rules. The Commission is granted extensive investigatory powers and under Article 9 of the Merger Treaty (now see the Treaty of Amsterdam, Article 9(2)) the Commission may exercise powers and functions that include enforcing the **2–110**

Treaty provisions and initiating Community policy through administering the community budget. In the case of a state breaching Community law there is a set
procedure.

2–111   This is a two-stage process. First, the Commission must deliver a reasoned Opinion
and ensure that the State concerned has an opportunity to submit its observations on
the question of whether the Member State has failed to fulfil its Treaty obligations.
Second, if the State does not comply with the Opinion within a specified period, the
Commission may go to the Court of Justice. An example in terms of enforcement
proceedings taken by the Commission against the United Kingdom was a case[32]
involving equal pay between men and women, a principle of the EEC Treaty under
Article 119. The outcome of the judgment delivered by the Court of Justice required
the United Kingdom Government to introduce new legislation to give effect to the
Equal Pay Directive. This involved amending the Equal Pay Act 1970 by the Equal Pay
(Amendment) Regulations 1983 as the relevant statutory instrument.[33]

2–112   This is a good illustration of the interconnection between overall policy objectives
contained in the EC Treaty and the force of law and interpretation by the Court of
Justice. In the case of equal wages the United Kingdom had not fully implemented the
Equal Pay Directive. The United Kingdom had argued that Article 1 of the Directive
was silent on the point and therefore did not require the determination of equal pay by
a job classification system. Further, it was argued that the worker could not insist on a
comparative evaluation of different work.

2–113   The work of the Commission is divided into approximately 24 Directorates
(currently under review). The Directorates may vary in size from large such as
Personnel and Administration (DGIX) employing 2,500, to small such as Enterprise
Policy (DGXXIII) employing about 80 people. The size of the Commission currently
stands at about 18,000 out of a total staff of about 26,400 for the European Union's
administration. The Commission may take action as guardian of the Treaties. For
example it may, under Articles 92–94 take action on what it regards as unacceptable
state action in the subsidisation of industry. In July 1990 it took action to recover £44.4
million worth of concessions given to British Aerospace at the time of the acquisition
of Rover cars. Eventually in May 1993 it recovered £57.6 million, the additional
amount due because of lost interest calculated from August 1990.

2–114   The Commission received considerable criticism over allegations of corruption
leading to the resignation of Jacques Santer. This has seriously weakened the
Commission and provided an opportunity for the Parliament to assert its role.
Increasingly the Commission is engaged in external relations which, in certain areas
must be carried out with the agreement of the European Parliament under Article
300(3).

The Council of the European Union

2–115   Under Articles 202–210 (Articles 145–154 amended) and Art. 9(2) of the Treaty of
Amsterdam, the Council of the European Union, hitherto the Council of the
European Communities, consists of the various ministers representing the Member

---

[32] Case 61/81 *Commission of the European Communities v UK* [1982] E.C.R. 2601.
[33] Equal Pay (Amendment) Regulations 1983 (SI 1983/1794).

States' governments. The limit on membership is one from each Member State. Thus its membership varies according to the subject area under discussion and the jurisdiction of the minister concerned. Unlike the Commission, where national self-interest of Member States is subservient to Community interests, the Council represents the collective views of each Member State as part of settling the objectives of the Treaties. Thus the Council is often engaged in bargaining and compromising national self-interest which is forged into Community policy. Foreign ministers meet as a General Council. There is a Presidency of the Council held in turn by each of the Member States for six months on a rotational basis. Increasing importance is given to the meeting of Heads of State and this is now recognised under Article 2 of the Single European Act.

The main role of the Council is contained in Article 202 and is primarily a co-ordinating role and a deliberative function to consult with the Commission. The Council has the final say on most secondary legislation and this provides opportunity for the more powerful Member States. The Council may override Parliament's opposition to a measure on a unanimous vote, which is required to amend proposals made by the Commission. Voting by the Council may be by a unanimous, qualified majority or a simple majority vote. The latter is not usually used. The use of a unanimous vote procedure was common in the early life of the Treaties to safeguard the Treaty areas that might have been amended. As the Community has developed, the use of qualified majority voting has become more prevalent. This is a sign of political maturity but also of the need for consensus-building to allow the Community to develop. **2–116**

Voting in the Council of Ministers by qualified majority takes place with votes weighted according to the size of each country. The weighting has changed as the Community has expanded. Article 205 EC provided that a new allocation of votes might be introduced, whereby 10 votes are allocated to the larger countries such as the United Kingdom, Germany, France and Italy; Spain has eight votes; Portugal, Belgium, Greece and the Netherlands each have five votes; Austria and Sweden have four votes each; and three votes each are accorded to Denmark, Finland and Ireland. Luxembourg has only two votes. The arrangement is that for a measure to be adopted, 62 votes are required. This represents 71 per cent of the votes. Where the Act is not a proposal from the Commission, an additional 10 votes are required. **2–117**

After the Single European Act 1986 and the Maastricht Treaty, the use of qualified majority vote was extended to apply to a greater range of matters concerned with the internal market. The Council operates on compromise but uncertainty exists as to the question of when unanimity is required and when national interest is said to apply. It remains to be seen the extent to which that potential will be realised. The scope for development is considerable. Considerable progress has been made especially in the use of qualified majority voting which includes the environment Article 175. The Council has roughly 2,500 personnel in permanent posts and 18 temporary posts. **2–118**

The European Parliament

The Treaties establishing the EC envisaged an assembly or representative body to represent the people of the Community. The past forty years has seen the role and function of the Parliament transformed. Since 1962 the European Parliament (Articles **2–119**

189–201, (Articles 137–144 EC as amended)) became its designated name and the Single European Act 1986 refers to such a body. Currently it has 626 members elected for a five-year term by the Member States. Each country is allocated a number of seats based on its size: Germany has 99 members; France, the United Kingdom and Italy each have 87 members; Spain has 64; the Netherlands, 31; Belgium, Greece and Portugal, 25; Sweden, 22; Austria, 21; Denmark and Finland, 16; Ireland, 15; and Luxembourg, 6. Direct elections from each Member State have existed since 1979. After the Amsterdam Treaty the number was expanded to a maximum of 700 and the Treaty of Nice forecasts an expansion to 738 to take account of the expansion in Member States. Initially the United Kingdom adopted a first-past-the-post system to elect its M.E.P.s (with the exception of Northern Ireland where proportional representation is used). In 1999 the closed regional list system was used . The voter is unable to identify his or her M.E.P. under the regional list system. This may cause a lack of Community support or electorate identification and support for the M.E.P. The regional list system also corresponds to the electoral arrangements for the regional chambers in England, and also elections to the devolved institutions in Scotland and Wales.

2–120   Occasionally a member of the national parliament may also be a "Euro MP" at the same time. There are concerns about the effectiveness of multi-membership in the hands of a single individual and steps are being considered to limit the number of bodies for which membership may be held simultaneously. There are also concerns about the low turnout at European elections in the United Kingdom. In 1999 the turnout was 24 per cent when the EU average turnout is 49.4 per cent. The low turnout for elections is a problem that has not been fully addressed. It may be a sign of voter apathy or disillusionment with the institutions of the European Union.

2–121   It is a mistake to regard the European Parliament as primarily a legislative body. Its function is "advisory" and supervisory. Many of the powers conferred on the Council require consultation with the Parliament. New powers enhance its role and include participation in the legislative process, budgetary responsibilities and a role in the election of the Commission. The Single European Act 1986 has developed the potential to change fundamentally the European Parliament's role. There is a co-operation procedure with the Council requiring the Parliament to give an opinion and, on a second reading stage, Parliament may approve, reject or amend the views contained in the legislation. Once agreed, the Act is formally the Council's measure and may be so adopted.

2–122   It is generally agreed that the Single European Act 1986 has long-term and far-reaching potential for expanding Parliament's role. One area which has already seen an increase in influence is the debate on the Community budget where the Parliament since 1988 has reached an inter-institutional agreement between itself, the Commission and the Council to set limits for Community expenditure; these cannot be altered without Parliamentary consent. Under Article 192 (Article 138d EC) the Parliament may take an initiative on behalf of a majority of its members. Considerable expansion in the Parliament's work on human rights has taken place over the past few years. There is a sub-committee to identify and tackle instances of abuse. The European Parliament also has the power to hear petitions from individual citizens or groups. The fact that the Parliament's role is expanding is clear as it has sufficient standing to challenge acts of the Council or the Commission,[34] powers to set up a system of

---

[34] *Roquette Freres SA v Council* case 138/79.

ombudsmen to investigate maladministration, and committees of inquiry[35] to review and investigate any allegations of misconduct. In 1999 following the Parliament's inquiry into allegations of abuse and fraud and corruption against the Commission, the Parliament's report[36] resulted in the resignation of the Commission. The Parliament's report into BSE, for example, is another high profile investigation. It is clear that there is considerable scope for altering the balance of powers between the Commission, the Council and the Parliament. It may be envisaged that there should be greater democratic accountability through an increase in parliamentary powers.

The Court of Justice

Under Articles 220–245 (formerly Articles 164–168), the Court of Justice, more formally the Court of Justice of the European Communities, ensures that the interpretation and application of Treaty law is observed. It sits as a supreme authority on all questions of Community law. The Court is comprised of 15 judges appointed from the Member States. There are six Advocates-General appointed by the Member States (Article 223) to act "with complete impartiality and independence, to make, in open court, reasoned submissions on cases brought before the Court of Justice". Sharing the same status, independence and security as the 15 judges, the 8 Advocates-General give a view of the case and although the court is not bound to accept their opinion, it often does so (Article 222). **2–123**

The procedure of the Court is discussed in more detail in chapter 9. It is sufficient to note that the Court's jurisdiction includes preliminary rulings under Article 234 (formerly Article 177) this requires any final court but permits any lower court jurisdiction over Community law arising in national courts and tribunals. Specific questions of Community law might be referred where relevant to the general issues in the case being heard before the national court. There is also a Court of First Instance (operational from November 1, 1989) with jurisdiction that extends to disputes between the Community and its employees, applications for judicial review and damages. There is the right of appeal on matters of law to the ECJ. The ECJ acts as an appeal court, a review court and a means to refer matters for consideration. It is intended that the Treaty of Nice will provide that the Court of Justice will consist of one judge for each Member State and an increase in the number of Advocates-General. At first instance there may be judicial panels to cope with additional workload problems. The scope of first instance jurisdiction has expanded to include a reference to the court for the determination of any dispute regarding any community obligation. **2–124**

The Court of Auditors

The Court of Auditors was established in 1977 after the Treaty amending Certain Financial Provisions of the Treaties 1975 came into force. After Maastricht the Court became recognised as a Community institution. Its task is to examine the accounts of **2–125**

---

[35] General Report of the European Parliament, 1996.
[36] *First Report on Allegations regarding Fraud, Mismanagement and Nepotism* in the European Commission, March 15, 1999. The second report followed on September 10, 1999.

the revenue and expenditure of community institutions and bodies funded by the Community. The Court of Auditors acts closely with the audit authorities of the Member States and has negotiated audit agreements as the basis for supervising Community funds that fall within the budget systems of the Member States' budgets. It is composed of 15 members unanimously appointed by the Council in consultation with the European Parliament. Renewable terms of office are in force for up to six years.

Change and Expansion of the European Union

2–126 The Treaty on European Union signed on February 7, 1992 at Maastricht was ratified by all Member States of the Community and adopted into the United Kingdom by the European Communities (Amendment) Act 1993. The Treaty establishes a European Union wider than the Economic Community. It amends the Treaty of Rome and thereby changes the name from the EEC Treaty to the EC Treaty. The Union contains two fields of activity; a Common Foreign and Security Policy, and Justice and Home Affairs.

2–127 Changes have been made to the EC's legislative procedures, most notably the introduction of a veto vested in the European Parliament. The Treaty on European Union is supplemented by a number of protocols, primarily in the field of developing the European Monetary System. The creation of a monetary Union has fallen into a number of stages under Articles 98–124. The first phase was the completion of the internal market and the removal of controls on the movement of capital. The second phase, begun in January 1994, ensured that there were economic criteria for convergence and this led to the creation of a single currency within the majority of Member States. The states that have opted out of the single currency are Denmark and the United Kingdom. It is expected that in the next five years, both these countries will join.

2–128 Forever evolving, the EU has continued along the pathway set in 1992. The Treaty of Amsterdam was signed on October 2, 1997 and came into force on May 1, 1999. This has led to a renumbering of the Treaties (as indicated above) and has strengthened the three pillars of the Union. As noted by many commentators, the Treaty of Amsterdam and the Treaty of Nice mark a broader political evolution of the European Union beyond the purely economic and market-driven focus of the early years of the European Community. Lasok[37] has noted that changes are:

> ". . . of such magnitude as the Treaty of European Union is not explicit enough to create a federal state or government. Therefore at this stage the Union is merely an organization of sovereign states with a strong federal potential."

Finally the United Kingdom has legislation bringing into force the changes in the community introduced since the Treaty of Nice under the European Communities (Amendment) Act 2002.

Sovereignty and the United Kingdom Parliament

2–129 Dicey's analysis of parliamentary sovereignty faces a severe challenge, when the outline of the EC discussed above is considered. His formulation gave Parliament ultimate sovereignty with potentially unlimited power. Even Dicey accepted that in exercising

---

[37] K.P.E. Lasok, *Law and Institutions of the European Union* (7th ed., Butterworths, London, 2001), p.36.

such powers Parliament's democratic basis might mean limitations on how future powers were exercised. Nevertheless, Dicey held the view that, however theoretical was the power of Parliament, this had overarching effect even when confronting practical problems. Membership of the European Union poses a severe test to United Kingdom sovereignty. As a result the courts have adjusted their conceptual language and understanding to adapt to change. The United Kingdom's membership of the EU is without a written constitution, dependent on ss.2 and 3 of the European Communities Act 1972. Community law in the United Kingdom may be said to be derived from this Act. S.2(4) permits Community law to be given priority to any United Kingdom legislation passed prior to 1973:

> "Any enactment passed or to be passed, other than one contained in this part of the Act, shall be construed and have effect subject to the . . . provisions of this section."

While s.2(1) provides for the direct applicability of Community law in the United Kingdom, and s.2(2) grants a general power for the future implementation of Community obligations by means of secondary legislation, there remains the question as to statutes passed after 1972 and the application of Community law. Where there may be inconsistencies or contradiction, Dicey's analysis would argue for the United Kingdom statute to be given priority by the courts over Community law.   **2–130**

A close reading of s.2(4) might suggest that in those terms Parliament in 1972 had given authority for priority to be given to Community law after 1972 and that even where there is conflict with a United Kingdom statute, community law must prevail. Dicey's traditional view is that parliamentary sovereignty does not leave Parliament free to bind its successors. Priority for Community law is not consistent with parliamentary sovereignty because entrenchment of Community law is impossible.   **2–131**

Craig[38] suggests that two possibilities might be adopted by the courts to resolve the problem. One is to modify Dicey's doctrine and accept that Community law has priority as part of the United Kingdom's membership conditions. The second possibility is to adopt an interpretation that Parliament is presumed not to intend statutes to override Community law, so that it is assumed that statutes passed after 1972 are impliedly consistent with community law.   **2–132**

Both possibilities have their respective merits. The second of Craig's options generally describes the direction the United Kingdom's courts have adopted until recently. The first requires consideration in the light of a recent House of Lords decision. The House of Lords referred to the European Court the issue of whether Community law was compatible with the Merchant Shipping Act 1988 in the *Factortame* case.[39] The 1988 Act had established a new register of British fishing vessels to ensure that fishing quotas under the Common Fisheries Policy were exploited by vessels which were truly linked to the United Kingdom's fishing economy. The result of the Act was that a number of Spanish-owned British Companies could not be registered on the register of British fishing vessels. As a result the Spanish fishermen   **2–133**

---

[38] Paul Craig, *Administrative Law* (4th ed., Sweet & Maxwell, London, 1999). Also see P. Craig, "Britain in the European Union" in *The Changing Constitution* (J. Jowell and D. Oliver ed., Oxford University Press, Oxford, 2000), p.61.
[39] [1991] 1 A.C. 603 at 659. Case C–213/89, [1990] E.C.R. I–2433; [1990] 3 C.M.L.R. 375.

sought a declaration that the 1988 Act was incompatible with the Community Treaty. The European Court and the Advocate-General gave their opinion that national courts must ensure compliance with EC law even where this might lead the national court not to apply an Act of Parliament. Lord Bridge[40] in the House of Lords responded to the European Court's ruling as follows:

> "Under the terms of the Act of 1972 it has always been clear that it was the duty of a United Kingdom court, when delivering final judgment to override any rule of national law, found to be in conflict with any directly enforceable rule of Community law . . . . Thus there is nothing in any way novel in according supremacy to rules of Community law in those areas to which they apply and to insist that, in the protection of rights under Community law national courts must not be inhibited by rules of national law from granting interim relief in appropriate cases, is no more than a logical recognition of that supremacy."

2–134   *Factortame*[41] is the clearest indication that EC membership is no longer compatible with Dicey's classical doctrine of Parliamentary sovereignty. The House of Lords has, in effect, abandoned Dicey's view in favour of a construction which indicates a willingness to apply Community law even where it may conflict with national law.

2–135   The *Factortame* case also makes clear the compatibility of Community law and international law or customary law. Britain had unsuccessfully relied on the Article 5 provisions of the Geneva Convention to make its case. Thus a Member State of the European Union cannot rely upon its rights even if granted under international treaty law to justify non-compliance with the rules of the Community.

2–136   The British courts in a number of cases have taken account of Community law. In the case of *Garden Cottage Foods v Milk Marketing Board*[42] a party injured by another's abuse of a dominant position, may be entitled to damages under Article 86. Directly applicable rights and obligations created by the Community Treaty take precedence over national law as has been accepted in *Simmenthal*[43] and more recently in *Factortame*.[44] Equally significant is the recognition by UK courts of the availability of damages in respect of liability for legislative breaches of Community law.[45] The acceptance by the courts of the *Francovich*[46] principle, whereby damages are available, broadens the range and scope of Community law. Inevitably this may lead to a rights agenda incorporated into the institutions of the United Kingdom.[47] This extends beyond the boundaries of public law to private law and the issues raised by commercial observance of the EU's competition rules. Thus the Francovich principle applies to all breaches of Community law whether committed by a Member State or other entity.[48]

---

[40] Lord Bridge in *Factortame* [1991] 1 A.C. 603 at 659.
[41] *R. v Secretary of State for Transport Ex p. Factortame Ltd* (No.2) [1991] 1 A.C. 603; Case C–213/89; [1990] E.C.R. I–2433; [1990] 3 C.M.L.R. 375.
[42] [1984] A.C. 130; [1984] 3 W.L.R. 143.
[43] Case 106/77 *Amministrazione v Simmenthal*: [1978] E.C.R. 629; [1978] 3 C.M.L.R. 263; *Emmott v Minister for Social Welfare* [1993] I.C.R. 8.
[44] [1991] 1 A.C. 603; Case C–213/89, [1990] E.C.R. I–2433; [1990] 3 C.M.L.R. 1.
[45] *R. v Secretary of State for the Home Department Ex p. Gallagher* [1996] 2 C.M.L.R. 951.
[46] *Francovich v Italy* Cases C–6 & 9/90) [1991] E.C.R. I–5357; [1992] I.R.D.L.R. 84.
[47] *Bowden v South West Water Services* [1999] 3 C.M.L.R. 180.
[48] *Crehan* case (C–453/99, *Crehan* unreported [2001].

THE FUTURE CONSTITUTIONAL ARRANGEMENTS IN THE UK: SOME CONCLUSIONS

We have seen throughout this chapter how the United Kingdom's constitutional   **2–137** arrangements have undergone change and transformation. Is now the time for a rethink? In 1973 the Royal Commission on the Constitution[49] (known as the Kilbrandon Commission) considered the structure and organisation of the United Kingdom's constitution. It recommended the creation of subordinate Parliaments in Scotland, and Wales, on the model of devolution under the Northern Ireland Constitution. No recommendation was made for a written constitution nor a fundamental reconsideration of our constitutional arrangements. The granting of devolution to England, Wales, Scotland, Northern Ireland and London provides a new constitutional framework for the United Kingdom.

The United Kingdom's membership of the EC applies a whole variety of different   **2–138** laws to the United Kingdom. Regulations bind all Member States and take effect without the need for further implementation. Directives are binding on Member States but leave the choice to national authorities as to the form and method. They are not directly applicable, but in certain circumstances can be directly applied by the courts. Decisions made by the European Court are directly applicable and binding on those to whom they are addressed. This provides for the strengthening of EC policy over a wide variety of issues of national concern.

The development of Community institutions such as the Council, Commission and   **2–139** Parliament leads after 1992 to a single European market and has gradually shifted more power to the European Parliament. The "Luxembourg Six" as they are known refers to the accession of Poland, the Czech Republic, Hungary, Slovenia, Estonia and Cyprus and the timetable is likely to be before 2005. The expansion of the European Union to 27 members will have enormous significance. Some favour adopting a federal States of Europe perspective with the necessary constitutional changes in both European and national institutions. The traditional doctrines of the United Kingdom's constitution which help explain our present constitutional arrangements do not necessarily help us to understand the future of our existing institutions. EC policy influences our laws on competition policy, the free movement of goods, state aids, and the free movement of persons throughout the Community. Energy, the environment, agriculture and fisheries, transport, social security and sex discrimination have also been important areas in the development of EC law. National sovereignty is so bound up with these areas that Parliament's authority to legislate has become integrated with EC legislative policy. The application of Community law seems no longer dependent on Dicey's perception of where Parliament's power ultimately lies.

SUMMARY AND CONCLUSIONS

- The constitutional history and sovereignty of the United Kingdom is defined   **2–140** by the creation of the various Acts of Union with Wales, Scotland and Ireland. Relations with the Commonwealth have helped delineate parliamentary and political power.

[49] Cmnd.5460 (1973).

- Membership of the EU is a major influence in formulating legal, economic and political decision making. The EU is not static and membership provides a *process* for future development and an agenda for change. Expansion of its membership is likely to bring about further consideration of a European Constitution with wide-ranging implications. While it is often difficult to predict future developments it is certain that EU law is more integral to the legal system of the United Kingdom than anyone might have foreseen or understood.
- Devolution is also the beginning of a *process*. While maintaining the idea of legal sovereignty in the United Kingdom Parliament, it is likely that devolution will be led by pressure for change at the regions.

FURTHER READING

Introductory books include: Anthony King, *Does the United Kingdom still have a Constitution?* (D. Oliver and G. Drewry ed., Sweet & Maxwell, London, 2001); *The Law and Parliament* (Butterworth, London, 1998); G. Ganz, *Understanding Public Law* (3rd ed., Sweet & Maxwell, London, 2001); Paul Silk and Rhodri Walters, *How Parliament Works* (4th ed. Longman, Essex, 1999.

Useful textbooks include: de Smith, *Constitutional and Administrative Law* (Rodney Brazier ed., 8th ed., Penguin, London, 1998); E.C.S. Wade and A.W. Bradley, *Constitutional and Administrative Law* (12th ed., Longman, Essex, 1998). For an historical dimension see: W. Cornish, *Law and Society in England and Wales 1750–1950* (Sweet & Maxwell, London, 1989); A.V. Dicey, *Introduction to the Study of the Law of the Constitution* (Macmillan, 1885); C. Munro, *Studies in Constitutional Law* (2nd ed., Butterworths, 1999), p.3; *The Changing Constitution* (J. Jowell and D. Oliver ed., 4th ed., Oxford University Press, Oxford, 2001).

For a theoretical perspective see: Martin Loughlin, *Sword and Scales* (Hart Publishing, Oxford, 2000).

A useful political science perspective may be found in: Ian Budge, Ivor Crewe, David McKay and Ken Newton, *The New British Politics* (2nd ed., Longman, Essex, 2001); Bill Jones, Denos Kavangah, Michael Moran and Philip Norton, *Politics UK* (4th ed., Longman, Essex, 2001).

On devolution see: N. Burrows, *Devolution* (Sweet & Maxwell, London, 2000); Aidan O'Neill, "Judicial Politics and the Judicial Committee: The Devolution Jurisprudence of the Privy Council" (2001) 64 *Modern Law Review* 603.

On Europe see: Josephine Steiner and Lorna Woods, *Textbook on EC Law* (7th ed., Blackstone, London, 2000).

Chapter 3

Parliament

Introduction

The role of Parliament and its fundamental importance in the Constitution is considered in this chapter. Technically, Parliament consists of the Queen, the House of Commons which is a directly elected body and the House of Lords which is appointed but is currently being reformed. Reform of the House of Lords has been a recurring theme throughout the past century. The difficulty of reform is in achieving a balance between the continuity of the past, whereby patronage provided access to the Lords, and the changes needed to make the Lords a modern second chamber. It is broadly accepted that the role of the Lords is as a revising chamber, thus the pre-eminence of the Commons is unchallenged. The first stage of Lords' reform was achieved under the House of Lords Act 1999 which provided for 92 hereditary peers 90 to be elected from among hereditary peers to sit temporarily in a transitional House of Lords. The elected hereditary peers signal the end of the hereditary peerage once the final composition of the House of Lords is settled. Currently, there are 695 members of the Lords, 92 hereditary peers, 549 life peers, 28 Law Lords and 26 bishops and archbishops. **3–001**

The United Kingdom's system of government in formal terms is described as a constitutional monarchy. Parliamentary government describes the fact that the Government's authority depends on the confidence of the House of Commons. By virtue of having no formal written constitution, Government operates within the boundaries set by a variety of laws, conventions and understandings. In fact the United Kingdom's constitutional arrangements provide largely unfettered powers to the government of the day who are able through their majority in Parliament to exercise control over Parliament and its procedures relatively free from any restraint. **3–002**

As a result the Government of the day may appear to enjoy unparalleled freedoms compared to countries with a written constitution. The source of government power may be traced to the relationship between Government and Parliament. Government within the United Kingdom's constitutional arrangements is said to be limited and responsible. This means that the Government is accountable to Parliament and, through elections, representative. As explained in the previous chapter, the sovereignty of Parliament may become too easily the sovereignty of the House of Commons. The political reality of power is that the government, having the majority of seats in the Commons, has the overall influence and authority over how decisions are to be taken. Political legitimacy flows from the authority of elections and the control of government business in the Commons allows the government to exert influence over Parliament **3–003** itself. Lord Hailsham saw the danger[1] that "the sovereignty of the Commons has increasingly become, in practice the sovereignty of the government". There are few countries that have government able to exercise political power through legislation that is largely unfettered by the concerns of judicial challenge or institutional intervention. The point is well summarised by Ewing[2]:

"British constitutional arrangements nevertheless provided the best means for social reform in the sense that there were no institutional restraints on a legally sovereign legislature and a politically sovereign electorate. And the best means also for social reform in the sense that the hierarchy of rights in the British constitution did not distinguish between rights according to their substance, but only according to their source. So unlike in other constitutional regimes, there was no priority in the British constitution for civil and political rights over social and economic rights."

3–004   An important feature of the government's day-to-day use of political power is the use of the party Whips in the system of whipping, which places pressure on M.P.s to vote according to party policy. This is an important mechanism in the hands of the government to force M.P.s on the government side to vote the government's Bills into law. A similar system among the opposition parties has the effect of strengthening party solidarity in opposition to government policy. Party political power is therefore an important influence on the workings and practices of the House of Commons. An added dimension to government is the use and appointment of political advisors within government to project the government's message in the media. The art of government is rapidly becoming the task of media presentation. This represents a paradigm shift from a focus on Parliament and its procedures to the media and presentational skills. This shift may not endure beyond the life-time of one or more governments but it signals a remarkable re-formulation of political power. In medieval times the general use of the term *parliament* meant[3] "any meeting for speech or conference". In that sense the institution of Parliament is linked to the popular idiom of the day—thus the media and presentation are given such importance.

3–005   In this chapter the focus is on the functions of Parliament, explaining its role in passing legislation, and in the debate and scrutiny of government. The role and possible reform of the House of Lords is considered. Finally, the privileges of Parliament are examined in the context of the rights and immunities of Members of Parliament and the work of the Committee on Standards in Public Life begun by Lord Nolan, now chaired by Sir Nigel Wicks. The new Select Committee of the House of Commons on Standards and Privileges was established in 1995 as a response to the setting-up of a Standing Committee on Standards in Public Life chaired by Lord Nolan in October 1994 following newspaper allegations concerning M.P's who may have accepted payment for putting down parliamentary questions. Allegations of corruption and sleaze have necessitated an investigatory role for the Committee rather than depending on the form of self-regulation that appeared to be acceptable in the past.

[1] Lord Hailsham, *Elective Dictatorship* (*The Listener Dimbleby lecture*, London, 1976) 1976, pp.430–431.
[2] Keith Ewing, "The Unbalanced Constitution" in *Sceptical Essays on Human Rights* (T. Campbell, K. Ewing and A. Tomkins, ed., Oxford University Press, Oxford, 2001), p.104.
[3] J. Griffith and M. Ryle, *Parliament* (Sweet & Maxwell, London, 1989), p.3.

The creation of a Parliamentary Commissioner for Standards, removable only by a resolution of the House, became necessary in order to maintain the register of M.P.s interests and to investigate any compliant made about an individual M.P. In addition to these investigative powers, there are powers to oversee a Code of Conduct and to liaise with the Committee on Standards and Privileges in Misconduct Cases.

PARLIAMENT, GOVERNMENT AND THE DOCTRINE OF THE SEPARATION OF POWERS

Griffith and Ryle[4] explain the meaning of the term "Parliament" in its broadest sense "to refer to the House of Commons and the House of Lords, and the institution called the Executive or the Government." This explanation draws attention to the constitutional relationship between Parliament and Government. The ability of Government to control Parliament is a striking characteristic of the United Kingdom's constitutional arrangements and a sign of the strength of party politics. That such control may exist reflects the strength of political power over the institutions of the United Kingdom's Constitution.   **3–006**

Strictly speaking unlike most countries with a written constitution, the United Kingdom's constitutional arrangements do not operate under the formal requirements of the doctrine of the separation of powers. This may help explain the fact that Cabinet Government operates with a parliamentary Executive; and that the Law Lords may act as both legislators and judges, although in practice the Law Lords abstain from party political matters in debates in the House of Lords.   **3–007**

The doctrine of the separation of powers is based on the theory that the separation of the legislative, executive and judicial functions provide the best means to restrain or prevent any abuse of governmental power. Originally the idea of separation of powers emanates from ancient Greece, and Aristotle believed in the ideals of government according to law. Associated with the ideals of accountable government was the perspective that more than one interest in government must be withheld from a single individual. This gave rise to the theory of mixed government, to avoid absolute power and to divide powers thus preventing any monopolistic tendencies. Writers such as Bolingbroke viewed the constitution as dependent on "balance" and in the eighteenth century government was limited by the idea of balance between the different organs of government, by ensuring that each part should work in balance with the other. In the seventeenth and eighteenth centuries the philosophy of Locke and Montesquieu[5] became influential. The philosophy was largely descriptive unlike its modern formulation which has become prescriptive of how government should govern. Munro[6] draws a sharp distinction between the doctrine as a " prescription" of what ought to be done and the description of how the constitution may exhibit certain characteristics. The separation of powers doctrine was adopted in countries with written constitutions,   **3–008**

---

[4] *ibid.*

[5] Locke, *Second Treatise of Civil Government* (1690) and Montesquieu, *The Spirit of Laws* (1748). T.R.S. Allan, *Law, Liberty and Justice* (1993), pp.48–64. M.J.C. Vile, *Constitutionalism and the Separation of Powers* (1967).

[6] C. Munro, *Studies in Constitutional Law* (2nd ed., 1999), p.303.

most notably in America in the Federal Constitution of 1798. As a theory of government in the United Kingdom, it has been influential but not as an absolute and rigid rule. In essence the doctrine describes how power should be exercised rather than the realities of how power is enjoyed. As the Donoughmore Committee[7] commented, within the United Kingdom's constitutional arrangements "there is no such thing as the absolute separation of powers". Opposition to the theory of a separation of powers doctrine in England came from the view that a balanced constitution controlled by checks and balances affords the best protection against abuse. On this view all the different elements within the constitutional arrangements may be held in equilibrium. Reliance on a balanced constitution emerged in the context of the development of parliamentary democracy. The pre-eminence of political power, the organic nature of the constitution itself and the reliance on conventional rules defeated any demand for a separation of powers doctrine in the eighteenth and nineteenth centuries.

3–009   There was support for the theory of the separation of powers in the works of William Blackstone in his influential *Commentaries on the Laws of England*. Blackstone's influence did not succeed in elevating the separation of powers into a fundamental design for the constitution. In modern Britain the doctrine is deficient as an accurate description of present day constitutional arrangements. However, in modern times, the doctrine does retain important value as a descripion of how the different elements of our constitution might or should operate as independent from each other. This makes the value of the doctrine of the separation of powers an important element in the protection of the judiciary and its independence. As Lord Templeman explained in *Re M*,[8]:

"... Parliament makes the law, the executive carry the law into effect and the judiciary enforce the law."

3–010   The question arises as to how the doctrine stands in relationship to the actual working constitution. A useful insight is in the office of Lord Chancellor. Appointment is in the patronage of the Prime Minister of the day and the office holder has a seat in cabinet. The Lord Chancellor combines executive, legislative and judicial functions. Constitutional reform is also within his remit. As a member of the executive he is in charge of an important government department with a large budget and responsibility for the administration of justice. He is accountable to Parliament for his department and bound by the doctrine of ministerial and cabinet responsibility. As a senior member of the House of Lords he is given a peerage on appointment and assumes for the Lords the role of the Speaker in the House of Commons. He participates in debates and promotes legislation on the part of the government. He votes and speaks for the government. As a senior judge, the Lord Chancellor sits on the judicial committees of the House of Lords and Privy Council. He is President of the Supreme Court in England and of the Chancery Division. *Ex officio* the Lord Chancellor is a Judge of the Court of Appeal. The question arises as to how all three functions may be discharged by the office holder. Law Lords as a general rule rarely speak in debate in the Lords. In the past few years, the current holder of the office of Lord Chancellor has had a

---

[7] *Report of the Committee on Ministers' Powers*, Cmd.4060 (1932), pp.4–5.
[8] *M, Re* [1993] 3 W.L.R. 433.

relatively minor role in appeals. Annually there are about 65 appeals in the House of Lords and 60 appeals in the Privy Council. It is estimated that since May 1997 the Lord Chancellor has sat in only one case in the Privy Council and in the Appellate Committee in about 8 cases. Significantly, in 1999, the Lord Chancellor was challenged when he attempted to sit in a case involving police liability for the death of a prisoner in police cells. It was argued that his participation in the panel to hear the appeal might breach the fair trial provision under Article 6 of the European Convention on Human Rights.[9] As a result the Lord Chancellor declined to sit. It might be suggested that the doctrine of the separation of powers is influential, although not binding on the way the powers of the Lord Chancellor are exercised today. As a result it is difficult to predict how the Lord Chancellor is expected to behave. At a minimum it might be suggested that, taking account of the sensitivity of the position of government policy on legal issues, it is impossible for the Lord Chancellor to sit in any of the major cases coming before the Lords that involves a review of government policy however oblique. This may be an over-cautious view but the impact of the Human Rights Act 1998 makes it unlikely that cases covering the wide ambit of governmental powers that fall within public law, devolution or human rights, are able to be determined by any panel including of the Lord Chancellor. The influence of the separation of powers doctrine is likely to become greater and not less in the coming years.

PARLIAMENT'S ROLE

Walter Bagehot in *The English Constitution*[10] identified the role and function of Parliament to provide an expression of the will of the people, to provide information and to have an educative value. These roles are in addition to the functions of providing legislation and finance. A brief historical overview allows us to see all these roles emerge as part of the evolution of parliamentary democracy. Parliament's legal and political authority developed historically, and explains the close relationship between government and legislature as part of Parliament's evolution.   **3–011**

The early medieval meaning given to *Parliament* was that of "any meeting for speech or conference." In its law-making function Parliament shared judicial and legislative business. In the thirteenth century a common practice was to use parliamentary power to redress specific grievances contained in petitions presented to Parliament. Earlier kings asserted a wide power to redress grievances to individuals and a system of petitions was well established by 1280. Edward I was able to exploit the granting of petitions to extend his influence over even the most powerful of his subjects via the King's Council in his Parliament.   **3–012**

During the reign of Edward III (1327–77), the use of regular petitions being presented to the Commons was established. The Crown made law through parliamentary legislation as a means to expedite petitions in a similar way that Government Bills may be introduced in Parliament today.   **3–013**

[9] D. Woodhouse, *The Office of Lord Chancellor* (2001) p.127.
[10] Walter Bagehot, *The English Constitution* with an introduction by R. Crossman (1963).

3–014   During the fourteenth century Parliament gained influence through a variety of practices which assisted in the development of parliamentary power. Taxation required the consent of both Houses of Parliament and hence also required regular meetings. Parliaments, by the statutes of 1330 and 1362, were required to be held frequently. Although this was not always followed, Parliament began to meet regularly and developed a constitutional basis of "making law". By the end of the fifteenth century the institution of Parliament had replaced the Great Council of the King.

3–015   In the seventeenth century Parliament's powers grew in importance and influence as its constitutional status developed. The Petition of Right 1627 established that taxation was not to be levied without the consent of Parliament. In the seventeenth century, events of constitutional significance included: the English Civil War (1642-49); the defeat of the King and his execution; and the operation by Cromwell of a protectorate (1653). These events resembled a revolution. In 1661, however, the "convention Parliament of Lords and Commons" restored the monarchy by inviting Charles II to take the throne. The restoration settlement legitimated the conventions developed by Parliament under Cromwell but also asserted the King's authority in Parliament under the Constitution. Parliament's authority ensured its continued supremacy. An uneasy settlement between King and Parliament led to the Bill of Rights 1688 which curtailed royal power under Parliament's authority. James II (1685-88) abdicated and fled, but constitutional change was accomplished by Parliament's acceptance of the Bill of Rights and, under William and Mary, by Royal Assent to Parliament's authority.

3–016   The term "Queen in Parliament" has the technical significance of the power to make laws vested in the Queen, Lords and Commons and may be found in the enacting words of an Act of Parliament. In common usage "Parliament" is often used as a term to denote that authority.

3–017   The eighteenth and nineteenth centuries saw the continued development of Parliament's legislative activities. It had an important role in the life of the nation even though the franchise was narrow and unrepresentative of popular support, because few were allowed to vote. The Septennial Act 1715 provided for an election every seven years. During the eighteenth century the principal advisors of the King formed a cabinet and by convention were members of one or other House of Parliament. Support for policies was often obtained through corrupt practices and seldom through popularity. The offices of state, such as Prime Minister, emerged as royal influence replaced royal power. In more modern times monarchy has endured even after the abdication crisis in 1936 when Edward VIII abdicated the throne.

3–018   The nineteenth century with the two major Reform Acts of 1832 and 1867 gave the franchise to a wider section of the population than ever before, and allowed all male urban householders to vote. Similarly, in 1880 county householders were granted the vote.

3–019   Parliament's legislative activities were greatly altered and change was brought about by various political, economic and social factors rather than constitutional reform. It is noteworthy that no general review of the Constitution occurred. Change was organic and often unpredictable. Constitutional arrangements preserved what was needed and discarded the unnecessary.

3–020   The style and content of legislation deserves mention. Up until the end of the nineteenth century, legislation was narrow in scope and covered matters of local and even temporary significance. Watson[11] observes that there was "a paucity of general statutes covering what we would term private law or mercantile law". Subjects covered included such matters as divorce through Acts of Parliament, patents, and the incorporation of companies with limited liability. Rarely were general statutes passed and as codification was resisted in the common law tradition, there were only a few statutes which "consolidated" rather than codified the law, such as the Offences Against the Person Act 1861. Such statutes often expressed in statutory language the development by the judges of the main principles through the common law.

Dicey observed that Parliament had become the repository of all public power with Parliament overseeing a unitary state and legislating on particular issues no matter how local or specific. On this view Parliament exercised all public power. Craig refers to Dicey's analysis as "parliamentary monopoly"; a belief that Parliament's legislative power in all matters was accompanied by the equally important view that the Commons could and should control the Executive. This has given rise to a strong tradition setting out "the order of things" which has been influential in the study of the Constitution.   **3–021**

The period of transformation from Parliament acting through legislation to deal with individual problems and grievances into a more collective action on social, economic and political problems may be said to have begun in the mid-nineteenth century. Precise dates are difficult to provide but it is generally agreed that between 1830 and 1850 central government expanded its functions to include railways, factories, poor law, public health and licensing. Legislation concerning these areas may be identified to indicate the growth in government activities and administration. Government policies were proactive in providing the impetus for change in society in the industrial and agrarian revolution of the period.   **3–022**

Simultaneous with the growth of central government activities, local and municipal government also changed. The Reform Act 1832 had broadened the franchise for central government. A Royal Commission reported on municipal corporations and their defects led to the Municipal Corporations Act 1835, which extended the franchise for local government. The result was that after 1835 the franchise included a wider range of people than before, bringing urban middle class interests into the activities of local government. Local government was further reformed, after the 1867 and 1884 central government franchise was expanded; the Local Government Act 1888 instituted a two-tier system of government in the metropolis.   **3–023**

Craig[12] points out that the local government system developed in the nineteenth century survived virtually unchanged until 1972:   **3–024**

> "The metropolis had a two-tier system with the London County Council at the top and metropolitan boroughs providing the second tier. County boroughs, the larger towns, were single purpose authorities. The counties were slightly more complex. The County Council was the main authority for the area. Beneath it existed three

[11] A. Watson, *Failures of the Legal Imagination* (Edinburgh, 1988), pp.39–40; A. Watson, *Society and Legal Change* (Edinburgh, 1977); Milsom, *Historical Foundations of the English Common Law* (2nd ed., 1981); F. Pollock and F.W. Maitland, *The History of English Law* (Cambridge, 1968); A. Watson, *The Evolution of Law* (Johns Hopkins, 1985); P.S. Atiyah and R.S. Summers, *Form and Substance in Anglo-American Law* (Oxford, 1987); M. Lobban, *The Common Law and English Jurisprudence 1760–1850* (Oxford, 1991).
[12] P. Craig, *Administrative Law* (2nd ed., 1989), pp.34–51. Brebner, "Laissez-faire and State Intervention in nineteenth century Britain" (1948) 8 *Journal of Economic History* 61.

types of institution: non County boroughs; urban districts; and rural districts. The last of these could have parish councils within its area, thereby providing a third tier of authority."

3–025   Local government is a good example of the extensive legislative powers granted by Parliament to enable local authorities to expand their activities and diversify their interests.

3–026   Changes also occurred in parliamentary procedures for legislation, reflecting a change in the policies and directions of the government. Private Bill procedures and private Members' Bills gave way to Public General Acts of Parliament.

3–027   Craig notes two further trends in the centralisation of legislative power. The first is the use of standing committees of the whole House, which favoured discussion by the Government of policy in detail and helped expedite busy legislative programmes. Added to this was the increase in Cabinet Committees to discuss and debate any legislative proposals, thus preparing the way for the safe passage of proposals knowing that agreement and party political support would most likely be given. The second is the growth of delegated legislation which considerably broadened the scope of government powers and ministerial discretion; this is discussed in more detail in Chapter 10.

3–028   The growth of party politics is also significant in the development of Parliament's political authority. The extension of the franchise broadened Parliament's appeal and rooted its legitimacy in its responsiveness to the popular vote. This could easily detract from the power and authority of Parliament itself, if voting patterns were not focused on group activity and electoral manifestos. Successive governments responded by tightening control over party political policies and discipline which included the use of guillotine procedures, the whip system of party voting and the selection of members of Parliament to sit in committees. Electoral choices through elections replaced appointments through patronage, but patronage returned in a different guise as a means of operating party politics effectively.

3–029   The development of the parliamentary system of government is an important part of the discussion of administrative law. It also provides a perspective on the constitutional arrangements for the United Kingdom in its relations within the European Community.

THE FORMS OF LEGISLATION

3–030   Both Houses of Parliament follow set procedures and rules. The machinery of both Houses through the Officers constitute an important element in ensuring that in exercising its functions Parliament acts correctly. The rules of procedure may be traced back to the fourteenth century; they have been revised and updated in the light of experience and practice. One of the most important areas is in the procedures on legislation. In 1997 the creation of a Select Committee on the Modernisation of the House of Commons is a welcome sign that some attention is being given to the way in which legislation is debated and scrutinised.

3–031   In defining Parliament's major role, attention is given to using the general term "legislation." The term legislation may be used in three senses. First, it refers to "Acts of Parliament." These are primary rules contained in government legislation and called "Public General Acts". Erskine May[13] defined such an Act as "a law affecting the whole public, one which belongs to the *jus generale publicae*": generally today we would recognise such Acts as forming the bulk of Government policy and as reflecting a major part of the legislative role of Parliament. Second, the term may refer to private Acts of Parliament. Erskine May[14] referred to such Acts as being "in the form of an Act of Parliament, some special rule affecting only a special section of the nation, what may be called *jus particulor*". Private Acts of Parliament were once an important device to promote specific interests—local authorities, railways, companies—and even to circumvent the existing law on planning matters. Since 1987 criticism of the use of private Bill procedures in the planning system led to a recommendation[15] that private legislation should be available only as a last resort and not as an alternative to established statutory procedures. In fact, the increase in Public General Acts has reduced the quantity of private Bills. A specialised procedure is required for the introduction and debate of private Bills which is expensive and time-consuming.

Private Bills may be introduced by members of Parliament and are usually termed "private Members' Bills". There are primarily two methods or procedures which may be used. The first is a ballot of Members of Parliament held each session giving 20 Members the opportunity to introduce a private Bill in the limited time available. Since 1972 the Government has allocated annually £200 towards drafting expenses but even this modest change has little impact. In 1982 Norman St. John Stevas M.P. successfully introduced his private Members' Bill, Parliamentary Control of Expenditure (Reform Bill). This Bill was later adopted by the Government of the day in return for a number of changes which were duly made. The new revised Bill successfully became law as the National Audit Act 1983. Nevertheless the experience was far from satisfactory, illustrating the dependence of the success of a private Members' Bill on government assistance and drafting. **3–032**

The second procedure is under "the Ten Minute Rule". Members of Parliament **3–033** unsuccessful in the ballot may set down a motion for leave to introduce a Bill on Tuesdays and Wednesdays. Three weeks' notice is usually required and the majority of such Bills have been allowed to lapse and are unsuccessful. It is estimated that only 10 to 12 private Members' Bills become law each session. The ballot procedure is usually the best chance of a private Member's Bill becoming law.

In constitutional terms there is no legal distinction between the authority of a **3–034** private Act and a public general Act. The courts are unwilling to allow a challenge to the validity of either a public or private Act as explained in 1974 in *Pickin v British Railways Board*.[16] This marks out the limits of judicial scrutiny under the United Kingdom's constitutional arrangements. This does not, however, prevent the Courts from taking account of EC law and whenever there is a conflict between a United Kingdom Act of Parliament and EC law, resolving the conflict in favour of the latter. This includes the recent *Factortame*[17] case illustrating the overriding of a United Kingdom Act of Parliament in subservience to EC law.

[13] T. Erskine May, *Parliamentary Practice* (London, 1997). Also see D. Miers and A. Page, *Legislation* (2nd ed., 1990).
[14] *ibid.*
[15] *Report of the Joint Committee on Private Bill Procedure 1987–88* (1988 HC 625; HL 97).
[16] [1974] A.C. 765.
[17] [1991] 1 A.C. 603; Case C–213/89, [1990] E.C.R. I–2433; [1990] 3 C.M.L.R. 375.

3–035   The term legislation may also apply to a third category of Bill known as a "hybrid Bill". It is difficult to provide an exact definition of a hybrid Bill. Erskine May[18] defines it as legislation which "affects a particular private interest in a manner different from the private interests of other persons or bodies of the same category or class".

3–036   One caveat to introducing a private Bill whether or not it is a hybrid Bill, is Standing Order No.48 of the House of Commons, namely that the main object of such a Bill may not create a charge on public funds, as this lies within the allocation of ministerial power only. In the case of a dispute over the exact procedure for a Bill, the matter may be adjudicated by the Clerk of Public Bills and the Members concerned.

3–037   The vast majority of government legislation is to be found in legislation introduced into the House of Commons. However, it is possible for the government to introduce legislation in the Lords for tactical reasons. Two important examples of this are the Crime and Disorder Act 1998 and the Human Rights Act 1998. The former makes changes to the sentencing and criminal procedure in England and Wales and to the substantive criminal law in Scotland. The latter incorporates the bulk of the European Convention on Human Rights into domestic law. In addition to primary legislation, the legislative output of the Government also includes a vast number of statutory instruments which are loosely described by the phrase "delegated legislation". Generally the average number of public general Acts in any one year is 63; a corresponding assessment of the number of statutory instruments comes to over 6,000. Since 1900 the growth in legislation has been a remarkable feature of Parliament's activities. Griffith and Ryle conclude[19]: "In our opinion the growth of work and activity is the most noteworthy change in the functioning of the House of Commons in this century".

3–038   As we shall see in Chapter 10 the growth in legislation has had an effect on the procedures, character and nature of the House of Commons and this includes the use of select committees. Backbench Members of Parliament have been given a greater role through the formation of the numerous select committees to expedite legislation.

3–039   A distinctive feature of English law has been the formal structures and procedures adopted. Atiyah and Summers identified the heavy reliance on statute law[20]:

> ". . . the English political-legal system relies more heavily than the American on statute law and less on case-law, and that, because statute law is more formal than case-law, this is one factor which makes English law more formal."

3–040   The authors conclude that to a large extent the wide use of legislation in the United Kingdom is a reflection of the constitutional arrangements present under the parliamentary system of government. The characteristics of the parliamentary system may be enumerated as follows: strong centralised political institutions; the English judiciary has a relatively weak role as compared with the centralised executive-legislative machinery; strong ministerial influence has a powerful control over the legislature; the United Kingdom parliamentary system combines executive and legislative powers; party political influence may strengthen cabinet government and this in

---

[18] T. Erskine May, *Parliamentary Practice* (London, 1997).
[19] Griffith and Ryle, *Parliament* (1989), pp.229, 312.
[20] P.S. Atiyah and R.S. Summers, *Form and Substance in Anglo-American Law* (Oxford, 1987), p.298. See *The Role of the Legislature in Western Democracies* (N.J. Ornstein ed., American Enterprise Institute for Public Policy Research, Washington, 1981).

turn strengthens the ministerial fiat; Ministers are effectively in control of making most delegated legislation and it is uncommon for government-supported legislation not to be successfully passed through Parliament.

Concern about delegated legislation led to the Donoughmore Committee on **3–041** Ministers Powers in 1932 which recognised the problem of scrutiny over delegated legislation. Many of these problems remain. S.A. Walkland noted[21]:

> "Much of the suspicion of delegated legislation is aroused by the fact that civil servants are intimately associated with its procedures, and that the opportunities for participation in the process by representative and politically responsible members of the House of Commons are necessarily limited."

There are two areas where Parliament gives special attention to legislation. The first is **3–042** Community legislation and the second is in the area of human rights. Special consideration is given to European Community legislation; since 1972 the United Kingdom's accession into the EC has committed her to adopting a variety of EC legislation. In 1972 both the House of Commons and the House of Lords provided new committees to scrutinise proposals for Community legislation and consider how best they might be adopted. The role of the United Kingdom Parliament with such legislation is to ensure that the domestic law is made consistent with EC Law. Thus, the committee does not consider the substantive merits of legislative proposals or other EC documents. Its role does not include any formal input into the Community's own law-making processes. United Kingdom ministries participate in legislation through the Council of Ministers. Thus there is no direct means for the United Kingdom Parliament to adopt a formal role in the law-making process of the EC.

It is noticeable that the remit of the House of Lords Scrutiny Committee over EC **3–043** legislation is wider than the House of Commons Committee; the former's terms of reference allow for a limited inquiry into "the merits of community proposals". More time is devoted in the House of Lords Committee than in the Commons Committee and the Lords reports are generally accepted as authoritative and providing well-argued analysis. It is noteworthy that the Lords have taken the innovative step of setting up, on February 8, 2001, a Select Committee on the Constitution, chaired by Professor Lord Norton, a leading expert in this area.[22]

The second area where special attention is given is human rights. The Human **3–044** Rights Act 1998 incorporates the main provisions of the European Convention on Human Rights. While the Act falls short of allowing the courts to hold an Act of Parliament illegal or to strike down legislation, s.10 of the Act allows ministers to introduce remedial orders to amend any part of the legislation that is held by the courts to be incompatible with the Human Rights Act. This is regarded as an extreme situation. In order to avoid any potential conflict between the Human Rights Act and legislation, s.19 of the 1998 Act provides that ministers are required to make a statement of compatibility accompanying the Bill before the second reading of the Bill. In cases where such a statement cannot be made then the Minister in charge of the Bill

---

[21] S.A. Walkland, *The Legislative Process in Great Britain* (1968), pp.16–17. *Machinery of Government Committee* Cd.9230 (1918); Hewart, *New Despotism* (1929); *Report of the Committee on Ministers' Powers*, Cmd. 4060 (1932).

[22] *Reviewing the Constitution; terms of reference and methods of working*, First Report (2001–02 HL 11).

must indicate where the potential conflict or incompatibility with the Act may arise. There is a Joint Committee on Human Rights; this is a Select Committee of both Houses of Parliament established in February 2001. The government rejected the idea of a Human Rights Commission modelled on the Northern Ireland experience. Instead there is a Human Rights Advisor who provides the Joint Committee with advice on the implications of the Act. These arrangements complement the monitoring of the Human Rights Act undertaken by a special unit set up within the Lord Chancellor's department. Before the 1998 Act came into force in England and Wales in October 2001, resources were provided for government departments and Parliament to develop systems of administration to ensure that the law was compatible with the implications of the new legislation. The landmark decision of *Pepper v Hart*[23] remains influential. This permits the courts to read the debates in Parliament as reported in Hansard when interpreting legislation. In that regard s.3 of the Human Rights Act 1998 provides that "as far as it is possible to do so" primary and secondary legislation must be read and given effect so as to render the law compatible with the human rights requirements under the Act. This includes legislation enacted before and after the 1998 Act. In formal legal terms the Human Rights Act 1998 attempts to introduce a rights-based culture into the working of the Constitution while preserving the pre-eminence of the House of Commons. In so doing the courts must take into account the jurisprudence of the European Court of Human Rights, and courts along with other public authorities have a duty to conform to the European Convention on Human Rights itself. At the heart of this ambitious objective of bringing rights into the centre of decision-making is the need to interpret the Convention and assimilate Convention rights into the law. The plain meaning of statutes must be interpreted alongside the rights culture contained in the Human Rights Act. As Campbell[24] points out this has wider implications than simply giving effect to legal rules alone:

> "it will be necessary to hold onto a plain-meaning approach to the interpretation of statutes, and to openly acknowledge that interpreting the ECHR is a matter of moral reasoning in which courts have no special expertise and in connection with which their decisions have no political legitimacy.

3–045 How this is likely to work out in the future is still uncertain. Amid uncertainty there is a degree of responsiveness to change.

Drafting and Interpreting Legislation

3–046 It is clear that in the drafting of legislation, human rights is likely to be taken into account. An important but often neglected subject is the question of how legislation is drafted. The existence of the Parliamentary Counsel Office is all too often ignored. The office came into existence in 1869 during Gladstone's first administration. Previously Acts of Parliament were drafted either by the judges or by practising lawyers or by Members of Parliament. The creation of the Parliamentary Counsel Office regularised the drafting of Bills.

---

[23] [1993] A.C. 593.
[24] T. Campbell, "Incorporation through Interpretation" in *Sceptical Essays on Human Rights* (Campbell, Ewing and Tomkins ed., Oxford University Press, Oxford, 2001), p.99.

Parliamentary Counsel work out of the Parliamentary Counsel Office and are   **3–047**
responsible for the drafting of the majority of Government Bills. Counsel are involved
in advising government departments on aspects of Parliamentary procedure and in the
drafting of amendments. The staff of the Office of Parliamentary Counsel in Whitehall,
London comprise over 30 members headed by the First Parliamentary Counsel. The
Finance Bill 1996 was subjected to external drafting through a contract awarded
outside the Office of the Parliamentary Counsel. Such use of external drafting is an
important development in terms of diversity. The Lord Chancellor is charged with the
responsibility of codification and making suggestions for reform under the Law
Commission Act 1965. This remit includes keeping the law under review. Reports are
received from the Law Commission and the Lord Chancellor is required to consider
these reports. An example of some controversy was the Public Order Act 1986, the
result of recommendations made by the English Law Commission.

The Law Commission provides important input into the drafting of new legislation   **3–048**
through its work on law reform and its duty to keep the statute book under review. It
publishes consultation papers and its reports contain draft Bills incorporating details of
law reform proposals. There is a Common Law and Public Law team within the Law
Commission engaged in an overview of public law matters. Recently human rights has
taken on an important emphasis. Although there is a special parliamentary procedure
for Law Commission Bills there is no special status attached to such Bills to ensure
that they are taken into the parliamentary timetable or to ensure that they become law.
The need to check Bills as to their compatibility with the European Convention on
Human Rights receives special attention. This is in addition to the work of the Judicial
Studies Board in providing intensive training and courses on the implications of the
Act throughout all parts of the legal system. In the past two years the addition of
Explanatory Notes to Acts provides a much needed guide to an understanding of the
main elements of the legislation. This is a welcome development in an era where the
complexity of legislation is an obstacle to understanding its significance.

Increasingly important in the techniques of drafting Bills are the rules of statutory   **3–049**
interpretation. It is more common than in the past for the courts to look at reports of
Parliamentary debates in *Hansard* as an aid to interpretation. The use of *Hansard* in
certain circumstances as an aid to interpretation[25] has been approved by the House of
Lords in *Pepper v Hart*.[26] The discussion and analysis contained in the reports
of Parliamentary Select Committees is also very helpful. However, the availability of
Parliamentary debates as an aid to interpretation should be distinguished from the bar
on the courts questioning the proceedings in Parliament. As Lord Browne-Wilkinson
explained in *Prebble v Television New Zealand Ltd*[27]:

> "So far as the courts are concerned they will not allow any challenge to be made
> to what is said or done within the walls of Parliament in performance of its
> legislative functions and protection of its established principles."

There are various aids in the interpretation of statutes. These consist of rules or   **3–050**
presumptions about how words in a statute may be interpreted. Taken together they

---

[25] Lord Lester, "Pepper v Hart Revisited" (1992) 15 (1) *Statutory Law Review* (1994) 10.
[26] [1993] A.C. 593.
[27] [1995] A.C. 321 at 323D.

form what are called principles of statutory interpretation that are generally applied in English law. Different rules apply in the interpretation of European Community law. The continental style of drafting only sets out general broad principles. This leaves the exact details to be filled in by the judges, who are expected to promote the general legislative purpose of the law. Similarly the Human Rights Act 1998 in the United Kingdom will bring its own style of interpretation as the law begins to be developed on a case by case basis.

3–051   In English law the principles of statutory interpretation consist of rules and presumptions and at the discretion of the judge may be applied when seeking to understand the meaning of a statute. The following are the main rules to aid interpretation.

(i) The Literal Rule

The literal rule refers to the method of interpretation of words in a statute by giving words their plain, ordinary or literal meaning. Courts attempt to find the parliamentary intention behind the statute. As an aid to interpretation the dictionary meaning of words may be used.

(ii) The Golden Rule

The golden rule when applied is used to modify the literal rule by seeking to avoid any absurdity. If the words used in legislation are ambiguous, the golden rule allows the court to avoid the absurdity and adopt a meaning that is suitable for the purpose intended rather than permit some absurd outcome. The application of the golden rule is at the discretion of the court. It may be used in preference to the literal rule. Where the courts decide that public policy requires an interpretation beyond the literal interpretation of the words, the golden rule may ensure effect is given to public policy. In public law cases the golden rule is frequently used to understand the nature of the legislation.

(iii) The Mischief Rule

The mischief rule, otherwise referred to as the rule in *Heydon's Case*[28] allows the courts to examine the law before the statute was made in order to ascertain the nature of the mischief which the statute was intended to remedy. The mischief rule allows the courts some discretion in finding the construction of the statute that best applies to the facts of the case. In public law cases the mischief rule provides the courts with the means to look behind the policy and objectives of the legislation.

(iv) The *Ejusdem Generis* rule

In applying the rules of interpretation the court may read the statute as a whole to understand the overall context of the law. Normally the courts give attention to the *ejusdem generis* rule, meaning that general words which follow particular words are limited in meaning to those of the particular words. The courts may follow certain presumptions when interpreting a statute. Property rights or private rights are not implicitly interfered with unless there are very clear words. The individual's liberty is presumed not to be interfered with unless Parliament has provided clear words.

---

[28] (1584) 3 Co. Rep. 7a.

Parliament is assumed not to have altered the common law unless the statute expressly makes this clear. There are also presumptions that for a criminal offence there must be proof of the requisite intention or guilty mind before the accused may be convicted. Statutes are generally presumed not to have retrospective effect. The courts presume that crimes are not to be created by Parliament retrospectively because it would be oppressive or abhorrent to do so.[29]

(v) Human Rights as an Aid to Interpretation

The question of statutory interpretation arises in the context of the Human Rights Act 1998. The point is explained by Sedley J. in *R. v Broadcasting Complaints Commission, Ex p. Barclay*,[30] that when considering the Convention and the Human Rights Act 1998 it might be relevant for the court to consider the clear Parliamentary intention and in doing so it might be relevant to consider the Convention.

> "Here the respective roles of Hansard and the Convention as aids to construction are likely to be complex and the court will not be assisted by a doctrinal ranking of one source above the other.

Lord Woolf[31] has suggested that a broad and purposive approach should be adopted   **3–052** when considering human rights and noted that this had been the way the Hong Kong Bill of Rights had been interpreted by the courts. Lord Steyn[32] hoped that the way the Human Rights Act ought to be interpreted reflected "a disciplined approach" to the law. An indication of this discipline is that the Act should not be given retrospective effect.[33]

Adopting the principles[34] of *Pepper v Hart* it is important to remember that the use   **3–053** of *Hansard* is available in three circumstances set out by Lord Browne-Wilkinson as follows:

- the legislation is ambiguous, obscure or leads to an absurdity;

- the material relied upon consists of one or more statements by a minister or other promoter of the Bill together with such other Parliamentary material as is necessary to understand such statements and their effect;

- the statements relied upon are clear.

As already mentioned there is no hard and fast rule as to the rule of interpretation or   **3–054** presumption[35] the courts may wish to follow. Courts exercise a discretion according to the context of the law and the facts of the case. Statutory interpretation is aided in the

---

[29] *R. v Secretary of State for the Home Department Ex p. Leech* [1993] 4 All E.R. 539 upholding the citizen's right to the free flow of communication between a solicitor and client.
[30] (1997) 9 Admin. L.R. 265 at 272C–D.
[31] *R. v Director of Public Prosecutions Ex p. Kebilene* [2000] 2 A.C. 326; also see *R. Lambert* [2001] 2 W.L.R. 211.
[32] *ibid.* at 371G.
[33] *R. v Secretary of State for the Environment Ex p. Challenger* [2001] Env. L.R. 209.
[34] *Chief Adjudication Officer v Forster* [1993] A.C. 593.
[35] See *R. v Secretary of State for the Environment, Transport and the Regions Ex p. Spath Holme* [2001] 2 W.L.R. 15.

way the statute is drafted. The preamble to the Act sets forth the need for the legislation and sometimes the effect the legislation is intended to have. The long title of an Act may assist the court in cases of ambiguity. It explains the purpose behind the legislation. The short title to an Act provides a general description of the Act but rarely is a guide to interpretation. Modern Acts of Parliament may have headings delineating particular sections or parts of the Act. There are marginal notes and side-notes. These are not part of the Act and are not discussed in Parliament. They may provide some help in finding the sense of a difficult section but are not normally used by the courts. Finally there are schedules to many modern Acts. There is an increasing tendency to use the schedules to contain more detail than is possible in the main part of the Act. This is to avoid the main part of the Act becoming unduly cluttered. This has the disadvantage that often reference must be made to the schedules of the Act to understand the main content of each of the sections.

Deregulation

3–055   The acknowledged technical complexity of the law and the growth in legislation has seen a trend in favour of deregulation where it is shown that regulation may be unnecessary. Attempts to simplify legislation may fall under the new procedures under the Deregulation and Contracting Out Act 1994. This allows for ministerial Order by affirmative resolution to amend or repeal existing primary legislation. The draft of the proposed Order must be scrutinised by the Deregulation Committee in the House of Commons and by the Delegated Powers Scrutiny Committee in the House of Lords.

3–056   There is a Deregulation Task Force. Its remit is to identify regulatory burdens on industry and make recommendations for their removal. In its first report, the Task Force identifies some of the areas where business is carrying a heavy regulatory burden. The 1994 Act has begun a trend in favour of simplification and providing a speedier means to make law through Order than through Act of Parliament. The Regulatory Reform Act 2001 allows amending powers to primary legislation to be introduced by Order. The requirements are that the primary legislation is amended to impose new burdens or increase an existing burden. The remit of the 2001 Act is sufficiently wide as to extend the powers available to ministers to include any person "in the carrying on of any activity". The width of the power extends to public bodies, charities and businesses. The use of the Order procedure is intended to speed up the process of change and facilitate a more efficient use of departmental resources. This has implications for the work of the various committees of the House.

Debate and Scrutiny

3–057   Parliament's role is not confined to the passage of legislation. It performs a number of other functions—it informs, debates, scrutinises and approves. It is widely accepted that as the Commons has limited influence over the substance of legislation (since most governments can almost always ensure that their legislation becomes law), these other functions may be of questionable significance. Even though a government with a large working majority will nearly always ensure that its legislation is passed, the House of Commons provides, through its procedures and processes, legitimation for legislation. Debates, votes and censure are the life-blood of party politics and the House of Commons provides the opposition with a forum to censure the Government of the day. Opposition M.P.s may introduce Bills, ask questions, introduce amendments, table motions and attend as members of select committees to oversee the activities of government departments.

The development of select committees has been piece-meal. The most prestigious is **3–058** the Public Accounts Committee (PAC) established in 1861 to ensure the financial scrutiny of Government activities, and uniquely placed among the other select committees because the Comptroller and Auditor General may give evidence to this Committee, prepare reports and assist the Committee in its work. Once the Auditor General makes a report, there is an opportunity for the PAC to respond in the form of a report followed by the Treasury, on behalf of the Government department, setting out in a Treasury minute its own findings. Parliamentary scrutiny of government finance is a specialised area of activity, and one that emphasises Parliament's authority to approve expenditure. Public finance is examined in detail in Chapter 12.

Since 1979 "new select committees" were introduced in a reform of existing **3–059** committee procedures. The new committees are intended to scrutinise the departments of government, covering all aspects of the departments' roles and adopting investigative techniques as a means of control. It was expected that the select committee system would help the House of Commons to exercise some control over Government activities. A major sanction comes from an adverse report which might later be reported to the House of Commons and lead to ministerial embarrassment.

The number of Select Committees may change over time and are regulated by **3–060** standing order. In May 1, 1997 there were 18 House of Commons select committees covering all the main departments of government. In addition there were 25 other committees including the Committee on Standards and Privileges, the Committee of Public Accounts, the Joint Committee on Consolidation, Bills, etc. and the Select Committee on European Legislation. In July 2002 there are 16 committees[36] and 20 other committees. There is a Liaison Committee made up of the chairs of the various select committees. The Liaison Committee has a pivotal role in keeping under review the working of the select committee system as a whole.[37] From July 2002, the Prime Minister agreed to appear before this committee, composed of the chairs of the other select committees, and answer questions.

The 16 departmental select committees include Culture, Media and Sport; Defence; **3–061** Education and Skills; Environment, Food and Rural Affairs; Foreign Affairs; Health; Home Affairs; International Development; Northern Ireland Affairs; Science and Technology; Scottish Affairs; Trade and Industry; Transport; Local Government and the Regions; Treasury; Welsh Affairs; and Work and Pensions.

The composition of select committees allows back-bench M.P.s the opportunity to **3–062** take an active role in the scrutiny of government. There is an all-party Committee of Selection which makes nominations for appointment to select committees, having regard to the balance of parties in the House. However, the fear of domination by party politics and the system of Whips is a real one. Accusations that the Whips will only support government sympathisers or loyal backbenchers make it seem that the

---

[36] *First Report of the Liaison Committee* (2000–01 HC 321).
[37] Examples of recent reports include: Liaison Committee, First Report (1999–2000 HC 300; 1999–2000 HC 748: 2000–2001 HC 321).

government of the day has an overriding influence over the composition of select committees. There is a need to ensure that party policy may be represented in the selection of M.P.s for the committees. M.P.s who are outspoken or too independently minded may be persuaded not to stand for election. This is seen as an inevitable weakness in the present arrangements. Composition of select committees is one of the areas where proposals for reform have been forthcoming. To date little has been achieved in securing a greater independence for committees from the government of the day.

3–063 Technically, a select committee has power "to send for persons, papers and records" but this power is subject to practical restraints. The private citizen may choose to claim his right to silence, especially if there is a possibility of criminal proceedings pending. Although attendance may be made compulsory, replies to questions are largely left to the citizen's discretion.

3–064 In the case of civil servants, negotiation is required between the Minister responsible for the department and the committee, if a civil servant is to be allowed to give evidence. Questions asked of civil servants by the committee are constrained by the embargo Ministers may place on civil servants over matters of confidentiality, policy questions or the individual conduct of an official. The attendance of a particular civil servant, even though requested by the committee, is ultimately decided by Ministers. In the *Westland* affair,[38] which raised issues relating to the leaking of a confidential letter of the Solicitor General, the Defence Committee was refused the attendance of five civil servants. The Westland company supplied helicopters to the Ministry of Defence and required re-organisation in the light of new market conditions. Rival financial packages from US and European companies caused intense debate within the Government and the Cabinet. The leaking of the confidential letter of the Solicitor General involved certain civil servants, allegedly acting under the direction of a Cabinet Minister.[39]

3–065 Since then directions issued to civil servants, reminding them of their duty of loyalty to ministers and the government of the day, have raised doubts about the ability of select committees to penetrate the relationship between civil servants and Ministers. In strict constitutional theory, this relationship supports the doctrine of ministerial responsibility whereby Ministers, and not civil servants, are accountable directly to Parliament. *The Code of Practice on Access to Government Information* (1997) provides some guidance on when information may be withheld from select committees that would harm national security or defence or where information is provided in confidence. In 1998 the Foreign Affairs Select Committee was able to require the Government to debate its refusal to supply information on arms to Sierra Leone. In a rare example of its kind the Government conceded the release of confidential information but was able to defeat a motion of criticism over the government's conditions for the release of information.[40]

3–066 In addition to the new select committees there are a plethora of other committees of the House of Commons. Amazingly these amount to 30 select committees in total

---

[38] Michael Heseltine, then Secretary of State for Defence resigned over his allegation that he had been excluded from various Cabinet committees. See *The Observer*, January 12, 1986. Also see Marshall [1986] P.L. 184. Discussion of the affair may be found in the Defence Select Committee (1985–86 HC 519); Cm.9916 (1986) and Cm.9841 (1986).

[39] *Memorandum of Guidance for Officials Appearing before Select Committees*, Cm.78 (1987).

[40] *Hansard*, HC Vol.315, col.865–959 (July 7, 1998).

(including the new committees) dealing with a variety of matters such as the Committee of Privileges, and the Select Committee on the Parliamentary Commissioner.

The assessment of the impact of select committees on government behaviour is **3–067** difficult and is considered in further detail in Chapter 11. On the one hand, in favour of their role there is a fact-finding and information contribution, which undoubtedly exists, because of the select committee system. We know more and have more information about government as a result. On the other hand, there is a lack of success in bringing measurable differences in the way that government is conducted. Ministers and civil servants may, through careful briefing, actually second guess the committee's work. Often committees are *ex post facto* inquiries and they depend on the enthusiasm and skill of the individual M.P.s for their success. A lot may depend in the tenacity of the chairman and his skill in avoiding the division of opinion in the committee along party political lines. This system may be too random and haphazard to be relied upon. Ultimately political issues may intervene in the work of the select committees, as when back-bench M.P.s attempt to use a select committee's findings in debates in the House of Commons to criticise or defend Government policy. There is the added concern that strengthening select committees moves the locus of power away from the House of Commons to back-room committees. Reassurance on this point has come from the televising of proceedings of select committee hearings, which has done much to publicise their work and gain recognition for their important role. Finally, it may be conceded that select committees in this country look less impressive than the US Congressional Committees with which they are commonly compared. This seems an unfair comparison given the difference in the constitutional role of each.

Select committees have a further function, that is they provide a scrutiny over the **3–068** financial affairs of the government. We have already discussed the PAC, but the role of each select committee includes within its remit scrutiny of departmental expenditures. Flegmann[41] and others have noted that only limited interest has been shown in the select committees' development of financial scrutiny over departments.

Parliamentary debate is often party political and adversarial in style whereas select **3–069** committees are intended to be bi-partisan and inquisitorial. Craig observes[42]:

> "Select committees run counter to both of these tenets: they seek to strengthen the power of Parliament as against the executive, and to proceed by a more non-partisan approach."

The essence of committees, however, is that they are "committees of the whole **3–070** House". Any weakening of that fundamental link might leave committees untrusted as an unrepresentative intrusion into government decision-taking and even a usurpation of parliamentary control. The tightrope existence between committees as "independent" scrutineers of government activities, and the application of party politics is difficult to explain. The further committees expand their independent scrutiny, the more tension may arise between their role and the government of the day. This may expose the constitutional limitations which surround their role.

---

[41] V. Flegman, "The Public Accounts Committee; A Successful Select Committee?" XXXIII Parliamentary Affairs (1980).
[42] Craig, *Administrative Law* (2nd ed., 1989), pp.68–69.

Modernisation of the House of Commons

3–071 A number of reports and proposals have attempted to strengthen the select committee system in the context of modernising the way Parliament works. The Hansard Society Commission Report *Making the Law* in 1993 is influential. More recently, the Hansard Society Report on *Strengthening Parliament* also calls for a greater role for select committees. The Liaison Committee[43] in 1999 made recommendations as to the composition and role of select committees. The Modernisation Committee in its report[44] of February 12, 2002 followed through with recommendations for reform.

3–072 The main focus of parliamentary reform has followed two strands. The first is improving the role of select committees and the second is organising the activities of the Commons more efficiently through the timetabling of Bills and the regulation of sitting times.

Modernising Select Committees

3–073 The nomination of members to serve on select committees is crucial to the success of the committee. As mentioned above the influence of the party whips has led to committees having a mixed function—allegiance to party, and critical scrutiny of the government. The Modernisation Committee's Report[45] on *Select Committees* proposed that the duty of selecting names for nomination should be given to a Committee of Nomination drawn from the Chairmen's panel, a group of senior M.P.s who are chairs of the Standing Committees. Membership of the panel would also include the most senior M.P. (the father of the House). The chairs of the Standing Committee are chosen by the Speaker of the House and are therefore independent from party nomination. The role of the Nomination Committee is seen as a last resort as it leaves the nominations for membership with the political parties but exercises an ultimate control over the nomination list. In addition to the proposal about nomination matters, the Modernisation Committee also includes recommendations about the role of the committees as a whole: the strengthening of supportive specialist staff, the payment of an additional salary to the Chair of a committee, and that the size of the committee should be expanded from 11 to 15. It is recommended that no one should serve as a chair for more than two full parliaments. Support for the Modernisation Committee's proposals may be found in the Liaison Committee's own report[46] and the Hansard Commission Report[47] in 2000. There is general support for such proposals as a means of making select committees a fulcrum for backbench activity, and providing a career plan for backbenchers who are unlikely to be chosen for the front bench. Despite the arguments in favour, the proposals as a whole were rejected; specifically the core proposal on the reform of the nomination system for committees was defeated by 209 votes to 195. There is some prospect that an increase in the size of committees might be followed up. The term limit for chairs of committees was accepted and the question of salary may be reviewed by the Review Body on Senior Salaries. One important

---

[43] (1999–2000 HC 300). For response see Cm.4737.
[44] (2001–2002 HC 224–I and II).
[45] *ibid.*
[46] *Select Committees: Modernisation Proposals*, Second Report (2001–2002 HC 692).
[47] Report of the Hansard Society Commission on Parliamentary Scrutiny: *The Challenge for Parliament: Making Government Accountable* (2001).

innovation is the agreement of the Prime Minister to appear before the Liaison Committee and answer questions. This is seen as an important breakthrough in terms of openness and will help deflect arguments that the Prime Minister is unaccountable. It is also a response to the criticism that in reducing Prime Minister's question time to a weekly rather than twice-weekly event, the Prime Minister is not interested in parliamentary accountability.

The Programming of Bills

The Hansard Commission Report, *Making the Law* in 1993 provided the basis for ideas   **3–074** for reform in the modernisation of the legislative process. Some ideas were readily accepted, such as in 1997 the use of explanatory notes to Bills to replace the sketchy memorandum used previously. Also adopted is the use of special standing committees on Bills such as the Immigration and Asylum Bill in 1998–99. More controversial is the setting of an agreed legislative timetable for Bills. The idea is that each Bill would be provided with a set timetable thus allowing an agreement between the political parties as to how to efficiently manage the Bill through the various stages of parliamentary debate and scrutiny. The means to achieve this is through the use of programme orders. In 1998 there were 11 of these but in 1999 the number reduced to 5 and by 2000 there were only 3. There appears to be a lack of co-ordination on the political level and although the idea has resulted in the successful passage of legislation such as devolution and the Human Rights Act 1998, there is a suspicion that in the hands of the government of the day the programming order may become a new form of guillotine rather than reflecting the consensus between political parties that the legislation should be passed. The idea of programming is also related to an 18-month period for the legislation to be passed. This idea has not met with party political support and is dropped in favour of Bills being accorded a slot for their passage of a fixed period of months. There is a general question about whether Bills could be carried over from one session to another. This is a facility favoured by the government because it would allow government business to be transacted but perhaps not so keenly supported by opposition parties. The problem with timetabling is that in the final analysis it requires a consensus and the means to enforce the agreed timetable.

Finally, some attention has been given to the use of Westminster Hall and the use of   **3–075** more socially acceptable hours for sittings of the Commons and the Lords. The aim is to make Parliament more effective as well as to modernise its timetable.[48]

PARLIAMENT, THE CROWN AND PREROGATIVE

In a constitutional sense the Government's law-making powers are exercised by the   **3–076** Crown in Parliament. Today, legislation in its various forms is the most common source of the Government's legal powers. The powers of government may also exist by virtue of custom and derived from the common law. These provide the sources for the Crown's discretionary powers vested in the government of the day and known as the royal prerogative.

---

[48] Research Paper 02/41, June 27, 2002, *Modernisation of the House of Commons: Sitting Hours.*

3–077   The significance of the royal prerogative as a source of governmental power is examined in detail in Chapter 5 in the discussion of the powers and practices of government. It is sufficient here to mention how Parliament's legislative authority was established through limiting, by law, the authority of the Crown, but maintaining the continuity of the royal prerogative.

3–078   Munro[49] has defined the royal prerogative as "those attributes peculiar to the Crown which are derived from common law, not statute, and which still survive". In origin they appear based on custom and in the recognition given to them by the common law. The prerogative had an external use in waging war, but also a domestic application in Royal patronage. Attempts to extend their scope in the fourteenth and fifteenth centuries were largely successful, even if resisted. A variety of Royal powers were appended to the use of the prerogative, including the controversial one of levying different forms of taxation. Such powers were occasionally upheld by the courts but the matter was never finally settled until the Bill of Rights 1688. By abolishing a number of prerogatives and amending others, the Crown's powers were curtailed but at the same time maintained.

3–079   Parliamentary control once asserted has remained intact; but as Munro[50] observes:

> "It is not surprising that modern governments have found it useful to retain such broad discretionary powers to act, which enable action to be taken without the necessity of prior parliamentary approval."

3–080   Gap-filling and residual powers are apt descriptions of how the prerogative may be perceived by modern government. Parliament moreover has condoned the use of the prerogative in this way and has sometimes replaced prerogative powers with statute.

3–081   Parliament has the power to regulate succession to the throne as it thinks fit. Title to the throne is determined under the Act of Settlement 1700 upholding the right of primogeniture; males are preferred over females. The right of succession to the Crown is restricted to Protestants. The Act of Settlement disqualifies Roman Catholics and those who marry Roman Catholics. The Sovereign must swear to uphold allegiance and maintain the Churches of England and Scotland. Proposals to amend the Act of Settlement and remove the discriminatory nature of the provisions were defeated in December 1999. The government is currently reviewing the Act of Settlement and it is likely that before long there will be changes proposed to the Act. There are also proposals to reform the law of treason. The Treason Felony Act 1848 provides a very broad definition that covers writing or overt acts that envisage or intend to deprive or depose the Queen from the Throne. The punishment for treason was, until s.36 of the Crime and Disorder Act 1998, the death penalty. The 1998 Act has abolished the death penalty under s.1 of the Treason Act 1814 and made conviction for treason subject to life imprisonment.

3–082   Parliament has regulated succession to the throne, as in 1936 under His Majesty's Declaration of Abdication Act 1936 permitting Edward VIII's brother to become King George VI. Parliament has also made special provision under the Regency Acts 1937–53 for the Sovereign's minority, incapacity or absence from the Realm. In recent years public controversy has surrounded the role of the Monarchy. In common with

---

[49] See Munro, *Studies in Constitutional Law* (2nd ed. 1999), p.256.
[50] *ibid.*, p.271.

almost all aspects of public life there are pressures to modernise the Monarchy and make it more accountable. The provision by Parliament of a Civil List of public money for the upkeep of the Royal Family has attracted attention to the role and function of the modern Monarchy. The Civil List Act 1952 provided that a sum of money was annually voted to the Monarch. This sum was amended by the Civil List Act 1972 increasing the sum allocated and requiring an annual report from the Royal Trustees on the current state of the royal finances. The Civil List Act 1975 built into the sum allocated a Treasury power to increase the sum to take account of inflation. In 1991 the Government agreed a 10-year arrangement whereby an annual sum for the Civil List, approximately £8 million, would be paid from the Consolidated Fund.

The Queen's personal wealth and income is distinguished from official income and expenditure. Estimates of the Queen's personal wealth appear unreliable as private wealth is not officially disclosed to the public. Since 1992 the Queen undertook responsibility to make provision for certain members of the Royal family out of her private wealth. With effect from 1993 the Queen undertook to pay income tax on her private income. This is a voluntary agreement as the Crown is not liable to pay taxes unless Parliament has expressly so provided. In 1999 the decommissioning of the Royal Yacht saved £12 million and further substantial savings are expected in travel costs. In 2002, the year of the Golden Jubilee, more detailed accounts of royal finances were made public. The death of the Queen Mother in 2002 encountered no taxation being payable on the passing of wealth from one sovereign to another within the Royal Family. The government contributes to the up keep of royal palaces and building with a grant of nearly £35 million. The popularity of the Monarchy endures with periods of intense criticism followed by popular acclaim. The future of the Monarchy is vested in the fulfilment of the function of Head of State and in relations with the Commonwealth.[51] How far the fickle nature of public opinion may be relied upon to maintain the existing status quo is anyone's guess.

3–082a

THE HOUSE OF LORDS

Historical developments outlined in the previous chapter explain how relations between the Commons and Lords were acrimonious. Even in the late-nineteenth century, the Lords attempted to assert its authority against the will of the elected and newly enfranchised House of Commons. The right to veto Money Bills was the main issue in 1860 when a measure for the repeal of paper duty was accepted in the Commons, but rejected by the Lords. Gladstone, as Chancellor of the Exchequer, had embarked on a major re-organisation of taxes, simplifying and clarifying their collection. According to Gladstone's Political Memorandum (May 26, 1860), rejection by the Lords[52]:

3–083

"amounted to the establishment of a revising power over the House of Commons in its most vital function long declared exclusively its own, and to a divided responsibility in fixing the revenue and charge of the country for the year."

[51] A. Marr, *Ruling Britannica* (Michael Joseph, London, 1995).
[52] Quoted and discussed in John Morley, *Life of Gladstone* (London, 1903), Vol.II, p.33.

3–084 The outcome of the Lords' rejection was for the Commons to pass a resolution containing the assertion of principle, namely that:

> "in its own hands [the House of Commons] had the power to remit and impose taxes and that the right to frame Bills of supply in its own measure, manner and time is a right to be kept inviolable."

3–085 The solution came in the form of presenting a single Bill to the Lords containing the various financial proposals, and thereby forcing the Lords to accept or reject the whole Bill. This procedure did not prevent debate of the content of the Bill, but it made rejection difficult.

3–086 The House of Lords opposed Gladstone's Church Bill in 1869, but the Bill was eventually passed. Irish Home Rule was similarly resisted in 1886 and 1893. Eventually the Commons acted to curtail the powers of the House of Lords by passing the Parliament Acts 1911 and 1949. This was achieved after some resistance from the Lords. In 1909 the Lords rejected the Finance Bill, but agreed to pass it on return of the Liberals after the election. After a second General Election in 1910, the passage of certain Bills was achieved only when the Government threatened to swamp the Lords with newly created peers. The Lords finally agreed to pass the Parliament Bill curtailing their powers.

3–087 Both Parliament Acts are relevant to the powers of the House of Lords today. The 1911 Act achieved three major alterations in the law. The Lords' powers to veto or delay Money Bills were abolished. In the case of other public Bills, the Lords' absolute veto was abolished, and a power to delay legislation for two years was substituted. Finally, the life of Parliament was reduced from seven to five years.

3–088 The two-year period of delay still permitted the Lords an influence over the political policy of the government of the day. In certain circumstances this might become crucial and amount to an effective veto if the delay was timed to coincide with the period before a General Election.

3–089 Further reforms of the Lords were considered and resulted in the Parliament Act 1949. The results of the 1949 legislation may be outlined as follows. Together, the Parliament Acts 1911 and 1949, provide that Bills may receive the Royal Assent if approved only by the Commons. This may occur either if the Lords fail within one month to pass a Bill which has passed the Commons and been endorsed by the Speaker as a Money Bill, or where the Lords refuse in two successive sessions to pass a Public Bill other than a Bill certified as a Money Bill. This last situation includes a Bill to extend the maximum duration of Parliament beyond five years which has been passed by the Commons in those two sessions, provided that one year has elapsed between the date of the Bill's second reading in the Commons, in the first of those sessions, and the date of its third reading in that House, in the second of those sessions.

3–090 The definition of a Money Bill, as contained in the Acts (s.1 of the 1911 Act, as amended by the 1949 Act), and by the National Loans Act 1968, refers to a Public Bill which the Speaker certifies, and covers:

> "the important, repeal, remission, alteration or regulation of taxation; the imposition of charges on the Consolidated Fund or the National Loans Fund or

on money provided by Parliament for the payment of debt or other financial purposes or the variation or repeal of such charges, supply, the appropriation, receipt custody, issue or audit of public accounts or the raising or guarantee or repayment of loans."

A strict interpretation applies and rarely are certificates issued, even the Finance Bill presented annually does not often meet the above criteria.   **3–091**

The restrictions set out above on the Lords' powers seldom apply in practice and thus, the basic principle that "the Crown demands money, the Commons grant it, and the Lords assent to the grant" remains true today. The fact that the Speaker's certificate, once issued, is conclusive proof of the status of a Bill, means that it may not be questioned in any court of law. The poll tax legislation, the Local Government Finance Bill 1988, did not qualify as a Money Bill. It was debated and amended in the Lords but passed after the Government defeated an amendment that the Bill should take account of poll tax payers' incomes.   **3–092**

In fact, few Bills have been introduced invoking the 1911 Act procedure. The examples often cited include the Government of Ireland Act 1914, the Welsh Church Act 1914 and the Parliament Act 1949 itself.   **3–093**

In 1990-91 the War Crimes Bill, retrospectively authorising prosecutions in Britain in respect of war crimes in Germany or German-occupied territory during the Second World War, resulted in sufficient controversy for the Government to invoke the Parliament Acts. The Bill was passed after being twice defeated in the Lords but agreed in the Commons on a free vote. This example clearly illustrates the use of the Parliament Acts to ensure the ultimate authority of the Commons over the Lords. More recently the European Elections Act 1999 and the Sexual Offences (Amendment) Act 2000 were passed following the procedure.   **3–094**

Ironically there is a dispute over the question of whether the 1911 Act procedure was capable of allowing the change introduced by the 1949 Act. The principle objection to using the 1911 Act is that a power conferred for one purpose should not be used for another purpose. Given the fact that the 1949 Act consolidated and amended the 1911 Act this may be seen as a step in the direction originally taken by the 1911 Act and therefore the 1949 Act is consistent with the 1911 Act.   **3–095**

Reforming the House of Lords

Before 1999

Attempts to reform the House of Lords have continued since 1949. Discussion of the aims and objectives of the Lords have been included in a White Paper on House of Lords Reform[53] in 1968. The functions performed by the Lords may be summarised as follows: **3–096**

• debate and discussion;

• the consideration of legislation including delegated legislation;

---

[53] Cmnd.3799 (1968).

- the initiation of pubic legislation including both Government and private Members' Bills;

- the revision of public Bills received from the Commons;

- the general scrutiny of Government and of private legislation;

- the work of select committees such as the Select Committee on the Constitution, the European Communities Select Committee and, finally;

- in its judicial capacity as the Supreme Court of Appeal in domestic matters, excluding the law of the European Community.

3–097   Taken together, such functions contribute to the process of legislation and the general debate about government and its powers. The Lords were the first to allow radio and television to broadcast their debates. Generally it is accepted that the quality and standard of debate is high. This is attributable partly to the fact that many of their Lordships hold or have held prominent positions in life, and partly to the individual expertise the Lords may bring to the discussion.

3–098   The fact that appointent to the Lords was appointed by patronage leads to the view that it does not have equal political legitimacy to the Commons. The limited role of revising legislation is one reason why the Lords is subservient to the Commons. Ultimately the Commons may overrule the Lords. Norton[54] offers the analysis that many of Parliament's functions may be formulated within six categories:

- legislative scrutiny;

- latent legitimisation;

- scrutiny and influence;

- tension release;

- support mobilisation, and;

- providing the personnel of government.

Taking each of the six categories, their relevance to the House of Lords may be seen as follows.

3–099   Legislative scrutiny includes similar procedures in the Lords as in the Commons for the reading of Bills, debate and scrutiny. It is said that the less crowded political agenda and the absence of party political divisions favours a more constructive role for the Lords in terms of scrutiny of the Executive, because of the greater influence of ideas and learned opinion from eminent experts in their field. All this may seem to add up to a "constitutional safeguard" provided by the Lords.

3–100   Latent legitimisation is of more doubtful relevance to the Lords. The fact that it meets regularly and without interruption may provide a source of legitimacy; but the Commons undoubtedly is seen to offer legitimacy to government because it has claims to electoral support. In recent years the Lords has adopted a robust approach to the policies of the government of the day.

[54] *Parliament in the 1980s* (P. Norton, ed., 1985). Also see: D.R. Shell, "The House of Lords and the Thatcher Government", *Parliamentary Affairs* XXXVIII, pp.16–32; Janet Morgan, *The House of Lords and the Labour Government 1964–1970* (1975).

In addition to Bills introduced into the Lords, the opportunity for revision comes in **3–101** the form of amendments to Bills. One estimate[55] is that:

". . . the number of amendments made has increased from an average per session of 511 under the 1964–5 Labour adminstration to 788 per session from 1970–74, 645 per session for 1976–79 and 1,061 per session in 1979–86."

The Lords may be said to fit into Norton's category of scrutiny and influence. In that **3–102** connection, because the Lords are largely independent of party politics, they may have "a limited tension release function". Particular causes may be debated and pressure groups given a voice which may not be easily accommodated within the agenda of the House of Commons. This does not go so far as to provide "support mobilisation" in Norton's terminology, meaning popular support, because of the Lords' lack of political legitimacy.

The last remaining function identified by Norton is the role of the Lords in **3–103** contributing to the personnel of government through providing junior ministers (normally about 10). It is also customary that some peers have a seat in the Cabinet (normally about two).

Finally, by supplying a judicial function through the Law Lords, the House of Lords **3–104** contributes to the judicial function under the Constitution.

The potential for acrimony between the Lords and Commons rose throughout the **3–105** period when Mrs Thatcher was Prime Minister. Norton notes[56]:

"The Thatcher administration was defeated more than one hundred times, several of the defeats taking place on contentious political issues including the 1980 Education (No. 2) Bill and the 1984 Paving Bill for the abolition of the Greater London Council."

A number of explanations may be offered: **3–106**

- a growing criticism of the style and management of Mrs Thatcher's government found support in the Lords, especially as a number of ex-Cabinet ministers were given seats in the Lords;

- an influx of new life peers more willing to adopt an active role in the criticism of government, and;

- the difficulty of finding the appropriate formula for reform of the House of Lords may have added to its need to find a more robust and publicly acknowledged role.

This last point carries weight as, since the reforms in 1999 discussed below the Lords appears robust in opposing government Bills when considered to be necessary.

The United Kingdom's Parliament has a bicameral system, with the House of Lords **3–107** forming the second chamber to the Commons. The Parliament Acts 1911 and 1949

[55] Griffith and Ryle, *Parliament* (1989), pp.490–491.
[56] P. Norton, *Politics UK* Longman, London, 2001, p.380.

made the Lords subsidiary to the pre-eminent House of Commons. The Lords have only a limited power to delay most legislation, and a Money Bill may be passed by the Commons acting alone. Long-standing questions are: what is the role of the Lords? and how should this House be composed to reflect its role and function? These questions have been consistently fudged by successive governments. An inter-party conference in 1948 reached limited agreement that the Lords should be complementary to the Commons. In 1967 another all-party conference was held with limited success.

After the House of Lords Act 1999

3–108 The new Labour Government in 1997 determined to tackle first the problem of composition. The House of Lords Act 1999 abolished hereditary peers but allowed for 92 to be retained comprising 90 elected from existing hereditary peers. The abolition of the hereditary element is a big step. It abolishes the potential in-built Conservative majority and moves the House of Lords to the position of having only life members. The elected hereditary element in the transitional House is as much as has yet been achieved, but the past history of the House as a revising and debating chamber has been retained. It is clear that there is consensus over the House retaining only a revising role. There are no plans to increase its powers or change its function. There is a sense of renewal permeating the work of the revised House of Lords. There is also a growing self-confidence to speak out and criticise government Bills and introduce amendments both on technical matters and on substantive points.

Composition

3–109 The composition of the House of Lords reflects its historic past. After 1999 four categories of membership exist. First the Church of England, including the 26 Lords Spiritual comprising the Archbishops of Canterbury and York, plus the Bishops of London, Durham and Winchester together with 21 Senior Bishops of the Church of England. Other ecclesiastical groupings may be represented through nomination as Life Peers. The Roman Catholic Archbishop of Westminster is not included and only recently the Chief Rabbi, head of the Jewish faith, has been made a Life Peer. The second category of membership includes 90 elected hereditary peers. The Earl Marshal and Lord Great Chamberlain are retained making in total 92 hereditary peers. Thirdly there are 549 life peers appointed under the Life Peerages Act 1958. Since 2000 there is an Appointments Commission as an advisory body to oversee the appointment of peers. It is ultimately to take over from the Prime Minister the function of nominating sufficient cross-bench peers to fill vacancies. The trend is in favour of inviting nominations and obtaining greater transparency in the way appointments are made. Fourthly, there are a maximum of 12 serving Lords of Appeal in Ordinary under s.1(1) (a) of the Administration of Justice Act 1968.

Select Committees

3–110 An active role for the Lords may be found in the business of the Lords Select Committees in areas of specialisation such as EC law and practice, where the Lords have established a good reputation for the authority of their reports.

3–111 The use of select committees in the House of Lords is noteworthy in its role as scrutineer of the Executive. Unlike the House of Commons, which has departmental select committees, the Lords has developed only three types of committee. Before

1970, these consisted of investigative committees on general matters, committees on public Bills, and public committees. Investigative committees covered a wide range of public affairs, but the practice of setting up such committees has gradually fallen into disuse.

Since 1970, the role of specific committees identified with particular bills was rarely used and there is a tendency to make use of investigative committees of the old style to cover a variety of ad hoc matters; examples include committees on unemployment (1979–82), overseas trade (1984–85), and on private Members' Bills. These illustrate the variety and type of activities which come under scrutiny. In fact life has been rekindled into the use of investigative committees as a form which adds stature to the Lords. Especially important in the public's perception of the House of Lords at work are the televised hearings of such committees. **3–112**

In December 1972, the Lords set up an investigation into how best to carry out scrutiny of EC legislation. The result was the European Communities Committee, first appointed in 1974, and since then appointed every session. In addition a number of sub-committees have been appointed to carry out a review in specialist areas of activity connected with the work of the main committee. The authority of the European Select Committee has been established, and it has been described as performing "an essential role" and making "a unique contribution to the process of European scrutiny by national Parliaments". Finally the setting-up of the Lords Select Committee on the Constitution appears a timely moment to take stock of current developments in constitutional matters in the United Kingdom. It is precisely this sort of role that the Lords excels in, standing back from party political in-fighting to take a broader look at developments to see the larger picture. **3–113**

The Current State of House of Lords Reform

Proposals for reform of the House of Lords date back to the period since the passage of the Parliament Act 1911. Even before that time there were hints that reform was necessary. The debate on Gladstone's paper duty in 1866 produced an objection to the right of the Lords to interfere with the activities of the Commons. John Bright complained[57] that the House of Lords "have not behaved even with fair honour towards the House of Commons". That sentiment may appear to be at the heart of the objections to an unelected chamber having a legislative role alongside the Commons, an elected chamber. The future reform of the Lords is problematic. The House of Lords Act 1999 and the abolition of the hereditary peerages began the first stage of reform. The question of how the next stage of Lords reform might be undertaken then came to the fore. In March 1999 a Royal Commission[58] under the chairmanship of Lord Wakeham was set up with limited terms of reference to recommend reforms. The terms of reference were set in the context of maintaining the existing powers of the Lords as follows: **3–114**

"Having regard to the need to maintain the position of the House of Commons as the pre-eminent chamber of Parliament and taking particular account of the constitutional settlement, including the newly devolved institutions, the impact of the Human Rights Act and developing relations with the European Union:

---

[57] Parl.Deb. (July 6, 1860). See also John Bright, *Speeches* (1868).
[58] *A House for the Future*, Cm.4534, (January 2000).

(a) To consider and make recommendations on the role and functions of a second chamber;

(b) To make recommendations on the method or combination of methods of composition required to constitute a second chamber fit for that role and those functions;

(c) To report by 31st December 1999."

3–115 The Wakeham Commission reported in January 2000 and made various proposals about the future of the Lords. Three characteristics were identified for the Lords:

- it should be authoritative, capable of holding the executive to account and scrutinising government;

- it should be sufficiently confident to use its powers and act effectively;

- ideally it should be representative of British society as a whole.

3–116 The Wakeham Commission recommended lengthy terms of non-renewable membership of up to 15 years, salaries for members, and an independent commission with the ultimate right to decide which party nominees are suitable for membership. Wakeham also recommended that there should be an elected element of up to 35 per cent of members and the continuation of appointed members. Thus he rejected making a straight choice between elected or appointed members by recommending a compromise. It was suggested that a regional list system might assist in ensuring local representation. The present House of Lords consists of about 750 members including the 15 Law Lords and 26 Lords Spiritual. Wakeham recommended a smaller House composed of up to 550 members.

3–117 Recently the Government published a White Paper on Lords reform.[59] While the main recommendations of the Wakeham Commission were accepted, it is clear that there are serious points of difference between the White Paper and Wakeham. The government appears to favour only 20 per cent elected members, and that the nominees of the party leaders should be put forward in consultation with the Appointments Commission but with the final say to the party leaders. Instead of the 15-year non-renewable terms proposed by Wakeham, the White Paper considers shorter renewable terms of 5–10 years. The size of the House is to be capped at 600, and the present 750 will remain for the next 10 years or so.

3–118 Lords reform is a symptom of the dilemma that faces the constitution under modernisation. Legitimacy is best conferred through elections, and this is a strong argument for having a wholly elected House of Lords. The concern is that such a House might behave along party political lines and mirror the behaviour and activities of the Commons. Successive governments have sought to inhibit the Lords by pointing to its position of weakness—its lack of a satisfactory electoral mandate. Yet, in order to secure a more independent House of Lords, it is necessary to advance appointments through an independent and transparent system. Expertise thus appointed will allow the Lords to fulfil its role of scrutiny and advice separate from the pressure of party politics. This is an argument for preserving the appointed elements to the Lords. A

[59] *The House of Lords—Completing the Reform*, Cm.5291, (November 2000).

compromise may result in an unsatisfactory outcome.[60] Members who are elected may appear to have a greater mandate than those members appointed because of their expertise. A two-tier House of Lords may gain neither authority nor self-confidence and certainly may never *represent* British society as a whole. Lords reform appears to have become more difficult than the government first realised. The government, sensing the problem of deadlock, has referred Lords reform to a Joint Committee of both Houses. This may provide a rare opportunity for Parliament to take the initiative. This is reminiscent of difficulties in 1911, 1949 and in the 1960s when all-party agreement was difficult to achieve.

Parliamentary Privileges

The Nature of Privileges

In considering the function and role of Parliament, account must be taken of the individual Members of Parliament. The medieval history of the House of Commons and House of Lords is reflected in the retention of ancient privileges. As the title "the High Court of Parliament" reminds us, laws and customs of Parliament developed historically. Parliament was and still is a court. As the highest court in the land many of Parliament's procedures remain from its historical origins. Hood Phillips links parliamentary privileges with the royal prerogative as part of the common law. Parliamentary privileges are the rights that are[61] "recognised by the courts and are deemed necessary to maintain the dignity and proper function of Parliament". In 1967 the House of Commons Report from the Committee of Privileges suggested that the term "privileges" should be replaced by "rights and immunities". This suggestion appears attractive because it expresses more clearly the reality of the various "privileges" today.   **3–119**

The important privileges of the House of Commons, may be divided into two: first, freedom of speech and debate; and second, freedom from arrest.   **3–120**

In the case of freedom of speech this may be traced back to medieval times and is accepted by the courts. The Bill of Rights 1688 asserted the freedom of speech of Members of Parliament by providing that "debates or proceedings in Parliament ought not to be impeached or queried in any court or place out of Parliament".   **3–121**

Freedom of speech is interpreted to mean that Members of Parliament are free from civil suits for defamation and are granted immunity in criminal law for words spoken in the course of parliamentary proceedings. Any threat of prosecution would itself be viewed as a contempt of the House. The House has its own internal rules and procedures and the office of the Speaker, on behalf of the House, can control debate within the House. Freedom of speech is, therefore, subject to adjudication by the House itself.   **3–122**

The term "proceedings in Parliament" is open to a variety of interpretations. Does the term refer only to debates as proceedings within the Chamber? The Committee of Privileges in 1938 accepted that immunity applied to the asking of questions or the   **3–123**

[60] *House of Lords Reform—the 2001 White Paper*, House of Commons Research Papers 02/002, January 8, 2002. *www.parliament.uk.*
[61] T. Erskine May, *Parliamentary Practice* (London, 1997), p.70. May defined privileges as "the sum of peculiar rights enjoyed by each House collectively and by Members of each House individually."

giving of notice of questions. However in 1957, a letter from a constituent to his Member of Parliament was held[62] not to be a proceeding in Parliament. An attempt to show a film about security matters in a committee room of the House of Commons that was banned by an interim injunction obtained by the Attorney-General, was considered not to be immune. The Speaker intervened to issue an order to ban the film, when a judge in chambers declined to issue an injunction applying to the Member of Parliament[63] or the House Committee.

3–124   It is unlikely that the privileges of the House may be used to protect Members from criminal proceedings in respect of crime or a breach of the peace committed within the House.

3–125   Uncertainty may surround the operation of the immunities permitting free speech, but the procedure of referring doubtful or hotly disputed cases to the Committee of Privileges allows an important element of debate and discussion to take place. The strength of the system is therefore to be found in the autonomy of Parliament in these matters. On average at least a dozen cases appear to require the views of the Committee each year, which may or may not be adopted on report to the full House of Commons.

3–126   The Defamation Act 1996 provides the right for M.P.s and others to waive parliamentary privilege in order to pursue actions for defamation in the courts. S.13 of the 1996 Act provides that the protection of parliamentary privilege afforded by art.9 of the Bill of Rights 1688 might be waived. This important amendment was prompted by the case taken by Neil Hamilton, then an M.P., who wished to pursue an action against the Guardian newspaper over allegations that he had received cash for asking parliamentary questions, an allegation he has strongly denied. In the course of legal proceedings the newspaper argued that it could not offer an adequate defence when it was unable to examine parliamentary proceedings in court.[64] Subsequently, Mr Hamilton withdrew his action but continued to claim his innocence. The Commons appointed Sir Gordon Downey to act as the first Parliamentary Commissioner for Standards to examine the conduct of M.P.s. The allegations against Mr Hamilton came under investigation. The calling of the General Election for May 1, 1997 took place before Sir Gordon could produce his final report. The definition of proceedings in Parliament may be considered by the courts and cover matters relating to the reports of the Parliamentary Commissioner for Standards.[65] It was held in *Hamilton v Al Fayed*[66] that the courts, in the words of Lord Woolf ". . . exercise a self-denying ordinace in relation to interfering with the proceedings of Parliament". It may be questioned as to whether this self-restraint will always endure.

3–127   There are important issues raised by the increasing use of the internet, televised parliament and the opening up of debates in Parliament to judicial scrutiny since *Pepper v Hart*. S.13 of the Defamation Act 1996 opens up the use of proceedings in civil cases. An alternative is to repeal s.13 and provide the House with statutory authority to waive privilege on the basis of facts or on the merits of a particular case.

---

[62] (1957/58 HC 227, HC 305), George Strauss, M.P.
[63] See Hansard, HL Vol.575, col.52.
[64] *Prebble v Television New Zealand* [1994] 3 W.L.R. 970. A Privy Council discussion of what constitutes activity outside and inside Parliament. Also see *Rost v Edwards* [1990] 2 Q.B. 460. For the Standing Orders see *Hansard*, Vol. 265 HC, 610–12 (November 1995).
[65] P.M. Leopold, "Free Speech in Parliament and the Courts" (1995) 15 *Legal Studies* 204.
[66] [2001] 1 A.C. 395.

The likelihood is that the question of privilege needs to be reconsidered in the light of s.3 of the Human Rights Act 1998. This means that art.9 of the Bill of Rights must now be read as compatible with Convention rights. Although Parliament is not regarded as behaving illegally if incompatible with Convention rights, it nevertheless needs to take account of Convention rights when resolving its historic privileges with rights under the Convention. The statutory protection provided under the Parliamentary Papers Act 1840 remains and this applies to the publication of papers printed by order of both Houses or under their authority. This protection was afforded to the Scott inquiry when it was published as a Parliamentary Paper.[67]

The second freedom claimed is that of arrest. This used to refer to arrest for civil **3–128** cases, but this is of little effect as this procedure is rarely used today. Members of Parliament cannot claim immunity from criminal charges, arrest or imprisonment. It appears that arrest may even occur within the House itself, provided the House has given leave when it is a "sitting day".

It may be concluded that freedoms enjoyed by Members of Parliament may be **3–129** greater than those itemised above as falling within the classification of the "proceedings of Parliament." Redlich in 1908 noted that[68]:

> "Parliamentary government as a system of law is intimately connected with parliamentary government as a political system determined by history and by national and social characteristics." There are compelling arguments for the removal of this privilege and its abolition has been advocated for some time.[69]

Regulating Financial and Other Interests

The disclosure of M.P.s' interests in the matters on which they may vote has become a **3–130** matter of considerable importance. A House of Commons resolution on May 25, 1974 refers to the disclosure of "any relevant pecuniary interest or benefit." Members of Parliament from June 1975 are expected to register any such interest in a register of members' interests maintained by a senior clerk of the House who acts as Registrar. A Select Committee on Members' Interests may examine any matter arising from a failure to disclose an interest. The scope of the registration is all-embracing to include any pecuniary interest or benefit which a member may receive which

> "might be thought to affect his conduct as a member or influence his actions, speeches or vote in Parliament. Financial sponsorship, directorships, ownership of land, payments from clients, occupational or professional conduct or consultancies"

should be included. Registration of an interest does not absolve the member from stating in debate whenever he has a relevant interest in the matter. Sanctions against any member in default are rare and limited. In serious cases it may be regarded as a contempt. In 1990 John Browne M.P. failed to register his financial interests in a

---

[67] The Rt Hon. Sir Richard Scott, The Vice-Chancellor, *Return to an Address of the Honourable House of Commons dated February 1996. Report of the Inquiry into the Export of Defence Equipment and Dual-use Goods to Iraq and Related Prosecutions.*
[68] See Redlich, *The Procedure of the House of Commons* (1908).
[69] (1998–99 HL 43; 1998–89 HC 214).

company. The Select Committee found the case proven and the House of Commons suspended[70] Browne for 20 days. Browne did not seek re-election in 1992. While this example illustrates the serious nature of a breach of the duty on members to disclose their interest, the policing of the register is left too often to the good faith of members. The influence of professional lobbyists is so all-embracing that the register and its operation should be re-examined in the light of modern practice.

3–131   Allegations of political corruption and sleaze have centred on the question of whether M.P.s have been willing to table questions in Parliament in return for financial rewards. The outcome was the setting-up of the Nolan Committee under the chairmanship of Lord Nolan, a Law Lord. The Select Committee on Standards and Privileges was set up after the Nolan report recommended a Parliamentary Code of Conduct. The Committee on Standards in Public Life is a standing committee, first chaired by Lord Nolan, then Lord Neill and, since 2001, by Sir Nigel Wicks. The Nolan Committee in their first report enunciated the seven principles of public life:

- selflessness: holders of public office should act not solely in terms of the public interest but also in a way that avoids financial gain or other material benefits for themselves or their families;

- integrity: holders of public office should not put themselves in a position that permits others to exercise an outside influence on behalf of individuals or organisations that may seek to influence how they perform their public duty;

- objectivity: holders of public office should seek to make choices on merit and not on other criteria;

- accountability: holders of public office should hold themselves accountable for their decisions and their actions;

- openness: reasons for decisions should be given and information only restricted when the wider public interest demands such restrictions;

- honesty: holders of public office should declare any private interest relating to their public duties;

- leadership: leadership should be provided by example, and these principles should be applied.

3–132   In addition to the Committee on Standards in Public Life, there is the Parliamentary Commissioner for Standards tasked to maintain the register of members interests and to operate a Code of Conduct. This includes investigative powers to examine any complaint and report to the House, including powers to conduct an oral hearing as well as to undertake a review of written submissions. The Code of Conduct is generally seen as an example of self-regulation and was adopted by joint resolution. It was agreed in July 2001 that the House of Lords should similarly adopt a Code of Conduct and the Lords register their interests on the basis of the Code. The non-statutory basis for regulation of both Houses may not remain for long as growing public disquiet about the financial interests of MPs may require satisfaction.

[70] *Hansard*, HC Vol.506, col.108 (1989–90); *Hansard*, HC, col.213.

SUMMARY AND CONCLUSIONS

It may be concluded that modern parliamentary government in the United Kingdom **3–133** has continued to develop, albeit alongside Parliament's medieval inheritance. Preserving the balance of the Constitution, whereby in Blackstone's analysis "the executive power should be a branch, though not the whole of the legislature" remains a perplexing and constant challenge to the institution of Parliament.

- The reality of constitutional power, beginning in the latter part of the nineteenth century in Britain, endures today. Government has expanded its role from its traditional preserve of raising revenue, entering foreign relations and maintaining peace throughout the realm. Legislation, including the redefinition of Parliament's powers in the Parliament Acts of 1911 and 1949, expanded to cover a wide range of social issues such as health, education, local government, factories, railways and, in the 1930s, malnutrition. This provided a radical transformation in the role of government and the state.

- The growth of party politics and the strengthening of cabinet decision-making altered the classical principles underlying Dicey's explanation of the Constitution, namely that Parliament could control the Executive.

- Parliamentary forms of control appear weak and ineffective while judicial influence and power has increased incrementally.

- Reform of the House of Lords is yet to be determined and the question of a wholly elected chamber requires careful consideration.

FURTHER READING

The House of Lords: Its Parliamentary and Judicial Roles (B. Dickson and P. Carmichael eds., Hart Publishing, Oxford, 1999).

P. Evans, *Handbook of Commons Procedure* (Vacher Dod Publishing, London, 1997).

P. Norton, *Does Parliament Matter?* (Harvester Wheatsheaf, London, 1993).

D. Oliver and Gavin Drewry, *The Law and Parliament* (Butterworths, London, 1998).

Report of the Hansard Society Commission on Parliamentary Scrutiny: *The Challenge for Parliament: Making Government Accountable* (Hansard Society, Vacher Dod Publishing Ltd, London 2001).

Royal Commission on Reform of the House of Lords, *A House for the Future*, Cm.4534 (2000) (Stationary Office, London).

Parliament and Pressure Politics (M. Rush ed., Clarendon Press, Oxford, 1990).

P. Silk and Rhoderi Walters, *How Parliament Works* (4th ed., Longman, London, 1999).

Sir R. Scott, *Report: Return to an Address of the Honourable House of Commons dated 15th February 1996. Report of the Inquiry into the Export of Defence Equipment and Dual-Use Goods to Iraq and Related Prosecutions The Rt Hon Sir Richard Scott, The Vice-Chancellor* (1996 HC 115).

Lord Justice Sedley, *Freedom, Law and Justice*, 50th Hamlyn Lectures (Sweet & Maxwell, London 1999).

Chapter 4

GOVERNMENT

INTRODUCTION

Government is carried out through Ministers of the Crown answerable to Parliament. **4–001**
Under the United Kingdom's constitutional arrangements, with the Queen as Head of
State, government is carried on in her name as is fitting for a country with a
constitutional monarchy.

The system of government in the United Kingdom is often referred to as **4–002**
responsible government. In that sense there is a degree of self-limitation in how
government may operate its legal authority. This is partly attributable to party
politics but also to the theoretical possibility at least that the government may lose
the confidence of the House of Commons. The government requires the authority of
Parliament for the passage of legislation and the expenditure of money. Government
in the United Kingdom is highly centralised and although local government is an
elected tier below central government, its practical autonomy has been greatly
eroded in recent times. As outlined in Chapter 2 devolution since 1998 has
introduced a new tier of government for London, Scotland, Wales and Northern
Ireland with the prospect of further devolution in England. Government in the
United Kingdom must also take account of the changes in membership of the
European Union which comprises 15 Member States and 370 million people and is
considered in detail in Chapter 8. Many government decisions are made in alliance
with other Member States and are implemented more formally through Community
law.

Any consideration of the powers and role of government involves explaining how it **4–003**
is carried out. This is discussed in both this chapter and the next. In this chapter, first
consideration is given to the prerogative powers of government which are a source of
governmental power in addition to the extensive reliance on legislation already
discussed in Chapter 3. Secondly, the role of the Cabinet and Prime Minister and the
administration of the government through the civil service is discussed. The institutions
of government also include a wide variety of bodies connected with administrative
decision-taking and these are discussed more fully in Chapter 6.

Government is carried out according to the conventions of the Constitution and the **4–004**
rule of law, which prescribe how government ought to exercise power. Consideration is
given to the importance of conventions and the rule of law in Chapter 5.

GOVERNMENT AND THE CONSTITUTION

4–005 A legal perspective of Britain's constitutional arrangements may be said to be too narrowly defined and to focus only on a narrow legal and technical explanation of parliamentary sovereignty, which Dicey attributed in 1885 as Parliament's "right to make or unmake any law whatever". In the sense that Dicey ascribed such wide powers to Parliament, it might be asked whether the United Kingdom in fact possesses a Constitution. Thomas Paine's analysis of the Rights of Man[1] which was influential in the drafting of the present American Constitution, noted the characteristics which defined a constitution.

> "A Constitution is not the act of a government, but of a people constituting a government, and a government without a constitution is power without right . . ."

4–006 Paine's analysis causes us to consider the question of where power and authority lie. Daintith and Page[2] summarise two elements: first the general neglect given to the question of who governs and how government works and secondly that in the absence of fundamental constitutional laws most commentators devote little attention to the powers and status of ministers and their importance.

> "The executive governs us; it comprises the individuals—mostly ministers and civil servants—who actually control, from day to day, the state's instruments of coercion, wealth and information. The idea that it might not be constitutionally important would seem too bizarre to mention, were it not for the fact that the literature of constitutional law is remarkably reticent on the subject."

4–007 The relevance of this point has been noted by a number of political scientists. F.F. Ridley[3] argues that because of the width of government powers Britain "does not really have a constitution at all, merely a system of government, even if some parts of it are more important to our democratic order than others. . .". This statement pre-dates the Human Rights Act 1998 but it is a perceptive analysis of how the common law system of government may appear.

4–008 Ridley calls in aid the views of James Bryce in the latter part of the nineteenth century when he argued that

> ". . . there is no text to discriminate between constitutional and less than constitutional elements since labelling has no defined consequence, unlike countries where constitutions are a higher form of law."

[1] T. Paine, "Rights of Man" in *The Complete Works of Thomas Paine* (1791–92), pp.302–303. Also see the discussion in C.H. McIlwain, *Constitutionalism Ancient and Modern* (1947), pp.8–10; Rousseau, *Le Contrat Social* (1762).
[2] T. Daintith and A. Page, *The Executive in the Constitution* (Oxford, 1999), p.2.
[3] F.F. Ridley, "There is no British Constitution: A Dangerous Case of the Emperor's Clothes" (1981) 41 *Parliamentary Affairs* 340–345; Samuel H. Beer, *Modern British Politics* (3rd ed., Faber & Faber, 1982); Max Beloff and Gillian Peele, *The Government of the U.K.: Political Authority in a Changing Society* (2nd ed., Weidenfeld and Nicolson, 1985); Nevil Johnson, *In Search of the Constitution: Reflections on State and Society in Britain* (1977); *Introduction to Constitutions in Democratic Politics* (Bogdanor, ed., 1988); J.M. Schaar, "Legitimacy in the Modern State" in *Legitimacy and the State* (Connolly *et al.*, 1984).

The idea of confronting government power with some superior rule of obligation is commonly accepted in written constitutions.[4] Equally there is no panacea to be found in a written constitution as the framers of the constitution may not accurately address the problems of where power and its abuse may be found. However written constitutions may settle the relationship between local and central government, the role of the courts and the separation of powers within the framework of the constitution. Ridley identifies four characteristics which he suggests are important and without which it is impossible to say a country has a constitution "in the current international sense of the word." He explained that the four characteristics are as follows:

• The constitution establishes the system of government. This is taken to mean that the system of government depends on the constitution for its rules and is not independent from the constitution.

• The constitution sets the authority outside the order it establishes. The meaning intended is that the constitution should provide the legitimacy for law and the governmental system. Common to modern constitutions like the Japanese or Irish, there is some reference to "the people" in whom ultimate authority is derived for the constitution to gain legitimacy.

• The constitution is a form of law superior to other laws. This authority is partly due to the point made above, but also the principle of hierarchy admits the possibility of judicial review of ordinary legislation to test its constitutional validity.

• The constitution is entrenched which thereby admits its general purpose, to limit the power of government; and because of its higher form of authority, this makes the constitution safe from political intervention. It is usual that only special procedures may be used to seek amendment and in such cases protection is afforded by requiring some form of popular consultation.

Ridley's analysis has some force when it is considered that in the absence of a written constitution in the United Kingdom, there is an omission in our present arrangements which fail to address Ridley's four characteristics. One answer might be that this is not surprising, as Ridley has in mind the formula for written constitutions which he is unfairly applying to our "unwritten arrangements". There remains, however, the question of what is fundamental in the United Kingdom's Constitution and how government might be made to conform to fundamental principles.   **4–009**

One answer is to consider how there may be what Daintith and Page[5] refer to as "external" and "internal" controls. External controls may be regulatory systems such as the courts or Parliament or through external contracts and financial controls. Internal systems may be found through the institutions of government providing their own internal "checks and balances". Civil servants and ministers operate within important conventions, principles and understandings. Occasionally these procedures have a legal   **4–010**

---

[4] M. Loughlin, *Public Law and Political Theory*, pp.16–17. Loughlin notes the Diceyan legacy, namely that constitutional law is too formalistically defined by lawyers.
[5] T. Daintith and A. Page, *The Executive in the Constitution* (Oxford, 1999), p.3.

framework such as the processes and procedures used by government to account for public money. Often the procedures come in the form of minutes, letters, circulars and public statements. Inevitably there are restraints which are never made public but exist beneath the surface—personal promotion, professional standards and ultimately self-advancement all serve to provide standards in the machinery of government decision-taking.

4-011   None of these arrangements, however, will guarantee that government conforms to the acceptable and high standards which should reasonably be expected. Occasionally civil servants and ministers may be subject to scrutiny such as before a select committee or in a parliamentary debate. Even here the ultimate sanction may not be found in resignation or judicial rebuke, but in the day-to-day political life of the nation. Newspapers and the news media have a contribution to make through investigative journalism in providing information and critical analysis of government activities.

4-012   Counterbalancing any checks and balances that this combination of factors may have is the secrecy which surrounds government in Britain. It begins with the need for collective Cabinet decision-taking and the anonymity of civil servants. Supported by both the civil and criminal law, Britain's secrecy laws have penetrated deeply inside the very culture of the machinery of government. Commercial confidentiality between government and business or industry in their contractual relationships also provides a reason for secrecy in many government activities. Recent attempts to provide open government through a newly enacted Freedom of Information Act 2000 have been tempered by the various exemptions in the Act. While the Act imposes a duty on public authorities and regional public authorities in England, Wales and Northern Ireland to respond to requests for information, the procedures are subject to a fee being payable and a long list of exemptions which are very broadly defined. Ironically the Act may be more effective in terms of public authorities outside central government. In the case of Scotland there are plans to have a wider Act than the Freedom of Information Act 2000.

4-013   Finally, emphasis should be given to the ultimate check on government through elections which determine the fate of government policies. Political parties, individual politicians and pressure groups all promote the political agenda of the nation. In a constitutional sense political parties look to the electorate for a mandate to govern. Local as well as central government has to account to electoral choices determined by popular support.

4-014   The weakness about elections serving as a mainstay of fundamental principles is that the results are not necessarily representative of public opinion. There is a sizeable number, estimated in 1981 at 2.5 million, of eligible electors who are not registered to vote. The turnout at central government elections fluctuates from 70 per cent to 85 per cent of the electorate. More significantly the British electoral system does not favour fairness between the number of votes cast at the election in favour of one particular party and the number of seats held in Parliament by that party. The statistical returns of all the general elections since the franchise was reformed in the nineteenth century show how "the first past the post system" may distort electoral preferences. For example, at the general election in 1992, the Conservative and Labour parties respectively won 42 per cent and 34 per cent of the votes, each winning 336 and 271 seats. The Liberal Democrats won 18 per cent of the vote but only 20 seats. These results are used to support the claim that the current plurality system (as it is known) or two-party system may discriminate against a third party or minority parties. More importantly, while the present electoral system may favour strong government, *i.e.* a government which holds a majority overall in the House of Commons, this may be at the expense of representative government. To the extent that this is true it may considerably weaken the case for relying on electoral choice as a mainstay of constitutional protection of fundamental principles. Daintith and Page[6] also note a further weakness in the electoral mandate:

> "'Democratic' control of the executive through the legislature may be a mixed blessing if the legislature's instincts are more populist or nationalistic than those of the executive, or if the legislature's key institutional values amount to no more than expediency and survival."

A further point is the time-delay for the impact of policies to be fully understood or appreciated by the electorate. Government policies over a five-year term may fail to be effective and this limitation may curtail medium- or long-term planning.   **4–015**

The conclusion which may be drawn from the above analysis is that while there are many important and disparate elements containing fundamental principles in the working of the United Kingdom's Constitution, political scientists have been correct to point out to constitutional lawyers that the Constitution does not fit easily within the ideas of constitutionalism resulting from the experience of modern written constitutions. It may seem surprising that British constitutional lawyers who have written many constitutions throughout the world should be reluctant to adopt a written constitution for Britain. Perhaps this distils the essence of constitutional law in the United Kingdom; systems of external and internal control are exercised within the limits of political power; rules and procedures are exercised within an overall framework of legislative authority and statutory powers, and are no less the working constitution than the law that may be found in other countries with a written constitution.   **4–016**

DEFINING CENTRAL AND LOCAL GOVERNMENT

No special status is accorded to government within the United Kingdom's constitutional arrangements. The term "government" is not given a precise legal meaning and not accorded any special pre-eminence. It may occasionally be found in a statute but rarely does the legal status or significance of government receive specific judicial evaluation. An example of reference to the word "minister" and the word "state" in the context of government may be found in the House of Commons Disqualification Act 1975 and in the Ministers of the Crown Act 1975. Both Acts contain technical rules applicable to government ministers, without explaining the powers, duties and responsibilities of ministers or the role of government.   **4–017**

Government may be defined in a variety of ways. Some definitions express the significance of the State, the way the State is governed, while other definitions may more generally refer to the executive powers enjoyed by the Cabinet and Prime   **4–018**

---

[6] T. Daintith and A. Page, *The Executive in the Constitution* (Oxford, 1999), p.394.

Minister. Government carries out a wide range of activities with its own policies and ideas developed to administer public money or implement its election promises.

4–019   Government enjoys a wide range of powers of patronage and influence. Legal powers may be derived from statute, the prerogative or from the legal obligations arising from the European Community. External affairs such as foreign relations and signing treaties, or maintaining diplomatic relations, may be carried out through the Crown's prerogative in foreign affairs.

4–020   Government is also capable of forming contractual relations. Given the Government's vast economic power it can wield considerable influence as an economic contractor. Statutory authority is not normally required for the Crown to enter into contracts, though prior statutory authority is often necessary for the approval of expenditure. In the case of departments making contracts, this is achieved through the authority of a civil servant acting on behalf of the Crown and no statutory authority is needed. Increasingly central government has viewed itself as a commercial enterprise, freely entering into contracts, or as a regulator overseeing contract activities.

4–021   Government is amenable to the jurisdiction of the courts. Lord Templeman has observed[7]: "Parliament makes the law, the executive carry the law into effect and the judiciary enforce the law". A finding of contempt may be made against a government department or a Minister of the Crown. In *M v Home Office* the House of Lords upheld a finding of contempt against a Minister of the Crown for not complying with an injunction. The injunction was granted ordering M to be returned to this country after the Home Office rejected his claim for asylum. Lord Templeman concluded[8]:

> "To enforce the law the courts have power to grant remedies including injunctions against a minister in his official capacity. . . For the purpose of enforcing the law against all persons and institutions, including ministers in their official capacity and in their personal capacity, the courts are armed with coercive powers exercisable in proceedings for contempt of court."

4–022   Lord Woolf in the House of Lords considered that it would rarely be justified to make use of injunctions against government departments in judicial review proceedings.

4–023   The generic term "government" requires further clarification. It is important to distinguish between central and local government. All the powers discussed above refer to central government. Local government has no special status under the United Kingdom's constitutional arrangements, even though it is elected and provides an enormous variety of services and activities for the community. Since the nineteenth century, local government has gained considerable statutory powers, which have been granted by central government enabling local government to carry out tasks and responsibilities in the provision of public health, education, planning, policing and other services.

4–024   Local government is perceived to be an agent of central government carrying out its tasks as a unique administrative agency. Each local authority has its own distinct legal personality from other local authorities. In law, local authority status as a body corporate gives it considerable financial autonomy within the framework of its legal

---

[7] *M v Home Office* [1993] 3 W.L.R. 433 at 437.
[8] *ibid.*

powers. Local authority elections offer the local community an opportunity to participate in a different tier of government distinct from central government. Councillors, as local authority representatives, may carry out their policies subject to the legal controls set by central government.

Compared to central government, local authorities do not operate as an emanation   **4–025**
of the Crown. As statutory corporations, local authorities must act within their powers according to law. Local authorities do not all conform to a single model of government as central government may appear to. The role, function and organisation of local government is examined in more detail in Chapter 13.

CROWN AND PREROGATIVE

Definition and Review

In addition to the various forms of legislation outlined in the previous chapter on   **4–026**
Parliament, an important source of governmental powers may arise from the use of prerogative powers. Various definitions are applied to the prerogative. Dicey defined the royal prerogative[9] as "the residue of discretionary or arbitrary authority which at any given time is legally left in the hands of the Crown"; de Smith attributed to the Crown "inherent legal attributes" which belong to the Queen as a person, and to the institution called the Crown. The latter may be defined to include Her Majesty's Government or the State. Defining the prerogative in legal terms is always difficult. This is largely because of the complexities of its historical evolution and uncertainties about its present usage. Dicey's description of the prerogative as a "residue" of powers should be confined to powers or privileges that are unique to the Crown. A wider description of the prerogative meaning all the powers of the Crown that have their source in the common law is inaccurate. Powers or privileges enjoyed by private persons are not strictly speaking part of the prerogative. Some writers find it convenient to classify power under the prerogative as "personal" and distinguish this from "political" prerogatives. The former are exercised by the Queen as a person, the latter apply as Head of State. Personal prerogatives refer to the immunities and property rights of the Sovereign which survive today, such as a right not to be sued or prosecuted in the courts. Personal estates such as the Crown's Private Estates are vested in the Sovereign.

Political prerogatives are arrogated to the Crown whereby the Queen may act in her   **4–027**
personal capacity, such as in the choice of the Prime Minister. Today the prerogative powers of the Crown are largely exercised by ministers reponsible to Parliament who in theory act on behalf of the Crown. The Courts have recognised prerogative powers as early as the *Case of Proclamations*[10] (1610), but have from time to time restricted their scope and attempted to define their meaning.

The royal prerogative is regarded as part of the common law powers of the Crown.   **4–028**
It consists mainly of executive government powers such as the conduct of foreign

---

[9] Dicey, *Law of the Constitution*, p.424. Lord Reid in *Burmah Oil v Lord Advocate* [1965] A.C. 75, 99. See also *Laker Airways Ltd v Department of Trade* [1977] Q.B. 643.
[10] (1610) 2 St. Tr. 723.

affairs, the making of war and peace, the appointment of Ministers, the dissolution of Parliament and the assent to Bills. The difficulty of exact legal definition may have prompted Dicey to define the prerogative in very broad terms[11]:

"Every act which the executive government can lawfully do without the authority of the Act of Parliament is done in virtue of the prerogative. . ."

4–029   The difficulty of precise legal definition and the breadth of Dicey's vision of the extent of prerogative powers has not been helped by any clarity to be found in legal cases. The history of prerogative powers is the history of relations between the King and Parliament and the attempts by the courts to mediate.

4–030   The historical origins of the prerogative may be traced back to medieval times. The inherent powers of the King to govern the realm rested on the prerogative. Legal definitions appeared unhelpful as they may have attempted to expand or limit the powers of the King. Advice sought was usually influenced by the expected outcome in terms of defining the King's powers. Blackstone[12] identified the pre-eminence accorded to the prerogative in English law:

". . . [i]t signified in its etymology (from prae and rogo) something that is required or demanded before, or in preference to, all others."

4–031   Maitland[13] cautions us about the "often great uncertainty as to the exact limits of the royal prerogative". His suggestion that there is "no such doctrine as that a prerogative may cease to exist because it is not used", may not easily fit within modern representative government with extensive statutory powers.

4–032   Keir and Lawson[14] make the important distinction between the powers enjoyed by the King at common law and those powers conferred by statute. Statutes have restricted prerogative powers and in some cases statutes either repeal the prerogative completely or overlap with prerogative powers. An example where statutory authority has replaced prerogative powers are the powers of the sovereign to spend money or raise taxation prior to the seventeenth century. Such powers are today ceded to Parliament and statutory authority. Another example is the Crown Proceedings Act 1947 which abolished the Crown's absolute immunity from legal suit in contract and tort.

4–033   In adapting to changing circumstances the courts may be required to give further thought to long accepted principles. Until recently it was commonly assumed that injunctions were not available against the Crown. In *M v Home Office*[15] the House of Lords clarified the position regarding the availability of injunctions against the Crown. Lord Woolf, giving the views of the House, held that injunctions including interim injunctions were available against Ministers of the Crown. A Minister could be personally liable for wrongs done by the Minister when acting in an official capacity. The importance of the case lies in the clarification over the use of injunctions against

[11] Dicey, *Law of the Constitution*, p.424.
[12] Blackstone, *Commentaries*, Bk 1, p.239.
[13] Maitland, *Constitutional History of England* (Cambridge, 1908), p.418.
[14] Keir and Lawson, *Cases in Constitutional Law* (Oxford, 1967), pp.72–80.
[15] [1993] 3 All E.R. 537.

the Crown. The current law lays emphasis on the limited circumstances where it is considered appropriate to grant an injunction against the Crown.

How relevant is the prerogative to modern government when it is of such ancient   **4–034** origin? Present-day prerogative powers may be found in: the Executive's power to conclude treaties with Sovereign States; the power to declare war; to provide for the security of the Realm; to grant pardons to convicted criminals or reprieve a sentence; to mint the currency; and to appoint Commissions by Royal Warrant. Some prerogative powers remain in the personal control of the Sovereign such as power to dismiss and appoint a Prime Minister and the power of dissolution of Parliament. Undoubtedly the prerogative is a "residual" power as it can be removed, altered or amended by an Act of Parliament. No new prerogatives may be created but surprisingly old prerogatives have an "elastic quality" which allows their adaption into modern government. Lord Roskill in *Council of Civil Service Unions v Minister for the Civil Service*[16] considers that there are various prerogatives where the courts appear not to be able to review, such as the prerogative that applies to the "making of treaties, the defence of the realm, the prerogative of mercy, the grant of honours, the dissolution of Parliament and the appointment of ministers". These are evidently not amenable to judicial review because of their nature, and it should be noted that the list is not an exhaustive one. More recently the courts appear to have taken a different approach than Lord Roskill's. Arising from the application of the prerogative of mercy, it appears that the fairness of sentencing that fall under the exercise of the powers of remission of sentencing under the prerogative may be reviewed.[17] Similarly matters of defence are not wholly outside the power of judicial review, such as including the admission of gay people into the armed forces[18] and the use of an ordinance to remove island people to allow a US military base to be set up.[19] This change in emphasis is partly due to the nature of the rights agenda set by the Human Rights Act but also because increasingly the courts are invited to review all public power whatever its source. It remains the case that there will always be a reluctance to review prerogative powers that underline government policy in the defence of the realm.

Some examples may be given of the use of the prerogative. A prerogative power was   **4–035** claimed as the basis for setting up a scheme for compensation payable to victims of violent crime. The Criminal Injuries Compensation Board has recently received statutory authority and recognition under the Criminal Justice Act 1988, s.108; but in 1964, it was set up by prerogative powers subject to express statutory approval by Parliament of the necessary government expenditure under the annual Appropriation Act.

In *Secretary of State for the Home Department Ex p. Fire Brigades Union*,[20] despite the   **4–036** existence of the statutory scheme under the Criminal Justice Act 1988, the Home Secretary attempted to introduce a tariff scheme under the prerogative. The tariff scheme was different from the statutory one and the Home Secretary purported to exercise powers under s.171 of the Criminal Justice Act 1988 which gave the Home

[16] [1985] A.C. 374 at 418B–C.
[17] *R. (on the application of Quinn) v Secretary of State for the Home Department* [2001] A.C.D. 258.
[18] *R v Ministry of Defence Ex p. Smith* [1996] Q.B. 517.
[19] *R. (on the application of Bancoult) v Secretary of State for the Foreign and Commonwealth Office* [2001] 2 W.L.R. 1219.
[20] [1995] 2 All E.R. 244.

Secretary discretion as to when to bring the statutory scheme into operation. It was accepted by Lord Browne-Wilkinson that the tariff scheme was inconsistent with the statutory scheme. In effect it might involve the winding up of the old Criminal Injuries Compensation Board and the creation of a new body, the Criminal Injuries Compensation Authority. The House of Lords by a majority held that such a tariff scheme introduced under the prerogative was unlawful. The tariff scheme under the prerogative was inconsistent with parliamentary intent established under Pt VII of the Criminal Justice Act 1988. This case is important because it establishes the important relationship between statute and prerogative. Lord Browne-Wilkinson stated that[21] "the existence of legislation basically affects the mode in which such prerogative powers can be lawfully exercised". The case restored the validity of the scheme under the Criminal Injuries Compensation Board. As a result of the House of Lords decision, the Home Secretary introduced new legislation providing for the introduction of a new scheme of compensation under the Criminal Injuries Compensation Act 1995. In the final analysis the Government won the day but the entire episode illustrates the pre-eminence of statutory powers over the prerogative.

4-037 The civil service falls under prerogative influence in the sense that the Crown has historically the power to appoint or dismiss its servants at pleasure. This power may be identified as a prerogative power. The civil service is regulated not by statute, though statutes may apply to civil servants, but by Orders in Council made under the royal prerogative, notably the Civil Service Order in Council 1982 which determines a code of regulations in pay and conditions of service. The Order in Council also empowers the Minister for the Civil Service and the Treasury to make regulations for the conduct of the civil service. There are plans to provide a new statutory basis for the civil service and remove the vagueness associated with unwritten rules or doubts over the enforceability of Codes of Practice.

4-038 The prerogative power in the Crown to establish courts to administer the common law has fallen into disuse as new courts are created by statute. The Crown may pardon convicted prisoners. The Attorney-General may enter a *nolle prosequi* in prosecutions on indictment. However under s.23 of the Prosecution of Offences Act 1985, the Crown Prosecution Service has statutory powers to discontinue cases without the leave of the court.

4-039 The versatility of the prerogative is demonstrated by Turpin's[22] reference to orders in council such as the 1982 Order, as "prerogative legislation". This is an apt but perhaps misleading phrase. It is the case that during the two World Wars many prerogative orders in council were adopted without statutory authority. The Reprisals Orders in Council of 1915 and 1917, and more recently in 1982 the requisitioning of ships on account of the Falklands war, was achieved through the prerogative. The misleading part of the phrase is the word "legislation" when used alongside the word prerogative. This implies parliamentary approval and scrutiny which may be misleading, because no such detailed scrutiny is undertaken. However, in the general sense legislation may mean the power to make rules for others. The prerogative may clearly fall within this meaning.

4-040 Prerogative powers that apply in relation to Parliament include the power to summon, to dissolve or to prorogue Parliament. The Royal Assent to Bills is also a

---

[21] See *Compensating Victims of Violent Crime. Changes to the Criminal Injuries Compensation Scheme* (Cm.2434 (December 1993).
[22] Turpin, *British Government and the Constitution*, p.382.

prerogative power. Prerogative powers are not subject to the processes of scrutiny of the House of Commons, nor is it always clear when a prerogative power is being used. Such doubts can give rise to questions about the relationship between prerogative powers and statute. Wade suggests somewhat tentatively[23] that: "Prerogative powers may also, it seems, be atrophied by mere disuse".

As to the exact nature or remit of the prerogative Nourse, L.J. explained[24]:   **4–041**

> "It has not at any stage in our history been practicable to identify all the prerogative powers of the Crown. It is only by a process of piecemeal decision over a period of centuries that particular powers are seen to exist or not to exist, as the case may be. From time to time a need for more exact definition arises. The present need arose from a difference of view between the Secretary of State and a police authority over what is necessary to maintain public order, a phenomenon which has been observed only in recent times. There has probably never been a comparable occasion for investigating a prerogative of keeping the peace within the realm."

This sets the potential scope for future development of the prerogative to be largely discretionary, save for the fact that "no new prerogative" may be created.

Some doubts may be advanced as to the desirability of such a wide discretion. Does   **4–042** the Executive have a choice as to when *it* may rely on prerogative powers or require statute? Does the prerogative overlap with statute or co-exist with statutory authority? Conventional wisdom has drawn back from the creation of new prerogative powers to revive an existing statute or create new prerogatives. It is settled law that in the *Case of Proclamations*[25] the Crown has no prerogative to create new wrongs; but in *Malone v MPC*[26] Megarry V.C. accepted that the limited power to authorise telephone-tapping under the prerogative was derived from the extension of the power to open articles sent through the post. Today such powers have a firmer statutory foundation under the Interception of Communications Act 1985. This followed the decision in *Malone* after a decision of the European Court of Human Rights[27] which held that the absence of legal controls over the circumstances in which phone-tap warrants could be issued was incompatible with Article 8 of the Convention.

It might be suggested that statutory authority is preferable to reliance on prerogative   **4–043** powers thus enabling debate and parliamentary scrutiny to take place. This form of democratic check on the Executive provides a visible and public forum for discussion. In the *Council of Civil Service Unions v Minister for the Civil Service*[28] known as the *GCHQ Case*, in 1985, the House of Lords held that in legal principle the prerogative could be subject to judicial review in much the same way as an Act of Parliament or delegated legislation made under the Act. The Prime Minister relied on an Order in Council made under the prerogative to ban trade union membership by staff at the Government Communications Headquarters. Reliance on the Order in Council was

[23] William Wade, *Constitutional Fundamentals* (1989), pp.58–64.
[24] *R. v Secretary of State for the Home Department Ex p. Northumbria Police Authority* [1989] Q.B. 26.
[25] (1610) 2 St. Tr. 723.
[26] [1979] Ch. 344.
[27] (1985) 7 E.H.R.R. 14.
[28] [1985] A.C. 374 at 418B–C.

claimed on the basis of national security. In the past prerogative powers had not always been amenable to judicial review, and *GCHQ* has settled the question of justiciability. However, the judges have shown reluctance to offer a fundamental reconsideration of how such review might operate. The wide discretion given to the Executive in their use of prerogative powers in the *Northumbria Police Authority* case may indicate a judicial willingness to support executive powers.

4–044   The supply of CS gas and baton rounds to the Northumbria Police Authority was open to the Home Secretary as a prerogative power "to supply equipment reasonably required by police forces to discharge their functions". The provision of equipment was authorised by the Police Act 1964 but also by the prerogative. Such a prerogative may be found in the Crown's right to prevent crime and maintain justice. This is an example of a prerogative being updated to the needs of modern society.

4–045   In *Secretary of State for the Home Department Ex p. Fire Brigades Union*[29] the House of Lords acknowledged the importance of statutory authority over the prerogative. The case concerned the attempt by the Home Secretary to introduce a tariff system of compensation under prerogative powers in preference to the system of compensation established under the Criminal Justice Act 1988. The House of Lords held that this was an abuse of prerogative powers and unlawful.

4–046   Prerogative powers may appear to sit uneasily with the legislative functions provided by a democratically elected Parliament. Nevertheless the importance of the prerogative is undiminished. Consider, for example, the prerogative of mercy, one of the personal prerogatives of the Crown which is exercised theoretically by the Sovereign on advice of the Home Secretary. A pardon so granted may be free or conditional. It may be regarded as an essential power, a necessary part of the criminal process to remedy mistakes either at trials or appeal. At present such a power appears as a final determination made by the Home Secretary and to date the courts have been reluctant to provide review of how it is exercised. Arguments for and against such a review may be made but the question is, should such a power of pardon remain a prerogative and not a statutory power?

4–047   The preference for a legislative rather than a prerogative power is intended to regularise and bring up-to-date ancient practice and provide clarification of a vague and uncertain area of the law.

4–048   The courts have been willing to define the existence of the prerogative and its applicability. But in the *GCHQ* case the House of Lords were reluctant to extend judicial scrutiny to the question of whether prerogative powers should or should not be exercised. This potentially leaves a wide discretion as to whether statutory or prerogative powers should be used, which apparently does not fall within the remit of judicial scrutiny.

4–049   The example of the *Northumbria* case[30] has shown the use of the prerogative to secure a particularly broad discretion to preserve the peace. Since the Second World War, legislation such as the Emergency Powers (Defence) Acts and various Public Order Acts such as the consolidation in the Public Order Act 1986 and the Prevention of Terrorism (Temporary Provisions) Act 1984 on terrorism in the United Kingdom has shown the wide powers required for the maintenance of peace. But despite the

[29] [1995] 2 All E.R. 244.
[30] 1989] Q.B. 26.

width of these wide statutory powers, they do not preclude the future use of the prerogative.

An alternative perspective offers a more restrictive use of prerogative powers. On this perspective, if statutory powers exist which apply to the same activities as a prerogative power, the statutory powers should be used. In *Attorney-General v De Keysers Royal Hotel Ltd*[31] the House of Lords preferred a statutory basis for possession of a London hotel for Staff Officers during the First World War, as opposed to the use of prerogative powers. Lord Moulton explained: **4–050**

> "There can be no excuse for reverting to prerogative powers simpliciter—if indeed they even did exist in such a form as would cover the proposed acquisition, a matter which is far from clear in such a case as the present—when the legislative has given to the Crown statutory powers which are wider than anyone pretends that it possessed under the prerogative . . ."

In *Burmah Oil Co v Lord Advocate*[32] the House of Lords accepted that the use of the prerogative did not prevent a claim for compensation even where the destruction of oil installations was required to prevent the enemy from using a valuable resource. After the decision of the House of Lords, the War Damage Act 1965 retroactively removed the subjects' rights to compensation. **4–051**

Prerogative powers allow the Crown the power of incorporation, such as the incorporation of universities, professional societies and even the British Broadcasting Corporation. Additional powers required are usually statutory and the prerogative is confined to the power to hold property, enter contracts and engage in the terms of the activities contained in the Royal Charter. In most cases today, statutory authority is provided in the relevant legislation which is adapted to ensure the corporate entity has sufficient legal powers. Historically this "incorporation" of local authorities such as Parish, District and County Councils provided the early basis of local government. **4–052**

The prerogative in foreign affairs

Foreign relations often involve international agreements and are primarily conducted under prerogative powers. International agreements cover a wide range of activities contained in treaties, conventions, agreements, protocols or charters. While often binding in international law, their application as part of the United Kingdom's domestic law requires an Act of Parliament. While the Crown has no prerogative powers to enforce treaties as part of English law, the Crown possesses wide prerogative powers in foreign affairs where the Crown in an action for tort liability may plead the defence of "act of state" for acts performed abroad. This defence is strictly confined to acts done "abroad" and not within domestic jurisdiction. **4–053**

The term "act of state" is itself a complex expression which does not facilitate easy definition in constitutional law. Jackson and Leopold[33] define that the term act of state: **4–054**

---

[31] [1920] A.C. 508.
[32] 1965] A.C. 75.
[33] P. Jackson and P. Leopold, *O'Hood Phillips and Jackson, Constitutional and Administrative Law* (2001) p.321.

". . .is generally used for an act done by the Crown as a matter of policy in relation to another state, or in relation to an individual who is not within the allegiance to the Crown."

4-055   In *Laker Airways v Dept of Trade*[34] Lord Denning considered the use of the prerogative in connection with the designation of an airline. The Bermuda Agreement 1946, a Treaty between the United States and the United Kingdom, stated that designated carriers would be able to obtain a foreign air-carrier permit from the United States Civil Aeronautical Board which was subject to Presidential signature. On the part of the United Kingdom, the Civil Aviation Act 1971 permitted the Civil Aviation Authority (CAA) to issue an air transport licence to provide a designated carrier permission. The case arose when Laker Airlines, who had been granted a licence for its low-cost transatlantic air service, found that a change of government resulted in the Secretary of State issuing the CAA guidelines effectively withdrawing the licence designation from Laker. The Secretary of State claimed both statutory and prerogative powers. Lord Denning in an *obiter dicta* rejected the use of prerogative powers "to deprive the subject of a right conferred on him by statute". Once a licence had been granted under the 1971 Act, it could not be removed by prerogative powers.

4-056   Where an act of state is more directly relevant is where the Crown may use its authority to protect itself from action at the suit of a private individual. Here the courts may examine the facts to decide whether an act of state may be pleaded and whether done within the limits of the discretion. It has been held that a wrong committed by a Crown servant against a British citizen in a British territory has no defence of act of state. However this view is not always accepted by the courts and each case would seem to depend on its own particular facts. Particularly confusing is the question of the definition of "British citizen" under the British Nationality Act 1981; does it mean the same as British subject, or those "who owe allegiance to the Crown"?

4-057   In defining the limits of the prerogative and its reviewability, the courts have broadened their review to the issuing of passports which are Crown property issued at the discretion of the Secretary of State. In *R. v Secretary of State for Foreign and Commonwealth Affairs Ex p. Everett*[35] the Court of Appeal reviewed the Secretary of State's refusal to issue a passport under the prerogative. Taylor, L.J. explained that:

> "the grant or refusal of a passport is . . . a matter of administrative decision, affecting the rights of individuals and their freedom of travel. It raises issues which are just as justiciable as, for example, the issues arising in immigration cases."

4-058   This view rejected the argument that the issuing of passports fell within the category of foreign affairs involving executive functions and therefore outside the power of the courts to review.

4-059   The prerogative in foreign affairs developed historically and continues to exist as an important "residuary" power of the Crown.

[34] [1977] Q.B. 643.
[35] [1989] Q.B. 811.

Some general conclusions might be made about the prerogative. Although the **4–060** existence and precise limits of the prerogative are at times vague and unchartered, it is subject to judicial review and the remit of its use may be subject to judicial control. Many of the conventions, characteristic of the United Kingdom's Constitution, owe their origins to ancient prerogative powers. The principal convention, for example, is that the Queen shall exercise her formal legal powers only in accordance with the advice of Ministers. However, there are some prerogative powers such as choice of Prime Minister in the event of a hung Parliament, which leave the Sovereign a degree of discretion when deciding who is likely to command the support of the House of Commons.

Total abolition of the prerogative and its replacement with statutory powers would, **4–061** out of necessity, require codification of rules covering many of the areas it currently regulates. This may prove difficult and more challenging than might appear at first glance. Any codified arrangement would need to retain some degree of discretion in defining when prerogative powers may be used.

A major advantage is the inherent flexibility and versatility of the prerogative. For **4–062** example the prerogative of mercy may remove "all pains, penalties and punishment". In foreign affairs, diplomatic relations and representation have their source in prerogative and not statutory powers. Democratic accountability is argued in favour of statutory powers over the prerogative because statutory authority is more visible, clearly defined and subject to the parliamentary process. It is also clear that prerogative powers when claimed to give sovereign immunity are subject to review. A detailed restriction on the immunities enjoyed by foreign governments is provided by the State Immunity Act 1978. It includes situations where civil actions may lie against foreign states that fall within the jurisdiction of the British courts. This covers commercial transactions and contracts, liability in tort, and patents. None of the provisions of the 1978 Act are intended to affect the immunities given to embassies and consular services of foreign diplomats under the Diplomatic Privileges Act 1964 and the Consular Relations Act 1968. A significant decision of the House of Lords on the limits and extent of sovereign immunity may be found in *R. v Bow Street Magistrate Ex p. Pinochet (nos.1 and 2)*, known as the *Pinochet case*.[36] The use of a claim of sovereign immunity to protect General Pinochet from arrest and extradiction was considered in detail by the House of Lords. The case against Pinochet was that, while Head of State in Chile, he had acted unlawfully in authorising torture and other illegal acts. The claim of sovereign immunity was held by a majority in the House of Lords to only afford protection to legal acts and not illegal ones. A distinction appears to have been drawn between the full immunity enjoyed by current and serving diplomats and Heads of State and the partial immunity enjoyed after service. The illegality complained about, the breach of human rights, fell under s.134 of the Criminal Justice Act 1988 which incorporated into British law the Convention on Torture. The application for extradition was made by Spain. General Pinochet is not a British citizen and the crimes alleged to have been committed were outside the United Kingdom. The majority in the House of Lords appear to construct the responsibilities of the courts in England and Wales as giving effect to international obligations on human rights. This

---

[36] *R. v Bow Street Magistrate Ex p. Pinochet (no.1)* [2000] 1 A.C. 61; also see *Pinochet (No.2)* [2000] 1 A.C. 119.

is a trend that is noticeably moving the courts towards a universal jurisdiction over crimes committed under international law and the upholding of international human rights. The majority appear to have rejected the idea of upholding any protection afforded by sovereign immunity when human rights abuses were alleged against a former Head of State.[37]

THE CROWN AND THE GOVERNMENT

4–063 The Monarch as Head of State performs many ceremonial functions. The money to finance the Royal Family is separate from the expenses of maintaining the Government. Since George III's time, in return for the surrender to Parliament of the ancient hereditary revenues of the Crown and any income from Crown land, Parliament has made provision for the salaries and other expenses of the Royal Family. The Civil List Act 1952 provided for a fixed annual sum but the Civil List Act 1972 provided that the sum may be varied by Treasury Order. In 1975 the effects of inflation caused the Civil List Act 1975 to be passed allowing supplements to be paid. This remains the case today although from 1991 it was agreed that a fixed annual payment of about £8 million per annum would be made. The result, it was hoped, would avoid any need for incremental increases and would mean that Royal finances would fall into line with the principles of ordinary departmental expenditure. Increasingly the Royal Family is being treated like any other government department. Indeed some expenses such as the royal yacht before its decommissioning in 1999 were paid out of departmental expenses. In 1992 the Queen agreed to pay for certain members of the Royal Family out of her own funds. The Prince of Wales has never received any money from the Civil List as provision is made for income out of the Duchy of Cornwall. Also in 1992 the Queen agreed for the first time to pay income tax in respect of her private income.

4–064   While some favour abolition of the Monarchy claiming that it is unrepresentative or out of touch with ordinary people, the trend is more in favour of incremental modernisation. How to make the monarchy compatible with a modern and vibrant democracy is less easy to achieve. Hereditary office appears inconsistent with elected and open competition. Today there is less tolerance of the ancient relics of the Constitution and it is generally accepted that the Monarchy's survival depends on the wish of the British people to maintain a Monarchy. This debate should not undervalue the importance of the Monarchy in the terms of Walter Bagehot's defined roles[38]: "the right to be consulted, the right to encourage and the right to warn". In these matters the Monarch is ruled by convention.

The Personal Powers of the Sovereign

4–065 Some of the personal powers of the Queen have been touched upon above. Three require some special mention. First the appointment of the Prime Minister, secondly the dismissal of Ministers, and finally the dissolution of Parliament. In the case of the

---

[37] Kriangsak Kittichaisaree, *International Criminal Law* (Oxford, 2001), pp.56–61.
[38] Walter Bagehot, *The English Constitution* (Fontana, 1963), p.111.

appointment of the Prime Minister, the Monarch's choice is governed by the convention that the person appointed must have the confidence of the House of Commons. The judgment as to who fulfils this criterion is usually straightforward: the party leader with the majority of seats is appointed as the Prime Minister. Where a party leader resigns or dies in office then the election of the leader falls to the rules of the political party in power. The resignation of Mrs Thatcher as Prime Minister in 1990 resulted in the Conservative Party's election of Mr Major as the leader of the Conservative Party, the party with the largest number of seats, and he therefore became Prime Minister.

If there is an election which results in a "hung Parliament", that is where no one 4–066 party is in the majority the choice of the Monarch as to who should be asked to form a Government may become the crucial issue. There is a general convention that the Monarch will seek a wide canvass of views but there is in the final analysis a personal choice to be made within the boundaries of the question of who is most likely to be able to form a government. This residual discretion may in practice be delegated to political leaders as to their advice or to the Queen's personal advisers. A more transparent system of decision-making may be more appropriate.

The second prerogative power relates to the dismissal of Ministers. This is 4–067 undertaken on the advice of the Prime Minister. This in turn must rest on the political reality of most government power, the ability to command the support of the political party in power. It is unlikely that today the Queen could exercise a personal choice over the dismissal of the Prime Minister or Ministers. It is clear that the reality of public opinion must caution any interference with democratic choices made by the electorate.

Finally, there is the question of the prerogative of dissolution. The advice of the 4–068 Prime Minister is normally accepted in these matters. A Cabinet decision is unnecessary before any request is made and it is accepted convention that the request for a dissolution should not be refused nor has one been refused over the past century.

The question of whether the Monarch's prerogative powers should be codified in a 4–069 written constitution or provided for in a statute has been raised in several reform proposals. In the case of dissolution there is an additional argument in favour of fixed-term Parliaments.

CABINET AND PRIME MINISTER

Powers and functions

Executive powers in the United Kingdom are carried out by the Cabinet and Prime 4–070 Minister. Crick, writing in 1964 commented[39]:

> "Of all Governments of countries with free political institutions, British government exhibits the greatest concentration of power and authority. Nowhere else is a Government normally so free to act decisively, so unfettered by formal restraints of constitutional law."

[39] B. Crick, *The Reform of Parliament (1964)* (2nd ed., 1968), p.16.

4–071 Crick's analysis appears equally valid in recent times. The Government enjoys considerable powers and rights over the citizen through a wide variety of sources. Statutory, prerogative or EC Directives or Regulations may permit the Government or its agents to carry out different tasks and functions. Such extensive powers are said to be exercised according to the law. In this respect it may be noted that the courts' role in overseeing ministerial decision-taking becomes important when ministerial decisions are challenged in the courts. The function of judicial review in the oversight of government involves the broader question of how government is made accountable, and the different techniques both legal and political involved in the scrutiny of government.

4–072 The executive powers of government in the United Kingdom are exercised by or on behalf of Ministers of the Crown who are members of the Cabinet. The Cabinet as an institution of government has its origins in the seventeenth and eighteenth centuries. No exact date for its beginning may be given as it evolved around confidential advisers to the Monarch. The Cabinet's independence from Royal influence was gradual and probably due to the incapacity of various Monarchs rather than a revolutionary break with tradition.[40]

4–073 Historical traces of the exact form the eighteenth-century Cabinet may have taken are obscure. References in 1740 as to the existence of the inner Cabinet bear similarities to the modern Cabinet system of today. As the role of domestic government expanded beyond the collection of finance, the regulation of the State became a shared enterprise not solely within royal power. Various departments of State may be identified with specific responsibilities such as the Lords Commissioners of the Treasury. Hennessy[41] identifies the Privy Council as the model of how the earliest Cabinet took shape. Some writers are reluctant[42] to link the modern Cabinet with any particular committee such as the Foreign Committee or Intelligence Committee of the Privy Council in the 1660s and 1670s.

4–074 Blackstone[43] linked the Monarch with exclusive executive powers. Advice taken by the Monarch came from the Privy Council. Cornish notes[44]:

> "Queen Ann had held regular 'Cabinets' and the idea persisted, dividing at some stages into inner and outer works, but still contributing to a process in which the monarch would play a decisive personal role. The Chief among these Ministers, forerunner of the modern Prime Minister, remained so long as he kept the royal confidence, though it was already part of that favour that he should also enjoy the support of the Commons on most issues."

4–075 Bagehot, writing of the English Constitution in 1867, identified the principal characteristics which linked the legislature and executive elements of the Constitution. He acknowledged "the efficient secret of the English Constitution" as the close union and complete fusion between the executive and legislative powers. The Prime Minister was

[40] The cabinet is fully discussed in: J.P. Mackintosh, *The British Cabinet* (1977); Ivor Jennings, *Cabinet Government* (1959); Patrick Gordon Walker, *The Cabinet* (1972); Douglas Wass, *Government and the Governed* (1984).
[41] P. Hennessy, *Cabinet* (1986), pp.100–103.
[42] I. Jennings, *Cabinet Government* (3rd ed., 1959), p.86.
[43] Blackstone, *Commentaries*, BkI., Ch.6.
[44] W.R. Cornish and G. de Clark, *Law and Society in England 1750–1950*, pp.10–14.

at the head of the "efficient" part of the Constitution. Bagehot distinguished the "efficient" from the "dignified". The Queen was head of the "dignified" part of the Constitution. The "efficient" were the parts of the Constitution "by which it, in fact works and rules". The "dignified" parts were those which "executed and preserved the reverence of the population".

Bagehot's classification that the Cabinet and Prime Minister performed the "efficient" elements of the Constitution, endures today as a classic explanation of the theory of Cabinet government[45]: **4–076**

> "A Cabinet is a combining committee—a hyphen which joins, a buckle which fosters, the legislative part of the State to the executive part of the State. In its origin it belongs to the one, in its functions it belongs to the other."

Cabinet government has continued to develop, conforming to the theory of Bagehot's definition, but in recent times evolving modern characteristics. **4–077**

Cabinet size and the allocation of seats within Cabinet does not conform to a rigid convention but, through the choice exercised by the Prime Minister of the day. Since the Second World War the size of the Cabinet has varied. The smallest modern Cabinet of 16 members was achieved by Churchill by excluding Ministers of Education and Agriculture and Fisheries. The recent experience of Cabinet Government suggests between 22 and 24 members. Mrs Thatcher's Cabinet had 22 members, Mr Wilson's 24, and Mr Blair has 23 members. **4–078**

However, the House of Commons Disqualification Act 1975 and the Ministerial and other Salaries Act 1975 allow no more than 95 holders of ministerial office to sit and vote in the Commons. In addition the Prime Minister may appoint between 20 and 30 parliamentary private secretaries. Such appointments are largely held by supporters of the Government in the Commons. **4–079**

The working of the Cabinet, as distinct from its membership, has always been cloaked with secrecy. Gladstone, when Prime Minister, sent copies of Cabinet discussions to the Queen with personal notes and suggestions added. Glimpses of the Cabinet at work in recent times have emerged from the published diaries of ex-Cabinet Ministers, most notably Richard Crossman's Diaries.[46] Often such diaries reveal more about individual ministers than the exact functioning of the Cabinet, which remains secret. The 30-year rule allows the disclosure of Cabinet documents, but this is subject to "weeding" out those that remain sensitive or too confidential to be made available to the public. Some of the more confidential papers may be withheld for a longer period than the 30-year rule may provide. The confidentiality of Cabinet deliberations receives protection in a number of ways. S.8(4) of the Parliamentary Commissioner Act 1967 protects the information that relates to the proceedings of the cabinet. S.28 of the Data Protection Act 1998 provides exemptions for information from the data protection provisions of the Act if the minister's a member of the cabinet. **4–080**

The Haldane Report[47] (1918) is one of the few reports that tackle the issue of what is the role and function of the Cabinet. Its description is a classic formulation of the theory and practice of Cabinet government. The Cabinet's functions include the **4–081**

---

[45] Bagehot, *The English Constitution* (1867).
[46] *Att.-Gen. v Jonathan Cape Ltd* [1976] Q.B. 752.
[47] Report of the Machinery of Government Committee, Cd.9230 (1918).

determination of policy to be submitted to Parliament, the control of the national Executive in accordance with policy presented by Parliament and "the continuous co-ordination and delineation of the activities of several Departments of State". A noticeable part of Haldane's description of the Cabinet function is the parliamentary aspect of the Cabinet's role, thus acknowledging Parliament's ultimate authority.

4–082   Since the *Haldane Report*, the Cabinet has continued to change reflecting the party political aspects of its development. In 1986 Peter Hennessy[48] published a confidential government memorandum which reveals how the modern Cabinet has developed. In *Questions on Procedure for Ministers, A Guide for Cabinet Ministers* (1986, as amended in 1994) the business of the Cabinet is identified as:

> "(a)   questions which engage the collective responsibility of the Government, either because they raise major issues of policy or because they are likely to occasion public comment or criticism;
>
> (b)   questions on which there is an unresolved conflict of interest between departments."

4–083   In addition, financial proposals are submitted to the Cabinet and Ministers may set out their views on general issues of policy before the Cabinet. Advice may be given by the Secretary to the Cabinet, who is also the Head of the Civil Service, as to the question of when matters which may be suitable for the discussion of the whole Cabinet may be raised. The Prime Minister's consent must be sought if an individual Minister wishes to raise a matter at Cabinet.

4–084   A noticeable distinction is drawn between the individual work of Ministers in departments and general policy issues to be put before Cabinet. Defining such a distinction is clearly problematic but leaves the setting of the tone, culture and overall policy of the Cabinet within the Prime Minister's ambit.

4–085   The evolution of the modern Cabinet through incremental change from the nineteenth century to the modern style of management, is a remarkable demonstration of the inherent flexibility in constitutional arrangements. Constitutional innovation may take place without any general reconsideration.

4–086   One innovation of modern Cabinets has been the gradual increase in the Prime Minister's influence. Crossman[49] believed that the era of Prime Ministerial government was the reality of modern government. The outcome, he feared, was to relegate the Cabinet from the "efficient" to the "dignified" according to the Bagehot classification.

4–087   Examples cited of the so-called "decline" in the decision-making role of the Cabinet include the announcement that the first British A-bomb was tested without the Cabinet having made a formal decision on the matter, when the Atlee Government commissioned its development with only the Prime Minister and a number of close Cabinet colleagues consulted.

4–088   In 1984 the decision of the Government to ban trade union membership at GCHQ Cheltenham was made by a small group of Cabinet Ministers rather than the Cabinet

---

[48] Hennessy, *Cabinet* (1986), pp.8–13. Also published in *The New Statesman*, February 14, 18, 21 (1986).
[49] R.H.S. Crossman, *Memoirs of a Cabinet Minister* (London, 1976), 3 vols. Also see Turpin, *British Government and the Constitution* (1990), pp.168–70; G.W. Jones, "Development of the Cabinet" in *The Modernisation of British Government* (W. Thornhill ed., 1975).

as a whole. In 1986 Mr Heseltine, the Secretary of State for Defence, complained and later resigned because the Cabinet had not discussed a key policy issue over the future of Westland plc, a major defence supplier of helicopters. His resignation came at a Cabinet meeting, when it was decided that Ministers' statements on the affair should first be submitted to the Cabinet Office for clearance as to their consistency with Government policy.[50]

In the final analysis, Westland may be seen as the assertion of Cabinet decision-making. However in the initial stages the problem may have arisen because of the use of Cabinet committees, the restricted membership of each committee preventing a full debate of the issues before the full Cabinet. Mrs Thatcher's resignation in 1990 may have underlined the importance of Cabinet support, even when the Prime Minister appears popular and successful. **4–089**

Committees of the Cabinet are of nineteenth-century origin. Their use has evolved over time in an ad hoc way. Some committees are chaired by the Prime Minister, others by senior Ministers. Some are referred to as standing committees which are permanent for the duration of the Prime Minister's period in office. Others are called ad hoc committees because they have specific and particular issues to exercise. One good example of this was known as the "Star Chamber", well known because it used to meet each autumn to reconcile the competing claims made by the various spending departments. Membership of the Star Chamber included the Chief Secretary to the Treasury and the Chancellor of the Exchequer. Since 1992 the Star Chamber has not met. Its current role is undertaken as part of the Comprehensive Spending Review which settles government expenditure over a three-year period and concludes its deliberations by July. There is a third category known as ministerial committees which are composed only of civil servants. The existence of such committees has been, until recently, kept within the inner workings of No.10 Downing Street. However, the committees and their operation are now more openly publicised and acknowledged. In 1999 it was discovered that there were well over 13 committees, 11 sub-committees and seven ministerial groups. The range of activities covered by such committees is comprehensive: Economic Affairs, Energy Policy, Public Services and Expenditure, Environment, Local Government, London, Home and Social Affairs, Women's Issues, Legislation, Constitutional Reform, Devolution, Northern Ireland, Intelligence Services, Food Safety and Utility Regulation. The existence of a committee reflects the ebb and flow of government policy. **4–090**

Such committees have added to the debate on the question of Cabinet or Prime Ministerial government. The influence of the Prime Minister is seen as a key element in their functioning, appointment and operation. In theory, Ministers have access to the full Cabinet should they require approval against the wishes of the Committee but only where the Committee chairman gives approval. Mrs Thatcher when Prime Minister continued the procedure of her predecessors by using committees to make key decisions. In 1980, the decision to replace Polaris with Trident was taken by an ad hoc committee with the Defence Secretary, Foreign Secretary, Chancellor of the Exchequer and Home Secretary present. The granting of independence to the Bank of England in 1997 through powers to set interest rates also appears as a decision undertaken without formal Cabinet discussion. The Bank of England Act 1998 **4–091**

[50] Heseltine, Resignation statement, *The Times*, January 10, 1986.

contains the legislative framework to implement this reform and creates an independent Bank of England.

4–092   In addition to the above committees, there is conclusive evidence that Prime
Ministers in recent times have developed the habit of summoning an "inner Cabinet"
of key Ministers. Clement Atlee, Chamberlain, Churchill, Eden and Wilson throughout
their premierships made use of a small group of close friends or allies drawn from the
Cabinet. In a constitutional sense the existence of such an inner Cabinet is not
recognised in our formal constitutional arrangements. However its existence is a
political fact, reflecting the way in which Prime Ministers may wish to function. During
periods of crisis such as the Falklands or Gulf Wars, small war cabinets exist
containing key Ministers relevant to the success of wartime operations.

4–093   The question arises as to whether such "inner cabinets" are consistent with Prime
Ministerial government which may conform to a Presidential style or should be
compared to collective decision-taking through Cabinet government. The existence of
the inner Cabinet and various committees of the Cabinet, such as the Defence and
Overseas Policy Committee; the Economic Strategy Committee; the Legislation
Committee and a Home and Social Offices Committee is used as evidence to
strengthen the view that Prime Ministerial influence is paramount.

4–094   Crossman wrote[51] in 1972 that Prime Ministerial government arose because the
Prime Minister decides the membership of the Cabinet, sets the agenda of Cabinet
discussion and organises Cabinet committees. An opposing view to Crossman is
provided by Jones,[52] who doubts that the evidence against Cabinet government is
conclusive. Jones offers the analysis that trends in favour of Prime Ministerial
government may just as easily be interpreted to show that the Cabinet's survival
depends on effective delegation to cope with a growing bureaucracy in government. In
recent years, Mrs Thatcher's style and method dominated the work of the Cabinet. Her
years as Prime Minister seemed to support the view that "collective decision-making in
Cabinet" had suffered a decline and a shift to a Presidential style.

4–095   Mrs Thatcher came under the accusation that in all but name the style was
presidential rather than Prime Ministerial.[53] The same analysis is offered about Mr
Blair. The reduction of Prime Minister's Question Time to one occasion in the week
rather than the twice-weekly tradition of past Prime Ministers is viewed as an example
of the shift in style. Research[54] has shown that Mr Blair has voted in only 5 per cent of
House of Commons divisions since May 1997. This is an indication of the setting of
priorities away from Parliament. The use of political advisers and an active role for the
Press Secretary to supplement a relatively small number of civil servants in the Prime
Minister's office is seen as further evidence of a shift in the direction of Presidential
style. The small number of full Cabinet meetings and the delegation of policy to the
various committees mentioned above suggest a shift in emphasis, if not in substance.
The shift towards any Presidential style is vigorously denied by the Prime Minister. It is
argued that it is a perception about modern government rather than any substantive
change in the nature of cabinet government.

---

[51] Crossman, *Inside View* (1972), pp.62–67.
[52] G.W. Jones, "The Prime Minister's power" in *The British Prime Minister* (A. King ed., Macmillan,
London, 1985), p.216.
[53] M. Foley, "Presidential Politics in Britain" (1994) 6(3) *Talking Politics* 141.
[54] B. Jones *et al., Politics UK* (4th ed.), p.419.

Another dimension to the debate is the party political nature of government's **4–096** decision-taking. Prime Ministers are simultaneously leaders of their party. At a party political level, the choices exercised by the Prime Minister must ensure electoral success. The timing of the election and the decision to dissolve Parliament are at the discretion of the Prime Minister and choosing wrongly may have the penalty of losing the election and political power.

The ebb and flow of Prime Ministerial influence through Cabinet reshuffles and **4–097** policy decision-making is often constrained by the realities of political life. In the case of Mrs Thatcher, the epitome of the shift to a Presidential-style Prime Minister, her demise as Prime Minister was the signal of ultimate Cabinet and therefore party control.[55]

It may be concluded that in recent years the shifts in style and management **4–098** techniques between the Cabinet and Prime Minister do not necessarily signal institutional change in the role of the Cabinet. The Prime Minister remains *primus inter pares* with considerable powers to influence the Cabinet and ultimately the success or failure of the Government.

The Cabinet Office provides the Cabinet and Prime Minister with the administrative **4–099** services necessary for the circulation of the Cabinet's agenda reports and recording the Cabinet's conclusion. It is headed by the Secretary to the Cabinet who serves as a Principal Private Secretary to the Prime Minister and is Head of the Civil Service. Contained within the Cabinet Office from 1970 to 1983 was the Cabinet "think-tank" as it was known or more precisely the Central Policy Review Staff (CPRS). The CPRS has the role to cross-departmental activities and take a long-term view of the policies and strategies to be recommended. It was staffed by non-civil servants and abolished by Mrs Thatcher in 1983. It was replaced by a Downing Street Policy Unit which operates as part of the Prime Minister's Office. There is a communications and strategy section within No. 10 to concentrate on media relations.

Also within the working of No.10, there are various political staff attached to the **4–100** Prime Minister, including a Principal Private Secretary, press agent and various advisers. Political advisers have in recent years had an increasingly important role within government departments as well as within the Prime Minister's Office. Their role has increased under Mr Blair as Prime Minister. The image of the Prime Minister, in terms of media profile and in the international arena, has given rise to an increasing sense of presidential powers. The implications of the terrorist attacks on September 11, 2001 and the use of an inner war cabinet to deal with the "war against terrorism" supports the view that for moments in the life-cycle of party politics, the Prime Minister is in charge rather than the Cabinet. It is difficult to predict whether this represents a paradigm shift in the relations between cabinet and prime minister. Large parliamentary majorities provide for differences in approach and both Mrs Thatcher and Mr Blair had successive majorities overall. In contrast Mr Major did not, and so adopted a more inclusive style of cabinet deliberation.

---

[55] B. Jones, "Thatcher and After" in *Politics UK* (Jones *et al.*, 1991), pp.588–597.

Collective and Individual Ministerial Responsibility

4–101　Individual ministerial responsibility is the cornerstone of our constitutional arrangements. The responsibility arises from convention and is defined to mean that Ministers are responsible, i.e. accountable, or answerable to Parliament. In modern times it has been interpreted to mean that Ministers take responsibility for their departments and for the consequences of what has been decided as a matter of policy. Turpin has identified the meaning of responsibility and the question of how sanctions might apply to uphold responsibility.[56]

> "The obligations to answer, to submit to scrutiny, and to redress grievances may seem in practice to lack the support of any coercive rule or sanction. Undoubtedly these obligations are imperfect, resting as they do upon conventions, practices, and procedures which are liable to change and to be variously interpreted and applied, and which depend ultimately upon the political culture."

4–102　Ministerial responsibility has been acknowledged by the courts as a guiding principle of the Constitution. It provides constitutional principles as the basis for the Parliamentary scrutiny of the Executive. Ministers may appear before Select Committees to answer questions or before the whole House of Commons. It has been invoked as the basis of ministerial resignation, for example, Lord Carrington over the Falklands invasion by Argentina in 1982; and the resignation of Mr Leon Brittan in 1986, after he authorised the improper release of a confidential letter written by the Solicitor-General to the Secretary of State for Defence.

4–103　In the classic case of resignation, that of Sir Thomas Dugdale in 1954 over the sale of land[57] in Devon compulsorily acquired during the War, resignation is seen not as an automatic or inevitable sanction, but as the basis of what the Prime Minister regards as the interests of the Government. The *Crichel Down* case is often referred to as supporting the convention of ministerial resignation for the acts of civil servants. Since 1984, official and private papers on the affair have cast doubts over whether the facts in 1954 support ministerial resignation over the alleged failure of civil servants to act correctly over the application of Commander Marten. It seems that the civil servants had not been negligent; rather, they acted according to the wishes of the Minister.[58] In fact it may be argued that the Crichel Down example is atypical. Resignation is rarely used today for ministerial errors. It is unlikely that ministers would resign in similar circumstances today. The complexity of government and the difficult matter of linking ministerial policy with the complaint of failure have weakened the system of holding ministers to account. A single departmental budget may be worth several billions of pounds, and it is difficult to see how ministers may be able to exercise scrutiny over all the activities of their departments. Ministers are often in their job for a limited time

---

[56] C. Turpin, "Ministerial Responsibility: Myth or Reality?" in *The Changing Constitution* (J. Jowell and D. Oliver ed., 2nd ed., 1989), pp.55–60. See D. Woodhouse, "Ministerial Responsibility in the 1990s: When Do Ministers Resign?" [1993] 46 *Parliamentary Affairs* 277. See Chap.4 for a fuller discussion of conventions.

[57] *Report of the Public Inquiry into the Disposal of Land at Crichel Down*, Cmd.9176 (1954). See also I.F. Nicolson, *The Mystery of Crichel Down* (1986).

[58] I.F. Nicolson, *The Mystery of Crichel Down*, 1986.

and consequently have limited opportunities to discover whether or not their policy is working or is defective. In the Crichel Down affair ministerial resignations came about because of political embarrassment caused by revelations about ministerial impropriety in supervising the conduct of their respective departments.

Ministers may resign after appearing before Select Committees or the whole House of Commons to answer questions. For example, Mr Leon Brittan resigned in 1986, after it was alleged that he authorised the improper release of a confidential letter written by the Solicitor-General to the Secretary of State for Defence. The resignation of Mr Brittan as Secretary of State for Trade and Industry typifies the modern approach to ministerial errors. Resignation appears to have been a means of protecting the government of the day from serious political damage and also a way for Mrs Thatcher, the then Prime Minister, to survive.   **4–104**

In theory, ministerial resignation might also follow from serious policy misjudge-ments, errors within a government department, or personal error arising from a minister's private life. Instances where some degree of fault is perceived to lie with the minister have been unusually numerous in the past twenty years. However, the fault is usually connected with the private life of the minister rather than an error of government policy. David Mellor in 1992 and Cecil Parkinson in 1985 resigned over sexual affairs, while Patrick Nicholls, Under-Secretary of State for the Environment, resigned in 1990 after being arrested for drunk-driving, and Tim Yeo resigned in 1994 for personal reasons during a period when public opinion became critical of the personal morality of ministers and members of Parliament. Ron Davies, the Secretary of State for Wales, resigned in 1998 because of his private life, as did Lord Caithness, Minister of State for Transport, in 1994. Two resignations in 1998, those of Peter Mandelson, the Minister without Portfolio, and Geoffrey Robinson, Paymaster General, were due to an undeclared personal loan made by Robinson to Mandelson.   **4–105**

Ministerial responsibility came under scrutiny in 1992. This followed the collapse of the Matrix Churchill trial and led to the first modern, in-depth investigation of government decision-making, legal powers and administration, and the effectiveness of the Parliamentary process for holding government to account.   **4–106**

The Scott Report and Ministerial Responsibility

In November 1992 the trial of three former executives of the machine-tool manufac-turer Matrix Churchill for the illegal export of arms to Iraq collapsed after a former minister, Alan Clark, gave testimony. He revealed that government departments had been aware of the nature of the equipment when export licences were granted. Despite this fact, four ministers had signed public interest immunity certificates intended to prevent confidential documents from being revealed to the defence at the trial. It was also revealed that one of the defendants had provided information to the Secret Service over a number of years. Signing the certificates also prevented full parliamen-tary disclosure of the reality of government policy. Soon after the trial collapsed, and following public disquiet about the way it had been conducted, the Prime Minister set up an inquiry under Sir Richard Scott. Its aim was to find out the circumstances leading up to the trial and the role of government ministers.   **4–107**

The inquiry was not set up under the Tribunals and Inquiries Act 1921. Instead it was an independent inquiry entrusted to a single judge, on behalf of the Prime   **4–108**

Minister, with its own procedures determined by the inquiry chairman, Sir Richard Scott, and put into practical operation by a team attached to the inquiry. The inquiry concerned the role of the Attorney-General, thus preventing the Attorney-General fulfilling his customary role of acting as legal adviser to the inquiry. Independent counsel was appointed[59] and carried out the role of investigator and adversarial ally to the chairman of the inquiry. As a result the inquiry incorporated both inquisitorial and adversarial techniques. The inquiry lasted over three years.

4–109   The Scott Report into the "arms to Iraq" affair consists of five indexed volumes. Amounting to over 1,800 pages, it was published in February 1996 as a House of Commons paper. The conclusions reached in the Scott Report go to the heart of government accountability. Trade and its regulation fall under the provisions of the Export and Customs Powers (Defence) Act 1939, passed on the outbreak of the Second World War. Until the Scott Report was published, this was a little-known but vital piece of legislation that had remained unrepealed and largely unnoticed. Successive governments enjoyed the benefits of the legislation without amending or reforming its basic provisions for fear that amending legislation would draw public attention to existing practice and lead to contentious debate. This fact alone drawn from the Scott Report confronts one of the basic assumptions made about parliamentary democracy—that when in doubt, the government of the day will seek parliamentary authority for its actions. Legislation should be updated to take account of changing circumstances, and keeping quiet about legislation that in modern times ought to have been revised is a serious flaw in the system of internal checks and balances.

4–110   In fact, the Scott Report leads to the conclusion that the operating assumption within the inner workings of government is that government has the necessary legal powers until specifically and categorically prohibited by legislation. This assumption or working practice is seriously called into question and challenged by the Scott Report. It is a fundamental weakness of existing systems of parliamentary scrutiny that internal checks and balances very often fail to alert Parliament to the necessity for law reform.

4–111   More immediately, the facts leading up to the Matrix Churchill trial[60] in November 1992 that precipitated the Scott inquiry go back to the circumstances surrounding the outbreak of war between Iran and Iraq in 1980. The outbreak of war resulted in a speedy assurance from the government that no lethal weapons would be supplied through licensed sales to either side. This trade embargo was applied on the basis of the 1939 legislation, and a government statement made public the restrictions on sales to Iran and Iraq. Though ambiguously worded, these restrictions were added to by the government in 1981 with the view that every opportunity should be taken to exploit Iraq's potential as a promising purchaser of defence equipment, with the exception of lethal weapons interpreted in the narrowest sense.

4–112   In 1984 what became known as the Howe guidelines were promulgated and made public. The guidelines contained four restrictions, namely: that the consistent refusal to supply lethal weapons to either side should be maintained; that existing contracts and obligations should be fulfilled; that no new orders should be sanctioned for any defence equipment which might significantly enhance the capability of either side to

[59] Presiley Baxendale Q.C.
[60] See D Leigh, *Betrayed: The Real Story of the Matrix Churchill Trial* (1993).

the conflict; and that all applications for export licences for the supply of defence equipment to Iran or Iraq should be scrutinised with great care.

The Howe guidelines were certainly intended to tighten up and strengthen existing practice. However, they left considerable doubt as to the actual restrictions to be observed. The restriction on lethal weapons was vaguely expressed; the acceptance that defence equipment might be provided was equally unclear; and the juxtaposition of both concepts appeared contradictory. Defence equipment might indeed include lethal weapons, and lethal weapons might be required for defence purposes. Government policy as represented in the Howe guidelines appeared sufficiently ambiguous and flexible to provide very little difficulty in their observance. According to the Scott Report, up until August 1988 they appeared to be an accurate reflection of government policy.   **4–113**

The cessation of the Gulf war in 1988 brought to an end the apparent mischief that the Howe guidelines were intended to deal with. The signal given by the government, including Lord Howe himself, was that the end of the war and the cease-fire could allow economic opportunities to be exploited to the full.   **4–113a**

It is clear, with the benefit of hindsight, that what was required was a full-scale review of the guidelines, the applicable law, and how arms sales are regulated. What occurred instead was incremental change through stealth, rather than a fundamental review. A more flexible approach over arms sales appeared to be necessary, and the government exploited the ambiguous guidelines to that end. A number of key government departments had responsibilities over arms sales.   **4–114**

The Foreign Office appeared reluctant to allow fundamental changes to the guidelines. The system of licensing required formal approval from the Department of Trade and Industry (DTI), which had overall responsibility for exports, and the DTI appeared willing to embrace a more open policy of trade. The Foreign Office attempted to keep the government advised of long-term strategies. Pressure from British companies intensified for a share in the arms trade and the economic opportunities of trade amid intense competition from foreign companies. The Ministry of Defence broadly favoured a more market-based approach and supported the DTI in a more flexible interpretation of the Howe guidelines. The guidelines were subtly amended. The original 1984 Howe guidelines contained the following: **4–115**

"... we should not in future approve or sanction new orders for any defence equipment which in our view would significantly enhance the capability of either side to prolong or exacerbate the conflict. . . [61]

The revised 1988 guidelines included:

"... we should not in future approve new orders for any defence equipment which in our view would be of *direct and significant assistance to either country in the conduct of offensive operations in breach of the ceasefire. . .*" (author's emphasis).

Interpretation of the revised guidelines appeared to offer more flexibility than the original guidelines. Given the sensitive nature of the arms trade, the revised guidelines   **4–116**

[61] *Hansard*, HC Vol.84, col.450w.

were not published or announced in Parliament. Incongruous though it sounds, it was naively believed by the government of the day that shifts in policy would probably be detected by the public at large, and so the revised guidelines would receive tacit public approval once they were operative. It was tacitly assumed that the government was prepared to withstand robust questioning on its policy both inside and outside Parliament. On the other hand it was assumed that, if the government made the guidelines public, then great public debate would arise, possibly resulting in political embarrassment. The Government might be forced into an unwelcome review of the entire arms licensing system. This had major implications for Britain's reputation abroad and might put at risk future arms sales.

4–117   Scott considered that the guidelines on arms sales constituted a statement of policy and that revising the guidelines reflected a change in government policy. Government statements made in 1989 and 1990 about policy on arms exports[62] "consistently failed to discharge the obligations imposed by the constitutional principle of Ministerial responsibility".

4–118   Sir Richard Scott also found that the Attorney-General was at fault in not making clear to the court at the trial of the Matrix Churchill directors that Mr Heseltine, then President of the Board of Trade, was reluctant to agree to signing the certificate claiming public interest immunity.[63] A second criticism was that the Attorney-General had mistakenly interpreted the law on public interest certificates when he claimed that ministers were bound to sign such certificates when requested to do so. Criticism was also made of a number of ministers for the reasons they gave for signing certificates.

4–119   Aside from such criticisms, Sir Richard considers that ministers were, albeit perhaps mistakenly, engaged in acting in what they took to be the national, and therefore the public, interest. Ministers gained no direct benefits from the arms sales and had been influenced by the need to operate within the competitive conditions of the market. The information available to ministers at the time was less than the information available with the benefit of hindsight. Ministers and civil servants are to be judged by what they knew and believed then. At the heart of the ministerial defence on arms exports was the claim that ministers had applied the spirit of the guidelines out of necessity. In short, ministers could rely on their subjective assessment as a defence. They may now appear to have been mistaken but at the time they acted in good faith and with the public interest in mind. In effect, parliamentary answers left Parliament and the public at best confused and at worst misled about the government's true policy on arms sales. The question of whether ministers were to blame for this state of affairs was a central issue of importance for the Scott Report. Scott approaches this issue with some degree of dexterity. He provides throughout the report an elaborate and detailed analysis of the facts and evidence that justify the main conclusions reached in the report. In so doing he read, digested and had access to more secret information than possibly any other single individual in recent times. Far from being captivated by the ethos of secrecy, Scott adopts a stance highly critical of the conduct of government.

4–120   Scott provides detailed and systematic evidence about government indifference to Parliament and the public. Three ministers deliberately failed to inform Parliament

---

[62] See The Rt. Hon Sir Richard Scott, The Vice-Chancellor, *Return to an Address of the Honourable House of Commons dated 15th February 1996. Report of the Inquiry into the Export of Defence Equipment and Dual-use Goods to Iraq and related Prosecutions* (1996 HC 115) (hereinafter the Scott Report), para.D4.63.

[63] See John F. McEldowney, "The Scott Report: Inquiries, Parliamentary Accountability and Government Control in Britain" (1997) 4:4 Winter *Democratization* 135–56.

about sales of arms to Iraq for fear of the public outcry that might result. On the sensitive issue of whether Parliament was misled, Scott found that, with regard to the policy on exports, Parliament and MPs were[64] "designedly led to believe that a stricter policy was applied than was the case". Scott does not accept that the Attorney-General was not personally at fault. The Department's attitude to disclosure of information was consistently grudging. The letters on exports to Iraq conveyed the idea that no military equipment had been sold to Iraq during the Gulf Conflict. This assertion could not truthfully be made.

Following its publication, the Scott Report was considered in debate in the House of Commons. No minister resigned, and by a majority of one, ministerial censure or resignation was avoided. The Scott Report provides an important summary of ministerial accountability where the focus is not on resignation but on the requirement to give information to Parliament. The Scott Report underlines the importance attached to information. It is expected that ministers should not knowingly mislead Parliament and that they should be as open as possible in the giving of information. However, the lack of any obligation on ministers to volunteer information when it is not specifically requested may result in their responsibility appearing too weak and inadequate if they are prepared to be economical in their answers. A more worrying legacy of the Scott Report is that ministers may be able to rely on a subjective defence. In other words ministers, when questioned, may be mistaken in their answers, but so long as they act in good faith and with the public interest in mind, they should not be held at fault. This leaves a remarkable void. Very often, only ministers will know whether their answers may mislead. Without an obligation to provide a full answer, full ministerial responsibility may remain elusive.   **4–121**

What is the long-term significance of the Scott Report? At the time there was much controversy over the procedures adopted by the inquiry. Criticism focused on the absence of the right to allow lawyers to cross-examine witnesses about information revealed during the day-to-day hearings at the inquiry.[65] Sir Richard came under intense public scrutiny. An inquiry headed by a single judge inevitably led to consideration of his personal views. The juristic techniques available to the inquiry, the careful collection of evidence, and the technical consideration of detailed Civil Service documents were often overlooked as the melodrama of the inquiry played out in public hearings and the media when the Attorney-General, Mrs Thatcher and Mr Major gave evidence. The political debate captured the public's attention and distracted attention from the main issues.   **4–122**

The criticism that the inquiry had departed from the conventional wisdom of allowing cross-examination gained support from the authority of the six principles adopted by Lord Salmon in 1966 among criteria to guide future inquiries. Cross-examination is seen as one of the strengths of the oral tradition of advocacy at the Bar. This point was used to great effect as a means of criticising the report. However, Scott's rebuttal of any unfairness is equally cogent. The inquiry provided funds for legal advice and the large numbers of written submissions that were received made cross-examination impractical if the inquiry was to report within a reasonable time. The oral part was only a small fraction of the work of the inquiry. Scott's defence of   **4–122a**

---

[64] Scott, *op.cit.*, para.G117.
[65] Lord Howe of Aberavon, "Procedure at the Scott Inquiry" [1996] *Public Law* 445.

the procedures adopted received support from the Council on Tribunals after the inquiry findings were made public.

4–123　A more serious matter raised by the holding of the inquiry is the propriety of an inquiry on behalf of the prime minister of the day about the government of the day rather than an inquiry on behalf of Parliament. Parliament appears to have divided along party political lines, favouring the government of the day. The facts and circumstances surrounding the Scott inquiry raised fundamental issues about Parliament and its role. What Scott had found was that Parliament had been unable to hold government to account in a satisfactory way. It had been misled, and had consistently failed to detect any alteration in government policy or, through the select committee system, exercise enough scrutiny to deter practices that were inconsistent with the original guidelines. Parliament also appeared weak and ineffectual when the Scott Report came to be debated. It had failed to set the agenda and felt honour-bound to vote on the Report, not according to any principles of parliamentary etiquette, but on party political lines. The greatest irony is that, to protect the findings from legal proceedings, the Report was given the protection of parliamentary privilege by being published as a report of the House of Commons.

4–124　Sir Richard's exhaustive inquiry allowed an outsider into the secret world of the Civil Service and the administration. As an outsider, was he qualified for the task in hand? Professor Martin Loughlin queries Scott's role and expertise[66]:

> "Scott was obliged to examine a sphere of government decision-making, which generally remains secret, and his background in commercial law may not have been ideal training for the task. The conduct of foreign relations is an area in which "ambiguity often seems the safest course". . . From this perspective, reminded of the circuitous ways of foreign relations, Scott indeed may have been rather naive.

4–125　Further criticism is that a judge caught up in the internal politics of party government is liable to become politicised as a result.[67] There is clearly a danger when judges are involved in public inquiries that inevitably lead to party political controversy.

4–126　This may explain why the Scott inquiry showed differences of opinion between government ministers and Sir Richard, reflecting differences in culture and attitude. On Sir Richard's part there is the forensic role of law and lawyers applying prescriptive rules to facts and finding exemptions or exceptions. On the part of ministers there is a culture of secrecy, and an attitude that the role of law is one of enabling and facilitating the conduct of government policy—that unless an action is prohibited by law, it is permissible.

4–127　A more formidable issue is the fact that the Scott inquiry appeared to trespass on the role of Parliament itself and its internal functioning. While this may have been inadvertently undertaken, nevertheless the appearance is that the Scott inquiry roamed into the proceedings of Parliament strictly protected from outside inquiry under art.9 of the Bill of Rights. Art.9, respected by the courts, is followed in many leading cases. In the Privy Council case of *Prebble v Television New Zealand*[68] it was held, in an action

---

[66] Martin Loughlin, *Sword and Scales* (2000), p.43.
[67] Rodney Brazier, "It *is* a Constitutional Issue: Fitness for Ministerial Office in the 1990s" [1994] *Public Law* 431.
[68] [1995] 1 A.C. 321.

which cited proceedings in Parliament, that if the action questioned parliamentary proceedings then it would have to be stayed.[69] What constitutes proceedings of Parliament is an elastic concept. While the Register of Members' Interests does not,[70] it is clear that resolutions of the House, the reports from the committees of the House, and subsequent inquiries and reports do come within the category of proceedings.[71] According to Erskine May,[72] "everything that is said or done" within the precincts of the House forms part of the proceedings in Parliament. Patricia Leopold asks whether the Scott inquiry fell into this category, and concludes:

> "[i]n his report, Sir Richard severely criticised various aspect of parliamentary proceedings—the veracity of answers to parliamentary questions; a statement in the House of Commons by a minister; evidence to a select committee by a minister and a civil servant; and the choice of departmental witnesses for a select committee inquiry. But if Sir Richard had been debarred from making these criticisms, he would have been unable to do his job. However, the contrast is marked between the freedom he possessed as a one-man tribunal and the restrictions he would have had to observe as a judge in a court hearing. A Nelsonian blind eye has been turned to the problem. . ."[73]

It may be concluded that Sir Richard's report followed the trail to its logical conclusions. He exposed the weakness of government decision-making for which the government escaped the censure of resignation. He also exposed the fundamental weakness of Parliament itself, which Parliament has refrained from properly addressing.[74]   **4–128**

Collective responsibility

Historically ministerial responsibility has been formulated to include the whole Ministry responsible for all official acts of the individual Ministers. This carries the implication of collective responsibility when a Minister is acting on behalf of the Government[75] as a whole. Undoubtedly collective responsibility means collective resignation, should there be a no confidence vote in the House of Commons in the government of the day. Such votes are rare. This leaves unanswered the precise formulation of collective responsibility, as inevitably different views within the Cabinet may lead to lack of unanimity over the precise nature of government policy.   **4–129**

Collective responsibility may have a different aspect other than explaining how the Cabinet is responsible to Parliament. It may explain the process which ties the Cabinet   **4–130**

[69] Also see *In Re Parliamentary Privilege Act 1770* [1958] A.C. 331.
[70] *Rost v Edwards* [1990] 2 Q.B. 460.
[71] *Hamilton v Al Fayed* [1999] 3 All E.R. 317, [2001] A.C. 395.
[72] Erskine May, *Parliamentary Practice* (Sir David Limon ed., 22nd ed., Butterworths, London, 1997).
[73] Patricia Leopold, "The Application of the Civil and Criminal Law to Members of Parliament and Parliamentary Proceedings", in *Law and Parliament* (G. Drewry and D. Oliver ed., 1998), pp.71–87.
[74] S.13 of the Defamation Act 1996 was passed to allow M.P.s to pursue legal claims for defamation where the conduct of a person, in or in relation to proceedings in, Parliament is in issue. Immunity may be waived whereby the protection of parliamentary privilege prevented the courts from questioning what was said or done in Parliament.
[75] *Falkland Islands Review*, Cmnd.8787 (1983).

to confidentiality in its decision-making. Thus dissenting voices are silenced once a decision has been agreed in Cabinet.

4–131   The confidentiality aspect of Cabinet deliberations was acknowledged in the *Crossman diaries* case, *Attorney-General v Jonathan Cape Ltd*[76] when the Attorney-General attempted unsuccessfully to prevent the posthumous publication of Cross-man's diaries compiled while he was a Cabinet Minister. The view of Lord Widgery C.J. was that opinions by Cabinet Ministers in the course of Cabinet discussions were protected by confidentiality, and in the public interest, publication could be prohibited by the courts. On the facts of the *Crossman* case a period of 10 years had elapsed and it was considered unlikely that publication would damage the doctrine of joint Cabinet responsibility. Lord Widgery C.J. rejected the view that the diaries should not be published because they disclosed advice given by senior civil servants.

4–132   The *Crossman* case should not be interpreted to mean that in every case publication of diaries would be accepted by the courts. Instead, the case lays the foundation for protecting Cabinet discussion on the basis of confidentiality and therefore the law of confidence. Thus, a claim that disclosure would not be in the public interest is usually sufficient to maintain confidentiality.

4–133   In 1976, after the *Crossman* case, Lord Radcliffe considered the publication of ministerial memoirs as Chairman of a Committee of Privy Counsellors on Ministerial Memoirs.[77] The Report identified working principles as to "the public interest" especially matters which in the international sphere might be detrimental to relations with other nations; or in the domestic sphere, information which would destroy the trust between Ministers or between Minister or advisers or private bodies.

4–134   Since publication of the *Crossman* diaries, the diaries of other ex-Cabinet Ministers, notably Barbara Castle and Tony Benn, have been successfully published in what might be regarded as against the spirit of the Radcliffe rules. Recent publications have also included diaries of ex-civil servants and advisers. Even the Former Head of MI5 has managed to have her diaries published albeit with reluctance on the part of the civil service and ministers. Retired Prime Ministers find a lucrative market among publishers willing to provide large cash advances for publication of diaries or reflections made during the period of office. Nevertheless the confidentiality of the Cabinet has been used to prevent publication, by civil servants and others, of Cabinet discussion. The *Spycatcher* litigation[78] relating to the attempts by the British Government to prevent publication of the memoirs of Peter Wright who had been a scientific officer in counter-espionage from 1955 to 1973 ran the gauntlet of the use of injunctions and potential use of the criminal law. However, in the end it was found that as publication had taken place abroad it was impossible to make an injunction effective.[79] The global use of the internet and other facilities renders the enforcement of the law problematic.

4–135   The conclusion must be that stemming from the doctrine of collective cabinet responsibility, the secrecy of the system of government emanates from the principles of cabinet government. Mr Justice McCowan in *R. v Ponting*[80] directed the jury that Clive

[76] [1976] Q.B. 752.
[77] Cmnd.6386 (1976).
[78] *Att.-Gen. v Guardian Newspapers Ltd (No.2)* [1990] 1 A.C. 109.
[79] *Att.-Gen. v Guardian Newspapers Ltd* [1987] 1 W.L.R. 1248; [1987] 3 All E.R. 316.
[80] [1985] Crim.L.R. 318.

Ponting, an Assistant Secretary of the Ministry of Defence, could not rely on his belief that the government deliberately misled Parliament over the sinking of the Argentine warship, the *General Belgrano*, during the Falklands war, in order to leak documents to Tam Dalyell M.P., a critic of government policy. The Human Rights Act 1998 opens up possibilities that the courts may have to balance the right of the public to know, as against the interests of the government of the day to protect the state. The law is in somewhat of a state of flux. As rights are now available to ensure freedom of expression and open up the ethos of secrecy, government lawyers have become ingenious in attempting to frustrate memoirs in the Peter Wright tradition by seeking to use injunctions to seize assets or prevent any monetary benefit accruing from publication. In *Att.-Gen. v Blake*[81] the House of Lords refused to allow the government an injunction to seize the royalties of the former spy George Blake from the sale of his published memoirs. It was noted that Blake had not been convicted of an offence and that publication probably breached s.1 of the Official Secrets Act 1989. As there had been no conviction there was no statutory power to confiscate his assets. However, the majority of the Lords accepted that the former spy had a fiduciary duty which he breached and, had he been within the jurisdiction of the courts, they would have granted a permanent injunction against the memoirs. It was accepted that given the passage of time there was little in the book that was truly confidential but he was liable to provide an account of profits. This forms a separate form of action from the use of an injunction and opens up the possibility of acting as a deterrent to publication. Another possibility is that publication may breach copyright and this may further be used to restrict publication. At the heart of the government's anxiety is the prevention of embarrassing revelations but also the upholding of cabinet confidentiality.

The cases illustrate how government may be conceived as both a political entity and a constitutional institution. In that sense collective Cabinet decision-making is an effective means of allowing political debate and discussion to take place, while the inner workings of the Cabinet are protected from external scrutiny and accountability.[82] The Scott Report exposed the problems of working within the ethos of secrecy when using immunity certificates to restrict information available to the courts. The next few years will see the development of convention rights expressed through Art.6(1) as setting standards for the courts to review the balance of interests of the litigant as against the protection of the public interest. **4–136**

THE CIVIL SERVICE

There are currently fewer than 500,000 civil servants and over two-thirds of them work in executive agencies. It is expected that by the next five years over 90 per cent of the civil service will be found in executive agencies. A brief overview of the role and function of the civil service is considered here. In Chapter 11 executive agencies are explained and defined in some detail. **4–137**

---

[81] [2000] 3 W.L.R. 625.
[82] *Falkland Islands Review*, Cmnd.8787 (1983).

Definition

4–138   The civil service is permanent and appointed on merit. Described[83] as "the ultimate monster to stop governments changing things," the civil service provides the main administration for the activities of the government of the day. Civil servants may be defined in general terms as servants of the Crown employed in government departments. The Fulton Committee[84] in 1968 added certain exclusions:

> "servants of the Crown, other than holders of political or judicial officers, who are employed in a civil capacity and whose remuneration is paid wholly and directly out of monies voted by Parliament."

4–139   In most discussions about civil servants; the judiciary, Ministers of the Crown, the army, police, officials in local government or National Health Service, are excluded. Commonly-used terms to describe civil servants are: "public officials"; public servants; administrators or crown servants. The latter term has found acceptance in law, as describing the employment relationship and sometimes status of civil servants.

4–140   Civil servants are regulated by many different Acts of Parliament such as the Official Secrets Acts 1911 and 1989 and the Superannuation Act 1972. This is piece-meal legislation; none of the Acts clarifies the legal status, duties, obligations or rights of civil servants. In addition, there are numerous memoranda, such as instructions to civil servants when appearing before select committees or when acting under the Royal prerogative. There are also regulations and instructions made by the Treasury and the Minister for the Civil Service under the Civil Service Order in Council 1982. Civil servants receive a code containing details of their service and pay, entitled: "The Civil Service Pay and Conditions of Service Code". The Code is supplemented by regulations made by each government department for its staff.

4–141   There has always been difficulty in precisely categorising the legal status of civil servants in their employment situation. Modern employment legislation has been applied to civil servants, granting rights in common with other employees regarding unfair dismissal. At common law, service as a civil servant was at the pleasure of the Crown. The exact basis of this rule is a mixture of constitutional law and public policy. The latter has always been difficult to estimate and predict. This is partly due to the fact that "there is in law no universally applicable definition of civil servant or civil service. The most important distinguishing characteristic is service on behalf of the Crown." There is difficulty in expressing a legal implication for such service.

4–142   In addition to the 1978 Employment Protection Consolidation Act, Pt V and s.138 on unfair dismissal, numerous other recent employment legislation also applies. The Equal Pay Act 1970, the Sex Discrimination Act 1975 and the Race Relations Act 1976, all apply to civil servants.

4–143   Civil servants are also regulated by a wide variety of regulations, rules, codes of practice, disciplinary codes and Orders in Council; specifically the Civil Service Order in Council 1982 made under the royal prerogative. Wide powers are granted under the 1982 Order art.4 entitles the Minister for the Civil Service "to give instructions . . . for

---

[83] Quoted in the preface in P. Hennessy, *Whitehall* (1989), p.xiii.
[84] Cmnd.3638 (1968).

controlling the Conduct of the Service, and providing for . . . the conditions of service."

Pay and conditions of civil servants are negotiated through the Civil Service National Whitley Council, dating from 1919. National pay bargaining has gradually broken up and individual negotiations with trade unions are not uncommon. Employment conditions are likely to be further delegated to departments and agencies after the setting-up of "Agencies under The Next Steps" in 1988. The Civil Service (Management of Functions) Act 1992 facilitates this system of delegation. **4–144**

Some doubt has been expressed about whether there is a contractual relationship between the civil servant and the employer, the Crown. It seemed to be accepted in the *GCHQ*[85] case that a contractual relationship did not exist; or at any rate, in arguing for or against retraction of trade union membership, this issue of contract was not relied upon. **4–145**

Mr Justice Otton considered the issue in *R. v Civil Service Appeal Board Ex p. Cunningham.*[86] A prison officer, because of his status as a civil servant and constable, had forfeited his rights by not appearing before an industrial tribunal but had been given an assurance in the Civil Service Pay and Conditions of Service that he would not be "less favourably" treated as a result. Whether contractual rights existed was unclear. This matter of contract rights becomes important because of the present law on how an aggrieved citizen may seek remedies in the courts, through the procedure known as judicial review. Such a procedure must relate to public law matters, and normally disciplinary procedures of a purely domestic nature were not amenable to judicial review. A civil servant may have private contractual rights but also, as a public official, rights under the civil service Pay and Conditions of Service Code. Do such rights fall into the category of public law rights or are they entirely private law rights based on contract? The case law has not provided a clear answer to this question. **4–146**

There is in existence a Civil Service Appeal Board (CSAB) set up under the prerogative which may hear appeals against disciplinary action. In *R. v Civil Service Appeal Board Ex p. Bruce,*[87] Bruce, a civil servant, was an Inland Revenue employee who appealed to the CSAB against his dismissal. The Court of Appeal and the Divisonal Court accepted that the CSAB was amenable to judicial review even though in that particular case an alternative remedy could have been sought. There was some doubt as to whether a contract might exist, as no intention to create legal relations existed. This point was *obiter dictum* and the *Bruce* case did not decide whether civil servants had contracts of employment. Earlier in *McClaren v Home Office,*[88] again *obiter dictum* Woolf L.J. stated that "an employee of a public body is normally in the same position as other employees". The *McClaren* case concerned the appointment of prison officers, appointed under the Prison Act 1952 rather than the prerogative, so the case may be unhelpful when it is applied to civil servants normally appointed under the prerogative. **4–147**

The uncertainty in the law leaves unanswered the fundamental question of whether civil servants have contractual rights. The answer to this question may prove elusive, in the absence of any legislative intervention. **4–148**

---

[85] [1984] 3 All E.R. 935.
[86] [1991] 4 All E.R. 310.
[87] [1988] 3 All E.R. 686.
[88] [1990] I.C.R. 824; [1990] I.R.L.R. 338.

Role and Function of the Civil Service

4–149 The convention of ministerial responsibility applies not only to the relationship between Ministers and the House of Commons but also to that between Ministers and civil servants. The formulation of this principle may take a number of forms.

4–150 First, civil servants owe a duty to Ministers. Here there is no distinction between the Government of the day and the role of the civil service. The civil servant is answerable to the Minister and through the Minister, to Parliament.

4–151 Secondly, Ministers do not normally reveal the role played by civil servants in formulating policy. Even when advice is problematic, rarely do Ministers reveal the identity of civil servants.

4–152 Thirdly, civil servants may advise Ministers on policy but in theory they are not called upon to act politically. Where a civil servant has doubts or misgivings about the instructions received from Ministers, the *Armstrong Memorandum* in 1987, since revised, provides guidelines as to how civil servants should behave. Especially when questions of constitutional propriety or legality are involved or even politically embarrassing decisions are made, civil servants should seek redress or resolution of such doubts within the civil servant's own department. This may be achieved through appeal to the senior officer in the department, or to the legal adviser to the department in question. There is the addition of the Public Disclosure Act 1998 which covers "whistleblowers" and provides protection for private, public and voluntary sectors. The Act is confined to matters of malpractice and on the basis of that affords protection to the whistleblower. In order to qualify for protection there is a good faith requirement and a factual basis must be established for the basis of the whistle blower's belief to cover an external disclosure.

4–153 Criticism of the *Armstrong Guidelines* points to doubts over the effectiveness of such arrangements especially after the Westland affair. Differences between Government Ministers were being resolved by the disclosure of a confidential letter, between the Solicitor General and the then Secretary of State for Defence (Mr Heseltine), by the civil servants acting with the authority of the Secretary of State for Trade and Industry (Mr Britton). This disclosure broke the convention of strict confidentiality over the letters and advice of law officers. Civil servants did not seem able to prevent such disclosure and there may have been no option in the circumstances but to have complied with the instructions of the Minister. Civil servants in this matter were prohibited from appearing before select committees or giving interviews to the press.

4–154 Ministers may claim to know what is in the best interests of the public as well as in the interests of the Government. Ministers are self-authorising over the publication of confidential information. Leaks may be authorised by a Minister. Oddly, what appears to be a means of holding ministers to account, the doctrine of ministerial accountability, may allow a wide exercise of ministerial discretion.

SUMMARY AND CONCLUSIONS

- Prime ministerial government has the appearance of a presidential style despite the tradition of cabinet decision-making. The Presidential style of Prime

Ministerial decision-making is often because the government of the day has a large parliamentary majority.

● The civil service undertakes the conduct of government amid the glare of media attention and the appointment of political advisers to act as a link between government and the electorate.

● The exercise of prerogative powers is subject to review by the courts.

● Accountable and responsible government requires strengthening of select committees and the power of Parliament.

● The Crichel Down affair in 1954 raised the possibility that ministerial resignation might follow the acts of civil servants. Since 1984 the papers, official and private, on the affair have cast doubts over whether the facts as believed in 1954 support ministerial resignation on the basis of the alleged failure of civil servants to act correctly over the application of Commander Marten to buy or rent land originally compulsorily acquired by the Air Ministry in 1938. It seems that the civil servants had not been negligent, rather that they acted according to the wishes of the Minister. In both the Westland affair and in *Crichel Down*, ministerial resignation came about because of political embarrassment caused in both cases by revelations about ministerial impropriety in supervising the conduct of their respective departments.

● The role and function of the modern civil service is undergoing considerable change. A useful contrast may be drawn between the Victorian legacy of the civil service and the modern tendency to transfer civil servant activities to Next Step agencies.

● Ministers have increasingly sought advice from outside the civil service through the appointment of advisers sympathetic to the policies of the Government. This is a trend which was noticeable in the Wilson Government in 1974. The trend has continued and prompted a former retired civil servant to suggest that[89] "a large number of senior civil servants" might be replaced with politically appointed officials on contracts. Political neutrality, permanence, independence and professionalism are seen as advantages in the recruitment and ethos of public service. Such an ethos is under detailed scrutiny today. Currently there are over 90 special advisers acting for the government of the day and, as a result, in the public mind blurring the distinction between impartiality and political spin. This development represents one of the greatest challenges for the future of the civil service. Diversity in its role, the modern Civil Service has to address the inclination of the government of the day to develop policy that is sold to the electorate in a media-friendly way.

---

[89] John Hoskyns, "Whitehall and Westminster: An Outsider's View" (1983) 36 *Parliamentary Affairs*, 137–147.

FURTHER READING

T. Daintith and A. Page, *The Executive in the Constitution* (Oxford University Press, Oxford, 1999).

G. Drewry, "The New Public Management" in *The Changing Constitution* (J. Jowell and D. Oliver ed., 4th ed., Oxford University Press, Oxford, 2001), pp.168–189.

EU, *Improving Management in Government: The Next Steps* (Stationery Office, London, 1988).

Making the Most of Next Steps: The Management of Ministers' Departments and their Executive Agencies (Stationery Office, London, 1991).

G. Ganz, *Understanding Public Law* (3rd ed., Sweet & Maxwell, London, 2001).

C. Harlow and R. Rawlings, *Law and Administration* (2nd ed., Butterworths, London, 1997).

P. Hennessy, *The Blair Centre: A Question of Command and Control?* (Public Management Foundation, London, 1999).

The Secret State: Whitehall and the Cold War (Allen Lane, London, 2002).

Does the United Kingdom Still have a Constitution? (A. King ed., Sweet & Maxwell, London, 2001).

C. Munro, *Studies in Constitutional Law* (2nd ed., Butterworths, London, 1999).

Chapter 5

THE RULE OF LAW AND CONSTITUTIONAL CONVENTIONS

INTRODUCTION

Constitutional conventions[1] are an important part of the United Kingdom's constitutional arrangements. Conventions may explain the common practices and workings of government and how the United Kingdom's unwritten Constitution accommodates change.   **5–001**

Dicey's influence has led constitutional lawyers to regard conventions as a means for past practices to be examined in order to determine future conduct. In that sense conventions appear to link the ancient, medieval Constitution with the modern and present-day Constitution. Conventions may provide some order to practices which are, by their nature, forms of political behaviour and therefore difficult to categorise in any strictly legal or constitutional sense. Conventions are usually descriptive of a particular practice.   **5–002**

Conventions have been likened to rules or laws in many of their characteristics, with the exception that conventions are not enforceable by the courts. There is however some ambiguity about the meaning of enforceable, because the courts acknowledge the existence of conventions as aids to interpretation.[2] Frequently, conventions may appear to be objective or neutral in the exposition of a rule or understanding. This may be misleading as conventions often contain value judgements prescribing how certain conduct of government or officials should take place. Conventions commonly recognise the political facts of life and help explain the political workings of the Constitution.   **5–003**

Conventions have grown historically as unwritten rules, and may adapt to the changing methods of modern government. That is their enduring quality. They are not the product of either judicial or legislative intervention, but rather of custom, usage, habit and common practice. The most formative period for their development was probably in the eighteenth and towards the end of the nineteenth century. Conventions have the shortcoming that they reflect the values of mid-Victorian Government, and   **5–004**

---

[1] The most useful account may be found in G. Marshall, *Constitutional Conventions* (1984). See also Hood Phillips, *Constitutional and Administrative Law* (London, 1987), Chap.6; C.R. Munro, *Studies in Constitutional Law* (Butterworths, 1987).

[2] See the *Crossman Diaries* case: *Att.-Gen. v Jonathan Cape Ltd* [1976] Q.B. 752. Discussion of conventions may be found in *Ex p. Notts C.C.* [1988] A.C. 240. The Canadian Courts have discussed conventions. See *Reference Re Amendment of the Constitution of Canada* (1982) 125 D.L.R. (3d) 1.

perhaps fail to take account of modern party political realities. The growth in the complexity of the machinery of government may make accountability through conventions more of a myth than a reality. Many important practices are part of the internal working of government and it is difficult to give internal working practices special value or elevation to the status of convention.[3]

5–005 In this chapter the value and significance of conventions is examined. This is followed by an account of the influence of Dicey in defining and explaining the rule of law. The United Kingdom's constitutional arrangements provide that government is subject to law and may only exercise its powers according to law. The discussion on the rule of law leads into the question of the role of the courts, preparatory to the discussion on administrative law in Chapter 6.

CONVENTIONS

Perhaps the most influential legal writer on the nature of conventions is A.V. Dicey who defined conventions[4] as "the rules which make up constitutional law" that made the United Kingdom distinctive. The use of the term "rules" is deliberate. In Dicey's definition he distinguished "laws" from "conventions". The former he defined as comprising, in the strictest sense, laws such as statute, judge-made law and common law doctrines which are enforceable by the courts. The latter, conventions, are "understandings, habits and practices which are not enforced by the courts but which regulate the conduct of members of the sovereign power".

5–006 Dicey's emphasis on the "non-enforcement" of conventions by the courts is suitably ambiguous to create controversy over whether in principle there is any real distinction between laws and conventions. Since not all laws are enforceable by the court, as some are enforceable by tribunals, and some through discretion bestowed upon Ministers after inquiries, the distinction may seem a curious one today. Despite this reservation it is possible to see the usefulness of the distinction that laws are given effect to, or are recognised by, the courts whereas conventions may not be recognised.

5–007 Dicey's views about conventions appear to have been influenced[5] by John Austin (1790–1859), who distinguished non-legal rules from legal rules and believed in the general value of rules made for the guidance of man. Austin pioneered the analytical form of jurisprudence which was influential in Dicey's analysis of the Constitution. Conventions are regarded in Austin's analysis as part of "positive morality". But conventions do not appear to fit within Austin's definition of law as no clear sanction or enforcement accompanies any breach of a convention; they do however fit in with the idea of morality. Dicey followed this analysis when describing conventions as "the morality of the constitution".

---

[3] C. Turpin, "Ministerial Responsibilty: Myth or Reality?" in *The Changing Constitution* (J. Jowell and D. Oliver ed., 2nd ed., 1989), pp.55–57.

[4] A.V. Dicey, *Law of the Constitution*, Chaps.14 and 15. Dicey tends to provide general principles in the early part of his text which he then re-capitulates later on as he reflects more deeply on their meaning. This may give rise to problems of interpretation (see pp.24, 28–32). Generally, see R.A. Cosgrove, *The Rule of Law, Albert Venn Dicey Victorian Jurist* (1981), pp.87–90.

[5] C.R. Munro, *Studies in Constitutional Law* (1987), Chap.3, pp.35–52. Also Munro, "Laws and Conventions Distinguished" (1975) 91 *Law Quarterly Review* 218; Munro, "Dicey on Constitutional Conventions" [1985] *Public Law* 637. J. Austin, *The Province of Jurisprudence Determined (1832); G. Marshall, Constitutional Conventions* (1984).

However, taking a different perspective from Dicey, Jennings[6] doubted whether the distinction between laws and convention was of any "substance or nature". This might appear to place conventions in a diminished role in the Constitution. Perhaps Jennings doubted the validity of the distinction between laws and conventions to be determined by the courts alone. **5–008**

Jennings' views however would seem to ignore the working practices of most courts who appear to follow Dicey's distinction that conventions may be recognised but not enforced. Rarely have the courts in the United Kingdom used a convention as an enforceable rule. Some leading cases illustrate how the courts are reluctant to treat conventions as enforceable. This does not prevent the courts from recognising the existence of a convention and such acknowledgement may at times appear to be similar to enforcement. **5–009**

In *Madzimbamuto v Lardner-Burke*,[7] the Privy Council had to consider a convention contained in a 1961 declaration that the Westminster Parliament was not to legislate for Southern Rhodesia. Lord Reid commented that the convention, although important, had no legal effect "in limiting the legal power of Parliament". **5–010**

A similar convention of legislative self-restraint was said to have developed historically over Northern Ireland affairs. The Government of Ireland Act 1920, now repealed, provided for a Parliament for Northern Ireland. Over the years a practice developed, that in the House of Commons at Westminster ministerial responsibility excluded any discussion of Northern Ireland transferred matters, that is discussion of matters which were transferred to the competence of the Northern Ireland Parliament. Calvert explains[8]: **5–011**

> "In this sense and in this sense only can these be said to be a convention, but its scope is somewhat limited. It is a convention only as to administrative practice. It does not inhibit legislation or discussion of a bill on a special motion. It operates only within the sphere of questions and other debates and only in relation to matters in respect of which there is, for the time being no ministerial responsibility at Westminster."

Another example of where the courts have recognised the existence of conventions, in *Att.-Gen. v Jonathan Cape Ltd.*[9] Here the case involved the recognition of the important convention of collective ministerial responsibility. Richard Crossman, a Labour Minister from 1964 to 1970, had maintained a daily political diary with a view to publication after his death. Crossman died in 1974 and his executors published the diaries and also extracts from his diaries in the *Sunday Times*. The Attorney-General argued that collective Cabinet responsibility provided a fundamental requirement of Cabinet secrecy which should be enforced through an injunction. Lord Widgery C.J. concluded that a convention could not be enforced in that way if it was "an obligation founded in conscience only" but in general terms the courts might be willing to enforce Cabinet confidences when "the improper publication of such information can be restrained by the court". Redress might therefore be available for a breach of a conventional rule. **5–012**

---

[6] Jennings, *The Law and the Constitution* (5th ed., 1959).
[7] [1969] 1 A.C. 645.
[8] H. Calvert, *Constitutional Law in Northern Ireland* (1968), pp.103, 110.
[9] [1976] Q.B. 752. See also Crossman, *Diaries of a Cabinet Minister* (London, 1976), Vol.2.

5–013   Another example is provided in Canada. The British North American Act 1867 passed by the United Kingdom Parliament left Canada, after the Statute of Westminster 1931, an independent State but with little or no competence to amend the 1867 Act. Amendments had to be through the United Kingdom Parliament, usually at the request of the Canadian Parliament. In 1980 the Federal Canadian Government decided to end the power of the United Kingdom Parliament to legislate, and to incorporate the Charter of Rights as part of its independence. The question arose as to the legal powers of the United Kingdom Government when faced with a desire to change the existing status of the Canadian Constitution arising out of representations made from the Federal Government, when only two Canadian Provinces, Ontario and New Brunswick, agreed. The remaining Canadian Provinces objected to the Federal Government's terms.

5–014   The Federal Canadian Government claimed that the United Kingdom Parliament was bound to accede to its request. This raised the question of what the United Kingdom Parliament was required by convention to undertake under the Statute of Westminster 1931. Doubts were expressed as to the existence of such a convention and, if one existed, should it be enforced? The Foreign Affairs Committee in its report to the House of Commons 1980–81, concluded that there was no binding convention upon the United Kingdom Parliament to accede to the request of the Federal Canadian Government. The matter was put to the Supreme Court of Canada.[10] A majority decision concluded that there was no legal objection to the Federal Government position to petition the Queen for agreement without the consent of the Provinces, but "at least a substantial measure of provincial consent" was required, and as this was not present it was unconstitutional for the Federal Parliament to act. In the end nine Provinces (with the exception of Quebec) did agree and the Canadian Bill 1982 was passed. The Canadian example raised a great deal of discussion about how conventions arose, who decided on their importance and what role the court performed.

5–015   A recurring theme in most of the discussion is Dicey's distinction between laws and conventions and how this might be observed. Unlike common law rules made by judges, conventions are established by the institution of government. Conventional rules might conflict with formal legal rules and therefore are difficult to enforce. Perhaps the courts' search for conventions, and judicial "recognition" of their existence is, as some writers concluded, "enforcing the convention"? Strictly speaking recognition does not mean enforcement in the same way as a statute or byelaw. The question of why conventions are obeyed is difficult to answer.

5–016   Conventions seem to arise in ordinary day usage and develop over a period of time culminating in their general recognition and acceptance. Once a convention is accepted and then followed, it becomes an acceptable form of good practice. Little is known about why conventions are actually obeyed. They do not normally imply any sanction for their breach and as Turpin has noted, they have a remarkable ability to survive and change[11]:

---

[10] *Reference Re Amendment of the Constitution of Canada* (1982) 125 D.L.R. (3d) 1. C. Munro, *Studies in Constitutional Law*, p.45; P. Hogg, *Constitutional Law of Canada* (1992), p.795; Heard, Canadian *Constitutional Conventions* (1991).
[11] Turpin, *British Government and the Constitution*, p.99.

"Conventions are always emerging, crystallizing and dissolving, and it is some-times questionable whether a convention has been broken or has simply changed."

It is a mistake to confine the discussion of conventions merely to good political   **5–017**
practices and thereby beyond constitutional significance. Although unwritten in form
and unclear in existence, they offer important guidance over the behaviour of
government.

Some significant constitutional conventions may be briefly mentioned. Dicey noted   **5–018**
the importance of both ministerial and Cabinet responsibility. The convention that a
government that loses the confidence of the House of Commons must resign or advise
dissolution has a significance in the constitutional history of the United Kingdom.
Brazier[12] notes how such conventions have a certain vagueness and uncertainty about
when they apply. When may a government be said to have lost the confidence of the
House? How major or significant has a "policy" defeat to be before a principle of
confidence is raised? Marshall's conclusion on these matters explains how old or even
outmoded conventions may undergo change.

"In the 1960's and 1970's, in any event, governments seem to have been following
a new rule, according to which only votes specifically stated by the Government to
be matters of confidence or votes of no confidence by the Opposition are allowed
to count. Just conceivably one can imagine amongst recent Prime Ministers those
who might have felt it their duties to soldier on in the general interest even in the
face of such a vote."

The most important convention, which Dicey recognised, is collective responsibility of   **5–019**
individual Ministers and of the Cabinet. As discussed in the previous chapter,
individual ministerial responsibility is traditionally defined to mean that a Minister is
responsible for his private conduct and that of his department, including the acts of the
civil servants in his department. The latter suggests some degree of responsibility for
civil servant incompetence or negligence. One example is the ministerial resignation of
Thomas Dugdale in 1954 following the Crichel Down inquiry which concluded that the
Department of Agriculture had acted in an arbitrary manner. Various civil servants
were criticised and the Minister, Thomas Dugdale, resigned. This resignation at the
time was perceived to be a triumph over the bureaucracy of irresponsible civil servants.
More recently, fresh evidence has suggested that ministerial resignation came about
because of the government's embarrassment. As Peter Carrington, then joint Parliamentary Secretary, explained[13] in *Reflect on Things Past*, he and Dick Nuggent had
offered their resignation to Churchill who agreed they should carry on. In such
circumstances Ministers may resign or retain office simply because the Prime Minister
concedes it is in the government's interests.

Ministerial resignations since 1960 have appeared to arise from differences in policy   **5–020**
over government collective decisions such as entering into the European Communities
or disputes over government policy. An eclectic assortment of reasons may be offered
to support the convention of resignation which meets the needs of the government of

---

[12] R. Brazier, *Constitutional Texts* (Oxford, 1990), pp.345–389. Also see de Smith, *Constitutional and Administrative Law* (1989), pp.28–47.
[13] P. Carrington, *Reflect on Things Past*; P. Cosgrove, *Carrington: A Life and a Policy* (1989), pp.55, 57.

the day as much as any principle of accountability to Parliament. Nevertheless responsibility of Ministers means that mistakes, blunders or the incompetence of Ministers are issues which may be raised as matters for the debate and scrutiny of the House of Commons where resignation is rarely the sanction. Instead criticism, rebuke or embarrassment may be the stimulus for Ministers to improve. Overall the standing of the government of the day may decline when poor ministerial judgement is exposed to the glare of publicity. Constitutional conventions may give rise to greater political effects than have constitutional significance. This underlines the remarkable feature of the United Kingdom's unwritten Constitution which often leaves political judgement to determine the outcome of constitutional practices. To countries with a written constitution, this appears an unusual characteristic of the United Kingdom's Constitution where much political power resides and determines constitutional practice.[14]

5–021   Conventions have invariably attracted a wide spectrum of opinion from lawyers and political scientists. Why have conventions, and what purpose do they fulfil? Hood Phillips and other writers have remarked that conventions are really based on[15] "the wishes of the majority of the electors".

5–022   Examples supporting this view are: the conventions relating to the choice of government which is formed from the majority party in the Commons; the convention that the Queen should act on the advice of Ministers; or the convention that the Queen will not refuse Royal Assent to a Bill.

5–023   On more mundane matters such as a request by the Leader of the Opposition for the recall of Parliament during recess, the position is regulated by both convention and the Standing Orders of the House of Commons. Standing Order No.12 allows Ministers to recall Parliament should the Speaker be satisfied by representations that[16] "the public interest does so require". In fact convention seems to indicate that requests by opposition M.P.s to recall Parliament in recent years have been invariably refused. Emergency recall has been rejected on four occasions in the past 20 years. However, since 1945 Parliament has been recalled 14 times: in 1950 to discuss military involvement in Korea, the Suez crisis in 1956, and the Berlin crisis in 1961. More recently recall was granted over the Falklands invasion in 1982 and the Gulf war in 1990. A request for a recall in 1992 on the economy and the sending of British troops to Bosnia was refused. Parliament was recalled to debate the consequences of the terrorist attack in the United States on September 11, 2001.

5–024   Conventions as precedent for past practice may, in the examples shown, not provide much guidance as to future practice. The government may find it easy to make up its mind on the basis of the facts in each case.

5–025   Academic writers have discussed[17] the question of whether conventions might be codified. It is suggested that the importance of conventions is such that they should be collected together into a single code which would attempt to be comprehensive. The attraction of such a code would be to end uncertainty and vagueness associated with knowing whether a particular convention exists or not. The disadvantage is that a code

[14] D. Oliver and R. Austin, "Political and Constitutional Aspects of the Westland Affair" (1987) 40 *Parliamentary Affairs* 20. Also see D. Woodhouse, *Ministers and Parliament* (Oxford, 1994).
[15] Hood Phillips, *Constitutional and Administrative Law* (London, 1987), p.119; R. Brazier, "Choosing a Prime Minister" [1982] *Public Law* 395.
[16] Standing Order of the House of Commons No.12 (1948).
[17] Marshall has discussed codification as has Brazier in de Smith, *Constitutional and Administrative Law* (1985), p.46 and in new edition (1989), pp.34–37.

might lead to rigidity; once codified, would a convention lose its flexibility to change and so become fixed at one period in time? Are all conventions capable of enforcement by the courts? This might invariably follow once a convention became written and adopted in a code.

Attempts at the classification of the subject matter of conventions have identified conventions arising in the exercise of prerogative powers, the workings of Cabinet, the proceedings in Parliament and relations between Lords and Commons, and finally, in relations between the United Kingdom and Commonwealth. This list is not exhaustive. **5–026**

Conventions may be adopted into statute, such as the convention of the United Kingdom not legislating for a former dependent territory in the preamble and s.4 of the Statute of Westminster 1931. **5–027**

The survival of conventions owes much to their general acceptance and the requirement of constitutional government with ultimate electoral accountability. When a convention is breached, the convention is usually sufficiently flexible to survive, even though there may be doubt as to its value once it is discovered that the convention was unable to prevent the breach in the first place. It is ultimately the electorate who will determine the government's worth if there are flagrant breaches of constitutional convention.[18] The courts remain reluctant to enforce conventions. In 1981 Lord Diplock in *R. v Inland Revenue Commissioners Ex p. National Federation of Self-Employed and Small Businesses Ltd*[19] made clear that while Ministers were responsible to both Parliament and the Courts, there was an important distinction. This distinction he explained in terms of law and policy: **5–028**

> "They [Ministers] are accountable to Parliament for what they do so far as regards efficiency and policy; and of that Parliament is the only judge; they are responsible to a court of justice for the lawfulness of what they do and of that the court is the only judge."

Lord Diplock's distinction recognises the differences between Parliament's role to oversee conventions and the courts' authority to determine what is lawful. **5–029**

Some reflections may be offered on the value of conventions. Constitutional lawyers face great difficulty when attempting to understand the different practices of government. Such practices do not easily conform to legal analysis and present problems of ordering, classifying and describing. Constitutional conventions provide a useful organising category, permitting the discussion of government behaviour and activities elevated to constitutional consideration rather than party politics. Loughlin warns that conventions may appear too neatly packaged and therefore may give a distorted analysis[20]: **5–030**

> "It leads too easily to a false ascription of meaning to events and, by trying to generalise from the exceptional cases and ignoring the common case (in which resignation does not occur) has a distortive effect."

Taking Loughlin's caveat seriously, however, there is still value in studying and understanding conventions, although their limitations ought to be admitted. Conven- **5–031**

[18] N. Johnson, *In Search of the Constitution* (1977), pp.31–33.
[19] [1982] A.C. 617.
[20] M. Loughlin, *Public Law and Political Theory* (Oxford, 1992), p.53.

tions may appear descriptive, but in fact they are also normative and interpretative. Perhaps too great an expectation is placed on conventions to fill the gaps in the unwritten Constitution.

5–032   Johnson reflects that perhaps the place given to conventions within the United Kingdom's constitutional arrangements is misplaced and over-optimistic? This may arise from the changing nature of social life and the speed and variety of such change. Johnson notes[21] that:

> "there is no longer that degree of commitment to particular procedures, that respect for traditional values and habits, nor that breadth of agreement about how political authority should be exercised and for what purposes, which would justify the belief that convention alone is a sheet anchor on which we can rely for the protection of civil rights or for the survival of a particular form of government."

5–033   If in the past conventions appeared to offer predictability in the conduct of government activities it is doubtful if this remains so today. In a general way this reflects on the workings of an unwritten constitution. Johnson warns that the qualities of flexibility and adaptability in the Constitution may become simply a means for executive power to increase.

5–034   Perhaps the most positive opinion about conventions is that of T.R.S. Allan who observes that conventions might provide[22] "a primary source of legal principle". Allan also argues that such principles might inform how the rule of law might develop.

THE RULE OF LAW

5–035   Government in the United Kingdom is highly centralised and carried out within a unitary state. Governmental power is not confined by a written constitution or a domestically entrenched Bill of Rights. Government is said to be both accountable and responsible. Responsible government is carried out according to constitutional conventions, international obligations such as the European Convention on Human Rights, obligations through membership of the European Community and the rule of law. Great significance has been given to the rule of law within the United Kingdom's Constitution.

5–036   Constitutional lawyers continue to be influenced by Dicey's explanation of the rule of law contained in his *Introduction to the Law of the Constitution*. The term "rule of law" Dicey acknowledged was not originally his own but taken from the writings of William Hearn[23] (1826–88). Hearn, in fact, acknowledged that his understanding of the rule of law owed much to his analysis of the ideal of government, according to law, from the debates on English government in the seventeenth century. Hearn suggests that the rule of law is of ancient origin and may be found in the literature on the role of the State in society. One of the earliest writings on the ideal of the authority of the

---

[21] N. Johnson, *op.cit.*, n.30, p.33. Jeffrey Jowell, "The Rule of Law Today" in *The Changing Constitution* (J. Jowell and D. Oliver ed., 3rd ed., Oxford, 1994), pp.58–62.
[22] T.R.S. Allan, *Law, Liberty and Justice* (Oxford University Press, 1993).
[23] W. Hearn, *The Government of England, its Structure and Development* (1867).

State acting according to pre-existing laws and not arbitrarily, may be found in Plato's Laws.

Similar ethical considerations apply in various writings in the twelfth and fourteenth   **5–037**
centuries of how rulers or the State should apply the law and subordinate their authority to the law. In the thirteenth century in England, there was strong resistance to the idea that the King should be above the law. Considerable ambiguity surrounds the implications of Magna Carta (1215) when conceded by King John. Some of its chapters place the law of the land as paramount. By implication rather than expressly, the King's acceptance of Magna Carta was also acceptance of the principle of subservience to the law.[24] Sir John Fortescue (1394–1476), an English judge and early English authority on the rule of law, wrote that the King could not override the law as judges must decide according to law, even when commanded to do otherwise.

As mentioned above, Hearn's inspiration for his ideas on the rule of law lay in the   **5–038**
constitutional conflicts of the seventeenth century. James I claimed royal authority over law despite much acknowledged advice to the contrary. The claim against such royal authority lay in its arbitrary nature and even though Monarchy was restored after the Civil Wars, royal authority was not. John Locke (1632–1704) articulated the principles which Hearn was later to rely on, namely that government should be exercised according to the law "promulgated and known to the people" as opposed to extraordinary powers dispensed through proclamation. It is noteworthy that Locke's clear analysis of how the governed should be governed, is less clear over how government itself should be subject to law. While accepting the ultimate authority of law, Locke conceded that discretion was a necessary element in rules and that the prerogative may be a required power for the ruler. Since it was impossible to make full provision for all problems, arguably, much discretion may be considered necessary.

Dicey's own reasoning about the existence of the rule of law depended in large part   **5–039**
on the work of Blackstone, Coke and John Austin. In common with his views on conventions, it was Austin's analysis that had the greatest influence on Dicey, and in particular Austin's views on the ultimate omnipotence of Parliament. Dicey recognised the difficulty of resolving the operation of constitutional conventions and the compatibility of parliamentary sovereignty with the rule of law.

Parliamentary sovereignty had both a legal and a political dimension. Parliament   **5–040**
was susceptible to change through the extension of the franchise and what Dicey perceived as "the working class vote". Dicey, somewhat grudgingly, accepted what he termed "the progress to democracy", but he admitted the potential for conflict between Parliament's sovereignty and reforming legislation which might radically alter the Union or challenge the fundamental characteristics of the Constitution. Dicey believed in the rule of law and the use of conventions as essential mechanisms against abuse, especially of discretionary power. Conventions recognised public "morality" which self-limited the power of Parliament.

In the absence of any formal doctrine of the separation of powers or a written   **5–041**
constitution limiting the powers of the Executive within the State, the rule of law provided a convenient means to express concern over the uncontrolled powers of a newly enfranchised Parliament. Dicey feared the growth in incremental powers to the

---

[24] Bracton, *De legibus et consuetudinibus*. Fortescue, *De Natura legis naturae*, Bk.1 p.16. Coke in *Prohibitions Del Roy* (1607) 12 Co. Rep. 63.

State—in particular, legislation which might interfere with individual liberty, particularly property rights.

5–042   The rule of law is susceptible to a number of different meanings often based on value judgements. In its broadest sense it may be viewed as a general political doctrine. The rule of law is both descriptive and prescriptive, characteristics it shares with conventions of the Constitution. Dicey found three meanings for the rule of law to be considered as part of the constitutional order of the United Kingdom.

5–043   First, Dicey insisted on the predominance of "ordinary law". Government power, especially when it affects the citizen, must be accompanied by observance of the correct legal rules and have the authority of law. Secondly, discretionary power however broadly based must not be abused or used in an unrestricted way to circumvent the legislative authority of Parliament. The Executive should be amenable to parliamentary control. Thirdly, Dicey believed that the enforcement of the principles of the rule of law was best achieved through the ordinary courts and not as part of a written constitution or through the setting-up of a special system of courts. Dicey assumed that civil liberties were best protected through the system of remedies which had developed historically through the courts. Parliamentary sovereignty, which could at a whim destroy the delicate nature of the rule of law, was instead in Dicey's view intended to compliment and reinforce the rule of law. Concerns about the potential for the abuse of sovereignty were offset by Dicey's focus on the elected accountability of Parliament. Craig explains how Dicey attempted to reconcile the apparent contradiction that sovereignty might threaten the rule of law[25]:

> "The two main elements of Dicey's rule of law possesses both a descriptive and a normative content. In descriptive terms it was assumed that the regular law predominated, that exercise of broad discretionary power was absent, and that all people were subject to the ordinary law of the realm. Public power resided with Parliament. In normative terms it was assumed that this was indeed a better system than that which existed in France, where special rules and a distinctive regime existed for public law matters."

5–044   Dicey's belief in the rule of law assumed fundamental importance in his understanding of the Constitution. A jaundiced view might be that Dicey hoped the rule of law might be a valuable tool in his attempt to argue against major political changes, to which he was personally opposed. Home Rule for Ireland, votes for women, and social legislation might be postponed if they offended the rule of law.

5–045   How might Dicey's vision of the rule of law apply today? A major misunderstanding in Dicey's belief in the rule of law was the scope of ministerial power and its delegation to a wide variety of other agents. Even in Dicey's time there was a miscellaneous number of administrative institutions outside the ordinary courts; their existence was not fully appreciated by Dicey which greatly weakened the cogency of his arguments about the rule of law and the role of the courts. The nature of the errors in Dicey's misconceptions are explained more fully in Chapter 8. However, this should not detract from the eloquence of Dicey's views on the rule of law and the importance of Dicey's influence on the development of administrative law.

[25] P. Craig, *Public Law and Democracy in the U.K. and U.S.A.* (Oxford, 1990), p.21. Also see Harlow and Rawlings, *Law and Administration* (1984), pp.1–6, 15–19.

As remarkable as his description of the rule of law is, Dicey's analytical method, **5–046** employed in the formulation of legal principles, also deserves mention. Dicey's method involved abstracting basic principles from legal materials. His style was to begin his text with generalised principles, discussed in more detail later in the work. At times the clarity of his original principles became obscured by the later discussion and contradictions may obscure the principle.

Dicey's critics have identified such weaknesses and some of Dicey's views have been **5–047** revised and re-examined. The challenge mounted by his critics is to expose Dicey's analytical method and the political values upon which his theory rests. Both parliamentary sovereignty and the rule of law have been subjected to such criticism. Loughlin suggests that Dicey was mistaken in his perception of administrative power[26]:

> "In general public law should ensure that the legal framework within which government operated provided an effective and equitable structure for the implementation of the public good, as expressed in the positive functions of the State. From this perspective delegated legislation and administrative adjudication was not a symptom of despotic power but of the changing role of the state."

It may be concluded that Dicey's perception of the role of central government in 1885 **5–048** was influenced by the centralising tendencies of government power and his belief that such powers could be adequately controlled. This depended on his view of the courts enforcing the rule of law as a means of keeping in check the boundaries of parliamentary power. This raises the question of the role of the courts in applying and upholding the rule of law. There is a perception that the common law offers a tradition of fundamental human rights or norms.

The courts adopted different strategies depending on their perception of procedural **5–049** rules, the nature and complexity of the law and remedies and the nature of the issues they were invited to consider, at the time. The emergence in the late seventeenth century of judicial review was largely free from doctrinal development, and reflected the changing nature of parliamentary power. Craig explains[27]:

> "On the one hand, the judiciary began to justify the exercise of jurisdictional control more specifically in terms of ensuring that the authority in question did not usurp or extend the area over which the legislature had granted it jurisdiction. The objective was to ensure that the agency did not assume authority to regulate behaviour or to legislate in areas outside those delegated to it by Parliament. On the other hand, the courts become more aware, in form at least, of the legitimate limits to the exercise of their judicial power."

Craig's thesis is that the courts often adopted conflicting directions and interpretations **5–050** over the nature of legislative powers, the delegation of such powers to inferior bodies and the precise discretionary nature of their own judicial powers.[28] A number of cases may be cited in support of this view. A common theme is the question of whether the delegated body has competence to determine its own decisions. Accordingly the power

---

[26] M. Loughlin, *Public Law and Political Theory* (Oxford, 1992), p.168.
[27] Craig, *op.cit.*, p.22.
[28] See P. Craig, "Formal and sustantive conception of the Rule of Law" [1997] *Public Law* 467.

of appeal to a court of law is distinguished from a review. The former examines the correctness of the decision while the latter the legality.

5–051   This leaves the courts with a less certain role in evaluating the activities of inferior bodies, and gives rise to a perception that the courts' powers of review are limited to technical or procedural requirements as distinct from substantive review. Nevertheless there are a number of legal cases where the courts have sought to curtail the unfettered exercise of State power. In *Entick v Carrington*,[29] Lord Camden in the Court of Common Pleas examined the legal power of the Secretary of State to arrest John Entick, an alleged author of seditious writings, to seize his papers and books and use these as evidence. Entick successfully sued the officers and obtained damages when Lord Camden held that the warrant was illegal and void. The legal reasoning in the case depended on the absence of any legal authority supporting the legal claim that the warrants were lawful. The result was to leave the courts with a power of review but subject to the legislative authority of Parliament. Statutes which expressly confer the rights of arrest or seizure may leave the courts with a minimal role in finding any legal grounds to support the rights of the citizen beyond the narrow scope of the wording of the Act of Parliament.

5–052   There may be a number of limitations on the role of the courts. The "intention of Parliament" is open to interpretation by the Courts. The courts may be limited in the scope of their interpretation. Acts of Parliament cannot be held to be unconstitutional, severely limiting the extent of judicial intervention. Constraints on judicial activism in reviewing informal bodies often depend on the type of body, and their powers under review.

5–053   Implicit in our current unwritten constitutional arrangements is that there is no hierarchy of rights such that any one of them is more entrenched by the law than any other. This point is explained by Mr Justice Laws in *R. v Lord Chancellor Ex p. Witham*[30]:

> "The common law does not generally speak in the language of constitutional rights, for the good reason that in the absence of any sovereign text, a written constitution which is logically and legally prior to the power of legislature, executive and judiciary alike there is on the face of it no hierarchy of rights such that anyone of them is more entrenched by the law than any other. And if the concept of a constitutional right is to have any meaning, it must surely sound in the protection which the law affords to it. Where a written constitution guarantees a right there is no conceptual difficulty. The state authorities must give way to it save to the extent that the constitution allows them to deny it."

5–054   It may be fair to conclude that in the unwritten constitution where the common law accords legislative supremacy to Parliament, the existence of rights for the citizen may be difficult to imagine.[31]

5–055   Local government is not only an elected element of government but possesses wide statutory authority to carry out activities including the promotion of private Bill

---

[29] (1765) 19 St. Tr. 1030.
[30] [1997] 2 All E.R. 779 at 783f–j.
[31] J. Jowell, "The Rule of Law Today" in *The Changing Constitution* J. Jowell and D. Oliver ed., (1989), pp.3–23. See T.R.S. Allan, *Constitutional Justice: A Liberal Theory of the Rule of Law* Oxford University Press, Oxford, 2001.

legislation, the enforcement of criminal sanctions and the expenditure of public money. The courts have held that a local authority acts unreasonably "if no reasonable public body" could have made a decision. The Wednesbury Corporation was empowered to grant licences for Sunday entertainment subject to conditions which it thought fit. The condition—that no children under 15 be admitted to a cinema—was challenged as unreasonable and *ultra vires*; Lord Greene accepted that the courts could not substitute its policy for that of the local authority—an inherent limit on the jurisdiction of the courts. However the courts may intervene as to the legality of the decision on the basis of applying a test of reasonableness. Within the scope of unreasonableness the courts have a wide discretion as to the legality of the powers under review. In *Associated Picture Houses Ltd v Wednesbury Corporation*[32] Lord Greene acknowledged both the jurisdiction of review of the courts and the jurisdiction of the decision-maker to make decisions.

A final dimension to the issue of the remit and scope of the rule of law arises with the Human Rights Act 1998. For the first time Convention rights may be enjoyed by citizens through interpretation of the European Convention by the courts. This creates tensions between the traditional role of the judiciary to interpret and apply the rule of law within the boundaries of statutory enactment, and the significance of constitutional rights that must be given compatibility with our existing law. This shifts the analysis about the rule of law to a rights-based order seeking to locate and secure rights amid a plethora of regulation and complex administrative machinery. Will rights endure? Are such rights sufficiently powerful to endure beyond the necessity of the moment or the emergency of war or civil unrest? Only time will tell. This is, after all, not only uncharted waters, but also a glimpse at real politics when judicial decisions will be seized upon as evidence of political judgment and morality rather than of technical law alone. Rights are likely to be seen as a means of holding to account and an opportunity to create challenges rather than providing a means to seek better government or administration. The pivotal role of the courts depends on the sensitive exercise of discretion, and the hope is that the rule of law will ultimately mean not just justiciable rights but improvements in the policy implementation of decision-makers.[33] Underpinning rights are questions about how the common law development of the idea of the rule of law is likely to survive? Allan in his recent writing, *Constitutional Justice: Liberal Theory of the Rule of Law* has identified how the common law may take the high ground for the articulation of the ideas and conceptual framework that represents the reasoning of the common law embodying the ideals of justice. Rationality and justice operate under a common thread linking the medieval inheritance with the reality of the common law today. Thus the rule of law stands for principles that reflect fundamental values of society and these will endure beyond the life cycle of party politics or political whims. In his thought-provoking analysis the question may be asked as to whether seeing the courts as the delivery system of such values as the rule of law, locates litigation with the protection of the value system. It is equally clear that governmental and non-governmental decision-makers, including business and commerce, through contract employment and a plethora of regulation impact on the day-to-day lives of many people. In so doing the value systems may very well locate rights

5–056

---

[32] [1948] 1 K.B. 223.
[33] See Martin Loughlin, "Rights, Democracy and Law" in *Sceptical Essays on Human Rights* (T. Campbell, K. Ewing and A. Tomkins ed., Oxford University Press, Oxford, 2001).

and protection but they are also going to make-profit making decisions, and risk analysis may well prioritise market gain over any fundamental values. The courts certainly have a part to play in developing the fundamental values in society but it may be peripheral and spasmodic rather than pivotal and predictable.

SUMMARY AND CONCLUSIONS

5–057   Dicey's belief in the rule of law paradoxically inhibited the courts for many years from developing a coherent system of administrative law. His objection to the French *droit administratif* was more generally interpreted as an objection to administrative law, a view which Dicey later retracted.

5–058   Dicey also failed in his analysis of the rule of law to take account of the "body of special rights, prerogatives and immunities". Dicey considered that these no longer existed when in fact government powers include not only the statutory variety discussed above, but prerogative powers and common law rights. We have seen that the courts have developed, in recent years, powers of review over the prerogative, but Dicey failed to appreciate the extent of government or State powers exercised through prerogative powers and therefore largely outside the controls implied in the rule of law.

5–059   Dicey's understanding of the rule of law has had an important effect on the perceptions of many generations of lawyers. In one sense the rule of law may be synonymous with equality before the law and the protection of civil and religious liberty. It also acts as a restraint on power and its abuse. Dicey's analysis was clearly rooted in procedural and technical observance of the law; as a consequence, indirectly Dicey helped to promote the idea that law, politics and the outcome of legal rules should be separated from the legal rules themselves. As Sugarman has observed[34]:

> "Dicey's rule of law endeavoured to create a new procedural natural law or Bill of Rights which could be used to ensure that legal change was slow paced and conservative."

FURTHER READING

T.R.S. Allan, "The Rule of Law as the rule of reason: consent and constitutionalism" (1999) 115 L.Q.R. 221.

T.R.S. Allan, *Constitutional Justice: A Liberal Theory of the Rule of Law* (Oxford University Press, Oxford, 2001).

The Changing Constitution (J. Jowell and D. Oliver ed., 4th ed., Oxford University Press, Oxford, 2000).

I. Loveland, *Constitutional Law* (2nd ed., Butterworths, London, 2000).

---

[34] D. Sugarman, "The Legal Boundaries of Liberty: Dicey, Liberalism and Legal Science" (1983) M.L.R. 102 at 110.

G. Marshall, *Constitutional Conventions. The Rules and Forms of Political Account-ability* (Oxford University Press, Oxford, 1984).

Colin Munro, *Studies in Constitutional Law* (2nd ed., Butterworths, London, 1999).

A.W.B. Simpson, *Human Rights and the End of Empire. Britain and the Genesis of the European Convention* (Oxford University Press, Oxford, 2001).

Chapter 6

AN INTRODUCTION TO ADMINISTRATIVE LAW

In the preceding chapters the outline, structures and principles of the United **6–001** Kingdom's Constitution have been examined, including the role of central government and the civil service. This chapter is intended to explain the development of administrative law: its nature, purpose and significance within the context of the United Kingdom's constitutional arrangements.

This chapter introduces students to the basic framework of administrative law in **6–002** outline, including the impact of the procedures under the Human Rights Act 1998. In Pt III of the book, chapters will be found covering local government, judicial review, remedies and citizens' grievances in more detail. It is hoped that the reader will find the explanation contained in this chapter useful background reading before the more advanced discussion undertaken in Pt III.

INTRODUCTION

Administrative law may be defined as the law relating to the control of government **6–003** power including the detailed rules which govern the exercise of administrative decision-taking. A wide variety of institutions and bodies are subject to administrative law: the Executive and central government; local authorities; tribunals; inquiries; fringe bodies or non-departmental bodies such as quangos and even inferior courts.

A.V. Dicey was reluctant in his *Law of the Constitution* in 1885 to accept the idea of **6–004** specialised and specific legal rules governing administrative decision-making. Nevertheless English law has developed administrative law especially through the growth in case law over the last 30 years. Lord Diplock in *R. v Inland Revenue Commissioners Ex p. National Federation of Self-Employed and Small Businesses Ltd*[1] regarded the development of English administrative law "as having been the greatest achievement of the English Courts in my judicial lifetime".

Account must be taken of changes that have been made to the procedures and rules **6–005** that apply to administrative law as part of the general modernisation of procedures. These changes are in line with the changes introduced under the Woolf reforms to the civil justice system as a whole. The Civil Procedure Rules, specifically from October 2, 2000, known as Civil Procedure Rules CPR Pt 54 Judicial Review and various practice Directions and Pre-action Protocols apply. The term Administrative Law Court is used

---

[1] [1982] A.C. 617.

to describe the jurisdiction of the Divisional Court in matters of judicial review, with new case names and an amalgamated form of Practice Direction[2] intended to stream-line and modernise the system of review.[3] In addition to the creation of an Administrative Law Court, there are changes to the names of the various remedies, certiorari is a quashing order, prohibition is a prohibiting order, *mandamus* is a mandatory order.

6–006   In this introductory chapter we examine the historical development of administrative law, the allocation of functions, the role of the courts and the function of tribunals and inquiries. There are noticeable underlying trends in the development of administrative law. First, as noted by Daintith[4] "text-book writers have tended to see governmental power more as a threat to the individual than as the means of implementing public policy". The cause of this tendency is an emphasis on parliamentary sovereignty, and the inspiration for the study of many of the rules of administrative law has been through the study of judicial review. This only represents one "mode" of government activity and usually one that is conflict-ridden and problematic. Thus, the temptation is for lawyers not to see administrative law not as a means to achieve good administrative decision-making, but as power which requires control either through legislation or the courts.

6–007   Secondly, an over-emphasis on case law may avoid consideration of the different techniques of decision-taking. Daintith identifies the Government's powers of bargain-ing and economic regulation as examples of how implementation of governmental policy may be achieved. This is a recurring theme which is returned to in Pt III of the textbook. An understanding of administration as well as administrative law is necessary in the context of how government activities are carried out. Thirdly, there is a further dimension in the development of a rights focus to judicial interpretation under the Human Rights Act 1998. This is likely to encourage a litigious approach to problem-solving. In part this may question the adequacy of administrative law, developed before the 1998 Act came into force. It may be questioned whether the common law tests for legality or unreasonableness[5] are adequate to the standards of human rights.[6] The creation of an Administrative Law Court may lead to greater conceptual coherence in the development of judicial review. The aspirational quality of rights should not be underestimated in encouraging greater attention to legal rules and their application than hitherto. Even if the courts decide to take a cautious and self-disciplined approach in interpreting the Human Rights Act, it is clear that an important turning point has been reached in the public law of this country.[7] It may in fact prove to strengthen the common law system of analysis and provide greater potential for judicial decision making than at any time in its long history.

---

[2] [2001] 1 W.L.R. 1001.
[3] Michael Fordham, *Judicial Review Handbook* (3rd ed., Hart Publishing, Oxford, 2001).
[4] Daintith, "The Executive Power Today: Bargaining and Economic Control" in *The Changing Constitution* (J. Jowell and D. Oliver ed., Oxford University Press, Oxford, 1989), p.194.
[5] J. Jowell and A. Lester, "Beyond Wednesbury: Substantive Principles of Administrative Law" (1987) *Public Law* 368.
[6] P. Craig, "Ultra Vires and the Foundations of Judicial Review" (1998) 57 *Cambridge Law Journal* 63.
[7] Sir J. Laws, "The Constitution: Morals and Rights" (1996) *Public Law* 622.

ADMINISTRATIVE LAW AND ADMINISTRATION IN ITS HISTORICAL PERSPECTIVE

Administrative law may be examined from the perspective of the phenomenon of modern government possessing a vast array of State powers which may[8] affect the lives of the ordinary citizen, in both domestic and foreign affairs. A sharp contrast is obvious if the nineteenth century is compared to the present day: the size, shape and functions of government have greatly changed. Public expenditure in the 1870s represented less than 10 per cent of the gross national product. Today it is nearly 50 per cent of the gross domestic product. The size and activities of the civil service, even with restraints and cutbacks, is larger today than in 1900. In 1900 there were 50,000 civil servants; by 1980 this had risen to 548,600. Outside central government today there are some 600,000 local government officials, and 100,000 administering the Health Service. Similarly a rapid increase in the legal activities of the State[9] such as in the growth of legislation may also be recognised when compared to the period before and after 1900.[10]   **6–008**

Thus in 1900 Acts of Parliament covered 198 pages of the Statute Book; in 1935, 1515 pages; and in 1975, 2,800 pages. As for regulations these were comparatively few before the First World War: in 1947 statutory instruments covered 2,678 pages; in 1975, 8,442.   **6–009**

Commensurate with the changes in government activities there have been changes in the habits, customs and expectations of citizens. Voting at elections before the Great Reform Act of 1832 was a mere 652,000 out of a population of 13.9 million. Today under universal franchise there is an electorate of over 43 million with a turnout at general elections fluctuating between 72 per cent and 84 per cent of the electorate. Party politics from the latter part of the nineteenth century dominate the exercise of political and therefore governmental powers.   **6–010**

What legacy remains from the formative period of administrative law in the nineteenth century? This question deserves close attention, as developments in the nineteenth century provide much of the explanation of how administrative law developed in England. Craig explains that[11]:   **6–011**

> "the period between 1830 and 1850 witnessed a considerable expansion in the functions performed by central government. Reform in four main areas provides the basis for this expansion: factory legislation, the Poor Law, railways and public health."

---

[8] D.L. Keir, *The Constitutional History of Modern Britain* (1938) provides a useful historical overview. Also see W.R. Cornish, G. de N. Clark, *Law and Society in England 1250–1950* (1989).

[9] H. Parris, *Constitutional Bureaucracy* (1969); D. Roberts, *Victorian Origins of the British Welfare State* (1960); W. Robson, *Justice and Administrative Law*; *The Dynamics of Victorian Business* (Roy Church ed., 1980). O. MacDonagh, *Early Victorian Government* (1977).

[10] *Justice/All Souls Review* 1981, paras.18–22 and cited in Harlow and Rawlings, *Law and Administration*, pp.6–7.

[11] Craig, *Administrative Law* (2nd ed., 1989), p.45.

6–012   These reforms were a result of the growing industrialisation in Britain. Administrative lawyers consider that administrative law developed on a pragmatic and often sporadic basis. There are a number of points to note. First, administrative law depended very largely on statutory intervention. In addition, regulation of many activities was carried on in an informal way sometimes using contract or through procedures avoiding the direct use of legal powers. Major administrative developments were carried out through legislative initiatives or in certain cases, legislative acceptance of rules or existing arrangements.

6–013   Secondly, there was no single or coherent model which applied uniformly. Different forms of adjudication, fact-finding, decision-taking and policy-making were used and made to fit particular circumstances. Debate focused on the nature of the growth in the legislative and judicial powers of the Executive. The categorisation of legal powers was a major preoccupation from the mid-nineteenth century until the 1930s and the setting-up of the Donoughmore Committee on Ministers Powers.[12]

6–013a   Thirdly, the courts' role in developing different techniques to overview administrative decision-taking was often marginal and limited by technicalities. One example of a legal technicality[13] is the difficulty of suing the Crown in tort, which remained problematic until the Crown Proceedings Act 1947. The Crown was allowed certain excepted privileges and this applied to central government ministries, thus precluding the courts' intervention. Crown servants could be sued individually for any wrong, but this did not offer an effective basis for establishing administrative law.

6–014   Fourthly, most State intervention through legislation directly interfered with private property rights and market forces. This is a legacy which remains today when courts are faced with the task of reconciling newly created public statutory rights of State interests with traditional private rights in contract and property law. In the nineteenth century interpretation of statutory arrangements appeared unfamiliar and restrictive to judges instructed in the art of advocacy and in the technicalities of property law. An additional difficulty was the recognition of the different forms of State intervention with the growth in local government as a means of delivery of the many services needed for a locality.

6–015   Finally, the nature of legal rights changed remarkably during this period. Dicey described the nature of the change as a gradual shift from "individualism" to "collectivism". Developments in the growth of administration during the nineteenth century were greatly influenced by utilitarian ideology.

State Intervention and Legislation

6–016   The early development of state intervention provides important clues as to the regulatory techniques that were created. It also helps to explain the mixture of political, legal and social controls that took shape. The relationship between local and central government, the use of inspectorates and the role of the courts may be seen from the foundations set out in the middle part of the nineteenth century. Mac-

---

[12] Cmd.4060 (1932).

[13] *R. v Commissioners of Income Tax* (1888) 21 Q.B.D. 313; G.E. Robinson, *Public Authorities and Legal Liability* (1925). See G.S. Robertson, *Civil Proceedings by and against the Crown* (1908).

Donagh[14] identifies the pattern for the growth in government activities in the nineteenth century. He believes it was based on a practical response borne out of identifying problems and suggesting solutions. Beginning with social problems and their amelioration, various legal responses were applied. General legal prohibition or regulation was attempted, followed by the creation of an administrative body charged with improving the efficiency of decision-taking. Gradually the newly formed administrative body adopted strategies to inform, persuade or encourage compliance with its directions. If necessary central government powers were used, and ultimately ministerial decision-taking might be adopted. Compliance techniques ranged from prosecutions to licensing strategies which might be used to achieve policy implementation and direct compliance. This called for further legislation in order to meet new problems or gaps in the law identified by the new administrative bodies. There was a cycle of formation, growth and demise of administrative bodies.

MacDonagh's analysis is not universally accepted. The main tenets of his analysis **6–017** suggest that administrative developments depend on factual necessity rather than any ideological influences. Critics of MacDonagh argue that he failed to take sufficient account of such influences as Bentham's utilitarian principles. His main critic in this regard is Parris[15] who argues that nineteenth-century government must be seen as a function both of organic change and contemporary political and ideological thought, one of the main currents of which was Benthamism.

The debate between MacDonagh and Parris is largely unresolved. Their contribution **6–018** to our understanding of administration in the nineteenth century is that pragmatic developments in administrative law may be due to the nature of changing administrative bodies. A number of influences may be involved in that development such as practical necessity, ideological belief and enthusiasm for change.

A significant influence on government policy and law reform in mid-Victorian **6–019** Britain was the existence of the statistical movement. The collection of official statistics prepared by government departments complemented the activities of various private statistical societies. The first association for the study of statistics was the statistical section of the British Association formed in Cambridge in 1833. Various statistical societies were formed in other parts of the United Kingdom, with lawyers a dominant influence in the membership. The first, in Manchester in September 1833, was later followed by societies in London, Ulster and Dublin. Building on Brougham's famous law reform speech in 1828, which suggested that Britain's social problems could be identified and remedies proposed, the first meeting of the Association for the Promotion of Social Sciences was held in 1857. The collection of civil and criminal judicial statistics assisted in establishing the operation of laws and practices which had hitherto remained obscure. Similarly finding "facts" on births, deaths and marriages led to greater knowledge about population growth, its distribution and public health.

Statistical study achieved a factual basis for law reforms to be proposed. "Objective **6–020** facts" were used to ascertain needs; a major focus of attention were the social, economic and political problems arising from urbanisation. Victorian idealism often lacked coherence. The dogma of benevolence and good works was unsystematic and often counter-productive. Empirical research, achieved through statistical inquiry,

[14] O. MacDonagh, *A Pattern of Government Growth: The Passenger Acts and their Enforcement 1800–1860* (1961).
[15] H. Parris, *Government and the Railways in Nineteenth Century Britain* (1965).

informed the work of countless inquiries and Royal Commissions held in the nineteenth century. The activities of organisations such as the statistical societies were variously described as "volunteer legislators" or outdoor Parliament. Prominent intellectuals, politicians and civil servants were members of the main statistical societies.

6–021   The outcome of statistical study may be seen in a large number of legislative initiatives which became the political agenda for the growth in Victorian liberalism. In the administrative law field, the variety and diversity of the different forms such as legislative initiative took, may be shortly explained through a number of examples illustrating the use of commissions, boards, inspectors and Ministers.[16]

6–022   A number of examples may be used to illustrate the distinctive nature and the variety of regulatory style adopted. The poor law, revised after the Poor Law Report 1834 and influenced by Edwin Chadwick[17] and Nassau Senior, shifted the role poor law relief was expected to perform. High costs and the lack of tangible benefits from the input of resources had left the old system of poor law relief discredited. Originally, under the jurisdiction of the Justice of the Peace who combined judicial office with administrative functions, the Poor Law Amendment Act 1834 introduced a three-man Commission, independent from Parliament. This model of administration had its earliest origins in the eighteenth century in the creation of Boards, designed to prevent individual excess or corruption and provide checks and balances through its reports and published activities.

6–023   Cornish[18] explains how the Boards system was transformed after 1832, when it developed some of its own independence: ". . . it was conceived as a way of conferring semi-autonomous authority for a particular function; this achieved a certain distinction from the immediately political."

6–024   In the creation of the Poor Law Commissioners after 1832, a wide variety of legal powers accompanied their role. Prosecutions, legal action through *mandamus* and an appointment power of local officers in workhouses were all combined in their functions. It is noticeable that the Poor Law Commissioners neatly linked central government with local government activities. Also noteworthy is that the granting of such powers was couched in general terms with the agreement of a Minister and Parliament in general rule-making. The Commissioners had the ability to make their own rules and regulations as part of their powers.

6–025   Experimentation was invariably involved in the choice of administrative body adopted for any particular activity. Cornish notes[19]:

> "The Railway Department in the Board of Trade (1840) was to become a 'Board' (still departmental—1844) and a Commission (independent—1846) before being re-absorbed de facto (1849) and then de jure (1851) into the Board of Trade. Between the 1850s and 1906 those boards which constitutionally remained distinct from ministries were all important cases placed under some form of ministerial supervision."

6–026   Another model of administrative body was the inspectorates. Examples which came under the jurisdiction of the Home Office were factories, prisons, mining and burial

---

[16] J.F. McEldowney, "Administration and Law in England in the 18th and 19th Centuries" 8 Jahrbuch Für Europäische Verwaltungsgeschichte (1996), pp.19–36.
[17] S.E. Finer, *Life and Times of Sir Edwin Chadwick* (1952).
[18] Cornish, *et al.*, *op.cit.* pp.55–58.
[19] *ibid.*, p.58

inspectors. Inspectorates were fact-finders, investigators and adjudicators. They possessed limited powers to impose fines and prosecutions, but their role of serving notices and enforcing standards relied on voluntary compliance as much as coercive sanctions. Very often their activities involved some form of compromise because of hostility to the use of their powers and a reluctance to comply with the imposition of an external standard. The Factory Inspectors, in particular, adjusted their powers to meet opposition or objections. Inspectors had the status of magistrates, but the Home Office in 1844 directed inspectors not to use their enforcement jurisdiction by introducing a new Factories Act 1844 which constrained their powers.

Public Health was another area of administrative growth and an example of **6–027** administrative decision-making which directly interfered with property rights. It is also illustrative of the use of private law techniques, such as actions in nuisance, combined with statutory powers. In administrative decision-making, findings from various reports and commissions of inquiry had confirmed the existence of disease and poverty among the poor. Health hazards were directly linked to urbanisation and industrialisation. Sanitary improvements were required and introduced on a piecemeal basis; first in 1848, then in 1872 and 1875 various Public Health Acts were passed giving legislative powers to various sanitary authorities to set standards and achieve improvements in living conditions.

Public health legislation directly interfered with property rights and substantially **6–028** overlapped with the use of nuisance law in cases where an injury was caused by a neighbour's occupation of land. The role of the courts in applying and developing such remedies was largely a pragmatic one, taking each case on its own particular facts.

As industrialisation spread new processes and industry throughout the country, **6–029** regulation of these activities was left to individual initiative in the first instance. By 1869 the judges had at last concluded that nuisance from noise, dirt and pollution from railways permitted an occupier of premises affected by the nuisance to seek legal redress.

Finally, another source of administrative growth was in the development of local **6–030** government. Local corporations and parishes developed a myriad of legal powers to deliver many of the new responsibilities that gradually became entrusted to local authority control. A major source of income came through the raising of local taxes and rates. Slowly, incremental changes occurred to the various newly established administrative bodies, but eventually they were to come under local authority control. The Poor Law Commissioners shifted from a Board to a Tribunal of Appeal in 1847. In 1868 it could appoint district auditors, who in 1879 became civil servants on the creation of the Local Government Board.

Local authorities gained the administrative function of delivering what were termed **6–031** "public goods". First the Municipal Corporations Act 1835 provided elected local authorities. From 1843 to 1929 local authorities gained responsibility for such "public goods", including water, gas, transport, education, housing and health services.

A distinctive feature of these developments was the acceptance of local political **6–032** accountability through local elections and Parliament's willingness to encourage local legislation, to enable local authorities to carry out their tasks. Local authorities developed considerable legal powers through private Bill legislation.

Courts, Lawyers and Legal Techniques

6–033   The growth in administrative bodies and their wide diversity broadened the scope of legal powers and raised questions about accountability and control. Arthurs[20] notes how a number of constraints were invoked to prevent abuses. Statutes or regulations often required ministerial approval for their implementation. Ministerial responsibility to Parliament constrained administrators from acting without recourse to political authority and observance of legal rules. Government Law Officers restrained and inhibited any internal decision-making since account had to be taken of their legal opinions.

6–034   Despite such constraints it is recognised that wide discretionary powers were enjoyed by many officials. Such powers[21] were often resented and, when in conflict with the landed interest or the new wealth industrialists, led to conflicts. Self-interest and protection led many administrative bodies to adopt codes of conduct and practice to ease the application of their rules.

6–035   The period of Victorian growth in administrative bodies led to distrust over the considerable powers enjoyed by administrators. Victorian lawyers seemed deeply suspicious of the new powers possessed by the State. The broad discretionary powers favoured in the new legislation were seen as delegating wide powers to administrators, without obvious checks and balances. Some of these powers were necessary, some were the product of legislative draftsmen unaccustomed to the new-found administrative bodies, and some drafted in the spirit of enthusiasm for the newly found reforms. Perhaps the most important reason for the way legal powers were drafted was the narrow and limited role performed by lawyers. Lawyers drafted legislation without much experience of how legal powers were exercised. The most eminent lawyers were members of the statistical societies which did most to promote reform and law codification or amendments. Lawyers acted as legal advisers to the government of the day. In 1860, Henry Thring[22] was appointed Counsel to the Home Office and nine years later became head of the new office of Parliamentary Counsel to the Treasury. Eventually this office became responsible for drafting all Government Bills. Lawyers appeared in court, gave legal advice and, as judges in the higher courts, adjudicated disputes. A noticeable gap in their lawyerly activities was that they were rarely called upon to implement legislation. Their experience of administration was necessarily limited.

6–036   A further consideration was the question of how best to supervise such administrative bodies. Many lawyers believed that this task was best performed by the ordinary courts. The preference for the use of the ordinary courts as opposed to the use of special administrative courts was reinforced by Dicey's scepticism of the benefits of *droit administratif*, the French system of specialised administrative courts. Dicey feared that the formation of administrative courts might encourage the encroachment on the private rights of citizens by governmental powers in the interests of the State, a

---

[20] H.W. Arthurs, *"Without the Law": Administrative Justice and Legal Pluralism in 19th Century England* (1985).

[21] Robson, "The Report of the Committee on Administrative Powers" (1932) 3 *Political Quarterly* 346.

[22] Also see J.E. Pemberton, *British Official Publications* (1971); Sir C. Ilbert, *Legislative Methods and Forms* (1901); G. Drewry, "Lawyers in the UK Civil Service" (1981) 59 *Public Administration* 15–46.

hangover from the period of the Crown's extensive use of arbitrary powers. Dicey believed that the ordinary courts afforded the best protection against any incremental growth in the powers of government intervention.

Dicey's analysis has since been subject to criticism but his powerful influence has endured. de Smith described how Dicey's assumptions about the role of the courts may have misled English administrative lawyers into complacency after the nineteenth century[23]:   **6–037**

> "Representative and responsible Government was securely founded: political and administrative morality was unusually high; the administration of justice by the ordinary courts was even-handed and uncorrupt; the common law, itself pre-eminently pragmatic was tenacious but adaptable. Such an environment bred the assumption that England had little to learn from other countries in matters of public law. Moreover the absence of judicial review of the constitutionality of legislation conduced to a lack of informed interests among practising lawyers in the judicial problems of government. And the role assigned to constitutional and administrative law in legal education was conspicuously modest."

Throughout the period of growth in administrative bodies, it is noteworthy that the courts retained exclusive jurisdiction over the criminal law. Government had carefully circumvented any attack on the courts' powers in this area.   **6–038**

The fact that the courts had an unbroken historical past which could be traced back to the thirteenth century further encouraged the government to refrain from interfering with the role of the courts. To the extent that central government perceived the role of the courts, the question of judicial intervention depended on the nature of the body exercising powers. Limited immunity to the Crown preserved Crown activities from judicial supervision. Ministerial accountability to Parliament allowed discretion to be exercised and largely escape judicial scrutiny. Moreover the growth in legislative powers enjoyed by Parliament as law-makers left the courts fewer facilities to exercise law-making powers of their own. The massive effort towards the enforcement of the new legislation was in the hands of an administrative bureaucracy and occasionally, local magistrates. The superior courts' role in enforcement declined in proportion to the spread of administrative decision-taking. Belief in the rule of law and the jurisdiction of the ordinary courts implied that Ministers, officials and citizens were amenable to the same law. Moving to a new form of administrative law, supervision was seen as inconsistent with the supremacy of the law even as late as 1932. The Committee on Ministers' Powers found the proposal for such an administrative court inconsistent with the supervisory jurisdiction of the High Court and a threat to the rule of law. Such reservations over the development of administrative law have remained influential among lawyers in the United Kingdom until more recent times.   **6–039**

In addition to the role of the courts, other procedures are noteworthy. The various techniques of decision-making, adjudication, discretion, fact-finding and inquiries were supplemented by the development of statutory inquiries. Techniques of inquiry and investigation were commonplace in the work of the Royal Commission and even in some of the administrative tasks entrusted to Justices of the Peace, such as wage-bargaining in the eighteenth and early-nineteenth centuries.   **6–040**

[23] de Smith, *Judicial Review of Administrative Action* (4th ed., 1980), p.7.

6–041   Statutory inquiries may be found in the 1801 Enclosure Act with ad hoc Commissions of Inquiry appointed. Some explanation may be advanced as to why such procedures were adopted. The use of private Bills or public Acts of Parliament did not always provide the necessary coverage of all the issues to be decided. Wade[24] attributes this fact as a reason for adopting inquiries outside Parliament. The procedures of parliamentary committees, already existing inside Parliament and familiar in the passage of legislation, were conveniently adopted and employed.

6–042   Special law-making procedures were available through provisional orders. The provisional order procedure under an Act of Parliament granted powers to some statutory authorities to make a provisional order once an inquiry had been held and objections considered.

6–043   Special procedures were introduced applicable to enclosures to overcome the need for provisional orders. In 1845, the General Enclosure Act required publication of the enclosure scheme and a public meeting "to their objections". Similar procedures were permitted under the Local Government Acts 1858–1933 and various Public Health Acts 1848–1931. Eventually the need to make a provisional order was abandoned, allowing the order to take effect in the absence of any objections or opposition, as in the Statutory Orders (Special Procedure) Act 1945.

6–044   Another variation to provisional orders may be found in the Local Government Act 1894 whereby county councils could acquire land under a public inquiry procedure. The Council could make an order followed by a local inquiry if opposition to the order was made in a memorial to the Council.

6–045   The development of tribunals as a means of adjudication is also noteworthy. Railway companies were compelled in 1854 to afford "reasonable facilities and preferences" to particular traders, in an effort to prevent railways achieving a virtual monopoly. Complaints could be made to the Court of Common Pleas but this was unsatisfactory and in 1893 a tribunal of commissioners was appointed. Fifteen years later it was reformulated into a Railing and Canal Commission. Appointment was through the Home Secretary on the recommendation of the President of the Board of Trade. The Chancellor could nominate a High Court Judge. The Commission adjudicated, found facts and achieved decisions on a judicial basis, having many of the formalities of a Court of Law.

6–046   Similar techniques[25] were employed in 1897 when workmen's compensation was payable. The use of tribunals developed an importance in the resolution of disputes over workmen's compensation. This has remained today.

6–047   Finally, a neglected but important element in nineteenth-century administration was the use of audit procedures as a check on financial arrangements. Central government audit combined judicial and administrative decision-making. The medieval Court of Exchequer responsible for carrying out the audit of public expenditure was identified by Holdsworth as analogous to "an administrative court". The decline of judicial scrutiny over public expenditure began in the sixteenth century when Parliament assumed responsibility for the power of appropriation. The nineteenth century saw the introduction of the modern office of Comptroller and Auditor General with responsibility given to the Public Accounts Committee to oversee public expenditure. Audit techniques included investigation, certification and reporting of accounts.

---

[24] H.W.R. Wade, *Administrative Law* (6th ed., Oxford, 1988).
[25] The Exchequer and Audit Departments Act 1866.

Local government audit may be traced to the fifteenth century with the records of a **6–048** Commission for the hearing of the accounts of the collectors of money. Audit techniques included investigation, certification and where necessary the power "to charge" on the defaulters where sums were found improperly in their possession.

The development of the poor law in the sixteenth century and the consolidation of **6–049** the Poor Relief Act 1601 provided safeguards in the form of audit undertaken by Justices of the Peace. In the eighteenth century the principles of modern audit procedure in local government evolved. The Poor Relief Act 1743 required church wardens and overseers to keep "a just, true and perfect account in writing fairly entered in a book or books . . .".

The requirements of signed and verified accounts were combined with the rights of **6–050** rate payers to inspect accounts. Over a hundred years later the Poor Law Amendment Act 1844 introduced the office of district auditor with powers to deal with illegality and misconduct. The techniques of certification were supplemented by powers to examine, audit and disallow accounts. In cases where misconduct was identified, legal remedies could be provided by the High Court. The role of the Justice of the Peace in these matters of audit was finally ended with the transfer of their functions to the district auditor. As Jones notes[26]:

> "The audit remained judicial in nature; indeed, in comparison with the 1834 provision, the 1844 system was markedly more complete in its judicial character by virtue of the procedure for appeal to the High Court. It was also more effective in its precise statutory power to compel restitution and in its provisions for increasing the independence of the auditor."

Strengthening of the audit system was achieved by the District Auditors Act 1879, **6–051** which provided for the payment of district auditors, partly out of central funds and partly from fees collected from the audited authorities. Adaptations of the principles of the audit system were continually made as changes were introduced to the system of local government.

In terms of administration and law, the nineteenth-century legacy may be shortly **6–052** stated: the assortment of different agencies, administrative bodies and the variety of institutions ranging from courts, inquiries, tribunals, inspectors, commissions and boards represent the "untidiness of the British Administrative System". The form and substance of judicial scrutiny offered by the courts as fact-finders, combined with adjudicatory and judicial functions, may be found replicated in the wide variety of bodies charged with regulating administrative bodies.

The role of the courts requires some additional consideration. Two distinctive roles **6–053** were apparent. First, the courts[27] applied principles of law to the activities of the body under review. Historically, points of law could be raised on the record by the various prerogative writs, most notably certiorari for "error of law on the face of the record". Review in certain circumstances might also include *mandamus*, applied for by inspectors such as the mines inspectors, to compel the determination of charges made against mine owners and heard before magistrates.

---

[26] R. Jones, *Local Government Audit Law* (2nd ed., 1985). See Local Government Finance Act 1982, ss.19 and 20.
[27] Memoranda submitted by Government Depts. (HMSO, 6 vols.) to the Franks Committee (1957).

6–054   Judicial decision-making established by the superior courts assisted in the development of the grounds for judicial review. Through the system of remedies, rights were gradually established. These included establishing procedures at hearings, rights of consultation and representation among the parties, knowing the case against the defendant and their right to an unbiased hearing.

6–055   Second, the courts had an extensive appeal jurisdiction. Since 1857 the Summary Proceedings Act provided an appeal by way of a case stated to the superior courts against errors of law by magistrates. Appeals through the use of the Factories Acts also permitted the courts a role in shaping standards for the performance of individual acts of the inspectors.

6–056   Taken together, both appeal and judicial review gave rise to an expectation that a greater role might be mapped out for the courts. This was slow in developing and only became more significant later in the present century. In the nineteenth century, Parliament created statutes with summary jurisdiction, such as the Summary Jurisdiction Act 1848, which made it impossible for the courts to correct errors of law except those which were within the technical question of jurisdiction. After the 1870s the use of certiorari for errors of law on the face of record was rarely obtained. Various technical problems inhibited the development of judicial review by the courts, most notably Dicey's perspective that the existing "rule of law" was adequate to the tasks of the new administrative bodies, when it was clear that it was not.

6–057   Lawyers and courts, while providing useful procedures to oversee administrative decisions, did not necessarily benefit administrators. Lawyers gained influence through drafting laws, representation in Parliament, advising on the law and representing commercial and industrial interests. However, the superior courts were not actively engaged in regulating administrative decisions. Nor were lawyers developing legal principles to make administration effective. Once lawyers' techniques appeared unhelpful or unsatisfactory, they could be circumvented. Higher priority was given to the economic, political and social activities than to the vested interests of lawyers. Legal rules may not be taken as indicative of how administrative bodies make decisions. They may, however, act as legitimatising principles which allow administrative decision-making of a broad, discretionary kind to take place under a veneer of legality.

ALLOCATION OF FUNCTIONS

6–058   Modern administrative law remains influenced by the legacy of the past and the often bewildering development of various institutions, techniques and strategies to carry out administrative decisions. It is convenient to attempt to classify administrative decision-taking in a way which may help identify the relevant legal powers, on whom the powers are granted and how those powers are exercised. Identifying these issues assists in clarifying the procedures and rules which govern the making of decisions, the methods of accountability and the role of the courts, if any.

6–059   The classification of government institutions and various functions vested in those institutions is probably easier under a written constitution than under the arrangements in the United Kingdom. Under a written Constitution the citizen may be provided with legally enforceable rights. In the United Kingdom the citizen relies on

the availability of remedies depending on the nature of the decision. The citizen
be affected by a decision-maker in different ways—such as whether there is an app
procedure or whether review may be obtained through the courts or there is a tribu __.
Decision-making itself involves broad discretion. Fact-finding and applying rules are
discretionary elements in decision-making. Officials or administrators exercising their
powers operate within a broad discretion in both the interpretation of rules and their
application. Value judgements may be required as to the application of rules and how
they are to be interpreted. Ganz makes the point that Parliament may make the value
judgements and embody these in precise rules in Statutes. The degree of freedom of
choice left to the decision-maker may vary according to the type of rule, the context
and extent to which discretion may be exercised.

The definition of "discretion" is difficult. It is not a precise word with a clearly **6–060**
defined legal meaning and the context in which it is found may change its meaning.
Discretion describes how value judgments, rules and procedures may be combined in
the decision-maker.

In discussing the allocation of functions, consider first the form the relevant legal **6–061**
powers may take. These consist of first, primary legislation and delegated legislation;
and second, there are prerogative powers, licences and contract.[28] An explanation of
each is helpful within the context of administrative decision-making.

Legislation, Guidance, Codes of Practice and Delegated Legislation

Parliament's law-making powers are exercised through Acts of Parliament which **6–062**
broadly provide the main policy and general details of the law. This leaves Ministers,
local authorities, corporations or other bodies to make rules, orders and regulations
setting out in greater detail the technical and precise rules. Such delegated rules may
take different forms and are known as delegated legislation.

The Queen in Council may make Statutory Orders in Council such as under the **6–063**
Emergency Powers Act 1920. Ministers and heads of government departments may
make departmental rules or ministerial regulations under Act of Parliament. Similarly,
local authorities may have wide powers to make regulations such as under the Local
Government Act 1972. Various public bodies or even private bodies have been granted
legal powers to carry out their activities. These may take the form of regulations,
byelaws or Orders. The courts also enjoy a variety of rule-making procedures such as
the Rules of the Supreme Court under the Supreme Court Act 1981. There is a
County Court Rule Committee, under the County Courts Act 1984, s.75 which make
rules for the County Court. The introduction of changes to civil procedure following
the Woolf reforms[29] is illustrative of various rule making powers of the courts
contained in the Civil Procedure Rules.

Powers may be conferred to the Church of England under the Church of England **6–064**
(Assembly) Powers Act 1919, allowing measures in the form of delegated legislation to
be enacted. Such measures may amend or repeal the whole or any part of any Act of
Parliament. There are a multitude of Special Procedure Orders under the Statutory

---

[28] J. Golding, "The Impact of Statutes on the Royal Prerogative" (1974) 48 A.L.J. 434.
[29] Access to Justice (Final Report) 1996. See M. Zander, "The Government Plans on Civil Justice" (1998)
61 *Modern Law Review* 382.

Orders (Special Procedure) Act 1945. A special joint committee of both Houses considers any objections and allows an opportunity for objections to a proposed order to be heard at a local inquiry. This procedure is particularly valuable for water, planning and various other statutory activities.

6–065   Delegated legislation might also loosely describe various codes of practice. These have legal effect because of the statutory provisions which permit their introduction. The Health and Safety at Work Act 1974 permits the Health and Safety Commission to approve a Health and Safety at Work Code which is issued under ss.16 and 17 of the Act. Guidance, codes, recommendations, directions and determinations describe the wide variety of types of delegated powers which operate in modern administrative law.

6–066   The rationale for delegated legislation is wide-ranging. The Committee on Ministers' Powers 1932,[30] identified six reasons in favour of the "necessity for delegation", while admitting the need for safeguards and with the provision "that the statutory powers are exercised and the statutory functions performed in the right way". The six reasons are: that pressure upon parliamentary time is too great; the subject matter of modern legislation is technical; it is difficult to include all the details in a single Act; constant adaptation may take place without the necessity of amending legislation, thus flexibility is encouraged; experimenting with new ideas is possible and lessons from past experience learnt. Sixthly, in a modern state, delegated legislation provides a convenient and speedy remedy when there may be either emergency or urgency in the matters covered by the legislation.

6–067   The Deregulation and Contracting Out Act 1994, supplemented by the considerably broader in scope Regulatory Reform Act 2001, intended to reduce the burdens on business and industry by reducing the level of government regulation of industry. The 1994 Act was used 48 times by April 2001 and involves the use of two powers contained in Ch.1 of Pt 1 of the Act. First, there is a power to amend or repeal by ministerial order any primary legislation that is deemed to impose an unnecessary burden on business. Secondly, there are powers to improve enforcement procedures consistent with fairness and transparency. The unusual nature of the legislation is that it allows a Minister to use an order to suspend an Act of Parliament, a power previously seldom used in peace-time. This is usually referred to as a Henry VIII clause. Such a clause grants a wide power in the legislation that gives general discretion to a Minister including amendment powers without any additional primary legislation. There is a code of good enforcement practice introduced into the 1994 Act procedure for good practice in respect of the deregulation order.

6–068   The arrangements under the Regulatory Reform Act 2001 are similar to the 1994 Act. Regulatory reform orders follow the affirmative procedure route and have a specific mechanism for parliamentary scrutiny in both houses of Parliament. The Regulatory Reform Act extends the powers where an order may be made and allows minor changes to the draft order while it is being scrutinised. It also requires that any burdens under the Act must be proportionate to the benefits expected from them. Ministers must provide fuller information than under the 1994 Act to lay the basis for the order to be made and since January 2001 there is a Code of Practice on written consultation as to when an order may be made.

6–069   A form of delegated legislation which has become more popular in recent years is what Ganz[31] refers to as "quasi-legislation". Unlike statutory instruments or orders, the

---

[30] Cmnd.4060 (1932).

[31] Ganz, *Quasi-Legislation: Recent Developments in Secondary Legislation* (Sweet & Maxwell, 1987).

legal force of much "quasi-legislation" depends on the enabling Act of Parliament. Quasi-legislation may be defined to mean "codes of conduct, guidelines, circulars and a miscellany of rules". No one is quite sure of the extent and scope of quasi-legislation because it does not always conform to the clearest pattern of organisation. Some examples illustrate the meaning of the term. The Highway Code lays down general guidance and advice to motorists. Breach of any of its guidance does not make the offender subject to a criminal prosecution. However it may be used in either civil or criminal proceedings as relevant to the consideration before the court. Equally there are other examples where it is not intended that powers exercised should form the basis of litigation but may provide general guidance to the public. The newly created Food Standards Agency under the Food Standards Act 1999 provides powers for the new Agency to issue reports and advise the public on standards in food. In exercising such widely defined powers the Agency must under s.23 of the Act consider the costs and benefits of any exercise or non-exercise of its powers and the giving of advice or information. This must be undertaken within the general provisions of s.22 namely, the publication of a statement of general objectives the Agency intends to pursue and the general practice it intends to adopt.

The Police and Criminal Evidence Act 1984 (PACE) provides the police with various codes of conduct. Breach of any of the guidance in the code makes the police liable to disciplinary proceedings but not prosecution. Under the Utilities Act 2000 various codes of practice set out the conditions for Public Electricity Suppliers. These may be relevant in the Determinations made by the regulator. Additionally, voluntary codes of practice have been agreed by the various electricity companies regarding their disconnection powers and rights of consumers. Such codes operate within the legal framework set by the Act and may form the framework for the regulator to implement policies.   **6–070**

As Ganz observed, one of the dangers inherent in quasi-legislation is that codes of practice may occupy a wider breadth of activity than originally intended by Parliament. One example is the Code of Practice on Picketing, which limited the number to six pickets. The enabling Act, the Employment Act 1980, did not include such a number but the practice of limiting the number of pickets to six has been accepted by the police and the courts.   **6–071**

Delegated legislation may be considered by the courts as to its legality, under the enabling legislation. Great care must be taken when ministerial circulars or advice are issued because such advice may pre-judge an individual case or a particular issue. Each case must be considered on its merits.   **6–072**

Prerogative Powers, Licences and Contracts

The prerogative is an important source of governmental legal powers. In *Malone v Metropolitan Police Commissioner*[32] the Vice-Chancellor, Sir Robert Megarry, recognised that the Home Secretary had a limited power to authorise telephone-tapping. This power was a residue of the power to open articles through the post, said to exist through the prerogative. Such powers have been made statutory under the Interception   **6–073**

---

[32] [1979] Ch. 344.

of Telecommunications Act 1985, but the case is illustrative of the prerogative as a source of legal powers applied in modern circumstances.

6–074   In the *GCHQ* case, the House of Lords accepted the prerogative as the basis of legal powers to ban trade unions at the Government Communications Headquarters. The courts have expressed their willingness to review prerogative powers. Some doubts were expressed in the case as to the nature of the prerogative powers. The exact issue of the legal powers depended on seeing an Order in Council as derived from the authority of the prerogative or under Act of Parliament.

6–075   This is a characteristic of prerogative powers. Their exact nature, scope and extent are often difficult to review or define. Occasionally this may give rise to difficulty when there are statutory powers which are incomplete or inadequate and the question arises as to whether the prerogative may supplement these powers.

6–076   In *R. v Secretary of State for the Home Department Ex p. Northumbrian Police Authority*[33] the Court of Appeal was willing to supplement the Home Secretary's powers under the Police Act 1964 to permit the issuing of a circular providing plastic bullets and CS gas to local police forces. Relying on the prerogative power "to keep the peace", the Court of Appeal concluded that this entitled the Home Secretary to all that was "reasonably necessary to preserve the peace of the realm". This entitled the Home Secretary to rely on the prerogative powers even though the statutory arrangements appeared comprehensive and conclusive in the matter. The case has been heavily criticised but it represents an indication of how important it is to clarify the nature of legal powers.

6–077   Sources of legal powers are not restricted to legislation, quasi-legislation or prerogative powers. Increasingly public bodies rely on contracts or licences to establish the legal authority and powers necessary to carry out their activities. Such powers operate within a statutory framework but are undeniably private law powers.

6–078   In the case of gas, telecommunications, electricity and water, the newly privatised companies require licences issued by the Secretary of State to carry out their activities. Such licences, under the relevant legislation, provide criminal sanctions for anyone attempting to carry out specified activities without a licence. The licence conditions are detailed and technical. They contain legal powers, duties and conditions which must be performed.

6–079   The novelty of the use of licences in the newly privatised industries leaves the prospect of negotiation and modification a matter for political decision-making as well as legal powers. References to the Competition Commission are possible by any one of the new regulatory agencies set up to regulate utilities such as gas, electricity, water or telecommunications. The merger of gas and electricity regulation into a single regulator, OFGEM, is supplemented by the power of the new authority to modify licences following a Competition Commission reference. The statutory posts of the Directors-General of Electricity Supply and Gas Supply are merged into a single body called GEMA, the Gas and Electricity Markets Authority. Existing responsibility is shared between the Secretary of State and the regulators over how the industry is to be regulated and a division of powers for enforcing licences and their conditions is made. Such a framework requires careful consideration as to the exact nature of the legal powers, how they are to be exercised and by whom. Under the Utilities Act 2000 it is clear that economic regulation is combined with legal rules that are enforceable in the courts.

[33] [1988] 2 W.L.R. 590.

Monitoring the tariff charges of the various utilities also involves the legal powers of   **6–080**
the regulators. Careful consideration of the economic and social aspects involved in
the price formula is required, to balance the efficiency of the industry with consumer
protection.

Contractual powers offer the most demanding and interesting use of legal powers in   **6–081**
the allocation of functions of public bodies. As a source of power, there is usually some
legislative authority permitting the use of contract. One example is the contractual
powers of local authorities. Recent legislation such as the Local Government Act 1988
requires local authorities to subject to competitive tendering a number of services such
as street-cleaning, vehicle maintenance, schools and welfare catering, refuse collection,
and the management of sports and leisure facilities. The law requires that private
companies be permitted to bid for the work involved. Setting performance standards
and competitive tendering are included in the Local Government Act 1992. Such legal
powers are intended to encourage contracts and competition and to increase the
effectiveness of local authority powers.

Some doubts as to the legal powers to enter financial contracts arose in *Hazell v*   **6–082**
Hammersmith and Fulham.[34] The local authority had invested substantial sums in
various investments known as "interest rate swaps" in order to finance expenditure,
during a period when central government financial support to local authorities had
diminished. In order to invest in such activities as interest rate swaps, the local
authority relied on s.111(1) of the Local Government Act 1972, which empowered
local authorities to borrow according to what was "calculated to facilitate or conducive
or incidental to, the discharge of any of their functions". Doubts over the legality of
such powers were raised by the District Auditor. The House of Lords held that the
local authority borrowing powers under s.111(1) were curtailed by Sch.13 to the 1972
Act. It was concluded that the local authority had no contractual power to enter the
swap market.

In *Credit Suisse v Allerdale B.C.*[35] the Court of Appeal considered the operation of a   **6–082a**
local authority company and whether the establishment of the company was consistent
with Sch.13, s.111 of the 1972 Act. The local authority wished to establish a leisure
pool complex. The setting-up of a company for such a purpose was regarded as a
means of overcoming statutory borrowing restrictions. The company was formed and
borrowed £6 million from Credit Suisse. The recession caused the company to fail and
the bank claimed repayment of the loan. In considering the express and implied
powers of the local authority, the Court of Appeal concluded that the local authority
had no powers to set up a company for the purposes of borrowing the requisite finance
for the various recreational activities favoured by the local authority. The Court of
Appeal followed the approach in *Hazell v Hammersmith*. It acknowledged that local
authorities were empowered under s.19(1) of the Local Government (Miscellaneous
Provisions) Act 1976 to provide recreational facilities. Such authorisation, however,
does not apply to borrowing. Thus the purported borrowing contract was *ultra vires*.

The method of statutory construction given by the Court of Appeal to the 1972 Act   **6–083**
follows the pattern observed in previous decisions regarding local government. Unless
there are clear words the courts will not imply any discretion or general assumptions

---

[34] [1990] 2 W.L.R. 1038.
[35] *Credit Suisse v Allerdale BC* [1996] 4 All E.R. 129.

concerning local authority powers. Indeed the nature of *ultra vires* contracts are such that they cannot be enforced.

6–084   In another case, *Credit Suisse v Waltham Forest*[36] the same judges considered a claim against a local authority which had guaranteed a bank loan to a company. The Court of Appeal followed the *Allerdale* case and held that the borrowing was *ultra vires*.

6–085   Contractual powers may be the main source of legal powers for a particular activity. This may give rise to questions of the reviewability of the activities in question. In *R. v Panel on Take-overs and Mergers Ex p. Datafin*,[37] the Take-overs Panel, a non-statutory body involved in regulating city take-overs and mergers, was provided with regulatory powers by contract. The courts regarded the take-over panel as an important element in the regulation of take-overs. The Government, together with the Bank of England, approved the appointment of the Chairman even though no statutory basis existed for the Panel. The Court of Appeal regarded the "authority of the government" as sufficiently relevant to give the Panel a public law dimension. In that way, the Courts were prepared to offer judicial review of the Panel's activities.

6–086   Contracts are likely to become an increasingly important source of legal powers. Daintith[38] explains how government has a number of powers available to carry on its activities. These powers divide into two: *imperium* and *dominium*. Under *imperium* the government may prohibit through legislation or promote through existing legal powers, various activities. Under *dominium* it might offer subsidies or purchasing agreements or licensing arrangements favouring one activity or another. The vast range of possibilities makes classification of the legal powers involved an important element in understanding how powers are allocated.

CENTRAL AND LOCAL GOVERNMENT

6–087   Identical legal powers may be viewed differently depending on who exercises the power and how the power is exercised. There are a variety of factors relevant in the choice of decision-making bodies.

6–088   In the context of administrative decision-making, central government may be distinguished from local government even though both share the common feature of being directly elected. Local authorities represent local interests and are accountable to the local electorate. However, since the nineteenth century, the wide range of activities carried out by local authorities for housing, education, police and public health have required increasing statutory activity. Diversity in size and in politics have given local authorities a great deal of autonomy. However, local authority activities are not the only way to judge the role of local government. Viewed from the perspective of central government, local activities are carried out on behalf of central government policy-making. The sovereignty of Parliament suggests that local authorities' powers are allocated by central government. There is no independence or constitutional autonomy given to local authorities other than that presented by Acts of Parliament. Legal powers from Acts of Parliament give the government of the day authority to lay

[36] *Credit Suisse v Waltham Forest* [1996] 4 All E.R. 176.
[37] [1987] Q.B. 815.
[38] Daintith, *op.cit.*, p.194.

down policy and prescribe local authority activities. Legal powers may also be found through appeals by laws and circulars.

Many local authority activities, such as in the area of planning, leave the right of appeal to a Minister after a refusal of planning permission by a local authority. Byelaws made by a local authority require ministerial approval. Central government circulars may set policy guidance for local authorities.[39]   **6–089**

In the area of local authority finance, central government had extensive powers to place a legal "cap" on the amount of Community Charge which may be levied by the local authority. Ultimately, powers granted to local authorities may be removed by central government, such as the abolition of the Greater London Council and the Metropolitan counties, under the Local Government Act 1985. The successor to the Community Charge under s.1 of the Local Government Finance Act 1992 came into effect on April 1, 1993. The Secretary of State has powers under s.54 to determine the maximum budgetary requirement of each local authority and to place a "cap" on local authority expenditure.   **6–090**

Ministerial discretion provides extensive powers for central government decision-taking. Reserve powers are provided in many statutes allowing the Secretary of State authority to make decisions, delegate powers or allocate powers to other bodies. Central government powers operate within the framework of ministerial responsibility to Parliament; Ministers alone may raise public expenditure through Act of Parliament. This power of taxation is exclusively controlled by the government of the day on the authority of Parliament.   **6–091**

Allocating functions between central and local government raises important issues about where political, legal and judicial powers ought to reside.   **6–092**

Types of Agencies

In public law the names of particular institutions that are hived off from government follow no exact science. The civil service organised around the various departments of central government is undergoing radical change. On April 1, 1996 there were 494,292 permanent civil servants. Since 1988 the Next Steps initiative has been in operation intended to deliver better services within available resources. By April 1, 1996 there were 102 Next Steps agencies in the Home Civil Service. In addition there are agencies within HM Customs and Excise and the Inland Revenue. Taken together this amounts to 71 per cent of the civil service, approximately 350,126 permanent staff. Two years later there were 138 agencies over 76 per cent of the Civil Service. The powers and responsibilities of such agencies fall within the "Framework Documents" setting up the agency. Such agencies come within Treasury guidance and financial control. The increase in the number of agencies has required the re-writing of the Treasury Handbook on Government Accounting. In 1998 the White Paper *Modern Public Services*[40] advanced the idea of benchmarking or the setting of standards of best practice. The chief executive of the agency has responsibility for the day-to-day management and decision-making of the agency. In theory this leaves ministerial responsibility confined to the overall policy of the agency.   **6–093**

---

[39] Under the Education Act 1944, as amended. S.H. Bailey, "Central and Local Government and the Courts" [1983] *Public Law* 8.
[40] Cm.4011.

6–094   The Next Steps agencies need to be distinguished from other forms of agency established independently from the Next Steps arrangements. Such agencies may appear to share some similarities with the Next Steps type of agency. However, unlike Next Steps agencies these are usually set up under statute. For the purposes of convenience they may be given the generic title of fringe organisations.

Fringe Organisations and Statutory Bodies

6–095   The allocation of powers may be entrusted to various non-governmental organisations (quangos).[41] Most have a statutory framework such as the Equal Opportunities Commission, the Civil Aviation Authority, the Gaming Board, the Monopolies and Mergers Commission, and the Health and Safety Commission. Many of their activities are directly related to carrying out statutory powers, but their remit outside government departments gives scope for a broader view of their activities. In 1993 the Cabinet Office listed four types of Non-Departmental Public Bodies (NDPs). Annual reports are published by the Cabinet Office providing statistical information and data. In common usage these bodies are often referred to as fringe organisations or quangos. Such bodies have a role in the process of national government but are not part of a department and operate at arm's length from Ministers.

6–096   The first type are Executive Bodies. They employ staff and have their own budget. Some may have the status of a public corporation. In 1979 there were 492 such bodies employing 217,000 staff and spending £6,150 million. In 1993 there were 358 employing 111,300 staff and spending £15,410 million. In 1996 there were 309 with expenditure of £21,420 million. Executive Bodies range in size and diversity, such as the Agricultural Training Board, to the Higher Education Funding Council for England and Wales with wide statutory powers.

6–096a   The second type are Advisory Bodies. This group consists mainly of bodies set up by Ministers to advise them and their departments on matters requiring specialist expertise. Included in this category are Royal Commissions. Generally advisory bodies do not employ their own staff or incur their own expenditure. In 1979 there were 1,485 advisory bodies; in 1993 there were 829; in 1996, 674.

6–097   The third type are a variety of administrative tribunals. In this category are bodies with licensing and appeal functions. Generally they are serviced by staff from the sponsoring department. In 1979 there were 70, and in 1993 there were 68. In 1996 this had increased to 75.

6–098   Finally, there are a miscellaneous group of other bodies comprising the boards of visitors to penal establishments in Great Britain and boards of visitors and visiting committees in Northern Ireland.

6–099   The four types of NDPs are not an exhaustive list of fringe organisations. Privatisation of many nationalised industries has increased the range and scope of specialised statutory bodies. Mention has been made above to OFGEM that covers electricity and gas. In the case of Railways, under the 1993 Railways Act there is the Office of Passenger Rail Franchising (OPRAF) and the Office of the Railway Regulator (ORR). Some regulatory agencies fall into different categories. For example the Office of Standards in Education (OFSTED) has a staff of 500 and a budget of £56m. It is set up to monitor the four-yearly inspection of schools and advise the Secretary of State for Education on the quality of schools.

[41] See *The Civil Service Yearbook 2002* (Stationery Office, London).

Baldwin and McCrudden have identified reasons for the creation of the wide variety **6–100** of regulatory agencies. Hiving off government work may be more efficient and reduce the size of the civil service. Particular expertise is sought outside a government ministry. Independence from government may be required to develop the necessary experience and expertise. Delegation of rule-making functions may be required in order to facilitate giving technical detail. Constant up-dating and adjustment are more suited to such bodies than government departments. Interest groups, industry and policy formulation may be assisted through the creation of such agencies. Funding from outside government sources may be easier to achieve. Treasury interference or inter-departmental rivalries may be more easily resisted through the creation of regulatory agencies.

There are also a wide variety of functions discharged by such agencies. Baldwin and **6–101** McCrudden[42] identify five different governmental functions present: first, the prevention of undesirable activities; secondly, the provision of techniques to the various parties to reach agreement or compromise; thirdly, the provision and allocation of various benefits such as particular services or ensuring good standards such as competitive and economical industries; fourthly, setting standards through legal mechanism; and finally, providing dispute facilities.

Decision-making bodies may be influenced by the need to provide some elements of **6–102** adjudication in the decision-maker. Adjudication may be informal or formal. Informal adjudication may take place without lawyers and be confined to internal procedures. Formal methods of adjudication inevitably involve the use of the courts, tribunals or inquiries. Lawyers tend to become a dominant influence. Jowell[43] described this process as "judicialisation". The choice to be made is to consider the role of courts and the function of tribunals and inquiries.

Courts

The Judiciary and the Administration of Justice

Openness, integrity, impartiality and fairness are some of the characteristics necessary **6–103** for a decision-maker to follow when adjudicating disputes. Courts appear to offer such characteristics. Although historically England had a large number of special local courts, these have now been displaced by a centrally organised system of courts: the High Court including the Administrative Court, Court of Appeal and House of Lords for civil matters.

The courts gained independence in the seventeenth century and although proposed **6–104** in the nineteenth century, a Minister of Justice covering judicial appointments, law reform and the legal profession, was never implemented. The jurisdiction of the High Court has developed as a place where the legality of acts and decisions of public bodies may be challenged.

It is the adjudicatory nature of the courts' role, with its implied independence and **6–105** appearance of non-political decision-making, that makes the facility of the courts an important model for allocating powers. The value of the court may come from

[42] R. Baldwin and McCrudden, *Regulation and Public Law* (1987).
[43] Jowell, "Courts and Administration in Britain: Standard, Principles and Rights" (1988) *Israel Law Review* 409.

techniques for dealing with law and facts. An illustration of this valuable role is provided by the employment of High Court judges in chairing inquiries or investigations.

6–106   The use of the courts' techniques may require adaptation to meet specialised needs. The Restrictive Trade Practices Act 1956 was passed after debate in the House of Commons on the value of a tribunal rather than a court. The former was answerable to the Minister while the latter was not. In the end a tribunal was favoured. The hallmark of courts such as rules of evidence, representation, cross-examination, and oral hearings have been adapted to the way certain tribunals and inquiries may function. Courts are seen in many instances to provide a useful means of protecting civil liberties and citizens' rights.

6–107   In England and Wales the High Court exercises a civil jurisdiction. There are three divisions: Queen's Bench, Chancery and Family. On appeal there is the Court of Appeal, Civil Division. The Supreme Court comprises the High Court, the Court of Appeal and the Crown Court. Appeals lie to the House of Lords, sitting as a court, from the Court of Appeal and in some instances direct from the High Court. There is a limited civil jurisdiction exercised by the county courts and by the magistrates' court. The Lord Chancellor may extend the jurisdiction of county courts under the Courts and Legal Services Act 1990. See Fig. 1.

6–108   Criminal jurisdiction is provided for summary offences before the magistrates' courts and in jury trials before the Crown Court. Criminal appeals may be taken to the Queen's Bench Divisional Court or to the High Court or to the Court of Appeal, Criminal Division. A further appeal on matters of law may lie to the House of Lords. See Fig. 2.

6–109   The House of Lords when sitting as a court may be composed of up to 12 Lords of Appeal in Ordinary. Usually appeals are heard by five judges and in exceptional cases, seven judges may sit. Since 1844, by convention[44] no lay peer should take part in appellate work of the Lords. The hearing of appeals is carried out by an appellate committee sitting as one or two appellate committees of the House. Appeals may be heard irrespective of whether Parliament is sitting or not. Since 1966 the House of Lords is not bound by its previous decisions though it does not depart from former decisions which it regards as normally binding.

6–110   Judicial appointments are made by the Executive. Appointments to senior judicial positions such as Lord Chief Justice, Master of the Rolls and President of the Family Division are made by the Crown on the advice of the Prime Minister. Appointments for High Court judges, recorders and circuit judges are made by the Crown on the advice of the Lord Chancellor. The Courts and Legal Services Act 1990 has changed the qualifications necessary for judicial appointments. Before 1990 judges of the High Court had to be barristers of at least 10 years' standing. After the 1990 Act it is possible for solicitors with rights of audience in the High Court and for circuit court judges to be appointed. Appointment as a Lord Justice of Appeal to the Court of Appeal previously required standing as a barrister of at least 15 years or previous appointment as a High Court judge. After 1990 solicitors with rights of audience in the High Court are eligible and the 15 years has been reduced to 10 years. Non-practising barristers may in certain circumstances be appointed High Court judges, where there is a particular specialism required.

[44] See the discussion in *O'Connell v R.* (1844) 11 Cl. & F. 155.

Criticism of the selection process is related to the role of the Lord Chancellor in   **6–111**
advising and making judicial appointments. In practical terms the Lord Chancellor
operates under advice from civil servants in his own department and leading lawyers
including practitioners and judges. Since 1994 appointments to the circuit court follow
advertisement of the position available. In 1998 the principle of advertisement was
extended to High Court appointments and the job description of magistrates. One of
the tasks of the Lord Chancellor is to make an annual report to Parliament. An
innovation in 2000 is the setting-up of an independent judicial Appointment Commissioner with the role to oversee and monitor appointments. This falls short of the
demand to set up an independent appointments commission free to make recommendations on appointments. The question of judicial appointment is particularly
sensitive given the broad remit the judges have been given to their powers under the
Human Rights Act 1998. One of the early cases on the Human Rights Act 1998 in
Scotland was that the appointment of temporary sheriffs was an infringement of
Article 6 of the European Convention on Human Rights.[45]

There are few senior judges who are women and there is an under-representation on   **6–112**
the judicial bench as a whole from the Black or Asian communities. As of September
2001, the Lord Chancellor's Department *Annual Report on Judicial Appointments*
shows that out of the 12 Lords of Appeal there are no women. There is one woman
head of Division and out of 35 Lord Justices of Appeal there are two women. In the
High Court, there are eight women High Court Judges from a total of 105. On the
Circuit Court only 47 Circuit Judges out of a total of 476 are women. The higher
judiciary from the High Court or above has no Black or Asian representation. The
expectation is that in the future the judiciary will be composed of people from
different ethnic and cultural backgrounds.

The independence[46] of the judiciary provides important safeguards. Judges must be   **6–113**
free from political pressures when deciding cases. The terms and conditions of judicial
appointments are therefore important in contributing to the independence of the
judiciary. Judges have security of tenure. Judges of the High Court, Court of Appeal
and Lords of Appeal hold office during good behaviour, subject to the power of
removal by the Queen on an address presented to both Houses of Parliament.

Judicial appointments are made for life but since 1959 statutory retirement ages   **6–114**
have been introduced: 72 for a circuit judge and 75 for a High Court judge. This was
modified in 1993 when the Judicial Pensions and Retirement Act 1993 introduced a
new retirement age of 70 which may be extended to 75. Since 1973 there are
procedures for determining judicial incapacity and grounds of retirement.

Judicial salaries are charged permanently from the Consolidated Fund, relieving   **6–115**
Parliament of the obligation of approving salaries every year. Salaries fall under the
review procedure set up by the government for review by the advisory Review Body on
Top Salaries. The Lord Chancellor with Prime Ministerial approval may increase
salaries in line with the recommendations from the Review Body.

As noted above the Lord Chancellor is concerned with all judicial appointments,   **6–116**
including the magistracy, circuit court judges and High Court judges. The general
administration of the Supreme Court is also his responsibility. The Rule Committee

---

[45] *Starrs v Ruxton* 2000 S.L.T. 42 and the subsequent legislation, Judicial Appointments etc. (Scotland) Act
2000.
[46] See Robert Stevens, *The Independence of the Judiciary* (Oxford, 1993).

consisting of the Lord Chancellor and other judges, together with practising barristers and solicitors provides the Rules of the Supreme Court. The Lord Chancellor is also responsible for the allocation of business between the High Court and county courts. The administration and management of the magistrates' courts was transferred from the Home Secretary to the Lord Chancellor in April 1992. In addition to his judicial functions, the Lord Chancellor is speaker of the House of Lords and is a member of the Cabinet. The Lord Chancellor is also important in promoting law reform and appoints for England and Wales members of the Law Commission.

6–117   The Law Commission has statutory responsibility to keep under systematic review the law including codification, simplification and where relevant modernisation of the law. There is a Judicial Studies Board and since coming into force its responsibilities include training on sentencing, criminal law, family law, civil matters and the Human Rights Act 1998.

6–118   The latter formed an impressive agenda for a sustained period of training for all members of the judiciary on the implications of the new Act. In the midst of considerable uncertainty, intensive preparations were made for the 1998 Act's coming into force in England and Wales and an extra £60 million allocated for legal aid and court costs. The judiciary at all levels from magistrates' courts to the appeals courts have undergone intensive education and training programmes on the Act. A central issue is the extent of the application of Convention rights and the implications of a rights-based culture in English law. Courses organised by the Judicial Studies Board have explained the remit of the 1998 Act and how it might be interpreted. Similarly, administrators and civil servants have undergone training on the impact of the Act. The courts now have the difficult task of interpreting the proper procedures and merits of administrative decisions. While there were fears that the number of cases under the Act might overwhelm the court administration, a sensible case-by-case approach has been adopted. As Professor Anthony King has pointed out, there can be little doubt that[47] ". . . many of the changes in our traditional constitution are permanent and irreversible". It is an opportune moment to take stock of the direction a more rights-orientated public law will take us. There are some words of caution. While conceding, as everyone must, that human rights are intrinsic to our democratic system, there is room for consideration of the boundaries of judicial power as a custodian of rights. What degree of self-regulation should be exercised by judges when they are granted such overarching powers? How should decision-makers be advised to achieve good decisions when individual rights may serve to inhibit risk-taking and long-term strategies?

6–119   The Human Rights Act holds obvious pitfalls for the unwary. Judges in the House of Lords may find it difficult to take part in debates on legislation and might be advised to refrain from publishing their views on controversial issues. Judges are expected to exercise self-restraint and maintain the independence of the judiciary.

6–120   Judges must exercise great care to ensure that a judge is not a party to a case and is free from any personal interest or bias in a case heard before him. The ordinary rules of natural justice apply. In the *Pinochet*[48] litigation, because of his status as chair of a trust set up by Amnesty International, Lord Hoffman had an interest in the proceedings and so should not have been a member of the panel that heard the case.

---

[47] Anthony King, *Does the United Kingdom Still Have a Constitution?* (2001), p.90.
[48] *R. v Bow Street Magistrates Ex p. Pinochet No.2* [2000] 1 A.C. 119.

Judges are often required to preside over royal commissions or inquiries set up **6–121** under the Tribunals of Inquiry (Evidence) Act 1921. Ad hoc inquiries set up in the public interest are often chaired by a High Court judge. Judicial involvement in such a role is often accompanied by great publicity. The subject matter of many inquiries is often controversial and may indirectly involve judges in political issues of the day. Lord Widgery, then Lord Chief Justice, undertook an inquiry into events in Northern Ireland leading up to "Bloody Sunday". Lord Saville is re-investigating those events in an inquiry set up in 1998. The involvement of senior judges in highly controversial issues has its dangers. The public may find it difficult to draw a distinction between the primary judicial function of judges and their role in inquiries set up by the government of the day.

In recent years the public and media attention on the procedures and outcome of **6–122** the Scott inquiry[49] was particularly intense. There were a number of reasons for this heightened and at times almost hysterical attention given by the media to the inquiry. First, the nature of the inquiry itself and the undoubted public interest in its contents. Secondly, the public standing of the witnesses including the Attorney-General; senior Government Ministers including the then serving Prime Minister Mr Major; and Mrs Thatcher, the previous Prime Minister. Thirdly, the nature of public cross-examination attracted media attention. The undoubted charisma of Sir Richard Scott and the appointment of a Counsel to the inquiry, Presiley Baxendale Q.C., all added a sense of drama to proceedings. Finally, the political parties seized on every opportunity afforded by the inquiry to embarrass government Ministers about the potential findings of the inquiry. In the end the Government was able to use the charges laid by the opposition parties as a means to deflect criticism. This allowed media attention to diminish once any ministerial resignation was defeated in the House of Commons. All this served to illustrate the delicate nature of judicial independence, public scrutiny and media attention.

Judges often have a difficult task in ensuring that they are perceived by the public as **6–123** independent. The diversity of the tasks entrusted to judges by the government of the day only reinforces the importance of judicial independence. Judges are regularly invited to chair the Security Commission which investigates the workings of British Intelligence.

Judges observe the convention that they must not become involved in party political **6–124** activities. They must not engage in conduct which is likely to bring the judiciary into disrepute. Members of the government, and civil servants are constrained by convention not to criticise a judicial decision by attacking the competence or credibility of the judge. Similarly M.P.s exercise self-restraint in their criticism of judges. Parliamentary debate is expected to observe the *sub judice* rule when matters awaiting judicial decision are brought before the courts. At times this may seem an undue fetter on the freedom of the House of Commons to debate, but it is generally accepted as a necessary protection of the judiciary.[50]

Judges are protected at common law from any action for acts done or words spoken **6–125** in their judicial capacity in a court of justice.[51] This protection appears extensive. It

[49] *Return to an Address of the Honourable House of Commons dated 15th February 1996. Report of the Inquiry into the Export of Defence Equipment and Dual-use Goods to Iraq and Related Prosecutions* The Rt Hon. Sir Richard Scott, The Vice-Chancellor (1996 HC 115) (HMSO, London,
[50] See *Hansard*, HC Vol. 365, 1986–87, p.6, col.710 (July 13, 1987).
[51] A. Olowofoyeku, *Suing Judges* (Oxford, 1993); *Sirros v Moore* [1975] Q.B. 118.

may even cover anything done or said however corrupt, oppressive or malicious. In recent years the protection afforded to superior court judges is increasingly applied to lower courts such as magistrates. The Courts and Legal Services Act 1990 provides that a magistrate will not be liable for any acts done within his jurisdiction nor for any acts outside his jurisdiction unless bad faith may be shown. Judicial incompetence which may result in a wrongful conviction does not render the judge liable in either civil or criminal law. Negligence or poor judgment does not result in disciplinary action. There is at least some extension of judicial immunity to the vast array of inferior tribunals where the duties involve judicial rather than administrative decisions. It may be questioned whether absolute judicial immunity outlined above is entirely defensible.

6–126   The immunity of advocates from actions for negligence has been re-examined by the House of Lords. In *Arthur J.S.Hall and Co (a firm) v Simmons*[52] the House of Lords rejected the argument that the administration of justice required that advocates should be protected. The immunity of the past appears to have no place in a modern society and for that reason immunity was removed for advocates in civil cases.

6–127   Finally, it is important to note that the courts have extensive powers in respect of contempt of court. Contempt of court allows the courts to punish conduct that threatens, obstructs or prejudices the administration of justice. The law has been amended in the Contempt of Court Act 1981. Civil contempt is the failure to obey the order of a superior court that has prescribed conduct for a party to a civil action. Criminal contempt may arise where there is conduct calculated to interfere with proceedings which are in their nature criminal proceedings. However, both civil and criminal courts have jurisdiction over criminal contempt. Obedience to the orders of the court is required against litigants. In the case of the Crown or government departments, the courts may issue injunctions against officers of the court and the contempt jurisdiction of the courts extends to Ministers. Contempt proceedings may be invoked for matters that are said to scandalise the court, or where there are threats made in the face of the court. Contempt proceedings may arise from publications that are held to prejudice the course of justice or other acts that interfere with the course of justice.

6–128   Securing judicial independence is a continuous process which at times involves judicial self-restraint and critical self-analysis. Judges are expected to be active members of society participating in discussion, and demonstrating that their independence does not mean isolation. Increased media scrutiny is likely to continue and require judges to observe the etiquette of careful judgment and thoughtful comment. The law of contempt is subject to the Human Rights Act 1998 and this raises the question of the fairness of procedures used in contempt findings and their compatibility with Articles 6 and 10 of the European Convention on Human Rights. In the future the creation of a new Supreme Court with a constitutional jurisdiction might be welcomed. The advantage would be that by separating the judicial functions from the House of Lords it would create a clear distinction between an independent judicial role from that of the legislature. It would also modernise the office of Lord Chancellor and create a separation between judicial and executive functions. A new Supreme Court might require repeal of the Appellate Jurisdiction Act 1876 and the expansion of the number of Law Lords beyond the existing 12. The new Supreme Court might build on

---

[52] [2000] 3 All E.R. 673.

the wealth of experience developed from appeals to the Privy Council and the rich inheritance of the common law.

THE DEVELOPMENT OF JUDICIAL REVIEW

In the previous chapter, mention was made of Dicey's influential *Law of the Constitution* (1885), in which he suggested that the fundamental safeguard in the United Kingdom's Constitution against abuse of power was the doctrine of the rule of law. Rights, for example, to personal liberty or to hold public meetings arise "as the result of judicial decisions determining the rights of private persons in particular cases brought before the courts". The rule of law expresses the idea that the independence of the judiciary is part of a fundamental legal doctrine that government must be conducted according to law. Disputed cases require judicial decisions according to detailed rules in both substance and procedure.   **6–129**

The courts are uniquely placed to consider the relationship between the citizen and the State. The variety of roles that fall to the courts provides an opportunity for the courts to settle disputes. This includes the interpretation of statutes, reviewing discretion, sometimes adjudicating between different government departments, or in local and central relations and supervising regulatory agencies—all fall within the broad remit of the supervisory jurisdiction of the High Court.   **6–130**

Before 1977, litigants or "aggrieved citizens" as they are termed, had to choose which of a number of ancient prerogative writs was suited to their needs. These included habeas corpus, certiorari (a quashing order), prohibition (a prohibiting order) and *mandamus* (a mandatory order). Habeas corpus is still referred to as a writ; all the rest are now orders since the Administration of Justice (Miscellaneous Provisions) Acts 1933 and 1938. Such orders could not be "mixed" with other remedies such as declaration, damages or injunctions. Technical rules of standing (*locus standi*) applied to each remedy. Different grounds for seeking each remedy also applied. In the case of certiorari (a quashing order) and prohibition (a prohibiting order), the availability of the remedy depended on the body performing the function complained about.   **6–131**

Proposals to reform the procedures and the substantive law of remedies were made by the Law Commission in 1969, which recommended a comprehensive review of administrative law by a Royal Commission or body of comparable status. Although this advice was persuasively argued, it was rejected. In 1969 the Law Commission was instructed to study the law of remedies, which led to recommendations in 1977, contained in Order 53 and now s.31 of the Supreme Court Act 1981. These procedures, commonly known as Order 53, provide for the application for judicial review. The rules of procedure are to be found under the CPR Part 54 Judicial Review and various practice Directions and Pre-action Protocols apply. Currently, the Crown Office, responsible for the administration of applications for judicial review, has recorded nearly 3,000 applications, of which 20 per cent are planning or statutory procedures. In 1992–93, there had been an 18 per cent increase in the number of cases on current figures. The 1998 Act is likely to increase the use of judicial review[53] and nearly 20 per cent of all judicial review cases raise a human rights issue.   **6–132**

---

[53] Practice Statement [2002] 1 All E.R. 633. It is noted that from October 2 to December 31, 2001 some 19 per cent of judicial review cases raised an issue of human rights. In numerical terms judicial review receipts for 2001 showed an overall increase of 11 per cent on 2000.

6–133   An application for judicial review is made to the Administrative Law Court with the leave of the Court. The first stage is to request leave and if this is refused a second application may be made to a Judge in open court. All applications must be made to the Administrative Law Court, formerly the Divisional Court of the Queen's Bench Division. Leave is based on the applicant showing grounds which the court considers to be of "sufficient interest". The first stage for leave must be made within three months of the grievance occurring. Once leave is granted, the second stage is a full hearing. Usually the first stage is on affidavit evidence and only one party, the applicant, is present. Remedies may be granted at the Court's discretion and remedies may be mixed; damages are available. The decision to grant a remedy is discretionary, depending on the nature of the body under review and the powers reviewed. Normally the application for judicial review is confined to "public law" matters, a term which is difficult to define and is often hard to reconcile with the various decisions made by the courts.[54]

6–134   Judicial review does not always afford the citizen redress. Parliament may entrust certain types of decision-making powers to Ministers and not the courts. In *R. v Secretary of State for Education and Science Ex p. Avon CC*,[55] the Court of Appeal reviewing the powers granted to the Minister of Education under the 1988 Education Reform Act, noted that:

> "Parliament did not entrust the making of that judgement, the Minister's approval for grant maintained status of a school to the Court but to the Minister who was answerable to Parliament."

6–135   The role of the courts may be limited or excluded in the allocation of functions by Parliament. In terms of subject matter, judicial review covers a wide range of activities. Sunkin[56] and research for the Public Law Project have identified the average case-load of applications for judicial review to be approximately 2,600 applications per annum. The bulk of the case-load relates to "immigration, housing, planning and licensing" cases. Education, homelessness and prisoners' rights are also fairly widely represented in applications.

6–136   Historically, grounds for judicial review include review of a tribunal or official where there is an error of law. A description applied to review of such matters is "illegality". This ground has been considerably broadened in recent years to correct mistakes of law made by inferior bodies, where there was not necessarily any right of appeal. Even where there may be an overlap between an appeal and a review, the courts have a discretion to offer review. A second ground for review is where there is "irrationality". This is defined to mean, as Lord Diplock explained, where the decision[57]:

> "is so outrageous in its defiance of logic or of accepted moral standards that no sensible person who had applied his mind to the question to be decided could have arrived at it."

---

[54] See M. Sunkin, "What is Happening to Applications for Judicial Review?" (1987) 50 *Modern Law Review* 432. Lee Bridges *et al.*, *Judicial Review in Perspective* (2nd ed., Public Law Project, Cavendish, 1995).
[55] [1991] 1 All E.R. 282.
[56] M. Sunkin, "The Judicial Review Case-load 1987–89" [1992] *Public Law* 490.
[57] *Council for Civil Service Unions v Minister for Civil Service* [1985] A.C. 374.

This ground affords the opportunity to review the exercise of statutory powers or **6–137** discretion. The test of "reasonableness" leaves considerable judicial flexibility in how to apply for review which even extends to reviewing inferior courts such as the legal powers of magistrates.

The third ground for judicial review identified by Lord Diplock, is "procedural **6–138** impropriety". On this ground the correct procedure has not been properly followed. A broader interpretation of procedural impropriety is where the rules of natural justice have been broken. There are two rules of natural justice. The first is to hear both sides of the case; giving an opportunity to hear each side is a fundamental part of the common law principles developed by the courts. The second is that no one should be a judge in his own cause. Decisions must be made in an unbiased way. An open mind and unprejudiced thinking before the case is presented, is required. Both rules of natural justice require fairness of decision-makers and apply to a wide range of public bodies especially when required by the interests of the litigant. If there is a "legitimate expectation" or if rights are affected then the courts have a discretion to apply such rules.

The application for judicial review may succeed if any of the grounds for review **6–139** outlined above are proven to the court. The granting of a remedy and the ultimate success of the application is nevertheless discretionary.

THE HUMAN RIGHTS ACT 1998

The Human Rights Act is examined in some detail in chapter 15. Suffice to mention **6–140** here that under s.3 of the Act "so far as it is possible to do so" primary and secondary legislation must be interpreted and enacted in a way that is compatible with Convention rights under the European Convention on Human Rights (ECHR). The Act falls short of allowing the courts to hold that an Act of Parliament is unconstitutional or illegal. The most the courts may do is rule on incompatibility[58] between the 1998 Act and the legislation under review. Since the Act came into force there have been three declarations of incompatibility.[59] It is then for Parliament, not the courts, to resolve any incompatibility. The courts are not *bound* by the jurisprudence of the Strasbourg Court of Human Rights but may give effect to those decisions. The impact of the Act is that under s.6 it is unlawful for a public authority to act in a way incompatible with Convention rights. S.7 permits an individual to bring a claim under s.6 in an appropriate court or tribunal and to rely on a Convention right in any proceedings if a victim of the unlawful act. In a claim that a judicial act infringes a Convention right, then s.9 of the Human Rights Act requires that proceedings should be brought by way of an appeal or judicial review. Remedies that are available include under s.8(4) payment of compensation or an order for damages.

It will be for the courts to consider how to interpret the Convention rights under the **6–141** Human Rights Act 1998. In *Alconbury*, the first case of its kind, the House of Lords

---

[58] There is no United Kingdom equivalent of the United States Supreme Court decision in *Roe v Wade* 410 U.S. 113 (1973).
[59] See *R. (on the application of Alconbury Developments Ltd) v Secretary of State for the Environment, Transport and the Regions* [2001] 2 W.L.R. 1389; *Wilson v First County Trust Ltd* [2001] 3 All E.R. 229; *R. (on the application of H) v North and East Region Mental Health Review Tribunal* [2001] 3 W.L.R. 512.

considered how rights set out under Article 6 of the ECHR may have an impact on how planning decisions are made. Article 6 provides that ". . . everyone is entitled to a fair and public hearing within a reasonable time by an *independent and impartial tribunal. . .*" (italics added). The case is examined in some detail in Chapter 16 but it is sufficient here to explain that an applicant for planning permission has a right of appeal to the Secretary of State against any refusal or condition of planning permission. The planning system effectively gives the final say to the Secretary of State, an elected politician, who may include matters of policy as part of the overarching responsibility to ensure that policy issues are considered as part of the system. The Secretary of State's decision may be appealed to the High Court on the same basis as judicial review. The appeal is seen as confined to legal issues, and the courts do not consider the merits of the policy behind the decision. The Secretary of State is in theory responsible to Parliament for policy matters.

6–142   The House of Lords considered the full implications of human rights introduced under the 1998 Act for the planning system and concluded that the court should not have every aspect of planning law fall under the scope of review. To ensure that the relevant human rights procedures are followed, it was sufficient that there should be a review of the legality of the decision. It fell within the Secretary of State's remit, including policy matters, to determine appeals. Thus, while the House of Lords recognise the requirements of the Human Rights Act, this Act does not require judicial intervention in every aspect of the planning system, which is already suscept-ible to judicial review. This illustrates the court's sensible case-by-case approach.

6–143   It is also important to recognise that legal rights developed under the Human Rights Act 1998 have the potential to shift Britain's constitutional arrangements in a new direction. The Court of Appeal[60] in October 2001 in a series of significant judgments outlined the significance of the Human Rights Act in terms of the powers of the courts to issue injunctions in matters of planning disputes. Issues of proportionality need to be considered by the courts before an injunction for threatened breaches of the law may be exercised under the discretionary powers of the courts. This is one example of the importance of the rights culture becoming an integral part of the judicial process.

6–144   Professor Ewing notes the danger of the unelected (judges) making important decisions over the elected (ministers):

> "We now have a constitutional system in which the output of the democratic process can avoid successful challenge and possible censure only if it can pass a test of democracy developed by a group of public officials who have escaped all forms of democratic scrutiny and accountability."[61]

TRIBUNALS AND INQUIRIES

6–145   One of the distinctive parts of the early development of English administrative law is the existence of tribunals. The nineteenth century witnessed the growth[62] in various forms of adjudication. The Railway and Canal Commission, set up in 1888, was a good

---

[60] *South Bucks DC v Porter* October 12, 2001. See ENDS [Environmental Data Services] Report 323, p.57; *www.ends.co.uk/index.htm.*

[61] K. Ewing, "The Unbalanced Constitution" in Campbell, Ewing and Tomkins, pp.116–117.

[62] W.A. Robson, "Administrative Justice and Injustice: A Commentary on the Franks Report" [1958] *Public Law* 12; W.A. Robson, "Justice and Administrative Law reconsidered" (1979) 32 *Current Legal Problems* 107.

example of the use of a specialised tribunal, sharing some of the characteristics of a court but specialised in its findings and activities. The Railway and Canal Commission consisted of two members appointed by the Home Secretary, and a High Court judge nominated by the Lord Chancellor. The Commission was judicial in form and the proceedings resembled those of a court.

In the nineteenth century the use of specialised commissions or tribunals was fairly common but not universal. Not all tribunals conformed to a single pattern. Often there were appeals to the courts. Even the county courts were used occasionally to undertake dispute settlement such as workers' compensation disputes.   **6–146**

While the pattern of growth in adjudicating procedures was uneven, the necessity for adjudication became greater as the Welfare State took shape. State-contributed funds for unemployment benefit or sickness benefit to workers increased the scale of state expenditure and also the need for fair and reasonable procedures to solve disputes. The National Insurance Act 1911 provided state benefits and adjudication procedures over unemployment pay were deputed to Insurance Officers appointed by the Board of Trade. Appeals lay to a Court of Referees representing employers, employees and a chairman appointed by the Board of Trade. Often the procedures were cumbersome, complicated and bureaucratic with several levels of decision-making.   **6–147**

Both World Wars had significant consequences in shaping the role of government and responsibilities accepted by the State. State responsibility or involvement covered pensions payable to the disabled and dependants of the dead killed in action. A plethora of local tribunals assisted in the administration of appeals, known as the Pensions Appeal Tribunals.   **6–148**

Reconstruction of the inter-war economy saw the reorganisation of transport, both road and rail, and the streamlining of freight to assist in the regulation of trade and industry. Tribunals were commonplace as an effective way to administer such changes. The Second World War further increased the growth in government powers and the need for new tribunals. The reason was not seen as a reactive one, but proactive, as a means of increasing the availability of welfare services based on need. Tribunals could introduce new policies and new regulatory legislation.   **6–149**

Tribunals mirrored government activities, as the Franks Committee observed[63]:   **6–150**

> "The continuing extension of governmental activity and responsibility for the general well-being of the community has greatly multiplied the occasions on which an individual may be at issue with the administration or with another citizen or body, as to his rights and the post war years have seen a substantial growth in the importance and activities of tribunals."

The introduction of the modern Welfare State after the Second World War increased benefits payable by the State under the National Insurance Acts 1946 and 1948. Tribunals proliferated with the inherent dangers of increasing government powers. Warnings that the State was too powerful were not slow in coming. First in 1928 with W.A. Robson's *Justice and Administrative Law* which warned against the growth of judicial powers exercised by Ministers and tribunals. A year later Lord Hewart C.J.,   **6–151**

---

[63] D.G.T. Williams, "Public Local Inquiries—Formal Administrative Adjudication" (1980) 29 *International and Comparative Law Quarterly* L.Q. 701. Franks Committee, Cmnd.218 (1957).

author of *The New Despotism*, and who had held the offices of Attorney-General and Solicitor General in the post-war Liberal Government, warned, for different political reasons to Robson, of the increase in civil service power and influence.

6–152   The concern over the use of the civil service in the machinery of tribunals was taken up by the Donoughmore[64] Committee on Ministers' Powers 1932. The Committee made recommendations in an attempt to find some rationalisation of the administrative system. Some tribunals were categorised as "specialised courts of law", others were called "ministerial tribunals". While recognising the value of each, the Committee recommended the use of the former rather than the latter, thus preserving the ad hoc development of the English tribunal system. The Committee left unresolved the value and the merits of tribunals as against courts.

6–153   The Second World War had incrementally increased the powers granted to Ministers to operate the wartime emergency. Tribunals were required to cope with compensation claims for war damages, disability and bereaved persons. Arising out of the question of land acquistion, the Crichel Down affair caused the Government embarrassment. The outcome led to the setting-up of a Committee of Administrative Tribunals and Inquiries under Sir Oliver Franks (the Franks Committee), only 25 years after the Donoughmore Committee.

6–154   The Franks Committee considered the Constitution and the workings of tribunals other than the ordinary courts of law, and examined the workings of such administrative procedures for holding inquiries by or on behalf of the Minister. This was the first occasion that the question of allocation was fairly grasped. The Committee examined the distinction between Ministers' powers and tribunals. Franks concluded[64a] that both decision-making Ministers and tribunals should share characteristics of openness, fairness and impartiality. Tribunals were "not ordinary courts" and not appendages of government departments. Tribunals were set up for adjudication and were not part of the machinery of administration.

6–155   The outcome was the Tribunals and Inquiries Act 1958 which was later amended in 1966 and consolidated in the Tribunals and Inquiries Act 1971, and 1992. Today there are over 2,000 tribunals covering, as Ganz explains[65] "such diverse areas as social security, immigration, employment, rents, taxation, rates and the National Health Service". The existence of such an extensive number of tribunals is a practical response to the need for an adjudication system other than the ordinary courts. Their practical advantages are cheapness, less formality than courts, and speed of operation. However, procedures vary according to the tribunal in question and the activity to be regulated. Many are chaired by lawyers and legal representation is not uncommon. There is a Council on Tribunals set up to oversee the operation of tribunals and also inquiries. It has been compared to a Departmental Committee; membership is unpaid and part-time. An annual report is published and the Council operates as a watchdog. There are proposals for its reform and expansion to meet the growing needs and changes in the role of tribunals. In May 2000 a Review of Tribunals was undertaken by Sir Andrew Legatt to provide a coherent structure for the organisation of the tribunal system. The complexity of much of the work of tribunals is due in part to the technical complexity of the law.

[64] Cmd.4060 (1932).
[64a] Franks Committee Cmd. 218 (1957).
[65] *Quasi-Legislation* (Sweet and Maxwell, London 1987) Ganz, G.

The Franks Committee also included inquiries within its remit. It separated **6–156** consideration of inquiries from tribunals but this separation is difficult to make in practice, and the legislation currently in force covers both tribunals and inquiries.

The purpose of inquiries, outlined by Franks,[66] is: **6–157**

> "to ensure that the interests of the citizens closely affected should be protected by the grant to them of a statutory right to be heard in support of their objections and to ensure that thereby the Minister should be better informed about the facts of the case."

The contrast between tribunals and inquiries is explained by Wade,[67] who offers a **6–158** distinction between the respective role of each. Wade argues that a tribunal "finds facts and decides the case by applying legal rules laid down by statute or regulation". An inquiry hears evidence, finds facts "but the person conducting it finally makes a recommendation to a Minister as to how the Minister should act in some question of policy."

However plain this distinction may appear, Parliament has experimented with many **6–159** different procedures which share the characteristics of inquiries and those that share the characteristics of tribunals. Thus the distinction may not always be easy to find. Particularly prevalent in recent years has been the use of public local inquiries associated with housing, town and country planning, motorways and the compulsory acquisition of land. D.G.T. Williams has found no fewer than 105 statutory provisions incorporating mandatory inquiries. Public local inquiries can be seen as large in scale, expensive in outlay and slow in reaching conclusions when major issues are at stake— for example, the third London Airport, the Sizewell B inquiry into nuclear power generation, and a variety of large inquiries on motorway planning. Many of the issues at such inquiries have required intervention by the courts to review the procedures at the inquiries, admissibility of evidence and fairness in cross-examination of witnesses. There is also the ultimate question of whether the Minister ought to accept the decision of the inquiry if there are errors in the conduct of the inquiry.

Both inquiries and tribunals provide for the citizen's consultation and participation **6–160** in the decision-making process. This may be seen as supplementary to the decision of Ministers and the role of Parliament. There are plans to modernise the planning system.[68] In particular the government is actively considering plans to revise the way large public inquiries may be used, preferring instead to use a new parliamentary inquiry for major projects rather than the long-drawn-out process, delay and expense of an inquiry.

SUMMARY AND CONCLUSIONS

Modernisation of the administration of justice has resulted in the creation of an **6–161** Administrative Law Court, the streamlining of procedures for judicial review and the development of administration. The spirit of the age of constitutional reform and

---

[66] Franks Committee, Cmnd.218 (1957).
[67] Wade, *Administrative Law* (6th ed., 1988).
[68] Planning Green Paper: Delivering a Fundamental Change December, 2001 and New Parliamentary Procedures for processing major infrastructure projects, December 2001. 323 Ends Report 39–40, December 2001.

changes to the system of judicial review are in part judge-led, as well as judge-designed. An increase in judicial power has been accomplished through innovative ideas and thinking about the development of judicial review and its application to the ordinary citizen. The transformation of judicial power has also involved assimilation of many European elements into United Kingdom law, including the enactment of the Human Rights Act 1998, incorporating most of the European Convention on Human Rights. In matters concerning the European Union the judiciary, and not the United Kingdom Parliament, has the final say.

6–162   It may be concluded that, at the apex of constitutional power, judges now command the heights, controlling how power—generally defined—is allocated, reviewed and assessed. It is tempting to see the judicial role increasing further to fill the void left by the weakening of parliamentary authority.

Further Reading

P. Cane, *An Introduction to Administrative Law (3rd ed., Oxford, 1998).*

G. Ganz, Understanding Public Law (Sweet & Maxwell, London, 2001).

Lord Justice Sedley, *Freedom, Law and Justice* 50th Hamlyn Lectures (Sweet & Maxwell, London, 1999).

C. Turpin, *British Government and the Constitution (4th ed., Butterworths, London, 1999).*

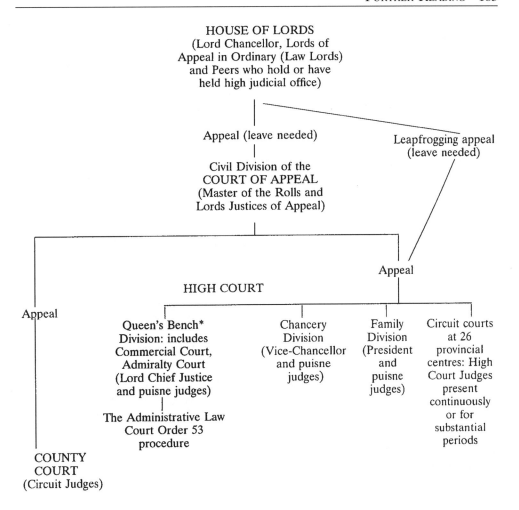

Fig. 1. The civil jurisdiction and appeal structure. (Reproduced from p. 39 Spencer, J.R. (1989) *Jackson's Machinery of Justice* by kind permission of the author and Cambridge University Press. © Cambridge University Press 1989). *Order 53 Procedure.

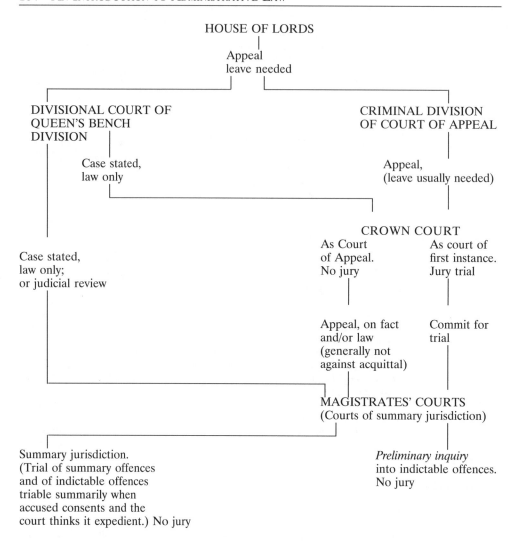

Fig. 2. The criminal jurisdiction and appeal structure. (Reproduced from p. 211 Spencer, J.R. (1989) *Jackson's Machinery of Justice* by kind permission of the author and Cambridge University Press. © Cambridge University Press 1989).

Part II

PUBLIC LAW, POLITICS, IDEAS AND INFLUENCES

Part II consists of three chapters. In Chapter 7 the electoral system is discussed in **II–001** terms of representative government. The question of political influences on the institutions of government is examined as part of the overall theme of accountable government. Chapter 8 provides an explanation of the ideas and influences which have shaped the development of public law in the United Kingdom. Chapter 9 explains the European dimension to the United Kingdom's constitutional arrangements with membership of the European Union.

Chapter 7

The Electorate, Politics and the Constitution

Introduction

Representative democracy is one of the most important measurements to judge the success of an electoral system.[1] In the United Kingdom the trust that resides in Parliament to hold government to account also gives rise to the idea that citizens have a right to participate in the electoral process for the selection of members of the House of Commons. Change and modernisation to electoral law are taking place, since the election of the new Labour Government in 1997. There are changes to the electoral system for European, local and parliamentary elections and the introduction of diversity in the electoral systems used; financial controls over party political funding; and improvements to the administration of elections through the creation of a new Electoral Commission. The development of regional government, through systems of devolution to Scotland, Wales, and Northern Ireland and the introduction of mayoral elections for London, has introduced different proportional systems of elections into the United Kingdom. The traditional, "winner takes all", First Past the Post (FPP) system remains for Parliamentary elections and local elections in England and Wales and Scotland. Elections to the European Parliament are conducted on the basis of a regional list system. The additional member system is used for the Scottish Parliament and Welsh Assembly, and the London Assembly. A supplementary vote system is used for the London mayoral election, and Northern Ireland operates a single transferable vote (STV) system for all elections with the exception of elections to the UK Parliament from Northern Ireland. The plethora of new voting systems only serves to show the striking anomaly which is the FPP system for the British general election to Westminster. In time this is likely to be amended, though in what way is less than certain.

7–001

It is also clear that referendums have an important role in the transition to new constitutional structures. In 1975 a referendum was used to confirm Britain's entry into the European Community, undertaken two years later. Again referendums were used, with limited success in 1978 but more successfully in 1997, for devolution to Scotland and Wales. A referendum on both sides of the border in the Republic of Ireland and Northern Ireland confirmed the peace process in 1998 for Northern Ireland. A

7–002

---

[1] Robert Blackburn, *The Electoral System in Britain* (Macmillan, St Martin's Press, 1995).

referendum is promised for entry into the single European currency, at a time when the economic conditions are considered to be appropriate.

7–003   In addition to the formal and institutional changes noted above, a shift has occurred in the traditional balance of powers between elected and non-elected elements. First, general dissatisfaction with the standards of politics and the public perception about the poor standing of the political parties is shown by the poor turnout at elections: at the last general election in 2001, turnout was disappointingly low at only 59.4 per cent, well below the average of 70 per cent. Yet the United Kingdom today has more systems of election and more opportunities for electoral choices than ever in its history. Despite this mis-match between the opportunities for citizen participation and voter satisfaction with the result, there is an ever-increasing quest for an accurate assessment of the political mood of the nation. Finally, in 1999 the abolition of the hereditary principle for membership of the House of Lords resulted in 92 hereditary members, 90, being elected from the list of the soon to be abolished hereditary peers. The future composition of the House of Lords is yet to be determined, but rests on the question of what percentage of the Lords should continue to be appointed and what percentage elected.

WHAT ARE ELECTORAL SYSTEMS INTENDED TO ACHIEVE?

7–004   The concepts of citizenship and participation depend on an effective electoral system. As Blackburn[2] has observed:

> "The crucial democratic link between politicians and people—or government and the governed—is the electoral system. The quality of that electoral system itself determines the quality of our democracy."

7–005   Yet oddly for many commentators in the United Kingdom, supreme authority has never resided in the people.[3] Over the past few decades great attention has been given to the question of whether the current electoral system in the United Kingdom lives up to these high ideals. No one can doubt that the debate on electoral reform is an important element in any healthy democracy. In the United Kingdom that debate has been added to by the demand for a referendum for the introduction of the common currency under the European Monetary System.

7–006   The United Kingdom is described as having representative and responsible government within a parliamentary democracy. The nature of that democracy depends on the electoral system. The relative political stability of the United Kingdom is attributed to the electoral system and the development of strong political parties. The fact that a government is able to command a strong majority sets the remit on how government governs and their attitude to party political power and parliament itself.

7–007   It must be remembered that the modern system of parliamentary elections gradually evolved from the nineteenth century. Progress towards universal adult franchise and the elimination of election corruption was gradual. The development of the present

[2] *ibid.* p.1.
[3] See C. Turpin, *British Government and the Constitution* (3rd ed., Butterworths, 1995), p.417.

electoral system is due more to pragmatism than the adoption of a theoretical ideal system. No pretence is made that present arrangements are ideal, rather that they produce strong government and therefore are seen to leave choice with the electorate.

Elected government raises questions about accountability, the representative nature **7–008** of government and the powers of government in the House of Commons. Also important are the growth and influence of political parties and the use of the electoral manifesto and public opinion when considering how the policies of government are made. Increasingly relevant are the influences of pressure groups, the media and the press on government policy-making.

Constitutional lawyers are particularly concerned with the question of how parlia- **7–009** mentary accountability and sovereignty are compatible; this raises one of the most difficult issues under the United Kingdom's constitutional arrangements. Johnson, writing[4] in 1975, fears that over the years there has been "a retreat from constitutional ways of thinking in Britain". This makes it more difficult to set limits on the powers of government and uncertainty arises as to the principles which govern many of "the institutions and practices, political habits and modes of behaviour".

In recent times criticism of the electoral system has focused on two issues. First, **7–010** what may be termed "institutional" criticism summarised by Ganz[5] to mean:

"that the elected part of Parliament, namely the House of Commons, having achieved supremacy over the unelected parts, namely the Queen and the House of Lords have summoned its sovereignty to the government which controls it through the party machine."

This represents a profound challenge to the idea of elected and accountable **7–011** democratic government. Secondly, criticism is made that the United Kingdom's electoral system of "first past the post" has a discriminatory effect against minority parties. The United Kingdom and recently Italy, stand out from other European countries in adopting a first past the post system of elections for central government. This is said to favour strong government with a decisive majority. In fact, coalition governments were not uncommon before the Second World War when governments were formed on a multi-party arrangement. Election results, since the Second World War, show a marked disparity between votes cast and seats gained in the House of Commons. Turpin notes that a party can be put in power with far less than a majority of votes and may govern without having to accommodate its policies to the interests of a majority of voters represented by the other parties in Parliament. Such alleged unfairness in the voting system has resulted in calls for reform of the current electoral system for central government, and the introduction of some form of proportional representation. The question of further progress largely depends on the judgment of the major political parties and the government of the day.

[4] N. Johnson, *In Search of the Constitution* (1977), pp.vii–viii. See table 1, p.212.
[5] G. Ganz, *Understanding Public Law* (3rd ed.), p.4.

PARLIAMENTARY DEMOCRACY, ORIGINS, IDEAS AND INFLUENCES

7–012   Different meanings are accorded to the idea of democracy. In countries with written constitutions, it is customary to locate the sources of power, the authority of the constitution and the basis of law as resting on the people.[6] This is an aspiration, even an ideal that may be unattainable given the reality of how power is in fact exercised. Such constitutional idealism places individual rights at the centre of the values which are sought to be protected. This creates a constitutional tradition where the political and legal institutions are made to conform to set values and rights. In such a tradition the protection of minorities or diverse groups is made an aspiration as part of the creation of a stable and diverse community. Such a tradition of constitutional idealism is illustrated in countries such as the United States which offer individual rights and constitutional protections as part of their constitutional arrangements. Even countries with one-party states may offer constitutional arrangements which appear to give democratic authority to the people as a means of providing some form of legitimacy for government.

7–013   In the United Kingdom, history and tradition have contributed to a different political tradition than the constitutional idealism discussed above. Solutions are worked out according to experience and institutions are expected to operate flexibly and develop as a response to experience and the needs of the time. The United Kingdom's tradition developed historically and the principles which have influenced its development, such as parliamentary sovereignty, conventions and majority government, are a reflection of that political development.

7–014   The evolution of parliamentary democracy and the ideals of democracy fit uneasily within the doctrine of parliamentary sovereignty. This is better understood when two different meanings of sovereignty are compared. First, legal sovereignty, as outlined in earlier chapters, is far removed from the people, as it is vested to the Crown in Parliament. A government with an overall majority is more free than in most other democratic countries to introduce its own legislative programmes with the likelihood of their passage into law. As in theory Parliament is free "to make or unmake any law", this provides considerable scope for government to exercise public power.

7–015   Secondly, there is political sovereignty. Political sovereignty emphasises the elected nature and authority of government. Political scientists[7] find it helpful to understand that the legitimacy of government depends on its elected and representative nature. Constitutional lawyers have been greatly influenced by Dicey's attempts to reconcile parliamentary sovereignty with popular franchise.

DICEY, PARLIAMENTARY SOVEREIGNTY AND POPULAR DEMOCRACY

7–016   Reforms in the electoral franchise in 1832 and 1867 gradually moved the United Kingdom towards a popular franchise. Existing governmental institutions survived but were subtly changed. Effectively the House of Commons became the centre of political

---

[6] See the United States Constitution, and the Japanese Constitution drafted on the American model in 1946.
[7] Ben Syed "Electoral Systems and Party Funding" in *The Changing Constitution*, (J. Jowell and D. Oliver ed., 4th ed., Oxford University Press, Oxford, 2000), p.293.

power and determined the composition of the government. There was no fixed idea of democratic government and no theoretical model to which political and legal institutions were expected to conform. Instead parliamentary democracy gradually evolved.

Dicey's vision of constitutional and administrative law in the United Kingdom, and   **7–017** how any extension of the franchise might be accommodated within existing frameworks and institutions, is relevant in understanding how parliamentary sovereignty and popular franchise challenged the established order. Dicey recognised the importance of legal sovereignty but conveniently distinguished legal from political sovereignty. In his essay[8] "Democracy in England in 1880", Dicey outlined his belief that "English democracy depended on love of order, the spirit of ordinary morality as the guide to public life and of constitutional morality" and in Dicey's view secured the sovereignty of the people. The clear implication was that political power must be tempered by obedience to the norms of the constitution—a view advanced out of fear that popular franchise posed a threat to the natural order maintained under the Constitution.

Dicey's attempt to reconcile his vision of democracy with his description of the main   **7–018** constitutional doctrines in the Constitution was fundamentally challenged both by his contemporaries and recent writers. His thesis rested on two premises: first, that the power of Parliament could be used to control government because "the will of the nation" was represented in the House of Commons; secondly, that democracy could be "self-correcting" namely, the flexibility inherent in an unwritten constitution allowed change but preserved the sovereignty of Parliament and the rule of law.

The challenge to Dicey's views came from contemporary writers of the period and   **7–019** succeeded in convincing Dicey of some errors in his views, which received a belated acknowledgement from Dicey in his later writing. However this did not cause any major re-think of the propositions Dicey advanced. Dicey's attempted reconciliation of the rule of law and sovereignty of Parliament revealed further weaknesses in his own analysis.

A number of conclusions may be deduced from Dicey's formulation of constitutional   **7–020** principles with the experience of democratic, elected and popular government. First, when the rule of law is challenged by Parliament, it is parliamentary sovereignty which remains supreme. Craig observes[9]:

> "If the majority within Parliament does enact legislation which is detrimental to minority interests, no sanctions can be expected from the Common law. When representative democracy proves incapable of aligning the interests of the elected representatives with the nation as a whole, so that some are constitutionally disadvantaged, the oppressed can but hope for a shift in their political fortune."

Secondly, the "advance in democracy" whereby the franchise was broadened, hastened   **7–021** the development of party politics. Votes were won rather than bought. The Executive demanded more control over the activities of the Commons as Cabinet Committees proliferated; delegated legislation increased in range and extent and gradually power moved from the Commons to the Executive. These developments put strain on Dicey's

[8] A.V. Dicey, June 13, 1880 *Nation*; J.F. McEldowney, "Dicey in Historical Perspective—A Review Essay" in *Law, Legitimacy and the Constitution* (McEldowney and McAuslan ed., 1985), pp.47–60.
[9] P. Craig, "Dicey, Unitary, Self-Correcting Democracy" (Jan., 1990) 106 *Law Quarterly Review* 105–143.

vision of the ideal constitution to the extent that it may be questioned whether it destroyed the vision entirely. In Dicey's later writings contained in his lectures[10] on the relation between law and public opinion in England during the nineteenth century, Dicey refined and broadened his understanding of democracy as including either a social condition or a form of government. The former he drew from de Tocqueville, that democracy created "a state of things under which there exists a general equality of rights and a similarity of conditions of thoughts, of sentiments and of ideals". The latter, influenced by Austin, he defined in its "older sense" to mean "a form of government; namely a constitution under which sovereign power is possessed by the numerical majority of the male citizens".

7–022   Dicey recognised the changes brought about by the extension of the franchise but he found it difficult to assess their significance within the conceptual framework of the Constitution. He explained the "advance of democracy" as a fitting description for the transfer of "supreme power" from either a single person, or from a privileged and limited class, to the majority of the citizens. Throughout his life and in his writings, Dicey attempted to reconcile both the conflicting nature of the United Kingdom's constitutional arrangements and conflicts in his own thinking. Dicey warned about the dangers of democracy in action. While supporting the extension of the franchise in 1832, he began to doubt its efficiency in 1867 and 1884 when Irish Home Rule and the demands for the franchise for women became part of the political agenda. He warned of the dangers of strict party discipline, and feared the restriction of individual liberty and the growth of administrative bureaucracy.

7–023   Dicey found the referendum mechanism a useful tool to counter-balance the tendency to party politics in government which he feared contributed to the decline of Parliament's prestige. A referendum also emphasised the role of the people as part of the political sovereignty of the nation. Dicey's vision of the unity of the United Kingdom provides a link between elections to Parliament and, through the House of Commons, the authority of the government of the day. That vision is an uncomplicated vision of a single unitary State wherein change could easily be accommodated through the politics of the day, while guarded against by the morality of the Constitution through the supremacy of the law. Conventions of the Constitution provided "a modern code" but undoubtedly it distracted the balance implicit in Dicey's "self correcting" vision of the Constitution.

7–024   Contemporary writers such as Bagehot[11] realised that parliamentary democracy did not always entail the "election of just and moderate men". Legislation might distort and change the fundamentals of the Constitution. Instead of representative democracy, policies became party political dominated by a single leader controlling a Cabinet government. Belatedly, Dicey recognised this threat in the form of Home Rule in Ireland and in the passage of administrative legislation granting wide discretion, largely unsupervised, to administrators.

7–025   Craig[12] concludes how Dicey's influence has endured despite much criticism and weakness in his analysis:

[10] A.V. Dicey, *Lectures on the Relation between Law and Public Opinion in England during the Nineteenth Century* (1905).

[11] W. Bagehot, (R.S. Crossman (ed.)), *The English Constitution* (1867) (London and Glasgow, 1963).

[12] P. Craig, "Dicey, Unitary, Self-Correcting Democracy" (Jan., 1990) 106 *Law Quarterly Review* 105–143.

"The realisation that political and social developments had undermined many of the premises upon which Dicey has built his constitutional doctrine was never truly appreciated by the immediate successors to Dicey in the field of constitutional scholarship. They were content to draw upon Dicey's conclusions without ever evaluating the reasoning through which those conclusions were reached."

By the end of the nineteenth century, parliamentary democracy brought with it the recognition that party discipline might curtail the independence of individual M.P.s; that debate in the House of Commons may be curtailed by procedures which favoured the Executive; and that the Cabinet rather than the House of Commons exercised real political power. This leaves unresolved the question raised by Turpin that "if the people were acknowledged in constitutional theory as the source of political authority debates on these matters would be conducted in different terms". In a similar way Keir writing about parliamentary democracy for the period 1867–1937 identified the[13] "distinctive characteristics" within the United Kingdom's constitutional arrangements which may influence future developments[14]: **7–026**

"In the modern state, an extended executive able to make, enforce, and interpret law, has come into being under imperfect parliamentary and judicial control. The principles of the separation of powers have been violated. Considerations of "policy and government" as they would have been called in the seventeenth century, have been accorded a larger place in the constitution than they have held for two hundred years."

The life cycle of politics means that political power is constantly shifting, while the institutions of government remain remarkably static. **7–027**

One of the remarkable features of the United Kingdom's political system is the two-party system. Government and a single "official opposition" is mainly a reflection of the electoral system and has a physical manifestation in the architectural design and shape of the House of Commons. Thus adversarial politics are encouraged and seen as part of the political culture of the country. The failure of smaller parties to make any inroads into the power of the Conservative or Labour party is also a feature of the existing state of the political parties. The major parties seem remarkably agile at providing a broad range of options to favour the widest possible appeal. In fact, as Colley has observed[15]: **7–028**

". . . since 1885 the Conservatives have been the single dominant party for 85 years. By contrast, in only 18 of these 107 years has a single party other than the Conservatives had a clear Commons majority. In other words, the one party dominance that characterised British politics so often in the 18th and 19th centuries has become if anything still more pronounced in this century."

[13] Keir, *Constitutional History of Modern Britain* (1938), p.520.
[14] *ibid.*, p.520.
[15] Linda Colley, "The Illusion of a Two-Party State" *Independent*, October 28, 1992.

PARLIAMENTARY FRANCHISE 1832–1948

7–029   The Representation of the People Act 1832, known as the Great Reform Act, represents the starting point for modern elected government. The 1832 Act was intended to broaden the franchise and introduce a more fair and representative system of elections. Keir described the reforms as introducing[16]:

> "organic changes which reflected the increasing ascendancy of the radical thought stimulated by Bentham and reinforced by the democratic impulse received from the doctrine of the French revolution."

7–030   The Act maintained the influence of property rights, but property other than land fulfilled the qualification necessary to be included within the franchise. Old boroughs were abolished, and the population shift to the towns was for the first time represented in the franchise. New boroughs were created and this process of reform applied throughout the country. The 40-shilling freeholder was retained but an additional residence qualification was added. New qualifications in terms of copyholders, leaseholders and tenants at will with rent not less than £50, were included.

7–031   In counties, tenants at will were retained and this preserved and continued the landlord's influence. An entirely new qualification, that of the £10 occupier, was created. The outcome of these reforms was to increase the electorate by 50 per cent, adding 217,000 to the electoral total of those qualified to vote.

7–032   The significance of the 1832 Act was remarkable. In previous chapters we have noted how, in constitutional terms, incremental change accompanied organic growth. Reform of the electorate introduced by the 1832 Act resulted in a marked shift in political power and influence from the unelected to the elected. This change only became noticeable gradually. In the case of patronage and royal influence the decline in royal power over the Cabinet had been gradual. In 1834 after royal attempts to influence the appointment of the Prime Minister and Ministers through the selection of Sir Robert Peel, Peel failed to obtain a majority at a general election and royal influence was rejected.

7–033   The 1832 Act also introduced a new procedure for registration of voters. This began a process of law reform which proved significant in shaping the modern law.

7–034   In 1867 the Representation of the People Act introduced the vote for many urban workers and extended new categories of eligible voters in boroughs to include lodgers and certain occupations. Even after 1867, the electorate was entirely male and this principle had been upheld by the courts. A further extension of the franchise was achieved under the 1884 Representation of the People Act which, by extending the franchise to certain householders in counties, enfranchised agricultural workers.

7–035   It is difficult to estimate the effects of both the 1867 Act and the 1884 Representation of the People Act as many qualified voters may have failed to register. It is estimated that apparently only 60 per cent of adult males were on the register before 1914.

7–036   In 1918 a considerable achievement was made in introducing universal adult male suffrage, by sweeping away the old complex property qualification. Instead of property,

[16] D. Keir, *Constitutional History of Modern Britain* (1948), p.595.

there was a residence qualification, requiring living in the constituency or adjoining constituency six months before a qualifying date. There was also a business and university qualification. This shift from property to residence as the basis of the qualification significantly broadened the franchise. For the first time a limited franchise for women over 30 was granted and, in 1928, for women over 21.

In 1945 the Representation of the People Act joined the local government franchise   **7–037** to that of central government. Three years later the business and university franchise was removed thus introducing the principle of "one man one vote". The 1948 Representation of the People Act also provided that only one member of Parliament should be returned for each constituency. The modern system of popular vote or universal franchise had been achieved.

THE ELECTORATE

There are major statutory reforms to electoral law. The Representation of the People   **7–038** Act 2000 has reformed the registration of voters for both parliamentary and local elections. In addition there have been changes on party political funding and the administration of the electoral system introduced by the Political Parties, Elections and Referendums Act 2000. The potential impact of Article 3 of the European Convention on Human Rights on free elections, and Article 10 on the freedom of expression has to be taken into account in electoral law under the Human Rights Act 1998. Since 1948 a number of changes in the franchise have been made in the direction of further extending the principle of universal franchise. First, the voting age was lowered from 21 to 18 in 1969 under the Representation of the People Act 1969. The age period for entitlement to be on the electoral register is based on whether the citizen reaches 18 during the period of the register. As soon as the citizen reaches 18, he or she may vote. Secondly, for the first time under the 1969 Act, merchant seamen may register as if they were resident at a home address or hostel. Thirdly, the Representation of the People Act 1985 introduced overseas voting. Any British citizen resident overseas, provided their residence in the United Kingdom was within the preceding five years, is entitled to vote.[17] Fourthly, the Representation of the People Act 2000 provides changes to the system of registration and introduces flexibility to the electoral register by allowing names to be added or deleted. It is possible for an elector to become registered during the year, replacing the concept of a fixed electoral register. In order to be qualified as an elector, s.1 of the Representation of the People Act 1983 stipulates that:

- you must be registered on the register of parliamentary electors for the constituency and you are only entitled to vote once in any parliamentary constituency and you cannot vote in more than one constituency and;

- electors must be 18 years or above on the date of the poll, be either a Commonwealth citizen or a citizen of the Republic of Ireland and not be subject to any legal incapacity to vote.

[17] Representation of the People Act 1985, ss.1–3. See s.59 of the Representation of the People Act 1993.

7–039   The Representation of the People Act 1983 provided, under s.5 criteria to judge the circumstances for a person to be in residence. The Representation of the People Act 2000 adds to the criteria. The courts have taken a broad and purposive interpretation under Article 3 of the Convention in *Hipperstone v Newbury Electoral Officer*.[18] This permitted protestors at Greenham Common to claim that their makeshift temporary accommodation used while making their protest was sufficient to allow them to register as voters.

7–040   The Representation of the People Act 2000 makes more generous provision to qualify as a voter:

- service voters, on making a service declaration may be qualified to register in the normal way or as an overseas voter;

- overseas voters on making an overseas elector's declaration may be qualified;

- mental patients may be registered provided they fulfil the requirement of residence in their mental institution;

- prisoners remanded in custody may be eligible to vote subject to the requirements of residence;

- remand prisoners and patients in mental hospitals may be registered;

- homeless people provided there is an available address for night or day will be eligible to become registered;

- postal votes are available to any eligible voter. This makes postal voting a viable option for many people who in the past were unable to qualify. At the last election it is estimated that 1.4 million used a postal vote, an increase from 738,614 postal votes issued in 1997.

7–041   Disqualification includes aliens, minors under 18, peers and hereditary peers no longer able to sit in the House of Lords, convicted persons detained in penal institutions, and those disqualified for five years because of a corrupt practice.

CONSTITUENCY BOUNDARIES

7–042   Since 1911, s.7 of the Parliament Act 1911 has required the maximum duration of Parliament to be five years. Any extension of the five-year period may be provided only through Act of Parliament. The number of constituencies is divided up between the different parts of the United Kingdom. It is intended not to be substantially greater or less than 613 for Great Britain, at least 71 for Scotland, 35 for Wales and 17 for Northern Ireland. There is provision in the Scotland Act 1998 for a reduction in the number of Scottish seats in the House of Commons to take account of the introduction of devolution to a Scottish Parliament. Currently the United Kingdom is divided into 659 constituencies, each sending one Member of Parliament to the House of

---

[18] [1985] Q.B. 1060.

Commons. Scotland is allocated 72 seats, 40 seats for Wales, and 19 seats for Northern Ireland. Constituency size is roughly 60,000 people though there are variations on this. The drawing-up of constituency boundaries, a key feature of the reformed electoral arrangements since 1832, is one of the most controversial issues of electoral practice. Electoral boundaries have a critical influence on determining electoral results.

Since 1944, for central government there are four permanent and independent **7–043** Boundary Commissions for England, Scotland, Wales and Northern Ireland. This system is to be changed by the creation of an Electoral Commission set out below. The Speaker is chairman of each Commission with a deputy chairman appointed from the High Court. Reports from the Boundary Commission are laid before the House of Commons by the Secretary of State together with a draft Order in Council to give effect to the Commissions' recommendations. The draft Order must be approved by resolution of each House before the final order is approved by the Queen in Council. This process is not without problems. In 1969 the then Labour government was in receipt of the Commissions' recommendations in April. No action was taken until June, notwithstanding the obligation to take action "as soon as may be" possible to lay a resolution before the House of Commons. When the resolutions were laid, no attendant Orders in Council accompanied the proposals. A Bill intended to implement the proposals and providing the Home Secretary with immunity because of any breach of duty was introduced. The Bill did not pass the House of Lords.

Mandamus was sought by an elector, Mr McWhirter,[19] to compel the Home **7–044** Secretary to lay a draft Order in Council in accordance with the 1949 and 1958 Acts. The Home Secretary duly agreed to comply and the *mandamus* application was withdrawn. In the event a Bill was introduced with a positive recommendation by the Government to reject it. The Government used its majority and in that event the Bill was rejected. The Government had made use of its majority to influence the outcome, when the spirit of the arrangements was intended to prevent direct political intervention by the government of the day. The ensuing election had to be fought on the old 1954 boundaries and not the new ones. After 1970 when the Conservative Government was returned the new boundaries were implemented.

The controversial nature of the drawing-up of the boundaries was recognised when **7–045** Parliament set up the Boundary Commission[20] with rules contained in the 1949 and 1958 Acts. The events outlined above showed how a cynical use of power could frustrate Parliament's intentions.

There is no exact science in drawing up constituency boundaries, and predicting the **7–046** outcome of any proposed changes is often difficult. An attempt to set out legislative rules for the line drawing of constituency boundaries was made in 1986. The Parliamentary Constituencies Act 1986 consolidated previous legislation, and in Sch.2 contains rules for the redistribution of seats. Each Commission must carry out a general review of constituency boundaries in its part of the United Kingdom at intervals of not less than 10 or more than 15 years. Particular areas may be given an interim review. Such an interim report was made in 1989 recommending changes to Milton Keynes in Buckinghamshire because of population growth.

---

[19] *R. v Home Secretary Ex p. McWhirter, The Times*, October 20, 1969.
[20] *R. v Boundary Commission for England Ex p. Foot* [1983] 1 Q.B. 600 at 603.

7–047   The rules are complex and difficult to interpret. Broadly they are as follows: Rule 1 sets the number of seats for each of the four parts of the United Kingdom; Rule 2 requires that only one member may be retained for each constituency; Rule 3 applies to the city of London only; Rules 4–6 set out how boundaries are to be drawn for each constituency; Rule 7 provides for any variation or departure from the rules set out in Rules 4–6, but there is considerable scope for interpretation of each of the rules.

7–048   At present the rules provide that there are a minimum number of seats. This means a minimum of not substantially greater or less than 613 seats for England, 71 for Scotland, 35 for Wales and from 16 to 18 seats for Northern Ireland. Controversy surrounds the interpretation of Rule 1, as the rules may appear to give undue preference to Scotland, Wales and Northern Ireland. Calculations if based on the removal of each region's guaranteed minimum would mean reductions: Scotland 12 seats, Northern Ireland 1, Wales 6; and England would gain 19. In 1991 the average electorate in constituencies in England was 69,279, in Wales 58,086 and in Scotland 54,369. Rawlings has pointed out[21]:

> "the Commission will clearly be well advised not to allow an excessive growth in Welsh and Scottish constituencies given that the seat minimum set out in rule 1 even if not exceeded, still incorporate a substantial measure of over-representation."

7–049   Such imbalance may appear odd in a modern electoral system, but this is a reflection of the historical development of electoral rules. Northern Ireland received additional seats after the demise of the system of self-government with its own elected Parliament under the Government of Ireland Act 1920. The introduction of devolution in 1998 has not resulted in any re-adjustment. However, in the future it is clear that adjustments to the seats accorded to the four geographical regions may have to be made after the introduction of devolution in Northern Ireland, Scotland and Wales.

7–050   Interpretation of Rules 4 and 5 involves how the boundaries of each seat should be determined. Rule 4 provides principles for local government boundaries. Rule 5 provides the objective for the drawing-up of the boundaries, namely the achievement of equal-sized constituencies in numerical numbers of electors.

7–051   Reconciliation of Rules 4 and 5 is controversial and was the basis of an important challenge in the courts by the Labour Party in 1983. Some explanation of each rule is required.

7–052   Rule 4 involves the Commission determining an electoral boundary for each constituency taking account of local government boundaries. Since 1976 the changes in population growth and in the movement from inner cities to outlying regions caused distortion in the sizes of constituency electorates. This resulted in disparity between constituencies, with nearly 30 per cent over quota in one example of the proposed constituencies of Hornsey & Wood Green and nearly 15 per cent under quota in Hendon South.

7–053   Rule 5 involves the Commission setting an electoral quota taking account "as far as is practicable" of the geographical limits set for the local government boundaries. The application of this principle of equal constituencies, in terms of number of electors,

---

[21] See H.F. Rawlings, *Law and the Electoral Process* (London, 1988), pp.24–72.

was rendered almost impossible by the requirements of the local government boundaries set out in Rule 4.

In 1982 the Commission completed its review and made proposals to correct **7–054** imbalances between constituencies taking account of the demographic changes mentioned above. A number of constituencies were removed from the Greater London Council area. In order to keep within the physical limitations of Rule 5, great distortion arose in the constituency size in terms of the number of voters represented. The two examples of Hornsey & Wood Green, and Hendon South showed the disparity. Criticism was made that the Commission's proposals violated the principle of one vote having equal value in every constituency.

The Labour party believed the proposals were unfavourable to their electoral **7–055** prospects. Before the Boundary Commission Report was brought before Parliament, and to avoid exclusion from judicial review by the courts once the Report was approved, the Labour party through its then leader, Mr Foot, sought the remedies of prohibition and injunction against the Boundary Commission. Their contention was based on two arguments:

> (1) that the Commission had failed to give proper weight to Rule 5 containing the principle of equal representation between constituencies;
> (2) The Commission was failing in its duty to propose constituencies which crossed county and London Borough boundaries. The point of this argument was to insist that the Commission ought to give primacy to Rule 5 in practice.

Unsuccessful in the Divisional Court, the applicants appealed to the Court of Appeal. **7–056** Sir John Donaldson first asserted the correctness of the courts' powers to check whether Ministers or local authorities or other bodies including the Commission had exercised their powers according to law—"the courts can and will interfere in the defence of the ordinary citizen". He went on to conclude[22] as between Rules 4 and 5:

> "The requirement of electoral equality (Rule 5) is, subject to the second limb of Rule 5, subservient to the requirements that constituencies shall not cross county or London Borough boundaries."

The second limb of Rule 5 authorises departure from Rule 4 only where[23] "it is **7–057** desirable to avoid an excessive disparity between the electorate of any constituency and the electoral quota". However in the argument advanced by the Labour Party it was claimed that the Commission had exercised their discretion wrongly. The Court of Appeal concluded that the Commission had exercised such a discretion but it was exercised on sufficient grounds. Any objection based on this argument was rejected by the court.

The Court of Appeal upheld the Commission's proposals and rejected the appli- **7–058** cation, leave was later refused to the House of Lords.

One effect of the courts' interpretation is the primacy and respect for local **7–059** government boundaries (Rule 4) over equal representation between constituencies

[22] *R. v Boundary Commission for England Ex p. Foot* [1983] 1 Q.B. 600 at 603.
[23] *ibid.*

(Rule 5). However, the Court of Appeal entered a *caveat* in certain circumstances where disparity between electoral boundaries might be unacceptable[24]:

> "the theoretical possibility that in a given instance the disparity between the electorate of a proposed constituency and the electoral quota might be so grotesquely large as to make it obvious in the figures that no reasonable commission which had paid any attention at all to rule 5 could possibly have made such a proposal."

7–060   Leaving open the possibility of reviewing any disparity in the electoral quota which is "grotesquely large" for the future, must cause the Boundary Commission difficulty for the years ahead in the balance needed between Rules 4 and 5. In fact up until the *Foot* case the courts have shown remarkable consistency in self-restraint in this area. This is shown in the judgement of Oliver L.J. in the *Foot* case arguing that judicial intervention is inappropriate in boundary disputes. For the future it might be advisable to reconsider the formula "as near the electoral quota as possible" and substitute precise guidelines to the Boundary Commission in terms of the percentage of divergence which is permissible.

7–061   Such criticisms are not shared by all commentators. As M.P.s are said to be constituency trained, they will not favour cross-boundary constituency work which may entail two or more local authorities. Departure from local boundaries adds to the Boundary Commission's task and complexity. Perhaps the most difficult problem at the heart of the matter is how to preserve community participation in electoral activities, when shifts in population change the nature of the community. However, popularity of voting has not been inhibited by boundary changes. Electoral turn-out at central government elections is well over 70 per cent of the electorate so it may be asked, do electoral boundaries really matter? The answer depends largely on party politics. It is rather difficult to find any precise constitutional basis for any objection to the electoral system. There is a sense of constitutional propriety, meaning that government may lose its political authority if it does not pay sufficient attention to the electorate.[25] In theory government is said to be representative, even if in practice the Commission appears to need to be given greater priority to achieve equality between constituencies.

THE ELECTORAL COMMISSION

7–062   The creation of an independent body to oversee the regulation of elections and electoral administration has been advocated by a number of reports.[26] The details of the new Electoral Commission are contained in Pt 1 of the Political Parties, Elections and Referendums Act 2000. The new Electoral Commission was set up in October 2000 and is expected to oversee the work of the Boundary Commission, gradually absorbing that role within its remit. It is also required to set up Boundary Committees for England, Scotland and Northern Ireland. The Secretary of State will no longer be

---

[24] *ibid.*
[25] See R. Blackburn, *The Electoral System in Britain* (1995).
[26] The *Jenkins Commission* Cm.4090 (1998) and the *Neill Committee* Cm.4057.

able to modify the Commission's recommendations regarding constituency boundaries. Recommendations are expected to be laid before Parliament by draft Order in Council. It is expected that by 2006, electronic voting will be possible and the Electoral Commission are expected to develop strategies to implement that goal. The main functions of the Electoral Commission are:

- to oversee regulation of the political process such as spending arrangements and the preparation of an annual report on all elections;

- reviewing and reporting on election law and related matters, referendums, distribution of seats at parliamentary elections, boundary changes, and the registration of political parties;

- to be consulted on any reforms on electoral law;

- to keep the public informed of electoral systems and the method of elections for the different tiers of government and for Europe.

The status of the Electoral Commission is comparable to the National Audit Office. Appointments to the Commission are formally made by the Queen, but by approval of the Speaker of the House. There is scope for party political representation with the establishment of a Parliamentary Parties Panel to provide input into the deliberations of the Commission. The Electoral Commission will consist of between five and nine office holders but they must not have had any connection with a political party 10 years prior to their appointment.   **7–063**

ELECTION CAMPAIGN AND FINANCE

Registration

Regulation of the conduct of elections is provided for by a number of statutes. The Representation of the People Acts 1983 and 1985 apply to election campaigns, election expenditure and the conduct of elections. The Political Parties, Elections and Referendums Act 2000 makes substantial changes to the law. Underpinning the new system of regulation is a requirement that political parties should be registered, building on the principles set out in the Registration of Political Parties Act 1998. If the candidate is not a member of a political party then they must describe themselves as independent. There is also a requirement that each political party must register a treasurer responsible for compliance with Pts III and IV of the 2000 Act. It is expected that each political party should have a campaign manager and if one is not appointed then the treasurer is responsible. Nomination papers must be submitted to a returning officer signed by the proposer and seconder, and containing eight other electors. A system of deposits is used; these are forfeited if the candidate fails to obtain one-twentieth of the votes cast. The deposit is usually set at £500. Proposals to increase this amount have received a mixed reaction. In addition each candidate must make an election return including any details of donations of £50 or more. Candidates are entitled to make use of public rooms for election meetings. Selecting a candidate to   **7–064** represent a political party is an important part of the work of the constituency party. In *Jephson v Labour Party*[27] an industrial tribunal found that a women-only shortlist proposed by the Labour party breached the Sex Discrimination Act 1975. This had the potential of restraining the selection of candidates through some form of positive discrimination. The Sex Discrimination (Election Candidates) Act 2002 provides a change retrospectively to the Sex Discrimination Act 1975 and removes the application of the 1975 Act to the measures adopted by political parties to reduce inequality in the numbers of men and women selected as candidates. The new arrangements apply to registered political parties and apply to elections held in Northern Ireland as well as Scotland and Wales.

Election Expenses and Accounting Requirements

7–065   A long-standing controversial issue, and one of considerable importance in the winning of elections, is the question of election expenditure. Since the end of the nineteenth century, the Corrupt and Illegal Practices Prevention Act 1883 established a limit on election expenses for each candidate.[28] It is estimated that in the 1997 election both Conservative and Labour Parties spent £54 million, an all-time high. Pts III and IV of the Political Parties, Elections and Referendums Act 2000 impose new duties on political parties with legal controls on the regulation of donations and campaign expenditure.

- Duties are imposed on the treasurer of a political party. These duties vary according to the amount of expenditure. Accounts have to be prepared using a set formula approved by the Electoral Commission where expenditure is greater than £250,000 or less than £5,000. Above £250,000 accounts must be audited. Wide powers are given to the Electoral Commission to monitor these arrangements.

- Controls on Donations to Registered Parties are contained in Pt IV of the Political Parties, Elections and Referendums Act 2000. The most fundamental change is that, following the Neill Committee's recommendation[29] anonymous and foreign donations are banned. The identity of donors must be known and donation is widely defined to cover gifts of money, property or sponsorship of services at less than commercial rate. Donations below £200 may be disregarded and political parties are required to make quarterly returns of donations received in excess of £5,000 from individual donors in any one year. The Electoral Commission is expected to prepare a register of all donations. There are special provisions for Northern Ireland taking account of the impracticality of banning foreign funding.

- Controls on campaign expenditure are in place for the first time, setting a limit on the ability of the political parties to spend in relation to election campaigns. There is a limit of £30,000 to be spent in any one constituency up to a

[27] [1996] I.R.L.R. 116.
[28] The present limit for each candidate is approximately £3,648 plus an additional 4.1p for every registered voter in a County constituency or 3.1p in a Borough constituency.
[29] 5th *Report from the Committee on Standards in Public Life* (October, 1998).

maximum limit of £810,000 in England, £120,000 in Scotland and £60,000 in Wales for United Kingdom Parliamentary elections. In practical terms this means that the limit for the party that fights every seat in each constituency is over £19 million. There is defined a "relevant time " for the calculation of election expenditure and for general elections it is a period of one year before the poll. The definition of campaign expenditure is generously defined to include market research, opinion polls and rallies, transport and the provision of facilities to engage in electioneering. Sch. 9 of the Act makes similar provision for European elections and elections to the Scottish Parliament and Welsh Assembly. There are also controls on the involvement of third parties covering individuals or groups. This includes expenses by third parties or groups in connection with election material and in any way promoting or procuring the election of a registered party. Limits are placed on what is termed "controlled expenditure".

● Controls on political donations and expenditure by companies are also applicable. Ss.139–140 of the Political Parties, Elections and Referendums Act 2000 provide for the first time that shareholders must give approval before making a donation to a political party. This brings the position of company donations into line with an earlier change in the law applying to trade unions. Trade union contributions are covered by the Trade Union Act 1984. Political funds may only be established and maintained after balloted approval has been obtained from the membership within the last 10 years. Funds for political objects are affected and the term "political objects" is defined in the 1984 Act as to "relate to activity designed to secure and maintain a candidate in elected office". It is possible that once approved under the 1984 Act, the individual trade union member may opt out of the donation. The means to exercise this right must not cause discrimination among trade union members.

ELECTIONS AND THE MEDIA

Unlike the USA, in the United Kingdom expenditure on TV is precluded, although the parties are entitled to purchase advertising in the press. In the United Kingdom, election broadcasting is regulated by the BBC and ITC, the Independent Television Commission (the predecessor of the IBA for independent TV), for Party Election Broadcasts. Supplementary coverage is provided in news and current affairs programmes, interviews with candidates and general discussion programmes. Both the BBC and ITC seek to establish impartiality in the conduct of election broadcasts and news reports. There is an informal non-statutory Committee on Political Broadcasting which is chaired by the Prime Minister and comprises the senior management of the BBC and ITC. Unofficial in status, unpublished in determinations and unknown in terms of reference, the decisions of this Committee find their way into the allocation of "slots" for each political party.[30] In 1997 it was decided by the BBC and Independent Television to deal directly   **7–066**

[30] *R. v Tronoh Mines Ltd* [1952] 1 All E.R. 697. Unauthorised election expenditure did not extend to general propaganda made by a political party even if it assisted individual candidates, an example of the difficulty in determining legal expenditure in the media.

with political parties rather than with the Committee. Ss.11 of the Political Parties, Elections and Referendums Act 2000 provides that broadcasters must consider input from the Electoral Commission before setting out their rules or protocols.

7–067   The general test of entitlement to a single electoral broadcast is based on the number of candidates fielded at the election—currently 50—though the question of the allocation of broadcast time between the main parties is more difficult to ascertain. One view is that it is based on the allocation of seats in the House of Commons at the dissolution. Another view is that the allocation should be based not only on seats won but also on votes obtained.

7–068   A number of legal challenges to the criteria have been made. The Communist Party unsuccessfully challenged the BBC in its allocation of broadcasts. It was argued that the BBC assisted the candidates who were permitted broadcasts and that such expenditure for TV programmes should count against each individual candidate's election expenses. S.9(4) of the Representation of the People Act 1969 as amended by s.75(1)(c) permits broadcasting authorities to present to the electorate party figures who happen to be candidates, without incurring the problem of each candidate's expenditure maximum for elections.[31]

7–069   The fact that allocation decisions over election broadcasting are amenable to judicial review provides an important safeguard. However many issues are unresolved. The time schedules of programmes, the content of interviews, the perspective of the interviewer may all contribute to give one party more favourable exposure than another. The major political parties engage in monitoring television programmes and make claims of political bias whenever appropriate. Claims are made by the smaller parties that the present arrangements favour the two larger parties. Little may be expected to change, as the present arrangements are unlikely to be reformed if they continue to favour the larger parties. One change is that s.144 of the Political Parties, Elections and Referendums Act 2000 provides that each broadcasting authority must adopt a code of practice on local election broadcasting during an election period. The Human Rights Act 1998 introduces the dimension of fairness in the exercise of freedom of expression, for example, under Article 10. In *Bowman v UK*[32] an election rule under s.75 of the Representation of the People Act 1983 making it an offence for someone other than a candidate to spend more than £5 on campaigns to elect a candidate, effectively prevented an anti-abortion worker from campaigning at an election. The European Court held this was a violation of Article 10. Care must therefore be exercised in assessing the impact of regulating elections to avoid an unfair or discriminatory practice.

7–070   Newspapers also have a dominant role in the election campaigns of the various political parties. Supervising newspaper coverage is equally problematic. Unlike the BBC and ITC which claim impartiality, newspapers are free to be partisan. The Press Council is the body charged with the self-regulation of the newspaper industry. This raises the question of whether there is the need for privacy laws to protect public figures from an intrusive invasion of their personal and private lives. Politicians accept the glare of publicity as a necessary part of their profession, but recent complaints about press behaviour have raised the issue of whether private and personal affairs of public figures should be kept from public scrutiny in the press.

---

[31] *Grieve v Douglas-Home* [1965] S.C. 315.
[32] 26 E.H.R.R. 1.

Many complaints and criticisms are made of press coverage[33] during elections. The **7–071** fact that newspapers legally support one political party as against another may lead to gross distortions in the news and unfairness to the other parties. Generally it is accepted that newspapers favourable to the Conservatives outnumber those favourable to Labour. Equally clear is that minority parties may not be represented by the large national newspapers.

Support for each party brings large-scale donations. In the case of the Conservatives, **7–072** almost 30 per cent comes from company donations. In the case of the Labour party, almost 55 per cent comes from trade union donations with a political levy. Donations have fallen as trade union membership has diminished.

The 1976 Committee on Financial Aid to Political Parties recommended annual **7–073** grants should be payable from the Exchequer funds to the central organisations of the parties. No immediate action is forthcoming on this proposal.

Individual donations once free from much controversy or legal controls are now made **7–074** more transparently as all the main political parties have agreed to make public donations. In the past the conditions which may attach to such contributions were hidden from public scrutiny and the implication of this might well be serious if the information regarding conditions was made public. A particularly sensitive question is the suggestion that there might be a link between political donations by individuals or companies and the granting of personal honours by the Monarch on the advice of the Prime Minister.

Party politics is the lifeblood of the working Constitution. Political rivalry occupies a **7–074a** central feature of the competition for electoral victory. Fairness ought to be a prominent feature in how parties are funded and how they carry out their activities. Financial advantage to the two larger parties may effectively deprive smaller parties of a fair opportunity to put their case to the electorate.[34]

EUROPE

In 1979, direct elections to the European Assembly, now called the European **7–075** Parliament, were first held. Prolonged negotiations had taken place within the Community to settle the question of the allocation of seats in each Member State. Once the allocation of seats was carried out, each Member State was left to introduce the necessary domestic election law and machinery. In the United Kingdom responsibility rested on the Boundary Commission to draw up Assembly boundaries. In Northern Ireland arrangements in place before 1979 had introduced a system of elections for the Northern Ireland Assembly and these arrangements were sufficiently flexible to accommodate European Assembly elections. The arrangement of the electoral system in Northern Ireland was changed to meet the needs of the minority Catholic population by the use of proportional representation rather than the first past the post system.

The European Assembly Elections Act 1978, as amended, provides the main legal **7–076** framework for elections. The European Parliament Act 1999 amends the law and

---

[33] *R. v Broadcasting Complaints Commission Ex p. Owen* [1985] Q.B. 1153; Rawlings, *op.cit.* p.207.
[34] See Rawlings, *op.cit.* p.207. See Trade Union Act 1913, s.3(1)(b); *Report of the Committee on Financial Aid to Political Parties*, Cmnd.6601 (1976); C. Munro, "Elections and Expenditure" [1976] *Public Law* 300; *Conservative and Unionist Central Office v Burrell* [1982] 2 All E.R. 1.

replaces the system of first past the post with a regional list system for Scotland, Wales and England. In Northern Ireland the single transferable vote system is used. At the Edinburgh summit in December 1992, it was agreed to increase representation to reflect German unification. The European Parliamentary Elections Act 1993 increases the number of representatives for the United Kingdom to be elected to the European Parliament. There are 87 seats for the United Kingdom. Representation for Scotland and Northern Ireland remains unchanged. The 1993 Act sets up a European Parliamentary Constituencies Committees for each of England and Wales. The work of the Committee is in drawing up constituency boundaries for European Parliamentary Constituencies. Draft recommendations approved by the Secretary of State have to be laid before Parliament for approval. The Treaty of Nice expands the size of the Parliament to 738, to reflect the planned expansion in membership. It is expected that the United Kingdom will lose 13 seats to accommodate the change.

7–077   Doubts about the legality of adopting the British electoral system were raised in Scotland in a court case[35] taken by the Social Democratic Party/Liberal Alliance, that the first past the post system was discriminatory, and was in conflict with the spirit of Article 138 of the Treaty, which implied equality of voting procedures throughout the Community. The United Kingdom is alone among other Member States in not having an electoral system based on some form of proportional representation. The Scottish Court refused the application, as *inter alia* it was doubtful if enforceable rights were created under Article 138. There were additional procedural objections to making a reference under Article 177 which were not in the applicant's favour owing to problems with how the pleadings were drafted.

7–078   This leaves unresolved the question of whether the United Kingdom's electoral system is a fair one and ultimately, the question of whether, in the period of debate after the drawing-up of the Maastricht Treaty, the United Kingdom's electoral system is sufficiently representative. Voter turnout at European Parliament elections was 32.6 per cent in 1979 and 1984, 36.2 per cent in 1989 and 1994. This is relatively low when compared to central government elections.

MANIFESTO, MANDATE AND PRESSURE GROUPS

Manifesto and Mandate

7–079   Political parties aspire to become the government. The relationship between the electoral process which influences the selection of the government and the policies of the government once elected, is one of intense and continuous debate. Governments are free to depart from any electoral promise but they do so at the expense of their own popularity. The question of allowing the electorate some influence over the functioning of the government of the day is not easy to address. By-elections caused by the death, illness or retirement of M.P.s, give an opportunity for the popularity of the Government's policies to be judged by the electorate. Normally a by-election is held within three months of the vacancy occurring. However successful opposition parties

---

[35] *Prince v Secretary of State for Scotland* [1984] 1 C.M.L.R. 723; [1985] S.L.T. 74.

may be in winning by-elections, it is difficult to regard such results as accurate predictions of the outcome of a general election or of government popularity. Opinion polls may help gauge public opinion but are not always reliable.

The electorate may exercise some influence over the government of the day through **7–080** the implications of the electoral policies contained in the party manifesto. Is there a mandate to govern? The idea of electoral mandates has its appeal. It stresses the principle of representative government and that an M.P. is somehow a "delegate" of the people. However popular this view may appear, it does not accord with historical precedent. Turpin notes the resolution in 1947 of the House of Commons that members of the House of Commons are not delegates[36]

> " . . . the duty of member being to his constituents, and to the country as a whole rather than to any particular section thereof."

The independence of M.P.s is a zealous guarantee of an individual's right to vote **7–081** according to conscience but the reality of political power seems oddly inconsistent with individual M.P.s voting according to free will. Party government is the modern form of government and M.P.s are expected to conform.

A more realistic view of the practical role attributed to the M.P.'s function is **7–082** provided by Griffith and Ryle[37]:

> "When a voter at a general election, in that hiatus between Parliaments, puts his cross against the name of a candidate, he is (most often) consciously performing two functions: seeking to return a particular person to the House of Commons as Member for that Constituency; and seeking to return to power as the Government of the country a group of individuals of the same party as that particular person. The voter votes for a representative and a Government."

Griffith and Ryle's analysis places emphasis on representation as well as government. **7–083** Not all M.P.s can be involved in government even if their own Party wins the election. The role an M.P. may adopt may involve membership of a select committee or one of the many backbench committees formed to promote the interests of particular causes. The Conservative Party "1922 Committee" is a good example of the function such a committee may perform. It may warn and criticise. It provides a conduit for party workers in constituencies to make their views known to the government of the day when the Conservative Party is in power. As a critic of the government, an M.P. must be prepared to both maintain the government in power and scrutinise its activities.

From the perspective of the M.P., the idea of government possessing a mandate **7–084** seems strangely inconsistent with his own role and function. From the perspective of the political party, an electoral mandate or manifesto promise may control party members, focus the activities of M.P.s, and help unite the party. From the perspective of the electorate, the manifesto may appear to clarify the policies of each political party and thereby allow choice of support.

The courts may take account of the manifesto in elections. In *Bromley*[38] the House **7–085** of Lords considered the now defunct Greater London Council's manifesto promise to

---

[36] Turpin, *op.cit.* pp.535–539. *Hansard*, HC Vol.440, col.365 (July 15, 1947), quoted in Turpin, p.535.
[37] Griffith and Ryle, *Parliament: Functions, Practice and Proceedings* (1989), p.69.
[38] *Bromley LBC v Greater London Council* [1983] 1 A.C. 768.

reduce fares on public transport in London. Lord Diplock was clear that the manifesto did not provide a local authority with a mandatory requirement to carry out policies. Members of a local authority must not "treat themselves as irrevocably bound to carry out pre-announced policies" in election manifestos.

7–086   However this view is not always consistently followed. In *Tameside*,[39] Lord Wilberforce regarded the electoral policy of the Conservative local authority to retain grammar schools as one which "bound" the authority to carry out its task.

7–087   The current view of the courts is more likely to follow the direction set by *Bromley*. In terms of central and local government relations the view of Lord Templeman in *Nottingham C.C. v Secretary of State for the Environment*[40] is similar to the strict "allocation of power" analysis made out by Lord Diplock in *Bromley*. The analysis is based on the theory that legal powers should be exercised not according to their political agenda but according to law. The role of the courts is confined to determining the law and not the politics or policy of the law. Policy may only be questioned in Parliament and not the courts[41]:

> "Where Parliament has legislated that the action to be taken by the Secretary of State must, before it is taken be approved by the House of Commons, it is no part of the judges's role to declare that the action proposed is unfair, unless it constitutes an abuse of power the sense of which I have explained; for Parliament has enacted that one of its Houses is responsible. Judicial review is a great weapon in the hands of the judges; but the judges must observe the constitutional limits set by our parliamentary system on their exercise of this beneficent power."

7–088   The distinction between review according to law and review as to policy may be difficult to make, but the implications are clear: party politics set certain boundaries for the courts in determining the extent of their review powers. An example of policy dispute between a local authority and the relevant Minister is found in *R. v Secretary of State for Education and Science Ex p. Avon C*. Lord Justice Ralf Gibson explained[42]:

> ". . . The application was misconceived in so far as it asked the court to intervene in what was analysed, a dispute as to educational policies between Avon [the local authority] and the minister . . ."

7–089   In a concurring judgment Lord Justice Nicholls commented:

> "Given the notice of the subject matter of the decision, it was difficult to see how the Council's challenge on the ground of 'irrationality' could ever get off the ground."

7–090   Both judgments stressed how inappropriate it was to review the Minister's decision in such circumstances.

7–091   The courts assume that policy questions are under the doctrine of ministerial responsibility, a matter for parliamentary discussion and debate. The formulation of

---

[39] *Secretary of State for Education and Science v Tameside Metropolitan Borough Council* [1977] A.C. 1014.
[40] *Nottinghamshire C.C. v Secretary of State for the Environment* [1986] A.C. 240, 255–1.
[41] *ibid.*, Lord Scarman, pp.250–251.
[42] *Independent*, May 25, 1990, C.A.; (1990) 49 L.G.R. 498.

party policy through the manifesto gives electors an opportunity to see the shape of their Government's policies. Rarely are such manifesto promises seen as an enforceable mandate in the legal sense, against party policy changes or shifts in government policy.

The influence of party manifestos has perceptibly increased since 1979. The government of the day's adoption of more radical policies such as privatisation and reforms in education, the health service and local government highlights the importance of the manifesto in government policy. Careful drafting of manifesto promises is seen as an important political expedient. The calculating of "keeping pledges" is a way to continue keeping faith with the electorate.   **7–092**

It is equally clear that the courts will adopt a robust view when confronting corruption. Lord Scott explained in the recent House of Lords decision of *Porter v Magill*[43] how political corruption might take a variety of forms: **7–093**

> "Gerrymandering, the manipulation of constituency boundaries for party political advantage, is a clear form of political corruption. So, too would be any misuse of municipal powers, intended for use in the general public interest but used instead for party political advantage."

The case concerned allegations made by Mr Magill, the District Auditor for Westminster City Council, against three officers and three councillors, that through wilful misconduct they had jointly and severally lost £31 million to the Council. The Council operated a housing policy that was alleged to favour voters more likely to vote Conservative. Council-owned residential properties were being sold in such a way as to enhance the political chances of the Conservative party at election time. The House of Lords held that it was unlawful to dispose of property for the purpose of promoting the electoral advantage of any party represented on the Council.   **7–094**

Pressure Groups

Pressure groups are an important part of the political life of Britain. Broadly defined by Grant[44] as "groups that seek to influence public policy", this definition recognises such characteristics as a defined membership, with stated objectives in terms of public policy and paid staff. Pressure groups may create their own social movement, and self-interest in promoting their cause. The question is to what extent pressure groups contribute to democracy.   **7–095**

The first point to note is that pressure groups are not a modern phenomenon. Patricia Hollis has written that pressure groups in the nineteenth century came from two groupings, those that lobby for an interest and those that adopt a crusade for a cause. The lobby of a vested interest may be seen as "within" the establishment, the crusade for a cause may be perceived as coming from outside the establishment and thus distinct from vested interest.   **7–096**

---

[43] (1990) 49 L.G.R. 498, [2002] 2 W.L.R. 37 p.515, para.132. See Anti-Terrorism, Crime and Security Act 2001 containing tougher laws on corruption.
[44] Wyn Grant, *Pressure Groups, Politics and Democracy in Britain* (Philip Allan, 1989), p.3; C. Harlow and R. Rawlings, *Pressure Through Law* (London, 1992).

7–097   In the nineteenth century, after the 1832 Reform Act, Parliament became increasingly responsive to public opinion. Claiming to speak for public opinion gave pressure groups a legitimacy. Hollis concludes that pressure groups significantly contributed to the life of the nation.[45]

> "Nineteenth century pressure from without did have some effect on legislation; it had a marked effect on class harmony and social tranquillity; and both enlarged the realm of government and the breadth and base of government."

7–098   Hollis makes a number of further observations, namely that pressure groups depend on "a sense of political pluralism". Their purpose is to provide an alternative means to express political ideas. There is a belief that this alternative strengthens the existing political institutions and the political health of society. There is also a sense that pressure groups may exert greater flexibility into existing political institutions and therefore provide an important channel of action or alternative political strategy.

7–099   In modern times there are a number of distinctive pressure groups which are easily identifiable and have well-known campaigners prominent among their membership. Groups such as Greenpeace (an environmental group) and Campaign for Nuclear Disarmament (CND, a group campaigning for no nuclear weapons) fit into the category of protest groups and are good examples of their kind. Also important but not seen as protest groups, are the various bodies representing "sectional" interests such as the Law Society, Bar Council, British Medical Association and the like. Grant notes that business alone has over 1,800 associations representing their interests. Added to these are groups such as the Confederation of British Industry (CBI) and the various trade unions, which all contribute to the activities of persuasion and representation of their interests. Particularly useful by way of analysis are the various farmers' unions representing the agricultural sector. These have been successful in representing their interests in the government's attitude to the Common Agricultural Policy of the European Union.

7–100   In recent years various consumers' associations and "the consumer" have become a target for pressure group activation. The National Consumer Council set up in 1975 is partly funded by government but it carries out intensive lobbying activities.

7–101   The variety of pressure groups has grown in recent years and the more active and aggressive areas such as Animal Rights have warranted criticism against pressure group activity over allegations that some of their members take part in direct action. Wilson[46] believes that pressure groups contribute to democracy.

7–102   The argument in favour rests on a number of assumptions. First, there "is more to democracy than an occasional vote"; pressure groups engage in "participatory democracy". Secondly, pressure groups are specialised to the particular issues and therefore provide more effective opposition than the main opposition party. This permits minority parties or views to be better represented.

7–103   Criticism of pressure groups casts doubts on their effectiveness as agents of democracy. Brittan has argued that because of the entrenched nature of the various

---

[45] P. Hollis, *Pressure from Without* (1975), p.IX.
[46] See D. Wilson, *Pressure: The A to Z of Campaigning in Britain* (Heineman, 1984). Also see M. Olson, *The Logic of Collective Action* (Harvard, 1965); M. Olson, *The Rise and Decline of Nations* (Yale University Press, 1982).

"industrial, economic and political interest groups"[47] this will limit what may be achieved by any form of economic management, new or old, attempted by the government of the day.

Brittan's argument is that democracy should not be seen as[47a] "an unprincipled auction to satisfy rival organised groups who can never in the long run be appeased because their demands are mutually incompatible".   **7–104**

There is value in Brittan's observations, not least because of the unreliable nature of any accountability over the activities of pressure groups. Grant warns of the damages of allowing pressure groups too much influence. In the competition for public opinion, there is no guarantee that pressure groups will not eventually run into political issues and as a consequence either misunderstand or misrepresent the issues. This is often the point of criticism raised by government ministers or the main political parties. In that sense pressure groups may be held in check by political parties and their policies.   **7–105**

Grant concludes with a useful analysis of pressure group activities and results[48]:   **7–106**

"Pressure group power is limited: it is based on the ability to persuade and to influence, rather than to take decisions or, with certain exceptions, to veto them."

The contribution of pressure groups is an eclectic one. Through their activities the government of the day may be influenced and their contributions may improve the quality of policy-making and decision-taking. However there are dangers. Inside groups may achieve unwarranted influence and unduly tip the balance against a more open style of government. Within political parties, pressure groups may operate largely undetected and provide a counterbalance to the public debate outside.   **7–107**

In the final analysis pressure groups may be seen as an inevitable result of the close bargaining of party politics. Not everyone may join in and the temptation is to split off and join a group representing only one's interests. Taken to extreme levels, the damages of pressure group activity should be recognised; but pressure groups perform a valuable task of ensuring that the distance between government and the governed does not become too great.   **7–108**

ELECTORAL REFORM

The United Kingdom, until changes introduced in Italy in 1993, was unique among other Member States of the European Union in adopting for central and local government elections the "first past the post" (FPP) or "plurality" system. Northern Ireland has had its own separate electoral system with proportional representation on the single transferable vote system for local government elections since 1973, as well as for elections to the Northern Ireland assembly. Since the introduction of devolution the United Kingdom has the experience of a number of electoral systems. This is a remarkable change undertaken in a short period of time. Voting systems are complex and there is no single formula which translates votes into seats.   **7–109**

---

[47] S. Brittan, "The Economic Contradictions of Democracy", *British Journal of Political Science*, Vol.5, pp.129–159.
[47a] *ibid*.
[48] Grant, Pressure Groups, *Politics and Democracy in Britain* (Philip Allan, 1989), p.163.

First Past the Post

7–110   Characteristics:

- Used for Parliamentary and Local Government elections in England, Wales and Scotland.

- One constituency for each member to be elected and each elector has only one vote. The most votes wins. Losing votes are not counted in terms of seats.

7–111   Criticism of the United Kingdom's present electoral arrangement has come from the smaller parties, who point to the electoral results of past general elections to show that their share of the popular vote is not reflected in terms of the number of seats obtained in the House of Commons. The disproportion of votes to seats is also clear when it is recognised that rarely does the winning party which forms the government, with a majority of seats, win with more than 50 per cent of the total vote. Thus the Conservatives in 1983 with 42.4 per cent of the vote, in 1987 with 42.3 per cent of the vote, and in 1992 with 41.86 per cent had the majority of seats to form a government. Turpin draws attention to the "strikingly demonstrated disproportionality" which may result[49]:

> "In each of the two 1974 elections the Liberals with over 18 per cent of the total vote, won only 2 per cent of the seats, and it was observed that more than ten times as many votes were needed to elect a Liberal M.P., as to elect a Labour or Conservative M.P."

7–112   In 1983, election statistics show that the Liberal/SDP alliance received 25.4 per cent of the vote and only 23 seats, while Labour received 27.6 per cent of the vote but 209 seats. The pattern of disproportion has continued in the 1987, 1992, 1997 and 2001 elections.

7–113   From time to time a Speaker's Conference on electoral law may be convened to secure all-party support for any reform proposals. The conference is usually in private and proceedings are not usually published. Recommendations, if any, are not binding on the Government.

7–114   The conclusion drawn by many critics is that the "first past the post system" does discriminate unfairly against smaller parties. Conversely it favours the two major parties.

7–115   Proposals for reform have come from the Liberal Democrats, the Institute of Public Policy Research, and the Hansard Society Commission on electoral reform. Of the two major parties, the Labour Party is currently considering the question of an alternative system in the form of proportional representation, in a wide ranging-review of the electoral system.

The Aims and Objectives of the Electoral System

7–116   In considering the question of electoral reform it is important to identify the aims and objectives of any electoral system. A number of different expectations may be said to arise from the electoral system. These are: that the result produces a legislature

---

[49] C. Turpin, *British Government and the Constitution* (3rd ed. Butterworths, 1995) p.440.

reflecting the main trends and views of the electorate; that the government is able to act according to the wishes of the majority of the electorate; that government is strong and stable and; that the representatives chosen by the electorate are sufficiently competent to perform their task of governing and legislating.

Many of these expectations will not be met, or an electoral system cannot be agreed to that will deliver conflicting aims and objectives, in any single electoral system. Representativeness, good government and electoral choice may be claimed by a variety of different electoral systems. It is often difficult to anticipate in advance the effect of a particular system in terms of the electoral outcome. Thus competing demands are made, often partisan and inclined to favour one system as against another, without much evidence to judge or make conclusions as to the most suitable system.   **7–116a**

Bogdanor has argued that the United Kingdom's electoral system is no longer   **7–117** justifiable. This view points to the "adversarial" nature of British politics and the arrangement of a two-party system. The first past the post plurality system has favoured strong majority government. This means the electorate make a clear decisive choice and that the electoral system discourages coalition government or compromise politics. Bogdanor[50] points out that election results in Britain do not necessarily reflect the pressure of popular support for or against policies among the electorate. Distortions in the seats gained through the votes cast means that the electorate who do not vote for a winning candidate have little chance to have their votes counted and their opinion is not represented in the overall outcome of the election.

Bogdanor identifies particular groups such as women and minorities within the   **7–118** United Kingdom as being disadvantaged by the present arrangements. Co-operation between the political parties is handicapped, consensus is difficult to attain and compromise is shunned. However, it may be pointed out that for a lengthy period since the Second World War the electoral system has permitted strong and responsible government. Radical changes in policy, for example privatisation of the nationalised industries introduced since 1979, would have been more difficult to accommodate under any other electoral system. Thus change and continuity, the hallmark of the United Kingdom's unwritten Constitution, may be combined and strengthened under the present electoral arrangements. Nevertheless, criticism of the electoral system has been strengthened by the argument that since 1979, the Government has abandoned consensus policies in favour of strong non-consultative government. Critics of Mrs Thatcher attribute the cause of her "style and intent of government" to the electoral success of a large-seat majority.

The suggestion is made that some form of proportional representation is to be   **7–119** preferred. How far does present dissatisfaction go in terms of popular demand for reform? Stuart Weir[51] has completed empirical research into this question. He concludes that:

> "The survey showed that dissatisfaction with the governing system was at 63 per cent, as high in 1991, as in the crisis torn mid-1970s. Most voters agreed that government power is too centralised (60 per cent to 18 per cent) that rights are too easily changed (54 per cent to 22 per cent) and that Parliament does not have enough control over government (50 per cent to 23 per cent)."

[50] V. Bogdanor, *The People and the Party System* (1981), p.205.
[51] Stuart Weir, "Waiting for Change: Public Opinion and Electoral Reform" (June 1992) 63 *Political Quarterly* 197 at 216.

7–120   If these findings are borne out by subsequent research then they indicate that there is both popular and intellectual demand for reform of the United Kingdom's electoral system. However, if reform is required what reforms might be adopted?

7–121   There is a great lack of clarity, not only in the form of any new arrangements, but also in their expected results. This is hardly surprising given the complex task of divising a new electoral system.

Single Transferable Vote

7–122   Characteristics:

● In use in elections in Northern Ireland and the Republic of Ireland. In Northern Ireland it applies to the Northern Assembly, the European Parliament and local government.

● Voters are entitled to as many votes as candidates. Preferences are allowed and each voter may state their preference. Election is based on there being a quota and once a candidate reaches the quota they are elected. The candidate with the lowest number of first preferences drops out.The surplus votes are re-allocated to the second preference candidate until the seats allocated for the constituency are filled.

7–123   The single transferable vote (STV) system is currently in use in Northern Ireland and in the Republic of Ireland. This system is based on redrawing existing constituencies into larger multi-member constituencies. This would create five member constituencies based on the electoral quota of about 3 million voters. Voting on the ballot paper is undertaken by indicating an order of preference for each candidate. Winning an election according to this system requires setting an "electoral quota." Broadly this means setting a proportion of votes expressed as a percentage which must be achieved before a member is returned for that constituency. Depending on the number of seats for each constituency the successful candidate will require 16.6 per cent of the vote whereas in a two-member constituency 33.3 per cent of the vote is required. Once a candidate passes the electoral quota, the candidate wins. Passing the electoral quota is determined by the returning officer counting the number of first preference votes. It is possible that often a candidate will achieve a sufficient number of first preference votes. On this basis the number of seats will determine the number of winning candidates. Once a sufficient number of first preference votes are achieved, the returning officer counts all the second preferences recorded by the voters who gave first preference votes. In this way no votes are wasted. Once the second preference votes are counted, the returning officer transfers a proportion of the preferences given to each candidate. This may permit another candidate to achieve the electoral quota or better. The process is continued permitting all the candidates who reach the electoral quota to be elected.

7–124   In theory the advantage of such a system is to provide a coincidence between the distribution of votes among parties and the distribution of seats. Variables in such a system will depend on the size of constituencies determined by the number of voters and the number of seats in each constituency. It is assumed that the smaller the number of constituencies, the greater the degree of representativeness possible. If the entire country were treated as a single constituency this would amount to the minimum distortion. Only in Israel and the Netherlands does this arrangement operate.

Regional List System

Characteristics: 7–125

- In use in elections for the European Parliament;

- Electors vote for a party list of candidates; the emphasis is on the party rather than the candidate. Seats are allocated in the basis of a proportion of the vote won by the political party.

An alternative to STV is the list system, popular in Western Europe. Votes are cast for   7–126
parties, seats are distributed according to the parties' proportion of their share of the votes. Candidates are thus elected on the allocation of votes in the order of preference. Modification of these arrangements is usually introduced by a "cut-off point" being applied. If a party fails to reach this barrier it will not be qualified to receive any seats.

Additional Member System

Characteristics: 7–127

- In use for the Scottish Parliament, Welsh Assembly and Greater London Authority.

- Voters have two votes; one vote is used to elect a constituency member, the other vote is used to vote for the political party.

- Constituency votes are counted on the basis of first past the post.

- Party vote is counted on the basis of a fair share of seats based on a distribution of votes. The total number of seats won by the party is intended to reflect the votes cast for the party.

The first use of the additional member system was in the election of the Scottish   7–128
Parliament, Welsh Assembly and Greater London Authority.

Supplementary Vote

Characteristics: 7–129

- In use for the election of the London Mayor.

- Voters have a first and second preference, the aim being to achieve a vote that records for the winner more than 50 per cent of the votes cast. Failing this the candidate with the highest percentage of first votes goes through to a second round, the aim being that the winning candidate secures 50 per cent of the vote.

7–130   The first use of the supplementary vote system resulted in Ken Livingstone being elected London Mayor. The system is suitable for the election of an individual.

Alternative Vote

7–131   Characteristics:

• Proposed by the Jenkins Commission for Parliamentary elections to the House of Commons.

• Voters have two votes; one vote might be recorded using the alternative vote system for an MP for an individual constituency, the second vote might be used to vote for either a party or a candidate. The first vote would result in roughly 80 to 85 per cent of M.P.s elected. The second vote would fill the remaining seats.

• One person is elected on the basis of a majority. Voters have more than one preference. The winner is the candidate with the majority of first preferences. In the event that there is no outright winner, the candidate with the lowest number of first preferences drops out, second preference votes are then re-distributed.

7–132   The Jenkins Report made a number of recommendations for electoral reform. The key point is the adoption of a variant of the alternative vote system. Seyd explains[52]:

"The Jenkins Commission recommended a variant of AV—AV Top-Up—which combined the Alternative Vote in single member constituencies (80–85 per cent of the total) with small top up areas with members elected from lists (15–20 per cent of the total). The inclusion of top ups was intended to ensure that the system was more proportional than straight AV."

7–133   The complexity of different proportional voting systems is clear. One distinguishing feature is that voters are given a choice between political parties rather than for candidates.

7–134   Proportional representation has many advocates. Critics point to the fear that a government elected under such a system may not have a worthy overall majority. Weak government, proliferation of small parties and a constant need to go to the electorate are seen as characteristics of the proportional representation systems in countries such as Italy, Holland and Israel. Critics further argue that there is a high likelihood of a hung parliament. Coalition between the parties is inevitable and there is a greater likelihood for the need for coalition government.

7–135   Proportional representation does pose major questions in terms of many of the constitutional conventions, the role of political parties and ultimately how Parliament might function. This is not always appreciated. Membership of the Cabinet is currently *de facto*, restricted to the government of the day. Inclusion of opposition-nominated M.P.s and members of smaller parties might change the nature and role of the Cabinet. Cabinet secrecy and collective decisions might be more difficult to achieve.

---

[52] Ben Syed, "Electoral Systems and Party Funding" in *The Changing Constitution* (J. Jowell and D. Oliver ed., Oxford University Press, Oxford, 2000), p.318.

M.P.s would be freer from the importance of strict party discipline and the power of the whips which might change the relationship between M.P. and party.

Many of these changes might be seen as beneficial but undoubtedly they may flow **7–136** from proportional representation. David Butler concludes[53]:

"In these and many other matters the rules of the game of British politics would be transformed if appeals to the people no longer produced single party parliamentary majorities. A change in voting procedures would have fundamental consequences. Electoral systems are not matters of technical detail. They lie at the very heart of a nation's arrangements."

The future likelihood of electoral reform is difficult to assess for Parliamentary or local **7–137** government elections. The Government is not committed to the introduction of proportional representation in the foreseeable future and it is suspected that opposition parties are unsure of the exact effects of its introduction, although the Liberal Democrats are most enthusiastic about its introduction. The debate is likely to continue. The winning party under the first past the post system has a vested interest to perpetuate the existing FPP system.

REFERENDUMS

Referendums have an important role in any well functioning democracy. Dicey in the **7–138** late nineteenth century was an eventual convert to the value of a referendum.[54] His main ground for seeing the value of the referendum was that it avoided the "evils" of the party system and the conflict between political parties; Dicey regarded party political conflicts as an impediment to the consensus necessary for the effective working of the political system. In the aftermath of the Irish Home Rule debate in 1886 and in 1894 when a new Home Rule Bill was introduced for Ireland, Dicey supported a referendum as a device to avoid "extreme" legislation. At the time the influential National Review held a symposium on the merits of the referendum. Dicey believed its role on matters of fundamental constitutional importance was invaluable. There were few converts to this idea. On the whole, the value of a referendum was not seen in terms of a generally applicable principle, but it was conceded that on some matters of constitutional importance, a referendum might have a role. This view did not hold sway in the debates on the Parliament Act 1911. Then the opposition were unsuccessful in the demand for a referendum to affirm the changes in the role of the House of Lords.

In contemporary times in the Northern Ireland (Border Poll) Act 1972, referendum **7–139** was approved to allow the electors of Northern Ireland to vote on whether Northern Ireland should remain part of the United Kingdom or join with the Irish Republic. There was also express provision in the Northern Ireland Constitution Act 1973 for holding a referendum on the status of Northern Ireland. We have seen the use of referendum in the adoption of devolution.

[53] D. Butler, "Electoral Reform" in *The Changing Constitution* (J. Jowell and D. Oliver ed., Oxford University Press, Oxford, 1989), p.383.
[54] See Richard Cosgrove, *The Rule of Law Albert Venn Dicey, Victorian Jurist* (Macmillan, 1980), pp.105–110.

7–140   The decision to join the European Community in 1972 was taken without a referendum. However, the political controversy about joining has remained a sensitive issue in British politics. The Referendum Act 1975 was seen as an attempt to avoid internal party political disagreements and allowed the electorate to vote on June 5, 1975 on the question of whether the United Kingdom should stay in the European Community. The majority, 67.2 per cent, voted for staying in the Community out of an electoral turnout of 65 per cent. The referendum has not settled the question of membership of the European Community. The signing of the Maastricht Treaty was accompanied by demands for a referendum, although a Bill proposing this course of action failed in the House of Commons. The 1997 general election campaign saw the renewed efforts of the Referendum Party, formed in 1994, to have a referendum to consider membership of the Community. The Referendum Party failed to attract significant electoral support.

7–141   The use of referendums was at the centre of the debate on devolution in 1978. Both the Scotland Act 1978 and the Wales Act 1978 allowed for a referendum on the matter of devolution. The test of agreement was a threshold requirement of 40 per cent of the electorate. If this failed to be achieved, then both the 1978 Acts had to be repealed. While a majority of those that voted in Scotland favoured devolution, this amounted to only 32.9 per cent of the electorate. Devolution failed to be implemented in Scotland. In Wales only 20.2 per cent were in favour, representing only 11.9 per cent of the electorate. Devolution also failed to be implemented in Wales. The referendum may have tested the wishes of the electorate on the form of devolution on offer rather than on the principle of devolution *per se*. The limitations of the referendum are found in the way the question is posed and on the timing of the referendum. These matters may be influential with the electorate. Referendums are not necessarily a good barometer of public opinion; rather they may provide politicians with a way forward when party political loyalties are divided. In all the examples mentioned above the referendum has not proved conclusive.

7–142   However, having gained from the lessons of 1978, the government adopted a different and altogether more straightforward approach to devolution in 1997. In September 1997 referendums were held in Scotland and Wales. The result was that in Scotland 75 per cent of the voters were in favour, on a 60 per cent turnout. In Wales support for devolution was more marginal, and on a turnout of around 50 per cent the majority were in favour but by the narrowest of margins (0.6 per cent). The new Labour Government with a secure Parliamentary majority at Westminster could afford to be radical.

7–143   There are two matters that may fall to the referendum device over the next few years. First, the Government has promised to hold a referendum in the United Kingdom to consider the introduction of the Euro, the common currency for the European Union, as part of the development of the European Community. Secondly, if electoral reform to the Westminster system of parliamentary elections is proposed it may be achieved through the device of a referendum. The timing of the referendum is seen as critical in the government's future policy strategy. In both examples, the argument in favour of using the referendum device is that some matter of constitutional importance is involved. However, it is noteworthy that reform of the House of Lords does not appear to be a matter that may call for the use of a referendum. Determining what is or what is not of constitutional significance is unclear. For example, a proposal to introduce some form of proportional representation is likely to be accompanied by the requirement of a referendum.[55] There is some difficulty in knowing whether a referendum is suitable or appropriate for any particular issue. A referendum on the restoration of capital punishment may provide a clear outcome in favour, but leave politicians and the judiciary with uncompromising choices. When a referendum is used it is very often because political parties have to respond to internal disagreements. The referendum may not be wholly satisfactory, as party divisions may emerge later and all the referendum has done is provide a brief respite.

There are some limitations in the use of the referendum mechanism as seen with the **7–144** devolution issue in 1978; determining the ground rules for holding a referendum is itself controversial. The initiative lies with the government of the day and the outcome of the referendum may be unduly influenced by the way the question is drafted and the rules relating to how the electorate's choice may be counted. There is also a question of how fully informed the electorate may be in determining the choices represented in the referendum. The way information is presented may provide a biased account. The media and advertising may distort the values of the arguments presented by different groups.

In principle there is great merit in the use of the referendum. The idea behind the **7–145** referendum may appear to be an attractive one, namely that it appeals to the authority of the electorate rather than relying on political choices decided in Parliament. This may be misleading. The nature of the United Kingdom's current constitutional arrangements are that the referendum may disguise where real political power and authority actually reside.

SUMMARY AND CONCLUSIONS

It is remarkable that in the last decade, parliamentary power in the hands of **7–146** governments with large majorities has contributed to the substantial enlargement of the statute book. The scope and range of legislative intervention are substantial and appear to come from the British voters' confidence in either of the two main political parties. Although the dogma of the parties may sharply differ, there is striking similarity in the accretion of political power to the Prime Minister of the day under both Conservative and Labour administrations. It is equally clear that despite the long history of voting for either of the two major parties to form the government, voter apathy and dissatisfaction is today more apparent than ever. As Professor Anthony King shrewdly observes:

"... at all ten general elections—held between 1931 and 1970 the Conservative and Labour parties have always won more than 85% of the popular vote and frequently more than 90%. Nothing like that has happened since. At the seven general elections held between February 1974 and May 1997, the two main parties never won as much as 85% of the vote, and on five of the seven occasions their combined share of the vote fell to 75% or less."[56]

---

[55] R. Blackburn, *The Electoral System in Britain* (Macmillan, St Martin's Press, 1995) p.427.
[56] Anthony King, *Does the United Kingdom Still Have a Constitution?* (2001), p.61.

7–147   Voter apathy and political inertia are some of the major challenges facing political parties and the future of the electoral system. Some progress has been made in the modernisation of the British electoral system. The challenge remains as to how to reform the electoral system for Parliamentary and local elections. The question of voter apathy also needs to be fully addressed by the political parties.

FURTHER READING

R. Blackburn, *The Electoral System in Britain* (Macmillan, London, 1995).

R. Blackburn, "Electoral Law and Administration" in *Constitutional Reform: The Labour Government's Constitutional Reform Agenda* (R. Blackburn and R. Plant ed., 1999).

I. Budge, I. Crewe *et al.*, *The New British Politics* (2nd ed., Longman, London, 2001).

Ben Seyd, "Electoral Systems and Party Funding" in *The Changing Constitution* (J. Jowell and D. Oliver ed., Oxford University Press, Oxford, 2000), pp.292–315.

General Election Results 1945–2001

Year	Party	Votes%	Seats%
1945	Labour	47.7	61.4
	Conservative	39.7	32.8
	Liberal	9.0	1.9
	Others*	3.6	3.9
1950	Labour	46.1	50.4
	Conservative	43.4	47.4
	Liberal	9.1	1.4
	Others	1.3	0.5
1951	Labour	48.8	47.2
	Conservative	48.0	51.3
	Liberal	2.5	0.9
	Others	0.7	0.5
1955	Labour	46.4	44.0
	Conservative	49.7	54.8
	Liberal	2.7	0.9
	Others	1.2	0.3
1959	Labour	43.8	40.9
	Conservative	49.4	57.9
	Liberal	5.9	0.9
	Others	0.9	0.2

General Election Results 1945–2001—*continued*

Year	Party	Votes%	Seats%
1964	Labour	44.1	50.3
	Conservative	43.4	48.3
	Liberal	11.2	1.4
	Others	1.3	0.0
1966	Labour	48.0	57.8
	Conservative	41.9	40.1
	Liberal	8.5	1.9
	Others	1.5	0.1
1970	Labour	43.1	45.7
	Conservative	46.4	52.4
	Liberal	7.5	0.9
	Others	3.0	1.0
1974 (Feb)	Labour	37.2	47.4
	Conservative	37.9	46.8
	Liberal	19.3	2.2
	Others	5.6	3.6
1974 (Oct)	Labour	39.2	50.2
	Conservative	35.8	43.6
	Liberal	18.3	2.0
	Others	7.7	4.1
1979	Labour	36.9	42.4
	Conservative	43.9	53.4
	Liberal	13.8	1.7
	Others	5.4	2.5
1983	Labour	27.6	32.2
	Conservative	42.4	61.1
	Liberal/SDP	25.4	3.5
	Others	4.6	3.2
1987	Labour	30.8	35.2
	Conservative	42.3	57.8
	Liberal/SDP	22.6	3.4
	Others	4.3	3.6
1992	Labour	34.4	41.6
	Conservative	41.9	51.6
	Liberal Dem.	17.8	3.1
	Others	5.9	3.7

General Election Results 1945–2001—*continued*

Year	Party	Votes%	Seats%
1997	Labour	43.2	63.4
	Conservative	30.7	25.0
	Liberal Dems	16.8	7.0
	Others	9.3	4.6
2001	Labour	40.7	62.5
	Conservative	31.7	25.2
	Liberal Dems	18.3	7.9
	Others*	9.3	4.4

*others include Green Party, Plaid Cymru, SNP, N. Irish Parties, Independent Labour, Commonwealth, Independents, etc.

Number of Seats, Electorate Size, Percentage of Electorate Turnout

Year	Total Number of seats	Total electorate	Turnout %
1945	640	33,240,391	72.8
1950	625	34,412,255	83.9
1951	625	34,919,331	82.6
1955	630	34,852,179	76.8
1959	630	35,397,304	78.7
1964	630	35,894,054	77.1
1966	630	35,957,245	75.8
1970	630	39,342,013	72.0
1974 (Feb)	635	39,753,863	78.8
1974 (Oct)	635	40,072,970	72.8
1979	635	41,095,649	76.0
1983	650	42,192,99	72.7
1987	650	43,180,753	75.3
1992	651	43,249,721	77.7
1997	659	44,863,488	71.5
2001	659	44,403,238	59.4

Chapter 8

PUBLIC LAW AND LEGAL THOUGHT

INTRODUCTION

As Van Caenegem[1] reminds us: "the concept of public law is itself somewhat **8–001** problematic". He describes how continental jurisprudence developed a system of public law distinguished as a separate field of study from private law. In marked contrast, England, he observed, did not conform to such a separation or distinction[2]:

> "Until the nineteenth century, and even beyond, English doctrine proudly maintained that, unlike the continent, England knew no separate public law or public-law courts; the traditional common law assumed that the law was indivisible in the sense that the same body of rules applied to the government and its agents as well as to private citizens."

The absence of a separate public law jurisprudence in England did not inhibit the **8–002** growth of a common law inheritance, as outlined in the preceding chapters, through the contributions of various writers and their ideas, influential in the development of the United Kingdom's constitutional arrangements. Albert Venn Dicey (1835–1922) and his contemporaries are perhaps the most influential and their importance endures in understanding the present constitutional arrangements, if only to see how ideas have been changed or have moved on. This chapter is intended to examine the major, legal and philosophical thinking, influential in the development of public law.

Attention in the past has focused mainly on Dicey and his critics. Today there is a **8–003** vast literature on contemporary legal thought and its influence on public law, a reflection of a growing interest in thinking about public law. There are a number of reasons for public law becoming a major influence that extends to conceptions about law and the nature of the legal system. One perception is that public law may become dominant when thinking about legal principles particularly in the growth of a public law contract or in contractual relations in public administration.[3] There is a growth in public–private partnerships and the introduction of many commercial ideas into

---

[1] R.C. Van Caenegem, *An Historical Introduction to Western Constitutional Law* (Cambridge University Press, 1995), p.1.
[2] *ibid.*, p.3.
[3] See M. Freedland, "Government by Contract and Public Law" [1994] *Public Law* 86. See also T.R.S. Allan, "Pragmatism and Theory in Public Law" (1988) 104 *Law Quarterly Review* 422; Allan, "Constitutional Rights and Common Law" (1991) 11 *Oxford Journal of Legal Studies* 453; T.R.S. Allan, *Law, Liberty and Justice* (Oxford, 1993).

government, for example resource accounting and budgeting with its roots in company accounts and market valuation. Borrowing from the private sector and the creation of a purchaser–provider relationship provides the beginnings of a new legal framework in the public sector.[4] There is a view that a "public law of contract" is discernible from the analysis of legal principles that apply to government by contract.[5]

8–004   There is also a general interest in the theoretical underpinnings of public law. Craig[6] examines the theme of how constitutional and administrative law are inter-related. Craig also explains how the background of political theory assists in understanding both how society and law have developed, and how the contribution of different commentators on the United Kingdom's constitutional arrangements may be assessed. Loughlin[7] discusses the connection between public law and politics. He explores the development of ideas and influences in public law, specifically addressing an inquiry into the nature and distinctiveness of public law. In his later work, *Sword and Scales*[8] he locates changes in our perception about both law and politics and recognises the ascendancy of rights that permeate our understanding of relationships within society.

> "In modern times, however, politics has undergone a radical shift in perspective. Rather than being concerned with the rights of citizens and the duties of subjects, it is scarcely an exaggeration to suggest that modern politics is primarily concerned with the rights of citizens and the obligations of government. Alongside this shift in perspective, we also see a transformation in our understanding of law. Both the conceptions of law as a set of customary practices of governance and of law as the command of the sovereign are able to be accommodated within the traditional approach to politics. With the inversion of political perspective, however, we see a revolution in our understanding of law. Once treated as a code based on duties, law now presents itself as being founded on rights."

8–005   In addition, the Human Rights Act 1998 has generated an unprecedented literature on aspects of human rights and how this may impact on the law. The scope of human rights law is difficult to discern and the traditional boundaries between private and public law may not be helpful in attempting to understand the range and scope of rights and their impact on the citizen. Tort lawyers[9] familiar with the *Osman*[10] case are also aware that the European Convention on Human Rights has a significance in the development of tort law in England and a rights influence is likely to endure for some time to come. Public law has become an important forum to probe the boundaries between law, theory and politics.[11] The latter may underpin many of the moral considerations that underline public law principles.

8–006   This chapter is an attempt to outline some current discussion and debate about public law. Whether, as Loughlin believes, there is a crisis in "public law thought" may

[4] I. Harden, *The Contracting State* (Open University Press, Buckingham, 1992).
[5] A.C.L. Davies, *Accountability: A Public Law Analysis of Government by Contract* (Oxford University Press, Oxford, 2001).
[6] P. Craig, *Public Law and Democracy in the United Kingdom and the United States of America* (1990). Also see H. Arthurs, *Without the Law* (Toronto, 1985).
[7] M. Loughlin, *Public Law and Political Theory* (1992).
[8] M. Loughlin, *Sword and Scales* (Hart Publishing, Oxford, 2000). pp.232–234.
[9] Jane Wright, *Tort Law and Human Rights* (Hart Publishing, Oxford, 2001).
[10] *Osman v UK* (2000) 29 E.H.R.R. 245.
[11] John Griffith, "The Brave New World of Sir John Laws" (2000) 63 MLR 159.

be open to conjecture, but there is certainly a sustained and important debate concerning the nature of public law, the value of a theoretical approach to the subject and its future development. Or whether, as Allan has powerfully argued,[12] that the common law represents a superior form of constitutionalism, placing the rule of law at the apex of political power, and that the common law approach to public law may be compared to the view of public law from the civil law perspective. It is hoped that the brief introduction to legal thought in this chapter will facilitate the analysis and inquiry undertaken in the remainder of this textbook. What are the aims and objectives of public law? Is public law a distinctive subject? What are its boundaries? How do public lawyers differ in their approach to problems or disputes from private lawyers? Discussion of these questions is essential to understanding the value and nature of public law.

THE COMMON LAW TRADITION

Constitutional and administrative law evolved historically, mainly from tradition and the general development of the common law. The common law tradition is the subject of specialist works of legal history such as Milsom's *Historical Foundations of the English Common Law*.[13] Such accounts are instructive in the insights they provide on the role of lawyers in the development of the common law, particularly in terms of the adoption of legal techniques and methods of analysis. However, rarely are substantive issues of constitutional and administrative law made distinctive. Legal skills are explained and analysed but the emphasis in such works is on the development of the common law in terms of courts and procedures, property law, including both land law and equity, contract, and occasionally the criminal law. Legal methods and techniques developed in the area of property relations are relevant to understanding the traditions of the common law. As English law did not develop a separate jurisdiction over matters of constitutional and administrative law, however, the same common law techniques are helpful in understanding the role of the State and its relationship with the citizen.   **8–007**

General assumptions about the nature of law informed the mind of common lawyers. One such assumption was that law is perceived as having universal application. No special status is awarded to the State or to the Constitution and disputes between the citizen and the State are not seen as peculiar or different. Thus, English law failed to recognise any intrinsic differences between disputes arising out of the law of contract between two private citizens and contractual disputes where the contract is between the citizen and the State.   **8–008**

The fact that today courts make a distinction between public and private law has come about in the context where English law in the past failed to draw any such distinction. The absence of any special group of rules or analysis associated with public law in its early development creates difficulties in defining public law and delineating its boundaries with private law. The question of what is the distinctiveness of public law, assuming that it is possible to identify such, is not readily answered.   **8–009**

---

[12] T.R.S. Allan, *Constitutional Justice: A Liberal Theory of the Rule of Law* (Oxford University Press, Oxford, 2001).
[13] (2nd ed., Butterworths, London, 1980).

8–010   However, despite such difficulties it is possible to identify some of the characteristics found in the common law tradition which are important in understanding public law. Atiyah and Summers[14] identified formal reasoning and pragmatism as major influences in English law.

8–011   Formal reasoning contains a number of influences which relate to how law is perceived and developed. Interestingly, both contract and property law provide the most useful analysis and examples of formal reasoning. How might formal reasoning be explained? First, rules are recognised as legally authoritative, that is by their context or status, their validity is accepted. Formal reasoning may place emphasis on certain requirements such as a seal, or registration of title, a signature of a witness or the requirements of writing. Technical correctness is a hallmark of the precision associated with formality and the idea that problems may be reduced to a study of the rules alone.

8–012   Second, formal reasoning places weight on the value of coherence. That the law is a unified body of law lies at the heart of the judges relying on previous decisions and on the authority of the particular court. The creation of legal principles through points of law or legal doctrine further supports the view that law is internally coherent. The influence of *stare decisis* makes clear the distinction between judgments which are binding and those that are merely persuasive. As law reporting developed, the tradition of authoritative decision-making in the higher courts on points of legal technicalities influenced the lower courts in their decisions. Assumptions underlying this unified operation of law is that law provides protection to the individual and that reverence, universality and respect are provided by the legal process.

8–013   Pragmatism[15] is not inconsistent with formalism and when combined, seems influential in helping to develop legal principles. How formalism and pragmatism may be combined is illustrated in the example of administrative law. Writing in the second edition of his work on *Judicial Review of Administrative Action*, de Smith observed that as English law originally failed to admit the existence of administrative law, its existence today has been influenced by pragmatic development. His analysis is equally valid if applied to the whole enterprise of public law as he explained[16]:

> "... in place of integrated coherence we have an asymmetrical hotch potch, developed pragmatically by legislation and judicial decisions in particular contexts, blending fitfully with private law and magisterial law, alternately blurred and jagged in its outlines, still partly secreted in the interstices of medieval forms of action."

8–014   de Smith found that administrative law lacked clear principles and noted that the "dearth of coherent principles of administrative law" is an example of looking for

---

[14] Useful background reading may be found in M.A. Eisenberg, *The Nature of Common Law* (1988); Atiyah and Summers, *Form and Substance in Anglo–American Law* (Oxford, 1987); S.F.C. Milsom, "Reason in the Development of the Common Law" in *Studies in the History of the Common Law* (1989); D. Sugarman, "Legal Theory, the Common Law Mind and the Making of the Textbook Tradition" in *Legal Theory and Common Law* (W. Twining ed., Blackwell, 1986), pp.26–61. There is an excellent explanation of the role of the textbook in P. Birks, *Introduction to the Law of Restitution* (Oxford, 1992), pp.1–3.

[15] See Brian Simpson, "The Common Law and Legal Theory" in *Legal Theory and Common Law* (W. Twining ed., Blackwell, 1986), pp.8–25. *Stare decisis* in its modern meaning binds courts to agreed legal principles. In historical terms the common law tradition had developed based on customary rules rather than formal law.

[16] de Smith, *Judicial Review of Administrative Action* (2nd ed.), p.4.

formalism in the quest for certainty, clarity and reason through principle. de Smith's explanation that administrative courts were opposed to the traditions of the English common law in the seventeenth century, is compelling. Suspicion was commonly held that any encroachment by a specialised court in the sphere of public law might re-kindle the arbitrary powers of the discredited court of Star Chamber and the prerogative courts in medieval times.

The void left by no separate administrative law court was rapidly filled by ad hoc developments. The strongly held view was that the ordinary courts may control the Executive and its agents in much the same way as any other legal dispute might be resolved by the courts. **8–015**

Pragmatism and formalism encapsulate the essential qualities of the common law. How influential have such characteristics been in shaping public law? Some writers link the formalism, explained above, to "the common law frame of mind". This seeks "to dig deep" to find coherent and unified rules amid the irrational, the chaotic or the exceptional. Generalisations are drawn to create principles with the appearance of objectivity and coherence. Such techniques of analysis are familiar to lawyers and are applied to find great principles or define legal issues and are particularly suited to case law analysis. Lawyers make use of judicial decisions and seek to explain their relevance as a coherent set of rules available to be applied to a new set of problems or facts. The mastery of techniques of case law analysis depends, whenever relevant, on drawing distinctions, recognising exceptions and if necessary special circumstances in order to categorise and create a coherent set of legal rules. **8–016**

Like any model of analysis it may be readily adapted for different purposes. Applied to judicial decisions by lawyers it is also applied by academic lawyers in their textbooks. The influence of the "common law mind" is seen particularly in the development of legal education in the mid-nineteenth century. **8–017**

The law schools in the major universities became influential not only in the role they began to perform of educating lawyers, but also in the textbooks written by the leading academics of the period. An example of the role of the textbook in the study of public law is Dicey's *Introduction to the Law of the Constitution*. Dicey's lectures which formed the core of the book were constructed around the idea of analysing, defining, and creating a uniformity of legal rules based on coherent principles. Dicey's achievement, in both the clarity of his style and the presentation of principles in the form of a working constitutional code, all contributed to the influence of the textbook in the development of public law. Textbooks readily filled a gap in the uncodified system of English law. They appeared to bridge the gap between the needs of the practitioner in the courts who required a compendium of relevant cases and precedents, and the academic study of law which required a coherent synthesis of the law. The standing of academic lawyers remained low, and the precedent value of their opinions was not readily accepted before the courts. **8–018**

Aside from the influence of textbooks, other characteristics of the common law are striking when the common law tradition is compared to the civil law. English law in the public law area developed a system of remedies rather than rights. Remedies may be traced to the development of legal actions in the early history of the common law. The inheritance of the medieval Constitution focused on Parliament's powers and their development, to supersede the King's powers to make law and influence affairs of State through patronage. Once Parliament's authority was resolved the question of rights was regarded as a residual matter. **8–019**

8–020   The judges, responsive to the need to develop legal rules, attempted to interpret the needs and problems of society through flexible solutions applied in individual cases. Much of the development of English law depended on the ability of the law to grant a suitable remedy in an individual case. While remedies may have offered solutions to practical problems, often these were constructed in narrowly defined ways and limited by procedure and form. No codified set of statutes or codified doctrine existed.

8–021   The English common law was particularly influenced by the practitioner's concerns. This may explain how its survival and the haphazard nature of its development was achieved. The common law was remarkably anti-theoretical in its approach. Notions of policy, justice and legal doctrine found in the common law were determined by procedure and form rather than through reasoned or theoretical principles. From an impartial view the law had to find an appropriate remedy to solve the case.

8–022   Opposition to codification also marked out the English common law tradition as distinctive. This was particularly striking in the case of the criminal law in the nineteenth century. Bentham's *Principles of Penal Law* set out basic principles of law, both in theory and in substance, and contained a draft criminal code. Generally, codification was not proceeded with even after Brougham, as Lord Chancellor, appointed Criminal Law Commissioners to consider consolidation of existing common law principles and statutes into one coherent set of rules. Continental systems[17] of law more easily adopted codified systems of law influenced by the French *Code Napoleon* and the Roman law tradition found in the *Corpus Juris Civilis*. In part this may be a reflection of the differing political developments in England compared with European countries. But evaluation is difficult because the common law rarely articulated explanations of its own developments in contrast to scholars proposing and formulating codes.

8–023   Another distinctive feature of the common law tradition bearing on the development of public law is the development of statute law. Parliament's role as a regular source of legal change was bound up with the theory of the sovereignty of Parliament. The eighteenth-century Constitution emphasised a balance between the Executive and Parliament freely admitting that parliamentary power might become governmental power. The nineteenth-century Constitution with an extended franchise made Parliament a major source of law through legislation.

8–024   Statutory law was an important source of formal reasoning that maintained the sovereignty of Parliament. As Atiyah and Summers note[18]:

> "England has a long tradition of narrow, detailed drafting; the English draftsman has always (or at any rate for at least two centuries) tried to produce language which is capable of neutral, non-purposive interpretation. An English statute has traditionally been drafted in such detail that it can be said to be a catalogue of rules."

8–025   The strong orientation in favour of hard and fast rules contained in the mass of technical statutory law reflects the traditions of English government, based on a single

---

[17] In contrast in Germany, Anton Thibaut (1772–1840) a Law professor, Heidelberg, argued in his essay "On the Necessity for a General Civil Code for Germany". Reservations about the universal nature of such a code were made by Friedrich Carl Von Savigny (1779–1861). R.C. Van Caenegem, *Judges, Legislators and Professors: Chapters in European Legal History* (1987). I. Loveland, *Constitutional law* (2nd ed., Butterworths, 2001).

[18] Atiyah and Summers, *Form and Substance in Anglo–American Law* (1988), p.323.

winning party with strong political objectives presented in legislative form and passed by Parliament. There is an equally strong tradition of skilled parliamentary drafting carried out by professional lawyers, with skills developed through the experience of permanent officials over a period of time. Most of this expertise remains confined to the resources of government departments.

The traditions of parliamentary sovereignty are therefore reinforced by the absence **8–026** of any judicial power to review the legality of Acts of Parliament and until recently in the context of European Community law, this tradition remains strong. While public lawyers in the United Kingdom require the skills of reading cases and interpreting judicial decisions, equal and perhaps more important are the interpretative skills over complex, technical and precisely drafted statutes. Public law in the United Kingdom is to be found more in a statutory form than in the decisions of decided cases by judges.

Statutory developments have been so extensive that, it will be appreciated, this has **8–027** added to the diffuse nature of the subject. Specialisms developed in public law where statutory developments have been extensive include such subjects as local government, housing, planning law, immigration and the environment. The specialist nature of these subject areas make any generalisations of legal principle difficult. Moreover, any generalisations that attempt to explain the context where government activity takes place, such as housing, immigration or social security law, invariably become entangled in a mass of technical and complex rules that add further difficulty to understanding the nature of public law in the United Kingdom.

A similar problem arises in the examination of principles of judicial review. Judicial **8–028** review of administrative decisions lacks any detailed code of general principles. Any attempt to formulate such a code is frustrated by the pragmatic and often sporadic nature of judical review. Arguably, legal principles derived from a small number of legal cases are limited in their general application.

The eclectic and diffuse nature of public law, the absence of clearly defined **8–029** principles and the historical legacy of an unwritten constitution have affected the development of public law. Public lawyers engage in a certain amount of gap-filling. This means finding solutions from past experiences which do not always fit the challenges posed by new problems. Hence the attention given to conventions, understandings or practices which explain the working of the Constitution, but which may in reality be little more than the political habits of the government of the day. The attraction of accomplishing legal changes relatively easily within an unwritten constitution compared to a written constitution may be misleading. Equally important is the possibility at least that the flexibility of an unwritten constitution may be adapted to the needs of government anxious to extend public power potentially unlimited or uncontrolled by any constitutional brake or device.

The main characteristics of the United Kingdom's common law tradition may be **8–030** briefly summarised. The unitary and centralised nature of the State, the formality and pragmatism of English law, the continuity offered by an unwritten constitution have their origins in the historical influences of the past and notably in the last century. As McCrudden observed[19]:

[19] C. McCrudden, "Northern Ireland and the British Constitution" in *The Changing Constitution* (J. Jowell and D. Oliver ed., 2nd ed., 1989), p.298; (J. Jowell and D. Oliver ed., 3rd ed., 1994) pp.323–379.

"An important theme running through British thought concentrates on history and tradition when evaluating the processes by which political and legal decisions are made. Problems are solved, in this empiricist tradition, on the basis of experience. Solutions are what works and what lasts. Institutions should therefore operate flexibly, learn from the past and develop to suit the conditions of their time. This is the essence of the common law tradition."

The Historical Legacy

8–031   The question arises as to the influences public law has experienced throughout its development. Arguably, the content of public law which is found in statutes, common law principles, conventions, rules and institutions may only be understood in the broader context of the ideas and influences which a society experiences. Most contemporary legal writers would accept that it is impossible to understand administrative law as a distinct subject without recognising the close inter-relationship between the constitutional arrangements within which administrative law must operate.

8–032   There is no complete congruence between legal theory or the ideas of political scientists or philosophers and public law. Differing assumptions about the role of the State, the exercise of power and the role of law itself make any informed discussion of legal theory and public law difficult to achieve. A further *caveat* is that traditionally lawyers have reacted against broadening the nature of their inquiry beyond the confines of legally enforceable rights and the study of purely technical legal rules. This is a reflection of an approach confined to the study of court orientated rules. However, the nature of public law is such that many issues are not justiciable before the courts and depend not on legally enforceable rights, but on an understanding of the nature of law and political power under democratic and accountable government.

8–033   The task of assessing the influence of legal thinking on public law may be facilitated by the division of the discussion into two parts: first, consideration of the historical influences and second, an introduction to contemporary discourse on public law. It is not possible to account for the development of all political theory in the nineteenth century. A selection is necessary of the influences confined to explaining some of the main developments in public law.

8–034   The eighteenth-century enlightenment is a convenient starting point to begin to trace the influences of legal thinking, theory and philosophy on public law. The United Kingdom had established, without revolution, effective change by the end of the seventeenth century, contained in the Bill of Rights (1689), the Act of Settlement (1701) and the Act of Union (1707). Taken to be the framework of modern constitutional arrangements, the shape, function and operating practices of the Constitution remained to be defined and clarified.

8–035   Montesquieu's (1689–1755) influence was remarkable.[20] Influential in the idea that institutions of the State both political and legal might be criticised, he advanced the view that law was linked to the needs of society. His studies in England from 1729–31, and particularly the influence of the writings of John Locke (1632–1704) led him to

---

[20] Montesquieu, *L'Esprit des Lois* (1748); *Defense de l'Esprit des Lois* (1750).

believe that natural law rights determined through constitutional law, the liberty of the individual. Montesquieu found attractive the liberalism of the English Constitution and this promoted the value of the United Kingdom's constitutional arrangements in Europe.

Montesquieu's influence became known in terms of social contract theory which **8–036** linked the civil state, the laws and constitutions to the general state of society. Montesquieu helped promote belief in the doctrine of separation of powers setting out how government ought to carry out its legislative, executive and judicial functions, each working independently. Undoubtedly these ideas became influential as to how government was perceived to act within a framework contained in the eighteenth-century Constitution. Building on Locke's thesis of the sovereignty or supremacy of Parliament, Montesquieu identified the various functions of government such as the legislative, executive and judicial. Believing in "checks and balances" Montesquieu also identified the necessary balance between the different elements of government to achieve some degree of self-regulation.

Many of the assumptions underlying Montesquieu's analysis found recognition in the **8–037** works of later writers.[21] Recent contemporary writers such as Robson adopt Montesquieu's analysis when describing the working of the modern Constitution.

The quest for order in society[22] is a familiar theme among constitutional writing in **8–038** the eighteenth century. This theme was developed in the writings of William Blackstone (1723–80) in his *Commentaries on the Laws of England*. Blackstone asserted the sovereignty of Parliament but this did not prevent him from accepting some natural law ideas as a means of achieving enforcement. Natural law concepts formed part of various social contract theories in an attempt to reconcile Parliament's legislative supremacy and individual justice. At times, there emerges in Blackstone's writing an explanation of constitutional "rights". These are asserted as part of the general protection afforded to the citizen under the law. Arguably such statements appear idealistic rather than practical and there is no acknowledgement of the difficulty of attempting to put their meaning into practice. We shall see below the importance of Blackstone in the development of the science of law.

Nevertheless, natural law concepts were significant for many eighteenth-century **8–039** legal writers because a law of nature conveniently fitted the natural reasoning of the period. Certainly in European legal philosophy, natural law concepts helped form international law, and provide a strong tradition for a debate over the role of law in society. Both Montesquieu and Blackstone contributed to the discussion of natural law concepts in England. Blackstone's formal presentation of the law and formidable understanding of legal principles helped make the influence of his Commentaries extend beyond a small legal audience, to become part of "the literature of England". In the English courts, during the period when codification took root in Germany and France, principles of English law became solidified. The question arises as to what were the influences at work in the decisions of the courts during the seventeenth and eighteenth centuries?

Developments in public law included some early seventeenth-century cases that laid **8–040** the foundations of natural justice and standards of reasonableness as principles of the

---

[21] A discussion of such influences may be found in Kelly, *A Short History of Western Legal Theory* (Oxford, 1992). Also see M.J. Horwitz, *The Transformation of American Law 1870–1960 (Oxford, 1992).*
[22] See the letter from Dicey to Leo Maxse, September 25, 1909. Quoted in Richard Cosgrove, *The Rule of Law: Albert Venn Dicey, Victorian Jurist* (Macmillan, 1980), p.62.

common law. The explanation for such judicial creativity came from the separate development of "natural rights" from natural law. Political writers in the eighteenth century influenced by Locke's explanation of and justification for the English revolution, developed more sophisticated understandings of rights being created through legal rules. Legal writers such as Coke (1552–1634) had linked property to rights and both Locke and Coke contributed to the views on the rule of law and natural rights which were later influential among French writers prior to the French Revolution. Locke's thinking on the rule of law had an important influence on Blackstone, whose analysis of the royal prerogative included the view that the Crown should not enjoy any immunity from civil liability by virtue of the nature of the prerogative.

8–041   Judicial developments in the eighteenth century were about the relationship between law, the State and moral authority. One of the leading eighteenth-century cases of *Entick v Carrington* (1765)[23] applied, in a practical way, the principle of individual rights as a protection against the implementation of a general warrant of arrest against John Wilkes which the courts declared illegal.

8–042   It will be apparent that a number of themes, recognisable from the discussion in Pt I of the textbook, emerge from the eighteenth-century writings on legal theory and political thought. These include the doctrine of the separation of powers, the rule of law and natural rights. Such constitutional principles become relevant in understanding the English Constitution. Particularly important was the influence of the doctrine of separation of powers as a protection against abuse and tyranny. By the end of the eighteenth century the role of the courts in developing common law principles had become articulated in disputes between the King and the judges over taxation and in the legality of arrest, search and seizure. The focus on principles of the common good were identified as an objective of law and good government. These principles became more fully developed at the beginning of the nineteenth century as pertinent to the questions raised about the increasing use of legislation.

The Science of Law

8–043   Attempts to systemise English law came from two directions. One approach, influenced by Blackstone, attempted to add continental ideas about rights to the reasoning implied in the common law. The other approach dominated by Jeremy Bentham (1748–1832) aimed to provide a codification of principles. While different directions may be detected in both approaches, there was common ground. The methodology of science and the reasoning of statistical study were influential in the writings of both Blackstone and Bentham. This ensured that scientific methodology was integral to the analytical methodology and the legal reasoning employed in the development of the common law.

8–044   Blackstone encouraged the idea that English law was "a science which distinguished the criterion of right and wrong".[24] His attempts to reconcile the historical develop-

---

[23] *Entick v Carrington* (1765) 19 St. Tr. 1030.
[24] See Griffiths, "The Political Constitution" (1979) 42 *Modern Law Review* 1; and *The Politics of the Judiciary* (London, 1991). Echoes of Jennings' view are apparent in Loughlin's thesis: see Jennings, *The Law and the Constitution* (1942), p.300: "The process of explanation is the function of constitutional law (or jurisprudence) or of that part of political science which is concerned with the actual workings of institutes; the process of justification belongs to political theory (or the philosophy of law) or to that part of political science which relates to the theory of institutes."

ment of the common law with a flexible and rule-bound system gave rise to an analytical method. This proved to be very influential especially when later adopted by Dicey in his analysis of the English Constitution. The essential of Blackstone's legacy found that English law could be understood from a deductive system of reasoning incorporating natural law principles. This required a mathematical approach to law through a deductive method of analysis. It favoured the formality of legal rules and the formal reduction to specific points of the resolution of any dispute.

It is not surprising to find that at the end of the eighteenth century many lawyers had become empiricists at a time when scientific discovery and science attracted the attention of the age. Whether this was coincidence or not is difficult to determine. What was remarkable was that lawyers found that through detailed empirical investigation, law was treated as practical and relevant rather than theoretical and abstract. The law on pleading was a clear example of the view that the legal system was a functioning set of rules that provided the tools for the practitioner to fashion remedies for the client. Writers considered "the science of pleading" rooted in the belief that the precision of rules would give rise to the revelation of truth. The system of writs accentuated the idea that correct procedure gave rise to an accurate record and this laid the foundations of law.

8–045

On a broader analysis empirical methodgy lay at the root of deciding cases. The development of case law followed from the efforts to systematise. The idea that English law could be found in decided cases rested on the development of a reliable and comprehensive system of law reports. The system of *stare decisis* and the doctrine of precedent rested on judicial reasoning being applied by analogy to cases with similar facts. Technical and formal rules applied in an analytical and scientific way rooted the common law to the empiricist tradition and the logic of the judges.

8–046

Within this tradition lay considerable self-doubt and disenchantment. The desire for a clearly defined set of rules for judges to apply prompted many English lawyers to examine the value of the civil law as a source of principles and jurisprudence. Generally there was considerable reluctance to reconcile the common law with the civil law system in all its forms.

8–047

Bentham's disillusionment with the common law identified in his later writings came from the inadequacy of the procedural rules, the absence of clear principles and the lack of comprehensiveness. His pursuit of universal codification of English law proved a life-time work which ultimately ended in frustration. There is evidence to show that in determing the contents of codes and their application, Bentham shared the techniques implied in the scientific method as a means to determine concepts and ideas. Lobban explains[25]:

8–048

> "An Introduction [to the Principles of Morals and legislation] was perceived by Bentham to be a 'metaphysical' work, standing in relation to the substantive law as a treatise of pure mathematics stood to natural philosophy."

Bentham's codification project was ultimately rejected despite many attempts through numerous Royal Commissions and law reform initiatives. Bentham had sought to

8–049

---

[25] M. Lobban, *The Common Law and English Jurisprudence 1760–1850* (Clarendon Press, Oxford, 1991) p.155.

devise a science of principles derived from the immutable laws of human nature. In his principles of utility may be found the science of law reform. Diagnosing a wide range of social reforms from prisons to the workhouse, from education to the courts and from the substantive criminal law to a codified constitution, Bentham's ambitious aim was that through codification a legislative solution to the problems of society may be found.

8–050   The measurement of law against some standard or criterion was the dominant theme in Bentham's pioneering work, *A Fragment of Government*, (1776) followed by his *Introduction to the Principles of Morals and Legislation* (1789). Bentham's[26] task, to develop a science of human action, began with a search for fundamental meaning in defining legal terms. His initial inquiry disputed the basic assumptions underlying Blackstone's *Commentaries* that all law was to be accepted without questioning its utility. Bentham questioned not only how law might be defined but what law should be. Bentham divided law into two categories: the first, that of the legislator, he described as "authoritative law"; and the second, law that was unauthoritative. By this means he questioned the quality of law according to his theory of utility, namely the greatest happiness principle. This became an important theme developed at great length in his book *A Fragment of Government*. Bentham's influence became apparent in the impact of his ideas on how legislation was to be appraised by lawyers in the nineteenth century. Bentham insisted that legislation should encourage the general good and to that end linguistic analysis might be called in aid of statutory interpretation. Weak laws might be avoided by an accurate analysis of legal terminology and an understanding "of the art of legislation."

8–051   Bentham's influence was wide-ranging. His philosophy was read by a wide range of interested disciplines beyond law. In particular he was influential in fostering the idea that law might create improvements if subjected to an analytical approach and careful appraisal. The full importance of Bentham's work became clear in the nineteenth century as Bentham's legislative principles became influential. One explanation of Bentham's influence was the interpretation given to Bentham's writing by John Austin (1790–1859). Austin's lectures on jurisprudence were first published in *The Province of Jurisprudence Determined* (1832) which were later amended and expanded by a number of editors after his death. In terms of thinking about issues of public law, Austin's influence was probably the most significant in the nineteenth century, partly because his lectures appeared in the style of a textbook and in the absence of a major rival, Austin's views dominated jurisprudence.

8–052   Comparing Austin to Bentham is difficult, but it is generally accepted that Austin's view of law was narrower than Bentham's. It is also suggested that had Bentham published in his lifetime his work *Of Laws in General*, this might have established Bentham's pre-eminence over Austin. The narrowness of Austin's analysis is due to the distinction he drew between the analysis of legal terms and reform of the law. Bentham conveniently drew both together, while Austin's desire to strictly interpret the law came from his definition of law to be "a command supported with a sanction".

[26] P. Schofield, "Jeremy Bentham and Nineteenth Century English Jurisprudence" (May 1991) 12, *Journal of Legal History* No.1, 58–88. Also see S. Collini, D. Winch, J. Burrow, *That Noble Science of Politics: A Study in Nineteenth Century Intellectual History* (Cambridge, 1983); *A Comment on the Commentaries and A Fragment on Government* (J.M. Burns and H.L.A. Hart ed., London, 1977); J. Dinwiddy, "Early Nineteenth Century Reactions to Benthamism", Transactions of the Royal Historical Society XXXIV (1984), pp.47–69; *The Works of Jeremy Bentham* (J. Bowring ed., 11 vols). See *The Limits of Jurisprudence Defined* (1945).

The essential clarity of the conception of law helped later writers, such as Dicey, to **8–053** distinguish laws from conventions. Austin, along with Bentham, promised an analytical form of jurisprudence. Laws could be considered by jurists through defining their meaning and explaining their terms. Austin was less concerned than Bentham with considering what laws ought to consist of. Nonetheless both were influential in the development of public law in the nineteenth century.

Both Austin and Bentham belonged to the analytical school of jurisprudence. The **8–054** analytical jurists classified, defined and expressed laws freed from any normative analysis. An equally significant influence in nineteenth-century jurisprudence came from the historical school of jurisprudence. The historical school disputed that all law might be resolved as a command of a sovereign and insisted that custom, history, and opinion might be important sources of law. In contrast to the analytical school, the historical school, founded by Savigny (1779–1861) and influenced by Maine's (1822–88) *Ancient Law* (1861) and *Early Law and Custom* (1883), examined the relationship between law and morality. This inquiry questioned how existing practices and institutions reflected moral ideas and influences.

Both analytical and historical[27] schools came under various attempts to combine the **8–055** strengths of each at different times throughout the nineteenth century but with limited success. Taken generally there emerged a "science of jurisprudence", as an attempt to combine the virtues of both analytical and historical schools. Methodology became an important means to bridge the differences between each of the philosophical schools of thought.

The science of law united both analytical and historical schools in the study of **8–056** legislation. Denis Caulfield Heron (1825–1881) in his work, *An Introduction to the History of Jurisprudence*[28] wrote how legislation was a "compromise between history and philosophy". The influence of codification in Europe encouraged consideration of law as a means of setting standards. While codification itself was rejected in England, the search for some reasonable standard to judge law united the historical method of the historical school with the analytical style and method of the analytical school.

In the nineteenth century the development of public law came under similar **8–057** influences as other areas of knowledge. Generally, it was commonly assumed that law could be regarded in the same way as other disciplines. In particular the science of law influenced how writers such as Dicey came to consider Parliament's role in developing legislation. Public law was influenced by the popularity of law reform. Law reform became a major catalyst for change and in the late nineteenth-century became the forum for debate as to precisely the extent of Parliament's role.[29] The Reform Acts of 1832 and 1867 by extending the franchise, considerably broadened the franchise and the scope for change through an extended scope for Parliament's legislative authority.

As a result, English law resisted the attempt to provide a single jurisprudence of **8–058** rights and remedies. The jurisprudence of Blackstone, Bentham, Austin and Dicey

---

[27] J.M. Kelly, *A Short History of Western Legal Theory* (Oxford, 1992), pp.312–325.
[28] D.C. Heron, *An Introduction to the History of Jurisprudence* London, 1860.
[29] Denis Caulfield Heron (1825–1881), Professor of Jurisprudence and Political Economy, Queen's College, Galway, 1849–1859, Q.C. 1860, MP for Tipperary 1868–74, Third Sergeant-at-Law 1880, Vice-President, Social Inquiry and Statistical Society of Ireland (1871–81). T. Porter, *The Rise of Statistical Thinking 1820–1900* (Princeton, 1986); John A. Hannigan, *Environmental Sociology* (Routledge, 1995). See Martin Loughlin, "The Pathways of Public Law Scholarship" in *Frontiers of Legal Scholarship* (G.P. Wilson, John Wiley, 1996), pp.163–188.

allowed lawyers to conceive law through an analytical jurisprudence rooted in an empirical tradition bearing many characteristics of scientific proof. Strict procedural rules determined the precise point of dispute for deliberation by the court. Judges attempted to discover through deductive reasoning the resolution of the dispute from the material facts presented by the litigants in each case. So much lay outside the control of any single system of rule. The litigant determined the cases that came to court and the facts each case presented. The judges responded to the challenge in a haphazard way drawing on a wide range of sources and ideas to find solutions. The jury added to the lack of predictability of outcome. The common law built on the reasoning common to "ordinary men" and the rules of procedure that guided the discourse set the agenda for judges. The absence of a systemised English law and a coherent theoretical underpinning of the principles of law underlines the importance of the analytical method used in the common law.

The Statistical Movement

8–058a   Schofield noted[30] that the science of law had two parts:

> "the first an analysis and a classification of the general principles which are to be found in advanced systems of law, and the second the discovery of the origin and growth of legal notions."

8–059   Public law was greatly influenced by both the methods of analysis and the search for principles in the growth and development of the common law tradition. Equating law and its study with other disciplines was encouraged by the development of the statistical movement in Britain.

8–060   Statistical study had its origins in the seventeenth century in the development of a scientific approach in the work of William Petty (1623–87). Petty applied "political arithmetic" to the study of social problems. Collective phenomena could be investigated on the basis of a statistical method which permitted reasoning through the use of numbers. Statistical information could be collected and in 1835, Quételet[31] identified the "average man" in his essay *Sur l'Homme* which related a number of examples to an assessment of what was average.

8–061   This combination of ascertaining "facts" through statistics and quantifying the "average" had wide application. The study of statistical phenomena attracted the formation of various statistical societies. One of the first such associations was the study of statistics undertaken by the British Association for the Advancement of Science in Cambridge in 1833. The Manchester Statistical Society first met in September 1833 and soon after, in the 1840s, statistical societies appeared in Bristol, Ulster and in other parts of the United Kingdom.

8–062   An important source of statistical study came from official statistics prepared by government departments. The General Register Office and the Board of Trade became a major centre for statistical study in Britain. Parliamentary Committees of

---

[30] Philip Schofield, "Jeremy Bentham and Nineteenth Century English Jurisprudence" (May 1991) 12 *Journal of Legal History* No.1 at 58–88.
[31] L. Quételet (1796–1874), L'Anthropométrie (1871).

Inquiry sat during the nineteenth century, received evidence and collected statistical data.

The attractions of statistical study and its affect on public law require explanation. A **8–063** number of factors are evident from the influence of statistical study. The first is that "statistical facts" offered not only curiosity to the uninformed, but also the basis of knowledge and ultimately power to those with influence. Secondly, official support for statistical study through various official departmental studies created an important database for government to make projections as to the future. Statistics contributed to an estimation of the problems confronting society such as crime, public health, education, literacy and housing. Thirdly, statistical study provided "an era of enthusiasm". A new sense of optimism or enthusiasm for law reform in the hope for future improvement combined with statistical study. Industrial progress could be vindicated by laying the blame for many social problems on other causes such as alcohol abuse, moral degeneration or urban life, linked to crime and destitution.

A recurrent theme of statistical study was the use of "objective facts" to provide **8–064** persuasive evidence to encourage legislative reform. This added to the persuasive authority of Brougham (1778–1868) who founded the Social Science Association in 1857 and favoured law reforms on a large scale. A speech to Parliament in 1828 on law reform led to the investigation of law reform by the Common Law Commissioners. In 1864 this led to the setting-up of a Law Amendment Society. Thirty years later new Civil Judicial Statistics were published, the inspiration of that Society and Brougham's influence.

The statistical movement attracted an eclectic group of followers: intellectuals, **8–065** largely middle class but inter-disciplinary, combining the study of mathematics, the natural sciences, economics, law, philosophy and jurisprudence. The prominent role of the Social Science Association in promoting law reform on a wide variety of issues from education, public health, criminal and penal reform to the poor law, led it to be described as an "outdoor parliament" or "unofficial parliament". Such "volunteer legislators" were influenced by Bentham's principle that social, economic and political problems might be solved through legislation.[32]

Statistical study greatly contributed to the general development of political thought **8–066** in mid-Victorian Britain. As a period of liberal influence, a growing professionalism in techniques of analysis and expertise was evident in the use of scientific analysis when applied to social problems.

Victorian idealism often lacked coherence. The dogma of benevolence and good **8–067** works was unsystematic and could easily be counterproductive. Philosophical ideas required a practical output and scientific method appealed to a wide cross section of the main disciplines of the period. Law received an enhanced reputation when worked up into a practical science. Especially so when the economic laws of production and wealth and the main theories of political economists appeared too abstract to be relevant.[33] Social science, through statistical study, appeared to offer a way forward in

[32] Also see P.G. Stein, *Legal Evolution: the Story of an Idea* (Cambridge, 1980); Alexander Henry, *Jurisprudence: or, The Science of Law, Its Objects and Methods. An Introductory Lecture delivered at University College, London (November 2, 1883)*, (London, 1884); R. Smith, The *Fontana History of the Human Science* (1997).
[33] J. Harris, "Political Thought and the Welfare State 1870–1940: An Intellectual Framework for British Social Policy" (May 1992) 135 *Past and Present* 116–141.

diagnosing both the cause of social problems as well as solutions through legislation. Statistical study provided lawyers with a new role for Parliament and therefore public law. A vast variety of welfare legislation from the 1870s to the 1940s came under the influence of the statistical movement. The Statistical movement was aimed at first establishing an empirical basis for reform; such reforms were intended to ameliorate social distress. Such changes were gradual and found favour within government departments and through the influences of law teachers in universities.

Dicey and his Contemporaries

8–068   The emergence of an influential group of academic lawyers in the late nineteenth-century must be set against a background of neglect in legal education. The 1846 Select Committee on legal education described[34] "the lamentable state of legal education" and criticised the teaching of law in the universities of Oxford and Cambridge. Practical training in articles or pupillage was not well regulated or examined. Only gradually did change occur, first in 1852, with the establishment of the Council of Legal Education to regulate education of Bar students. Then in 1877, the Law Society succeeded in establishing solicitors' qualifying examinations and eventually in 1903, a School of Law in London.

8–069   The Royal Commission Report, in 1856, continued demands for reform and the preference that universities should concentrate on the theoretical and philosophical study of law, leaving the teaching of practical law to the profession.[35]

8–070   The creation of new courses and posts in Oxford and Cambridge in the latter half of the nineteenth century brought a new intellectual influence. The question was how to establish a role for academic lawyers which numbered Maine (1822–88); Whewell, Professor of International Law in Cambridge, 1887; Bryce (1838–1922), Regius Professor of Civil Law at Oxford 1870–93; Anson (1843–1914), Warden of All Souls, Oxford 1899–1914; Holland (1835–1926), Chichele Professor of International Law and Diplomacy, Oxford 1874–1910; and Dicey (1835–1922), Vinerian Professor of Law, Oxford 1882–1909.

8–071   The answer came from analytical jurisprudence; so influential in shaping legislation, it also influenced academic law.[36] Academic lawyers faced two pressures: one from within university education where academic respectability required a body of expertise and coherence; the other came from the legal profession which required understanding of legal principle, and practical explanation. As already mentioned above, academic lawyers found that legal textbooks offered a suitable solution. This permitted an exposition of the law as a coherent whole, together with an analysis of legal doctrine consistent with the tasks of legal education and scholarship. In the field of public law, Dicey's writings came to dominate.

8–072   It has already been noted that Dicey's lectures at Oxford came to be published in 1885 in his *Introduction to the Law of the Constitution*. Influenced by the analytical

[34] J.H. Baker, "University College and Legal Education 1826–1976" (1977) 30 *Current Legal Problems*, pp.1–13. See D. Sugarman in *Legal Theory and the Common Law* (W.L. Twining ed., 1986), Chap.3.
[35] Philip Schofield, "Jeremy Bentham and Nineteenth Century English Jurisprudence" (May 1991) 12 *Journal of Legal History* No.1 at 58–88.
[36] Henry Maine, *Ancient Law: its Connection with the Early History of Society and its Relation to Modern Ideas* (London, 1861).

school of thought, Dicey carefully set out the legal principles which guided the student of the Constitution. Originality of thought was not claimed, but by identifying the guiding principles which underpinned the unwritten constitution he created a legal textbook for lawyers devoid of much historical explanation.

Dicey's contribution to public law and his enduring influence may be examined in two respects. First, Dicey's method of analysis and its significance when interpreting the law of the Constitution. Secondly, Dicey's explanation of the Constitution, especially his description of the legislative sovereignty of Parliament, the rule of law and the role of constitutional conventions, may be noted as to its significance for the study of public law. Throughout this textbook various references may be found to the explanation of basic principles provided by Dicey. Even though his ideas remain controversial, they are nevertheless influential. **8–073**

Dicey's analytical method was based on Austin's analytical approach to legal thinking. The analytical method of inquiry favoured abstracting basic principles from legal material and subjecting constitutional law to scientific study. Dicey presented a vision of constitutional law corresponding to the earlier influences of Blackstone, Bagehot and Montesquieu. The English Constitution when subjected to Dicey's analysis appears as a triumph of achievement. Dicey's formulation of principles have the hallmark of a codified constitution providing uniformity, and formality through the application of Dicey's analytical method. Dicey's achievement was to provide the required exposition, conceptualisation and systematisation of constitutional law in the United Kingdom. In short, Dicey's *Law of the Constitution* filled a gap without encroaching upon law reform or the codification movement. **8–074**

The enduring qualities of Dicey's analysis are reflected in his formulation of constitutional principles. It is useful to draw together the main elements in Dicey's thinking which remain influential today. It is readily apparent that Dicey borrowed many of his ideas from the various schools of jurisprudence mentioned above. Here we are concerned with general principles only; the details of many of these principles are discussed in the appropriate part of the textbook. **8–075**

Dicey's vision of constitutional and administrative law begins with his analysis of sovereignty, both political and legal. Dicey acknowledged that Parliament could "make or unmake any law" but accepted that political and legal sovereignty could be distinguished. Political sovereignty placed certain influence with the majority of the electorate but this was to be entirely self-adjusting. Craig noted[37]: **8–076**

"The absence of constitutional review and the Diceyan conception of sovereignty are therefore firmly embedded within a conception of self-correcting majoritarian democracy."

Dicey's idealism led him to believe that a unitary state embodying elected government might reinforce the rule of law. Paradoxically, the rule of law which later commentators considered the weak element in Dicey's analysis, came to reinforce sovereignty. The assumption is that the Commons might control the government. Dicey's style of analysis at first appears descriptive. His focus on principles and analytical style appears **8–077**

[37] P.P.Craig, *Public Law and Democracy in the United Kingdom and the United States of America* (1990) pp.15–16. Also see D. Sugarman, "The Legal Boundaries of Liberty: Dicey, Liberalism and Legal Science" (1983) 46 *Modern Law Review* 102–111.

to offer a neutral perspective of the Constitution. Beneath the level of general description there are strong elements of value judgement. Dicey assumed that the English model of the Constitution was a better model than France or Germany or Switzerland, whose Constitutions Dicey had studied in great detail.

8–078   Dicey's rule of law adopted ideas from William Hearn (1826–1888) in his work *The Government of England, its Structure and its Development* (London, 1867); and his understanding of conventions came from Edward Freeman (1823–1892) in his work *Growth of the English Constitution* (London, 1877). The essentials of Dicey's analysis are as follows: the rule of law depended on the absence of broad discretionary power and that all public power resided with Parliament. The courts' power to review legislation was inappropriate when Parliament's role was to keep government under scrutiny. Judicial review did not require a separate or distinct system of courts when the Commons might control the Executive and the direction of all governmental power was through Parliament.

8–079   Such assumptions lie behind Dicey's vision of judicial intervention being limited only to legislative intention. Even when the development of judicial scrutiny began in areas where the legislature had jurisdiction, Dicey was reluctant to envisage the courts developing beyond a narrow and defined remit, namely to ensure that the authority or power was exercised within its jurisdiction.

8–080   Conventions come under the same tension as the rule of law when threatened by the sovereignty of Parliament. Dicey's reconciliation of conventions to a "modern code of constitutional morality" and thereby representative democracy, linked the power of Parliament to that of democracy. Government was believed to be representative.

8–081   However, democracy was narrowly defined as confined to male citizens. The dangers of popular opinion when it called for trade union reform, Home Rule for Ireland or votes for women were seen as threats to the single unitary model of the Constitution. Dicey's later writing reflected his concerns about the break-up of the constituent parts of the United Kingdom through any federal constitutional arrangement.

8–082   To summarise, Dicey's skill at linking the historical roots of the common law tradition to constitutional change in the nineteenth century gave coherence to his vision of constitutional law. Adept at combining the influences of both the analytical and historical schools of jurisprudence, Dicey's work on the Constitution became influential. This was due to the combination of Dicey's analytical and expository style and the effect of providing in a codified form, a set of principles to guide discussion of constitutional law. Dicey had recognised a gap in textbook writing in constitutional law and by skilful analysis he provided a legacy for future generations of lawyers. Eight editions of the work were published during Dicey's lifetime. None were given substantial revision, though his last edition in 1914 received a revised introduction. By that time the shortcomings in Dicey's analysis had been noted and recognised.

8–083   The growth in delegated powers and in party government extended beyond any of Dicey's ideas of representative government. The ability of the Commons to control the Executive was doubted. Dicey also doubted whether the rule of law could survive given the combination of party politics and weak parliamentary control. The growth in legislation, and especially the debate over Irish Home Rule, had pointed to a growing tension between Dicey's model of the ideal constitution formulated in 1885 and the reality of the Constitution in 1914.

8–084   Such acknowledged defects in Dicey's vision of the constitution, apparent even to Dicey himself, did not lessen the importance of the Law of the Constitution.

Paradoxically, the more defective the work was shown to be, the more influence it seemed to hold over lawyers and public law.

The most glaring weakness in Dicey's analysis was his failure to recognise the **8–085** development of administrative law and his misunderstanding of French *droit administratif* which he erroneously saw as equivalent to tyranny and something alien and Continental. English traditions were seen as superior to French traditions and the character of English law and its institutions influenced Dicey's vision of English administrative law.[38] In 1915 Dicey belatedly recognised administrative law as a branch of English public law. In so doing Dicey identified a role for the courts in overseeing the exercise of powers by government departments. Relying on cases such as *Local Government Board v Arlidge* and the *Board of Education v Rice*, Dicey believed that the courts offered greater guarantees of the rule of law than ministerial responsibility.

"But any man who will look plain facts in the face will see in a moment that ministerial liability to the censure not in fact by Parliament, not even by the House of Commons, but by the party majority who keep the Government in office, is a very feeble guarantee indeed against the action which evades the authority of the law courts."

Despite his earlier reservations about judicial review, Dicey gave the impression that **8–086** the courts might provide the best protection of liberties within existing constitutional arrangements.[39] Dicey's death in 1922 left unanswered in any detail whether this revision of his earlier views might have altered the fundamental principles of the constitution he explained in 1885. Dicey's contemporaries at Oxford—Bryce, Pollock, Holland and Anson—also wrote textbooks setting out principles in a coherent and lawyerly fashion. However, it is Dicey, alone among his contemporaries, whose influence became the most significant.

CONTEMPORARY WRITERS AND PUBLIC LAW

Robson and Laski

Over one hundred years have passed since publication of the *Law of the Constitution*. **8–087** During this period public law has continued to be influenced by Dicey's work. No less an influence came from writers challenging Dicey's vision of the Constitution.

The period after the First World War witnessed an enormous growth in the role of **8–088** both central and local government which had continued from the nineteenth century. Major political developments such as the growth in party politics and coalition government had already put a strain on Dicey's views of the Constitution. Legal developments included an extension of governmental powers and functions, and the growth of public Health and welfare provisions. This growth in administration had not

[38] A.V. Dicey, "The Development of Administrative Law in England" (1915) 31 *Law Quarterly Review* 148. See F.H. Lawson, "Dicey Revisited', (1959) *Political Quarterly* 109–126.
[39] H. Arthurs, *Without the Law: Administrative Justice and Legal Pluralism in Nineteenth Century England* (Toronto, 1985); H. Arthurs, "Rethinking Administrative Law" (1979) *Osgoode Hall Law Journal* 1–45.

been accompanied by any re-think of how the rights of the citizen and the role of the State might be held in balance.

8–089   Criticisms of administrative bureaucracy and inefficiencies at the expense of individual freedom were made in the late 1920s and throughout the period leading to the Second World War. William Robson[40] was influential in re-considering the Dicey model of the Constitution which he complained lacked an adequate administrative law to meet the demands of an extensive administrative State. A source of major concern was the "acquisition of legislative and judicial functions by the Executive". Shortcomings in the system of tribunals, then in existence, were pointed out. Other writers criticised Dicey's analysis that administrative law was foreign or alien to English law. Particularly forthright in pointing out the errors in Dicey's analysis and understanding of French administrative law, Jennings asserted that administrative law had a valuable role in a country with a highly developed sense of political organisation. Jennings also disputed Dicey's analysis of sovereignty and questioned the value of individual rights contained in the rule of law as outlined by Dicey. In general Jennings favoured a broader, more sociological approach to public law. Dicey had analysed public law in terms of applying private law concepts and principles to government, sovereignty and the State. Jennings adopted a different approach, preferring to develop public law concepts in terms of duties, powers and responsibilites by adopting a "sociological method."

8–090   Jennings defined the role of the lawyer interested in the Constitution as different from the practitioner[41]:

> "The sociological process is simply to examine the facts, including the ideas of any given society. A jurist or a constitutional lawyer, unlike the practising lawyer is not concerned with the set of ideas possessed by lawyers alone, but with the ideas of people generally."

8–091   Broadening the debate as to the relationship between the nature of law and the State brought more influences in the development of public law. The most formidable was the work of Harold Laski[42] (1893–1950), whose influence on the theory of the State called into question assumptions behind the liberal State and the exercise of political power. Laski was greatly influenced by American jurists such as Holmes and Pound. By rejecting high theory he argued for practical, common-sense and realistic assessments to be made of the reasoning behind judicial decisions and an exposition of assumptions which lay behind the value judgements contained in policy decisions.

8–092   Laski also questioned the single, unitary view of the State favoured by Dicey. Far removed from Dicey's idealism of the perfection he found in the Constitution, Laski sought justification for the consequences of government power and linked economic

---

[40] W.A. Robson, *Justice and Administrative Law* (London 1928). Also see W.A. Robson, "The Report of the Committee on Ministers' Powers" (1932) 3 *Political Quarterly* 346.
[41] I. Jennings, *The Law and the Constitution* (London, 1933). See Jennings, "The Report on Ministers' Powers" (1932) 10 *Public Administration* 333; Jennings, "In praise of Dicey 1885–1935" (1935) 13 *Public Administration* 123; Jennings, *The Law and the Constitution* (London, 1933).
[42] H. Laski, *Studies in the Problem of Sovereignty* (1917); *Authority in the Modern State* (1919); "The Growth of Administrative Discretion" (1923) 1 *Journal of Public Administration* 92; *Report of the Committee on Ministers' Powers*, Cmd. 4060 (1932), Annex V. H. Laski, *Studies in the Problem of Sovereignty* (London, 1917). H. Laski, "Judicial Review of Social Policy in England" (1926) 39 *Harvard Law Review* 839.

and social power to legal authority. Developing these ideas caused Laski to challenge the liberal theory of the State with the result that his sociological approach found support in the writings of Jennings and Robson.

Variations in Laski's reasoning, especially in his later works, have echoes of the **8–093** influences of pragmatism which may also be found in other writers of the period. No single, coherent theme may be identified from among all of Dicey's critics but the debate about the nature of public law had changed remarkably from Dicey's influence. The period 1928–1932 marked an intense debate about public law.

Robson's influential *Justice and Administrative Law* was published in 1928. A year **8–094** later the Lord Chief Justice, Lord Hewart had published *The New Despotism*[43] and a year after came F.J. Port's *Administrative Law*.[44] Hewart's warning of "administrative lawlessness" feared that government had become too powerful and, in common with Dicey's fears voiced in 1915, Hewart feared that the rule of law might become meaningless. All these influences came to the fore when in 1929 the Donoughmore Committee was set up inquiring into Ministers' powers, the use of delegated legislation and judicial decision-making. The Report was published in 1932 and Laski was included among the membership of the Committee. Hewart's *New Despotism* claimed that the power of government had expanded[45]:

> "The official is anonymous, he is not bound by any course of procedure nor by any rules of evidence, nor is he obliged to give any reasons for his decision . . . The exercise of arbitrary power is neither law nor justice, administrative or at all."

English administrative law with its distinctive use of administrative tribunals and **8–095** inquiries was ill co-ordinated and lacked rationality.

Despite such strictures little was achieved by the Donoughmore Committee in terms **8–096** of unifying the hotchpotch of administrative tribunals into a coherent whole. After Donoughmore, tribunals grew in an uncontrolled and bureaucratic way with specialised and complex rules accompanying their development.

The rejection of Robson and Laski's analysis which favoured an independent **8–097** tribunal system may be attributed to *droit administratif* and Dicey's objections. The Committee feared that setting up a uniform and independent tribunal system amounted to a rival form of administrative law to the ordinary courts and especially so if judicial review was excluded. While Dicey's influence still inhibited the growth of administrative law, it was only after the Second World War that the opportunity to break with the past arose. The Franks Committee in 1957, set up after the Crichel Down affair, reported in favour of creating a proper system of tribunals with clearly defined objectives and procedures under the Council of Tribunals. In effect this abandoned Dicey's opposition to such a system.

Recognition that administrative law had a proper place in English law came slowly. **8–098** In 1964 Lord Reid observed,[46] "We do not have a developed system of administrative law—perhaps because until fairly recently we did not need it." Thereafter doubts about

---

[43] G. Hewart, *New Despotism* (1929), pp.43–44.
[44] F.J. Port, *Administrative Law* (1930).
[45] Hewart, *op.cit.*, pp.43–44.
[46] *Ridge v Baldwin* [1964] A.C. 40. See H.W.R. Wade, *Administrative Law*; and "Law, Opinion and Administration" (1962) 78 *Law Quarterly Review* 188; and *Constitutional Fundamentals* (1980).

the existence and need for administrative law slowly dispelled. What remained, however, was a fundamental debate about the role of the courts in the future development of administrative law.

8–099   Dicey's rule of law asserted that the ordinary law should be supreme and that the ordinary courts should act as the cornerstone of the rule of law. Expanding the role of the courts through increased judicial intervention as the means of developing administrative law seemed to many to be supporting Dicey's rule of law. Under this view administrative law came to mean only judicial review. Remedies available to the litigant were narrowly and often procedurally defined and restricted to issues which to the courts appeared similar to settling contract or tort liability disputes in the private sector. This comparison of administrative law to actions in the private sector is useful when understanding how judicial review in the early development of administrative law remained restricted and constrained by narrow and technical concerns.

8–100   While Laski, Robson and Jennings had set a new agenda for the development of public law, judicial attitudes seemed to reflect Dicey's influence. One reason lay in the historical development of remedies and the narrow confines of statutory intention in terms only of legislative intent. The courts were presented with individual rights and specific remedies with the requirements of a specific *locus standi* rather than any broader inquiry into how powers were exercised. No conceptual framework for administrative law was put in place once administrative law became an established part of English law.

8–101   Another reason may be gleaned from the nature of Dicey's inheritance bequeathed to lawyers. With hindsight Dicey's original principles seem untenable given the nature of political and economic changes since 1885. Later writers had successfully shown contradictions in Dicey's principles and even Dicey's later revisions failed to support his original premise. Despite these flaws and rather like a many-headed hydra, Dicey's influence was not confined to his written text but his vision of constitutional arrangements triumphed over past practices and early history. Errors or flaws in Dicey's principles seemed to have been overlooked or distinguished as if they represented old precedents, which allowed Dicey's vision to continue and *Law of the Constitution* to remain a significant textbook for the study of constitutional and administrative law. Dicey's analytical method, which owes much to the empirical tradition in law, has also remained influential in the style of public law scholarship.

PUBLIC LAW AND POLITICAL CHANGE

8–102   Robson and Laski invigorated the study of public law by broadening the terms of inquiry into the nature of power and how power is exercised by the State. Economic, social and political issues became relevant in understanding public law. Further advances in understanding public law came from the influence of philosophy on law, which underwent a remarkable transformation under the influence of H.L.A. Hart.

8–103   Dicey, following Austin and Bentham, defined law as the command of a sovereign. After the Second World War jurisprudence became influenced by linguistic analysis from the writing of Wittgenstein and Gilbert Ryle.[47] The Oxford lawyer and philoso-

[47] Kelly, *A Short History of Western Theory* (Oxford, 1992), pp.403–447.

pher H.L.A. Hart[48] questioned the Austin view of sovereignty and law, pointing out inadequacies in the understanding "of all law as a command". This contributed further to the discourse on public law by bringing questions of morality and explicit notions of adjudication in seeking to explain why laws are obeyed. Distinguishing legal from moral rules, Hart argued, depends on how society views the status of a particular rule.

The diversity of the influences in the development of public law includes contribu- **8–104** tions from political science, international studies and sociology. The blurring of subject categories as well as legal categories further complicates the question of whether public law is a distinctive subject. Daintith observes that a noticeable trend in writing about public law[49] "is the prevailing descriptive and eclectic mode of writing about the United Kingdom's constitution and public law". The various influences currently at work in public law scholarship may be noted as follows.

Dicey's influence and analytical method may find familiarity in public law writing **8–105** today. Some writers see the present development of administrative law as a product of Dicey's influence and the furtherance of the rule of law. Other writers take their point of reference from Laski and Robson and seek to expand the study of public law through an analysis of present day problems supported by detailed empirical investigation.

HUMAN RIGHTS AND PUBLIC LAW

The Human Rights Act 1998 for the first time allows British citizens to use domestic **8–106** courts to enforce Convention rights. British law is entering a period of considerable uncertainty as the transition to a rights-based culture is undertaken through cases decided by the judges. This is likely to be a painful process as age-old constitutional assumptions are held up for inspection. It is possible that many institutions and practices may be found wanting.

In the midst of considerable uncertainty, intensive preparations were made for the **8–107** 1998 Act's coming into force in England and Wales and an extra £60 million allocated for legal aid and court costs. The judiciary at all levels from magistrates' courts to the appeals courts have undergone intensive education and training programmes. A central issue is the extent of the application of Convention rights and the implications of a rights-based culture in English law. Courses organised by the Judicial Studies Board have explained the remit of the 1998 Act and how it might be interpreted. Similarly, administrators and civil servants have undergone training on the impact of the Act. The courts now have the difficult task of interpreting the proper procedures and merits of administrative decisions. While there were fears that the number of cases under the Act might overwhelm the court administration, a sensible case-by-case approach has been adopted. As Professor Anthony King has pointed out, there can be little doubt that[50] ". . .many of the changes in our traditional constitution are

---

[48] H.L.A. Hart, *The Concept of Law* (Oxford, 1961); "Definition and Theory in Jurisprudence" (1954) 70 *Law Quarterly Review* 37. See also J. Raz, *The Morality of Freedom*.
[49] T. Daintith, "Political Programmes and the Content of the Constitution" in *Edinburgh Essays in Public Law* (Finnie, Himsworth and Walker ed., 1991), pp.41–55. Laswell and MacDougal, "Legal Education and Public Policy" (1943) 52 *Yale Law Journal* 203.
[50] Anthony King, *Does the United Kingdom Still Have a Constitution?* (2001), p.90.

permanent and irreversible". It is an opportune moment to take stock of the direction a more rights-orientated public law will take us. There are some words of caution.

8–108   While conceding, as everyone must, that human rights are intrinsic to our democratic system, there is room for consideration of the boundaries of judicial power as a custodian of rights. What degree of self-regulation should be exercised by judges when they are granted such overarching powers? How should decision-makers be advised to achieve good decisions when individual rights may serve to inhibit risk-taking and the development of long-term strategies?

8–109   One example of judicial creativity surrounds the development of a right to privacy in the United Kingdom. In *Kaye v Robertson*[51] the Court of Appeal denied that there is a right to privacy in English law. This view was upheld by the House of Lords in *R. v Brown*.[52] Lord Hoffman commented that the common law did not recognise such a right and that Parliament was reluctant to introduce one. In court decisions after the introduction of the Human Rights Act 1998, the courts have gone to great lengths to create such a right. In *Douglas v Hello Ltd*[53] the courts acknowledged the possibility of an arguable right to privacy. This decision has the potential[54] of developing into a full right of privacy even though in the past, the judges had been reluctant to do so. This is an example of how the Human Rights Act may provide judges with new perspectives and allow the common law to be supplemented by a "rights" jurisprudence.

8–110   There is another example of how rights from a European perspective may infiltrate into English institutions and the legal system. In *Osman v United Kingdom*[55] the claimants, Mr and Mrs Osman were the son and wife of a man who had been shot and killed by a Mr Paget-Lewis. The claimants alleged negligence, on the part of a consultant psychiatrist and the Commissioner of the Metropolitan Police, that resulted in suffering loss and damage. The allegations arose from the alleged failure of the police to apprehend Mr Paget-Lewis prior to shootings that he was involved in. The facts of the case involve events leading up to the tragic death of the man who was shot and killed by Mr Paget-Lewis, a school teacher who had become infatuated with the son while teaching him. The events leading up to this tragedy began with various incidents reported to the police alleged to have been caused by the actions of Paget-Lewis. Despite the fact that the Local Education Authority had arranged for a psychiatric assessment of Paget-Lewis and despite evidence of the increasing use of harassment against the Osmans, there appeared to be insufficient evidence to warrant a prosecution. After a short period away from the school, Paget-Lewis returned and took part in a number of killings. He killed the father of the boy, Mr Osman, injured the son, wounded a teacher in the school and also killed the teacher's son. The applicants, Mrs Osman and her son, alleged that the police were negligent in failing to arrest Paget-Lewis earlier and to take steps to prevent any harm to the Osmans. In English law the existing case law on liability against the police rested on the operation of an immunity[56] in the public interest. This immunity might be rebutted in circumstances where it could be shown that there was some form of a "relationship of

---

[51] [1991] F.S.R. 62.
[52] [1996] 1 All E.R. 545.
[53] [2001] 2 All E.R. 289.
[54] See: *Earl Spencer v UK* (1998) 25 E.H.R.R. CD 105 before the 1998 Act came into force.
[55] [1999] 1 F.L.R. 193.
[56] *Hill v Chief Constable of West Yorkshire* [1989] A.C. 53.

proximity" between the police and the applicants. The police claimed this immunity and unsuccessfully applied to the first instant court to have the case dismissed as having no reasonable cause of action. The police appealed to the Court of Appeal. The appeal was successful in the Court of Appeal applying the case of *Hill v Chief Constable of West Yorkshire*[57] and holding that there was not a sufficient proximity, thus upholding police immunity. Though one of the Appeal Court judges, McGowan L.J. took the view that there was a possible proximate relationship. The House of Lords refused leave to appeal. The applicants, the Osmans took their case to the European Court of Human Rights. It was argued that Articles 2, 6 and 8 of the Convention applied. Article 2 provides an obligation on the authorities to take steps to safeguard citizens within their jurisdiction. The European Court held that Article 2 was not breached. However, under Article 6 the applicants argued that they were entitled to have the full matter of their case considered and not dismissed on the basis of a procedural rule or of no case to answer on the basis of the immunity set out in the *Hill* decision. The application of Article 6 required that the Osmans were entitled to a full determination of their case on its merits and a full assessment of whether or not they fell within the proximity test. The European Court of Human Rights found that Article 6 had been breached. The Court awarded damages of £10,000 to each applicant and a sum of £30,000 in costs. Their Article 6 rights had been insufficiently protected by the courts. In considering the case the European Court of Human Rights ruled that the Court of Appeal in England when considering the Osmans' case had breached Article 6. The English courts considered that the applicants' case fell under an immunity granted to the police in previous case law.

In this case Convention rights are seen to have an impact on the law of tort. It is **8–111** quite likely that depending on the scope of rights, the law of contract may be similarly treated. McKendrick[58] suggests that the impact may be significant. Consider the situation where, because of an illegal contract unenforceable by the courts, the party concerned argues that Convention rights require some remedy. It is equally the case that the role of human rights and the role of contracts within the public sector are changing the shape of how government governs. *Osman* is an example that confronts the central core of the way law is developing. Driven by a human rights agenda, the Human Rights Court adopts a posture and position that is distinctive from the equivalent attitude of the United Kingdom courts. The civil law tradition of investigatory and inquisitorial procedures of inquiry confront the common law world where adversarial proceedings through cross-examination and oral hearings are the norm. The resolution of differences in culture and tradition makes the future uncertain. The *Osman* case provides an indication of the future direction rights are likely to enforce in the development of the English common law. The impact of the *Osman* case is far-Reaching. At one level it suggests that English courts when applying procedural rules must take into consideration their likely impact and scope in terms of human rights. Secondly, that the overriding presumption of the European Court of Human Rights is to assess the fairness of procedures and substantive law giving pre-eminence to the protection of rights rather than adopting the presumption of immunity on the part of public authorities. Since *Osman* the European Court of Human Rights has narrowly

[57] *Hill v Chief Constable of West Yorkshire* [1989] A.C. 53.
[58] E. McKendrick, *Contract Law* (Macmillan, London, 2000), p.15.

interpreted its application[59] and limited its scope. However, the attitude and approach of the English courts is markedly different than the European Court of Human Rights. This raises considerable doubts as to the strict compatibility in the way rights are interpreted in the common law and in civil law systems. At the minimum it is clear that immunities devised to fit the English system of accountability and control are incompatible with the rights-based culture of the European Convention on Human Rights.[60]

8–112   The Human Rights Act also creates the question of the range and scope of rights. The potential for the Act to have a "horizontal" effect arises because under s.6 of the Act, the courts are public authorities and have a duty to make decisions that are compatible with the Convention.[61]

8–113   Mapping the future impact of rights that are integrated into the English common law is the subject of controversy and differing perspectives. As previous chapters have shown there are a number of discernible trends. Linking past thinking with the current vogue for a pre-eminence of human rights in legal disputes may cause a substantial re-think about the boundaries of public law and political decision-making. Trust, the axiom of ministerial responsibility, is likely to be displaced by a more juridical formulation. The role of ancient institutions, the reverential style of past generations and respect for dignity and status are being replaced by a modernisation process that appears to know no boundaries. Public power, however exercised, is to be made more accountable and subject to regulatory structures and rules. This increases the role and variety of legal work for lawyers and puts legality at the centre of the decision-making process. The role of the civil service is likely to become more transparent and placed on a statutory basis. Despite resistance it is inevitable that the role of the office of Lord Chancellor should receive clarification. Support for a modern Supreme Court is accompanied by demands for a representative bench.[62] Change and modernisation are working together to provide the need for greater use of comparative analysis and an evaluation of the shift from political power and its systems of control to judicial power and the processes of judicial accountability.

SUMMARY AND CONCLUSIONS

8–114   Contemporary writing on constitutional and administrative law has reflected the fast-developing specialisms[63] which may conveniently fit within the broadest definition of public law. These include planning law, environmental law, housing law and welfare law. In addition there is a growing interest in cross-boundary disciplinary study.

---

[59] *Z v UK* Application no. 29392/95, May 10, 2001 and *TP and KM v UK* Application no. 28945/95, May 10, 2001.
[60] E. McKendrick, "Negligence and Human Rights: Re-considering Osman" in *Human Rights in Private Law* (D. Friedmann and D. Barak-Erez ed., Hart Publishing, Oxford, 2001), p.331.
[61] M. Hunt, "The Horizontal Effect of the Human Rights Act" [1998] *Public Law* 423; and another perspective: Buxton L.J., "The Human Rights Act and Private Law" (2000) 116 *Law Quarterly Review* 48.
[62] K. Ewing, "The Unbalanced Constitution" in *Sceptical Essays on Human Rights* (T. Campbell, K. Ewing and A. Tomkins ed., Oxford University Press, Oxford 2001), p.117.
[63] T. Daintith, "Political Programmes and the Content of the Constitution" in *Edinburgh Essays in Public Law* (Finnie, Himsworth and Walker ed., 1991), pp.41–55. J. Mitchell, "The Causes and Effects of the Absence of a System of Public Law in the United Kingdom" [1965] *Public Law* 95.

Regulation and how the public sector is subject to economic indices and rules provide important insights into the development of public law. Such subjects receive separate treatment in specialised texts but the nature of the subject matter raises questions about government powers, administrative decision-taking and the role of the courts. Generalisations made from the study of such specialisms about public law require careful elucidation.

Also noticeable is the trend to develop expertise within public law itself. Subjects **8–115** include privatisation, regulation, European Community law, local and central government, and public finance. Public law issues are therefore increasingly perceived as involving not only the courts but a range of institutions and bodies, some with quasi-governmental functions. Another significant influence on the development of public law is the increasingly relevant writings undertaken by political scientists. A good example is N. Johnson's *In Search of the Constitution*, which critically examines the existing constitutional arrangements in the United Kingdom in 1975. Johnson notes[64]:

> "It becomes more and more difficult to set limits to the powers of government; there is growing uncertainty about the terms in which public bodies are expected to act: the authority of those in political life is weakened; and it becomes steadily harder to justify political action by reference to constitutional norms."

Political scientists found common cause with lawyers in the discussion of devolution **8–116** proposals made in the Kilbrandon Report in 1979. A range of important topics such as the select committees, electoral reform, reform of the House of Lords, freedom of information, police accountability, central-local relations and emergency powers in Northern Ireland represent major areas where political scientists and lawyers have had a fruitful dialogue. Parliament, its function and role has also attracted multi-disciplinary attention.

Two areas in particular may be mentioned as coming under intense scrutiny as part **8–117** of the socio–legal approach and analysis of public law issues. First, is the subject of non-judicial means of dispute resolution between citizens and administration. Attention is given to tribunals, inquiries, ombudsmen and M.P.s as part of the dispute procedures involved in grievance machinery. Empirical research, case studies and theoretical analysis are often combined in research projects covering a wide range of institutions. Although the Law Commission declined in 1965 to undertake a detailed analysis of administrative law, the studies carried out over the last 25 years provide an important resource if such a study were to be undertaken in the future.

Secondly, and related to the first, regulation of the newly privatised utilities has set a **8–118** new direction for public lawyers. Hybrid powers involving statutory authorities, licences, contracts and Company Act company agreements, provide the main means for carrying out many of the main activities in the provision of telecommunications, water, gas and electricity. Research into these fields involves economists, political scientists and lawyers.

The "descriptive and eclectic" mode of writing about public law has also extended to **8–119** a more radical critique of the United Kingdom's constitutional arrangements. Public lawyers have become increasingly aware of the political origins and nature of the

[64] N. Johnson, *In Search of the Constitution* (1977), p.viii.

changes in society as reflected in the legislation passed as a result of the policies of the government of the day. As a result a large body of literature attempts to set the boundaries of public law within the framework of theoretical debate. Attempts to provide new criteria or norms to evaluate the "legitimacy" of government action or principle to direct critical analysis of government decision-taking have not been wholly successful. However frustrated such attempts have been there is merit in setting out to improve the analysis of values and techniques intended to provide for more open and accountable government.

8–120   As part of this development of more theoretical-based studies there is a growing unease about the futility of the operation. Loughlin's expectation that legal theory helps us to render explicit the styles of public law thinking is somewhat blunted by the difficulty of finding a suitable vocabulary to provide public lawyers with an appropriate agenda for the future. There is in fact a veritable hotchpotch of theories and ideas competing for influence in setting public law on a clear direction for the future. Loughlin summarises his vision for the future[65]:

"In confronting these important issues concerning the relationship between government and law, the functional logic of modern law must be accepted. This means that any contribution which public law may provide to the development of effective and accountable structures of government should be based on a sociological orientation.[66] Studies need to be rooted in a socially constructed field and, from that perspective, should investigate the interplay of cognitive and normative considerations. The normative structure of law should be recognised. But unlike the normatist approach, the question of laws' normative structure is itself an object of inquiry."

8–121   Other writers have sensed the need for new directions but have been reluctant to set out an agenda for the future.

8–122   The breadth of the inquiry presently undertaken by public lawyers is formidable. As Daintith has observed, "the conscientious search for a structure of constitutional obligation might well show that we possess no reliable rules over large areas of public life".

8–123   The focus of public law scholarship extends from the legal to the non-legal. Because many of the informal rules or understandings which guide public institutions are important, the task in hand extends beyond the ordinary remit of legal training. Political science, history, sociology and economics have a relevance to the future direction of public law within the United Kingdom even if that relevance requires justification and explanation to fit each task under review.

8–124   The inquiry is not narrowly confined to the United Kingdom. Comparative evaluation of constitutional arrangements in Canada, Australia and the USA have provided useful influences in understanding common law systems and their adaptation. There is also an increasing europeanisation of law through membership of the European Union. The European Union and Community institutions are important for the future of public law in the United Kingdom and are considered in more detail in the chapter which follows.

---

[65] M. Loughlin, *Public Law and Political Theory* (Clarendon Press: Oxford, 1992), p.262.
[66] T. Daintith, "Political Programmes and the Content of the Constitution" in *Edinburgh Essays in Public Law* (Finnie, Himsworth and Walker ed., 1991), pp.41–55.

FURTHER READING

T.R.S. Allan, *Constitutional Justice: A Liberal Theory of the Rule of Law* (Oxford University Press, Oxford, 2001).

P. Craig, "Public Law, Political Theory and Legal Theory" [2000] *Public Law* 211.

P. Craig, "Competing Models of Judicial Review" (1999) *Public Law* 428.

M. Loughlin, *Sword and Scales* (Hart Publishing, Oxford, 2000).

D. Oliver, "The Underlying Values of Public and Private Law" in M. Taggart ed., *The Province of Administrative Law* (M. Taggart ed., Hart Publishing, Oxford, 1997).

Chapter 9

THE EUROPEAN UNION

INTRODUCTION

The European Union comprises 15 Member States and stands on three pillars. The **9–001** Community pillar governs the operation of the various institutions such as the Commission, Parliament, the Council and the Court of Justice which involves managing the internal market and common polices of the Community. The two remaining pillars were introduced under the Maastricht Treaty (Treaty on European Union) which came into force on November 1, 1993. Foreign and security policy forms one and the other is formed around asylum and immigration policy, the police and justice. Since Maastricht, there are important reforms introduced in 1999 under the Treaty of Amsterdam and in 2001 the Treaty of Nice agreed on February 26, 2001. At times proposals raised by the institutions of the EU set grand expectations, including ambitious plans for expansion of the number of Member States by the year 2010 so that the EU could comprise 27 Member States. In the foreseeable future it is hoped to provide Member States of the European Union with a Charter of Fundamental Rights of the European Union. A draft Charter of Fundamental Rights[1] was agreed in Biarritz in October 2000. However, at Nice it was agreed that the Charter should become for the time being a declaratory agreement, pending the future expansion of the European Union. As outlined briefly in Chapter 2, (para.2–106), the Laeken Declaration on the Future of Europe concluded in December 2001 the setting-up of a Convention on Europe to devise a future strategy for Europe. It is hoped that there will be an Intergovernmental Conference in 2004 to take matters to the next stage, including in all probability some form of new charter of rights or constitution for Europe.

The European Union is undergoing change to expand its size to around 27 members **9–002** and also complete economic and monetary union. The majority of the Member States, after satisfying certain economic criteria and the maintenance of sound financial management have created a common currency, the Euro, and agreed fixed exchange rates. This has led to the development of a central bank and the introduction of a new exchange rate mechanism. The United Kingdom is one of the three including Denmark and Norway that are not in the Euro. In October 1997 the Chancellor of the Exchequer drew up five economic tests for Britain joining the single currency. These are:

[1] See Neil Waker, "Human Rights in a Postnational Order: reconciling Political and Constitutional Pluralism" in *Sceptical Essays on Human Rights* (T. Campbell , K. Ewing and A. Tomkins ed., Oxford University Press, Oxford, 2001), p.119.

- sustainable convergence between the British economy and the economies of a single currency;

- sufficient flexibility to accommodate economic change;

- the effect on investment;

- the impact on financial services; and

- whether it is good for employment.

9–003   It is intended that there should be a referendum before legislation permitting entry into the single currency is passed. No date has been set for the referendum and there are conflicting views as to whether Britain will meet the five criteria. The aim of this chapter is to examine European influences on the United Kingdom's system of public law taking account of the developing rights jurisprudence of the Community.

EVOLVING EUROPE

9–004   Since January 1, 1973, when the European Communities Act 1972 took effect, the United Kingdom became a member of the European Community.[2] The United Kingdom's membership of the Community is not a single event nor is it static. Membership is part of an ongoing process. Change within the Community is both evolutionary and pragmatic in the creation of a new European legal order. Intense political debate and controversy very often accompany discussion of the future direction of the Community The United Kingdom is an important, albeit at times reluctant part of a single market, a major economic and social unit which has as its objective, benefits for the economies of the Member States. The development of a true single market among Member States is the ambition of the Single European Act, signed by all Member States in 1986. Slowly this ambition is being realised. Membership of the Community has raised significant implications for the United Kingdom's existing constitutional arrangements. Many of these issues, such as the impact of membership on the United Kingdom's sovereignty, are being addressed. There are also noticeable cultural changes, difficult to assess and quantify when it is remembered how new directions and influences may come into national law from European ideas and influences. Milsom[3] reminds us that the development of a system of law into a legal system is a rare occurrence:

> "It has happened twice only that the customs of European peoples were worked up into intellectual systems of law; and much of the world today is governed by laws derived from the one or the other."

[2] The term European Community and its abbreviation (EC) requirers explanation: there are three distinct communities, namely the European Coal and Steel Community, the European Economic Community, and the European Atomic Energy Community, and as a result it is common to refer to the EC. Finally a fourth was added by the Treaty on European Union has created a European Union (EU) wider than the Economic Community. Currently EC membership comprises: the UK, France, Germany, Italy, Republic of Ireland, Denmark, Netherlands, Belgium, Luxembourg, Portugal, Greece, Spain, Austria, Finland and Sweden. In Ch.1 the structures of the EC have been shortly outlined. A more comprehensive analysis is provided in P.J.G. Kapteyn and P. Verloren Van Themaat, *Introduction to the Law of the European Communities* (Laurence Gormley ed., English ed., Kluwer, 1990).
[3] S.F.C. Milsom, *Historical Foundations of the Common Law* (2nd ed., 1981), p.1.

The apparent fusion of the civil and common law systems within the integration of   **9–005**
European law gives rise to a new understanding of what is a legal system. It would
appear that we are witnessing the birth of a new European "federation" with
widespread implications for the future of our legal system and public law.

Historical Influences

Many European countries, with the exception of the United Kingdom, adopted a civil   **9–006**
law tradition as part of their development. The civil law tradition cast a rich inheritance
of law, morality and culture which was also influential in English law but there it did not
take root and endure. From early European history it is possible to trace common
influences across Europe. The growth of European trade in the Middle Ages had
encouraged the development of various rules of European law which began to become
collected and recognised as part of a legal order which transcended individual states.[4]
These influences were particularly significant for trade and commercial dealings.

Some examples of European influences on law may be identified. The beginnings of   **9–007**
modern contract doctrine may be found in a shared origin between common lawyers
and civil lawyers based on a "similar doctrinal structure based on similar legal
concepts". This shared inheritance owes much to the philosophy of the *Corpus Juris
Civilis*, but in the later development of contract, civil and common lawyers separated.
Leaving behind their shared inheritance, the outcome of reformulation in the
nineteenth century was two distinct systems. The fact that the theoretical and
philosophical home of English contract law is derived from the European legal model
is often overlooked by English lawyers.[5]

More closely related to the role of the State was the influence of codification.   **9–008**
Relying on inspiration from continental theorists, English law drew ideas from Roman
law, especially from the writings of Savigny (1779–1861)[6] Maine's (1822–88)[6a] general
legal theory about the law and State owed much to the influence of Roman law and
this in turn presented codes as part of an evolutionary process in the development of
society. As Stein has noted[7] "English law has always been strong on its legal rules, but
weak on its legal theory". Nevertheless, English legal theory especially for Austin and
Bentham, drew insights from Roman law and the codification favoured by civil lawyers.

Membership of the Community injects into English law a European civil tradition.   **9–009**
Mitchell[8] was one of the few lawyers to foresee the possibility that British and

---

[4] See J.H. Merryman, *The Civil Law Tradition* (Stanford University Press, 1985), p.1. Also see A. Von
Mehren, *The Civil Law System* (Little Brown, 1957). On French law and the code system see R. David,
H.P. de Vries, *The French Legal System* (Oceana, 1958); P. Stein, *Legal Evolution* (Cambridge, 1980); John
Austin (1790–1859), Henry Maine (1822–88), Fredrich Carl von Savigny (1779–1861); Albert Bleckman, "Le
Droit Européen Commun dans le Domaine du Droit Administratif" in *Le Droit Commun de l'Europe et
l'Avenir de l'Enseignement Juridique* (Bruno de Witte and Caroline Forden ed., Kluwer, 1992); R.C. Van
Caenegem, *Judges, Legislators and Professors: Chapters in European Legal History* (Cambridge, 1987);
P.S. Atiyah, *Pragmatism and Theory in English Law* (London, 1987); J.M. Kelly, *A Short History of Western
Legal Theory* (Oxford University Press, 1992), pp.156–157.
[5] J. Gordley, *The Philosophical Origins of Modern Contract Doctrine* (Oxford, 1991). Also see R.C. Van
Caenegem, *The Birth of the English Common Law* (2nd ed., 1988). Also in Europe a *jus commune* was
established, namely a European common law influenced by Roman law.
[6] Savigny, *System of Roman Law* (1840–49).
[6a] H.S. Maine *Ancient Law* (London, 1881).
[7] P. Stein, *op.cit.*, p.123.
[8] J.D. Mitchell, "The State of Public Law in the UK" (1966) 15 *International and Comparative Law Quarterly*
133. Also see "The Causes and Effects of the Absence of a System of Public Law in the United Kingdom"
[1965] *Public Law* 95.

Continental legal systems might combine with significant results. While the majority of United Kingdom lawyers failed to understand this particular consequence of Community membership, it is likely that Mitchell's analysis will prove far-sighted. Already in one particular instance the influence of the European tradition has been acknowledged as helpful. On the question of the distinction between public law and private law, the experience of the civil law where such a distinction has developed has been acknowledged as a fruitful source for ideas.[9]

9–010   The civil law tradition is more fully developed in defining the significance of the distinction between public and private law. Public law is concerned with the interests of the whole community, the preservation of the State and the maintenance of order. Private law is concerned with property rights and the resolution of such disputes. At work in developing such a distinction is the desire to give property ownership, and its enjoyment, maximum protection according to the law. The philosophical tradition found in the jurisprudence of civil law lays the theoretical basis of private and public law. It might be considered that this influence has already helped to draw a distinction between public and private law in recent court cases[10] in the United Kingdom. Still further, it is possible to foresee that the new legal order borne out of the European Community may require a re-interpretation of the United Kingdom's basic understanding of constitutional and administrative law.

9–011   On the question of national sovereignty, Mitchell's view, that the United Kingdom's sovereignty had been altered on entry into the Community and that this would lead inevitably to recognition by the courts of the primacy of Community law, has to some extent been realised. The *Factortame*[11] case confirms Mitchell's view by ascertaining the supremacy of Community law over a United Kingdom Act of Parliament. If this aspect of sovereignty has been settled, there remains the question of the future influence Community membership might have on the United Kingdom's constitutional and administrative law.

MEMBERSHIP OF THE EUROPEAN UNION

9–012   The United Kingdom's membership[12] of the Community has undergone significant change as the Community has adopted ,[13] new policies and objectives. The original treaty arrangements envisaged four areas where economic freedoms within a common market might be established. These include goods, persons, services and capital. An important area of policy concerned with fundamental principle is the development of a common agricultural policy which has proved controversial and difficult.

9–013   Additional areas of substantive Community law include provisions covering competition and harmonisation of laws, social policy, research, technological development and

[9] Francis Jacobs, "Human Rights in Europe: New Dimensions" (1992) *The King's College Law Journal* 49.
[10] *O'Reilly v Mackman* [1983] 2 A.C. 237; *Cocks v Thanet DC* [1983] 2 A.C. 286; *Davy v Spelthorne BC* [1984] A.C. 262; *Wandsworth v Winder* [1985] A.C. 461.
[11] Case C–213/89, Factortame: [1990] E.C.R. I–2433, [1990] 3 C.M.L.R. 375; Weatherill and Beaumont, *EU Law* Penguin Books, London, 1999, pp.318–322. J. Hanna, "Community Rights all at Sea" (1990) *Law Quarterly Review* 2.
[12] Josephine Steiner, *Textbook on EEC Law* (7th ed., 2000).
[13] Gordon Slynn, *Introducing a European Legal Order* (Hamlyn Lecture, 1992), pp.41–62.

environmental policy. Provisions covering commercial policy are intended to facilitate major political, economic and institutional reform.

In 1986, reforms towards a single market among Member States were introduced through the Single European Act 1986. The 1986 Act was intended to remove any remaining barriers as obstacles to a single internal market. The form of the 1986 Act was a Treaty which was later ratified into United Kingdom domestic law by legislation.   **9–014**

The main objective of the 1986 Act was to achieve a single internal market by the end of 1992. Community competence is therefore extended into a wide variety of new areas including environment, energy, regional policy, and a common commercial policy. A significant part of these reforms are institutional and procedural in terms of giving more potential for the European Parliament to exert some influence in certain areas of Community law.   **9–015**

Equally important is the establishment of a new European marketing system leading to harmonisation of economic and monetary policy. Since 1969 the development of economic and monetary union has been advocated. Ten years later the European Monetary System (EMS) came into operation with all Member States including the United Kingdom and also latterly Greece, Spain and Portugal joining after they became members of the Community.   **9–016**

Four elements are included[14] in the EMS; membership entitles Member States to participate in but not necessarily join each of the elements of the EMS. The four elements are: the exchange rate mechanism, which obliges members to maintain exchange rates within certain limits; the European Currency Unit, which calculates the value of Community currencies pending the development of the euro (this role has been superseded by the introduction of the Euro and the establishment of a central bank); the European Monetary Co-operation Fund, which regulates the issues of the ECU (European Currency Unit) throughout the Community, and fourthly, to allow short-term credit facilities among Member States.   **9–017**

In 1989, the Delors Report proposed a three-stage approach to Member States within the Economic Monetary Union (EMU). These proposals have important economic and political implications for Member States.   **9–018**

Stage 1 seeks to achieve a single market among Member States in goods, services and capital. This assumes a strengthening of competition policy, reduction of state aids and a close co-ordination of economic and monetary policies.   **9–019**

Stage 2 is a transitional state, involving setting up the European System of Central Banks, while retaining within Member States elements of ultimate policy-making responsibility.   **9–020**

Stage 3, the most controversial, envisages the removal of the economic formulation and implementation of monetary policy to the European System of Central Banks which is intended to act as a regulator of exchange rate and currency markets.   **9–021**

The implications of Stage 3 are so wide-ranging that they would involve amendment to the Treaty of Rome. Stage 3 implies binding restraints on national budgets and the Community of Member States acting as a single entity in terms of international policy measures. The role of the Central Bank would be critical in the setting of exchange rates, currency market intervention and the management of official reserves. In the United Kingdom this power had rested with the Bank of England under Treasury   **9–022**

---

[14] *Economic and Monetary Union: An Evolutionary Approach* (December 1989). *Economic Progress Report* (Treasury, 1989).

control and ministerial influence. The result of adopting the substance of Stage 3 would be a severe curtailment of the national banks of Member States. In the United Kingdom this resulted in independence being granted to the Bank of England over interest rates under the Bank of England Act 1998.

9–023   The United Kingdom agreed to enter the Exchange Rate Mechanism at the first stage. This was intended to enable the United Kingdom to plan implementation, on an incremental basis, of the next two stages. However, events during September 1992 resulted in an unexpected and dramatic change when the United Kingdom was forced to leave the ERM as the pound came under severe pressure from the financial markets. Similar factors caused other Member States to leave the ERM.

9–024   At the heart of the debate on the EMU is the question of the role of the European System of Central Banks. It appears that for some time there was some reluctance in the United Kingdom to vest control in the European Central Bank away from the Bank of England[15]:

> "The Delors plan [Stages 1–3] would take the control of monetary policy away from National governments while leaving those governments answerable to their electorate for policies over which they would have no control."

9–025   As a result, it is likely to be some time before the full implementation of Economic and Monetary Union with the United Kingdom as a leading participant is completed. The fact that the Community has its own legal personality and political systems gives it a life of its own. The European Parliament has favoured progress towards European union and this direction is likely to be pursued for the foreseeable future. As mentioned above no date has been fixed for Britain's entry into the Euro.

9–026   Finally there is a unique quality to the European Union. No other collection of international treaties has been so extensive in delivering a wide variety of social policies, obligations, rights and enforceable laws within the Member States' own courts. The Court of Justice has developed its own jurisprudence and applied a degree of creativity in helping to pursue the general objective and policies of the European Union. As the European Union expands in size and scope it is clear that reliance on the various Community institutions is increasing. The Treaties set out the general framework. This leaves the institutions, the Commission, Council, Parliament and Court of Justice, to settle many details through delegated powers. Member States face new challenges as the Union embarks on its expansion. In the immediate future the new Member States include Bulgaria, the Czech Republic, Hungary, Poland, Romania, Slovakia, Estonia, Latvia, Lithuania, Cyprus, Malta and Turkey.

INSTITUTIONS AND STRUCTURES

9–027   It is necessary to outline in more detail the role and function of the various institutions of the European Union.

Council and Commission

9–028   The Council, established in December 1974, is comprised of representatives of the governments of the various Member States. As the Council has some control over the various legislative initiatives, the system of representation gives Member States an

---

[15] Bank of England *Economic and Monetary Union* (December 1989).

influence. The Council concludes international agreements on behalf of the Community. It may also lay down budgetary procedures. Usually it acts on the basis of consultation with the Commission. There are rules of procedure and a body known as a Committee of Permanent Representatives, composed of ambassadors, as head of the Permanent Representatives of each of the Member States in the Community. This body advises, prepares the agenda and sets the co-ordinates of policy (Article 203ex. 146).

Various specialised meetings of the Council may take place permitting Ministers **9–029** responsible for particular areas of expertise to take part. Regular meetings of Finance Ministers take place outside the Council's normal meetings.

The Single European Act 1986 provides that Heads of State and Foreign Ministers, **9–030** together with the President of the Commission are to meet at least twice a year. The Commission has initiated major reforms such as direct elections to the European Parliament, the setting-up of the European Monetary System (outlined above) and various policies on Value Added Tax. There is a sense that because of the links between the Heads of Government of the different Member States and the Council, a higher priority and influence is given to the Council when compared to the Commission. The Council acts as a co-ordinator, settling national policies between Member States, administering common policies not settled in the Treaties and, with the Commission and the European Parliament, ensuring that the Treaties are observed and implemented, and extending the scope and proposing revision of the treaties.

Voting procedures within the Council of Ministers may vary. Decisions require a **9–031** unanimous vote, a qualified majority (on proposals from the Commission) or a simple majority vote. The latter is extended by the Treaty on European Union into various areas such as environmental protection, consumer affairs and public health. There are six monthly meetings of the Council in the form of European Summit Meetings. The European Council consists of the Heads of State or government of the Member States and the President of the Commission. It first met in 1975 and since then has met regularly. This is an example of powers evolving rather than being established by any of the Community Treaties. The chairmanship of the European Council rotates every six months with the Presidency of the Council. The European Council submits a report to the European Parliament after each meeting. As outlined in Chapter 2, the decision-making procedures have been altered by the Maastricht Treaty. Unanimity is now required only in respect of the two pillars of the Community that cover Common Foreign and Security Policy and Justice and Home Affairs. Unanimity will also apply where the Council wishes to amend a Commission proposal and this is against the Commission's wishes. Qualified majority voting now applies to most types of decisions covering the main policy issues of the European Union. The Council acts in Community matters with the co-operation of the Commission whose duty is to serve the general interest of the Community as a whole.

Presently the Commission consists of 20 members, who must be nationals of a **9–032** Member State. The aim of national governments is to ensure that the Commission reflects the balance of European political interests. Members of the Commission serve a term of four years in office, enjoy various privileges and immunities to ensure that their duties are carried out unimpeded. The independence of the Commission is important and, although Commissioners are drawn from Member States, they must not be seen to act in a partisan way.

9–033   The Commission acts as an independent body, is headed by a President and is the "watchdog" of the Community. Its key function is to ensure that it makes proposals and acts as the engine room of the Community. The Council has power to request the Commission to undertake studies but otherwise it has remarkable freedom to set policy, implement studies and formulate proposals, together with the Council. It must ensure under Article 211 (ex. 155) that the Treaties are being applied. In certain areas such as competition policy it has enforcement powers over its own policy. Under Article 226 (ex. 169) it may take action to ensure compliance against a Member State including legal action in the European Court.

9–034   The Commission has a President, six Vice-Presidents and each member of the Commission has a personal staff, namely his cabinet, and Chefs de Cabinet who meet regularly to discuss the role and objectives of Commission policy. Collaboration between the Council and the Commission is required. In particular Article 15 of the Merger Treaty provides they must "consult" and "decide by common accord". One view is that recently the Commission has tended to see itself less as[16] "an embryonic European Government" than in earlier times. This marks a shift in the fortunes of the European Parliament which has had direct elections since 1979.

9–035   Powers granted to the Commission and the Council permit the taking of decisions which become legally binding on Member States and individuals within the Community. The formulation of such powers gives the initiative to the Council, on a proposal from the Commission and after consultation with the European Parliament, to take appropriate legal measures. In theory there is great scope for the broadening of such powers under Article 235 based on the doctrine of "implied power", namely that filling a gap in express powers may fit within the generally granted power if it is implied or necessary. There are doubts as to the precise scope and requirements for such powers. The Commission acts as an "overseer" of the interests of the Community and Article 5 obliges it to take appropriate measures to ensure "fulfilment of the obligations" from the Treaty. Extensive investigative powers are granted to the Commission which require Member States and even individuals to provide information allowing the Commission to carry out its task.

9–036   A number of specific policy areas fall within the jurisdiction of the Commission such as the competition policy of the Community and the implementation of the Common Agricultural Policy. This delegates to specific commissioners wide-ranging powers and activities.

The European Parliament

9–037   Directly elected since 1979, the Parliament was originally perceived as having an advisory role. Today it has 626 M.E.P.s directly elected from the 15 Member States. Increasingly important are the political groups and the lobbying that is carried out. There are 17 standing committees with a specialist focus and an elected chair. The formal powers of the Parliament such as dismissal of the Commission or rejecting the budget for the Community institutions proposed by the Commission may only be exercised on the basis of a two-thirds majority. In the 1980s the European Parliament

---

[16] See N. Nugent, *The Government and Politics of the European Community* (3rd. ed., Macmillan, 1994).

rejected the budget for a total of five years, as a signal of growing impatience over budgetary spending within the European Union. The power to dismiss the Commission is not a theoretical one, as this power was used to force the Commission to resign in 1999. Parliament took the initiative in ensuring the dismissal of the Commission because of allegations of wrongdoing. It has powers under Article 201 (ex. 144) to dismiss the Commission by a majority vote. The Parliament is required by various articles of the Treaty to be consulted but this is procedural in many instances. The Parliament meets in plenary session 12 to 14 times a year. Members sit and vote in political groupings rather than according to national allegiance.

Since 1977 various conciliation procedures have existed to promote co-operation **9–038** between Parliament, Council and Commission. This allows the Parliament a second opportunity to examine legislation. Amendments may be proposed and sent to the Commission but, even if rejected by the Commission, the amendments may be adopted by the Council by a unanimous vote.

The European Parliament may assist in the scrutiny of the Commission, who are **9–039** required to give answers to questions raised by the Parliament. The Council sends reports to the Parliament and three times every year Parliament provides a review of the Council's activities.

In terms of future developments in the European Community it is likely that the **9–040** Parliament will perform an increasingly important role. The European Parliament holds a number of characteristics which make its existence difficult to reconcile with the traditional idea of a democratically elected and accountable United Kingdom Parliament. There is no equivalent ministerial responsibility or full legislative power. The European Parliament is distinctive. For example, it can refer matters to the Court of Justice if the Council or the Commission infringe Community rules. Article 232 (ex. 175) provides the Parliament and other institutions with the power to bring actions to establish if there is an infringement of a Treaty obligation. Article 193 (ex. 138c) provides the Parliament with the power to set up a Committee of inquiry to review or investigate any matter of maladministration in the implementation of community law. The establishment of a European Ombudsman appointed by the Parliament allows it to receive reports and inquire into maladministration. Article 192 (ex. 138b) provides Parliament with a power to request the Commission to make appropriate proposals that are necessary for the implementation of Treaty obligations. Together with Article 251 (ex. 189b) the Parliament has the right of co-decision with the Council on certain limited and defined areas—in essence a veto power that may apply to areas such as health, and consumer affairs. Parliament may also ask questions and the Commission is required to reply. Parliament is consulted on an advisory basis at the pre-legislative stage to ensure that deliberations are complete.

The European Court

The Court of Justice, commonly called the European Court, ensures that the Treaty **9–041** and its obligations are interpreted.[17] There are 15 judges appointed with the agreement of the Member States. The number of judges may be expanded to meet the growth in

---

[17] *Reflections on the Future Development of the Community Judicial System, by the Court of First Instance of the European Community* (1991) 16 Vol.3 *European Law Review* 175–189.

the number of Member States. A wide range of matters comes within its remit ranging from social, economic, constitutional and administrative law. The jurisprudence of the court is influenced by the civil law tradition. Its workload has increased. Slynn notes[18]:

> "Not far short of 400 new cases have been arriving at the Court each year, though in 1990/91 the number was down to 355. Allowing for 200 judgments and, on average, 130 withdrawals or summary dismissals, the backlog can only increase, and by September 1991, the 'stock' of cases before the Court and the Court of First Instance amounted to 782, of which 614 were before the Court."

9–042   Current delays can amount to over 24 months, commensurate with the scope and range of the court's activities which are broader and more linked to the economic, political and social issues than would be commonly found in English judicial decisions. The Treaty of Nice provides that Article 221 will be amended so that the number of judges in the court will reflect expansion in the number of Member States so that there will be one judge for each Member State.

9–043   Article 230 (ex. 173) EC provides that the European Court of Justice may review all measures adopted by the institutions and consider their intended consequences and effect. Standing is given to Member States, the Council and the Commission and, since the Treaty of Amsterdam, a limited standing has been given to the Court of Auditors.

9–044   The 1986 Single European Act introduced a new Court of First Instance which may be called the Tribunal (its full title is Tribunal de Premiere Instance). The aim was to share some of the workload of the European Court. In the case of the Court of First Instance, each Member State provides a judge. The Court of First Instance operates principally in chambers of three or five judges and its first proceedings began on September 1, 1989. The Treaty of Nice permits an expansion in the number of judges to at least one judge per Member State. One innovation is that judicial panels might hear cases at first instance with a right of appeal on law or law and fact to the Court of First Instance. Also, the Court of First Instance jurisdiction is broadened considerably by including the interpretation of the Treaty and the creation of judicial panels to hear cases. However, it retains exclusive jurisdiction over direct action between the Member State and the organs of the Community.

The Jurisprudence of the European Court

9–045   The jurisprudence of the European Court has significant effects on the United Kingdom's constitutional and administrative law and legal system. The jurisdiction of the European Court is provided under Article 234 (ex. 177), which permits the European Court to give preliminary rulings on Community law. A preliminary ruling may be requested by the courts of the Member States. For example at the level of the magistrates' court it is possible for a direct approach to be made to the European Court under Article 177. The European Court is competent to interpret the Treaty, to consider the validity and interpretation of acts of the various Community institutions, noted above, and to consider the constitution of any of the bodies set up by the Council of the Community.

[18] Gordon Slynn, *Introducing a European Legal Order* (Hamlyn Lecture, 1992), pp.136–137.

Guidelines were provided for the United Kingdom's courts in *Bulmer v Bollinger*,[19] **9–046**
and although criticised, they provide the general approach adopted by the United
Kingdom's courts. In deciding whether to refer to the European court, Lord Denning
explained that: (i) the decision must be necessary; (ii) the decision must be conclusive
of the case, and if necessary; (iii) the court has to exercise its discretion to determine
all the circumstances and consideration given to matters such as the delay involved,
difficulty of the issues, the expense involved and the burden on the court. The main
area of dispute arising from Lord Denning's three categories was the issue of
"conclusive". On a narrow interpretation this might inhibit an English judge from
referring a matter if there was doubt as to the suitability of the European Court
resolving the dispute before it with sufficient clarity. On a broad interpretation, as
Community law is part of domestic law it might be considered that any domestic court
of the Member State of the European Community is entitled to receive the opinion of
the European Court. Lord Denning explained that the facts should first be established
by the English courts before a reference might be made. He added that if the law was
clear then it was unnecessary to refer the matter to the European Court. This point is
also open to question, as some argue that it is perfectly acceptable to receive an
interpretation of a clear point of law just as it is for an unclear one. Article 234 (ex.
177) permits a preliminary reference made by "any court or tribunal."

Another possibility covered in the Article 177 procedure, is where there can never **9–047**
be an appeal. This applies in the case of the House of Lords, because it is the final
appellate court within the United Kingdom where the House of Lords is bound to
refer such a question to the Court. But the procedure applies to decisions where there
are no further domestic remedies available. There is therefore an important role given
to the House of Lords. In *Chiron Corp v Murex Diagnostics Ltd*,[20] it is regarded as the
court against which there is no judicial remedy. Reference to the European Court will
be made where the question is required for the decision in the case. If there is already
case law on the matter or where the Court of Justice has already resolved the issue
then no reference is required.

In addition to preliminary rulings it is possible for references to be made directly by **9–048**
the House of Lords. In such cases the requirements are that the principles in dispute,
or raising matters of Community law, should be set out in the reference. This
invariably involves the formulation of specific questions to be taken before the
European Court.

In England the first reference arising for the House of Lords was a case in 1981, *R. v* **9–049**
Henn[21] which raised the question of whether importing obscene or indecent articles,
which was a criminal offence in the United Kingdom, amounted to a restriction of
imports within Article 30 and whether this was justifiable under Article 30. The
European Court accepted the judgment in terms of Article 36 relating to "public
morality, public policy or public security".

References to the European Court may be made by the Employment Appeal **9–050**
Tribunal, the High Court and by the magistrates' court. Criminal law matters often

---

[19] [1974] Ch. 401. Also see *R. v Henn* [1981] A.C. 580 and *R. v Plymouth Justice Ex p. Rogers* [1982] Q.B. 863.
See McEldowney, "Pigs Marketing Board for Northern Ireland v Redmond" [1980] *Northern Ireland Legal
Quarterly* 165–172, Case 83/78: [1978] E.C.R. 2347; [1979] 1 C.M.L.R. 177. See [1997] E.C. 1 ECJ.
[20] [1995] All E.R. (EC) 88.
[21] [1980] A.C. 850.

raise issues of European Community law. Increasingly the interpretation of Community law forms part of the law of the United Kingdom. Courts and tribunals are adopting a positive approach towards the interpretation of Community law and there is general satisfaction that the United Kingdom courts are showing such a positive view.[22]

9–051   In Northern Ireland the first reference made by the Magistrates' Court concerned the prosecution of Redmond, a pig dealer, under the Northern Ireland Movement of Pigs Regulations 1972, enforced by the Pigs Marketing Board, which was set up under a scheme requiring local pig producers to sell to the Board, bacon produced by pigs in Northern Ireland.[23]

9–052   The European Court determined that the prosecution was inconsistent with Community law and the Board's powers unlawfully interfered with the Community market in pigmeat. A similar fate awaited other marketing boards, but the reference illustrated the flexibility of the European Court's procedures. In marked contrast to the formality of English procedure, the European Court greatly assisted the magistrates in the formulation of the issues involving Community law raised in the case. This raises the question of how Community law takes effect in the United Kingdom. The Community legal order consists of Regulations, Articles, Directives and Decisions and how each takes effect in the United Kingdom requires explanation.

9–053   In *Bulmer v Bollinger*[24] the United Kingdom's courts have acknowledged, as Lord Denning explained, that "rights or obligations created by the Treaty are to be given legal effect". More recently, Lord Bridge in *Factortame*[25] declared:

> "It has always been clear that it was the duty of a United Kingdom Court, when delivering final judgment, to override any rule of national law found to be in conflict with any directly enforceable rule of Community law."

Sources of Community Law

9–054   As explained above the European Court provides an important source of Community law. This raises the question of the concept of "direct effect" and its meaning as to the "rights or obligations" which are enforceable rights by individuals or Member States within the Community. The answer may depend on the interpretation of "direct effect". Ambiguously worded, the term may be found in international law as well as Community law. In international law the term refers to the concept of national courts applying at the suit of individuals rights and obligations.

9–055   In addition to the sources of Community law provided by the European Court's jurisprudence there are rules, regulations and laws arising under the various Treaties. Regulations under Article 249 (ex. 189), as amended by the Treaty on European Union are directly applicable but little further guidance is provided other than the fact that they bind Member States in their entirety without further implementation. Occasionally regulations may be drafted in a conditional or provisional mode,

---

[22] *Sixth Annual Report to the European Parliament on Commission Monitoring of the Application of Community Law* COM (89) 411 final, Appendix pp.31–34.
[23] See McEldowney, "Pigs Marketing Board for Northern Ireland v Redmond [1980] *Northern Ireland Legal Quarterly* 165–172, Case 83/78: [1978] E.C.R. 2347; [1979] 1 C.M.L.R. 177. See [1997] E.C. 1 ECJ.
[24] [1974] Ch. 401.
[25] *Factortame (No.1)* [1990] 2 A.C. 85, *Factortame (No.2)* [1991] A.C. 603, 658–9. See Case 26/62 *Van Gend en Loos v Nederlandse Administratie der Belastingen*: [1963] E.C.R. 1, C.M.L.R. 105.

requiring further action for their implementation, but generally they apply with immediate effect. This means that they may create individual rights enforceable before national courts.

Articles of the Treaty are said to have internal effect in the Member States of the Community. However, doubts exist as to when all Articles of the Treaty would be so treated. Over time the European Court has held many of the Articles of the Treaty to be directly applicable. Directives are described under Article 249 (ex. 189) as being "directly applicable". It was once thought that only regulations might have "direct effect" as distinct from "direct applicability". The latter term was interpreted to mean that direct effect was not given. However, in a number of Decisions[26] the European Court took the view that some Directives might have "direct effect".   **9–056**

While not all Directives might be said to have "direct effect", in the *Marshall Case*[27] it was decided that Directives might be relied upon by individuals within Member States against any part of the "state." The question of direct effect depends on the subject matter and whether the wording is "unconditional and sufficiently precise". Not every national court has accepted the view that Directives may have direct effect. Not all Directives before the courts may fall into the category of direct application because of a further ambiguity caused by the concept of the "state". This term is not precisely defined but may be generally used to mean a public body or agency of the State. It is difficult to put this characteristic of such bodies into categories which give rise to general principles of universal application.   **9–057**

A broad interpretation was adopted by the House of Lords in *Foster v British Gas*[28] as to a body "which has been made responsible pursuant to a measure adopted by the State for providing a public service under the control of the state". Such a body might be granted "special powers" which differentiate it from any individual. On such an interpretation the State could be all-embracing as to include any entity which had legal powers over individuals and this might cover a Company Act company. On such an interpretation, noticeably broader than in other areas of law, the House of Lords held that the then British Gas Corporation under the Gas Act 1972, then a nationalised industry, fell within the definition.   **9–058**

A further possibility over direct effect has been mooted by the European Court which is to allow a Directive to have an application in domestic law indirectly, as a means to interpret national law as part of Community law.[29] The possibilities of interpretation make this area of law subject to intense discussion and debate. Particularly so, since many of the Community's most significant social and economic policies are enacted into legislative form through the means of Directives.   **9–059**

---

[26] Case 9/70, *Grad v Finanzamt Traunstein* [1970] E.C.R. 825; [1971] C.M.L.R. 1. *Van Duyn v Home Office* [1974] E.C.R. 1337. Also see Case 222/84 *Johnston v The Chief Constable of the Royal Ulster Constabulary* [1986] E.C.R. 1651; [1986] 3 C.M.L.R. 240.
[27] Case 152/84 *Marshall v Southampton and South West Hampshire AHA (Teaching)* [1986] E.C.R. II–723, 748; [1986] 1 C.M.L.R. 688; [1986] 2 All E.R. 584.
[28] [1990] 3 All E.R. 897, 922.
[29] Known as the Von Colson principle (Case 14/83). See Grainne de Burca, "Giving effect to European Community Directives" 1992 *Modern Law Review* 215 and Steiner "Coming to terms with EEC Directives" (1990) 106 *Law Quarterly Review* 144.

9–060   An important dimension arises from the *Francovich*[30] principles where a failure by the Member State to implement Community law or comply with their obligations under Community law might provide the individual citizen with a remedy in damages. This might include damages for example for failure to implement a Directive.

9–061   The United Kingdom courts face a formidable challenge in developing their interpretative skills to overcome the difficulties mentioned above. Not least is the difficulty that even if a Directive is held to be directly applicable, thereby conferring on an individual various rights against the State, there is not always an available remedy in domestic law open to the court. This leaves a considerable gap in the jurisprudence of the ECJ in the development of the principle that there is a strong obligation on Member States to enforce Directives through domestic courts.[31]

9–062   Finally there are decisions of the Community which are binding under Article 249 (ex. 189). This is largely unproblematic as the decision is addressed to a specific issue or problem and may be made to an individual or Member State. The assumption is made that because the decision is made to address an individual or Member State it should be integrated and enforced as a binding rule. Lord Denning's reference in *Bulmer v Bollinger* to "rights or obligations" under Community law raises a different expectation than simply the interpretation and application of Regulations, Decisions or Directives. Perhaps the European Court in interpreting the Treaty and its obligations might create its own jurisprudence of fundamental rights to supplement national courts and constitutions?

9–063   In the early years of the Community, the European Court rejected the idea that fundamental rights might be protected directly by the Court's interpretation of Community law. Instead reliance was placed on national courts and constitutions developing their own jurisprudence of fundamental rights. However, in subsequent years and more recently is the question of the activities of the European Court in interpreting and discussing Community law[32] requiring national courts to accept the status of Community law. The question of compatibility between the law of the Member State and Community law has been reviewed in a protracted series of cases arising from the *Factortame* litigation.[33]

9–064   The facts of *Factortame* are as follows. In 1988 the Divisional Court requested a preliminary ruling under Article 177 from the European Court to determine the compatibility of the Merchant Shipping Act 1988 and the provisions of the Community Treaty. The 1988 Act and subsequent regulations required shipping vessels previously registered under a nineteenth-century statute to re-register with new conditions to prevent Spanish fishing vessels entering the register and thereby gaining access to British fishing areas which are under Community quota regulation. Registration was thereby conditional on a nationality requirement. Spanish fishing vessel owners sought

---

[30] See Case C–6/90, C–9/90, *Francovich v Italian Republic* [1991] E.C.R. I–5357; [1993] 2 C.M.L.R. 66; N. Gravells, "Disapplying an Act of Parliament pending a Preliminary Ruling: Constitutional Enormity or Community Law Right?" [1989] P.L. 568; Barav (1989) 26 C.M.L. Rev. 369; Churchill (1989) 14 *European Law Rev.* 470.

[31] N. O'Loan, "U.K. Implementation of the Services Directive 92/50" (1994) 3 *Public Procurement Law Review* 60; the Public Service Contracts Regulations 1993 (SI 1993/3228).

[32] UK's Sunday Trading laws—trading on Sunday. See Case 145/88, *Torfaen BC v B&Q plc* [1990] 1 All E.R. 129; [1989] E.C.R. 3851; [1990] 1 C.M.L.R. 337. On disablement benefits under the UK's Social Security Act 1975 see *Thomas v Adjudication Officer* [1991] 2 Q.B. 164.

[33] See: *R. v Employment Secretary, Ex p. EOC* [1995] 1 A.C. 1.

to challenge the legality of the 1988 Act in terms of the Community law and sought an interim injunction by way of judicial review.

A secondary issue in the *Factortame*[34] case arose in connection with the grant of interim relief. The Court of Appeal set aside an interim injunction granted by the Divisional Court pending the outcome of the European Court. The House of Lords upheld the Court of Appeal's decision, because it reasoned that English courts could not grant an interim injunction against the Crown. However, this question of whether Community law obliged national courts to grant interim protection of Community rights was also referred to the European Court. Pending the outcome of the decision, the European Court gave interim relief and the United Kingdom government introduced an Order in Council amending the relevant s.14 of the 1988 Act. **9–065**

The ruling of the European Court examined two issues: first, the issue of sovereignty, the validity of a United Kingdom statute and subordinate legislation as against Community law; second, the issue of interim relief, in the form of injunctions against the Crown. **9–066**

On the first question of sovereignty, the European Court reasoned that Community law prevailed over United Kingdom law even if the result meant abrogation of the 1988 Act. Because of the extent to which the 1988 Act offended against Community law, it was inapplicable and ineffective. This outcome asserts the right of the European Court to disapply national legislation. On the second question, on the availability of interim relief against the Crown, it would appear that interim relief must be available to give full effect to Community law. It appears that injunctions and interim injunctions are available against the Crown when an issue of Community law arises.[35] **9–067**

The *Factortame* decision supports those who view the European Communities as creating a new era for the jurisprudence of the United Kingdom This much is acknowledged by the House of Lords and it appears not to be confined to cases involving the application of Community law. In the *GCHQ* case, Lord Diplock accepted the concept of proportionality as part of English Administrative Law, which suggests[36] borrowing from the French system of administrative law. More recently Lord Goff[37] discussed the concept of Leichtfertigkeit, or recklessness, in German law in his discussion of the English law on recklessness. The development of human rights jurisprudence and the influence of the European Union is set to continue to find relevance in the United Kingdom's domestic law and institutions. **9–068**

There are general principles of Community law to be found under Article 220 (ex. 164) as a means of interpretation and since the Treaty on European Union this includes for example human rights under Article 6[F]. **9–069**

---

[34] See Case C–6/90, C–9/90, *Francovich v Italian Republic* [1991] E.C.R. I–5357; [1993] 2 C.M.L.R. 66; N. Gravells, "Disapplying an Act of Parliament pending a Preliminary Ruling: Constitutional Enormity or Community Law Right?" [1989] P.L. 568; Barav (1989) 26 C.M.L. Rev. 369; Churchill, (1989) 14 E.L. Rev. 470.

[35] See *M v Home Office* [1992] Q.B. 270; [1993] 3 W.L.R. 433. The House of Lords held that the courts had jurisdiction to issue injunctions against officers of the Crown.

[36] [1985] A.C. 374. See Sophie Boyron, "Proportionality in English Administrative Law: A Faulty Translation?" (1992) 12 *Oxford Journal of Legal Studies* 237–264.

[37] *R. v Reid* [1992] 3 All E.R. 673 at 689.

The Court of Auditors

9-070   The Court of Auditors,[38] established under the 1975 Treaty amending Certain Financial Provisions of the Treaties became, under Article 4 of the Maastricht Treaty, an institution of the Community. The Court is based in Luxembourg and it has important functions for ensuring that the finances of the Community are properly accounted for. Each Member State is entitled to one member of the Court appointed by a unanimous vote of the Council of Ministers and in consultation with the European Parliament. Members of the Court must act in a non-partisan way. There are approximately 412 permanent members and 91 temporary posts.

9-071   The activities of the Court centre around the task of examining the accounts of all revenue and expenditure of the various Community bodies and of the finances of the Community. This covers the general budget of the European Union. The Court also monitors the work of DGXX, the Directorate that is concerned with Financial Control within the Community. Audit arrangements include both internal and external audits. There is also an important initiative over the past five years to combat fraud within the Community. The Court must liaise with the audit arrangements and procedures in Member States. Once Community funds are transferred to Member States the scrutiny of the Community money falls under the budget arrangements of the Member States. This means that 15 separate budget systems have to be considered by DGXX and also by the Court.

9-072   Various strategies for the improvement of the accountability of the Community budget in Member States may be considered such as the Commission's Anti-Fraud Strategy and Work Programme. There is a Unit for the Co-ordination of Fraud Prevention with extensive legal powers. There are further additional measures to consider in order to achieve sound financial management of the Community that emerge from the United Kingdom budgetary system. Many of the main suggestions are usefully summarised in a Treasury Report.[39] The main principles that may be considered that emerge from an analysis of the report are as follows:

- use of targeting according to risk of fraud;

- setting precise goals and targets in the anti-fraud action programme of the Commission;

- enhanced co-ordination of anti-fraud measures;

- fraud-proofing new legislative proposals;

- periodic review of all budgetary operations;

- all Community expenditure should be subject to principles of sound public finance;

- Prior appraisal should precede the commitment of Community money in order to assess whether economic benefits are in keeping with the resources deployed.

[38] D. O'Keefe, "The Court of Auditors" in *Institutional Dynamics of European Integration* (D. Curtin and T. Heukels ed., Kluwer, London, 1994).
[39] HM Treasury, *European Community Finances*, Cm.2824 (April 1995), p.14, para.50.

Emphasis is placed on budgetary controls and discipline. Also since 1996, there are **9–073** frequent use of spot checks to prevent and deter fraud.[40]

Following on from this analysis and in line with the problems of corruption found in **9–074** the operation of the Commission after a report on mismanagement and sleaze, which led to the resignation of the Commission in 1999, there are more robust arrangements to scrutinise expenditure. This led to the creation of a European Anti-fraud Office[41] with extensive investigative powers. The aim is to provide extensive preventative arrangements against fraud as well as creating a culture where fraud is unacceptable.

EUROPEANISATION AND THE CREATION OF A EUROPEAN PUBLIC LAW

The constitutional and political complications of the Treaty on European Union[42] may **9–075** cause the United Kingdom to consider once more the question of its own parliamentary sovereignty. While it is doubtful if the Treaty fundamentally alters the United Kingdom's constitutional relationship with the Community since this was established in the Single European Act, it is less clear what effects the Treaty may have on political decision-making.[43]

In evidence to the House of Commons Select Committee on Foreign Affairs it was **9–076** argued that greater political power may be transferred from the Government in the United Kingdom to the Community. This may be due to economic and social factors as much as to the Treaty. However, it is likely to rekindle a debate about the nature of political power in the United Kingdom. In evidence to the Commons Foreign Affairs Committee, Paul Taylor explained that:

> "For political reasons, however, members of the executive who are opposed to the development of closer relations with the Community would like it to be believed that the legislation is equally a victim—to conjure up a common enemy is to strengthen an alliance."

Political and constitutional issues are easily intertwined but it is clear that national **9–077** governments of Member States in the Council of Ministers may veto proposed legislation of which they disapprove. Member States may continue to pursue their own policies within the Community and subsidiarity permits regional differences to be retained.[44]

Sovereignty, whether political or legal, is not the only issue raised by the proposals **9–078** for a European Union. Harlow[45] has raised the question of how the Community as a

---

[40] Regulation 2185/96.
[41] Commission Decision 1999/352. Also see OJ 1999 L136 and Council Decision 1999/394, OJ 1999, L149.
[42] Second Report of the Foreign Affairs Select Committee: Europe after Maastricht, Minutes of Evidence, Vol.II (1991/92 HC 223–ii).
[43] T. Koopmans, "European Public Law: Reality and Prospect" [1991] P.L. 53–63.
[44] C. Harlow, "A Community of Interests? Making the Most of European Law" (1992) 55 M.L.R. 331–350. Justin Greeenwood, *Representing Interests in the European Union* (Macmillan, 1997).
[45] *ibid.*, p.344.

common market has created its own internal political system of "pressure group politics and its attendant professions of lobbyist and public relations expert". Her view is that the Community's origins as a transnational organisation has produced "the 'wheeler/dealer' style of Brussels politics" borrowed from the world of diplomacy and the influence of American-style business with its forms of professional lobbyists and interest group politics. There is a need for further research on the question of how decision-making is transparent within the European Union.

9–079   This gives rise to questions about how far "open" government and, among decision-makers, accountability may be found within the Community? The answers may not easily be found in any institutional changes nor in the policy formulations involved in European Union. Harlow argues that the United Kingdom's parliamentary system may provide a valuable contribution to how a more open and democratic community may evolve.

THE EUROPEAN CONVENTION ON HUMAN RIGHTS AND FUNDAMENTAL FREEDOMS AND COMMUNITY LAW

9–080   Human rights provide an example of the importance of wider European influences and are not confined simply to membership of the Community. In 1949 European States, including the 15 currently existing members of the Community, founded an international organisation known as the Council of Europe. This was an attempt to form a "unified" Europe and address the problem of human rights. The outcome was a treaty known as the European Convention on Human Rights (ECHR). Further, it was hoped that such an organisation might act as a "watchdog" against human rights atrocities and, through Community action, as a deterrent preventing further atrocities from taking place. This primary function of the Council of Europe has gone into abeyance, leaving the ECHR as a means to raise legal issues in the Member States of the co-signatories. Out of the 25 Member States, 23 formed an agreement and put into force, in 1952, the ECHR. The main objectives of the Convention are to secure civil and political rights. Other social rights are protected under a separate arrangement known as the European Social Charter signed in 1961. A number of important decisions made by the European Court of Human Rights under the ECHR concern Northern Ireland[46] and the question of interrogation techniques and methods. The Court held that such techniques did not constitute a "practice of ill-treatment", but held that certain techniques disclosed "torture" and other "inhuman treatment".

9–081   Many of the techniques continued to be used after the judgment of the Court, nevertheless new procedures were introduced for the interrogation of suspects. Public opinion was greatly influenced by the significance of the findings.

9–082   The general expectation is that the existence of the ECHR helps to establish a "new legal order" as part of the desire to deal with domestic problems on a European rather than a State basis. However, there are problems in integrating the ECHR with the European Union.

9–083   Almost as a parallel development to the ECHR, the Treaty of Maastricht and, following on from that, the Treaty of Amsterdam have created a new Article 6(2) of

---

[46] *Ireland v UK* European Court H.R. Series A, Vol.25, January 18, 1978, 2 E.H.R.R. 25.

the Social Chapter of the original Treaty of Rome, to provide employment rights and social security rights. The incoming Labour government adopted the Social Charter as part of the substantive law of the United Kingdom by the Treaty of Amsterdam in 1997. The Amsterdam Treaty further extended the jurisidiction of the Court of Justice of the European Union to include justice and home affairs. A whole raft of issues covering social, environmental and consumer protection are integrated into Community policy-making covering aspects of discrimination including sex, racial or ethnic origin. In December 2000 there is a new EU Charter of Fundamental Rights including social rights and civil and political rights. Building on these developments, there is an EC Council Directive implementing the Principle of Equal Treatment between Persons Irrespective of Racial or Ethnic Origins.[47] This considerably broadens the definition of indirect discrimination under s.2 of the Race Relations Act 1976. Covered by the Directive are any practices that place anyone from one racial or ethnic origin at a disadvantage to others. Excluded from the remit of the Directive are immigration or residential criteria for employment or the rights of third-party nationals and stateless persons. There is an EU Framework Directive on Discrimination[48] for protection from discrimination against religion, disability, age or sexual orientation. The full implications are being considered by Member States.

At the same time there are developments towards a Constitution for Europe   **9–084** including a new Charter of Rights which is pending consideration of its status at the Intergovernmental Conference in 2004. The development of the Convention and the jurisprudence of the European Court of Human Rights throughout many of the Member States has increased awareness of human rights. In the past the European Union has been slightly ambivalent about how far it should pursue a rights focus as part of the obligations of Member States. The drawing up of a new Charter is a promising development but it comes at a time when the work of the European Court of Human Rights is at an all time high with an enlargement of its membership and an increase in its workload. The obvious concern is that the European Union may not develop in parallel but as a rival. This might seem incongruous, but the creation of rights within the European Union Treaties will inevitably lead to a need for some form of synergy of ideas and processes with the ECHR. Blackburn proposes that the solution is for the European Union to accede to the Convention as a contracting party.[49]

> "The effect of EU accession to the ECHR would be that all decisions, laws, and actions by Community and Union bodies would become subject to review by the European Court of Human Rights for their compatibility with the ECHR."

Inevitably this idea would mean that the European Court of Justice and its decisions   **9–085** would become subordinate to the European Court of Human Rights. The hierarchical nature of the relationship might cause disquiet and resistance. The way forward might be through some form of assimilation of rights. For example the Human Rights Act 1998 provides courts in the United Kingdom with the opportunity to interpret the

---

[47] Directive 2000/43 [2000] OJ L180/22.
[48] Council Directive 2000/78 EC (November 27, 2000).
[49] *Fundamental Rights in Europe* (R. Blackburn, and Jorg Polakiewicz ed., Oxford University Press, Oxford, 2001), pp.96–97.

Convention. S.3 of the 1998 Act provides that the courts are obliged to interpret s.2 of the European Communities Act in a way that is compatible with Convention rights. This does not preclude the European Union expanding or developing rights beyond the minimum standards set by the Convention. One concern is that the delivery of rights protection will become over complex and this may prove counterproductive. Simplification of technical legal rules is required as a means of delivering rights to all citizens.

CONCLUSIONS AND SUMMARY

9–086 The question arises as to the possible development of a European public law. European Community influences on the United Kingdom's domestic legal system have already been noted. A growing jurisprudence exists in the European Court of Justice and in the United Kingdom's adaptation of Community law. Principles of French or German law may be found, explained and examined in English courts' decisions at the highest levels. Influences such as the European Convention on Human Rights are also relevant and important. Koopmans[50] has written that common influences may be detectable even amid differences between Member States. Citizens are more litigious[51] and perhaps more likely to challenge authority in some European countries than in others. While different Member States may adopt Directives of the Community in distinct ways, the European Court may receive an overview of the activities of all the Member States. His conclusion is that despite differences[52]:

> "We are bound to come to one European system. The integration process cannot be discontinued."

9–087 The differences and diversity of the Member States of the European Union may remain but are there signs that there is newly emerging a common law of Europe?

9–088   The answer to this question may well depend on the development of future policies and objectives within the European Union. Expansion of the Union may strain existing institutions to cope with new challenges and expectations. This may weaken the Community institutions and cast doubt on their effectiveness.

FURTHER READING

P. Alston *et al.*, *The EU and Human Rights* (Oxford University Press, Oxford, 1999).

Fundamental Rights in Europe (R. Blackburn and J. Polakiewicz, ed., Oxford University Press, Oxford, 2001).

D. Feldman, *Civil Liberties and Human Rights in England and Wales* (Oxford University Press, Oxford, 2002).

[50] T. Koopmans, "European Public Law: Reality and Prospect" [1991] P.L. 53–63.
[51] Case 222/84, *Johnston v Chief Constable of the RUC* [1986] E.C.R. V–1651; [1986] 3 C.M.L.R. 240.
[52] Koopmans, *op.cit.*, p.63.

J. Gordley and Von Meheren, *The Civil Law System: An Introduction to the Comparative Study of Law* (2nd ed., University Press, Boston, 1977).

K.P.E. Lasok, *Law and Institutions of the European Union* (7th ed., Butterworths, London, 2001).

The Europeanisation of Law (F. Snyder ed., Hart Publishing, Oxford, 2000).
Josephine Steiner, *Textbook on EEC Law* (7th ed., Blackstone, London, 2000).
S. Weatherill and P. Beaumont, *EU Law* (Penguin, London, 1999).

Part III

GOVERNMENT, REGULATION AND ACCOUNTABILITY

The preceding chapters in Parts I and II of the textbook have been primarily **III–001** concerned with providing an introductory framework of the constitutional and administrative law of the United Kingdom, including the ideas and influences which have shaped its development. Part III of the textbook comprises an examination in more detail of some of the increasingly specialist areas of public law in the United Kingdom. Chapters 10-12 are intended to explain, respectively, how present day government operates within the parliamentary system of accountability, how the civil service is managed and how public finance is scrutinised. Chapter 13 comprises an analysis of local government and its relationship with central government. Chapter 14 outlines some of the new regulatory arrangements after privatisation of the major utilities.

Chapter 10

GOVERNMENT AND ACCOUNTABILITY

INTRODUCTION

In previous chapters the roles of government and Parliament have been discussed in **10–001** outline. In this chapter it is intended to explain how in theory and in practice government may be made accountable. Accountability takes many forms. A wide variety of techniques and institutions are involved in the scrutiny of government, including the work of parliamentary select committees and courts. The system of government is essentially one of party government and the political process may exert influences on the style of government and public affairs. Also relevant in how government may be held to account for its actions, is the work of the various audit bodies such as the National Audit Office and, in the case of local government, the Audit Commission. Reference to their role may be found in Chapters 12 and 13 respectively.

How government may formulate its policies and how it carries out the tasks of **10–002** government may place strain on existing constitutional arrangements. In recent years an increasing trend towards centralisation of government powers has coincided with a period of government with a large working parliamentary majority. The size of the government's parliamentary majority may affect the ability of Parliament to scrutinise effectively the Executive. In fact governments with a large parliamentary majority may raise questions about the effectiveness of constitutional arrangements to hold government to account.

ACCOUNTABILITY DEFINED

To be accountable[1] is to give reasons and explanations for actions or decisions taken. **10–003** The characteristic of medieval accountability was the direct responsibility of the individual servant to the King.[2] The idea of accountability may be traced back to the earliest form of organised government. Normanton has pointed out how accountability has[3] "an historical connection between administrative secrecy and the hierarchical

[1] See 1st Report of the Public Service Select Committee, *Ministerial Accountability and Responsibility*, (1996–97 H.C. 234).
[2] E. Normanton, *The Accountability and Audit of Governments* (1966), p.2.
[3] *ibid.*, p.4.

state". Such a connection may arise where the State is a hierarchy and all account-ability is to the head. Accountability as a means of authorisation control may promote secrecy[4]:

> "The ruler must learn what his servants have been doing, so that he can promote or punish; private persons need know nothing of the secrets and errors of administration, and within unitary states they are rarely allowed to do so. Government is an authoritarian mystery."

10–004 The link between secrecy and accountability has not entirely ended with medieval government. Present day government may be described as responsible government, but this does not always give rise to open or adequate accountability. One explanation is that accountability may be both internal and external. Internal accountability relates to internal guidance within government departments based on rules of conduct that are not statutory, and some may not be widely published. A good example is the use of Treasury Solicitor's Guidance or Treasury Memorandum as a means of checking on government expenditure and accounts. Internal accountability may prove effective, but it is often hidden from external scrutiny and to some extent this may perpetuate secrecy as the nature of internal review involves confidential and sensitive information.[5]

10–005 External accountability relates to the idea that Ministers are "responsible" or "answerable" to Parliament. This covers such matters as appearing before select committees or answering parliamentary questions. Information provided through parliamentary debate and media coverage contributes to the functions of holding Ministers to account and also controlling government. Advice tendered to civil servants as to their duties and responsibilities in attending before select committees, sets out lines of responsibility between civil servants and Ministers. However such advice, if invoked, might be considered restrictive of more open government.

10–006 Accountability also involves legal redress. The appeal to courts or tribunals or the establishment of an inquiry with investigative powers with the right to examine evidence and establish facts provides an external assessment of government actions. As part of the fact-finding process a court, tribunal or inquiry may seek to establish reasons or justifications for action taken. The giving of reasons becomes an important element for establishing the grounds for decision-making. This is aimed at remedying citizens' grievances but it also assists in improving the quality of administration. Well reasoned and considered decisions with recourse to advice and consultation are the hallmark of good government. Recent judicial decisions appear to be in sympathy with those aims. In *Rowling v Takaro Properties Ltd*[6] the Privy Council considered how Ministers may be liable under a duty of care, in an action for negligence arising out of their public duties as Ministers. Considering whether such a duty may be imposed was a question of "an intensely pragmatic character". In *Lonhro v. Tebbit*[7] the Court of Appeal accepted this point and affirmed the role of the court to consider the issue. In *M v. Home Office*[8] the House of Lords held that the contempt jurisdiction of the courts extended to Ministers of the Crown.

---

[4] *ibid.*
[5] See T. Daintith and A. Page, *The Executive in the Constitution* Oxford University Press, Oxford, 1999).
[6] [1988] 1 All E.R. 163 at 172.
[7] [1992] 4 All E.R. 280.
[8] *M v Home Office* [1992] Q.B. 270; [1992] 4 All E.R. 97, [1994] 1 A.C. 377.

There are also various forms of accountability involved in achieving better admin-   **10–007**
istration. In addition to the courts these involve various audits carried out by the
Comptroller and Auditor General and the National Audit Office, or the Audit
Commission in the case of local government. There are various ombudsmen, namely
the Commissioner for Local Administration in the case of local authorities, or the
Parliamentary Commissioner for Administration in the case of central government.
Ombudsmen perform important investigative functions.

Responsible government also implies parliamentary control as Turpin has noted[9]:   **10–008**

> "The notion of 'responsible government' implies both acceptance of responsibility
> for things done and 'responsiveness' to influence, persuasion, and pressure for
> modifications of policy. Activist parliamentarians of our day aim to 'redress the
> balance' of the constitution in favour of Parliament by strengthening both control
> and responsibility of the executive, without making a fine discrimination between
> these concepts."

There are further attempts to clarify different forms of accountability. Sir Robin   **10–009**
Butler, when Head of the Civil Service, made a distinction between "the duty to give
an account" and "the obligation to accept responsibility". This formulation may be
found in the booklet produced as guidance to ministers known as *Questions of
Procedures for Ministers*. This document has no legal status but it sets out current
thinking on such matters. The question arises as to how the distinction made by Sir
Robin Butler works in practice. The answer may be found in considering the findings
of the Scott Inquiry.[10] Clearly Sir Richard Scott accepted the basis of the distinction
but then reaches a number of conclusions that find difficulty in drawing any clear line
between the duty to give an account and the obligation to accept responsibility. If the
findings of the Scott inquiry are closely examined it is apparent that the following
conclusions are reached. Sir Richard Scott considered that the guidelines on arms
sales, known as the Howe Guidelines, were conceived as a statement of policy and that
as a result of revising the guidelines this reflected the actuality that policy had been
changed. Government statements made in 1989 and 1990 about policy on arms exports
"consistently failed to discharge the obligations imposed by the constitutional principle
of Ministerial responsibility".[11]

As outlined in Chapter 4, Sir Richard Scott also found that the Attorney-General   **10–010**
was at fault in not making clear to the court at the trial of the Matrix Churchill
directors that Mr Heseltine, then President of the Board of Trade, was reluctant to
agree signing the certificate claiming public interest immunity.[12] A second criticism was
that the Attorney-General had mistakenly interpreted the law on public interest
certificates when he claimed that Ministers were bound to sign such certificates when
requested to do so. Criticism was also made of a number of Ministers for the reasons
they gave for signing certificates.[13]

---

[9] Turpin, "Ministerial Responsibility: Myth or Reality" in *The Changing Constitution* (J. Jowell and
D. Oliver ed., 1989) (2nd ed., 1994), p.56.
[10] The Scott Report: The Rt Hon. Sir Richard Scott, The Vice-Chancellor, *Return to an Address of the
Honourable House of Commons dated 15th February 1996. Report of the Inquiry into the Export of Defence
Equipment and Dual-use Goods to Iraq and Related Prosecutions* (1996 H.C. 115), (HMSO, London, 1996).
[11] Scott Report, D4.63.
[12] See the Scott Report, G13.69–72.
[13] See the Scott Report, G54, 67, 106, 117, 125.

10–011   It is clear that Sir Richard considers that Ministers were, albeit perhaps mistakenly, engaged in acting in what they took to be the national and therefore the public interest. Ministers gained no direct benefits from the arms sales and had been influenced by the need to operate within the competitive conditions of the market. The information available to Ministers at the time was less than the information which is now available with the benefit of hindsight. As outlined in Chapter 4 above Ministers and civil servants are to be judged by what they then knew and on the basis of what they believed at that time. At the heart of the ministerial defence on arms exports was the claim that Ministers had applied the spirit of the guidelines of necessity. In short, Ministers could rely on their subjective defence. They may now appear to have been mistaken but at the time they acted in good faith and with the public interest in mind.

10–012   While Scott reserves strongest criticism for the failure of Ministers in not publishing the revised guidelines and giving Parliament the opportunity to debate them, but stops short of laying blame having found faults in the conduct of government. Could Scott have come to conclusions on the same evidence that would have forced ministerial resignation?

10–013   It is possible to read the Scott findings and evidence and apply a different standard of blameworthiness than the one applied by Scott. If Ministers knew that they had misled Parliament because the revised guidelines remained concealed from Parliament and the public, were they then not to blame? Whether Ministers had the intention to mislead Parliament or not is irrelevant if the course of conduct they adopted led inexorably to the outcome that Parliament and the public believed that the original Howe Guidelines were still in place. In the language of strict liability, Ministers must be presumed to have sufficient knowledge of the effects of their actions whether they intended those effects or not. On this basis a more blameworthy conclusion might be reached with the requirement that the ultimate sanction of resignation should have been applied. The fact that Scott chose to apply a subjective standard based on what Ministers claimed they believed, left the report devoid of any positive recommendation that resignations of any Minister should follow from the findings in the Report.

10–014   There are thus several important implications to be drawn from Scott's findings on government wrongdoing. Ministers might consider that they have obtained the best "get out" clause possible from ministerial blameworthiness, that their view of events may be accepted as the best judge of establishing the limits of their own responsibility. After all it was a Minister, Mr Alan Clark, who precipitated the discovery that the guidelines had been revised from his frank disclosure at the "arms to Iraq" trial that the guidelines were regularly bypassed. The Scott report carefully finds blame to be attached to the actions of several Ministers but the question of fault-finding and ultimate resignation is left to the political arena. If there are shortcomings on blame it is Parliament that must act not tribunals of inquiry. For the future it would appear that a Freedom of Information Act might be the only effective way to police ministerial integrity in these matters.

10–015   The publication of a new Civil Service Code[14] appears to confirm the existing orthodoxy.[15] One way forward is proposed by Diane Woodhouse[16]:

10–016   "Moving into the twenty-first century, the convention of ministerial responsibility can be defined loosely as requiring, first, information rather than resignation;

[14] *Hansard*, HC, cols.273–293 (February 12, 1997).
[15] *Hansard*, HL (January 9, 1996); Written Answers 21 (January 1, 1996).
[16] Diane Woodhouse "Ministerial Responsibility: Something Old, Something New" [1997] *Public Law* 262.

secondly, ministerial 'accountability' for everything but 'responsibility' for only some things; thirdly, civil servant 'responsibility' for some things but 'accountability' only when this suits ministerial interests.

The added dimension to parliamentary control is political accountability to the electorate. This raises questions about how party politics influence government.   **10–017**

The Scott Report and Parliament

The Scott inquiry raises a serious question about the propriety of an inquiry on behalf of the prime minister of the day about the government of the day rather than an inquiry on behalf of Parliament. It was inevitable that Parliament would divide along party political lines, favouring the government of the day. In the media battle over presenting the findings of the inquiry the main findings of the Scott inquiry appear to have been overlooked. The Scott inquiry had found that Parliament was unable to hold government to account in any satisfactory way. Parliament had been misled, and had consistently failed to detect any alteration in government policy or, through the select committee system, exercise enough scrutiny to deter practices that were inconsistent with the original guidelines. It is clear that Parliament also appeared weak and ineffectual when the Scott report came to be debated. Parliament had failed to set the agenda and felt honour bound to vote on the report, not according to any principles of parliamentary etiquette, but on party political lines. Both opposition and government used the report to claim political advantage. The greatest irony is that, to protect the findings from legal proceedings, the report was given the protection of parliamentary privilege by being published as a report of the House of Commons. Sir Richard's exhaustive inquiry allowed an outsider into the secret world of the civil service and the administration. As an outsider, was he qualified for the task in hand? Professor Martin Loughlin queries Scott's role and expertise[17] and questions whether a single judge sitting independently without any expert assessors appreciated the realities of government decision making and the dilemma of ministerial discretion. Sir Richard is probably the first independent person to have had complete access to the secret world of the civil service and their relations with ministers. There is also a further concern that a judge caught up in the internal politics of party government is liable to become politicised as a result.[18] There is clearly a danger when judges are involved in public inquiries that inevitably lead to party political controversy.   **10–018**

The different style and culture involved in decision making between the judicial, ministerial and administrative may explain why the Scott inquiry showed differences of opinion between government ministers and Sir Richard, reflecting differences in culture and attitude. On Sir Richard's part there is the forensic role of law and lawyers applying prescriptive rules to facts and finding exemptions or exceptions. On the part of ministers there is a culture of secrecy, and an attitude that the role of law is one of enabling and facilitating the conduct of government policy—that unless an action is prohibited by law, it is permissible.   **10–019**

---

[17] Martin Loughlin, *Sword and Scales*, 2000, p.43.
[18] Rodney Brazier, "It *is* a Constitutional Issue: Fitness for Ministerial Office in the 1990s" [1994] *Public Law* 431.

10–020   There are also questions raising constitutional issues surrounding the fact that the Scott inquiry appeared to trespass on the role of Parliament itself and its internal functioning. The concern is that Sir Richard may have inadvertently trespassed into the proceedings of Parliament strictly protected under Article 9 of the Bill of Rights from outside inquiry. As already discussed in Chapter 4, Article 9, is followed in many leading cases and is applied in the Privy Council case of *Prebble v Television New Zealand*.[19] It was held, that in an action which cited proceedings in Parliament, if the action questioned parliamentary proceedings then it would have to be stayed.[20] It is not always exactly clear what constitutes proceedings of Parliament. The concept is an elastic and flexible one. The Register of Members' Interests is not,[21] it is clear that resolutions of the House, the reports from the committees of the House, and subsequent inquiries and reports do come within the category of proceedings.[22] Erskine May,[23] notes that "everything that is said or done" within the precincts of the House forms part of the proceedings in Parliament. Patricia Leopold queries whether the Scott inquiry fell into the category that would exclude him from inquiring into the "proceedings in Parliament". Leopold concludes that it was necessary for Sir Richard to make the inquiries that he undertook otherwise:

> ". . . But if Sir Richard had been debarred from making these criticisms, he would have been unable to do his job. However, the contrast is marked between the freedom he possessed as a one-man tribunal and the restrictions he would have had to observe as a judge in a court hearing. A Nelsonian blind eye has been turned to the problem."[24]

The delicate question of the remit of Sir Richard's inquiry and parliamentary proceedings does not appear to have been addressed in setting up the inquiry. Sir Richard exposed the weakness of government decision-making for which the government escaped the censure of resignation. He also exposed the fundamental weakness of Parliament itself, which Parliament has refrained from properly addressing.[25]

THE PARTY SYSTEM

10–021   Political parties engage in policy formulation and in setting the agenda for the period they hope to occupy government. In the case of the Conservative Party, policies are determined through a variety of advisers through the co-ordination of the Conservative

---

[19] [1995] 1 A.C. 321.
[20] Also see *In Re Parliamentary Privilege Act 1770* [1958] A.C. 331.
[21] *Rost v Edwards* [1990] 2 Q.B. 460.
[22] *Hamilton v Al Fayed* [1999] 3 All E.R. 317, [2001] A.C. 395.
[23] Erskine May, *Parliamentary Practice* (Sir David Limon ed., 22nd ed., Butterworths, London, 1997).
[24] Patricia Leopold, "The Application of the Civil and Criminal Law to Members of Parliament and Parliamentary Proceedings", chap.5 in *Law and Parliament* (G. Drewry and D. Oliver ed., 1998), pp.71–87.
[25] S.13 of the Defamation Act 1996 was passed to allow M.P.s to pursue legal claims for defamation where the conduct of a person in or in relation to proceedings in Parliament is in issue. Immunity may be waived whereby the protection of parliamentary privilege prevented the courts from questioning what was said or done in Parliament.

Research Department. Included are the Institute of Economic Affairs, the Centre for Policy Studies founded in 1974 by Sir Keith Joseph, and the Adam Smith Institute. The annual party conference rarely sets the scene for the formulation of policy, rather it acts as a fulcrum of support for the party leadership. Historically, a key feature of the procedure for the selection of the Leader of the Conservative Party was the role of the influential backbench 1922 Committee whose chairman, not the chairman of the Conservative Party, was responsible for the conduct of all ballots. The timetable for election was within 28 days of the opening of the new session of Parliament. The process of election was by a secret ballot system among all the elected M.P.s holding the party whip and who were members of the Conservative Party. The elected candidate who becomes Leader of the Party and, if the party is the government of the day, the Prime Minister, was the one candidate who:

"[i] both receives an overall majority of the votes of those entitled to vote and (ii) receives 15 per cent. more of the votes of those entitled to vote than any other candidate."

The second ballot was more straightforward with the winner declared on the basis of an outright majority.

Descriptions of the election of Mr Heath in 1965, following the resignation of Sir **10–022** Alex Douglas Home, show how the victory of Mr Heath over other candidates came through careful electioneering, well-managed campaigns and well-focused appeals to backbench loyalties. The leadership election of Mrs Thatcher in 1975 showed similar tactics in winning loyalty from backbench M.P.s. Clearly party leaders who then become Prime Minister have the reality of party support as the basis of exercising power.

On November 19, 1990 the premature resignation of Mrs Thatcher as Prime **10–023** Minister reinforced the power of party politics and underlined the collective force of Cabinet government. Nigel Lawson in his memoirs[26] explains the consequences of the Prime Minister's political unpopularity:

"It was unprecedented: yet there were good reasons why no fewer than 45 per cent of her parliamentary colleagues felt unable to support their leader of the previous fifteen years and more in the first ballot—and among the 55 per cent who did there were many, particularly among her ministerial colleagues, who had allowed their loyalty to get the better of their judgement in the first ballot but would not have done so in the second. Those reasons essentially boiled down to one: the conviction that Margaret had become an electoral liability and that the Conservative Party could win the coming general election only under a new leader."

Nicholas Ridley[27] attributed Mrs Thatcher's failure to gain sufficient votes in the first **10–024** ballot to win the leadership to bad tactics. The first error was the timing of the election to coincide with a period when the Prime Minister had to be out of the country while

[26] Nigel Lawson, *The View From No. 11* (London, 1992), pp.1000–1001.
[27] Nicholas Ridley, *My Style of Government* (1992), pp.241–242.

attending a conference in Paris. Secondly, there was a clear mistake in deciding "to appoint a weak campaign team."

10–025   The team contained five ex-Cabinet Ministers who Ridley believes did "not know large numbers of M.P.s". The team merely canvassed opinion and did not seek to persuade. This example underlines the point already noted of the careful relationship required between the political party and the leadership.

10–026   The election of the leader of the Conservative Party following the defeat of Mr John Major at the General Election on May 1, 1997 highlighted the problems of the lack of input into the constituency party. The election of Mr William Hague took three ballots, although the canvass of constituency support was in favour of Mr Kenneth Clarke. The constituency associations were not part of the ballot which was confined to Conservative M.P.s. Following the defeat of the Conservative Party in the 2001 election, Mr Hague resigned the leadership. The election of a new leader followed new rules drawn up in 1998 and used for the first time, whereby the parliamentary party had a major role replacing the 1922 Committee. Conservative M.P.s determine from a list of those who wish to stand the names of two candidates. In 2001 at the first stage the ballot reduced the field to two candidates from five that stood. The two names are subject to election by the whole party membership on the basis of one member, one vote. In 2001, a final ballot took place leaving Mr Iain Duncan Smith the leader of the party. There was a turnout of 79 per cent of party members and Mr Duncan Smith received 60 per cent of the vote.

10–027   In the case of the Labour Party, unlike the Conservative Party, the formulation of policy is partly carried out through the party conference. Thus, "direction and control" of the work of the party is in theory left to the conference. This body provides a wide canvass for Labour Party support. The trade unions and other affiliated groups comprise about 90 per cent of the conference votes. There is a National Executive Committee elected by the party conference which sets out the main developments and direction of policy. There are various sub-committees which carry out the actual work of devising policy. The manifesto is jointly arrived at by the National Executive Committee and the leadership of the parliamentary party comprising the party leader, deputy leader and shadow Cabinet, if out of government. Advice to the Labour Party comes from a wide variety of sources including the Adam Smith Institute, the Institute for Public Policy Research and various trade union-funded advisers.

10–028   Attempts to shift control from the parliamentary party leadership to the National Executive Committee have been unsuccessful. Given the fact that the Labour Party had been unsuccessful in gaining office in the General Elections from 1978 to 1992, the Labour Parliamentary Party has resisted attempts to have the annual conference impose control over its policy. In fact centralising tendencies within the party have adopted a more directed approach to policy than hitherto. This has resulted in policy initiatives largely controlled by the party leadership. The election victory in May 1997 confirmed strict party discipline as an element in election success. Similarly the victory in 2001 continued the tradition of strong party discipline.

10–029   Nominations for leadership must be supported by 20 per cent of the Commons members of the Parliamentary Labour Party. There are three constituencies entitled to participate in voting. The votes for each nominee in a section are to be calculated as a percentage of the total votes cast in that section and apportioned according to a set percentage. First for the Commons members of the Parliamentary Labour Party, the apportioned vote is 30 per cent. Second, for delegates from affiliated Constituency Labour Parties present at party conference, the apportioned vote is 30 per cent. Third, for delegates from affiliated trade unions, and various related societies and interest groups, the apportioned vote is 40 per cent. There is in addition, once the votes have been apportioned according to the percentage noted above, the requirement that[28]:

> "the candidate receiving more than half of the votes shall be declared elected and if no candidate reaches this total on the first ballot further ballots should be held on an elimination basis."

The above procedure with its weighting in favour of, respectively, affiliated labour organisations, the Constituency Labour Party and the Parliamentary Labour Party, makes the question of the manifesto a difficult issue in the development of the policies of any future Labour Government. Attempts by the National Executive Committee to mandate the Parliamentary Labour Party with an election manifesto drawn up by the National Executive Committee would leave any future Labour Government with little discretion over their policies. This would pose a serious question about the propriety of a future Labour Government being bound by the National Executive Committee, a body that is not responsible for the implementation of any policies. One tactic has been to have annual elections to the National Executive Committee and this has given the party leadership greater influence.   **10–030**

The Social and Liberal Democratic Party has a Federal Party for matters of policy common to England, Scotland and Wales. For specific matters within each of the regions, there is a State Party for each region. The Federal Party determines issues which overlap with policies decided in each of the regions. There is a Federal Policy Committee, responsible for research and development. Ultimate authority is found to vest within the Federal Conference which has representatives from the local party. Election of party leader is by the system of a Single Transferable Vote (STV) and by secret ballot. Nominations must be supported by 200 members and the nominee must be a member of the Parliamentary Party in the House of Commons.   **10–031**

The internal organisation of political parties may well have repercussions on the government's treatment of various issues and in the organisation of the government itself. Accountability of the government of the day to political parties emphasises the nature of party government. Thus it is likely that the policies created through the political process will also have an effect on the institutions of government itself.[29] In that way different forms of accountability are continually evolving. For example, impeachment of Ministers preceded the development of political accountability to Parliament. The fact that one form of accountability gives way to some new idea is recognised by Marshall who identifies a number of elements in the continuous development of constitutional practice. Marshall identifies "removability", "answerability" and resignation as elements in this process.   **10–032**

Accountability involves the principles of Cabinet and individual responsibility to Parliament, the role of Parliament may be examined from this perspective.   **10–033**

---

[28] Constitution of the Labour Party. The death of Mr John Smith Q.C. in 1994 resulted in the election of a new leader of the Labour Party adopting for the first time the new electoral procedures outlined above.
[29] Geoffrey Marshall, "The Evolving Practice of Parliamentary Accountability: Writing Down the Rules" (1991) *Parliamentary Affairs* 460–469.

THE ROLE OF PARLIAMENT

10–034   Parliament provides the framework for government accountability but it also provides the government with the means to carry out its policies through legislation. Current concern is that the legislature has become too dominated by the Executive. Some commentators have attributed Parliament's role[30] to merely one of influencing policy. While others believe that there is little need to refer to Parliament when the vast majority of government work is accepted into law.

10–035   The increase in the volume of legislation passing through Parliament illustrates the problems of modern government. New legislation is complex and detailed, often amending previous Acts of Parliament and seeking to meet every contingency. The problem of increasing governmental powers gives rise to increasing administrative bureaucracy. Reid noted[31]:

> "In 1913 there were 38 new statutes occupying only 301 pages. In 1956, there were 59 new statutes occupying 1,016 pages. In 1988, 55 statutes were passed and in 1989, 46 statutes in 2,489 large pages. Those statutes cover primary legislation."

10–036   In addition, in the last decade it is estimated that over 7,000 Orders in Council had been made through which Ministers may be given power to issue rules, and on an annual basis around 1,000 statutory instruments are issued. Most primary legislation emanates from central government while local authority and public corporation byelaws, departmental rules and regulations or decisions, add to the increase in legal powers and the breadth of their distribution.

10–037   Parliamentary accountability offers a wide variety of forms of control over government. One form is in the scrutiny of legislation, another is through the work of the new departmentally-related select committees, and a third is through parliamentary debate and ministerial responsibility.

Scrutiny and Passage of Legislation

10–038   Parliament's role in the scrutiny of primary legislation involves debate at the various stages of the Bill. Scrutiny of legislation provides a good example of both procedural rules and debate used as a means of scrutiny. The first reading is purely formal: the title of the Bill is approved.

10–039   The second reading may be referred to a Second Reading Committee which is a Standing Committee, nominated for the consideration of the Bill referred to it. It is intended to save time allowing a number of non-controversial Bills to proceed through the House of Commons with the minimum of time spent in debate in the Chamber of the House. The procedure is open to objection by at least 20 members of the House.[32] After second reading, the Bill goes to one of the standing committees unless the House

[30] P. Norton, "Independence, Scrutiny and Rationalisation: a Decade of Changes in the House of Commons" in *Political Institutions in Britain: Development and Change* (L. Robins ed., Longman, 1986), pp.58–86.
[31] Wiliam K. Reid "Changing Notions of Public Accountability" (1992) *Public Administration* 81–87.
[32] See Lord Renton, "Modern Acts of Parliament" in *The House Magazine*, February 11, 1991, p.14.

disagrees. It is possible for some parts of the Bill to be examined by t̸
committee while the remainder is examined by a committee of the entire
procedure in committee can be painstaking and involve consideration li..
each clause of the Bill.

Once through the committee stage the Bill, if amended, is reported to the House. **10–040**
There then follows the third reading. At this stage the debate is confined to general
principles only and verbal amendments may be moved. Once carried by vote, the Bill is
then sent to the House of Lords for consideration. There the procedure generally
follows that of the Commons. After the Lords, the Bill is returned. It is then subject to
assent by the Commons including any amendments introduced by the Lords.

Parliamentary scrutiny of delegated legislation is less uniform when compared to **10–041**
primary legislation. There is no requirement to comply with a single standard
procedure. The explanation for the lack of standardisation in procedure lies in the fact
that delegated powers are exercised by a very wide variety of bodies and fall within
specialised rules according to the nature of the powers involved.

The procedures which may be invoked, according to the nature of the regulations or **10–042**
orders to be enacted, are as follows. The first procedure is that of laying the delegated
legislation or instrument before Parliament. Invariably this procedure applies to
statutory instruments but the requirement of laying does not apply to all such
instruments, even those that fall within the Statutory Instruments Act 1946.

Statutory instruments may take effect immediately but are subject to annulment by **10–043**
Order in Council of either House. S.5 of the 1946 Act prescribes a period of 40 days
before laying where an instrument subject to a negative resolution may be annulled.
Excluded from the time-period are days when Parliament is dissolved, prorogued or
adjourned. Statutory instruments may be laid in draft before Parliament and made
subject to a resolution that no further proceedings need be taken.

Statutory instruments may be subject to affirmative parliamentary procedure. These **10–044**
may be laid before Parliament either in draft or completed form, but do not take effect
until approved. This requires government time, as normally a Minister must present
the instrument and there are no amendments possible. Occasionally an instrument may
be laid to have immediate effect but will cease to have this effect unless approved by
resolution within a prescribed time period. There are, in uncommon examples,
procedures for laying instruments and Parliament is only to be informed of the action
to be taken, thus leaving Ministers in control. There is also a lack of clarity over the
precise legal requirements of laying instruments. One view is that in the cases of
instruments subject to negative resolution and possibly those requiring positive
resolution, the requirement is directory and not mandatory. This leaves uncertain a key
issue of requiring appropriate sanctions over the government in the exercise of
parliamentary control.

The second procedure involved in the parliamentary supervision of delegated **10–045**
legislation is the use of scrutinising committees. The Select Committee on Statutory
Instruments usually meets with a Lords Committee to form a Joint Committee. Its role
and function is to bring some improvement to the form and content of statutory
instruments. A small number of instruments gave rise to a referral to the House. The
terms of reference of the Joint Committee were agreed in 1973 and include
consideration of any instrument to decide whether special attention of the House
needs to be drawn to any matter coming within any one of eight categories. These are

as follows: Does the instrument impose any charge on the public revenues or any fee to a public authority for services or a licence? Does the instrument made in pursuance of an Act of Parliament exclude challenge by the courts? Does the instrument have retrospective effect in circumstances where the parent Act does not confer any such authority? Has there been any unjustifiable delay in the publication of the instruments or in the laying procedure before Parliament? Are there unjustifiable delays in informing the Speaker in the case of instruments in operation because of a matter of urgency and before Parliament was informed? Are there doubts as to the legality of the instrument? Is the drafting in order and not defective? Could the wording or construction of the instrument require additional explanation?

10–046   An important innovation since 1973 has been the power to refer instruments to a Standing Committee on Statutory Instruments to question their merits. However it appears that the referral is limited as each committee meets only once, is limited to one and a half hours of debate, and cannot reject an instrument or secure a debate in the Commons. The Committee may take evidence only from government officials or HMSO. Some commentators claim that the main benefit of the Standing Committee is that the government has made use of its role to save time on the floor of the House. In 1989–90, the *Select Committee on Procedure*[33] received evidence recommending that: debate in the House of Commons on instruments subject to affirmative resolution should not proceed until the Committee reported on the instrument; the remit of the Committee should extend to include Northern Ireland instruments requiring negative resolution; the Committee should be free to take evidence from any source; and that codes of practice should be more regularly open to scrutiny. Finally greater regard should be taken of the Committee by other departmental committees.

10–047   An additional check on the procedures for Statutory Instruments is the requirement of publicity. First in 1893 under the Rules Publication Act, and now under the Statutory Instruments Act 1946, there are specific requirements for the printing and publication of statutory instruments, *i.e.* "they should be printed and sold as soon as possible".

10–048   The use of statutory instruments extends from rules relating to national insurance contributions, welfare benefits and employment protection procedures affecting the everyday lives of many people. Normally security and taxation matters are outside the remit of statutory instruments, with the exception of Northern Ireland since 1972 where direct rule has been carried out through the use of statutory instruments. This leaves many major issues largely under-debated in the House of Commons and therefore not subject to the normal scrutiny of parliamentary debate.

10–049   A controversial innovation is contained in the Deregulation and Contracting Out Bill introduced in January 1994. If enacted the Bill would allow a Minister to make an order to amend or repeal primary legislation which imposes an unnecessary burden on a trade or business provided necessary protection in the original Act of Parliament is not removed. The Select Committee on Procedure has recommended that there should be a new Scrutiny Committee in each House to allow debate over deregulation proposals.

---

[33] See *Commission on the Legislative Process* (Hansard Society, 1992).

Select Committees

One of the main functions of the House of Commons is to scrutinise the policies of the   **10–050**
government of the day. Accountability may therefore be achieved through a number of
select committees which carry out this task. Such committees are normally appointed
under the permanent Standing Orders of the House. Committees have a long history
that may be traced back almost 400 years. Following consideration of the committees
in use in the House of Commons, reforms were introduced and adopted in 1979. The
"new" select committees, as they are often referred to, are directly related to the
departments they oversee. The initiative for the formation of the new select committees owed much to the then leader of the House, Norman St John Stevas, who
pledged support from the government in the operation of the new committee system.[34]

In theory the new select committees are independent from party politics. However,   **10–051**
in practice the nomination for the selection of backbench M.P.s to serve on a
committee through the Committee of Selection has seen some party political activity.
The convention has developed that the names of members of the two main parties go
forward, but the party whips are consulted as to who to appoint. Concern has been
expressed that party discussion overshadows the selection process to the detriment of
the independence of the work of the committees. Each committee has either nine or
11 members. Normally there is a majority of backbench M.P.s from the government
party.

Membership of the select committee endures for the lifetime of the Parliament. The   **10–052**
chairmanship of committees is shared between the opposition and the government.
The procedure allows each committee to elect its own chairman but the party of the
chairman has been agreed beforehand. The powers of the committees are to send for
papers, persons and records. In their work the committees are department-led.

After the election of the new Labour government on May 1, 1997, a 15-member   **10–053**
Select Committee to consider modernisation of the work of the House of Commons
was set up.

The new select committees do not review systematically how Acts of Parliament are   **10–054**
in fact operating. However, select committees have a role in overseeing some aspects
of public expenditure, but the main work in this area is delegated to the Public
Accounts Committee, a specialist scrutiny committee. The view put forward by *Ryle*[35]
is that there is a case for expanding the role of departmental select committees into the
questions of choices over public expenditure plans. This expanded role might also lead
to a greater contribution to the various debates on Finance Bills and detailed tax
proposals. This idea is further considered below in the recommendations put forward
by the Hansard Commission.

The advantages of the new select committees include better information for   **10–055**
Members of Parliament, and this informs the quality of scrutiny offered in the
Commons debate. Public understanding and knowledge is thereby increased in the
work of the select committee. The examination of witnesses, especially since the most
topical issues when examined by the committee are televised, has increased the public

---

[34] P. Giddings, "What has been achieved?" in *The New Select Committees: A Study of the 1979 Reforms*
(Drewry ed., 2nd ed., Oxford University Press, Oxford, 1995).
[35] *Memorandum by Michael Ryle on The Select Committee System*, Select Committee on Procedure (1989–90
HC 19–II).

awareness of the work of the committees. This gives expert witnesses and pressure groups an opportunity to be heard. The fact that reports are not normally aired in the House of Commons suggests that the government may not face the full extent of the pressure generated by the Reports of the Select Committee.

10–056 A central question in the role of the committees in providing scrutiny of government policies is the attendance of witnesses before the committees. Gavin Drewry[36] has identified that there are instances "where select committees have faced difficulties in summoning witnesses and compelling disclosure of documents". Some instances of these difficulties may be noted. In 1984, the Government declined to allow the Director of the Government Communications Headquarters (GCHQ) to give evidence to the Select Committee on Employment.[37] In the notable Westland Affair, in 1986, officials of the Department of Trade and Industry were refused permission to give evidence to the Defence Committee, although the Head of the Civil Service appeared and gave answers to specified questions.

10–057 More recently, the attendance of witnesses has raised questions about whether the right to silence or the protection against self-incrimination might apply. The aftermath of the death of Robert Maxwell raised such questions over the refusal of his sons to answer the questions put to them by the Select Committee on Social Services.

10–058 The attendance of civil servants may be at the committees' compulsion but there is no duty on the part of civil servants to answer questions. The relationship between civil servants and the committee is explained in the *Memorandum of Guidance for Officials Appearing before Select Committees*. While officials are to be helpful to the work of the committee, the principle is that officials appear before the committee "on behalf of Ministers". Ministerial instruction may be given to officials as to how they should conduct their appearance before the committee.

10–059 The question arises as to how successful the new select committees are in the scrutiny of government and, perhaps as important, how success may be measured. There are two opposing views of their effectiveness. George Jones argues[38] that the committees have failed to fulfil their terms of reference and therefore they are not worth pursuing. The opposing view appears from much of the evidence received by the Select Committee on Procedure, which is generally praiseworthy of the performance of the committees and only minor adjustments are recommended.

10–060 In setting out the criteria for evaluation, both opposing views are vague in explaining how the work of the committee may be properly tested.

10–061 Philip Norton, in evidence to the Committee on Procedure provides a more comprehensive evaluation and suggests that "select committees are now the essential agents for such scrutiny of Parliament in subjecting government to informed, detailed and continuous scrutiny". The latter point is perhaps one of the most essential elements in any system of accountability. Continuous scrutiny allows past experience to be supplemented. Norton notes how techniques of questioning and cross-examination of Ministers have improved and how[39]:

[36] *Memorandum from Gavin Drewry, Reform of the Select Committee System* submitted on behalf of the Study of Parliament Group. Select Committee on Procedure (1989–90 HC 19–II).
[37] *First Report from the Employment Committee* (1983–84; HC 238), paras 6–7.
[38] G.W. Jones, "Send the Watchdogs Packing" *The Times*, November 4, 1989.
[39] P. Norton, *Memorandum to the Select Committee on Procedure* (1989–90 HC 19-11), p.139.

"there is sufficient evidence to demonstrate changes in public policy, changes that would not have taken place but for the recommendations of the committees".

Norton also draws attention to the value for money offered by the select committee system which has meagre resources and financial assistance. The key to the success or failure of the committee system appears to be the development of the political will to make the system effective. Norton identifies some shortcomings such as: limited interest by members in committee reports; limited time and resources; absence of career development in the select committee structure; finally, the committees do not appear to have a sufficiently strong link with the chamber of the House of Commons. Additional pressure on the select committee system may come from government in terms of the need to pass large volumes of legislation and from the career demands and self interests of the backbench M.P.s who serve on the committees. It may be concluded that while the new committees have not radically altered the relationship between Parliament and the Executive, they have provided information and knowledge about the internal workings of government. There is also the contribution made by the committees in keeping a clear focus on the work of backbench M.P.s. The decision by the Prime Minister to appear before the Liaison Committee is a step in the direction of giving select committees a greater role.   **10–062**

Parliamentary Reform: The Way Forward?

While successive governments have shown an apparent lack of interest in the effectiveness of parliamentary procedures, a recently published Hansard Society Commission Report[40] sets out an analysis of current weaknesses together with recommendations to improve the effectiveness of Parliament. This is a timely moment to focus attention on Parliament, neglected in the general pattern of constitutional reforms introduced since the election of a new Labour Government in 1997. The report, *The Challenge for Parliament: Making Government Accountable*, raises the central question of how effectively Westminster scrutinizes the executive. In the Commission's view, Parliament "has been left behind by far-reaching changes to the constitution, government and society in the past two decades". The Commission undertakes an analysis of the various procedures and mechanisms used by the Commons and Lords in their pursuit of accountability—debates, ministerial statements, select committees and inquiries, and the work of the ombudsman and the National Audit Office. Also included are the role of the courts and the work of inspectors and regulators. The report provides both an authoritative account of problems in filling the "serious gaps and weaknesses" identified in the system of accountability, and a "vision" of how a reformed Parliament might work. In doing this, the Commission adopts seven principles for reform, summarised below.   **10–063**

Parliament at the apex[41]

Under this principle, Parliament is seen as providing a framework for the different bodies and functions developed to ensure accountability of the executive. In summary: **10–064**

[40] Report of the Hansard Society Commission on Parliamentary Scrutiny: *The Challenge for Parliament: Making Government Accountable* (2001). Hereinafter the *Hansard Commission*. www.hansardsociety. org.uk
[41] *ibid.*, p.107.

"[our] recommendations aim to create a more formal and organised relationship between outside bodies and Parliament, to promote more systematic scrutiny by both the Commons and the Lords."[42]

Parliament must develop a culture of scrutiny[43]

10–065　This principle is aimed at strengthening the culture of politicians, changing attitudes and beliefs to ensure scrutiny and accountability of the executive.

Committees should play a more influential role within Parliament[44]

10–066　The introduction of departmental select committees in 1979 is reviewed, and the role and functioning of the various select committees are closely examined. The conclusions and recommendations are intended to give committees a more influential role within Parliament and lead to better scrutiny of the executive.

> "The role of the committees needs to be more closely defined, so that each has a set of core responsibilities and a set of certain pre-agreed and public goals. Their reach should be extended to provide regular scrutiny of regulators, executive agencies, quangos and the like. Committee structures should adopt new methods of work through sub-committees and perhaps the use of rapporteurs. In return, committee service should provide rewards for MPs—chairing a select committee needs to be recognised as a political position comparable to being a minister, and be paid accordingly. In addition, the committees should be given the staffing and resources needed to oversee the areas for which they are responsible."[45]

The Chamber should remain central to accountability[46]

10–067　The Hansard Report underlines the importance of the Chamber as the main forum where ministers are held to account. The main principle is that the Chamber should be more responsive to issues of public concern. A number of procedural reforms may assist in achieving this goal. Lengthy debates are of questionable value; M.P.s should have more opportunity to question ministers on recent select committee reports; the opposition and backbench M.P.s should have more opportunities to call ministers to account through ministerial statements or Private Notice Questions; and there should be the opportunity to undertake short, cross-party "public interest debates".

Financial scrutiny should be central to accountability[47]

10–068　The importance of financial scrutiny is underlined. The Hansard Society Commission concluded that

> "[f]inancial scrutiny should be central to the work of the Commons since it underpins all other forms of accountability. The procedures of the Commons need to be adapted to ensure that all committees, and hence all MPs have the scope and resources to ensure proper financial accountability."[48]

[42] *ibid.*, pp.107–108.
[43] *ibid.*, p.107.
[44] *ibid.*, p.107.
[45] *ibid.*, pp.108–109.
[46] *ibid.*, p.109.
[47] *ibid.*, p.110.
[48] *ibid.*, p.xii.

The House of Lords should complement the Commons[49]

10–069 The role of the Lords, whatever its position after any further reforms, is seen as complementary to the Commons. Close co-operation and co-ordination between the two Houses is required in an effort to provide support for greater scrutiny.

Parliament must communicate more effectively with the public[50]

10–070 The principle that Parliament must be seen to have a public voice is identified as essential to the public's positive perception of Parliament. Recommendations made to achieve this include: a general improvement in its procedures and hours, to allow media coverage and to make parliamentary business more comprehensible to the public; improvement in the organisation and structure of the work of committees; and the setting-up and operation of a designated press office, to maintain media interest in Parliament.

10–071 Finally, the report contains detailed conclusions and recommendations intended to implement each of the seven principles outlined above. It is clear that the Hansard Society Commission Report makes a significant contribution to the question of how effectively Parliament may scrutinise the Executive. Now that the report has set the agenda, it must be actively discussed—outside Parliament, as well as within it.

Parliamentary Debate and Ministerial Responsibility

10–072 Accountability for the actions and policy of the government of the day involves public debate in the media and in Parliament. The question arises as to how effective parliamentary debate may be in changing the opinion of the government or in forming a separate policy agenda from the government of the day. The answer may depend on the size of the parliamentary majority enjoyed by the government. There are only a small number of examples where the outcome of a speech made in a debate has been influential for the course of legislation. The Immigration Rules under the Immigration Act 1971[50a] resulted in a government defeat because of speeches made by several Conservative M.P.s and the failure of the Foreign Secretary to give concessions. In 1986 the Shops Bill was lost in a second reading despite the government's overall majority. Speeches made by many Conservative M.P.s resulted in the unprecedented loss in modern times of a government Bill after second reading. The paucity of such examples serve to show that Parliamentary debate may have limitations in terms of accountability over government policy.

10–073 Political opinion and support for the government in office requires that the government must take account of its political standing. In constitutional terms, a government that loses the confidence of the House of Commons must either resign or advise dissolution. For example in 1924, under Ramsay Macdonald, and in 1979 under James Callaghan, the Government was defeated in a confidence motion and advised dissolution. Similarly the classic formulation of ministerial responsibility attributes to the entire Ministry responsibility for all official acts performed by individual Ministers. Turpin concludes that accountability of government through ministerial responsibility[51]:

---

[49] *ibid.*, p.xii.
[50] *ibid.*, p.xiii.
[50a] Immigration (leave to Enter and Remain) Regulations Order 2000 (SI 2000/1161).
[51] Turpin, "Ministerial Responsibility: Myth or Reality?" in *The Changing Constitution* (Jowell and D. Oliver ed., 1989), p.85.

". . . depends upon procedure and custom, upon intangible understandings and traditions, and upon political circumstances and the government's need for the co-operation of Opposition and backbenchers. Ministerial responsibility, both collective and individual, in large part involves conflicts of interests between the government on the one hand and Parliament and the public on the other."

Brazier,[52] writing in 1990, records that since 1960, there have been 24 ministerial resignations on grounds of collective responsibility. In the case of individual responsibility there have been 12. It is not uncommon for Ministers to resign because of private and personal matters. While Ministers are responsible for their private conduct, the conduct of their department and acts of their civil servants, this does not always give rise to resignation. The resignation of Mr Stephen Byers, the Transport Secretary, came about because of internal conflict over policy and the role of advisors in his department. Resignation was not an inevitable outcome, but resulted from a general sense of lack of control and command over his department. History is rich in examples where resignation does not follow when there has been a perceived ministerial failing.

10–074   In 1982, the then Home Secretary Mr Whitelaw did not resign even though a breach in security allowed an intruder into the Queen's private bedroom. A year later, in 1983, the then Secretary of State for Northern Ireland, Mr Prior, did not resign because of a break-out at the Maze prison in Northern Ireland owing to security lapses. The Hennessey Report into the escape of prisoners concluded that there were no policy mistakes responsible.

10–075   The question of ministerial resignation has as much to do with damage limitation by the Prime Minister of the day as with accountability to Parliament. In that sense the Prime Minister's judgment of what may be acceptable to the House of Commons for the survival of the government may depend on parliamentary debate. A reasonably wide latitude appears to be given to Ministers given the pressure of work many endure. In 1971–72, the collapse of the Vehicle and General Insurance Company did not lead to ministerial resignation. There was criticism of civil servants and the acceptance that Ministers may experience a steady turnover of appointments and departments, and that the actual percentage of matters within departments which are referred to Ministers for personal attention is very small. In the case of the Vehicle and General collapse in 1971, less than 1 per cent of the department workload was referred to the Minister; and there had been since 1964, six different Ministers appointed.[53] In the debate, following the inquiry into the collapse of the insurance company, the Home Secretary explained[54]:

"In my own department we get 1 1/2 million letters a year, any one of which may lead to disaster. It is no minimising of the responsibility of Ministers to Parliament to say that a Minister cannot be blamed for a mistake made if he did not make it himself and if he has not failed to ensure that that sort of mistake ought not to be made."

[52] Brazier, *Constitutional Texts* (Oxford, 1990), pp.359–360.
[53] *Hansard*, HC Debs. Vol.831, col.419 (February 16, 1972). See *Report of the Tribunal of Inquiry into the Cessation of Trading of the Vehicle and General Insurance Co.* (1971–72 HC 133); (1972 HL 80), February 15, 1972.
[54] *Hansard*, HC Debs. Vol.836, col.33 (May 1, 1972). C. Turpin "Ministerial Responsibility" in *The Changing Constitution* (Jowell and Oliver ed., 3rd ed., 1994).

One example is the dismissal of Derek Lewis as Head of the Prison Service following **10–076** the report by Sir John Learmont into prison escapes from Parkhurst.[55] The then Home Secretary Michael Howard refused to resign, drawing on the distinction between operational and policy matters; he claimed that as the Home Secretary was responsible for policy and no policy had been found to be at fault, he was entitled to rely on this fact and not resign. On this fine distinction, the question of responsibility is confined to the duty to be accountable. Thus it may be argued that ministerial responsibility for the acts of civil servants appears to be non-existent.

Ministerial responsibility is susceptible to the ebb and flow of political debate. What **10–077** may appear settled may, on reflection, seem less clear. For example the resignation of Thomas Dugdale, over the sale of land at Crichel Down in 1954, was attributed to criticism of his civil servants' behaviour. With the benefit of hindsight and access to official papers it appears that the civil servants who were blamed were the victims of ministerial indecision and policy changes. Resignation came from backbench pressure and the Prime Minister's political judgment.[56] Ministerial responsibility that leads to resignation may ultimately depend on public opinion and political judgment.

GOVERNMENT AND THE CROWN

Ministers and Public Interest Immunity

Accountability, it has been noted from the foregoing discussion, may also be linked to **10–078** secrecy. As Birkinshaw some years ago noted,[57] in historical terms Parliament saw secrecy for its proceedings "as a necessary protection against the Crown's absolutist tendencies". The struggle for information became the centre of the desire for control. This legacy remains. So does the status of the Crown. A great deal of secrecy and mystique still surrounds the Crown, both as to the personal wealth and fortune of members of the Royal family and also as to the relationship and role of the Monarch with the government of the day.

Ministers are chosen by the Prime Minister but appointed by the Queen; in **10–079** constitutional theory they are servants of the Crown. Major public powers remain vested in the Crown or in Ministers who act as servants of the Crown. Civil servants under ministerial direction remain servants of the Crown. The creation of modern government has not dispensed with the various common law powers, privileges and immunities that were ascribed to royal power but today they are exercised by the government of the day with few powers remaining personal to the Queen.

In the appointment of Prime Minister, the convention of whether the person to be **10–080** appointed commands the confidence of the House of Commons is left to the Queen and her advisers. Normally the leader of the largest party is selected, but in making a choice the Queen may face difficult judgments when there is no overall majority party and the choice of person is less obvious.

In the dismissal of Ministers, the Queen's prerogative is exercisable by convention, **10–081** on the advice of the Prime Minister, but the retention of this prerogative maintains the

[55] *Hansard*, HC Vol.264, cols.502–506 (November 18, 1995).
[56] P. Carrington, *Reflect on Things Past*, pp.90–93.
[57] P. Birkinshaw, *Freedom of Information* (London, 1988), p.63.

role of the Crown in constitutional matters.[58] Finally in the dissolution of Parliament the normal convention is that in the exercise of the prerogative of dissolution, the Queen acts on the advice of the Prime Minister.

10–082   The Crown's exercise of powers does not readily conform to the normal arrangements for accountability. The Crown has traditionally enjoyed certain Crown privileges. Before the Crown Proceedings Act 1947, claims against the Crown for breach of contract were brought through Petition of Right, thus providing that the Home Secretary's agreement had to be sought before proceedings could begin. In addition in constitutional law, the presumption of statutory construction is that the Crown is not bound by an Act of Parliament. This does not prevent the Crown from benefiting from statutory powers. The Crown Proceedings Act 1947 permits claims formerly made by Petition of Right to be made and enforceable through ordinary civil proceedings instituted in county courts. This does not affect the taking of proceedings against the Queen in her own personal capacity, which remain by way of Petition of Right.

10–083   The Crown retains certain privileges which may be beneficial to the government of the day in the exercise of Crown powers. The remedies of injunction and specific performance were traditionally not available against the Crown. Crown Servants may be sued personally for civil wrongs committed by them even when they are acting in their official capacity at the time. The House of Lords held in *M v. Home Office*[59] that the courts could issue injunctions against Crown officers in judicial review proceedings. Ministers are amenable to the contempt jurisdiction of the courts. The use of prerogative powers is amenable to judicial scrutiny by way of judicial review, but prerogative powers give considerable powers to the government of the day in addition to any statutory authority. In the exercise of Executive powers to allocate licences, approve appointments to public office, engage in contracts, undertake research and development and provide loans and subsidies, the carrying out of government is by nature confidential and often removed from direct accountability. It is in the nature of government that some of its most important activities are free from direct parliamentary scrutiny or control.

10–084   Crown immunity or public interest immunity as it is more commonly called, provides the government of the day with an important claim in the event of legal proceedings. Crown privilege or immunity[60] may be claimed as the basis for the non-disclosure of documents which are confidential. The Crown may argue that to disclose such documents in legal proceedings may be "injurious to the public interest". Most of the authorities on Crown immunity involve civil proceedings rather than criminal prosecutions.

10–085   In the House of Lords in 1942 in *Duncan v Cammell Laird & Co Ltd*,[61] the basis of such a claim was made clear: Crown privilege may be claimed in respect of two alternative grounds. First that the disclosure of the contents of a particular document would injure the public interest such as endangering national security or prejudicing diplomatic relations with other countries. Secondly, that the document comes within a

---

[58] See The Petitions of Right Act 1860, repealed by the Crown Proceedings Act 1947.
[59] [1993] 3 W.L.R. 433.
[60] The terminology currently used by the courts is public interest immunity. This term is preferred over Crown Privilege. See *Rogers v Secretary of State for Home Department* [1973] A.C. 388. See *Alfred Crompton Amusement Machines Ltd v Customs and Excise Commissioners No.2* [1974] A.C. 405.
[61] [1942] A.C. 624. In *Glasgow Corp v Central Land Board* (1956) S.C. 1 (H.L.) the House of Lords held that *Duncan v Cammell Laird* did not apply in Scotland.

certain category, or "class" of document which by its nature should be withheld to ensure the proper working of the public service. In the first ground the Crown had to satisfy the court of the nature of the contents of the particular document. In the second ground, the category of documents that fitted the particular class of documents for which immunity was sought, was very broad. In seeking to find a balance between freedom of information and protection of the State, the class of documents was reviewed. A statement made by a Minister in the proper form could claim immunity and establish within which of the two categories the document came. The *Duncan* case concerned a civil action undertaken by the widow of one of the sailors drowned when the submarine Thetis sank whilst undergoing sea trials. In order to pursue her action in negligence, the plaintiff claimed from the Ministry of Defence documents such as the plans of the submarine. The effect of the *Duncan* case considerably restricted the official documents allowed to be admitted in evidence in legal proceedings, giving the Crown a wider discretion to withhold documents than had previously been accepted.

Under s.28 of the Crown Proceedings Act 1947 the courts may make an order for discovery of documents or require the Crown to answer interrogatories. However, this power did not affect an existing rule of law that the Crown may refuse to disclose any documents or answer any questions on the ground that this would be injurious to the public interest. **10–086**

In 1968 the House of Lords considered the law in *Conway v Rimmer*[62] which concerned a number of documents being withheld in a civil action undertaken by a probationary police constable. The Secretary of State objected on the grounds that the reports fell into classes of documents where disclosure would not be in the public interest. The reports related to the conduct of individual officers and investigation into particular crimes. In reaching a conclusion on these matters the House of Lords rejected the approach in *Duncan* as restrictive in admitting documents, preferring instead to assert a judicial power to consider and decide on whether the documents should be excluded. Lord Reid distinguishing *Duncan* asserted the judicial role "to hold the balance between the public interest, as expressed by a Minister, to withhold certain documents or other evidence and the public interest in ensuring the proper administration of justice". **10–087**

The House of Lords also accepted the need to give the greatest weight to the Minister's opinions. However the question arises as to whether the courts will always be prepared to exercise their judgment by balancing the interests of the Minister against the interests of disclosure. It appears that certain classes of documents ought never to be disclosed. For example Lord Widgery in *Att.-Gen. v Jonathan Cape Ltd*[63] claimed that "no court will compel the production of cabinet papers in the course of discovery in an action". Thus routine or less sensitive documents may be more likely to be admitted in evidence than higher grade or more secret documents. **10–088**

Following *Conway* the House of Lords have further considered how to strike the balance of interests between competing claims of the Minister and the need to disclose information. In *Burmah Oil Co Ltd v Bank of England*,[64] the Chief Secretary to the Treasury signed a certificate that the production of documents would be "injurious to the public interest." The documents related to negotiations between the Bank of **10–089**

---

[62] [1968] A.C. 910.
[63] [1976] Q.B. 752.
[64] [1980] A.C. 1090.

England, Burmah Oil and the Government over the purchase by the Bank of England of stock in British Petroleum (BP) owned by Burmah at a specific price per unit of stock. Within a year the value of the stock had doubled and Burmah brought an action against the Bank of England with regard to the sale on the ground that it was unreasonable and unconscionable. The sale took place at a time when Burmah experienced financial difficulties and the Government insisted that they could not share in any profit from the resale of the BP shares by the Bank of England. It had originally been intended that some profit in any sale of the shares might be shared between the Bank and Burmah.

10–090   The House of Lords concluded that on judicial inspection of the documents they did not contain material which was necessary for a fair consideration of the case. The case establishes a number of points.

10–091   First, no class of document is entirely excluded from the process of balancing the different interests between the Minister and the need to disclose information. Secondly, that the courts had a power of inspection of documents. This includes deciding the category or class of document to which the documents may belong, whether disclosure is necesssary for a fair trial of the issues in the case and whether the balance of interests criteria, outlined above, has been satisfied to permit disclosure. In these matters it is not always clear at what stage inspection is used. It is not always the case that the court will order inspection. When inspection is required, is it fair to both parties that the judge should examine documents which one of the parties has not seen?

10–092   The third point to emerge in *Burmah Oil* is that the courts are unwilling to grant immunity from disclosure simply because the documents contain matters of "candour", though it may be regarded as a factor which might be useful in deciding on the balance of interests criteria. The courts are sensitive to arguments in favour of more open government that may lead to a fishing expedition for information. Speculative claims are unlikely to gain favour with the judges.

10–093   When public interest immunity is pleaded the other party faces a difficult task to persuade the judge to admit the documents in question. What standard of case must be made out? In the *Burmah Oil* case the judges differed in their choice of criteria to be satisfied before disclosure is granted. Some judges preferred a real likelihood, others, reasonable probability; and Lord Wilberforce who dissented, suggested that a positive case must be shown before the documents would be admitted. What must be shown is that the documents must be necessary for "fairly disposing the case".

10–094   There are various matters relevant to deciding how the balance of interests is to be calculated. In *D v. National Society for the Prevention of Cruelty to Children*,[65] D's application to have NSPCC documents admitted was refused because of the nature of the NSPCC; its voluntary status, statutory powers and the receipt of information on a confidential basis, required immunity. In *R. v Chief Constable Ex p. Wiley*[66] the House of Lords held that public interest immunity in police complaints proceedings did not extend to the use in civil proceedings of information generated through the complaint proceedings. Public interest immunity did not in a general way extend to the use of the documents or information contained in the police files. All relevant documents ought to be capable of disclosure unless it might cause substantial harm.

[65] [1978] A.C. 171.
[66] [1995] 1 A.C. 274.

In *Halford v. Sharples*[67] a claim was made by Alison Halford, then Assistant Chief   **10–095**
Constable of Merseyside, that her promotion within the police was blocked because of
sex discrimination. In support of her claim she wished to have access to confidential
files but one was refused by the Court of Appeal. The reasoning that there was an
overwhelming public interest in maintaining the integrity of police complaints and
disciplinary files prevented disclosure of the files to Alison Halford but it also
prevented the Chief Constable from relying on information on the files. An important
element in the reasoning in this case came from reliance on an earlier Court of Appeal
case, *Makanjoula v Commissioner of Police for the Metropolis*.[68] In *Makanjoula*,
statements that had been given to the police by witnesses were withheld from the
court, even when the witnesses might have given their consent. Bingham L.J. said[69]:

> "Where a litigant asserts that documents are immune from production or
> disclosure on public interest grounds he is not (if the claim is well founded)
> claiming a right but observing a duty. Public interest immunity is not a trump card
> vouchsafed to certain privileged players to play when and as they wish. It is an
> exclusionary rule, imposed on parties in certain circumstances even where it is to
> their disadvantage."

Interpretation of "observing a duty" in the judgment of Bingham L.J. in *Makanjoula*   **10–096**
became the central issue in the recent *Matrix Churchill* case. Criminal prosecutions
taken against certain directors of Matrix Churchill by Customs and Excise, over
allegations that the company had broken trade sanctions in the sales of weapons to
Iraq, resulted in public interest immunity being claimed by Ministers over confidential
documents relating to the government's policy on arms sales. The Ministers concerned
claimed that they had "a duty" to sign the certificates and were advised to do so by the
Attorney-General. One minister, Michael Heseltine, only signed the certificate after he
was instructed that he was under a clear duty to do so.

Some support for this view that Ministers are under a duty to sign public interest   **10–097**
immunity certificates, is taken from what was said by Bingham L.J. in *Makanjoula*.
However, a further reading of the judgment of Bingham L.J. reveals further clarification on whether there is a duty in all cases to assert an immunity claim. Bingham L.J.
added[70]:

> "This does not mean that in any case where a party holds a document in a class
> prima facie immune he is bound to persist in an assertion of immunity even where
> it is held that, on any weighing of the public interest, in withholding the document
> against the public interest in disclosure for the purpose of furthering the
> administration of justice, there is a clear balance in favour of the latter."

There is a division of opinion over the interpretation of the judgment of Bingham L.J.   **10–098**
In the *Matrix Churchill* case Ministers claimed that at the time the certificates were

[67] [1992] 1 W.L.R. 736.
[68] [1992] 3 All E.R. 617.
[69] *ibid*. at 623.
[70] [1992] 3 All E.R. 617 at 623g–h.

signed they had no choice but to sign the certificates. Some legal opinion takes the view that there is no obligation or duty on Ministers to make a claim. Ministers are free to authorise disclosure to the public of confidential documents and by analogy are free to decide whether to sign certificates or not.

10–099   The better view is that Ministers have a discretion as to whether to claim public interest immunity or not. They are not bound to sign a certificate even where there is a *prima facie* case that the documents may belong to a class where public interest immunity may be sought. The courts decide "where the balance of public interest lies" in such cases.

10–100   Since the Matrix Churchill trial, the House of Lords have now accepted in *Ex p. Wiley*[71] a number of propositions about public interest immunity. The view that there is a class of documents which may guarantee exclusion from disclosure is no longer tenable. This view has been made clear by the Lord Chancellor and the Attorney-General in changes that have been announced to the administration of public interest immunity certificates.[72] Furthermore it is considered that in criminal cases the scales of justice have to be more keenly balanced to protect the accused. The House of Lords in *Ex p. Wiley* also rejects the proposition that there is a duty on Ministers to sign public interest immunity certificates. From the above discussion, it may be concluded that the Attorney-General's interpretation is unsound in principle and wrong in its potential effects on the accused.

10–101   A further consideration is whether there is any distinction between civil and criminal cases. In a criminal trial, accused persons may be convicted notwithstanding that there is evidence showing their innocence. This appears inconsistent with the public interest. In criminal litigation the courts have been concerned about the balance of interests and the protection of the accused when public interest immunity is claimed by the prosecution. In *R. v Governor of Brixton Prison Ex p. Osman*[73] Lord Justice Mann accepted that public interest immunity may be claimed in criminal proceedings but he noted ". . . that the application of the public immunity doctrine in criminal proceedings will involve a different balancing of interest to that in civil proceedings". Relying on a number of authorities including *Marks v Beyfus*,[74] Lord Justice Mann noted that the privilege of public interest immunity

> "cannot prevail if the evidence is necessary for the prevention of a miscarriage of justice. No balance is called for. If admission is necessary to prevent miscarriage of justice, balance does not arise."[75]

10–102   The courts have not always been consistent in their approach. In *R. v Lewes Justices Ex p. Home Secretary*[76] concerning criminal libel, the House of Lords upheld a claim for Crown privilege in respect of police documents relied upon by the Gaming Board. An applicant had been unsuccessful in applying to the Gaming Board for a licence for a Bingo Club. He alleged that the police had sent the Gaming Board a libellous letter

---

[71] *R. v Chief Constable of the West Midlands Ex p. Wiley* [1994] 3 All E.R. 420 at 423.
[72] *Hansard*, HL Vol.576, col.1507, and *Hansard*, HC Vol.287, col.949 (December 18, 1996).
[73] [1992] 1 All E.R. 108.
[74] (1890) 25 Q.B.D. 494.
[75] [1992] 1 All E.R. 108 at 118a–b.
[76] [1973] A.C. 388, HL.

and for this reason he had been unsuccessful in his application. Lord Reid reasoned that much of the information came from a letter from the police based on information from sources that must be protected. The nature of the information may disclose the source and this required protection. This case is open to a narrow interpretation. Although the House of Lords upheld the claim made on public interest immunity to prevent disclosure of documents, the case may be said to have raised special facts. Lord Reid noted that the documents were not intended to deprive the applicant of any legal right. The only reason the documents came into existence was because the applicant "is asking for a privilege and is submitting his character and reputation to scrutiny". It is significant that Lord Reid upheld the important principle that should be observed in public interest immunity cases namely that the "course of justice should not be impeded by the withholding of evidence".

In *Ward*[77] the Court of Appeal observed that there were requirements laid upon the   **10–103** prosecution if they wished to claim public interest immunity. First, notice must be given to the defence if the prosecution wished to rely on immunity and that the prosecution are applying to the court for a ruling. Secondly, the defence must be given some idea of the category of information involved. Thirdly, the defence must be given the opportunity to make representations. Lord Justice Glidewell made clear that it was for the court to make the ultimate decision as to whether evidence is to be disclosed. This does not prevent the Crown Prosecution Service deciding in exceptional cases to volunteer information without obtaining a court order.

The courts have generally been sensitive in criminal prosecutions to prevent the   **10–104** claim of public interest immunity from interfering with the rights of the accused. Lord Justice Mann in *Ex p. Osman (No.1)*[78] noted that: "it may be that prosecutions are not initiated where material is not to be exposed, or it may be that the force of the balance is recognised by prosecuting authorities and the immunity is never claimed". In *Neilson v Laugharne*[79] Lord Justice Oliver said: "If public policy prevents disclosure, it prevents it, in my judgement, in all legal circumstances except to establish innocence in criminal proceeding."

In the *Matrix Churchill* case, which involved a criminal prosecution, the trial judge   **10–105** allowed the documents to be admitted in the case and this, together with evidence from a former Minister, led to the failure of the prosecution case. The furore caused by the case in Parliament and the broader implications that Ministers may have misled Parliament led to the setting up of an inquiry under Lord Justice Scott. The higher appellate courts had until *Ex p. Wiley*[80] been mainly concerned with civil proceedings. The use of public interest immunity certificates in criminal cases has given rise to a clear difference of opinion on the part of the Government's legal advisers and the Scott report on this issue. Sir Richard Scott recommended that class claims should no longer be used in criminal litigation and seldom used in civil litigation.[81] However in the Government's response,[82] the view of government advisers remained as follows:

> "The understanding of those advising Government was and is that the general principles of PII [Public Interest Immunity] apply in the same way in criminal

[77] *R. v Ward* [1993] 2 All E.R. 577. Also see *R. v Davis* [1993] 2 All E.R. 643.
[78] [1992] 1 All E.R. 108 at 116.
[79] [1981] 1 All E.R. 829 at 839h. See Adam Tomkins, "Public Interest Immunity after Matrix Churchill" [1993] *P.L.* 650.
[80] *R. v Chief Constable of the West Midlands Ex p. Wiley* [1994] 3 All E.R. 420.
[81] The Scott Report, Vol.III, para.G18.86 at 1525.
[82] *Government's Response*, para.3.1, p.14.

proceedings as they do in civil proceedings. In each case both class and contents claims can properly be advanced; and in each case the public interest in non-disclosure falls to be balanced (at the material time, by the court) against the public interest in disclosure for the purposes of the administration of justice. The balance is much more likely to come down in favour of disclosure in criminal proceedings, and procedural differences exist, but the general principles are the same."

10–106   However, in *Ex p. Wiley* Lord Templeman explained[83]:

"Prosecution authorities know which documents are relevant to the prosecution but they cannot know for certain which documents will be relevant to the defence. . . In order to avoid criticism and a miscarriage of justice one way or the other, the police authorities now feel obliged to disclose documents of doubtful relevance and materiality."

10–107   In the light of these differences, criminal cases involving public interest immunity claims have to be considered in a different context than cases where civil issues are resolved.

10–108   The Criminal Procedure and Investigations Act 1996 contains a Code of Practice which lays down the basis for documents relevant to the investigation to become available to the defence. The 1996 Act does not make substantive changes to the case law on public interest immunity. The Act strengthens the view put forward by Scott that in criminal cases the issue of disclosure of information is whether it might be of relevance to the defence. The Act introduces the requirement of defence disclosure. Paradoxically the Act will limit the role of the judge as there will be few occasions when the judge will have to rule on disclosure because the Act will require disclosure of most material.

10–109   In summary the following appears to be the current law. As already mentioned the view that there is a class of documents which may guarantee exclusion from disclosure is no longer tenable. This view has been made clear by the Lord Chancellor and the Attorney-General in changes that have been announced to the administration of public interest immunity certificates. Furthermore, Ministers will only claim public interest immunity when it is believed that disclosure of a document would cause real damage or harm to the public interest. Contained in the certificate will be an explanation of how disclosure could cause real damage to the public interest. Although these changes apply to the use of public interest immunity certificates claimed by the government, it is expected that the changes will have wider application.

GOVERNMENT AND SECRECY

10–110   The ethos of secrecy is an intrinsic part of government. While Cabinet government requires and maintains the confidence of the House of Commons, its deliberations and decisions are bound together through collective Cabinet responsibility. This is intended to ensure confidentiality of decision-making as much as responsibility.

---

[83] *R. v Chief Constable of the West Midlands Ex p. Wiley* [1994] 3 All E.R. 420 at 423. See T.R.S. Allan, "Public Interest Immunity and Ministers' Responsibilities" (1993) *Criminal Law Review* 660; A.W. Bradley, "Justice, Good Government and Public Interest Immunity" (1992) *Public Law* 514; G. Ganz, "Matrix Churchill and Public Interest Immunity" (1993) 56 *Modern Law Review* 564.

Many of the rules of the Cabinet are confidential. Ministers are not expected to   **10–111**
divulge the existence of cabinet committees, or the membership of the committees or
the rules under which the committees operate. Such confidentiality appears to favour
Prime Ministerial influence, the exchange of information on a need-to-know basis
within government, and the protection of the civil servants in giving advice. Confidentiality is also required in the contractual and financial relations undertaken by the
government of the day. For example in January 1985 a leak of information on the
Government's policy on foreign exchange rates resulted in a story in the *Sunday
Times*.[84] Nigel Lawson, then Chancellor of the Exchequer, recalls in his memoirs[85] how
the leak came from Bernard Ingham, then Press Secretary to the Prime Minister. The
leak cost the government a great deal of upheaval in the exchange markets and
confidence in the City. This is an illustration of the need for confidentiality within
government and this example also underlines the influence of the press and media over
the government's economic policies.

The ethos of secrecy in government is maintained through the use of various   **10–112**
restraints on free access to information. The most formidable are the various legal
restraints such as s.2 of the Official Secrets Act 1911. The breadth of this section was
illustrated in 1984 by the prosecution of Sarah Tisdell, a civil service clerk convicted
for leaking the Government's plans for policing and keeping order at Greenham
Common, the base intended to receive Cruise Missiles. Clive Ponting, a senior civil
servant, was prosecuted under this section for leaking documents relating to the
sinking of the Argentinian warship The General Belgrano during the Falklands War.
Although the jury was instructed that Ponting had no defence because he claimed that
he owed a duty to Parliament to provide information, the jury, to his surprise,
acquitted.

In addition to s.2, there are a variety of devices such as "D" notices, available to   **10–113**
indicate to the press and media that publication may not be within the law. An official
committee of press and broadcasting representatives known as the Defence, Press and
Broadcasting Committee acts as a scrutineer of the system.

Conventions that Ministers do not reveal the inner workings of government remain.   **10–114**
However, since the *Crossman Diary* case,[86] which permitted the posthumous publication of Richard Crossman's diaries, a number of former Cabinet Ministers have
published their diaries, even when the diaries were made contemporaneously with
their official duties.

Actions for breach of confidence may also be involved to protect official secrets such   **10–115**
as in the litigation arising out of the Spycatcher book.[87] This book contained the
memoirs of Peter Wright, a former member of MI5, revealing details of the inner
workings and operations of the security services.

The question arises as to the compatibility of open government with confidentiality.   **10–116**
This question is considered in more detail in Chap.20, but it is apparent that the
United Kingdom does not benefit from any general presumption in favour of access to
official information. This gives rise to the question of how effective government
accountability may be within the restrictions imposed on information. The ethos of

---

[84] *Sunday Times*, January 6, 1985.
[85] N. Lawson, *The View from No. 11.* (Bantam Press, London 1992), pp.1–469.
[86] *Att.-Gen. v Jonathan Cape Ltd* [1976] Q.B. 752.
[87] *Att.-Gen. v Guardian Newspapers Ltd (No.2)* [1990] 1 A.C. 109; [1988] 3 W.L.R. 776.

secrecy pervades the culture of how government conducts its business. Limitations on the flow of information available to the public restricts the opportunities for the critical analysis of government policy. This may have a detrimental effect on how effective government and its related agencies may be in making policy decisions. The decision to release more information on Treasury forecasting of the economy in September 1992 was made in an effort to gain greater credibility for government ministers in managing the economy. This is a good illustration of the obvious benefits to be gained by making more information available allowing more informed judgements. The use of the National Audit Office to check on government and Treasury forecasting is an example of transparency.

10–117   Gradually through public and media pressure, advances are being made to create greater openness in government. A step in the direction of greater openness came in 1993 with publication of the White Paper on Open Government[88] and a proposed relaxation of the laws prohibiting disclosure of information. There is a *Code of Practice on Access to Government Information*[89] issued in 1994 and revised in 1997. This Code sets out how a complaint may be made and how there are five commitments to open government. These are: to supply the facts and analysis with major policy decisions; to open up internal guidelines about departments' dealings with the public; to supply reasons for administrative decisions; to provide information under the Citizen's Charter about public services; and to respond to requests for information. A formal request may be made for information with a guarantee of a reply within 20 working days. Citizens should be able to clarify information and check its accuracy. For example the Data Protection Act 1984 requires that information must be obtained and processed fairly and lawfully, it must be held only for specific purposes and not used or disclosed in any way incompatible with those purposes. The Data Protection Registrar set up under the Act along with the Data Protection Tribunal, oversees the regulation of information used and classified under the 1984 Act.

10–118   Citizens may view access to more information as a means of redressing grievances but also there is the greater opportunity to participate in government decision-making. Government consultation through White Papers, Royal Commissions, and committees of inquiry, all contribute to the provision of more information as well as to the general level of government accountability.

10–119   Some steps in the direction of greater accountability have taken place. The new select committees discussed above have made an important contribution in this area. In 1977 the then Head of the Civil Service issued what has become known as "the Croham" Directive, namely that background material on policy matters should be published unless ministers specifically object. This system has declined in use since 1979 but it is illustrative of how important initiatives may be taken.

10–120   Clearly the Human Rights Act 1998 is likely to have an impact on how access to information is considered by the courts. Article 8 of the Convention provides respect for family life and the home. The right to receive information is to be found under Article 10(1) but this has not given rise to a substantive right to know. The boundaries of the protections and rights under a rights-based focus have to be considered in the context of providing from public bodies access to official information.

---

[88] Cm.2290 (1993).
[89] Cabinet Office, Whitehall, London.

At the same time there are obvious limitations on a general policy on openness. **10–121**
Private citizens may wish to have some degree of privacy protection. Commercial
organisations may wish to have copyrights and patents protected and government as a
major contractor may be inhibited from open access. Setting the boundaries is not
easy. The Freedom of Information Act 2000, which applies to England and Wales but
not Scotland, where separate arrangements are being considered, is an attempt to
provide some general principles such as a general right of access to information but
subject to general limitations and exceptions. However, it is not currently in force. It
will be phased in, first with central government in November 2000 and then later the
entire Act will be in force by July 2005. The Act builds on previous attempts at greater
transparency especially with the Data Protection Act 1998, Access to Medical Records
Act 1988 and the Environmental Information Regulations 1992.[90] Critics see the Act as
a disappointment because of the extensive exceptions and exemptions. However, as
Feldman explains[91]:

> "All one can say in favour of the Act is that it represents a small and extremely
> tentative first step towards making real openness in government the norm."

S.1 of the Act provides a general right of access to information held by public **10–122**
authorities. The definition of a public authority includes central government departments, local government including health authorities and maintained schools. There
are a variety of other bodies including the British Council who are included. In terms
of positive rights the citizen is provided with the right to information because there is a
duty on public authorities to respond to a request for information. The request must
be in writing and, within 20 working days, once confirmed that the information is with
the public authority there is a right to access to the information. A fee may be payable
and there appears no obligation to become proactive in tracing the information or
investigating whether the information is in fact in the possession of the public
authority. The exemption categories are all-embracing. S.14 provides grounds for
refusing the request if it is regarded as vexatious or would be too expensive to provide.
There is a raft of exclusions including where the information is available through other
means. Some of the main areas where information does not have to be disclosed are if
the information would:

- be prejudicial to defence or the capability of the security or armed forces;
- be prejudicial to the interests of relations with other countries;
- be prejudicial to the economic interests of the country;
- infringe the privileges of Parliament;
- be prejudicial to the audit functions of public authorities discharging their
  functions.

It is difficult to qualify the term "prejudicial" and how this might be interpreted by the **10–123**
courts. Information does not have to be disclosed if it is likely to be actionable and a
breach of confidence or prejudicial to commercial interests, or would be subject to
legal professional privilege.

---

[90] Environmental Information Regulations SI 1992/3240.
[91] D. Feldman, *Civil Liberties and Human Rights in England and Wales* (2nd ed., Oxford University Press,
Oxford, 2002), p.786.

10–124   The Act also has an enforcement procedure. The Data Protection Commissioner is renamed under s.18 as the Information Commissioner. The Data Protection Tribunal is renamed the Information Tribunal.

SUMMARY AND CONCLUSIONS

10–125   Access to more information and knowledge of government strategy is an important element in the ideals of democratic government. We live in an information age. The political life of the nation is focused on presentation to the media and the management of information. Good government depends on access to information, informed public debate and reasoned analysis. There are positive signs. The Citizen's Charter[92] which sets out standards for the delivery and quality of a wide range of public services provides expectations and greater openness in the process of government. The Freedom of Information Act 2000 provides a development in favour of open government and access to information. It falls short of the expectation of making government accountable through greater transparency.

FURTHER READING

R. Butler, "The Evolution of the Civil Service—A Progress Report" (1993) 71 *Public Administration* 395–406.

Cabinet Office, *Public Bodies* (Stationery Office, London, 2001–2002).

The Civil Service Yearbook 2001 (Stationery Office, London, 2001–2002).

T. Daintith and A. Page, *The Executive in the Constitution* (Oxford University Press, Oxford, 1999).

Hansard Society, *Report of the Hansard Society Commission on Parliamentary Scrutiny: The Challenge for Parliament: Making Government Accountable* (Hansard Society, Vacher Dod Publishing Ltd, London, 2001).

D. Oliver and G. Drewry, *Public Service Reform: issues of Accountability and Public Law* (Pinter, London, 1996).

Law and Parliament (D. Oliver and G. Drewry ed., Butterworths, London, 1998).

[92] Cm.1599 (1991).

Chapter 11

THE NEW PUBLIC MANAGEMENT

INTRODUCTION

The civil service, over the past 30 years, has come under detailed scrutiny. The Fulton **11–001** Report in 1969 examined the lack of effective management in the civil service that has given rise to concern. Demands for greater efficiency and effectiveness in the civil service has become a theme of the relations between the government and the civil service. Senior civil servants advise Ministers on major policy issues, take many policy decisions, implement and co-ordinate complex administrative schemes and manage large departments. Such tasks require not only high administrative skills, but also managerial ability. Perceived deficiencies in the structures and management techniques within the civil service have led to change and a break with the past traditions of public service.

Also related to change within the civil service has been recognition that long-term or **11–002** strategic planning was absent from the system of Cabinet government. Civil servants recognised that seldom was the impact of government policies fully reviewed, discussed and considered in the light of future policies, by the Cabinet.

In this chapter the changes introduced into the civil service will be discussed, such as **11–003** the introduction of Next Steps Agencies. These have challenged some of the principles of the civil service established since the Northcote-Trevelyan Report in 1853 which may be taken to be the beginning of the modern development of the civil service. Since Fulton, the aims, objectives and management of the civil service have undergone intense scrutiny. The steps taken to introduce management techniques into the civil service will be examined and the setting-up of the Next Steps agencies, by hiving off department activities, is explained in terms of the constitutional implications for parliamentary accountability. Such fundamental changes to the civil service have raised questions about the future direction and development of the civil service. Questions about Agency Status have raised issues about the criteria used to measure their success and the value of agencies in the efficiency of service provision.

The civil service, its organisation and status provide an important dimension on how **11–004** government governs. Modernisation of government has had incremental effects on the civil service. Since 1997 there are discernible trends. The appointment of special advisers by the government of the day blurs the distinction between political influence and civil service neutrality. Currently the number of special advisers stands at over 80 in total. The Office of Press Secretary has become increasingly controversial as has the Prime Minister's Chief of Staff at No.10. Both are technically special advisers and technically fall within the category of civil service. A special Order in Council was made to provide the legal arrangements surrounding the appointment. The creation of a new Strategic Communications Unit in No.10 heightens concerns of a presidential style. Government is one of the largest purchasers of advertising in the country. The question is whether the trend towards special advisers[1] will inevitably politicise the civil service and jeopardise its political neutrality, the bedrock of the system. This chapter traces the evolution of the civil service and the changes that are taking place to its role and status.

CIVIL SERVICE—EVOLUTION AND REFORM

11–005   Since the nineteenth century, the civil service has been the focus of attempts to reform its role and function. Prior to Mrs Thatcher becoming Prime Minister in 1979, the civil service had largely withstood major reforms to its organisation and management. These comprise Plowden in 1961, Fulton in 1968 and reforms under Mr Heath in 1970 in hiving off departments.

11–006   In 1961 the Plowden Report[2] on the public expenditure process introduced the Public Expenditure Survey (PES) which was aimed at changing the financial procedures involved in planning government strategy. This involved "regular surveys" of public expenditure as a whole over a period of years ahead. Decisions "should be taken in the light of those surveys". The creation of a continuous programme of the spending objectives for the medium term was intended to allow bilateral discussions in Cabinet at the beginning of the autumn. It also encouraged civil service efficiency within a framework directed by Ministers. In reaching policy decisions within departments the civil service was expected to be more cost effective and better informed of the economic advice tendered to Ministers. However the civil service proved resistant to any fundamental changes and the PES ran into major economic problems during periods of inflation and itself came under considerable change.

11–007   In 1968 the Fulton Report[3] on the civil service made recommendations for major changes. When it reported, the civil service had grown to 20 times the size of the civil service in 1854. Arguably the increase in size reflected larger departments and a greater workload with an increasingly complex system of government. Both its size and the variety of work expected from civil servants confirmed the need to re-consider how the civil service was managed. Particularly important throughout the last two decades has been the need to improve strategic planning and management of resources.

11–008   Fulton was the first major inquiry into the civil service since the Northcote-Trevelyan inquiry in the nineteenth century. The report offered both an analysis of the structure, management and organisation of the civil service and provided recommendations for reform. It recognised a number of defects concerning how the civil service was organised. At one level the nineteenth century had ensured fair and open competition, selection on merit, the ethos of public service, political neutrality and

[1] See Sixth Report of the Committee on Standards in Public Life, *Reinforcing Standards*, Cm.4557 (January 2000). *Government Response*: Cm.4817 (July 2000).
[2] Plowden Report, *The Control of Public Expenditure*, Cmnd.1432 (1961).
[3] Fulton Report, Cmnd.3638 (1968).

professionalism. At another level the system of classes, clerical, executive and administrative, impeded the work of the civil service. There was a proliferation of specialists within a complex departmental structure. Fulton also recognised that the "generalist" dominated the service, and this may have contributed to the undervalue given to specialist skills. More significantly, Fulton recognised the lack of management skills, the exclusive nature of the service which resulted in the lack of contact between the service and the rest of the community. Poor personal management stifled the most gifted and this led to problems within the complicated class structure.

Fulton made 158 recommendations and this led to the creation of the civil service department which stopped the control of the civil service from being the direct responsibility of the Treasury. It is suggested that many of Fulton's other proposals were undermined[4] by senior civil servants who did not desire change. The establishment of a Civil Service College, the recruitment of graduates and the abolition of classes were successfully introduced. However successful these changes were in restructuring the civil service, by 1980 there were still 700,000 civil servants serving over 100 ministers. **11–009**

One major omission in the Fulton Report was the absence of a clear answer to the question of the future role of the modern civil service. To a large extent the answer to this question emerged in the late 1980s as a result of a number of developments in the way the civil service carries out its functions. Today, there remains the need for a clear and unambiguous explanation of the role of the Civil Service in a period of new challenges and unprecedented demands on the civil service. This is one area where modernisation of the public sector has come about through a radical re-think of how the civil service ought to deliver public services. The process of modernisation in this instance began with Mrs Thatcher in 1979, drawing together many ideas for change first mooted in the Fulton Report. **11–010**

On becoming Prime Minister, Mrs Thatcher identified a number of shortcomings in the existing Civil Service. Led by private managerial techniques perceived to avoid waste and save money, Mrs Thatcher's Government adopted the strategy of applying private management to the public sector. **11–011**

The initial stage was to target 100,000 civil service jobs by April 1984, reducing the civil service to 630,000. In 1993 the number of civil servants fell below 600,000. Numbers have continued to decline to below 500,000. Reducing the size of the civil service was only a first step; the most fundamental development was to build on the reforms of the past and develop an efficiency strategy. The main themes involved in this strategy will be examined below. **11–012**

The origins of the Efficiency Strategy may be found in the appointment of Sir Derek Rayner in 1974, and later Sir Robin Ibbs as the Prime Minister's Special Adviser on Efficiency. The Rayner efficiency studies had their origins in the work undertaken after Fulton during the 1970s, under Edward Heath's proposals for creating "super" departments and hiving off through the Central Policy Review Staff, major policy decision-taking. A Programme Analysis and Review System designed to enhance the strategy of the decision-making powers of the Cabinet was introduced. **11–013**

Rayner's analysis brought private management skills into government coupled with a series of scrutinies aimed at identifying and eliminating areas of cost, inefficiency, **11–014**

---

[4] Sir Douglas Wass, *Government and the Governed* (1984). Also see Wass, "Checks and Balances in Public Policy Making" [1987] P.L. 181–201. P. Kellner and Lord Crowther-Hunt, *The Civil Servants: An Inquiry into Britain's Ruling Class* (1980), p.220.

duplication and overlap. Such scrutinies differed from past attempts to reform the civil service because generally the studies were carried out in a spirit of co-operation within the civil service. Department civil servants identified areas of administrative work where gains might be introduced cheaply and efficiently. Once specific areas were identified in reports, the second part of the efficiency strategy was introduced. The second part of the strategy was intended to consolidate and integrate evidence gained from individual scrutiny based on such findings; a major reform initiative was expected to take place with more far-reaching and long-lasting consequences than merely departmental savings.

11–015   Another significant difference in the Rayner studies was that reforms were focused on internal processes rather than external review. Beginning with Rayner as an efficiency adviser, the Prime Minister set up an Efficiency Unit as part of the Prime Minister's Office. This comprised a small unit located in the Cabinet Office. When the Civil Service Department was abolished in November 1981, introduced as one of the Fulton reforms, the responsibility for managing the civil service was divided between the Treasury and a newly-created Management and Personnel Office. The under-secretary who headed the Efficiency Unit was responsible for the management and efficiency division of the Management and Personnel Office. Thus the impetus for civil service reform came from within rather than from without.

11–016   The Rayner efficiency programme also accommodated the other policies of the Government. Pledged to provide value for money throughout the public sector, the Government set to work in an ambitious privatisation programme which moved the major nationalised utilities into Public Act Companies in the private sector. Internal reforms within the civil service picked up the guiding philosophy of the period, a world[5]:

> ". . . where bureaucrats (and ministers) are redefined as accountable managers, public sector operatives sub-divided into businesses, and the public seen as the customer."

11–017   The period to the end of 1982 saw the first results of the 133 Rayner Scrutinies and when Sir Derek Rayner relinquished the post, his successor, Sir Robin Ibbs, continued the process begun by Rayner. An estimate of the savings accomplished by Rayner and the reforms recommended for adoption is put at[6]:

> "Once and for all savings of £56 million and recurrent savings of £400 million and 21,000 posts per annum. Firm decisions had been reached on £29 million once and for all savings, with annual savings of £180 million and 12,000 posts. The recurrent savings recommended by October 1985 were £600 million, of which £300 million have actually been achieved. A further £145 million have been rejected, and the rest are somewhere in the pipeline."

11–018   Some mention should be made of the techniques adopted in the Rayner scrutiny. Specific objectives included:

[5] Sir Douglas Wass, Government and the Governed (1984). Also see Wass, "Checks and Balances in Public Policy Making" [1987] P.L. 181–201. P. Kellner and Lord Crowther-Hunt, The Civil Servants: An Inquiry into Britain's Ruling Class (1980), p.220.
[6] Les Metcalfe and Sue Richards, Improving Public Management (2nd ed., 1990), p.10.

- the examination of a specific policy or activity, including the investigation of all work normally taken for granted;

- recommendations for solutions seeking to achieve savings and cut costs, thus improving the efficiency and effectiveness of policies;

- implementation of agreed solutions with a clear knowledge of the implications of any solution proposed and its cost.

There are five main stages to setting up an efficiency scrutiny. First, topics for scrutiny are regularly suggested from within departments; secondly, investigations are carried out by departmental staff according to a set timetable, usually 90 working before reports should be submitted to Ministers; thirdly, action plans set out savings to be approved within three months of the report; fourthly, implementation which is the responsibility of the departmental permanent secretary; and finally, action taken, savings made and achieved are included in a report to be produced within two years of the start of the scrutiny.   **11–019**

A number of side effects are evident as a result of the Rayner scrutiny. Metcalfe and Richards have noted[7] that scrutineers within departments continue to carry out their role even after their study has been completed. This has led to some departments instigating their own form of scrutiny. The advantages of continuous monitoring become obvious over a long period of time.   **11–020**

Also noted has been the ability of the Efficiency Unit to make cross-department comparisons. This has helped to highlight difficulties within particular departments and encouraged ministerial kudos for making savings and carrying out waste reduction policies. This has given an increasing management function to the permanent secretary and deputy secretaries in each department.   **11–021**

The question arises as to whether such changes in the ethos of public service to the better managing of public resources has been accompanied by any cultural change within the civil service.   **11–022**

Throughout the Rayner efficiency studies the dominant theme has been to improve management structure within the civil service. Spearheading by a Prime Minister committed to saving money was a necessary pre-condition to finding the necessary will to undertake the studies in the first place. However, as Metcalfe and Richards note[8]: "Relying on political clout underestimates the extent to which the obstacles to reform are specifically cultural."   **11–023**

The reliance on a politically-driven and motivated efficiency system has given rise to some reservations about the lasting impact of Rayner's reforms. Johnson noted that there was a remarkable continuity between existing prescriptions for better management under the Rayner Scrutinies and earlier prescriptions for administrative improvement. It is suggested that the narrow perception of management found in the studies might suggest that all government administration was concerned with "controlling and supervising". The focus on economy, efficiency and effectiveness gives rise to what Metcalfe and Richards refer to as the limited "role of public managers to programmed implementation of predetermined policies. They disregard the problems of adapting policies and organisations to environmental change."   **11–024**

---

[7] Les Metcalfe and Sue Richards, *Improving Public Management* (2nd ed., 1990), p.10.
[8] *ibid*.

11–025   A comparison between public sector and business management techniques reveals that different management roles are preferred by different layers of management. Top management in the private sector deals with strategy, policy in new opportunities and even areas of uncertainty where a surprise change in the business environment may threaten existing arrangements. In public sector management little adaptation and learning are built into the processes and no clear differentiation is made between layers of management.

11–026   Metcalfe and Richards are sceptical as to whether Whitehall has learnt any lessons from business and little attention is given to questions about the machinery of government. By 1985 a total of 266 reviews were conducted amounting to annual savings of £600 million, with an additional £67 million as one-off savings. The Public Accounts Committee noted in 1986 that savings of £950 million had been made at a cost of only £5 million in scrutiny costs. As we shall see, impressive though such savings are, further steps were required in an effort to bring more long-term progress. In terms of civil service management and reform, first Rayner and then Ibbs had dramatically changed the conventional wisdom of how the civil service might perform its role.

MANAGEMENT TECHNIQUES

11–026a   The Rayner efficiency studies have encouraged the development of management techniques in the civil service. Since 1980 further changes introduced into the civil service have continued the development of new structures and organisation in the civil service. The changes in the 1980s have laid the foundations of a new public management strategy.The following is an account of how and why the techniques of managing business have become part of the ethos of the civil service.

11–027   In 1980, following the introduction of the Rayner efficiency studies, a more broadly-based initiative began to introduce structural changes within public management inside the civil service. This initiative, known as the Management Information System for Ministers (MINIS) identified the need to obtain information as one of the most important elements in exercising control and scrutiny and therefore avoiding waste.

11–028   The introduction of MINIS came from the pioneering efforts of Michael Heseltine, then Secretary of State at the Department of the Environment. The essential objectives of MINIS were to ascertain departmental economic targets, how they were set and how the department was carrying out its activities. MINIS was intended to remedy the defects in the chain of responsibility and to ascertain the data needed for decision-making. There was also an important role given in MINIS to the Minister—that of manager, assembling information and ensuring that the Minister was fully in charge of the department for which he was responsible. Soon MINIS became a commitment about information systems in public management.

11–029   MINIS involves three stages: First, each section head prepares a statement of activities with details of staff numbers, achievements and potential for future activities. Secondly, statements agreed within departments are considered by Ministers and management. Section heads are called to give evidence and subject to cross-examination on the policies contained in the statements. Finally, implementation of the second stage is carried out. The three-stage process is conducted annually. Each "cycle" of MINIS activity allows annual activites to be monitored.

The potential for MINIS is far-reaching. Staffing and expenditure may be more **11–030** accurately assessed, expenditure cuts offered and while most audit systems are normally *ex post facto*, MINIS attempts to be proactive and forward thinking. However, MINIS is not entirely innovatory. Many departments had experimented with some system of information retrieval; MINIS is simply more rigorous and streamlined. Fulton had advocated a MINIS-type initiative with specific cost centres working with allocated budgets. This had proved difficult to implement.

To civil servants MINIS offers an opportunity to find out exactly the true potential **11–031** of their departments and despite initial opposition to Heseltine's initiative in 1982 all departments were expected to develop a similar management system.

MINIS and its introduction throughout Whitehall bore some similarities to the **11–032** Rayner and Ibbs Efficiency Unit mentioned above. The success in introducing MINIS came from the initative of a strong Minister supported politically by the Prime Minister. In its initial stages the political rhetoric about its introduction may have facilitated some civil service resistance to its full effect. MINIS simply defines objectives, gives greater importance and focus to responsibilities and, in theory at least, supports the constitutional position of ministerial responsibility and civil service duty. This last matter has involved some serious questions about the relationship between civil servants and Ministers.

Three events have served to underline the idea of civil servants owing a duty to the **11–033** government of the day rather than directly to Parliament. These are the Maze prison breakout in 1983, the Clive Ponting trial in 1985 and the Westland affair in 1985-86, which brought greater attention to the role of civil servants than ever before. In the Maze prison breakout, civil servants were found at fault for a major failure in security at the Maze prison for which the Governor was held responsible. No Minister resigned because the escape was not attributed to any failure of policy but the Governor of the Maze did resign.

In the case of Clive Ponting, a civil servant was prosecuted under the Official Secrets **11–034** Act for releasing the text of a memorandum on the sinking of the *Belgrano* during the Falklands War. Although acquitted by a jury, the trial judge stated that civil servants owed a duty to Ministers as "the government of the day" rather than Parliament. In 1985–86 Mr Leon Britton, then Secretary of State for Trade and Industry, resigned after he authorised civil servants to take the improper action of releasing a confidential letter written by the Solicitor General to the Secretary of State for Defence.[9]

As MINIS was developing so was media interest in government and civil service **11–035** activities. The fact that MINIS appeared to release greater information about government came as a surprise to many commentators and increased interest in how government departments were organised. The civil servants involved in the examples mentioned above received greater publicity about their role in the conduct of government than ever before. The later litigation on the *Spycatcher* book containing the memoirs of Peter Wright, a former MI 5 officer and the evidence in Australia from the then Head of the civil service, Lord Armstrong, maintained at a high level, public interest in the civil service.[10] The civil service has continued to enjoy greater publicity than at any time in their history.

---

[9] Marshall, "Cabinet Government and the Westland Affair" [1986] P.L. 184; Oliver and Austin, "Political and Constitutional Aspects of the Westland Affair" (1987) 40 *Parliamentary Affairs* 20; Hennessy Report: Report of an Inquiry by H.M. Chief Inspector of Prisons into the Security Arrangements at H.M. Prison Maze (1983–84 HC 203).
[10] *Att.-Gen. v Guardian Newspapers Ltd (No.2)* [1988] 3 W.L.R. 776.

11–036   While MINIS kept parliamentary interest engaged in changes in attitude to management structures within the Civil Service, it was the introduction of the Financial Management Initiatives (FMI) in 1982 that secured a stronger niche for MINIS itself. The idea behind FMI was to promote a management accounting system within the civil service. This linked the activities of managing the civil service to the question of public expenditure surveys and estimates. These matters are discussed in more detail in the following chapter on Public Finance.

11–037   The aims of the FMI comprised three objectives. First, to set objectives and assess through the measurement of outputs of performance the achievement of the objectives. Secondly, to consider how resources are best managed, especially through value for money studies. Thirdly and finally, to set out costs, information on training and access to expertise to ensure that objectives are met.

11–038   This linked the management of the civil service to wider issues involving public expenditure built on the successes found in MINIS and in the early Rayner efficiency studies. It was no accident that Rayner pioneered the FMI system before he left in 1983 to return to Marks and Spencer. FMI was co-ordinated by a specially created unit of the Cabinet Office. Along with the Treasury later in 1985 this was replaced by a Treasury Cabinet Office Joint Management Unit.

11–039   The significance of MINIS and FMI was that for the first time the techniques of business management adapted to the public sector actually created changes in the structure and management of the civil service. MINIS may be perceived as usefully establishing a more accountable management structure. Clearer delegation of authority and levels of policy decision-making have been introduced. Another perception is that MINIS actually encouraged disclosure of information. More open government was encouraged. Published information provided opportunities for greater accountability for government activities.

11–040   A number of side-effects arising from the introduction of FMI may also be noted. The FMI strategy appeared to offer a counterbalancing effect on decision-taking against the prevailing tendency towards centralisation of government powers. Delegation and decentralisation were encouraged as part of cost-centre management. This led to the introduction in April 1988 of new running costs imposed on departments with cash limits set on individual civil service managers.

11–041   Any assessment of MINIS must take into consideration the frustrated attempts in earlier years to make management information systems part of the culture of the civil service. But this should be seen as only a first step towards a process which ultimately might lead to greater accountable management within departments. Injecting new ideas and innovatory ways to manage the public sector faces stiff opposition from the continuity fostered by the public service ethos, a legacy of the Victorian past. The Government's own assessment of FMI and further consideration of the steps to be taken for the future awaited a Report from the Government's Efficiency Unit begun in 1986, but not published until 1988 and known as The Next Steps.

THE NEXT STEPS

11–042   The background to the development of the Next Steps Initiative began after Robin Ibbs succeeded Derek Rayner as Head of the Efficiency Unit in 1983. While anxious to maintain the momentum set by Rayner, Ibbs shared the same drive for greater

efficiency inside the management structure set within the civil service. The main
question was how to assess FMI and how might initiatives to remedy any problems
with the FMI system be introduced.

The period from 1983 to 1986 was dominated by the attempt to implement FMI. In   **11–043**
theory FMI, by delegating executive responsibility to managerial decision-makers at a
local level, gave more budgeting control to individual civil servants, who would become
largely autonomous and removed from the direct oversight of ministerial control. Civil
servants, at least in the potential given to them to set and manage their own policy,
seemed remarkably freed from the tight hierarchical control favoured within the
traditional civil service. No major structural reforms had been introduced to implement the major changes such delegation may produce and not surprisingly difficulties
were experienced in the full implementation of FMI.

Many reasons for "this patchy development" of FMI have been suggested. A   **11–044**
number of institutions had overlapping jurisdictions and the fragmented institutional
arrangements within central government led to problems of identifying the respective
roles of each element in the management chain. Some departments adjusted more
easily to the demands of FMI than others. Progress on some elements in FMI was
greater than in other elements. For example, Wilson and Greenwood note[11]:

> "Progress was greater, for example, with developing management systems than
> with defining objectives, decentralization was developed more readily in field
> offices than in headquarters and policy divisions, and performance measurement
> applied more easily to inputs than outputs, and to administrative roles rather than
> programme expenditure."

Nevertheless FMI proved more durable than might have at first been supposed. This   **11–045**
was a political initiative taken by a Government agreeable to the introduction of the
business management ethos, into the civil service. Inter-government research on FMI
surveys has shown that the introduction of FMI has been accepted by the civil service.
It is likely therefore to survive beyond the political views of one particular government.
The success in persuading departments that "efficient management" is a necessary
prerequisite of the civil service seems accepted by most commentators.

In 1986 the Public Accounts Committee report noted that a new momentum was   **11–046**
required to speed up implementation of FMI. This touched a sensitive issue. It appears
that some reservations among top civil servants and even Government Ministers about
Robin Ibbs's views on spending within government departments may have contributed
to problems in implementing FMI.

A new initiative, in the form of a scrutiny report, begun in 1986 by Sir Robin Ibbs   **11–047**
was published in 1988. The report from the Efficiency Unit, *Improving Management in
Government: The Next Steps* suggested, to the surprise at least of Nigel Lawson, then
Chancellor of the Exchequer, that executive functions of government should be hived
off into separate executive agencies to be run like businesses by chief executives.

The evaluation underlying[12] this recommendation was that delegating budgeting, the   **11–048**
basis of FMI, was difficult to implement because of many of the traditions of the civil

---

[11] J. Greenwood and D. Wilson, *Public Administration in Britain Today* (2nd ed., 1989), p.135.
[12] Nigel Lawson, *The View from No. 11*, pp.390–392.

service. One problem identified in the report was the lack of management experience in top civil servants. This appeared to originate from top civil servants supporting policy advice to Ministers in Parliament rather than focusing on managing their departments. In order to change such administrative traditions, Ibbs suggested three main priorities. First, each department should reorganise its activities to ensure that the systems and structure provided for the effective delivery of policies and services. Second, the management of each department must ensure that their staff had the relevant experience, skills and abilities required to undertake tasks that are essential to effective government. Third, each department should have value for money in the delivery of its policies and services. In achieving value for money there should be continuous pressure to secure that objective throughout the department.

11–049   Setting objectives, however well formulated, did not guarantee their success, and Ibbs went one step further than before. The Next Steps scrutiny team in their report recommended that agencies should be established to carry out some of the executive functions of government. Departments could set the general policy and resources, but agencies should be developed to carry out the tasks allocated.

11–050   The Next Steps agencies, as they were referred to, were to be set up but as Nigel Lawson noted this left unresolved two major questions[13]:

"It was clear that Ibbs had not addressed the two principal problems involved in a change of this kind, however sensible the concept may have been. The first was the question of Parliamentary accountability. Members of Parliament would not take kindly to the idea of a Minister being able to shrug off a constituent's complaint as being nothing to do with him since the wrong suffered by the constituent had been inflicted by an autonomous agency, whose head was, according to the original Ibbs blueprint, effectively accountable to no-one."

11–051   The second problem identified by Lawson was that of maintaining effective financial control over the agencies' expenditure. Resolution of this problem came through an agreement reached with the Treasury and the appointment of Peter Kemp as manager of the Next Steps project with the status of Second Permanent Secretary.

11–052   The Ibbs Report implied that once Next Steps agencies were put in place, the role of the civil service would change. Changes introduced through the development of agencies might include differences in the allocation of resources and greater demands for value for money.

11–053   On the question of accountability[14] the creation of Next Steps agencies gave rise to fundamental questions about the relationship between the agencies, the civil service and the role of Ministers.

Administrative Agencies

11–054   In February 1988 a small cohesive Next Steps Unit was set up under Peter Kemp in the Office of the Minister for the Civil Service. By 1991 it was estimated that over 50 executive agencies, comprising 200,000 civil servants had been set up. Currently over 80 per cent of the civil service are in such agencies.

[13] Nigel Lawson, *The View from No. 11*, pp.390–392.
[14] The Next Steps Initiative, (HMSO, 1988). Cm.1761 (1991). The Government's reply to the Seventh Report from the Treasury and Civil Service Committee, (1990–91; HC 496).

The first agency created under Peter Kemp was the Vehicle Inspectorate, respon- **11–055** sible to the Department of Transport for heavy goods vehicles and licensees of garages. The model adopted became the standard practice. Responsibility for the day-to-day operations of each agency were delegated to a Chief Executive. The Chief Executive was responsible for management within a framework of policy objectives and resources set by the responsible Minister in consultation with the Treasury. Some other executive agencies were created with Her Majesty's Stationery Office (one of the largest), the Central Office of Information, the Land Registry and the Passport Office.

By December 31, 1996 there were 348,529 civil servants working in Next Steps **11–056** agencies amounting to 129 agencies. In addition, HM Customs and Excise, organised in 24 Executive Units, and the Inland Revenue, organised in 25 Executive Units, brought the total figure of 421,679 civil servants working on Next Steps lines. A further 27 Next Steps agencies are being planned. Further developments include the appropriate training and development of the civil service on the basis of the White Paper *Development and Training for Civil Servants: A Framework for Action.*[15] This initiative is accompanied by the plan to maintain the standards of the civil service while adapting to change. Managing the Civil Service in an area of change also has to confront the stereotype as explained by Gillian Peele[16]:

> "The bias at the higher levels towards graduates of Oxford and Cambridge has not, however, been the only concern about the civil service's composition. It was clear from the Cassells Report of 1983 that although almost half of the civil service were women, they formed a much higher proportion of the junior grades than of the senior one . . . The evidence on recent developments with respect to the role of women in the civil service is somewhat mixed. By 1994 very few of the top 38 posts at permanent secretary rank were held by women . . ."

The innovatory nature of the agency arrangements has given rise to a number of initial **11–057** problems. Prior to the grant of agency status a business plan and corporate identity requires careful consideration. The term Chief Executive carries high expectations of managerial control and business initiative. However, in public sector activities these may appear illusory because detailed financial control may still rest with the Treasury. Thus it took some time before bonus payments based on group and not individual initiative were accepted. This required protracted negotiation in the Vehicle Inspectorate before it was agreed. Chief executives are generally drawn from the civil service and this may continue old interests and pressures in the new guise of agency status. Similiarities with business appear inapplicable when it is recognised that ultimately financial failure is not a sanction.

Lawson notes that[17] "the main practical advantage . . . is that by creating accounts, **11–058** boards of directors and saleable assets, future privatisation may prove less difficult." It may be well within the scope of future governments to provide privatisation of civil service activities as the ultimate reform of the civil service. Therefore the idea that agency status is "second best to privatisation" may suggest that the Next Steps may be only one step in the progress toward complete privatisation.

[15] *The Civil Service: Taking Forward Continuity and Change,* Cm.2748 (July 1996).
[16] Gillian Peele, *Governing the United Kingdom* (3rd ed., Blackwell, 1995), p.137.
[17] N. Lawson, *The View from No. 11.* (Bantam Press, London, 1992), pp.390–392.

11–059   Agency status remains in its early stages of development. The Employment Service agency is an example of one of the largest agency arrangements and employs over 34,500 staff. The largest agency created is the Social Security Benefits agency employing over 89,248 staff. The Prison Service employs over 38,936 staff.

11–060   It is therefore no exaggeration to claim that[18] "Next Steps is radically altering the organisation of the Civil Service". It will also require careful scrutiny to determine if any of the desired changes in the management of civil service activities is actually achieved through agency status.

11–061   Initial studies contained in research work by Elizabeth Mellon into the working of a number of Executive Agencies have suggested criteria for evaluating an Agency. Three methods of evaluation may be adopted. First, an examination of performance measures from inside and outside the organisation may determine whether available resources have delivered services more efficiently and effectively. In this assessment an examination of cutting costs, and the performance criteria set out in the originating framework documents may be helpful. Secondly, to test the extent to which control has been given to members of staff inside agencies, which may assist in determining how leadership and responsibility within the agency may have changed. Thirdly, the introduction of the concept of "customers" within the civil service may allow feedback from customers, and responsiveness to customer needs may be quantified and tested.

11–062   Useful as such criteria may be, there are doubts as to whether agency status in itself may produce significant change to the operating practices of civil servants.

Agencies, Accountability and Control

11–063   Agency status has raised questions regarding accountability and control. How do agencies fit into the structure of constitutional oversight offered by select committees, ministerial responsibility and the existing status of the civil service. The answer to these questions has been raised, not only within the civil service and the government, but also in Parliament. At the forefront of discussion is the Parliamentary Select Committee on the Treasury and Civil Service. Reports since 1987–88 have both monitored and contributed to the information available on the role of agencies. It is now accepted that agencies have a bi-partisan approach from the political parties, and that the Committee itself has a role in monitoring arrangements on an annual basis. The Government has continued to provide assistance to the Committee on the subject of agencies.

11–064   In their fourth report 1990/91, the Select Committee on the Treasury and Civil Service noted that while agency status increased, the core departments in central government should continue to exercise "general responsibility for the oversight of the Civil Service".

11–065   In allocating agency status, the chief executive is required to manage the agency effectively[19] "to achieve the ends dictated by the Minister responsible". The chief executive is a civil servant in formal terms. The chief executive may appear before select committees responsible directly for the work as head of an agency. Thus the

---

[18] Elizabeth Mellon, Memorandum, Appendix 1 in *Evidence to the Treasury and Civil Service Committee Seventh Report, The Next Steps Initiative* (1990–91 HC 496).
[19] Cm.1263 (1990), p.3; *Hansard*, HC Vol.186, cols.270–2W.

chief executive appears to give evidence to select committees like any other civil servant on the minister's behalf. While this preserves the constitutional continuity between agency and civil service, Select Committees have voiced concern that in effect chief executives are not like any other civil servant because their responsibility as chief executives, laid down in framework documents differs from ordinary delegated authority given to the civil service by Ministers.

Parliamentary accountability for agencies appears to continue to rest on the Minister who is responsible to Parliament. Accountability also follows from this, through scrutiny by select committee, and individual M.P.s may ask parliamentary questions about areas within ministerial control.   **11–066**

Parliamentary questions[20] and procedures have proved difficult for agencies to fit into existing practices. Ministers normally reply to questions by promising to write to the M.P. When a parliamentary answer states that an executive agency will write, the letters written are to be sent to the Department of the Library, House of Commons. However, on detailed financial policy where the agency chief executive is responsible, Ministers may have little scope for reply. Inconsistency of approach between different agencies and departments may arise. One recommendation is that all replies from chief executives should be included in the Official Report. In this way access to all replies either from ministers or chief executives would conform to a common method.   **11–067**

In conclusion, the formulation of how Next Steps agencies fit within the conventional arrangements for ministerial responsibility appear to follow the distinction between operational and policy matters. Chief executives may answer for operational or day-to-day decisions, while ministers retain responsibility for policy matters. Even when ministers may interfere in operational matters, unless there are clear policy issues at stake, chief executives shoulder the burden of responsibility.   **11–068**

Undoubtedly one of the benefits attributable to agency status has been a growth in publications concerning the function of the agencies. Detailed accounts, future plans, corporate strategy, reviews of activities over the past financial year, objectives and key performance targets have all been included in a mass of agency annual reports. One criticism raises questions about the variety and lack of standardisation in the way such reports are produced, and the details of information they contain. Such inconsistency may give rise to confusion. Generally publications from agencies have been welcomed as providing additional information to Parliament.   **11–069**

A key factor in determining control over agencies is the question of budget management and financial scrutiny. The chief executive of an agency is appointed an Accountancy Officer or Agency Accounting Officer and is therefore accountable to the Committee of Public Accounts for the financial budgets of the agency. The Treasury has issued a note of guidance setting out the obligation for annual reports and accounts. This accountability through the publication of annual reports and accounts is also provided by the work of the National Audit Office.   **11–070**

The financial arrangements for agencies fall under direct vote, that is supply financed by the relevant government department or under trading fund arrangements. Supply financed agencies cover a wide spectrum of activities. Some agencies rely entirely on voted expenditure to cover only operating and capital requirements while   **11–071**

---

[20] Third Report of the Select Committee on Procedure, *Parliamentary Questions*, (1990–91 HC 178), para.125.

some agencies may cover all their costs. Supply financed agencies are cash limited in the normal departmental appropriation accounts. In such cases the departmental Accounting Officer remains accountable for all payments to the agency for votes for which he accounts.

11–072   In the case of trading fund agencies, the Treasury has published a guide to the Establishment and Operation of Trading Funds.[21] This guide sets out the criteria for the use of trading funds for:

> "certain kinds of operations within Government, particularly those where the outputs of the organisation are financed from related receipts and the demand for output fluctuates, for which cash control based on inputs can inhibit effective management."

11–073   Trading funds therefore provide agencies with greater flexibility than the normal restrictions implied in vote finance. In particular the financing framework covers all operating costs, receipts, capital expenditure, borrowing and cash flow. Compared to voted expenditure, trading funds have standing authority to meet outgoings from receipts and do not require advance approval by Parliament of income and expenditure. Such a fund may borrow and create reserves, thus maintaining a higher degree of flexibility than voted expenditure which may have difficulty meeting unexpected demands.

11–074   Agencies set up under the Trading Fund arrangements fall under the detailed requirements of the Government Trading Act 1990, which amends the Government Trading Funds Act 1973. The 1990 Act broadened the statutory criteria for setting up such funds. This necessitates removal from the normal parliamentary supply controls of the fund's expenditure and receipts. Before setting up such a fund parliamentary approval by affirmative Order is required, setting overall limits on borrowing.

11–075   The statutory tests are that: first, operations to be financed by a trading fund must already be carried out by a government department. Secondly, revenues of the fund must primarily consist of receipts "in respect of goods or services provided". This means that funds arise from payment for goods, services rendered and not through block grants or taxation. Finally, the funds must be established in the interests of "improved management, efficiency and effectiveness".

11–076   The enabling powers under both the 1973 and 1990 Acts are supplemented under s.2 of the 1973 Act, which provides administrative suitability for each fund to be worked out with the Treasury and the sponsoring government department responsible. Trading funds are therefore more likely to provide greater flexibility for agencies than voted accounts.

11–077   Accountability is driven through both the internal structures and accounting practices of each agency as well as external information to parliamentary select committees and published reports. An added incentive is that the Citizen's Charter[22] envisages standard-setting for the delivery of goods and services. All agencies within the Citizen's Charter remit must comply with the principles of the Charter including

[21] Appendix 10: Memorandum submitted by H.M. Treasury, *Guide to the Establishment and Operation of Trading Funds*, Seventh Report of the Treasury and Civil Service Committee, The Next Steps Initiative (1990–91; HC 496), p.123.
[22] *Citizen's Charter*, Cm.1599 (1991), pp.36–38.

complaints procedures, consultation with customers and clients, and compiling track records of their activities.

CIVIL SERVANTS AND MINISTERS

Curiously there has been great reluctance to set out a statutory framework for the civil service. The Civil Service (Management Functions) Act 1992 provides one of the few Acts of Parliament that apply. Ministers may delegate various powers for the pay, conditions and regulation of the civil service. The need for statutory protection to secure the independence of the civil service ought to receive some attention. The Armstrong Memorandum in 1985 asserted that the duty of the individual civil servant is "first and foremost" to the Minister of the Crown.[23] The Civil Service Code (1996) was further revised in 1999 and takes account of the Official Secrets Act 1989, the role of civil service in their relationship with ministers and in giving evidence before select committees. The code contains the requirement that civil servants should not deceive or knowingly mislead Parliament or the public. This has given rise to questions concerning the procedures to be adopted in the event of a dispute between a civil servant and a Minister. While the legal position is clear that civil servants do not owe any direct duty to Parliament but absolute loyalty to Ministers, there is concern that the public interest does not always coincide with the law. In effect civil servants may find that they are covering up for ministerial mistakes or bad policy decisions. This raises questions about the role of Parliament in its holding of civil servants to account. No satisfactory solution to this question appears given the convention of ministerial responsibility.

11–078

The Treasury and Civil Service Select Committee[24] has received detailed evidence on the question of accountability of Next Steps agencies chief executives. One view was that the chief executive for an agency might have some form of parallel responsibility to that of the Minister and thus fit into a separate category of direct accountability to Parliament from the Minister. This view was rejected as inconsistent with the doctrine of ministerial accountability. The example of Derek Lewis, the former Director-General of the Prison Service, who resigned following the report by Sir John Learmont inquiring into prison escapes from Parkhurst.[25] The then Home Secretary Michael Howard refused to resign, drawing on the distinction between operational and policy matters. He claimed that as the Home Secretary was responsible for policy and no policy had been found to be at fault, he was entitled to rely on this fact and not resign. The Lewis case shows how difficult it would be to "force" agency chief executives to hold Ministers to account. In the case of the Next Steps agency there is greater transparency between administrators and policy-makers, and Ministers and chief executives. The relationship between Ministers and chief executives is contained in the framework documents subject to review every three years. The "quasi-contractual nature" of that

11–079

---

[23] Sir Robert Armstrong, *The Duties and Responsibilities of Civil Servants in Relation to Ministers: Note by the Head of the Home Civil Service* (1985 HC Official Report, Vol.74).
[24] Minutes of Evidence taken before the Treasury and Civil Service Select Committee (1993–94 HC 27), November 23, 1993.
[25] *Hansard*, HC Vol.264, cols.502–506 (November 18, 1995).

relationship may give rise to questions of adequate decision-making and accountability for any policy or management mistakes giving rise to claims in negligence.

BSE—a Case Study of Crisis Management

11–080   The relationship between civil servants, advisors and ministers comes under detailed scrutiny during a period of crisis. Two examples serve to show the problems of tackling policy under intense political controversy and media attention. The first is the foot-and-mouth epidemic and the second is the BSE crisis. The first example showed how managing a crisis in the absence of an up-to-date emergency plan tests resources to their limits with the result that panic and confusion took over and policy was not proactive but reactive. Decisions when to order a cull of cattle and make use of the Army were taken often too late and with poor direction. In the second case the bovine spongiform encephalopathy (BSE) crisis in Britain over the past decade highlights the important link between scientific research, regulation and government decision-making. It serves to illustrate the dilemma faced when regulatory decisions to protect the environment, agriculture and human health must be based on uncertain scientific knowledge. It also starkly demonstrates the economic cost and the possible human cost of regulatory inaction owing to scientific uncertainty.

11–081   In 1999 the roles of the main institutional actors in the crisis, including the Ministry of Agriculture, Fisheries and Food (MAFF), the scientific community, government research scientists and ministers were the subject of an independent inquiry chaired by Lord Phillips, a senior judge.[26] The remit for the Inquiry was to establish and review the history of the BSE epidemic (a prion disease of cattle) and variant Creutzfeld-Jakob Disease (vCJD, the human form of the disease). The Inquiry was also to establish what action had been taken in response to the BSE epidemic and present recommendations for the future. A number of key findings were made by the Inquiry that raised questions over both the scientific advice and the role of decision-makers in developing a suitable regulatory regime in response to BSE. The aim of the Inquiry was not to apportion fault but to understand the nature of advice given and the lessons to be learnt.

11–082   The Phillips Inquiry found that BSE was not caused by scrapie in sheep, but was probably the result of a chance appearance of a new spongiform encephalopathy in a single animal during the 1970s. The original hypothesis made by a senior government vet, that BSE was the result of cattle being fed scrapie-infected meat and bone meal, was based on the best available information at the time. It was not, however, subsequently questioned by scientists even though there was increasing evidence that this may not be the case. The assessment that BSE was very unlikely to jump the species barrier and cause disease in humans was largely based on this assumption. The Phillips Inquiry's assessment of scientific evidence found that an exceptionally small dose of infective material, potentially as little as a gram, is needed for the transmission of BSE between animals. Evidence for this was found relatively early in the BSE epidemic but was largely overlooked by scientists, even though it had large implications in terms of the potential for transmission and the epidemiology of BSE. Phillips also

---

[26] *The BSE Inquiry. The Inquiry into BSE and variant CJD in the United Kingdom* (Stationery Office, 1999). Also available on *www.bseinquiry.gov.uk*

found that senior government scientists including the Chief Medical Officer continued   **11–083**
to inform the public that BSE could not pass the species barrier and was not
transmissible to humans as late in the epidemic as 1990. This was despite growing
evidence and concern that this may not be the case and came after the discovery of an
infected cat. It was never indicated that reassurances that beef was safe to eat were
based on the fact that the most infective material was removed from the meat
carcasses.

The Southwood Report[26a] was the subject of criticism in arriving at conclusions that   **11–084**
were claimed to be unfounded and unwarranted. A further criticism of the Southwood
Report is that information was considered to be, on occasions, poorly communicated
in the Report. In particular the statement that:

> "From the present evidence, it is likely that cattle will prove a 'dead-end host' for
> the disease agent and most unlikely that BSE will have any implications for
> human health. Nevertheless, if our assessment of these likelihoods are incorrect,
> the implications would be extremely serious."

The Phillips Inquiry also made a number of findings that went to the nature of the   **11–085**
response by the Ministry of Agriculture, Fisheries and Food (MAFF) and Government
ministers to the BSE crisis. Firstly, there was an atmosphere of secrecy and a lack of
openness on the part of Government departments. This affected not only the
information available to the public but the ability of government departments to work
together. Indeed, in general throughout the crisis, Government departments failed to
communicate and work together. The BSE epidemic and the potential spread of a
spongiform encephalopathy to humans were problems that fell within the remit of
several departments including the Department of Health, MAFF and, once large scale
slaughter and disposal of carcasses began, the Department of Environment, Transport
and the Regions. A lack of co-operation between departments reduced the speed and
effectiveness of the Government's response to the BSE epidemic. For example,
although by late 1987 MAFF officials were concerned about the prospect of meat from
diseased cattle entering the human food chain, they did not pass on their concerns to
the Department of Health. Similarly the Department of Health was not informed as to
MAFF's concerns about the incorporation of cattle products in medicines. It is
noteworthy that the lesson of communication and co-operation between departments
appears still not to be learnt. In the recent foot-and-mouth epidemic MAFF did not
initially discuss with the Environment Agency the environmental risks associated with
mass incineration or burial of animal carcasses; nor have all the mass burial sites used
by MAFF for disposal of carcasses been authorised, as required by the 1998
groundwater regulations, by the Environment Agency.[27]

The Phillips Inquiry also found that there were excessive delays in Government   **11–086**
departments acting on clear scientific advice. For example, nearly three years elapsed
between the Spongiform Encephalopathy Advisory Committee (SEAC)[28] advising that

---

[26a] The Southwood Report, Report of the Working Party on BSE (The Southwood Report (1989)
Department of Health, London 1989).
[27] See 'Confusion reigns over foot and mouth burial sites' in *The Ends Report*, No.320, p.9.
[28] The Spongiform Encephalopathy Advisory Committee (SEAC) was established in 1990 as a standing
committee reporting to MAFF and the Department of Health on spongiform encephalopathy.

schools should be warned of the risks associated with dissecting bovine eyeballs and schools actually being warned.

11–087   The Phillips Inquiry found that research indicating that BSE was a new disease was withheld by MAFF. For example, the Chief Veterinary Officer refused permission for research work undertaken on BSE to be submitted to a scientific journal. Such non-submission could, of course, be for a number of reasons, *e.g.* a poorly prepared article or poor data, but given the serious nature of the BSE epidemic it would seem essential to address any such faults speedily and release material for publication. Withholding research information had a number of consequences. First there was a lack of accurate information in the public domain; and second the dissemination of scientific information to the broader scientific community was inhibited. Any impediment to the communication of scientific data to as wide a scientific community as possible would inevitably slow understanding of the risks posed by BSE.

11–088   It was found that measures to halt the spread of BSE and limit any potential transmission to humans were inadequate and misconceived. In part this probably arose because of the nature of BSE and the large uncertainties with regard to the risks posed to humans by the disease. The Inquiry Report puts this dilemma in the following terms: "At the heart of the BSE story lie questions of how to handle hazard—a known hazard to cattle and an unknown hazard to humans".

11–089   Finally the Phillip's Inquiry found that the public was generally insufficiently informed about BSE and any risks to humans associated with the disease in cows. There was a marked lack of openness and transparency in the availability of information to the public. In the early stages this may have arisen to avoid perhaps unwarranted public concern affecting both home and export markets for an economically important industry. It may have become perpetuated by the uncertainties remaining unresolved, while balanced against a large and highly evident economic cost of full disclosure of information.[29]

11–090   The BSE crisis highlights some of the challenges facing modern government. A previously unseen risk that has unpredictable consequences and outcomes challenged the decision-making functions of both ministers and civil servants. Ministers, while relying on expert specialist advice, appeared to delegate the key decisions to experts, without recognising that the public interest required sound political and economic judgements to be made—most importantly to inform the public of the full facts. Failure to engage in an open debate about risk left the public losing confidence in ministers and in the process of government. Parliament also appears to have been left on the side-lines while centre stage was given to media attention and hype.

THE NEW PUBLIC MANAGEMENT

11–091   As Gavin Drewry has pointed out:

> "Public administration has been displaced—at least in part—by a 'new public management' (NPM) which rejects bureaucratic methods and structures in favour of market-based and business-like regimes of public service."[30]

[29] I am grateful to Sharron McEldowney for the details of the above case study.
[30] Gavin Drewry, "The New Public Management" in *The Changing Constitution*, (D. Oliver and J. Jowell ed., 4th ed., 2001), pp.168–189.

This may be regarded as a global phenomenon or, as Hughes[31] refers to it, "a new **11–092** global paradigm".

This new paradigm for public management sharply contrasts with the early **11–093** foundations of the modern civil service. The Northcote-Trevelyan Report and reforms of 1853 set the standard for the service to be built on public trust and stewardship of public funds. Replacing the earlier form, based on patronage and appointment on favour, the new civil service after the Northcote-Trevelyan reforms was characterised by political neutrality, appointment on merit, and permanence, and was generally admired and respected. The establishment in 1969 of the Civil Service College and an internal code of discipline further enhanced its reputation. Rarely was the criminal law required, except in the case of some well-publicised breaches of the Official Secrets Act 1911, 1920–1939 later amended in 1989. As explained in the previous chapter there is a new Freedom of Information Act 2000, but it remains to be seen whether the Act will provide more open government.

Changes in approach to the management of the civil service began when Margaret **11–094** Thatcher was Prime Minister. First there was a drop in civil service staffing levels and a reduction in the status of the Civil Service. Drewry estimates that:

> "[i]n 1979 there were 732,000 civil servants; ten years later the figure stood at 570,000; by 1999 it was around 450,000. The early Thatcher years saw a substantial squeeze on civil service pay, and subsequently there have been moves in many parts of the public sector away from traditional, more or less automatic incremental pay increases towards more performance-related pay regimes."[32]

Changes were also introduced in the management of the civil service. The Next Steps **11–095** initiative provided a change in structure and organisation. The unitary structure of the past was replaced by the use of agencies—an idea that appears to have been considered many years previously, in the Fulton Report[33] of 1968. However, it was not until 1979 that a substantial reconsideration of the organisation of the civil service was undertaken.

At the heart of the organisational reforms is the separation between the policy **11–096** functions of the civil service (undertaken by about 20,000 civil servants working in close collaboration with ministers) and the delivery of services. The latter would be undertaken by agencies that operate at arm's length from government or the policy-making side of the civil service. The distinction between policy making, for which ministers are in theory accountable to Parliament, and operational decisions, which are undertaken by civil servants in agencies and for which ministers appear not to be directly accountable, was—ironically—in vogue when the nationalised industries were in public ownership. The distinction, such as it is, forms one of the main boundaries between those situations that call for ministerial resignation and those in which the fault is seen as lying with civil servants. An example is the distinction between the role of the Home Office and of the police. The former sets guidelines, while the latter is free to interpret and implement guidelines depending on operational needs.

Next Steps agencies have proliferated. Gavin Drewry estimates: **11–097**

---

[31] O. Hughes, *Public Management and Administration* (2nd ed., 1998), quoted in Drewry.
[32] Drewry, *op.cit.*, p.169.
[33] Fulton Report: *The Civil Service*, Cmnd.3638, 1968.

"By 1st April 1997 there were 110 agencies in the Home Civil Service, plus Customs and Excise, Inland Revenue, the Crown Prosecution Service, and the Serious Fraud Office, operating on next steps lines: these bodies covered nearly 77 per cent of the civil service—364,163 permanent staff."[34]

11–098   Each Next Steps agency is headed by a chief executive whose role is equivalent to that of the head of a medium-sized company, with performance targets for the delivery of their services and budget responsibility in many cases as trading funds. The transformation of the civil service into agencies has had profound implications for the culture of the civil service and the system of accountability and control. Civil service culture fits under the traditional—and some would argue, malleable—concept of ministerial responsibility, while accountability and control fall under the scrutiny of the National Audit Office and the various select committees of the House of Commons.

11–099   The Citizen's Charter initiative seeks to empower citizens as regulators and thus create a form of popular accountability. Agencies, and public services generally, are to provide information to the citizen, who is to assess the value and quality of public services on the basis of consumer choice and quality testing.

11–100   The direction set for public services may be found in the March 1999 White Paper of the Blair Government, *Modernising Government*.[35] The aim is for government to fulfil a more strategic role, to be more forward-thinking and to make the users of public services the focus of strategy and reforms. Instruments to ensure the implementation of this strategy include the development of best practice; the use of close targets and monitoring; the adoption of best value on an economic and financial evaluation, across all aspects of public service; and the integration of stronger business principles into the working of government.

11–101   It cannot be denied that many of the changes outlined above create a new era for the civil service. How might this be characterised? The current orthodoxy within the civil service is that the service remains "unified but not uniform", driven by the demands of consumer service, and negotiating contracts with the citizen as consumer and regulator of those services.

11–102   There is a clear tension between the culture of the traditional civil service and the role of advisers, exemplified in recent problems arising from the resignation of Jo Moores, a political advisor in the Department of Transport, Local Government and the Regions.[36] There is a need for a new statutory framework for the civil service setting out in a clear way the relationship between civil servants, advisers and ministers. All these changes need to be placed within the overall context of constitutional change.

11–103   There is a public perception of increasing prime ministerial power, and concern about an increasingly presidential style, at a time when devolution to the regions and the fragmentation of the party system is at its keenest. This increase in prime ministerial power has not been matched by a commensurate change in the scrutiny functions of Parliament. In fact the converse appears to be the case. Parliament and its structures appear weakened, and parliamentary accountability appears diminished in value. As already noted, at the same time that there appears to be a diminution in

[34] Drewry, *op.cit.*, p.177.
[35] *Modernising Government*, Cm.4310, 1999.
[36] *Guardian*, February 27, 2002.

Parliamentary accountability there is an increase in the powers of the courts, not least through the development of judicial review and the coming into force of the Human Rights Act 1998.

SUMMARY AND CONCLUSIONS

A number of important changes have been brought about by the new Labour government elected in 1997 and for a second term in 2001. The emphasis is on modernisation. The White Paper *Modernising Government*[37] provides for more joined-up government and consolidates ideas of the citizen as a regulator as well as consumer of goods and services. This is perceived as introducing greater flexibility in working with the private and public sectors to develop "joined up" government. It includes initiatives to avoid "borrowing to spend", in favour of policies of prudent resource allocation, low inflation and low unemployment. Modernisation has also given rise to a number of major constitutional initiatives inside government itself. These include the centralisation of the Cabinet Office, with greater use of advisers and others appointed to guide the government in its policy-making. Although technically civil servants, the advisers are political appointees and have not been recruited on the basis of an open system of appointment. Neither do they fall under the Civil Service Code, and they will probably leave their position with any change of prime minister.   **11–104**

In management terms the civil service as a public sector institution is going through a creative time, developing new ideas on public management. However, two *caveats* require consideration. First, public management is not necessarily best described as a business because of the added dimension of greater accountability. Such pressures for accountability need to be accommodated within public sector management techniques. As Metcalfe and Richards point out: **11–105**

> "Pouring new managerial wine into old accountability bottles may have explosive consequences. Part of the future agenda of public management will be designing accountability systems."

The second *caveat* is that government itself, by hiving off activities to agencies, remains subject to the question of how best to develop for the future. This may pose the most demanding challenge for the civil service especially as past experience has shown that administrative change has been gradual, piecemeal and incremental.   **11–106**

The role of the senior civil servant in advising Ministers retains civil service power and influence. Ministers often seek the support of outside advisers to provide political and specialist support in carrying out their policies. It has been argued that identifying civil servants, often named to the public, with particular government policies impairs the political neutrality of civil servants[38]:   **11–107**

> "Individual senior civil servants are already associated with particular government policies. The present government's recent appointments at senior levels of the

[37] *Op.cit.*
[38] L. Metcalfe and S. Richards, *Improving Public Management* Sage, Open University, London, 2nd ed. 1990, p.236.

civil service acknowledge and reflect this political reality by the selection of civil servants committed to the formulation and effective implementation of specific policies consistent with the general framework of government policy. Civil servants have become, in a sense, political advocates, capable of arguing the case for and implementing different sets of policies depending upon the political complexion of the government of the day."

11–108 One effect of agencies in the civil service is to allow greater scrutiny to be given to civil service activities as an indirect result of establishing new agencies. In this new environment civil service secrecy and confidentiality comes increasingly under threat. Annual reports from agencies provide much more information than previously available from within government departments. The business of government and the management of administration are now closely combined with results that are still to be fully determined.

FURTHER READING

Gavin Drewry, "The New Public Management" in *The Changing Constitution* (J. Jowell and D. Oliver ed., 4th ed., Oxford University Press, Oxford, 2001), pp.168–189

O. Hughes, *Public Management and Administration* (Macmillan, London, 1998).

The Civil Service (Management Functions) Act 1992.

The Civil Service Code (revised May 1999).

T. Daintith and A. Page, *The Executive in the Constitution* (Oxford University Press, Oxford, 1999).

P. Hennessy, *Whitehall* (Secker and Warburg, London, 1989).

N. Lawson, *The View from No. 11*, (Bantam Press, London, 1992).

Chapter 12

PUBLIC FINANCE

INTRODUCTION

Public finance refers to the government's requirements in relation to raising and **12–001** spending money. The House of Commons performs the important function of authorising public expenditure and taxation. In the management of the economy, government exercises wide powers through economic policy, and controls through its influence on the economy and the Bank of England. Money supply, interest rates and the economic policy of the government of the day are often linked to the various international financial institutions such as the International Monetary Fund and the World Bank.

Since 1969 the Member States of the European Community have been discussing **12–002** economic and monetary union. Ten years later the European Monetary System (EMS) came into operation. Membership of the EMS is open to all Member States. The United Kingdom is currently a member. Members of the EMS take part in discussions on the future functioning and development of the system. In January 2002 the successful introduction of the new coins and notes of the Euro is seen as a triumph of policy. One of the key issues for the future will be the United Kingdom's decision whether or not to introduce the Euro. The five tests for joining and the promise of a referendum are the mechanism chosen by the Government to determine whether or not to join. The determination of the criteria is linked to a political judgement when to hold a referendum as a condition precedent to joining. Increasingly, issues raised about public finance are linked to the development of economic policy and relations within the European Community and external relations with other countries notably the United States and the value of the dollar.

Modernisation of government has also continued apace in the changes introduced in **12–003** the area of public finance. Major innovations include independence granted to the Bank of England in the Bank of England Act 1998 over interest rates, and the creation of a Monetary Policy Committee as part of the preparation for Britain's eventual acceptance of the Euro. Incremental changes include the phased introduction of resource accounting which currently operates within the system of Estimates and Appropriation Accounts until 2001. After this, resource budgeting was introduced.

Improvements have been made in various consultation processes. Since 1997 the **12–004** introduction of the Chancellor's Pre-Budget Consultation Process in November allows some months of scrutiny before final budget decisions are taken and the budget is presented in April. *A Handbook on Regularity and Propriety* (1997), *A Code for Fiscal*

Stability (1998), a *Resource Accounting Manual* (2002) and up-dating supplements to *Government Accounting* (1989–, currently 2002) have been published. The Fundamental Expenditure Review introduced by the Treasury in 1993 continues to advise departments as to whether their spending trends over the long term are sustainable and appropriate. The purpose of this chapter is to examine the main procedures and institutions used to manage, control and hold to account public expenditure. The starting point is to provide an introductory outline of first, the sources of government revenue and second, the structures for the control and planning of public expenditure.

THE SYSTEM OF PLANNING AND FINANCIAL CONTROL

12–005   The development of a system of financial control has evolved over centuries on an ad hoc basis. The procedures for financial control are of great complexity with numerous changes and additions added as need arises. In recent years the pace of change has quickened and in response the Treasury provides a number of manuals containing detailed accounts of the main financial rules and procedures for government departments. Part of the reason for such complexity lies in the nature and diversity of the assortment of rules. Many rules are developed as constitutional conventions or customs. Some are to be found in primary legislation. Most are contained in codes and memoranda addressed to the system of internal checks and balances that are intended to ensure that financial probity and propriety is observed. In the absence of express statutory authority, the legality of many of the rules rests on the prerogative powers of the Crown. Filling the gaps in this way has provided a time-honoured contribution to the diversity of the British Constitution. In fact the area of public finance provides an opportunity to examine regulation that is applied as internal rules and practices within government itself and through external rules and systems of accountability.

12–006   The authoritative source for parliamentary practice is Erskine May's *Treatise on the Law, Privileges, Proceedings and Usage of Parliament* which has undergone revision through a number of editions. Additional rules and codes are to be found through Treasury guidance developed over the years and in *Government Accounting*, a regularly updated guide to the procedures and rules that apply to financial control.

Public Revenue

12–007   Government raises taxes in order to finance public spending. Public expenditure currently runs at about 40 per cent of the entire economy's national income. This amounts to approximately £418.4 billion. Taxation takes many forms and must be authorised by Act of Parliament. An annual Finance Act sets the limits of the amount payable each year. The courts have been vigilant in ensuring that legal authority has been correctly granted. In *Bowles v Bank of England*,[1] Bowles was successful in suing the Bank of England for a declaration that income tax could not be deducted by virtue of a budget resolution alone and until such tax had been imposed by Act of

---

[1] [1913] 1 Ch. 57. Also see *British Oxygen v Board of Trade* [1971] A.C. 610; *Burmah Oil v Bank of England* [1980] A.C. 1090.

Parliament, he was not required to pay it. The case led to the Provisional Collection of Taxes Act 1968 which gives statutory force for a limited time to resolutions of the House of Commons varying taxation levels and soon to be made part of the Finance Act.

In 1975, in *Congreve v Home Office*[2] the Court of Appeal held that it was unlawful for the Home Office to make use of its revocation powers under the Wireless Telegraphy Act 1949, to revoke the TV licence to prevent licence holders benefiting from an overlapping licence purchased to avoid an increase in the licence fee. Congreve and about 20,000 other licence holders had purchased a second licence while their existing licence was still valid, in anticipation of an increase in the licence fee. Lord Denning claimed that the Bill of Rights 1689 had been infringed as a levying of money without grant of Parliament. There is some doubt on this interpretation. Congreve had sought avoidance of a tax through the purchase of a second licence, clearly not intended by the Wireless Telegraphy Act. However the case illustrates how the judges will adapt statutory interpretation to uphold the principle of authorisation.

12–008

In *Woolwich Building Society v Inland Revenue Commissioner (No.2)*[3] the House of Lords considered the general principle that money paid to a public authority pursuant to an *ultra vires* demand should be repayable as of right. The case arose out of an Inland Revenue demand for tax from the Woolwich Building Society, which was later declared by the courts to have no lawful basis. It was accepted that the money paid to the Revenue was not paid under any mistake of law on the part of the tax payer; but the Woolwich Building Society had no express statutory right to repayment of the money. The House of Lords held that money pursuant to an *ultra vires* demand was *prima facie* repayable as a common law right of the subject. Lord Goff considered how far the principle might[4]:

12–009

"... extend to embrace cases in which the tax or other levy has been wrongly exacted by a public authority not because the demand was ultra vires but for other reasons, for example because the authority has misconstrued a relevant statute or regulation."

Lord Goff's views, although *obiter dicta* emphasise the vigour with which the courts may review the taxation powers of the revenue. In the *Woolwich* case the payment of tax amounted to almost £57 million with interest and dividends, an illustration of the role of the courts in revenue matters with an indirect effect on expenditure totals. The government has estimated that the total cost of repaying composite rate tax to all Building Societies which had overpaid amounted to £250 million.[5]

12–010

The annual cycle of raising and spending money continues the tradition of established constitutional practice. The government, in the name of the Crown demands money, the Commons grant it and the Lords give assent. Central government has the important long-term role of managing the economy. The government receives

12–011

---

[2] [1976] Q.B. 629.
[3] [1992] 3 All E.R. 737.
[4] [1992] 3 All E.R. 737 at 764d–e. (See also Lord Slynn at p.783, for example). See J. Beatson, "Restitution of Taxes, Levies and Other Imposts: Defining the Extent of the Woolwich Principle" [1993] *L.Q.R.* 401.
[5] Beatson, *op.cit.*, p.428. Beatson also notes the effect of the decision in *Pepper v Hart* [1993] 1 All E.R. 86 on the taxation of benefits in kind which may lead to £30 million in refunds of tax.

direct taxes levied on income or capital and indirect taxes levied on spending. The Inland Revenue under the authority, direction and control of the Treasury, collects direct taxes and Her Majesty's Customs and Excise are responsible for collecting customs duties on goods entering the European Community and most excise duties. They also collect value added tax (VAT). There is an increase in the use of indirect taxation varying from petrol duties to airport taxes. In addition to taxation, the government may borrow money to finance its expenditure. This may be achieved through borrowing from the International Monetary Fund or World Bank. The government may also obtain receipts from the sale of assets. For example, receipts from privatisation sales have netted over £50 billion since 1981. An additional source of income has been revenue from the Crown Estates, about £70 million, in return for which the Queen is paid a fixed annual sum called the Civil List—approximately £24 million for the upkeep of Royal Palaces and over £12 million on the Queen and other members of the Royal Family. From November 1992 it was agreed that the Queen would pay income tax on a voluntary basis, though it is difficult to know for certain how much her private investments are worth. It was said that £100 million was too wild an estimate.

12–012   All public revenue is paid into the Consolidated Fund. In addition the National Loans Acts 1968–73 and extended by the Government Trading Act 1990, established a National Loans Fund as the central government account for all government borrowing and most domestic lending operations. Loans from the Fund require statutory authority.

The Treasury, Planning and Financial Control

12–013   The Treasury[6] is the main department under the Chancellor of the Exchequer responsible for the management of the economy. The Haldane Report[7] in 1918 identified a number of functions that describe the modern Treasury. In addition to the management of the economy, the Treasury, with the authority of Parliament, imposes and regulates taxation, arranges funds to meet day-to-day demands for public services and manages and controls the national debt. Finally in the control of public expenditure the Treasury supervises and prepares the supply estimates.

12–014   The Treasury combines the work of a government department with the role of exercising internal financial control over government departments. Control is usually *a priori* because the Treasury prepares, monitors, audits, and authorises under parliamentary authority, the expenditure of money. The rules relating to public finance have a miscellany of sources. The Treasury produces a large looseleaf guide to *Government Accounting* which is regularly updated with amendments. Conventions, practices and statutory arrangements are noted and described. In addition, and dating back to 1934, with a revision in 1977, there is a *Treasury Handbook: Supply and other Financial Procedures of the House of Commons*. This is a foundation document for the *Government Accounting* manual.

12–015   The Treasury may act as a guide to departments in terms of advice and consultation. In preparing legislation, departments are required to keep the Treasury informed of

---

[6] An excellent account of the Treasury may be found in Henry Roseveare, *The Treasury* (Penguin, 1969); M. Wright, *Treasury Control of the Civil Service 1854–1974* (Oxford, 1969).
[7] Cd.9230 1918.

any proposals for legislation with a financial implication. Consultation is expected at an early stage and the amendments to Bills should be included if they affect the financial arrangements. This represents a major influence over how departments consider spending public money.

The key official within departments, who exercises considerable responsibilities for **12–016** public finance, is the Accounting Officer. The Accounting Officer is appointed by the Treasury and their responsibilities are contained in a detailed Memorandum which they each receive on appointment. Accounting Officers are in effect expected to combine their task of ensuring a high standard of financial management in their department with the duty to serve their Minister. An Accounting Officer is appointed for every vote account in compliance with s.22 of the Exchequer and Audit Departments Act 1866, and s.4(6) of the Government Trading Funds Act 1973 and the Trading Fund Act 1990 provide for the appointment of a departmental Accounting Officer by the Treasury for Trading Accounts. The Accounting Officer is given responsibility for signing accounts and appearing as the principal witness on behalf of the department before the Committee of Public Accounts (PAC).

The Accounting Officer has the crucial role of ensuring that Treasury sanction is **12–017** obtained for expenditure and that funds are applied to the extent and for the purposes authorised by Parliament. The internal network of Treasury control over expenditure depends on his exercise of authority. He is a powerful ally to both Government, Treasury and the PAC in controlling expenditure and ensuring propriety. He provides the link between internal control and the external audit carried out by the Comptroller and Auditor General (C&AG) and the Public Accounts Committee, while maintaining his independent status. It can be appreciated that in practical terms the effectiveness of the C&AG depends on his obtaining the co-operation of Accounting Officers and Government departments. The latter role is of crucial importance to the Treasury system of internal audit. There is a specialised manual for Government Internal Audit. This contains the basic standards for the Treasury's internal audit representing good practice. An internal audit is an independent appraisal within a department as a service to management in measuring and evaluating standards within the department.

Through the system of internal audit the Accounting Officer may be assisted in his **12–018** task. Internal audit is not however seen as a substitute for line management; it is a means to ensure that appraisal within a department is properly carried out. It is usual practice to carry out such appraisal by the appointment of a unit charged with responsibility to the Accounting Officer. As the Accounting Officer is usually the permanent head of the department this "reflects the view that finance and policy cannot be considered separately". Thus good management is the key to his function. He must ensure compliance with parliamentary requirements in the control of public expenditure. In his role he is to avoid waste and extravagance and to seek economy, efficiency and effectiveness in the use of all the resources made available to the department.

It would appear that the Accounting Officer carries out internally as part of his **12–019** management function, a similar function to the external examinations carried out by the C&AG. Achieving internal audit in these terms means having a clear view of objectives and the use of resources, assigning well-defined responsibilities and processing the correct information particularly about costs in the training and expertise required. However the Accounting Officer is also expressly concerned with policy. He has responsibility to advise Ministers on all "matters of financial propriety and regularity" and to ensure that departmental expenditure is justified to the PAC. In matters where a Minister may disagree, he is free to set out his own advice and the overruling of it by the Minister. He is free to point out to Ministers the possibility of the department receiving criticism by the PAC.

12–020   Procedures exist for an Accounting Officer to notify the Comptroller and Auditor General should his advice be overruled. An example of this practice is in the *Pergau Dam* case[8] discussed below. More recently, Ministers overruled the Accounting Officer on additional expenditure to up-rate motorway access to Silverstone, as part of the Government's strategy to keep the Formula 1 Grand Prix in Britain.

12–021   There are important responsibilities to ensure that appropriate advice is tendered to Ministers "on all matters of financial propriety and regularity and more broadly as to all considerations of prudent and economical administration, efficiency and effectiveness". Thus where the Accounting Officer is unhappy with a course of action, he is free to draw the attention of the Minister to his advice. If overruled then "he should ensure that both his advice and the overruling of it are apparent clearly from the papers".[9] Controversy surrounding the payment of any money by the Treasury may be raised by the PAC, or the C&AG may inquire into accounts. In 1992, contributions were made out of public funds to the legal expenses of Norman Lamont, the then Chancellor of the Exchequer. The Chancellor's legal expenses arose from the eviction of a tenant from his private residence. The payments caused a furore that resulted in investigation of the payment by the C&AG. It is also possible for department-led select committees to inquire into such matters. For example the Treasury and Civil Service Committee decided to investigate the Chancellor's legal expenses. In the course of press coverage of the affair, the Treasury revealed hitherto unpublished internal guidance, Treasury Solicitor's Rules on *Defamation of Ministers and Civil Servants* relating to the conduct of Ministers in the performance of their official duties. It appears that[10]:

> "if a minister applies to his department for financial assistance in taking [legal] proceedings, assistance may be given to him if the department decided after consultation with its legal advisers that it is in the department's interests that proceedings should be instigated."

Planning and Controlling Public Expenditure

12–022   The Treasury's annual Public Expenditure Survey (PES) is the central factor in planning and controlling public expenditure. Since 1963, following the Plowden Report[11] which recommended that decisions on public expenditure should be taken "in the light of surveys of public expenditure as a whole over a period of years, and in relation to prospective resources", there has been an annual survey published as the Public Expenditure White Paper. This sets out the aims and objectives of all

[8] Pergau Hydro-Electric Project (1994–95 HC 155).
[9] *Government Accounting Amendment* 4/1992, para.6.1.5.13. Amendment 7/1997 (3/97).
[10] *Guardian*, December 1, 1992. See Committee of Public Accounts: *Payments to meet legal expenses incurred by the Chancellor of the Exchequer and other Ministers* (1992–93 HC 386–ii).
[11] Plowden Report, Cmnd.1432 (1961).

government spending for the forthcoming three financial years for central government departments and local government. The Public Expenditure White Paper published in the 1980s contained two volumes. Volume I contained an outline of the general spending policies of the Government and became in 1988–89 merged in an expanded version of the Autumn Statement. A supplement containing the statistical information of the aggregate of departmental spending is published along with the Autumn Statement in an Autumn Statement Statistical Supplement. Volume II, which had covered individual departments, has been replaced by a series of separate papers published by departments in 1988–89. A further refinement in 1991–92 has been the publication of departmental reports. The Public Expenditure White Paper has now effectively been replaced by the Autumn Statement Statistical Supplement and Departmental Reports.

The planning of public expenditure sets the agenda between differing departmental demands for money. There is a Comprehensive Spending Review setting out the winners and losers over a three-year period on government planning. Since 1979 the Government developed the objectives of limiting the amount of money supply in the economy and cutting public spending and taxation. Greater efficiencies were required and the Government, as we have already noted in the previous chapter, adopted a wide range of techniques within government departments such as the Rayner Efficiency Studies (1979), the Financial Management Initiative (FMI) (1983) and the Next Steps (1988) to achieve this. Such strategies are designed to reduce cost, improve the economy and efficiency of government, avoid waste and provide greater value for money. Accountancy techniques and business practices have been adopted as principles of government policy replacing the traditional Whitehall model in the organisation and management of government departments. **12–023**

Following withdrawal from the Exchange Rate Mechanism in September 1992, the Government's Autumn statement introduced a number of changes to the system of public expenditure control through the introduction of a New Control Total. This replaces the planning total and differs from it by excluding the main elements of cyclical social security and privatisation proceeds; it includes local authority self-financed expenditure. Cyclical social security expenditure is excluded as recognition of the fact that this element of spending is very difficult to control. Privatisation proceeds are excluded at a time when proceeds have fallen to less than 3 per cent of the planning total, but they were included in the planning total when proceeds were high and expanding. The inclusion of local government self-financed expenditure reflects the significance of an important area of public finance currently estimated to be £1.4 billion. The intention of the New Control Total is to insulate the planning process from fluctuations in the cycle of economic growth and for the Government to have a more accurate assessment of expenditure plans. This, it is hoped, will lend greater stability to the planning process over the long term—a persistent criticism made about the old planning total was that it failed in its objectives of long-term planning. **12–024**

The Treasury also performs an important policy function in advising, through economic forecasts, the state of the economy and the prospects for inflation, unemployment and growth. Criticism has been made of the accuracy of the Treasury forecasts and the failure to identify in the late 1980s and in the 1990s the increase in credit and housing inflation. The Treasury, possibly because of its dual role as both a government department and as an important constitutional control over government **12–025** expenditure, is itself more scrutinised than most other departments of government. It retains its power and influence and expertly manages confidential and, from an economic perspective, sensitive information. Since 1997, the sensitive issue of setting interest rates belongs to the newly independent Bank of England described below.

The Bank of England

12–026   The Bank of England is the United Kingdom's central bank and acts as banker to the government. The accounts held in the Bank of England on the government's behalf are the Consolidated Fund and the National Loans Fund. Also held are the accounts of the Inland Revenue and Customs and Excise (the Revenue departments), the National Debt Commissioners and the Paymaster General. The Bank of England is also a full member of the clearing system with the other major banks.

12–027   Various other public sector enterprises have accounts at the Bank but the tendency is for departments to consider carefully whether in situations where there is no statutory duty to make use of the Bank of England, there are any advantages to be gained in using the Bank of England. Since April 1, 1989 departments and public bodies are required to pay "explicit charges" to the Bank of England to cover the costs of holding accounts or undertaking other financial services.

12–028   A list of banks is published by the Treasury and if departments wish to open an account with a bank not on the list then the Treasury must be consulted. Banks accredited with the Bank of England are not necessarily good investment institutions, as a number of creditors and local authorities found when a major bank collapsed.

12–029   Detailed internal rules exist for the various financial transactions carried out by central government departments including the use of credit cards, debit cards and in the handling of receipts and payments.

12–030   The Bank of England is not a government department and exercises independent advice. The Bank and its functions fall within the remit of the Treasury and Civil Service Select Committee. The Governor and his staff may be called to give evidence and be cross-examined before the Committee. The independence of the Bank of England became a major political question when its scrutiny of the economy and its past regulatory role over financial institutions was considered. The question of membership of the Exchange Rate Mechanism requires that there should be an independent central bank.

12–031   Nigel Lawson in his memoirs made public the text of a minute to the Prime Minister of November 25, 1988 arguing for a fully independent Bank. The Lawson proposal rests on a division of responsibility as follows[12]:

> "(a) The bank would assume sole responsibility for the operation of monetary policy, with a statutory duty to protect and maintain the value of the currency. It would thus be responsible for setting short-term interest rates and monetary targets.
>
> (b) The Government would remain responsible for determining the exchange rate framework—for example, whether we were part of any international agreement,

---

[12] Nigel Lawson, *The View from No. 11* (1992), p.1060. See H.C. Treasury and Civil Service Committee: *The Role of the Bank of England* (1993–94 HC 98–I).

of whatever kind, formal or informal. The bank would then be responsible for the conduct of exchange rate policy within that framework."

The Chancellor of the Exchequer in the new Labour Government formed after the general election on May 1, 1997 announced that the Bank of England would set interest rates on an assessment independent from the Government. The Bank of England Act 1998 provides that the Bank would be given operational responsibility to achieve an inflation target and this would be set by the Government for the Bank. The inflation target would be reviewed annually and announced in the Budget. A new panel of advisers would be appointed to sit with the Governor of the Bank of England to undertake this task. The new panel named the Monetary Policy Committee meets regularly to review interest rates. Regular publications of the minutes of the meetings provide a measure of financial scrutiny and transparency. A further reform under the Bank of England Act 1998 is that the Bank of England's Banking Supervision department would be transferred to the regulation of the Financial Services Authority. This sector has expanded through the creation of new Banks from the old mutual societies, formerly the Building Societies.

12–032

The Private Finance Initiative

The Private Finance Initiative (PFI) was launched in 1992. Its aims are to improve the quality and quantity of public sector capital projects. As from September 1, 2001 there were over 450 PFI agreements worth a total capital value of £20 billion. Indirectly the number of PFI arrangements is likely to influence government expenditure through additional support for the projects given by the government to the private sector. The aims of PFI are to secure funding for all public sector procurement. This means that all central government departments and sponsored bodies should screen all capital projects for PFI potential. Areas that are likely to receive sympathetic consideration include roads, prisons, tunnels, light railway systems, health facilities and major equipment and office accommodation. Joint ventures between the public and private sectors are also included. PFI developed the twin objectives of encouraging value for money in any public sector expenditure and placing the financial risks on the private sector.

12–033

PFI has undergone a number of important incremental changes. In the early development of PFI there was a PFI panel charged with the responsibility of vetting projects such as lease arrangements, the joint financing of projects between the public and private sectors, or the sale of private sector services to the public sector. In 1995 over £9 billion of "priority projects" were identified and a handbook of procedures and contractual mechanisms was published. In April 1996 PFIs that involved local government came under more liberal rules intended to facilitate local government engaging in PFI arrangements. Arising out of PFI arrangements is the Public Private Partnerships Programme, intended to encourage rationalisation and upgrading of local authority property, to improve value for money, to encourage the use of joint ventures, and to remove unnecessary obstacles to partnership.

12–034

PFI falls under Treasury rules and has been reviewed in 1997 and again in 1999. The aim is to further streamline and simplify the rules for PFI. A Taskforce was set up in September 1997 with this purpose linked to the creation, from April 2000, of an Office

12–035

of Government Commerce within the Treasury aimed to provide procurement skills and resources for the public sector. The Office replaces the Treasury Taskforce and reports to the Chief Secretary of the Treasury. There is a supervisory board chaired by the Chief Secretary and composed of Permanent Secretaries and the Head of the National Audit Office. The Government Resources and Accounts Act 2000 makes specific provision for the setting-up of Partnerships UK, from June 2000, as a link to the provision of commercial skills within the public sector. This new body is a private sector company drawn from a wide cross section of the financial services industry with access to private and public finance. It is intended to bring greater financial know-how into the management of PFI ventures.

12–036   PFI has grown in scale since 1992. Such changes are intended to provide departments with a strategic framework and access to expertise. Additional changes are envisaged. Taken as a whole it is estimated that "investment in the private sector under the PFI is equivalent to 17 per cent of total public sector investment under the three-year period covered by the Comprehensive Spending Review". It is expected that PFI will secure £3 billion *per annum* over the next three years.

Devolution and Funding of the Scottish Parliament, National Assembly for Wales and the Northern Ireland Assembly

12–037   The creation of the Scottish Parliament, National Assembly for Wales and Northern Ireland Assembly requires consideration of the financial relationship between the United Kingdom's financial system of control and the new devolved administrations. The general principles are contained in *A Statement of Funding Policy*[13] issued by the Treasury. These are: that responsibility for overall fiscal policy, and in the drawing-up of budgets and public expenditure allocation is retained within the United Kingdom's Treasury; that the United Kingdom Government funding of devolution will normally be determined through departmental spending reviews and that devolved administrations will make decisions for programmes within the overall totals.

12–038   The United Kingdom Parliament will vote the relevant provision for the devolved administration by means of a grant. At the devolved level additional elements of the budget will come from locally financed expenditure, funds from the European Commission and borrowing undertaken by local authorities. In the case of Scotland, additional funds will arise from tax-raising powers under the Scottish Variable Rate of Income Tax and also through non-domestic rates.

12–039   It is clear that the United Kingdom government rigorously retains a number of techniques for overall financial control. These include the right to make adjustments to the budgets to devolved administrations, and the assumption that devolved administrations will carry the burden of any additional or unforeseen financial burdens. Responsibilities for the receipt and disbursement of funds from the European Community is retained by the United Kingdom Government.

12–040   It is generally assumed that any changes in the budgets for devolved administrations funded from the UK's tax revenues or by borrowing will depend on the spending plans of the comparable departments of the United Kingdom. The requirement of apparent

[13] HM Treasury, March 31, 1999.

"parity" will be achieved in general through an ingenious formula known as the Barnett formula. This may be summarised as follows[14]: The Barnett Formula determines changes to expenditure within the assigned budgets of the devolved administrations. Under the Formula, Scotland, Wales and Northern Ireland receive a population-based proportion of changes in planned spending on comparable United Kingdom Government services in England, England and Wales or Great Britain as appropriate.

The formula works on the principle that changes to the planned spending of departments of the United Kingdom government is calculated and applied against a comparability percentage and against each country's population as a proportion of the United Kingdom's population. **12–041**

Services under the control of the devolved administration will be fully accountable within the devolved arrangements. This includes value for money, audit and accountability. Taken together accountability falls on the devolved administration, with the United Kingdom Treasury operating under the system of financial control. **12–042**

Parliament and the Control of Public Expenditure

Parliamentary control of expenditure rests on principles and procedures known as the "Supply Procedure" which may be briefly outlined as follows: the Executive requests Parliament for funds to meet the expenditure by Government departments and related bodies. This request comes in the form of supply estimates. Most of the money required to finance the services of Government departments is covered by supply estimates.[15] Once the supply estimates are approved by the House of Commons they form the basis of the statutory authority for the appropriation of funds. This allows the Treasury to authorise funds out of the Consolidated Fund Act through the authority of the Appropriation Act. Significantly, in respect of formal supply resolutions approved by the House of Commons there is a formal requirement for legislative authority. Issues of money from the Consolidated Fund are authorised by the Consolidated Fund Act. Authority for the appropriation of money for the various purposes contained in the estimates is granted in the annual Appropriation Act. The timetable set out (see: para.12–062) below, refers to the various stages in the financial cycle. It will be observed that the financial timetable does not follow the logic of the calendar year. Instead the current financial year which runs from April is being considered after January with the next financial year. Annual Departmental Reports relate to the current financial year with the addition of forward planning over the next three years. **12–043**

Powers to Incur Expenditure

In considering the financial procedures of the House of Commons it is necessary to set out the general principles and the legal authority that underpins the main work and constitutional role of the House of Commons. The House of Commons does not itself initiate expenditure. The Crown, namely the executive government, is charged with the management of all the revenue of the State. The Crown demands money, the House of Commons grant it and the House of Lords assent to the grant. The House of **12–044**

[14] *ibid.*, para.3.3 The Barnett formula is named after Joed Barnett, then Chief Secretary to the Treasury.
[15] Certain specific activities subject to certain criteria may be financed by a trading fund under the Government Trading Act 1973.

Commons have accepted the Crown's initiative in public expenditure in Standing Orders No.46 and No.47 of the House of Commons.[16] This means that neither the official Opposition nor a private member are able to propose increased charges on public funds. The power of spending and raising taxation rests on the initiative of the government of the day.

Legal Authority for Expenditure

12–045   *Government Accounting* (HMSO, 1988 with supplementary revisions to December 2001) already noted above is the handbook published by the Treasury which outlines the detailed working arrangements for the Parliamentary supervision of expenditure. Para.2.2.2 (Amendment No.6 Government Accounting 8/94 and amendments to December 1999), provides the following advice:

> "There are many instances in which statutory powers have been conferred on Ministers and there are frequently questions on whether an express statutory provision conferring particular powers does not by implication have a restrictive effect in the field in which those powers have been granted. Whether or not such an implication ought to be drawn in any particular case must always be a question of construction to be determined on the wording of the relevant statutes, but the governing principle is that express statutory provision is not generally necessary to enable a Minister to exercise functions."

12–046   This advice sets out the general scope of ministerial powers in the United Kingdom.[17] However, while a Minister "may generally do anything which he is not precluded from doing" there is a requirement that Parliamentary approval is necessary under the normal supply procedure, namely the Supply Estimates and the confirmation of supply in the Appropriation Act. Although awkwardly expressed the principle of parliamentary approval is rigidly adhered to. In general the majority of services provided by Government Departments are financed from money voted annually by Parliament through the Supply Estimates. This is brought to account in the Annual Appropriation Accounts. The Parliamentary timetable takes account of the current financial procedures of the House. Changes over the past few years include an experiment of having a unified budget. This was during a brief period from November 1993 which ended in March 1998 when there was a unified budgetary system with an Autumn unified budget containing taxation and expenditure proposals. The experiment ended in March 1998, reverting to an April budget statement.

12–047   There are two other regimes provided by Parliament for the financing of public services. First there are Consolidated Fund Standing Services. These are payments for services that are "once and for all" and that Parliament has accepted shall be met

[16] No.46: This House will receive no petition for any sum relating to public service or proceed upon any motion for a grant upon the public revenue, whether payable out of the Consolidated Fund of the National Loans Fund or out of money to be provided by Parliament, or for releasing or compounding any sum of money owing to the Crown, unless recommended from the Crown.
   No. 47 Any charge upon the public revenue whether payable out of the Consolidated Fund of the National Loans Fund or out of money to be provided by Parliament including any provision for releasing or compounding any sum of money owing to the Crown shall be authorised by resolution of the House.
[17] See *R. v Secretary of State for Foreign Affairs Ex p. World Development Movement* (the *Pergau Dam* case) [1995] 1 All E.R. 611.

directly from the Consolidated Fund. Thus they fall outside the annual authorisation of supply expenditure and the Supply Estimates. An example of payments, and by far the largest, is payment to the National Loans Fund in respect of the National Debt. Other examples are issues to the Contingencies Fund, which require re-payment of any amounts drawn on the Fund and consist of 2 per cent of the previous year's total Estimates provision, the Civil List salaries and salaries and pensions of Judges and various individuals such as the Comptroller and Auditor General.

The other regime is Trading Funds. Various activities of Government Departments **12–048** may fall under the criteria for finance to be made available as a trading fund under the Government Trading Funds Act 1973. Trading Funds are subject to special rules that fall outside the normal Supply procedures.[18] It is significant that Executive Agencies, otherwise known as Next Step agencies, may be funded either as a Supply Service through a vote or votes or by means of a Trading Fund[19] under the Government Trading Funds Act 1973 as amended by the Government Trading Act 1990. Each Next Steps agency has a framework document that sets out the specific day-to-day operations of the agency and the relevant responsibilities. Agencies, in common with Government Departments, are expected to conform to the standards of accounting and the requirements of propriety and regularity. Trading Funds therefore are not subject to the same Parliamentary scrutiny as the Supply Estimates. Given the increasing use of Next Steps agencies there appears to be a trend away from direct Parliamentary authorisation in favour of more indirect means. A noticeable aspect of the Next Steps agencies has been a debate about the Departmental Accounting Officer and the role of the National Audit Office in the scrutiny of the Agencies.[20] The Private Finance Initiative (PFI) also fits into the overall description of Parliamentary control.

Treasury Approval

Treasury guidance contained in *Government Accounting*[21] provides that "no expendi- **12–049** ture can properly be incurred without the approval of the Treasury". Supply Estimates require Treasury approval before they are presented to Parliament. In fact the central responsibility within government for financial relations with Parliament is the Treasury. The Treasury[22] is also the main department under the Chancellor of the Exchequer responsible[23] for the management of the economy. The Haldane Report[24] in 1918 identified a number of functions which describe the modern Treasury. In addition to the management of the economy the Treasury, with the authority of Parliament, imposes and regulates taxation, arranges funds to meet day-to-day demands for public services, manages and controls the national debt. Finally, in the control of public expenditure the Treasury supervises and prepares the supply estimates.

---

[18] See Chap.17, *Government Accounting, Amendment No.6 8/94* (HMSO, 1994).
[19] See *The Financing and Accountability of Next Step Agencies* Cm.914 (December 1989) Also see: Chap.16, *Government Accounting, Amendment No.6 8/94* (HMSO, 1994).
[20] See P. Giddings, Parliamentary Accountability (Macmillan, 1995) especially Chap.4 (by Philip Giddings) and Chap.5 (by Priscilla Baines). The area of financial scrutiny should be kept under review.
[21] See Chap.2, *Government Acounting, Amendment* No.6 8/94 (HMSO, 1994), para.2.4.1.
[22] The Treasury from the earliest record dated about 1635 began exercising control through warrants and written orders to the officers of the Exchequer. From about 1660 the Treasury had offices in Whitehall and its own permanent staff from the Exchequer.
[23] An excellent account of the Treasury may be found in Henry Roseveare, *The Treasury* (Penguin, 1969), M. Wright, *Treasury Control of the Civil Service 1854–1974* (Oxford, 1969).
[24] Cd.9230.

Planning and Controlling Public Expenditure

12–050   The Treasury's annual Public Expenditure Survey (PES) is the central factor in planning and controlling public expenditure. Since 1963, following the Plowden Report[25] which recommended that decisions on public expenditure should be taken "in the light of surveys of public expenditure as a whole over a period of years, and in relation to prospective resources", there has been an annual survey published as the Public Expenditure White Paper setting out the aims and objectives of all government spending for the forthcoming three financial years for central government departments and local government. This is an example where changes to the presentation of departmental expenditure are significant. The Public Expenditure White Paper published in the 1980s contained two volumes. Volume I contained an outline of the general spending policies of the government and became in 1988–89 merged in an expanded version of the Autumn Statement. A supplement containing the statistical information of the aggregate of departmental spending is published along with the Autumn Statement in an Autumn Statement Statistical Supplement. Volume II, which had covered individual departments has been replaced by a series of separate papers published by departments in 1988–89. A further refinement in 1991–92 has been the publication of Departmental Reports. Reports are laid before Parliament by the Government in February and March each year. Such Reports[26] "are valuable quarries of information for MPs and for departmental select committees in particular". The planning of public expenditure sets the agenda between differing departmental demands for money. Between the end of the PES round in October and the Autumn statement in November, winners and losers in the expenditure debate are settled. Since the late 1990s the procedure for the final settlement of expenditure occurs through a new Cabinet Committee on Public Expenditure chaired by the Chancellor of the Exchequer with the Chief Secretary as a member. Recommendations are approved in a meeting involving all spending ministers in the full cabinet.

12–051   Driven by the desire to reduce the public sector borrowing requirement the Treasury evolved better techniques of accounting[27] in the public sector in the control of public expenditure as an essential means to defeat inflation. Since the mid 1970s the introduction of cash limits[28] and the dispensing with volume planned public expenditure in favour of cash planning in 1983, has attempted to avoid incremental budgeting and introduce restraints on the costs of goods and services in the public sector. Since 1979 the government developed the objectives of limiting the amount of money supply in the economy, and cutting public spending and taxation. Greater efficiencies were required, and the government adopted a wide range of techniques within government departments such as the Rayner Efficiency Studies (1979),[29] the Financial Management

---

[25] Plowden Report, Cmnd.1432.
[26] Paul Silk and Rhoderi Walters, *How Parliament Works* (4th ed., Longman, London, 1999) p.161.
[27] Generally see John J. Glynn, *Public Sector Financial Control and Accounting* (Basil Blackwell, 1987). Sir G. Downey, "Public accountability: fact or myth" (1986) 6(1)*Public Money* 35–39. D. Henley, C. Holtham, A. Likierman, *Public Sector Accounting and Financial Control* (1986); J.F. McEldowney, "The control of Public Expenditure" in *The Changing Constitution* (J. Jowell and D. Oliver ed., 3rd. ed., Oxford, 1994).
[28] R.G. Bevan, "Cash limits" (1980) *Fiscal Studies*; Colin Thain and Maurice Wright, "The Advent of cash planning" 5(3) *Financial Accountability and Management* Autumn 1989, 149–162.
[29] Headed by Lord Rayner, later headed by Sir Robin Ibbs and now Sir Angus Fraser. See Andrew Flynn, Andrew Gray and William Jenkins, "The Next Steps and the Management of Government" 1990. *Parliamentary Affairs* 43(2), 159–178. Also see Committee on Public Accounts, 39th Report (1985–86, HC 322). *The Rayner Scrutiny Programmes* 1979–83, 13th Report (1987–88, HC 61) *The Financial Management Initiative.*

Initiative[30] (FMI) (1983) and the Next Steps (1988).[31] Such strategies are designed to reduce cost, improve the economy and efficiency of government, avoid waste and provide greater value for money. Accountancy techniques and business practices have been adopted as principles of government policy replacing the traditional Whitehall model in the organisation and management of government departments. This is reflected in the management of the Treasury and in the *Fundamental Review of Running Costs*[32] in 1994. The Treasury also performs an important policy function in advising through economic forecasts the state of the economy and the prospects for inflation, unemployment and growth.

Parliamentary Procedures and timetable

The central importance of parliamentary procedures is found in the supply estimates which give the House of Commons the necessary information to provide the government with funds from the Consolidated Fund. The supply estimates must be approved by the date of the Budget.   **12–052**

Parliamentary statutory authority for funds to be drawn from the Consolidated Fund are approved by Acts of Parliament known as Consolidated Fund Acts and by an annual Appropriation Act. There is a principle known as "annuality" whereby funds voted by Parliament under the Consolidated Fund Acts and the Appropriation Act are available for expenditure during the financial year which runs from 1 April to 31 March. Supply estimates are based on cash accounting. The normal convention is that money voted to meet expenditure chargeable in one year is surrendered to the Consolidated Fund and cannot be carried forward into the next financial year.   **12–053**

Estimates of departmental expenditure are drawn up and must be approved by resolutions of the Commons for the necessary release of funds from the Consolidated Fund. Since 1986, the supply estimates have been divided into about 20 major categories with detailed sub-clauses within the various votes for each department. The estimates provide the majority, over 70 per cent, of annual public expenditure. There is an annual Appropriation Act[33] enacted by July/August each year authorising the Bank of England to make payments from the Consolidated Fund. The Estimates must conform to Treasury format and approval, and must not be altered unless Treasury authority has been granted. The audit carried out by the Comptroller and Auditor General is focused on the estimates which when divided into heads of expenditure appear as "votes".   **12–054**

Each estimate presented to Parliament is in two parts. Part I sets out the services and purposes for which the estimate is presented. Eventually Part I will form part of the Appropriation Act and provide the statutory description contained in the Act for the purposes for which supply is granted. Part II sets out the subheads under which the   **12–055**

---

[30] Progress in Financial Management in Government Departments Cmnd.9297 (1984); L. Metcalfe and S. Richards, *Improving Public Management* (1987). See Helco and Wildavsky, *The Private Government of Public Money* (1981).

[31] Gavin Drewry "The Next Steps: The Pace Falters" [1990] *PL* 322; and Gavin Drewry "Forward from F.M.I. The Next Steps" [1988] *PL* 505.

[32] *Fundamental Review of Running Costs: A Report to the Chancellor of the Exchequer* (HM Treasury, October 1994).

[33] The Appropriaton Act begins life as the Consolidated Fund (Appropriation) Bill.

Treasury requires expenditure to be accounted for. This forms the basis of Parliamentary scrutiny of expenditure of the individual services provided by each Government department. The Treasury has powers of *virement* between the various subheads of the service in question.

12–056   Departments work on the supply estimates in the Summer or early Autumn of each financial year. On or about the time of the Budget each year, the estimates are published. If a department's needs exceed that of the estimates then a supplementary estimate may be passed subject to Treasury and Parliamentary approval. The Standing Orders of the Commons provide three opportunities to introduce a supplementary estimate with the benefit of a guillotine procedure ensuring their speedy passage: supplementaries for Summer are presented in June, for Winter in November, and for Spring in February. Estimates may be submitted at other times of the year but without the benefit of the guillotine procedure.

12–057   The following timetable sets out the three periods for Parliament's consideration of the estimates; special supplementary estimates are debated whenever they arise.

March–July for the main estimates, June–July for the summer supplementary estimates. Estimate day debates take place in July and at the time of the Appropriation Act.
November–December for the winter supplementary estimates followed by any debates and a Consolidated Fund Act.
February–March for the spring supplementary estimates followed by any debates on the Consolidated Fund Act.

12–058   Since 1982, the Financial Management Initiative requires that good financial management should be part of the financial decision-making within departments.

12–059   The requirement for statutory authority for authorisation of public expenditure is seriously regarded by the Treasury. *The Treasury Handbook* insists on this principle that statutory authority for the payment of expenditure out of moneys provided by Parliament[34] "must be and can only be given year by year by means of votes and the Appropriation Act". A minister[35] "when exercising functions which may involve the expenditure of money may only do what he does if Parliament votes him the money".

12–060   Parliamentary debate on individual estimates is undertaken by departmentally-related Select Committees charged with the task of scrutiny of the department. The Committee may examine individual main, revised or supplementary estimates. Officials may be cross-examined and further information may be provided to aid the departmental Committee in its scrutiny role.

12–061   Since 1982 there have been three specific days to consider the estimates. The Commons may only reduce the estimates but even this is unlikely if the government of

---

[34] *Treasury Handbook*, paras 47–49.
[35] *ibid.* The Public Accounts Committee considered in 1932 the question of whether the Appropriation Act is sufficient authority for the expenditure, whether there is or not specific statutory authority for the service concerned. In concluding that the Appropriation Act is sufficient in itself for such authority, known as the 1932 PAC Concordat, the Treasury have accepted that provided the government of the day undertakes to ask Parliament for authorisation services under the Appropriation Act this would come within the PAC Concordat. However it is preferable to seek specific statutory authority.

the day has an overall majority. Parliament is unable to initiate its own expenditure on its own behalf rather than the Government's. The scrutiny function over the estimates appears a limited one. While the presentation of the estimates has become more attractive and readable, little has been achieved in restoring earlier practice to modern times of making debate and scrutiny a substantive control of the Commons over the executive.

Each department provides an annual report in February separate from both the **12–062** estimates and the Appropriation Accounts. The annual report is both prospective seeking to justify the estimates for the department and reflective seeking to outline past performance. One criticism of the current arrangements is that it is often difficult for Parliament to track expenditure from one document to another. In particular it is difficult to link the Department's annual report to the estimates.

TIMETABLE for the Conduct of Financial Business in the House of Commons[36]

November. The publication of the Pre-Budget Statement takes place known as the Green Budget. This contains a general overview of the direction and policy of the government's financial plans and predictions for the future. Only the government of the day is authorised to introduce a Bill, for which the main purpose is to increase expenditure. November is also the month when the winter supplementary estimates are approved.

December. The Consolidated Fund Bill is passed. Taxation revenue is paid into the Consolidated Fund. These receipts include fees and services paid to the Government. In the case of money that is borrowed by the Government this forms a separate fund, namely the National Loans Fund. There is a close link between the operation of the two Funds.

February. The estimates, explained in detail below, are approved by 6 February. This incudes the winter supplementary estimates and the spring supplementary estimates. Also the defence votes are presented. In February or March of every year the *Departmental Reports* are published containing details of the financial information available to departments involved in their own spending plans. The aim of this information is to provide a comparative basis with the estimates. Aims and objectives are included and there is a commentary of the targets to be achieved, efficiency gains and future activities that are linked to meeting planned targets. The Appropriation Act authorises the issue and appropriation of Supply grants for the two preceding financial years and the main and summer supplementary grants for the current financial year. The Appropriation Act is usually introduced and has completed all its stages before the Summer Recess when Parliament adjourns.

March. The Chancellor of the Exchequer presents the Budget Statement for the year. At this time the Finance Bill is presented containing the main provisions for implementing the Budget. Departmental Annual Reports are published and the Consolidated Fund Bill is passed.

April. The second reading of the Finance Bill is taken.

---

[36] This timetable is drawn from: Paul Evans, *Handbook of House of Commons Procedure* (Vacher Dod Publishing, London, 1999), pp.94–96.

May. Finance Bill is taken in Committee; the summer supplementary estimates are taken and revised. Estimates are presented.

June. Finance Bill reaches its Committee Stage and Report Stage of the Bill to the House.

July. Finance Bill Report stage given third reading and Royal Assent. Main estimates are passed and the Appropriation Act is passed.

August. Main estimates, the Appropriation Act and the Finance Bill must be passed by 5 August.

October. Debate on the Reports of the Public Accounts Committee, and the Appropriation Accounts for the year are presented up to Christmas.

Financial reporting to Parliament

12–063   Financial reporting to Parliament has undergone intense debate[37] over the past ten years. Reports from the Committee of Public Accounts[38] and from the Treasury and Civil Service Committee[39] have resulted in a debate about any changes to the presentation of the estimates and the desire to see improvements in the information available to Parliament on the aims and objectives of departmental expenditure[40]. In July 1994 the Treasury published a Green Paper[41] *Better Accounting for the Taxpayer's Money: Resource Accounting and Budgeting in Government* which contains far-reaching proposals for the introduction of accrual-based resource accounts to supplement current cash-based accounts. There are also proposals from the Treasury to revise the format of the estimates[42] as part of the Treasury's on-going Fundamental Expenditure Review. This is intended to provide more effective controls over public expenditure. These proposals have been considered by both the Committee of Public Accounts and the Treasury and Civil Service Committee.[43]

12–064   Consideration of the most effective means of providing financial information for Parliament is not confined to the United Kingdom. There is also a similar and important comparative analysis being undertaken of the New Zealand system of financial reporting and budgeting.[44]

[37] See Report of the Comptroller and Auditor General, *Financial Reporting to Parliament* (1985–86 HC 576).
[38] There are also various reports from the Commmittee of Public Accounts: *Financial Reporting to Parliament* 8th Report (1986–87) HC 98; *Financial Reporting to Parliament* 18th Report (1988–89 HC 354); *Central Funds and Accountability and the Exchange Equalisation Account* 8th Report (1989–90 HC 267); *Financial Reporting to Parliament: Changes in the Format of the Supply Estimates* 25th Report (1993–94, HC 386); *Resource Accounting and Budgeting in Government* 15th report 1994–95 HC 407).
[39] There are Treasury and Civil Service Committee Reports: *The Form of the Estimates* 6th Report (1980–81 HC 325); *Efficiency and Effectiveness in the Civil Service* 3rd report (1981–82 HC 236); *The Structure and Form of Financial Documents Presented to Parliament* 2nd, 7th and 10th Reports (1984–85 HC 110, 322, & 544); *Financial Reporting to Parliament* 6th Report (1987–88 HC 614); *The Form of the Estimates: The Government's Response to the Third Report from the Committeee* 3rd Report (1993–94 HC 192); 3rd Special Report (1993–94 HC 441); *Simplified Estimates and Resource Accounting* 4th Report (1994–95 HC 212).
[40] See Appendix A, NAO Report, *Resource Accounting and Budgeting in Government* (1994–95 HC 123).
[41] Cm.2626.
[42] Memorandum submitted by the Treasury to the Treasury and Civil Service Committee in the Treasury and Civil Service Committee 3rd Report (1993–94 HC 192), minutes of evidence, pp.1–2.
[43] See the Treasury and Civil Service Committee 3rd Report (1993–94 HC 192); 3rd Special Report (1993–94 HC 441); and see the Public Accounts Committee, *Financial Reporting to Parliament: Changes in the Format of the Supply Estimates* 25th Report (1993–94 HC 386); *Resource Accounting and Budgeting in Government* 15th Report (1994–95 HC 407).
[44] See for example New Zealand Fiscal Responsibility Act 1994 No.17.

Resource Accounting

The 1995 NAO report[45] usefully defines resource accounting as involving two elements: **12–065**

- a set of accruals-based techniques for accounting and reporting on the expenditure of UK central government; and

- a framework for analysing expenditure by departmental objectives, related to outputs wherever possible.

Currently cash-based accounts provide the main way for government accounting. **12–066** There is no requirement to match expenditure with revenues for the period to which they relate. There is no framework for the valuation of assets and liabilities. Capital spending is made to account wholly in the year in which the capital purchase or disposal is made. In contrast it is argued that accruals accounting makes up for these deficiencies. The NAO Report summarises the main benefits of accruals accounting over the existing cash accounting system:

- accruals accounting records expenditure and income in the accounting period to which they relate;

- accruals accounting spreads the cost of capital items across their useful lives;

- accruals accounting provides a detailed snapshot of the assets, liabilities and net worth of an organisation at a given moment of time and through a Balance Sheet provides a better picture of the true cost of departments' activities.

- accruals accounting is intended to increase information and detailed inventories of departmental holdings, deployment and stewardship of assets.

Resource accounting based on an accruals accounting system is intended to match **12–067** more closely the resources used to departmental objectives. The outputs of departmental activities can then be used to measure departmental achievements. It is intended that departments will in future provide a schedule showing the true cost of resources consumed and a schedule measuring output performance against each main objective. Introducing such a system has depended on the adoption of the UK Generally Accepted Accounting Practice[46] supplemented by specific requirements developed for departmental accounts. The Government Resources and Accounts Act 2000 sets out the necessary statutory authority for the principles of resources accounting. The Treasury provides useful templates as to how accounts should be prepared and how these might be analysed.

The Contingencies Fund

There is a Contingencies Fund which may be used to finance urgent expenditure. The **12–068** fund is a reserve fund intended to meet unforeseen items of expenditure. In technical terms it is used "to meet payments for urgent services in anticipation of Parliamentary

[45] NAO Report, *Resource Accounting and Budgeting in Government* (1994–95 HC 123) para.10.
[46] This is defined as the accounting standards required of the Companies Act 1985 and the accounting standards set by the Accounting Standards Board.

provisions for those services becoming available." Total advances outstanding from the Fund should not exceed 2 per cent of the previous year's total estimates provision. Money withdrawn from the Fund must be repaid. The Treasury may authorise payment out of the Fund subject to the limit of 2 per cent set under the Contingencies Fund Act 1974. The use of the Fund is regarded as "exceptional" particularly if the Fund is used for a new service. The instructions contained in Government Accounting state:

> "The criterion is not convenience, but urgency in the public interest. If the amount of money involved, or the potentially contentious nature of the proposal is such as to create special difficulty in justifying anticipation of specific Parliamentary approval, it may be necessary to consider the alternative of immediate presentation of a Supplementary Estimate, outside the normal time-table, to be followed by a special Consolidated Fund Bill."

12–069   The Contingencies Fund offers an unusual example where the main scrutiny of the government's use of the Fund largely depends on effective Treasury control. Legislation giving authority for the expenditure involved must be introduced at the earliest possible time and ought never be postponed. Additional guidance issued in 1992 makes clear that the government of the day must be prepared "to take the responsibility of assuming that legislation being considered by Parliament will pass into law". In 1974 the then Financial Secretary to the Treasury explained that:

> "The Contingencies Fund cannot be drawn upon for any purpose for which the statutory authority of Parliament is required until legislation seeking that authority has been given a Second Reading."

12–070   The Contingencies Fund has been used for a variety of purposes: the relief of national disasters, the manufacture of the first Atomic Bomb, victory celebrations and, at time of war, for financing urgent supplies. Concern about the use of the Contingencies Fund is focused on the question of Parliamentary accountability. The total expenditure from the Fund, within the resources available to the Fund, is considerable. There are no clear statutory conditions for expenditure being advanced from the Fund. Reliance is placed on the system of internal Treasury control and audit. No select committee directly monitors the use of the Fund. In the area of policy there are no satisfactory means to inquire into the policy behind the government's use of the Fund prior to the Fund being used. Any *ex post facto* inquiry is difficult since the money has already been used. The fact that the money is to be repaid hardly seems an adequate safeguard to question the purpose for which the Fund has been used.

12–071   Doubts about the legality of the existence of the Fund were raised in 1983 but have been seemingly resolved and the Fund is assumed by the Treasury to be legal. The Contingencies Fund is an example of where Parliament has, through inactivity, allowed an exception to the principle that Parliament should vote money before expenditure is incurred. There is also tacit acceptance that Treasury control may be more effective in this instance than Parliamentary scrutiny.[47]

---

[47] See McEldowney "The Contingencies Fund and the Parliamentary Scrutiny of Public Finance" [1988] *Public Law* 232–245.

The Committee of Public Accounts (PAC), the New Select Committees and the Comptroller and Auditor General (C&AG)

Once expenditure is settled then the question of scrutiny and audit arises. Since 1861 **12–072** the Committee of Public Accounts (PAC) acts on behalf of Parliament to examine and report on accounts and the regularity and propriety of expenditure which are matters usually covered by the Comptroller and Auditor General's (C&AG) certification audit. In more recent times value for money audit (VFM) examinations have become a major part of the work of the PAC. In that regard the PAC works with the assistance of the C&AG. The constitutional importance of the PAC is beyond question. It has traditionally been seen as the doyen of all select committees with its worldwide prestige and the reputation of being the terror of the departments. No other select committee has the same authority, clarity of remit and breadth and depth of advice available to it.

Select committees generally, may exercise *ex post facto* control over public expendi- **12–073** ture. The Select Committee on Procedure and the Treasury and Civil Service Committee have been particularly active in assisting in the development of strategies for greater availability of information on public expenditure and its more effective control. The PAC's authority and remit differs from other select committees mentioned in previous chapters, because of two factors. The first is the non-party political approach it devotes to its task, the fact that it is chaired by a senior opposition M.P. and has no more than 15 members. The second is that its inquiries are almost all audit-based and it receives expert assistance from the C&AG. In the case of VFM examinations its reports to Parliament carry considerable weight.

One criticism of the PAC is that in its scrutiny its *ex post facto* review leaves much to **12–074** be desired. An example of the work of the PAC is the investigation carried out in 1984 into the use of public money invested in Delorean Cars[48] in Northern Ireland. Over £77 million was invested; a large proportion of this was found to have been improperly used. The PAC called for tighter rules on the use of public money for business ventures in private companies. Particularly difficult has been the area of defence contracts where costs may quite easily overrun earlier estimates.[49] In April 1986 the resignation of Michael Heseltine, over the Westland affair, resulted in the appointment of George Younger as Defence Secretary. This made possible the removal of the block grant system for defence spending and its replacement by an expenditure round on an item by item basis supervised by the Treasury. The agreement was in the form of an "unrecorded concordat" between the ministers and officials.

Another difficulty is that the size of the task under consideration invariably leads to **12–075** an emphasis on small examples of bureaucratic blunder which are easier to pick up and debate than larger examples of overspending which may have inherent causes in the procedures.

Although the PAC rarely divides on party political lines, it is made up of busy M.P.s **12–076** who may find it difficult to give the complexities of the National Audit Office reports their full attention. By implication matters of importance may be missed in the outlook

---

[48] J. Redwood, *Going For Broke* (1984), Chap.2.
[49] PAC Ninth Report on the Chevaline Ministry of Defence Expenditure (1981–82 HC). Costs on the chevaline project were not properly disclosed. Treasury Minute Cmnd.8759 (1982).

for the PAC which is targeted to parliamentary debate and acceptability. An added complication is that the new departmental select committees, introduced since 1979, have a sufficiently wide remit which invariably brings the reports of the PAC and the C&AG within their jurisdiction. In 1988–89 the House of Commons Select Committee on Procedure recommended, and the Government accepted, that departmental select committees should take greater consideration of the analysis of broad expenditure priorities. Unlike the PAC the membership of these committees is such that party politics may intrude in their analysis. At least one commentator has been critical of the way in which the success or failure of the new select committee depends not so much on the institution itself but on the willingness of individual M.P.s to work on complex, technical and intricate detail. Few political rewards are obvious from such time-consuming work. The combination of the PAC and the new select committees may pose a fresh challenge for the C&AG. In exercising his independent audit function he must be sensitive to the problem that the PAC should not divide on party lines when discussing his reports. On the other hand, the new select committees, the news media and individual backbench M.P.s are likely to seize every opportunity to take political advantage from a report critical of a department's use of public funds. Parliamentary debate is both a method for publicising the findings of the C&AG and an opportunity for political debate. While the C&AG may rely on both as a sanction against an obdurate government department, he must remain independent.

12–077   Finally it should be recognised that as an external form of audit, the independent status of the C&AG means that he relies heavily on co-operation with departments and their Accounting Officers who exercise internal control. The C&AG Reports contain findings of facts and opinions in the case of VFM examinations as to how performance is related to objectives set. It is often a delicate calculation as how best to preserve the privileges of access to confidential information with conclusions on the outcome of his examination.

12–078   The constitutional protection awarded to the C&AG determines his independence and status. However, it is the C&AG's discretion which determines the scope of his remit for VFM examinations of privatisation sales. These have been developed within the framework of the above analysis of the constitutional role and jurisdiction of the C&AG.

The National Audit Office

12–079   The constitutional status of the Comptroller and Auditor General (C&AG) provides that in carrying out his functions he acts on behalf of Parliament. The independence and constitutional status of the C&AG may now be considered.[50] Since the Exchequer and Audit Act 1866 the C&AG is required to examine accounts on behalf of the House of Commons. The 1983 National Audit Act recognised the constitutional implications of this requirement and made the C&AG an Officer of the House of Commons and provided for his appointment. The C&AG is head of the National

---

[50] *The Role of the Comptroller and Auditor General* Cmnd.8323. Also see Eleventh Report from the Expenditure Committee Session 1976–77 (HC 535); First Report from the Select Committee on Procedure Session 1977–78 (HC 588); Second Special Report from the Committee of Public Accounts, Session 1978–79 (HC 330).

Audit Office (NAO),which was created under the 1983 Act, and replaced the Exchequer and Audit Department. The C&AG appoints staff and subject to the 1983 Act determines grading, pay and conditions. The C&AG is independent from party politics or the political influence of the government of the day.

The NAO is itself independent from the Civil Service and may recruit and train its own staff usually qualified by the Chartered Institute of Public Finance and Accountancy or the Institute of Chartered Accountants in England and Wales. Recently the NAO has been able to adopt its own in house training scheme (TOPS) for professional Chartered Accountants on a par with the City commercial accountancy firms. The NAO is free to hire outside experts and consultants as required.

12–080

The NAO is itself subject to audit by the Public Accounts Commission, a body appointed for this purpose under s.2 of the 1983 Act and which came into existence on January 1, 1984. The Commission comprises nine members of the House of Commons—two are *ex officio* members, one being the Leader of the House of Commons, the other the Chairman of the PAC. None of the members may be Ministers of the Crown.

12–081

The purpose of the Public Accounts Commission is threefold: first, to appoint a suitable Accounting Officer for the appropriation accounts of the NAO; second to appoint auditors; and third, to examine estimates and take advice from the Treasury or the PAC. In the case of certification audit, the C&AG carries out on behalf of the House of Commons the audit and certification of all Government departments and a wide range of public sector bodies. These include appropriation accounts of departments. Receipts for privatisation and expenses are presented to Parliament in the form of a standard Government Appropriation Account relevant to the government department responsible for the sale. In such cases the C&AG provides an audit certificate which states his opinion as to whether either (a) the "account properly presents" the expenditure and receipts of the vote and payments of the organisation; or (b) the account presents a "true and fair view" where accounts are prepared on an income and expenditure basis.

12–082

This form of audit is "departmental led",[51] that is, it is focused on the departments' responsibilities. The C&AG may seek an explanation from the sponsoring department concerned if he is dissatisfied with any aspect of the accounts and may qualify his certificate with his reservations. The primary focus of such an audit is to assess whether accounts are accurate or whether they may mislead someone relying on the accounts. In particular, if there is expenditure which requires Treasury authority which has not been given, the matter is reported to the Treasury.

12–083

Normally the audit work involved in certication audit is confined to the proper presentation of receipts and expenditure. In common with most of the auditing work of the NAO it is scrutiny *ex post facto* with the implication that any past errors may provide lessons for the future. This is open to the criticism that an *a priori* examination might offer a means of avoiding mistakes and therefore save public money.[52]

12–084

In the case of Value For Money (VFM) examinations, this is potentially a more far-reaching means of accounting.[53] S.6 of the 1983 Act provides a statutory basis for VFM

12–085

[51] Chris Beauchamp "National Audit Office: its role in privatisation" *Public Money and Management*, Summer 1990, 55–58. Hereinafter Beauchamp. *A Framework for Value for Money Audits* (National Audit Office).
[52] C. Graham and T. Prosser, *Privatizing Public Enterprises* (Oxford, 1991), pp.59–64.
[53] Generally see P. Anand, "Monitoring and Auditing Value for Money in the U.K.: The Scope for Quantitative Analysis, Financial Accountability and Management (Winter 1988), pp.253–270.

examinations at the discretion of the C&AG. Included within this jurisdiction are Government departments and other public bodies where the C&AG has statutory rights of inspection or where he is the statutory auditor. VFM audit is not extended to the nationalised industries.[54] For many years the Committee of Public Accounts (PAC) encouraged the C&AG to examine expenditure and receipts in departments and to bring to the notice of Parliament weakness of the system which appeared "to involve imprudent, uneconomical or extravagant expenditure of waste". The 1983 Act placed such examinations on a statutory basis. However the Act makes an important proviso that VFM examination shall not be construed as entitling the C&AG to question the merits of the policy objectives of the department[55] or body concerned.

12–086   Some of the most important VFM studies have been into the major privatisations, are carried out at the C&AG's discretion and are subject to the important restraint that the merits of the policy is outside the jurisdiction of the C&AG.

12–087   S.6 of the National Audit Act 1983 provides the statutory authority for the NAO to carry out Value for Money examinations of departmental activities. The 1983 Act simply defines such examinations in terms of "economy, efficiency and effectiveness". As the words are contained in a statute it might be assumed that they carry a precise legal meaning and certainly a court might be called upon to give legal effect to the phrase. In the example of privatisation sales, their size and scale posed a challenge to sponsoring departments and their relationship with the NAO. At least 20 per cent of NAO staff and consultants are engaged in VFM examinations which is a significant proportion of its activity.[56]

12–088   Evaluating efficiency and effectiveness is a common theme in recent years[57] in the development of government policy objectives. It has become a commonplace that Government borrows techniques, methods and objectives from business or commerce. How to measure efficiency and effectiveness is the key issue, and evaluation may be as difficult as setting the objectives in the first place. In 1981 the Treasury and Civil Service Committee in its Report on Efficiency and Effectiveness set out some criteria for evaluating efficiency and effectiveness.[58] The criteria include clarifying the intention of the programme, and setting objectives which are quantified as targets. Objectives may be assessed in terms of output. An efficient programme is one where the target is achieved with the least use of resources and instruments for change. An effective programme is one where the intention of the programme is being achieved. This means that the intention is contained in operational objectives which are set as defined targets. Thus the output of the programme is equal to the target set. In this way an effective and efficient programme may be evaluated.

---

[54] E.L. Normanton, "Reform in the field of public accountability and audit: a progress report" (1980) 51 *Political Quarterly* 175—99.
[55] *Hansard*, HC 357–360 (April 27, 1990), Written Answers. The Prime Minister Stated: "*Twenty-nine major businesses have been privatised and around 800,000 jobs have been transferred to the private sector. Receipts so far amount to some £27.5 billion with future sales projected at a rate of about £5 billion a year.*"
[56] Annual Report Comptroller and Auditor General 1989/90.
[57] See *The Reorganisation of Central Government*, Cmnd.4506 (1970); *Financial Management in Government Departments*, Cmnd.9058 (1983); and *Progress in Financial Management in Government Departments*, Cmnd.9297 (1984).
[58] *Treasury and Civil Service Committee: Efficiency and Effectiveness in the Civil Service* (1981 HC 236). Also see *Helping Managers Manage* (Cabinet Office Efficiency Unit, 1984).

Such criteria are similar to those in use within the NAO in carrying out a VFM **12–089** examination. This is defined to mean economy, efficiency and effectiveness which the NAO explain as follows[59]:

> "Economy is concerned with minimising the cost of resources acquired with regard to appropriate quality.
>
> Efficiency is concerned with the relationship between output of goods, services or other results and the resources used.
>
> Effectiveness is concerned with the relationship between intended results and the actual results of targets."

The NAO has developed[60] VFM strategies which emphasise the avoidance of waste, **12–090** the setting of clearly defined policy objectives and obtaining good value for the tax-payers. There is a duty on government departments to consider the NAO's reports and the PAC recommendations and to provide replies to the House of Commons on matters raised in the reports.[61] VFM examinations would seem to be a blend of conventional auditing skills with management consulting techniques.

The former benefits from a degree of independence and objectivity and the **12–091** ascertaining of facts through the skills of an auditor. The latter draws on the analytical skills of the management consultant. In comparison to ordinary certification auditing, VFM takes the opportunity to understand the effects of policy and whether those effects relate to the intention behind the policy. The NAO's experience has increased given the large number of VFM studies since 1983.

Particularly difficult to categorise is the distinction to be drawn between the **12–092** implementation of policy, a legitimate concern of VFM, and the merits of policy which is outside the jurisdiction of the NAO.

THE COURTS

The courts have accepted Parliament's role in the matter of financial control. Viscount **12–093** Haldane in *Auckland Harbour Board v The King*,[62] a Privy Council case, noted that payments out of the Consolidated Fund without parliamentary authority were illegal. Direct challenges to central government on constitutional issues raised by public expenditure issues are not commonplace. The major disputes involving public finance arise on the supply side involving issues of taxation. However there are cases which do raise issues which may indirectly affect public spending. For example in *Metzger v Department of Health and Social Security*[63] the duty of the Secretary of State for Social

---

[59] See *A Framework for Value for Money Audits (National Audit Office)* Cmnd.9755; Treasury Minute on the First Four Reports from the Committee of Public Accounts Session 1985–86, paras 21–23. See Cmnd.8413, para.87.
[60] A. Hopwood "Accounting and the Pursuit of Efficiency", chap.9 in *Issues in Public Sector Accounting* (A. Hopwood and C. Tomkins ed., 1984).
[61] Government Accounting, paras 7.1.38–7.1.40.
[62] [1925] A.C. 318, 326.
[63] [1977] 3 All E.R. 444.

Services to carry out reviews of the rates of pension payable under the Social Security Act 1975, was considered and the cost of uprating pension benefits ascertained. The impact on public expenditure was large if the court decided to grant a declaration which it refused.

12–094   The impact of the Human Rights Act 1998 in this area is likely to be directed to the scope of Article 6 (right to a fair trial) and the impact of this on procedures for the adjudication of taxation disputes. However, in *Ferrazini v Italy*[64] the European Court of Human Rights showed reluctance to interpret taxation liability as falling within the obligations under Article 6(1). However in criminal proceedings the courts may adopt a different perspective.[65]

12–095   The role of the courts generally in decisions on public expenditure of central government has been minimal. This is in contrast to the audit of local authorities in cases such as *Roberts v Hopwood* [66] or more recently in *Hazell v Hammersmith*,[67] where the House of Lords considered the investment powers of local authorities in the swap markets.

12–096   In *Bromley CBC v GLC*[68] the concept of fiduciary duty was developed and extended to apply to the duty owed by a local authority to its ratepayers. The case involved the now defunct Greater London Council and its policy of providing cheap fares for London Transport. Having regard to the term "economic" in ss.1 and 5 of the Transport (London) Act 1969, the House of Lords held that the GLC was not empowered to adopt a fares policy unduly beneficial to transport users at a cost to ratepayers in London. The interpretation of "economic" involved careful judicial consideration of the benefits and costs involved.

12–097   The courts have also pursued a robust attitude to the development of their scrutiny of public money. Recently the House of Lords upheld the findings of political corruption in *Porter v Magill*.[69] The case concerned allegations made by Mr Magill, the District Auditor for Westminster City Council, against three officers and three councillors that through wilful misconduct they had jointly and severally lost £31 million to the Council. The Council operated a housing policy that was alleged to favour voters more likely to vote Conservative. Council-owned residential properties were being sold in such a way as to enhance the political chances of the Conservative party at election time. The House of Lords held that it was unlawful to dispose of property for the purpose of promoting the electoral advantage of any party represented on the Council.

12–098   The scope for such judicial intervention, as has been shown with the local authority cases, is very wide with regard to the expression "economy, efficiency and effectiveness". However, the National Audit Act is silent as to the exact meaning of the terms used in the phrase, leaving the courts free to develop a legal definition of the phrase.

[64] [2001] S.T.C. 1314.
[65] *R. v Allen (No.2)* [2001] 4 All E.R. 768. Also see *Georgiou (trading as Marios Chippery) v UK* [2001] S.T.C. 80.
[66] [1925] A.C. 578.
[67] [1991] 1 All E.R. 545. But see *Bromley CBC v GLC* [1983] 1 A.C. 768 on the meaning of "economic". See Loughlin, "Innovative Financing in Local Government: The Limits of Legal Instrumentation—Part I" (1990) *P.L.* 372–405. Also C. Holtham "Local Government: Internal Control and External Reporting" in *Public Sector Accounting and Financial Control* (D. Henley *et al.* ed., 1983).
[68] [1982] 1 A.C. 768.
[69] [2002] W.L.R. 37. See: Anti-Terrorism, Crime and Security Act 2001 containing tougher laws on corruption.

The result is that although many judicial elements, which were the hallmark of the early history of public audit, remain, there has been little modern judicial creativity in this area.

The National Audit Office has a discretion both as to how to carry out VFM examinations and when to embark on such an examination. The law merely defines the broad terms of reference of its inquiries by setting a legal framework. A decision to carry out VFM examinations of privatisation sales is made by the C&AG.   **12–099**

One of the most significant cases in recent years is *R v Secretary of State for Foreign Affairs Ex p. World Development Movement*.[70] The World Development Movement, a well-known and internationally recognised pressure group, sought judicial review to challenge the decision by the Foreign Secretary to make a payment of aid under the Overseas Development and Co-operation Act 1980 to the Malaysian government. The case is an important authority on the law of standing, but it is also an important case on the question of financial authority. In granting standing the factors that weighed heavily with the court were the necessity to uphold the rule of law, the nature of the breach of the duty complained about and the importance of aid.   **12–100**

The Divisional Court found that the grant of aid for the Pergau Dam project was economically unsound. It therefore did not satisfy the criteria set out in s.1 of the 1980 Act and it was therefore unlawful. A declaration was granted that the grant was unlawful. In reaching this conclusion Lord Justice Rose considered the proceedings of the Public Accounts Committee and the findings of a National Audit Office scrutiny. The case is a landmark for the use of pressure groups. The pressure group relied on information obtained through a National Audit Office report and information gleaned from debates within, and evidence taken by, the Public Accounts Committee and the Foreign Affairs Committee.[71] The National Audit Office and the Public Accounts Committee assumed the legality of the aid but criticised aspects of its value for money. The National Audit Office regarded the allocation of money as falling under policy matters within the remit of ministers. This excluded from its consideration the merits of the policy. However, it appeared that the Accounting Officer had serious reservations about the project. As Lord Justice Rose noted, the accounting officer's view was that the Pergau project was "an abuse of the aid programme in the terms that this is an uneconomic project" and that "it was not a sound development project."[72] Despite such reservations, written ministerial instructions were given to proceed with the financial aid. The Pergau project was funded, purportedly under s.1 of the Overseas Development and Co-operation Act 1980. Considering whether the aid for the Pergau dam fell within the ambit of the 1980 Act, Lord Justice Rose concluded: **12–101**

> "[a]ccordingly, where, as here, the contemplated development is, on the evidence, so economically unsound that there is no economic argument in favour of the case, it is not, in my judgment, possible to draw any material distinction between questions of propriety and regularity on the one hand and questions of economy and efficiency of public expenditure on the other."[73]

---

[70] The Pergau Dam case see: [1995] 1 All E.R. 611.
[71] Pergau Hydro–Electric Project (1994–95 HC 155). See F. White, I. Harden and K. Donnelly, "Audit, Accounting Officers and Accountability: The Pergau Dam Affair" [1994] *Public Law* 526.
[72] [1995] 1 All E.R. 611 at 617A–B.
[73] [1995] 1 All E.R. 611 at 626J–627B.

12–102   The Secretary of State under s.1(1) of the 1980 Act had extensive powers as follows:

> "The Secretary of State shall have power, for the purpose of promoting the development or maintaining the economy of a country or territory outside the United Kingdom, or the welfare of its people, to furnish any person or body with assistance, whether financial, technical or of any other nature."

12–103   The case hinged on the interpretation of this section. Was the grant in question "for the purpose of promoting the development" of Malaysia? This depended on whether the aid flowed into a development that might be described, according to the Foreign Office test for funding development, as one that was "sound, financially viable and [would] bring economic benefits". As doubts had been expressed within the consultation process within the government departments, the divisional court held that the provision of aid was *ultra vires* the 1980 Act. As a result of this decision, the Comptroller and Auditor General qualified his opinion of the aid on the basis of irregularity.

12–104   Despite this finding and the decision of the Divisional Court, the government found the necessary additional aid required to finance the Dam from a repayable charge on the Contingency Fund. Eventually the money was found from the Reserve Fund.

12–105   The World Development Movement was able to show how the Dam project had limited use in terms of promoting development but had enormous potential for encouraging arms sales and potential markets for UK companies. The project also failed on the criteria of its potential damage to the environment and limited benefits for the community. Evidence used in the case provided a broad cost–benefit analysis of the project, beyond the narrow view of the government in favour of economic trade.

12–106   The case signifies that issues of the legality of public expenditure may involve questions of value for money. There is a stark warning here. As Lord Justice Rose noted, the Government had taken no legal advice in the first instance on the legality of the aid; and as Daintith and Page observe:

> "The question of the relationship between the legislation and the Department's power to incur expenditure subject only to the authority of the Appropriation Act does not appear to have been raised or discussed."[74]

12–107   Clearly the case provides a good example of the range of judicial review today that includes an evaluation of the economic as distinct from the political and social merits of decisions. A powerful tool in the hands of the litigant is the work of the various parliamentary watchdogs such as the Committee of Public Accounts.

SUMMARY AND CONCLUSIONS

12–108   In the United Kingdom there is considerable debate about how effective are the current arrangements for the financial reporting of government expenditure. Too often the systems of audit and control reveal problems after the events have taken place, the

---

[74] T. Daintith and A Page, *The Executive in the Constitution* (1999) p.35.

money has been spent or the mistake made. Designing new systems of control requires setting targets and taking pre-emptive action to prevent mistakes.

There are a number of principles that apply to the way Parliament exercises control over expenditure: **12–109**

- The purposes of expenditure must be clearly identified. It is a principle of Parliamentary authority that Parliament approves expenditure for specific purposes. Sums appropriated for a specific service cannot be used for another service. Estimates presented to Parliament provide details of the information necessary for Parliamentary approval. Supplementary estimates must be used for new services in cases where Government departments require a new service that is not covered by the ambit of existing authority.

- The principle that voted sums authorised by Parliament cannot be exceeded. Departments cannot exceed the sums authorised in the annual Appropriation Act without Parliamentary authority. This may be in the form of a revised or supplementary estimate or by presenting an excess vote to Parliament which is subsequently authorised in the Appropriation Act. In the latter case there must be a report from the Comptroller and Auditor General setting out the reasons for the excess.

- The principle of annuality: the sums authorised by Parliament are only available in the financial year for which they are appropriated. This principle is intended to ensure that departmental expenditure is subject to regular Parliamentary review and authorisation. Subject to Treasury rules about the carry-forward of underspends, this principle helps to maintain annual Parliamentary authority.

- The principle of good stewardship: departments are expected to provide Parliament, through various departmental select committees, with information as the basis for the examination of the departments' performance in carrying out policies, functions, projects and programmes. In addition Parliament has to be provided with information to measure the performance of departmental expenditure. This is achieved through the work of the National Audit Office in measuring departmental performance in terms of the economy, efficiency and effectiveness with which departments are operating services and through value for money examinations.

FURTHER READING

Terence Daintith and Alan Page, *The Executive in the Constitution* (Oxford University Press, Oxford, 2000).

Paul Evans, *Handbook of House of Commons Procedure* (Vacher Dod Publishing, London, 1997).

Andrew Likierman, *Public Expenditure* (Penguin, London, 1988).

T. Erskine May, *Parliamentary Practice* (22nd ed., Butterworths, London, 1997).

Paul Silk and Rhoderi Walters, *How Parliament Works* (4th ed., Longman, London, 1999).

Colin Thain and Maurice Wright, *The Treasury and Whitehall* (Clarendon Press, Oxford, 1995).

HM Treasury, *Resource Accounting Manual* (The Stationery Office, London, 2000).

HM Treasury, *Government Accounting: A Guide on Accounting and Financial Procedures for the Use of Government* (The Stationery Office updated with supplements from 1989–2002).

HM Treasury, *Supply Estimates*, (London).

HM Treasury, *Regularity and Propriety* (London, 1997).

HM Treasury, *Code for Fiscal Stability* (London, 1998).

Fidelma White and Kathryn Hollingsworth, *Audit, Accountability and Government* (Oxford University Press, Oxford, 1999).

Chapter 13

LOCAL GOVERNMENT

INTRODUCTION

The United Kingdom's development as a unitary state results in no special constitu- **13–001** tional status being awarded to local government. The term asymmetrical constitution is appropriate. A remarkable feature of Parliamentary power has been its centralisation in the hands of successive governments. This gives central government ultimate legal authority over local government. In the absence of any federal system offering local government an entrenched protection, local government may be amended or modified at the whim of central government. Similarly, newly devolved government to Wales, Scotland and Northern Ireland is subject to Parliamentary authority. In strict constitutional theory devolution may be retracted, modified, suspended or amended. As noted in earlier chapters in the book, the term asymmetrical seems appropriate to describe current arrangements since devolution. Centralised and ultimate sovereignty continues to rest with the United Kingdom Parliament, with subordinate law-making powers delegated to Scotland, Wales, Northern Ireland and the London Mayor. Local government has only the powers that have been conferred on it by Parliament. Devolution is outlined in Chapter 2. It provides an additional tier of government leaving local government to continue to deliver diverse public services. Local government in the United Kingdom provides a means to allocate decision-making that is different from central government. Locally elected authorities provide citizens with a large range of services which have a degree of local autonomy. Local authority activities are wide-ranging across a range of public services from the police, public health to education and street cleaning. Superficially, local government may appear uncomplicated. In fact, because of the political nature of changes in the way local government is financed and its role and function being determined by the life cycle of party politics, the law and regulation of local authorities is unduly complex and technical. It deserves a more coherent treatment and a major simplification of the law is long overdue.

Elected local authorities have wide statutory powers including powers of local **13–002** taxation. They also receive large financial support from central government, roughly 60 per cent of their expenditure. As an administrative agency, local government appears similar to other agencies with statutory powers and duties. In law, local authorities are statutory corporations. They are subject to judicial review, and accountable for their expenditure to the Audit Commission, an independent statutory body with a similar role for local government as the National Audit Office provides to Parliament for central government. Local government is also accountable to the Commissioner for Local Administration, with similar functions to the Parliamentary Commissioner for Administration. Local authorities may develop their own politics and policies within the legal powers they possess. Because of their elected nature, local authorities are accountable to their electorate for their policies and spending plans. This form of electoral accountability may give rise to political and ideological differences with central government. Conflicts between the centre and local authorities are not easily reconciled, and this has increased the centralising tendencies of the legislation passed for local government.

13–003   This chapter is intended firstly to explain the role and function of local authorities in a period of change and modernisation. The account is limited to England and Wales, as Scotland has its own system of law applicable to local government, and Northern Ireland's arrangements are distinctive to that region. Secondly, to explain relations between local and central government that has set new challenges for the courts. Finally, it is intended to outline the role of the Audit Commission in the accountability of local authorities.

MODERNISATION AND CHANGE

Phase One: 1979–1997

13–004   In the past thirty years, local government has come under intense change and increased scrutiny often in conflicting directions depending on the political ideology of the government of the day. The first phase under the Conservative government of Mrs Thatcher sought to reduce local authority expenditure and bring tighter controls over public services provided by local authorities. At that time there were many conflicts between local and central government over local government finance, and the role and functions of local authorities. A number of disputes involving financial issues led to litigation. A significant increase in the number of applications for judicial review— roughly one third are disputes involving local authorities—illustrated how the judicial element in resolving the conflict took on its own momentum. This includes cases taken against a local authority as well as local authorities seeking judicial redress against central government or other agencies including other local authorities. The Conservative Government appeared to see the elected element of the local authority as less important than the legal powers used to hold local government to account. There were attempts to give the citizen greater opportunities to challenge local authority decisions. The Committee of Inquiry in 1986 under the Chairmanship of David Widdicombe (hereinafter the Widdicombe Report),[1] recommended that the right of objection to accounts should be extended to all ratepayers and that greater publicity should be given to the auditors' reports. The latter recommendation became law under the Local Government Finance (Publicity for Auditors Reports) Act 1991. As a result changes took place in the way local authorities are expected to manage their own affairs, including their control of their financial arrangements. Traditionally local authorities

---

[1] Widdicombe Report (Cm.9797, 1986).

have employed the necessary staff to carry out the services for which they are responsible. This includes, for example, social service staff, teachers, and refuse collection. The Local Government Act 1988 required local authorities to subject a number of services such as street cleaning, vehicle maintenance, schools and welfare catering, refuse collection and the management of sports and leisure facilities to competition. Competition has set new management challenges and has had profound effects on the way local authorities manage themselves. The law requires that private companies must be permitted to bid for the work involved and this element of competition within public service provision sets new directions for the future of local authorities. The Local Government Act has been amended by the Local Government Act 2000 removing the requirement on compulsory competitive tendering.

In May 1991 the Secretary of State for the Environment instigated a review of local **13–005** government and following this a number of consultative documents were published. The outcome was the Local Government Act 1992 that includes changes to introduce performance standards for local authorities and increased powers for competitive tendering in line with the provisions in the Citizen's Charter.[2] These developments were in line with the idea of constraining local government's expenditure plans and making local government more responsive to the market.

Perceptible changes are evident in the role of local authorities as a result of these **13–006** developments. First, there is a tendency towards centralisation of powers and policy decision-making. Secondly, there is a challenge to the effectiveness of local authorities being accountable to their own electorate. Current government thinking questions the efficiency of local government elections as an adequate means of accountability over local government. Since 1979 the bi-partisan approach of the major political parties to local authority decision-making has been abandoned. Local authorities are perceived as "instruments of social welfare" and therefore seen as acting in opposition to the policies of central government. Thirdly, there is a tendency to envisage local authorities developing management styles more consistent with regulating local authority activities rather than delivering the services. Fourthly, there is a perceptible shift in the variety and type of legislation which local authorities are required to follow. The Victorian style of legislation, containing broadly drafted wide discretion with enabling powers, has continued in modern times supplemented with complex, technical and precisely formulated provisions which require enforcement. Legal rules have replaced broad discretion. Detailed regulations, codes of practice and rules proliferate. The courts are expected to enforce such rules even if they may be in conflict with policy objectives of the duly elected local authority.[3]

Phase two: 1997–2002

The new Labour Government in 1997 embarked on an ambitious programme of **13–007** modernisation and reform. The White Paper *Modern Local Government—in Touch with the People*[4] provides the long-term goal of the government to provide a new sense

---

[2] Citizen's Charter, Cm.1599 (1991).
[3] See *Report of the Committee of Enquiry into Local Government Finance*, Cmnd.6453 (1976). (The Layfield Report.)
[4] Cm.4014 (1998).

of community leadership. There followed two major statutory reforms. The Local Government Act 1999 repeals the compulsory competitive tendering arrangements, which is outlined below in more detail. A second part of the 1999 Act is the introduction of a new "best value" concept. Detailed regulations followed outlining how the concept was to be implemented. Over the past two years, local authorities have been expected to develop a Performance Plan for the local authority implementing best value. Best value reviews are conducted to ensure that performance targets are reached and the management of the local authority is up to standard.

13–008   The system of best value review has the following component parts[5]:

- identifying the current position of the service looking at performance and the market;
- determining the scope of the review to ensure that all aspects are covered and addressing priorities;
- consultation and comparison with customers and other providers;
- challenging the service and demonstrating it is competitive so that a gap analysis may be undertaken;
- development of an action plan to ensure continuous improvement.

13–009   It is clear that all local authorities must meet the best value requirements of the legislation. This is a vague concept defined in the DETR paper as[6] ". . . about the cost and quality of services that meet the aspirations of the people". Local authorities must meet the centrally set performance indicators established by central government. They must publish an annual performance target and publish how they meet the standards of performance. Fundamental reviews must take place and this represents a further extension of regulation, command and control. The Best Value Inspectorate within the Audit Commission is required to monitor, report and take steps to ensure that best value is achieved.

13–010   There are also detailed powers under the 1999 Act dealing with the capping powers over local government council tax. These are powers exercised by central government "to cap" or restrict the increases in council tax levied by local authorities. In theory the 1999 Act might mean a relaxation of the capping powers which are considered to be an excessive use of central government discretion since they were first introduced in 1992 when the council tax was introduced. In fact, on closer examination it is clear that the 1999 Act retains the power of the Secretary of State to cap the local authority's council tax. In s.30 and sch.1 there are powers to identify local authorities that are thought to be spending excessively. The Secretary of State is free to categorise a local authority and warn the relevant authority to take measures to prevent excessive spending. Once warned then there are extensive powers for calculating the amount of expenditure that is excessive and the Secretary of State may then nominate the authority for action to be taken. This may take the form of setting a sum for the authority's annual budget and for the incoming financial year setting targets to be met. In extreme circumstances where there is evidence of serious mismanagement it would be possible for central government to bring in their own management team to take over the management of

---

[5] *Warwick District Council Best Value Performance Plan 2002–3.*
[6] DETR, *Best Value in Housing Framework* (1999), paras:1.3, 2.4.

the local authority. In July 2002, Hull City Council received criticism from an Inspector's report that may lead to central government operating its powers.

In addition to the introduction of best value there is also a new management agenda contained in the Local Government Act 2000. The question of the governance of local authorities has not received much attention since the Widdicombe Committee last inquired into the business of local government in 1986. The aim of local authorities performing their role for the community is being strengthened by the idea that by April 2002 all local authorities are expected to introduce a new management structure. The idea is to introduce some form of democratic renewal as set out in the White Paper, *Strong Local Leadership: Quality Public Services*.[7] There is no single prescribed model. Local authorities are expected to choose the model that is agreed through consultation with the local community. What models are on offer ? One model is to be found in the London elected mayoral system. Another model might be to set up a cabinet form of executive decision-making and variations on this theme might be employed. In total there are three models on offer as follows: **13–011**

- Mayor and cabinet with a directly elected mayor;

- a mayor and council manager executive, the mayor being directly elected and the authority appointed by the council as a council manager;

- a leader and cabinet as an executive.

Local authorities have not adopted the mayoral model, though the emerging trends are difficult to predict. Only one electoral mayor other than London is proposed by referendum at Watford; only 13 authorities have held mayor referendums and only 7 voted in favour. In May 2002 local elections were held; seven mayoral elections were held, five referendums were held on mayoral elections.   **13–012**

Pt II of the Local Government Act 2000 provides that there should be improvements in the management and efficiency of local authorities. Each local authority should have a management committee appointed to take decisions on behalf of the authority. The management committee is composed of between 5 and 9 leading councillors. Pt III of the Act makes changes to the audit arrangements and in particular removes the power of surcharge. Auditors will be able to seek advisory notices rather than a prohibition order as in the past.   **13–013**

Many of the new arrangements, such as the new management structures, are taking effect and it is too soon to evaluate them as the transitional arrangements are being put into place. The policy underlining the changes, however, is that a responsive and community-managed local authority will be more democratic. Despite this optimism that changes will be successful there is much local voter apathy and a belief that while local consultation may be improved, public service delivery is beyond the capacity and the structure of local authorities.   **13–014**

THE ROLE AND FUNCTION OF LOCAL GOVERNMENT

It is necessary to consider the historical evolution of local government and how the pattern of growth has broadly followed the increase in the delivery of public services at the local level from the nineteenth century until the present day. Local government is   **13–015**

[7] Cm.5237 (December 2001).

very much a reflection of the life cycle of central government policies and this has led to uncertainty about its role. As public services have come under the spotlight of modernisation, so have local authorities. It will be interesting to discover what impact if any devolution will have in terms of weakening or strengthening local government.

The History of Local Government

13–016   The historical background provides an explanation of the development of modern local government. The nineteenth century brought a growth in towns and new laws to deal with problems such as health, housing, sanitation, law and order, and education. The Municipal Corporations Act 1835 created elected local authorities, but local authorities' statutory powers developed during the remainder of the century on an ad hoc basis. Diane Dawson explains the considerable growth in local authority responsibilities during the nineteenth century as an important stage in the development of local government in Britain[8]:

> "From 1843 to 1929, the assumption of responsibility for water, gas, transport, education, housing and health services was a perceived response to the inadequacy or inefficiency of private enterprise and voluntary organisations in supplying these services."

13–017   By the end of the nineteenth century elected councils were established for counties, county boroughs, urban and rural districts and most parishes. Local authorities had become as Robson described[9] "the most effective instrument of social welfare in our national life."

13–018   Over the years local authorities have gained wide and extensive statutory powers. They may initiate their own private Bill legislation and possess wide secondary law-making powers made in the form of byelaws. They have limited but important powers to raise rates, a form of local taxation. The present structure, organisation and legal framework of local government for local authority activities in England and Wales is derived from the Local Government Act 1972.

1972 Re-organisation

13–019   The 1972 Act introduced major re-organisations in the size and shape of local government in England and Wales which were put into operation after intense debate in 1974. The report of the Redcliffe–Maud Committee[10] in 1969 favoured 58 unitary authorities but in major conurbations such as Liverpool, Manchester and Birmingham it favoured a two-tier system. The 1972 Act departed from this recommendation and established a two-tier system with a different distribution of functions. London was treated separately under the London Government Act 1963 following a Royal Commission on Local Government in 1960. The 1963 Act created the Greater London

---

[8] Diane Dawson, "Economic Change and the Changing Role of Local Government" in M. Loughlin *et al.*, *Half a Century of Municipal Decline 1935–1985* (M. Loughlin, *et al.*, London, 1985), pp.26–99.
[9] *ibid.*, quoted in Dawson *op.cit.*
[10] Report of the Royal Commission on Local Government in England, Cmnd.4040 (1969). [Redcliffe–Maud.] See Local Government Acts 1963, 1972 and 1985.

Council and 32 larger boroughs and the City of London within the area defined as Greater London. The 1972 Act also defined the boundaries of the metropolitan counties and districts and the non-metropolitan or "shire" counties. A local Government Boundary Commission was also established to review electoral arrangements and boundaries.

Altogether there were 514 principal local authorities in Great Britain, Northern **13–020** Ireland is treated differently and does not fall within this structure. There are 404 authorities in England, 65 in Scotland and 45 in Wales. The two-tier system operates throughout the "shire" areas in England, in all of Wales and on the mainland in Scotland. The two-tier system comprises an upper tier and a lower tier. In England and Wales the upper tier is known as counties where there were 47 counties (38 in England and 9 in Wales), and in Scotland as regions where there were 9 regions. The lower tier authorities are known as districts. There were 53 districts in Scotland, 37 in Wales and 296 in the shire areas of England.

In Greater London and the six metropolitan counties of England[11] a different system **13–021** prevailed. In London, the upper tier comprised the Greater London Council and the lower tier comprised 32 London boroughs and the City of London. In the case of the six metropolitan counties of England, the upper tier comprised six county councils, and the lower tier consisted of 36 district councils. The Local Government Act 1985 from April 1, 1986 abolished the Greater London Council and the six metropolitan county councils. The result of these changes left functions distributed to the remaining tier of government and some functions were shared with new single-purpose joint authorities. In the case of Inner London a new directly elected education authority was created.

Current Organisation and Structure

The movement in favour of unitary local government authorities has gathered **13–022** momentum. The re-drawing of local government took considerable time to implement. The Local Government (Wales) Act 1994 and the Local Government etc. (Scotland) Act 1994 provided for unitary authorities in Wales and Scotland replacing the dual authority system inherited and re-organised in the 1970s.

- Scotland: 32 unitary authorities
- Wales: 22 unitary authorities.

There has been no equivalent legislation to introduce unitary authorities for every **13–023** local authority in England. As a result there are the following local authorities:

England

- 46 new unitary authorities;
- 34 county councils;
- 238 district councils.

---

[11] In London specific changes were made on April 1, 1986, to the London and Metropolitan Counties. This tier of local government including the Greater London Council was abolished.

London

- 33 London Boroughs;

- 1 Greater London Authority and 1 elected Mayor under devolution arrangements.

13–024   Under the Local Government Act 1992 the Local Government Commission for England was established with the task of undertaking a review of local government areas. Matters of such party political sensitivity exposed the ground rules of the Commission, given in the form of guidance, to a great deal of controversy. Matters of s.13(6) of the 1992 Act that should guide the Commission included preference to be given to "natural communities" and that account should be taken of peoples' preferences. However, the government insisted in its revised guidance issued in 1993 that the aim of having a unitary system of local authority should be considered. In *R. v. Secretary of State for the Environment Ex p. Lancashire C*[12] the guidance that sought to give undue weight to the Government's preference for unitary authorities was unlawful.

13–025   The approach taken thereafter was to consider the introduction of unitary authorities on a consultation basis. This process, begun in 1992, has proved more time-consuming and complex than was first envisaged. In addition, periodic electoral review is undertaken to rectify electoral imbalances in a local authority area. The Commission completed its review in early 1995. In the end, 50 all-purpose unitary authorities were proposed. Since March 1996 over 30 local authorities have been considered and the results of these deliberations will be forthcoming in the form of further consultation papers. The preference for an overwhelming number of unitary local authorities appears to have been held in check.

Role and Function of Local Authorities

13–026   The role and function of local authorities was examined in the Widdicombe Report (1986). The main characteristics of the modern local authority were identified. These include its diversity, the opportunities given for local democracy, the responsiveness to local needs through the delivery of services and finally its contribution to the national political system through its diversity of politics.

13–027   Diversity comes about through the geographical size and management style in different local authorities. The size of local authorities varies throughout the country and this includes the geographical areas covered, the size of population (from as few as 25,000 to over 1.5 million), and the amount of local authority expenditure which varies considerably from one authority to another. The Widdicombe Report drew attention to the difficult question of the role of local authorities. There remains intense debate as to how local authorities with such diversity in politics, size, finance and policy priorities may best develop relations with central government. In 1976 the Layfield Report[13] on local government finance identified two opposing views of local authority activities which were relevant to the Widdicombe inquiry.

---

[12] [1994] 4 All E.R. 165.
[13] Report of the Committee of Enquiry into Local Government Finance, Cmnd.6453 (1976). (The Layfield Report.)

The "centralist" view is that local authorities act as agents for central government. **13–028** As custodians of the interests of the local community they mitigate the dangers of remoteness and bureaucratic organisation which would occur if government were entirely centralised. On this view emphasis is placed not on the elected element in local authority activities, but on the sovereignty of Parliament to direct local authorities to carry out activities on behalf of central government policy-making. On this view local authorities are less free to develop their own distinctive policies which may conflict with central government's general direction and policy-making.

The opposing view is the "localist" view, that local authorities are decentralised with **13–029** real political authority and power in respect of the functions which can appropriately be performed at the local level. On this view emphasis is placed on the statutory duties local authorities are expected and, in many cases, required to perform. Local authorities are entitled to develop their own strategies and are free to promote their own distinctive policies even if these might conflict with the policy of the government of the day.

The Widdicombe Report found this dichotomy of views unhelpful in the sense that **13–030** the true constitutional status of local authorities was that they derived all their powers, not as autonomous entities with an entrenched constitutional status, but from Parliament. The view of central government and the tendency towards centralism in the past policies of central government left local authorities no option but to accept "as a fact of life" the reality of central government's legal authority. Today the debate remains just as intense and crosses party political lines. Those who favour reducing the power of the state desire a streamlined and slim local authority component. Those that favour public service delivery see local authorities as part of the delivery system, providing for the community a responsive public service.

As Grant has argued[14]: **13–031**

"The constitutional element of the central-local relations debate is potentially empty and barren, and neither of the two approaches [one that gives formal constitutional protection to local government and the other that gives limited protection to local government, providing for a more consensus political arrangement for the distribution of functions between central–local relations] has overcome the initial problems. The constitutional debate is not only potentially empty in itself because of the tendency inherent in it to attach a priori values and attributes to legal institutions and to pursue principles more for their traditional value than their contemporary utility. But also, because of its focus upon the formal relationships between government bodies it threatens to overlook the broader grounds of recent central-local conflict."

Grant's analysis has greater acceptance today in the current approaches to local **13–032** government. We shall see that the differences between centralism and localism have an ideological effect on the cultures of local authorities. Many local authorities are steeped in the idealism of localism which has been partly fostered by the sense that the local authority delivers public services and in that way fits Robson's description of

---

[14] M. Grant, "Central–local Relations: The Balance of Power" in *The Changing Constitution* (J. Jowell and D. Oliver ed., 1989), pp.251–252.

acting as "an instrument of social welfare". Local authorities that adopted the welfare view of their functions found that after 1979 they came into conflict with central government policies. This led to disputes over local authority finance and in some cases litigation between local and central government.

13–033   There are many instances where the traditional functions of local authorities are being changed. In education the Education Reform Act 1988 with its national based curriculum and key learning stages gave greater parental choice and this has allowed some schools to opt out of local authority control. There are further plans to make School Heads and Governors budget holders. In housing, the compulsory right to buy gave council tenants the right to opt out of local government control.[15]

13–034   Local authorities possess some widely drawn statutory powers in addition to many specific statutory duties. A few examples illustrate how local authorities may be provided with wide statutory powers. Any local authority may exercise under s.111 of the Local Government Act 1972 general powers "to do anything which is calculated to facilitate or is conducive or incidental to, the discharge of any of their functions". Such powers, especially if used to raise money by borrowing or lending money, must also conform to detailed rules regulating these activities. S.137 of the Local Government Act 1972 is a general power to incur expenditure subject to an annual financial limit. Such a power is intended to be used where there is no other statutory power available. More recently, the Local Government and Housing Act 1989 provides local authorities with a general power to promote economic development and considerable flexibility in carrying out their plans. Regulations assist in setting the limits of the permitted activities which may fall within their powers. The Local Government (Amendment) Act 1993 extends local authority powers to make grants to ethnic minorities by extending their powers under s.11 of the Local Government Act 1966. There are general powers under s.2 of the Local Government Act 2000 for the promotion of the economic, social and environmental wellbeing of the area. This is more broadly drafted than s.137 of the Local Government Act 1972 meaning that the benefit does not have to be commensurate with the expenditure.

Elections

13–035   The Local Government Act 1972 provides arrangements for the return of local councillors for each electoral area, that is at county, district or parish level. Electoral areas are designated according to the different levels of local government. There is a Local Government Boundary Commission, established under the 1972 Act for the purposes of keeping under review the "electoral arrangements" of the principal authorities. The Commission may also determine the number of councillors that may be returned for each constituency. The aim in carrying out both functions is the same, namely to provide arrangements "in the interests of effective and convenient local government".

13–036   Pt II of the Local Government Act 1992 establishes a Local Government Commission. One of its tasks is to take over the responsibilities of the Local Government Boundary Commission for England in the conduct of periodic reviews of electoral

[15] T. Byrne, *Local Government in Britain* (7th ed., rev. ed., Penguin, London, 2000).

arrangements. Directions or guidance may be given to the Commission by the Secretary of State. The setting-up of the Commission is intended to review matters concerning elections, boundaries and the structure of local government without recourse to a Royal Commission or similar inquiry. Three advantages are claimed from a unitary system of local government. First, a unitary system might promote local democracy by increasing the accountability of local authority communities. Secondly, a unitary system might reduce bureaucracy and administrative costs inherent in the duplication of central management at county and district level. Thirdly, a unitary system offers the opportunity for improved co-ordination and cost-effectiveness in the delivery of local government services.

Under the 1972 Local Government Act the structure of local authorities is as follows. In the case of the county councils the area is divided into electoral divisions, with one council member returned for each division. Elections must be held every four years with each member retiring simultaneously. **13–037**

In the case of the Shire district councils, the area is divided into electoral wards with three members normally returned for each ward. All the members of the council retire simultaneously, but it is possible to opt for a system of election based on one-third of the council retiring at a time. Voting takes place only in those wards where a member is retiring. In wards where there are only one or two members returned, it is not possible to vote every year. **13–038**

In the case of the metropolitan district councils, the electoral area is divided into wards with three members for each ward. One-third of the members stand for election and elections are commonly held in three years out of four. On the principle that a member retires in each ward at each election, the entire electorate has the opportunity to vote. **13–039**

In the case of the Parish or Community Council, any number of councillors may be elected. There is no maximum number for the size of the Parish Council, but the minimum is set at five. There are requirements under the Representation of the People Act 1983 that each District Council or London Borough Council must appoint an electoral officer. Responsibility falls on the electoral registration officer to prepare and publish each year an electoral register for both parliamentary and local government elections. **13–040**

The electoral qualification for local government is similar to central government. However disqualification is more widely drawn. Tenure of any office of profit at the disposal of a local authority or any of its committees is a disqualification for office as a councillor. Also bankruptcy, surcharge by the auditor or conviction for corrupt or illegal practices and incurring imprisonment within five years of an election is also a disqualification. **13–041**

The electoral registration officer must also publish notice of the election, receive nominations and co-ordinate the arrangements for polling day. Turnout at local government elections is usually significantly less than at elections for central government—on average 40–50 per cent, compared to 75 per cent at a general election. In the elections held in May 2002, the turnout was 34.4 per cent. There are about 23,000 councillors in Britain. They appear to be untypical of the cross—section of the community. Byrne[16] notes how many are older than the age of 54, predomi- **13–042**

---

[16] Byrne, *op.cit.*, pp.196–199.

nantly male, a large majority are owner-occupiers, white collar in occupation and most were well educated, to A level or above. Also a high proportion were among the better paid.

CHANGE AND STRUCTURE IN LOCAL GOVERNMENT

Structure and Organisation

13–043   Unlike central government with a clearly defined executive, up until the Local Government Act 2000 there was no clearly defined concept of providing through different models some form of executive branch for local government. It will be for local authorities to opt for one of the models identified above. However, unlike central government there is no equivalent of ministerial responsibility, leaving a gap in the arrangements for accountability which in the past have been filled by the development of a separate Audit Commission in 1982 and the creation of a local government ombudsman. It will be interesting to speculate whether an elected Mayor will embrace a prime ministerial or presidential style of leadership where this model of governance is adopted. This is likely to be only in a minority of local authorities The development of an executive element is likely to be the most popular and under this model the question of decision making and accountability is evolving.

13–044   Local government may be described as combining an elected element, namely the councillors, and an administrative staff comprising, at the most senior level, professional officers. The council chairman is annually elected; decisions are taken by resolutions of the council or through officials acting with delegated authority. The council usually works through a large number of committees. Standing orders and minutes are kept of the conduct of meetings and under the Public Bodies (Admission to Meetings) Act 1960 members of the public are normally admitted.[17] The Chairman has power to exclude the public in cases of disorderly conduct[18] and meetings may be kept confidential and closed to the public where the nature of business or public interest requires.

13–045   Following the Widdicombe Committee report legislation was introduced to bring greater openness into the conduct of local authority business. The Local Government (Access to Information) Act 1985 requires councils to give public notice of meetings, make available certain relevant documents and make the agenda, minutes and relevant reports public. The main *caveat* is that they do not have to be disclosed if confidential information relating to government departments or the like is disclosed. Reports and background papers are open to inspection by members of the public for four years in the case of any background papers and six years for other papers.

13–046   Excluded from open access are matters relating to personal information about members of staff in connection with employment and this restriction includes access to information regarding wages and the payment of benefits.

13–047   The Widdicombe Committee paid particular attention to the role of the principal officer of a local authority and the committee structure of local authority decision-

---

[17] See *R. v Liverpool City Council Ex p. Liverpool Taxi Fleet Operators Association* [1975] 1 W.L.R. 701, which discusses the rights of the public to attend meetings.
[18] *R. v Brent HA Ex p. Francis* [1985] Q.B. 869.

making. The aim of the Widdicombe Committee was to strengthen the system of democratic accountability. For example *R. v Waltham Forest LBC, Ex p. Baxter*[19] illustrated how leading councillors and local political activists met and later attended meetings of the council. The link between ideology and local authority decision-making seemed complete. This link was criticised by the courts.

The Local Government and Housing Act 1989 provides important changes to the organisation and management of committees ensuring that representation on committees and sub-committees comprises various political groups. There are provisions to prevent officers from serving on more than one local authority and for the non-voting of non-elected and appointed members of committees. Some provision is made for the appointment of political advisers. The changes introduced in 1989 were less than those recommended by the Widdicombe Report. **13–048**

Competitive Tendering for Local Authority Services

The history of competitive tendering and its reform under the new Labour Government may be outlined as follows: the shift in focus from local authorities in the 1980s as[20] "providers of services" to local authorities as "enablers and regulators" is well illustrated by the introduction of competitive tendering. For a period up until 2000, Britain was the only European country in which competitive tendering for certain local authority services was compulsory. The British experience probably represented the most systematic and comprehensive experience of compulsory tendering. The stages adopted in the use of competitive tendering began in the National Health Service prior to 1988 and introduced catering, domestic and laundry services to competitive tendering. Individual health authorities extended various support services such as porters and ground maintenance to competitive tendering. In various central government departments such as the Ministry of Defence and also in the civil service competitive tendering has been extensively used. **13–049**

In 1980, the Local Government Planning and Land Act 1980 (Pt III) required certain local authority construction and maintenance work to be made subject to competitive tendering. Highways and building work were included. Traditionally for such work local authorities operated their own Direct Labour Organisations (DLO). After 1980 DLOs could continue to carry our their work but on the basis of winning a competitive contract not on an automatic basis. **13–050**

In 1985 the Government issued a White Paper: Competition in the Provision of Local Authority Service[21] (February 1985) which argued for an extension of competitive tendering to a wider range of activities such as catering, refuse collection, building, cleaning schools, welfare catering and sporting and leisure activities. The Local Government Act 1988 required local authorities to provide competition for the above services. DLOs are permitted to bid for contracts but are not given any preferential treatment. Services subject to contract bids were expected to be subject to competition at six month intervals between August 1, 1989 and January 1, 1992. The extension of **13–051**

---

[19] [1988] Q.B. 419.
[20] (1989) Municipal Review, (April, 1989) p.9. See Byrne, *op.cit.*, Chaps.9 and 10. Also see The New Local Authorities: Management and Structure (the Bains Report), (HMSO 1972).
[21] See: HMSO, Audit Commission, *Competitiveness and Contracting Out of Local Authorities Services* HMSO, 1987.

competition into local authority activities is set to continue. Parallel legislation such as the Education Reform Act 1988 and the Local Government and Housing Act 1989 continued to introduce competitive elements into education and local authority companies.

PFI Projects

13–052 The Government has taken steps to encourage private finance to be invested in public sector activities. Since November 1992 the Private Finance Initiative (PFI) allows private finance to be used for public sector capital activities including buildings, computer technology, know-how and new management systems. The most notable examples of PFI are in the Channel Tunnel Rail Link and other new construction projects. HM Treasury have insisted that their criteria for a PFI project is that "the genuine risk" is transferred to the private sector and the project represents value for money when public sector finance is involved. The idea behind the PFI strategy is that of a public–private partnership allowing some degree of contracting out where public services are contracted from the private sector. PFI has the potential to transform the problems of long-term capital under-funding in local government. In the context of local authorities PFI requires careful supervision because of the restrictive nature of local authority powers. PFI has been used extensively throughout the country for about 450 major projects such as new hospital buildings, roads, prisons, education and Northern Line Trains. The supervision of each project is vested in a central government department.

Central–Local Government Relations

13–053 As outlined above, relations between local and central government have proved controversial, especially when there may be ideological differences about role and function. Central government has sought greater accountability over the provision of public services, especially with regard to local government finance. It is therefore not surprising that the main focus in the relationship between central and local government is finance.

Local Authority Finance

13–054 Local government finance is highly complex and the complexity has not diminished in recent years. As already noted, local authority spending is at least 60 per cent of public spending. The vast amount of expenditure is taken up with education, housing, and personal social services.

13–055 The structures of local government's financial arrangements are complex and have undergone considerable change. In outline the following description is an attempt to explain the main features of the system, from the old system of rating valuation to the new system of community charge, in operation until April 1, 1993, and afterwards its replacement by the Council tax.[22]

---

[22] C.M.G. Himsworth, "Poll Tax Capping and Judicial Review" [1991] *Public Law* 76–92. Also see C.M.G. Himsworth and N.C. Walker, "After Rates? The Community Charge in Scotland" [1987] *Public Law* 586.

Historically local authorities were given wide discretion and a degree of self-regulation over the financial arrangements and accounting practices in use in local government. Local authority expenditure is divided between revenue and capital. Revenue expenditure refers to short-term matters such as salaries and office supplies and is funded out of current income; capital expenditure refers to longer term spending such as buildings and is funded from borrowing. The latter has caused central government to restrict and control the extent of local government borrowing in order to control public spending as part of its long-term policy.   **13–056**

Local authority finance is often complicated and beset by technical and detailed legal rules. Current expenditure is funded from three main sources of income: charges made by local government for services, etc.; central government grants; and, up until 1990, rates. Of the three, the main sources of local authority income came from rates (now replaced by the Council tax) and grants from central government.   **13–057**

Rates were based on a property valuation and were levied on both domestic and business occupancy. Their origin may be traced to the earliest development of local authorities. In the Vagabonds Act 1535, churchwardens were responsible for the administration of the poor through relief charged upon each parish. The Poor Relief Act 1597 recognised the growing scale of the amount of relief and introduced a general system of local rating. Compulsory rating, enforced through distress and sale of chattels for non-payment, was accompanied by a system of audit, later through a district auditor under the Poor Law Amendment Act 1866, and proper accounting introduced by the Poor Relief Act 1601. Consolidation of enforcement procedures was further provided in the General Rates Act 1967. The basis of the rating system depended on regular valuation of property values. Property values, which set the basis of the rating system, had not been revalued since April 1973 in England, and any revaluation was seen as problematic, which prompted the Government to consider changes in the rating system of local government finance.   **13–058**

A further complication arose when local authorities increased the amount of revenue from the rates by sharply increasing rate levels. By 1974 this had caused a "crisis in local government finance which led to the setting up of the Layfield Committee[23] into local government finance which reported after two years of deliberations in 1976."   **13–059**

An additional complication to the rating system was the need for major financial support from central government through a rate support grant under the Local Government Act 1966 and later amended by the Local Government, Planning and Land Act 1980, Pt VI. In the mid-1970s the extent of central government grants received by local authorities exceeded the amount raised by rates. Over 60 per cent of local authority funding came through central government grant, an indication of the dependency of local authorities on central government. The form of grant, the rate support grant (RSG), was as a block grant which left local authorities free to determine how spending priorities could be identified within their statutory duties imposed on local authorities. Local authorities could increase the level of their rates to take account of their expenditure.   **13–060**

Central government desired to impose a new financial discipline on local authorities and imposed a revision of the RSG system on each local authority. The revision was   **13–061**

[23] Reports of the Layfield Committee, Cmnd.6453 (1976).

set out according to the assessment of each local authority spending conducted by central government under the Local Government, Planning and Land Act 1980. Included under the 1980 Act were controls on local government capital expenditure in an effort to reduce local government expenditure and curtail the freedom of local authorities to depart from the financial policies of central government.

13–062   The theory behind the 1980 Act was that differences in local authority spending habits might be identified and controls applied to the more prolific spending authorities. Further refinements to the 1980 Act were provided by the Local Government Finance Act 1982 by setting spending targets and penalties on local authorities. The 1982 Act introduced the Audit Commission to improve the financial management of local authorities. The 1982 Act also abolished supplementary rates.

13–063   Local authority ingenuity contrived to avoid the effects of central government's initiatives at control. Setting targets for local authority spending did not prove effective and in 1984 the Rates Act included powers to the Secretary of State to control the making of rates and the issuing of precepts. This introduced the concept of "rate capping" whereby the Secretary of State could determine the rates of "over-spending" authorities and limit their rate levels. This led to further "creative accounting" by local authorities. Central government found the making of regulations and their enforcement a complex and expensive game of "cat and mouse" between local and central government.

13–064   The abolition of the Greater London Council and the six Metropolitan Counties took place in 1985 as a further attempt to curtail the more irritating excesses of local government. However these changes and the adaptation of the rates system to bring it within central government control failed to address the central issue of how to provide a satisfactory system for the finance of local government.

13–065   The Layfield Committee in 1976 in reviewing local government rating, had noted the difficulty of re-valuation of property based on notional rental values. The Layfield Committee recommended that re-valuation should take place on the basis of property sale price. The system of rating remained unchanged, although the government in its election manifestos from 1979 promised to introduce reforms to the rating system. The Department of Environment published in December 1981 a Green Paper entitled *Alternatives to Domestic Rates* which examined the three options possible for reform: a local sales tax, a local income tax, and a poll tax. There were, however, considerable doubts about the desirability and cost of the poll tax, not least from the then Chancellor of the Exchequer Nigel Lawson who "was unequivocal" in his opposition to the Poll Tax, and who noted that the Poll Tax was chosen as the best option for the reform of local government finance. Nigel Lawson in his memoirs stated[24]:

> "The Poll Tax was then given fresh momentum by the removal of Patrick Jenkin as Environment Secretary in the first week of September 1985 and his replacement by Kenneth Baker, who as Minister of State in charge of local government was part-author of the original proposal."

13–066   Dissatisfaction with the rating system resulted in its abolition and replacement with the Community Charge, commonly called the Poll Tax, under the Local Government

[24] Nigel Lawson, *The View from No. 11* (1992), pp.561–585.

Finance Act 1988 and the Local Government and Housing Act 1989. The responsibilities of local authorities included the conduct of a canvass of properties in their areas, allocating between charge-payers the various categories of charge such as the personal or collective community charge, maintaining a register and a public extract, imposing penalties and demanding payments.

The introduction of the Community Charge was intended to remove the need for the complex rate-capping procedures and the acrimonious relations between local and central government. The tax was essentially on each of the electors in each local authority. All adults were expected to pay the tax and it was first implemented in Scotland in 1989 in advance of England and Wales. Originally in 1988 the charge was estimated at £200 per capita but by 1990 when the tax came to be implemented the average tax was around £400. The business rates remained unaffected by the introduction of the Community Charge. **13–067**

Complications in the implementation of the charge added to the general dissatisfaction over the tax. Non-payment of the tax, difficulty of enforcing court orders against defaulters and massive administrative costs of keeping the register up to date made the tax difficult and cumbersome to collect. Anomalies arose in the way the charge was calculated leading to larger than expected charges. Some Conservative local authorities, considered to be well run and managed, found charges over 30 per cent greater than had been expected. In others the cost was up to 36 per cent greater. As a result the Secretary of State was forced to use his charge-capping powers with a formula, which proved controversial, to limit the amount of the charge on certain local authorities. In 1990, 21 local authorities were charge-capped. Extra assistance from the Treasury only served to reinforce the earlier doubts about the efficacy of the Community Charge. Invariably the Government's popularity diminished which may have contributed to the leadership crisis leading to the resignation of Mrs Thatcher. **13–068**

The dissatisfaction with the Community Charge caused the Government to reconsider once more the basis of taxation for local government. A Council Tax took effect from April 1, 1993 under the Local Government Finance Act 1992, involving an element of property valuation in the setting of the charge. Ironically this has required the valuation of the entire housing stock in order to implement the changes introduced by the new tax. The tax is based on the banded capital value of domestic property, with discounts for the number and status of the adults who are resident in the property. There are provisions for people on low incomes. There is a Valuation Office Agency responsible for the valuation of domestic property for the Council Tax. **13–069**

The current law is to be found in the Local Government Finance Act 1992. The Council Tax may best be described as "a hybrid". It is not wholly a property tax but in part bears some resemblance to the Community Charge as it has some elements of "a household tax", because of the use of rebates depending on the income of the occupier. The property element comes from the fact that the Council Tax is based on a valuation of property in which the person lives on April 1, 1991. There are eight property bands with different limits in England, Scotland and Wales to take account of differentials in the property market. In theory the higher band tax payer will pay about three times as much as the lower band payer. The household element comes from a rebate scheme based on income. This element is intended to mitigate the poverty of the household in cases of small or no income. Thus the household will be unaffected by the tax set by the Council if the means of the occupants of the property are such **13–070** that there is a reduction in tax. There are, in addition, certain groups specifically exempted.

THE COURTS AND LOCAL AUTHORITY ACTIVITIES

13–071   Local authorities are subject to the rules of administrative law in the same way as any other administrative decision-maker that has statutory powers. In fact some of the most important principles of administrative law emerged in cases involving local authorities. In *Associated Picture Houses Ltd v Wednesbury Corp*[25] the courts tested the condition of a licence, restricting children under 15 to admission to Sunday perfor-mances in a cinema, according to whether the condition was unreasonable or not. In upholding the condition of the local authority as legal the courts established a test of reasonableness which has been influential in the development of administrative law. The test is known as *Wednesbury* unreasonableness when the authority has come to a conclusion "so unreasonable that no reasonable authority could ever have come to it". Judicial review of discretionary powers exercised by local authorities involves ensuring that the purpose, policy and objectives of a statute should not be frustrated in the exercise of statutory powers. Irrelevant considerations should not be taken when making decisions. Ignoring facts or errors of law or fact, may give rise to a ground for challenge.[26]

13–072   Judicial review may be seen as an important means to check on the legality of local authority activities. It also provides for the resolution of disputes between the parties especially in the resolution of disputes between central and local government.[27] Sunkin[28] has estimated that "approximately 20 per cent were challenges to decisions of other local authorities." A sizeable proportion of the applications for judicial review involve the local authority in areas such as homeless persons, education disputes, matters involving planning and the environment, and the internal affairs of local authorities.

13–073   Local authorities have also a role in representing the public interest and a limited role in seeking to protect rights narrower but analogous with the Attorney-General's role. S.222 of the Local Government Act 1972 contains legal powers for the "promotion and protection of the interests of the inhabitants of their area." A local authority is competent to take proceedings in its own name without the consent of the Attorney-General. Proceedings by local authorities have included action against illegal trading under the Shops Act 1950, the control of noise pollution and trading in breach of controls over sex shops.[29] The constitutional importance of judicial review is underlined by the authors of the study as follows[30]:

> "There are lessons to be drawn here about the constitutional significance of judicial review. Judicial review is often depicted as a weapon in the hands of the

[25] [1948] 1 K.B. 223.
[26] *Secretary of State for Education and Science v Tameside MBC* [1977] A.C. 1014.
[27] *ibid.*
[28] M. Sunkin, "The Judicial Review Case-load 1987–89" [1991] *Public Law* 490 at 498.
[29] See *Solihull MBC v Maxfern Ltd* [1977] 1 W.L.R. 127 also B. Hough "Local Authorities as Guardians of the Public Interest" [1992] *Public Law* 130.
[30] *ibid.*, pp.193–194.

citizen against the over-mighty powers of central government, and it has certainly performed this role in a number of recent high profile cases. Our data suggests, however, that over the past decade it has been used more often as a weapon to further limit the autonomy of local government rather than as a constraint on the power of the central state."

Public lawyers interested in local government will consider that the recent Court of Appeal decision in *Credit Suisse v Allerdale BC*[31] is significant. Allerdale local authority engaged in a joint venture through a number of companies set up by the local authority, technically known as "local government influenced companies", to build and operate a leisure complex. A time-share scheme was envisaged as the best means to operate the complex. Credit Suisse, a leading international banking institution, provided substantial loans repayable over a fixed period. The district auditor queried the legality of the local authority joint venture companies, the local authority involvement and the investment of Credit Suisse. This arose when the ability of the local authority companies to repay the loans came into doubt. The case involved legal consideration of the powers and duties of the local authority and its relationship to Credit Suisse. The Court of Appeal held that the arrangements with the joint-venture companies was *ultra vires* the powers of the local authority. **13–074**

The Court of Appeal has therefore adopted a highly restrictive approach in the interpretation of local government powers. The result of the case left Credit Suisse largely exposed to debts and liabilities that arise from the *ultra vires* transaction. This will seriously inhibit local government joint ventures with the private sector. **13–075**

Local authorities possess wide statutory enforcement powers which may give rise to litigation. In *Kirklees MBC v Wickes Building Supplies Ltd*[32] the local authority sought an interlocutory injunction under s.222 of the Local Government Act 1972 restraining a DIY shop from trading contrary to s.47 of the Shops Act 1950. Criminal prosecutions under the Shops Act 1950 had little deterrent effect with large stores prepared to pay fines as a "tax" on Sunday opening. The use of an injunction by the local authority was an attempt to enforce the law when criminal prosecutions were ineffective. The use of injunctions is a common practice for local authorities in a range of circumstances where the criminal law may be of dubious value in terms of its effectiveness. In such cases the question arises as to the making of a cross-undertaking in damages. In the *Kirklees* case the local authority declined, most likely because such an undertaking might result in large liabilities for the local authority should the case be finally resolved in favour of the shops. Lord Goff in the House of Lords accepted that a local authority could be treated in the same way as the Crown and not be required to give an undertaking in damages. **13–076**

Occasionally major issues of policy are raised involving the precise nature and role of the local authority. In *Bromley LBC v GLC*[33] the House of Lords held unlawful the subsidy of the now defunct GLC to the London Transport Executive. The majority group in the GLC had regarded themselves bound by an election manifesto and had accordingly fettered their discretion unreasonably. The subsidy supported a reduction in fares of 25 per cent and this was regarded by the House of Lords as an improper **13–077**

---

[31] [1997] Q.B. 306.
[32] [1992] 3 All E.R. 717.
[33] [1983] 1 A.C. 768.

exercise of discretion. The majority in the House of Lords also held that local authorities owed a general fiduciary duty to their rate payers.

13–078   Local authorities are statutory corporations. They may enter contracts and freely negotiate commercial arrangements. Local authorities are subject to their own statutory powers and the *ultra vires* rule. This rule means that a local authority should not act outside its statutory powers. Each local authority has its own legal personality[34] and may make use of Private Bill legislation to enhance its powers. Private Bills are a regular means for local authority powers to be extended—though it is doubtful if a local authority can sue for libel in respect of its governing or administrative reputation. However a local authority or[35] "any corporation, whether trading or non-trading, which can show that it has a corporate reputation (as distinct from that of its members) which is capable of being damaged by a defamatory statement, can sue in libel to protect that reputation, in the same way as can a natural person, although there will of course be certain types of statement which cannot defame an artificial person."

13–079   Loughlin[36] has reviewed the increase in the use of legal rules settling disputes over the functions, structures and financial arrangements of local government. One area which illustrates this phenomenon are disputes over local government finance, particularly over the rate support system under the rating system replaced by the Community Charge and later the Council Tax.

13–080   The Secretary of State was obliged to follow complex rules to set the amount of rate support grant available for the year. A report had to be prepared and laid before the House of Commons before the individual local authority grant could be determined. Disputes on the policy which informed the Secretary of State's view of the aggregation rules gave use to court cases challenging the application of the rules. In one such case however, *R. v Secretary of State for the Environment Ex p. Nottinghamshire C*[37] the House of Lords showed reluctance to interfere in the discretion of the Secretary of State who was making a "political judgment". Only in exceptional cases would judicial review be available and only if the Secretary of State had failed to consult or ignored matters expressly listed in the legislation. Local authorities have continued to seek to exploit ambiguities, "loopholes" or uncertainties in the law in order to increase the revenue available to their needs. Often Labour-controlled authorities have spearheaded the manipulation of financial rules to meet expenditure programmes. The court's willingness to declare some of the more speculative local authorities schemes as unlawful may be seen in *Stockdale v Haringey* LBC.[37a] The Court of Appeal struck out as unlawful the use of Haringey LBC's loans fund to maintain its expenditure programmes.

13–081   Local authorities have continually resorted to new techniques to find additional revenue and as these techniques are put in place, so central government rules are introduced to attempt to control prolific spending by local authorities through "innovative financing". Central government's frustrations were not helped by the additional complexity of the rules and the excessive legalism of their application. The

---

[34] *per* Balcombe L.J. in *Derbyshire C v Times Newspapers* [1992] 3 All E.R. 65 at 75.
[35] *ibid*.
[36] M. Loughlin, "Innovative Financing in Local Government: The Limits of Legal Instrumentalism" Pts I and II [1990] *Public Law* 372–407 and [1991] *Public Law* 568–599.
[37] [1986] 2 W.L.R. 1.
[37a] (1989) 88 L.G.R. 7.

growth in litigation and the need for expensive legal opinions before decisions could be reached contributed to the decision to replace local authority rates with first the Community Charge and then the Council Tax.

CONTROLS OVER LOCAL GOVERNMENT EXPENDITURE

A particularly difficult area was the power of central government to "rate cap" local authorities for excessive spending. The "rate cap" was a fiscal device used by central government to prevent an individual local authority from increasing its revenue by increasing the rates charged to inhabitants within its area. This was a bitterly contested power under the Rates Act 1984 which it was hoped the introduction of the Community Charge would end. In theory the Community Charge was a *per capita* tax, allowing a substantial level of autonomy to local authorities. Local authorities with large expenditure totals would charge their inhabitants more than local authorities with lower expenditure requirements. Central government labelled local authorities who were high spenders as wasteful. It was expected that such local authorities would be electorally unpopular as inhabitants would suffer higher Poll Tax Bills. Potentially the Poll Tax had the political significance of giving electoral advantage to the Conservative- rather than the Labour-controlled local authority. Labour-controlled authorities were alleged to need to spend large amounts of public money to provide their services. **13–082**

The introduction of the Community Charge, first in Scotland, then in England, required the Government to introduce "charge capping powers". These were similar to the rate-capping powers abolished with the rates. They were proved necessary because the Government undertook a review of the appropriate level of total standard spending of all local authorities which resulted in an allocation of the appropriate spending needed for each individual local authority. The result of that exercise showed that a number of local authorities' Community Charge Bills exceeded the expectations of the central government based on their predictions and calculation of the requirements for each local authority. **13–083**

In *Hammersmith and Fulham LBC v Secretary of State for the Environment*[38] the House of Lords considered the legality and the operation of the Poll Tax capping rules. Two arguments were made by Hammersmith and Fulham against the Secretary of State's decision to cap the local authority Poll Tax charge. First, that the Secretary of State should satisfy himself that the authority's budget was excessive; and secondly the Secretary of State should consider whether the authority's budget should be designated as requiring the application of the Poll Tax cap. Both arguments were rejected by Lord Bridge. In upholding the legality of the Secretary of State's powers the House of Lords left the subjective judgment of the Secretary of State intact. The judicial viewpoint was that there was no objective criterion which could be used to determine excessive expenditure. No "procedural impropriety" could be found in the Secretary of State's decision. As a result, separate and therefore different levels of expenditure applied in different local authorities. In applying this criterion the Secretary of State admitted that differences based on political considerations might **13–084**

[38] [1990] 3 All E.R. 589.

apply. This gave rise to inconsistencies in the level of the "cap" with the political implication that Labour-controlled local authorities were not fairly treated. However the courts were unwilling to offer any review of the criteria. The House of Lords concluded that the Secretary of State was the best judge of the differences and was free to set his own principles. There was no obligation to set out the reasons behind the principles.

13–085   The *Hammersmith and Fulham* decision raises important questions about the use of judicial review. The local authority perspective is that the role of the courts is to act as a fetter on the potentially unrestrained powers of central government. Statutory interpretation should be sufficiently creative to allow the courts an opportunity to intervene. From the courts' perspective, however, there is difficulty in finding suitable and acceptable standards which may be used to adjudicate between central and local government. Courts have found this area of the law to be complex. Especially so when the doctrine of ministerial responsibilty applies in the case of central government Ministers who are accountable to Parliament.

13–086   The complexity of the legal rules, the vagueness of standards of judicial review and the political nature of local authority decision-making, give the courts wide discretion when reviewing the powers of local authorities. The courts are in a sensitive area of having to adjudicate between central and local government over matters involving the fundamental role of local authorities.

13–087   Local authority speculation in the swaps market highlights another dimension to judicial review. In *Hazell v Hammersmith and Fulham LBC*,[39] Hammersmith had invested substantial sums in the swaps market in order to find investment income to finance expenditure. The basic principle of the swaps market is that a borrower at a fixed interest rate contracts with a third party to pay or receive the difference between his interest liability and what it would have been at a variable interest. Many local authorities became active in this lucrative market. Hammersmith had gained up to £37 million in interest premiums by the end of 1989. But with the rise in interest rates on local authority borrowings and the loss of confidence in the stock market, it was estimated that Hammersmith might lose between £74 million and £186 million. A large number of other local authorities had similarly invested. The precise legality of the investments was open to doubt.

13–088   The local authority relied on s.111(1) of the Local Government Act 1972 which empowered local authorities certain borrowing powers: "calculated to facilitate, or conducive or incidental to, the discharge of any of their functions." The local government auditor challenged the legality of local authority investment in the swaps market as being unlawful. This court case initiated by the auditor was opposed by the banks and financial institutions who wished to show the transactions were lawful.

13–089   If the transactions were held to be unlawful, the banks would have to bear the burden of the debts because local authority liability could not extend to transactions which were potentially void because of their illegality. In a curiosity of the case, the local authorities who at first argued for the lawfulness of the transactions found that their best interests would be served if the transactions were declared void. This would leave the local authority free of the bulk of any debt liability.

13–090   The House of Lords concluded that Hammersmith's swap transactions were *ultra vires*. Their reasoning relied on the statutory interpretation of s.111(1). Particular

---

[39] [1990] 2 W.L.R. 1038; [1991] 2 W.L.R. 372.

emphasis was placed on Pt 1 to Sch. 13 of the 1972 Act[40] which limited the general powers of borrowing given to local authorities under s.111(1). Lord Templeman concluded that the Schedule was "inconsistent with any incidental power to enter into swaps transactions."

The case had far-reaching effects. Local authority debts arising out of the swaps market were generally taken up by banks and financial institutions through protracted litigation in an attempt to unravel the nature of many individual swaps transactions. Currently, uncertainty arises as to the liability of financial advisers and lawyers advising local authorities to enter the swap market.   **13–091**

Loughlin[41] criticises the courts. He argues that in reaching their decisions the Lords adopted a "strict constructionist line" and were affected by their perceptions both of the nature of the swaps market and the reasons for local authority investment in it. This raises the question of how suitable the courts may be in developing "a managerial role" over local authorities. Loughlin questions whether the courts have sufficiently developed techniques to interpret complex regulatory and financial issues. There is also the question of the adjudicative functions performed by courts and their suitablility in enforcing legal rules of such complexity involving financial management.   **13–092**

In this regard the characteristics of legislation affecting local authorities in the 1980s deserve mention. Loughlin describes this as "a new style of legislation" namely, precise directive powers setting out a comprehensive regulatory structure. Such legislation gives the courts little opportunity not to apply the exact wording and letter of the law to local authorities. Courts are, in effect, required to exercise a regulatory role over local authorities.   **13–093**

Against this criticism there is the counterbalancing argument that the courts are effectively the only fair way to determine what the law is. In the decision of the auditor to seek a judicial remedy lies the question of whether the legal rules were correctly applied by the local authority. Ultimately such legal issues require the courts to clarify the law however inconvenient or overridden with policy issues.   **13–094**

The question of the management of local government sets new challenges for the courts. The traditional value of the courts in developing procedural redress on the basis of *Wednesbury* unreasonableness or where local authority councillors may be surcharged as in *Roberts v Hopwood*[42] is only a starting point. Courts are increasingly required to develop their legal techniques of review and are required to make more exacting judgment on the regulation of decision-making in local authorities. This raises questions about how best local authorities may be managed.   **13–095**

---

[40] This section should be read alongside Sched.13 which limits s.111(1): The terms of Sched.13 are such that Lord Templeman (at p.387) stated: "Schedule 13 establishes a comprehensive code which defines and limits the powers of a local authority with regard to its borrowing. The Schedule is in my view inconsistent with any incidental power to enter into swaps transactions." "1. Without prejudice to section III above—(a) a principal council may borrow money for the purpose of lending money to another authority . . . (b) a local authority . . . may borrow money for any other purpose of class of purpose approved for the purposes of this sub-paragraph by the Secretary of State and in accordance with any conditions subject to which the approval is given . . ." "However this general power is negatived by the provision of para. 7 and is subject to regulation 7.-(1). Where expenditure incurred by a local authority for any purpose is defrayed by borrowing, the local authority shall . . . debit the account from which that expenditure would otherwise fall to be defrayed with a sum equivalent to an instalment of principal and interest combined such that if paid annually it would secure the payment of interest at the due rate on the outstanding principal together with the repayment of the principal not later than the end of the fixed period [of the loan]."

[41] Loughlin, [1991] *Public Law* 568–599. Also see N. Deakin, "Local Government; Some recent change and future Prospects" [1991] *Parliamentary Affairs* 493–504.

[42] *Roberts v Hopwood* [1925] A.C. 578; *Pickwell v Camden LBC* [1983] Q.B. 962.

13–096   The role of the courts is often problematic. Increasingly called upon to enforce legal controls over local authority activities, the complexities of financial management, social, economic and political issues expose the inadequacies of many legal techniques of analysis. Invariably courts offer *ex post facto* review, limited to highly technical and procedural problems which may not fit the management requirements which the law adopts when used as a regulating mechanism. Techniques of statutory construction in use by the ordinary courts pose the question raised by Loughlin. Do the courts possess "the cognitive conceptual and material resources" to enable them to perform the functions expected?

13–097   The challenge for the future development of judicial review is reminiscent of the challenge identified in 1947 by William Robson which then formed the development of administrative law. Robson explained that administrative law had to respond[43]:

> "to the creation of new types of offences against the community, the growth of a new conception of social rights, an enhanced solicitude for the common good and a lessening of that belief in the divinity of extreme individualistic rights which was envinced in the early 19th century."

13–098   Today the courts face a growing belief in the market as a regulator, the preference for individual choice, and scepticism about the ability of local government to manage and deliver services as part of their statutory responsibility.

AUDIT COMMISSION AND ACCOUNTABILITY

13–099   Pt III of the Local Government Finance Act 1982 established the Audit Commission for local authorities in England and Wales. The Audit Commission built on the established system of local authority audit with its modern origins in the late nineteenth century. However the earliest origins of auditing may be traced back to the fifteenth century. District Auditors for each local authority are appointed by the Audit Commission. Auditors may be either officers of the Commission or appointed private firms of accountants. The status of the Commission rests on its professionalism and statutory powers. It is not directly responsible to any Minister but makes annual reports to Parliament. The Commisson is itself subject to audit by the National Audit Office. There are provisions in the 1982 Act for co-ordination between the Commission and the National Audit Office. The Commission is not a servant of the Crown and its staff are not Crown servants. Radford has pointed out that the Audit Commission was appointed[44]:

> "with the twin objectives of emphasising the independence of the audit process and greater value for money in local authority spending, the government being of the view that 'improving public sector efficiency is still in large measure a matter of improving scrutiny, monitoring and management within the context of existing institutions'."

[43] W.A. Robson, *Justice and Administrative Law* (London, 1947), p.31.
[44] Mike Radford, "Auditing for Change: Local Government and the Audit Commission" [1991] *M.L.R.* 144.

The Audit Commission is responsible for the drawing-up of a code of practice for local **13–100** authorities subject to parliamentary approval. This code has been extended by the National Health Service and Community Care Act 1990 to the National Health Service in England and Wales. The Code contains "what appears to the Commission to be the best professional practice" with respect to the audit responsibilities of the auditors concerned. The Commission may undertake studies for economy, efficiency and effectiveness in local authorities. This power clarified an area where the District Auditor had been active in the past. Powers to report on any matter which came within the notice of the auditors was also clarified. All auditors were given the same powers that the District Auditor had enjoyed, namely the power to make objections to the accounts on the basis of illegality, failure to account or gross misconduct. It must publish an annual report and the Commission publishes the studies it has undertaken.

Auditors appointed by the Audit Commission must ensure in the word of Lord **13–101** Sumner in *Roberts v Hopwood* that[45]:

> "The purpose of the whole audit is to ensure wise and prudent administration and to recover for the council's funds money that should not have been taken out of them."

The Audit Commission was further strengthened after the review undertaken by the **13–102** Widdicombe Committeee in 1986. Various powers enjoyed by the Auditors under ss.19 and 20 of the Local Government Finance Act 1982 were transferred to the Audit Commission. S.19 concerned unlawful items of account and s.20 related to loss due to misconduct, and both sections envisaged procedures which might lead to surcharge or disqualification.

Additional powers were also granted to the Audit Commission. The Local Govern- **13–103** ment Act 1988 inserted new sections into the 1982 Act which empowered the auditor to issue a prohibition order preventing a body or officer under audit from carrying out any particular decision or action which might lead to an unlawful account or is likely to cause a loss or deficit. An innovation under the 1989 Act was the power granted to the Audit Commission to seek a judicial review of any decision of a body under review by the Commission. Thus the Audit Commission has been granted statutory *locus standi* to take action in the courts.

Audit Commission and Local Authority Audit

In carrying out its tasks as auditors the Commission has followed a similar *modus* **13–104** *operandi* to the National Audit Office. The Commission conducts an inspection audit focused on the regularity of accounts where local authority accounts are examined for any defects in accounting, misconduct, illegal payments or unlawful expenditure.

In addition to the regularity audit, the Commission may carry out value for money **13–105** examinations. Similar considerations apply to the conduct of value for money examinations in central and local government but there are important differences. Local authorities do not operate on the basis of departmental decision-making or

---

[45] [1925] A.C. 578.

under the doctrine of ministerial responsibility to Parliament. Local authorities do, however, have various legal duties and responsibilities.

13–106   The Audit (Miscellaneous Provisions) Act 1996 provides for an extension of the functions of the Audit Commission and the National Health Service in England and Wales. Amendments under the 1996 Act include powers to undertake collaborative studies of social services and to permit publication of information on performance indicators. All these changes are intended to facilitate greater openness in accounting.

13–107   In 1983 the House of Lords in *Bromley LBC v GLC*,[46] established that local authorities had a fiduciary duty to their ratepayers. Lord Diplock noted that such a duty was "not to spend money thriftlessly" but make full use of the financial resources available. In the context of establishing good guidance for local authorities, the Commission has followed this principle and has attempted to apply it to the development of strategies for the future of local authorities.

13–108   The Audit Commission may advise on the legality of local authority investments or financial plans. This is an important task and, as discussed above, illustrates the watchdog function the Commission performed in the example of *Hazell v Hammersmith*[47] which was initiated by the District Auditor. In giving advice the Audit Commission is primarily addressing the Auditors under its control, although this does not preclude the advice becoming widely known to the local authority.

13–109   The most controversial investigation recently carried out by the District Auditor is into the policy of Council house sales undertaken by Westminster City Council. The Auditor's report makes allegations of political bias and illegality in the operation of the right-to-buy scheme for Council housing. The House of Lords have upheld the Auditor's report in *Porter v Magill*.[48] The case concerned allegations made by Mr Magill, the District Auditor for Westminster City Council, against three officers and three councillors that through wilful misconduct they had jointly and severally lost £31 million to the Council. The Council operated a housing policy that was alleged to favour voters more likely to vote Conservative. Council owned residential properties were being sold in such a way as to enhance the political chances of the Conservative party at election time. The House of Lords held that it was unlawful to dispose of property for the purpose of promoting the electoral advantage of any party represented on the Council. The power to levy a surcharge has been abolished by Pt V of the Local Government Act 2000.

13–110   An equally controversial and difficult area in the giving of legal advice is cross-boundary competitive tendering, where the Commission has considered such arrangements as of dubious legality on the basis that local authorities have no legal powers to enter into municipal trading for a profit.[49] The Audit Commission tends to combine two functions, watching and checking accounts and warning of future problems ahead. In this proactive role the Commission seeks to influence local authorities into providing greater efficiency and effectiveness as good value for money.

13–111   In developing value for money examinations the Audit Commission has established its own methodology. First it provides a statistical profile of each local authority;

---

[46] [1983] 1 A.C. 768.
[47] [1991] 1 All E.R. 545.
[48] [2002] 2 W.L.R. 37.
[49] Report of the Audit Commission: "*Cross Boundary Tendering: Local Authorities doing work for One Another*" (Audit Commission Technical Release 23/90, London, 1990).

secondly it undertakes on an annual basis a comparative evaluation on a national level of the activities of local authorities leading to various special studies to raise good practices and set out issues for the future. The Commission has sought to change the culture of local authorities and introduce innovations in management. Pt V of the Local Government Act 2000 provides for a new system of advisory notices that may be issued by the auditor that also allows the courts to give a declaration on the legality of the proposed local authority action. The auditor's power to issue a prohibition order was repealed. There are also powers provided for the local authority to give compensation to the citizen who has suffered as a result of maladministration by the local authority.

The Commission has provided its own definition of value for money[50] in terms of economy, efficiency and effectiveness. Economy sets the terms under which an authority acquires human and material resources; efficiency sets the relationship between goods or services in terms of inputs needed to produce them and outputs found and measured in the product itself; and effectiveness determines the assessment of how well a programme achieves its aims and objectives. Some commentators believe[51] that in setting out to provide value for money examinations, the Commission has neglected effectiveness in favour of economy and efficiency. It may be argued that this is because the Commission is itself attempting to set its own objectives for local authorities rather than accept the objectives determined by the local authorities. In this respect the Audit Commission is creating its own form of public sector management with an emphasis on management consultancy and innovative competition in the development of local authorities.

13–112

SUMMARY AND CONCLUSIONS

The developing role and function of the local authority as a regulator of services and the demand for better management of public money poses new challenges to the use of law and techniques of legal analysis. The courts, Audit Commission and central government are required to work in a harmonious relationship in the complex task of regulating local government. Ultimately the future shape of local government depends on the success of that relationship. Uniquely, the continuity fostered by the British Constitution may be overwhelmed by change.

13–113

The agenda for change in local government is set to continue in the present decade. On the external management of local authorities' decision-taking, the role of the Audit Commission has been set to develop new strategies in improving performance in terms of efficiency, effectiveness and economy. These strategies are consistent with the approach taken in the Citizen's Charter and competition in local authority tendering. In assessing the goods and services undertaken by local authorities, the Audit Commission provides a league table of local authorities and a direction setting

13–114

---

[50] Report of the Audit Commission: *Improving Economy, Efficiency and Effectiveness in Local Government in England and Wales*" (London, 1984); J. Gyford, "Local Authority Audit: An Alternative Tradition" (1989) *Local Government Studies* 9.
[51] A. Neilson, "Value for Money Auditing in Local Government" (1986) 6 *Public Money* 52; Arthur Midwinter, "The Politics of Local Fiscal Reform" (1989) 4 *Public Policy and Administration* 2–9.

performance targets for each financial year. Local authorities are subject to a common mixture of techniques found throughout most parts of the public sector. These include the following: Value for Money audits, a private style of competition and market strategies, the setting of targets and a performance evaluation. The new style of "best value" attempts to provide coherence and strategy with a community focus and a legalistic style of accountability. Local government is expected to deliver public services more efficiently than in the past. At the same time, key elements of local government territory such as health, education and social services are being subjected to privatisation and private sector techniques. The challenge for the future will be to make sense of an overly complex and highly technical element of government considerably weakened by poor electoral turnouts.

FURTHER READING

T. Blair, *Leading the Way: A New Vision for Local Government* (Institute for Public Policy Research, 1998).

G. Boyne, "External regulation and Best Value in Local Government" (2000) *Public Money and Management*, 7.

T. Byrne, *Local Government in Britain* (7th ed., Penguin, London, 2000).

D. Wilson, "Local Government: Balancing Diversity and Uniformity" (2001) *Parliamentary Affairs* 289–307.

Chapter 14

PRIVATISATION AND REGULATION

INTRODUCTION

Privatisation policies have continued to evolve since the 1980s. The major nationalised **14–001** utility industries have been transformed into Company Act Companies. New regulatory agencies and a legal framework to regulate the utilities have been put in place. A wide range of statutory powers, contracts, licences and conditions provide the main legal mechanisms which govern the relationship between regulator, the company and the consumer. Largely discretionary, but also of great importance to the future of each industry is the role of the relevant Secretary of State and the complex legal powers which are devoted to the relationship between the regulator and the Secretary of State. Regulating the privatised utilities has proved to be more complex and detailed than at first predicted. The legislative framework of the original privatisation arrangements has had to be amended to take account of problems as they occurred. The result is a complex hotchpotch of legislation, regulation, rules, guidance, codes and licences, far removed from the consolidation and simplification that it was hoped might result after privatisation.

There have been a number of stages in the strategy to regulate the privatisation of **14–002** public corporations that had been under state ownership after nationalisation in the 1940s and 50s. Regulation has a long history in the United Kingdom and it was required throughout the period of nationalisation. It was often at arm's length with the operational decisions being taken by the industry itself. A series of White Papers in the 1960s and 70s attempted to provide some transparency in the control of the nationalised industries. The first stage of privatisation began in the 1980s and 90s with the adoption of a privatisation strategy intended to remove Government from the business economics of the different industries. This period is concerned with the transfer of the nationalised companies into Company Act Companies with as wide as possible shareholding.

The enabling legislation also had a number of features: the setting-up of individual **14–003** regulators for the main utilities; the creation of licences and pricing arrangements; the development of a regulation strategy including the challenge of replacing the past ethos of "self-regulation" with greater competition; the liaison between individual regulators and the Monopolies and Mergers Commission (MMC), now replaced by the Competition Commission under the Competition Act 1998, over competition policy; and protection of the interests of consumers and the creation of rather weak but vocal consumer groups to represent consumers. The regulatory agencies that emerged from the early legislation include the Office of Telecommunications (OFTEL), the Office of Gas Supply (OFGAS), the Office of Electricity Regulation (OFFER), the Office of Water Services (OFWAT) and the Office of the Rail Regulator (ORR). The second stage in the regulation of the privatised utilities has come about more recently. In order to align United Kingdom competition policy more closely with the EU, the Competition Act 1998 replaces the MMC with the Competition Commission and relevant to co-ordinating the competition policy in the utility sector is the cross-utility panel. Replacing the single regulators for gas and electricity is the merger of OFGAS and OFFER into OFGEM under the Utilities Act 2000. The Office of Communications Act 2002 provides for the establishment of OFCOM to replace five existing regulators: Office of Telecommunications (OFTEL), the Independent Television Commission, the Broadcasting Standards Commission, the Radio Authority and Radio-communications Agency. It is intended that a separate Communications Bill will be law by the Autumn of 2002 providing rules for mergers, takeovers and more details of regulation for TV channels and communication.

14–004   Some privatisations have not followed the model outlined above. For example, air traffic control was created in 1996 into a company, National Air Services. The Transport Act 2000 provided for the sale of up to 51 per cent of the shares (now owned by the major airlines) with the government retaining a golden share.

14–005   This chapter is focused only on the major utilities and how utility regulation has developed since nationalisation. Regulation provides public lawyers with an important dimension to the development of public administration. In contrast to other countries, most notably the United States, regulation is done in the main without recourse to the courts. This reluctance to use courts is intended to provide regulators within the boundaries of their legal powers quite wide discretion over policy and its implementation. There are issues about accountability and how the traditional vehicle for accountability such as ministerial accountability to Parliament may appear ill-suited to the problems that arise from regulating the privatised utilities. The early stages of the development of OFGAS, OFFER and OFTEL were highly personalised; the individual regulator provided the lead and this set the relationship between regulation and the industry. The new structure underpinning OFGEM is that the personality of the regulator is less important and that the procedural rules for regulation become more transparent and are more objective in their application. The focus of regulation has also shifted. In the early stage it was mainly concerned with creating effective Company Act Companies with shareholders well rewarded through high dividends. The fact that many privatised utilities remained as monopolies gave rise to problems over competition policy. One attempt to tackle this problem was the introduction of additional regulatory powers under the Competition and Service (Utilities) Act 1992. However, a more fundamental re-think took place in the Utilities Act 2000 with a new emphasis being given to the protection of consumer interests and the promotion of efficient competition. Making both these objectives compatible with one another is going to prove to be difficult.

NATIONALISATION POLICY AND STRUCTURES

Nationalisation or state ownership requires some explanation and a brief outline of the **14–006** attempts by successive governments to provide effective controls and ensure that the nationalised industries were run efficiently. Thirty years ago, William Robson in the first edition of *Nationalised Industries and Public Ownership*[1] defined the meaning of nationalised industry in Britain as:

> "State intervention of a positive kind in the ownership, operation or regulation of industries and services in a vast movement of world wide dimension."

Robson listed the public undertakings which fell within his definition. These included **14–007** the major utilities such as water, gas, electricity, transport including rail, bus and air. It also covered the British Steel Corporation, the Post Office and the United Kingdom Atomic Energy Authority.

Nationalisation is of unquestionable political, economic and social significance. **14–008** Constitutional lawyers have recognised that nationalisation has posed questions about the role of law and constitutional questions on the effectiveness of ministerial accountability for the industries.

The creation of public corporations created the nationalised industries with a wide **14–009** range of statutory powers granted by Parliament to allow their particular activities to flourish. Statutory powers usually included the grant of a monopoly over the supply of the utilities to the sectors served and a framework which effectively separated the day-to-day working of the corporation from government intervention. A wide range of statutory formulations existed to achieve these characteristics. Sometimes the government took a major shareholding in an existing company, in other examples regulatory mechanisms were placed through the structure of the corporation itself.

As Nigel Lawson[2] summarises in his memoirs, five arguments were advanced in **14–010** favour of nationalisation during the 1940s. These included: the improvement of industrial relations; the promotion of full employment; the gain in productivity from the removal of absentee ownership; the efficient regulation of monopolies; and the replacement of short-term profit-maximisation by wider national and social priorities. Ideological reasons for public ownership were if anything more important than the desire to remedy defects.

Labour Party thinking emphasised the belief that certain activities were essential to **14–011** the well-being of the nation and should be run by the State. Industries with a natural monopoly were an obvious target for nationalisation. Accompanying the desire to run the natural monopolies was the idea that excessive profits should not be accumulated by exploiting a monopoly. Added to this there was a strong belief that industry should be working to the benefit of the nation and provide services rather than relying on the market as a regulator.

[1] W. Robson, *Nationalised Industry and Public Ownership* (1960) (2nd ed., 1962), p.17. Also see L. Gordon, *The Public Corporation in Great Britain* (London, 1938); E. Goodwin, *Forms of Public Control and Ownership* (London, 1951); T. Prosser, *Nationalised Industries and Public Control* (Blackwell, 1986); T. Prosser, M.E. Dimook, *British Public Utilities and National Development* (1983, Chester), p.3; L. Hannah, *Electricity Before Nationalisation* (Electricity Council, 1929); H. Ballin, *The Organisation of Electricity Supply in Great Britain* (1946).
[2] N. Lawson, *The View From No. 11* (1992), pp.201–202.

Government as a Regulator of the Nationalised Industries

14–012   The model adopted for most nationalised industries followed the Morrisonian[3] model named after Herbert Morrison whose ideas were the most influential. Thus the public corporation was the chosen form with statutory powers to provide services for the newly nationalised industries. Such arrangements were heavily influenced by ideology[4]:

> "The public corporation must not be a capitalist business . . . It must have a different atmosphere at its board table from that of a shareholders meeting; the board and its officers must regard themselves as high custodians of the public interest."

14–013   A number of influences could be directed by Ministers upon the nationalised industry. Such influences included the power of appointment to the boards of nationalised industries, the issuing of general directions as to policy, and specific ministerial approval over financial planning. Also included were ideas about encouraging the buying of British goods, an emphasis on the direction of returns on profits which could be ploughed back into the industry and overall policy objectives on employment conditions such as wage bargaining. The theory of ministerial supervision could in practice allow Ministers to "run the industry". Critics of the nationalised industries feared that such intervention might interfere with the efficiency of the industry itself.

14–014   Nationalisation however did not come about as a coherent and well considered plan. Initially corporations were given little guidance on the policies they were to follow. There was general uncertainty as to the precise role such industries should play in the economy, and confusion over the extent to which government influence should dictate managerial decisions. In general it was considered sufficient to appoint prudent managers to allow the industries to run themselves. The major issue was whether the nationalised industries required more direct intervention. The answer to this question was slow in coming.

14–015   The government of the day located the running of the nationalised industries as an important part of the general economy. Three government White Papers,[5] in 1961, 1967 and 1978 set out policy considerations which were influential. The 1961 White Paper set out financial targets to be achieved, specified as a rate of return on assets set by Ministers. The formula used was crudely expressed; each nationalised industry was required to manage their affairs with the requirement of taking one year with notice to be sufficient to meet all items chargeable to revenue account. Thus "targets" were set for the industry to pay its way. Within this framework the industries were remarkably free to develop their own management strategies.

14–016   The 1967 White Paper marked a more significant development in providing detailed guidelines as to how the nationalised industries were to perform. Specific financial targets were set with a requirement on capital investment projects of a certain

---

[3] H. Morrison, *Socialisation of Transport* (1933).
[4] R. Molyneux and D. Thompson, "Nationalised Industry Performance: Still Third Rate?" (1987) 18 *Fiscal Studies* (1987), p.48.
[5] *Financial and Economic Obligations of the Nationalised Industries*, Cmnd.1337 (1961); *Nationalised Industries: A Review of Economic and Financial Objectives*, Cmnd.3437 (1967); and *The Nationalised Industries*, Cmnd.7131 (1978).

minimum rate of return fixed for all the industries by the Government. The means to monitor the operation of the 1967 White Paper was the Prices and Incomes Board. A weakness in the arrangements was the emphasis on financial instruments and little attention devoted to productive efficiency. A major concern was the potential power of Ministers to intervene, thus causing confusion over the exact boundaries of decision-taking between Ministers and the nationalised industries.

A further deficiency was that in the early 1970s Government policy to counter inflation required public corporations to hold down prices at a level which made productivity uneconomic. Compensation for this policy appeared in the form of subsidies, paid to the industry in order to mitigate the economic consequences of loss-making activities. Critics regarded the Government's short-term limited objectives based on political choices as inconsistent with the need to develop efficient industries.   **14–017**

The 1978 White Paper went further than the two previous White Papers and set various targets for the nationalised industries in an attempt to provide for the weaknesses in government policy. In effect the targets set were intended to make the nationalised industries more efficient and avoid the problem of recurring losses. Although the 1978 White Paper was broadly unclear as to how the level of financial targets was to be estimated, there was ample opportunity for Ministers to intervene on the basis of determining "each industry's target in the light of general policy objectives, including consideration of social, sectoral and counter-inflation policy."   **14–018**

The 1978 White Paper had resulted in a major shift towards auditing the efficiency of the nationalised industries. The 1980 Competition Act allowed the Monopolies and Mergers Commission (MMC) to undertake efficiency audits at the request of Ministers. Productive efficiency became the basis of the overall financial controls set on each industry. The "non-commercial objective" of the nationalised industries characterised by the Labour Party[6] in its early nationalisation policies were set to one side in favour of greater financial scrutiny through efficiency audit. Craig has observed[7]: "The tension between the exercise of commercial freedom and the utilisation of public corporations as part of a broader governmental strategy is apparent once again."   **14–019**

Although individual statutory arrangements differed, depending on the particular industry involved, nevertheless some common features may be noted. A degree of day-to-day autonomy was granted to each industry leaving Ministers overall policy and direction. Ministers could influence the membership of the boards of the industry through individual appointment and the giving of general directions. Financial control, especially over borrowing and in major development programmes, was largely dependent on ministerial discretion and sanction. Generally, the role of the nationalised industries was vague and uncertain and left to the policies of successive governments. Rarely were legal powers invoked or actually used in the relationship between Ministers acting as an "arm's length" regulator and responsible to Parliament through ministerial responsibility. Financial target-setting after the 1978 White Paper heralded a new breakthrough whereby sponsoring government departments assessed individual efficiency of each government industry through scrutiny of the financial targets of the   **14–020**

---

[6] Graham and Prosser, "Privatising Nationalised Industries: Constitutional Issues and New Legal Techniques" (1987) 50 *Modern Law Review* 16; T. Prosser, *The Privatisation of Public Enterprises in France and Great Britain; The State, Constitution and Public Policy*, EUR Working Paper No.88/364 (1988), p.37.
[7] P. Craig, *Administrative Law* (2nd ed., 1989), pp.84–87.

relevant industry. The question of the annual debt of each nationalised industry and the amount of public expenditure became a key aspect of ministerial policy. Such issues gave rise to relatively few legal disputes and were subordinated to the day-to-day management of the industry and the government's overall economic policies. A common complaint of nationalisation was the lack of information and knowledge of the working of the industry concerned. Studies[8] of the nationalised industries prior to privatisation have indicated that after a long struggle by successive governments the nationalised industries had become more efficient and well run. It is open to controversy whether this was because of the preparation for privatisation or simply a process of providing better management and targets through the White Papers mentioned above.

PRIVATISATION, POLICY AND OBJECTIVES

14–021   Privatisation shared with nationalisation strong ideological reasons for its introduction. As Craig noted[9]:

> "The reasons for privatisation are, like those for nationalisation, eclectic. They include the following; improving efficiency, reducing government involvement in decision-making of industry, ordinary share ownership, encouraging share ownership by employees, alleviating problems of public sector pay determinate, reducing the public sector borrowing requirement and the enhancement of economic freedom."

14–022   Driven by strong ideological beliefs that the nationalised industries required dramatic reconstruction, the Government also desired to widen share ownership. Privatisation began with a crucial distinction between smaller privatised companies and larger activities. For example smaller companies such as Amersham International, Jaguar, Sealink and British Aerospace operate within a competitive framework and pose little concern to the constitutional lawyer as to how their activities may be regulated. The Government's initial forays into implementing its privatisation policy were based on identifying these smaller activities which were privatised as the first phase of the Government's policy. In contrast the larger privatisations such as British Telecom in 1984, British Gas in 1985, and electricity in 1989 required a regulatory framework which attempts to deal with the larger market to which the newly privatised industry belongs. The popularity of wider share ownership, the removal of large companies dependent in the past on government support into the private sector has resulted in privatisation strategies being continued under the new Labour Government elected in 1997. Mention has been made of the Private Finance Initiative in previous chapters and this has involved private public partnerships. Contracting-out strategies have been in operation in local and central government and within the National Health Service. There is also the popularity of management buy-outs such as may be found in the

---

[8] M. Bishop and J. Kay, *Does Privatisation Work?* (London Business School, 1988); J. Kay *et al.*, *Privatisation and Regulation—the UK Experience* (Oxford, 1986).
[9] Craig, *op.cit.*

examples of parts of British Coal and in the National Freight Corporation. The Government has sold some of its remaining shareholdings and added new privatisations to its list. Since the first privatisation, remaining shares have been sold in British Telecom and in the electricity industry there has been the sell-off of British Nuclear Fuels. New privatisations include British Coal under the British Coal Act 1993 and the Coal Industry Act 1994; British Rail under the Railways Act 1993 and amended by the Transport Act 2000 and H.M. Stationery Office.

The relative success of many privatisations has drawn worldwide attention to the   **14–023** United Kingdom's experience of privatisation. However, rail privatisation has proved disappointing. Mounting criticism of the investments required in the industry, a series of major accidents and reports dealing with poor infrastructure and maintenance left the Government with a major crisis leading to Railtrack, the owner of the infrastructure, being taken into receivership in the autumn of 2001. The Transport Act 2000 provides for the creation of a new Strategic Rail Authority (SRA). The aims of the SRA are to secure development of the rail network and contribute to an integrated transport system. SRA has a number of objectives:

- to protect the interests of consumers;

- to contribute to sustainable development;

- to promote efficiency and economy in the rail network;

- to provide the minimum necessary restrictions on rail operators;

- to enable providers of rail services to make future plans and business decisions with some degree of certainty;

- to promote the use of the railway through ticketing.

In the unlikely event of any wide-scale re-nationalisation, the Transport Act 2000   **14–024** reflects a bargain between business use for profit and public service use for customers. In recent years there has been a shift in regulation with an emphasis in protecting the consumer and environmental concerns.

Privatisation policy has not always been successfully implemented by the Govern-   **14–025** ment even when it is desired. Since 1992 there have been plans to privatise the Post Office. The proposed sale of Parcel Force, a major part of the mail service, and the Royal Mail has been considered, proposed and rejected. Post Office Counters Ltd was created, a type of private–public partnership covering an agency function for many government departments such as Transport, Social Security and the Passport Agency; it was intended to be sold but this proved impossible. Privatisation has been put on hold as public opinion and support is doubtful. The Postal Service Act 2000 is an attempt to modernise the Post Office. It falls short of privatisation but it permits market competition and unlike previous proposals maintains the Post Office as a single entity. The Post Office is formed into a limited liability company under Crown ownership. The Act also takes account of the EU Directive on Common Rules for the Development of the Internal Market of Community Postal Services and the Improvement of Quality of Service.[10] Consumers are provided with a statutory framework for

[10] Directive 97/67.

the Consumer Council for Postal Services replacing the old Post Office Users' Councils. There is to be a new regulator, the Postal Services Commission, and a five-year strategic business plan. The new regulator is expected to encourage competition and regulate the market in postal services. In the short term the Post Office is unlikely to face full-scale privatisation, but through a number of economic devices it is expected to become more competitive.[11]

REGULATION, STRUCTURES AND TECHNIQUES

14–026 The characteristics[12] of the British approach to legal regulation have a long history and have evolved gradually on a case by case basis. It is useful to place the newly created regulatory bodies in the context of the approach to regulation adopted in the United Kingdom. Historically the regulation and scrutiny of industry in Britain developed from the nineteenth century. Legal powers were first granted through Private Acts of Parliament in return for statutory responsibilities assumed by the industries—the railways and the electricity companies are two good examples. Also relevant is the experience of the early Poor Law Commission in 1834 which struck a balance between central and local government. This early form of government regulation permitted commissioners to determine the qualification and duties of local poor law guardians and they, in turn, appointed paid officers to administer relief, subject to the Poor Law Commission. The establishment of Boards, which acted in a quasi-ministerial manner combined administrative decision-taking and both non-political or semi-independent status. A number of examples such as railways and the factories inspectorate, illustrate the experiment of placing certain activities beyond the direct reach of political intervention. Eventually these activities succumbed to ministerial control but attempts at combining or isolating ministerial intervention with regulation were made. In the example of the railways, the Railway Department in the Board of Trade in 1840 was a department board in 1844, a Commission in 1846 before absorption into the Board of Trade in 1851.

14–027 A wide variety of powers were enjoyed by such regulators; invariably, a statutory framework would set the general shape and scope of the individual Board or inspectorate. Additionally codes of practice, circulars, directions, rules, regulations were all included as part of that legal framework. Occasionally a feature of regulation involved enforcement procedures through adjudication processes which invariably might involve a fine or criminal sanction. For example the early factory inspectorate under the Factories Act 1934 had the status of a magistrate with corresponding legal powers. Inevitably claims of partisanship and bias were made against individuals in carrying out their duties and activities. One of the characteristics of the nineteenth century was a remarkable degree of detail and openness in the reports published by the various Boards, departments and agencies. This characteristic gradually diminished as the nationalisation process took place in the post-Second World War period which was

---

[11] John Cooper, "Delivering Change—The Beginnings of Postal Services Reform in the United Kingdom" 12 [2001/2] *Utilities Law Review* 46.
[12] See R. Baldwin and C. McCrudden, *Regulation and Public Law* (1987). W. Cornish, G. de N. Clark, *Law and Society in England 1850–1950* (1989).

characterised by secrecy and lack of information on the actual performance of each industry.

The Role of the Courts

Overviewing the activities of Boards, inspectors and Ministries, the courts had a limited but important role. Various devices such as Crown immunity up until 1947 were used to prevent law suits in the case of torts and the amenability to judicial review depended to some extent on the remedy sought. In the case of *mandamus*, for example a Crown servant could not be compelled to perform a duty solely owed to the Crown. A wide array of legal powers were available. For example, the Poor Law Commission were advised to keep within the rules of natural justice and when they acted all their members had to be present. The courts were unpredictable in their application of the rules of natural justice. Technical distinctions were the hallmark of this area of the law. At one time the courts appeared to apply distinctions based on the classification of the bureaucratic function as "judicial", "quasi-judicial", "legislative" or "administrative". In 1964 the House of Lords adopted a more permissive approach in the landmark case of *Ridge v Baldwin*[13] and thereby abolished the technical distinctions which inhibited the development of judicial review.

14–028

In summary, the characteristics of regulation such as judicial scrutiny, adjudication of disputes and ministerial accountability were all in place during the lifetime of nationalisation. No coherent system existed to oversee and monitor the system of regulation, as development was ad hoc and pragmatic. The legal controls that there were, seldom became the subject of litigation. Few lawyers were involved apart from internal law advisers over the Company Act provisions and the requirements of the specific statutory authority of each of the nationalised industries. The paucity of legal cases is an example of where the role of the court is limited by the nature of the regulatory structure. Challenges to the regulator's role are reluctantly taken by the courts.[14] There is a tacit assumption that within the boundaries of legality the regulator has a broad discretion.[15] Although judicial review is available even when a matter of private law is involved the courts may intervene.

14–029

In the unreported decision of the divisional court *R. v Director-General of Gas Supply Ex p. Smith*,[16] Mr Justice Pill applied the rules of national justice to the investigative powers of the Director-General of Gas Supply in his role in determining whether British Gas was justified in using its disconnection powers where it suspected an offence was committed. Relying on the main legal authorities such as *O'Reilly v Mackman*[17] the courts have developed the potential for intervention to review the decision of regulators or Ministers where it is thought unreasonable, procedurally inconvenient or on some grounds of unfairness. The danger of the courts substituting its view for that of the designated authority who have been given that authority by

14–030

[13] [1964] A.C. 40.
[14] *R. v Independent Television Commission Ex p. TSW Broadcasting Ltd* [1996] E.M.L.R. 318.
[15] See *Mercury Communications v DG of Telecommunications* [1996] 1 All E.R. 575.
[16] CO/1398/88. See J. McEldowney "Theft and meter tampering and the gas and electricity utilities" (Autumn 1991) *Utilities Law Review* 122–126. Also see *R. v British Coal Corporation and the Secretary of State for Trade Ex p. Vardy* [1993] I.R.L.R. 104.
[17] [1983] 2 A.C. 237.

Parliament was recognised by Lord Justice Watkins in *R. v Secretary of State for Trade and Industry Ex p. Lonrho*.[18] The boundary of the courts' jurisdiction would seem to be that the courts should not "arrogate to themselves executive or administrative decisions". Interpretation of this phrase is difficult to predict and open to narrow or broad interpretations.[19]

14–031   The remaining question to be addressed is the likely future direction of legal techniques of regulation in Britain. An obvious influence is likely to be the application of EC law in the fast developing area of environment (environmental impact assessment), energy policy and regulation of competition practices. An example is *Foster v British Gas plc European Court*.[20] Here the European Court interpreted a dispute concerning the implementation of an EC Directive 76/207 (February 9, 1976) on equal treatment for men and women as regards access to employment working conditions and promotion. The case has implications for anybody that engages in supply services such as privatised industries, quangos and civil servants. Under the principle of the *Marshall case*,[21] if the British Gas Corporation were a public body then the corporation were in breach of the Directive. British Gas plc as successors would have to accept liability for the unfair dismissal. More important was the question of how Community law is applied by the national courts as EC Directives cannot be directly applied by national courts and tribunals, but where a private individual has a complaint against a state body a Directive will be directly enforceable. The judgment of the European Court has left to the national courts their ideas of public service and the application of criteria laid down by the courts. This leaves a degree of uncertainty for the future as to the precise nature of the criteria and the likely result. There is confusion in the courts as to how directly and indirectly effective Directives may be applied.

Regulating and Privatising the Utilities

British Telecom

14–032   The privatisation of British Telecom in 1984 and the Telecommunications Act 1984 were the first major reforms of a public utility industry which had been from 1912 until 1981 a State-owned monopoly. In 1981 the first stage, prior to privatisation, took place when legislation, the British Telecommunications Act 1981, separated telecommunications from postal services thereby establishing British Telecom as a public corporation. The 1981 stage relaxed the restrictions of supply of customers' equipment and allowed licensing of other telecommunications systems. The 1984 Telecommunications Act created a Director-General of Telecommunications (DGT) with regulatory powers based on guidelines as to how the DGT is expected to perform his duties. The

---

[18] [1989] 1 W.L.R. 525.
[19] *R. v Panel on Takeovers and Mergers Ex p. Datafin plc* [1987] 1 Q.B. 815.
[20] Case C-188/89, *Foster v British Gas* [1990] 1 E.C.R. 3313; [1990] 2 C.M.L.R. 833.
[21] Case 152/84, *Marshall v Southampton and South West Hampshire AHA* (No.1) C152/84 [1986] E.C.R. 723; [1986] 1 C.M.L.R. 688. R. Nobles, "Application of E.C. Law to Supply Services" (1990) *Utilities Law Review* 127–129; B. Fitzpatrick, "Direct Effect of Directives" (1991) *Utilities Law Review* 34–38.

hallmark of this particular privatisation was the need to find a suitable competitor for British Telecom. The Government effectively promoted the creation of a competitive rival, Mercury, which is the only competitor licensed to date to compete with British Telecom. The experience of nationalisation may be seen in the power under the 1984 Act to refer, for example, British Telecom to the Monopolies and Mergers Commission and the matter is one which operates against the public interest.

The legal structure of the 1984 Act is significant because it provided a model for   **14–033** future privatisation. The characteristics of the 1984 Act are the use of an independent regulator (OFTEL) appointed by the Secretary of State (s.1 of the 1984 Act), and that the operators of telecommunications systems must possess a licence granted by the Director-General of OFTEL and the Secretary of State. There is a power to refer matters to the Monopolies and Mergers Commission (MMC) to decide if the matter referred is in the public interest. The Director-General of Fair Trading has powers to supervise and investigate any possible anti-competitive practices or abuses of market power. Included in the regulation is a price formula designed "to cap" the prices charged to consumers for services. Privatisation of water (OFWAT) and electricity (OFFER) followed similar principles.

Another characteristic is the requirement to build a pricing structure into the   **14–034** regulatory arrangements. Currently BT cannot increase prices by more than the Retail Price Index minus 3 per cent. The success of the pricing mechanism is to be gauged on how efficient and cost-effective the industry may be, and this remains to be seen. The creation of the Director-General of Telecommunications as a means to secure effective competition, economy, efficiency and growth and development of the telecommunications business in the United Kingdom both national and international depends on how effective the regulatory system might be. Criticism of the 1984 Act focuses on three matters. First, the legislation fails to provide any requirement that adequate information is available to the DGT. Secondly, there is concern that the resources of the DGT may not be adequate to maintain supervision of the organisation and, thirdly, that the DGT and Office of Telecommunications (OFTEL) may be perceived as too closely linked with the industry. Thus their independence and impartiality might be questioned if their perceived role became too protective of the industry.

The Government's strategy for privatisation also addressed the question of the value   **14–035** of the market as a regulator of the newly privatised activity. Rather than simply privatise a monopoly, some liberalisation was attempted both before and after privatisation. This policy required legal powers to regulate the market. In the case of telecommunications, competition between Mercury and BT was created when Mercury was set up to provide an element of competition. The duopoly that resulted has itself been subject to criticism and review. OFTEL has been concerned with the terms of Mercury's network connection with BT. After delays and intervention by the courts, OFTEL ruled that the two networks should have full interconnection charges based on BT's costs and a time-scale was set for the implementation of connection arrangements. This applied to both national and international calls. In March 1991 the long-awaited White Paper[22] on the duopoly review was published. Its main conclusion, that all applications for new licences to provide new telecommunications systems would be considered, and this would include both national and international services. This may

---

[22] *Competition and Choice: Telecommunications Policy for the 1990s*, Cm.1461 (1991).

be seen as broadening the possibilities for competition beyond the original framework of the 1984 Act.

14–036   The 1984 telecommunications regulatory structure was perceived to be weak. Additional powers have been introduced under the Competition and Services (Utilities) Act 1992 intended to set a uniform standard of regulation for the utilities, and in the case of telecommunications, gas and water, greater competition. Thus the 1992 Act introduces additional powers for the Director of Telecommunications to set standards for levels of performance, provide greater information to the Director on the working of the industry, to determine disputes between the customer and the industry, and to make provisions relating to consumer protection such as disconnection charges. Many of these proposals arise out of the Citizen's Charter.[23]

The Office of Communications Act 2002

14–036a   The various regulatory bodies covering telecommunications, television and radio are to be merged into a single regulator OFCOM under the Office of Communications Act 2002. The five bodies covered by OFCOM are the Office of Telecommunications (OFTEL), the Independent Television Commission, the Broadcasting Standards Commission, the Radio Authority and Radio-communications Agency. This followed the removal of telecommunications from the original Utilities Bill in 2000. The winding-up of the existing regulators will take place in a new Communications Bill currently being debated. OFTEL was a pioneering regulator, as it was the first established under the privatisation legislation. As such it was expected to create the necessary competition in the communications market and ultimately it was hoped that this would be the best form of regulation of the industry. The Office of Telecommunications Act 2002 contains seven sections and establishes OFCOM and provides general duties to be set out in detail in the forthcoming Communications Bill. The Act also provides for the management of OFCOM and its organisation and finance.

Energy and Natural Resources Utilities

Gas

14–037   The privatisation of the gas industry faced similar regulatory problems as identified in the case of telecommunications. In 1985 the Government decided to privatise British Gas and the question of how competition and efficiency might be achieved was given serious consideration but with limited and disappointing results.

14–038   The nationalisation of the British gas industry in 1948 and its centralisation in 1962 had created a single industry centralised under a public corporation responsible for the activities of 12 area boards who were autonomous over the manufacture and supply of gas. Sole rights to purchase gas from producers had been granted to the corporation in 1982 and pricing had been characteristically low with a resultant lack of investment.

[23] Citizen's Charter, Cm.1599 (1991). On telecommunications see NAO, *The Office of Telecommunications: Licence Compliance and Consumer Protection* (1993; HC 529), HMSO; NAO, *The Sale of the Second Tranche of Shares in British Telecommunications plc*, (1993 HC 568), HMSO. See Scott, [1993] *Utilities Law Review* 183.

This lack of investment has been attributed to poor policy direction by the government of the day.

Privatisation was undertaken by the Gas Act 1986 which followed the model set by telecommunications in 1984. A regulatory structure was set up under a Director-General of supply (OFGAS) and an OFGAS office. The newly created Company, British Gas, did not have any competition and unlike BT and Mercury none was created by the 1986 Act for the Gas Industry. No attempt was made to restructure the industry in the 1986 Act. The 12 regional boards could have become gas companies with a company to control the distribution system. The strong ideological belief that the timetable of the Government's privatisation strategy should not be altered or slowed down meant that restructuring of the gas industry was avoided.   **14–039**

It is clear that the Gas Act 1986 in practical effect insulated British Gas from competition. As no new competitor was created it was difficult not to see the monopoly of British Gas as virtually impregnable by any new entrant to the market.   **14–040**

Finally the 1986 Act provided a complex formula for pricing supervised by the Director-General of Gas Supply (DGGS) and OFGAS. Legal powers similar to OFTEL were provided to OFGAS to promote efficiency to gas suppliers and users. The DGGS might impose conditions upon the grant of authorisation to a public gas supplier and there is a possibility of a referral to the Monopolies and Mergers Commission to specify any modification to the authorisation. Compliance powers granted to the DGGS and investigative powers over conditions granted in the authorisation were all part of the regulatory framework.   **14–041**

The powers of the regulator were considerably less than the powers possessed by British Gas. For example under the 1986 Act it was impossible for the DGGS to alter the legal structure of the gas industry. Some doubts existed, at the time, as to the powers of the DGGS to provide transparency of pricing and in opening up the transmission system through supplies to third parties.   **14–042**

In the case of gas the Director-General had powers to promote competition within the contract market, *i.e.* over 25,000 therms *per annum*, but lacked a general duty to promote competition overall. In contrast the Director-General of Electricity has such powers which are widely drawn but not easily interpreted with a precise and clear meaning. Gas privatisation had resulted in a virtual monopoly for British Gas; unlike the telecommunications industry with Mercury, no competitors were established at the time of privatisation. British Gas was in a strong market position post privatisation with the resultant effect that the regulator (OFGAS) became a surrogate competitor in its attempts to regulate the gas industry effectively. A major threat to any monopolistic conduct is the use of the Fair Trading Act 1973 (Sch.8) in requiring the MMC to consider whether such conduct militates against the public interest. A wide range of remedial action is available including adjusting contracts, the formation or winding-up of a company and consideration of the division of the business "by the sale of any part of the undertaking or assets or otherwise". . . .".   **14–043**

In the early stages of the newly privatised life of British Gas, it was apparent that a number of grounds for dissatisfaction existed. These included: individual prices were unclear and companies had difficulty estimating future gas costs; a wide variation in prices was experienced between customers with the same or similar levels of requirement; tendering for contracts lasted for only three-month periods at a time, and future gas costs were difficult to estimate, given the lack of transparency in pricing;   **14–044**

British Gas was reluctant to quote prices for interruptible supplies and required in many cases the installation of dual-fired equipment which was costly; British Gas were also unwilling to offer supply to certain types of companies which would close down when supplies were interrupted.

14–045   Such complaints were reviewed by the MMC after OFGAS made a reference on the basis of there being a monopoly enjoyed by British Gas. The MMC upheld this view of a monopoly and concluded that greater competition was required. An additional finding was that the only effective means of remedying adverse consequences flowing from the monopoly status of British Gas was direct gas to gas competition. A long list of recommendations relating to the pricing and tendering of gas, third party access to the gas transmission system operated by British Gas, and transparency in the system of gas schedules were also made by the MMC.

14–046   Inevitably the MMC findings in 1988 required a reorganisation of the gas market and provided the regulator with increased powers in terms of enhancing his status and in securing compliance with his objectives. Ultimately the Secretary of State's wide powers under Sch.9 of the Fair Trading Act provide a threat hanging over the industry should the monopolistic practices be continued. As a result British Gas in February 1990 entered into a number of undertakings which included: not to purchase more than 90 per cent of gas on offer; not to require the inclusion of contract terms which could frustrate that objective; to provide common carriage quotations within a four-week period. In addition price schedules were introduced for firm and interruptible contract customers to prevent British Gas from blocking market entry by a strategy of discriminatory pricing.

14–047   In July 1991 the effectiveness of the remedies applied by British Gas after the MMC Report (1985) was referred to the Office of Fair Trading (OFT) for consideration. The result of that review was published in October 1991 and concluded that although British Gas had complied with its undertakings, nevertheless the dominance of British Gas in the market had remained. British Gas, because of its size and market dominance was able to assert its influence. Thus it could cross-subsidise, act in a predatory manner on pipeline competition and set price levels in the indemnities market that a competitor could not match. All these factors led the OFT to conclude that the behaviour of British Gas should lead to a fundamental reconsideration of the market position of British Gas. In 1993 the MMC published two reports on Gas. Some conclusions may be reached from a reading of the reports. First that competition had been attempted in the gas industry before privatisation but with very limited success. The Oil and Gas (Enterprise) Act 1982 initiated competition in gas supply by allowing competing gas suppliers access to British Gas's pipelines. In fact no agreement was ever reached. The 1986 Gas Act as outlined above, preserved the *de facto* monopoly of British Gas. Even though the 1986 Act gave freedom of competition to suppliers of large industrial and commercial customers above 25,000 therms, this did not remove the monopoly position of British Gas. In 1995 a new Gas Act was passed that gave additional powers to the regulator to allow for a more radical re-structuring of British Gas to provide additional competition for suppliers to domestic customers and for access to the gas pipeline. This new structure had the following features:

(a)   the setting up of Trans Co, British Gas's transportation and storage business with assets inclusive of about £17.4 billion;

(b)   from March 1995 separation of Trans Co from British Gas;

(c)   the Gas Act 1995 came into force on March 1, 1995.

The 1995 Act sets up a new structure for the licensing of gas supply. The main features   **14–048**
of the 1995 Act are that access is now available to the pipeline owned by British Gas
for any licensed supplier. There are licences for the following:

(a)   Public Gas Transporter (PGT) for firms that operate a pipeline system and
       contract with gas shippers;

(b)   gas shipper licences for licence holders who contract to provide a public gas
       transporter to be conveyed through the pipeline of the PGT;

(c)   gas supplier licences for companies that sell at the meter gas which has been
       delivered through pipelines by a shipper. This includes supply to domestic
       customers.

The introduction of licensed suppliers into the domestic market is a gradual one. The   **14–049**
above analysis of the British Gas example points to inherent structural problems in the
way British Gas was privatised. Splitting up the distribution side from the production
of gas supply might have avoided the problems of monopoly mentioned above. The
model for such a restructuring may be seen in the Electricity Act 1989 (discussed
below) where the transmission grid was separated from the production and distribution
system.

Additional powers have been granted to the Director of Gas Supply under the   **14–050**
Competition and Service (Utilities) Act 1992. These include the powers to set
standards, improve the procedures for complaints by customers and set regulations to
determine disputes over the accuracy of bills. An increase in competition in the gas
market is intended by reducing the gas monopoly threshold of 15,000 therms to a
lower amount or to abolition of the threshold altogether. These changes are the result
of the introduction of proposals contained in the Citizen's Charter.

The Citizen's Charter Report on an annual basis sets out the achievements of the   **14–051**
Charter.[24] In the Report there is a list of a wide range of achievements including
setting up Codes of Practice, setting standards for dealing with complaints and
arranging for payments for failure to meet standards. For example in 1994 British Gas
paid a total of £2,439,272 in compensation. The bulk of this went to a single domestic
user. The Public Electricity Suppliers in 1994 paid £115,000 and the water companies
paid £267,900.

In addition to the Citizen's Charter the government has embarked on new   **14–052**
procedures to simplify existing regulations and unnecessary rules. The Deregulation
and Contracting Out Act 1994 provides that amending orders, called deregulation
orders, may be introduced to amend delegated legislation or where necessary primary
legislation. This procedure is a novel way to lift the burden of unnecessary regulation
from industry.

The British Gas example also shows the flexibility inherent in the legal mechanisms   **14–053**
used to regulate the industry. The legal basis for referral to the MMC and the resultant

---

[24] *Citizen's Charter Improving Service*, Cm.2970 (September 1995).

modification of the authorisation allowed gradual changes to be introduced. The existing legal framework is also sufficiently flexible to realise the creation of a separate gas transmission subsidiary company. This could be achieved by British Gas voluntarily adopting the recommendations of the OFT. In the event of non-compliance the regulatory structure is sufficiently flexible to hold the threat of referral to the MMC. The combination of regulatory supervision by OFGAS, overview by the OFT and MMC combines wide legal powers with oversight by the relevant Secretary of State.

Electricity

14–054   The experience gained from gas and telecommunications privatisations proved to be insufficient to meet the challenge posed by electricity privatisation. The Government's proposals to privatise the electricity supply industry faced a sterner test because the electricity industry was the largest of the United Kingdom's nationalised industries in terms of turnover and capital employed.

14–055   Electricity privatisation also posed some of the most complex legal problems. Electricity is a natural monopoly, involves the use of fuels as diverse as solar power and nuclear energy, and is a heavy polluter of the environment. Under nationalisation the generation, supply and transmission of electricity were integrated by the 1957 Electricity Act. The Central Electricity Generating Board (CEGB) was put in charge of both generation and transmission. A national grid was created with 12 Area Boards for distribution purposes. These purposes were left to the autonomy of the boards particularly in respect of financial matters. Consumers' interests in England and Wales were represented by 13 district organisations. There were 12 Area Electricity Consultative Councils, one for each Area Board and an Electricity Consumers' Council.

14–056   The privatisation strategy adopted by the Government was contained in the White Paper *Privatising Electricity*[25] which set out six objectives to be followed, namely: the needs of customers should be considered an important part of the industry; competition is an essential guarantee of customers' interests; regulation was required to promote competition, oversee prices and protect customers' interests; security and safety should be maintained; customers should be given new rights; and share ownership should include those who work for the company.

14–057   In the case of electricity privatisation the experience of both British Gas and Telecommunications suggested that a different model should be adopted to provide increased competition as part of the legal structure for the newly privatised industry. The electricity supply industry (ESI) is a key industry in the energy field—especially in promoting energy efficiency and addressing environmental concerns.

14–058   Despite objections to the White Paper proposals and the belated recognition that the nuclear power side of generation was too much of a high risk in terms of economic cost (partly owing to decommissioning costs), the Government pushed ahead with the existing proposals. In October 1989 and after the Electricity Act 1989 had been passed for the privatisation of the industry, the Government reluctantly removed the nuclear side of the industry from privatisation and it will remain in Government control. A separate company called Nuclear Power was set up under Government ownership. A nuclear levy, known as the non-fossil fuel levy acts as a subsidy to nuclear electricity, and is payable by all users of electricity.

[25] Cm.322 (1988).

The Electricity Act 1989 adopted a combination of licensing, contractual and **14–059** statutory powers to regulate and operate the newly created structure under the post-privatisation arrangements. Licensing is a power which combines the work of both Secretary of State and the Director. Wider reserve powers are given to the Secretary of State in the case of electricity than in gas or telecommunications. Such reserve powers given to the Secretary of State (s.96) are for preserving the security of electricity supply, the maintenance and the security of buildings or installations used for the purposes connected with the generation, transmission or supply of electricity. The Secretary of State may set the percentage of electricity required from non-fossil fuel after consultation with the Director-General of electricity and suppliers; such order is subject only to negative resolution in the procedure of laying the order before Parliament.

The Director-General of electricity with the consent of the Secretary of State and **14–060** after consulting public electricity suppliers and affected individuals may set individual and overall standards of performance. The Director-General of electricity was required to publish information which is expedient to provide information for customers of public electricity supplies.

This wide range of statutory powers is also reinforced by licensing conditions such as **14–060a** the avoidance of cross-subsidisation and the separation of accounts between different businesses.

The 1989 Act follows the pattern in the privatisation of British Gas which allows the **14–061** DGES a discretion to make a reference to the Monopolies and Mergers Commission (MMC). But the Secretary of State for Energy can direct the MMC not to proceed with the reference. Once a report is prepared the Secretary of State may prohibit publication of "any matter" if it appears to him that it would be against the public or commercial interest of "any person".

The Secretary of State possesses wide powers to keep a register of information on **14–062** licences, modifications and the like. Effectively placing the Secretary of State as the electricity supply industry's licensing authority, the 1989 Act allows intervention in the work of the DGES as a regulator that challenges any sense of independence or freedom from political influence which the DGES may want to develop. While the DGES has a duty to review the "carrying on" of electricity generation, transmission and supply, the Secretary of State may give the DGES directions as to the priorities or matters which form the DGES's remit.

The Secretary of State's powers extend to the day-to-day operations of the **14–063** Electricity Supply Industry. The constitution of generating stations and the consents required may be supervised by the Secretary of State, under s.36 of the Act. The use of fuel stocks, and the requirement that electricity is available from non-fossil fuel sources are all part of the wide powers possessed by the Secretary of State.

The management functions of the person operating the generating station could be **14–064** directed by the Secretary of State as well as the "specified objectives" which may be given to the National Grid Company to operate the transmission system. It is clear that the legal powers contained in the 1989 Act provide the Secretary of State with the means to take over the operational management of the industry. Finally, wide emergency powers are included in Pt III of the 1989 Act which provide the Secretary of State with extensive powers to give directions to the industry. The term "civil emergency" is widely defined in subjective terms in s.96 of the 1989 Act. It includes any national disaster or other emergency which in the opinion of the Secretary of State is against the interest of national security or commercial interests. The power to give directions does not contain any requirement of laying the direction before Parliament. The 1989 Act provides the Secretary of State unparalleled powers in the history of the electricity supply industry to intervene in the day-to-day running of the industry. Electricity privatisation provided more extensive regulatory powers than previous privatisations. The few changes introduced by the Competition and Service (Utilities) Act 1992 include standards of performance, complaints and disputes, the level of achievement of each public electricity supplier, and the power for the Director to make determinations regarding the accuracy of bills.

The Utilities Act 2000

14–065   Reports on the various utilities pointed out the strengths and weaknesses of the arrangements.[26] The Utilities Act 2000 reflected the ideas contained in the DTI Green Paper *A Fair Deal for Consumers: Modernising the Framework for Utility Regulation*.[27] The act achieves four aims and objectives as follows:

- the merger of OFGAS and OFFER into a single regulatory body OFGEM;

- to provide for a fair deal and greater consumer protection than in the past;

- to meet more widely defined social and environmental objectives;

- to provide and implement more transparent trading arrangements.

14–066   In order to meet these new objectives there are a number of changes to the licensing regime for electricity. The 14 PES licences and second-tier licences are to be abolished and there will be a single-tier licence. The separation of supply and distribution will result in the distribution business being sold off to companies under the Companies Act. Distribution licences are likely to remain but subject to tighter control and supervision. There are also powers to standardise licence conditions and provide a more coherent framework for modification. The aim is to provide some stability and consistency to allow licence holders to develop their future strategic plans.

14–067   The new Utilities Act 2000 also brings additional regulatory controls over electricity companies in the following areas:

- the powers to introduce efficiency standards of performance on both suppliers and distributors;

- a requirement to meet greater transparency through the disclosure of directors' pay and remuneration in terms of meeting performance standards;

- a requirement on suppliers to have a certain percentage of electricity to come from renewable supply;

---

[26] See National Audit Office, *The Work of the Directors General of Telecommunications, Gas Supply*, Water Services and Electricity Supply (1995–96 HC 645).
[27] DTI (March, 1998).

- a power to raise a cross-subsidy to meet the needs of various identifiable groups.

The Utilities Act 2000 introduces a revision of the Gas Act 1986 in favour of **14–068** consumers. A specific requirement is to ensure that the disabled, or the chronically sick and those who are pensioners or live on low incomes in rural areas are given protection. The consumers' interests are to be somehow reconciled with different categories of consumer and at the same time fit within the general duties of the regulator and the Secretary of State to promote efficiency and economy in the use of gas. The licensing scheme under the Gas Act 1995 and the Electricity Act 1989 are brought into alignment by the Utilities Act 2000. The Competition Commission appears to have the final say on whether to modify licence conditions, replacing the previously held OFGAS power of referral.

Water

The privatisation of water also proved a greater problem than gas or telecommunica- **14–069** tions. Water privatisation had to address one of the most complex[28] legal arrangements for water services. In the case of water, 10 public water authorities and 29 private water companies comprised the water industry before privatisation. The Water Act 1989 had to address the problem of not only the new structure under privatisation but the question of merger and investment in the water industry, which also included major health and evironmental issues. In the run up to privatisation, concern among the water authorities was expressed because of the fear of predatory takeovers by French water companies.

Privatisation was carried out under the Water Act 1989 which created a new public **14–070** body, the National Rivers Authorities (NRA) now subsumed under the Environment Agency under the Environment Act 1995 with the rights and liabilities of the existing water authorities divided between the NRA and successor companies. The 29 statutory water companies are retained as water undertakers for their areas. The successor companies inherit the responsibilities of sewerage and water subject to the terms of the instruments of appointment. The various commercial companies as water and sewerage undertakers have received powers under the Water Industry Act 1991. The duty to maintain and develop an efficient and economical water supply and sewerage system falls under ss.37 and 94 of the 1991 Act. The supply of water for domestic purposes must be wholesome and of adequate quality. There is a Water Services Office with a Director-General of Water Services.

NRA, within the Environment Agency, has responsibilities for the control of river **14–071** and coastal water pollution, water resource management, land drainage, fisheries, navigation and flood defence. A major feature of the legislation is a complex pricing formula, detailed environmental protection arrangements, and a new regulatory body under the Director-General of Water Services. The latter is required in effect to balance the protection of the consumer from monopoly exploitation and the efficient running of the utility.

---

[28] See MacRory, The Water Act 1989 *Current Law Statutes* (1989); Byatt, "The Office of Water Services: Structure and Policy" [1990] *Utilities Law Review* 85–90.

14–072   The Water Act 1989 (s.230(3)) gives the Monopolies and Mergers Commission (MMC), now the Competition Commission, power to consider whether any proposed merger might prejudice the Director-General of Water Services' ability to regulate the industry and whether the proposed merger was against the public interest.

14–073   A merger must fulfil the requirements that:

(a) either it must not reduce the number of companies under independent control; or

(b) the merger must achieve some other benefit of greater significance.

14–074   The latter may be achieved by a substantial benefit to customers. Nevertheless a large number of the existing water companies had received French investment before the Act was in force, thus the regulatory protection appeared too late to be effective.

14–075   The Water Act 1989, however, broadly follows some of the legal characteristics of the post-privatisation arrangements of the other main utilities. The main regulatory instrument is the licence which contains a regulatory mechanism which "caps" the price companies may charge their customers. The annual increase is restricted to the "RPI plus an additional factor K allocated to the companies on an individual basis for each of the next 10 years." This is designed according to Director-General of Water, Ian Byatt "to off-set the significant investment programmes which have been necessary to achieve the higher standards which we all seek."

14–076   In the case of water, reference to the MMC may be made by the Secretary of State for Trade and Industry following advice from the Office of Fair Trading (OFT). The water companies may appeal to the MMC if they wish to contest the action of the Director-General of Water Services in respect of determining the "K" factor in the price cap, amendments to their licences and accounting guidelines.

14–077   The actual management of the industry is, subject to the legal framework identified above, left to the individual water companies to develop. Within OFWAT's remit is a periodic review every 10 years of the company, investment programme, management plan, efficiency standards and the regulatory regime in general.

14–078   Additional powers and responsibilities were added under the Competition and Services (Utilities) Act 1992. S.39 of the 1992 Act makes changes to the mergers procedures, under the Water Industry Act 1991, as to the matters which the MMC must take into account, such as the number of companies in separate ownership, in considering water mergers referred to the MMC. In addition the 1992 Act provides the giving of greater information on research, consumer views and an improved complaints system for customers as part of the proposals contained in the Citizen's Charter. Clearly the water privatisation plans present yet another example of problems in terms of efficiency and accountability. The present statutory formulation would seem to do little to achieve competition between the different parts of the industry.

A New Water Bill 2002

14–079   Since November 2000 a new Water Bill has been planned by the Government. The details of the proposed Bill are currently under consultation but it is envisaged that there will be a number of features common to OFGEM. Originally it was thought that a single regulator might be retained thus OFWAT would have survived. Current thinking is in favour of a regulatory board following the OFGEM model. The new Bill would also cover the following:

- changes in the regulation for supervising the financial probity of water companies;

- a new duty on OFWAT to take into account sustainable development and environmental and social matters;

- a limited protection for water companies of confidentiality to ensure that competition between the companies is encouraged;

- resolution of the problems of liability for water companies involved in abstracting water which causes damage.

There are also plans to include new regulatory controls to prevent pollution and to bring into force the EU Water Framework Directive. **14–080**

THE BROADER REGULATORY STRUCTURE

In addition to the regulatory agencies put in place post privatisation, mention should also be made of the various "quasi-governmental agencies" or non-departmental public bodies. There is a wide range and a large number of such bodies ranging from the Gaming Board, the Advisory Conciliation and Arbitration Service, Health and Safety at Work, Civil Aviation Authority, the Office of Fair Trading, the Competition Commission, to the Environment Agency. Their diversity and size is reflected in their ad hoc development. **14–081**

Innovatory procedures and specialisms give rise to new agencies such as the Human Fertilisation and Embryology Authority under the Human Fertilisation and Embryology Act 1990. Regulating professional standards of various occupations may require statutory interventions. The Osteopaths Act 1993 establishes a new body known as the General Osteopathic Council. This Council will regulate the professional education and conduct of around 2,000 persons in the United Kingdom in the delivery of osteopathic treatment. **14–082**

The reasons for creating such agencies and the likelihood that they will continue to be favoured as a means of exercising administrative powers are varied. Studies undertaken as to why fringe bodies are created have identified a number of reasons.[29] Fringe organisations may protect certain activities from direct political intervention. As they are outside the departmental system of government they may provide access to expertise and greater independence in decision-making. They may permit and encourage new initiatives away from the restrictions of both civil service and ministerial direction. Fringe organisations appear to lessen the grip of a single bureaucracy and allow greater diversity in decision-making. All the advantages claimed for such bodies make them attractive to successive governments as a means of spreading patronage in the appointment and selection of the management of such bodies. **14–083**

[29] *Public Policy and Private Interests: The Institutions of Compromise* (Hague, McKenzie and Barker, ed., 1975).

14–084   Fringe organisations give rise to questions about accountability[30] and patronage as well as concerns about their effectiveness. Accountability may vary with the organisation concerned. It may be to a Minister or to a select committee of Parliament. Occasionally there is accountability to the courts, although the exact outcome of judicial review may depend on the statutory arrangements setting out the relationship between Ministers and the agency.

SUMMARY AND CONCLUSIONS

14–085   Privatisation has provided public lawyers with new challenges in extending their knowledge of regulation into areas of contract and licensing, which involve private law techiques in drafting and understanding legal rules. The British experience of regulation began in an ad hoc manner—there is no coherent policy-making to achieve a consistent approach among regulators, combining accountability with performance indicators. Modernisation of the law has been attempted through the Utilities Act 2000 but it remains to be seen how effective this will be.

14–086   At the outset of privatisation the political dimension of each regulator's role was concealed in discussions about ownership, and debates about efficiency and effectiveness of the nationalised industries. It is only now by clarifying the political dimension that full assessment of the privatisation programme will emerge. Changes in the regulatory culture have significance for the way utility companies operate. Doubts remain about the effectiveness of privatisation strategies when competition may require re-structuring of the utility industries. Even breaking up natural monopolies may not promise a solution to the problem of competition. The monopoly operator may provide economies of scale not available to smaller operators. A smaller operator may not provide economic efficiency because it may lack expertise or sufficient bargaining power through the contracts it makes with larger units. A smaller operator may wish to develop into a larger single unit and through its internal organisation provide more efficient organisation of the external contracts it once entered into. Complexity and confusion emerge from the regulation of the utilities that may cast doubt on the value of the British experience of privatisation as a model for the future.

14–087   Privatisation has provided an important agenda for developing innovative and creative legislation concerning the regulation and the day-to-day running of the newly privatised enterprises. It is a phenomenon of global significance. The United Kingdom has led the way in developing strategies and innovation. The United Kingdom model has been used throughout Europe, North America and Japan and also among developing and newly-industrialised countries.[31]

---

[30] See *Laker Airways Ltd v Department of Trade* [1977] Q.B. 643. This case provides a good case study of the complexity in the legal arrangements which provide for the giving of directions and guidance to the Civil Aviation Authority, CAA, under the Civil Aviation Act 1971. The Court of Appeal held that the Secretary of State's guidance was *ultra vires* because it apeared that the policy guidance given to the CAA contradicted the precise objectives set out in the 1971 Act. It was unclear how the contradiction was made out. The effect of the decision was to permit Mr Laker to run his Skytrain service to the United States of America. Subsequently Laker Airlines went bankrupt; the Civil Aviation legislation was amended by the Civil Aviation Act 1982.

[31] See Istvan Pogany, "Privatisation and Regulatory Change in Hungary" *Privatization and Regulatory Change in Europe* (M. Moran and T. Prosser ed., Open University Press, 1994). Also see Jacques Pelkmans and Norbert Wagner, *Privatization and Deregulation in Asean and EC* (1990, Institute of Southeast Asia Studies); and L. Gray Cowan, *Privatization in the Developing World* (Prager, New York West Port, Connecticut, London, 1990).

There is also the question of the precise techniques available to public lawyers when **14–088** regulating privatised industries and seeking to achieve a balance of interests between consumers, the market, the industry, and the role of government. A number of issues arise. First, reliance on the use of licences and contracts has involved legal drafting in the technical side of formally operating the industry. Complex and detailed licences have required skilled interpretation and careful drafting. In the case of utilities in general they run to many hundreds of pages and provide in formal, legal language the mechanisms of running the industry. This has given rise to a number of determinations made by the Director-General over the interpretation of various licence conditions and statutory powers. Secondly, the outcome of increasing complexity in the regulation and supervision of the private utility companies provides work for many of the leading London firms of solicitors with an ever-demanding appetite for well trained and educated lawyers. The combination of contract and licences has stretched the demands on public lawyers to understand legal regulation in a broader context than before.

Further Reading

Cosmo Graham, *Regulating Public Utilities* (Hart Publishing, Oxford, 2000).

Hansard Commission Report, *The Report of the Commission on the Regulation of Privatised Utilities* (London, 1996).

T. Prosser, *Law and the Regulators* (Clarendon Press, Oxford, 1997).

T. Prosser, "Regulation, Markets, and Legitimacy" in *The Changing Constitution* (J. Jowell and D. Oliver ed., Oxford University Press, Oxford, 2000), p.228.

D. Vogel, *National Style of Regulation* (Cornell Press, London, 1986).

Part IV

CITIZENS' GRIEVANCES, HUMAN RIGHTS AND CIVIL LIBERTIES

Chapters 15–18 take account of the development of civil liberties and human rights in the United Kingdom. Chapter 15 is an analysis of how citizens' grievances are considered. The chapter covers the various mechanisms in use other than the courts. This includes tribunals, inquiries and the ombudsman system. Informal mechanisms are also discussed. Chapter 16 explains the impact of the Human Rights Act 1998 and chapters 17–18 are concerned with judicial review and obtaining remedies through judicial review in the Administrative Law Court. **IV–001**

Chapter 15

CITIZENS' GRIEVANCES

INTRODUCTION

The purpose of this chapter is to consider the opportunities for the citizen either **15–001** individually or collectively to make complaints about public bodies and seek redress. The focus of the chapter is on the means to resolve disputes other than recourse to the courts. The courts and judicial review are examined in detail in subsequent chapters. It is likely that attitudes to complaints will change as the importance of human rights and the opportunities the Human Rights Act 1998 provides for citizens to enforce their rights begins to take effect. The Act will undoubtedly create a rights-based legal culture whereby legal powers will be subjected to rigorous scrutiny as to the potential for challenge. Significant though this will be, the traditional use of tackling citizens' grievances should not be overlooked. This chapter is focused on the complaints industry outside the use of review in the administrative law court.

Administrative law should have the means to hold the administration accountable. **15–002** Responsible government is also accountable government. The Canadian Law Reform Commission's Report states that public administration constantly produces and applies rules which, even though they are not legislation, nonetheless govern the activities of administrators[1]:

> "Control of administrative action is a function that can be shared among many institutions or types of decision-makers. Law and bodies entrusted with law application and creation are primary candidates for organizing control. However a plurality of independent modes, bodies and procedural regimes that reflect the diverse nature of the control function, is called for. For instance, legal control can address jurisdiction only, or questions of law; control through an appeal can reach facts and the merits of a decision. Non-legal control bears not upon the legality of a decision, but upon its regularity, expediency or financial soundness. A legal dispute may involve several parties, or simply an individual and a decision-maker. This we call a contentious procedure. It implies adversariness which is treated by following a trial-type procedure. The suitability of that model for all legal controls is questionable."

---

[1] *Towards a Modern Federal Administrative Law* (Law Reform Commission of Canada, 1987), p.23. Also see Working Paper 51, *Policy Implementation, Compliance and Administrative Law* (Law Reform Commission of Canada, 1986).

15–003   The vast array of grievance mechanisms include adversarial as well as inquisitorial methods. This may involve some form of investigatory function, for example under the jurisdiction of the ombudsman. Inquisitorial procedures are seen in the work of inquiries such as the Scott inquiry or in the inquiry into BSE undertaken by Lord Phillips discussed in previous chapters.

15–004   There are a range of formal investigative powers entrusted to specific bodies to deal with citizens' complaints. Such bodies have "specialist grievance" procedures for dealing with complaints arising out of particular areas of activity. Some examples are as follows. Complaints related to the various public utilities such as gas, water, electricity, and telecommunications may be made to the relevant regulatory body. Recent statutory arrangements under the Utilities Act 2000 have improved access and transparency. In the case of data protection set up under the Data Protection Act 1984, replaced by the Data Protection Act 1998, a complaint may be made to the Data Protection Registrar. The 1998 Act has been amended by the Freedom of Information Act 2000 and the Data Protection Commissioner given greater powers and re-named the Information Commissioner. Complaints about the police may be made to the Police Complaints Authority which has a duty to supervise the complaint, and it may invite an officer from a constabulary other than the one under investigation to carry out an investigation into the complaint.[2] In reality there is a complaints industry offering a formula for handling public sector complaints ranging from education to health. There are a wide variety of techniques available for handling complaints from independent investigation to internal responses or the use of an ombudsman system.

15–005   The chapter is focused on alternatives to the courts and the importance of informal and internal means to redress disputes involving the administration. This includes the use of tribunals, inquiries and ombudsmen. The Justice-All Souls review in 1988 recognised the problem that there is no single institution within the United Kingdom[3] "to keep under constant review all the procedures and institutions whereby the individual may challenge administrative action". This deficiency led to their recommendation that there should be an independent body separate from the Executive charged with the responsibility of reviewing all aspects of administrative law. This proposal might take the form of a standing Royal Commission or even an extended role for the Council on Tribunals discussed below.

INFORMAL MECHANISMS OF COMPLAINT AND M.P.S

15–006   An aggrieved citizen may find that the first avenue of redress concerning a public body is to make a formal complaint to the body concerned. In fact the citizen may find that the help of their constituency M.P. is a necessary first step in making any complaint because of the complexity of complaining. Many M.P.s feel that they play a significant role in "troubleshooting" on behalf of their constituents. Accurate estimates of the extent that M.P.s engage in this watchdog function are difficult to make. It is estimated

---

[2] Established under the Police Act 1984 and amended by the Police Act 1996 and Police (Conduct) Regulations; SI 1999/730.
[3] Justice–All Souls Review: *Administrative Justice: Some Necessary Reforms* (Oxford, 1988), Chap.4, pp.75–84.

that approximately 10,000 letters a month are written to Ministers by M.P.s on behalf of their constituents. Corresponding with Ministers is an efficient way to have matters raised and may solicit an effective remedy. Letters are usually kept private away from the glare of publicity, often invite some form of response from the Minister and allow departments to be alerted to particular problems and difficulties before any public action needs to be taken. Birkinshaw notes that[4]:

> "In 1981, the Department of Employment received in the region of 8,000 letters from M.P.s dealing with constituent's complaints. The D.H.S.S. stated their average to be 22,000–25,000 per annum and the Home Office 22,500 letters from M.P.s in 1981, though some of these were requests for information and concerned bodies other than central departments."

M.P.s may also take advantage of various contacts they may have on select committees, within government departments and among Cabinet Ministers. If a letter from an M.P. fails to provoke a satisfactory response then an M.P. may raise the issue in a parliamentary question or during a debate in the House of Commons or during a half-hour adjournment debate. **15–007**

An M.P. may make use of an Early Day Motion, as a means to raise a complaint from a constituent. This acts as an accurate "notice board" for any grievances raised by M.P.s especially when there is a common cause of complaint affecting many constituents or involving several constituencies. If the matter is very contentious the debate may be accompanied by the collection of a large number of signatures supporting the debate. Topics included in Early Day Motions are very broad and through debate, grievances may be aired on a regular basis during each parliamentary session. **15–008**

Enthusiasm for the M.P. system as a form of redress should be tempered by the problem that many citizens may not know their M.P., may fail to understand the role of an M.P., and may not have confidence in the M.P.'s abilities to remedy any grievance. Disputes may fall outside the remit of the M.P. when there are legal proceedings imminent or where the matter may be more properly dealt with by an alternative means of redress. Various studies have suggested that the work of M.P.s may be obscure to the average constituent. The inadequacy of the M.P. as an effective watchdog was partly acknowledged in the setting-up of the central government Parliamentary Commissioner for Administration. **15–009**

In terms of informal means to redress grievances, there are a wide number of pressure groups or trade unions who may act as a watchdog for the citizen. There are about 850 local Citizens Advice Bureaux, mostly staffed with volunteers who provide information and advice on access to both formal and informal means to redress grievances. Since the opening of the first Law Centre in 1970 there has been a steady development in their work and activities, although recently their funding and support has been put in doubt. Law Centres provide legal advice and may specialise on specific problem areas which require specialist advice such as housing and immigration problems. Some times the matter complained about involves some form of consumer redress such as a housing problem which may fit in the category of a private law **15–010**

---

[4] P. Birkinshaw, *Grievances Remedies and the State* (2nd ed., London, 1985), pp.24–25.

problem between the landlord and tenant or, if there is a public body involved, local authority and tenant. The hybrid nature of such problems makes a knowledge of both public and private law essential.

15–011   Citizens' grievances in the public law arena may benefit from newspaper or media coverage to force officials to take account of the citizen's grievance. This may involve "in depth" investigative journalism or simply drawing attention to the nature of the disputes.

15–011a   The first report of the Government's Citizen's Charter[5] initiative announced the intention of setting up a Complaints Task Force to examine and advise on setting up and improving complaints systems in the public sector. Guidance issued to the Task Force by the Council on Tribunals from June 1993 includes advice on complaints investigation procedures. Such procedures require access to official information. There are some important developments in open government under the Code of Practice on Access to Government Information, revised 1997, and the Freedom of Information Act 2000 is also relevant in providing access to information. The Environment Information Regulations amended in 1998 provide access to information on environmental matters. The Public Disclosure Act 1998 provides some protection for whistleblowers.

TRIBUNALS AND INQUIRIES

Tribunals

15–012   In considering alternatives to the courts in the adjudication of disputes, importance must be given to the work of tribunals. Tribunals were commonly in use in the nineteenth century. Today they perform a wide variety of functions and may take a number of forms for redressing the citizen's grievances. The Employment Appeals Tribunal is a superior Court of Record. The Local Valuation Court set up under s.88 of the General Rate Act 1967, hears appeals on land drainage, and before the Community Charge and Council Tax, valuation courts heard a whole range of rating matters with appeals to the Land Tribunal; valuation courts appear to have all the formalities of a court of law. It is clear that the coming into force of the Human Rights Act 1998 requires that tribunals must take account of the requirement under Article 6 of the Convention to a fair trial and public hearing in terms of the procedures and processes in use in a tribunal.

15–013   The Franks Committee[6] in 1957 recommended the creation of the Council of Tribunals to keep under review the working and the constitution of tribunals. The work of the Council closely monitors the development of the system of administrative tribunals "to provide some consistent principles" to guide the work of tribunals. Since the Tribunal and Inquiries Act 1958 following the recommendations of the Franks Committee, the number of tribunals which fall within the jurisdiction of the Council on Tribunals exceeds a total of 83. The Legatt Review[7] estimated that the total number of

---

[5] Cm.2101 (1992).

[6] *Report of the Committee on Administrative Tribunals and Enquiries*, Cmnd.218 (1957).

[7] Sir Andrew Legatt, *Tribunals for Users One System, One Service: Report of the Review of Tribunals*, March 2001.

tribunals may be more than their estimate of 137. Franks regarded tribunals as part of the machinery provided by Parliament for the purposes of adjudication rather than as part of the machinery of the administration. A wide variety of bodies and institutions rely on the work of tribunals.

It is impossible to provide any coherent organising principles to group the work of tribunals. However on the basis of the jurisdiction of the Council on Tribunals, the following examples give an indication of the activities covered by tribunals. Sch.1 to the Tribunals and Inquiries Act 1992 contains a list of the tribunals falling under the direct supervision of the Council on Tribunals. **15–014**

The Report by Sir Andrew Legatt into the *Review of Tribunals*[8] has made a number of recommendations in an attempt to bring coherence to the system of tribunals and to provide coherence between one part of the civil justice system, the courts and the system of tribunals. The courts came under the Woolf reforms while the latter do not. As Sir Andrew noted[9]: **15–015**

> "The last 50 years have brought an accelerating accumulation of tribunals as bodies whose function it is to decide disputes that would otherwise go to the courts. Together they form the largest part of the civil justice system in England and Wales, hearing about one million cases each year. That number of cases alone makes their work of great importance to our society, since more of us bring a case before a tribunal than go to any other part of the justice system. Their collective impact is immense."

It is the variety of types of tribunal and their different uses that is also striking. Various disciplinary bodies may take the form of a tribunal. For example, the General Dental Council, the Central Council for Nursing, Midwifery and Health Visiting,[10] the General Medical Council and the Architects Registration Council for the United Kingdom exercise a variety of disciplinary powers within a statutory framework. Licensing also forms an important function of the work of tribunals such as the Civil Aviation Authority, or the Consumer Credit Licensing Hearings. As Hendry has noted[11]: **15–016**

> ". . . a multiplicity of tribunals each operating within the bounds of a confined jurisdiction and each directed toward disposing of claims and arguments arising out of a particular statutory scheme."

Specialised and comprehensive rules are now provided in Pt III of the Trade Union Reform and Employment Rights Act 1993, now the Employment Tribunals Act 1996, for the constitution of industrial tribunals. The 1993 Act established for the first time in primary legislation the basic constitution of industrial tribunals. **15–017**

Taxation in its various forms has also created the need for a number of tribunals. For example the General and Special Commissioners of Income Tax through the various Income Tax Acts dating back to 1816 hears appeals against assessments to tax, **15–018**

[8] *ibid.*
[9] *ibid.*, para.1.1.
[10] Dentists Act 1984, s.27.
[11] K.H. Hendry, "The Tasks of Tribunals: Some Thoughts" (1982) 1 *Civil Justice Quarterly* 253.

relief against tax and oversees the administration of the taxation system in the United Kingdom. In the case of value added tax an appeal jurisdiction exists with the various Value Added Tax Tribunals set up under the Finance Act 1972 and subsequent amendments.

15–019   There is also the introduction in 1993 of the Revenue Adjudicator, entrusted to investigate complaints about the Inland Revenue. This jurisdiction was expanded in 1995 to include Customs and Excise and the Contributions Agency. The idea of an adjudicator is also adopted in respect of prisons, and Companies House. Adjudicators build on the experience of a variety of different tribunals by filling any perceived "gaps" in the system. Dissatisfaction in existing methods of redress for taxation matters favoured what Morris has described as[12]:

> "In short there was a pressing need for a speedy, user-friendly, cheap but independent complaints mechanism whereby tax payers could ventilate grievances regarding the manner in which the revenue has exercised its powers, and an Adjudicator scheme was seized upon as the ideal solution."

15–020   Some areas of tribunal activity have come under particular scrutiny by the courts, partly because of the nature of the work involved. For example the Prison Board of Visitors with its origins in the Prison Act 1898 appears to have developed into a tribunal in all but name when performing a wide adjudicative function on charges of offences under the Prison Act 1952 and amendments. The disciplinary function can be vast as over 81,000 disciplinary offences were punished in the year 1989. Such disciplinary proceedings are subject to judicial review by the courts. There is concern that legal representation should be available at such hearings as the powers of the Board of Visitors have been compared to the jurisdiction of the magistrates' courts. In *R. v Board of Visitors of HM Prison, the Maze, Ex p. Hone*[13] Lord Goff noted the observations made on behalf of the appellant:

> "a hearing before a board of visitors is a sophisticated hearing. In particular, he [counsel for the appellant] submitted there is an oral hearing; a formal plea is entered; cross-examination is allowed and witnesses are called; the onus and standard of proof are the same as in a criminal trial; free legal aid is available; punishments are imposed; a plea in mitigation can be entered, and the board has greater powers of punishment than those exercised by magistrates' courts."

15–021   The House of Lords rejected the submission that those appearing before the Prison Board had a right to legal representation by a lawyer. The courts have consistently upheld the principle that the rules of natural justice apply to the Board of Prison Visitors in making their adjudications. It may be expected that the Human Rights Act 1998 will have implications in the way decision-making is reached in terms of Article 6 (right to a fair hearing) under the Convention. Article 8 of the Convention applies to the correspondence of prisoners[14] including interviews with journalists.

15–022   Immigration appeals also fall under the work of a tribunal, the Immigration Appeal Tribunal[15] with considerable discretionary powers. The detailed rules are contained in

[12] See P.E. Morris, "The Revenue Adjudicator—The First Two Years" [1996] *Public Law* 309–32.
[13] [1988] A.C. 379; [1988] 2 W.L.R. 177; *Hone v Maze Prison Visitors* [1988] 1 All E.R. 321.
[14] *R. v Secretary of State for the Home Department Ex p. Simms* [2000] 2 A.C. 15.
[15] Immigration Act 1971, s.12.

the Immigration and Asylum Act 1999 and various rules made under the Act known as Immigration Rules.

Social welfare rights created a number of statutory bodies which have the designa- **15–023** tion of a tribunal. This is a vast area where adjudication lies at the heart of the many social welfare provisions introduced since the setting-up of the modern Welfare State. Social Security Appeal Tribunals[16] now unified under the Unified Appeal Tribunals Social Security Act 1998 hear a whole range of matters relating to social welfare benefits. In outline the system depends first on civil servants appointed as local adjudication officers working in the local offices of the Department of Health and Social Services. Their tasks are to adjudicate claims affecting the payments of a wide range of benefits, collecting evidence on claims, and acting independently of the Department in their interpretation and application of the law.

The Social Security Appeal Tribunals are normally chaired by a lawyer of not less **15–024** than five years' standing and two persons selected from a panel made up of representatives from employers and employed persons. There may be a further appeal to the Social Security Commissioners. In 1980 the Social Security Act introduced for the first time an appeal on a point of law from the decision of Commissioners to the High Court.

The Council on Tribunals has fought hard for an increased role and additional **15–025** powers to carry out its role. The original legislation, the Tribunals and Inquiries Act 1958, was subsequently modified and later consolidated in 1992. The 1958 Act set up the Council and its composition combines practising lawyers and academic lawyers with non-lawyers who are in the majority. All members are appointed by the Lord Chancellor or the Lord Advocate for Scotland. The Council has presently no jurisdiction in Northern Ireland.

An important function of the Council on Tribunals is providing detailed considera- **15–026** tion of draft rules and procedures of individual tribunals. Foulkes has noted[17] how a limited but important role is performed by the Council in considering areas of dispute settlement in the recent privatisation legislation for electricity and water, where the legislation gave the respective Directors-General a role in the determination of disputes. The Council has a role in overseeing the rules laid down for the procedures in the conduct of determinations made by the regulators. In 1991 the Council published a Report on Model Rules of Procedure for Tribunals.[18] The report contained guidance in setting up adjudication procedures. In general such guidance is to ensure that there are fair procedures and reasons for decisions are made known as part of those procedures.

The Council has been active in setting the standards of how rights and procedures **15–027** might be efficiently combined into the operation of the tribunal system. This includes the rules of evidence, the award of costs, the rights of appearance of witnesses, the rules relating to the disclosure of confidential information and the time-limits for appeals and such matters. During the course of its work a number of issues have been raised by the Council, most notably the need to avoid the proliferation and expansion of the number of tribunals without careful consideration. This has led to the suggestion that tribunals might be consolidated to give greater efficiency to the system overall.

[16] See the Health and Social Services and Social Security Adjudication Act 1983.
[17] D. Foulkes, "The Council on Tribunals and the Utilities" [1990] *Utilities Law Review* 145.
[18] Cm.1434 (1991).

15–028   In 1980 in a special report[19] the Council considered the functions of the Council and how best to develop them for the future. The Council argued for an advisory role over "the whole area of administrative adjudication". There is currently no obligation on ministers to consult with the Council at any stage when Bills are being prepared which may establish new tribunals or affect existing ones. The Council considered that this deficiency should be remedied. The Government's response considered that it would be inappropriate to lay a statutory duty on ministers to consult the Council on Tribunals on the legislation that they were considering. Consultation on an ad hoc basis might be encouraged and subsequently a Code of Practice[20] was formulated by the Council for the guidance of officials involved in drafting legislation when to consult with the Council. However the Code has not been given any statutory endorsement. The Council has noted that despite the Code being reissued in 1986 it is not always followed by every government department.

15–029   The Council has also raised a further shortcoming in its arrangements for edealing with any complaints which may be made to it about the working of tribunals. The Council has not got the statutory powers to deal with major complaints even though they may raise fundamental issues.

15–030   While the Council historically believes its role is to consider "openness, fairness and impartiality" in the tribunal system, it also has to meet new demands for "efficiency, effectiveness, and economy". Settling the inevitable tensions between the differing standards expected of the Council is a challenge for the future. While the Council has embarked on providing a research register of those interested in tribunals and inquiries through the appointment of a part-time research co-ordinator in 1987, it admits that its largest deficiency is the lack of manpower and the resources to provide a detailed knowledge of the working of the system of tribunals.

15–031   Tribunals are often compared to courts and may appear to perform the work of departments in adjudications. However, the Franks Report was clear[21]: "tribunals . . . are not ordinary courts, but neither are they appendages of Government Departments . . .".

15–032   Defining the role and objectives of tribunals presents formidable problems given the great diversity of their work and the lack of uniformity in their functions. All tribunals which deal with disputes between the citizen and the government are concerned with administrative power and how it may properly be exercised. The Justice All Souls review noted[22]:

> ". . . that the true role of the courts is restricted to a review of legality and the judges are not concerned with the merits in the sense of the rightness (or wrongness) of the decision. Tribunals on the other hand, are given a different role. Very commonly they are concerned with the merits of the decision and typically they will be given the task of deciding, as between citizen and the state, whether an official has dealt correctly with a claim or application."

---

[19] *The Functions of the Council on Tribunals: Special Report*, Cmnd.7805 (1980).
[20] See Appendix C to the *Annual Report of the Council on Tribunals 1986/87* (1987–88 HC 234). See *Annual Report of the Council on Tribunals 1992/93* (1992–93 HC 78).
[21] Franks, *Report of the Committee on Administrative Tribunals and Enquiries* Cmnd 218 (1957), para.40.
[22] Justice All Souls Review, p.212.

Tribunals may also exercise similar decision-making functions as Ministers. Franks **15–033** expressed a preference for tribunals over the largely discretionary powers of Ministers and preferred courts over tribunals. In the allocation of functions it appears quite difficult to decide the advantages of one over the other. However it is possible to set out some of the reasons for creating independent statutory tribunals.

The main reasons and by implication the advantages claimed for a system of **15–034** tribunals are the following. Tribunals provide access to expert and specialist knowledge of complex areas of law and practice. The forum of a tribunal allows a wider degree of expertise than would normally be possible with the courts. In addition tribunals are claimed to provide cheap, reasonably speedy and efficient means for the resolution of disputes. The procedures may claim to be less formal than courts though as pointed out above, some tribunals appear to have inherited procedures almost identical to the courts. Another claimed advantage is that tribunals are not bound by very complex and legalistic rules of evidence and the decisions reached at tribunals may cover more widely developed considerations than the courts.

This raises the broader question of whether tribunals may offer a distinctive system **15–035** of adjudication that is not orientated to the adversarial process in the way that the courts are. Lord Denning in *R. v National Insurance Commr, Ex p. Viscusi*[23] suggested that tribunals were "more in the nature of an inquiry before an investigating body charged with the task of finding out what happened".

However, with the question of representation at tribunals, almost all tribunals permit **15–036** legal representation, and the desirability of legal aid for all tribunals, advocated by the Lord Chancellor's Advisory Committee,[24] there is a temptation to see tribunals moving under the influences of lawyers into an adversarial role. Investigating the characteristics of tribunal procedures and whether they represent a distinctly inquisitorial system is an important issue in the light of recent doubts about miscarriages of justice in the criminal courts.

Tribunals fall under the jurisdiction of the courts. Ss.10–12 of the Tribunals and **15–037** Inquiries Act 1992 provides that tribunals must "furnish a statement either written or oral, of the reasons for the decision", Under s.13 of the Tribunals and Inquiries Act 1971, now s.11 of the 1992 Act, a party dissatisfied on a point of law with a decision of the tribunal may appeal or make a case stated to the High Court if the tribunal falls in the category of a Sch.1 tribunal listed in the Act.

Great difficulty is experienced in identifying with any clarity the meaning of "a point **15–038** of law" which has to be settled by the courts. Errors of law may include the misinterpretation of a statute, taking irrelevant considerations into account, or an abuse of discretion. But distinguishing a point of law from one of fact appears to be made on the basis of each case. Craig suggests that[25]:

> "Two questions can arise which are not always properly distinguished. The first is whether the error alleged involves any question of law at all. Presuming an affirmative answer to this first question, the second is by what standard will the courts determine whether there has been an erroneous construction of this legal term?"

[23] [1974] 1 W.L.R. 646.
[24] Lord Chancellor's Advisory Committee 24th Annual Report (1973–74 HC 20).
[25] P. Craig, *Administrative Law* (1989), p.124.

15–039   The problem may also be seen in terms of the latitude the courts are willing to allow the decision-maker and the extent to which intervention by the courts substitutes judicial decision-making for the tribunal. Wade distinguishes[26] between two rival approaches followed by the courts on the distinction between facts and law. One approach suggests that matters of fact may be confined to the primary facts of the case. Once such facts are established the question of whether they satisfy some legal definition must be a question of law. "The facts themselves not being in dispute, the conclusion is a matter of legal inference." The other approach proceeds on the assumption that the "meaning of an ordinary word in the English language is not a question of law" unless the interpretation given to it by the tribunal is unreasonable. Wade shows that the courts have not been consistent in their approach and this leaves considerable discretion in the interpretation of this complex issue.

15–040   Tribunals in reaching their decisions must keep within their legal powers. The Court of Appeal declined to allow a review of the validity of income support regulations through the statutory appeal system. The Social Security Commissioner had held on an appeal from a Social Security Tribunal that its decision was *ultra vires* and contrary to law.[27] The Court held that such a finding is inconsistent with the role of the Commissioner. The House of Lords has reversed the decision of the Court of Appeal and held that a Commissioner has jurisdiction to determine any challenge to the *vires* of a provision in regulations when considering if a decision order appeal was an error in law. This raises the possibility of appeals raising identical issues to that of review. The scope for development in this area requires further consideration by the courts. A distinction should be drawn between an appellate and a judicial review jurisdiction. Normally the courts will not permit *vires* to be raised on appeal, though this may depend on the nature of the body involved as there are some decided cases which do accept this possibility.

The Legatt Proposals for the Reform of the Tribunal System

15–041   The Legatt Report on tribunals was published on August 16, 2001 and comprises a number of important recommendations covering the reform of the tribunal system. One area given specific attention was the employment tribunal. The main recommendations cover the transfer of the tribunal system into the work of the Lord Chancellor's department. This includes the development of rules for tribunals to follow the rules set out in the Civil Justice Review by Lord Woolf into the working of the civil court system. The aim of the Legatt Report was to retain characteristics of the tribunal rather than the idea of an "industrial court". Thus while legal aid may be available, it was not recommended to be introduced generally for tribunals, but rather on the basis of need or complexity. One idea was that the employment tribunal system might be extended to cover all employment related disputes and all discrimination cases. Appropriate powers might be given to transfer relevant cases to the county court in particular circumstances.

15–042   The specialist nature of the Employment Tribunal gives rise to an interesting comparison between a court and a tribunal. Employment law is exceptionally complex

---

[26] See *Edwards v Bristow* [1956] A.C. 14 for the discussion of the principles involved in facts and law distinctions. Wade, *Administrative Law* (6th ed., 1988), pp.940–943.

[27] *Chief Adjudication Officer v Foster* [1992] Q.B. 31; [1993] 1 All E.R. 705.

and the advantage of a tribunal over a court is that there are dedicated members who have developed as specialists in this area of law. The composition of an Employment Tribunal may include members who are drawn from outside the legal profession and this wide cross-section may bring benefits to the work of the Tribunal itself. While wishing to maintain and enhance this role, the Legatt proposals take care to keep courts and tribunals separate. The Legatt recommendations are very detailed and canvass a large series of technical reforms designed to make all tribunals meet the standards of delivering a good service to the public in handling disputes, notably the creation of a unified appeal structure to include full-time judges to supervise offenders.

Inquiries

Aggrieved citizens may find that the forum which allows their viewpoint or objections to be most clearly expressed and openly considered is through the use of inquiries. Compared to tribunals, where there is a need to adjudicate disputes between the citizen and the State, inquiries developed historically as an alternative to the Private Bill procedure where proposals for powers by government in matters involving public authority were investigated through parliamentary committees. Inquiries, developed from different considerations than the tribunal system. Wade notes[28]:   **15–043**

> "The typical tribunal finds facts and decides the case by applying legal rules laid down by statute or regulation. The typical inquiry hears evidence and finds facts, but the person conducting it finally makes a recommendation to a minister as to how the minister should act on some question of policy, eg, whether he should grant planning permission for some development scheme."

In essence inquiries allow the citizen the right to a hearing before an important administrative decision may be made. This means that inquiries allow more public participation than would otherwise be possible especially in the planning law area where there is controversy over the location of an airport, a power station or a major motorway.   **15–044**

Traditionally inquiries are limited to an investigative role, usually through the provision of evidential material to allow a Minister to reach an ultimate decision. Rarely do they make the actual decision. Inquiries have developed in an ad hoc way. As a valuable technique in administrative law, the basic elements of independent investigation, presentation of evidence and the making of recommendations allow for great flexibility. Inquiries also have the potential to cross the boundary between public law and private law issues. For example the Department of Trade enjoy wide powers to appoint inspectors to investigate companies which include, under s.177(1) of the Financial Services Act 1986, the power to appoint inspectors if it appears to the Secretary of State that there is a breach of the Company Securities (Insider Dealing) Act 1985.   **15–045**

Inquiries into accidents may be set up under various statutory powers. S.466 of the Merchant Shipping Act 1894 gives powers to hold an inquiry into a collision of a ship at sea;[29] there are various statutory powers to hold inquiries into railway accidents, gas   **15–046**

---

[28] Wade, *Administrative Law* (6th ed, Oxford, 1988), p.900.
[29] The Report was carried out by Mr Justice Sheen, with assessors and published in July 1987. Also see J. McEldowney, "Public Inquiry into the Piper Alpha Disaster" [1991] *Utilities Law Review* 2.

explosions, or nuclear installations. The normal formulation of the terms of reference of such inquiries includes questions of why did the accident occur, and what lessons may be gained from past mistakes? In some instances the basis of the inquiry may give rise to criminal prosecutions or disciplinary procedures.

15–047   Civil liability may therefore be largely dependent on the outcome of an accident inquiry and this raises questions about the confidentiality of evidence and the rights of witnesses who give evidence and afterwards find that criminal prosecutions are taken. In that respect account needs to be taken of the possibility, now accepted but at one time doubted, that in English criminal law a corporation could be convicted of manslaughter. In P&O European Ferries Ltd, Mr Justice Turner held that an indictment for manslaughter might lie against P&O Ferries after the Zeebrugge disaster.[30] The evidence which may form the basis of any criminal prosecution may come from the evidence obtained as part of the findings of the inquiry into the disaster. The Sheen Report[31] found that from the Board of Directors: "through the managers of the marine department down to the Junior Superintendents' fault could be established." The conclusion reached in the report was that: "From top to bottom the body corporate was infected with the disease of sloppiness."

15–048   Inquiries may also have an important role in establishing facts arising from social problems such as child abuse. Such inquiries may come under s.26 of the Child Care Act 1980 or inquiries undertaken by review panels appointed by local authorities or local agencies. The standing of the person appointed to hold the inquiry and the nature of the recommendation may prove influential with the government of the day even though there is no obligation to accept any of the recommendations made in the report prepared by the inquiry. Not everyone favours the inquiry as an investigative technique in such cases. In 1981 the Annual General Meeting of the British Association of Social Workers rejected the use of committees of inquiry in such cases. Dissatisfaction of the Association has focused on the showpiece nature of the inquiry and the feeling that those under investigation are perceived by the media as "on trial".

15–049   The principles identified by Franks that ought to apply to inquiries such as openness, fairness and impartiality, have been recognised in the Tribunals and Inquiries Acts 1958 and in s.11 of the 1971 Act and their consolidation in the Tribunals and Inquiries Act 1992. This legislation permits the Lord Chancellor to make various procedural rules for the conduct of inquiries. An example of these rules may be found in the Town and Country Planning (Inquiries Procedure) Rules 1988.[31a] In drawing up such rules the Council on Tribunals may be consulted; such rules are advisory only.

15–050   In addition to the above procedures there are a miscellaneous number of statutory provisions which permit the holding of inquiries. Formal powers for the investigation of improper official behaviour of officials in 1921 were enacted under the Tribunals of Inquiry (Evidence) Act 1921. The 1921 Act is sparingly used for such matters of "urgent public importance". It has been estimated that these powers have only been used in fewer than 20 occasions in the past. There are also a variety of non-statutory inquiries where it is desired to carry out an investigation and a statutory inquiry is not required. The best known example of this is the Crichel Down inquiry,[32] and the

---

[30] *R. v Coroner for Kent Ex p. Spooner* (1989) 88 Cr.App.R. 10.
[31] See McEldowney [1991] *Utilities Law Review* 2.
[31a] Town and Country Planning (Inquiry Procedure) Rules 1988 (SI 1988/944).
[32] *Report of the Public Inquiry into the Disposal of Land at Crichel Down*, Cmnd.9176 (1954). See Chap.3 for a fuller discussion.

Stansted inquiry into the location of London's third airport. Inquiries may be set up where there are public concerns about the role of Ministers. In 1963 Lord Denning's inquiry into the Profumo affair was set up informally and had no statutory powers. The Salmon Commission later recommended that such inquiries should not normally be used in matters of such public concern. Perhaps the most controversial and intrusive into the internal working of government is the Scott inquiry. The inquiry was established after the collapse of the trial of three former executives of the machine tool company Matrix Churchill charged with deception in obtaining export licences led to the setting-up of an inquiry chaired by Lord Justice Scott. At the trial the prosecution had alleged that the intended use of the machine tools supplied to Iraq was for weapons. The defence claimed that the government was fully aware of the use of the machine tools which had been subject to a licence application. Evidence given by Alan Clark, the former Minister of State at the Department of Trade and Industry confirmed that there was no deception as the Government were aware of the intended use of the machine tools. The judge quashed public interest immunity certificates served by the prosecution to prevent disclosure of intelligence information. The documents released at the trial revealed how high-level departmental and ministerial contact had taken place over the licence application. Controversy surrounds the use of public interest immunity certificates and the role of government Ministers in signing the certificates. Also of significance is the question of the legal advice tendered by the Attorney-General that Ministers were under a duty to sign the certificates. The role of Customs and Excise in bringing the prosecutions is also questioned.

The terms of reference of the Scott inquiry were announced by the Prime Minister[33] **15–051** "to examine and report on decisions taken by the prosecuting authority and those signing public interest immunity certificates in *R. v Henderson* and any other similar cases that he considers relevant to the inquiry; and to make recommendations." The Chairman of the inquiry appointed an independent counsel to the inquiry who in practice took the main burden of asking questions of witnesses. The inquiry has heard evidence in public and the evidence is available from the Public Records Office.

The Scott inquiry was not set up under the Tribunals and Inquiry (Evidence) Act **15–052** 1921 and thus it did not have statutory powers to *subpoena* witnesses. The Prime Minister gave assurances that civil servants and Ministers would be required to give evidence. Former Ministers accepted invitations to attend including Lady Thatcher, the former Prime Minister. John Major also gave evidence as serving Prime Minister. Witnesses had been given immunity from prosecution for their evidence given at the inquiry.

As an *ad hoc* inquiry with no express statutory powers, this gave Sir Richard Scott **15–053** the freedom to determine the procedures to be adopted at the inquiry itself. The procedures adopted at the Scott inquiry proved as controversial as the subject of the inquiry itself. The starting point is to consider the six cardinal principles adopted by Lord Salmon as guidance for inquiries laid down by the Royal Commission 1966 under the chairmanship of Lord Salmon.[34] The six Salmon principles are as follows:

> 1. Before any person becomes involved in an inquiry the Tribunal must be satisfied that there are circumstances which affect him and which the tribunal proposes to investigate.

[33] *Hansard*, HC Vol.214, col.74 (November 16, 1992). *R. v Henderson*, unreported, November, 1992. Also see D. Leigh, *Betrayed: The Real Story of the Matrix Churchill Trial (London, 1993).*
[34] Cmnd.3121 (1966).

2. Before any person who is involved in an inquiry is called as a witness he should be informed of any allegations which are made against him and the substance of the evidence in support of them.

3. He should be given an adequate opportunity of preparing his case and of being advised by legal advisers; his legal expenses should normally be met out of public funds.

4. He should have the opportunity of being examined by his own solicitor or counsel and of stating his case in public at the inquiry.

5. Any material witnesses he wishes to be called at the inquiry should, if reasonably practicable be heard.

6. He should have the opportunity of testing by cross-examination conducted by his own solicitor or counsel any evidence which may affect him.

15–054   It is important to remember that the six principles, outlined above, are not rules of law but guidance which might be followed. The Salmon principles were intended to provide the basis for Tribunals operating under the Tribunals of Inquiries Act 1921. While many commentators see the principles as a matter of fundamental fairness,[35] the Scott inquiry was free to depart from them. The approach taken by Scott was to acknowledge that as far as possible the principles should be applied and followed. However, the nature of the Scott inquiry required both adversarial and inquisitorial techniques. In the end the procedures that were adopted of necessity reflected the inquisitorial approach taken by the inquiry. Scott rapidly discovered that if the inquiry adopted all of the six Salmon principles it might take a considerable time to complete. The principle that caused most controversy relates to the question of cross-examination and legal representation at the inquiry. In the past, notable inquiries such as Lord Justice Crom-Johnson into the Crown Agents affair took considerable time and were subject to extensive delay. Cross-examination by lawyers at the inquiry was held largely responsible for that delay.

15–055   The question of whether Scott was correct in adopting an inquisitorial approach remains highly debated. Criticism focused on the argument that the inquisitive nature of the procedures were inappropriate when conducted in public hearings, left witnesses unprotected and put due process in jeopardy. Scott's response to such criticisms, notably from Lord Howe,[36] was to point to the increasingly large amount of written submissions received throughout the entire period of the inquiry, the fact that oral proceedings were only a small fraction of the inquiry's work and that witnesses were granted legal advice at considerable cost to the taxpayer though admittedly not cross-examination. This last point, the absence of cross-examination rights remains a contentious issue. In its recent consideration of the Scott procedures, the Council on Tribunals broadly favoured the Scott approach whenever inquisitorial procedures were involved. There remain some lurking doubts that perhaps the procedures were in some way defective because the key element of cross-examination by lawyers was absent. There was also the sheer scale of the work generated by the inquiry. Lord Howe makes the following observations[37]:

---

[35] Lord Howe, "Procedure at the Scott Inquiry" [1996] *Public Law* 445–460.
[36] *ibid.*
[37] *ibid.*

"My own case may be seen as a useful illustration. Unrepresented as I was until very near the end (only my closing submissions were prepared by counsel and solicitors rather than myself), I struggled to keep abreast of the mountains of transcripts that filled the months before and after I gave evidence, and over the years during which I was obliged to comment on several distinct batches of preliminary conclusions. I estimate that I spent at least 30 unrewarding (and unrewarded) days, testifying to or preparing the increasingly prolix questionnaires, which they had to inflict upon others as well as themselves. By contrast with this prolonged ordeal, Lord Justice Edmund Davis's Aberfan report was published within nine months of the disaster. So too was Lord Justice Bingham's Report on the collapse of BCCI."

Following on from Lord Howe's strong reservations about the Scott inquiry procedures, the Council on Tribunals has considered the way forward. In general terms the key objectives of an inquiry are effectiveness, fairness, speed and economy. No single constitution or model set of rules are possible to achieve these goals. However, the Council did recommend "that inquiry reports of any length should provide for an executive summary of the findings and recommendations".[38]   **15–056**

More commonly used are powers under the compulsory acquisitions of land legislation to hold a public local inquiry. The Acquisition of Land Act 1981 provides an opportunity for objectors to make their case heard in the case of the compulsory purchase of land. However the role of the inquiry is not confined to this objective alone, as the effect of such inquiries is to provide administrators with a sense of the public interest. The courts have upheld this view of the inquiry as a means of providing authorisation for the use of land for public use. In this sense the inquiry procedure legitimates and informs government decision-making in addition to providing the citizen with a means of redress.   **15–057**

Planning appeals require that the Secretary of State should allow the appellant and the local planning authority an opportunity of putting their case. Invariably, though not necessarily, this may mean holding an inquiry under powers granted to the Secretary of State under the Local Government Act 1972 to direct that a local inquiry should be held. Planning appeals arise when planning permission has been refused or is granted subject to conditions. Public local inquiries have recognisable characteristics. They are held in the locality where the proposed schemes are situated. The inspector is normally appointed by the Minister with the relevant statutory authority. Currently the Department of the Environment has a corps of nearly 400 inspectors responsible for over 3,000 inquiries each year. The subject matter of the inquiry relates to the objections to the proposed scheme received by the Minister from private parties or local authorities. The purpose of the inquiry is to provide the relevant Minister with the necessary information to allow the Minister to consider the scheme in light of the public benefit to be derived from the scheme if implemented. Weighing up all the material factors is greatly assisted by the inquiry process. However this does not preclude taking other matters into consideration, including the policy of the government, advice from experts or departmental considerations.   **15–058**

---

[38] Advice to the Lord Chancellor on the procedural issues arising in the conduct of public inquiries set up by Ministers Council on Tribunals, July 1996.

15–059   A particularly controversial area of planning are highways inquiries into large motorway projects. Detailed rules exist as to the conduct of these inquiries and efforts are made to improve the information available to objectors.

15–060   Distinct from planning appeals the planning system adopts inquiries as a means to allow public participation in the planning process. Local plan inquiries allow objectors to raise issues surrounding the publication of local plans or structure plans prepared under Pt II of the Town and Country Planning Act 1971. The Town and Country Planning (Costs of Inquiries etc.) Act 1995 authorises the Secretary of State to recover from local planning authorities the costs borne by the Secretary of State in relation to the appointment of inspectors to hold local public inquiries. The 1995 Act provides express powers for the defrayment of such expenses.

15–061   The inquiry procedure is a key issue for planning and administrative lawyers. Inquiries may resemble a court where the trial of the issues involves the presentation of the appellant's case after the inspector makes introductory comments. The appellant has a right of final reply, and often the legal representation at inquiries ensures that the proceedings are formal and may appear over-legalistic. The adversarial nature of the proceedings is characterised by the cross-examination of witnesses who may be experts in their field. Witnesses who give evidence are protected from actions for defamation because they enjoy absolute privilege. However, the inspector has the right to intervene, ask questions, and re-examine witnesses. The extent that an inspector adopts an inquisitorial style may be due to the style and personality of the inspector. An inquiry may attract news media and unlike a court does not have contempt powers, thus the issues tested at an inquiry may well be simultaneously examined in the media. The inspector is at a disadvantage compared to the courts in controlling outbursts of anger or strong feelings among the participants. The Planning Inquiries (Attendance of Public) Act 1976 provides that in principle oral evidence should be given in public and that documentary evidence should be open to inspection.

15–062   Inquiries may be seen as a safety valve for the views of the community and local opinion is often organised to put their case. In theory, at the discretion of the inspector, anyone may attend an inquiry, while certain groups are entitled to appear such as the National Park Committee where the land is situated in a National Park. However the giving of evidence is left to the discretion of the inspector.

15–063   The nature of the discretion exercised by the inquiry inspector is subject to statutory rules such as the Town and Country Planning (Inquiries Procedure) Rules 1988.[38a] Evidence may be taken on oath and may require the attendance of persons and documents. A timetable for the inquiry may be drawn up with a pre-inquiry meeting to ensure that the inquiry is held efficiently and expeditiously. This allows the Secretary of State to serve notice of the issues which are likely to be relevant and to be considered. The date fixed for the inquiry must be within eight weeks of the conclusion of a pre-inquiry meeting and not later than 22 weeks after the date of notification of the holding of an inquiry. The 1988 rules also allow the Secretary of State an influence in the appointment of assessors and to indicate the weight to be attached to their opinion.

15–064   After the inquiry is held and the inspector's report is made to the Secretary of State, r.16(4) provides the basis for the resolution of any disagreement between the inspector's report and the Secretary of State. Generally, the Secretary of State is free,

---

[38a] SI 1988/944.

provided the procedures are correctly followed and due weight is attached to the inspector's findings, to make his own conclusion. Then the Secretary of State must notify all the parties to the inquiry of his decision and his reasons under r.16(5) of the 1988 rules. The applicant may make further representations within 21 days, and if necessary the Secretary of State may re-open the inquiry.

The courts have exercised vigilance over the conduct of inquiries, the findings of fact **15–065** made by the inspector and the observance of natural justice throughout the inquiry proceedings. It would also be possible to argue that the Human Rights Act 1998 has importance in ensuring that the procedures of the inquiry are fair and that human rights are protected.

The Franks Committee envisaged that inquiries would be informal, accessible and **15–066** open. Legal representation gives rise to the question about legal aid and advice. Legal advice and assistance but not legal aid is normally available at inquiries on the same basis as tribunals. S.250 of the Local Government Act 1972 empowers the award of costs in connection with statutory public inquiries. There is little guidance in the section as to how this power may be exercised. There is considerable debate about how this wide discretion may be exercised; though restrictive in the present exercise of this discretion, some argue that the rules should be permissive to permit the speedier resolution of matters when one party delays or acts inefficiently. Examples of where it may be used include where one party refuses to discuss the matter or provide information or has been unable to support their decision by the necessary evidence.

In contrast to the use of inquiries at a local level, inquiries into large-scale developments **15–067** place greater stress and strain on the system of inquiries. The model of the public local inquiry seems ill-suited to dealing with these major issues. For example the inquiry concerned with the Greater London Development Plan in 1970 took 240 days. The inquiry into the Sizewell B Power Station[39] lasted 340 days. In the case of the Third London Airport inquiry chaired by Lord Roskill, a non-statutory inquiry was set up with 11 Commissioners with both investigative and adjudicative powers. These procedures offered an alternative to a planning application with a site chosen and a public local inquiry focused on the suitability of the site. Instead a more wide-ranging investigation could be undertaken reviewing a whole range of possibilities and hearing local evidence about the site in anticipation of any decision. The inquiry was able to carry out its own evaluation of air patterns and regional transport planning. Evaluating all this information and any objections provided an invaluable source of information for the Secretary of State.

However as Grant has observed[40]:   **15–068**

"But the crucial question which in fact subsequently determined that action taken by the government, was excluded from the Commission's terms of reference. It was the question of the need for the airport at all."

This suggests that there are serious weaknesses in such a format of inquiry if the main **15–069** issue does not come under the terms of reference of the inquiry. There are more serious questions raised.

The final stage in the long running saga of a third London airport has been reached **15–070** quite recently. Yet another public inquiry was held, looking into the more modest

[39] T. O'Riordan, R. Kemp, and M. Purdue, *Sizewell B: An Anatomy of the Inquiry* (1988). The inquiry was chaired by Sir Frank Layfield.
[40] M. Grant, *Urban Planning Law* (1982), p.603.

proposal that there should be a new Terminal 5 for Heathrow. The inquiry lasted four years with an estimated cost of £84 million. Its recommendation that there should be a new Terminal 5 was finally approved by the Secretary of State in November 2001. The long delays, large expense and the complexity of the inquiry format has led to concerns about the efficiency of the system of inquiries.

15–071   However as to the procedures, public participation is an important goal of the inquiry system and the use of large inquiries gives opportunities for the public to object, hear evidence and find out more information on complex issues. At the same time as the Roskill inquiry, the government introduced procedures for a Planning Inquiry Commission in the Town and Country Planning Act 1968. The arrangements consist of a two-stage process. The first stage is analogous to a Royal Commission and consists of a general investigation and only at the second stage do objections come to be considered. The Planning Inquiry Commission procedure has not been implemented, partly because it was considered unfair that having taken part in the first stage, to hear objections in the second stage might not appear to offer objectors a fair hearing. The Sizewell B inquiry, already mentioned above, was carried out under the Electric Lighting Act 1909 into the Central Electricity Generating Board's (CEGB) proposal to build a nuclear generating station at Sizewell, Suffolk. The investigation examined the merits of different types of nuclear generating stations, and assessed the British-designed steam-generated heavy-water reactors compared to the more popular American-designed Pressurised Water Reactor (PWR). The decision to recommend the building of the PWR followed after the Layfield inquiry. The Sizewell B inquiry was the longest public inquiry ever held; surprisingly the full costs of nuclear electricity only became apparent when the Government later embarked on its electricity privatisation scheme. As Nigel Lawson, for a time Energy Secretary, noted in his memoirs[41]:

> "It turned out that for years the CEGB, wittingly or unwittingly, had been making a deceptive case in favour of the economics of nuclear power that had taken in even Frank Layfield and was not finally exposed until the government was in the final stages of the privatisation of the industry in 1989, and a detailed prospectus had to be drafted."

15–072   The scale of the deception appears staggering, as the CEGB had in 1989 estimated decommissioning costs at £3.7 billion whereas in 1990 the costs were estimated to be in excess of £15 billion. The virtues of the inquiry had quickly turned into shortcomings as ministerial suspicion over the true cost of decommissioning were not satisfied until the Layfield inquiry was completed and then the decision to go ahead with the building of Sizewell B was taken without the matter being given a satisfactory analysis.

15–073   Such shortcomings in the inquiry system may be because the ultimate decision depends on political and ministerial discretion which is outside the control of any inquiry. Inquiries may be regarded as providing important techniques in the administrative system of decision-making. O'Riordan has identified some procedural techniques in use at the Layfield inquiry. The investigative nature of the proceedings was supported by the appointment of a counsel to the inquiry. This enabled evidence to be

---

[41] N. Lawson, *The View from No. 11* (1992).

sifted on behalf of the inspector and its presentation made more ordered. There was also a pre-inquiry stage to allow for the strategic planning of the inquiry. Since Sizewell, a Code of Practice has been published containing details of how a pre-inquiry meeting is to be held, should the Secretary of State require one.

The use of inquiries, albeit with some of the shortcomings mentioned above, is seen   **15–074** as an important element in allowing public participation in the administrative process. The findings of inquiries do not have to be followed as in the Vale of Belvoir inquiry where the Energy Secretary rejected the inspector's report. Doubts about inquiries have focused on the delay, expense and the postponement of decisions because of the need to consult and the requirements of inquiries. Frustration over the inquiry process may have led the government to support a hybrid Bill which became the Channel Tunnel Act 1987, to allow the building of the Channel Tunnel construction project between Britain and France. No inquiry was therefore necessary and the tunnel could be constructed without delays in the planning process. This procedure, although criticised, was more speedy and efficient than the procedures under a public inquiry but at the expense of public participation.

Current government thinking on the future of large scale inquiries is towards some   **15–075** form of reform. The Government Planning Green Paper *Planning: Delivering a Fundamental Change*[42] considered major changes to the planning system alongside a consultation paper on the new procedure for major projects. The latter envisaged a new system of parliamentary inquiry. The procedure would rest on the initiative of the Secretary of State who would ask Parliament to approve the principle of the need for a particular designated project. There would follow a draft Order and interested parties would have 42 days in which to make representations. The developer would be given 21 days to submit an environmental statement including the wider economic benefits. Following Parliamentary debate the project might go to a public inquiry on precise issues such as the nature of legal agreements, and the layout of the proposed project. The final decision would rest with the Secretary of State. The assumption would be in favour of the project and only in exceptional circumstances would there be a refusal. The problem with adopting a parliamentary procedure is that the Government currently prefers using a select committee model rather than the private Bill procedure. The latter is used for certain types of projects but may be long and is expensive involving time-consuming cross-examination by lawyers. This is precisely the main concern with the present system of public inquiry for large projects. The government is considering how best to proceed. Inevitably reforms will be forthcoming in the next year or so.

Inspectorates

Finally in the general context of tribunals and inquiries an additional technique   **15–076** adopted in administrative law for the examination of a complaint is through the use of inspection powers. Inspectorates have a history extending back into the nineteenth century such as the development of factory inspectors. A modern example is the use of inspectors to provide information on prisons through the report of the HM Chief

---

[42] HMSO, December 12, 2001.

Inspector of Prisons, or since 1987, the formation of HM Inspectorate of Pollution which, although independent from government, incorporates the industrial Air Pollution Inspectorate and the Radiochemical and Hazardous Waste Inspectorate from the Department of the Environment. Powers granted to the HM Inspectorate of Pollution under the Environmental Protection Act 1990 (now under the Environment Agency) are comprehensive, including the power to make examinations and investigations, take samples, test articles and substances found on premises and require information. Inspection along with licensing powers may provide greater sanctions for the enforcement of standards than the traditional role of fact-finding and distributing blame from the use of an inquiry.

OMBUDSMEN: LOCAL AND CENTRAL

Central Government

15–077   The system for citizens' complaints about the administration was considered in 1961 in an influential report by *Justice*.[43] Many complaints do not warrant the full-scale use of an inquiry, or indeed give rise to an action in the courts. The expense, uncertainty and the difficulty in always establishing facts may leave the ordinary citizen aggrieved and without a satisfactory remedy. An illustration of the deficiency in the system for citizens' grievances came in the *Crichel Down* case, which highlighted the difficulty of finding a suitable means of redress. Even the use of Members of Parliament may be unsatisfactory as a means of investigating and finding the facts needed to establish redress. *Crichel Down* also illustrated the sheer impossibility in many cases of establishing the exact nature of the mistake or the basis for the policy where the decision is politically sensitive and where access to information is impossible for the ordinary citizen.

15–078   The 1961 Justice report recommended the introduction of the Scandinavian idea of an officer or commissioner with investigative powers known as an ombudsman. The technique depends on the receipt of a complaint by the ombudsman who may enter government departments and inspect correspondence, discuss matters with officials and ascertain what has taken place and why.

15–079   The Parliamentary Commissioner Act 1967 established a Parliamentary Commissioner for Administration or ombudsman. Soon after, further commissioners were established including a Commissioner for Local Government, discussed below. The exact nature and jurisdiction of the ombudsman for central government may be considered.

15–080   The Parliamentary Commissioner for Administration (PCA) must be considered, not as a replacement of the parliamentary system and Ministerial accountability, but as a supplement. Thus the PCA receives complaints through M.P.s and appears before the House of Commons Select Committee on the Parliamentary Commissioner. The Chairman of that Select Committee may be consulted on the appointment of the PCA who holds office under the Crown. The PCA holds office during good behaviour, but

---

[43] Justice, *The Citizen and the Administration* (1961).

he may be removed by the Crown following addresses by both Houses of Parliament. The PCA is an *ex officio* member of the Council on Tribunals. The PCA is assisted by a staff of about 90, appointed with the approval of the Civil Service Department. Unlike the Comptroller and Auditor General, the PCA is not an officer of the House of Commons.

The PCA is likened to an agency of Parliament; the holders of the office to date have been lawyers or ex-civil servants. The appointment of a civil servant carries the advantage of someone who may understand the system from within, but the disadvantage of being perceived as too close to the body that is being investigated. The appointment of a lawyer has the advantage of bringing independent legal analysis and techniques to bear on the complainant's case and the disadvantage of an over-formalistic and legalistic approach to complaints. **15–081**

The 1967 Act gave the PCA jurisdiction over central government departments. There is a list, contained in Sch.2 to the Act, which sets out the various departments and bodies which fall within the PCA's jurisdiction. It is noteworthy that Ministers fall within the PCA's jurisdiction. Government departments include the Home Office, the Treasury, Department of Transport and Environment, Ministry of Defence, and the Foreign Office, etc. This list did not include various governmental quangos but in 1987, under the Parliamentary and Health Service Commissioners Act 1987, over 50 such bodies were included within the PCA's jurisdiction. These additions include the Arts Council, the various research councils and tourist boards. The list may be amended by Order in Council. But there are restrictions on the scope of such an Order in Council. An entry to the schedule may be inserted provided it relates to a government department whose functions are exercised by the Crown, or if it relates to a body established by a Minister, and all or some of its members are appointed by the Crown and at least half the revenue is provided by Parliament. Excluded are bodies which act in a predominantly commercial manner or a corporation carrying on an industrial undertaking under public ownership. **15–082**

Complaints have been rejected as not falling within the jurisdiction of the PCA such as against the Parole Board, local authorities, the courts, the police and nationalised industries. There is a Sch.3 list of excluded matters outside the PCA's remit of investigation. Exclusions included in the list cover matters of foreign affairs, the commencement or conduct of civil or criminal proceedings and the prerogative of mercy. Contractual and commercial relations and personnel matters are excluded as are the grant or award of honours, awards, privileges or charters. Despite criticism of the exclusion of government contractual matters from the remit of the PCA, the Government has maintained opposition to their inclusion. The main argument for their inclusion rests on the absence of practical remedies or adequate ways to investigate an individual's grievance as opposed to the departmental scrutiny offered by the National Audit Office. **15–083**

The hospital service was excluded under the 1967 Act from the jurisdiction of the PCA mainly because it was organised by local authorities. Separate provision was made under the National Health Service Reorganisation Act 1973 for the appointment of Health Service Commissioners. Direct access is allowed for complaints to the Service Commissioners whose office is held by the PCA. The complaint must be made by the person aggrieved or in certain circumstance where he is unable to make a complaint, by a member of the same family or representative appointed for the **15–084** purpose. Health Service Commissioners may investigate any alleged failure in a service provided by the authority, or a failure in a service provided on its behalf or other action it may have taken. The complainant must show that injustice or hardship resulted from any alleged failure in the service taken by the Authority or taken on its behalf. In respect of any other action taken by the Authority, maladministration must be shown. The precise meaning of this term is discussed below.

15–085   Finally, the National Health Service Commissioner reports to the Secretary of State, rather than to Parliament as is the case with the PCA. The Health Service Commissioners Act 1993 is a consolidation of the law relating to the Health Service Commissioners. The Act is intended to facilitate consultation between the Health Service Commissioners and other Commissioners including the Local Commissioners for Administration. The Health Service Commissioners remain empowered to examine complaints made directly to them. Complaints that may be considered are those that relate to maladministration, failure in the provision of a service to be provided by a health service body. The complaints may relate to delays in admission to hospital, a failure to indicate that patients may refuse to be examined in front of medical students and inadequate or illegible medical notes. However there remains no jurisdiction to investigate matters solely from the exercise of clinical judgment.

15–086   The Health Service Commissioners (Amendment) Act 2000, which began life as a Private Member's Bill, extends the jurisdiction of the Health Service Commissioners to investigate complaints against doctors, and other health service providers. The list includes pharmacists, dentists, and ophthalmic surgeons. A loophole is closed by the Act which in the past allowed doctors and other health care workers to avoid investigation after they retired from the National Health Service.

15–087   Provided the body to be investigated falls within the PCA's jurisdiction then an investigation may be undertaken but it is assumed that the investigation may only concern the administrative functions of the department. This appears to exclude the department's legislative role, although the interpretation of legislation falls within the remit of an administrative function. Also excluded might be any judicial function of a department, as tribunals and courts are outside the jurisdiction of the PCA. However, after considerable debate s.110 of the Courts and Legal Services Act 1990 provides that administrative functions undertaken by staff of courts or tribunals appointed by the Lord Chancellor, shall be deemed to fall within the remit of the Lord Chancellor's department and therefore fall within the jurisdiction of the PCA. Remaining outside the PCA's jurisdiction will be action taken under the direction or authority of a person acting in a judicial capacity.

15–088   The PCA is not a substitute for legal action in the courts, or the remedies available through a tribunal. Where the complainant has a right of appeal or remedy in law it is not normal for the PCA to investigate. However a proviso to the 1967 Act in s.5(2) may permit an investigation if the PCA is satisfied that in the particular circumstances it is not reasonable to expect the right or remedy to be investigated or invoked. It is possible therefore to see the PCA as an alternative to the courts but it may be the case that an overlapping jurisdiction is required. In *Congreve v Home Office*[44] a complaint to the PCA was accompanied by legal redress through the courts which eventually was granted by the Court of Appeal in the matter of overlapping television licences. This

[44] [1976] Q.B. 629.

appears an unusual case as the PCA may have doubted, until the Court of Appeal decision was made, that the complainant had a legal remedy and had this been clear in the first instance may not have felt able to offer an investigation.

In the leading case, *R. v Inland Revenue Commissioners Ex p. National Federation of Self-Employed and Small Businesses Ltd*,[45] on the rules of standing in administrative law, the House of Lords considered the boundaries between maladministration and legality. Lord Roskill considered "that there was an important boundary between administration whether good or bad which is lawful and what is unlawful performance of a statutory duty". Injustices caused by maladministration fell within the remit of the Ombudsman while illegality and its consequences fell within the review power of the courts. It is possible to have a complaint that raises both issues about legality and maladministration. As the courts are the most suitable means for redress the Ombudsman may decline to investigate. Most likely the question of whether to accept jurisdiction is for the Ombudsman's discretion. **11–088a**

A complainant must have "sustained injustice in consequence of maladministration". The term maladministration is not defined in the 1967 Act but in the debate on the second reading of the 1967 Bill, Richard Crossman explained that maladministration[46] "might include bias, neglect, inattention, delay, incompetence, ineptitude, perversity, turpitude, arbitrariness and so on." The word injustice was used in the legislation in preference to "loss or damage" which might be construed with legal overtones too restrictive to the spirit of the legislation. **15–089**

The PCA is not entitled to question the merits of the policy of a "decision taken without maladministration" under s.12(3) of the 1967 Act. This is a difficult section to interpret, and at one time was given a restrictive meaning that the quality of discretionary decisions could not be questioned even when it was shown that they contained bias or perversity. However after prompting from the Select Committee, the PCA was willing to criticise decisions which were bad on their merits. **15–090**

Studies of the meaning given to the term maladministration have indicated that drawing any useful distinction between merits and maladministration is pointless. The lack of merits is surely grounds for maladministration? Reform proposals made in 1977 by Justice said that[47] "maladministration" might be replaced by "unreasonable, unjust, or oppressive action" by government departments. This proposal was rejected[48] by the Select Committee on the PCA and later in 1988 the Justice All Souls report declined to make any recommendation for change. **15–091**

Complaints received by the PCA each year are on average approximately 700, though there was a significant increase in 1991 bringing the total for that year to over 800. The procedure of referring the complaint through a Member of Parliament, a requirement of the current law, has been subject to much debate and criticism. In theory the addition of this requirement keeps in place the principle of ministerial responsibility to Parliament by linking the investigation of complaints to the role of the M.P. The number of M.P.s who refer complaints each year stands at around 400. The PCA receives just as many direct complaints as from M.P.s. In practice the complainant may be referred back to his or her M.P. by the PCA and the complaint is then **15–092**

---

[45] [1982] A.C. 617 at 663 C–E.
[46] Hansard HC Deb, Ser.5, 734 col.42.
[47] (1967–68 HC 350), para.36. G. Marshall, "Maladministration" [1973] *P.L.* 32.
[48] *Review of Access and Jurisdiction* (1977–78 HC 615).

correctly made through the M.P. Nevertheless the use of the M.P. filter is seen as a curtailment in the role of the PCA and perhaps the office is unduly inhibited from developing its full potential. On the other hand the concern is that the removal of the M.P. filter might cause the PCA's workload to expand to an unacceptably high level. The removal of the M.P. filter is recommended in a recent Cabinet Office Review of the ombudsman discussed below.

15–093   The debate on access raises fundamental questions about the role of the PCA. The procedures adopted by the PCA are investigative and targeted on individual case files and this is costly and time-consuming. Presently it is estimated that the average time taken by the PCA is over 15 months to complete an investigation. Is such an investigative system capable of handling very large numbers of complaints? How far could an expanded role be met by the necessary expertise and resources? Only when both these questions are satisfactorily answered will the role of the PCA be adequately considered.

15–094   There is no rule that the complainant must be a British citizen but there is under s.6(4) of the 1967 Act a requirement of residence. There is also a time-limit. S.6(3) provides that the PCA must be informed of the complaint within 12 months from the date when the citizen had notice of the matter complained of. Special circumstance may permit an extension of time.

15–095   The PCA in carrying out its investigation may hold formal hearings and allow legal representation in the course of the investigation. S.8 of the 1967 Act allows access to official documents and papers and the PCA's powers are analogous to those of the High Court. A limitation is provided under s.8(4) which permits the issuing of a certificate of immunity in respect of Cabinet papers issued by the Secretary to the Cabinet.

15–096   The remedies available to the PCA are first under s.10 of the 1967 Act to make a report which is normally sent to the M.P. who raised the complaint. A copy of the report is sent to the principal officer of the department concerned. An annual report is prepared by the PCA and laid before Parliament. That report details the PCA's activities for the year. In detailing his findings, departments are subject to scrutiny by Parliament and this provides a major source of the PCA's influence. Departments may conform to his recommendations under threat of an adverse report. Under s.10(3) of the 1967 Act, the PCA may lay a special report before Parliament giving details of the complaint, attempts to resolve it and the outcome. Secondly, the PCA operates through negotiation and conciliation. There are no formal powers to enforce the PCA's decision. Thus a department in the legal sense cannot be compelled to pay money, to take action or to refrain from a particular practice. However departments may make administrative changes as a result of the findings of the PCA; the Driving and Vehicle Licensing Centre introduced changes to deal with delays for applicants for driving licences.[49]

15–097   The co-operation necessary for the PCA to gain access and a working relationship with the department concerned may make it difficult to give the PCA sanctions with an enforcement power. The PCA depends on negotiation and following the exposure of maladministration it is hoped will give rise to a remedy. The PCA has succeeded in

[49] See Gregory, "The Select Committee on the Parliamentary Commissioner for Administration 1967–80" [1982] *P.L.* 49–88.

gaining financial settlements for the citizen in a variety of tax cases where repayment was made by the department concerned. In the *Sachsenhausen* case the PCA criticised decisions made by Ministers not to allow compensation to be payable to the victims of Nazi atrocities applying the rules laid down by the then Foreign secretary R.A. Butler, that compensation was only payable to those detained in concentration camps or equivalent conditions.[50] This led to compensation payable as a result of the PCA's intervention. The Barlow Clowes Affair investigation in 1988 conducted by the Ombudsman did lead "99 per cent. of investors to receive at least 85 per cent. of their capital" and came about through the findings of the PCA's investigation.

However there are grounds for concern that perhaps such examples reflect an increasing problem of finding maladministration. In the first few years after 1967 only 10 per cent of cases investigated resulted in such a finding being made. In the 1970s this increased to about 30 per cent and in the 1980s 40 per cent. In the mid–1980s about 75 complaints annually are found to show maladministration. The main departments concerned are Social Security and the Inland Revenue.   **15–098**

An important development in the PCA's role is the growth in recent years of case studies containing advice on administrative practices. Potentially this may create the most significant contribution of the Ombudsman system. Through this means the individual complainant receives the benefit of the PCA's interpretation of the rules, and the existence of principles within government departments. This provides a blend of external scrutiny and internal review; fact-finding through investigation combined with administrative guidance.   **15–099**

The attraction of using the PCA for the citizen is that the costs are borne by the PCA, not by the complainant, and the investigative role of the PCA may be crucial where there are no other remedies available for redress. An assessment of the effectiveness of the PCA is a mixed one. While the PCA has shortcomings there are sufficient successes to suggest that the PCA has made a worthwhile contribution in providing citizens redress where before none existed. Recently the Prime Minister is said to have blocked the release of information agreed by the Ombudsman in a case concerning the deputy Prime Minister after a complaint was made to the Ombudsman when a citizen was refused information on how many conflicts of interest had been disclosed by ministers. The information was released from many government departments with the exception of Mr Prescott's.[51]   **15–100**

The techniques of the PCA have proved valuable and have been copied in a wide variety of areas in the private sector including insurance, newspapers, building societies and banking. A more difficult question is the value of the investigative techniques employed by the PCA. As a contrast to the adversarial style of courts, are the PCA's inquisitorial powers more effective in finding facts and evaluating behaviour? Has the PCA encouraged good administration and affected the existing culture within government departments?   **15–101**

The PCA is susceptible to judicial review[52] and must comply with the Human Rights Act 1998. However the courts are reluctant to intervene when the PCA acts in   **15–102**

---

[50] The PCA was influential in obtaining changes to the 1974 and 1975 Finance Acts for the repayment of interest for delayed tax repayments.
Third Report of the Parliamentary Commissioner 1967–68. The report was debated February 5, 1968; *Hansard*, HC Vol.5, col.108.
[51] *The Guardian*, July 27, 2002.
[52] *R. v Parliamentary Comr Ex p. Dyer* [1994] 1 All E.R. 375. N. Marsh, "The Extent and Depth of Judicial Review of the Decisions of the Parliamentary Commissioner for Administration" (1994) *Public Law* 347–50.

accordance with his own discretion whether to initiate, continue or discontinue an investigation (s.5(5) of the 1967 Act) or decide the procedures to be adopted in any investigation (s.7(2) of the 1967 Act).

Local Commissioners for Administration

15–103   Redress of citizens' grievances in local government is provided by the appointment of Local Commissioners for Administration under the Local Government Act 1974 following the influential Justice report in 1969 on the creation of a local government ombudsman. There are three Local Commissioners for Administration for England and one for Wales under two separate Commissions, one for England and the other for Wales. The Local Government Commissioner (LGC) does not act under the same constitutional relationship as the PCA does for central government, who is acting through ministerial responsibility and complaints through the complainant's M.P.

15–104   The jurisdiction of the LGC is similar to the 1967 Act and the PCA, and the powers of investigation are the same as the PCA. The LGC may investigate complaints where a member of the public has "sustained injustice in consequence of maladministration." The number of complaints has steadily increased over the years. In 1983–84 there were approximately 3,000 complaints but in 1990–91 the number had increased to over 9,000. Originally there was a councillor filter equivalent to the M.P. filter for the PCA discussed above. The Widdicombe Report[53] recommended and the Government accepted the desirability of allowing direct access and this was granted under the Local Government Act 1988. In terms of jurisdiction, in common with the PCA the LGC may not inquire into contractual or commercial matters. The Widdicombe Committee recommended reform to allow these areas to be investigated but this was not implemented by the Government. The Widdicombe Report also favoured the LGC to be given powers to initiate investigations on their own behalf but this was also rejected. The Government was concerned that if such powers were given the LGC might have problems in their relations with local authorities. However, under procedures introduced by the Local Government and Housing Act 1989, the LGC may issue codes of practice on good administrative procedures for local authorities. In particular, s.31 of the 1989 Act allows the Secretary of State to publish a code to be laid and approved by a resolution of each House of Parliament.

15–105   Maladministration is interpreted by the LGC in a similar way to the PCA. In *R. v Local Commissioner for Administration for the North and East Area of England Ex p. Bradford Metropolitan City Council*,[54] Lord Denning considered that the LGC is concerned in matters of maladministration, with the manner in which decisions are reached and the manner in which they may or may not be implemented. The nature, quality and reasonableness of the decision are not part of the LGC remit. The subject matter of investigations conducted by the LGC covers a wide cross-section of local authority activities; housing, planning and education comprise a large proportion of the case-load of the LGC. Ss.266–269 and Sch.16 of the 1993 Education Act extend the LGC's remit to appeal committees in grant-maintained schools. Complaints are made within 12 months from the day the complainant has notice of the matter complained of, although there is a discretion to investigate complaints out of time.

[53] Cm.9797 (1986).
[54] [1979] Q.B. 287.

A Commission may not investigate a complaint which affects all or nearly all of the   **15–106**
inhabitants of a local authority. Complaints about public passenger transport and the
internal management of local authority schools are also excluded from this jurisdiction.

The remedies offered by the LGC comprise, first, a report of the investigation   **15–107**
showing maladministration is made available for public inspection for three weeks. If
the local authority fails to take account of the report, the LGC may make a further
report. Secondly, the LGC having made a report and attempted to persuade the local
authority to comply with the terms of the report, the local authority is, under s.26 of
the Local Government and Housing Act 1989, under a duty to consider the LGC's
report and must within three months respond to it. A further report may be made by
the LGC and if the local authority does not take satisfactory action, the report may be
published in a local newspaper with the local authority's reasons for not implementing
the report.

The LGC is unable to take any further action to enforce its report. Unlike the PCA   **15–108**
who has recourse to the House of Commons, there is no satisfactory equivalent for the
LGC, although under s.5 of the Local Government and Housing Act 1989, a local
authority must appoint a monitoring officer to report on findings of maladministration.

Despite strong advice to the Widdicombe Committee in favour of giving the LGC   **15–109**
power to seek judicial review, this was not favoured by the Committee in its report.
Instead the Widdicombe Report recommended that following an adverse report in
favour of the complainant, the complainant should be able to go to the County Court
for a remedy.

Compared to the Audit Commission, the LGC has less proactive powers to seek   **15–110**
enforcement for its findings. This may indicate that the role of the LGC is a more
difficult one, as the experience of non-enforcement of the LGC reports by some local
authorities may indicate. Legal powers to enforce the LGC findings may be counterproductive and give rise to disputes between local authorities and the LGC in the
courts.

The possibility for judicial review of the LGC's findings was envisaged when the   **15–111**
1974 Act was debated in the House of Commons. A number of challenges to the
jurisdiction of the LGC have resulted in judicial scrutiny, of the powers of the LGC.
These decisions have focused on the role of the LGC. The first is *R. v Local
Commissioner for Administration for the South Ex p. Eastleigh B.C.*[55] After a complaint
to the LGC from a householder that Eastleigh B.C. failed to properly inspect sewers in
accordance with the Building Regulations 1976,[55a] the LGC found maladministration
and that the householder had suffered maladministration. However the LGC accepted
that even if the inspection of the sewers had been carried out diligently it was unclear
that the defects would have been spotted. Consequently Eastleigh should pay only part
of the costs of any remedial action. Eastleigh B.C. sought judicial review. Lord
Donaldson in the Court of Appeal reinforced the earlier observations of Lord
Denning[56] when he distinguished between the merits or reasonableness of a decision of
a local authority and the means adopted by the local authority. The Court of Appeal
accepted the legality of the LGC's report but granted Eastleigh B.C. a declaration on
the basis that the LGC's report did not justify his findings.

[55] [1988] Q.B. 855.
[55a] Now see: Town and Country Planning (General Permitted Development) Order 1995 (SI 1995/418).
[56] [1979] Q.B. 287.

15–112   Lord Donaldson considered judicial review of the LGC's reports as unusual and "unlikely to succeed". Soon after *Eastleigh*, Woolf L.J. in the High Court found that a report made in 1986 by the LGC in *R. v Commissioner for Local Administration Ex p. Croydon LBC*[57] was *ultra vires*. The case arose out of an unsuccessful appeal by parents against the decision of Croydon LBC as to the school their daughter should attend. The appeal was heard by the Education Appeal Committee established by Croydon. The LGC investigated a complaint by the parents about the outcome of the appeal. The LGC found maladaministration in the way the Appeal Committee gave weight to Croydon's policy on education. The Council sought judicial review of the LGC's investigation. In holding that the LGC acted *ultra vires*, several grounds for review were considered. First, that the possibility of legal action by the parents should have been considered by the LGC throughout his investigation, and this might have resulted in the LGC declining jurisdiction in the matter. Secondly, the Appeal Committee had evaluated the evidence and based its decision on the merits of the case. The LGC had no grounds for finding maladministration in such circumstances.

15–113   One of the difficult issues raised in the case is the suitability of using the courts compared to the LGC. Lord Justice Woolf concluded that the courts were more appropriate in cases such as the *Croydon* case where the issues demanded an understanding of the relevant law and legal obligations. The preference for using the courts for legal disputes is important in clarifying the jurisdiction of the LGC, even though it is unclear where the boundaries may be set.

15–114   There have been other cases. In *R. v Lambeth BC Ex p. Crookes*[58] it was considered that a complaint of maladministration might be made before a challenge involving procedural irregularity. This fits with the idea that judicial review should be the mechanism of last resort as explained in *R. v Hammersmith and Fulham LBC Ex p. Burkett*.[59] Maladministration will rarely provide the grounds for judicial review as a form of redress. However, this does not preclude judicial review being used nor should the availability of judicial review prevent a complaint of maladministration.[60] One possible solution is for the LGC or the PCA to refer matters to the High Court when legal issues arise in the course of their investigation.

15–115   The *Croydon* case firmly establishes the principle that the LGC's reports are subject to judicial review. In both cases of *Eastleigh* and *Croydon* the courts appear to deal with the review of the LGC's powers rather than reviewing the exercise of the LGC's discretion. However in *Ex p. Dyer* in the Divisional Court, Lord Justice Simon Brown concluded that judicial review is available to review the LGC's discretion. This result may not be entirely satisfactory. The threat of judicial review, however rare, may inhibit the working of the LGC when confronted by local authorities prepared to use the courts to challenge the LGC's decisions. This may have the unfortunate consequence of damaging the standing and investigative functions of the LGC and the citizen may be less certain of having a grievance remedied. The likelihood of many cases being challenged in the courts is small; nevertheless, the LGC must take account of the possibility of judicial review when writing their reports.

---

[57] [1989] 1 All E.R. 1033.
[58] [1997] 29 H.L.R. 28.
[59] [2001] Env. L.R. 684.
[60] *R. v Local Commissioner for Administration in North and North East England Ex p. Liverpool City Council* [2001] 1 All E.R. 462 and *R. v Local Commissioner for Administration Ex p. H.* [1999] C.O.D. 382.

An assessment of the value of the LGC has been conducted in a number of studies **15–116** with favourable results. The quality and scope of investigations are of a high standard. The investigations are based on individual complaints and the extent to which local authorities can learn from the various case studies of individual complaints. The question arises as to whether the reports of the LGCs may lead to better administration within local authorities. There is a question of co-ordinating complaints mechanisms within local authorities. The Widdicombe Committee heard evidence of the extensive system of internal complaints procedures within local authorities. Is there a case for greater co-ordination of the work of the LGC with the internal system of complaints resolution within local authorities?

The European Ombudsman

The European Parliament may appoint an Ombudsman under EC Article 195 (ex. **15–117** Article 138e) to receive complaints of instances of maladministration against the activities of the Community institutions or bodies. The European Ombudsman[61] was established in July 1995 and has an establishment of 16 including five legal officers. Although based in Strasbourg there is an office in Brussels from February 1997. Since its inception there have been over 1,000 complaints. There have been a large number arising out of the French nuclear tests in the Pacific. The limitations on the remit of the European Ombudsman are that his jurisdiction does not extend to allegations against national governments of the Member States. However, it is possible for him to initiate complaints himself and he may gain the co-operation of Community institutions in pursuing his investigations. The Ombudsman may act on his own initiative or may receive complaints directly through an M.E.P. The remit is confined to maladministration of Community institutions and there are formal Rules of Procedure that govern how he may carry out his tasks. The Ombudsman may be dismissed by the Court of Justice at the request of the European Parliament.

The Citizen's Charter

Citizens with specific grievances arising out of public services may find that the **15–118** Citizen's Charter provides redress for complaints. The Citizen's Charter is focused on how public services are delivered and managed. In that sense the aim is to provide such economy, efficiency and effectiveness in the high quality of services that complaints will become a means to ensure standards as well as dealing with the grievances of the citizen. This approach is consumer-orientated, and extends complaints mechanisms and the right to redress when services fall below certain targets. It also raises expectations and by suggesting "rights" rather than remedies, reverses the tradition in English law which focuses on remedies.

The Citizen's Charter sets high expectations and provides well-publicised complaints **15–119** procedures, some based entirely on contractual rights, others enforced through

---

[61] The current post holder is Jakob Soderman from Finland. The author is grateful to Professor Ian Harden, the European Ombudsman's Principal Officer, for all his help and advice and for much of the information on the European Ombudsman. Views expressed are the author's.

standards set by legislation such as the Competition and Service (Utilities) Act 1992 in respect of the main utilities such as water, gas, electricity and telecommunications. Support for quality standards comes through the award of performance related targets for each service. Accreditation through the standard of the British Standards Institute is common as many local authorities require accreditation to BS 5750 as a contract condition. Competitive tendering is another element in ensuring contract compliance with the standards expected from the Charter. Compensation paid to the customer when the quality of a service falls below a certain standard, is another means to ensure better standards.

15–120   The aim of the Citizen's Charter is "to give more power to the people". Information, accessibility, openness and standards are involved in the Charter's techniques to provide the citizen with a benchmark to gauge the quality of the services provided. Potentially the Citizen's Charter may have far-reaching effects on the public's perception about complaints and their resolution. This remains to be seen. Incrementally the Citizen's Charter may have a wider effect on the procedures for the resolution of grievances within the United Kingdom, than was envisaged or perhaps originally intended. In the current run-up to enactment of a modern Bill of Rights, the Citizen's Charter is a first step in a direction for change that has heralded an emphasis in rights in the United Kingdom.

Reforming the Ombudsman System

15–121   A review of the role and organisation of the central and local government system together with the Health Service Commissioner was carried out by the Cabinet Office[62] as part of the Modernising Government[63] strategy. Its findings called for a more coherent and fused system of ombudsmen. Recommendations include removing the M.P. filter for the central government ombudsmen, re-modelling the ombudsman system to take account of the changes in the way government is conducted and improvements in streamlining the legislation. A single commission involving all three ombudsmen might be more focused with a coherent set of priorities and working practices. Greater emphasis is recommended to be given to the process of informal adjudication and a less confrontational style in favour of a more conciliatory approach. The idea of setting up partnerships with a community-based focus on the Community Legal Service and the Community Health Councils is aimed at providing citizens with a more holistic approach to complaints. The organisation of the Commission should also reflect more community-based representation. The outcome is intended to align the ombudsman system with the new public management style of governance. One interesting idea is that the proposed new Commission might be able to refer a matter raising an issue of law to the courts for legal consideration.

SUMMARY AND CONCLUSIONS

15–122   The plethora of systems for dealing with citizens' complaints has developed on an ad hoc basis. Modernisation of the system of tribunals and the use of large public inquiries is being considered by the government. Reform proposals for the system of

---

[62] P. Collcutt and M. Hourihan, *Review of the Public Sector Ombudsman in England* (Cabinet Office, London, 2000).
[63] *Modernising Government*, Cm.4310 (1999).

public sector ombudsman also illustrate how change and modernisation are being considered. The importance of providing alternatives to the courts is at the heart of the system of grievance procedures. The compelling idea is that the courts are not always suitable for dealing with citizens' grievances and the diversity of the system of tribunals is an example of how valuable the alternatives appear to be.

Further Reading

Citizen's Charter Complaints Taskforce, *Service First How to Deal with Complaints* London: (Cabinet Office, London, 1998).

C. Harlow and R. Rawlings, *Law and Administration* (2nd ed., Butterworths, London, 1997).

Justice, The Citizen and the Administration: The Redress of Grievances (The Whyatt Report), (Stevens, London, 1961).

B. Thompson "Integrated Ombudsmanry: Joined-up to a Point" (2001) *MLR* 459.

Chapter 16

HUMAN RIGHTS AND CIVIL LIBERTIES

INTRODUCTION

The subject of this chapter is the citizen and civil liberties. For many centuries the protection of civil liberties in the United Kingdom formed "a patchwork", rather than a coherent code of rights. Freedoms were perceived in terms of remedies enforceable through the courts. Rights were intended as a specific protection granted to a minority or as a response to a specific set of problems or to remedy an injustice. There was also a perception that civil liberties were better protected through the development of institutions rather than the enforcement of written fundamental rights. It was widely believed that institutions under parliamentary authority, including Parliament, would provide adequate protection. It was assumed that the courts, through the development of remedies for individual cases, were more likely to protect the liberty of the citizen than reliance on written documents that may become worthless if not supported by the institutions of the Constitution. In a broader sense there is acknowledgment that "political and social pressures" may be more effective in protecting liberty than purely legal rights. Many of these perceptions remain today, including concerns that by enacting the Human Rights Act 1998 judges are placed in the unenviable position of having the final say as to whether or not rights have been infringed.

16–001

The Labour Government fulfilled its manifesto promise by enacting the Human Rights Act 1998 which came into force in October 2000 in England and Wales, a far-reaching major constitutional change. The Act makes Convention rights under the European Convention on Human Rights available to citizens in the United Kingdom.

16–002

The Human Rights Act 1998 creates opportunities for the development of a new culture of rights in the United Kingdom at an important stage in the development of constitutional change and reform. Debates about human rights are truly global in scale[1] and significance. The United Kingdom joins Canada (1982) and New Zealand (1990) in having recently introduced a new Bill of Rights. The growing importance of rights in countries with new constitutions is seen in South Africa and the countries that have emerged from the old Soviet Union. As already noted, the European Union (EU) is considering a new Charter of Rights. The movement in favour of a positive rights approach creates added responsibilities on the judiciary. This also comes about from creating the jurisdiction of the International Criminal Court,[2] and ensures that the

16–003

[1] Foreign and Commonwealth Office Annual Report, *Human Rights*, Cm.5211 (September, 2001).
[2] Agreed in Rome July 15 and 17, 1998. Also see Preparatory Commission for the International Criminal Court, June 30, 2000.

judges play a significant role in the protection of human rights at national and international levels.

THE HUMAN RIGHTS ACT 1998

The Method of Incorporation of the European Convention on Human Rights

16–004 The United Kingdom was the first Government among the member countries of the Council of Europe to ratify the European Convention on Human Rights (ECHR) in 1951. The Convention was itself drafted with the aid of British lawyers and it adopts an English style of drafting commonly found among legal draftsmen of the time. As a result many of the Articles are broadly defined in terms of freedoms that are for the most part negatively expressed. In 1966 the Government accepted the right of individual petition under the European Convention. In the past the reluctance to embrace full integration of the Convention into domestic law came from a profound belief that Parliament and the rule of law would secure the protection of rights unaided by the Convention. In the past successive governments were consistent in their scepticism about rights, fearing that to incorporate the Convention would transfer to the courts overarching powers that would usurp Parliament's authority. The tide in favour of incorporating the Convention turned gradually and perceptibly. The House of Lords Select Committee on a Bill of Rights in 1978 recommended in favour of incorporation.[3] A year earlier the Standing Advisory Commission on Human Rights recommended a Bill of Rights for Northern Ireland. Support for a Bill of Rights has emerged from a variety of different groups and prominent individuals, particularly senior members of the judiciary.[4]

16–005 The Human Rights Act 1998 came into force on October 2, 2000 in England and Wales. The Act requires courts to apply most[5] of the European Convention on Human Rights as Convention rights within the legal system. For the first time this provides the citizen with Convention rights directly available in domestic legal proceedings against public authorities. As noted in previous chapters, this marks a major constitutional change in the United Kingdom as there has previously been no comparable legislation on human rights in domestic law. The Act fits the overall modernisation strategy of the Government. The period leading up to the Act coming into force provided an opportunity for preparation.

---

[3] *Legislation on Human Rights with Particular Reference to the European Convention: A Discussion Document* (HMSO, 1976). See Lester *et al.*, *A British Bill of Rights Constitution Paper No.1* (Institute of Public Policy Research, 1990), pp.16–18. *Report of the House of Lords Select Committee on a Bill of Rights* (1978).

[4] Scarman, *English Law—the New Dimension* (1974), Sir John Laws, "Is the High Court the Guardian of Fundamental Constitutional Rights" (1993) *Public Law* 63; Sir John Laws, "Judicial Remedies and the Constitution" (1994) 57 *Modern Law Review* 213; Sir S. Sedley, "The Sound of Silence: Constitutional Lawyers without a Constitution" (1994) 110 *Law Quarterly Review* 270; Lord Taylor, Richard Dimbleby Lecture: The Judiciary in the Nineties (BBC Education, 1992); Sir H. Woolf, *Protection of the Public—A New Challenge* (Stevens, London, 1992); Sir H. Woolf, "Judicial review: A possible programme for reform" (1992) *Public Law* 221; Sir K. Schiemann, "Locus Standi" (1990) *Public Law* 342; Lord Scarman, "The Development of Administrative Law: Obstacles and Opportunities" (1990) *Public Law* 490.

[5] Article 13 of the Convention which guarantees anyone an effective remedy does not apply under the Human Rights Act 1998.

In an unprecedented way judicial training was undertaken at all levels of the legal   **16–006**
system. Public authorities undertook a review of procedures and practices to ensure
compliance with the Act.

S.3 of the Act provides that the courts will be required to uphold Convention rights   **16–007**
unless the legislation is so clearly incompatible with the Convention that it is
impossible to do so. This means that when interpreting primary or secondary
legislation it must be read in a way that "so far as it is possible to do so" it is
compatible with Convention rights. S.4 of the Act provides that when s.3 has been
applied if it is the case that the provision is incompatible with a Convention right, then
the superior courts have a power to make a declaration of incompatibility. In so doing
the Human Rights Act 1998 is consistent with the traditions of Parliamentary
sovereignty and there are no powers under the Act to strike down legislation for
incompatibility. It was hoped that the formulation of the Act in this way would avoid
the implications of the European Communities Act 1972 and the impact of the
Factortame[6] decision. This may not prevail as it is not unlikely that Convention rights
will be given legal authority were the EU to incorporate the ECHR. S.10 of the
Human Rights Act is consistent in attempting to uphold Parliamentary sovereignty
through the powers of amendment where there has been a holding that a provision is
incompatible. The relevant minister is given powers under s.10 of the Act to amend the
legislation that the courts have considered is incompatible by remedial order. There is
no mandatory legal requirement to introduce a remedial order. Sched.2 of the Act
provides that a remedial order may only be made if there are "compelling" reasons.
There is a special fast-track procedure laid down for remedial orders involving a
timetable for the order to be laid in draft before Parliament for 60 days. The Draft
Order must include an approved explanatory statement by the Commons and Lords.
Only in an urgent case can the requirement of the draft be waived and this is subject to
approval by joint resolution of both Commons and Lords.

It is expected that Bills prepared after the Human Rights Act came into force will be   **16–008**
compatible with the Act. S.19 of the Act provides that the relevant minister should
provide a statement of compatibility before the second reading of the Bill. In the event
that this is not possible then a statement to this effect is also possible under s.19.
Parliament is free to enact legislation where the implications are that there is
incompatibility. The Human Rights Act is not entrenched and so it may be amended
by subsequent legislation. In common with there being no mandatory requirement to
introduce a remedial order, there remains scope for ministers and parliament to have
the final say. While there is a mandatory duty on the courts to give effect to
Convention rights, as far as it is practicable, the jurisprudence of the European Court
of Human Rights at Strasbourg is highly authoritative, but it is not judicially binding. It
might be possible to depart from a Strasbourg decision but this is likely to be unusual.
It is also thought unlikely for legislation to be passed to amend the Human Rights Act
1998 or for the courts to find many instances where a declaration of incompatibility is
required. In the first 18 months of the Act coming into force there have only been
three cases where a declaration of incompatibility[7] has been given. There is a fourth
case pending decision.

[6] [1990] 2 A.C. 85.
[7] See *R. (on the application of Alconbury Developments Ltd) v Secretary of State for the Environment,
Transport and the Regions* [2001] 2 W.L.R. 1389; *Wilson v First County Trust Ltd* [2001] 3 All E.R. 229; *R. (on
the application of H) v North and East Region Mental Health Review Tribunal* [2001] 3 W.L.R. 512.

Legal Proceedings Under the Act

16–009   S.6 of the Human Rights Act 1998 stipulates that it is unlawful for a public authority to act in a way that is incompatible with a Convention right. The term public authority is ambiguous and this opens up the question of whether the Human Rights Act applies in litigation between private parties or to a dispute outside the confines of public law. This question has been put in terms of whether the Act is intended to have vertical or horizontal effect. The wider horizontal effect is favoured by Professor Sir William Wade.[8] On the other hand the narrower vertical effect is supported by arguing that the Act is intended to bring public authorities under Convention rights and that such rights have rarely if ever been applied to situations involving private rights alone. Indeed the terms vertical and horizontal may be unhelpful and fail to address the question of the scope of the Act. This is a question of great debate[9] and will ultimately depend upon the courts. A public authority is defined by the Act to include a court or tribunal. In private litigation it could be argued that the court or tribunal as a public body is itself required to apply the Convention. This interpretation considerably broadens the potential scope of the application of Convention rights under the Human Rights Act. Lord Justice Sedley considered how the common law might be interpreted in discussing the scope of any potential law on privacy when applying the Human Rights Act in *Douglas v Hello! Ltd*.[10] In *Venables v News Group Newspapers*[11] it was noted that the court as a public authority was obliged to act in a way that is compatible with Convention rights when adjudicating a common law cause of action.

16–010   A public authority is not liable in legal proceedings if it can be shown that there is a statutory requirement upon it to act in the way it has. It would therefore be open to the court to consider the statutory requirement as to whether it may be made compatible or to issue a declaration of incompatibility. Proceedings for a person who claims a human rights infringement or breach of the Convention may be by way of appeal or judicial review. S.7 provides that proceedings should be brought within one year. The person must satisfy the "victim" test for the purposes of Article 34 of the Convention. This is the same test of standing that applies before the European Court of Human Rights. It is generally agreed that the "victim" test is narrower and more restrictive than the more liberal rules of standing in the United Kingdom that a claimant has to overcome for judicial review.[12] Pressure groups appear precluded from taking proceedings under the victim test but they would not be precluded by the rules of standing for judicial review.

16–011   S.8 of the Human Rights Act provides a general remedial discretion to a court or tribunal which finds that a public authority has acted unlawfully under s.6. The Act does not create any new powers; the remedial discretion is one the court or tribunal must act on according to law. Damages may be awarded but consistent with the jurisprudence of the ECHR.

---

[8] Sir William Wade, "Human Rights and the Judiciary" *European Human Rights Law Review* (1998) 520.
[9] Buxton, L.J. "The Human Rights Act and Private law" (2000) 116 *LQR* 48.
[10] [2001] 2 W.L.R. 992 at [129].
[11] [2001] 2 W.L.R. 1038.
[12] See Chap.18. Mark Elliott, "The Human Rights Act 1998 and the Standard of Substantive Review" [2001] *Cambridge Law Journal* 301. See: *D.G. of Financial Trading v Proprietary Association of Great Britain* [2001] UKHR 429.

Concerns were expressed during the passage of the Act about the extension of the **16–012** Act to the mass media and to religious groups. S.12 accords the media special protections, most notably in warning if an injunction is likely to be made, but also the court is expected to give particular attention to the balance between personal protection and privacy. S.13 of the Act provides that the court must take account of religious freedoms and when applying Convention rights give effect to that freedom. The Church of England appears uniquely to qualify as a public authority and may fall within the protection of s.13. It is doubtful if other churches are in a similar position. The way the Act is to be interpreted will largely determine its scope and importance. As noted in previous chapters the courts have taken a cautious, restrictive interpretation preparing the way on a case-by-case basis to develop Convention rights into the existing public law culture.

Early indications of how the Act is to be interpreted come from some recent **16–013** decisions. In *R. v Lambert*[13] it was held that the Human Rights Act did not have retrospective effect. There has been significant progress in determining the full impact of Article 6 (right to a fair trial) in cases involving the use of temporary sheriffs in Scotland,[14] and in procedures for Mental Health Tribunals.[15]

Significantly, an applicant for planning permission has a right of appeal to the **16–014** Secretary of State against any refusal or condition of planning permission. The Secretary of State is part of the planning process and hears appeals on the main issues of planning applications. When considering such appeals the Secretary of State may bring broader government policy to bear. Effectively this gives the Secretary of State the ultimate decision over planning policy and its implementation. There are no express rights for third parties and no right of appeal against a grant of planning permission. The Secretary of State's decision may be appealed to the High Court on the same basis of judicial review. Such an appeal is confined to legal issues; the courts do not intervene on the grounds of fact or policy.

In the *Alconbury Case* the High Court first examined the application of Article 6 to **16–015** the Secretary of State's powers. Article 6 requires that " . . . everyone is entitled to a fair and public hearing within a reasonable time by an independent and impartial tribunal. . .". Specifically at issue were the Secretary of State's powers to "call in" an application for consideration either on his or her own initiative or on the initiative of the planning inspectorate. The number of call-in powers is very small compared to the number of planning applications.[16] The High Court concluded that the Secretary of State's powers were inconsistent with Article 6. It was reasoned that the Secretary of State acted as both a policy-maker and a decision-maker. Judicial review was an inadequate protection because the courts had limited powers of intervention and there was not a full appeal on the merits. The House of Lords considered the full implications of civil rights and the planning system. It was held:

- that disputes involving planning matters such as compulsory purchase orders and the determination of planning conditions did involve rights protected by the Convention;

[13] [2001] 3 W.L.R. 206.
[14] *Starrs v Procurator-Fiscal (Linlithgow)* (2000) JC 208.
[15] *R(H) v Mental Health Tribunal, North and East London Region* [2001] H.R.L.R. 752 and *R(C) v Mental Health Review Tribunal* (July 11, 2001).
[16] Richard Macrory estimates that there are about 130 call-ins out of some 500,000 applications and only 100 recovered cases out of 13,000 appeals.

- that the House of Lords reviewed many cases determined under the Convention where ministers take decisions and are answerable to Parliament. However, Article 6 does not require the court to have full jurisdiction over every aspect of the powers of those making decisions on planning matters. Lord Hoffman reasoned that the jurisdiction of the courts was one that related to a full jurisdiction to deal with the case as the nature of the decision requires;

- that it was not appropriate nor required that the court should have every aspect of planning law fall under the review; it was sufficient that there should be a review of the legality of the decision and of the relevant procedures followed;

- that the extent to which judicial review had been expanded over recent years was sufficient to provide the necessary protection for the individual.[17]

16–016   The decision of the House of Lords marks a significant development in how rights may be attached to our existing system of planning and environmental protection. The Lords recognise the development of a rights-based culture, but the area of policy and its implementation appears to fall under parliamentary accountability.

16–017   A number of important outcomes follow from the case. First, the development of a new system of planning appeals—be it a tribunal or a court—may be undertaken, but not at the insistence of the courts. Second, rights impact on the way decisions are reached, the factual basis of the decision, and the legal principles that apply. Rights and ethics are to be found not simply through a formalistic application of rules but also through the development of policy. The *Alconbury Case* underlines the role that a rights-based analysis may play in the future development of environmental law.

16–018   After *Alconbury* it might be concluded that the courts are likely to adopt a relatively restrictive interpretation of the Human Rights Act at least in terms of attempting to integrate rights into the national legal culture. A similarly restrictive approach has been taken in *R. (on the application of Vetterlein) v Hampshire C*.[18] In a judicial review in the administrative court, a challenge under Article 8 (protecting the right to home and family life) was rejected. The facts concerned local taxpayers whose claim was that a proposed incinerator was a threat to the enjoyment of their home. The decision reinforces the need to show a strong connection between the harm complained of and the protection offered by Article 8.

16–019   Article 8 was invoked in *Marcic v Thames Water Utilities Ltd*.[19] The case involved the protection that should be afforded to householders in areas prone to repeated flooding from nearby streams. The statutory water authority was aware of the potential for flooding but had not listed the remedial works as an immediate priority. The homeowner had carried out substantial preventative measures funded out of his own resources. It was common ground that major works were required before the threat of flooding could be prevented. In fact, as the problem of flooding is so common throughout the country, it was very unlikely that the statutory water authority would carry out any work. It was estimated that the total cost of such projects was £1,000 million.

[17] Text of a Public Lecture delivered in New Zealand in the Summer of 2001.
[18] [2001] All E.R. (D) 146 (June 2001).
[19] [2002] 2 All E.R. 55.

The issue in the case taken by the homeowner was whether a suitable remedy was   **16–020**
available. Under the common law, the principle of the law of nuisance, the rule in
Rylands v Fletcher, and negligence afforded some limited protection against pollution.
However, the statute—the Water Industry Act 1991—authorising the sewerage
arrangements for the area did not provide for any direct form of compensation.
Instead there is under s.18 a duty, enforceable only through an order by the Secretary
of State or the Director of Water Services. A breach of the order might give rise under
s.22 to an action by someone who has suffered loss or damage as a result. As no order
had been made, this left the complainant with potentially no remedy. The Human
Rights Act 1998 might provide a solution. This gap in the statutory provision might be
filled by the use of Article 6 (fair procedure) and Article 8. The case is on appeal but
the first-instance decision was in favour of the homeowners. The court held that s.18
arrangements did not prevent the use of the various actions in common law and that
the human rights implications gave the court the discretion to consider the question of
why the statutory water authority had not carried out remedial work. Investigation of
the merits system used by water companies in determining the allocation of their
resources and their system of establishing priorities provides an important role for the
courts in their scrutiny of policy and the circumstances where priorities are to be set.
The case is illustrative of the potential provided by a human rights view of legal
concepts. The individual with rights is regarded differently from a complainant with
remedies.

This difference is also highlighted in the case recently decided by the European   **16–021**
Court of Human Rights, *Hatton v UK*[20] October 2, 2001. The issue in the case was the
noise implications of night flights over Heathrow. Since 1962 late night flights were
banned between 11.30 pm and 6.00 am. In 1993 a quota system was introduced, and in
1998 a consultation paper on noise pollution was published by the Government. The
applicants argued that the levels of noise and the recurrent use of night flights
interfered with their rights under Article 8 of the Convention. The argument in favour
of night flights and used to justify their continuation was that it was in the interests of
the economy to allow such flights to occur. The Court reviewed the policy behind the
restrictions set up in 1993, the working of the quota system, and the measure adopted
to limit the noise of aircraft flights. By a majority of five to two the Court considered
that Article 8 had been breached. Significantly, the case points to a review and
evaluation by the courts of the processes at work in the determination of policy, and
economic arguments, including competing claims, are also evaluated. For example, the
complainants might be free to move house or accept that living in the vicinity of an
airport carries with it the likelihood of aircraft noise. The *Hatton* case, like *Marcic*,
resolves a common approach to human rights and the environment.

Finally, the Court of Appeal has recently considered the significance of the Human   **16–022**
Rights Act in terms of the discretion exercised by the courts when considering whether
or not to issue injunctions for breaches of planning control. The use of an injunction is
a powerful remedy for the enforcement of the law. S.187B of the Town and Country
Planning Act 1990 empowers a local authority "where it considers it necessary or
expedient" to apply for an injunction. The breach of an injunction carries with it the
sanction that a breach may amount to a contempt of court with severe penalties such

---

[20] Application 36022/97, European Court of Human Rights, October 2, 2001.

as imprisonment or a fine. In four cases, *South Bucks DC v Porter, Chichester v Searle, Wrexham v Berry* and *Herstmere BC v Harty*[21] the Court of Appeal considered whether the grant of injunctions in the lower courts was compatible with Art.8(1) of the Human Rights Act 1998. The question of an individual's rights under Article 8 ". . . to respect for his private and family life, his home. . ." was relevant when an injunction was granted to preserve the environment. The Court had to balance individual rights under Article 8 with the local authority's desire, on behalf of the community as a whole, to protect the environment. In considering the appropriateness of issuing an injunction, was the court required to consider the full merits of the planning dispute or the much narrower question of whether the law had been breached? The question of the full planning merits of any dispute was a matter for the planning authorities. However, if the grant of an injunction interfered, as it almost invariably would, with individual rights under Article 8, how far did the court have to consider the merits of the planning case before granting an injunction? The Court of Appeal reasoned that rights were now a relevant matter for consideration when deciding whether or not to award an injunction.

16–023   Proportionality requires that the injunction should be appropriate and necessary for the objectives to be achieved. In deciding the four cases, the Court of Appeal remitted three for reconsideration by the lower courts, holding that the lower courts had been too inclined in their approach in favour of issuing an injunction. In the fourth case (*Harty*) the Court of Appeal had adopted the correct test and the use of the injunction was upheld.

16–024   The broader rights-based approach adopted by the Court of Appeal is indicative of the changing culture of rights that pervades judicial thinking. The case law set out above has a number of distinctive attributes:

- the courts are limiting their own overt intervention in the political processes of decision-making, and the application of the principle of proportionality allows the judges the discretion to maintain this approach;
- legal rules and conventional practices appear to require that rights should be assimilated within the operating discretion and principles that guide decision-makers;
- the courts are likely to develop this area of the law on the pragmatic techniques of common law reasoning, case by case.

THE EUROPEAN CONVENTION ON HUMAN RIGHTS (ECHR)

16–025   The jurisprudence of the ECHR is highly authoritative in the interpretation courts must give to Convention rights under the Human Rights Act 1998. The content of the ECHR specifies basic rights and liberties agreed in the early 1950s. The ECHR was signed at Rome in 1950, ratified by the United Kingdom in 1951 and came into force in the states that ratified the Convention in 1953. The ECHR is an international treaty and has the force of international law.[22] Read in that light, the ECHR appears

---

[21] Court of Appeal, October 12, 2001. [2002] 1 All E.R. 425.
[22] See C. Gearty, "The European Court of Human rights and the Protection of Civil Liberties" [1993] *Cambridge Law Journal* 89.

enthusiastic and idealistic representing expectations about rights that may not always result in practical realities given high unemployment or economic depression. Nevertheless such rights provide a rich jurisprudence arising from the ECHR. The First Protocol covers Article 1 which provides for the citizen the peaceful enjoyment of his possessions and Articles 2 and 3 respectively provide the right to education and to take part in free elections. Convention rights are broadly expressed and cover in consecutive order: the right to life (Article 2); freedom from torture or degrading treatment, or punishment (Article 3); freedom from slavery or forced labour (Article 4); the right to liberty and security of the person (Article 5); the right to a fair trial (Article 6); the prohibition of retrospective laws (Article 7); the right to respect for family life, home and correspondence (Article 8); freedom of thought and religion (Article 9); freedom of expression (Article 10) and freedom to join a trade union and to engage in peaceful assembly (Article 11); and finally the right to marry and found a family (Article 12). The ECHR omits general economic and social rights which may cause political controversy.

There are specific provisions permitting the derogation from such provisions at times of emergency such as in Northern Ireland or following September 11 attacks on New York and Washington. It is not possible to derogate from freedom from torture, or inhuman or degrading treatment (Article 3), or from slavery (Article 4) and on retroactive criminal offences (Article 7). In time of war or grave public emergency a state may under Article 15 derogate from the right to life but this only applies to lawful acts of war.   **16–026**

In addition to the main articles of the ECHR, there are a number of protocols signed by the Member States which allow Member States to enter a reservation. For example under the Education Acts in force in the United Kingdom there is a reservation to Article 2 of the First Protocol to the Convention as to the right to education. This stipulates so far as it is "compatible with the provision of efficient instruction and training and the avoidance of unreasonable public expenditure." Many of the rights are qualified by provisos or exceptions and are subject to judicial interpretation.   **16–027**

The procedures are complex and time-consuming. To some extent the ECHR is a victim of its own success as the world's most important human rights court. The time factor has now become quite acute. It is estimated that it may take over six years from commencing proceedings to completion of the case after it has been considered by the Court. The popularity of individual petitions has led to a backlog of over 2,500 applications. This may lead to abuse being uncorrected and the delay in hearing cases may cause remedies to be too delayed to be effective.   **16–028**

A case may be taken by one State party as against another under Article 24 or in the case of the United Kingdom since 1966, at the petition of an individual against his own State under Article 25. In 1998 the pre-existing institutions of the European Commission of Human Rights and the European Court of Human Rights were superseded by a new full-time European Court of Human Rights. All applications go directly to the Court and the right of individual petition became mandatory for all Member States since 1998.   **16–029**

The question of whether the petition is admissible depends on the exhaustion of domestic remedies the petition must be presented within six months of the particular decision and any petition which is ill-founded or an abuse of the rights of the   **16–029a** petitioner will be rejected. The petition must not under Article 27 be incompatible with the ECHR and must raise a violation as a matter of law.

16–030   Blackburn has estimated[23] that "the total number of judgments of the Court in its entire history to 1998 was 903; yet in the first nine months of 1999 alone the figure was 108". The evidence is that the number of registered applications is increasing. Blackburn has found that on June 26, 1999 there were[24] "10,000 registered applications and more than 47,000 provisional files, as well as around 700 letters and more than 200 overseas phone calls per day".

16–031   The Court of Justice at Strasbourg is composed of 41 judges. The force of international law and inter-state relations means that in practice Member States do tend to follow the findings of the Court. Changes introduced in the United Kingdom as a result of decisions of the Court include the Contempt of Court Act 1981, the Interception of Communications Act 1985 and in Northern Ireland, the Homosexual Offences (Northern Ireland) Order 1982.[24a]

16–032   There have been a number of cases taken against the United Kingdom alleging a breach of the ECHR. In over a dozen cases the Court has ruled against the United Kingdom government.

16–033   The first case against the United Kingdom from an individual petition was *Golder*[25] where a former prisoner claimed under Article 8 the right to privacy for his private correspondence and under Article 6, a fair hearing. Golder had been refused access to a solicitor under the Prison Rules and denied the opportunity to bring an action against a police officer. The Court held that the Prison Rules were inconsistent with the ECHR and later this resulted in a change in the Prison Rules. The Court has also held that the censorship by the prison authorities of prisoners' correspondence was in breach of Article 8 in *Silver v UK*[26] and that there was a lack of an effective remedy under national law. The procedures for the hearing of charges made against prisoners by the Prison Boards of Visitors was found to be in breach of Article 6 relating to the right to a fair trial in *Campbell and Fell v UK*.[27]

16–034   The use of birching in the Isle of Man was held in *Tyrer*[28] to be a degrading punishment under Article 3. Since 1976 when the United Kingdom's declaration under Article 25 was renewed, the Isle of Man was excluded from individual petitions although under Article 63 the ECHR may still apply to the Isle of Man. The United Kingdom has brought the *Tyrer* judgment to the attention of the Isle of Man authorities thus satisfying the United Kingdom's obligations under the judgment but no law preventing judicial corporal punishment of juveniles has been enacted.

16–035   The Court has considered the use of corporal punishment in schools in the cases of *Campbell and Cosans*.[29] While the Court could not find any breach of Article 3 on inhuman and degrading treatment, they were prepared to hold that there was a breach

---

[23] R. Blackburn "Current Developments, Assessment and Prospects" in *Fundamental Rights in Europe* (R. Blackburn and Jorg Polakiewicz ed., Oxford University Press, Oxford, 2001), p.77.
[24] *ibid.*
[24a] Homosexual Offences (Northern Ireland) Order (SI 1982/1536).
[25] *Golder v UK* (1975) 1 E.H.R.R. 524.
[26] (1983) 5 E.H.R.R. 347.
[27] (1985) 7 E.H.R.R. 165.
[28] *Tyrer v UK* (1978) 2 E.H.R.R. 1.
[29] (1982) 4 E.H.R.R. 293. See *Teare v O'Callaghan* (1982) 4 E.H.R.R. 232. The Isle of Man High Court quashed the decision of Magistrates over corporal punishment in line with the ECHR.

of Article 2 of the First Protocol, which requires the State to "respect the rights of parents to ensure such education and teaching in conformity with their own religious and philosophical convictions." Since 1986, corporal punishment in State Schools has been abolished in England, Wales and Scotland. This applies to publicly-funded pupils of independent schools but not to the independent schools sector as a whole.

Individual rights such as under Article 8, the right to privacy and family life, have been the subject of individual petition. In *Dudgeon*[30] the Court held that various laws in Northern Ireland making homosexual practices illegal[30a] between consenting males was a breach of his privacy and the law in Northern Ireland was subsequently changed to fall into line with the decision of the Court. The *Dudgeon* case has been applied by the courts in their interpretation of the law in the Irish Republic.   **16–036**

In *Gaskin v UK*[31] the release of confidential records for the period the applicant was in care were refused. The Court accepted that this refusal was a breach of Article 8 because there was inadequate provision for an independent review of what should or should not be disclosed.   **16–037**

The Court has also considered the law of contempt in *Sunday Times v UK*.[32] This case arose out of the House of Lords decision in *Att.-Gen. v Times Newspapers Ltd*[33] over the legality of the *Sunday Times* publication of articles relating to the drug thalidomide. The Commission had held by a majority that the injunction granted by the House of Lords against the *Sunday Times* was in breach of Article 10, the right to freedom of information. The Court ruled by a majority of 11 votes to 9 that the injunction was inconsistent with the ECHR. This was the first time that the Court had to consider consistency between a common law rule of contempt of Court and the ECHR. The difference in approach in the case taken by the House of Lords and the Court of Justice represents a marked contrast in the jurisprudence of each. While the House of Lords attempted to balance the differing interests between the parties, the Court of Justice focused on the application of freedom of expression to the issues raised in the case.   **16–038**

The Court has not refrained from considering the question of pornography in the context of freedom of expression under Article 20. In *Handyside*[34] the Court considered the legality of the English courts order to destroy copies of the *Little Red Schoolbook* under the Obscene Publications Act. The book, aimed at children, contained explicit sexual information which had led to the conviction of the applicant under the Obscene Publications Act. The Court held that the conviction was not a breach of Article 10, on freedom of speech.   **16–039**

The procedure for the release of mental patients under s.66(3) of the Mental Health Act 1959 was held to be a breach of Article 5 of the ECHR in *X v UK*.[35] The case was notable because the Court had viewed habeas corpus available in the English courts as not a sufficient remedy. Recourse to the Mental Health Review Tribunal was also regarded as inadequate because the tribunal had powers only to make a recommendation. The Mental Health (Amendment) Act 1982 brought English law into line with the judgment of the Court.   **16–040**

---

[30] *Dudgeon v UK* (1981) 4 E.H.R.R. 149. See Homosexual Offences (Northern Ireland) Order 1982.
[30a] Homosexual Offences (Northern Ireland) Order (SI 1982/1536).
[31] (1989) 12 E.H.R.R. 36.
[32] (1979) 2 E.H.R.R. 245.
[33] [1973] 3 All E.R. 54.
[34] *Handyside v UK* (1976) 1 E.H.R.R. 737.
[35] (1981) 4 E.H.R.R. 188.

16–041   The Court considered the provisions of the Trade Union and Labour Relations Act 1974 and their compatibility with Article 11 of the ECHR in the *Young James and Webster cases*.[36] Three British Rail employees refused to become members of a closed shop agreement entered into by British Rail and the Unions in 1975. The closed shop agreement was held to violate the freedom of association protected under Article 11. Since the case was decided, the law relating to trade unions has been substantially altered. In the case of the Government Communications Headquarters where 7,000 civil servants were deprived of their rights to join a trade union, the Commission ruled the application inadmissible.[37]

16–042   In *Malone v UK*,[38] telephone tapping was held by the Court to be a violation of Article 8 on the right to privacy. Since then the law has been changed to take account of the Court's decision which revealed how the regulation of telephone tapping was carried out through administrative guidance rather than a statutory basis.

16–043   In *McCann, Farrell and Savage v UK*[39] the shooting of IRA suspects in Gibraltar was not disproportionate to the aim of defending life and protecting property from unlawful violence. However, it was accepted by a majority of 10 to 9 that the killing of the IRA members breached the victims' Article 2 rights to life. The majority held that the inefficient organisation of the undercover operation made their deaths likely, though avoidable. However, the compensation that was payable was only confined to the costs of the applicants.

16–044   Aside from the use of the individual petition procedure it is possible for action to be taken by another State against the United Kingdom. The first such case was the *Republic of Ireland v UK*.[40] In 1971, Ireland lodged complaints with the Commission alleging that there had been a failure by the security forces to protect life under Article 2 over deaths which arose in Londonderry in 1972, that detained suspects were subject to treatment which amounted to torture, inhuman and degrading treatment contrary to Article 3, and that internment without trial violated Articles 5 and 6, and in its operation it violated Article 14. Finally the allegation was made that the United Kingdom Government had failed to honour the rights and freedoms contained in Article 1 of the ECHR.

16–045   The Court upheld complaints relating to interrogation methods as a breach of Article 3. In addition the Court rejected discrimination contrary to Articles 4 and 5 by accepting that the focus of internment was justifiable against Republican terrorists because of the level of violence from that element in the community. As a result of the Court's decision, the United Kingdom Government sought to incorporate the substance of Article 3 into the domestic law in Northern Ireland and enacted s.5 of the Northern Ireland (Emergency Provisions) Act 1987 which allows the courts in Northern Ireland to exclude evidence where there is *prima facie* evidence that the accused was subject to "torture, to inhuman or degrading treatment, or to any violence or threat of violence".

---

[36] (1982) 4 E.H.R.R. 38.
[37] See *Council for Civil Service Unions v Minister for the Civil Service* [1985] A.C. 374; (1988) 10 E.H.R.R. 269; (1985) 7 E.H.R.R. 14.
[38] (1984) 7 E.H.R.R. 14.
[39] Application 1894/91, (1991) Eur. Ct. HR.
[40] (1978) 2 E.H.R.R. 25. K. Boyle and H. Hannum, "Ireland in Strasbourg" (1976) *Irish Jurist* 243.

Northern Ireland has continued to prove a problem for the United Kingdom's   **16–046**
emergency laws and their compatibility with the ECHR. A wide variety of individual
applications have been received by the Commission. McCrudden notes[41]:

> "A wide variety of issues has been raised, ranging from allegations of breach of
> fair trial protections, to torture, from interference with correspondence, to
> internment, from arrest and detention under the PTA [Prevention of Terrorism
> Act] to the law on reasonable force, from discrimination to the voting system."

In *Brogan*[42] the Court considered Article 5 which protects the freedom of the person in   **16–047**
respect of arrests, questioning and detention for up to seven days under the Prevention
of Terrorism (Temporary Provisions) Act 1984. The question of the length of
detention was considered by the Court. While accepting the availability of habeas
corpus as a remedy, the Court considered that in respect of applicants detained for
more than five days the ECHR had been infringed. For applicants detained for up to
four or five days, the Court regarded their detention as not an infringement of the
ECHR. The outcome of the *Brogan* decision proved difficult for the United Kingdom
Government and the operational decisions of the police in Northern Ireland. Taking
such matters as general security into account, the United Kingdom Government
decided to derogate under Article 15 from its obligations under the ECHR. The
requirements under Article 5 that the accused should be charged "promptly" resulted
in the Court holding that Article 5 was infringed by the Prevention of Terrorism
(Temporary provisions) Act 1984.

Any assessment of the impact of the ECHR must take account of the pattern of civil   **16–048**
liberties protection within the United Kingdom. The Court has considerably greater
latitude in the interpretation of citizens' rights when the ECHR is focused primarily on
the interpretation of rights and fundamental freedoms. In contrast it appears that
courts in the United Kingdom face a more difficult task when confronted by legislation
which is not focused on citizens' rights. Palley notes how different legal systems may
address different priorities[43]:

> "Every legal system that recognises rights, whether in some form of Bill of Rights
> or in ordinary law, has to decide what rights to accord, how to adjust competing
> rights, whether to give particular rights priority, and whether to treat some as
> absolute."

Historically, United Kingdom courts have been reluctant to take account of inter-   **16–049**
national treaties or conventions when not required to do so. There is also a reluctance,
as in *Malone v Metropolitan Police Commissioner*, for the courts to use the ECHR to
legislate in new areas through judicial interpretation.

Conor Gearty neatly sums up the achievements to 1995 to be as follows[44]:   **16–050**

> "At the end of 1995, 30 of these 37 decisions [these are cases won in the
> European Court up to the end of 1995] had been the subject of resolutions of the

---

[41] C. McCrudden, "Northern Ireland and the British Constitution" in *The Changing Constitution* (J. Jowell
and D. Oliver ed., 2nd ed., 1989), pp.320–321.
[42] *Brogan v UK* (1989) 11 E.H.R.R. 117.
[43] C. Palley, *The United Kingdom and Human Rights* (Hamlyn Trust, 1991), p.159.
[44] *European Civil Liberties and the European Convention on Human Rights* (Conor Gearty ed., Kluwer, 1995).

Committee of Ministers under Article 54. In eight of these cases, it had been decided that no changes in United Kingdom law were required, either because the issue had already been dealt with by the legislature, or because on the facts all that was required was an assurance that no violation would occur, or because it was considered that the payment of compensation in accordance with the Court's ruling was a sufficient compliance with it."

16–051   It is clear that the experience of the ECHR provides an insight into the jurisprudence of the courts. It remains an intriguing question as to the future direction that is likely to be taken given the potential for community rights to be assimilated into the ECHR. An early indication is to be found in *R. v Human Fertilisation and Embryology Authority Ex p. Blood.*[45] The Court of Appeal held that the widow could seek medical treatment under Articles 59 and 60 of the EC Treaty which gave her directly enforceable rights. The facts of the case arose when the widow had requested sperm samples to be taken from her seriously ill husband who was in a coma so that at a later date the sperm could be used by her in treatment by artificial insemination. The husband was unable to give consent and later died. The Embryology Authority in the United Kingdom refused to allow the treatment to be carried out as they claimed it infringed the 1990 Human Fertilisation and Embryology Act.

Citizens' Rights and Citizenship

16–052   Citizens' rights may involve consideration of some of the freedoms identified under the ECHR such as the freedom of expression, the right to privacy, the freedom of religion and freedom from racial discrimination or the freedom of movement involving immigration and deportation. The citizen's freedom of expression also raises questions of censorship and obscenity. In outline the various laws that regulate and seek to control obscenity may be considered.

16–053   We have already seen that in *Handyside,* discussed above, the ECHR permits restraints on freedom of expression on the grounds of morality under Article 10(2). Attempts to regulate and control obscene publications since the eighteenth century moved the jurisdiction over obscene materials from the ecclesiastical to the common law courts. At common law, an offence punishable by the common law courts was the publication of obscene material. It was an offence to publish a book that tended to corrupt public morals and was against the King's peace. The Obscene Publications Act 1959 creates the statutory offence of publishing an obscene matter. The test of obscene is "if taken as a whole, such as to tend to deprave and corrupt persons who are likely, having regard to all relevant circumstances, to read, see or hear the matter contained or embodied in it." The question of what is obscene is subject to judicial interpretation[46] and originated in the common law. The issue of what is obscene is a matter for the jury properly instructed on the law. The legal meaning of obscene must be distinguished from the meaning given to the word by the ordinary layman. In the *Oz case*[47] the judge left the jury with the impression that obscene could be equated with

---

[45] [1997] 2 All E.R. 687.
[46] See Smith and Hogan, *Criminal Law* (4th ed., 1992), p.730.
[47] *R. v Oz* [1972] 1 Q.B. 509.

repulsive, lewd, or filthy material. The crucial question is not only whether a publication fulfils any of these conditions but whether it "has a tendency to deprave and corrupt". An article which is so filthy that causes revulsion may paradoxically not "deprave and corrupt." The conviction was quashed because the judge failed to make clear to the jury the requirement that the article must deprave and corrupt while making clear it may have been lewd. It is possible that an article may be deemed obscene if it had a tendency to deprave and corrupt but was not lewd.

The use of the Obscene Publications Act 1959 in not confined to sexual activities. **16–054** The publication of *Cain's Book* which highlighted the favourable effects of drug-taking fell within the scope of "deprave and corrupt". Smith and Hogan note[48]:

> "The difficulty about extending the notion of obscenity beyond sexual morality is that it is not now apparent where the law is to stop. It seems obvious that an article with a tendency to induce violence is now obscene, and if taking drugs is depravity, why not drinking, or, if evidence of its harmful effects accumulates, smoking?"

The scope of the 1959 Act also applies to a wide range of literature where readers may **16–055** engage in their own sexual fantasies without involving any overt sexual activity of any kind. It is possible that an article may be deemed obscene even when directed only to persons already depraved.

The Obscene Publications Act 1959 as amended by s.1(2) of the Obscene Publica- **16–056** tions Act 1964 also makes it an offence to publish an article for gain or not. The terms "publication for gain" shall mean "any publication with a view to gain, whether the gain is to accrue by way of consideration for the publication or any other way."

Despite the scope of the legislation, the 1959 and 1964 Acts preserve the common **16–057** law of conspiracy to corrupt public morals or outrage public decency. Scope for this offence is considerable given the vague nature of the crime of conspiracy and the potential for overlap with the Obscene Publications Acts. Assurances have been given that the use of conspiracy charges will not be used to circumvent the protections available under the Obscene Publications Acts. Such protections under the Obscene Publications Acts include the following. The defendant had not examined the article and had no reasonable cause to suspect that it was obscene and that publication of it would be an offence under s.2 of the Acts. There is also a defence of public good. Once the jury have determined that the article or book is obscene, the defendant may show that publication of the article in question "is in the interests of science, literature, art or learning, or of other objects of general concern."

There is considerable debate as to the application of the Obscene Publications Acts **16–058** to works of literature or art. The line to be drawn between what is acceptable and what is not is based not on the intention of the author, but whether the article or book is obscene. The article or book "must be taken as a whole" and considered by the jury after direction by the judge. Very often the jury may find the judge's direction influential as to the outcome of the case.

The Obscene Publications Act 1857 provided that on summary procedure obscene **16–059** articles may be forfeited. S.3 of the Obscene Publications Act 1959 provides that on an

---

[48] Smith and Hogan, *op.cit.*, p.731. *R. v Anderson* and *R. v Oz* [1972] 1 Q.B. 304. *Calder (John) Publications Ltd v Powell* [1965] 1 Q.B. 509.

oath made before a magistrate a warrant may be issued authorising search and seizure of goods which may be obscene and are intended to be published for gain. The owner may appear and present his case as to why the offending article should not be forfeited with a right of appeal to the Crown Court. This may give rise to inconsistencies between different attitudes among different magistrates. There is no national or uniform standard, although the advice of the police and the Director of Public Prosecutions may be taken when considering whether to forfeit articles.

16–060   There are a range of offences connected with posting indecent or obscene material. The test is objective, namely offending against recognised standards of propriety, and includes sending unsolicited matter describing human sexual techniques. It is possible to interpret indecent and obscene in this context to extend beyond the sexual area. S.49 of the Customs and Excise Management Act 1979 permits customs officers to seize and destroy "indecent or obscene books" and other articles imported into the United Kingdom. The test is whether an article offends current standards of propriety.

16–061   Reform of the Obscene Publications Acts has been recommended by the Williams[49] Committee in 1979. A clear distinction should be drawn between material which should be prohibited and denied access to by anyone who wishes to see it. Restricted material should be available to those who wished to see it but not available to the general public. The Committee stressed the need to protect young people and therefore restrict the material that is available. The Williams Committee would effectively remove the categorisation of obscene, indecent or violent in favour of a clearer distinction based on access to material.

16–062   Protecting the public from obscene material also extends to videos[50] and the cinema. The Cinemas Act 1985 provides for the licensing of premises for film exhibitions. There is a British Board of Film Censors, founded in 1912 and given statutory powers to act on behalf of local authorities in setting standards and the censorship of films. The Board, renamed the British Board of Film Classification, has led to an age group category awarded to every film and the extension of this system to videos was made in 1984 under the Video Recordings Act 1984 and amended by the Video Recordings Act 1993. Videos are controlled as to the content and the classification of the material. In 1988 the enforcement of the 1984 Act was vested in the Weights and Measures Authorities at local level. Local authorities are responsible for licensing sex establishments in their locality under the Local Government (Miscellaneous Provisions) Act 1982. Indecent photographs of children under 16 are prohibited under the Protection of Children Act 1978.

16–063   Under the Theatres Act 1968 it is an offence to present or direct the performance of a play which is obscene. The term obscene is taken from the Obscene Publications Act 1959 which applies. This means that if taken as a whole the work's effect was such as to deprave and corrupt persons in all the circumstances likely to attend it.

Religion and Race

16–064   The freedom of religion involves the freedom to practice religion, freedom of discrimination between religions and equal treatment of different religions. In the United Kingdom older laws failed to grant religious toleration but many disabilities

---

[49] Cmnd.7772 (1979). *DPP v Whyte* [1972] 3 All E.R. 12. See *Knuller v DPP* [1973] A.C. 435. See *Hansard*, HC Vol.695, col.1212 (June 3, 1964) and *Hansard*, HC Vol.698, cols.315–316 (July 7, 1864). Post Office Act 1953, s.11. *Stanley* [1965] 2 Q.B. 327. And the Unsolicited Goods and Services Act 1971, s.4.
[50] Video Recordings Act 1984.

have now been removed within the framework of a State-recognised established Church. The question of religious belief and the legal recognition of a religion may arise in connection with charitable status with the Charity Commissioners and under the Places or Worship Registration Act 1855 for purposes of celebrating marriages, taxation arrangements and charitable status.

Various fringe religious groups or factions have attempted and sometimes succeeded   **16–065** in securing charitable status. The law may find it difficult to categorise such groups and to distinguish religious cults from a recognised religion. The value judgments inherent in such a distinction are difficult to make.[51]

The existence of an established religion, the Church of England, has ensured   **16–066** through successive statutes that the Sovereign is "the Supreme Governor of the Realm in all spiritual and ecclesiastical causes as well as temporal". It is therefore required that the Sovereign is a member of the Church of England and marriage to a Roman Catholic is grounds for disqualification.

A major issue is the teaching of religion in schools, compulsory under the National   **16–067** Curriculum under s.2(1)(a) and (8) of the Education Reform Act 1988; and the designation of religious schools. Recognition of religious affiliation is contained in ss.6 and 7 of the Education Reform Act 1988. Schools may be divided into county and voluntary schools. In the case of county schools under s.9(1) of the Education Act 1944, county schools are state schools owned and maintained by local education authorities. Maintained schools as they are commonly referred to, are required to have a daily act of worship under s.7(1) of the Education Reform Act 1988, "wholly or mainly of a broadly Christian character". Exemptions to reflect a particular form of worship may be obtained. Generally the law permits a child's religion and education to be matters for parents until the age of discretion.[52]

Voluntary schools are either controlled, aided, or special agreement schools, each   **16–068** with their own specialised sets of rules. Most of the voluntary schools have a religious affiliation such as Church of England, Roman Catholic, Methodist or Jewish. The daily act of worship will therefore be denominational. There are powers under s.13 of the Education Act 1980 to approve schools within the voluntary status such as Muslim Schools. This is a delicate issue. The freedom of Muslims to participate in their own schools has to be balanced against the need to have a racially balanced education system free from sectarian differences which may be exacerbated by the separation of education on the basis of religion. A voluntary-aided school may adopt a religious admission policy by giving account to s.6(3)(a) of the Education Act 1980. This applies where the school is over-subscribed. The House of Lords ruled that the parental wishes of some parents could be defeated on the basis of the School's own admission policy. In effect this may protect the religious preferences of some parents at the expense of others. The parents of two girls one a Hindu, the other a Muslim were unsuccessful in their application to enter a Roman Catholic School which favoured Roman Catholic and other Christian girls as part of the school's admission policy.

---

[51] Lord Chancellor (Tenure of Office and Discharge of Ecclesiastical Functions) Act 1974 allowing the Office of Lord Chancellor to be held by a Roman Catholic. *Re South Place Ethical Society: Barralet v Attorney-General* [1980] 3 All E.R. 918. See *Ex p. Segerdal* [1970] 2 Q.B. 697. For example the Unification Church known as the "Moonies" which has charitable status but has caused questions to be raised about its activities and suitability, see *Hansard*, HC Vol.926, cols.1597–1598 (February 23, 1977).
[52] *Ex p. Choudhury* [1991] 1 All E.R. 306.

16–069   The protection of the Christian religion is acknowledged in the law of blasphemy and in various statutes protecting Sunday. Acceptance of religious belief is also recognised in laws which exempt Sikhs from wearing crash helmets on motorcycles and on construction sites.[53] Such arrangements are minor exceptions to the general assumptions that the law is mainly concerned with the Christian or Jewish religions.

16–070   Euthanasia has largely been opposed by religious groups and this opposition has been upheld by the courts. The question of the use of pain-killing drugs by doctors raises religious and ethical issues. In *Adams*[54] Devlin J. expressed a traditional but not exclusively Christian position that doctors should not prescribe drugs which would shorten life. In *Airedale NHS Trust v Bland*,[55] the House of Lords was still opposed to euthanasia but held that in the case of an insensate patient with no hope of recovery when it was known that stopping medical treatment would result in death, there was no criminal act provided it was in the patient's best interests not to prolong his life. The courts would provide guidance in the form of a declaratory judgement to doctors in cases of withholding life-prolonging treatment. A minority of judges considered that it was important that Parliament should consider the moral, social and legal issues involved in such cases. In *Pretty v UK*[56] the European Court of Human Rights (ECtHR) rejected the applicant suffering from an incurable degenerative illness who was appealing against the refusal of the Director of Public Prosecutions to grant her husband immunity from prosecution if he assisted in her suicide. Her claim on the basis of Articles 2, 3, 8, 9 and 14 of the Convention was unanimously rejected. The ECtHR has consistently upheld the obligation of the State to protect life.

16–071   Freedom of religious belief may be considered in the context of the criminal law. In *Blaue*[57] the victim of a stabbing was a member of the Jehovah's Witnesses. She was told that unless she received a blood transfusion, which was the recommended standard medical treatment, she would die. She refused the treatment on religious grounds and her assailant was found guilty of her manslaughter. Lawton L.J. recognised that the religious belief of the victim, whether reasonable or not, had to be accepted as part of the principle that the defendant had to take the victim as he found her. The victim in legal terms was defined to include physical attributes such as an "egg shell skull", and also the religious beliefs of the victim.

16–072   However, in *R. v Senior*[58] in the case of a child in need of medical treatment, it was held that to withhold medical treatment from the child on the grounds of religious belief was manslaughter. Religious belief may be expressly recognised in a statute such as s.4 of the Abortion Act 1967 which recognises religious belief not to participate in an abortion on the ground of conscientious objection.

16–073   Religious discrimination is expressly prohibited in Northern Ireland, on the grounds of employment, education and the provision of services to the public. Similar provisions do not apply in other parts of the United Kingdom.

---

[53] Motorcycle Crash-helmets (Religious Exemption) Act 1976 and s.1 of the Employment Act 1988.
[54] [1957] Crim. L.R. 365.
[55] [1993] 1 All E.R. 821.
[56] [2002] All E.R. (D) 286.
[57] [1975] 1 W.L.R. 1411; [1975] 3 All E.R. 446.
[58] [1899] 1 Q.B. 283.

Freedom from racial discrimination is an example of piecemeal reform to meet   **16–074**
particular problems. Since the 1950s and 60s the number of immigrants from India,
Pakistan and the West Indies seeking employment in the United Kingdom focused
attention on the multi-racial and multi-ethnic nature of the United Kingdom. Three
Acts of Parliament have been extended to cover race relations while immigration
policy has been tightened and reviewed. The current legislation is the Race Relations
Act 1976 which strengthens and extends legislation passed in 1965 and 1968. The first
attempt at legislation in 1965 made it illegal to discriminate against a person on the
grounds of race in certain places of public access such as hotels, restaurants, theatres,
sports grounds, places of entertainment, pubs and dance halls, and under s.5, in the
disposal of tenancies and also in the creation of the offence of racial discrimination.
The difficulty of proving intent to stir up racial hatred made this part of the Act largely
ineffective. The Act created a new conciliatory procedure operated by the Race
Relations Board (RRB) which made an annual report to Parliament. Failure to
achieve a satisfactory settlement of a dispute might result in action by the Attorney-
General who could take action in the High Court or County Court through an
injunction.

Following criticism of the 1965 Act, the Race Relations Act 1968 was enacted. The   **16–075**
Act allowed the RRB to take cases to court rather than having to rely on the Attorney-
General. The Act also extended the application of the law to a wider range of activities
such as goods, facilities and services, employment, housing and advertisements. The
Act also extended to the Crown. Interpretation of the Act by the courts gave rise to a
number of difficulties. Certain private social or political clubs which operated a bar on
the basis of race were held to escape the provisions of the legislation. Discrimination
against a person on the grounds of a person's nationality as distinct from national
origins was not contrary to the Act. The RRB could take action on its own initiative to
investigate suspected cases of discrimination. Working on informal techniques of
compromise the RRB could attempt to find a solution. The 1968 Act had failed to be
effective and after a White Paper, a new Act was passed in 1976. Building on the
experience of the previous legislation, the 1976 Act set out to remedy some of the
shortcomings mentioned above.

The 1976 Act extended the scope of the 1968 Act to cover partnerships and clubs,   **16–076**
contract workers and discrimination on the grounds of nationality rather than national
origins. Direct and indirect discrimination and discriminatory practices such as
victimisation are also included within the scope of the Act. Such practices are illegal if
they fall within employment, education, goods and services, housing, clubs, or
advertisements.[59]

The definition of discrimination remains the same, namely a person discriminates if   **16–077**
on racial grounds he treats another less favourably than he treats or would treat other
persons. It is an offence to incite, instruct or induce someone to act in a discriminatory
way. The courts appear to have developed a relatively simple test; would the
complainant have received the same treatment from the defendant but for his or her
racial background?

---

[59] Racial Discrimination, Cmnd.6234 (1975).

16–078   The 1976 Act allows direct access to the individual who feels that there is a grievance. Assistance is then given by the Commission for Racial Equality (CRE) which replaced the Race Relations Board and the Community Relations Commission. The CRE may give advice or assistance and if necessary instigate proceedings in the County Court by seeking an injunction. It has considerable powers to require the furnishing of information and the production of documents and if necessary seek court orders to enforce the production of documents. The CRE is appointed by the Home Secretary and it makes an annual report to the Home Secretary which is laid before Parliament. It has 15 members and is independent from government.

16–079   Discrimination is unlawful in employment except where there is a particular racial group where this is a specified qualification for a specific job such as the theatre. Employment in a private household is not included under the Act.

16–080   In the case of employment where there are allegations of discrimination, the complainant must complain to an industrial tribunal. The burden lies on the complainant, and if successful the complainant may achieve compensation, or reversal of the policy or act of discrimination. Enforcement in the field of employment depends on the victim of discrimination complaining to an industrial tribunal with an appeal on a point of law to the Employment Appeal Tribunal.

16–081   As a result of the difficulty of proving intention under the 1965 Act for the offence of inciting racial hatred, the 1976 Act replaced the requirement of intention with an objective test. The defendant, if his conduct was judged to stir up racial hatred, was guilty of the offence irrespective of whether he intended to do so or not. Further refinement to the law was achieved under Pt III of the Public Order Act 1986 which added seven further offences to the offence of stirring up racial hatred. In the field of racial discrimination some advocate a different approach than that outlined in the 1976 Act. Positive discrimination or reverse discrimination is intended to encourage affirmative action to provide positive steps to redress any racial discrimination in society. For example in employment or education, one possibility is to allocate places on the basis of race or ethnic origin thus ensuring that there is a fair balance to the opportunities available to ethnic groups. The definition of discrimination under s.1 of the Race Relations Act makes affirmative action illegal. There are some exceptions such as ss.35–38 which may permit a particular group to be granted education, training and special needs. Introduction into the United Kingdom of a full programme of affirmative action requires careful consideration and research.

16–082   Following the findings of racism by the Macpherson Report into the death of Stephen Lawrence, the Race Relations (Amendment) Act 2000 applies to the Police. The effect of the Act is to broaden the impact of the previous Acts and make it a requirement that there is a public duty on all public authorities to eliminate unlawful discrimination and this includes direct or indirect discrimination or victimisation. The act makes Chief Officers of Police vicariously liable for acts of racial discrimination by police officers under their direction and control. The exemption for national security found in the Race Relations Act 1976 is amended to make it compatible with the Convention. The Act blurs any distinction between public and private as it brings within its scope public functions carried out by private sector organisations.

Work

The United Kingdom enacted specific laws to oppose sex discrimination. There are   **16–083**
two statutes relevant to sex discrimination, first the Equal Pay Act 1970 and secondly
the Sex Discrimination Act 1975. The Equal Pay Act is intended to provide women
with equal pay when undertaking equal work, or where a job evaluation scheme has
been carried out and the work is rated as equivalent to a man's work. In the case of a
collective bargain agreement between employer and trade union that provides different
rates for men and women, the collective agreement may be referred to an Industrial
Arbitration Board for the removal of any clause which is unfair or discriminatory.

Women who believe that they are not getting equal pay may refer their claim to an   **16–084**
industrial tribunal. The onus of proof is that she has to show that her work is similar to
that of a man's. Once this element of proof has been discharged the onus is then on
the employer to show that there are material differences between the man's work and
the woman's work. Compensation is payable of up to two years' arrears of pay. The
Equal Pay Act has also a more general application to a woman's terms and conditions
of employment including sickness pay and holiday bonuses. For example Lloyds' Bank
Ltd operated a pension scheme which in *Worringham and Humphreys v Lloyds' Bank
Ltd (No.2)*[60] was held by the European Court of Justice to be a violation of Article 19.
Male employees over 25 were expected to contribute 5 per cent of their salary to the
pension fund while female employees of the same age were not required to make any
contribution. The male employees over 55 received extra salary to compensate them
and if they left before 55 they received a full refund.

The Sex Discrimination Act 1975 bears similarity to the scope of the provisions of   **16–085**
the Race Relations Act 1976. In the case of sex discrimination, Pt II of the 1975 Act
prohibits discrimination in employment and applies to the arrangements for the terms
and conditions of employment, access to training, promotion and benefits and to
dismissal. This includes job advertisements and includes that a refusal or deliberate
omission to offer employment because of a person's sex is unlawful.

There are a number of exceptions to the Act such as employment in private   **16–086**
households, and genuine examples where the job may only be performed by someone
of a certain sex. The Equal Opportunities Commission has powers to bring proceedings in the County Court and extensive powers to carry out formal investigations into
employers' policies and practices. In cases where it establishes that there is discrimination or contravention of the equal pay provisions, it may issue a non-discrimination
notice. Codes of Practice may be issued or inquiries may be carried out into a specific
complaint provided the Commission is satisfied that there has been a breach of the
statute before embarking on the inquiry.

The Disability Rights Commission Act 1999 set up a Commission to replace the   **16–087**
National Disability Council established under the Disability Discrimination Act 1995.
The Commission is a non-departmental body with the majority of its members
disabled. The Commission has similar functions to the Equal Opportunities Commission and may take formal investigations and issue non-discrimination notices, provide
assistance in relation to agreements and facilitate the resolution of disputes.

---

[60] [1982] 3 All E.R. 373.

IMMIGRATION, CITIZENSHIP AND EXTRADITION

Citizenship and the Right of Abode

16–088   The Treaty on European Union provides for the first time in the context of the Community, the formulation of rights for the Citizen of the European Union. The first of the rights pertaining to European citizenship conferred by the new Treaty is the right to move and reside freely throughout the territory of the Member States. The concept of citizenship is an important one for the bestowal of rights and the ascertainment of responsibilities. Race relations in the United Kingdom are not exclusively determined by the Race Relations Acts. In fact an important aspect of immigration policy has been the question of the rights of immigrants to enter and remain within the United Kingdom. Restrictions may be imposed on British subjects.

16–089   At common law a British subject was synonymous with allegiance to the Crown within His Majesty's dominions. Aliens owed a temporary allegiance. Historical reasons influenced the categorisation of British subjects to be defined as including the United Kingdom and Colonies. The status of British subject became the basis of citizenship and this was recognised under the British Nationality Act 1948. Historical reasons also combined with economic factors to influence restrictions on the freedom of Commonwealth citizens to enter and live in the United Kingdom. For example after a period of growth in emigration from India, Pakistan and the West Indies in the 1950s, there followed a period of restriction, first under the Commonwealth Immigrants Act 1962 and secondly, under the Immigration Act 1971. Thus holding citizenship does not qualify one for living within the United Kingdom.

16–090   A major change in the law took place under the British Nationality Act 1981 which came into force in 1983. At the end of 1982 anyone who was a citizen of the United Kingdom and Colonies under the 1971 Act and had the right to abode in the United Kingdom became a British citizen.[61] Those that did not have a right of abode but had some connection with a British dependent territory became British dependent territories citizens. Those who did not qualify as either British citizens or British dependent territories citizens become British overseas citizens. So although the 1981 Act introduces the requirement of citizenship as the basis of immigration control, the concept of citizenship is defined to include all those who had the right of abode prior to the 1981 Act. The right to abode is specified in detailed provisions of the 1981 Act. From 1983 onwards birth in the United Kingdom ceased to be a qualification for British citizenship. At the time of birth, if either parent is either a British citizen or ordinarily resident, *i.e.* "settled" in the United Kingdom, then British citizenship is acquired. A minor who is adopted becomes a British citizen if the order is made by a United Kingdom court and either adoptive parent is a British citizen on the date of the Order of adoption. In other cases those born in the United Kingdom acquire British citizenship through registration if they have spent the first 10 years of their life in the United Kingdom. British citizenship may be gained through a system of naturalisation.[62] The Home Secretary has a discretion to naturalise certain categories of

---

[61] If a parent subsequently becomes a citizen or is ordinarily resident here while the child is still a minor the child is a citizen of the UK. A child adopted through a United Kingdom court order becomes a British citizen if the adopter is a British citizen.
[62] S.6 and Sch.1, British Nationality Act 1981.

applicant but there is no appeal against his refusal. Those married to a British citizen or with a five years' residence in the United Kingdom may be included as naturalised citizens.

The question raised under the Immigration Act 1971 and the British Nationality Act 1981, in force since 1983, together with a variety of immigration rules and regulations is whether a person has a right of abode in the United Kingdom. This question will determine whether the person is subject to immigration control. Those who are subject to control, that is they do not have the right to abode, may be classified as those who are expected to be permitted to enter and remain and those that have no such expectation. Determination of such a category depends on the application of immigration rules under s.3(2) of the Immigration Act 1971. This section provides that either House of Parliament may disapprove of a statement of rules within 40 days of such resolution. S.39(2) of the 1981 Act provides that all British citizens have a right of abode. Commonwealth citizens before 1981 have a right of abode satisfied on the production of a certificate of entitlement. The right of abode also extends to citizens of the European Community. Two countries where immigration have proved problematic are the Falkland Islands and Hong Kong. First is the case of the Falklands. After the Falklands War the Government passed the British Nationality (Falkland Islands) Act 1983. Those born in the Falklands to parents who were settled there have become British citizens. Second is the case of Hong Kong where the potential for large-scale immigration into the United Kingdom has increased after the period of British rule and the handing over of the colony to China. The Hong Kong Act 1985 provides a unique category of "British Nationals (Overseas)", after July 1997. This category carries no rights to United Kingdom residence. However a small category of Hong Kong citizens have been granted British citizenship with entry rights intended to encourage them to remain in Hong Kong with the knowledge that they may leave Hong Kong and live in the United Kingdom as an assurance against unfavourable treatment by the Chinese. **16–091**

Further changes to the status and registration of British citizens comes from The British Overseas Territories Act 2002. This Act follows discussion and consultation with the fourteen British overseas territories[63] resulting in a White Paper in March 1999. The fourteen British overseas territories include: Anguilla, Bermuda, British Antarctic Territory, British Indian Ocean Territory, British Virgin Islands, Cayman Islands, Falkland Islands, Gibraltar, Montserrat, Pitcairn Islands, St Helena and Dependencies, South Georgia and the South Sandwich Islands, the Sovereign Base Areas of Akrotiri and Dhekelia in Cyprus, and the Turks and Caicos Islands. The aim of the Act is to give British citizenship with the right of abode to the British Dependant Territories on the same basis as granted to the Falkland Islands in 1983. **16–092**

Immigration Rules and Procedures

Administration of the immigration rules represents an important example of administrative discretion. This is an area of great political controversy and it is the subject of much legislative change. Ss.1 and 2 of the Immigration Act 1971 provides that all **16–093**

---

[63] *Partnership for Progress and Prosperity: Britain and the Overseas Territories*, Cm.4264 (March 1999).

persons who have a right to abode are free to come and go. S.3(2) of the 1971 Act provides for immigration rules and procedures to regulate entry into the United Kingdom and providing powers for immigration officials to ensure that the requirements of the immigrations rules are fulfilled. A person who fails to meet the requirements of the rules or does not have the right of abode may be refused leave. The immigration rules are in effect given the force of law and may form the basis of a legal challenge in the High Court on the basis that the rules have been incorrectly interpreted or applied. The question of judicial review is related to the question of whether there are available alternative remedies. The immigration rules are also supplemented by instructions issued from time to time by the Home Office.

16–094   Nationals of the European Community once free to enter are free from any restrictions on employment or occupation and no work permit is required for prospective workers. Community nationals and their families enjoy generous rights within Member States subject to refusal on the grounds of personal unacceptability such as public security or public health. Citizens of the Republic of Ireland are part of a Common Travel Area permitting immigration-free travel within the specified area but subject to the provisions applying to emergency powers. New legislation passed in 1987, the Immigration (Carriers' Liability) Act 1987, makes it a criminal offence for the owner of a ship, aircraft or a carrier to allow any person who requires leave to enter the United Kingdom to arrive in the United Kingdom without any necessary passport and visa. The provisions of the 1987 Act make it difficult for asylum seekers as claims for asylum are made on arrival in the country of destination, and not prior to departure. Carriers may in certain circumstances have the penalty under the 1987 Act waived in cases where asylum is granted.

Asylum

16–095   This is one of the most complex and sensitive areas of the law. It is estimated[64] that in 1999 there were "71,160 applications for that year and 102,870 claims outstanding overall the highest number ever recorded". Asylum seekers appear to be on the increase, hence the sense of urgency for every new enactment. There are a plethora of rules and regulations and several major statutory requirements. A new Asylum Bill is being planned for the Autumn of 2002. As matters stand the Immigration Rules 1994, the Asylum and Immigration Appeals Act 1993, and the Asylum and Immigration Act 1996 amended by the Immigration and Asylum Act 1999 provide a comprehensive range of powers for asylum seekers. There are special considerations that apply where a person seeking entry claims asylum. Asylum may refer to political refugees, that is those "owing to a well-founded fear of being prosecuted for reasons of race, religion, nationality, membership of a particular group or political opinion". Making a judgment as to the presence of any of these factors in any particular case requires the discretion of the Secretary of State. Factors which may be considered are facts and information which the Secretary of State is aware of, even if such factors are unknown to the applicant. The question is whether there is "a real likelihood" of persecution which may be based on "substantial grounds" or a "serious possibility" of persecution.

---

[64] D. Stevens, "The Immigration and Asylum Act 1999: A Missed Opportunity?" [2001] *MLR* 413.

The House of Lords upheld the decision of the Secretary of State to refuse the asylum applications of the six applicants who were Tamils from Sri Lanka, but on appeal to the adjudicator the Tamils were successful on the basis of the findings of the adjudicator made from the evidence before him.[65]

16–096 The Asylum and Immigration Appeals Act 1993 was intended to accelerate the process of immigration control to cope with the growth in the numbers of asylum seekers and problems of blatant abuse. The rights of appeal of asylum seekers are also covered in the Act. New measures include powers under s.3 to undertake fingerprinting together with arrest powers granted to immigration officers. S.8 of the 1993 Act provides a right of appeal in cases where a claim for asylum has been refused. This is subject to the terms of the Asylum and Immigration Act 1996 and the Immigration and Asylum Act 1999 discussed below. In certain cases the Secretary of State may certify that in his opinion the asylum seeker's claim is without foundation. Special time-limits will apply in such cases. If the special adjudicator agrees with the Secretary of State's assessment there can be no further appeal to the Immigration Appeal Tribunal. S.9 provides for a right of appeal on a point of law to the Court of Appeal or in Scotland, the Court of Sessions, from a final determination of the Immigration Appeal Tribunal. The introduction of an appeal represents an important improvement, as hitherto an application for judicial review was the only way in which decisions of the Tribunals could be challenged. The right of appeal does not preclude judicial review. However the 1993 Act does remove long-established rights of appeal from would-be visitors and certain categories of students and their dependants. This means that judicial review may become overburdened with applications from visitors or certain categories of students deprived of the right of appeal under the Act. In addition to the above, the 1993 Act introduces changes to the Immigration Rules dated July 5, 1993. Member States are comparatively free to provide their own restrictive arrangements. At the time of adoption of the Single European Act, Member States adopted a General Declaration retaining the power of the Member States as regards the control of immigration from Third World countries and attempting to control the illicit traffic in drugs and the illegal market in antiques and art. There is also a Dublin Convention signed in June 1990 for asylum seekers suggesting a common approach to restricting asylum seekers throughout the Community, though it is doubtful if once asylum is granted by one Member State there is any free movement within the Community between Member States.

16–097 The Immigration Rules 1994 have been added to by the Asylum Appeals (Procedure) Rules 1996 and the Asylum and Immigration Act 1996. Further changes are made by the Immigration and Asylum Act 1999 explained below. The 1996 Act considerably strengthened the existing law. The 1996 Act has three aims, namely: to deal with any bogus claims for asylum expeditiously; to combat immigration racketeering through stronger powers, new offences and higher penalties; and finally to reduce the economic incentives which attract people to come to Britain in breach of the law.

16–098 The Act achieves these aims in several ways as follows. It excludes cases from appeals to the Immigration and Appeals Tribunal and substitutes appeals to a special adjudicator. There is a system of certification by the Secretary of State. The special adjudicator may conclude that the appellant does have a well-founded fear of prosecution and allow

[65] See *Ex p. Sivakumaran* [1988] A.C. 958; [1988] 1 All E.R. 193.

appeal against removal; or dismiss the appeal on the grounds that the special adjudicator is not satisfied that the appellant has a well-grounded fear of persecution at the date of the hearing. In the latter case the special adjudicator is free to accept or reject the certificate of the Secretary of State. Under these procedures there is no longer the possibility of making a reference back to the Secretary of State. There are changes to the law on removal to "safe third countries" certified as such by the Secretary of State. There is an appeal to a special adjudicator in such cases. There are new immigration offences of obtaining leave by deception under s.4 of the 1996 Act and assisting asylum claimants to obtain leave by deception. There are increased penalties and additional powers of arrest and search under s.7 of the 1996 Act. There is a draconian rule under s.9 that a person subject to immigration control is not eligible for a council tenancy, introduced after a number of cases struck down the attempt to impose this rule by statutory instrument. There are also provisions covering social security and child benefit.

16–099   The Immigration and Asylum Act 1999 makes the Home Office administratively responsible for providing support and accommodation for asylum seekers pending determination of their application. There is a new Home Office Agency, the National Asylum Support Service, and the Act provides a new system of appeals. The Act also allows new grounds for removal to Member States of the European Union or to other safe third countries. Extensive powers are granted to use new technology to record and process asylum seekers. There are additional powers for the running of detention centres and new offences for carriers of illegal immigrants, and for setting up "sham marriages". There is a new offence under s.4 of the Immigration and Asylum Act 1999 that pertains to an asylum claimant who remains in Britain, having gained asylum on the basis of a bogus claim. In these circumstances the asylum claimant continues to commit an offence while being in the country. Powers of detention include detaining vehicles and restrictions on only qualified persons under s.84 of the 1999 Act that may give immigration advice or offer immigration services. S.22 of the 1999 Act amends s.8 of the Asylum and Immigration Act 1996 which made it an offence for an employer to employ an illegal immigrant. The new powers under s.22 of the 1999 Act allow the Secretary of State to issue a code of practice setting out the steps employers are expected to take to meet their requirements under the Act.

16–100   The 1999 Act creates a reform and consolidation of the appeal system. The claims for asylum fall under new rules—the Immigration and Asylum Appeals (Procedure) Rules 2000.[65a] There is a new Human Rights Appeal procedure under s.65, namely that the authority has breached the asylum seeker's human rights. There is also under ss.74-78, the introduction of a single-tier appeal for consolidation of the grounds of appeal that would include the notice of additional grounds served on a person appealing a decision.

Deportation

16–101   Deportation of all who are not British citizens is currently regulated under the Immigration Act 1971 as amended by the British Nationality Act 1981 and the Immigration Act 1988 and the Immigration Rules 1990. Sch.14 of the immigration and

[65a] Immigration and Asylum Appeals (Procedure) Rules (SI 2000/2333).

Asylum Act 1999 makes further amendments. Anyone who is not a British citizen, with certain specified exceptions, is subject to deportation. There are generally four grounds: first if the Home Secretary deems it "conducive to the public good"; secondly, on the recommendation by a court on conviction of a person over 17 for an offence which is punishable by imprisonment; thirdly, where a person breaks any entry conditions or overstays the period of entry permitted by the immigration officer; fourthly, he or she is the infant child or wife of a person against whom a deportation order is made.

A deportation order may be used for a mixture of motives. In *Ex p. Soblen*[66] the deportation order was used to comply with a request from the United States for Soblen's return. This in effect amounted to extradition, in circumstances where extradition was not possible because Soblen's alleged crimes involved espionage and extradition was not available for such offences. The Court of Appeal upheld the deportation order even though it was apparent that the motives of the Secretary of State were not confined to deportation grounds and that extradition was acheived through the facility of deportation.

16–102

The breadth of the Secretary of State's discretion is also indicated by the phrase "conducive to public good" which is commonly used in respect of convicted offenders. This may occur even where the court does not recommend deportation but where the Secretary of State is convinced the presence of the individual is not conducive to the public good. Less easy to justify is the use of deportation powers where no cirminal prosecution has been taken and no conviction gained. In cases where the question of political activities of the individual arise, deportation on the basis of objections to such activities is open to criticism. For example the deportation of Rudi Deutschke to West Germany in 1969 and the deportation of journalists Agee and Hosenball[67] on national security grounds raises questions about the use of deportation powers.

16–103

There is an appeal system now consolidated under Pt IV of the Immigration and Asylum Act 1999, previously under ss.13–17 of the Immigration Act 1971 as amended by the British Nationality Act 1981 against refusal of entry, refusal of certificates of entitlement and refusal of entry clearances. The procedure for appeal lies against the decision of the immigration officer to an adjudicator and then with leave to an independent Immigration Appeal Tribunal. There is a presumption that appeal rights should be exhausted before judicial review is resorted to by the applicant. In a number of circumstances it is no longer possible to appeal against the merits of a deportation decision and appeal is thereby confined to matters of law. Further restrictions have received judicial approval by the House of Lords in *Oladehinde v Secretary of State of the Home Department*[68] where an adjudicator was not entitled to question the propriety of the Secretary of State's decision to make a deportation order.

16–104

PERSONAL FREEDOM

The citizen's personal liberty and freedom are often provided in rules of evidence and the right to a fair trial. Minimum safeguards are provided for the arrest, detention and trial of an accused on criminal charges. For example there may be the requirement

16–105

[66] *R. v. Brixton Prison Governor Ex p. Soblen* [1963] 2 Q.B. 243.
[67] See *Ex p. Hosenball* [1977] 3 All E.R. 452.
[68] [1990] 3 All E.R. 393.

that there should within a reasonable period of time be a trial before a court and a fair hearing. The rules of evidence at a criminal trial entitle a person accused to know the evidence against him; entitlement to some form of legal representation is also required as is assistance in the form of legal aid in the preparation of his case. The Human Rights Act 1998 is likely to have an impact on how personal freedoms are to be treated by the courts in the future.

16–106   The law relating to the powers of arrest, questioning of suspects and their rights is untidy and unduly complicated. In practical terms the scope of the citizen's freedom is often dependent on the exercise of police powers and in individual cases how the police officer exercises his discretion. The courts have not always followed a consistent approach of how to determine the exact scope of police powers. Judicial intervention has therefore been sporadic. Setting the delicate balance between protecting the suspect and allowing the police sufficient powers to undertake their duties is difficult. The Royal Commission on Criminal Procedure,[69] set up in 1977, reported in 1981. The outcome of the Royal Commission's deliberations is the Police and Criminal Evidence Act 1984 intended to transform many of the common law principles into a single coherent statute. At the same time, the Prosecution of Offences Act 1985 created the Crown Prosecution Service (CPS) headed by the Director of Public Prosecutions, organised on the basis of 31 areas, each headed by a Chief Crown Prosecutor covering at least one or two police forces for that area. The power of the private citizen to prosecute is retained but the bulk of prosecutions are taken by the CPS and the CPS may take over any private prosecution when it is regarded as in the public interest.

16–107   A further Royal Commission was set up[70] and its main recommendations are found in the Criminal Justice and Public Order Act 1994, and the Criminal Procedure and Investigations Act 1996. There are additional powers under the Crime and Disorder Act 1998 and the Criminal Justice and Police Act 2001. The Regulation and Investigatory Powers Act 2000 provides the police with surveillance powers. These powers are discussed in Chapter 20 on secrecy.

16–108   The Police and Criminal Evidence Act 1984, hereinafter referred to as PACE, generally extended police powers on the basis of additional statutory powers but introduced a number of requirements in the form of codes of practice made by the Home Secretary under s.66 of PACE and intended to act as safeguards for the accused. These safeguards include that those under the exercise of police powers should be informed of the reasons for the exercise of those powers, that reasons be recorded contemporaneously, that senior officers should undertake a review of the use of powers, and that various codes of conduct and practices should be set up to administer the exercise of police powers. There are also extensive provisions under s.58 which confer rights on suspects, such as access to legal advice at police stations.

16–109   The arrangements under PACE have recently been extended to Northern Ireland and research into the operation of arrangements under PACE has been undertaken. Questions concerning the efficacy of the safeguards under PACE have been raised.

---

[69] Cmnd.8092.
[70] See A. Sanders, "Constructing the Case for the Prosecution" (1987) 14 *Journal of Law and Society* 229. The Royal Commission on Criminal Justice, Cm.2263 (1993), chaired by Lord Runciman.

Arrest

The police have no general powers to detain suspects for questioning unless they are **16–110** arrested. Unlawful detention and arrest may amount to false imprisonment which may be actionable as well as a criminal offence. The exercise of arrest powers involves an element of compulsion, and requires that the person arrested is informed that he is under arrest. In effecting an arrest no more physical force must be used than is reasonably required. Unreasonable use of force becomes an actionable assault. The person arrested must be made aware of the fact of his arrest as soon as it is practicable, except where the arrest is by a private citizen and the ground of arrest is obvious. There are stop-and-search powers available under a number of statutes. Under s.23 of the Misuse of Drugs Act 1971 a constable may search and detain a suspect who he has reasonable grounds to believe to be in unlawful possession of a controlled drug. S.163 of the Road Traffic Act 1988 provides that a uniformed constable may require a driver of a motor vehicle or a cyclist to stop. Additional powers exist to require the production of insurance or motor licence. Powers of arrest under PACE fall into two categories: either without a warrant or with a warrant. Arrest without warrant is provided under s.24. The Royal Commission on Criminal Procedure envisaged that the police should be able to arrest an individual without a warrant if the crime suspected was an imprisonable offence rather than a fine. An additional safeguard was that arrest should be linked to one that is necessary. Necessary conditions may be found in the general arrest conditions in PACE. This is intended to be the main power for arrest without warrant. Any member of the public may arrest, without warrant, anyone who is in the act of committing an arrestable offence or where there are reasonable grounds for suspecting the committing of an arrestable offence. In addition, a constable may arrest, without warrant: anyone whom he has reasonable grounds for suspecting of having committed an arrestable offence, even though no such crime has been committed; and anyone who is about to commit an arrestable offence or he has reasonable grounds to believe is about to commit such a crime. A constable, with reasonable grounds, may arrest any person whom he suspects is committing or has committed or attempted an offence which is not an arrestable offence, provided that service of the summons is impracticable or inappropriate because certain general arrest conditions are satisfied.

The question of what is an arrestable offence is clarified in s.24, such as murder, **16–111** treason, and other crimes imprisonable for five years or more. However there are a number of offences which do not fit this category, such as offences relating to crimes against property and sexual offences, which are also made arrestable even though they may not carry prison sentences of five years or more. In fact, Sch.2 of PACE contains numerous provisions retained under s.26 of PACE and granting the power to arrest without warrant. Various inchoate offences such as conspiring, or attempting to commit or incite or procure the commission of any arrestable offence is also arrestable. The common law power to arrest for breach of the peace is also included.[71]

It may be concluded that the police have very wide powers to arrest without a **16–112** warrant. The requirements of arrest procedures are to be informed of the arrest and of

[71] For example, the Street Offences Act 1959, s.7(3); Immigration Act 1971, s.1(3). Since PACE there have been additions to the list such as: Sporting Events (Control of Alcohol etc.) Act 1985, Public Order Act 1986, s.3(6).

the ground of arrest. In *Abbassy v Metropolitan Police Commissioner*,[72] a civil case, the Court of Appeal accepted that an arrest for "unlawful possession" was sufficient as a reason to arrest for theft. Even when the arrest is unlawful initially, if the police failed to inform the suspect of the ground of arrest, the police may make a lawful arrest once they comply with this requirement. Arrest with a warrant as provided by statute, empowers the justice to either issue a summons requiring that person to appear before a magistrates' court or to issue a warrant to arrest the person to appear before the court. A warrant is obtained from a magistrate after information is made in writing and substantiated on oath. An arrest warrant may be executed through the use of reasonable force to enter and search premises. A warrant protects the police from liability for the search.

16–113   Aside from the powers of arrest, PACE provides powers of detention after arrest and before charge. Prior to PACE there was considerable doubt as to the legality of detention powers. Once the police decide that there is sufficient evidence to charge a person, he must be charged otherwise he must be released. PACE leaves considerable latitude to the police as to how this power may be interpreted. The maximum permitted period of detention is 96 hours but there is a vague expression as a rider to this such as "a person must normally be brought before a magistrates' court as soon as practicable". The time limit is taken from the moment the person arrives at the police station. This leaves the police time to interrogate before arrival at the police station. In *Parchment*[73] although the police may have broken various rules in their interrogation of a suspect if carried out at the police station, because the interrogation was carried out in the period before arrival at the police station, the court held that the police had not acted illegally.

16–114   In cases of serious arrestable offences a superintendent or above, may authorise detention for up to 36 hours. A magistrates' court may grant a further 36 hours provided the total time does not exceed 96 hours.

16–115   Safeguards are provided under various codes of practice which require that certain powers may be exercised only by senior officers or a designated custody officer, defined as being independent from the investigation. The custody officer has various responsibilities under PACE including informing suspects of their rights, keeping detailed custody records, authorising and releasing from detention and deciding whether suspects should be charged or not. Considerable variation appears to exist in how the rules are interpreted and the practices of different police stations throughout the country.

Search and Seizure

16–116   Powers of search and seizure are often provided on the basis of a valid arrest. Following an arrest, a police constable has the power to search a suspect to determine whether he may present a danger to himself or others or has evidence relating to suspected offences or has anything which might assist his escape. S.1 of PACE and additions provided by ss.139 and 140 of the Criminal Justice Act 1988 provide powers to stop and search for any offensive weapon, stolen goods or for equipment used in

---

[72] [1990] 1 W.L.R. 385; [1990] 1 All E.R. 193.
[73] [1989] Crim. L.R. 290.

offences such as a burglary. Extensive stop-and-search powers are also available under the Misuse of Drugs Act 1971 as well as a plethora of other legislative enactments. Powers exercised under PACE must comply with a Code of Practice. The suspect must be informed of the grounds for the search and that such "reasonable grounds" must be made out before and not after the stop-and-search powers are exercised. It is accepted that such stop-and-search powers are controversial and require tact, forbearance and understanding on the part of the police when exercising their powers in multi-ethnical or multi-racial societies.

Searching premises and seizing goods may arise under search warrant powers under **16–117** ss.8 and 9 of PACE. At common law the police had no general power to obtain warrants, and warrants could not be generally authorising of police powers to search and seize goods. Such restrictions have been largely removed by Pt II of PACE which consists of general powers to enter premises and search after an arrest, a general power of seizure, and general powers of entry. In addition a number of statutes provide quite specific powers for the police to search premises, for example in the areas of theft or drugs-related crimes.

Search without a warrant may arise following an arrest (s.32 of PACE) or, ancillary **16–118** to arrest powers, there is a power to search premises and finally, the power to search without a warrant the home of the arrested person (s.18 of PACE).

Interrogation of Suspects

A large part of the safeguards to be found in PACE for the interrogation of suspects in **16–119** custody depend on the actions of the custody officer. The arrival of the suspect at the police station under arrest or when he is arrested results in the custody officer informing the suspect of his right to have someone informed of his arrest; the right to consult privately with a solicitor; and the availability of free legal advice. There are detailed rules for the detention of suspects, including the conditions of cells and rooms. A search of the suspect may be carried out and any property may be retained by the custody officer. The right to consult a solicitor is stated in categorical terms under s.58(1) of PACE "to consult a solicitor privately at any time"; however the remaining subsections provide a number of *caveats* restricting this right. These allow for consultation to be "as soon as practicable". An officer of or above the rank of superintendent may delay access where the suspect is suspected of a serious arrestable offence and where the officer believes that one of four situations may arise: interference with or harm to evidence connected with a serious arrestable offence; interference with or physical injury to other persons; alerting other persons suspected of having committed such an offence but who have not been arrested for it; the hindering of the recovery of any property obtained as a result of such an offence.

While access to legal advice may only be delayed for up to 36 hours, the scope of the **16–120** delay provisions is sufficiently wide to enable the police to restrict the suspect's rights to consult a solicitor. Further, the term "serious arrestable offence" is sufficiently broad to encourage this category to be expanded and come within the terms of the delay power. The extent of police discretion relies on judicial supervision by the courts. In *Samuel* the defendant's request to see a solicitor was denied, and the police found incriminating evidence in various searches of his house. He was kept in the police station overnight and after an in-depth interrogation he later confessed to the offences of burglary; after he was charged, his solicitor's attempts to interview him were frustrated by the police. The Court of Appeal was critical of the police handling of the case and held that a suspect should always be able to see a solicitor after being charged. The confession obtained by the police was excluded by the Court and the defendant's conviction quashed.

16–121   Some qualification to the principles in *Samuel*[74] came in *Alladice*.[74a] The Court of Appeal accepted that a confession obtained by the police after refusal of access to a solicitor did not render the confession inadmissible. These cases illustrate some of the difficulties of oversight by the courts. Attempting to balance the interests of the police with those of the accused in the face of statutory provisions which are capable of wide and diffuse interpretation is difficult. Since *Alladice* the Divisional Court in *Robinson*[75] accepted that a solicitor's clerk may be refused access if the police believe that the clerk is unsuitable to give advice based on the capacity of the clerk in the view of the police to perform that function.

16–122   An important element in police practice is the requirement that the person arrested and charged must be brought before a magistrates' court. Release on bail may be granted by a custody sergeant following the arrest without warrant; or by the magistrate or by a High Court judge. Conditions of bail may include the accused being asked to enter his own recognisance to keep the peace. A general power remains, that magistrates may make it a condition of bail that the accused does not breach the peace and such bail conditions are open to rigorous enforcement by the courts. The practice of setting particularly restrictive bail conditions on striking miners in 1984 came to be regarded as "usual conditions". This power led to the criticism that the courts were exercising a system of group justice. There appears to be no direct appeal against such orders of the court and the restrictions imposed as bail conditions may be used to inhibit political agitation.

16–123   The outcome of the interrogation process is often a statement which has some damaging effect on the accused. This may be through the provision of information which may assist the police in the gathering of intelligence or the obtaining of additional evidence. In fact the possibility exists that the police may find it convenient to use such information to create a factual basis for the conclusions they may wish a court to reach. PACE covers the admission of confession evidence under ss.50–60 and 76–78 of the 1984 Act and the various codes of practice. There is a revised Code of Practice C (1995) for interviewing suspects. The courts have a general discretion at common law and under s.78 of PACE to exclude evidence, generally to ensure that the accused was not induced to incriminate himself by deception. S.78 has been used to exclude identification evidence in breach of the code of practice, and to exclude the evidence of previous convictions of persons other than the accused. However, it is unclear the extent to which this power may be used to exclude illegally obtained evidence.

16–124   S.76 covers the admissibility of confessions where the confession may have been obtained:

[74] *R. v Samuel* [1988] Q.B. 615.
[74a] *R. v Alladice* (1988) 87 Cr.App.R. 380.
[75] (1989) 139 N.L.J. 186.

"by oppression of the person who made it, in consequence of anything asaid or done which was likely in the circumstances existing at the time, to render unreliable any confession which might be made by him in consequence thereof."

Oppression is defined under s.76(8) of PACE as including "torture, inhuman or degrading treatment and the use or threat of violence". Lord Lane in *Fulling*[76] explained that the word should be given its ordinary meaning such as the   **16–125**

"exercise of authority or power in a burdensome, harsh, or wrongful manner; unjust or cruel treatment of subjects, inferiors etc. the imposition of unreasonable or unjust burdens."

Oppression is not satisfied merely by breaches of the law or the codes of practice under PACE, which do not necessarily amount to oppression. Unrealibility of a confession is used more often than the claim of oppression. Breaches of PACE, improperly conducted interviews, and improper inducement may lead to exclusion on the basis that the confession is unreliable.   **16–125a**

The right of the suspect to be silent in the face of police interrogation is a central principle of English law and is of long standing. The right to silence provides that no person may be required to give information to the police in the course of a criminal prosecution. This means that the suspect may decline to answer questions during interrogation. It also means that a person charged with a criminal offence cannot be required to give evidence in court at any stage of the trial. In the past no adverse inferences may be drawn from an accused's silence at an interview or failure to give evidence in court. In recent years the future of the right to silence has been the subject of intense debate, resulting in its removal in 1994. Ss.34–39 of the Criminal Justice and Public Order Act 1994 allows a court or jury to draw inferences from an accused's silence.   **16–126**

Following the discovery of a number of miscarriages of justice in the *Confait*, *Birmingham Six* and *Guildford Four* cases,[77] concern about police practices and the trial of criminal cases has led to discussion of the adversarial system at a criminal trial. Recent research has pointed to the inadequacy of accountability over the police and questioned the effectiveness of the adversarial system of trial. Even more worrying is the conclusion that "internal, legalistic reforms would leave untouched the class, gender and race biases of the system." The search for a suitable reform of the system of criminal justice is problematical. The same researchers conclude that the desire for greater accountability has little meaning as it is directed at providing after the fact explanations which can be simply self-serving to the police to construct the facts to meet the criteria of accountability. The research concludes[78]:   **16–127**

"Accountability, if it is to have any relevance to police-work practices, must be both prospective and able to penetrate the control networks which the police utilize to perpetuate police values and ideologies and screen out external inspection mechanisms."

[76] *R. v Fulling* [1987] 2 All E.R. 65.
[77] See M. McConville, A. Sanders and R. Leng, *The Case for the Prosecution* (Routledge, London, 1991).
[78] *ibid.*, pp.207–208.

Complaints Against the Police

16–128   The citizen may seek redress against the police through judicial review or in the defence of a criminal charge, or may seek to show that the police acted unlawfully. In the event of the acquittal of criminal charges because of evidence which shows police doing wrong, this may result in civil action against the police; the most common basis for such action is for assault or wrongful arrest. Extensive provisions contained in s.49 of the Police Act 1964 and ss.83–100 and 105 of PACE establishing a Police Complaints Authority (PCA) are now to be found in Pt IV of the Police Act 1996. The regulations that apply to complaints are provided in detail in the Police (Complaints) (General) Regulations 1985. A number of disciplinary offences such as abuse of authority, neglect of duty or using unnecessary violence are available against police officers. Informal resolution of complaint is favoured. The process of complaining involves the Chief Constable deciding whether it should be formally investigated. The PCA supervises the complaint and may appoint an officer from another force to investigate the complaint. The PCA report goes to the Chief Constable who may decide to refer the report to the Director of Public Prosecutions (DPP) with a view to prosecution. The PCA has the power to direct the Chief Constable to refer its report to the DPP. Disciplinary charges may be taken against the police officer involved. In such cases a fair hearing must be given to the officers concerned.

16–129   Criticism of the system of complaints is that the system relies too heavily on the police to investigate complaints against themselves. The PCA is concerned with delays in action being taken by the police and the tendency to retire officers early on ill health where there may be a case for disciplinary action. The rise in the number of civil actions against the police may test public confidence in the ability of the PCA to act efficiently.

16–130   Statements used in police disciplinary hearings are the subject of public interest immunity. This may prevent disclosure of information in civil or criminal proceedings. Documents generated under the police complaints procedures under s.49 of the Police Act 1964, now Pt IV of the Police Act 1996, are similarly regarded. Grievance procedures available through an application before an industrial tribunal on the grounds of racial and sexual victimisation may be treated differently. The police officer complained of sexual discrimination. In determining the case the Employment Appeal Tribunal distinguished grievance procedures for police officers from disciplinary proceedings. While in the former, the applicant was entitled to receive documents, in the latter she was not.

16–131   The police have a pivotal role in the personal freedoms of the citizen. The accountability of the police becomes a significant factor in protecting citizens' rights. More effective accountability may be found, not through greater political control as advocated by some writers, but through effective complaints procedures, and a wider discussion of police practice and culture. The United Kingdom's constitutional arrangements for the protection of civil liberties provides prohibitions and restrictions as well as freedoms and rights. Civil liberties are said to be facing a crisis; not readily cured by the enactment of a Bill of Rights nor easily amenable to any particular legislative reform. In the life cycle of political and constitutional affairs it may be that the most important protection afforded to civil liberties is that the political culture and institutions are continually questioned as to their efficacy in providing the citizen with an adequate enjoyment of civil liberties.

SUMMARY AND CONCLUSIONS

The Human Rights Act 1998 provides citizens with Convention rights as part of **16–132** domestic law. Courts face the daunting challenge of having to adapt discrete areas of human rights law into the domestic legal system through the interpretation of the jurisprudence of the European Court of Human Rights. They must also "as far as it is possible" give importance to the Convention when attempting to interpret and make compatible both primary and secondary legislation. Inevitably this will lead to fundamental changes in the way rights are approached and, as will be outlined in Chapters 17 and 18, in the development of judicial review. Human rights are significant in the way constitutional and administrative law is likely to develop in this country. The culture of public law is set to undergo change and that includes the variety of institutions and agencies that public law embraces—with the far reaching potential of trickling rights into areas of private law; or at the very least suggesting that the boundaries that may separate public and private law are not robust enough to withstand the influence of rights. The courts will continue to have to grapple with the delicate balance between intervention and agency autonomy or ministerial policy. The intrinsic and enduring quality of the common law is its ability to adapt to change. Problem-focused and responsive to needs, the common law has customised solutions to fit new circumstances.

FURTHER READING

S.H. Bailey, D.J. Harris, and B.L. Jones, *Civil Liberties: Cases and Materials* (5th ed., Butterworths, London, 2001).

R. Blackburn and J. Polakiewicz, *Fundamental Rights In Europe* (Oxford University Press, Oxford, 2001).

K. Ewing, "The Human Rights Act and Parliamentary Democracy" (1999) 62 *Modern Law Review* 79.

K. Ewing, "A Theory of Democratic Adjudication: Towards a Representative, Accountable and Independent Judiciary" (2000) 38 *Alberta Law Review* 708.

K. Ewing and C. Gearty, *The Struggle for Civil Liberties* (Oxford University Press, Oxford, 2000).

D. Feldman, *Civil Liberties and Human Rights in England and Wales* (Clarendon Press, Oxford, 1993).

European Civil Liberties and the European Convention on Human Rights (C. Gearty ed., Martinus Nijhoff Publishers, London, 1997).

C. Gearty, "What Are Judges For?" Unpublished inaugural lecture delivered at King's College, London, on Monday December 11, 2000.

J. Waldron, "A Rights-Based Critique of Constitutional Rights" (1993) 13 *Oxford Journal of Legal Studies* 18.

Chapter 17

JUDICIAL REVIEW

INTRODUCTION

The focus of this chapter is on judicial review where an aggrieved citizen may seek **17–001** redress against a public authority through the courts. Judicial review may also arise where there are inter-governmental disputes. This is where, for example, disputes arise between different government departments or between local and central government. This list is not exhaustive as administrative decisions cover a variety of powers and duties that are susceptible to judicial review. The role of the courts must be understood in the context of the administrative process itself. This may set boundaries on the availability of judicial review. For example judicial review does not normally extend to the policy and merits of elected Ministers. In such cases the conventional constitutional wisdom is that the political merits of decisions are accountable to Parliament and the political process, rather than the courts. Drawing the fine distinction between legal and political accountability is a difficult judgment that judges are called upon to make.

We have already seen[1] the wide range of institutions and procedures for the **17–002** resolution of grievances other than the courts. These alternatives range from informal mechanisms to tribunals, inquiries and ombudsmen. In this chapter the primary concern is the means the courts may use to hold the exercise of powers by authorities to account. Public authorities and bodies enjoy a vast array of statutory powers supplemented by a bewildering assortment of administrative rules such as licences, codes of practice, guidelines, regulations and contractual conditions. Public bodies are provided with a plethora of administrative powers. Their status and the context of the problem that they are called upon to address determines the allocation of powers and the systems of accountability that apply. The past two decades has witnessed an expansion in the variety and types of public bodies and agencies that have been created.

Traditionally courts offer a form of external check on the legality of administrative **17–003** powers. The courts may determine the nature of legal powers and how powers may be exercised. The focus is usually directed at resolving a dispute between the individual and the administration. In the United Kingdom, traditionally the litigant seeks a remedy in order to create rights. The Human Rights Act 1998 has added a dimension of rights and the litigant is able to rely on Convention rights to enforce remedies. This

---

[1] See Chap.15.

is a formative period for the transition of a rights-based emphasis into the legal culture of the country and will require some "self-restraint" on the part of the judiciary.[2]

17–004 At first glance judicial review may appear limited and offer a formal, technical and narrowly focused form of accountability. Too often this may appear negative in form, setting out what may or may not be done within the law. Thus judicial review may appear pragmatic and unsystematic. Normally courts offer *ex post facto* rather than *a priori* review, limited to remedies for wrongful actions rather than providing a prescription for the future conduct of administration. As a result it is difficult through the case law developed by the courts to develop principles of good administration.

17–005 Undoubtedly the impact of judicial rules over the long term may encourage a better understanding of keeping within the law.[3] There is also greater awareness today of the availability of judicial review, and the existence of pressure groups engaged in litigation has gained media and public attention. Judicial review has continued to expand during the 1990s. This is marked by a perceptible growth in judicial self-confidence in their role, and increased visibility in a number of headline cases[4] that have attracted public comment and media attention. The judges have exposed new areas of governmental power to judicial review.

17–006 Judicial review is not confined to the needs of the individual citizen. Government bodies may engage in judicial review as a means of establishing the basis of their relationship with the citizen, or with another public body. In the chapter on local government, it was noted how relations between local and central government were considered by the courts. Intra-governmental disputes between local and central government may be the basis of judicial review as much as the individual citizen seeking redress.

17–007 Judicial review must also be considered within the overall constitutional context of accountability of public bodies. There remains the broader question about the role of the courts in reviewing administrative action. Controlling administrative decisions is further complicated if the forms of political accountability appear weak and the role of the courts appears to be expanding. Are the courts able to respond to an expanded role in carrying out their functions? Such a role might lead to greater scrutiny of the judiciary and may bring judges more closely within the agenda of political debate.

THE CLASSIFICATION OF ADMINISTRATIVE DECISION-MAKING

17–008 The making of administrative decisions affects the lives of many citizens. In the context of the body making a decision, it is necessary to consider the various ways decision-making may be classified. A discretion whether or not to make a decision or pursue a course of action may be classified as a power to make the appropriate decision, whereas an obligation to take action may be classified as a duty to act or make a decision. There is a working presumption that provided the action is not prohibited by law, there is freedom to do anything. Determining what falls within the law involves

---

[2] *R. (on the application of Lichniak) v Secretary of State for the Home Department* [2001] 4 All E.R. 934.

[3] The pamphlet *The Judge Over Your Shoulder* has had a number of editions warning civil servants to act within the law.

[4] On the work of pressure groups see, for example *R. v Secretary of State for Foreign Affairs Ex p. World Development Movement Ltd* [1995] 1 All E.R. 611. *R. v Inspectorate of Pollution Ex p. Greenpeace Ltd (No.2)* [1994] 4 All E.R. 321.

careful consideration of the nature of the body making the decision, the nature of the legal powers involved, and the question of whether the correct procedures have been applied. The answer to these questions generally involves statutory interpretation as many legal powers have a statutory basis. In previous chapters we have noted how many governmental powers are derived from the prerogative which are reviewable by the courts. Contract or licences may also form the basis of legal powers. Disputes may involve civil action in tort or contract rather than judicial review. The courts may be confronted with a hybrid of powers, some statutory, contractual or prerogative.

Powers and duties provided by statute are open to interpretation by the courts. The courts' role in interpreting statutory enactments depends on resolving ambiguities through the interpretation of the meaning of words in the statute and giving account to parliamentary intention. There are differences in the style of drafting statutory provisions. The Victorian style was to encapsulate the common law position within a statutory framework. Modern statutory drafting may be more technical and detailed with narrowly defined powers and duties leaving little room for any creative statutory interpretation by the judges. There is also a judicial role in "filling in gaps", or seeking to give effect to Parliament's intentions through techniques of statutory interpretation. Government White Papers and official reports may be useful in construing parliamentary intention.   **17–009**

Recently the House of Lords accepted in *Pepper (Inspector of Taxes) v Hart*[5] that the rule prohibiting courts from reading parliamentary material as an aid to statutory construction should be relaxed. Where the legislation was ambiguous or obscure or the literal meaning led to an absurdity then it might be helpful to examine the relevant parliamentary materials, subject to questions regarding parliamentary privilege. This might include statements by a Minister or other promoter of the Bill which led to the enactment of the legislation, and other material which might be necessary to understand such statements provided the statements were clear. However the relaxation of the rule is confined to Ministers or promoters of the Bill which might exclude full parliamentary debates. Lord Browne-Wilkinson explained how the courts in construing statutory instruments had regard to the statements made by Ministers who may have initiated the debate on regulations.[6] Expanding this principle to primary legislation would enable the courts to understand the nature of the issues raised by the legislation.   **17–010**

Earlier cases had accepted that the courts might consider *Hansard* in ascertaining whether a statutory power had been used for an improper purpose. The House of Lords in *R. v Secretary of State for the Home Department Ex p. Brind*[7] attached importance to what the Minister had said in Parliament as an aid to interpretation. Indeed, in general matters of statutory interpretation beyond the ministerial remit, the courts may be called upon to draw a line between political and legal material that has to be interpreted by a regulatory agency. In *R. v Radio Authority Ex p. Bull*,[8] the Court of Appeal examined the decision of the Radio Authority to regard Amnesty International's campaign for human rights as mainly of a political nature. Under s.92(2)(a)(i) of the Broadcasting Act 1990 advertising of a political nature was banned   **17–011**

---

[5] [1993] 1 All E.R. 42.
[6] *Pickstone v Freemans plc* [1988] 2 All E.R. 803.
[7] [1991] 1 A.C. 696.
[8] *The Times Law Reports* (January 21, 1997).

from the radio. Interpretation of the political nature of human rights and the restrictions imposed by the 1990 Act required the Court of Appeal to make a careful value judgment of Amnesty's campaign, even though Lord Woolf accepted that such a campaign was "commendable".

17–012 The House of Lords relaxation of the rules regarding statutory interpretation is probably acceptance of practices that have been developing over the last 30 years. Does this make it more likely for the courts to question the merits of a decision? Traditionally the courts have refrained from overtly considering the merits of the case and judicial review may fall short of substituting judicial decision-making for that of the decision-maker entrusted by Parliament. The limits of judicial review were acknowledged by Lord Justice Watkins in *R. v Secretary of State for Trade and Industry Ex p. Lonrho*[9] when he suggested that the courts' role would not take on the responsibility of making "executive or administrative decisions". The dangers of an excessively interventionist approach by the courts were pointed out by Lord Scarman in *Nottingham C v Secretary of State for the Environment*[10]:

> "Judicial review is a great weapon in the hands of the judges; but the judges must observe the constitutional limits set by our parliamentary system upon the exercise of this beneficent power."

17–013 The courts in the United Kingdom cannot review the legality of a United Kingdom Act of Parliament in matters of strictly domestic law that does not involve matters of European Community law. S.2 of the Human Rights Act 1998 provides the power for courts when considering cases that raise issues of interpretation of a Convention right, to take into account judgments, decisions or advisory opinions of the European Court of Human Rights. They are not bound by the decisions but they must interpret them. Legislation may not be struck down by the United Kingdom's courts for incompatibility with Convention rights. The most the courts may do is to make a declaration of incompatibility under s.4(2) of the Act.

Statutory Appeals

17–014 The citizen may have available a right of appeal. Appeals provide the courts with an opportunity to rule on the legality of particular decisions and are as important as judicial review when considering the role of the courts and the procedures open to the citizen. Unlike judicial review which developed from common law origins, appeals are statutory in origin. The statutory formulation includes express provision usually setting out the grounds for appeal and the appellate jurisdiction of the courts. It is difficult to generalise any principles involved in appeals provided by statute. Parliamentary developments in creating appeals have been on a case by case basis depending on the nature of the issues expected to be raised on appeal. The Franks Committee noted[11] "the desirability of some form of appeal", but there is no universal principle setting out a minimum standard of when an appeal should be provided, nor the scope of an appeal once conferred by statute.

[9] [1989] 1 W.L.R. 525.
[10] [1986] A.C. 240, 250–251.
[11] Cmnd.218 (1957).

The existence of an appeal procedure raises the question of whether under an   **17–015**
appeal procedure, the legality of action may be challenged. The Law Commission has
noted that many judicial review applications were initiated as desperate and ill-
disguised attempts to appeal against the decision in question. Conversely, appeals may
be widely interpreted to include matters that could be reviewed. Occasionally the
courts have accepted a wider remit to the appeal system even where it may overlap
with the application for judicial review. An appeal against the decision of the district
auditor under the Local Government Finance Act 1982 raised questions of the legality
and fairness of the auditor's decision. Such matters, the Court of Appeal acknowledged, could also be the subject of an application for judicial review. In *Lloyd v
McMahon*[12] the Court of Appeal was content to allow the appeal in that instance, to
include issues of the legality of the auditor's decision. In the House of Lords, Lord
Bridge accepted the overlapping jurisdiction of an application for judicial review and
appeals under the 1982 Act, but preferred the wider grounds of an appeal to raise the
legality of the auditor's report.

In *Foster v Chief Adjudication Officer*[13] the House of Lords allowed a social security   **17–016**
claimant an appeal to a tribunal when a benefit claim was rejected but based on
consideration of whether the regulations were *ultra vires*. The Commissioners were
given jurisdiction to consider the question of *vires*, thus indicating a trend in favour of
plaintiffs raising, through private law claims in ordinary civil proceedings, issues of
legality.

Appeals are not normally provided against discretionary decisions involving Minis-   **17–017**
ters or policy matters involving the allocation of resources or the implementation of
Cabinet decisions. The absence of an appeal structure may be due to the political
nature of the policy where the appropriate forum is in Parliament. However, this may
not be a satisfactory reason to cover all cases where there is no appeal. In chapter 15,
criticisms made by the Council on Tribunals of the lack of a proper appeals system
following the replacement of supplementary benefit payments by payments from the
social fund made by social fund officers under the Social Security Act 1986, were
noted. The absence of an appeal procedure was perceived as creating unfairness. The
Council on Tribunals view judicial review as an inappropriate means of appeal from
tribunal decisions. For example, instead of judicial review of immigration cases the
Council on Tribunals favoured the introduction of an appeal on a point of law from
the Immigration Appeal Tribunal, under the Asylum and Immigration Appeals Act
1993 as amended by the Asylum and Immigration Act 1996 and the Immigration and
Asylum Act 1999.

Statutory appeals may be used as an alternative to an application for judicial review   **17–018**
which is subject to a three-month time-limit whereas some appeals are restricted to six
weeks. For example the Acquisition of Land Act 1981 forbids any challenge to a
compulsory purchase order other than under its s.23 appeal procedure to the High
Court on matters of law.

Appeals may consist of an appeal on questions of fact or on the merits of a decision.   **17–019**
Usually the right of appeal is confined to "persons aggrieved". The grounds of appeal
may vary according to the content of the statute. Lack of evidence and the failure to

---

[12] [1987] A.C. 625.
[13] [1993] 1 All E.R. 705.

give adequate reasons, may amount to an error of law which may be considered on appeal. A decision may be reversed on appeal to the courts on a point of law. The leading case of *Edwards v Bairstow*[14] concluded that a decision of the Inland Revenue Commissioners might be reversed by the courts where the facts did not justify the inference or conclusion of the Commissioners. In such instances the courts are willing to consider issues of fact giving rise to questions of law when no reasonable interpretation would support the finding of facts disputed in an appeal.

17–020   There is at present no satisfactory arrangement for standardising the grounds for an appeal, the availability of an appeal or the way appeals are considered by the courts. Lord Justice Woolf, as he then was, has suggested[15] that a more coherent appeals system might replace the present random and chaotic system.

Order 53 Procedure: Public and Private Law

17–021   The availability of judicial review allows a decision or action to be challenged in the courts on the basis of remedies available in public law. This means that the grounds for challenge depend on rules developed by the courts as grounds for review in public law. The distinction between public law and private law becomes important when considering the procedures known as the application for judicial review. In Chapter 6 judicial review was examined in outline. Recent changes to the procedures for the application for judicial review include CPR Pt 54 *Judicial Review* and various practice directions and protocols.[16] The Administrative Court, formerly the Divisional Court of the Queen's Bench Division, has the jurisdiction to hear applications for judicial review. The Crown Office is responsible for the administration of applications for judicial review. There are also changes to the terminology used. Applicants for judicial review are now referred to as claimants and the system of remedies to be discussed in Chapter 18 has been renamed; certiorari is a quashing order, prohibition, a prohibiting order and *mandamus*, a mandatory order.

17–022   There are 25 judges nominated to sit in the Administrative Court. On current figures[17] from October 2000 up until December 2001, the number of judicial review cases was 4,407; during 2002 there were 274 Divisional Court sitting days, 1,447 single judge sitting days and 102 deputy High Court judge sitting days. The average time for an application for permission to apply for judicial review was eight weeks and the average time waiting for a substantive determination was 20 weeks (from lodging to decision). In expedited cases hearings were held within a few weeks. There is a procedure for urgent cases to be dealt with set out in the practice statement.[18] There is a new *Pre-Action Protocol*[19] requiring that after March 4, 2002 all claims for judicial review must fall under the arrangements in the *Protocol*. The *Protocol* sets out a code of good practice that should be followed when making a claim for judicial review. There has been an overall increase by about 11 per cent of the number of judicial review cases in the period October 2000 to December 2001. This is mainly attributable to an increase in immigration cases (up 15

---

[14] [1956] A.C. 14.
[15] H. Woolf, "A Hotchpotch of Appeals—The Need for a Blender" (1988) 7 *Civil Justice Quarterly* 44.
[16] *Practice Statement* [2002] 1 All E.R. 633.
[17] *ibid.* at 634.
[18] *ibid.* at 635.
[19] [2002] All E.R. (D) Feb.

per cent) and Human Rights issues. It appears that some 19 per cent of all cases raise a human rights issue. However, these figures suggest that there has not been a flood of cases following the coming into force of the Human Rights Act 1998 in October 2000, which was feared by some commentators.

It is necessary to consider in greater detail, how the courts have developed an **17–023** exclusive jurisdiction for the application of judicial review for public law matters. This is central to an understanding of the position of the litigant who wishes to obtain remedies in public law. Perhaps the most significant sign of judicial self-confidence at work is the way procedural reforms have modernised judicial review. As will be demonstrated, most of the reforms are the work of judges operating within the shadow of Parliament with the tacit understanding that they are to be trusted in their creative role. The early development of the current procedures for application for judicial review may be traced back to the work of the Law Commission. In 1969 the government rejected proposals from the Law Commission[20] for a Royal Commission on administrative law, agreeing only to a study of the existing law of remedies for the judicial control of administrative action. As a result the opportunity was lost to conduct a review of the entire system of administrative law. The Law Commission made recommendations on the law of remedies,[21] and it was left to the Rules Committee of the Supreme Court to implement modest proposals for reforms in the application for judicial review, under Order 53 of the Rules of the Supreme Court. This reform received statutory modification in s.31 of the Supreme Court Act 1981.

Order 53 streamlined the procedures for obtaining remedies. An applicant is able to **17–024** seek any one or more of five remedies: *mandamus*, *certiorari*, prohibition, declaration or injunction. At the same time, interlocutory procedures such as discovery and interrogatories are theoretically available. In addition, the court may award damages if claimed by the applicant and if they could have been awarded in an action at the same time. The inclusion of declaration and injunction alongside the prerogative orders of *mandamus*, *certiorari* and prohibition was innovatory. For the first time traditionally private law remedies, that is remedies also available by ordinary writ, might be obtained alongside the traditional public law remedies of the prerogative orders of *mandamus*, *certiorari* and prohibition, under a single application for judicial review. The introduction of a uniform system made it easier to apply for judicial review. The first stage in the two-stage process. is obtaining the leave of the court, based on whether there is an arguable case. The aggrieved citizen has to overcome this hurdle in order to pursue a claim. Normally a single judge hears this first stage on affidavit evidence. A claim in judicial review must be made without "undue delay". As this falls under s.31(7) of the 1981 Act, the time-limit is three months. The second stage is a full hearing of the issues, when all the parties are heard. In developing the Order 53 procedure it soon became apparent that the distinction between public law and private law is critical when considering how the procedures work in practice.

The "exclusive nature of the application for judicial review" was expressed by Lord **17–025** Diplock in the House of Lords in *O'Reilly v Mackman*.[22] Lord Diplock made the distinction between public and private law and considered that it was an abuse of the

---

[20] The Law Commission was established by statute in 1965 to review the law and recommend codification. See Cmnd.4059 (1969).

[21] Law Commission Report no.73 (1976).

[22] [1983] 2 A.C. 237.

process of the court to use an ordinary action for a public law matter when it should have been taken under the application for judicial review. The House of Lords considered the actions brought by writ in the case of four plaintiffs who were prisoners in Hull Prison charged with various disciplinary offences arising out of riots in December 1976 and in 1979. The plaintiff claimed that the Board of Visitors, in the exercise of their disciplinary functions, had breached the rules of natural justice. Lord Diplock held that the prisoners' challenge to the legality of the Board's decisions could not be made by ordinary writ but should have been made through the application for judicial review under Order 53, amended by s.31 of the Supreme Court Act 1981, now CPR 54.

17–026   The reasoning in the case rested on the assumption that the prisoners' legitimate expectation of the rules of natural justice rested in public law, not private law. Lord Diplock established a general rule that an applicant seeking to establish rights recognised in public law was required to make use of the Order 53 procedure. His reasoning for this rule rested on a number of assumptions. First, Order 53 contains certain safeguards, such as the requirement of standing, the use of affidavits at the first stage in the application, and the time-limit of three months which sets a restriction on the period. These safeguards permit a legal challenge to be mounted. Second, Order 53 provides a speedy resolution of the issues. In theory, these procedures offer, in the public interest, safeguards to public bodies and third parties.

17–027   The question of distinguishing between public and private law came to be considered in a number of cases following *O'Reilly v Mackman*. In *Cocks v Thanet*[23] the House of Lords considered whether a declaration and injunction sought by the plaintiff, Cocks, in the county court, claiming that a local authority had breached its duty under the Housing (Homeless Persons) Act 1977, should have been brought under the Order 53 procedure for judicial review. The House of Lords, in a decision given on the same day as *O'Reilly v Mackman*, concluded that the issues raised by the plaintiff were public law matters. The local authority had a duty to inquire if the plaintiff might be made homeless and whether he was legally entitled to temporary or permanent accommodation. Such public law rights needed to be determined before any private rights such as the plaintiff may have could be established. Ironically, once the local authority established that the plaintiff was entitled to be housed, then private law rights existed. The court appeared to classify the decision-making function of the local authority as a public law matter when concerned with the question of whether the criteria in the 1977 Act were satisfied. Once the criteria were satisfied by the applicant and the local authority acted in its executive capacity in considering the rights of the applicant, this gave rise to an action in private law.

17–028   In *Davy v Spelthorne BC*[24] the plaintiff owned premises used to make pre-cast concrete. The plaintiff entered an agreement with the local planning authority not to appeal to the Secretary of State against an enforcement notice in respect of the use of the premises on condition that the authority would not seek to enforce the notice for three years. Two years after the notice was served and the time for an appeal had lapsed, the plaintiff brought an action in the Chancery division, claiming that the agreement was *ultra vires,* and also claiming damages in respect of negligent advice

[23] [1993] 2 A.C. 286.
[24] [1984] A.C. 262.

given to him by the local authority. The local authority applied to strike out the proceedings on the basis of the rule in *O'Reilly v Mackman*. The Court of Appeal followed *O'Reilly v Mackman* and struck out the plaintiff's claim for an injunction restraining the local authority from implementing the enforcement notice and an order that the enforcement notice should be set aside. However, the claim in damages could stand as a private law matter as it was based on a common law duty of care. The local authority appealed to the House of Lords on the basis that the claim for damages should also be struck out.

The argument that the claim for damages was linked to the exercise of a statutory **17–029** duty, and therefore a public law matter, was considered alongside the opposing argument that the plaintiff's common law rights had been infringed. The House of Lords decided that no public law issues were involved in the plaintiff's claim for damages for negligence. In reaching the decision in *Davy*, the House of Lords distinguished the decision in *Cocks*. In *Cocks* the challenge depended on public law rights under the 1977 Act being declared before any private law rights existed. In *Davy*, public law rights were not being exercised by the plaintiff, although the failure of the local authority to enforce the notice may have been a breach of its discretion. The plaintiff was claiming damages for negligent advice on the part of the local authority that resulted in his losing the opportunity to appeal the enforcement order. Thus, because the plaintiff did not seek to impugn the enforcement order it did not give rise to public law rights, and it was not an abuse of process to proceed in negligence against the local authority.

Does the approach of the House of Lords in *Davy* show some relaxation of the rule **17–030** in *O'Reilly v Mackman*? The most difficult analyses relate to cases raising a combination of public and private law issues. The decision in *Davy* shows the reluctance of the courts to interfere with the award of damages in an action in negligence by imposing Order 53 procedures on ordinary litigation. A similar approach appears evident in *Roy v Kensington and Chelsea and Westminster Family Practitioner Committee*.[25] In *Roy*, a general medical practitioner engaged in private consultancy work in addition to his National Health duties was considered by the Family Practitioner Committee to have spent too little time on his National Health duties, and his remuneration was accordingly reduced by 20 per cent. Roy brought an action against the decision of the Committee, and the Committee applied to strike the action out because it breached the exclusivity rule in *O'Reilly v Mackman*. The House of Lords refused to strike out the claim. Lord Bridge explained that the case involved the litigant asserting his rights in private law. Lord Lowry agreed but considered that it was possible to distinguish two different approaches in the interpretation of *O'Reilly v Mackman*:

> "The 'broad approach' was that the 'rule in *O'Reilly v Mackman*' did not apply generally against bringing actions to vindicate private rights in all circumstances in which those actions involved a challenge to a public law act or decision, but that it merely required the aggrieved person to proceed by judicial review only when private law rights were not at stake. The 'narrow approach' assumed that the rule applied generally to all proceedings in which public law acts or decisions were challenged, subject to some exceptions when private law rights were involved."

[25] [1992] 1 All E.R. 705.

17–031   Choosing between these approaches is not always possible, and Lord Lowry acknowledged that it might be preferable for the matters to be heard rather than conduct an analysis over procedure.

17–032   Difficulty in choosing how to apply the rule in *O'Reilly v Mackman* arises because in many cases litigants have "a bundle of rights".[26] In *Roy* these included "his private law rights against the committee, arising from the statute and regulations and including the very important private law right to be paid for the work he has done."[27] Since *O'Reilly v Mackman* the courts have developed a more flexible approach.

17–033   A welcome signal that the House of Lords is prepared to adopt a flexible approach to *O'Reilly* may be found in *Mercury Communications Ltd v Director General of Telecommunications*.[28] Lord Slynn delivered the unanimous view of the House. The case arose, not through Order 53 procedures, but in the Queen's Bench Division (Commercial Court) by originating summons seeking a declaration. The issue arose out of a licensing dispute between Mercury and British Telecommunications and the Director-General of Telecommunications under the Telecommunications Act 1984. Both the respondents, Mercury and British Telecommunications, claimed that the Director-General had misconstrued the licence and therefore raised matters of public law which should not properly fall under the originating summons procedure but instead should be taken under Order 53. The Director-General sought to enforce the licence under the originating summons as raising enforceable licence matters that came within the jurisdiction of the summons. The question that required consideration was whether a public law matter was involved; if this was the case, then the matter would have to be taken under Order 53 through new proceedings for judicial review. The difficulty with this question is the lack of a clear definition or distinction between public law and private law in English law.

17–034   A further difficulty in deciding between private and public law arises from some general exceptions to the rule established in *O'Reilly v Mackman*. Lord Diplock, while accepting that the application of the rule was to be determined case by case, envisaged two possible exceptions. First, where the parties agreed to use the ordinary writ procedure or summons to obtain a declaration or injunction, they might waive the rule in *O'Reilly v Mackman* and proceed with their case. Second, an exception to *O'Reilly v Mackman* might arise where the challenge is collateral, that is, when an issue of public law arises in the course of some other claim involving private law.

17–035   The exact nature of the collateral exception has been considered in a number of subsequent decisions. In *Wandsworth LBC v Winder*,[29] Wandsworth Borough Council was the landlord of a flat occupied by Winder. Winder had a contractual right to occupy the flat on standard conditions, including the condition that the rent would be paid. The local authority, using its statutory powers under the Housing Act 1957, increased the rent charged. Winder refused to pay the whole increase but continued to pay rent and only such increase as appeared reasonable to him. The local authority took proceedings in the county court for arrears of rent. The question of a collateral issue arose when Winder sought to defend his refusal to pay the rent increases by arguing that the increases were *ultra vires* and void. He counterclaimed for a

---

[26] [1992] 1 All E.R. 705 at 725H.
[27] *ibid*.
[28] [1996] 1 All E.R. 575.
[29] [1985] A.C. 461.

declaration that the only rent payable was the old rent. In the House of Lords, the authority argued that Winder's counter-claim should only be by way of judicial review. In fact Winder had applied for judicial review, but it had been refused because he was outside the time limit of three months. Did Winder's counter-claim come within the collateral exception to the rule in *O'Reilly v Mackman*? Lord Fraser in the House of Lords distinguished *Cocks* and *O'Reilly v Mackman*. *Winder* was distinctive from both cases and was based on private law rights, based on contract. Winder had not initiated litigation, but merely sought to defend the legal action taken against him. Lord Fraser considered that Winder's case did not fall into Lord Diplock's exception of a collateral matter to the rule in *O'Reilly v Mackman*. The House of Lords found in Winder's favour and allowed the *ultra vires* question to be considered even though it was not under the Order 53 procedure. In the event, Winder's defence later proved unsuccessful.

In a number of cases the courts have sought to distinguish *Winder*, adopting a case **17–036** by case approach in settling on whether to allow ordinary civil actions to raise matters of public law. In delineating between public and private law for the purposes of the rule in *O'Reilly v Mackman*, clear principles are hard to determine. The nature of the body must be considered alongside the activities the body performs.

O'Reilly v Mackman has provided a new direction for administrative law, but the **17–037** distinction between public and private law, and the question of whether a claim should be brought by ordinary action or by way of judicial review, causes litigants to bear enormous costs, as noted by Lord Saville in *British Steel v HM Commissioners of Customs and Excise*:

> "[t]he cost of this litigation, borne privately or through taxation, must be immense, with often the lawyers the only people to gain. Such litigation brings the law and our legal system into disrepute; and to my mind correctly so. It reinforces the view held by the ordinary person that the law and our legal system are slow, expensive and unsatisfactory. In this day and age it is surely possible to devise procedures which avoid this form of satellite litigation, while safeguarding both the private rights of individuals and companies and the position and responsibilities of public authorities."[30]

The public/private distinction[31] is an example of the problem of incremental develop- **17–038** ment case by case. In practical terms there are limits to the judicial power to self-regulate this area of law. No satisfactory solution will be forthcoming until the legislature defines the concept of public law and codifies administrative law as a whole.[32] In fact the nature of administrative law invites a broader question as to who should ultimately decide matters of public policy—politicians or lawyers? The demarcation between the merits of the decision, not generally reviewable by the courts, and the legality of the decision itself poses one of the most difficult issues for the courts.

What guidance may be provided in delineating public from private? The courts have **17–039** adopted a case by case approach in settling on whether to allow ordinary civil actions

[30] [1997] 2 All E.R. 366 at 379.
[31] See *Boddington v British Transport Police* [1992] 2 A.C. 143 allowing the legality of the criminal law to be considered in criminal proceedings.
[32] See *Steed v Secretary of State for the Home Department* [2000] 3 All E.R. 226

to raise matters of public law. In delineating between public and private law for the purposes of the rule in *O'Reilly v Mackman,* clear principles are hard to determine. The nature of the body must be considered alongside the activities the body performs. In the case of Walsh, who was employed by the East Berkshire Health Authority, even though the regulations of his employment were statutory, he was refused leave to challenge his dismissal through judicial review. The Court of Appeal in *R. v East Berkshire Health Authority Ex p. Walsh*[33] decided that mere employment by a public authority does not make the matter one of public law and therefore justiciable. Similarly if the decision-maker is mistakenly bound by a policy or previous practice may likewise be regarded as justiciable. This permits a court to consider if the case is suitable or not or where it might be inconvenient or inappropriate for judicial review to apply. It is noticeable, however that there are areas where the courts seem unwilling to offer review. In *Ex p. Puhlofer*[34] the House of Lords restricted access to judicial review to cases under the Housing (Homeless Persons) Act 1977. Similarly in *Ex p. Swati*[35] the discretion to refuse leave is operated when there are alternative remedies. In immigration cases there is adjudication by the Immigration Appeal Tribunal and appeal to the courts from that Tribunal under the Asylum and Immigration Appeals Act 1993.

17–040   In *Doyle v Northumbria Probation Committee*[36] which posed the question of raising matters of public law as a defence in a civil action by writ, the facts concerned probation officers who took action for breach of contract against their employers, a probation authority, a body corporate with statutory powers. The dispute raised matters of contract and the matter came to court within the time-limit set for an action in contract, namely six years. The defence argued that the case raised a fundamental question about the legal powers of the probation authority that should have been raised by judicial review. Henry J. considered that the plaintiff's claim was entirely based on private law rights and to decide otherwise left the plaintiffs out of time for judicial review. He concluded that there were three operating principles from the legal authorities.[37] First, for cases which fall within the *O'Reilly v Mackman* rule, the courts must "be astute" to see that there is no evasion of the protections afforded by Order 53 in cases which are unmeritorious. Secondly, there is no "overriding objection" to public law issues being litigated in writ actions. Thirdly, that in principle, Order 53 should not be used for the litigation of private law claims. A further qualification important to note is that where the parties agree, this will permit an ordinary action to raise matters of public law.

17–041   Drawing together some conclusions from the case law is difficult. Some examples serve to show how judicial decision-making is influenced very much on the facts of each case, the nature of the dispute involved and the application of the three operating principles noted by Henry J., in the *Doyle* case. In *Gillick*[38] an ordinary action challenging the health authority's guidance to medical practitioners on contraceptive advice was permitted to proceed even though an application for judicial review was possible. In *Ex p. Noble*[39] a deputy police surgeon sought to challenge his dismissal by

---

[33] [1985] Q.B. 152. Also see *R. v Lord Chancellors Dept. Ex p. Nangle* [1991] I.R.L.R. 343.
[34] [1986] A.C. 484; *Ex p. Benwell* [1985] 1 Q.B. 152. See *Ex p. Dew* [1987] 1 W.L.R. 881.
[35] [1986] 1 All E.R. 717.
[36] [1991] 4 All E.R. 294.
[37] See the discussion in *Gillick v West Norfolk and Wisbech AHA* [1986] A.C. 112.
[38] *ibid.*
[39] *R. v Derbyshire C Ex p. Noble* [1990] I.C.R. 808.

way of judicial review and this was dismissed on the grounds that a private action was more appropriate. Similarly this line of reasoning was applied in *McLaren v Home Office*[40] that an ordinary writ was appropriate for a declaration of a prison officer's employment conditions.

The exact nature of the distinction between public and private law is problematic and leaves the need for law reform to be greater than perhaps in 1969 when a Royal Commission was proposed but rejected. However, in 1988 an unofficial Royal Commission namely the Justice All Souls Review Committee[41] recommended reform of the rule in *O'Reilly v Mackman* and that the House of Lords should re-consider their decision. The report criticised the imprecision of the term "public law" and suggested that Parliament might wish to consider the circumstances where an applicant might be obliged to use Order 53 and be barred from proceeding by action or originating summons.   **17–042**

As matters stand the procedural rules under Order 53 are to be used by litigants who think that they have mainly a public law matter. If it later appears that this was the wrong procedure then Order 53, r.9(5) permits matters to continue as if the procedure had been by ordinary writ. This is only permitted if the applicant has sought an injunction, declaration or damages. However a litigant who commences an ordinary writ and then raises public law matters may only do so if the court exercises a discretion to proceed as if the issue had been raised by Order 53. That discretion is rarely exercised and would only be exercised if it would not be unfair to the respondent and where the court would be prepared to waive the safeguards included in the Order 53 procedure.   **17–042a**

It may be concluded that on the basis of procedural rules the distinction between public and private law is important to litigants. The signs are that the courts are beginning to recognise the problems in making such a distinction in cases, as in *Roy*, where the litigant has a "parcel of rights". Careful consideration is required of the question as to whether any great disadvantage seems to come from allowing the ordinary writ procedure to raise some matters of public law. However, great uncertainty surrounds the principles as to when the courts regard such cases as acceptable. One possible way forward is to consider clarifying the protections afforded under Order 53 to public bodies and consider extending these to the ordinary writ procedure.   **17–043**

Lord Woolf, writing extra-judicially in 1999, expressed the optimism that technical difficulties relating to the choice of the wrong procedure will be a problem of the past.[42] Lord Steyn in *Boddington v British Transport Police*[43] reiterated the view that the primary focus of *O'Reilly v Mackman*:   **17–044**

> "is situations in which an individual's sole aim was to challenge a public law act or decision. It does not apply in a civil case when an individual seeks to establish private law rights which cannot be determined without an examination of the validity of a public law decision. Nor does it apply where a defendant in a civil case simply seeks to defend himself by questioning the validity of a public law decision."

[40] [1990] I.C.R. 824.
[41] Justice Report: *Administrative Justice: Some Necessary Reforms* (Oxford University Press, 1988).
[42] (1998) 114 LQR 579.
[43] [1999] 2 A.C. 143 at 172G–H.

17–045   While the courts have shown some consistency in their flexible interpretation of the exclusivity principle, it should not be assumed that the law is straightforward. A clear case of a private law claim should be begun promptly by the private law procedure. Similarly a case involving public law should be begun by judicial review and a borderline or unclear case should sensibly begin with the judicial review claim.

Grounds for Review

17–046   Deciding the procedural route to take action in the courts depends on the nature of the dispute and the grounds for complaint. It is also necessary for the grounds for review applied by the superior courts to be considered. It is significant that there has not been any consolidation into statutory form of the different grounds available for review. This area has been left to develop on a case by case basis. Lord Diplock acknowledged the achievements of the courts in developing judicial review in the landmark decision in the *Council of Civil Service Unions v Minister for Civil Service*[44] when he suggested that "the English law relating to judicial control of administrative action has been developed upon a case by case basis which has virtually transformed it over the last three decades". In the same speech Lord Diplock referred to the grounds for judicial review as consisting of three "heads" upon which administrative law is subject to control. These have been considered in outline in Chapter 6 and are as follows: "illegality" meaning the decision-maker must understand the law and give effect to it; "irrationality" by which a decision which is unreasonable or so outrageous in its defiance of logic or of accepted moral standards that "no sensible person who applied his mind to the question to be decided could have arrived at it"; and finally there is "procedural impropriety" by which there is a failure to observe basic rules of natural justice or fail to act with procedural fairness towards the person who will be affected by the decision. A further possibility, that of proportionality was also mentioned. Here the courts have to balance the appropriateness of the various objectives set out in law, the adverse affects which its decision may have on the rights, the liberties or interests of the persons and purposes it pursues. Proportionality, while recognised fully in French, German and EC law has only become understood in its "application in English Administrative law in recent years" although it is a concept which has historical roots in much earlier cases. The above developments must be understood in the context of the absence of any codified system of administrative law.

17–047   The grounds for review may now be considered in further detail bearing in mind that Lord Diplock's classification is not exhaustive.

Ultra Vires and Excess of Jurisdiction

17–048   Lord Diplock's classification of illegality comprises a number of categories. Some categories may overlap and the classification is not exhaustive. As a general principle public bodies are expected to act within their legal powers. When a power is vested in a public body and the public body acts in excess of that power, its acts are invalid and *ultra vires*. The task of the courts, through judicial review is to consider the legal powers of public bodies at common law, statute or under the royal prerogative[45] and

---

[44] [1984] 3 All E.R. 935; [1985] A.C. 374.
[45] *R. v Wandsworth LBC Ex p. Beckwith* [1996] 1 All E.R. 129.

determine whether the public body has acted within its powers. Determining whether or not a public body is within its powers depends on statutory interpretation. The breadth of the powers contained in the statute will influence the courts' powers to intervene. Even broadly drafted powers are not immune to review. In *Hazell v Hammersmith*,[46] as noted in the chapters on local government and in the work of the Audit Commission, the House of Lords found that swap transactions were not authorised under Sch.13 to the Local Government Act 1972. This was notwithstanding a broadly drafted power contained in s.111 of the 1972 Act, namely that a local authority ". . . shall have power to do anything (whether or not involving the expenditure, borrowing or lending of money or the acquisition or disposal of any property or rights) which is calculated to facilitate, or is conducive or incidental, to the discharge of any of their functions."

The House of Lords viewed the swap transactions as speculative and therefore outside the remit of local authority powers. The extensive nature of s.111 has been increasingly narrowed by the courts in an attempt to keep local authorities within their legal powers. On the same approach to the interpretation of local government powers following the House of Lords in *Hazel* is the Court of Appeal in *Credit Suisse v Allerdale BC*.[47] Allerdale local authority engaged in a joint venture through a number of companies set up by the local authority, technically known as "local government influenced companies", to build and operate a leisure complex. A time-share scheme was envisaged as the best means to operate the complex. Credit Suisse, a leading international banking institution, provided substantial loans repayable over a fixed period. The district auditor queried the legality of the local authority joint venture companies, the local authority involvement and the investment of Credit Suisse. This arose when the ability of the local authority companies to repay the loans came into doubt. The case involved legal consideration of the powers and duties of the local authority and its relationship to Credit Suisse. The Court of Appeal held that the arrangements with the joint-venture companies were *ultra vires* the powers of the local authority. The result of the case left Credit Suisse largely exposed to debts and liabilities that arose from the *ultra vires* transaction. This will seriously inhibit local government joint ventures with the private sector.

17–049

Powers granted for one purpose cannot be assumed to provide powers for another purpose, even if closely related. In *Att.-Gen. v Fulham Corp*[48] Fulham Corporation had statutory powers under the Baths and Wash-houses Acts 1846-78 to establish baths and wash-houses. The question arose as to whether facilities for washing and drying clothes which included the operation of drying equipment by employees of the corporation, came within the powers of the legislation. The court held that the statutory powers only permitted the carrying out of clothes washing by customers themselves, and did not extend to operating a laundry service.

17–050

The review of statutory powers also extends to their exercise by Ministers. The Court of Appeal in *Laker Airways* held that the Secretary of State had acted *ultra vires*.[49] Guidance under the Civil Aviation Act 1971, subsequently amended, to the Civil Aviation Authority to the effect that British Airways should be the sole carrier on

17–051

[46] [1991] 2 W.L.R. 372.
[47] [1996] 4 All E.R. 129.
[48] [1921] 1 Ch. 440.
[49] [1977] Q.B. 643.

the Stansted to New York route, resulted in Laker Airways having their licence withdrawn. The guidance had been approved by both Houses of Parliament. The Court of Appeal regarded the guidance as effectively a directive power. The guidance was also contrary to the objectives given to the Civil Aviation Authority. Also the guidance was intended to explain and amplify the meaning of the objectives and not to replace them. The Court of Appeal considered that Laker Airways should be entitled to fly the New York route.

17–052   Local government provides another example of the power of the courts to review statutory powers. The courts may appear quite innovative in construing statutes when local authority powers are involved. In *Bromley*,[50] the House of Lords was asked to consider the "fair fares" policy of the GLC (now abolished). "Ordinary business principles" were applied to the reduction of fares and as the policy did not operate on those principles the proposed reduction in fares was *ultra vires*. Although the GLC had powers to make grants "for any purpose" to the London Transport Executive (LTE) the grant involving a supplementary rate was quashed because the purposes for which it was intended were *ultra vires*. There was "a fiduciary duty" on the GLC as a local authority, and the fares policy failed to live up to that standard which was owed to ratepayers. The Courts had to balance the GLC's duty owed to ratepayers against its wider power to provide reasonable transport facilities for transport users. The fact that a "fair fares" policy had been a manifesto condition in the election of the ruling party in the GLC was not relevant to the courts' powers of review, as such a condition was "not binding" on the local authority.

17–053   The application of any legal principles in this area of the law is always difficult. The courts may construe the statute as providing incidental powers within the jurisdiction of the body concerned provided the act is not expressly forbidden. In *Att.-Gen. v Crayford UDC*[51] the general powers of management of local authority housing under s.111(1) of the Housing Act 1957 were considered by the court in respect of a local authority decision to issue insurance policies to its tenants. Did such a scheme fall within "prudent management" by the local authority of its housing? The court held that the scheme was within the local authority's powers. The question of whether the scheme was *ultra vires* or not depended on whether it "may fairly be regarded as incidental to, or consequential upon" the powers granted to the authority under the 1957 Act.

17–054   A public authority must direct itself according to law and must not purport to exercise powers it does not have nor the powers that someone else may have. Statutes invariably provide that powers may only be exercised by a specific body or person or that the powers must operate within certain safeguards which must be obeyed. The *ultra vires* doctrine will apply where the delegation of powers is improper. Effectively the courts wish to ensure that discretion is properly exercised, free from pressure and unfettered in its application.

17–055   Some examples serve to illustrate the courts' review of the exercise of the delegation of discretion. In *Ex p. Brunyate*[52], the Court held that a local education authority may not use its powers to dismiss and appoint governors as a means of changing the educational policy of the Education Act 1944. The Court of Appeal in *R. v Monopolies*

---

[50] [1983] 1 A.C. 768.
[51] [1962] 1 Ch. 575.
[52] *R. v Inner London Education Authority Ex p. Brunyate* [1989] 1 W.L.R. 542.

and Mergers Commission Ex p. Argyll Group PLC[53] noted that the Monopolies and Mergers Commission, rather than its chairman should have decided whether to proceed with a reference made to it by the Secretary of State in the case of a takeover bid. The fact that the delegation of power to the chairman was *ultra vires* did not prevent the court from refusing to quash the chairman's decision.

In *R. v Waltham Forest LBC Ex p. Waltham Forest Ratepayers Action Group*[54] the courts struck down a decision of Waltham Forest councillors which was based on instructions from a pressure group known as the Local Government Group.   **17–056**

Over-reliance on rules, exercising a discretion when fettered by contract or pre-existing rules have all been regarded by the courts as examples of a failure to exercise discretionary powers correctly. Some latitude may be given to the correct delegation of ministerial powers to officials.[55] In *Carltona*[56] a wartime case arose when a factory owner challenged the Commissioners of Works over the exercise of requisition powers granted by statute. In fact the Commissioners never met and their powers were carried out by officials acting on their behalf. The Court of Appeal broadly interpreted delegation and upheld the legality of the procedures. Some official self-restraint must be taken not to extend the *Carltona* principle too broadly. In *Ex p. Oladehinde*[57] the House of Lords upheld the lawfulness of the Home Secretary's common practice to delegate to senior officials, namely immigration officers, his powers under the Immigration Act 1971 to serve notices of deportation. In such instances of delegation the House of Lords noted that care should be taken not to widen the delegation of powers unduly. Some caution must be exercised to establish that the officials are sufficiently senior and that they possess the necessary experience to carry out the statutory duties under the 1971 Act. The *Carltona* principle is applied to central government departments and the devolution of functions to civil servants.   **17–057**

In local government s.101 of the Local Government Act 1972 permits the delegation of wide powers to officials to carry out specific functions of the local authority. The nature of any delegated power must be given close scrutiny. If the power rests with an officer who may consult with members of the council, it is wrong for the powers to be actually exercised by the councillor rather than the officer.   **17–058**

A discretion which is mistakenly bound by a policy or previous practice may likewise be regarded as an abuse of discretion and subject to possible review by the courts. In *Bromley*,[58] discussed above, the local authority mistakenly felt bound by its election manifesto. The House of Lords held that this was an abuse of power. A contract to bind a public body and its successors to exercise its powers in a particular way is likely to be declared void by the courts.[59] In such cases the courts will consider the nature of the powers being exercised. A commercial body that enters a commercial undertaking not to increase its statutory charges was considered to be making an acceptable exercise of power by virtue of its status as a commercial undertaking.   **17–059**

The exercise of discretionary powers may be influenced by the doctrine of estoppel. Estoppel has been developed as part of private law; it is relevant in public law as   **17–060**

[53] [1986] 1 W.L.R. 763.
[54] *Ex p. Baxter* [1987] 3 All E.R. 671; [1988] Q.B. 419.
[55] *Lavender (H.) & Son Ltd v Minister of Housing and Local Government* [1970] 1 W.L.R. 1231. See *Local Government Board v Arlidge* [1915] A.C. 120.
[56] *Carltona v Commissioners of Works* [1943] 2 All E.R. 560.
[57] *R. v Secretary of State for the Home Department Ex p. Oladehinde* [1991] 2 A.C. 254.
[58] [1983] 1 A.C. 768.
[59] *Ayr Harbour Trustees v Oswald* (1883) L.R. 8 App. Cas. 623.

creating narrow and strictly defined exceptions to the strict application of the doctrine of *ultra vires*. The basis of estoppel was succinctly explained by Wade[60]:

> "a person who by some statement or representation of fact causes another to act to his detriment in reliance on the truth of it is not allowed to deny it later, even though it is wrong."

17–061 In private law, particularly in the law of contract, estoppel may prevent the enforcement of contractual rights where there was some undertaking not to enforce those rights in law. In the area of public law estoppel may arise where a citizen may be misled by advice from an official or public body and suffer detriment. However as a general principle estoppel cannot be used to give a public body powers which it would otherwise not have. In *Maritime Electric Co*[61] an electricity authority misread a customer's electricity meter and consequently undercharged the customer for two years. The authority had a statutory duty to collect the full amount and could not use the doctrine of estoppel to accept the lesser amount because it lacked the statutory powers to do so.

17–062 The question arises as to whether there are situations where the courts might be willing to enforce an *ultra vires* decision. Estoppel might assist an applicant when relying on advice. In *Western Fish Products*[62] where the power to make a decision was incorrectly delegated but where the plaintiff assumed it to be correctly delegated, then provided the courts are satisfied about the nature of the incorrect assumption, the plaintiff may in certain circumstances rely on the estoppel principle as an exception to what would otherwise be an *ultra vires* decision. The Court of Appeal asserted that estoppel could not prevent a statutory body from exercising its discretion or performing its duty.

17–063 Considerable difficulty surrounds defining the nature of the assumption made by the plaintiff that might be sufficient to satisfy the estoppel principle in public law cases. Two possibilities emerge from the *Western Fish Products* decision. First, estoppel may only operate when it reasonably appears to the plaintiff that the authority to make a decision has been correctly delegated to the relevant officer or body and where "there is some evidence" justifying the plaintiff in believing that the officer or body was binding the authority. Secondly, depending on the construction of the statute, Lord Justice Megaw explained that estoppel may arise where there is a procedural requirement in the statute waived by the statutory body in the exercise of its powers. For example, ". . . if a planning authority waives a procedural requirement relating to any application made to it for the exercise of its statutory powers, it may be estopped from relying on lack of formality."

17–064 In an earlier case, that of *Robertson v Minister of Pensions*,[63] where a citizen relied to his detriment on an assurance he was given that he was entitled to a military pension by someone who had no power to make the assurance, Denning J. advanced a wide interpretation that the plaintiff is entitled to rely upon a government department "having the authority which it assumes. He does not know and cannot be expected to know, the limits of that authority."

---

[60] Wade, *Administrative Law* (1988), p.261.
[61] *Maritime Electric Co v General Dairies Ltd* [1937] A.C. 610.
[62] *Western Fish Products Ltd v Penwith DC* [1981] 2 All E.R. 204.
[63] [1949] 1 K.B. 227.

However this wide interpretation was rejected in *Western Fish Products* and also by **17–065**
the House of Lords in *Howell v Falmouth Boat Construction Co Ltd*[64] which considered
that Denning's interpretation of the estoppel principle did not seem consistent with the
principle that legal authority cannot be delegated.

Estoppel may arise when a change of policy occurs and the result is to the detriment **17–066**
of the plaintiff. For example in *Lever Finance*[65] a planning officer, when asked by Lever
Finance as to whether fresh planning permission was required in respect of their
decision to alter the original plans of a housing scheme, concluded that no fresh
application was required. Lever Finance began construction but after neighbours
objected they were then advised that planning permission was required. Lever Finance
applied for planning permission which was then refused. The Court of Appeal
accepted that the planning officer had followed common practice, that Lever Finance
relied on the planning officer's advice, and therefore the planning officer had authority
to bind the council.

There has been criticism of the approach in *Lever Finance*. In *Western Fish Products* **17–067**
Ltd the Court of Appeal restricted the use of estoppel in planning matters as estoppel
could not prevent a statutory body from exercising its discretion or duty.

The law relating to estoppel in public law is unsatisfactory. This may be due to the **17–068**
difficulty of importing estoppel's private law characteristics into public law and of
reconciling the principles of estoppel with the overriding obligations found in statutes.
Even creative interpretations of statutory duties, discretions and procedural rules may
result in hard cases where there is no legal remedy.

One solution favoured by Wade[66] in seeking to find compatibility between the **17–069**
application of the *ultra vires* doctrine and fairness to the plaintiff, is to compensate the
plaintiff when the law must be enforced but injustice results. Compensation provides
the means of ensuring fairness while retaining the doctrine of *ultra vires*. However
compensation has been found to be equally difficult to apply in public law.

Instead of adhering to the strict application of the doctrine of *ultra vires*, consider **17–070**
whether balancing the different interests between the parties might provide a more
acceptable solution? This approach provides a more fundamental evaluation of the
true function of *ultra vires*. Thus a decision taken by a public body might be
enforceable even if it were *ultra vires* where the injury to the plaintiff was such that the
public interest would not be served by enforcing the decision. Invariably such an
approach invites considerable judicial discretion in setting the principles to be applied
in such cases. Also it might be considered inappropriate to re-consider the doctrine of
ultra vires in this way as the doctrine performs an important function of keeping a
check on the discretion of public bodies.

The *ultra vires* doctrine may apply where there are certain procedural requirements **17–071**
contained in the statute. Procedural requirements or conditions may be imposed
before specific statutory powers may be exercised. Procedural requirements may be
merely discretionary or mandatory. The latter is likely to lead to a decision being
quashed. In certain examples it may be helpful to classify the type of error or mistake
made by the public body. Some are minor and may not affect the jurisdiction of the
body making the decision. The courts' powers of supervision are usually intended to

[64] [1951] A.C. 837.
[65] *Lever Finance Ltd v Westminster (City) LBC* [1971] 1 Q.B. 222.
[66] Wade, *Administrative Law* (1988), p.385.

allow public bodies to make decisions within their jurisdiction. Thus in finding on the merits of a case the public body should be allowed to make mistakes that are not so fundamental that the jurisidiction of the body is impugned. Defining whether a mistake goes to jurisdiction or not is largely dependent on the role of the courts and the nature of the procedural rules.

17–072   In *Anisminic*[67] the United Kingdom Government received payment from the Egyptian Government of a sum of money intended to compensate for loss of British property sequestered. The Foreign Compensation Commission, on behalf of the United Kingdom Government, had the task of determining claims made against the money available. An Order in Council set out the conditions required before any payments could be made. The Commission concluded that Anisminic had not made out its case. The Commission's interpretation of the Order in Council required that Anisminic should be British and a "successor in title". Anisminic could fulfill the former but not the latter condition and challenged the Commission's interpretation of the Order in Council in the courts despite the ouster clause contained in s.4(4) of the Foreign Compensation Act 1950, namely that the Commission's determination "should not be questioned in any court of law". The House of Lords concluded that the Commission had erred in law in holding that Anisminic should be a "successor in title." The ouster clause was held not to protect "purported" determinations, only real determinations.

17–073   The question arises as to the nature of the error that is regarded as a jurisdictional error and therefore open to review by the courts. Are all errors jurisdictional? In *Anisminic*, the Foreign Compensation Commission had correctly interpreted its powers to consider Anisminic's application and inquire into the facts of the application. If the Commission had considered matters extraneous to its powers its determination would have been a nullity. Lord Roskill considered:

> "There are many cases where although the tribunal had jurisdiction to enter on the inquiry, it has done or failed to do something in the course of the inquiry which is of such a nature that its decision is a nullity."

17–074   Lord Reid identified those errors which may be considered as going to jurisdiction. These are: acting in bad faith; making decisions without the requisite powers; breaching the requirements of natural justice; failing to take into account relevant considerations; or taking into account irrelevant considerations. The list is not exhaustive, but it is based on the assumption that there is a distinction between those errors which do and those that do not go to jurisdiction.

17–075   The courts have considered the nature of such a distinction. In *Pearlman v Keepers and Governors of Harrow School*,[68] Lord Denning explained that any such distinction between errors which are jurisdictional and those that are not are so fine that the distinction may be discarded. Pearlman was a tenant who had installed central heating. He applied to the county court for a declaration that it constituted a "structural alteration" of the premises. The county court decided that it did not and Pearlman sought certiorari to quash this decision in the High Court, notwithstanding the fact that the county court decision was by statute "final and conclusive".

---

[67] *Anisminic Ltd v Foreign Compensation Commission* [1969] 2 A.C. 147.
[68] [1979] Q.B. 56. See *Williams v Bedwelty Justices* [1996] 3 All E.R. 737.

Lord Denning's attempts to render obsolete the distinction between errors within jurisdiction and those that were outside jurisdiction was rejected in the Privy Council case of *South East Asia Fire Bricks*[69] by Lord Fraser. Lord Diplock in *O'Reilly v Mackman*[70] believed that there was still an important distinction to be drawn between those bodies where error of law within jurisdiction remained relevant and bodies where it had become an unnecessary distinction. Inferior courts fell within the category of review such as tribunals and administrative agencies, while the ordinary courts such as the County Court in *Pearlman* were entitled to rely on the distinction between errors within jurisdiction which are not reviewable and errors outside jurisdiction which are subject to review.[71]   **17–076**

It may be concluded that such a distinction between errors that are within jurisdiction and those that are not, is necessary to safeguard the decision-maker and allow freedom to make the decision freed from over-rigid intervention by the courts. The courts are in turn allowed some discretion in setting the limits of their own jurisdiction. The most recent trend is in favour of removing any distinction between errors that are and those that are not jurisdictional ones. This is the approach of the court in *Palacegate Properties Ltd v Camden LBC*[72] suggesting that it was unnecessary to find a distinction between the different types of jurisdictional error.   **17–077**

Abuse of Discretion

Discretion exercised by a public body must not be exercised wrongly. Abuse of discretion may arise where the power has been exercised for a purpose not intended or expressed in the statute when the powers were conferred. The use of powers for improper purposes may result in the powers being declared *ultra vires* by the courts. For example, compulsory purchase powers should not be used for an ulterior or improper purpose. In *Sydney Municipal Council v Campbell*[73] compulsory purchase powers "to carry out improvements in remodelling any portion of the city" under the Sydney Corporation Amendment Act 1905 could not be used to secure a benefit of an increase in land values.   **17–078**

In construing a statute the courts may look at the "policy and objects" of the statute in order to consider whether the motivation for a decision and its outcome are within the powers conferred by Parliament. In *Padfield*[74] *mandamus* was granted by the House of Lords in favour of milk producers who had complained that the differential element, based on geographical areas, in the price fixed for their milk purchased by the Milk Marketing Board was too low. The Agricultural Marketing Act 1958 provided two methods of grievance resolution, arbitration and procedures under s.19 involving the setting-up of a committee of investigation. The first was accepted as unsuitable for the type of complaint. The second, the Minister declined to do. Padfield sought an order of *mandamus*. The House of Lords concluded that the Minister had misunderstood his powers and therefore frustrated the purpose of the Act. The terms of the   **17–079**

---

[69] *South East Asia Firebricks Sdn. Bhd. v Non-Metallic Mineral Products* [1981] A.C. 363.
[70] [1983] 2 A.C. 237. Lord Diplock drew a distinction between different bodies such as commissions and tribunals on the one hand and courts on the other. The former were open to review while the latter could rely on the principle of errors which are within jurisdiction as free from review.
[71] *R. v Greater Manchester Coroner Ex p. Tal* [1985] Q.B. 67.
[72] [2001] P.L.R. 59.
[73] [1925] A.C. 338.
[74] [1968] A.C. 997.

Minister's powers to refer the matter to a committee of investigation were if the Minister "in any case so directs". Lord Reid noted that this showed that the Minister had some discretion, but such a discretion must be in accordance with the intention of the statute. The courts, in considering whether discretion has been exercised reasonably, may consider reasons for the decision or in the absence of reasons, may infer whether the decision is a reasonable one or not.

17–080   In the event, after the House of Lords decision in *Padfield*, the Minister was compelled under the Agricultural Marketing Act 1958 to set up an inquiry in the form of a committee of investigation. This was duly convened and reported in favour of the complainants but the Minister's ultimate discretion allowed him to take no action.

17–081   In the exercise of discretion it is possible to take into account irrelevant considerations or fail to take account of relevant considerations. Abuse of discretion on these grounds may occur for the most altruistic reasons but may not conform to the relevant statutory requirements. In *Roberts v Hopwood Poplar BC*[75], the Borough Council introduced a "minimum wage" for its employees. The power to set wages under s.62 of the Metropolis Management Act 1855 contained the power to pay "such salaries and wages as . . . [the council] may think fit". This conferred a broad discretion on the local authority but the district auditor questioned the validity of the setting of a minimum wage and accordingly surcharged the local councillors. The House of Lords noted that the national average wage for similar workers was substantially less than the minimum wage set by the Council. The rationale for the minimum wage was based on an election mandate which the councillors felt bound to follow. However, the payment of the minimum wage was made without due regard for the interests of the ratepayers. The House of Lords viewed the minimum wage payments as amounting in effect to gifts to the workers which was an improper purpose and not intended by the legislation. The Council had not taken account of the wages paid to other workers and the result was that the minimum wage was unlawful. The House of Lords reached its conclusion by balancing the interests of the ratepayers with the statutory powers exercised by the local authority as to what is reasonable and a proper exercise of discretion.

17–082   A similar approach is evident in the *Bromley*[76] decision. The House of Lords held that the "fair fares" policy of the Greater London Council was *ultra vires* on the basis that the decision had not taken account of the fiduciary duty owed by the council to the ratepayers. In balancing the different interests of ratepayers, transport users and the duties of the local authority, the House of Lords concluded that the Council had acted unreasonably.

Unreasonableness is also a ground for holding that a discretion has been abused. In *Wednesbury Corp*[77] Lord Greene, M.R. considered the meaning of the term "unreasonable" and concluded that where an authority's decision "was so unreasonable that no reasonable authority" could ever come to the decision then it could be impugned by the courts. The courts are left with considerable discretion as to how to apply this direction. The question is whether a reasonable authority "could" ever come to the decision. What is the standard of the reasonable authority? On a narrow construction of the test, the courts should rarely intervene. As Lord Diplock recognised in the *Council of Civil Service Unions v Minister for the Civil Service*[78] the decision would have

---

[75] [1925] A.C. 578.
[76] [1983] 1 A.C. 768.
[77] *Associated Provincial Picture Houses Ltd v Wednesbury Corp* [1948] 1 K.B. 223.
[78] *Council of Civil Service Unions v Minister for the Civil Service* [1985] A.C. 374 at p.410.

to be so outrageous or in defiance of logic that no sensible person could come to such a decision. On this view, unreasonableness is unlikely to result in the courts intervening with the exercise of discretion. This appears to give decision-makers considerable latitude before offending against the criteria set by Lord Diplock. Unreasonableness will therefore provide a justification for upholding the exercise of discretion on the one hand but imposing self-restraint on the courts on the other. In *Nottingham C*[79] the view of Lord Scarman was that the decision must be so absurd that the decision-maker "must have taken leave of his senses".

An alternative to the narrow interpretation of *Wednesbury* unreasonableness is that   **17–083** the courts are prepared to seek more active intervention on the grounds of unreasonableness defined in terms of review in discretion where it is found to be illogical or against good sense. The courts are free to consider as in *Padfield* whether the policy and objects of the statute have been frustrated. In *Wheeler v Leicester City Council*[80] Lord Roskill considered whether the local authority's decision to terminate the agreement with the Leicester Rugby Football Club to make use of the council's recreation ground was "unreasonable." The Council had responded to the Club's decision to take part in a rugby tour of South Africa. Lord Roskill concluded that the Council had used an unfair means to achieve its objectives. Although the judges had failed in the lower courts to classify the decision of the local authority as *Wednesbury* unreasonableness, Lord Roskill was prepared to hold that the local authority had acted unreasonably.

Unreasonableness may be used to impugn a byelaw or delegated rule-making   **17–084** function.[81] Statutory interpretation provides the main basis for adopting the test of unreasonableness, though it may be the basis of a tort action in negligence against a public body. In addition to unreasonableness, vagueness or a lack of fair hearing such as is implied in the rules of natural justice may result in the courts holding that discretion has been abused.

The concept of "unreasonableness" is difficult to categorise satisfactorily. The courts   **17–085** are reluctant to review decisions on their merits and the policy behind decisions very often falls outside the courts' remit. One way forward is to see the role of the courts as providing a more systematic guide to the development of principles of good administration. Avoiding arbitrariness or inconsistency and ensuring that fair decision-making takes place might be further assisted if "unreasonableness" were focused on what constitutes good administration.

There have been a number of cases that have provided further elaboration of the   **17–086** *Wednesbury* principle. There are three cases where the breadth and possible objective standards implied in the *Wednesbury* test are discussed. In *R. v Chief Constable of the Devon and Cornwall Constabulary Ex p. Hay*,[82] Mr Justice Sedley granted certiorari and *mandamus* directing the Chief Constable to hear and determine disciplinary charges. Some irrelevant and extraneous matters had been taken into account but "it was in the public interest" that where there was unfairness the disciplinary proceedings should be reinstated. In *R. v Secretary of State for the Home Department Ex p. Onibiyo*,[83] the use of

[79] *Nottingham C v Secretary of State for the Environment* [1986] A.C. 240 at 247.
[80] [1985] A.C. 1054.
[81] *Kruse v Johnson* [1898] 2 Q.B. 91.
[82] [1996] 2 All E.R. 711.
[83] [1996] 2 All E.R. 901.

general *Wednesbury* principles was deployed in respect of an application for asylum. Sir Thomas Bingham noted that[84]

> ". . . the decision whether an asylum-seeker is a refugee is a question to be determined by the Secretary of State and the immigration appellate authorities whose determinations are susceptible to challenge only on *Wednesbury* principles."

17–087   In discussing *Wednesbury* principles Sir Thomas Bingham noted that[85] "on any *Wednesbury* ground of which irrationality is only one . . .". This is a useful reminder that strict categorisation of the grounds of review into self-contained compartments is to be avoided. *Wednesbury* principles may provide a "hard look" doctrine for the courts to discover if there is objectively any grounds for upholding a review. This approach favouring the overturning of any perverse decision making may be found in *R. v Wandsworth LBC Ex p. Mansor*,[86] a case on homeless persons.

17–088   The adequacy of *Wednesbury* unreasonableness was considered in the light of the Human Rights Act 1998. It is likely that over the coming years many of the grounds for judicial review will have to be considered within the broader canvass of Convention rights. Lord Steyn in *R. v Secretary of State for the Home Department Ex p. Daly*[87] drew attention to the necessity for courts to take account of the Convention when considering the intensity of the review applicable. In cases where it was appropriate to apply the test of *Wednesbury* unreasonableness it may be necessary to adjust the criteria of what is unreasonable in the light of the subject matter under review. Lord Steyn approved *R. (Mahmood) v Secretary of State for the Home Dept*[88] and the view of Laws, L.J. on the need to take account of the different "intensity of review" in a public law case. The courts may seek to adjust the scope of review available under *Wednesbury* and where appropriate expect a higher standard by public bodies. The use of the heading of proportionality may provide the courts with the opportunity to further develop judicial review by taking into account the human rights dimension.

Proportionality

17–089   Finally, in addition to the grounds of review already discussed consideration should be given to Lord Diplock's suggestion[89] that proportionality might be adopted as a ground for review in English law. The principle of proportionality provides the courts with the opportunity to consider whether the harmful effects of a particular exercise of power are disproportionate to any benefits which may occur. Support for the adoption of such a doctrine into English administrative law focuses on the opportunity it may provide the courts in evaluating what is fair.[90] In *Ex p. Brind*[91] the Home Secretary under the Broadcasting Act 1981 and under the powers under the BBC's licence agreements issued an order prohibiting the broadcasting of words spoken by members of certain

---

[84] [1996] 2 All E.R. 901 at 912 c–d.
[85] *ibid*. at p.912 f.
[86] [1996] 3 All E.R. 913.
[87] [2001] 3 All E.R. 433 at 445 g–h.
[88] [2001] 1 W.L.R. 840.
[89] *Council of Civil Service Unions v Minister for the Civil Service* [1985] A.C. 374.
[90] See Jowell and Lester, "Beyond Wednesbury: Substantive Principles of Administrative Law" [1987] P.L. 368. Jowell, "Beyond the Rule of Law: Towards Constitutional Judicial Review" [2000] *Public Law* 671.
[91] [1991] 1 A.C. 696.

proscribed organisations or their supporters. The applicants sought judicial review of the ban and argued that the effects of the ban might produce greater harm than any good that might result. The House of Lords considered the concept of proportionality but refused to recognise proportionality as a distinct principle from *Wednesbury* unreasonableness. The outcome of the case was that the ban was upheld. However, the reticence of the House of Lords to develop more fully a doctrine of proportionality seems well placed given the nature of French administrative law which has helped develop the concept of proportionality. Differences between the French and English legal systems as to standard of proof, method of legal reasoning and the constitutional role of the courts require more careful consideration before the concept may be assessed as to its value in English administrative law.

As matters stand it appears that under the principles of *Wednesbury* unreasonable-   **17–090** ness, the courts might consider the reasonable relationship between the objective which is sought to be achieved and the means used to achieve it. Proportionality, as a principle of European Community law, is therefore part of the law of the United Kingdom. It is unlikely that this concept will be expanded into a separate heading for review. It is more likely to infiltrate the thinking and approach of judges when confronted with cases where it is felt that it is disproportionate to grant judicial review.[92] In *Ex p. Daly*[93] Lord Steyn in the House of Lords canvassed the overlap between the traditional grounds for review and proportionality. The proportionality approach provided an intensity of review not available under the traditional headings of review. This suggests that the reviewing court may be required to "assess the balance which the decision maker has struck" and not merely consider if it falls within what is reasonable or unreasonable. The review court under the heading of proportionality may have to consider the "relative weight accorded to interests and considerations". Finally consideration should be given to the question raised[94] by the intensity of review[95]:

> "In other words, the intensity of the review, in similar cases, is guaranteed by the twin requirements that the limitation of the right was necessary in a democratic society, in the sense of meeting a pressing social need, and the question whether the interference was really proportionate to the legitimate aim pursued."

Natural Justice

Natural justice in administrative law is usually defined to include two rules. First there   **17–091** is the requirement to hear the other side of the case or give a fair hearing otherwise known as *audi alteram partem*. Secondly, there is the rule to avoid bias in the hearing or on the part of the decision maker, known as *nemo judex in sua causa*. Both rules provide the basis for procedural standards to be applied by the courts in the supervision of public bodies. Lord Diplock in the *Council of Civil Service Unions v*

---

[92] S. Boyron, "Proportionality in English Administrative Law: A Faulty Translation?" [1992] O.J.L.S. 237. Proportionality is found in many countries such as Germany, France, the USA and Canada.
[93] [2001] 3 All E.R. 433 at 445 g–h.
[94] See *R. v Ministry of Defence Ex p. Smith* [1996] 1 All E.R. 257.
[95] [2001] 3 All E.R. 433 at 446 h.

Minister for the Civil Service, [96]the GCHQ case, referred to the rules of natural justice as procedural impropriety. In that case procedural mistakes in not giving the Unions any consultation on the decision to ban Union membership at GCHQ, were regarded as a breach of a legitimate expectation to be consulted, and were amenable to judicial review. However, considerations of national security outweighed such legitimate expectations and the courts declined relief.

17–092   The sources of such rules of procedure vary according to the type of body and the relationship between the plaintiff and the decision-maker. In applying the rules of natural justice it is first necessary to inquire, does natural justice apply? The answer often depends on the nature of the body involved. Natural justice may be provided in a statutory form, or under contractual relations or through licences or even from a legitimate expectation that such rights may exist through the rather nebulous concept of private rights such as fiduciary relationships or quasi-contract. As Tucker, L.J. explained[97]:

> "The requirements of natural justice must depend on the circumstances of the case, the nature of the inquiry, the rules under which the tribunal is acting, the subject-matter that is being dealt with and so forth"

17–093   Natural justice is important in disciplinary hearings, employment disputes and in the rules of various regulatory authorities for sporting bodies.

17–094   In the early development of natural justice the courts developed principles on the basis of the common law. It was relatively easy to develop such principles when there was little statutory intervention. Gap-filling of this kind, however, is less common today. Statutory developments have became more comprehensive and often provide detailed rules relating to the conduct of hearings and the rights of parties.

17–095   The role of the courts has adapted to comprehensive statutory definitions setting out the principles of natural justice. This adaptation has been marked by a shift in focus from the rules of natural justice to the development by the courts of "the duty to act fairly". In *H(K) an infant, Re*[98] Lord Parker considered the decision of an immigration officer to meet the requirements of having to act fairly when refusing entry to K who was entitled to enter the United Kingdom provided he satisfied the immigration officer that he was under 16. The immigration officer relied on medical evidence that K was at least 16 but Lord Parker considered that K was entitled to know what had determined the matter in the mind of the immigration officer so that K would have the opportunity to answer the evidence. In fact the court found that the immigration officer had acted fairly.

17–096   The "duty to act fairly" may mark a shift in direction in judicial review.

17–097   At times the courts have considered the duty to act fairly as a substitute for the rules of natural justice. Lord Diplock in *GCHQ*, discussed above, considered that natural justice was replaced by the duty to act fairly. At other times, such as in *Ex p. Hosenball*[99] the courts continue to discuss the rules of natural justice.

---

[96] [1985] A.C. 374.
[97] *Russell v Duke of Norfolk* [1949] 1 All E.R. 109.
[98] [1967] 2 Q.B. 617. Also see *Pergamon Press Ltd, Re* [1971] Ch. 388.
[99] *Bushell v Secretary of State for the Environment* [1981] A.C. 75. Also *Pergamon Press Ltd, Re* [1971] Ch. 388.

The question arises as to whether the use of the duty to act fairly represents a **17–098** substantive change in the approach by the courts to applying principles of natural justice. Fairness appears a broader and more flexible concept than the rules of natural justice. It might appear to offer the courts the opportunity to look behind procedural rules and consider whether the outcome is fair. An alternative interpretation is to deny any difference between natural justice and the duty to act fairly. It is unclear whether the courts will adopt the duty to act fairly as a general expression of natural justice and the terms will be interchangeable.

The right to a hearing is one of the rules of natural justice. This may take a number **17–099** of forms: the right to put one's own side of the case, the right to be consulted, the right to make representations, or to submit reasoned arguments rebutting any allegations are all considered as elements in the duty imposed upon all decision-makers to act in good faith and listen fairly to each side of the case.

In *Ridge v Baldwin*,[1] Ridge, a Chief Constable was subject to disciplinary action by **17–100** the Watch Committee after he was acquitted of conspiracy to corrupt the course of justice. Remarks made by the trial judge critical of Ridge's conduct became the ground for disciplinary action. The Watch Committee decided to dismiss Ridge acting under s.191(4) of the Municipal Corporations Act 1882 without granting him a hearing. Ridge's solicitor requested and was granted a hearing and was permitted to appear before a later meeting of the Watch Committee. Ridge exercised his right of appeal to the Home Secretary but his appeal failed. He applied to the courts arguing that he had been given no opportunity to be heard and was not allowed to make representations. The House of Lords found in his favour and granted him a declaration that the decision of the Watch Committee was void and breached the rules of natural justice.

In disciplinary hearings for students, doctors, dentists and prisoners the rules of **17–101** natural justice have been applied. Natural justice may arise because the plaintiff's rights have been affected or because there is some legitimate expectation that consultation might take place. Particularly problematic has been a long established reticence on the part of the courts to review the internal disciplinary rules of sporting bodies. Examples of such bodies vary from the administration of boxing clubs by the British Board of Boxing Control, to the Jockey Club, and the Football Association. The courts' reluctance may stem from the rules themselves conforming to a certain minimum standard of natural justice and partly a concern that a large amount of litigation may result from active judicial intervention.[2]

Even where it may be established that natural justice applies it does not follow that **17–102** this includes the right to legal representation. The question of representations may arise because of the nature of the proceedings. For example in *Ex p. Hone*[3] the House of Lords considered whether legal representation was an absolute right. Lord Goff declined to accept that such a right existed in every case. The facts of *Hone* involved disciplinary charges against prisoners heard by the Board of Prison Visitors. The House of Lords accepted that there were circumstances where the need for legal representation might not be required. Matters which might be relevant in determining when to permit legal representation were outlined in *Ex p. Tarrant*[4] cited in opinion by

---

[1] [1964] A.C. 40.
[2] See "Mullan" (1975) 25 *University of Toronto Law Journal* 281.
[3] *R. v Board of Visitors of H.M. Prison the Maze Ex p. Hone* [1988] 1 A.C. 379.
[4] *R. v Secretary of State for the Home Department Ex p. Tarrant* [1985] Q.B. 251. *R. v Secretary of State for the Environment Ex p. Kirkstall Valley Campaign Ltd* [1996] 3 All E.R. 304.

Lord Goff. The list includes the serious nature of the charge, the question of whether any points of law are raised, the ability of the prisoner to make out his or her case, procedural questions of the difficulty of the rules, the need for reasonable efficiency in decision-making and finally fairness between prisoners. However while legal representation may be open to such considerations, the courts have maintained the view that cross-examination is an important element in a fair trial. Thus the plaintiff is nearly always entitled to this right.

17–103   It is not a requirement that an inquiry or investigation should always be in public. This appears from two cases, one involving the inquiry into murders carried out by Dr Shipman[5] and the other arising from the setting-up of three independent inquiries into the foot-and-mouth epidemic.[6]

17–104   The giving of reasons is also an important aspect of natural justice. The courts have been reluctant to provide a general duty to give reasons, but have considered that there must be sufficient reasons for the parties to know the nature of the case that has been considered. In *R. v Higher Education Funding Council Ex p. Institute of Dental Surgery*,[7] Mr Justice Sedley, as he then was, considered whether the University Funding Council, as it then was should be required to give reasons when making evaluations of the assessment of the quality of institutional research. He concluded that there was no general duty to give reasons but there are classes of case where a duty might arise. One example of such a class is where the subject matter is so highly regarded by the law, such as personal liberty, that reasons might be given as of right. Another class of case is where the decision appears aberrant. In the interests of fairness reasons may be required so that the recipient may know whether the aberration is in the legal sense real. In the case in question, a clear exercise of academic judgement does not fall within a decision which is challengeable only by reference to the reasons given for it.

17–105   An example where the House of Lords was prepared to require reasons is *Doody v Secretary of State for the Home Department*.[8] Prisoners convicted of murder and subject to a mandatory sentence of life imprisonment were entitled to be told by the Home Secretary what period or periods had been recommended by the judiciary to serve their sentence. The requirement to give reasons must therefore depend on the class of case involved and the role of the decision-maker under review. Some guidance may be found from the Court of Appeal decision in *English v Emery Reimbold and Strick Ltd*[9] as to the substantive details required when giving reasons to satisfy the requirements of natural justice.

17–106   The second rule of natural justice is the rule against bias. Pecuniary interests may disqualify a person from considering the case put before them. The courts have articulated this rule in the test of whether there is "a real likelihood of bias?" Direct pecuniary advantage extends to other forms of bias. Prejudice or direct involvement with one party as against another may amount to sufficient interest to be regarded as a breach of natural justice. A judge must not be the accuser or the prosecutor. In *Franklin*[10] the Minister appeared at a public meeting after he had prepared a draft

---

[5] *R. v Secretray of State for Health Ex p. Wagstaff* [2002] All E.R. (D) 1021.
[6] *Persey v Secretary of State for Environment, Food and Rural Affairs* [2002] All E.R. (D) (March).
[7] [1994] 1 All E.R. 651.
[8] [1993] 3 All E.R. 92.
[9] [2002] 3 All E.R. 385.
[10] *Dimes v Grand Junction Canal* (1852) 3 H.L. Cas. 759. *Metropolitan Properties v Lannon* [1969] 1 Q.B. 577. *Franklin v Minister of Town and Country Planning* [1948] A.C. 87.

order under the New Towns Act 1946 which designated Stevenage as a new town, and after he had decided to hold a public inquiry. At the meeting, amid strong objections from those who attended he said "It is no good your jeering: it is going to be done." This raised a challenge to the fairness of the Minister's judgment. The House of Lords accepted that there was no evidence that the Minister had not made a genuine consideration of the matters put before him and they upheld the legality of the Minister's approval of the order. Thus it is possible for the courts to accept that Ministers may follow a certain policy but in making their mind up as to the particular application of the policy a genuine consideration must be given to any objections.

Difficulty in establishing a satisfactory test for bias may stem from the question of the perspective to take when judging bias. The assumption behind the "real likelihood of bias" test is that the matter is to be judged by the standards of the reasonable man. However it may be necessary to consider a more subjective viewpoint. The perception of the plaintiff or others involved in the dispute may differ from the objective and balanced view of the hypothetical reasonable man. This may appear to be an equally valid perspective on the issue as the reasonable man. It may therefore appear necessary to consider both subjective and objective grounds as to whether there is bias or not.   **17–107**

The House of Lords in *Pinochet*[11] held that the issue of bias would apply where a judge might be thought to have a personal interest in the case. The real likelihood of bias test is set out in *R. v Gough*[12] and suggests that the court has to consider whether there is a danger or possibility of bias or injustice by taking account of all the circumstances.[13] As a result great care must be directed at providing in the membership of any disciplinary committee clear distinctions between the different levels of decision-making when disciplinary hearings are involved. The complainant should not be part of the adjudication committee and the appeal committee should not be tainted by the membership of the first instance committee. A separation between each function is important in such cases, especially involving closely knit groups within employment or in educational establishments. Most universities have well established internal rules to adjudicate disciplinary matters with representation for students and if necessary legal representation. The rules of natural justice must be read alongside Article 6 procedures.[14]   **17–108**

Given the problems that arose in the *Pinochet* case mentioned above, judges have become circumspect about how any interest in a case might give rise to a potential challenge. In *Taylor v Lawrence*[14a] the Court of Appeal gave consideration to the question of when bias might occur, especially when contacts between the judiciary and the legal profession may be close but in the normal way should not give rise to a possibility of bias. Where it was considered that "a fair minded and informed person" might regard the judge as biased it was important that disclosure should be made of any professional relationship or connection. In making a decision whether or not to withdraw from the case, the judge could hear from both parties and adopt the test of the perspective of a fair minded and informed person.   **17–109**

---

[11] *R. v Bow Street Metropolitan Stipendiary Magistrate Ex p. Pinochet Ugarte (No.2)* [2000] 1 A.C. 119.
[12] [1993] A.C. 646.
[13] *Nwabueze v General Medical Council* [2000] 1 W.L.R. 1760.
[14] See: *Director General of Financial Trading v Proprietary Association of Great Britain* [2001] UKHR 429.
[14a] [2002] 2 All E.R. 353.

Excluding Judicial Review

17–110 The High Court's supervisory role in the development of judicial review is derived from its common law powers of supervising "inferior bodies". In some examples there may be reasons for attempting to exclude the courts from interfering with the exercise of power or the application of the discretion of an inferior court or public body. While there is a presumption at common law in favour of the supervisory role of the courts, there are occasions when the courts may decline jurisdiction.

Judicial self-restraint or self-limitation may mean the courts do not intervene in reviewing the legal powers or the exercise of discretion of a public body. The courts' recognition of ministerial accountability to Parliament may result in not intervening in ministerial discretion. Similarly, invoking national security or the interests of the State will usually exclude the courts. The courts may decline to review the merits, policy or political choices of the decision-maker.

17–111 The courts may regard the existence of an appeal or other grievance mechanism adequate to the needs of the plaintiff. This may arise, for example, when the jurisdiction to consider grievances is given to a tribunal or a special body entrusted with particular responsibility. In *R. v Hull University Ex p. Page*[15] the House of Lords declined to exercise review over the jurisdiction of the Visitor in determining disputes arising under the domestic law of Hull University. The Visitor's jurisdiction included questions of fact or law and provided such powers were exercised within jurisdiction that the adjudication of disputes fell within the University rules, then the courts would refrain from intervening. If the Visitor acted outside his jurisdiction and acted in a manner incompatible with his judicial role or in breach of the rules of natural justice, then the courts might intervene. Lord Browne-Wilkinson explained[16]:

> "It is not only modern universities which have visitors: there are a substantial number of other long-established educational, ecclesiastical and eleemosynary bodies which have visitors. The advantages of having an informal system which produces a speedy, cheap and final answer to internal disputes has been repeatedly emphasised in the authorities . . ."

17–112 However as an illustration of an exception to the courts not reviewing such bodies, in *Ex p. Calder*[17] the Court of Appeal explained that judicial review was available against the disciplinary Tribunal of the Inns of Court. Judicial review jurisdiction also applied to the Visitors to the Inns of Court. In Calder's case the Visitors had misapprehended their role, and sat not as an appellate body but as a reviewing body.

17–113 The courts may decline to review on the basis that the right involves private law rights which are not susceptible to judicial review. In *R. v Disciplinary Committee of the Jockey Club Ex p. Aga Khan*[18] the Court of Appeal considered the role of the Jockey Club, incorporated by Royal Charter since 1970. The issue was whether a decision by the Jockey Club disqualifying a steward from chairmanship of a local panel was

---

[15] [1993] 1 All E.R. 102 [1993] A.C. 682.
[16] *ibid.* at 109. See *Patel v University of Bradford Senate* [1978] 3 All E.R. 841; and *Thomas v University of Bradford* [1987] 1 All E.R. 834 at p.850.
[17] *R. v Visitors to the Inns of Court Ex p. Calder; Ex p. Persaud* [1993] 2 All E.R. 876; *Independent*, January 29, 1993.
[18] [1993] 1 W.L.R. 909.

susceptible to review. The Court of Appeal held that the Rules were based on contractual agreement between the parties and owed their existence to private law rights. Thus they were not susceptible to review by the courts on the basis of judicial review. Undoubtedly if the Jockey Club had not provided such rules then Parliament would have had to intervene. This did not bring the matter within the category of a public body. Classification between public and private bodies provides a useful categorisation for the courts to decide whether the body is susceptible to review. However this does not always lead to consistency in approach. In *Datafin*[19] the takeover panel was susceptible to review notwithstanding that it was not created by statute or prerogative but because there was evidence that its powers would have been granted to the Department of Trade and Industry through legislation rather than through the informal rules set by the takeover panel. In this context there are similarities between the Jockey Club and the takeover panel. The former is not susceptible to review while the latter is.

Various techniques may be invoked to make judicial review either difficult or excluded altogether. The exclusion of the courts may occur when the wording of the statute contains such widely phrased powers that are couched in subjective terms that make review impossible. The form of words adopted may vary, such as "as the minister thinks fit", or "the minister's decision shall be conclusive" or the powers may be exercised "in such circumstances as the minister may believe". Faced with the prospect of subjective wording and unlimited discretion conferred on a Minister or public body, the courts require that the decision is made in good faith and that the powers are exercised fairly. Even faced with very wide discretionary powers, the courts may consider there is scope to intervene. In *Tameside*,[20] the Secretary of State for Education directed a local authority under s.68 of the Education Act 1944 to implement a 1975 scheme for the introduction of comprehensive education. Following a change in the political power of the local authority from Labour to Conservative the direction under s.68 of the 1944 Act was intended to prevent the Conservative-controlled local authority from implementing a selection process and retaining a number of grammar schools. The terms of s.68 of the 1944 Act were expressed in subjective terms, namely "If the Secretary of State is satisfied . . ." and ". . . give such directions as appear to him to be expedient . . .". The House of Lords concluded that there were matters which the Secretary of State had to address his mind to, before the powers under s.68 could be invoked. Lord Salmon interpreted the section to mean that the Secretary of State had to ask, could "any reasonable local authority act in the way, in which this authority have acted or is proposing to act?" The Secretary of State had failed to ask the right questions and therefore the decision was reviewable by the courts and the House of Lords held that the Secretary of State had acted unlawfully.

17–114

A further technique of avoiding the jurisdiction of the courts is to attempt to oust their jurisdiction. The most clear attempt to use an ouster clause may occur with the words: "shall not be called in question" in any court of law. In *Anisminic*,[21] already discussed above, the nature of the ouster clause was that under s.4(4) of the Foreign Compensation Act, the Commission's determinations "should not be questioned in any court of law whatsoever." The House of Lords considered that the ouster clause only

17–115

---

[19] *R. v Panel on Take-overs and Mergers Ex p. Datafin* [1987] Q.B. 815.
[20] *Secretary of State for Education v Tameside MBC* [1977] A.C. 1014.
[21] *Anisminic Ltd v Foreign Compensation Commission* [1969] 2 A.C. 147.

protected "real" determinations. The error of law made by the Commission in requiring Anisminic to be "a successor in title" resulted in the Commission's determination becoming a nullity and therefore the ouster clause was inoperative. Lord Reid regarded the purported determination of the Commission as in the eyes of the law one that had no existence. The courts had power to consider whether the determination made by the Commission was correct in law, notwithstanding the presence of an "ouster clause".

17–116   The success of ouster clauses may appear to be heavily qualified by the discretion of the courts in reviewing errors that go to the jurisdiction of the tribunal concerned. In *Johnston v Chief Constable of the Royal Ulster Constabulary*[22] it was noted that statutory ouster clauses could not be used to oust the jurisdiction of the courts in matters of EC law. In Johnston, a reserve police officer claimed sex discrimination by the failure of the RUC to renew her contract of employment. The reason given was that the RUC had a policy that women police constables should not carry firearms and there were sufficient full-time RUC officers to carry out all the jobs designated to women officers. The Secretary of State issued a certificate "that was conclusive" that she had been dismissed in the interests of national security. The European Court of Justice ruled that the order was inconsistent with EC law.

17–117   An alternative formulation to ousting the jurisdiction of the courts may be attempted. Instead of expressly stating that the courts are excluded a more subtle form of exclusion is used. Techniques of exclusion may vary but one method is to adopt the formula that a regulation or order "shall have effect as it enacted in this Act". A clause may provide that the confirmation of an order by a Minister is "conclusive evidence" of the requirements of the Act.

17–118   A widely used procedure is to limit the opportunity which allows a decision to be challenged in the courts. This may be achieved by specifying time-limits for taking legal action. One example of the use of time-limits is discussed in *Smith v East Elloe RDC*.[23] A person aggrieved with a compulsory purchase order made under the Acquisition of Land Act 1981 may apply to the High Court "within six weeks" for it to be quashed. Thereafter, the order could "not be questioned in any legal proceedings whatsoever". In the case of *Smith* the order was made five years before Smith decided to sue the Council claiming that the order was made in bad faith and therefore invalid. The House of Lords was divided on the matter, but the majority held that the time-limit effectively left the courts unable to review the order. Some of the judges advanced the view that had the proceedings been taken within the time-limit of six weeks and even if bad faith were proven, the courts could not intervene.

17–119   Reconciling the principles in *Smith* and *Anisminic* has been complicated by the lack of clarity in the *Smith* decision. *Ex p. Ostler*[24] held that the authority of *Smith* had not been diminished by *Anisminic*. The *Ostler* case effectively distinguished the *Anisminic* case: the former raised the question of a time-limit, while the latter was an ouster clause. The true interpretation of both the *Ostler* case and *Smith v East Elloe* rests on what is served by the public interest. Thus time-limits may retain their value as a protection in the public interest for some degree of finality to the judicial process. This leaves public bodies with some degree of certainty that projects once commenced may be safe from later review.

[22] [1987] Q.B. 129.
[23] [1956] A.C. 736.
[24] *R. v Secretary of State for the Environment Ex p. Ostler* [1976] 3 All E.R. 90.

University Procedures and Discipline

University procedures and discipline provide a good example where alternatives to the **17–120** courts may be sought and may be regarded as preferable in some circumstances, namely the area of student discipline. As mentioned above, universities or the Inns of Court have a Visitor with exclusive jurisdiction to consider matters within their jurisdiction. In *R v Hull University Visitor Ex p. Page*.[25] However for universities or colleges that do not have a Visitor, it is within the competence of the courts to review domestic procedures[26] even if the basis of the claim is made in contract and not public law. Internal procedures must be fair and reasonable.

The foundation document in this area is the *Report of the Task Force on Student* **17–121** *Disciplinary Procedures* chaired by Professor Graham Zellick.[27] The general principles involved in the use of university disciplinary proceedings are considered in the Zellick Report. There are however cases where it might be inappropriate to adopt internal disciplinary proceedings. Rape is given as an example of a serious offence where it might be considered that only in exceptional circumstances should university disciplinary proceedings be adopted. The Zellick Report offers the following advice[28]:

> "The police, Crown Prosecution Service or Procurator Fiscal Service may decide not to prosecute. Then the University may decide whether to proceed internally. However, it should do so only exceptionally and only where it is clear that the police or CPS decision is based on some special factor which has nothing to do with the quality of the evidence."

The prosecution authorities have a discretion to prosecute. In considering how to **17–122** exercise their discretion two questions are normally relevant. First, is there sufficient evidence to produce a "realistic prospect of a conviction"? Secondly, on the basis that there is sufficient evidence, is it in the public interest that a prosecution should be taken? The Zellick Report clearly sees the importance of keeping distinct the role of criminal prosecution and the use of disciplinary proceedings. Line-drawing of this sort is an important judgment to be made on the merits of each case.

Concerns about the expense and complexity of judicial review are evident in the **17–123** quest for many universities and colleges to seek internal procedures that permit student appeals and staff disputes to be resolved without recourse to the courts. In many instances it may be impossible to exclude the courts altogether. Another incentive for considering the question of appeals and disputes arises out of Lord Nolan's work on setting standards in public life.

Alternatives that might be considered include the use of arbitration or a panel of **17–124** independent persons to review cases on their merits. The following sets out some of the criteria which might be relevant in considering a system of complaints and appeals:

- Complaints procedures should provide a clear, simple and easy-to-operate system of handling complaints that is as far as possible transparent within the

---

[25] [1993] A.C. 682 at 704F.
[26] *Clark v University of Lincolnshire and Humberside* [2000] 1 W.L.R. 1988.
[27] *Final Report of the Task Force on Student Disciplinary Procedures*, chaired by Professor Graham Zellick, CVCP, December 1994.
[28] At para.15 on p.9 of the Zellick report.

confines of confidentiality. It is recognised that there is a minimum cost required to ensure that procedures are fair and are not weighted against the interests of any party. It is equally important that cost should not interfere with the attainment of justice. The aims of the complaints procedure ought to ensure that the financial burdens should not involve excessive expenditure through incurring legal fees or over-rigid formality.

● The system of complaints must be fair and impartial and meet all the requirements of natural justice.

● The system of complaints must command widespread support and respect throughout the university and avoid over-legalistic or procedural technicalities.

● The system of complaints should be capable of drawing on past university experience and should be flexible enough to accommodate changes in the culture of a modern university.

● The complaints system should have specific safeguards against abuse. Time-limits may be used at each stage of the deliberations.

● The administrative costs of the complaints procedures should be kept under review on an annual basis.

● There should be a link between the knowledge about administration gained through the complaints process and improvements in university administration.

17–125   The main principles that should govern the handling of complaints are:

● Complaints must be handled efficiently and within a reasonable time.

● The parties must be given an opportunity to give their side of the case and an opportunity to respond.

● Conciliation must be available at every stage of the complaints process.

● An annual report should be laid before the university setting out the lessons to be gained from the past experience of handling complaints.

● Any recommendations made in the report should be taken up for consideration by the relevant university committee and the various departments concerned.

● The complaints procedures cannot affect any legal rights of the complainant to go to court or seek judicial review. However, it is expected that if the complaints system meets all the criteria set out above, recourse to the courts will be avoided.

SUMMARY AND CONCLUSIONS

17–126   The fact that judicial review has come of age and found in the judiciary a robust self-confidence about its future, marks out the period of development of judicial review over the past 25 years. There remains considerable uncertainty about the values that inform judicial decision-making. This places the judiciary in the spotlight of speculation about the future. The Human Rights Act is likely to be influential in the future shape of judicial review.

Sunkin in his research on the case load of applications for judicial review has noted **17–127**
how judicial review has developed into an important and essential means for the
citizen to seek redress as well as for the courts to oversee the work of administrative
decision-making. His research findings underline the breadth, diversity and range of
issues which come before the courts. The statistical evidence in Sunkin's studies also
shows the use of judicial review by local authorities against central government. A
major proportion of judicial review cases come from litigation involving prisoners,
housing disputes including homeless persons, planning and licensing disputes. Immigration cases are also significant over the refusal of entry or challenging asylum
decisions. In two areas in particular, immigration and homelessness, judicial review has
grown in size. In other areas judicial review has been used sparingly. Judicial review is
used to challenge local government but its use in challenging the new generation of
non-departmental public bodies is uncertain at present.

Many of the conclusions to be drawn from Sunkin's study[29] underline the variables **17–128**
present in determining whether to seek judicial review. Variables include matters such
as the availability of legal aid, the existence of alternative remedies, the ability of
complainants to identify legal problems and lawyers to decide within the three month
time-limit to seek an application for judicial review. The availability of evidence, its
preparation and the willingness to litigate are all hidden factors in the availability of
judicial review.

An additional question in using the courts is whether the adversarial nature of the **17–129**
English judicial system provides an adequate basis to lay down normative principles for
the solution of administrative mistakes, inefficiencies or even in providing a grievance
resolution for citizens.

There is also the issue of how far formal legal rules may not only constrain officials **17–130**
but also condition or determine their behaviour. There is an increasing awareness
among public authorities and judges of the principles of judicial review and this
underlines the need for consistency in the approach adopted by the courts.

FURTHER READING

S.H. Bailey, D.J. Harris, and B.L. Jones, *Civil Liberties Cases and Materials* (5th ed.,
Butterworths, London, 2001).

P. Craig., *Administrative Law* (4th ed., Sweet and Maxwell, London, 1999).

de Smith, Woolf and J. Jowell, *Principles of Judicial Review* (Sweet & Maxwell,
London, 1999).

G. Ganz, *Understanding Public Law* (3rd ed., Sweet & Maxwell, London, 2001).

H.W.R. Wade and C.F Forsyth, *Administrative Law* (8th ed., Oxford University Press,
2000).

---

[29] M. Sunkin, "The Judicial Review Case-Load 1987–1989" [1991] *Public Law* 490–499; M. Sunkin, "What is
   happening to Applications for Judicial review?" (1987) 50 *Modern Law Review* 432.

Chapter 18

REMEDIES

INTRODUCTION

English law with its distinctive constitutional tradition, developed throughout the centuries an extensive system of remedies rather than a system of positive rights. Rights may arise in English law through the development of the common law and in express statutory enactments. Often such rights are expressed as negative rights to be protected in a particular way. The coming into force of the Human Rights Act 1998 is likely to be provide the courts with the opportunity to develop Convention rights supportive of the system of remedies. In many cases the availability of remedies is dependent on access to a lawyer. The availability of legal aid and advice may in the end become one of the factors that determines whether or not an application is made for a remedy. This chapter is focused on the role of the courts in the development of remedies. First, consideration is given to public law remedies and secondly, to remedies available in private law. The Order 53 procedure, discussed below and in Chapter 17, became Part 54 of the Civil Procedures Rules from October 2000. In much of the literature it is still referred to as Order 53. As noted previously, the other changes in line with the other procedural changes introduced to the civil justice system include applicants becoming "claimants" and the nomenclature of the prerogative, orders. The Queen's Bench Division of the High Court also known as the Divisional Court is now the Administrative Court.

18–001

FORMS OF RELIEF

Remedies may be statutory or non-statutory. In the case of statutory remedies, commonly this may take the form of an appeal to the High Court or of an application to a single judge of the High Court to quash or make an order depending on the terms of the statute. For example in the case of compulsory purchase orders there is an appeal to the High Court that the order may be *ultra vires*. Supervision by the courts of the planning process is an important and significant influence over how the planning system operates. Such rights of appeal originated in the 1947 Town and Country Planning Act and have been maintained under the 1971 Town and Country Planning legislation. Thus the validity of development plans and various other planning orders may be challenged in the High Court within a six-week period. In such cases the rights

18–002

of appeal are usually available to "any person aggrieved" by the plan or its amendment.

18–003   The provision of remedies through the system of appeals allows for the quashing of the decision at first instance. Generally appeals may be by rehearing, or on a point of law or by case stated. There are a number of procedural routes that may be taken to achieve an appeal. Many are derived from statutory provision or from the Rules of the Supreme Court. Appeals by way of rehearing under Order 55 give the appellate court powers to reverse the decision of the lower court. Appeals by way of case stated are usually from the magistrates' court to the High Court or specialist tribunals or the Crown Court to the High Court.

18–004   In the case of non-statutory remedies, the development of the various remedies available in administrative law may now be considered. In 1969 the Law Commission considered the law relating to the remedies available "for the judicial control of administrative acts or omissions with a view to evolving a simpler and more effective procedure". Following the Law Commission Report,[1] in 1977 the Order 53 procedure was introduced and took effect in 1978. The importance of this reform, and afterwards in 1981 its modification by s.31 of the Supreme Court Act 1981, was that the application for judicial review became the exclusive procedure for obtaining the prerogative writs. It was noted in the previous chapter that Order 53, r.9(5) empowers the court to order the transfer out of Order 53 in an appropriate case. However there is no provision for transfer into judicial review. The Law Commission is considering whether there ought to be a power to transfer a case which only raises issues of public law rights into the Queen's Bench Divisional Court. Also considered is whether there should be a power to join the two forms of proceedings so that all issues could be properly determined and the remedies provided in one court.

18–005   Prerogative remedies have a long history in English law. Certiorari according to Lord Atkin in *R. v Electricity Commissioners Ex p. London Electricity Joint Committee*[2] is available "whenever any body of persons having legal authority to determine questions affecting the rights of subjects, and having the duty to act judicially, act in excess of their jurisdiction". Certiorari is available to quash a decision in breach of the rules of natural justice or which is *ultra vires*. Prohibition is available to prevent action or the continuation of action which breaches the rules of natural justice or is in excess of jurisdiction. *Mandamus* compels the performance of a public duty. The prerogative remedies were first known as writs brought by the King against the offending official to compel the legal exercise of their powers. The Crown could ensure the performance of public duties and responsibilities by public authorities and inferior bodies kept within their jurisdiction. In 1933 the Administration of Justice (Miscellaneous Provisions) Act 1933 introduced a system whereby an ex parte motion had to be made to the High Court asking first for leave to apply for the remedy. The ex parte nature of the application resulted in only the applicant being represented and the other parties were not represented or given notice of the case. Rules of the Supreme Court laid down a time-limit of six months for seeking certiorari subject to the Court's discretion. The prerogative writs were subject to further change under s.7 of the Administration of

---

[1] *Report on Remedies in Administrative Law (Law Commission Paper No.73)* Cmnd.6407. Also see Law Commission Report No.226. Also see The Law Commission Consultation Paper No.126, *Administrative Law: Judicial Review and Statutory Appeals* (HMSO, 1993).
[2] [1924] 1 K.B. 171, 205.

Justice (Miscellaneous Provisions) Act 1938, which provided that the prerogative writs should be known as prerogative orders. Their development is part of the inherent supervisory jurisdiction of the High Court to review inferior bodies. Finally, there is also habeas corpus as a means of questioning the legality of detention exercised by administrative authorities and tribunals. The role of habeas corpus has diminished in use in recent years, but it still provides an important element of supervision over the detention powers of the executive.

In addition to the prerogative orders the citizen may seek a declaration and **18–006** injunction. Declarations set out the rights of the parties and could settle the legality of a particular cause or action, but it could not review cases where there was error of law on the face of the record. Injunctions provide the main remedy in private law prohibiting the commission of an unlawful act such as a breach of contract or a tort. It is a discretionary remedy and in origin owes its earlier existence to the Court of Chancery. The popularity of both declaration and injunction came to rival the use of the prerogative orders, specifically certiorari, traditionally regarded as the main order for keeping public bodies within their legal powers.[3] Litigants found a number of procedural drawbacks with the prerogative orders which may, in part, account for this development. First, that the prerogative orders did not provide for any interrogatories, normally available in any private action. Interrogatories included the lack of discovery of documents. Secondly, it was not possible to "mix" remedies. This means it was impossible to seek a certiorari along with damages or an injunction or declaration. Thirdly, the rules of standing varied according to the remedy sought and the circumstances differed where one remedy was available and another was unavailable.

Declaration provided the basis for establishing some of the most important **18–007** developments in administrative law and helped to shape and change the substantive law of judicial review. Declaration offered the litigant certain advantages. These included the absence of requirement of leave and the absence of a short time-limit for action such as the six-month time-limit for certiorari. Litigants' solicitors may have found the declaration a more attractive remedy because of its common use in many private law matters, whereas certiorari provided greater complexity concerning the nature of the decision that may be reviewed.

The Justice All Souls Review[4] identified the problems that existed before the **18–008** introduction of the Order 53 reforms as follows:

"The applicant, however, could not get sight of the relevant files of the authority nor could he cross-examine its witnesses. The general rule was that discovery of documents and interrogatories were not available and that evidence was confined to affidavit material. Different time-limits applied in relation to each remedy. If the applicant applied for the wrong remedy the whole proceedings would fail and he would have to start again (if still in time). The court had no power to award the right remedy."

In addition to declaration and injunction there is also an action for damages arising **18–009** out of a public authority's liability in tort or contract. Such remedies are discretionary

[3] *Congreve v Home Office* [1976] Q.B. 629. See de Smith, *Judicial Review of Administrative Action* (4th ed., 1980), Chap.10.
[4] *Administrative Justice Report of the Committee of the Justice—All Souls Review of Administrative Law in the United Kingdom* (Oxford, 1988), p.143.

and subject to rules relating to *locus standi.* Order 53 introduced significant reforms to the system of remedies. In public law matters an application for judicial review for *mandamus*, prohibition or certiorari, or declaration or injunction may be made to the High Court. Discovery may be ordered. Damages may be joined to the application for judicial review at the discretion of the Court. Before considering each of the remedies in more detail it is first necessary to explain the law of standing.

The Law of Standing

18–010   The law relating to standing, *locus standi*, is important in both private law claims and in the application made by claimants for judicial review. The rules of standing set out the entitlement of the aggrieved citizen to seek redress in the courts for the particular remedy sought. The rules of standing have a "gate-keeping" function as providing the means to exclude vexatious litigants or unworthy cases. Standing may appear as a procedural requirement but procedural rules in this instance are linked to substantive issues.

18–011   The arguments in favour of liberal rules of standing appear persuasive. Access to the courts should be open to the citizen as a means of complaint. Wide rules of standing permit the courts a large discretion in remedying the abuse of public power. Traditionally this fits Dicey's view that the rule of law requires that disputes as to the legality of acts of the government ought to be decided by judges independent of the Executive. This implies that illegal conduct should be prevented or stopped which is a necessary corollary of enforcing the law. Flouting of the law may occur where the procedures for redress are inadequate. If illegality is not checked then the law may be diminished in status.

18–012   What is the purpose of having rules of standing? One view is that standing rules provide administrators some protection against vexatious litigants and this protects the conduct of government business to be carried on unrestricted from outside inter-ference. Setting limits on who may litigate prevents government from an over-cautious and over-legalistic approach to problem-solving. Interest groups and organisations may be prevented from waging a political struggle by adopting legalistic techniques in order to challenge existing rules. There is a fear that politically motivated litigation may involve the courts in political struggles and the courts may regard such a use of judicial review as an unacceptable abuse of the courts' proper role. However, distinguishing acceptable from unacceptable motives in seeking litigation may not be easy and the need for flexible rules of standing may permit the courts a much needed discretion.

18–013   Standing may also permit public institutions to enforce the law. In the case of the Audit Commission, it is envisaged that under s.25(d) of the local Government Finance Act 1982 provided by s.30 and Sch.4 of the Local Government Act 1988, the auditor appointed in relation to the audit of accounts may apply for judicial review. This may arise where there is a failure by the body audited to act arising out of any decision where it might reasonably be considered that it would have an effect on the accounts of the local authority. Such powers to seek judicial review include the power to take action in anticipation of any breach of the law. In 1990 a Code of Audit Practice was published to facilitate the use of the auditor's legal powers and provides for consultation with the body under audit.

18–014   Local authorities under s.222(1) of the Local Government Act 1972 have, in respect of civil proceedings and where "it is expedient for the promotion or protection of the interests of their inhabitants", the right to institute proceedings. The use of injunctions in the case of the Sunday Trading laws is an example of this power.[5] In many instances such rights of standing have been used to enforce the law in respect of nuisance through stop-notices. In criminal matters local authorities are given wide powers to institute prosecutions for specific breaches of the criminal law that fall within their jurisdiction.

The Attorney-General occupies a unique role in terms of standing. As the guardian   **18–015** of the public interest, he has a special duty to enforce the law. The Attorney-General may agree to lend his name to the actions of a private citizen in seeking redress in the courts. When a private individual is unable to establish sufficient standing for the institution of a private action, which may involve public rights, the Attorney-General may permit the action to proceed as a "relator" action. Today the occasions to do this are rare as *locus standi* has been sufficiently broadened to permit the citizen direct access to the courts.[6] The use of the Attorney-General has expanded the role of injunction and declaration as providing a protection arising from private law for many public law grievances. The case for having a flexible approach to standing appears well made. However, permissive rules of standing may give rise to serious administrative problems in the organisation of the courts. The courts may become overburdened with the flow of cases and delays in having cases heard may lead to injustice. Currently, there is a delay of at least 15 months before an application for judicial review may be heard by a single judge. There are also questions about the cost of administering the system. In many instances the opportunities for litigation may depend on the availability of legal aid which is paid out of public funds. The cost of legal aid may become a consideration in the expense of operating the system of judicial review and pressure to reduce costs may require adjustments to the present arrangements.

Standing in Private Law

The rules of standing may be considered with respect to private actions. The use of   **18–016** remedies available in private law for public law wrongs requires there to be standing. In general in private law the entitlement to a remedy and the right to apply for the remedy are treated together. The most common remedies are the action for an injunction or declaration. In *Boyce v Paddington Corp*[7] the plaintiff brought an action to restrain the Council from constructing a hoarding adjacent to a building site, which would obstruct the plaintiff's right to light. The right to sue was accepted in respect of a public wrong where the plaintiff suffered damage to his private rights. This is capable of both narrow or broad interpretation depending on the nature of the issue.

In the case of a private action against a public authority in *Steeples v Derbyshire CC*[8]   **18–017** it was held that the plaintiff's action based on private propriety rights could provide sufficient *locus standi* when affected by the exercise of public law powers. The plaintiff was granted sufficient standing to challenge the grant of planning permission over two leisure complexes. The plaintiff claimed that his private rights such as enjoyment of his property as against nuisance caused by noise, or enjoyment of the use of a lane and the

---

[5] *Kirklees MBC v Wickes Building Supplies Ltd, The Times*, June 29, 1992; [1992] 3 All E.R. 717.
[6] Sir Harry Woolf, *Protection of the Public—A New Challenge* (Hamlyn Lecture, 1990). See *Gouriet v Union of Post Office Workers* [1978] A.C. 435.
[7] [1903] 1 Ch. 109.
[8] [1985] 1 W.L.R. 256.

risk of vandals or litter were infringed. He also claimed that there was a breach of natural justice in the granting of the planning permission. The grounds for standing arising out of both private rights were equivalent to those available to him to make an application for judicial review if necessary.

18–018 The courts may wish to restrict the availability of private law remedies only to those directly affected rather than to any citizen's sense of public spirit. In cases where the private person may lack the necessary standing, the Attorney-General may be requested to give his permission to a relator action. In *Gouriet*[9] Lord Wilberforce explained how a relator action, which allowed the Attorney-General at the suit of individuals to bring an action or assert a public right, might be used in a private action for an injunction to restrain a threatened breach of the criminal law by a trade union. However, such a relator action was at the discretion of the Attorney-General and the courts were unwilling to review such a discretion.

18–019 Similarly the courts are sensitive to the need to restrict the availability of remedies so as to exclude busybodies or unmeritorious cases. Invariably standing may be sought by ratepayers, taxpayers or "aggrieved citizens". Applying *Boyce v Paddington* such citizens may sue in their own name where a public right causes special damage. In *Barrs v Bethell*[10] some ratepayers from Camden sought an injunction against the local authority alleging that there had been various abuses of the discretion given to councillors and requiring that cuts should be made in services. It was decided that they could not sue in their own name but could seek a relator action through the Attorney-General.

Standing in Public Law

18–020 The application for judicial review under Order 53 requires consideration of the applicant's standing. It will be remembered that the procedure under Order 53 is a two-stage process. At the first stage there is a leave requirement. Obtaining leave requires that an arguable case is made out and if this is not found, leave may be refused. In practice this sets a low threshold but it may be seen as a procedural sieve or hurdle to be surmounted before the full hearing of the issues is considered at the second stage.

18–021 The Law Commission has noted[11]:

> "In 1980 there were 525 applications for leave to move for judicial review, in 1984 there were 918, and in 1991 there were 2089 such applications. This trend was maintained in 1992: in the first ten months there were 2034 applications for leave, compared with 1708 for the same period in 1991. In 1992 there were at any one time, on average two Divisional Courts and two (occasionally three) judges dealing with Crown office business, i.e.: with statutory appeals as well as judicial review."

18–022 There is no such leave requirement in ordinary civil actions and the leave requirement has been criticised as wrong in principle. However the requirement of leave may be

---

[9] *Gouriet v Union of Post Office Workers* [1978] A.C. 435.
[10] [1982] Ch. 294.
[11] Justice All Souls: *Administrative Justice: Some Necessary Reforms* (1988), pp.152–155. Also see A.P. Le Sueur and M. Sunkin, "Application for Judicial Review: The Requirement of Leave" [1992] P.L. 102.

justified as an important way to exclude vexatious litigants or busybodies. The leave requirement acts as a means to filter out hopeless or unmeritorious cases. In *Ex p. Doorga*[12] it was noted that leave should be granted where there are *prima facie* reasons for granting judicial review, but refused either when there is no *prima facie* case and where the case is wholly unarguable. In practical terms there are cases where the issues clearly appear arguable and those that require more detailed consideration to determine whether they are worth further consideration. In the former, leave will always be granted while the latter require more careful scrutiny.

At the first stage an application for leave normally is made ex parte to a single judge, usually on affidavits and subject to amendment at the discretion of the judge. The ex parte nature of the proceedings results in the absence of any representation from the defendant and this requires that the courts take time to ensure the accuracy of the affidavits. All relevant matters must be disclosed and there is a presumption of good faith on the part of the applicant. Thus if material facts are suppressed or withheld, the court may dismiss the application without reference to the merits of the case. In cases where the judge is uncertain of whether an arguable case is made out, it is possible for the judge to invite the defendant to appear in person and make representations on the nature of the case. An application may be made under the general jurisidiction of the court to set aside leave which has been granted. The criteria is whether the judge is satisfied that the case has no reasonable prospect of success.   **18–023**

The Law Commission has considered whether the leave requirement is required in the application for judicial review. Various suggestions might be considered such as an oral hearing from both sides with more comprehensive grounds stated as to why leave is refused. Where both parties agree that there is a serious issue to be tried, leave might be dispensed with. Refusal to grant leave for an application for judicial review may result in a renewal application made without a hearing to the Divisional Court in matters relating to criminal causes. In civil cases a refusal of leave may be renewed, but not appealed; the renewal may be made either before a single judge or to the Divisional Court. In cases where the refusal was made by the Divisional Court after an oral hearing, then the application may be renewed in the Court of Appeal. The right of access to the Court of Appeal is without leave and attempts to restrict this right in 1985 were defeated after intense debate in the House of Lords. There is no jurisdiction for the House of Lords to hear an appeal against the refusal of a renewed application for leave.[13]   **18–024**

The Order 53 procedure permits applying in a single application, for the prerogative remedies of *certiorari*, *mandamus* and prohibition, together with declaration, damages or injunction. The requirement of standing is now part of the leave requirement for the application for judicial review and is contained in s.31(3) of the Supreme Court Act 1981, "that the applicant has a sufficient interest in the matter to which the application relates".   **18–025**

Originally the Law Commission had envisaged that the standing rule should be part of the consideration of whether to grant any of the remedies sought. However as matters presently stand the question of standing may be raised as to the grant of leave   **18–026**

---

[12] *R. v Secretary of State for the Home Department Ex p. Doorga* [1990] C.O.D. 109.
[13] RSC, Ord. 32, r.6. See *R. v Governor of Pentonville Prison Ex p. Herbage (No.2)* [1987] Q.B. 1077; [1987] 2 W.L.R. 226. RSC, Ord. 53, r.3(4)(a). *Hansard*, HL Vol.461 cols.443–464 (March 19, 1985) and *Hansard*, HL Vol.459, cols.939–954 (February 5, 1985).

to apply for judicial review under s.31(3) of the 1981 Act but there remains the possibility that standing may be considered also at the second stage when there is a substantive hearing of the case. This possibility emerges from consideration given to the law of standing by the House of Lords in *R. v Inland Revenue Commissioners Ex p. National Federation of Self-Employed and Small Businesses*,[14] which may be conveniently referred to as the *Fleet Street Casuals* case. An application for judicial review was made by an association of taxpayers who objected to the Inland Revenue waiving the arrears of income tax for 6,000 workers in the printing industry in Fleet Street. The association objected to preferential treatment which it viewed as condoning illegality in newspaper practices in hiring casual labour for the printing industry in Fleet Street.

18–027   This case raises important issues over the interpretation of the existing law of standing but the decision unfortunately leaves uncertainty as to the precise legal principles which may apply. The case favoured a flexible and liberal approach to standing but failed to set out clear principles, preferring to leave a large measure of judicial discretion and policy-making.

18–028   The law of standing before the introduction of Order 53 varied according to the particular remedy sought. After the *Fleet Street Casuals* case there is still some doubt as to whether there is a single test for standing under the new procedures under Order 53. Thus it may still remain relevant to consider the nature of the particular remedy that is sought. However, it is generally accepted that in the *Fleet Street Casuals* case the general preference in judicial opinion was in favour of a uniform test for standing freed from any undue procedural or technical differences depending on the remedy sought. This preference emerges from the following opinions.

18–029   Lords Diplock, Scarman and Wilberforce agreed that standing had to be considered not in isolation but as part of the legal and factual context of the application. Lord Fraser dissented on this point but it was commonly agreed that the applicants had failed to show any breach of the duty of the Inland Revenue and that the Revenue had wide managerial powers which allowed them to make special agreements of this kind. Consequently the association according to Lord Scarman had failed to show sufficient interest to justify any further proceedings.

18–030   On the general matter of standing, Lords Diplock, Scarman and Roskill agreed that the law on standing was the same for all remedies. Lords Diplock and Scarman considered that *mandamus* was not stricter than certiorari and that injunction and declaration are available where certiorari would lie. The consensus of opinion in favour of liberal rules of standing raises the question about the nature of the rules that should apply to determine standing.

18–031   The judges refer to standing being determined as a question of "mixed law and fact". Statutory interpretation and the general context of the application are relevant to determine the nature of the applicant's interest in the case. Legal principles are expected to be applied to determine standing rather than general discretion, though Lord Diplock admitted that he regarded the judges as having an unfettered discretion to decide what sufficient interest may mean in a particular case. Searching for legal principles from the *Fleet Street Casuals* case, it emerges that every person who has a good case has standing. This might be interpreted to mean that standing no longer forms a distinct category as every good case will fulfil the standing requirement on its

---

[14] [1982] A.C. 617; [1981] 2 All E.R. 93.

merits. Standing only becomes a relevant issue for those cases where there is doubt about the merits of the decision. However this view does not find universal acceptance and the matter remains uncertain.

The *Fleet Street Casuals* case, by joining the issue of the applicant's status and   **18–032** interest to the merits of the case, appears to move in favour of presuming that citizens have the right of legal redress. However, this does not always guarantee that the citizen's action is approved of by the courts. Consistent principles in this area of the law are difficult to formulate. Factors that contribute to uncertainty include the use of the discretion of the courts and the fact that in some cases the Crown will waive any consideration of standing when issues arise that the Crown considers require adjudication by the courts.

Pressure Groups and Standing

In *Covent Garden Community Association Ltd v Greater London Council*,[15] the Covent   **18–033** Garden Community Association was a company formed to protect the rights and interests of Covent Garden residents. Woolf J. accepted that this gave the Association sufficient interest and therefore *locus standi* to challenge planning permission, but certiorari was refused on the merits of the case. A similar approach was evident in *R. v Hammersmith and Fulham BC Ex p. People Before Profit*[16] where a company limited by guarantee sought leave to object to the planning policy committee of the local borough's decision to grant planning permission after a planning report following a public inquiry had favoured objectors. *Locus standi* was established on the "legitimate" bona fide reason that any person was entitled to object to a planning matter. The status of a company did not provide sufficient ground to prevent standing. However the application was refused because the case was not a reasonable one.

A more fundamental objection to citizens challenging decisions appears from *R. v*   **18–034** *Secretary of State for the Environment Ex p. Rose Theatre Trust Co*[17] Schiemann J. considered the standing of a trust formed from local residents, well known and renowned archeological experts and leading actors, who applied for judicial review to preserve the remains of a site in London which was claimed to be the remains of the Rose Theatre and of great historical interest.

The case raised the fundamental question of the role of a pressure group and the   **18–035** law of standing. Leave was granted to apply for judicial review but the question of standing became a central issue at the full hearing of the application. Schiemann J. considered whether standing was established. He observed that, even after leave was granted, the court which hears the application ought to consider whether the applicant has sufficient interest. Whether an applicant has sufficient interest is not purely a matter for the court's discretion. Not every member of the public can complain of every breach of statutory duty. The fact that "some thousands of people join together and assert that they have an interest does not create an interest if the individuals did not have an interest". A company which has a particular power within its memorandum to pursue a particular objective does not create for a company an interest in the case. It remains to be seen whether this restrictive view of public interest litigation will be followed by the courts in future cases.

[15] 1981] J.P.L. 183.
[16] 80 L.G.R. 322.
[17] [1990] 1 Q.B. 504.

18–036   The *Rose Theatre Case* adopts an approach which emphasises the importance of establishing a sufficient interest even if the effect is to allow unchallenged the legality of the Secretary of State's powers. In deciding that the applicants failed to meet the standing requirement the question of who might have sufficient standing was also considered and it was concluded that "no individual has the standing to move for judicial review". This reasoning appears unduly protective of the powers of the Secretary of State, but it may arise from an unwillingness by the courts to become involved as an instrument of pressure group activity. This interpretation may arise from the particular statutory arrangements under s.1 of the Ancient Monuments and Archaeological Areas Act 1979 which did not envisage any appeal or review. However there is also an apparent reluctance from the case to develop public interest litigation. Two reasons may contribute to this reluctance. First, administrative pressures on the courts to cope with the increased volume of judicial review. Secondly, a concern that policy formulation is best left to parliamentary supervision rather than judicial review.

18–037   Is the law of standing in a satisfactory state? The answer depends on the earlier discussion about the precise role of the rules of standing. Galligan distinguishes standing which concerns an individual's capacity to seek judicial review where his private interest is in some way affected, from the position where a person seeks to challenge simply on the basis of the public interest in not allowing official power to be used improperly.

18–038   The current state of the law allows great flexibility in the courts and even though there are doubts about public interest challenge, such challenges have been allowed by the courts albeit on a restrictive basis. It is useful, for example, to contrast the use of public challenge to local authority decisions when compared to the use of public challenge to matters involving central government. The former was expressly approved by the Widdicombe Report[18] as a means to control local authority activities.

18–039   The importance of pressure groups at both the national and international level includes such well known groups as Friends of the Earth, Greenpeace and the World Development Movement. They have been active campaigners and have been active in the lobbying process for better protection of the environment and in challenging government policy. In *R v Secretary of State for Foreign and Commonwealth Affairs Ex p. World Development Movement*[19] the World Development Movement successfully challenged the payments from the overseas aid budget to build a dam in Malaysia.

18–040   The World Development Movement was described as "a non-partisan group, over 20 years old and limited by guarantee", that has 7,000 full voting members throughout the United Kingdom with a total supporter base of some 13,000. There are about 200 local groups, and campaign activities include letter writing and petitioning M.P.s.

18–041   The case marks an unusual and significant use of official documents and greater transparency in government decision-making. The pressure group relied on information obtained through a National Audit Office report and information gleaned from debates within, and evidence taken by, the Public Accounts Committee and the Foreign Affairs Committee.[20] The National Audit Office and the Public Accounts Committee assumed the legality of the aid but criticised aspects of its value for money.

---

[18] *The Conduct of Local Authority Business*, Cmd.9797 (1986).
[19] [1995] 1 All E.R. 615.
[20] *Pergau Hydro-Electric Project* (1994–95 HC 155). See F. White, I. Harden and K. Donnelly, "Audit, Accounting Officers and Accountability: The Pergau Dam Affair" [1994] *Public Law* 526.

The National Audit Office regarded the allocation of money as falling under policy matters within the remit of Ministers. This excluded from its consideration the merits of the policy. However, it appeared that the Accounting Officer had serious reservations about the project.

As Lord Justice Rose noted, the accounting officer's view was that the Pergau **18–042** project was "an abuse of the aid programme in the terms that this is an uneconomic project" and that "it was not a sound development project".[21] Despite such reservations, written ministerial instructions were given to proceed with the financial aid. The Pergau project was funded, purportedly under s.1 of the Overseas Development and Co-operation Act 1980. Considering whether the aid for the Pergau Dam fell within the ambit of the 1980 Act, Lord Justice Rose concluded:

> "[a]ccordingly, where, as here, the contemplated development is, on the evidence, so economically unsound that there is no economic argument in favour of the case, it is not, in my judgment, possible to draw any material distinction between questions of propriety and regularity on the one hand and questions of economy and efficiency of public expenditure on the other."[22]

The Secretary of State under s.1(1) of the 1980 Act had extensive powers as follows: **18–043**

> "The Secretary of State shall have power, for the purpose of promoting the development or maintaining the economy of a country or territory outside the United Kingdom, or the welfare of its people, to furnish any person or body with assistance, whether financial, technical or of any other nature."

The case hinged on the interpretation of this section. Was the grant in question "for **18–044** the purpose of promoting the development" of Malaysia? This depended on whether the aid flowed into a development that might be described, according to the Foreign Office test for funding development, as one that was "sound, financially viable and [would] bring economic benefits". As doubts had been expressed within the consultation process within the government departments, the divisional court held that the provision of aid was *ultra vires* the 1980 Act. As a result of this decision, the Comptroller and Auditor General qualified his opinion of the aid on the basis of irregularity. Despite this finding and the decision of the divisional court, the government found the necessary additional aid required to finance the Dam from a repayable charge on the Contingency Fund. Eventually the money was found from the Reserve Fund.

The World Development Movement were able to show how the dam project had **18–045** limited use in terms of promoting development but had enormous potential for encouraging arms sales and potential markets for UK companies. The project also failed on the criteria of its potential damage to the environment and limited benefits for the community. Evidence used in the case provided a broad cost–benefit analysis of the project, beyond the narrow view of the Government in favour of economic trade.

The case signifies that issues of the legality of public expenditure may involve **18–046** questions of value for money. There is a stark warning here. As Lord Justice Rose

---

[21] [1995] 1 All E.R. 611 at 617A–B.
[22] [1995] 1 All E.R. 611 at 626J–627B.

noted, the Government had taken no legal advice in the first instance on the legality of the aid; and as Daintith and Page observe:

> "The question of the relationship between the legislation and the Department's power to incur expenditure subject only to the authority of the Appropriation Act does not appear to have been raised or discussed. "[23]

18–047   Greenpeace has also been particularly active in monitoring radioactive waste. Mr Justice Otton in *R. v Pollution Inspectorate Ex p. Greenpeace*[24] described how the organisation had nearly 5 million supporters worldwide with 400,000 supporters in the United Kingdom of whom about 2,500 lived in the Cumbria region where the British Nuclear Fuels plant was situated.

18–048   The role of the pressure group or lobby group is often controversial. In recent years their importance has become more significant in the area of legal challenge. The Law Commission, in their recent report on administrative law,[25] acknowledged that interest groups may have good grounds for having standing, in the public interest, to make an application for judicial review. This might apply in cases where the pressure group feels that the public are adversely affected by an administrative decision of a government agency or government itself. Clearly there is evident flexibility in permitting pressure groups a role in bringing in the public interest matters before the courts.

18–049   The Law Commission has considered the use of standing in administrative law. Suggestions for reform include expressly linking public interest to the applicant's link with the case, as a basis for standing. Also considered might be the possibility of setting up a Director of Civil Proceedings as an alternative to individual public interest litigation.

18–050   Concern arises out of the *Rose Theatre Case*, if interpreted to mean that the ordinary citizen in the absence of an express statutory right is debarred from challenging decisions, even where it appears that there may be a public interest served by such a challenge. This may leave a gap in the arrangements for public challenge. There may be a role for the Attorney-General in such cases. But as Galligan notes the traditional role of the Attorney-General may be inappropriate to the needs of public interest litigation and therefore some means must be found for individuals to make a challenge.[26]

> "There is, however a serious flaw in the apparent symmetry between the object of review and the standing rules; the object of review is to ensure that officials act within their powers, while the point of standing is to determine who may bring an action. These are two different issues and the determination of the legality question is not linked in any logical way to the decision about who brings the action."

18–051   An important dimension to the law of standing in the United Kingdom is the development of European Community Law. Article 230 (ex. Article 173) provides

---

[23] T. Daintith and A. Page, *The Executive in the Constitution* (1999), p.35.
[24] [1994] 4 All E.R. 321 at 349.
[25] Law Commission No.226.
[26] D.J. Galligan, *Discretionary Powers* (Oxford, 1986), pp.379–382.

standing for individuals or one who is directly concerned by a decision, to challenge decisions made by Community institutions. National rules set down by Member States of the Community may not be used to inhibit the enforcement of a Community right.

The extension of this right has been recognised in *Factortame* and in *Francovich*[27] **18–052** where the European Court has created a remedy under Community law enforceable by individuals in their national courts against defaulting Member States. Thus any obstacle such as a restrictive view of standing may be placed to one side by the European Court in cases concerning Community law. In a particular context, for example European environmental law where Community environmental rights may be wider than domestic rights, the law on *locus standi* of the United Kingdom may Rbe more restrictive than that available under the law of the European Community. Inevitably reconciling domestic and European Community law may take some time, but in this particular example where the activities of pressure groups is high, there will be inevitable pressure to expand the rules of *locus standi* in favour of public interest litigation.

It is also inevitable that greater account will have to be taken of the provisions of **18–053** European Community law in the interpretation of Order 53 and s.31 of the Supreme Court Act 1981 in cases involving rights conferred by Community law.

Rules of Standing and the Role of the Courts

The law relating to standing, *locus standi*, is important in both private law actions and **18–054** the application for judicial review. The rules of standing set out the entitlement of the aggrieved citizen to seek redress in the courts for the particular remedy sought. The rules of standing have a "gate-keeping" function: they provide the means to exclude vexatious litigants or unworthy cases. Standing may appear to be a procedural requirement, but procedural rules in this instance are linked to substantive issues. The arguments in favour of liberal rules of standing appear persuasive.

Access to the courts should be open to the citizen as a means of complaint. Wide **18–055** rules of standing permit the courts a large discretion in remedying the abuse of public power. This fits Dicey's view, that the rule of law requires that disputes as to whether acts of the government are legal ought to be decided by judges independent of the Executive. This implies, as a necessary corollary of enforcing the law, that illegal conduct should be prevented or stopped. Flouting of the law may occur where the procedures for redress are inadequate. If illegality is not checked then the law may be diminished in status.

In the United Kingdom there are some notable examples[28] where an individual or **18–056** pressure group has taken legal action. In *Gillick*[29] the rights of an under-age schoolgirl to receive information on contraception were considered in a crusade against contraceptive advice being available to schoolgirls without the consent of their parents. The case was taken by Mrs Gillick and was broadly supported by religious groups and organisations. The pressure group tactic of pursuing legal cases is clear. The Pro-Life Alliance, an anti-abortion group, have pursued legal cases directly; recently, in an important legal case,[30] they were accepted as an intervention setting out moral issues as

[27] *Francovich v Italy* [1992] I.R.L.R. 84; [1993] 2 C.M.L.R. 66.
[28] See Carol Harlow, "Public Law and Popular Justice" (2001) 65 *Modern Law Review* 1. Also see D. Feldman, "Public Interest Litigtion and Constitutional Theory" (1992) *Modern Law Review* 44.
[29] *Gillick v W. Norfolk and Wisbech AHA* [1986] A.C. 112.
[30] *A (children) (Conjoined Twins: Surgical Separation), Re* [2001] 2 W.L.R. 480.

part of the court's consideration of the legality of a decision. Such tactics are unmistakably to make use of the courts in an effort to protect the unborn and to advance that cause through legal rights.

18–057   Increasingly the courts show willingness to allow interested parties or groups to represent their views in cases where the interpretation of law or international agreement might require explanation or expertise. The flexibility in allowing such a development appears from the introduction of new civil procedure rules. As Harlow has noted:

> "To sum up, we are seeing a shift away from the traditional bipolar and adversarial law suit familiar to common lawyers, to something more fluid, less formal and possibly less individualistic in character. By making access easier, judges are subtly changing the rules of the game. A novel public interest action is in the making, with the help of which campaigning groups are gaining entry to the legal process. No serious credentials in the form of "democratic stake" are required of them."[31]

18–058   The "rules of the game" include the possibility that public interest challenges, when they raise public law issues and the claimant has no private interest in the outcome of the case,[32] may be heard by the courts. However, though the number of applications for judicial review[33] has increased to 5,398 for the year 2001, these do not reflect a marked increase in pressure group activity. In fact judicial review cases neatly fall into three categories: those taken by homeless people, those arising out of immigration disputes, and those involving the police in relation to criminal matters and local authority cases.[34] One reason for pressure groups' small role in litigation is that, despite the liberalisation of the rules of standing, there is general reluctance on the part of the judiciary to encourage a widespread use of judicial review to settle disputes. There is marked sensitivity to maintaining strict discipline in applying the rules of procedure. The rules of standing are therefore important as a procedural route of access to the administrative court.

18–059   The Human Rights Act 1998 introduces a new dimension to the role of the courts. Rights issues may now be more openly addressed through legal action taken by pressure groups. There is a contrast between the "sufficient interest" test in judicial review, outlined above, and the restricted "victim" test for standing[35] adopted by s.7 of the Human Rights Act 1998 as part of the jurisprudence of the Strasbourg Court of Human Rights.[36] It would appear that various civil liberties groups or pressure groups may not meet the more difficult hurdle of the victim test than the lower requirement of " sufficient interest". This restriction may apply to trade unions or professional groups. This does not prevent financial resources being made available to meet the costs of litigation.

---

[31] Harlow, *op.cit.*, pp.7—8.
[32] *R. v Lord Chancellor Ex p. Child Poverty Action Group* [1999] 1 W.L.R. 347.
[33] *Practice Statement* [2002] 1 All E.R. 633.
[34] L. Bridges, G. Meszaros and M. Sunkin, *Judicial Review in Perspective* (1995).
[35] Mark Elliott, "The Human Rights Act 1998 and the Standard of Substantive Review (2001) *Cambridge Law Journal* 301.
[36] N. Garnham, "A Sufficient Victim?: Standing and the Human Rights Act 1998" [1999] JR 39. See *R. (on the application of Pelling) v Bow County Court* [2001] U.K.H.R.R. 165.

Public Law Remedies

Procedural Matters

In the previous chapter, attention was given to the exclusivity principle, namely that **18–060** after *O'Reilly v Mackman* the courts have required the Order 53 procedure to be exclusively confined to public law matters. Linked to this principle is the requirement of a time-limit in English law in which to make the application. Before Order 53 was introduced certiorari was the only prerogative remedy which required a time-limit, namely six months. While the courts had a limited discretion to review the six-month period this was rarely exercised. In the case of civil proceedings for declarations and injunction time-limits did not apply.

The law on time-limits for all applications for judicial review is contained in Order **18–061** 53, r.4 and also ss.31(6) and (7) of the Supreme Court Act 1981. Currently the time-limit is three months though there is a complexity in reconciling the terms of r.4 with s.31(6). R.4 applies only to applications for leave to apply for judicial review whereas s.31(6) applies to both applications for leave and applications for substantive relief. This adds to the complexity of the issue when it is also considered that r.4 is concerned with good reasons for extending the three-month time-limit whereas s.31(6) is confined to the effects of dealing with grounds for refusing relief either at the substantive stage or at the application stage.

The present law is unsatisfactory for two reasons. First, the law attempts to enforce a **18–062** rigid rule of three months but if the application is not made promptly, even if made within the three months the application may be refused.[37] Secondly, the date from which the time-limit may run is unclear. The circumstances where the court might exercise its discretion is unspecified.

The crucial issue is "promptness". In *Ex p. Caswell*[38] the House of Lords affirmed **18–063** the view that the three-month time-limit was not an entitlement. In cases where there is undue delay even within the three-month period, reasons must be given. Even where an extension of time is given at the first stage, that is, the application for leave, this may be considered at the full hearing after representations from both parties are heard. In *Ex p. Caswell* the applicants conceded that there had been undue delay. The House of Lords then had to consider whether the granting of relief would be likely to cause hardship or prejudice or would be detrimental to good administration. The answer to this question depended on the effect of whether after the lapse of time—the Dairy Produce Quota tribunal's decision had been made in 1985—it would be detrimental to good administration to grant relief. The House of Lords concluded that it would, and dismissed the appeal.

Time-limits under Order 53 and s.31 of the Supreme Court Act 1981, appear too **18–064** short and the ground of the courts discretion too vague. The question of whether it is desirable to retain a three-month time-limit or in general whether time-limits are needed is also under consideration.[39]

The question of time-limits was considered by the House of Lords in a planning case **18–065** involving analysis of the rule about going to the courts promptly and its compatibility

---

[37] *R. v Dairy Produce Tribunal Ex p. Caswell* [1990] 2 A.C. 738.
[38] *ibid.*
[39] *Law Commission Consultation Paper No.126*. On European Community law, see Case 209/83, *Ferriera Valsabbia Case* [1984] E.C.R. 3089.

with the Human Rights Act 1998. In *R. v Hammersmith and Fulham LBC Ex p. Burkett*[40] the House of Lords adopted a sensitive approach to the question of "promptness". The case involved a complex series of facts regarding a planning application for outline planning permission. In September 1999 the local authority planning committee decided to refer the application to the Secretary of State to make use of his call in plans. In February 2000, the Secretary of State declined to call in the application and outline planning permission was granted in May 2000. In April local residents issued judicial review proceedings to quash the decision to refer the matter in September 1999 to the Secretary of State. Their case rested on alleged failures on the part of the local authority planning committee to consider an environmental assessment.

18–066   The House of Lords reviewed the issues of promptness, as both the Court of Appeal and the High Court had considered this to be the main reason for dismissing the application for judicial review. The promptness rule, often interpreted to mean within three months, was considered by the House of Lords. Lord Steyn pointed out that going to court too quickly had often resulted in poorly considered cases and a reduction in the possibility of negotiated settlements. The uncertainty surrounding the exact nature of what promptness had actually meant in practice might be inconsistent with the Convention under the Human Rights Act. Lord Steyn also acknowledged that complex cases needed time for preparation and expressed unhappiness with a rigid three-month rule. It would appear that while there remains a need to go to court and prepare a case, the question of promptness has been given some latitude by the House of Lords. The way forward seems to be to give some certainty to the law and, even if this means tighter time-limits, to allow the court to consider the merits of each case.

The Discretionary Nature of Remedies

18–067   All the remedies available under the application for judicial review fall under the discretionary jurisdiction of the Divisional Court. There are no simple criteria on which this discretion is based. Generally the court will consider the availability of any alternative remedies such as appeals or the existence of a specialised tribunal before granting judicial review. As a general rule it is expected that the applicant will have attempted to make use of any available alternative remedies before coming to the court. In *Ex p. Calveley*,[41] Sir John Donaldson suggested that the courts would only rarely exercise their jurisdiction to grant judicial review in cases such as this one when there was an alternative appeal remedy available. Only in "exceptional circumstances" would review be accepted in preference to appeals available to the applicant. In *Ex p. Calveley*, in the case of police officers subject to disciplinary proceedings, certiorari was granted notwithstanding the existence of rights of appeal under the Police (Appeal) Rules 1977.[41a] This was a case where departure from the disciplinary procedures was such that on the merits, the courts would intervene by way of judicial review. But this exercise of judicial discretion is not always a predictable one. For example in *Puhlhoffer*[42] a local authority's decision that a person is not entitled to accommodation under the Housing (Homeless Persons) Act 1977 was not open to appeal. The House of Lords was clear that judicial review should be confined only to exceptional cases. In

[40] [2002] 3 All E.R. 97.
[41] *R. v Chief Constable of the Merseyside Police Ex p. Calveley* [1986] Q.B. 424.
[41a] Now see Police Regulations 1995 (SI 1995/215).
[42] *Puhlhoffer v Hillingdon LBC* [1986] A.C. 484; [1986] 1 All E.R. 467.

Ex p. Swati[43] a person refused leave to enter the United Kingdom was refused leave to apply for judicial review. The applicant would have to rely on his appeal rights only. However the circumstances which determined whether judicial review might be available appeared unquantifiable and appeared to "defy definition" in the case.

Considerations which may guide the exercise of the courts' discretion are very wide.   **18–068**
It may be that there is concern for the workload generated by judicial review in certain areas such as immigration cases or homeless persons. The courts' preference for seeking alternative remedies is in part recognition of the degree of specialist advice available to appeal tribunals. It is also recognition of the nature of many of the disputes which cover multi-disciplinary issues that the courts may wish to confine their jurisdiction and not usurp the jurisdiction of appellate bodies.

Another approach is to consider the balance of convenience. This is where the   **18–069**
courts regard proceedings taken by judicial review as an acceptable means to resolve the dispute because "in all the circumstances" it is the most cost-effective. Lord Justice Glidewell took this view in a number of cases following from the *Royco Homes Case*[44] in 1974. Lord Widgery explained that while a planning condition could be challenged on the basis of the statutory appeal structure, certiorari might lie where it was more efficient and effectual.

In exercising their discretion, the courts may also consider matters of delay and the   **18–070**
locus standi of the applicants. Both these matters may be considered at the full hearing stage as well as at the initial application for leave procedure. Indeed the entire boundary between public law and private law rights invites consideration of a whole range of questions which also admit the discretion of the court. This may include the subject matter of the dispute, the nature of the remedy sought and the implications for administrative decision-making. In this area of judicial discretion the courts find it difficult to explain why discretion is exercised in one case and not another. Consistency of approach should be important as well as the merits of the specific case, but courts are not always predictable.

There is an increasing judicial awareness of the cost–benefit analysis of judicial   **18–071**
review. This may mean considering the question of whether good administration is encouraged by the outcome of the decision. In *Ex p. Argyll Group*[45] the courts reluctance to quash the decision of the Chairman of the Monopolies and Mergers Commission, even though it was found to be illegal, was based on the needs of public administration. In assessing whether to exercise the courts' discretion it was noted that third parties had already acted on the decision and that the Commission would have made the same decision as its chairman. Lord Donaldson explained how the courts' discretion may be influenced by the following factors. Though not intended to be a complete catalogue they emphasise the importance of substance over form. These factors include a proper consideration: of the public interest; of the legitimate expectations of the individual citizens; of the financial interest involved; and finally of decisiveness and finality in decision-making. The speed of decision-making is also relevant. Decisiveness and finality are important virtues in the process of good administrative decisions.

[43] *R. v Secretary of State for the Home Department Ex p. Swati* [1986] 1 W.L.R. 477.
[44] *R. v Hillingdon LBC Ex p. Royco Homes Ltd* [1974] 1 Q.B. 720.
[45] *R. v Monopolies and Mergers Commission Ex p. Argyll Group plc* [1986] 1 W.L.R. 763; [1986] 2 All E.R. 257.

18–072   A final issue for consideration is the grant of legal aid. S.18(4) of the Legal Aid Act 1988 provides that the respondent must establish "severe financial hardship" unless an order is made. In matters involving judicial review there is consideration by both the courts when granting leave and the Legal Aid Board when considering legal aid, of the "appropriateness" of bringing the application. Two questions arise: first whether public bodies when they are involved in litigation should be able to receive legal aid, when presently they may not because they do not fall under the heading of "severe financial hardship"; secondly, whether the merits test as regards granting by the courts should be the same as the Legal Aid Board when granting legal aid. It is quite possible for the two different bodies to come to different conclusions when purporting to follow the same test.

Void and Voidable Administrative Action

18–073   A related and important question when considering remedies and the grounds for challenge either through judicial review or appeal is the question of the effect of an *ultra vires* decision. This question arises in connection with the effects of two types of error of law. One is jurisdictional and the other is non-jurisdictional. The former may render the decision void and having no legal effect. When the court decides to quash the decision, it does so in a retrospective way. The latter may have had some legal effect but because of some mistake in the law, it does not remain valid once the court decides to exercise its discretion and quash the decision. This is described as a voidable, as opposed to a void, decision. The court when quashing a voidable decision does so prospectively, because the decision is valid until the time comes for the court to quash the decision.

18–074   While there remains some doubt as to whether there is a distinction between jurisdisctional errors which render a decision void and not voidable, the concept of void and voidable is an additional element in judicial discretion. While it is not always easy to know whether an act is void or voidable, the categorisation may also have a direct result on a number of related issues. For example, the exercise of a right of appeal will not always cure the defect of a void act and the courts may wish not to consider an appeal against a void decision. A void act may be ignored by the person affected whereas a voidable act may not. If an act is potentially voidable, the courts may still regard the act as valid until it is declared invalid.

18–075   There are a variety of views as to the importance of the void and voidable distinction and there is a lack of consistency in the use of language when describing how void and voidable may apply to a decision. Judicial application of the distinction may not always be consistently applied. In *Anisminic*[46] the House of Lords accepted that an *ultra vires* act was void and a breach of natural justice was similarly void.

18–076   For the reasons outlined above, the void and voidable distinction appears important when considering the legal position of the parties and may affect the outcome of the decision.

Certiorari (a Quashing Order), Prohibition (a Prohibiting Order) and *Mandamus* (a Mandatory Order)

18–077   The main public law remedies may be briefly mentioned. Certiorari[47] has the effect of quashing a decision which may be done by an excess or abuse of power, whereas prohibition is intended to restrain a body from acting unlawfully in the future or

[46] *Anisminic Ltd v Foreign Compensation Commission* [1969] 2 A.C. 147.
[47] *R. v Electricity Commissioners Ex p. London Electricity Joint Committee Co (1920) Ltd* [1924] 1 K.B. 171.

preventing an excess or abuse of power. Certiorari and prohibition are similar and both are available as remedies in public law. The criteria for deciding which acts and decisions are subject to certiorari and prohibition was expressed by Lord Atkin in the *Electricity Commissioners case*[48]:

"... Wherever any body of persons having legal authority to determine questions affecting the rights of subjects, and having the duty to act judicially, act in excess of their legal authority they are subject to the controlling jurisdiction of the King's Bench Division."

The interpretation of the duty to act judicially has been widened considerably since the case was decided. Since *Ridge v Baldwin*[49] the courts have interpreted the phrase to include those bodies that have the power to decide and determine matters which affect the citizen. This means that certiorari generally may be available to review all administrative acts. This includes such variety of examples as a valuation officer, the grant of planning permission, the Criminal Injuries Compensation Board set up under the prerogative, and mandatory grants to students.[50] However certiorari was not available to quash a provisional order made by the Secretary of State for the compulsory purchase of land by the Hastings Board of Health.[51] **18–078**

The formulation of acting judicially commonly used today is that favoured by Lord Diplock in *O'Reilly v Mackman* that it is enough to show that the body or person has legal authority to determine questions affecting the common law or statutory rights of other persons. Historically it was assumed that certiorari would not be available for contractual matters or purely domestic disputes. **18–079**

Certiorari is available to quash decisions that are *ultra vires*, in breach of natural justice or where traditionally there has been an error of law on the face of the record. This includes most forms of *ultra vires* discussed in Chapter 17. As Lord Slynn suggested in *Page v Hull University Visitor*,[52] the scope of certiorari may be interpreted widely: **18–080**

"If it is accepted, as I believe it should be accepted, that certiorari goes not only for such an excess or abuse of power but also for a breach of the rules of natural justice."

Prohibition shares a similar scope to certiorari but it lies to restrain such action rather than quash it. It is important to emphasise that both certiorari and prohibition are discretionary remedies. While the law on *locus standi* has been discussed above with respect to the changes introduced by Order 53 it is worthwhile mentioning the law before Order 53, was introduced, as there is still the possibility that the courts may wish to consider the old law. *Locus standi* for certiorari distinguished between "persons aggrieved" and strangers. This distinction was left to the courts to define. A person **18–081**

---

[48] *R. v Electricity Commissioners Ex p. London Electricity Joint Committee Co (1920) Ltd* [1924] 1 K.B. 171.
[49] [1964] A.C. 40.
[50] *R. v Paddington Valuation Officer Ex p. Peachey Property Corporation Ltd* [1966] 1 Q.B. 380. *R. v Hillingdon LBC Ex p. Royco Homes Ltd* [1974] Q.B. 720. *R. v Criminal Injuries Compensation Board Ex p. Lain* [1967] 2 Q.B. 864; *Ex p. Nilish Shah* [1983] 2 A.C. 309.
[51] *R. v Hastings Board of Health* (1865) 6 B. & S. 401.
[52] [1993] 1 All E.R. 97 at 114b.

aggrieved was explained by Lord Denning in *Ex p. Liverpool Taxi*[53] as including any "person whose interests may be prejudicially affected". Strangers included busybodies interfering in matters which did not concern them.

18–082   *Mandamus* is a court order which commands the performance of a public duty. Public duty has been described as a concept which is "important but elusive". The courts have drawn attention to the distinction between a duty or a power. The former is enforced by *mandamus* while the latter is not. The question of what constitutes a duty is inconclusively defined by the courts. Statutory interpretation may depend on the purpose for which duties are to be exercised. Invariably the public character of the duty is crucial in the courts' discretion to make *mandamus* available. The source of a public duty may arise from the common law, prerogative or statute. It may also arise in respect of licences or contracts or from legal powers through charters or customs. The bodies amenable to *mandamus* include local authorities, the Metropolitan Police Commissioner and Ministers.[54]

18–083   Mandamus may lie where there is a breach of procedural jurisdiction or even where there is a discretion that involves public duties. In *Padfield*[55] the Minister was said by Lord Reid "to have a duty to act" even though such a duty was expressed in discretionary language, "if the minister in any case so directs". If such a power is used for an improper purpose or irrelevant considerations are taken into account, the courts may decide to grant *mandamus* to correct the misuse of power. *Mandamus* is a powerful remedy because it commands the performance of set obligations or responsibilities. Failure to obey the terms of *mandamus* may result in proceedings for contempt of court.

18–084   *Mandamus* usually required a strict rule of standing before Order 53 was introduced. In *R. v Lewisham Union*[56] standing required there to be a "legal specific right". The case raised particular facts relating to the attempt to compel the guardians of the poor to undertake compulsory vaccination to prevent outbreaks of smallpox. A less strict view was favoured in *Ex p. Blackburn*[56a] which favoured a public interest aspect to the enforcement of public rights created by the criminal law. This liberal trend has been further advanced by the House of Lords in the *Fleet Street Casuals Case* discussed above.

18–085   *Mandamus* may not lie against the Crown. This is a rule that has also been interpreted to include servants of the Crown. The rationale behind this rule owes its origins historically to the role of the courts in not commanding the Sovereign to command her own performance of any duty.[57] Crown immunity, however, does not appear to prevent *mandamus* being taken against the activities of the Crown, for example the Income Tax Commissioners in their function of revenue collection. The development of the declaration has limited the restrictions such a rule might appear to hold. *Mandamus* will also be refused where there are circumstances that suggest that all steps that could be taken have been taken and thus the courts' intervention would be inappropriate.

[53] *R. v Liverpool Corp Ex p. Liverpool Taxi Fleet Operators' Association* [1972] 2 Q.B. 299.
[54] See *R. v Camden LBC Ex p. Gillan* (1988) 21 H.L.R. 114. *R. v Metropolitan Police Commissioner Ex p. Blackburn* [1968] 2 Q.B. 118.
[55] *Padfield v Minister of Agriculture* [1968] A.C. 997.
[56] [1897] 1 Q.B. 498.
[56a] [1968] 2 Q.B. 118.
[57] *R. v Customs and Excise Commissioners Ex p. Cook* [1970] 1 W.L.R. 450.

Habeas Corpus

Habeas corpus is an ancient remedy which allows a person detained to challenge the **18–086** legality of detention. The law relating to habeas corpus has been kept outside the reforms introduced under Order 53 and consequently the remedy has been given less attention in recent years compared to its historical importance. Application is made to a Divisional Court of the Queen's Bench Division. The remedy is technical and narrow in scope as invariably other remedies have been developed to allow the detention of the applicant to be tested, such as the right of appeal or appearance before a magistrate. However there are circumstances where habeas corpus is the only remedy available to an applicant. In *X v UK*[58] the European Court of Human Rights expressed dissatisfaction about the procedures open to mental health patients to challenge their detention. The European Convention was not satisfied by the limited scope of the habeas corpus application.

Habeas corpus also appears to be useful in immigration cases. In *Khawaja*[59] the **18–087** House of Lords considered that common principles might be applied to habeas corpus and judicial review, but failed to clarify the scope of the courts' inquiry.

The Law Commission has considered the restrictive nature of habeas corpus **18–088** applications which are confined to the facts on which the detention is based. As Lord Donaldson noted in *Muboyai*,[60] the application for judicial review afforded a wider opportunity for challenging an administrative decision and this favoured using judicial review as opposed to habeas corpus. Perhaps the time has come to rationalise the relationship and set out the exact role that habeas corpus is expected to fulfil when reviewing powers of detention. One suggestion is to allow interim relief at the leave stage to allow the legality of detention to be questioned.

Private Law Remedies

Remedies such as declaration, injunction and damages are available in ordinary civil **18–089** proceedings. Order 53 provides that such remedies are added to the prerogative remedies of certiorari, prohibition and *mandamus*, and are available under the application for judicial review procedures in public law matters. In effect this gave the potential for an overlapping jurisdiction between the power to seek declaration and injunction in civil proceedings and under the application for judicial review. The limitations set by *O'Reilly v Mackman* have been considered in Chapter 17. It is important to consider in this section not only the remedies of declaration and injunction but also the special position of the Crown and the availability of tort and restitution remedies against public authorities.

Declaration and Injunction

A declaration or, as it is sometimes referred to, a declaratory judgment is an order of **18–090** the court. The procedure by way of originating summons is under RSC 1965, Ord. 5, r.2, or under Ord. 15, r.16, and it is also available under Order 53 on the application

[58] (1981) 4 E.H.R.R. 188.
[59] *R. v Secretary of State for the Home Department Ex p. Khawaja* [1984] A.C. 74.
[60] *R. v Secretary of State for the Home Department Ex p. Muboyai* [1992] Q.B. 244.

for judicial review for public law matters as defined in *O'Reilly v Mackman*. The preferred means of obtaining a declaration raising a public law matter is under the Order 53 procedure. In the case of an originating summons there is no power to grant an interim declaration of rights but some broadening of this rule has occurred under Ord. 5, r.4. Such a limitation does not arise under the Order 53 procedure.

18–091   Declaration is a wide ranging remedy. In *Dyson*[61] the applicant challenged the Inland Revenue's decision to require him under penalty to supply them with information. There was no cause of action and little authority for the use of the procedure under the then existing procedure, Ord. 25, r.5 which has since been amended by Ord. 15, r.16. The aim of providing a speedy and simple procedure in part underlines the reasons behind the *Dyson* decision. As a declaration is available against the Crown, this underlines the usefulness of this remedy.

18–092   The courts have not provided a complete list of situations or categories where a declaration may lie. In declaring rights there is the added implication that illegality will be established. This is useful in setting out the scope of a public body's duties, liabilities and lawfulness of decisions. In *Gillick*[62] advice on contraception for girls under 16 was considered as to its legality and the House of Lords upheld the advice as legal. Thus declaration may be useful for settling many doubtful matters relating to the exercise of legal powers. Planning permission, the work of the Boundary Commission, reports of public inquiries and the like are typical examples of the versatility of a declaration.

18–093   Despite the potential width and scope of a declaration there are limitations to its availability. In general terms a declaration will not be granted where the court considers that the statute retains an exclusive jurisdiction to the tribunal or other body provided in the statute. In *Barraclough v Brown*[63] the House of Lords held that the plaintiff's claim for declaration was one which arose under a statute and the statute had provided a procedure for grievances. The courts were confined by the procedures laid down in the statute and therefore declaration was not available. In contrast, in *Pyx Granite*[64] the House of Lords distinguished *Barraclough*. A declaration might be available notwithstanding any statutory rights where there remained common law rights. These may be enforced through a declaration.

18–094   A declaration will not be granted by the courts if its effect is to usurp the authority of the body under review. A declaration is not based on a speculative or hypothetical basis, it only issues as a ground of relief where relief is real and is needed. Unlike some countries where a written constitution permits a form of judicial preview, English law has historically been reluctant to take abstract or moot points as part of the remit of the courts. A declaration is available to the Equal Opportunities Commission for the purposes of determining whether the relevant provisions of the Employment Protection (Consolidation) Act 1978 are compatible with Community law.

18–095   The question of whether a declaration is available for an error of law is problematic. Such an error is usually regarded as resulting in a voidable and not a void decision. This means that the decision remains valid until action is taken to control or remedy the error. As a declaration merely declares what the rights of the parties may be and

[61] *Dyson v Att.-Gen.* [1911] 1 K.B. 410.
[62] *Gillick v West Norfolk and Wisbech AHA* [1986] A.C. 112.
[63] [1897] A.C. 614.
[64] *Pyx Granite Ltd v Ministry of Housing and Local Government* [1960] A.C. 260.

does not alter their position, this suggests that declaration would not be a useful means to control such an error of law. However this limitation may be less important with the availability of certiorari under the Order 53 procedure.

Injunctions are of equitable origin and may restrain a person or body from illegal **18–096** action. The equitable nature of the remedy makes the injunction a discretionary remedy in common with the prerogative remedies. Thus an injunction may be refused if there are alternative remedies available or where the court regards the granting of the injunction unnecessary. Injunctions may be prohibitory, or mandatory and may be expressed in terms of positive obligations or in the form of negative prohibition. Injunctions may be interim or interlocutory, that is, pending the outcome of the full hearing of an action, an injunction may be granted to preserve existing arrangements. The injunction as a form of interim relief is important. Under Order 53 the applicant may seek an order of *mandamus* or declaration, the main form of interim relief is through an interim injunction. When granted in the form of an interim injunction, the plaintiff is normally required to give an undertaking to indemnify the defendant for any loss he suffers as a result of the interim order. This practice does not always apply in the case of the Crown seeking an injunction.

The test applicable when interim relief is sought is based on principles developed in **18–097** the decision of the House of Lords in *American Cyanamid Co v Ethicon Ltd*.[65] The test is to decide if the applicant has a good arguable case and, if he has to take into account the balance of convenience when considering the duties owed by the public body and the interests of the public. An addition to this criteria is the inclusion of a *prima facie* case needed to justify the granting of relief when the court is exercising its discretion.

A good arguable case means one with a real chance of success, not necessarily a 51 **18–098** per cent chance. The balance of convenience may take into account the interest of the public.

Injunctions may be perpetual and granted at the end of the action. Injunctions are **18–099** available to one who has an arguable case, that is not frivolous or vexatious and that there is at least an arguable case which is likely to succeed. When considering such matters as the likelihood of success, the court may take account of the balance of convenience and the interests of the public.

The availability of injunctions may be by judicial review under Order 53 or in the **18–100** following circumstances where an injunction may lie at the suit of a private individual. In a private action, injunctions are available on the same basis of *locus standi* as a declaration, where some private right appears to be affected or where special damage peculiar to the private individual arises from an interference with a public right.

Injunctions are also available at the suit of the Attorney-General on behalf of the **18–101** Crown. This may arise where the protection of public rights or the interests of the public require the Attorney-General to take action to restrain breaches of the criminal law. Where a public body may be acting *ultra vires* the Attorney-General may intervene to prevent a threatened or immediate breach of the law.

The Attorney-General may take a relator action. Such action may arise where the **18–102** Attorney-General allows, at the suit of a private individual (the relator), his name to be joined to the action on the basis that he believes such action should be taken. The

---

[65] [1975] A.C. 396.

reponsibility of the relator is to ensure that the Attorney-General is satisified on the evidence that such an action should be taken. In *Gouriet v Union of Post Office Workers*[66] the House of Lords considered the refusal of the Attorney-General to agree to a relator action to enforce an injunction restraining a threatened breach of the criminal law. It is considered unlikely that the courts may wish to review the discretion of the Attorney-General in such matters.

18–103   The value of the relator action is less certain, since the general liberalisation of the rules of standing under Order 53, as the necessary standing may be given to the private individual in cases of judicial review. In the *Rose Theatre Case*[67] the Attorney-General did not agree to a relator action and so recourse to judicial review was necessary.

The Crown

18–104   One of the often discussed limitations on the use of the injunction is that it is not traditionally available against the Crown. This rule has a long historical development. S.21(1) of the Crown Proceedings Act 1947 expressly provides that the court shall not grant an injunction against the Crown. It had been generally accepted that this prohibition also applied to servants of the Crown. The reforms introduced under s.31(2) and Ord. 53, r.3(10) had possibly given the courts powers to grant injunctions, including interim injunctions, against Officers of the Crown and against government Ministers acting under statutory powers in their own names.

18–105   The House of Lords in *M, Re*[68] have, since *Factortame*,[69] considered the availability of injunctions against the Crown. Injunctions are generally available against departments or Ministers, although it was conceded that the use of injunctions against government departments would be rare.

Discovery, Damages and Restitution

18–106   Discovery of documents forms an important pre-trial preliminary in ordinary civil proceedings. The availability of discovery in public law matters under Order 53 allows for the cross-examination and appearance of affidavits. This is regarded as an important inclusion under the application for judicial review procedures. Since *O'Reilly v Mackman* the courts have generally adopted a common approach to the granting of discovery but in judicial review applications the courts have favoured a more restrictive approach and the careful exercise of discretion on the merits of each case. Not all documents will be relevant to the judicial review and those that are not will not normally be included in the granting of discovery. An additional issue is that the Crown is able to claim public interest immunity arising out of certain documents or indeed rely on the confidential nature of the papers as a means to prevent disclosure.[70]

18–107   Under Order 53 claims for damages may be joined to the application for judicial review. In England and Wales there is no provision for restitution proceedings. In *Woolwich Building Society v I.R.C. (No.2)*[71] the House of Lords considered the question

---

[66] [1978] A.C. 435.
[67] [1990] 1 Q.B. 504.
[68] See *M, Re* [1993] 3 All E.R. 537. See Lord Donaldson in *M v Home Office* [1992] Q.B. 270 at 306.
[69] *R. v Secretary of State for Transport Ex p. Factortame Ltd (No.2)* [1991] 1 A.C. 603.
[70] *Air Canada v Secretary of State for Trade* [1983] 2 A.C. 394.
[71] [1992] 3 All E.R. 737.

of restitution proceedings after an application for judicial review had established that the regulations on which the Revenue based its demand for tax payment against the Woolwich Building Society were illegal. The approach adopted by the House of Lords established the right of the citizen to recover money paid by the citizen under regulations which are *ultra vires*. The Law Commission is considering whether the application for judicial review should include proceedings for restitution.

Tort and Contract Liability of Public Authorities

A public body that acts *ultra vires* may be liable in tort in the same way as a private **18–108** citizen, provided a cause of action is established. S.2 of the Crown Proceedings Act 1947 permits the Crown to be sued on the same basis as private individuals, although the courts have a discretion whether to award damages or not, especially when policy issues may be concerned in the question of liability. Statutory interpretation is often difficult when it comes to the question of the application of tort principles to public bodies. When comparing public bodies to private individuals, the former usually possess wide statutory powers whereas the latter do not.

As a general principle, public bodies may be liable for the negligent exercise of their **18–109** powers. The courts in their discretion have attempted to apply similar principles to the liability of public officials and authorities, as apply to private persons. In the interpretation of statutory duties the courts may hold public bodies liable in damages for breach of their duty. For example a breach of a duty to provide housing for homeless people under the housing legislation may give rise to liability in damages. However it is a good defence to argue that the alleged tort is carried out according to express or implied statutory powers. In *Geddis*[72] the court accepted that even if the Act was authorised by the legislature, if carried out negligently it may give rise to liability. It is not easy to categorise how the courts will respond in each individual case. The courts have not found it easy to lay down clear principles when decisions amount to *ultra vires* and when decisions are to be regarded as negligent policy decisions to be reviewed by the courts, there is often uncertainty.

Principles of liability on the basis of *Anns v Merton LBC*[73] were established by the **18–110** House of Lords. The Council had statutory responsibility to regulate building regulations and requirements for the proper construction of property. The House of Lords accepted that the Council was liable in negligence for the cost of repairing buildings when the foundations had been improperly inspected or the inspector had negligently carried out inspections. Since *Anns* a more restrictive view of the extent of liability for economic loss has been accepted in *Murphy v Brentwood*[74] which distinguished *Anns* on the basis that there can be no liability in tort for the cost of repairing defective premises in anticipation of any personal injury or property liability.

Public bodies may be liable for nuisance but there is a presumption that statutory **18–111** powers are not intended to be exercised so as to cause nuisance. However, the

[72] *Geddis v Bann Reservoir Proprietors* (1878) L.R. 3 App. Cas. 430.
[73] [1978] A.C. 728. See the development by the courts of foreseen damage in *Cambridge Water Co Ltd v Eastern Counties Leather plc* [1994] 1 All E.R. 53.
[74] [1991] 1 A.C. 398.

question of whether a nuisance may be condoned in the exercise of statutory ypowers depends on the nature of the powers and their interpretation by the courts. In *Burgoin SA v Ministry of Agriculture*[75] the question arose out of the entitlement of a trader in a claim alleging liability because of a breach of European Community regulations against the Ministry of Agriculture. The courts were divided on the matter and decided in that instance that there was no liability; this is likely to become an important issue for the future.

18–112   Powers to engage in contracts are an important element in the activities of both central and local government. Such powers may be statutory or through the development of the European Community subject to public procurement directives. Increasingly such contracting powers are a means to enforce standards and this may provide remedies for the citizen. The financial controls over public bodies in their role of entering contractual relations are an important element of scrutiny. Local government powers to undertake competitive contracting are carefully proscribed under Pt 2 of the Local Government Act 1992.

18–113   The courts rarely intervene through judicial review to review the terms of contracts but the legal powers to enter contracts are carefully scrutinised. This may be achieved in two ways. First, has the public body the requisite legal authority to enter into the contract? If the court finds that the body has acted *ultra vires* the contract is void. Secondly, where there are sufficient legal powers to enter into a contract and the contract is not *ultra vires*, the question then falls to be determined under principles of ordinary contract law that the public body may be liable for any breach of contract.

18–114   The decision in *Osman v UK*[76] deserves mention[77] because it illustrates the potential for conflict between United Kingdom attitudes to litigation and the civil tradition of the European Court of Human Rights. A rule that effectively gives the police immunity from civil suit in respect of police powers to investigate crime was held to be under Article 6(1) a disproportionate interference with the applicant's rights to go to court. The case has been criticised[78] but it is illustrative of the differing perceptions about rules and their application.

18–115   Finally, Convention rights may provide remedies when in the past the English common law was lacking in a remedy. In *Marcic v Thames Water Utilities Ltd*[79] the Court of Appeal held that Thames Water's refusal to take measures to prevent flooding of Mr Marcic's property amounted to an infringement of his rights under Article 8 (the right to respect for private and family life). An award of damages in nuisance was available when in the past it is unlikely that any nuisance claim might have succeeded. This is a classic example of applying a rights-based formula to a minority of people who are liable to be flooded because of sewerage operations. The case is anticipatory of government proposals to undertake developments to prevent the increase in flooding.

---

[75] [1985] 3 All E.R. 585.
[76] (1998) 29 E.H.R.R. 245.
[77] C. Gearty, "Unravelling *Osman*" (2001) 64 MLR 159.
[78] *Barrett v Enfield LBC* [1999] 3 W.L.R. 79 at 85. Lord Browne-Wilkinson.
[79] [2002] 2 All E.R. 55.

SUMMARY AND CONCLUSIONS

Pressure goups or lobby groups often play a controversial role. In recent years their **18–116** activities have become more significant in the area of legal challenge. The Law Commission, in their recent report on administrative law,[80] acknowledged that interest groups may have good grounds for having standing in the public interest to make an application for judicial review. This might apply in cases where the pressure group feels that the public are adversely affected by an administrative decision of a government agency or government itself. Clearly there is some flexibility in permitting pressure groups a role in bringing public interest matters before the courts. Concern arises out of the *Rose Theatre Case*, however, if interpreted to mean that in the absence of an express statutory right the ordinary citizen is debarred from challenging decisions, even where it appears that there may be a public interest served by such a challenge. This may leave a gap in the arrangements for public challenge and may restrict standing to a few.

The broad liberalisation of the rules of standing since the *Fleet Street Casuals* case **18–117** raises the question of whether the rules of standing are required today. The Woolf Reforms on civil procedure provide a case management system sufficient to act as a gate-keeper function. Standing may therefore be seen less as a substantive hurdle to be overcome, but more as an unnecessary procedural requirement. In terms of developing systems for the simplification of the procedures for judicial review, rules of standing may be substituted by the exercise of a straightforward judicial discretion on the merits of each case.

There are a number of reform proposals, such as the possibility of setting up a **18–118** Director of Civil Proceedings[81] as an alternative to individual public interest litigation. The Lord Chancellor has argued that a Community Legal Service may provide sufficient cover to canvass issues of judicial review and human rights. However, lobbyists and pressure groups display unabated enthusiasm for litigation. Indeed, today there appear to be a plethora of groups and actors willing to campaign for individual rights as well as common causes. As Harlow has noted:

> "[a] new Public Interest Advisory Panel, designed to 'represent consumers', advises the Legal Service Commission and several leading public advocacy groups including the Public Law project, the Legal Action Group and JUSTICE have been involved. Some—Liberty, the Public Law Project and the Joint Council for the Welfare of Immigrants—have also signed contracts to provide back-up and training services to the Community Legal Service in their area of expertise and to maintain telephone help lines and web sites."[82]

There is an inherent problem in shifting democratic participation from the parliamen- **18–119** tary political process to courts. It might be argued in that context that, perhaps, the rules of standing are too liberal and require some refinement? That problem is exemplified in the *Pergau Dam* case, where government policy, however misconceived,

---

[80] Law Commission, *Administrative Law: Judicial Review and Statutory Appeals*, Report No.226 (1994).
[81] Sir Harry Woolf, "A Possible Programme for Reform" [1992] *Public Law* 221.
[82] Harlow, p.9.

eventually prevailed over the technical legal arguments accepted by the courts. The World Development Movement emerges as an effective group with international standing, and that can hardly be questioned, but as a representative group of the public at large it appears to be a small minority. However worthy its cause, pressure group activity has the potential for abuses of the legal process. Until the day the United Kingdom creates a constitutional court and a written constitution delineating the boundaries of legal and political power, the ultimate parliamentary authority and sovereignty vested in the government of the day prevails; meanwhile, confusion and lack of clarity remain over how legal and political authority may best be defined and where the boundaries between them should be drawn.

FURTHER READING

H. Arthurs, *"Without the Law": Administrative Justice and Legal Pluralism in Nineteenth Century England* (University of Toronto Press, Toronto, 1985).

P.P. Craig, *Administrative Law* (4th ed., Sweet and Maxwell, London, 1999).

de Smith, Woolf and Jowells, *Principles of Judicial Review* (Sweet and Maxwell, London, 1999).

C.R. Harlow and R.W. Rawlings, *Law and Administration* (2nd ed., Butterworths, London, 1997).

I. Loveland, *Constitutional Law: A Critical Introduction* (Butterworths, London, 1996 2nd ed. 1999).

Law Commission Report, *Remedies in Administrative Law: No.73* Cmnd.6407 (1976).

H.W.R. Wade, and C.F. Forsyth, *Administrative Law* (8th ed., Oxford University Press, Oxford, 2000).

Part V

PUBLIC LAW AND CONFLICT

Pt V of the textbook examines the role of law when tackling problems of public order, **V–001** terrorism, state secrecy and Northern Ireland. Chapter 19 addresses the issue of the law of public order. Chapter 20 is how secrecy is protected and Chapter 21 is devoted to the search for peace in Northern Ireland and constitutional responses to conflict and change in Northern Ireland. The final chapter attempts to assess the current state and future development of public law.

Chapter 19

PUBLIC ORDER AND THE FREEDOM OF ASSEMBLY

INTRODUCTION

The focus of this chapter is first, on how the law regulates public meetings, processions or demonstrations. A second focus is to consider emergency powers in the context of civil disturbance. Historically the development of popular protest gained important constitutional rights such as the broadening of the franchise, the right to vote for women; and in industrial relations, the rights of trades unions. Many rights gained through popular movements have endured. There is an important dimension to the discussion of public order. Freedoms associated with Convention rights under the Human Rights Act 1998 have now to be considered as part of the law. In particular, the right to freedom of peaceful assembly and association (Article 11) and the right to free expression (Article 10). Limitations on both freedoms must be prescribed by law and necessary in a democratic society. In addition the question of State interference with any freedom must be[1] "proportionate to the legitimate aim pursued". The onus rests on the State to show that the law meets this obligation.   **19–001**

In a democratic and accountable society that is open to change, the freedoms enjoyed by any particular group or the majority are dependent on how the law treats protests in the context of public order. A wide variety of political causes or beliefs may attract public protest which may take the form of public meeting, demonstration or protest. A responsibility rests on the police to fulfil their general function of keeping the peace. Their responsibility applies to a wide variety of public order problems as wide-ranging and as diverse as pop festivals, football crowds and political demonstrations.   **19–002**

As Lord Denning recognised in *Hubbard v Pitt*[2] "the right to demonstrate and the right to protest on matters of public concern . . . are often the only means by which grievances can be brought to the knowledge of those in authority". Detecting that the liberty of the individual to assemble is a hallmark of an open society, Lord Scarman noted[3] that while peaceful assembly is a fundamental right: **19–003**

> "A balance has to be struck, a compromise found that will accommodate the exercise of the right to protest within a framework of public order which enables

---

[1] *Steel v UK* (1998) 28 E.H.R.R. 603.
[2] [1976] 1 Q.B. 142.
[3] See D.G.T. Williams, *Keeping the Peace* (1967); R. Card, *Public Order The New Law* (Butterworths, 1987); A.T.H. Smith, *Offences Against Public Order* (1987).

ordinary citizens who are not protesting to go about their business and pleasure without obstruction or inconvenience."

19–004   In this area of law one of the most important questions is how police powers to maintain public order may be balanced in the interests of society to ensure freedom of assembly and association. Discussion of the freedom to protest, assemble or demonstrate within the context of the discussion of public order has undoubtedly facilitated more extensive powers to uphold public order. This fact reinforces the need to balance discussion of public order and the effect of those laws upon freedom of expression.

19–005   In recent years, one of the most notable periods for intense debate about public demonstrations was in the 1980s and the development of the peace movement as part of the Campaign for Nuclear Disarmament (CND). Another notable occasion for public protest which raised a number of public order issues came from an industrial conflict: a period of one year from March 1984 to 1985 when coal miners embarked on industrial action involved widespread picketing and protests at collieries throughout the country. The mobilisation of the police and the national co-ordination of police resources based on the National Reporting Centre at New Scotland Yard in London raised questions about policing in the 1980s. Subsequent prosecutions of the strikers were accompanied by the use of binding over orders and bail requirements to contain the activities of striking miners. The Public Order Act 1986 has been strengthened by the Criminal Justice and Public Order Act 1994.[4] Additional powers have been granted to the police when dealing with football disorder and young offenders.

HISTORICAL PERSPECTIVES

19–006   The setting-up of Sir Robert Peel's new police force in the nineteenth century was greatly advanced by the need to regulate popular protest. The historical role of policing—identified by Cornish[5] as covering a wide selection of popular issues and demands: "strikes, elections, political demands and periods of poor trade each contributed to spasmodic unrest"—also represented a significant opposition to military intervention in the internal maintenance of order in England. The lessons of policing developed through experience. Past mistakes were quickly overcome by a delicate mixture of Royal Commission and judicial oversight. The first attempt to provide comprehensive police powers to control public protest emerged in the Public Order Act 1936 which spearheaded the legal prohibition of "quasi-military organisations". The Act was passed at a period of high activity for the British Union of Fascists.

19–007   The importance of popular protest as providing pressure for reform had succeeded in gaining the vote for women, and greater trade union rights. Political authority gained from addressing the hustings and delivering directly to the electorate party political promises to gain election victory, has become an important feature of English democracy. Special arrangements are provided for policing the Metropolis with specific attention given to the rights of Parliament to sit unimpeded.

---

[4] Cm.2263 (July, 1993).
[5] W.R. Cornish, *Law and Society in England 1750–1850* (London, 1989); *Popular Protest and Public Order* (J. Stevenson and R. Qinault ed., 1974).

Policing is inextricably linked to public order. Public order requires high levels of **19–008** intelligence and surveillance activities.

Maintaining public order may involve the State in the use of extreme powers at **19–009** times of emergency or civil unrest. The benefits of Empire and the colonial experience informed English constitutional writing on martial law and states of emergency. Townshend noted[6]:

> "The whole drift of thinking about martial law, or emergency powers in general, was concerned with the problem of legality, and of ethical or political acceptability, not with that of practicality . . ."

Martial law may be defined as the common law duty of the executive to repel force **19–010** with force. The courts, after the event, could determine what was justified on the basis of what was reasonable. Set against this extreme, some doubted if martial law, meaning a state of seige, and the partial transfer of powers to the military might exist within English domestic law. Doubts about the effectiveness and acceptability of the use of the army in peacetime to control civil disorder on mainland Britain remain, and the onus is on the police as the primary agency to keep the peace.

Currently the law of public order is contained in the Public Order Act 1936 and **19–011** detailed powers granted to the police in the Public Order Act 1986 and the Criminal Justice and Public Order Act 1994. Other measures such as the Highways Act 1980 and Police Act 1964 are also relevant. Common law powers such as breach of the peace have also survived.

POLICE POWERS

Public Meetings and Assemblies

Various freedoms such as the right to take part in public meetings, processions and **19–012** demonstrations or to engage in political activities by joining trade unions or political clubs or associations may be discussed in the context of the powers the police have to preserve public order. For example the freedom to assemble and to engage in peaceful protest may be generally accepted as among[7] "our fundamental freedoms: they are numbered the touchstones which distinguish a free society from a totalitarian one . . ." However, the freedom to assemble is not unfettered. The law may regulate both the conduct and location of public assemblies. The policing of popular demonstrations and protests is often carried out in the glare of publicity with wide media coverage and reporting of meetings and demonstrations.

The various powers granted to the police to anticipate problems arising from **19–013** organisations and associations are both common law and statutory. The Public Order Act 1936 provides a number of relevant powers. S.1 prohibits the wearing of a uniform which has political objectives, introduced to prohibit the increasing use of uniforms by

---

[6] C. Townshend, *Political Violence in Ireland* (Oxford, 1983) on the use of military in Ireland.
[7] *R. v Jordan and Tyndall* [1963] Crim. L.R. 124.

political groups in the 1930s, with the rise of Fascists. In addition, s.2 of the 1936 Act prohibits the rise in quasi-military organisations by banning their organisation and association. Vigilante groups may fall within the category of proscribed organisation. In the absence of express statutory prohibition there is also the possibility of conspiracy offences arising out of an organisation set up to carry out illegal activities. The *caveat* to any prosecution is that the illegality must be capable of being committed by a single individual.

19–014   In the case of using the highway there are both statutory and common law offences regulating the conduct involved. S.137 of the Highways Act 1980 provides that "a person, without lawful authority or excuse, [who] in any way wilfully obstructs the free passage along the highway" is guilty of a criminal offence. The question of what constitutes a lawful excuse may be considered by the courts. In *Hirst v Chief Constable of West Yorkshire*,[8] animal rights supporters were convicted after they protested outside shops selling furs in Bradford city centre. Mr Justice Glidewell in the Divisional Court considered their appeal against conviction. In the earlier decision of *Nagy v Weston*,[9] Lord Parker considered the obstruction of the highway by a hot dog vendor. The question of whether it was a reasonable use:

> "depends upon all the circumstances, including the length of time the obstruction continues, the place where it occurs, the purpose for which it is done and of course whether it does in fact cause an actual obstruction as opposed to a potential obstruction."

19–015   Applying Lord Parker's dicta to the facts in *Hirst*, Glidewell L.J. considered three questions to be posed in such cases and quashed the convictions on the basis that the issues were not properly considered in the Crown Court. First, was there an obstruction? Any stopping on the highway could amount to an obstruction whether it is on the footpath or carriageway. Secondly, was the obstruction wilful? If the stopping was deliberate this could amount to wilful obstruction. Thirdly, was the activity complained about lawful? Lawful excuse requires the court to consider that "lawful excuse embraces activities otherwise lawful in themselves which may or may not be reasonable in all the circumstances". This leaves unclear the exact balance to be struck between activity such as obstructing the highway when a group of friends meet to discuss their holidays for 20 minutes or so, which is lawful, and that which is not. In the case of distributors advertising material or free periodicals outside major rail stations, this may raise issues of legality because it may appear to be unreasonable. The courts may regard conduct which is ancillary to the use of the highway as acceptable and reasonable, and that which is not as unreasonable.

19–016   The obstruction of the highway may constitute a public nuisance and it may also involve private nuisance and trespass. In the case of public nuisance, at common law this is a misdemeanour triable in either the Crown Court or before magistrates. The exact terms of the common law offence are broadly described as Smith and Hogan note[10] to include obstructing the highway and:

> ". . . it also includes a wide variety of other interferences with the public; for example the carrying on of an offensive trade which impregnates the air 'with

[8] (1987) 85 Cr.App.R. 143.
[9] [1965] 1 All E.R. 78.
[10] Smith and Hogan, *Criminal Law* (1992), p.762.

noisome offensive and stinking smoke' to the common nuisance of the public passing along the highway, polluting a river with gas so as to destroy the fish and render the water unfit for drinking . . ."

The interference in such cases must be substantial and unreasonable. The courts appear to have a discretion to decide where the limits lie between what is "reasonably incidental" to the right of passage on the highway and what is inconvenient. The degree of obstruction or inconvenience may determine the legality of what is permissible.   **19–017**

While it is not necessary to show that the defendant intended to create a nuisance, it is necessary to show that his actions constituted a nuisance. In criminal cases the defendant may be intentional or reckless in his actions. This may be more widely construed in the light of the *Caldwell*[11] criteria for recklessness which implies some degree of criminal liability for acts which are not foreseen by the defendant to involve risk but are foreseen to the reasonable man. This may in effect provide for criminal negligence as a basis for liability. In criminal cases of nuisance the prosecution must prove beyond a reasonable doubt, whereas in civil cases involving nuisance proof on a balance of probabilities is sufficient.   **19–018**

A public nuisance may be actionable in civil law, usually at the instance of the Attorney-General or a private citizen who must show special loss that is particular to the individual and not the public at large. It is necessary to distinguish civil cases from criminal cases although there has been considerable overlap arising from the grounds of nuisance liability. In *Southport Corp v Esso Petroleum*[12] Lord Denning observed how in a civil action once nuisance was proved and the defendant shown to have caused the act or omission constituting the nuisance, the legal burden shifts onto the defendant to justify or excuse his action.   **19–019**

A private nuisance is actionable at the instance of the private citizen who suffers a wilful interference with the enjoyment of land or rights over or in connection with the land. Sections 4 and 5 of the Protection of Harassment Act 1997 prevent harassment of a private citizen and may be used to prohibit conduct of a protestor. The Criminal Justice and Police Act 2001 restrains demonstrations outside a citizen's home.   **19–020**

Pt V of the Criminal Justice and Public Order Act 1994 gives additional and wide powers for the police to deal with squatters, large-scale trespass and those participating in raves or connected with hunt saboteurs. There is a new offence of aggravated trespass. This applies with trespass on land in the open air by those who seek to obstruct or disrupt those that are engaged in lawful activity.   **19–021**

There are powers to direct people to leave the land should the police have reasonable belief that the trespassers will disrupt a lawful activity. An offence is committed if a trespasser fails to obey a police direction. There are powers to prevent people attending raves or other events by stopping people and directing them to disperse. Failure to disperse is a criminal offence.   **19–022**

The police have powers to regulate what is called a "trespassery assembly". This is an assembly of 20 or more people on land to which the public has no right of access. There are powers to remove trespassers with six or more vehicles on land. Failure to comply with the directions of a police officer is a criminal offence.   **19–023**

---

[11] *Metropolitan Police Commissioner v Caldwell* [1982] A.C. 341.
[12] [1954] 2 Q.B. 182 at 197.

19–024   There are extensive remedies available under the Act which permits owners or occupiers to go to the County Court to require the squatter to leave the occupation of the land within 24 hours. The police are empowered to enforce this order. Finally, local authorities are given powers to direct unauthorised campers to leave the land. Failure to comply with this request is a criminal offence. An enforcement order may be obtained from the magistrates and the police may take reasonable steps to enforce the order including entering on the land and removing any vehicles. Obstructing the police in carrying out their duties is an offence.

19–025   Injunctions may be sought to prevent any threatened illegal assembly or picket. This is a common remedy used to enforce employment law and the rules about picketing.

19–026   The carrying on of a meeting or demonstration may be the subject of legal restrictions as to where the meeting may be held. It is a common law trespass to hold meetings on highways or in public places. Restrictions on holding meetings in open spaces such as parks or recreation areas may depend on the geographical location and therefore the jurisdiction such open space comes under. Byelaws empower local authorities to regulate such open spaces according to whether there is conduct amounting to a nuisance or the use of specific statutory powers for the good government of the area. In addition to these powers conditions may be imposed on such meetings by the police under the Public Order Act 1986 discussed below.

19–027   Pt IV of the Criminal Justice and Public Order Act 1994 gives the police extended powers to stop and search for offensive weapons or dangerous instruments. This power is constrained to a particular area for a specific and limited time provided a senior police officer reasonably believes that violence may break out.

19–028   Parliamentary candidates at elections have specific protection afforded to the traditional meetings carried out during the election period. Similar provisions apply to the carrying on of local government elections.[13]

19–029   The law also facilitates the carrying on of election meetings in public halls. The freedom of political discussion is an important responsibility which the governing bodies of universities and colleges of further education are expected to uphold, and take reasonable steps in order to ensure that there is freedom of speech afforded to visitors and members of the institution concerned. Interpretation of this provision can be extremely difficult when the university authorities are considering the likelihood of violence on the campus. In *Ex p. Caesar-Gordon*[14] the University of Liverpool granted permission to the student Conservative Association to hold a meeting. Restrictions were issued on the confidential nature of the organisational details of the meeting. The University considered that there was a threat of disorder because of the nature of the meeting and public feeling outside the University. These fears of disorder were in part because the University had little control over members of the public having access to University premises. Previously there had been widespread disorder in Toxteth, an area of Liverpool not far from the University. The Divisional Court granted a declaration and held that the University was not entitled to take account of the threat

---

[13] *Thomas v National Union of Mineworkers (South Wales Area)* [1985] 2 All E.R. 1; *Newsgroup Newspapers Ltd v Society of Graphical and Allied Trades '82 (No.2)* [1987] I.C.R. 181. See, for example: Open Spaces Act 1906, s.15; the various Public Health Acts 1875; and s.235 of the Local Government Act 1972; the Parks Regulations Act 1872. In London see the Trafalgar Square Regulations 1952 SI 1952/776. See s.95 of the Representation of the People Act 1983; s.96 of the Representation of the People Act 1983 as amended by Sch.4 para.38 of the Representation of the People Act 1985.

[14] *R. v University of Liverpool Ex p. Caesar-Gordon* [1990] 3 All E.R. 821.

of disorder other than on the University campus. This did not however invalidate the conditions imposed by the University. Each University is expected to publicise its own rules of conduct as codes of practice for public meetings within its own premises.

Extensive powers are provided under the Public Order Act 1936 to control public **19–030** processions. S.3 permits a chief officer of police who reasonably apprehends that a procession may "occasion serious public disorder" to apply in London to the Home Secretary for a banning order, or elsewhere, to a local authority; the order may be for a period up to three months. This power has been supplemented by Pt 1 of the Public Order Act 1986. The 1986 Act provides under s.11 for advance notice and s.12 regulates advance notice for processions. The Act includes the circumstances where there may be conditions attached to the permission to hold a procession, and under s.14 for the imposition of conditions on assemblies. Hitherto, the 1936 Public Order Act was silent as to the regulation of an assembly which is stationary and not engaged in a procession.

Imposing conditions on processions and assemblies arises out of the experience of **19–031** past years. During the 1960s and 70s an increase in political agitation led to a greater number of public demonstrations with their opposing counter-demonstrations. Popular causes have included the Vietnam War, apartheid, and the activities of the Campaign for Nuclear Disarmament. The National Front has also been actively contesting a number of parliamentary by-elections. Balancing the needs of each group to present its viewpoint requires careful judgment on the part of the police and the prosecuting authorities.

The police have at their disposal a wide range of possibilities. Re-routing pro- **19–032** cessions away from counter-demonstrations may be adopted. Conditions on the route of the procession may include a ban on using certain streets or thoroughfares. Matters which may be considered in regulating processions or meetings include the question of whether there might be serious damage to property, serious disruption to the life of the community and intimidation. In making any tactical judgment on these matters there is an added consideration which is the cost of policing, the manpower involved and the question of the most effective deployment of police resources. Public meetings may distract the police from other activities, engage a large amount of police overtime and increase the workload on the courts in any prosecutions taken as a result of disorder.

There are a number of offences which may be committed by those who take part in **19–033** or are engaged in the disruption of a public meeting or in certain circumstances carrying out a protest arising from a trade dispute. These include obstructing the police in the execution of their duty, criminal damage, the possession of offensive weapons, the use of threatening violence to enter premises, trespassing on premises, and failure to leave at the request of a displaced occupier, trespassing with an offensive weapon, and obstructing the court officers in the execution of their duty.

During the Miners' Strike in 1984, the police made use of powers under the Road **19–034** Traffic Act 1972 to stop vehicles. This was used to ascertain whether the occupants were engaged in picket duties. Failure to comply with a request by the police to re-route their journey and return home ran the risk of prosecution under s.51(3) of the Police Act 1964, namely obstructing a police officer in the execution of his duty.

The action taken by the police is usually left to their discretion. Even though the **19–035** courts may review that discretion, there is a reluctance to overturn police tactical decision-making. This reluctance may be traced back to cases decided at an earlier period though the courts may occasionally interpret the law to protect demonstrators. In *Beatty v Gillbanks*[15] members of the Salvation Army were subject to a binding over by magistrates not to assemble and hold a meeting. The binding over was the result of a police direction that the assembly might cause a breach of the peace because a rival and opposing organisation, the Skeleton Army, intended to counter-demonstrate against the Salvation Army. The Salvation Army appealed to the Divisional Court against the magistrates' order. Field J. concluded that the Salvation Army were wrongly bound over. There were no grounds for saying that the Salvation Army were holding an illegal protest. Any disturbance that was caused in the past had come from the Skeleton Army, and the Salvation Army did not incite or intentionally provoke a breach of the peace.

19–036 The case may be regarded as establishing an important principle that an assembly that is legal does not become illegal merely because it causes a counter-demonstration or when others threaten illegality. However, in practice how far might this principle be applied? It was possible for the court in *Beatty v Gillbanks* to clearly distinguish the motives or good faith of the Salvation Army from the Skeleton Army, but where this is not possible the principle may not easily be upheld.

19–037 There is also in Field J.'s formulation of the law, that if the natural and probable consequences of the action of the lawful assembly is to create a disturbance then there could legally be a binding over. It is hardly convincing that the Salavation Army did not share some element of responsibility. If their meeting were not held it is at least arguable that there would be no counter-demonstration.

19–038 Counter-demonstrations or protests were considered in *Wise v Dunning*.[16] A Protestant pastor George Wise, made provocative comments about Catholics in Liverpool and the majority of his meetings were held in Catholic areas of the city. He was bound over to keep the peace by magistrates and challenged the legality of the binding over. As breaches of the peace were likely to be the natural consequence of his meetings, the binding over was held by the Divisional Court to be legal.

19–039 In *Duncan v Jones*[17] Mrs Duncan, a communist, was about to make a speech at a public meeting in a quiet cul-de-sac in Deptford near the entrance to an unemployment centre. Duncan was convicted by magistrates of obstructing a police officer in the execution of his duty when she stepped on a box which she had placed on the road to deliver her speech. In a previous meeting held by Mrs Duncan fourteen months previously, there had been some disturbances. The Divisional Court upheld her conviction at Quarter Sessions. The case raises the possibility that because the police may fear a breach of the peace, even if none occurs, a peaceful meeting may be amenable to prosecution for the offence of obstructing the police in the execution of their duty. The far-reaching potential of *Duncan v Jones* means that the police may make use of the obstruction offence to regulate and control the activities of lawful pickets involved in trade disputes. The courts have been reluctant to challenge the day-to-day operational decisions of the police in these matters. Thus there appears to be little requirement on the police to prove that a threat to the peace is apprehended.

---

[15] (1882) 15 Cox C.C. 138, (1882) L.R. QBD 308.
[16] [1902] 1 K.B. 167.
[17] [1936] 1 K.B. 218. The case has been heavily criticised by Daintith ([1966] P.L. 248) and Williams, *Textbook of Criminal Law* (1983) p.203. See *Piddington v Bates* [1960] 3 All E.R. 660.

The role of the courts has proved problematic. On the one hand the courts may be   **19–040**
invited to consider the legality of police powers, especially the powers to seek a ban on
a public demonstration. On the other hand, the courts have not provided much
oversight of police operational practices, such as deciding how many demonstrators to
allow to attend a meeting or how many pickets to permit at the place of work of the
strikers. A code of practice exists[18] for industrial disputes, stating that in general the
number of pickets should not "exceed six at any entrance to a workplace; frequently a
smaller number will be appropriate."

In recent years an additional concern has been the policing of sports fixtures. The   **19–041**
Sporting Events (Control of Alcohol, etc.) Act 1985 regulates the sale of alcohol inside
sports grounds and at the entry to stadiums. Following the Hillsborough football
disaster,[19] the Football Spectators Act 1989 was passed enabling the courts to make
restriction orders preventing supporters from attending football matches if they have
been involved in hooligan activity. The Football Offences Act 1991 further strengthens
the law regulating crowds at football matches. Offences such as throwing missiles,
chanting indecent and racial abuse, running onto the pitch without any reasonable
excuse and selling tickets on the day of the match without the express authority of the
home club, are intended to provide preventive powers as well as enabling the police to
respond to incidents at football matches. There has been a spate of additional
legislation aimed at tackling the problems of football hooliganism. The Football
(Offences and Disorder) Act 1999 built on the foundations of the earlier legislation
and provided additional powers and closed loopholes in the law. Ss.1–5 provide powers
to tackle the international dimension of football hooligans, and banning orders are
now possible to prevent someone convicted of a football-related offence from
travelling to an international fixture. Additional powers are granted to the courts when
dealing with domestic football matches: a strengthening of penalties for breach of
court orders and a widening in the scope of the court orders available. Orders banning
supporters from attending football matches may be for a minimum of 12 months up to
a maximum of three years. The 1999 Act also clarifies various offences relating to
racism, obscenity and ticket touting. The Football (Disorder) Act 2000 makes further
changes to the law as an immediate response to football violence at the Euro 2000
competition. Banning orders are strengthened and the surrender of passports may be
required in connection with specific football matches held outside the United
Kingdom. Additional powers are given for the National Criminal Intelligence Service
to disclose information for the regulation of spectators. S.2 of the 2000 Act inserts this
power into the Police Act 1997.

Clarification of the scope and extent of the banning orders mentioned above is given   **19–042**
in yet another Act to regulate the problem of hooliganism and football. The Football
(Disorder) (Amendment) Act 2002 also deals with creating a new summary procedure
to prevent people from leaving the country during a control period when the police
become aware of likely disorder. The powers under the 2002 Act are broader than
before as they include disorder at departure rather than confined to disorder at the
football fixture. A limited power of detention of up to six hours may be used and the
police may make a requirement to appear before a magistrates'court.

---

[18] S.15 of the Trade Union and Labour Relations Act 1974 as amended by s.16(1) of the Employment Act
1980. Code of Practice on Picketing, see s.3(8) of the Employment Act 1980.
[19] Report on the Hillsborough Disaster, Cm.962 (1990).

Breach of the Peace

19-043   The police have common law powers of arrest for breach of the peace. If the police reasonably apprehend that the holding of a meeting or a demonstration will give rise to a breach of the peace, then such powers may be invoked. In *R. v Howell*[20] the Court of Appeal attempted to classify such powers, which have been distinctive in their breadth. Watkins L.J. held that there is a power of arrest for breach of the peace:

> "(1) where a breach of the peace is committed in the presence of the person making the arrest, or (2) the arrestor reasonably believes that such a breach of the peace will be committed in the immediate future by the person arrested although he has not yet committed any breach or (3) where a breach has been committed and it is reasonably believed that a renewal of it is threatened."

19-044   Relying on Halsbury[21] the Court of Appeal considered that a breach of the peace might be defined:

> ". . . where there is an actual assault, or where a public alarm and excitement are caused by a person's wrongful act. Mere annoyance and disturbance or insult to a person or abusive language or great heat and fury without personal violence are not generally sufficient."

19-045   This leaves unanswered the exact nature of the arrest powers available to the police because of the difficulty in defining breach of the peace. The elusive nature of any satisfactory definition of breach of the peace has received criticism. Peaceful behaviour in a public place may fall within the remit of a breach of the peace if the nature of the activity commands public attention and therefore a larger attendance of the public than if it were ignored. Lord Denning in *Ex p. Central Electricity Generating Board*[22] considered that a breach of the peace might arise if someone who is lawfully carrying out his work, is unlawfully and physically prevented from doing so, illustrating the potential for a wide police discretion in terms of arrest powers.

19-046   It was also accepted by the court that a person making an arrest is entitled to rely on what he reasonably believes. This raises the question of whether that belief relates to an actual breach of the peace or an apprehended breach of the peace. In *Howell* the possibility that an apprehended breach of the peace is sufficient considerably widens the arrest powers of the police.

19-047   In Ex p. Central Electricity Generating Board the Court of Appeal refused an application for *mandamus* requested by the Central Electricity Generating Board (CEGB) to require the Chief Constable to remove protesters encamped on private land with the intention of preventing the CEGB from carrying out a survey of the land for a nuclear power station. The question of the powers of the police in respect of a breach of the peace was considered, but as no breach of the peace had actually occurred the discussion was largely an academic one. The police appeared to have

---

[20] [1982] Q.B. 416. See *Colhoun v Friel* 1996 SSCR 497.
[21] See *Halsbury's Laws of England* (4th ed., 1976), Vol.11, para.108.
[22] *R. v Chief Constable of the Devon and Cornwall Constabulary Ex p. Central Electricity Generating Board* [1982] Q.B. 458. See Ewing and Gearty, *Freedom under Thatcher* (Oxford, 1990) p.90.

sufficient powers to intervene but the court was unwilling to substitute its judgment for that of the operational decision of the police, hence the decision not to grant *mandamus*. The Court of Appeal approved the test of whether an apprehended breach of the peace existed as this would be sufficient to constitute arrest powers as discussed in *Howell*. However at most this opinion is *obiter dicta* and the question of whether *Howell* will be followed remains unclear.

At common law the power of arrest for breach of the peace appears to extend to **19–048** private property. This point has been indirectly accepted in *McConnell v Chief Constable of the Greater Manchester Police*[23] and Glidewell L.J. rejected the idea that a breach of the peace on private premises had to have an external effect on public property before there could be an offence.

In addition to arrest powers for a breach of the peace, the police have powers of **19–049** arrest under s.24–26 of the Police and Criminal Evidence Act 1984 (PACE) which did not abolish the common law powers of arrest for breach of the peace, although it generally codified other arrest powers. S.26 allows an arrest for causing unlawful obstruction of the highway provided the arrest is necessary to prevent the unlawful obstruction continuing. Miscellaneous arrest powers are provided under s.25 of PACE arising out of offences under s.28 of the Town Police Clauses Act 1847.

The scope of breach of the peace is also relevant in defining the basis of the powers **19–050** of magistrates to bind over persons to keep the peace. This is a power of historical importance to the development of the magistracy. The power to bind over is that the person remains of good behaviour. Binding over may be used where there is a reasonable apprehension that a breach of the peace may occur. It has been accepted that a binding over power may be used where it is considered that there is no threat to peace but that public morality or "a good way of life" is threatened. The person who is bound over must enter a recognisance to be of good behaviour. The recognisance is forfeited on a breach in the conditions of the binding over. Such an order is both subject to an appeal and to review by the courts under Order 53. Binding over is a frequently used power to attempt to restrict the movement of potential trouble-makers. An additional power vested in magistrates is to set conditions on the grant of bail. Such bail conditions may set limits on the movements of the individual.

In addition to the above powers there is also the offence of threatening behaviour **19–051** under s.5 of the Public Order Act 1936. S.5 has been replaced later by s.4 of the Public Order Act 1986. This was the main public order offence commonly used by the police for 50 years in preference to charges of riot, unlawful assembly and affray. S.5 of the Public Order Act 1936 covered any person who in a public place or at any public meeting used threatening, abusive or insulting words or behaviour or distributed or displayed any writing, sign or other visible representation which was threatening, abusive or insulting. For a criminal offence to be proven, the conduct was required to be intended to be a breach of the peace or to be of such a nature that such a breach of the peace was threatened. This section has now been replaced by s.4 of the Public Order Act 1986 discussed below.

The powers of the police to enter private property are also related to the idea of **19–052** preserving the peace. In *Thomas v Sawkins*[24] Lord Hewart thought that the power of

---

[23] [1990] 1 W.L.R. 364.
[24] [1935] 2 K.B. 249.

the police to enter and if necessary remain on private property arose when the police officer had "reasonable ground for believing that an offence is imminent or is likely to be committed". Such generalised powers appear to be too widely expressed. The powers are vague as to when the police must have grounds for belief or the nature of the offence which falls within the police powers. If widely interpreted an extension of police powers in this way seems beyond the proper remit of judicial discretion. The powers of the police to enter on land to deal with nuisance or collective trespass have been strengthened under Pt V of the Criminal Justice and Public Order Act 1994.

19–053   A variety of innovative powers have been adopted to curb rowdy behaviour in public. There are rules for child curfew and anti-social behaviour orders under the Crime and Disorder Act 1998. Local authorities are required to formulate strategies for the prevention of crime and disorder with particular attention being paid to youth justice. The Criminal Justice and Police Act 2001 has powers to combat public drinking including drink-free zones.

Offences under the Public Order Act 1986

19–054   The experience gained from the Miners' Strike in 1984 and the policing of the peace movement led to consideration of the law on public order. The Public Order Act 1986 is largely based on the recommendations of the Law Commission.[25] The law was believed to be too complex and fragmented. This fact led to consideration of a single statute providing for greater clarity. The 1986 Act creates new statutory offences and abolishes the common law offences of riot, unlawful assembly and affray, and the offence under s.5 of the Public Order Act 1936. In fact the 1986 Act appears to add more powers to the police while retaining the miscellaneous powers outlined above and fails to clarify the concept of breach of the peace which remains largely dependent on judicial developments.

19–055   Each of the four new offences may be examined, namely: riot, violent disorder, affray, and causing fear or provocation of violence. At common law, riot consisted of three or more persons, together with a common purpose, with an intent to help one another by force if necessary against anyone who opposed their common purpose and such force or violence is displayed in such a manner as to cause alarm in at least one person of reasonable firmness and courage. Riot is one of the most serious offences and s.1 of the Public Order Act 1986 defines the offence in similar terms to the common law offence but with the requirement of 12 or more persons and not three. If 12 or more persons threaten violence through an unlawful purpose but only one person uses violence then there is a riot but only one rioter. The offence is indictable and punishable with 10 years' imprisonment.

19–056   Riot may be committed where the 12 assemble without any pre-arranged plan or by chance. Once they form together, all that is required is that they have a common purpose and at some point unlawful violence is used or there is a threat of violence. The common purpose may be inferred from conduct and need not be an unlawful one.

19–057   Violence is generally defined in s.8 of the 1986 Act to include, except in the context of affray, "violent conduct towards property as well as violent conduct towards

---

[25] Law Commission No.123.

persons". Violence is not restricted to conduct causing or intended to cause injury or damage but includes any other violent conduct (for example throwing at or towards a person a missile of a kind capable of causing injury which does not hit or falls short). But the threat of violence or the use of violence must be unlawful, and this appears to allow the excuse of violence used in self-defence. The courts may have a difficult task in establishing whether such force is believed to constitute self-defence when the force is used against the police. It has been held that when the police use force lawfully and that force is reasonable in the circumstances, in the prevention of crime or in the apprehension of suspects, then self-defence is not available against such force. But if the defendant uses force because he suspects that the police are terrorists or criminals, the defence might be available, even where the police might act lawfully.

The offence of riot is intended to provide for serious disorder where there has been **19–058** widespread civil unrest and the authorities are required to arrest large numbers of people. There remains considerable difficulty in obtaining convictions. This appears to stem from the mental element of the offence requiring proof of common purpose. It must be proved that the defendant intended to use violence or was aware that his conduct might be violent; being aware of whether one's conduct is violent or not appears a difficult concept to prove. This would appear to give the police evidential problems in proving the commission of the offence.

Compensation for riot under the Riot (Damages) Act 1886 is now construed under **19–059** the definition of riot under the Public Order Act 1986. The majority of cases involving riot raise issues associated with claims for compensation under the 1986 Act. Compensation is payable under the 1986 Act and regard is given to the conduct of the claimant. Relevant considerations are whether adequate precautions were taken by the claimant or whether he participated in the riot. In such circumstance compensation may be reduced.

Violent disorder under s.2 of the Public Order Act 1986 replaces the common law **19–060** offence of unlawful assembly, and is punishable on indictment or on summary conviction. This offence is commonly charged and used more frequently than the common law offence of unlawful assembly as a means to regulate crowd behaviour. For the offence to be proved there is a requirement that there is an assembly of three or more with a common purpose to commit a crime of violence or to achieve some other object whether lawful or not in such a way as to cause reasonable men to apprehend a breach of the peace. There need not be a common purpose as each of the three or more persons may have a different purpose or no purpose. The defendant must be proved to have threatened violence or must have been aware that his conduct might be violent and threaten violence. In *Mahroof*[26] three defendants were charged jointly on one indictment with violent disorder. Mahroof alone was convicted and appealed with the result that his conviction was quashed but a conviction on an alternative offence under s.4 was substituted. It was assumed that if three defendants to a violent disorder are involved and one of the three is acquitted, the others invariably but not necessarily must be acquitted. Invariably the acquittal of one may cause the jury to re-consider the evidence and may lead to the acquittal of the others.

S.3 of the Public Order Act 1986 replaces the common law offence of affray with a **19–061** new statutory equivalent. Affray under s.3 is triable either on indictment or on

[26] [1989] Crim. L.R. 72.

summary trial. The offence of affray requires three persons: the person using or threatening unlawful violence; a person towards whom the violence is directed; and a person of reasonable firmness who need not be, or be likely to be, at the scene. The use of affray is common in prosecutions of fights. The overlap in charging between ss.2 and 3 gives the police discretion in terms of differentiating pre-meditated violence charged under s.2 and spontaneous violence under s.3. It is also possible to charge defendants with a wide range of offences under the Offences Against the Person Act 1861, arising out of the same incident such as assault or causing grievous bodily harm.

19–062   S.4 of the Public Order Act 1986 contains the offence of using fear or provocation of violence. The purpose of s.4 was to replace the offence under s.5 of the Public Order Act 1936, noted above concerning using threatening behaviour. The new offence covers both private and public places, and is not confined to where a third party may be likely to be provoked into violence but where a third party fears violence. There is no requirement of proving that there is or has been a breach of the peace.

19–063   The phrase "threatening, abusive or insulting" is a component of the new offence which has been retained from the old offence under s.5 of the Public Order Act 1936. The ordinary meaning of English words is employed by the courts when seeking to interpret their meaning and apply them to the facts of a particular incident. However, the addition of the words "uses towards another person" did not appear in the old law and could be interpreted to narrow the offence.

19–064   In addition to the four offences noted above, s.5 of the Public Order Act 1986 creates a summary offence of harassment, alarm or distress. This section was intended to deal with minor acts of hooliganism causing rowdy behaviour, shouting abuse or obscenities. The width of the offence is due to the unspecific nature of the activity which may fall under its ambit. A wide range of fairly innocuous behaviour, including noisy behaviour and high spirits, may come within its scope. This may be committed where a person uses abusive, threatening or insulting words or behaviour, or displays any writing sign or other visible representation which is threatening, abusive or insulting. The person who may be affected by the conduct could be a policeman or bystander, and therefore to be harassed or alarmed must have the act performed within hearing or sight. It must be proved that the defendant intended his conduct to be threatening, abusive or insulting or disorderly and must be aware that it might be so construed. When drawing up any prosecutions under the Act the purpose of the Public Order Act must be considered when framing charges and the courts have been reluctant to accept charges under the Act for acts which are not intended to be covered by the legislation.

19–065   The width of s.5 allows the prosecution of a wide variety of activities including the wearing of tee shirts with particular slogans, the distribution of posters with unusual captions or emotive words. All such activities may fall under the criminal law. This raises the question of whether it is satisfactory to use the criminal law in this way. There is a power of arrest which accompanies the use of s.5 after a warning has been given, which extends police powers quite considerably in this area. The Public Order (Amendment) Act 1996 amends s.5(4) of the Public Order Act 1986. This permits a constable the power to arrest a person without warrant if he engages in conduct which the constable warns him to stop. The offensive conduct is set out in the Public Order Act 1986.

19–066   One of the striking features of the 1986 Act is that it does not set out rights for demonstrators or protestors. In terms of preventive powers for the purposes of controlling meetings or demonstrations, the new Act builds on the old law. Under s.11 of the Public Order Act 1986, the police, subject to few exceptions, must be given written notice of all public processions at least six days before they are due to take place. Reflecting the increase in the carrying out of public processions and meetings, the new law is intended to give the police advance warning and information about organisers, the type of procession, the date, time, route and destination of the march.

S.12 of the 1986 Act provides the police with powers to impose conditions on public assemblies, processions or meetings. The nature of the restrictions comes into operation once there is an assembly of 20 or more in a public place. The power to make conditions is a police power and not vested in magistrates, reflecting an emphasis on the operational control by the police of public meetings or assemblies. The grounds for imposing restrictions are much wider than the apprehension of a serious breach of the peace or public disorder. If the police reasonably believe that serious damage to property or serious disruption to the life of the community may occur then restrictions may be lawfully imposed by the police. Also if the police fear that intimidation of others may occur this may mean that restrictions may be imposed. The intimidation provision is intended to allow the police to distinguish between marches which are intended to persuade rather than intimidate. **19–067**

This distinction may not be at once apparent and thus the police have to make their own judgment in such matters. Intimidation may appear to follow from the size of the gathering rather than from the motive of those involved. In trades disputes picketing may seek to persuade but it may also have the effect of intimidating those that are a minority and are fearful of the results of refusing to strike. Line-drawing in these matters is exceptionally difficult. The police are in effect exercising a dual role. Facilitating processions may not be consistent with the maintenance of good order. **19–068**

The Act also includes powers of arrest and it is a criminal offence to disregard the instructions of a police officer acting under the powers contained in the Act. Conditions may be imposed at the scene of the meeting or procession that extend even to a fairly junior police officer as powers are conferred on "the senior police officer" present at the scene, and such a junior officer may be the most senior officer present. Conditions may be such as appear to the police officer to be necessary "to prevent such disorder, damage, disruption or intimidation, including conditions as to the route of the procession". **19–069**

The need for such powers may be justified in terms of the variety of public meetings and demonstrations the police are expected to regulate. The presumption built into the police powers under the Act is that disruption of the normal day-to-day lives of ordinary people should not be interfered with by public demonstrations. Thus there is an assumption that the police may need to regulate various forms of protest in favour of the more orthodox behaviour in society. Invariably this will mean that the unusual or unorthodox will receive little real protection under the law and are only free to demonstrate within the police tolerance of what is reasonable. Thus inconvenience will be tolerated only marginally subject to the availability of resources and the disposition of police policy. **19–070**

One example of where the police have regarded the inconvenience factor of public meetings as too great and have sought to use their powers is in the annual ritual meeting of the Druids at Stonehenge. A ban under the Public Order Act 1986 was imposed on meetings and assemblies during a period in June to coincide with the **19–071** summer solstice, the aim being to avoid disruption when travelling people descended on the area to take part in ceremonies at Stonehenge.

Police Organisation and Accountability

19–072 The importance of the police in the control of public protest and their extensive powers of arrest, search, seizure and entry requires some consideration to be given to the nature of the police in the United Kingdom.[27] At common law, the police have analogous powers to the ordinary citizen's powers of arrest. However, wide statutory powers such as those under the Public Order Act 1986 have resulted in the police acquiring a special status in terms of both organisation and resources.

19–073 Traditionally the role of prosecution vested with the private citizen. Gradually the police acquired the prosecution of offences as part of their investigation of crime and the interrogation of suspects. The private citizen rarely prosecuted while the police for over 150 years dominated the prosecution of offences. In terms of prosecution, the Prosecution of Offences Act 1985 created the Crown Prosecution Service headed by the Director of Public Prosecutions and organised into 31 areas, each under a Chief Crown Prosecutor. The powers of the ordinary citizen to prosecute are still retained but according to published guidelines, prosecutions are undertaken by the Crown Prosecution Service. The Crown Prosecution Inspectorate Act 2000 provides an external inspectorate to inspect the operation of the Crown Prosecution System. It is modelled on similar inspectorates for prisons, probation, magistrates' courts and constabulary.

19–074 In historical terms the absence of any centralised and controlled national police force has allowed the police to develop a large degree of local autonomy within fairly clear structures of accountability. This doctrine of "constabulary independence" governs the operational independence of the police in their day-to-day functions. As noted above the doctrine has been implicity accepted in the way the courts have shown a reluctance to interfere with police judgment arising out of the exercise of their discretion over crowd control and public order powers. However as Lord Steyn explained in *O'Hara v Chief Constable of the RUC*[28] where there is a power of arrest provided by legislation on an individual police officer, the fact that a superior officer has reasonable suspicion does not of itself provide the police officer the reasonable grounds that are required for a lawful arrest. The responsibility is an individual one and cannot be discharged through superior orders.

19–075 In London in the past the Metropolitan Police were uniquely accountable to the Home Secretary while other police forces are organised on a local authority basis and accountable to their respective Police Authority. Pts VI and VII of the Greater London Authority Act 1999 provide that the Metropolitan Police Service must fit within the overall framework laid down in the Police Act 1996. This means replacing the role of the Home Secretary with a police authority. There is a new Metropolitan Police Authority and under devolution Assembly members may become members of that Authority. The new Authority for London has similar powers to the reformed police authorities under the Police Act 1996. There are similar arrangements for a new

---

[27] Hay and Snyder, *Policing and Prosecution in Britain 1750–1850* (Oxford, 1989).
[28] [1997] 1 All E.R. 129.

body, the London Fire and Emergency Planning Authority, to replace the London Fire and Civil Defence Authority. The new body has a constitution and oversight powers.

The authority of the constable is that he is a public officer. The theory of maintaining public order and the Queen's peace gives the police constable wide discretion under the command of a Chief Constable. In reality many of the decisions at the scene of public disturbances are made by fairly junior officers who are under the command of more senior officers. Police officers may be sued or prosecuted as any other citizen. In the cases of negligence claims, the principle of vicarious liability attaches to the Chief Constable who may be indemnified out of public funds.   **19–076**

The office of Chief Constable is an onerous responsibility with considerable discretionary powers. However in legal terms the powers of the Chief Constable are often unclear and poorly defined. Reforms to the organisation and structure of the police under the Police Act 1964 leave questions about how the Chief Constable may be directed or made accountable. Each local police authority is composed of two-thirds local councillors, and one-third lay magistrates. The police authority appoints a Chief Constable, a deputy Chief Constable and assistant Chief Constables, which are subject to the agreement of the Home Secretary. The police authority has the power to require the retirement of those senior officers in the interests of efficiency of the police force. An inquiry may be commissioned by the Home Secretary when such powers are adopted to investigate a compulsory retirement. The officer must be given the right to a hearing and the investigation must conform to the rules of natural justice. Powers under the Police Act 1964 permit the Home Secretary to require an authority to retire a Chief Constable. In 1985 this power was used to require the retirement of the Chief Constable of Derbyshire in the interests of efficiency.   **19–077**

The Chief Constable may exercise disciplinary powers over senior officers, and has the power of promotion and the appointment of other ranks of officers in his force. Failure to give fair employment opportunities to women or ethnic minorities may result in legal action against the Chief Constable. A failure to promote the assistant Chief Constable of Merseyside, Alison Halford, gave rise to allegations of unlawful discrimination.[29]   **19–078**

While the Home Secretary is answerable for the activities of the Metropolitan Police to Parliament, this does not extend to operational matters for that police force which are in the hands of the Commissioner of the Metropolitan Police. There is no Ministry of Justice in the United Kingdom on the basis of a continental model, and the Home Office is not directly accountable for local police forces. However, increasing powers of the Home Office have raised the question of whether local authority accountability should remain a viable organisational basis for the police. The Home Secretary has powers in relation to regulations covering pensions, training, duties and equipment, including the decision to issue CS gas, baton rounds or matters of policy in the deployment of such equipment. In *R. v Secretary of State for the Home Department, Ex p. Northumbria Police Authority*,[30] the Police Authority was opposed to the issuing of CS gas and plastic bullets and applied for judicial review to require withdrawal by the Home Secretary from issuing guidance in the form of a circular to Chief Constables on the availability of such equipment. The Court of Appeal refused the Police Authority's   **19–079**

[29] *Halford v Sharples* [1992] 3 All E.R. 624.
[30] [1988] 2 W.L.R. 590.

application and upheld the Home Office powers to issue baton rounds as part of a general power under s.41 of the Police Act 1964 to provide police colleges and forensic evidence for the police. In addition the Court of Appeal recognised a prerogative power to keep the peace which might allow the Home Office to supply such equipment.

19–080   The contribution of the Home Office to the expenditure of police forces may represent 50 per cent of the net expenditure. The Home Secretary is advised by a Chief Inspector of Constabulary, who makes an annual report to him on matters such as the efficiency and effectiveness of the police force. If the Home Secretary is dissatisfied, he may withhold grants to the police authority. If necessary through a system of investigations and inquiries the Home Secretary has the potential to widen the remit of parliamentary accountability for the police. There is a widely drawn power under s.28 of the Police Act 1964 allows the Home Secretary to ensure that powers ". . . to such an extent as appears to him to be best calculated to promote the efficiency of the police." This power has been used sparingly as the traditional wisdom of Home Secretaries has been to allow police forces autonomy. However, there are signs that this attitude may change. Chief Constables come under considerable pressure from government controls over their expenditure. Increasingly seen like any other public sector body rather than a special case, police forces are becoming subject to more stringent financial controls. These may directly change the role of the police in their operational activities.

19–081   Such concerns about the efficiency of public expenditure on the police and the perceived increase in crime but reduction in detection and prosecution rates have resulted in the Home Secretary considering whether reform of the structure of the police is required. Criticism of the police in the interrogation of suspects led to the setting-up of a Royal Commission on Criminal Justice and an internal review of the organisation and structure of the police. It is likely that each police force may be required to publish efficiency studies of crime detection and "clear-up rates". On the principle that centralisation may be adopted in order to reform, it is likely that pressure for a national police force may grow. The setting-up of the National Reporting Centre in Scotland Yard in 1972 to co-ordinate the disposition of the police at times of crisis has set the trend for future development. The counter-intelligence tasks of the police have since 1992 been delegated to MI5 and this is intended to lead to better co-ordination of intelligence against terrorists. The setting up of the National Criminal Intelligence Service in 1992 is now regulated under the Police Act 1997.

19–082   The Criminal Justice and Public Order Act 1994 gives the police additional powers for cross-border co-operation between the police in Scotland and England and Wales. The police have in common with many other public bodies come under immense pressure to conform to the new style of public management. Two White Papers[31] in 1993 set out the basis for the Police and Magistrates' Courts Act 1994. The aims of the 1994 Act were to set performance standards for the police and instil a "business management" culture within policing. There are some examples of this new ethos in the Act such as provision for fixed-term contracts for the rank of superintendent and above. A movement in favour of free-standing police authorities removed from the

---

[31] *Police Reform: The Government's Proposals for the Police service in England and Wales*, Cm.2281 (1993), and *A New Framework for Local Justice*, Cm.1829 (1993).

necessity of local and elected control is finally consolidated in the new Police Act 1996. This 1996 Act consolidates the earlier law and introduces new statutory provisions for free-standing police authorities outside London. It maintains the distinction that metropolitan police forces are separately treated.

There was intense debate over the proposals for the composition of the new police authorities. Sch.2, para.1(1) provides that nine members are to be drawn from the relevant councils, five are to be independent members, and three are to be justices of the peace. Independent members are to be chosen from a short-list prepared by the Secretary of State and after nomination the candidates are submitted to the Secretary of State before appointment. **19–083**

It appears from research studies that in the area of public order[32] "the police put up with disorderliness only if it ceases on their arrival". The research has shown that police presence is usually effective; few arrests are made out of many of the disturbances attended by the police, but in periods of mass demonstrations such as the Miners' Strike, the powers of arrest are widely used. **19–084**

One important aspect of police powers is the desire to see that the police have their own authority accepted by the public. While most police officers may seek to avoid confrontations, when the police feel that their authority may be challenged it is more likely that they will wish to intervene even if there is a risk of physical violence. Aggressive police tactics may therefore be seen as a legitimate way to exert police authority and therefore respect for the law. **19–085**

THE INTELLIGENCE SERVICES' FUNCTIONS AND POLICING

There have been notable improvements in the way the intelligence services are organised and how they might be made accountable. The Security Services Act 1989 placed the activities of MI5 on a statutory basis. The Intelligence Services Act 1994 similarly places the Secret Intelligence Service MI6 and the Government Communications Headquarters (GCHQ) on a statutory basis. The security services are placed under the scrutiny of a tribunal, a Commissioner and a parliamentary committee, the Intelligence and Security Committee, which may not compel the attendance of witnesses and may not review operational matters. Policy is under the control of the Secretary of State. The Intelligence and Security Committee is required to make an annual report, but this is subject to vetting by the Prime Minister. There are powers for the Prime Minister to order a report from the committee and to exclude matters either from Parliament or from publication under s.10(7) of the 1994 Act. **19–086**

The link between the security services in the collection of information and intelligence and policing is made in the important Security Service Act 1996. This Act amends the Security Services Act 1989 and provides statutory authority for the security services including "the function of acting in support of the prevention and detection of serious crime". This is interpreted to mean "organised crime" involving serious criminal offences. However, there is no definition of what serious crime is and the role of the security services is only generally outlined. This leaves the impression that the **19–087**

---

[32] McCabe *et al.*, *Police, Public Order and Civil Liberties* (1988).

detail will not be made clear and will be left to the discretion of the police and the security services. As a result, the Act leaves little guidance on any checks or balances that may be in place to prevent abuse.

19–088   The 1996 Act is broadly drafted in another respect which gives a large discretion to the issuing of executive warrants. This is in principle contrary to the constitutional protection articulated in *Entick v Carrington*.[33] The general nature of the discretions contained in the Act may provide scope for its challenge as incompatible with the European Convention on Human Rights.

19–089   A variety of new statutory powers are in force intended to broaden the co-ordination of the different parts of the police and security services. In the 1990s the Security Service was also given responsibility for the protection of the State including its economic well being. The Security Services Act 1996 acknowledges this role. The Police Act 1997 and the Regulation of Investigatory Powers Act 2000 provide for a support function for the security services to act alongside the police. The Regulation of Investigatory Powers Act 2000 provides comprehensive regulation of the interception of communications and the processing of data. While the Act makes it a criminal offence to intercept a communication without lawful authority, lawful authority is very generously provided. Part of the rationale of the legislation was to fill the gap left when the European Court of Human Rights decided in *Khan v UK*[34] that the applicant's human rights under Article 8 had been breached mainly because the law did not regulate the use of secret listening devices.

Military Powers, States of Emergency and Terrorism

19–090   Public protest may give rise to a complete breakdown in law and order. With the exception of Northern Ireland, the experience has been rare and mainly confined to particular periods in history, when military power has been required to aid the civil power and restore order. Although the police are mainly unarmed, there is an increasing requirement for armed police to be involved where there is an emergency involving political terrorists. Terrorism poses a major threat to the lives of ordinary citizens and this factor may weigh heavily in the granting of additional powers to the police to maintain civil order.

19–091   The use of military assistance during periods of industrial disputes may involve troops in agricultural duties or in preserving public order as part of a general assistance to aid the civil power in preserving public order. The Emergency Powers Acts 1920 and 1964 permit the proclamation of a state of emergency where events have occurred or are likely to occur that are calculated to deprive the community, or a substantial part of the community, of the essentials of life by interference with the supply and distribution of food, water, fuel, or light, or the means of locomotion.

19–092   Industrial action in 1921, 1924 and 1926 at the time of the General Strike resulted in the proclamation of states of emergency. In more recent times, during the Heath Government in the 1970s, regulations were issued covering emergency supplies of electricity and powers to control the dock strike to ensure the essential supply of goods

[33] (1765) 19 St. Tr. 1030.
[34] 12 May 2000 and also [2000] Crim. L.R.

and services.[35] During widespread violence and disruption during the Miners' Strike in 1984–85, the police were utilised to the full and as already noted this brought to bear a wide variety of arrest powers which were later to prove controversial, especially the use of breach of the peace as the basis for stopping and re-directing strikers. The authorities appear reluctant to countenance the use of military powers for the purposes of industrial strikes. Largely this may be because the appearance of the use of the military is an emotive issue and may lose the government of the day much needed popular support.

Increasingly there is a preference for making use of the ordinary police to cope with civil disturbance and emergency. This is evidenced through the better training given to the police and the issuing of various riot control equipment. On the whole the police may prefer to take this responsibility as part of their general involvement in maintaining public order. However, the model of an unarmed civilian police force may become less credible if the police are required to make increasing use of their powers to control riots and civil disturbances.   **19–093**

In cases where there are serious breaches in the law and rioting becomes widespread and uncontrolled, resort may be had to the use of the military. Both the police and military may rely on the legal right to make use of force under s.3 of the Criminal Law Act 1967. This permits the use of reasonable force in all circumstances in the prevention of crime.   **19–094**

The judgment between when to make use of force by the police and when to consider the use of the army calls for careful consideration of the level of violence and its likely duration. A Chief Constable may then invite the Home Secretary, in consultation with the Prime Minister and Secretary of State for Defence, to consider the use of military aid to the civil power. Once the military are invited to restore order, then some form of martial law may be said to exist. Lord Diplock in *Attorney-General for Northern Ireland's Reference* explained that at common law:[36]   **19–095**

> "There is little authority in English law concerning the rights and duties of a member of the armed forces of the Crown when acting in aid of the civil power; and what little authority there is relates almost entirely to the duties of soldiers when troops are called on to assist in controlling a riotous assembly."

While there is a duty on the private citizen to assist in the maintenance of order, this becomes very difficult to put into practice when the nature of that duty is ill-defined and the citizen is acting under military command.   **19–096**

Martial law is in one sense the suspension of the ordinary law and the use of military command over the civil authorities. The term is therefore broad enough to cover the complete suspension of democratic government and its substitution by military orders. In the extreme example of the overthrow of the civilian authorities and the removal of democratic government, martial law may refer to the use of military law. This refers to the body of law under which military rules are administered by military officers through courts-martial. Such courts have military law powers and are subject to review and appeal to the ordinary courts. However, when courts-martial exercise martial law   **19–097**

---

[35] Emergency Powers Act 1964. Also see G. Morris, *Strikes in Essential Services* (1986).
[36] *Att.-Gen. for Northern Ireland's Reference (No.1 of 1975)* [1977] A.C. 105 at 136. See *Clifford, Re* [1921] 2 A.C. 570.

jurisdiction, they are not perceived of as "ordinary courts" but simply a form of military justice administered through a tribunal which may at a future date be subject to oversight by the ordinary courts. This may normally occur once civilian government has been restored.

19–098   The Armed Forces Act 1996 makes substantial changes to the military justice system. In general terms this is an attempt to modernise the military system, and improve the standards and quality of courts-martial procedures and the general powers of military investigation. The changes introduced under the 1996 Act occur partly because of the case of *Findlay v UK*[37] considered by the European Commission of Human Rights. It decided that Findlay had not received a fair hearing and this questioned the procedures of military discipline and courts-martial.

19–099   Similarly, a major revision of the law relating to reserve forces is contained in the Reserve Forces Act 1996. Taken together these changes provide an important modernisation of law and practice for the armed services. Consolidation and change in the law were introduced by the Armed Forces Discipline Act 2000. The Act regulates internal discipline within the armed forces and brings many of the procedures into compatibility with human rights requirements. Rules relating to trial and pre-trial and detailed rules about arrest, detention and the rules of procedure are provided in the Act.

19–100   The Act attempts to address some of the issues arising from the decision of the European Court of Human Rights in *Findlay v UK*[38] and *Hood v UK*.[39]

19–101   However, in civil emergencies, martial law may be used more generally to mean the state of affairs requiring the presence of the military under the direction of the civil authorities. This use of martial law has historical more than contemporary relevance. Given the extremely wide nature of emergency powers under the Emergency Powers Act 1920 and 1964, it is unnecessary for martial law to be resorted to in those circumstances. In addition, wide powers, under the Prevention of Terrorism (Temporary Provisions) Act 1989 subject to annual renewal, provide comprehensive powers to deal with most emergencies from any acts of terrorism.

19–102   The legal authorities on the existence of martial law and its review by the ordinary courts appear confined to the period during the Irish rebellion in 1916 and its aftermath in the creating of the Irish Republic. It appears to be settled law that the courts may at a later date determine that martial law based on the facts of the case, existed. The question of martial law may settle the legality of the jurisdiction of the military and the question of whether necessity is established justifying recourse to martial law. An important question is whether the civil or military authorities are liable in civil law for their actions. Thus it is often the experience of emergency powers that there is some form of Act of Indemnity[40] restricting civil and even criminal liability for acts done during war or civil emergency.

19–103   There is a presumption in favour of the ordinary courts, while still sitting, to have the jurisdiction to determine whether a state of war or martial law is in existence. It is normal for the courts to wait for the cessation of hostilities before determining any proceedings brought by citizens who wish to determine their rights and the liability of

[37] Application No.22107/93. (1996) 21 E.H.R.R. CD7.
[38] (1997) 24 E.H.R.R. 221.
[39] (2000) 29 E.H.R.R. 365.
[40] The Indemnity Act 1920.

the authorities. Military law is therefore seen as a last resort and not to be utilised when the ordinary civilian government is able to function.

War may require that the authorities exercise both prerogative and statutory powers. **19–104** The declaration of war and the conduct of the war is subject to the prerogative powers of the Crown and international law. Various powers for requisitioning supplies, ships, vehicles and material are provided in legislation passed during wartime. Such powers may be found in the Emergency Powers (Defence) Acts 1939 and 1940. The trial of civilians by special military courts may also be authorised by statute.

The Import, Export and Customs Powers (Defence) Act 1939 and The Import **19–105** Export Control Act 1990 provides the government of the day with powers to regulate through the issue of licences for manufactured goods for export. Powers under both Acts were the subject of inquiry in the Matrix Churchill affair under Sir Richard Scott.

Wartime powers to requisition property may be subject to claims for compensation. **19–106** Such claims may be subject to legislation which may deprive the citizen of any right of payment, as in the example of the War Damage Act 1965. Many of the major powers given to the authorities to protect the State may also be subject to judicial review by the courts. However, the courts have been reluctant to interfere with executive discretion when the interests of the State and national security are pre-eminent. In a number of wartime cases the courts have refused to review the exercise of executive powers.[41] The role of the courts and national security is examined in the next chapter.

The Terrorism Act 2000

The Terrorism Act 2000 provides a consolidation and reform of the law relating to **19–107** terrorism. It applies throughout the United Kingdom and covers terrorism whether at home, abroad or in relation to Northern Ireland. Some of the sections are entirely new while others are consolidations of previous law. S.1 defines terrorism very broadly to include " the use or threat of action where it is directed to influence the government or to intimidate the public or a section of the public and the use or threat is for the purpose of advancing a political, religious or ideological cause". The acts in question are broadly defined and the activity may occur overseas and which terrorises peoples and governments wherever they may be. The Act is certified to be compatible with the Human Rights Act 1998, though throughout debate on the Terrorism Act some doubts were expressed about this. The courts will have to consider whether the Act is compatible with Articles 10 and 11 of the European Convention on Human Rights. The Terrorism Act is extensive in range and scope. Various organisations are proscribed under Pt II, and Pt III of the Act sets out offences for the seizing of terrorist property and proscribes financial fund raising for terrorism. Additional powers are granted under Pt V for the police to investigate terrorist acts and this includes search powers, setting up road-blocks and a raft of counter-terrorist powers especially at ports and borders. The Act also creates offences relating to paramilitary activities and incitement to terrorism overseas. Powers of extradition and penalties for

---

[41] *Burmah Oil Co v Lord Advocate* [1965] A.C. 75. See *Liversidge v Anderson* [1942] A.C. 206, also R.F.V. Heuston "Liversidge v Anderson in Retrospect" (1970) 86 L.Q.R. 33. *R. v Home Secretary Ex p. Lees* [1941] 1 K.B. 72. In more recent times this reluctance of the courts to intervene has continued, see *McEldowney v Forde* [1971] A.C. 632.

the possession of information for terrorist purposes are also included. Financial institutions are required to provide information about terrorists during the investigation of any terrorist activities. There are powers under s.41 of the Act covering the detention and arrest of suspects.[42] One of the most controversial is the power under s.19, itself a replica of s.18A of the Prevention of Terrorism (Temporary Provisions) Act 1989, for disclosure of information about someone who the person may suspect of being a terrorist. This power may require journalists to disclose information and sources used in investigative journalism.

Anti-Terrorism, Crime and Security Act 2001

19–108   The terrorist events on September 11, 2001 in New York and Washington led the government to introduce legislation to strengthen the law to combat terrorist activities or the perceived threat of terrorist activities. The legislation has a number of elements to allow preventive action to be taken against any supposed threat of terrorism. This includes Pt 1 and Sch.1 and 2 to the Act providing measures to prevent terrorists making use of their funds and powers to freeze any funds used in terrorism. Tough requirements on financial institutions to provide information on financial accounts are included. There are additional powers under ss.17–19 to require public authorities to disclose information and enforcement provisions are provided for that purpose. One of the most controversial parts of the Act is the powers that cover immigration and asylum. Ss.21–32 of the Act give the Secretary of State powers to detain those who he certifies as threats to national security and who are suspected of being international terrorists. The detention powers are subject to independent review by the Special Immigration Appeals Commission (SIAC). There is an attempt to prevent judicial review of the decisions of SIAC by making SIAC a superior court of record. However, there is a right of appeal in law to the Court of Appeal. The detention powers have a limited life span as they must be renewed by November 10, 2006. There are also extensive powers covering the fingerprinting of suspects or asylum seekers. The Act also makes extensive provision controlling chemical, nuclear and biological weapons.

19–109   There are remaining doubts about the Act's compatibility with the Convention even though the United Kingdom, alone, had already opted out of Article 5 which bans detention without trial. Although the Act was said to be compatible during the debates on the legislation many regarded the Act as hurried and ill prepared.

19–110   In August 2002 SIAC ruled that the detention of 11 foreign suspects was illegal as it was discriminatory on the basis that it offended against Article 14 (which bans discrimination on the grounds of race or nationality) of the Convention. As already noted the Home Secretary had used derogation powers to opt out of Article 5 but had not similarly derogated from Article 14. The Act was aimed at foreigners and not British citizens. If British citizens fell within the legislation through its amendment then it might be compatible. The case is on appeal.

Summary and Conclusions

19–111   Many of the freedoms enjoyed by citizens in democratic countries have been hard won through centuries of case law amid efforts to restrain over-zealous or badly motivated officials. The breadth and scope of recent legislation, the Anti Terrorism Crime and

[42] *Legislation Against Terrorism* Cm.3420 (1996).

Security Act 2001 rests very wide discretion with public officials. The rule of law and protections against arbitrariness remain under judicial discretion and vigilance. In many ways the determination of liberty and the balance between the interests of the state, its protection and security and the right of the individual remains as precarious today as it did in the past.

It remains to be seen whether the Human Rights Act 1998 will live up to **19–112** expectation.

FURTHER READING

D. Feldman, *Civil Liberties and Human Rights* (2nd ed., Oxford University Press, Oxford, 2002).

R. Blackburn and J. Polakiewicz, *Fundamental Rights in Europe* (Oxford University Press, Oxford, 2001).

T. Campbell, K.D. Ewing and A. Tomkins., (eds) *Sceptical Essays on Human Rights* T. Campbell, K.D. Ewing and A. Tomkins ed., Oxford University Press, Oxford, 2001).

S. Davidson, *Human Rights* (Open University Press, Buckingham, 1993).

R. Dworkin, *Taking Rights Seriously* (Cambridge, Mass., 1977). *A Matter of Principle* (Cambridge, Mass., and London, 1985). *Law's Empire* (London, 1986). *A Bill of Rights for Britain* (London, 1990). *Freedom's Law: The Moral Reading of the American Constitution* (Clarendon Press, Oxford, 1996).

Chapter 20

SECRECY, FREEDOM OF EXPRESSION AND THE STATE

INTRODUCTION

Governmental secrecy and the interests of the State are considered in this chapter in   **20–001**
the context of freedom of information. Access to information has a crucial role in the
various systems of government accountability. Information is required to make
effective use of parliamentary questions and debate in the performance of select
committees and in the work of pressure groups. Information is also an essential
element in government decision-making and especially in the area of policy formulation. An open style of government encourages debate and discussion, and is helpful in
coming to a fully informed and reasoned analysis that is axiomatic to good decision-
making.

There is for the first time a Freedom of Information Act 2000 which will come into   **20–002**
force over the coming years. Government secrecy and freedom of information has to
be considered in the context of the various Convention rights that are available under
the Human Rights Act 1998. Article 10 recognises the freedom of expression, as well
as the right to receive and impart information that is free from interference from the
state. There is also protection from international treaties such as Article 19(2) of the
United Nations Covenant on Civil and Political Rights that recognises the freedom of
expression.

It will take some time before the impact of the Human Rights Act may be judged in   **20–003**
areas of controversy such as the media and press, or in the law relating to contempt, or
official secrets. The question of what restraints the State should impose on the media
and press commensurate with freedom of information is one of the most challenging
questions in public law.

There are also signs that since the adoption of the Convention under the Human   **20–004**
Rights Act 1998, the courts are developing a right to privacy. This is a good example of
judicial creativity under the influence of Convention rights in the United Kingdom.
Before the Human Rights Act 1998 was passed in *Kaye v Robertson*[1] the Court of
Appeal denied that there is a right to privacy in English law. This view was upheld by
the House of Lords in *R. v Brown*[2] by Lord Hoffman, in strong terms, who commented

---

[1] [1991] F.S.R. 62.
[2] [1996] 1 All E.R. 545.

that the common law did not recognise such a right and that Parliament was reluctant to introduce one. In court decisions after the introduction of the Human Rights Act 1998, the courts have gone to great lengths to create such a right. In *Douglas v Hello! Ltd*[3] the courts acknowledged the possibility of an arguable right to privacy. This decision has the potential[4] of developing into a full right of privacy when in the past judges had been reluctant. This is an example of how the Human Rights Act may provide judges with new perspectives and allow the common law to be supplemented by a "rights" jurisprudence. There is, however, no easy solution when balancing the right of the private citizen, press freedom and media attention with privacy.

20–005   One pressure for greater openness comes from the widely available access to the international media through the internet. Territorial protection of confidential information is increasingly difficult. Attempts in the United Kingdom to make government more open have resulted in the creation of a *Code of Practice on Access to Government Information* revised in 1997. There are a number of examples where the citizen has greater access to information than in the past such as through the Local Government (Access to Information) Act 1985, the Access to Personal Files Act 1987, the Access to Medical Reports Act 1988, the Environment and Safety Information Act 1990, the Access to Health Records Act 1990 and the Data Protection Act 1998. There are also the recommendations of a high-level group of experts, set up in May 1995, within the European Union, to examine the necessary changes that come about through an information society. There is the Commission's Information Society Project Office providing information about the Community. There is a strong desire in the Community to provide better information about decision-making.

20–006   The focus of this chapter is on the restrictions and inhibitions which are placed on the freedom of expression and on the access to information which permits the State to retain secrecy.

OPEN GOVERNMENT AND OFFICIAL SECRETS

20–007   Openness is a necessary prerequisite for accountable and responsible government. An open style of government permits Parliament, pressure groups and interested members of the public to participate in policy decision-making. A government that is more open is likely to be better informed than a government that is restrictive. A consequence of openness in government is that the quality of decision-making may be improved. Participation in the democratic process should not end with an election vote, but should continue to allow citizens the opportunity to contribute to the system of government decision-making.

20–008   There is a variety of legal rules and techniques relevant to the secrecy of government. For many years there has been a secrecy culture in the government and among public authorities in the United Kingdom. Before the Human Rights Act 1998 and latterly the passage of the Freedom of Information Act 2000, there was no legally enforceable right to information. But it would be misleading to attribute the culture of secrecy as owing to that single cause. Successive United Kingdom governments have

---

[3] [2001] 2 All E.R. 289.
[4] See *Earl Spencer v UK* (1998) 25 E.H.R.R. CD 105 before the 1998 Act came into force.

maintained secrecy as the hallmark of government decision-making. There are a number of factors that may contribute to this culture.

First, the civil service developed, during the Victorian era, the ethos of public **20–009** service. Hierarchical in structure, disciplined through promotion and advancement through public service, civil servants were kept hidden from public view and their contribution to government preserved under secrecy and the responsibility of Ministers to Parliament. The civil service sought to achieve influence but maintain political neutrality. As a result civil servants have contributed to the high degree of secrecy evident in government. Advice given to Ministers must remain confidential, sometimes because of the nature of the advice itself and also to protect the anonymity of the advice giver.

Secondly, the doctrine of collective Cabinet responsibility, intended to provide **20–010** collective decision-making and collective deliberations, ensures that the climate of secrecy becomes built into every structure of government. There is in fact a secretive character to the political culture of the United Kingdom. This is reinforced by the use of Cabinet collective decision-making, which binds the civil service and Ministers to confidentiality. The ethos of secrecy is also underlined by the way information is disseminated to the media. Official leaks of information concerning government policy may quite legally be given to newspapers through the process known as "the lobby system". This system has been in operation until 2002, when the Prime Minister has taken the initiative to meet the press on a regular basis for a press briefing adopting a question and answer format. Ministers may be self-authorising in releasing to the press details of government policy that may affect their department. Thirdly, individual ministerial responsibility serves to preserve the secrecy of government departmental decision-making. Ministers are directly accountable to Parliament but civil servants are not. Thus civil servants and Ministers may find secrecy the most effective buffer against outside intrusion or unwanted publicity.

Fourthly, governments are major providers of contracts. In the government's **20–011** relationship with the private sector there is a high degree of secrecy in contractual relationships. Relations between commercial enterprises seek to preserve confidentiality and protection against competitors through patenting industrial processes or copyright which contributes to the need to preserve price sensitive and commercially valuable information. Confidentiality of the commercial variety permeates the relationship between the private and public sectors.

The idea of freedom of discussion in the United Kingdom is no more than[5]: **20–012**

> "the freedom to write or say anything which is not a violation of the law as interpreted by the courts sometimes with, sometimes without, the aid of a jury."

Thus freedom of speech in the United Kingdom rests on the assumption that freedom **20–013** may exist outside any area prohibited by law. The list of offences and proscriptions are ill-defined and wide. This leaves considerable uncertainty as to where the boundaries of freedom to information may be drawn, as the extent of proscription may also depend on how rigorously the law is to be enforced.

[5] P. O'Higgins, *Censorship in Britain* (1972) p.16.

20–014   The historical origins of government secrecy may be traced back before the introduction of the first Official Secrets Act was passed in 1889. Medieval secrecy was provided on oaths of loyalty between the King and his advisers. Bound by loyalty, the enforcement of confidences was provided by widely interpreted treason laws. By the end of the seventeenth century with the restoration of the monarchy in 1660, Parliament had successfully limited prerogative powers of taxation such as ship-money impositions and other taxes. With the achievement of political and legal sovereignty Parliament had gained authority but not control over the central Executive which remained with the Crown. The decline of royal control over Ministers was gradual and ad hoc and even in the eighteenth century, the influence of the monarch over government endured during the period of Walpole's ministry which marked the birth of the office of modern Prime Minister. The secrecy of government was bound up with its mystique. Attempts to invigorate the system of government in the nineteenth century had to tread carefully around the controls over access to official papers.

20–015   The adoption of Royal Commissions of Inquiry and the greater use of select committees by both the House of Commons and the House of Lords provides a fascinating account of how modern government developed in the Victorian era. Reports from inspectors and the setting-up of various inspectorates also increased access to the workings of government. Such developments did not prove successful against the culture of secrecy. Inspectors were subject to ministerial responsibility and confidentiality was retained. The Treasury through the issuing of treasury minutes and memoranda influenced civil service attitudes to secrecy by preventing the disclosure of any official information without proper authority. The Victorian preoccupation with confidential information provides a culture which was receptive to instructions requiring non-disclosure. Equally clear is that attempts to circumvent legal controls were made and often were successful.[6]

20–016   The Victorian legacy remains today. As there is no public right to information various restrictions remain on the disclosure of information about the past activities of government. Public records in the Public Records Office are only available for inspection after a period of 30 years has elapsed. S.5(1) of the Public Records Act 1958 as amended by the Public Records Act 1967, provides that the Lord Chancellor may also proscribe different time periods for the disclosure of documents at the request of the Minister "or other person". Certain categories of papers may be subject to a longer time-scale. These are: "exceptionally sensitive papers, the disclosure of which would be contrary to the public interest whether on security or other grounds"; documents which contain information "supplied in confidence" the disclosure of which would or might constitute a breach of good faith; and documents containing information about individuals, "the disclosure of which would cause distress or danger to living persons or their immediate descendants".

20–017   In fact it is possible to prevent the disclosure of many documents by the simple expedient of "weeding" out those documents which may be too sensitive to publish, and their destruction amounts to their permanent removal from the records of government. Estimates as to the amount of weeding carried out are difficult to make with any degree of accuracy but it is also possible for papers to be destroyed at

---

[6] C. Roberts, *The Growth of Responsible Government in Stuart England* (1966). See William Cobbet and his pamphlets ensuring a constant flow of information on state trials and prosecutions. Wilson Report: *Modern Public Records: Selection and Access*, Cmnd.8204 (1981).

departmental level before they are ever put into the hands of the staff of the Public Records Office. The responsibility for the Public Records Office is with the Lord Chancellor who is a member of the Cabinet and at present is not answerable to Parliament through any departmental select committee. The assessment of the value of official papers in terms of their historical content is not included in the legislation. Thus it is possible and legal for government Ministers to order the destruction of official papers in the public interest. It is difficult to prevent the destruction of official papers. Would a longer time-limit beyond 30 years result in a different attitude towards publication? A longer time-limit may make the destruction of papers less likely but this may be at the expense of depriving the present generation of information about the activities of the government during their lifetime. Is this a price worth paying in the interests of preserving historical records? There is no guarantee that a longer time-limit would help to preserve official papers without some legal requirement of preservation.

While the 30-year rule is still in place, the Code of Practice on Access to **20–018** Government Information has provided a more liberal attitude to opening up files. Recent examples of such an approach may be found in the release of files on the German occupation of the Channel Islands and the release of the Rudolf Hess and Roger Casement papers. However, there have been surprises such as the revelation that in 1957 there had been a government decision to keep the details of an accident at the Windscale nuclear plant secret. This was revealed in papers released in January 1988.

An important source of information are ministerial memoirs. Previous Prime **20–019** Ministers and Cabinet Ministers often write biographies and memoirs of their period in office. Such publications usually obeyed certain conventions about confidential information. The advice tendered to the government of the day by the civil service usually fell into this category. However the memoirs of the late Richard Crossman who had been a Cabinet Minister in the Wilson Government 10 years previously created concerns about the revelation of official information. The text of the diaries contained detailed information about the deliberations of the Cabinet. Officials were identified as were the names and views of Ministers. Particularly significant was the advice given to Ministers by civil servants which was also given in great detail. The Attorney-General in 1976 attempted to prevent the publication of the diaries. The arguments made to prevent publication included the confidential nature of Cabinet information, that the public interest requires that publication should be restrained and that the courts had a duty to restrain publication. Lord Widgery took the unusual step of reading the diaries and concluded, that publication 10 years after the event would not inhibit Cabinet discussion and that publication would not harm the public interest. The result of the decision allowed publication of the Crossman Diaries and since then many ex-Cabinet Ministers have provided details of their period in office in a relatively short period after they left office. Such memoirs can often become an indispensable guide to the workings of government and the way in which modern government develops. Following the *Crossman* case,[7] Lord Radcliffe's committee of privy counsellors considered the advice tendered to Ministers about publication of their memoirs. In general the committee took a restrictive perspective on the publication of information which might

---

[7] *Att.-Gen. v Jonathan Cape Ltd* [1976] Q.B. 752.

put in jeopardy the "confidential relationships" between Ministers within the government. The committee concluded that the opinions or advice of civil servants or ministerial colleagues should not be revealed, nor should the advice of advisers, furthermore that criticism of policy or competence should not be made public. Such guidelines are much stricter than the *Crossman* case accepted. However, enforcement is left to the individual responsibility of each Minister and not through the courts. There is little sign that the Radcliffe view is being followed by Ministers today and it seems more commonly accepted that ministerial memoirs will be forthcoming and that their value as a means of understanding the work of government remains undiminished. The normal convention is that former Ministers or civil servants who wish to publish their memoirs should submit a full text to the Cabinet secretary in advance for clearance. Upon refusal of publication there is an appeal to the Prime Minister who has the final decision in the matter. There is a tacit acceptance that[8] after a period of 15 years, as the Government may no longer be in office, a fairly wide latitude may be shown to former Ministers[9].

20–020   Attempts have been made in recent years to encourage a more public disclosure of information. In 1977, the then Prime Minister James Callaghan introduced an initiative to make available to the public background studies and analytical information used when reaching key policy decisions. The text of this initiative became more generally known as the Croham Directive[10] which favoured a more open approach to giving information to the public. This view of greater openness was also espoused by Mrs Thatcher in 1981 when she accepted the Croham Directive and suggested that more information might be available.

20–021   Governments new to office are often enthusiastic supporters of more information being made publicly available but soon the experience of government may dull this enthusiasm. Although Mrs Thatcher was the first Prime Minister to publicly acknowledge the existence of MI5, her government took a strong line on leaks of information including the prosecution of Clive Ponting[11] for leaking secret information to M.P.s about the sinking of the Argentinian battleship *General Belgrano*, during the Falklands War in 1982.

20–022   The published memoirs of a former intelligence officer Peter Wright resulted in protracted litigation attempting to prevent the publication of his memoirs written in order to provide him with compensation and to settle a grievance he had with his former employer the British Government over his pension rights.

20–023   More recent attempts to provide greater public information have come from the initiative under the Citizen's Charter. Indirectly as a result of privatisation the public have been made more aware of the standards expected of the various public utility industries such as water, gas, electricity, and telecommunications industries. Charter Rights enable performance indicators to be published to allow the citizen to see the standards of service to be expected and the likely compensation payable should those standards not be met within a stipulated period and range of conditions. Such an approach has highlighted how many public services may be improved through greater access to information. The Citizen's Charter has an important significance in the way

[8] *Att.-Gen. v Guardian Newspapers Ltd (No.2)* [1990] 1 A.C. 109.
[9] Lord Radcliffe, *Committee of Privy Counsellors on Ministerial Memoirs*, Cmnd.6386 (1976).
[10] See *Hansard*, HC Vol.936, cols.699–700 (October 26, 1977).
[11] *R. v Ponting* [1985] Crim. L.R. 318.

public bodies may provide the public with information. The Next Step's agencies also have a more open approach to providing information than was previously available.

In 1993 the Government approved greater openness in a White Paper on Open Government. There is a Minister with responsibility for Open Government and the Citizen's Charter. This policy was implemented in the Code of Practice on Access to Government Information first published in 1994 and later revised in 1996.

20–024

Another initiative has come through the need for financial markets to obtain government confidence after the decision of the Government in summer 1992 to leave the European Monetary System of fixed exchange rates. As a result the Treasury have decided to give greater attention to publishing some of the working material which is used in government forecasting. In addition a group of leading economists has been appointed to advise the Chancellor of the Exchequer on economic policy. The names and views of these economists and their general advice are made public. In this example the Government believed it to be in its own interests to take these steps in order to encourage a more open style of decision-making and encourage greater confidence in the Government's intentions to manage the economy. There is also less latitude allowed to a government with a small majority compared to a government with a large majority. The former requires greater attention to the views of backbench M.P.s while the latter may encourage a degree of arrogance about how much information is really needed outside the government.

20–025

In contrast to various developments in favour of more open government there are some indications that government may from time to time prefer a more closed style of government. In the 1970s and 1980s experiments in government decision-making involving local government, notably the introduction of the Community Charge, in education reform, and in changes in the way schools are governed, have all been introduced in the absence of any Royal Commission or independent investigation or inquiry. This tendency has been viewed by some commentators as giving rise to "an authoritarian approach to law-making" and in some instances has led to major policy reversals for the Government.[12] A more open style of government may have avoided some of the more controversial mistakes in government policy.

20–026

It is often the more mundane and less sensationalist aspects of secrecy that may matter. In recent years a number of safety-related matters made public as a result of official reports are an illustration of the problems with excessive secrecy. For example the secrecy of fire brigade reports at British Rail stations was revealed in 1987, after Desmond Fennel Q.C. in his report on the King's Cross fire in 1987 revealed how public safety would have greatly benefited from the publication of such reports. Fire brigade inspections at London Underground stations are made public but British Rail had not made its own reports public. Rail Track, successor to British Rail, retained strict confidentiality over its own internal reports on commercial confidentiality.

20–027

Tests conducted on the safety of British cars undertaken by the Department of Transport's Vehicle Certification Agency on the basis of European Community safety and environmental standards are kept secret. If the information was made public this would allow the public to make choices based on the safety and effectiveness of different cars depending on the model range. Similarly the evidence suggests that a

20–028

---

[12] Cm.2290 (1993), White Paper on Open Government.

more open style of presentation of the scientific evidence would have assisted the government in handling the BSE crisis and the foot-and-mouth epidemic.

20–029   Progress in the United Kingdom on freedom of information has lagged behind developments in other countries—New Zealand, Canada, Australia and most notably the United States of America. Ironically information about the United Kingdom Government revealed under the Freedom of Information legislation in the United States is greater than under domestic United Kingdom law. Thus a major initiative to improve the United Kingdom's freedom of information is encouraged by the knowledge that the United Kingdom's Government cannot effectively prevent some information becoming available under the United States' laws. This may be counterproductive as the amount of information revealed under Freedom of Information legislation may be significantly greater than the Government may wish to accept in this country. This may act as an incentive towards more open government but equally it may also act as a deterrent against any future liberalisation of the law.

Official Secrets Legislation

20–030   Various laws and legal restrictions exist against the publication or dissemination of official information. At common law various offences such as blasphemy, sedition and conspiracy provided a structure for the prosecution of offences which were intended to limit the variety and content of published material available to the public. The criminal law exercised a crude form of censorship aimed at controlling booksellers, publishers and printers as well as authors. The nineteenth-century legacy of secrecy resulted in the passage of the Official Secrets Act 1889 which made it an offence to "improperly divulge official information" was so widely drawn that the requirement of proof of the mental elements of the crime made successful prosecutions difficult to achieve. At the end of the nineteenth century legal controls were ineffective whereby many breaches of the law went unpunished under the growing power and influence of newspapers. The need to tighten the law was recognised by the Official Secrets Act 1911. This Act was further refined and reformed by the Official Secrets Act 1920 and again reformed by the Official Secrets Act 1939.

20–031   S.1(1) of the 1911 Act makes it an offence for any person for any purpose prejudicial "to the safety or interests of the state" to engage in a number of activities. Those which are covered by the 1911 Act include: approaching or entering a prohibited place; making a sketch or plan calculated or intended to be useful to an enemy; obtaining, publishing, communicating such information, sketch, document or information which is calculated to or is intended to be useful to an enemy.

20–032   The purpose which is prejudicial to the interests of the State may be inferred from the circumstances. The purpose which is prejudicial refers to the intention of the accused and will be judged not on the actual effect but on what the accused intended. Thus in *Chandler v DPP*[13] demonstrators for the Campaign for Nuclear Disarmament who approached a military airfield were convicted under s.1 of the 1911 Act when it was proved that their intention was to disable the airfield. The House of Lords regarded a "prohibited place" as not confined to specific sites so designated by the

[13] [1964] A.C. 763.

Ministry of Defence but applied to places where information would be useful to an enemy. Thus the law, which was intended to cover acts during wartime, had a peacetime operational focus which included protestors, as well as spies, saboteurs or agitators. This broad construction of the Act seems perfectly consistent with the breadth of the language used in the legislation. However, was it correct to have brought such a prosecution under a section which was aimed at spies and saboteurs rather than protestors and demonstrators? This highlights one of the problems with broadly drafted and interpreted laws. Prosecutorial discretion seems to depend on whether the statute is broad enough to catch the undesirable activity, which in this case it was, rather than on whether the Official Secrets Act should be used for such a prosecution.

The defence in *Chandler* had argued that the purpose of the demonstrators was not **20–033** to prejudice the interests of the State but to draw attention to the use of nuclear weapons and thereby disarm the aircraft. Such direct action was unjustified and the courts rejected the defendants' arguments. Obstructing the lawful purpose of the armed services was held as prejudicial to the State even when the demonstrators held strongly their conviction that they were acting in the State's interests. The decision has been strongly criticised but the legal interpretation of the legislation is consistent with the words of the statute.

S.2 of the 1911 Act is intended to prevent the misuse of any sketch plan or model, **20–034** document or information. The section is aimed first at the holders of official information and makes it an offence to communicate this information except to a person authorised to receive the communication. A person who receives such information is also guilty of an offence if he has reasonable cause to believe that the information is in contravention of the Act. In *Crisp*[14] the scope of the section applied to a clerk in the War Office who handed to the director of a firm of tailors a copy of the clothing contract for the army. The clerk was not directly employed by the War Office but worked under the direction of the office-holder and this was sufficient.

S.2(1) of the 1911 Act was used to prosecute Sarah Tisdell, a civil service clerk in **20–035** 1984 for leaking to a newspaper a memorandum setting out the plans drawn up by the Government for maintaining public order when cruise missiles arrived at Greenham Common. Tisdell was sentenced to six months' imprisonment. S.2(1) was used in a prosecution against Clive Ponting, an assistant secretary in the Ministry of Defence, after he leaked a memorandum relating to the sinking of the Argentine battleship *General Belgrano*. Ponting admitted leaking the document but claimed that he owed a duty to the House of Commons, in their constitutional role to hold government accountable. The document contained highly embarrassing revelations which questioned the complete accuracy of the Prime Minister's account of the sinking to the House of Commons. Ponting[15] was acquitted after the jury were able to see the documents and the jury's verdict was a surprise to many after the judge's summing up pointed in favour of a conviction. Ponting had not been authorised to leak the documents. The trial judge explicitly rejected Ponting's argument that he was justified in leaking the documents as he could not be said to owe a duty to the House of Commons; such a duty was the duty of Ministers and not civil servants. This direction

[14] (1919) 83 J.P. 121.
[15] C. Ponting, *The Right to Know* (1986).

appears correct in constitutional law. Ponting had breached the confidential nature of his relationship with Ministers and, however altruistic his motives, this was not a breach that could be authorised in law. The Armstrong Memorandum[16] issued to civil servants soon after Ponting's acquittal is that civil servants may use the Head of the Civil Service as a form of appeal court to resort to after exhausting departmental means to remedy any conflict between the civil servant's duties and responsibilities and those of the Minister. The Armstrong Memorandum has been replaced by the Civil Service Code from January 1996, which was revised in 1999 to take account of devolution. However, another view is that Ponting exposed both the failure of the civil service to exercise sufficient control over Ministers in such cases of dispute and that civil servants ought to be able to appeal directly to Parliament as a means to hold Ministers to account. The latter is objected to because of the nature of the Minister's responsibility to Parliament. Undoubtedly Ponting's leak had the effect of breaching an important confidence between a civil servant and his Minister. Ponting's acquittal also highlighted patent defects in the Official Secrets Acts and this led to the Government's consideration of reform in preference to various private members' initiatives.

20–036   Criticism of s.2 had been of long standing, with the Franks Committee[17] (1972) having recommended its abolition. The broadly drafted legislation with its "catch-all" quality became so heavily criticised that it was seldom used. This Draconian law however was said to have a preventive effect and therefore was perceived as valuable. About one-third of prosecutions under the Act related to the use of police information improperly disclosed to journalists or private detectives. The Franks Committee made comprehensive proposals for replacing s.2 with a more modern and focused Act. Thus the use of criminal sanctions would be restricted to areas of major significance such as wrongful disclosure of information relating to the defence, security, foreign relations and reserves, Cabinet documents and the use of official information for private gain or information supplied about particular individuals. This reform proposal was accompanied by proposals to regularise the classification of documents, long regarded as the product of an over-protective civil service. Top secret would be restricted to defence, security, foreign relations and reserves. Prosecution would require a certificate from the responsible Minister and there would be some form of advisory committee advising on matters of classification. The Franks proposals received belated attention in the aftermath of the Ponting trial and consideration given to implementing some part of them in a White Paper.[18] The result was the introduction of the Official Secrets Act 1989.

20–037   The 1989 Act replaced s.2 of the 1911 Act and narrowed the protection of official information considerably. The use of the criminal law under the Act is restricted to various categories of information. While all Cabinet documents are not automatically protected under the Act, documents or information which falls under the following categories are subject to the criminal law.

20–038   It is an offence for a Crown servant or government contractor to disclose information which falls under any one of the following categories. The categories under ss.1–4 of the 1989 Act are: security and intelligence, defence, international

---

[16] Sir Robert Armstrong, *The Duties and Responsibilities of Civil Servants in relation to Ministers: Note by the Head of the Home Civil Service 1985* HC Official Report Vol.74 1984–85 (HMSO, 1985).
[17] *Departmental Committee on s.2 of the Official Secrets Act 1911* Cmnd.5104 (1972).
[18] Cm.408 (1988) and the debates at *Hansard*, HC Vol.137, cols.1412–1481.

relations, information obtained in confidence from other states or international organisations, information obtained by special investigations authorised by warrant. In the cases of security and intelligence information or where information is obtained by special investigations authorised by warrant, no damage need be proven for the offence to have been committed if the disclosure is made by an officer of the security and intelligence services. In cases where disclosure is made by a Crown servant or government contractor, damage must be proven for there to be an offence. However in the remaining categories covering defence and international relations, damage must be proven to have occurred where disclosure is made by someone other than a member of the security and intelligence services.

The 1989 Act also makes it a criminal offence for any person to make without **20–039** authority a damaging disclosure of information protected under the Act that has come into his possession following an unauthorised disclosure of information by a current Crown servant or government contractor. This applies to information which is made available in breach of a requirement of confidentiality or in breach of s.1 of the 1911 Official Secrets Act. While mere receipt of information is no longer an offence, it is an offence to make disclosure of information relating to security and intelligence, defence and international relations when the information is communicated in confidence by the United Kingdom to another State or international organisation.

S.8 of the 1989 Act makes it an offence to retain or fail to take care of protected **20–040** documents and articles or disclose information which may facilitate access to protected material.

In its effect, the 1989 Act means that there is a general prohibition against **20–041** disclosure of information by members of the security services or disclosure of information received from any authorised use of telephone tapping, irrespective of any damage proven. In such cases there is no public interest defence and no defence of prior publication. Raising a defence requires the burden of proof to rest on the accused and this may make a defence to such offences difficult to prove. The 1989 Act does not permit the disclosure of information even where it may reveal any unlawful behaviour. There is no general defence that disclosure was in the public interest thus excluding the type of defence argued by Ponting in his trial, but then rejected by the trial judge. Various defences under the 1989 Act are that in general it is a defence for the accused to prove that he did not know that any of the information fell into a prohibited category or, in certain circumstances indicated above where damage must be shown in relation to the disclosure, that damage did not occur.

The scope of the 1989 Act applies generally within the civil service and to some **20–042** outside bodies. The 1989 Act appears to move in a more liberal direction to official secrets compared to s.2 of the 1911 Act which it replaced. However, the 1989 Act falls short of providing access to information and its scope is supplemented by an increasing reliance on legal devices and techniques other than the criminal law, to prevent disclosures. Very often such techniques involve the use of the civil law.

As mentioned above for civil servants, the Civil Service Pay and Conditions of **20–043** Service Code has been revised to take account of the provisions of the 1989 Act and the details of the Armstrong Memorandum mentioned above. Thus civil servants are explicitly required under the terms and conditions of their employment as owing the Crown a duty of confidentiality. This duty applies even after the civil servant leaves his employment. In addition there is an obligation not to frustrate the policies or decisions of Ministers by the use or disclosure of information to which civil servants have access. Such requirements are intended to prevent leaks of information from civil servants who wish to disagree with the government's policy.

20–044   Civil servants who prove to be unreliable and untrustworthy are subject to disciplinary procedures which may result in dismissal from the Service. Promotion prospects are severely restricted when civil servants engage in activities incompatible with their duty of confidence to Ministers.

20–045   Recourse to the civil law either on the basis of breach of confidence or through the use of injunctions to protect copyright ownership avoids some of the difficulties encountered with the application of the criminal law. The disadvantages of using criminal prosecutions to punish leaks of information may be attributable to the unpredictable nature of jury trials for serious breaches of the Official Secrets Act and the publicity of court proceedings even when the proceedings may be held *in camera* or where disclosure is a contempt of court. The scope of contempt laws allows for restrictions on the access to information available to the court. Documents obtained by a solicitor and read out in open court in the course of litigation could not be used for any collateral or ancillary purpose. In *Home Office v Harman*[19] Harman, a solicitor for one of the parties in a civil action obtained documents by way of discovery which she later revealed to newspapers, was held by the House of Lords to have been in contempt of court for so doing in breach of the undertaking given for the disclosure of the documents to the court.

20–046   Civil proceedings have other advantages over criminal prosecutions. The burden of proof in criminal cases is higher than in civil cases which rests not on the standard of beyond a reasonable doubt but on the balance of probabilities. In civil cases the judiciary, and not the jury, performs the fact-finding role and this may facilitate the proof of the case against the defendant. Normally criminal proceedings are only used after the leak has occurred and the suspect detected. Civil proceedings can be activated in anticipation of any publication and offers prior restraint through the use of injunctions over any proposed publication. The ex parte nature of the interim injunction procedures means that the law may be readily applied and take effect as soon as the leak becomes apparent to the government.

20–047   However it is a mistake to assume that civil proceedings are a complete panacea when the government wishes to retain confidential information which has become available on a worldwide basis outside the United Kingdom and outside the jurisdiction of the United Kingdom's courts. The long running *Spycatcher* litigation exposed limitations in the use of law to enforce secrecy. The case is an example of the use of litigation to enforce the doctrine of breach of confidence. This doctrine owed its origins to private law and the enforcement of personal rights, including the enforcement of trade secrets and marital secrets. The potential for its use in public law owes its origins to the *obiter dicta* of Lord Widgery in the *Crossman Diaries Case*[20] discussed above. Then it was suggested that a breach of confidence might occur when government information was made public. The opportunity to apply this doctrine to its full potential, as an alternative to the use of the criminal law, arose in the *Spycatcher* case.

[19] [1983] 1 A.C. 280.
[20] [1976] Q.B. 752.

The saga began in 1985 when the Attorney-General commenced proceedings in   **20–048**
Australia against Peter Wright and his publisher seeking an injunction to prevent
publication of Wright's memoirs detailing the activities of the security services during
the period when Wright was a member of MI5. In the United Kingdom ex parte
injunctions were granted restraining the publication of extracts from the memoirs in
the *Guardian* and the *Observer*. After the trial of the issues in the Australian court, the
Attorney-General's action was dismissed and Wright's memoirs allowed to be published. Publication also took place in the United States from May 1987 after extracts
from the book were published in the *Washington Post*. The Attorney-General
continued to attempt to prevent publication in the United Kingdom and was granted
further interim injunctions against the *Sunday Times* and the *Independent*, the *Evening
Standard* and the *London Daily News*.

In the meantime an appeal against permission to publish was heard in the New   **20–049**
South Wales Court of Appeal where the Attorney-General was unsuccessful. Finally
after the *Independent*, the *Sunday Times* and the *News on Sunday* were fined £50,000
each for contempt of court, the House of Lords in 1990 decided that no injunction
would lie against the newspapers against any further serialisation of the book, nor
would the newspapers be liable for any financial account of profits to the Government
as the information contained in the *Spycatcher* book was now in the public domain and
thus could not be restrained.

The House of Lords' decision to permit publication indicated the ineffectiveness of   **20–050**
the law when attempting to restrain publication of information which has entered the
international arena. The case also highlights a number of further possibilities open to
the government interested in preventing publication. First the House of Lords
accepted that neither the publishers nor the author had copyright in the book as
copyright vested with the Crown. This gives rise to the possibility that the Crown might
seek damages and an account of profits to base its claim. In the future this is likely to
be a useful remedy. It could be argued that if a claim had been based on this ground,
the Government's attempts to prevent publication might have been more effective. It is
unlikely that any publisher would be willing to take such a risk of publication if the
profits from publication are put in jeopardy.

Secondly, the House of Lords considered whether reliance could be placed on   **20–051**
Wright's main defence that it was in the public interest to publish. The book was
claimed to establish wrongdoing and lack of accountability on the part of the security
services—claims which if proven might give rise to serious public concern about the
operational controls over the security services. In particular allegations were made that
MI5 had engaged in activities to destabilise the government when Harold Wilson was
Prime Minister. In the House of Lords, Lord Griffiths was prepared to concede that in
an extreme case the confidential nature of the trust between security service operatives
and the security services might be lifted so that the dangers of a serious abuse might be
made public.[21] However, such a justification did not appear to arise in the *Spycatcher*
case. The House of Lords appeared to accept that once the book was available in the
public domain, publication could not be prevented by an injunction. Such an injunction
would be "futile", as personal copies of the book had been purchased or received by
many United Kingdom citizens abroad and were imported into the United Kingdom.

[21] [1988] 3 All E.R. 545 at 650. See: P. Wright, *Spycatcher* (1987), p.54.

Despite the fact that Wright had a life-long duty of confidence, the reality was that such a duty was in practical terms unenforceable. This gave rise to the surprising result that Wright might be free to return to the United Kingdom and publish his memoirs without any prior restraint. The reality was that he would be prosecuted under the Official Secrets Act.

20–052   The effects of the *Spycatcher* litigation were far-reaching. The Government was seriously embarrassed by the revelations in the book, and attempts to restrict its publication had been unsuccessful. In the earlier consideration of an interim injunction, Lord Bridge in the House of Lords pointed to the absence of any Bill of Rights in the United Kingdom, at that time, when compared to many other countries. He indicated that the European Convention would most likely result in the unenforceable nature of any ban.

20–053   The defence of public interest was used by David Shayler, a former member of the security services who was charged with unlawful disclosure of documents under ss.1 and 4 of the Official Secrets Act 1989 In *R. v Shayler*[22] the House of Lords approved the use of a preparatory hearing to decide whether there was a public interest defence. This procedure is available under the Criminal Procedure and Investigations Act 1996 and the House of Lords held that the 1989 Official Secrets legislation was compatible with the Human Rights Act 1998.

The Security Services

20–054   The unwelcome glare of publicity resulting from the *Spycatcher* affair exposed many of the previously held secret activities of the security services. In particular the often quoted comment that Peter Wright and others "bugged and burgled our way across London at the State's behest, while pompous, bowler-hatted civil servants in Whitehall pretended to look the other way". In addition allegations made by Cathy Massiter that the phones of prominent CND activists and trade unionists were bugged confirmed the suspicion of many commentators that the security services were not under complete control.

20–055   The question of control over the security services is itself often shrouded in secrecy. In the 1940s a system of positive vetting developed which was aimed at preventing persons with a communist interest or affiliation from joining the civil service or the security services. This procedure applied to personnel mainly charged with handling sensitive information. It also applied to contractors engaged in work which may be similarly regarded as involving sensitive material.

20–056   The system of positive vetting developed as a means to purge the public service and contractors of any communists or sympathisers. Revisions to the system have been continuous since it was introduced in 1952. In 1990 it was revised once more and a written statement made by the Prime Minister defended the operation of the system.[23] The increasing use of positive vetting reflects the increasing complexity and sensitivity of government decision-making. Also the series of leaks by civil servants may cause a

---

[22] [2002] 2 All E.R. 477.
[23] See *Hansard*, HC Vol.448, cols.1703–1704 (March 14, 1948). See P. Hennessy and G. Brownfield, "Britain's Cold War Security purge: The Origins of Positive Vetting" (1982) 4(25) *The Historical Journal* 965–973. *Hansard*, HC Vol.177, cols.159–161 (July 24, 1990).

wider drawing of the boundaries as to who should or should not be included. The main focus of positive vetting is directed against anyone who might be involved in any activities which threaten national security, such as espionage, terrorism, sabotage, or actions "intended to overthrow or undermine Parliamentary democracy by political, industrial or violent means". Different levels of clearance are necessary for the various categories of secret information ranging from top secret to merely confidential information.

Judicial review for someone who is refused positive vetting clearance is limited as the courts have shown reluctance to engage in any substantial examination of what is in the national interest, but there is an appeal procedure to the three advisers constituted to hear cases where there are allegations against a public servant. There is a procedure which relies on the use of three advisers who may take account of the representations of the person affected. The recommendations of the three advisers are made to the Minister who may consider further evidence in the matter including representations from the person concerned.[24] Government contractors may also make use of the three advisers procedure since 1956.   **20–057**

In the aftermath of the *Spycatcher Case* the Government responded. The outcome was first to establish a staff counsellor for the security services to deal with matters relating to concerns of officers about the nature of their work and, if necessary, the counsellor could have access to the Head of the Civil Service in order to allay fears. Setting up some form of internal grievance mechanism in order to deal with legitimate concerns about the operational responsibilities of the security services was partly intended to restore morale to the service and also to re-build public confidence in the work of the service. The remit of the staff counsellor was later extended to include staff who were former members of the service. Dissatisfied members of the service could have recourse to the departmental Minister or the Prime Minister.   **20–058**

It is doubtful if such arrangements would be effective if they had been available to Peter Wright. In fact many of his allegations, especially that the one-time Head of MI5 was a double agent, had been considered but rejected by his superior officers. It is hard to envisage that an aggrieved officer would be satisfied by a polite refusal internally to take no further action. Thus the creation of a staff counsellor appears to have limited potential for effectiveness. However, the creation of this office further served to strengthen the secrecy binding all members of the security services. This culture of secrecy is further reinforced by the Official Secrets Act 1989.   **20–059**

In addition to the creation of a staff counsellor, the Government introduced a new Act, the Security Services Act 1989, to put the security services on a statutory basis. The new legislation marked an important departure in official recognition of MI5 under s.1 of the Act. However this Act did not include any of the other elements in the security services such as MI6, responsible for overseas intelligence activity in liaison with the Foreign Office. There is no mention of the Government Communications Headquarters (GCHQ) at Cheltenham nor any statutory basis for its existence in the legislation. Plans to put the intelligence service and GCHQ on a statutory basis are contained in the Intelligence Services Act 1994. The remit covering the activities of the security services is widely drawn. It includes under s.1(2) of the 1989 Act: **20–060**

---

[24] *R. v Director of Government Communications Headquarters Ex p. Hodges*, *Times* (July 26), 1988, DC. See Statement of the procedure to be followed when the reliability of a public servant is thought to be in doubt on security grounds. (Cabinet Office, 1985). Cmd.9715 (1956).

". . . the protection of national security and in particular, its protection against threats from espionage, terrorism, sabotage, from the activities of agents of foreign powers and from actions intended to overthrow or undermine parliamentary democracy by political, industrial or violent means."

20–061   In addition under s.1(3) the function of the security services includes "the economic well-being of the United Kingdom against threats posed by the actions or intentions of persons outside the British Islands". This is so broadly drafted that it might include any industrial commercial activity of foreign or international companies; in fact almost anything may be connected to this function. Criticism of this section has focused on the widely drawn nature of the section.

20–062   There is provision under the Act for the appointment of a Director-General by the Secretary of State. The statutory responsibility of the Director includes "the proper discharge of the functions of the service, for the purpose of preventing or detecting serious crime". The Director has to ensure that under s.2(2)b, the "service does not take any action to further the interests of any political party". The legislation, however, is vague on the arrangements for ministerial responsibility. The Government is presently agreed that some form of committee should be set up composed of Privy Councillors to oversee the work of the security services. There is little guidance in the legislation as to when Ministers ought be consulted or the relationship between the Minister and the Director. The implication is that the Director should have broad discretion in carrying out the various duties under the Act.

20–063   Prior to the passage of the Act it was common practice for the security services to operate alongside the Special Branch officers designated for that purpose by each police force. In 1992 the Government announced that the main responsibility for detecting terrorists would be devolved to MI5 away from the Special Branch and the Anti-terrorist branch of the Metropolitan Police. The supremacy of the intelligence officers over the police may be in part a refocusing of their activities in the aftermath of the collapse of the Soviet Union and a perceived end to the military threat of the Soviet Union.

20–064   The Security Services Act 1989 also contains considerable legal powers for the security services to carry out their activities. Prior to 1989, doubt was expressed about the legal powers of the security services to engage in covert activities. S.3 of the Act remedies such gaps which may have existed in the law by the use of warrants issued by the Home Secretary. A warrant may authorise entry onto property and the "taking of such action" as is specified in the warrant and thought to be necessary. The power to issue a warrant in such circumstances depends on whether the value of the information is likely "to be of substantial value in assisting the Service to discharge its functions" and "cannot reasonably be obtained by other means". This gives extremely wide powers first to the Home Secretary to authorise warrants and second to the security services to carry on their activities. Information obtained under a warrant may not be disclosed as the Security Services Act 1989 makes disclosures a criminal offence.

20–065   It is noteworthy that the powers are Executive-based and there is no recourse to a judicial element which is customary in the granting of warrants for example under PACE 1984. This leaves judicial review as the main means to challenge the decision of the Home Secretary or the activities of the security services. Judicial review[25] is limited

[25] See Leigh and Lustgarten "The Security Service Act 1989" (1989) 52 *Modern Law Review* 801; see also Cm.2523 (1994).

in such cases because historically judges have been reluctant to look behind the "national interest" and the opportunities for challenge will usually be confined to challenges after the warrants have been issued.

The procedure for granting warrants, which makes use of the Home Secretary's **20–066** powers, is likened to any other delegated authority without any special procedure for obtaining the Home Secretary's permission. There is no requirement to check the nature of the information, its source, reliability, the period for which the warrant may be issued and the places or people that may be affected. Critics of the Act have pointed to the systems in operation in both Canada and Australia which have greater accountability built into the system of granting of authority to the security services.

Although the statutory authority for warrants is very extensive, there is the question **20–067** of whether prerogative powers may co-exist with statutory authority. The scope of the prerogative is unclear and the question of whether prerogative powers remain after the statute is open to conjecture.

The Security Services Act 1989 also provides procedures for complaints. A tribunal **20–068** for the investigation of complaints against the security services is created with the Security Services Commissioner to undertake investigations with a duty on every member of the security services and every official of the Home Office to "disclose or give to the Commissioner such documents or information" as he may require for the purpose of enabling him to discharge his functions. Reports, including an annual report may be made to the Prime Minister and the Prime Minister is under a duty to lay the annual report before Parliament.[26]

The Intelligence Services Act 1994 performs similar functions for the Secret **20–68a** Intelligence Service (MI6) and the Government Communications Headquarters (GCHQ) as outlined under the Security Service Act 1989 for MI5. The 1994 Act attempts to strike a balance between more openness and the protection of the national interest. Ss.1(1) and 3(1) are very widely drawn setting out the remit of the operations of MI6 and their functions. Little information can be gained from the definition contained in the Act except its vagueness. For example one function is to protect the "economic well-being of the United Kingdom" and this finds its place alongside the function of "support of the prevention or detection of serious crime".

The Act establishes a committee composed of M.P.s and members of the House of **20–069** Lords to examine the administration, expenditure and policy of the three services MI5, MI6 and GCHQ. The committee is called the Intelligence and Security Committee. However, its function is not to review operational matters and it may not summon witnesses. In addition there is a tribunal for the purpose of investigating complaints against any one of the three services. The tribunal has no powers to compel the attendance of witnesses, its reasoning is kept confidential and its decisions are not open to challenge in the courts. S.9(4) of the 1994 Act stipulates that the decisions of the Tribunal and the Commissioner "shall not be subject to appeal or liable to be questioned in any court".

The Intelligence and Security Committee is intended to supplement the appoint- **20–070** ment of a Commissioner under the 1989 Act. The Commissioner's reports are delivered to the Prime Minister who acts as a filter before the release of the report to

[26] D. Cayley Chung (1985) 26 Harvard *International Law Journal* 234 and J.L.J. Edwards (1985) *Oxford Journal of Legal Studies* 143. H.P. Lee (1989) 38 *International and Comparative Legal Quarterly* 890. See Ewing and Gearty, *Freedom under Thatcher* (1990), pp.130–136.

Parliament. This allows the Prime Minister of the day to censor the contents of reports and clearly this provides an inadequate parliamentary check on the activities of the security services. Taken together the Security Services Act 1989 and the Intelligence Services Act 1994 provide a statutory framework for the security services.

20–071   The Security Service Act 1996 adds a further dimension to the law. The 1996 Act gives freedom to the security services to become involved in the "prevention and detection of serious crime". This inclusion of policing functions brings the activities of the security services into line with what many regarded as present day practice. As part of the programme to encourage a National Crime Squad the 1996 Act amends the Security Service Act 1989 and the Intelligence Services Act 1994. The Secretary of State may issue in certain specified circumstances general warrants to enter property or to interfere with wireless telegraphy in circumstances that would otherwise be unlawful. This represents a considerable extension of the legal powers of the security service but in a realistic way it may only reflect the reality of how powers were exercised in the past.

20–072   Reform of the law on surveillance such as telephone tapping and the interception of letters was introduced under the Interception of Communication Act 1985. The *Malone Case*[27] established that telephone tapping was in violation of Article 8 of the European Convention on Human Rights. The case drew attention to the regulation of such practices carried out in the United Kingdom through administrative practices. There was no direct statutory authority for phone tapping. It was argued that s.80 of the Post Office Act 1969 required the Post Office to make available to the police information gained through metering phone calls for the detection of criminal activity.

20–073   The 1985 Act creates a new offence of unlawful interception of communications by post or by means of a public telecommunications system. The offence is widely drawn and may be committed by journalists, newspapers or others in both the public or private sector. The assumption underlying the Act is that the Home Secretary will continue to make use of warrants authorising the interception of communications. S.2 of the Act authorises such warrants for the purposes of the interests of national security, preventing or detecting serious crime or for the purposes of safeguarding the economic well-being of the United Kingdom. Although attempts were made in Parliament to restrict the scope of the issuing of warrants to specific purposes such as the defence of the realm or to prevent subversions of terrorism or espionage, this was rejected in favour of the catch-all quality of the legislation. One troublesome concept is "national security", a phrase that is ideally suited to exclude much judicial scrutiny of the discretion of the Executive.

20–074   Also noteworthy is that the issuing of warrants remains vested in the relevant Secretary of State. In the past there was no judicial or independent element in the decision whether or not to issue a warrant and this has been objected to on the basis that it would be more desirable to subject such a power to judicial control. Since 1966 the Prime Minister has given assurances that the telephones of M.P.s were immune from interception. The issuing of warrants and the coverage of information obtained in the warrants leaves many critics of the system uneasy. The scope of the warrant may specify a single individual or organisation, but this would not prevent the tapping of many phones over a protracted period of time without any further need to re-apply for

---

[27] *Malone v UK*, Eur. Court H.R., Series A, No.82 (August 2, 1985); (1984) 7 E.H.R.R. 14.

a warrant. Bailey, Harris and Jones have noted that there were on average over 500 warrants, the majority for the interception of telephones[28]:

"Most warrants concerned 'serious crime'. 60% of the warrants requested by the police related to the importation or distribution of drugs. Just under 50% of all warrants issued at the request of the police have resulted directly or indirectly in arrests and in some cases in the recovery of property."

Under the 1985 Act there was a Commissioner appointed by the Prime Minister together with a quasi-judicial Tribunal to provide the main complaints procedures. The decision of the Tribunal is final and may not be reviewed by the courts though this may still leave open consideration by the European Convention on Human Rights. The membership of the Tribunal is for a limited fixed period of five years. The Tribunal has powers to determine whether a warrant to intercept information is properly issued under the Act. This refers to the question of whether there are adequate grounds for issuing the warrant and that statutory procedures are complied with. The means adopted to test the validity of the warrant procedure is akin to a court of law when exercising judicial review powers. This leaves considerable latitude with the security services as the courts are reluctant to apply more than a cursory consideration of national security matters. Indeed, on the basis of the *Wednesbury*[29] criteria of unreasonableness, in most cases ministerial discretion will be presumed to conform with the law unless it is so unreasonable that no reasonable Minister could have taken such a decision. The Commission has only found errors in the issuing of warrants of a minor and insubstantial nature. There has not been a finding that a warrant has been issued without cause. **20–075**

The Commissioner must report to the Prime Minister on an annual basis. It appears that the remit of the 1985 Act does not cover electronic bugging devices. This leaves open the questions of what controls may exist and whether such devices should be used by the authorities. The Commissioner has three functions and responsibilities under the 1985 Act. First, to keep under review the various functions carried out by the Home Secretary conferred by the Act. Secondly, to keep under review the arrangements for restricting the use of information obtained under the intercepted material. Thirdly, to give assistance to the Tribunal to carry out its statutory functions. These arrangements have now been changed by recent legislation. **20–076**

The Police Act 1997 has the limited objective of regulating surveillance that involves entry onto property or interference of property rights This regulates bugging devices where there is an interference in property rights. The Regulation of Investigatory Powers Act 2000 regulates the interception of communications that are made by postal service or telephone. S.1 provides that it is an offence to "intentionally or without lawful defence to interfere without lawful authority" with any communication in the course of its transmission by means of a public or private telecommunications system in the UK. A warrant may be issued and there is under Pt III of the Act provision for an Interception of Communication Commissioner, appointed by the Prime Minister, replacing the arrangements under the 1985 Act for a Commissioner. There is also an **20–077**

[28] Bailey, Harris and Jones, *Civil Liberties: Cases and Materials* p.517.
[29] [1948] 1 K.B. 223.

Intelligence Service Commissioner and an Investigatory Powers Commissioner for Northern Ireland.

20–078 S.65 creates a Tribunal to hear complaints in respect of matters that fall under the Act. There is also a statutory tort under s.1(3) for any unlawful interception in communication.

PRESS AND MEDIA

20–079 The press and media are subject to a wide variety of legal controls over what they may publish or broadcast. Newspapers are subject to the Defence Press and Broadcasting Committee. This Committee is generally referred to as "the D notice system". D notices may be addressed to radio, television and national and provincial editors of newspapers. In essence the system advises that publication or broadcasting of information would not be in the public interest. The composition of the D notice Committee is based on four government representatives, permanent civil servants, and other representatives of the press, both national and provincial, and the broadcasting agencies.

20–080 In practice the minority representatives from the Government were mainly influential in the work of the Committee. A tacit agreement up until 1967 provided that newspapers that accepted and implemented the advice of the Committee were provided with immunity from any prosecution under the Official Secrets Acts— although in fact there is no direct relationship between the D notice system and the Official Secrets Act. Editors cannot claim that because an item of news was cleared before the Committee that this absolved them of their statutory duties under the Official Secrets Acts.

20–081 In 1979–80 the system of D notices was reviewed[30] by the Defence Select Committee and evidence given which indicated that the system was not working effectively. Chapman Pincher, a journalist had revealed in 1978 that the D notice system was dependent on the Secretary of State indicating whether the story was covered by a D notice and if not then the journalist would not be prosecuted if the story was published. This had gained some press confidence in the system but once the Secretary of State declined to make any implied undertaking the system became virtually unused. As indicated in the discussion of the *Spycatcher* story, the international press makes it more difficult to retain stories within the national boundaries of the United Kingdom.

20–082 The Select Committee divided on the issue of whether the D notice system should be reformed. It agreed that some forms of secrecy required control over the press or broadcasting authorities. The Committee concluded that the essence of the D notice should be published as common practice was not to mention the use of the D notice system. After consideration of the Committee's report, the Government decided to retain the D Notice Committee but its operation may be revised at some future date.

[30] Third Report of the House of Commons Defence Committee, *The D Notice System: Observations Presented by the Secretary of State for Defence* Cmnd.8129 (1981). Fourth Report of the Defence Committee (1982–83): *Previous Recommendations of the Committee* (1982–83 HC 55). The programme "My Country Right or Wrong", see *Economical with the Truth* (Oliver and Kingsford-Smith ed., 1990). *Justice Report on Privacy and the Law* (1970); The Younger Committee Report, *Report of the Committee on Privacy* Cmnd.5012 (1972). *Report of the Committee on Privacy and Related Matters*, Cm.1102 (1990).

A general introduction to the work of the Committee was published and the Government have promised that the composition of the Committee might be reviewed in the future.

The advantage of the present system is that it allows representatives of the media to consider the matter in a reponsible manner. The disadvantage is that there is little openness in how the system actually works and the criteria used are far from clear. A more fundamental weakness of the system was revealed when the BBC attempted to broadcast a programme on the *Spycatcher* book. The programme had received clearance from the secretary to the D Notice Committee on the basis that it did not provide any material which was a threat to national security. However the Government sought and obtained injunctions to prevent the broadcast of interviews being held about the programme on the basis that there was a breach of confidence in the disclosure made in the programme. The explanation for the apparent disparity is that the Attorney-General based his injunction on breach of confidence whereas the secretary to the D Notice Committee based his clearance on the basis of national security. There is therefore some doubt about the effectiveness of the D Notice Committee when the Government is actively pursuing greater use of civil remedies rather than the use of the criminal law. **20–083**

There appears to be a case for maintaining some form of D Notice Committee. For the purposes of wartime expediency it would appear to offer a reasonably effective means to preserve some balance between freedom of the press to publish information and the protection of the public interest. But in peacetime it would appear to have become an anachronism, although it is influential with many newspapers and their reporters but in fact largely ignored when the availability of news on an international basis facilitates the dissemination of information so easily available instantaneously on fax machines. **20–084**

This raises the important question of the extent to which the right to privacy may exist in English law and how this right may be protected by the courts. The Calcutt Committee in 1990 concluded that the most appropriate definition of privacy might cover[31]: **20–085**

"The right of the individual to be protected against intrusion into his personal life or affairs, or those of his family, by direct physical means or by publication of information."

Following the recommendations of the Calcutt report the Press Complaints Commission was established in 1991, replacing the Press Council established in 1953. The Commission is a non-statutory body comprising a chairman and 15 members, one-third of whom are not associated with the press. Any person may complain to the press and the Commission may investigate and return findings such as an adverse adjudication which must be published by the newspapers in question. There is no legal obligation to publish and the criticism about the Commission is that it lacks sufficient legal powers and sanctions. **20–086**

Further reforms of the law have been considered by a second report carried out by the Calcutt[32] Committee. The second report went much further than previous reports **20–087**

---

[31] Calcutt Committee, First Report (1990).
[32] Calcutt Committee, Second Report (January 1993).

by recommending a statutory tribunal to replace the Press Commission. This favoured a move away from voluntary self-regulation in favour of statutory and legal regulation. The tribunal might be presided over by a senior judge appointed by the Lord Chancellor with powers to fine and place injunctions on newspapers. In addition Calcutt recommended that electronic eavesdropping and long-range photography on private property should be prohibited.

20–088   The press reacted unfavourably to proposals for tighter regulation. In that light the National Heritage Select Committee recommended that there should be a strengthening of the law both civil and criminal on privacy.[33] The Committee favoured the retention of some form of Press Complaints Commission but replacing the existing Press Complaints Commission with a Press Commission to uphold press freedom. The new commission should have powers to order fines and to order publication of apologies and in suitable cases the award of compensation. An appointed ombudsman to be appointed by the Lord Chancellor and funded by the Treasury to supervise adjudications of disputes, with the statutory power to compel newspapers to print apologies in a particular way, including the power of fines, is intended to strengthen supervision of the press. The Government has rejected the idea of Calcutt's statutory tribunal but is considering the best way forward in the light of the proposals. Recent newspaper articles on certain Government Ministers, and the private lives of the Royal Family and other public figures have drawn attention to the need to increase regulation of the press.

20–089   The press and media may come under considerable government influence in matters of national security. In the case of broadcasting, fear of prosecution under the Official Secrets Acts may result in television or radio programmes being withdrawn. In the same period as the Ponting trial, Channel 4 withdrew one of its television programmes "20/20 Vision" which contained detailed allegations made by Cathy Massiter about the use of MI5 but after a period of delay the programme was eventually shown.

20–090   The media is also subject to various search and seizure powers either under the Official Secrets Acts or under the ordinary law. For example there is a power for the police to search with a warrant under s.9 of the Official Secrets Act 1911 and this may be applied to discover journalists' information. In 1986, the BBC had commissioned a film series entitled "Secret Society" under the direction of Duncan Campbell, a journalist working in the intelligence field. The programme revealed the cost and extent of a secret Defence Ministry project to put a spy satellite into orbit. The programme was banned and an injunction obtained banning Campbell from publishing the story. A search of Campbell's home and offices, and also the Glasgow offices of the BBC, allowed the police to remove substantial numbers of documents. In Scotland, powers under s.9 of the Official Secrets Act 1911 were used, while in England, a warrant was issued under PACE 1984.

20–091   Little of substance was achieved in the use of these powers. Campbell had already published the story in the *New Statesman* before the injunction had been granted. The BBC eventually broadcast an agreed version of the programme.

20–092   The media is also subject to ordinary civil action in the form of actions for libel and defamation. In *Joyce v Sengupta*[34] the Court of Appeal accepted that a plaintiff could

---

[33] Report of the National Heritage Committee, *Privacy and Media Intrusion* (HMSO, March 1993).
[34] *Independent*, August 11, 1992.

establish more than one cause of action against a defendant and this might include both a claim for defamation and a claim for malicious falsehood. The latter gave rise to the possibility of legal aid, while the former did not. The plaintiff's claim arose out of a newspaper article which asserted that the plaintiff, then in the employment of the royal household, had stolen certain letters of an intimate character and had handed them to the national press. In such a case the plaintiff's intention in pursuing a claim in the courts was not dependent on the award of damages but the main means open to a plaintiff to clear her name.

Broadcasting in the United Kingdom is also the focus of State influence. Preserving independence for broadcasters is equally important as preserving the freedom of the press. In the case of the British Broadcasting Corporation (BBC), since 1926 it has been constituted by Royal Charter. The BBC provides public broadcasting on a non-commercial basis, funded through a licence fee payable by the public who have television sets. The BBC operates under its Charter, its Licence and Agreement[35] and where appropriate it receives directions under the relevant authority of the Charter or its licence from the Home Secretary. Failure to comply with such a direction might result in the withdrawal of the BBC's licence. The BBC is expected and required to act in a politically impartial manner and its programmes must be consistent with good taste and public opinion. The courts may be invited to consider whether the broadcasting authorities have complied with the standards of good taste.   **20–093**

The use of the Home Secretary's directions is rare. In 1927 in the early life of the BBC the corporation was forbidden to broadcast matters involving any religious, political or industrial controversy. There is a convention that the BBC should not derogate from the authority of Parliament in matters of public record. In recent years the televising of both Houses of Parliament has greatly assisted public information on the workings of Parliament and the broadcast of debates and the hearings of select committees is said to educate the public on the workings of democracy and this has been regarded as beneficial to the role of broadcasters.   **20–094**

In 1988 the Home Secretary announced a ban on the BBC and the independent broadcasting companies from broadcasting the spoken words of members of the IRA or its supporters including Sinn Fein. This ban was intended to prevent public support or sympathy for the IRA or like organisations.   **20–095**

The Government has been active in opposing programmes that in any way are regarded as promoting the cause of terrorism. Programmes which may be critical of the security services may indirectly appear supportive of the terrorist cause and the drawing of boundaries in such cases as to what is or is not permissible is often controversial. The Government has removed the ban on the broadcasting of Sinn Fein in an effort to expedite the peace process. The ban was seen as counterproductive, as the television authorities interpreted the ban as allowing actors' voices to replace the words of Sinn Fein spokesmen while broadcasting interviews.[36]   **20–096**

In recent years the focus of attention on the BBC is on the role of the Board of Governors. There is a full-time Chairman and a Deputy-Chairman with part-time members of the Board meeting usually at least once a month. Discussion has focused on the role of the Governor in the day-to-day affairs of the BBC, in particular in the question of operational decisions and the policy of the BBC.   **20–097**

[35] Cmnd.8313; Cmnd.8233.
[36] *R. v Secretary of State for the Home Deparment Ex p. Brind* [1991] 2 W.L.R. 588.

20–098   Political parties from all shades of opinion have from time to time alleged bias in reporting and presentation of political views. Particularly when the government of the day is loud in such accusations, the BBC has been placed on the defensive. The style and direction of the BBC is under pressure to provide greater accountability for the expenditure of public money. Quality assurance, better management style and greater attention to business principles have been encouraged in the run-up to the period for the renewal of the BBC's Charter.

20–099   In January 1993 the BBC Chairman and Deputy-Chairman were criticised for allowing the appointment of John Birt as a new Managing Director of the BBC to make his salary payable not under the PAYE scheme but to a company set up for this purpose. Resolution of this problem has called into question the organisation and structure of the management of the BBC.

20–100   In the case of commercial broadcasting, regulation is provided on a statutory basis. The Broadcasting Act 1990 replaced the old Independent Broadcasting Authority and, for cable television, the Cable Authority. A single authority, the Independent Television Commission (ITC) regulates and licences, with the exception of the BBC, all television, cable and satellite services. The process of franchising television licences depends on bids being made from commercial organisations to carry out the terms of the licence. The ITC is under a duty to consider whether the licence holder "is a fit and proper person to hold" a licence. There are restrictions on certain groups with political or religious connotations from holding a licence.

20–101   S.10 of the Broadcasting Act 1990 grants the relevant Minister or the Secretary of State powers to direct licence holders to include announcements or to make a notice to licence holders directing that certain specified matters may not be included in programmes. There is also a Programme Code[37] setting out the standards of broadcasting and the balance required in programming. This is in addition to the Broadcasting Standards Council, established as a consumer watchdog in 1988 to oversee broadcasters' activities in respect of violence, sex, taste and decency, and given statutory recognition under s.152 of the Broadcasting Act 1990.

20–102   In common with the BBC, commercial television has found controversy in its desire to broadcast investigative programmes involving terrorist activities and the security services. In 1988, Thames Television broadcast "Death on the Rock", an investigative programme into the shooting of three members of the IRA by members of the SAS in Gibraltar. The programme received criticism from the then Prime Minister and renewed debate began over whether there had been a shoot-to-kill policy on the part of the security forces. The criticism of the programme resulted in an inquiry into the objectivity and the factual basis of the programme.

20–103   Broadcasters face a climate of opinion which may favour further restrictions on reporting of terrorist activities especially when they involve the activities of the security services. The ban on broadcasting the spoken words of terrorist groups and Sinn Fein has contributed to a greater degree of "self-censorship" within broadcasting. In fact this has probably led to a more effective system of control than would have been possible through the passage of legislation prohibiting the broadcasting of a wide range of investigative programmes.

[37] February 1991.

FREEDOM OF EXPRESSION

The Public Interest Disclosure Act 1998 and the Freedom of Information Act 2000

Freedom of expression is commonly acknowledged to be a fundamental attribute of **20–104** many Western-style democracies. Because of the absence of any written constitutional protection of this fundamental concept, its existence may depend on the interpretation of various laws designed to protect the public in terms of blasphemy, defamation, obscenity and contempt of court. Street summarised the distinctive qualities of civil liberties in the United Kingdom[38]:

> "Civil liberties in Britain have been shown to be a patchwork. Some of them rest on the chance that citizens have sued each other and given the opportunity to declare some isolated legal rule. Some rest on sporadic legislation, often passed to meet some specific emergency real or imaginery. The extent of inroads on certain freedoms rests on the subtleties of ministerial responsibility and the muted insistence of Whitehall to be allowed to govern unhindered."

Secrecy and confidentiality discussed above operate in a society which is accustomed to **20–105** legal controls over information in the form of censorship. In that context the criminal law and in certain circumstances the civil law, has developed an extensive jurisdiction over the citizen's freedom to see, hear and read matter which is deemed unsuitable. Such freedoms are constrained on the basis of providing legal restraints justified in the public interest. A difficult balance must be struck in such cases between providing a remedy for the citizen to protect his or her rights and the right of freedom of information for the public. The law may also extend to cover actions for breach of copyright or breach of confidence. This may also form the basis of civil actions which allow for the use of injunctions to restrain publication of the information and for damages by way of compensation.[39]

The acknowledgment that an open society is in the public interest is in part the **20–106** reason for the Public Interest Disclosure Act 1998. The Act provides whistle-blowers with limited protection against dismissal or disciplinary action. Protection is provided by reading into the Employment Protection Act 1996 the protections as rights for employees. This means that a person who falls within the category of protection is regarded as unfairly dismissed or whose redundancy is regarded as unfair if based on the fact of disclosure. Not everyone in employment is included—the police and security services are excluded. Protection is provided on the basis of the following:

- A protected disclosure is one where on the basis of reasonable belief, a criminal offence has been committed; or a legal obligation has been breached; or that health and safety of a worker has been endangered; or that the environment is likely to be damaged.

[38] H. Street, *Freedom, Individual and the Law* (1982), p.307.
[39] Copyright, Designs and Patents Act 1988.

• A qualified disclosure is one where it is made in good faith to the discloser's employer; or in the course of legal advice; or made to a proscribed person such as the Health and Safety Executive; or is of an exceptionally serious nature.

20–107   The Freedom of Information Act 2000 attempts to build on past efforts to promote greater openness in government through the *Code of Practice on Access to Government Information*. Wider use of web pages and the internet by government departments and transparency through Next Steps agencies publishing information on their activities are encouraged. The Act is intended to be gradually phased into law and applies to England, Wales and Northern Ireland. The substantive change contained for the first time contained in s.1 is a general right of access to information held by public authorities. Rights under s.1 include the right to know if there is relevant information and, if it exists, the right to be given the information. There is a corresponding duty on public authorities to comply with these rights. Public authorities have been generally defined to cover local and central government and a list in Sch.1 may be further added to or amended by the Secretary of State. There is also a code of practice and Pt 1 of the Act requires that the Lord Chancellor should issue a code of good practice in the keeping, management and destruction of records. There is an Information Commissioner to whom complaints may be submitted and this role assumes responsibilities for the Data Protection Act 1998. However encouraging this innovation may be, it is provided with restrictions and limitations. There are limits set for the cost of compliance and if the limits are exceeded the public authority may refuse to comply with the request. If the request for information is regarded as vexatious then this may also be a ground for refusal. There is also a fee payable.

20–108   Pt II of the Act provides details of circumstances where information is exempt from disclosure and the duty to confirm or deny the existence of information does not apply. These are ss.26–29, ss.32–35, ss.38–39, and ss.42–44 of the Act. The range of matters covered includes defence, international relations and relations within the United Kingdom, the economy, court and audit records, matters of parliamentary privilege, the formulation of government policy, communications with Her Majesty the Queen, health and safety, the environment, information protected by legal professional privilege, commercial interests and circumstances under s.44 where information may be prohibited from disclosure such as contempt of court.

20–109   The extensive and vague nature of the exemptions gives rise to some disappointment that the Act will not do much to improve information flow and greater transparency.

Blasphemy and Defamation

20–110   At common law it is an offence to publish blasphemous matter whether orally or in writing. The definition of blasphemous is to deny the Christian religion, the Bible or the Book of Common Prayer. In *Whitehouse v Gay News Ltd*[40] the House of Lords held that it is a blasphemous publication if it is said to be indecent or offensive and is likely to outrage the general body of Christian believers. This was the first prosecution for 60

---

[40] [1979] A.C. 617.

years and the material in question was a poem which was accompanied by an illustration vilifying Christ in his life and crucifixion. While offensive to many people the material in question did not lead to a breach of the peace and there was no evidence that it was likely to provoke violence or civil disorder. Nevertheless a prosecution could be successful once it was shown that the general body of Christian believers might be shocked. The only mental requirements of the crime were proof that the defendants intended to publish the offending words.

More recently the question of applying the blasphemy laws to religions other than Christian ones was considered in *Ex p. Choudhury*[41] The material in question was the book *The Satanic Verses* by the author Salman Rushdie. The court held that the law only applied to the Christian religion. The Law Commission's recommendation[42] that the law could be abolished reflects a growing awareness that in a multi-national and multi-religious society, it is unfair to protect one religious group to the exclusion of any other.   **20–111**

Freedom of Expression under Article 10 of the Convention does admit the protection "of a reputation or rights of others". The law of defamation exists to protect citizens or the State against written or spoken words that expose the person to ridicule, or cause hatred or contempt. Defamatory words published in the course of a performance of a play amount to a criminal libel under ss.4 and 6 of the Theatres Act 1968. Defamatory matter usually consists of spoken words, but when written it is libel, and when accompanied by gestures is slander. Libel is writing which tends to vilify a person and bring them into hatred or contempt or ridicule.   **20–112**

Under s.5 of the Libel Act 1843, publication of a libel is a common law misdemeanour but it is rarely prosecuted. Normally criminal libel is focused only on serious matters. However sometimes, but not always, this may involve the question of whether a breach of the peace is involved. The use of the civil law is more frequent. The remedy usually lies in damages but the use of an interlocutory injunction may be more effective to prevent the dissemination of the offending material. It is a defence to show that the material published was true or was a fair comment or published in the public interest.   **20–113**

The Defamation Act 1996 categorises different protections in terms of privileged information. Absolute privilege at both common law and statute applies to circumstances whereby no proceedings may be brought in respect of them. Court proceedings or privileged statements such as the proceedings of the House of Commons will not allow for a civil action to be taken, but may well involve investigation by the Committee of Privileges should there be any abuse of the privileges of the House of Commons. Absolute privilege attaches to the judicial proceedings and communication between Officers of State.   **20–114**

Qualified privilege attaches to the communications between members of the public and M.P.s, M.P.s and Ministers, in the proceedings of public meetings of local councils, and in the administration of tribunals and inquiries. Before the Human Rights Act 1998 came into force the attempt to establish a new category of qualified privilege failed when Mr Reynolds, the former Irish Prime Minister sued the *Sunday Times* over a story suggesting he had lied to the Irish Parliament and misled his cabinet   **20–115**

---

[41] *R. v Chief Metropolitan Stipendiary Magistrate Ex p. Choudhury* [1991] 1 Q.B. 429.
[42] Law Commission No.145, *Offences Against Religion and Public Worship* (1985).

colleagues. The jury found that the newspaper had not acted maliciously in publishing the story but found that the statements were defamatory and untrue. In the event he received damages. There is reluctance to develop new categories of qualified privilege. It will be difficult for the courts to balance the protections under Article 10 of the Convention and the law on defamation.[43]

20–116   In *Loutchansky v Times (No. 2)*[44] the Court of Appeal considered the question of qualified privilege within the context of whether there was a duty on journalists to publish defamatory words at large; the standard to be applied is that of responsible journalism. If the publication attracted qualified privilege this would provide publishers with a complete defence. However in assessing journalists' standards, the court should consider that journalists should be rigorous and not lax in their approach to publication. However, it was important not to set the standard so high that newspapers would be unable to discharge their proper functions.

Contempt of Court

20–117   Contempt of court provides protection for the administration of justice to ensure that it is free from interference and obstruction. The fear of contempt proceedings may cause newspapers or the media not to publish or broadcast the details of their stories and this may interfere with the freedom of expression. A distinction is drawn by the English courts between civil and criminal contempt. In the case of civil contempt, this may arise in disobedience of a court order such as an injunction. Criminal contempt may arise where there are publications prejudicial to a fair trial or civil proceedings, publications which interfere with the course of justice, contempt in the face of the court or acts which interfere with the course of justice. Newspapers may often find that contempt proceedings are used against them. In *Att.-Gen. v Times Newspapers Ltd*,[45] the House of Lords considered contempt proceedings arising out of the publication by the *Sunday Times* of a series of investigative articles relating to the drug Thalidomide. The House of Lords held that the Attorney-General was the proper person to institute contempt proceedings and that injunctions could be granted to restrain publication of any articles which may be prejudicial to a fair hearing of the case.

20–118   The law of contempt may severely inhibit the freedom of the press to publish articles. Some reform but not codification of the common law rules of contempt was provided in the Contempt of Court Act 1981. This followed recommendations for reform of the law, after the Phillimore Committee Report[46] in 1974 and after the Thalidomide case was considered by the European Court of Human Rights, where the court held[47] that Article 10 of the Convention which concerns the right to freedom of expression had been infringed and the restrictions imposed by the injunction were not necessary in a democratic society.

20–119   Newspapers may attempt to protect their sources of information. In the case of Sarah Tisdell, the civil servant who copied documents relating to the defence

---

[43] *Loutchansky v Times Newspapers Ltd* [2001] 4 All E.R. 115.
[44] [2002] 1 All E.R. 652.
[45] [1974] A.C. 273.
[46] Cmnd.5794 (1974).
[47] *Sunday Times v UK* [1979] 2 E.H.R.R. 245.

arrangements for the reception of cruise missiles at RAF Greenham Common, and leaked the information to the *Guardian* newspaper, the identification of Tisdell followed after an investigation of the leak. The Government instituted proceedings for the return of the documents used by the newspaper. S.10 of the Contempt of Court Act 1981 provides that the court may not require disclosure of information "unless it be established to the satisfaction of the court that disclosure is necessary in the interests of justice or national security or for the prevention of disorder or crime". The Court of Appeal required the newspaper to return the documents which enabled the identity of Sarah Tisdell to be known and she was later successfully prosecuted. Later on the basis of the legal principles involved, the newspaper appealed to the House of Lords.[48] Lord Diplock pointed out that s.10 did not contain any reference to "the public interest." A majority of 3 to 2 concluded that the need to find the identity of the person who leaked the documents was in the national interest. The claim of national security appears sufficiently strong to provide justification for the courts to require disclosure of information by the press. In the *Tisdell* case, national security was accepted by the courts on the basis of an affidavit sworn by the Ministry of Defence establishment officer that national security required the return of the leaked documents.

The courts have accepted that on general principle a liberal interpretation should be given to s.10. However Lord Bridge in *X v Morgan-Grampian Publishers Ltd*[49] noted that in the balance to be struck between non-disclosure and disclosure, the courts would consider whether the information was obtained legitimately ("this will enhance the importance of protecting the source") whereas if the information is obtained illegally, this will diminish "the importance of protecting the source", unless there are counterbalancing factors such as "a clear public interest in the publication of the information, as in the classic case where the source has acted for the purpose of exposing iniquity." **20–120**

In this area the courts focus their attention on the legality and the motives behind the giving of information to newspapers. The question of the content of the material, its reliability and whether, on the merits of the information contained in the material, disclosure of the source of information is in the public interest appears a secondary consideration. **20–121**

Contempt of court protects the deliberations of jurors, the interference with witnesses and the course of justice. All are protected by the courts as part of their role in preventing any intentional contempt. In the case of jury deliberations, contempt of court proceedings were instituted after publication in the *New Statesman* of an interview carried out with a member of the jury in the trial of Jeremy Thorpe and others. Publications prejudicial to a criminal trial or civil proceedings are likely to fall within the remit of contempt.[50] There is some doubt as to whether contempt may apply to proceedings of a tribunal. The wording of s.19 of the Contempt of Court Act 1981 defines court as "any tribunal or body exercising the judicial power of the state". This has been narrowly interpreted by the courts in relation to a Mental Health Review **20–122**

[48] *Secretary of State for Defence v Guardian Newspapers Ltd* [1985] A.C. 339.
[49] [1991] 1 A.C. 1.
[50] *Att.-Gen. v New Statesman* [1981] Q.B. 1. Contempt of Court Act 1981, ss.2, 32 and Sched.1. *Att.-Gen. v News Groups Newspapers plc* [1989] Q.B. 110. *Att.-Gen. v Associated Newspapers Group plc* [1989] 1 All E.R. 604.

Tribunal; the Divisional Court held that the Tribunal was not a court for the purposes of the Contempt of Court Act.

20–123   Journalists are aware of the potential problems that may arise when required to disclose their sources. S.19 of the Terrorism Act 2000 may apply, thus this has the potential to restrict freedom of expression. There is a defence available under s.19(3) where there might be a reasonable excuse for not making the disclosure, for example if one's life is in danger but the scope of the defence is uncertain. Restrictions on freedom of expression that fall under s.19 must be read to be consistent with Article 10 of the Convention.

SUMMARY AND CONCLUSIONS

20–124   For many centuries the climate of secrecy has been endemic to the culture of government in the United Kingdom. Yet this must be set against a background of what many perceive to be a remarkably open and free society. This apparent contradiction appears to come from the fact that the United Kingdom has much less formal protection of fundamental rights and freedoms when compared to international standards. This situation is changing, especially with the Human Rights Act 1998. However, there is no room for complacency. A major obstacle towards greater openness comes from the private sector and the need to preserve confidential commercial information which is market sensitive and to balance disclosure that is in the public interest. It is clear that access to information is a key element in any democratic system. There is a perceptible change in the direction of greater openness as demonstrated by many new initiatives, not least the greater use of electronic information and websites. However there is little reason for complacency and it is unclear whether the Freedom of Information Act 2000 and the Public Interest Disclosure Act 1998 will change the culture of secrecy.

FURTHER READING

P. Birkinshaw, *Freedom of Information* (3rd ed., 2001).

D. Vincent, *The Culture of Secrecy; Britain 1832-1998* (1998).

White Paper, *Your Rights to know*, Cm.3818, (1997).

Chapter 21

NORTHERN IRELAND

INTRODUCTION

Northern Ireland's constitutional arrangements and the use of emergency powers in response to serious civil disturbance are considered in this chapter. Experience in Northern Ireland has tested many institutions and constitutional innovations inherited from the link with Britain. Northern Ireland has experienced devolution in different forms. First, under the Government of Ireland Act 1920 which was replaced by the Northern Ireland Constitution Act 1973 with a modern model of devolution. However, the 1973 Act was never implemented because of the lack of agreement over the future of Northern Ireland among politicians in the Province. More recently Northern Ireland was granted devolved government under the Northern Ireland Act 1998. Northern Ireland offers an important case study of conflict and attempts at its resolution. The rich literature about its history and current problems provides constitutional scholars with a study of the limitations of law as well as access to debates about constitutional innovation and change.

    Northern Ireland's constitutional history and current arrangements may be examined in three periods. The first period dates from 1800 to the creation of Northern Ireland and its efforts at self-government under the Government of Ireland Act 1920, until 1972. In the nineteenth century, the Act of Union 1800 united Britain and Ireland. Under the Union, laws were passed at Westminster for Ireland. Ireland's constitutional arrangements were unique within the United Kingdom. Irish government was centred in Dublin Castle which contained the main offices of administration, centralised and well organised with a professional civil service having administrative control over the local administration of law and government. At its head was an appointed Lord Lieutenant and General Governor of Ireland who represented the main link between the British Cabinet and Irish administration. He was assisted by an appointed Chief Secretary as adviser and assistant who directed the administration of justice aided by the Lord Chancellor of Ireland, and various law officers. Irish law continued to hold its own distinctiveness. Irish courts and judiciary were separate from the courts and judiciary of England and Wales. The Government of Ireland Act 1920 created a Parliament for Northern Ireland with a Prime Minister and Cabinet, modelled on Westminster. The government of Northern Ireland had extensive legislative and executive powers under a devolved system of government, that maintained the sovereignty of the United Kingdom Parliament.

    The second period begins with the end of self-government in 1972 and the beginning of direct rule from Westminster and culminates in 1998 with the creation of the

21–001

21–002

21–003

Northern Ireland Assembly and the peace process. Since the late 1960s serious terrorist violence has necessitated emergency powers, including the abolition of jury trial for specific scheduled offences. Extensive emergency powers allow wide powers of arrest, search, seizure and the right to silence is suspended for terrorist offences. Many of these powers were at one time unique to Northern Ireland; now they are common throughout the United Kingdom. Events since the terrorist attacks in the United States on September 11, 2001 have drawn attention to the global environment in which emergency powers are being exercised. The "war on terrorism" has resulted in considerable strengthening of the ordinary law. The existence of wide emergency powers raises the question of how compatible emergency powers may be with the protection of civil liberties. Northern Ireland has been compared to a[1]:

> . . . laboratory in which to assess the strengths and weaknesses of two approaches to the Constitution: a pragmatic empiricist approach which is traditionally British, and a constitutional idealist approach, more prevalent for example in the United States and Canada."

21–004   Experiments in providing Northern Ireland with limited devolution had been attempted under the Government of Ireland Act 1920. The Northern Ireland Constitution Act 1973 consisted of first the suspension and later the abolition of the Northern Ireland Government and a period of direct rule from Westminster which presently endures with a new system of devolution under the Northern Ireland Act 1998. In 1985 the Anglo-Irish Agreement was signed between the two Governments of Britain and Ireland and provides for the Government of the Republic of Ireland to have an influence over policy matters for Northern Ireland. The 1985 Anglo-Irish Agreement is examined as to its constitutional significance for the future of Northern Ireland.

21–005   Amid further sectarian violence in Northern Ireland of escalating ferocity, further constitutional initiatives have been attempted. On December 15, 1993, the British Prime Minister and the Taoiseach made a Joint Declaration. The declaration declared a number of constitutional principles and political realities for the future of Northern Ireland. Both Governments entered a commitment that "following a cessation of violence", democratically mandated parties which establish a commitment to exclusively peaceful methods "are free to participate in discussion between both Governments and the political parties on the way ahead". Significantly the Joint Declaration clarified that the British Government have "no selfish strategic or economic interest in Northern Ireland". However, Unionists are assured that unification between North and South in a united Ireland can only be by agreement of the two parts respectively. How such an agreement might be achieved or, once achieved, tested in a constitutional sense is left unclear. The Irish government accepts that it would be wrong to impose a United Ireland. They undertake to examine "any elements in the democratic life and organisation of the Irish state" which are feared by Unionists. The Joint Declaration helped to make way for a series of initiatives ultimately culminating in all-party talks and agreement for peace in 1998.

---

[1] C. McCrudden, "Northern Ireland and the British Constitution" in *The Changing Constitution* (J. Jowell and D. Oliver ed., 2nd ed., 1989), pp.297–342; (3rd ed., 1994).

The IRA declared a "complete cessation of violence" on August 31, 1994. Since **21–006**
then attempts to continue the peace process have included questions of decommissioning of terrorist weapons, and the setting up of all-party talks with the inclusion of Sinn
Fein subject to agreements about the end to violence and the complete renunciation of
terrorist activities. There are some relevant statutory provisions. The Northern Ireland
(Entry to Negotiations, etc.) Act 1996 provided for elections in Northern Ireland to
allow all-party negotiations. The decommissioning of arms has continued to attract
attention; the Northern Ireland Arms Decommissioning Act 1997 provides a statutory
framework, first for five years for arms' decommissioning, and later extended by the
Northern Ireland Arms Decommissioning (Amendment) Act 2002.

The third period is the peace process and the ongoing struggle during a period of **21–007**
constitutional change in Northern Ireland. Devolution has been set up under the
Northern Ireland Act 1998. Building on past legislation there are numerous reforms.
In the area of the police and policing, the Police (Northern Ireland) Act 1998 sets up a
Police Ombudsman. There is a new Police Service for Northern Ireland under the
Police (Northern Ireland) Act 2000 implementing the reforms recommended by the
Independent Commission on Policing for Northern Ireland chaired by Chris Patten.
There is also a codification of the terrorist legislation under the Terrorism Act 2000,
applicable in Northern Ireland and throughout the United Kingdom. There is a
Human Rights Commission set up under Pt VII of the Northern Ireland Act 1998 as
part of the Belfast (Good Friday) Agreement in 1998. Proposals for Northern Ireland
to have its own Bill of Rights have been made by the Commission[2] in its consultative
role.

Northern Ireland continues to attract attention. It provides a case study of law and **21–008**
conflict in the context of a multi-cultural and religious society. It has prompted
innovative constitutional devices and techniques used in an effort to achieve political
stability. Northern Ireland provides an example of the limits of legal and political
power and the dilemma of democratic institutions when faced with interrelated social,
economic and constitutional problems. The peace process is not based on a single
event nor is it capable on its own of providing a permanent resolution of Northern
Ireland's problems. Its strength rests on providing to be a flexible basis for continued
negotiations; its weakness is the fragility of the political process upon which it
ultimately depends. Fundamental institutional change in Northern Ireland is also
ongoing and this process is susceptible to weakening the institutions that are
fundamental to the proper functioning of the state.

A fine balance is required between institutional building and creating the cultural **21–009**
arrangements whereby differing communities may co-exist. There is also an under-
standable perception that whereas legal change may be relatively easily
accomplished—thus the enactment of many substantial reforms—such changes may
have little real impact in the day-to-day life of ordinary people. For the foreseeable
future the peace process is therefore likely to require continuous attention and
adjustment to take account of the changing political life of Northern Ireland.[3] This
may be the most difficult part of the process. Changing hearts and minds may take

[2] Northern Ireland Human Rights Commission, *Making a Bill of Rights for Northern Ireland* (September, 2001).
[3] B. O'Leary *et al.*, *Northern Ireland: Sharing Authority* (IPPR, 1993). J. McGarry and B. O'Leary, *Explaining Northern Ireland* (Blackwell, 1995).

many decades of effort and renewal in order to provide political stability and assurances. Northern Ireland is continuing to face new pressures. It is continually confronting its past while attempting to deal with its present in a way that was probably unthinkable even a few years ago. There are considerable dangers and risks. The core of constitutional re-thinking and re-shaping depends on a balanced and even-handed approach. Nationalists received a new Commission on policing and a Human Rights Commission. Paramilitary groups were given a phased release of prisoners coterminous with agreements to give up violence. Unionists obtained a repeal of the Irish Republic's territorial claim over Northern Ireland. The structure of the peace process is based on a series of interrelated strands or links. The danger is that if one link fails the entire enterprise may fall apart. This has not happened to date but there are on many occasions, signs that the process may stall or fail. The way forward is to disaggregate as far as possible the different strands and avoid the brinkmanship of one to threaten the collapse of the whole. As an example of constitutional innovation the peace process is an important development for the United Kingdom as a whole.

POLITICAL, ECONOMIC AND SOCIAL BACKGROUND

Historical Developments in the Formation of Northern Ireland

21–010   A brief account of Northern Ireland's past history may assist in explaining its present day constitutional status and government. In the nineteenth century the Act of Union created for the whole of Ireland a single "United Kingdom of Great Britain and Ireland". Ireland's own Parliament modelled on the English model was abolished and replaced with a legislative union with Britain. Thereafter Westminster legislation applied to Ireland, while taking account of Irish differences.[4]

21–011   In the eighteenth century, attempts to remedy Irish discontent caused the passage of various measures to ameliorate legal disadvantages among the Catholic population.[5] This process continued and by 1829 Catholic emancipation was granted. Catholics were entitled to hold land and vote at elections. Throughout the century, Irish discontent continued as the newly enfranchised population asserted rights translated into a demand for Home Rule. Famine and economic distress were at their height in severity in the 1840s. The population in 1851 estimated to be 6.5 million had increased to 8.3 million in 1841, but between 1841 and 1911 it fell by almost half to less than 4.4 million. Emigration and famine combined to cause such dramatic decline.

21–012   The quarter century after the famine years saw the build-up of resistance to English rule in Ireland. This manifested itself in the formation of local tenant societies set up in 1847 to agitate for improvement in the law on land-holding. These claims were

---

[4] See J.F. McEldowney, "Crown Prosecutions in Nineteenth-Century Ireland" in *Policing and Prosecution in Britain 1750–1850* (Hay and Snyder ed., Oxford, 1989), p.432. Also see M.R. Beames, "The Ribbon Societies: Lower Class Nationalism in Pre-famine Ireland" (1982) 47 *Past and Present* 131–132.
[5] K. Boyle and T. Hadden, *Ireland: A Positive Proposal* (1985); C. Palley, "Ways Forward; The Constitutional Options" in *The Constitution of Northern Ireland* (D. Watts ed., 1981); C. Palley, "The Evolution, Disintegration and Possible Reconstruction of the Northern Ireland Constitution" (1972) *Anglo American Law Review* 368; C. Palley, "Constitutional Solutions to the Irish Problem" (1980) 33 *Current Legal Problems* 121; C. Palley, *The United Kingdom and Human Rights* (London, 1991).

translated into demands for fair rent, fixity of tenure and free sale. The Land League appeared in 1850 to co-ordinate agitation for land reform, with a wider political agenda in national politics. Sectarian differences between the majority Catholic population and a Protestant ascendancy made the Irish land question a dominant issue. The granting of the franchise to some Catholics in 1829 after considerable pressure only heightened distrust of English law. Protestant resistance increased and Orange lodges feared the end to Protestant ascendancy and land ownership. Seen from the perspective of the British authorities, Protestant influence permeated the minds of magistrates and jurors, while Catholic tenants organised in secret societies and often neutralised the power of the landlord magistrates by intimidating jurors and witnesses. Prosecutions of crimes linked to political, religious or sectarian issues were often problematical.

The term "agrarian outrage", commonly used to describe offences arising out of disputes as to the occupation of land or arising out of political or religious antagonisms, was endemic in Ireland and affected almost every aspect of the administration of justice. The fact that crimes were motivated by political and religious allegiance meant that the idea of impartial justice received little support in Ireland.   **21–013**

The authorities in Dublin Castle struggled to find policies and laws to respond to widespread economic distress and agrarian outrage. Coercive powers enacted during the nineteenth century by special legislation included restrictions on movement, the possession of arms, suppression of organisations, meetings, publications and often the suspension of habeas corpus. Examples of coercive legislation varied but included in certain circumstances the suspension of jury trials in a proclaimed area.   **21–014**

Contemporaneous with coercive legislation, law reforms were introduced, intended to reduce violence and create economic and social stability. The attempt to govern Ireland at this time has been variously described as adopting a policy of coercion and conciliation. In 1881 Gladstone's major initiative, the Land Act 1881, granted fair rent, fixity of tenure and free sale of land. More ambitious reforms soon followed, building on the basis of the earlier 1870 Land Act to enable tenants to purchase land. One of the most innovative and far-reaching State interventions into the rights of private property was attempted with the formation of the Irish Land Commission. Interference with property rights on behalf of a once disenfranchised population was an unprecedented use of law in Ireland.[6]   **21–015**

The Land Commission acted on behalf of tenants and helped to underwrite their financial arrangements to purchase land and in 1881 received additional powers to provide almost three-quarters of the purchase price of land for the Irish tenants.   **21–016**

Land purchase schemes from 1881 to the end of the century provided tenants with ownership and property rights. Extensive legal powers and financial sources were provided to assist with purchase arrangements. Such initiatives, although surrounded with goodwill, failed to provide an enduring solution to the political question raised by tenant agitation which questioned the existence of the State and English governance. A strong Home Rule movement in Ireland, from its early origins in the 1850s gained widespread support and public acceptance. Home Rule, meaning a local parliament with independent powers from Westminster, became a vociferous demand from Irish   **21–017**

[6] P. Bew, "The Land League Ideal: Achievements and Contradictions" in P.J. Drudy (ed.), *"Ireland: Land, Politics and People* (1982); D. Bowen, *The Protestant Crusade in Ireland, 1800–70: A Study of Protestant–Catholic Relations between the Act of Union and Disestablishment* (Dublin, 1978).

nationalists, mainly Catholic and mainly tenant farmers. By the 1880s Home Rule had gained acceptance in the highest authorities within the British Cabinet including the British Prime Minister, William Gladstone.

21–018   Gladstone took the initiative in 1886 and introduced the first Home Rule Bill. Opposition from the mainly Protestant ascendancy helped secure the defeat of the Bill but a significant constitutional innovation had been attempted which went far beyond the attempt to make English law in Ireland more acceptable. The form of the 1886 Bill revealed important constitutional, technical, administrative and financial complexity in finding workable arrangements to meet Irish demands and maintain English support. The 1886 Bill drew on the experience gained in the drafting of federal and colonial constitutional laws. In that sense Ireland was compared to other colonial problems of the period.

21–019   The main innovation in the Bill was an Irish legislature in Dublin with extensive executive powers and responsibilities. Aside from excluded matters such as foreign affairs, defence and trade, the legislature in Dublin gained powers of taxation. The existing police forces, the Dublin Metropolitan Police and Royal Irish Constabulary remained but powers in the Bill allowed reorganisation and control under local authorities.[7]

21–020   Irish representation at Westminster was to cease but the Lord Lieutenant was retained and the police force remained subject to that authority. The 1886 Bill was perceived as creating a shift in the sovereignty of the United Kingdom's Parliament to an Irish Parliament with extensive legal powers. Doubts were raised at the extent to which, if the Bill was passed, residual sovereignty might reside with the Westminster Parliament.

21–021   The degree of autonomy contained in the Bill and the perception that Catholic domination might follow caused Irish Protestants to resist any form of Home Rule. Little relief came when the Bill was defeated. The success of Gladstone's conversion to Home Rule brought bitter disappointment to Unionist aspirations. In January 1886 the Ulster Loyalist Anti-Repeal Union was formed and this organisation linked the Orange Order and Protestant Churches in a unified opposition to Home Rule. It was particularly active in Ulster, one of four provinces in Ireland comprising nine counties situated in the North East of Ireland. In the same month as the formation of the Anti-Repeal Union, Ulster Unionist M.P.s formed themselves into a distinct parliamentary group at Westminster.

21–022   Gladstone's second Home Rule Bill in 1893 faced the same prospects of defeat as the failed attempts to introduce Home Rule in 1886. The 1893 Bill passed the House of Commons but was defeated in the House of Lords. The 1893 Bill clarified the issue of sovereignty by expressly stating that the Westminster Parliament created an Irish legislation "without impairing or restricting the supreme authority of Parliament". Irish representation was to be maintained at Westminster, including Irish peers in the House of Lords. The cornerstone of the Bill was the creation of an Irish legislature to legislate "for the peace order and good government of Ireland". More extensive financial powers retained greater autonomy to the Irish Exchequer and Consolidated Fund while customs duties were to be paid into the United Kingdom's Exchequer.

[7] An account is provided in B. Hadfield, *The Constitution of Northern Ireland* (Belfast SLS, 1989), pp.5–31. See K. Boyle and T. Hadden, *Northern Ireland: The Choice* (1994) and also *Frameworks for the Future* (1995).

Appeals to the Judicial Committee of the Privy Council were substituted for Irish **21–023** appeals to the House of Lords which would cease once the Bill came into effect. References arising out of the legal powers of the Irish legislature could be made by the Lord Lieutenant direct to the Judicial Committee. In common with previous attempts to introduce some form of local legislature, the attempt to introduce the terms of the 1893 Bill failed, a clear illustration of the strength and effectiveness of Unionist opposition. The opportunity to attempt a third Home Rule Bill in 1912 was made. This attempt was bound to be successful because the Parliament Act 1911 assured the authority of the House of Commons over the Lords. As the Lords' powers were reduced to the power of postponement, ultimately once the Bill had passed the Commons it would become law.

In 1912, Asquith introduced the Government of Ireland Bill modelled on the 1893 **21–024** Bill which the Lords had rejected. The proposed Irish legislature was given the title of Irish Parliament. It was bicameral in composition, to be elected under proportional representation and empowered to make laws "for peace order and good government". Extensive powers to regulate the police were to be transferred to the Irish Parliament after six years. The 1912 Bill also contained clauses intended to prevent religious inequality. Sovereignty was to be reserved to Westminster but the Irish legislative to be set up under the 1912 Bill would have commanded wide powers and autonomy. Opposition to the contents of the Bill moved outside Westminster into the public arena as the Bill's passage into law seemed inevitable. A voluntary military force was set up in Ulster to resist the imposition of Home Rule in Ireland. Separation was deemed possible with the setting-up of a "Provisional Government" in 1913 to take control of Ulster should Home Rule become a reality. Delays caused by Unionist opposition to the 1912 Bill resulted in the final passage of the Bill in September 1914. The 1914 Act received the Royal Assent but did not come into effect immediately. Implementation of the 1914 Act was delayed by the commencement of the First World War.

The protracted period of delays and frustrations caused by intense opposition to the **21–025** legislation had its effect on the popularity of Home Rule. In Ireland doubts as to the worth of Home Rule were caused by the lack of success in its implementation. Thus increased Nationalist demand for complete independence gained support. Protestant resistance to Home Rule had solidified into direct action which in the eyes of Irish nationalists had proved effective. English law was distrusted and paramilitary groups developed as part of the rising cycle of agrarian disorder. The culmination of frustrated political ambitions and resistance led to the armed uprising in 1916 on Easter Monday. At first the uprising lacked popular support and was unsuccessful in its ambition to defeat the British presence in Ireland. The execution of the uprising's ringleaders resulted in Nationalists finding common cause with the ambitions of the uprising, even though they were doubtful in giving it much support in 1916.

The attempt to find a constitutional settlement was resumed. The 1914 Government **21–026** of Ireland Act was restored to life as constitutional compromise was sought. Nationalists, finding common cause with the uprising in 1916 demanded nothing less than full independence. Unionists in Ulster would not accept any Irish national rule that denied the link with Britain. Negotiation for a settlement was attempted; an Irish Convention met for nine months from July 1916 to April 1917 but unionist aspirations were difficult to reconcile with nationalist independence. The end of the First World

War brought the dormant 1914 Government of Ireland Act into contention and inevitable implementation. Faced with the irreconcilable differences between Unionists and Nationalists a new Home Rule Bill was introduced in 1920. The Government of Ireland Bill 1920 attempted a constitutional compromise between Nationalists and Unionists. It sought to achieve, not the single Irish Parliament contained in the 1914 legislative proposals, but two Parliaments, one for Northern Ireland and the other for the remainder of Ireland. Northern Ireland was formed out of the ancient Province of Ulster but retained only six counties out of the nine. The remaining 26 counties in Ireland came under the jurisdiction of Southern Ireland. The 1920 Bill envisaged a Parliament for Northern Ireland which was proposed to sit in Belfast and a Parliament for Southern Ireland in Dublin.

21–027   Some elements of the 1914 Act were retained without change. Ultimate sovereignty for both Southern and Northern Ireland Parliaments was retained at Westminster. Ireland remained within the United Kingdom with a common High Court of Appeal for both Northern and Southern Ireland with final appeal to the House of Lords. It was ultimately intended that there should be a single Parliament for Ireland and to work towards that end a Council of Ireland was established with representatives from both Northern and Southern Ireland.

21–028   On December 23, 1920 the Royal Assent was granted to the Government of Ireland Act 1920. As a constitutional innovation for Ireland the 1920 Act effectively partitioned Ireland but failed to remove the Nationalists' aspirations of independence. Unionist aspirations for union with Britain were admittedly protected, but this only served to make the 1920 Act divisive with Nationalists. As Theodore Hoppen concluded[8]:

> "If partition represented the least bad and perhaps the only practical policy in the circumstances of the early 1920s it also ensured that many wounds would continue to be available for vituperative display by those in Ireland dedicated to rejecting the proposition that half a loaf is better than no bread."

21–029   The 1920 Act contained constitutional arrangements that satisfied no Irish aspiration entirely. In the South of Ireland division of opinion between Irish Nationalists and the British Government and inside the Nationalist movement itself led to violence and unrest. A provisional government set up in Dublin negotiated an Anglo-Irish Treaty in December 1921 which created the Irish Free State as a self-governing dominion. Northern Ireland accepted the constitutional arrangements under the Government of Ireland Act 1920 and this was formally accepted in December 1922 by the Northern Ireland Parliament.

21–030   This aftermath of the 1920 Act saw the birth of Northern Ireland united with Britain, and the status of an independent Ireland, later ratified by Act of Parliament. Northern Ireland's existence secured Unionist support while Nationalist aspirations sought unity of Ireland and independent status. Part of the 1921 Treaty Agreement envisaged the operation of a Boundary Commission to set boundary lines on the border between North and South. The expectation that the Boundary Commission would impugn the 1922 composition of the six counties forming Northern Ireland was

---

[8] K. Theodore Hoppen, Ireland since 1800 (Longman, 1992), p.173.

widely held by Nationalists. In the event the Boundary Commission broke down in 1924 and its powers were transferred to the Council of Ireland which never met. Northern Ireland was thus confirmed as comprising six counties with the Government of Ireland Act 1920 establishing a constitutional arrangement for the Northern Ireland Parliament with powers to make legislation for "the good government of Northern Ireland".

The Government of Northern Ireland 1920–1972

The creation of the State of Northern Ireland[9] and its Government under the Government of Ireland Act 1920 until the abolition of the Northern Ireland Parliament in 1972, may be examined in some detail. The 1920 Act is significant because it attempted to provide a workable parliamentary system adapted from the Westminster experience of government for Northern Ireland. The contents of the 1920 Act provide a useful case-study of the allocation of legislative, executive and judicial powers under a written constitution with a devolved system of government. Devolution on the basis of the 1920 Act provided Northern Ireland with a model of devolution that included legislative, executive and administrative powers. Sovereignty was ultimately retained by the Westminster Parliament. In this context the term devolution refers to the system whereby government powers are transferred from the Imperial Parliament to a subordinate but generally autonomous legislature.   **21–031**

Under the Government of Ireland Act 1920 Northern Ireland possessed a Parliament consisting of the Sovereign, represented by a Governor-General as Head of State, an elected House of Commons and a Senate comprising 24 senators elected by the Members of the House of Commons of Northern Ireland according to a proportional representation system. While the Government of Northern Ireland followed many of the procedures and practices of Cabinet and prime ministerial government in England, the Northern Ireland arrangements were nevertheless distinctive. Effectively the Northern Ireland Parliament had extensive powers subject to certain specified limitations.   **21–032**

In constitutional terms the Northern Ireland Parliament had powers to make laws for "the peace, order and good government of Northern Ireland". This grant of power was similar to many colonial arrangements, but it also laid down excepted or reserved matters outside the powers of the Northern Ireland Parliament and vested in the Imperial Parliament at Westminster.   **21–033**

Excepted matters ranged from those that were envisaged to be transferred to an all-Ireland Parliament and the making of laws which interfered with religious liberty which were illegal and outside the powers of the Northern Ireland Parliament. The taking of property without compensation was prohibited, although after 1962 the interpretation of this exception was doubted. The most significant restrictions were that the Northern Ireland Parliament could not make laws which encroached upon Acts of the United Kingdom Parliament and as the Sovereign Parliament, United Kingdom Acts of Parliament could prevail over Northern Ireland Acts, even if the area was one which came within the legal competence of the Northern Ireland Parliament. S.75 of the   **21–034**

[9] Claire Palley, "The Evolution, Disintegration and Possible Reconstruction of the Northern Ireland Constitution" (1972) *Anglo–American Law Review* 368–476 at 388–389.

Government of Ireland Act 1920 asserted that "the supreme authority of the Parliament of the United Kingdom shall remain unaffected and undiminished over all persons and things in Ireland and every part thereof."

21–035   Aside from such restrictions, and also that Acts of the Parliament of Northern Ireland were prohibited from having extra-territorial effect, the Northern Ireland Parliament enjoyed considerable autonomy. Claire Palley explained that the powers of the Northern Ireland Parliament were extensive[10]:

> "Put positively, the Northern Ireland Parliament may legislate on matters relating to law and order, to the police, to courts other than the Supreme Court, to civil and criminal law, to local government, to health and social services, to education, to planning and development, to commerce and industrial development and internal trade, to agriculture and to finance."

21–036   Northern Ireland's constitutional status could by analogy be compared to that of a Dominion Parliament before the Statute of Westminster, and there was early judicial acceptance of the idea that Northern Ireland's Parliament could exercise its own powers according to its own wishes within the powers conferred upon it. In addition to extensive parliamentary powers within Northern Ireland's own Parliament, Northern Ireland was entitled to representation at Westminster. Twelve members of Parliament represented Northern Ireland and were directly elected to their Westminster seats through constituency boundaries drawn up in Northern Ireland.

21–037   Viewed from the perspective of the United Kingdom's constitutional arrangement, Northern Ireland affairs seemed distant, remote and within the competence of Northern Ireland's own Parliament. A constitutional convention arose that Parliament at Westminster would not legislate in respect of matters transferred to the competence of the Parliament of Northern Ireland without the consent of the Government of Northern Ireland.

21–038   In matters of finance, Northern Ireland had its own exchequer but a complicated arrangement of taxation prevented Northern Ireland's autonomy in such matters. Major powers of taxation were vested in the Imperial Parliament and Northern Ireland received a share of reserved taxes after deductions of an "imperial contribution" and other necessary adjustments. Northern Ireland was given only limited entitlement to levy taxes on estate duty, licence fees, property rates, etc. Such financial dependency on the United Kingdom was misleading in terms of constitutional power being freely exercised by the Northern Ireland government but in accordance with the general economic direction and policy of the United Kingdom.

21–039   The strength of the constitutional arrangements set in place by the Government of Ireland Act 1920 appeared proven. As Palley noted[11]:

> "Observers of the Northern Ireland constitutional scene had in general evaluated the 1920 Act and its operation favourably, seeing it as providing for speedy action to settle regional problems, for ready access by citizens to a locally based administration and for opportunities to adapt central government legislation to

[10] Palley, *op.cit.*, p.389.
[11] Palley, *op.cit.*, p.406. The two books are: Mansergh, *The Government of Northern Ireland* (1936) and, D.P. Barritt and C.F. Carter, *The Northern Ireland Problem: A Study in Group Relations* (1962).

local needs. The Act was seen as a firm basis for the continuation of government in Northern Ireland, subject possibly to some minor modifications to secure greater efficiency in the government machine. Notes of disquiet had only been sounded in two important books. The Irish and Ulster Questions were generally seen by British statesmen as having been solved by the 1920 Act and the 1921 Treaty."

In political terms, and with the value of hindsight, the practice of Government in Northern Ireland was not in conformity with the Westminster model with its implication of democracy and a two-party system of government allowing alternative political policies to be adopted. In fact the sophistication of party politics allowing for different factions and interests groups to be represented failed to make significant impact in Northern Ireland. Party politics appeared sectarian in perspective. No comparable political divide between Socialist and Conservative politics enjoyed much success in Ireland when compared to politics within the United Kingdom in England, Wales or Scotland. **21–040**

The first Northern Irish Parliament met in June 1921 and consisted of 40 Unionists, and 6 Nationalists. Sinn Fein delegates failed to attend. Intermittent periods of abstention by Nationalist Members of Parliament was also accompanied by periodic but sustained periods of violence. Well organised and supported, extreme Nationalists did not recognise the State and sought its downfall. Equally intent in maintaining the Union, Protestant paramilitary organisations sought to defend and justify violence to maintain the State. **21–041**

Throughout its history the Northern Ireland Parliament was dominated by Unionist representation. This may fairly be said to have represented the majority of the population; with a population of 1.5 million roughly one-third were Catholics and the remaining two-thirds were Protestants. However such representation appeared one-sided when it retained influence over the major economic, social and political institutions in Northern Ireland. Justifications for the exclusion of Catholics from jobs, housing, and from positions of influence appeared reasonable in the absence of full Catholic participation in the State and the perception that Catholic Nationalists were prepared to destroy the State and seek independence with Ireland. Allegiances in Ireland were linked to religious, social and political habits, formed in the earlier centuries in Irish history but preserved in the folklore of popular history. **21–042**

Religious affiliation offered simple and readily recognisable labels which translated into action in terms of allegiance or non-allegiance with the State. The realities of political belief or religious understanding appeared far removed from the instincts of those brought up and educated in two separate cultures, one largely Catholic and Nationalist, the other largely Protestant and Unionist. **21–043**

An additional factor forever present in the minds of Unionists was the presence in the same island of another State, Ireland. In political terms, the Government of the Irish Republic was remarkably insensitive to Unionist concerns especially over issues such as divorce, contraception and abortion where the Catholic influences over the State were pervasive. The Republic of Ireland's Constitution also asserted sovereignty over Northern Ireland. **21–044**

The sense of identity fostered by Unionism appears remarkably narrow and isolated. The political and constitutional aspirations of Nationalists and Unionists were **21–045** mutually exclusive. Reconciliation of both identities and the hope of political compromise remained ultimately impossible given the continuation of violent unrest and substantial economic hardship as unemployment fluctuated between 20 per cent and 35 per cent.

21–046   The events leading up to the abolition of the Parliament of Northern Ireland and the introduction of direct rule cover the period from 1968 to 1972. Various explanations are offered for the failure of the Government of Ireland Act 1920.

21–047   The most immediate cause, that of escalating violence in Northern Ireland, shocked the Government both in Northern Ireland and in the United Kingdom, out of the complacency assumed from the appearance of a constitutional settlement in 1920. Civil unrest was not simply the outcry of a disaffected nationalism, its roots went deeply into the way the Catholic minority perceived its grievances had been treated by the Unionist majority.

21–048   The Report of the Cameron Commission[12] into civil disturbances testified to a "widespread sense of political and social grievances for long unaudited and therefore ignored by successive Governments of Northern Ireland". If such grievances appeared legitimate to the majority of Catholics, the justice of the cause offered an opportunity for exploitation among hardened Nationalists. The blurring of distinctions between political objectives to improve the conditions of Catholics within Northern Ireland and the complete overthrow of the State left room for violent means to become accepted. The illegal Irish Republican Army (IRA) divided into "official" and "provisional" groups allowing the extreme "provisional" to take a dominant influence.

21–049   The catalogue of constitutional and political deficiencies within the Northern Ireland Government identified in 1969 by the Cameron Report laid bare the unresolved matters left unanswered by the 1920 Act. Palley notes[13]:

> . . . The result of continuous one-party government from 1920 to 1968: an opposition never able to become a government tending to lose its sense of responsibility and a party in power never able to be turned out tending to complacency, insensitivity to criticism and refusal to accept change or reform."

21–050   An added dimension also identified in the Cameron Report was the problem of policing. Extensive police powers were granted to the Royal Ulster Constabulary (RUC) under the Civil Authorities (Special Powers) Act (Northern Ireland) 1922–43. Heavily armed, and in appearance paramilitary, the RUC were supported by auxiliary units known as "B" Specials. Although Catholics were encouraged to join the RUC and an allocation of places made to secure representation from the Catholic population, Catholic participation was small. The result was that the RUC appeared to identify with the Unionist rather than the Nationalist cause, the powers of the police were directed mainly against the Catholic population.

21–051   Civil disturbance, public protest and street demonstrations placed the RUC under extreme pressure. In the Summer of 1969 events moved exceedingly quickly. Catholic areas were attacked by Protestant mobs, demonstrations and unrest appeared out of control. On August 14, 1969 British troops were used to support the civil authorities.

---

[12] The Cameron Report, *Disturbances in Northern Ireland*, Cmnd. 532 (HMSO, Belfast, 1969).
[13] Palley, *op.cit.*, p.407.

In effect law and order was no longer in the hands of the police directed by the Northern Ireland Government but under the responsibility of the British military under control from the British Cabinet. The General Officer commanding the army in Northern Ireland took operational control of the police over security matters in Northern Ireland.

Attempts were made to restore normality to policing in Northern Ireland and these included the reorganisation of the RUC after a report in October 1969 into the organisation of the structure of the police.[14]   **21–052**

Events leading to the demise of the Northern Ireland Government came about during the period 1969 to 1972. The most significant constitutional change was direct involvement in Northern Ireland affairs by the British Cabinet. Encouraged to introduce wide-ranging reforms, the Government of Northern Ireland pledged support to "the views of Her Majesty's Government in the United Kingdom" which necessitated following a more open policy on encouraging the Catholic population to support the Government and police.   **21–053**

The scale of changes introduced by the Government of Northern Ireland were impressive and extensive. Reform of the electoral law in Northern Ireland brought Northern Ireland electoral practices and arrangements into line with those prevailing in the United Kingdom. Boundary changes were introduced to favour the principle of giving all citizens equal rights.[15] A Boundary Commission was set up to keep under review, representation in the House of Commons from Northern Ireland.   **21–054**

Local government reforms were initiated which introduced a restructured system, more streamlined and efficient, but with extensive powers delegated back to Central Government in Belfast from the party politics of local interests groups. Eventually in 1972 reforms were introduced to local government organisation following the Macrory Report[16] that involved the abolition of urban and rural district councils in municipalities and county borough councils. A more streamlined and compact system of local government was introduced. Altogether 26 new district councils were set up for Northern Ireland. In effect many activities of local government were transferred to Central Government departments or agencies.   **21–055**

Reforms dealing with citizens' grievances included the introduction of the office of Commissioner for Complaints in November 1969, with independent powers of investigation and bringing within its remit local government and public bodies and boards not subject to the newly established Parliamentary Commission for Administration (ombudsman). The office of ombudsman was established in Northern Ireland in 1969 closely modelled on the English equivalent set up in 1967.   **21–056**

The law on incitement to hatred was strengthened and a Community Relations Commission was established in 1969 which took proactive steps to encourage humane relations between the two communities. A number of additional bodies were established to oversee public activities which were contentious and had caused political controversy; the most notable was the setting-up of the Northern Ireland Housing Executive in 1971. This body, separated from ministerial intervention, set out to   **21–057**

---

[14] The Hunt Report, *Report of the Advisory Committee on Police in Northern Ireland*, Cmnd.535 (1969).
[15] Electoral Law Act (N.I.) 1969. The Local Government Act (N.I.) 1969. The Local Government Act (N.I.) 1972.
[16] Macrory Report *Report of the Review Body on Local Government in Northern Ireland*, Cmnd.517 (HMSO, Belfast, 1967, 1969, 1970).

provide an impartial and objective system of public housing allocation on a points system of allocation based on need.

21–058   While innovation and responsiveness were the hallmark of the reforms outlined above, without doubt the passage of these reforms was in favour of the Catholic minority, but this only further alienated Unionist opinion. The Unionist party, while historically cohesive, began to fragment into different groups. Nationalist politics were also fragmented but the formation of a new political group, the Social Democratic and Labour Party (SDLP), represented a new style of opposition politics. Prepared to work within existing institutions the SDLP became an articulate voice for moderate Catholic opinion. The SDLP ended the disparate and incoherent policies of the past and encouraged active constitutional participation. However, fragmentation of nationalist allegiance into support for the IRA, especially the more active Provisional IRA, created an efficient and well organised terrorist organisation which took offensive action against the security forces. Northern Ireland suffered a major setback when 13 citizens were shot in January 1972 by members of the British Army. Within three months of this incident the British Government asserted sovereignty over Northern Ireland and introduced direct rule in March 1972. The Government of Ireland Act 1920 had failed and the experiment in devolved government in Northern Ireland ended.

21–059   McCrudden attributes this situation to the failure of "the pragmatic empiricist tradition of constitutional developments", and thereby the failure of the common law tradition with its emphasis on flexibility, learning from past mistakes and developing solutions to meet future needs. After 1972 the opportunity to experiment with new constitutional arrangements for Northern Ireland came when it was probably least expected and most required.

Constitutional Arrangements in Flux

Northern Ireland Constitution Act 1973

21–060   Since 1972, until the setting-up of the Northern Ireland Assembly under the Northern Ireland Act 1998, Northern Ireland's Government has been carried out under "direct rule". This system has worked as follows: Orders in Council are prepared and, subject to affirmative resolution, are issued for Northern Ireland. These affirmative resolution procedures are open to criticism and McCrudden has written of the disadvantages of the procedure[17]:

> "The disadvantage of this mode is that Orders are not subject to amendment and are usually debated for a maximum of two and a half hours after 10pm. Government ministers available for Northern Ireland affairs in Parliament do not represent Northern Ireland constituencies."

21–061   Northern Ireland's representation at Westminster was increased to 18 M.P.s. Northern Ireland's M.P.s have little direct influence in the government of Northern Ireland,

[17] McCrudden, "Northern Ireland and the British Constitution" in Jowell and Oliver (eds.), *The Changing Constitution* (J. Jowell and D. Oliver ed., 2nd ed., 1989), pp.297–342; (3rd ed., 1994). pp.314–315.

whenever no Parliament or Assembly is operational in Northern Ireland and Westminster matters often overshadow discussion of Northern Ireland affairs. There is also the criticism that in the absence of a specific departmental select committee, Northern Ireland Ministers are not accountable for their actions in the same way as a comparable United Kingdom government department. This criticism also applied to civil servants in Northern Ireland who are not answerable to a specialised committee primarily concerned with Northern Ireland matters. In 1994 a Select Committee for Northern Ireland was set up.

The first period of direct rule covered the years 1972–1974. During this time future **21–062** constitutional innovations and adjustments were attempted amid increasing violence in Northern Ireland. Originally direct rule was conceived as a stop-gap measure but over time it became an accepted policy which soon appeared blighted with many of the shortcomings discussed above in connection with the earlier Home Rule debate.

In March 1973, a referendum was held on the issue of the Border between North **21–063** and South, and the result confirmed the majority population in favour of the union. Only 58.7 per cent of the electorate cast their votes; Nationalists and their supporters did not vote.

Attempts to fill the vacuum left by the suspension of the Northern Ireland **21–064** Parliament gave rise to a degree of "constitutional tinkering", a term which reflects the difficulty of proceeding with long-term initiatives. Events have always seemed to take the initiative in Northern Ireland and government policy has always lagged behind. However the fundamentals have remained largely unchanged. A majority favour union within the United Kingdom with a sizeable minority in favour of some form of United Ireland. A number of White Papers published at this time from 1972–74 attempted to set out Government thinking. Briefly, this involved (a) consideration of issues of security; (b) attempts to solve economic and social problems within Northern Ireland, and finally; (c) attempts to pursue a scheme of devolution whereby some form of government might be formed in Northern Ireland capable of achieving widespread community support. Broadly speaking these remain the current concerns of the attempts to find some solution in Northern Ireland.

Constitutional lawyers interested in the different forms of devolution will find the **21–065** Northern Ireland Constitution Act 1973 and the Northern Ireland Assembly Act 1973 useful models of modern devolved government. The 1973 Act envisaged an Assembly with legislative powers elected by proportional representation and an Executive drawn from parties representative of both communities. Within the framework of a link with the United Kingdom, Catholics were offered the opportunity to participate in power in a meaningful way for the first time. In return for Catholic acceptance of the Union, Unionists were expected to offer a power-sharing arrangement, a major departure from the idea of majority government. Guarantees of a regular series of border polls were built into these arrangements under the Northern Ireland Constitution Act 1973 in an effort to encourage dialogue but with a guarantee to maintain the Union as long as the majority so desired. As Catholics are ultimately expected to form a majority of the population within Northern Ireland, a period of power-sharing seemed inevitable and necessary in an attempt to reach compromise and consensus. It was envisaged that once a power-sharing government became firmly established legal powers devolved to the government of Northern Ireland might increase. The potential for further legal powers appeared unlimited and extended to a large measure of local autonomy.

21–066   The status of Northern Ireland expressed in s.1 of the 1973 Act contained a

"constitutional guarantee, that in no event will Northern Ireland or any part of it cease to be part of Her Majesty's dominions and of the United Kingdom without the consent of the majority of the people of Northern Ireland voting in a poll held for the purposes of this section."

S.2 of the 1973 Act was intended to replace the terms of s.1(2) of the Ireland Act 1949 which provides that "in no event will Northern Ireland . . . any part thereof cease to be part of Her Majesty's dominion and of the United Kingdom without the consent of the Parliament of Northern Ireland." The abolition of the Northern Ireland Parliament effectively left this guarantee as inoperative. Its replacement with the "consent of the majority of the people of Northern Ireland" transfers this aspect of political sovereignty from an institution and politicians to a referendum. This may in practice give less security to the Unionist majority especially as the geographical reality of political power may mean that large parts of the north-west which are nationalist, may wish to sever the link with the United Kingdom.

21–067   The question also arises as to the worth of this guarantee in terms of the constitutional status of Northern Ireland. The 1973 Act does not make any provision as to the course of action to be taken should consent for change be expressed in a border poll. Most Unionists correctly maintain the 1800 Act of Union as the basis of the Union between Great Britain and Ireland. This would indicate that even if Northern Ireland no longer remains a constitutional jurisdiction claimed by the Constitution of the Republic of Ireland, any future United Kingdom Parliament is free to alter both the terms of the guarantee and cede Northern Ireland to the Irish Republic. Unionists fears are that the current status of Northern Ireland is in fact no more than a leasehold arrangement rather than a freehold permanently protected within the United Kingdom. Parliament is not bound to follow the 1800 Act as an unalterable statement of legislative intent. This point becomes crucial later when evaluating the status and policy behind the Anglo-Irish Agreement between Dublin and London in 1985.

21–068   The Assembly set up under the 1973 Act was elected under proportional representation and duly formed a Government, the first of its kind comprising both Catholics and Protestants in a Cabinet of power-sharing Ministers. Unionist opposition to this form of government resulted in civil disturbance and in May 1974, the power-sharing Executive fell after a General Strike by Protestant workers. Direct rule was resumed under the Northern Ireland Act 1974 and remains in place.

21–069   Further attempts to provide a foundation for civil liberties come with the Fair Employment (Northern Ireland) Act 1976. The Act made discrimination on religious and poitical grounds unlawful in the public and private sector. The Act created the Fair Employment Agency to advise, monitor and investigate complaints.

21–070   A further attempt for a broadly based power-sharing government was attempted under the Northern Ireland Act 1982. This new scheme, referred to as "rolling devolution", provided a detailed committee structure to scrutinise the work of Northern Ireland departments. The Northern Ireland Assembly was granted powers to bring forward proposals for devolved government based on agreements between Unionists and Nationalists. In effect, the more agreement between the representatives of the two traditions, the more power was devolved. The Assembly failed to reach agreement beyond setting up a few committees to scrutinise legislation and in June 1986 it was dissolved by Order in Council. For the future, an Order in Council would be sufficient to revive it and bring it into operation depending on whether agreement could be reached.

Direct rule is retained in part under the devolved constitutional arrangements **21–071** consists of a Secretary of State for Northern Ireland together with a Minister of State and four parliamentary Under-Secretaries of State operating under direct rule. Orders in Council or primary Acts of the United Kingdom Parliament may be used to legislate for Northern Ireland. Although United Kingdom government departments are not directly responsible for Northern Ireland, departments' select committees include matters within the remit of the Northern Ireland Secretary of State.

The Anglo-Irish Agreement and the Peace Process

Northern Ireland's capacity to stimulate new initiatives brought a major departure in **21–072** 1985 from past attempts to solve Northern Ireland's status and constitutional arrangements, through the Anglo-Irish Agreement. Following an inter-governmental meeting[18] at Hillsborough Castle, Belfast on November 15, 1985, the Anglo-Irish Agreement was signed by the Governments of the United Kingdom and the Irish Republic. Unionist politicians were effectively excluded from the inter-governmental talks. The Agreement set out the status of Northern Ireland and recognised for the first time in an international Treaty the legitimacy of the competing aspirations of both Unionists and Nationalists.

Under the Agreement any change in the status of Northern Ireland would come **21–073** about only with the consent of a majority within Northern Ireland. This reiterates the status of Northern Ireland set out in the 1973 Act. However for the future, if a majority of the people of Northern Ireland "wish for and formally consent to the establishment of a United Ireland", then legislation would be introduced to give effect to those wishes. The Agreement also recognised that the majority of people in Northern Ireland desired no change in the status of Northern Ireland.

While the Agreement appeared to offer reassurance to Unionists in Northern **21–074** Ireland of the position of Northern Ireland within the United Kingdom, it also recognised the legitimacy of Catholics to aspire to a United Ireland. Another part of the Agreement wished to encourage inter-governmental co-operation between the North and South through an Inter-Governmental Conference consisting of British and Irish Ministers. In this forum, Irish Ministers assisted by a permanent secretariat in Northern Ireland could put forward views on political, security and legal matters. This device intended to bring Catholics into a closer recognition of the governmental process in Northern Ireland where in the past they had felt alienated. It also re-created the original idea of a Council of Ireland contained in the Government of Ireland Act 1920.

The Agreement also set out to encourage the introduction of some form of devolved **21–075** government. The sphere of influence of Irish Ministers would be curtailed where

---

[18] The Agreement was signed and later approved by both Parliaments in the United Kingdom and in the Republic of Ireland. Later it was lodged at the United Nations (November, 1985).

matters to be discussed were the responsibility of a devolved administration in Northern Ireland. The intention behind this arrangement was to encourage Unionists to accept devolution as a preferable policy to that of including Irish Ministers in discussions on Northern Ireland's domestic affairs. Thus the Agreement might stimulate greater realism and responsibility between Unionists and Nationalists in the political compromises needed to form a power-sharing administration.

21–076   Since the Agreement was signed, Unionists' opposition to the Agreement has been unrelenting. The inclusion of Irish Ministers and a secretariat in discussion of Northern Ireland's domestic affairs is seen as another step towards unification and a shift away from the Union with the United Kingdom. The Agreement itself was criticised by Unionists because they were excluded from the earlier discussions about its content.

21–077   The Agreement also contained a wide range of inter-governmental matters such as policing and security where it was hoped that greater co-operation might make for an effective security policy. Security problems are recognised as not being confined to geographical or political boundaries. The Agreement rests on the assumption that increased security might alleviate any Unionist discomfort from the terms of the Agreement. However, the level of violence has not returned to the 1972 period where it was at its worst, but has maintained on average about 80 deaths and over 1,500 shootings *per annum*. It is estimated that Britain contributed an average of nearly £2 billion *per annum* to the running of the Northern Ireland economy between 1983 and 1993.

21–078   The hope of an end to violence has not been realised and Unionist objection to the Agreement has remained constant. Nationalists' aspirations have been more fully expressed in the Agreement than at any time since the 1920 Act and the formation of Northern Ireland. Nevertheless, the hope that this might secure a shift to support for the Agreement and away from the terrorist IRA has not been fully realised among the Catholic population.

21–079   The question arises as to what significance should be attached to the Agreement. From a constitutional perspective the Agreement has a number of important ramifications.

21–080   First, the Government of the Irish Republic was given a direct influence over the domestic affairs of Northern Ireland. There is in effect a partnership agreement between the two Governments, external to Northern Ireland, to work together in its day-to-day running.

21–081   Secondly, that when Catholics in Northern Ireland form a sufficient majority in favour of a United Ireland,[19] there is a promise that the two Governments will secure legislation to put a United Ireland into effect. This in effect gives a time-period to the Unionist population to come to terms with Nationalists. Estimates vary as to the exact length of that time-limit, but at present the Catholic population has grown to at least 40 per cent and it is assumed in the next 40 years they may make up the deficit.

21–082   Thirdly, the Agreement has had some noticeable effects on many domestic issues in Northern Ireland such as industrial co-operation. The Agreement was reviewed by the

---

[19] "Catholics to be the Majority in Ulster," *Independent*, November 1, 1992. See P. Compton, Letters to the editor, *Independent*, November 4, 1992. Compton asserts the time-scale is 70 years.

courts[20] in both England and the Republic of Ireland, in challenges made to its constitutionality. Both cases upheld the Agreement as legal and effective.

Divisions within Northern Ireland society seem to remain as divided as the period **21–083** leading up to the creation of Northern Ireland itself. The experience of Northern Ireland's various attempts at constitutional change suggests that constitutional schemes are marginal. As Palley has pointed out[21]:

> "They may facilitate change or by their non-constructive nature provide safety valves for the expression of grievances. But they must by and large be in accordance with the facts of power, or in the currently fashionable phrases must 'be in accordance with political reality and must conform to the patterns established by institutionalized and non institutionalized force.' No constitution will be effective unless there is political will by the major power holders to work it."

Security problems are an intrinsic part of Northern Ireland's unresolved political social **21–084** and economic problems. Dickson has noted that[22]:

> ". . . from 1971 to 1977 an average of 252 persons were killed and 3,269 shootings have occurred each year; for the years 1978 to 1981 the averages have fallen, respectively, to 82 and 1,574."

Terrorist violence and an increasing sophistication in the means available to terrorists **21–085** including international support has tested Northern Ireland's emergency powers and posed difficult questions about the use of force by the state and the compatibility of emergency powers with civil liberties. Northern Ireland has provided an important case study in the use of emergency powers. How is the rule of law to be upheld while measures to defeat terrorism are pursued?

The Joint Declaration, December 1993 (The Downing Street Declaration)

The Joint Declaration agreed between the British and Irish Governments is contained **21–086** in a text consisting of 12 points, known as the Downing Street Declaration.

The declaration seeks to reinforce the Anglo-Irish Agreement but it goes much **21–087** further. The document actively seeks the cessation of terrorist violence and offers the opportunity for dialogue following the cessation of violence. For the first time, the British Government asserts that it has "no selfish, strategic or economic interest" in Northern Ireland. A number of commitments follow. First, that the British Government is neutral to the ultimate political outcome of Northern Ireland's constitutional arrangements. Secondly, that if the people of Northern Ireland agree to a United

---

[20] *Ex p. Molyneaux* [1986] 1 W.L.R. 331. The court refused leave to apply as an International Conference, the Statute of the Agreement, under the Agreement did not contravene any statute or rule of common law or constitutional convention. See *McGimpsey*, the unreported case in the courts of the Irish Republic.
[21] Palley, "The Evolution, Disintegration and Possible Reconstruction of the Northern Ireland Constitution", (1972) 1 *Anglo-American Law Review* 368–476, p.450.
[22] B. Dickson, "Northern Ireland's Emergency Legislation—The Wrong Medicine?" [1993] *P.L.* 592. The author acknowledges a debt of gratitude to Professor Dickson for useful information and advice on emergency powers.

Ireland, then the British Government will introduce the necessary legislation to implement that agreement. Thirdly, that the primary interest of the British government is to see peace, stability and reconciliation in Northern Ireland.

21–088   The Joint Declaration also provides a number of commitments from the Irish Government. First, that the Irish Government will examine "any elements in the democratic life and organisation of the Irish State" that can be represented to the Irish government as "not being fully consistent with a modern, democratic and pluralist society". Secondly, that the Irish Government accepts that "it would be wrong to attempt to impose a united Ireland, in the absence of the freely given consent of a majority of the people of Northern Ireland." There is also a strong commitment from the Joint Declaration that civil and religious liberties of both communities in Northern Ireland require respect. There is an implication that in any future political and constitutional arrangement, the respect of the liberties of both communities will be protected. This may be an indication that adopting a Bill of Rights for Northern Ireland will be considered.

21–089   Future discussion of the value of the Joint Declaration will focus on whether the IRA will find the document sufficiently attractive to end violence. The question of whether constitutional change and political debate will result in an end to conflict in Northern Ireland is uncertain.

The Good Friday Agreement

21–090   Building on the Downing Street Declaration and the Joint Declaration, on the IRA's announcement of the cessation of violence in 1994 and a multitude of discussions, the British and Irish Governments produced a Framework Document. This set out matters for further consideration including principles for non-violence, human rights and the parity of esteem for the expression of both national identities. It provided the basis for multi-party negotiations under the chairmanship ofSenator George Mitchell. After protracted discussions and uncertainties, agreement was reached on Good Friday, April 10, 1998. Simultaneous to the Agreement was the renewal of the various cease-fires and a reduction in paramilitary violence.

21–091   The Good Friday Agreement[23] marked a turning point in Northern Ireland's recent history. The Agreement is underpinned by a number of agreements reached by the Governments of the United Kingdom and the Irish Republic.[24] Referendums held in Northern Ireland and in the Republic of Ireland on May 22, 1998 resulted in acceptance of the Agreement. In Northern Ireland, there was a turnout of over 80 per cent and 71 per cent of those who voted accepted the Agreement. In the Republic of Ireland there was a lower turnout of nearly 56 per cent and 94 per cent of those who voted accepted the Agreement. In June 1998 elections to the Northern Ireland Assembly were held.

21–092   The Good Friday Agreement provides a number of interlinking strands. This is intended to strengthen the peace-process by interrelating the building of democratic institutions as an alternative to violence and the creation of new frameworks with the

---

[23] *The Agreement reached in multi-party negotiations* Cm.4292 (1998).
[24] See *Agreement Establishing Implementing Bodies*, Cm.4293 (1998); *Agreement Establishing a North–South Ministerial Council*, Cm.4294 (1998); *Agreement Establishing a British–Irish Council*, Cm.4296 (1998).

Irish Republic to recognise differences in religion and identity. Decommissioning of weapons and the total disarmament of paramilitary organisations is intended to allow for the normalisation of policing and the criminal justice system. An accelerated system of prisoner releases is intended to provide paramilitary organisations with a pathway to peace. Human rights are to set the standards for future decision-making removed from the past. In that regard a new Bill of Rights[25] specifically tailored to the needs of Northern Ireland is intended to assist the peace process, drawn up by the new Human Rights Commission for Northern Ireland. The proposals are widely drawn and build on the experience of the South African Bill of Rights. The proposals are at a consultative stage before a draft is agreed for consideration by the British Government.

The fragility of the system currently in place is that it is possible for one strand to fail thus putting in jeopardy the remainder. The different strands to the Agreement are as follows. **21–093**

First, there is a democratically elected Assembly set up under the Northern Ireland Act 1998 and the Northern Ireland (Elections) Act 1998, providing devolution for Northern Ireland. An executive with ministers from participating parties in the Assembly provides an elected First Minister and Deputy Minister. Secondly reaffirmation of the status of Northern Ireland is based on agreement. Thus the majority of the people of Northern Ireland are free to choose to remain within the United Kingdom or, with the agreement of the people of Ireland as a whole, to choose that a United Ireland should come into being. Thirdly, the Northern Ireland Assembly has legislative powers but subject to their compatibility with human rights including the Human Rights Act 1998 and the European Convention on Human Rights. Fourthly, there are two bodies intended to embed the peace process in the relationship with the United Kingdom and the Republic of Ireland. The North–South Ministerial Council and a British–Irish Council and Inter-governmental Conference provide for the discussion of issues of common concern. This is intended to provide a forum for debate and dialogue. **21–094**

Devolution Under the Northern Ireland Act 1998

The mechanics of devolution for Northern Ireland under the 1998 Act are examined in Chapter 2 of this book. Here it is necessary to note how devolution has had an erratic beginning. The necessary Devolution Order[25a] to bring devolution into existence in Northern Ireland was made in December 1999. This lasted for a short period when devolution was suspended under the Northern Ireland Act 2000 but was restored again in May 2000. A major strand of the peace process is decommissioning of weapons and slow progress in this area gave rise to major political problems. Matters came to a crisis once more in July 2001. The resignation of the First Minister because of frustrations over the decommissioning left a period of six weeks under s.16 of the Northern Ireland Act 1998 to find a solution before new elections to the offices of both First and Deputy First Minister. Under the rules of procedure setting up the devolved assembly, it was possible for a one-day suspension under the Northern Ireland Act **21–095**

---

[25] *Making a Bill of Rights for Northern Ireland* (Northern Ireland Human Rights Commission, September, 2001).
[25a] The Northern Ireland Act 1998 (Appointed Day) Order 1999 (SI 1999/3208).

2000 which allowed for an additional period of six weeks to provide time for the resolution of the decommissioning problem. Devolution was restored for a short time followed by another suspension on September 21, 2001 to allow for further talks. Eventually with some progress on decommissioning, devolution was restored and in November 2001 the First Minister and Deputy First Minister were elected again under circumstances that led to "the middle of the road" Alliance party being designated as Unionists in favour of the Agreement, to avoid the election of a Unionist who was against the Agreement.

21–096   The institutional frameworks and interconnected strands of the Agreement had provided sufficient flexibility to maintain the momentum of the peace process. However, it might be seen that the fragility of the process underlines the political underpinnings on which the entire process rests. The protracted delays in decommissioning has required the Northern Ireland Arms Decommissioning (Amendment) Act 2002 to be passed. This Act provides for an extension of the amnesty arrangements previously put in place under the Northern Ireland Arms Decommissioning Act 1997 to end before February 27, 2003 to be extended to February 26, 2007. If necessary the decommissioning arrangements may be extended by order of the Secretary of State.

21–097   Northern Ireland's future remains precariously tied to the activities of paramilitary organisations and the political parties that underpin the peace process. Devolution has provided an opportunity for self-government for the first time in Northern Ireland in many years. Unlike any other system of devolution it is linked to a peace process and is contingent on the supervision of the Secretary of State for Northern Ireland who has powers to suspend, amend or abandon devolution. The importance of direct rule is that it enables there to be a safety net if devolution fails or runs into difficulties. Thus the day-to-day legislative needs in Northern Ireland may be addressed through direct rule. For example the Electoral Fraud (Northern Ireland) Act 2002 gives effect to proposals set out in the White Paper[26] on electoral fraud in Northern Ireland in an attempt to combat fraud and impersonation at elections.

AN OVERVIEW OF EMERGENCY POWERS

The Historical Legacy

21–098   In 1922, with the creation of the State of Northern Ireland, emergency powers were deemed to be necessary and were immediately brought into operation. Historically emergency powers have formed an intrinsic part of the Government of Ireland. The Act of Union 1800 had been passed in the aftermath of the 1796 rebellion and the Government of Ireland Act 1920 had been passed after the Rebellion in 1916. Constitutional change and emergency powers were and remain inexorably linked.

21–099   In the nineteenth century the form of coercive powers, as they were referred to, varied. Suspension of the Habeas Corpus Acts 1781–82 was accompanied by a variety of miscellaneous powers including at times trial without jury for specified offences, extensive powers for search, arrest and seizure of goods. Deportation and internment without trial were also adopted with varying degrees of success.

[26] *Combating Electoral Fraud in Northern Ireland* (Cm.5080).

Agrarian crime, endemic in the nineteenth century, put the ordinary courts and the   **21–100**
administration of criminal justice under considerable strain. Ireland, in common with
Scotland but unlike England and Wales, developed a public Crown Prosecution system
where prosecutions were taken on behalf of victims of crime by Sessional Crown
Solicitors. The criminal law with its English origins depended on the lay magistrate and
jury trial but, under the extremes of Irish violence, required adjustment.

Stipendiary magistrates, legally qualified, were used to supplement the ineffective   **21–101**
and often criticised lay magistrates. By 1884, stipendiary magistrates were in the
majority, many with a military or police background, some with property or professional qualifications. At times of intense violence, magistrates received additional
powers which allowed for the proclamation of districts, the suspension of habeas
corpus and the arrest and detention of suspects.

At Dublin Castle, the judicial division, one of three divisions in the Irish civil service,   **21–102**
recorded the date, time and action taken against political and organised agitation.
Spies, informers and undercover agents communicated information to Dublin Castle
and assisted in the collection of evidence against suspects. Particularly difficult periods
of agrarian unrest and agitation resulted in disturbed parts of Ireland being proclaimed
and stipendiary magistrates received additional powers. For example in 1881 under the
Protection of Persons and Property Act 1881, suspension of habeas corpus, arrest and
detention of suspects was permitted.[27]

The Crimes Act 1887 allowed resident magistrates the power to admit into evidence   **21–103**
the accused's evidence even if it involved self-incrimination. This principle had been
first introduced by s.16 of the Prevention of Crimes Act 1882.

Difficulties in obtaining convictions before Irish juries resulted in the 1881 Select   **21–104**
Committee of the House of Lords recommending that jury trial might be suspended.[28]
The Prevention of Crimes Act 1882 in theory substituted trial by three judges for trial
by jury but in practice this section of the legislation was not implemented after a
resolution was passed by the Irish judiciary opposed to the abolition of jury trial.
However, many indictable crimes were made summary offences under the Act which
endured until 1898.

The Crimes Act 1887 was more permanent and provided special jury trials for   **21–105**
disturbed areas when unrest resulted in the area being proclaimed. Proclaimed areas
were subject to stronger legal powers. The experience of this Act encouraged the
listing of "dangerous associations" which were made illegal.

The outbreak of war on August 4, 1914 was followed by the Defence of the Realm   **21–106**
Act 1914. The 1914 Act represented a shift in emphasis from emergency legislation
confined to Ireland to legislation generally applicable throughout the United Kingdom
and Ireland. Regulations made under the Act provided extensive powers for serving
the public safety and "defence of the realm". This included martial law and trial by
court-martial of serious offences.

---

[27] J.F. McEldowney, "Crown Prosecutions in 19th Century Ireland" *Policing and Prosecution in Britain
1750–1850* (Hay and Snyder ed., Oxford, 1989), pp.427–457 (legislation included 44 & 45 Vict., c.4; 50 & 51
Vict. c.20; 45 & 46 Vict. c.25). See P. Hunt and B. Dickson, "Northern Ireland's Emergency Laws and
International Human Rights" (1993) 2 *National Quarterly Human Rights* 173.
[28] Parl. Pap. 1881 XI.1.I. S. Leadam, "Substitutes for Trial by Jury in Ireland" (May, 1882) 31 *Fortnightly
Review* 547–563.

Emergency powers since 1922

21–107   It is necessary to trace the development of emergency powers in Northern Ireland from the period of the inception of the State. Recently the law in Northern Ireland on emergency powers has been codified by the Northern Ireland (Emergency Provisions) Act 1996. This Act substantially re-enacts the Northern Ireland (Emergency Provisions) Act 1991. However, one part of the 1991 Act has not been re-enacted in the 1996 Act. That is matters relating to the confiscation of proceeds of terrorist-related activities. This will be the subject of a separate enactment. There is also the Prevention of Terrorism (Additional Powers) Act 1996 which relates to the law in areas where the police impose cordons in connection with the prevention of acts of terrorism following the bomb at South Quay in London in February 1996.

21–108   The Parliament of Northern Ireland shortly after the State was set up, enacted the Civil Authorities (Special Powers) Act 1922. Modelled on the Defence of the Realm Consolidation Act 1914 which only applied to making regulations during war, the Special Powers Act gave extensive regulation making powers for dealing with powers of arrest, search, detention, and seizure. The civil authority under the 1922 Act was widely defined to include a Northern Ireland Minister of Home Affairs, or any Parliamentary secretary or officer of the Royal Ulster Constabulary. In effect, the 1922 Act was so extensive that the powers conferred under the Act were considered as applicable to the army as well as the police in Northern Ireland.

21–109   This point was successfully challenged in the Northern Ireland courts in 1972 in *R. v Londonderry JJ. Ex p. Hume*[29] when the then Lord Chief Justice, Lord Lowry declared *ultra vires* regulations purporting to give powers to the armed forces. The United Kingdom Parliament was forced, in an all-night sitting, to pass the Northern Ireland Act 1972 retrospectively giving the army the powers which it was assumed they had always possessed. Although the Special Powers Act was intended to be of limited duration, its powers were added to and the life of the Act extended for the duration of the Northern Ireland Parliament until 1972. Since then there have been a number of emergency powers Acts, under the titles of the Northern Ireland (Emergency Provisions Act) 1973 and the Prevention of Terrorism Act 1974. The former replaced the 1922 Special Powers Act, the latter introduced in 1974, after the Birmingham bombing in November 1974. The Prevention of Terrorism (Temporary Provisions) Act 1974 was also passed.

21–110   Powers under both these Acts included a power to make regulation for detention without trial, power to detain for up to seven days, and powers to exclude persons moving from Great Britain to Northern Ireland and vice versa. The most extensive power is internment without trial.

21–111   The arguments in favour of internment rest on two assumptions. First, if properly pursued it may act as an efficient means of identifying and rounding up suspects who would remain at large in the community because of the lack of evidence for their arrest. Secondly, internment allows undercover intelligence to work in advance of the internment power and gives supremacy to intelligence-gathering over the routine of the police collecting evidence to put before the courts. Thus internment provides a

[29] [1972] N.I. 91. See Northern Ireland Act 1972, s.1; C. Walker (1989) 40 *Northern Ireland Legal Quarterly* 1; O'Higgins (1972) 35 *Modern Law Review* 295; *McElduff, Re.* [1972] N.I. 1.

strong military option and its widespread use may curtail terrorist organisations. Both assumptions stress the necessity of internment because of difficulties in using the ordinary courts.

The arguments against internment may similarly rest on two assumptions. First, **21–112** internment may cause public outcry and distrust of law and the legal authority of the Government. This may act as a catalyst for support of terrorist groups and deepen the sense of alienation in the local community. Secondly, internment has a finite existence and arrangements ending internment may become a major constraint on political activity. While this may appear a bargaining chip, it is usually heavily weighted in favour of the terrorist.

Opposition to internment involves arguments concerning the protection of individ- **21–113** ual liberty and against abuse of power. Any one-sided application of internment or the internment of suspects who are later believed innocent may make internment an unreliable and therefore an unjustified risk. In Northern Ireland, before the introduc- tion of direct rule, internment powers were used extensively in August 1971. The outcome of internment at that time was far from satisfactory. Alienation throughout the Catholic community was generally felt and a large number of allegations of torture and brutality were made, arising out of the interrogation techniques adopted by some members of the security forces. Violence increased and great disturbance arose out of the use of the internment power which was perceived as directed only against Catholic violence.

Internment powers once used may later be regarded as unjustified if there is no **21–114** direct reduction in violence. In Northern Ireland internment powers were found difficult to justify in terms of any cessation of violence and this led to a review of emergency powers, specifically the question of how internment might be replaced by some form of trial system. The review was carried out under the chairmanship of Lord Diplock. The Diplock Report[30] marked an important shift from internment by the Executive to judicial trial. Lord Diplock recommended that special courts (popularly named "Diplock courts") should be set up to deal with terrorist offences. The Diplock courts involve trial without jury before a single judge under the Northern Ireland (Emergency Provisions) Act 1973. Since 1973 Diplock courts have heard cases relating to terrorist offences without juries. Internment powers have not been used since 1971.

Scheduled offences triable before the Diplock courts include crimes commonly **21–115** committed by terrorists. These include murder, manslaughter, riot, kidnapping, false imprisonment, assault occasioning actual bodily harm, robbery involving weapons, theft, burglary or obtaining by deception and various firearms and explosives offences.

The schedule of offences that may be tried before the non-jury Diplock courts have **21–116** been extended under the Northern Ireland (Emergency Provisions) Act 1991. A new Pt IV to Sch.I includes any non-summary offence which an RUC officer above the rank of superintendent certifies has been charged as a result of an investigation into terrorist funds. This power to schedule an offence as a terrorist one is subject to the Attorney-General's discretion to order an offence not to be treated as scheduled. The width of the scheduling power—as it includes most offences involving dishonesty or deception—gives the police a wide discretion in the matter. Where an accused is charged with both a scheduled and non-scheduled offence, the mode of trial is

---

[30] Cmnd.5185 (1972).

determined by the more serious offence and it is therefore tried as a scheduled offence.

21–117   The powers to hold Diplock courts have been subjected to numerous amendments under ss.10 and 11 of the Northern Ireland (Emergency Provisions) Act 1996. The 1996 Act substantially re-enacted the Northern Ireland (Emergency Provisions) Act 1991. As noted below, Pt VII of the Terrorism Act 2000 provides for the continuation of the courts adopting a statutory formulation similar to the 1996 Act. Some points to note are as follows: in respect of the Diplock courts system, s.11 makes the requirement that the trial judge in a Diplock court must give full reasons for the conviction of an accused and subs.6 of s.11 gives an unfettered right of appeal from the verdict of the trial judge.

21–118   Concern about the low acquittal rates arising out of trials heard before the Diplock courts which, depending on the calculation used, may vary between 7.55 or 10.4 per cent, is focused on the question of the fairness of a criminal justice system where there is no jury, even though there is an automatic right of appeal from the decision of the single judge, this has not prevented general unease about the system. Specifically there is concern about some degree of case hardening of the judges in the Diplock courts, though this is not accepted by the periodic review carried out into the operation of the Diplock courts.

21–119   One of the major issues arising from any criminal trial, including the Diplock courts, is the admissibility of confession evidence. Following allegations of ill treatment, various inquiries investigated the use of effective policing methods and their compatibility with "the preservation of civil liberties and human rights". In 1975 Lord Gardiner's report[31] was clear in recommending that the continued "existence of emergency powers should be limited both in scope and duration". Certain methods of interrogation were outlawed after the Compton Report[32] and the Parker Committee[33] in 1972. The Gardiner report was equally sure that however effective security measures might be, Northern Ireland required a solution based "in political terms" and "must include further measures to promote social justice between classes and communities". A further set of recommendations contained in the Bennett Committee Report[34] tightened up procedures for interrogation by using tape recordings or even wider use of video evidence of suspects in custody under cross-examination. The use of Diplock courts has brought into question the rules of evidence available at the trial of suspected terrorists.

21–120   On interrogation procedures, the Bennett inquiry[35] in 1979, led to stricter controls over police interrogation procedures. The judiciary set tighter controls over the use of confession statements made by the accused. Judicial restrictions on the use of informants and scepticism about the value of such evidence in the absence of any corroboration has undoubtedly limited the effectiveness of informants and the use of confessions in obtaining convictions. In the past ten years, steps were taken to bring much of the ordinary criminal law and procedures under the Police and Criminal

---

[31] *Report of a Committee to consider in the context of civil liberties and human rights, measures to deal with terrorism in Northern Ireland*, Cmnd.5847 (1975). See C. Gearty, *Terrorism* (1991).
[32] Compton Report, Cmnd.4823 (1971).
[33] Parker Committee, Cmnd.4901 (1972).
[34] Bennett Committee Report, Cmnd.7497 (1979).
[35] S. Livingstone, "The House of Lords and the Northern Ireland Conflict" [1994] *Modern Law Review* 333.

Evidence (Northern Ireland) Order 1989.[35a] The peace process has brought reform of policing in Northern Ireland to the fore. The recommendations of the inquiry chaired by Chris Patten resulted in the setting-up of the Police Service for Northern Ireland replacing the Royal Ulster Constabulary.

The Terrorism Act 2000

Background and Context

Over the past decade regular reviews of emergency powers have been carried out and this led to replacing much of the 1978 and 1987 Acts by two statutes. The Northern Ireland (Emergency Provisions) Act 1991 and the Prevention of Terrorism (Temporary Provisions) Act 1989 consolidated reforms introduced in 1987. However the law became a virtual hotchpotch of temporary consolidations, some applied only to Northern Ireland and some to the United Kingdom as a whole. The approach taken has been to regard the powers necessary to deal with terrorism as temporary, and that such powers were exceptional and once the threat from terrorism subsided, there would be a restoration of "normal policing" powers.   **21–121**

The need for a review of all emergency powers as a whole has been pressing. Eventually the Terrorism Act was drafted following the recommendations[36] made by Lord Lloyd in 1996 and contained in the Government's White Paper, *Legislation Against Terrorism*.[37]   **21–122**

The Lloyd inquiry began with an assumption that the peace process in Northern Ireland would continue. In vol.2 of the inquiry report is a report into the present and future threat to the United Kingdom from international and domestic terrorism. A key element of the inquiry is the crucial comparison between ordinary police powers under the Police and Criminal Evidence Act 1984 and the special powers found in the Prevention of Terrorism (Temporary Provisions) Act 1984 and the Northern Ireland (Emergency Provisions) Act 1996.   **21–123**

The findings of the Lloyd inquiry were as follows. First there is a need for anti-terrorist legislation even if there is a lasting peace in Northern Ireland. A new definition of terrorism might include:[37a]   **21–124**

> "the use of serious violence against persons or property, or the threat to use such violence, to intimidate or coerce a government, the public or any section of the public, in order to promote political, social or ideological objectives."

There is a need at some time in the future to replace the existing emergency laws with measures that might appear in a new Act designed to supplement the ordinary criminal law. A number of powers require retention: the power to proscribe terrorist organisations; membership of such organisations to remain a criminal offence; arrest powers will be required with detention of up to 48 hours; powers to stop and search will be maintained; the power to examine people at ports will remain in force; and the powers to control and investigate terrorist funding are required.   **21–125**

[35a] Police and Criminal Evidence (Northern Ireland) Order (SI 1989/1341).
[36] Lloyd Report Inquiry into legislation against terrorism, Cm.3420 (1996).
[37] Cm.4178 (1998).
[37a] *Lloyd Report* Cm.3420 (1996) para. 5.23.

21–126   New powers should include: powers to enable the arrest and prosecution of those that conspire to commit terrorist acts abroad; the proposal that if a terrorist gives evidence in court "he should be entitled to receive a statutory discount of between one-third and two-thirds on the sentence which the court would otherwise have imposed". In the case of a charge of murder with a mandatory life sentence the discount could be reflected in the minimum period recommended to be served. Safeguards for the accused include the need for a special regime for the supervision of the detention of terrorist suspects. Included within these arrangements are the tape-recording of suspect interviews and access to solicitors. The power to examine people at ports should be the subject of a code of practice with specific needs set out such as targeting individual criminals or suspects. Examinations should be limited to a maximum of six hours rather than 24 at present.

21–127   The main justification for maintaining emergency powers is the problem of response time to states of emergency. Pre-planned legislation is therefore essential even if it may not be possible to maintain permanent legislation.

21–128   A number of key elements appear in Lord Lloyd's analysis. Once a lasting peace is established in Northern Ireland the existing system of Diplock courts for terrorist cases might be replaced. Transitional arrangements might be possible such as building into the process some element of flexibility by permitting some cases to be "certified out" from the Diplock court system into trial by jury.

21–129   The Lloyd inquiry provides an important context in which to discuss terrorism. Northern Ireland is examined within the context of international terrorism. In responding with legislation to deal with terrorism, four important guiding principles are identified:

• Legislation against terrorism should approximate as closely as possible to the ordinary criminal law and procedure.

• Additional statutory offences and powers may be justified, but only if they are necessary to meet the anticipated threat. They must then strike the right balance between the needs of security and the rights and liberties of the individual.

• The need for additional safeguards should be considered alongside any additional powers.

• The law should comply with the United Kingdom's obligations in international law.

21–130   The Terrorism Act 2000 completely reforms the law on terrorism and makes emergency powers permanent. Unlike other emergency powers against terrorism in the past, the Act as a whole is not subject to annual review as a basis of renewal, nor does the Act, with the exception of Pt VII which only applies to Northern Ireland, have a limited life expectancy. S.126 of the Act requires that Parliament should receive an annual report on the working of the Act. The Terrorism Act applies for the most part throughout the United Kingdom and Northern Ireland. The Act repealed the Prevention of Terrorism (Temporary Provisions) Act 1989 and the Northern Ireland (Emergency Provisions) Act 1996. However, matters are made complicated, as for practical purposes for Northern Ireland, steps have been taken to keep in place the main terrorist legislation consisting of the Prevention of Terrorism (Temporary

Provisions) Act 1989, the Northern Ireland (Emergency Provisions) Act 1996 and the Criminal Justice (Terrorism and Conspiracy) Act 1998. All three enactments were continued in force under Order in Council[38] with the coming into force of Sch.1 of the Terrorism Act 2000. This means that under Sch.1 of the Terrorism Act, the Secretary of State may continue the three statutes in force for 12 months.

Pt VII of the Terrorism Act only applies to Northern Ireland and applies for a **21–131** maximum life of five years from the date when it comes into force; and after five years it will expire. It is subject to continuing in force for 12 months at a time and then it must be renewed. Pt VII maintains the plethora of arrangements that cover the main mode of trial for terrorist offences in Northern Ireland under non-jury courts (known as Diplock courts) set up specifically to deal with Northern Ireland's emergency from 1972.

Although it is clear that the Terrorism Act 2000 is a new statute and does not **21–132** consolidate existing or past legislation, it is clear that its roots and ideas are drawn from the experience of emergency legislation enacted over the past fifty years.

It is generally accepted today that emergency powers in Northern Ireland are an **21–133** attempt to provide a greater balance between the security requirements of effective and widely drafted legal powers, and the need to provide suspects with acceptable standards of rights. The need to address the question of the rights of suspects has come from a number of inquiries including the decisions of the Court of Human Rights at Strasbourg[39] and judicial decisions in the courts in Northern Ireland. It is convenient to examine the use of emergency powers under three categories: police powers; trial and evidence; and the rule of law.

EMERGENCY POWERS AND THE PROTECTION OF CIVIL LIBERTIES

The Terrorism Act re-defines terrorism from previous legislation by considerably **21–134** broadening the scope and remit of what may be categorised as terrorism. The original idea embedded in the Prevention of Terrorism Act 1989 and the Emergency Provisions Act 1996 was the definition containing "the use of violence for political ends". S.1 of the Terrorism Act applies to serious violence but is all-embracing in the catalogue of causes that may be ideological and religious. This might include almost any organisation but what qualifies it as terrorism under the Act is " . . . action or threat of action which is designed to influence the Government or to intimidate the public or a section of the public". The action involved falls within the remit of the section if it:

- involves serious violence against a person;

- involves serious damage to property;

- endangers a person's life other than that of the person committing the action;

- creates a serious risk to the health or safety of the public or a section of the public; or

---

[38] Prevention of Terrorism (Temporary Provisions) Act 1989, (Continuance) Order 2000 (SI 2000/835).
[39] See the discussion in *Murray v UK* (1994) 19 E.H.R.R. 193.

- is designed seriously to interfere with or seriously to disrupt an electronic system.

21–135 Despite assurances given in the debate on the Terrorism Bill, it is possible to see such a wide definition covering industrial disputes, animal rights groups, or active engagement by religious or political causes. The underlying assumption is that the section is intended to apply to those who are seeking to undermine democracy.

21–136 Sch.6 of the Terrorism Act 2000 provides an extensive range of powers that cover financial institutions and ss.24 and 25 apply to the movement of cash between states, allowing the seizure of assets. The Act also retains the idea of proscribed organisations and under Pt II adds powers to Secretary of State to proscribe certain organisations connected with terrorism. There is a Proscribed Organisations Appeal Commission under s.5 to hear appeals against proscription. This provides an extensive set of procedures for de-proscription of a proscribed organisation. In the Northern Ireland context the IRA, the Ulster Freedom Fighters and other organisations have been proscribed and continue to be proscribed under the Terrorism Act 2000. Following the Act's coming into force in March 2001 various international organisations were also proscribed. The Northern Ireland experience would suggest that few individuals have been successfully prosecuted for membership of a proscribed organisation alone. Proscription may assist in identifying the funds and organisational structure of terrorist groups. It also may help proscribe fund-raising activities and information is required to be disclosed in respect of individuals who have suspected involvement with a proscribed organisation. Pt III of the Act also covers terrorist property and fund-raising.

Police Powers

21–137 Police powers to arrest, search and seize are provided under the emergency powers in force in Northern Ireland and under the Terrorism Act 2000 for the United Kingdom. These powers are intended to supplement the ordinary criminal law. In Northern Ireland there are occasions when the ordinary law is sufficiently wide to facilitate most emergency situations. For example under arts.42–45 of the Police and Criminal Evidence (Northern Ireland) Order 1989, detention is possible for up to 96 hours with at least two appearances before magistrates.

21–138 There is a long history of emergency arrest powers. S.11 of the Northern Ireland (Emergency Provisions) Act 1978 conferred powers to arrest on any constable "without warrant any person whom he suspects of being a terrorist". This arrest power was intended to be used as a means to begin procedures leading to detention without trial. As such the police had an extended time to detain suspects for questioning. Standard police procedures made use of s.11 powers notwithstanding the existence of arrest powers also under s.13 of the 1978 Act, replaced by s.17 of the 1991 Act or under s.2 of the Criminal Law Act (Northern Ireland) 1967 where detention powers were more heavily constrained.

21–139 S.11 of the 1978 Act was repealed by the Northern Ireland (Emergency Provisions) Act 1987. This leaves the police in Northern Ireland with arrest powers under s.14 of the Prevention of Terrorism (Temporary Provisions) Act 1989. This is the main arrest power in force in Northern Ireland and is also available throughout the United

Kingdom. In Northern Ireland, it is used more frequently than in England and Wales. Ss.40 and 41 of the Terrorism Act 2000 include arrest powers and Sch.8 of the Terrorism Act 2000 provides for extended detention that is similar to that found under s.14 of the 1989 Act.

The army in Northern Ireland has powers of arrest and detention up to four hours **21–140** under s.18 of the 1991 Act, re-enacted by s.19 of the Northern Ireland (Emergency Provisions) Act 1996. S.19(2) avoids the need to give the "ground of arrest" if the army states that the arrest is effected by a member of Her Majesty's Forces. Thus in effect the army have the power to arrest merely for interrogation purposes. S.19 also has the requirement that a contemporaneous account of the record of the search of premises must be made and supplied as soon as is practicable to the occupier of the premises searched. In *Murray v Ministry of Defence*[40] the House of Lords accepted that the giving of information concerning the reasons for the arrest could be delayed. While accepting there was no power to search for incriminating evidence, the House of Lords held that it "is a proper exercise of the power of search to" search every room for other occupants of the house in case there may be those who are disposed to resist arrest. However, this power was limited to arrest only and could not be used to carry out a search for incriminating evidence under s.14. It seems in practice that the army use their powers of arrest but within four hours all persons arrested are handed over to the police who may then re-arrest and give the appropriate reasons for the arrest. S.83(2) of the Terrorism Act 2000 provides powers of arrest and seizure to the armed forces in Northern Ireland, to s.19 of the 1996 Act in similar words. S.83(2) of the Terrorism Act 2000 provides, without warrant, powers for entry, search, seizure and arrest. Detention powers in connection with s.83 are for up to four hours. There are also extensive powers under Sch.10 of the Terrorism Act 2000 to search for munitions and scanning devices. S.87 provides that there are powers for the examination and search of documents and their retention.

The question of the reasonableness required to effect a lawful arrest has arisen in a **21–141** number of cases. In *McKee v Chief Constable of Northern Ireland*[41] the Court of Appeal in Northern Ireland as approved in the House of Lords, accepted that instructions given to a constable from a superior officer or an officer of equal status might be sufficient to entitle the officer to rely on the suspicion contained in his instructions. Since then it has been accepted that an officer giving the instruction should not necessarily have to be called as a witness in an action for false imprisonment.

The Northern Ireland Court of Appeal in the *McKee* case also considered whether **21–142** suspicion that a person was a member of a proscribed organisation was sufficient grounds to believe that the person was a terrorist as defined now under s.66 of the 1991 Act. The Court held that it required real suspicion of the commission or attempted commission of an act of terrorism or of directly organising or training of persons for terrorism. Thus suspicion of membership of a proscribed organisation did not satisfy that criterion.[42]

---

[40] [1988] 1 W.L.R. 692.
[41] [1983] 11 N.I.J.B. *Oscar v Chief Constable, RUC* [1993] 2 *Bulletin of Northern Ireland Law* 52 on the award of damages for any unlawful detention or arrest.
[42] See for civil liabililty requirements in *Stanford v Chief Constable of the Royal Ulster Constabulary* [1988] N.I. 361.

21–143   In *O'Hara v Chief Constable of the Royal Ulster Constabulary*[43] the House of Lords considered the arrest of a suspect under s.12(1)(b) of the Prevention of Terrorism (Temporary Provisions) Act 1984. The Court of Appeal in Northern Ireland had accepted, as had the trial judge, that the basis for the officer's reasonable suspicion was a briefing held by his superior officer. This satisfied the requirement of suspicion for the purposes of the Act. In fact the suspect was arrested based on the evidence of the briefing, but released two weeks later without being charged. He brought an action against the Chief Constable for wrongful arrest. A point of law of public importance was raised in an appeal to the House of Lords.

21–144   The House of Lords held that neither the trial judge nor the Court of Appeal in Northern Ireland had misdirected itself in construing the requirements of the Act. Lords Steyn and Hope concluded that:

>   (i)   The court was not required to look beyond what was in the arresting officer's mind. The grounds which were in the mind of the arresting officer at the time of the arrest were important.
>
>   (ii)   The officer's suspicion need not be based on his own observations but on the information he received from his briefing or anonymously. It was not necessary for him to prove what was known to his informant.
>
>   (iii)   The question of whether the information supplied at the briefing was a basis for reasonable grounds depended on its source and context and had to be viewed in the light of all the surrounding circumstances.

21–145   The case is important because many arrest powers commonly found in statutes have similar provisions that require reasonable suspicion. The case provides a useful analysis of this important arrest power.

21–146   Doubts surround the use of the above arrest powers for the purpose of gathering intelligence. A general power of intelligence gathering by arresting at random any person within a particular locality was not included in the legislation. Such "screening powers" of suspects are often advocated by military commentators but do not have legal authority under the emergency powers.

21–147   S.23 of the Northern Ireland (Emergency Provisions) Act 1991 re-enacted by s.25 of the Northern Ireland (Emergency Provisions) Act 1996 gives the police and army powers to stop and question any person about their identity, movements and what they may know about recent incidents such as explosions or injury to persons or killings. The breadth of interpretation of such powers may be of concern if there was a widespread practice to select areas for stop-and-search powers to be used indiscriminately.

21–148   Wide powers to proscribe terrorist organisations are contained in s.28 of the Northern Ireland (Emergency Provisions) Act 1991, re-enacted by s.29 of the Northern Ireland (Emergency Provisions) Act 1996, the list of proscribed organisations includes the Irish Republican Army and, recently added, the Ulster Volunteer Force. This power has been retained under the Terrorism Act 2000. Withholding information about acts of terrorism is an offence under s.18 of the Prevention of Terrorism (Temporary Provisions) Act 1989.

[43] [1997] 1 All E.R. 129.

Pt V of the Terrorism Act 2000 contains similar counter-terrorist powers as those **21–149** outlined under the 1989 Act. This includes detention and arrest powers The detention power proved controversial in use in Northern Ireland. In England and Wales the powers of detention fell under the Police and Criminal Evidence Act and various codes of practice. The use of audio-taping of interviews and access to legal advice are seen as important safeguards. The general welfare of the detained person is also important in providing a protection against any physical abuse.

In Northern Ireland various cases[44] alleging illegal treatment of suspects under **21–150** detention and interrogation led to the European Court of Human Rights reviewing arrangements. Afterwards the police adopted a code of practice under s.61 of the Emergency Provisions Act 1991. There is an Independent Commissioner for the Holding (detention centres) Centres. From March 1998 video-taping has been introduced without sound tracks. However, there are proposals that the video tape should include a sound track and this recommendation is expected to improve the accountability of police conduct over suspects in detention.

Access to legal advice in Northern Ireland is provided under s.45 of the Emergency **21–151** Provisions Act 1991 and s.47 of the Emergency Provisions Act 1996. Doubts have been expressed as to the legal implications of a failure to give a detained person access to a lawyer or a delay in giving access. There would appear to be no grounds for an action in damages[45] but there are possibilities of judicial review. The European Court of Human Rights has held in the leading case of *Magee v UK*[46] that in certain circumstances denial of access to a lawyer following an arrest, may constitute a breach of Article 6 of the Convention. On the facts of the case a confession statement was obtained before access to a lawyer was eventually allowed. The Human Rights Act 1998 strengthens the argument for account to be taken of Article 6 in designing the procedures for the detention and questioning of suspects . The detention of suspects in Northern Ireland has been reduced considerably with the operation of the peace process. This has resulted in the closure of the main detention centre and a significant reduction in the military presence in Northern Ireland. The aim is to provide as far as it is practicable "normal" policing arrangements.

Sch.8 of the Terrorism Act 2000 provides for the regulation and administration of **21–152** detention. This means that a person detained under the Act will rely on those procedures rather than the procedures available under PACE. Included within the arrangements for detention under the Act are codes of practice for the use of audio arrangements in interrogation. Account is taken under Sch.8 of the right of access to a solicitor and for the future there is the possibility of video-recording of questioning.

Wide powers to examine any person on arrival or departure from Great Britain or **21–153** Northern Ireland, by ship or aircraft, in travelling by land between Northern Ireland and the Republic, were contained in s.16, Sch.5 of the 1989 Act. Additional powers of investigation for the search of terrorist materials modelled on the Drugs Trafficking Offences Act 1986 are combined in s.17, Sch.7 of the 1989 Act. Such powers find their way generally into Pt V of the Terrorism Act 2000. Sch.7 of the Act provides powers for the examination and questioning of suspects at ports and borders and Sch.8 for their detention and treatment during investigation of their conduct. The Terrorism Act

[44] *Ireland v UK* (1978) (January, 1978).
[45] *R. v Lynch* (October 19, 1993) and *McKenna's Application, Re* [1992] N.I.J.B.
[46] June 6, 2000.

provide a comprehensive set of rules and codes of practice for the detention and questioning of suspects.

21–154   S.27 of the 1991 Act and s.29 of the Northern Ireland (Emergency Provisions) Act 1996 create one of the most widely drawn offences. The section makes it a criminal offence, a scheduled offence, for:

> "Any person who directs, at any level, the activities of an organisation which is concerned in the commission of acts of terrorism is guilty of an offence and liable on conviction on indictment to imprisonment for life."

21–155   The section is aimed at those who direct the activities of terrorism, but the section is capable of a broader interpretation to include those who appear to the security forces to have various tools or documents which may be useful to the commission of terrorist acts. This makes it difficult in law to distinguish degrees of support for terrorist organisations. On a wide interpretation of the section the link between a terrorist organisation and the activities sufficient to come within the Act need only be very slight. In fact any suspicious objects or activities may fall within the above classification giving wide discretion to the security forces. It is an offence under s.18(1)(b) of the Prevention of Terrorism (Temporary Provisions) Act 1989 to have information which a person knows might be of material assistance in securing the apprehension of any person involved in the commission, preparation or instigation of an act of terrorism and fail to disclose it to the police. S.31 of the 1991 Act, now s.33 of the Northern Ireland (Emergency Provisions) Act 1996 makes it a criminal offence to collect any information about police officers, soldiers, judges and court officials. The burden of proof shifts to the defendant showing lawful authority or reasonable excuse for the possession of such information.

21–156   Finally, internment powers were retained but are not in use under Pt IV and Sch.3 of the 1991 Act. These may be brought into force by the Secretary of State through the laying of a statutory instrument. Detailed detention orders may be made under Pt IV of the Northern Ireland (Emergency Provisions) Act 1996. There is no internment power under the Terrorism Act 2000 although the detention powers under the Act may provide similar arrangements.

The Use of Force

21–157   In a number of important cases the courts have interpreted s.3(1) of the Criminal Law Act (Northern Ireland) 1967 which is the Northern Ireland equivalent of the United Kingdom's s.3(1) of the Criminal Law Act 1967 relating to the use of force. This section authorises the use of reasonable force in making an arrest and the use of reasonable force to resist an unlawful arrest. The force authorised by law is "reasonable force". Reasonable force may mean that the minimum force necessary may be exceeded if it is reasonable. On this point the law in Northern Ireland appears to be the same as the rest of the United Kingdom.

21–158   In 1983 in London two policemen shot Stephen Waldorf in the belief, which later turned out to be mistaken, that he was a dangerous escaped prisoner. One officer was tried with attempted murder and wounding with intent to cause grievous bodily harm and the other officer, who assaulted Waldorf with his pistol after he had been shot, was charged in addition with causing grievous bodily harm with intent. The officers were acquitted after it was accepted that the policemen believed that Waldorf was a dangerous criminal. Such a belief was honestly held, albeit it was later discovered to have been a mistaken belief. Waldorf's shooting was a case of mistaken identity but this was not apparent to the police officers at the time. The case raised some important issues of legal principle. There is authority for the proposition that the defendant is to be judged on the facts as he believed them to be. *Gladstone Williams*[47] in the Court of Appeal has been approved by the Privy Council in *Beckford v R.*[48] The *Waldorf case*[49] allowed this defence to be used by the police officers and they were acquitted.

The defence of honest mistake is often joined to the defence of self-defence. On self-defence, the view put forward by Lowry L.C.J. in *Browne*[50] is that where a police officer acts lawfully and uses only reasonable force in effecting the lawful arrest of a suspect or an offender, then self-defence is not available to the defendant. This would appear to rule out the mistaken belief that the defendant is entitled to raise self-defence, if for example he thought the police officer was a gunman. Lord Lowry explained[51]:   **21–159**

> "The need to act must not have been created by the conduct of the accused in the immediate context of the incident which was likely to give rise to that need."

Perhaps the question of self-defence is too widely excluded in the *Browne* case. A mistaken belief as to self-defence is similar to a mistaken belief that the police officers raised in the *Waldorf* case. The question of reasonable and honest mistake was raised in the *Att.-Gen. for Northern Ireland's Reference (No.1 of 1975).*[52] The House of Lords examined two matters raised by the Court of Criminal Appeal in Northern Ireland. A soldier on patrol killed an unarmed man when he ran away after being challenged. A judge, without a jury, acquitted the soldier of murder as the prosecutor had failed to prove that the soldier either intended to kill or seriously injure. The killing was justifiable. The House of Lords held, first that whether the force used was reasonable was a matter of fact and whether the intention to kill was satisfied therefore did not arise.   **21–160**

The standard of reasonableness must take account of all the circumstances which gave rise to the use of force. In *R. v MacNaughton*[53] Lowry L.C.J. considered the facts surrounding the use of force. The fact of an explosion before the shooting, a danger of booby-traps and other suspected terrorists could be examined to consider whether the shooting was lawful.   **21–161**

Even where the arrest is lawful, are the security forces entitled to shoot to kill? Reconstructing the facts leading up to fatal shootings gives rise to many disputes[54] over exactly how the fatality occurred. However in Northern Ireland, arising out of a series   **21–162**

[47] (1984) 78 Cr.App.R. 276. See *Morgan* [1976] A.C. 182 and Smith & Hogan, *Criminal Law* (7th ed., 1992), pp.252–261.
[48] [1988] 3 A.C. 130.
[49] *The Times*, October 13–20, 1983.
[50] [1973] N.I. 96 at 107.
[51] *ibid.*
[52] [1977] A.C. 105; [1976] 2 All E.R. 937.
[53] [1976] 2 All E.R. 937; [1975] N.I. 203.
[54] *Farrell v Secretary of State for Defence* [1980] 1 All E.R. 166; *Farrell v UK* (1983) 5 E.H.R.R. 466. See also *Magill v Ministry of Defence* [1987] N.I. 194; *R. v Hegarty* [1986] N.I. 343; *Lynch v Ministry of Defence* [1983] N.I. 216; *McGuigan v Ministry of Defence* [1982] 19 N.I.J.B., Q.B.D (N.I.).

of incidents involving the police and the shooting of a number of terrorists, it was alleged that there was a shoot-to-kill policy but following a number of enquiries it was concluded that there was no evidence of a shoot-to-kill policy.[55] However, the number of incidents and the prosecution of a number of members of the security forces for killings using firearms, have given rise to the suspicion among members of the Nationalist community, that those engaged in covert operations had a clear understanding that lethal force might be used, but it was never proven that a shoot-to-kill policy was operated in Northern Ireland.

21–163   There have been a few successful prosecutions of members of the security forces. Two members of the Scots Guards regiment were convicted of the murder of Peter McBride. They unsuccessfully appealed to the House of Lords against conviction. It was held that they had had sufficient time to make a decision whether or not to use force and that Peter McBride when fired on posed no threat. Although convicted of murder the Army Board decided not to discharge the soldiers from the army; however, this decision was quashed on a judicial review taken by the deceased's mother.[56]

21–164   Two analyses may be drawn from the state of the law in this area. First, clearer guidelines are needed to set out the general circumstances where lethal force may be used. Currently, members of the security forces have "yellow card" guidelines on the use of force, but the details of the guidelines are not published and they do not have the force of law. The need to clarify s.3 of the 1967 Act is apparent when it is realised that the section states a rule of both civil and criminal law. The justification of force on the basis of "reasonable in the circumstances" removes the possibility of a successful civil action or the prosecution of the defendant in criminal proceedings.

21–165   Secondly, the Criminal Law Act 1967 is unclear as to the use of force in self-defence or against an unjustifiable attack. Such a defence exists in common law, and there is a question of whether self-defence is governed by s.3. It is most likely the case that s.3 governs the law of self-defence, but this should be made more clear. There is also a remarkable difference between civil and criminal liability in terms of evidential burden. Hutton J. in *McGuigan v Ministry of Defence*[57] noted that in criminal trials, once the accused raises a defence of reasonable force, the prosecution have the onus to prove beyond a reasonable doubt that the force used was unreasonable. In a civil case the defence have to rely on establishing on the balance of probabilities that a defence of reasonable force is proved. The call for a review of the law is supported by the United Nations' *Instrument on Basic Principles on the use of Force and Firearms by Law Enforcement Officials*, September 7, 1990. This is a area of law of particular sensitivity in Northern Ireland.

21–166   The shooting of 13 people by the Parachute Regiment on January 13, 1972 while attending a civil rights demonstration in Londonderry has caused enormous controversy and strong feelings. The inquiry[58] held by Lord Widgery, then the Lord Chief

---

[55] No evidence of a shoot-to-kill policy: see *Hansard*, HC Vol.126, cols.21–35 (January 25, 1983); J. Stalker, *Stalker* (1988). See also *Justice under Fire* (Jennings ed., 1990); D. Murphy, *The Stalker Affair and the Press* (1991). Mr Colin Simpson, Deputy Chief Constable of West Yorkshire, who completed the inquiry into shoot-to-kill after the removal of John Stalker.

[56] *McBride's Application for Judicial Review, Re* [1999] N.I. 299.

[57] [1982] 19 N.I.J.B.

[58] *Report of the Tribunal appointed to inquire into the events on Sunday 30th January 1972, which led to the loss of life in connection with the procession in Londonderry on that day by the lord Chief Justice Lord Widgery* (1972 HC 22).

Justice, largely exonerated the Parachute Regiment of any wrongdoing. In his findings it was accepted that some soldiers engaged in the shootings may have "bordered on the reckless". However, there were no prosecutions of any of those involved in the shooting. Evidence suggesting a link between any of the deceased and handling a firearm or a bomb has been discounted. The Widgery Report no longer holds much credibility and as a result it was agreed that a new Tribunal of Inquiry should be held. It began work in 1998 under the chairmanship of Lord Saville. The procedures of the Saville inquiry allow cross-examination and legal representation to the deceased's family and relatives. The procedures have been subject to judicial review[59] and this resulted in a reconsideration of the lifting of anonymity accorded to some soldiers when giving evidence. The inquiry is held in public with the latest technology to aid the dissemination of information and analysis. To date the inquiry is slow and cumbersome and is unlikely to be completed speedily. In the future it might be useful to review the precise procedural rules under which such an inquiry should take place. The sensitivity of the issues involved and the ongoing peace process provide the inquiry with enormous challenges: it has to avoid becoming a political tool in the peace process. The inquiry has the unenviable task of attempting to assess events that took place when circumstances and perceptions may have been different than today. There are many serious questions to be addressed. Was the Parachute Regiment given orders to open fire that were consistent with the rules of engagement then in force? Did individual soldiers respond with excessive force? Will the inquiry be able to reach a satisfactory resolution of the matters that fall within its remit and at the same time provide a means for the community to draw together rather than separate further in acrimony over its findings? Few inquiries will have had to confront some of the deeply held underlying political causes and strong beliefs. The implications of its findings will no doubt become an important element in the future political dialogue in Northern Ireland.

21–167 Members of the security forces are also amenable to the civil law.[60] In the case of the shootings in Londonderry, out-of-court settlements were made in civil actions. In *Copeland v Ministry of Defence*[61] vicarious liability applied to the Ministry of Defence in connection with the shooting of the plaintiff arising out of negligence on the part of an army corporal.

21–168 Another area of great difficulty in assessing the use of force is in connection with the use of plastic baton rounds or CS gas. Serious injury, even death has been caused by the use of such devices which are primarily intended to avoid the use of lethal force. In the case of using excessive force it is the criminal and civil liability of the individual policeman or soldier that is involved. There is no direct authority clearly stating the principle of where the borderline between superior orders and individual responsibility may lie. It is thought that it is no defence to a criminal charge to plead a duty to obey the commands of a superior where the orders are so manifestly illegal that the soldier must have recognised they are unlawful. Only when the orders are legal may the individual responsible hope to plead superior orders.

21–169 Controversy surrounding the use of force came to the fore in the case of *R. v Clegg*.[62] Over 350 deaths have been caused by the security forces in the course of their duties in

---

[59] *R. v Lord Saville of Newdigate Ex p. B (No.2)* [1999] 4 All E.R. 860.
[60] *McLaughlin v Ministry of Defence* (1978) 7 N.I.J.B.
[61] Unreported, Northern Ireland, May 19, 1999.
[62] June 4, 1993, [1995] 1 A.C. 482.

Northern Ireland. This has caused enormous controversy. The *Clegg* case highlights the problems for the prosecution authorities if there are grounds to consider that the use of force is unreasonable. The defendants were members of the British Army manning a road check-point. The victims were teenage joy-riders in a stolen car. Police evidence was given which challenged the army's version of the shooting incident arising out of the failure of the stolen car to stop at an army check-point. At the trial the judge held that the army was justified in firing shots at the car when speeding towards them but not justified in shooting after the car had passed the patrol. Two soldiers were convicted of murder. The Court of Appeal dismissed the appeal of one defendant, Clegg, but in the case of Aindow, the other defendant, substituted a conviction for malicious wounding for that of murder. The case went on appeal to the House of Lords which dismissed the appeal.[63] The controversy following has led to the release of Corporal Clegg on licence in July 1995.

21–170   Finally, in *McCann v UK*[64] the European Court of Human Rights considered whether the shooting of IRA suspects in Gibraltar violated the rights of the deceased under Article 2 of the European Convention. By a majority the Court held that there was no violation of Article 2 but the Court found that the UK had breached Article 2 in respect of the inadequacies of the investigations. The case highlights the importance of the human rights aspects of the use of force. There have been a number of cases taken under the European Convention on Human Rights arising out of deaths in Northern Ireland which test the compatibility of the use of force and the human rights of the deceased.[65]

Trial and Evidence

21–171   The Diplock courts[66] allow for the trial of scheduled offences before a single judge without a jury. The principle of using the judiciary in terrorist offences is seen as an attempt to provide a substitute for internment. The operation of the Diplock courts has been criticised because of the absence of jury trial and the resultant changes in the law of evidence. Fears that a single judge might become case hardened have been raised, and some evidence, though not conclusive, has been used to argue that low acquittal rates may be used as a means of testing judicial independence. Although comparisons of acquittal rates are not always valid, the fact that judges need to be alert to the possibility of becoming case hardened is a first step towards preventing this from happening. Suggestions for reform of the Diplock courts have ranged from using two or three judges or a judge with assessors or resident magistrates. Demands for return to jury trial have to date not been recommended in the reviews carried out into the operation of Diplock courts. Arguments in favour of restoring jury trial and providing protection for juries have been met with the argument that it is unsafe for jurors to perform their duty in Northern Ireland. The current arrangements under Pt VII of the

---

[63] [1995] 1 All E.R. 334.
[64] (1995) 21 E.H.R.R. 97.
[65] *McShane v UK*, Application no. 43290/98.
[66] Cmnd. 5185. See Greer (1980) 31 *Northern Ireland Legal Quarterly* 205; and Boyle, Current Law Statutes Annotated (1987); Boyle, Hadden and Hillyard, *Law and State* (1975). S. Greer and A. White, *Abolishing the Diplock Courts* (Cobden Trust, 1986); Hogan and Walker, *op.cit.*; A. Jennings and D. Wolchover (1984) 134 *New Law Journal* 659, 687.

Terrorism Act 2000 preserve the principles of the Diplock courts. S.65 creates schedule offences largely in line with the Northern Ireland legislation. While the Government is pledged to allow jury trial for all offences, the time appears not to be ripe to introduce this change. In fact the number of Diplock cases appears to be declining as the level of violence in Northern Ireland has diminished. However, events after September 11, 2001 put into doubt whether the government will wish to remove the Diplock court system from the statutory arrangements.

A number of evidential rules have been altered to meet the requirements of **21–172** emergency powers in Northern Ireland. In 1988 the Criminal Evidence (Northern Ireland) Order 1988[66a] abolished the defendants' privilege against self-incrimination. There is a history of defendants giving evidence from the late part of the nineteenth century. Under the Criminal Evidence Act 1898 defendants were first given the right to testify under oath. S.1(b) prohibited the prosecution from commenting upon the failure of the accused to testify. After the 1988 Order, the courts in Northern Ireland can place whatever weight they wish on the fact that a suspect refused to answer questions or refused to testify. As a result adverse inferences may be drawn from the accused's failure to mention a relevant fact during police questioning or when charged or giving evidence at trial. Inferences may also be drawn from his failure to account for his presence when found by a constable at a place at or about the time that the offence for which he was arrested was alleged to have been committed.

The most significant evidential rule in a criminal trial is the rule regarding **21–173** confessions. The detention and interrogation of suspects has given rise to allegations of coercion to obtain confessions. The law has to balance the interests of justice with the rights of the defendant. S.11 of the Northern Ireland (Emergency Provisions) Act 1991 re-enacts s.8 of the 1987 Northern Ireland (Emergency Provisions) Act. The 1987 Act broadened the range of conduct which makes confessions inadmissible. S.12 of the Northern Ireland (Emergency Provisions) Act 1996 provides that there are two important safeguards against the accused's self-incrimination under questioning. First, that admissions or confessions are excluded by the court where there is evidence that the accused was subjected "to torture, to inhuman or degrading treatment or to any violence or threat of violence (whether or not amounting to torture), in order to induce him to make a statement". Second, there is a judicial discretion to exclude rule. Violence or the threat of violence is a sufficient ground for the exclusion of a statement where the defendant is able to adduce *prima facie* evidence that he was subjected to such treatment. This is in addition to the exclusion of a confession obtained by any hope of advantage or fear of prejudice held out by a person in authority. Thus a confession obtained through the use of violence is almost always precluded, as s.12 of the 1996 Act precludes confessions obtained through "torture or inhuman or degrading treatment".

Once a *prima facie* case has been raised that the defendant has been subjected to **21–174** improper treatment, the Crown has the onus of proof beyond reasonable doubt that admissions were not obtained as a result of such treatment. However, two questions remain unclear. First, does s.12 preclude psychological or mental pressure as distinct from threats of violence? Second, the judges in Northern Ireland have accepted the need to have interrogation arrangements designed to obtain information from

[66a] Criminal Evidence (Northern Ireland) Order (SI 1988/1989).

unwilling suspects. If members of terrorist organisations are to be effectively questioned, how may their rights be best protected? How far do such arrangements offend against the test of oppression, *i.e.* torture, inhuman or degrading treatment and the use or threat of violence. S.12 of the 1996 Act is largely re-enacted under s.76 of the Terrorism Act 2000.

21–175   The House of Lords in *Murray v DPP for N.I.*[67] considered the interpretation of art.4 of the 1988 Order[67a] relating to inferences which may be drawn from the consequences of not giving evidence. The House of Lords held that the court must not only call upon the accused to give evidence but must tell him beforehand and explain the effect of failing to give evidence. The inferences that may be drawn from the accused are not confined to specific facts of the case but in a proper case may include drawing the inference that the accused is guilty of the events with which he is charged. The basis used to adduce guilt must be derived from the circumstances which justify such a finding. This includes the adequacy of the explanation or the failure of the accused to give an explanation. In the event the *Murray* case was considered by the European Court as regards Convention rights under Article 6. A majority of one held that there had been no violation of Article 6(1) and (2) as regards adverse inferences but that there had been a violation of Article 6(1) regarding access to a lawyer and during the first 48 hours of detention. Subsequently amendments have been made to the 1989 Order requiring that in a place of lawful detention an adverse inference may not be drawn if the accused had not been given the opportunity to consult a solicitor prior to questioning or charge or prior to the request to account for the relevant facts.[68]

21–176   Finally on admissibility of evidence it should be noted that s.12(2) of the 1996 Act states that there is a judicial discretion to exclude statements "if it appears to the court that it is appropriate to do so in order to avoid unfairness to the accused or otherwise in the interests of justice". The origins of subs.(3) may be found in s.8 of the 1978 Northern Ireland (Emergency Provisions) Act and s.8 was based on an earlier s.6 of the Northern Ireland (Emergency Provisions) Act 1973 as a re-statement of the common law discretion to exclude rule. Under s.12(3) of the 1996 Act there is some potential for the courts to exclude statements. Statements obtained by means falling short of torture, inhuman or degrading treatment and therefore admissible may be excluded. The application of this subs.(3) will be on a case by case basis. The view of Lowry L.C.J. in *O'Halloran*[69] was that the concept of voluntary confession at common law "is not by itself" a reason for the use of the discretion to exclude power.

21–177   In addition to rules of evidence on voluntary statements contained in the Emergency legislation in Northern Ireland, the PACE (Northern Ireland) Order 1989[69a] introduces the requirements of the PACE 1984 into Northern Ireland.

21–178   Ss.61 and 62 of the Emergency Provisions Act (Northern Ireland) 1991 and ss.52–54 of the 1996 Act provide that the Secretary of State must issue codes of practice in

---

[67] [1993] 7 *Bulletin of Northern Ireland Law* 44. See *R. v Dillon* [1984] N.I. 292.
[67a] Police and Criminal Evidence (Northern Ireland) Order (SI 1989/1341).
[68] Criminal Evidence (Northern Ireland) Order 1999 (SI 1999/2789, art.36).
[69] [1979] N.I. 45; Jackson, "Diplock and the Presumption Against Jury Trial: A Critique" [1992] *Criminal Law Review* 755. I am grateful to Mr Jackson for advice on a number of points regarding the criminal justice system in Northern Ireland; see Jackson [1991] *Criminal Law Review* 404; Jackson, (1989) 40 N.I.L.Q. 105, and the House of Lords decision in *R. v Murray*; [1993] 3 *Bulletin of Northern Ireland Law*. See *R. v Latimer* [1993] 3 *Bulletin of Northern Ireland Law* 45.
[69a] *ibid.*, see n.67a.

respect of detention, treatment, questioning and the identification of persons detained under the 1991 Act. Similarly, codes of practice must be issued on the powers of the police to stop, question, arrest, enter, search, seize and to close roads. Codes may be specifically issued to the army in Northern Ireland. The standing of such codes is such that breach of one of the provisions of the code may result in disciplinary proceedings against members of the army or police. This falls short of criminal prosecution.

The Role of Law and the Rule of Law

The emergency in Northern Ireland has raised fundamental questions about the role of constitutional law in attempting to provide solutions to a wide number of social, economic, religious and political problems. Specifically emergency powers are intended to protect society from terrorist activities, while at the same time providing support for law and order. Northern Ireland has witnessed widespread violence, civil unrest and destruction on a scale not seen or experienced in peacetime.   **21–179**

Northern Ireland has provided a case study of the limits of law and legality; the emergence of different sets of communities creates a sub-culture of "illegality" and self-imposed rules. There is a dangerous tendency to provide an apartheid culture between different communities and this is evident in parts of Belfast and some rural communities. Emergency powers have also tested the extent to which separate rules may apply to terrorist groups that question whether a more "rights"-orientated" approach to civil liberties might have resulted in a different perception about law. Or are there severe limitations in the role of law in dealing with civil emergencies in peacetime? Hadden[70] argues that instead of regarding emergency powers as a departure from the norm they should be seen as an integral part of modern constitutional law: **21–180**

> "The analysis of the rule of law in national systems and of human rights under international law is incomplete without a detailed consideration of the nature and extent of emergency powers and of the related derogations from human rights commitments, for it is precisely in these circumstances that the rule of law and the protection of individual human rights are most at risk."

In 1972 the then Lord Chief Justice, Lord MacDermott[71] warned of the dangers of the decline in the rule of law. His focus of concern was on Dicey's valuable strictures against "wide, arbitrary, or discretionary powers of constraint". One example of this decline and the potential for widespread abuse, is the problem of evidence obtained from "supergrasses". The use of "supergrasses" or paid informants, often as undercover agents, came to the attention of the courts in Northern Ireland in the 1980s. Such evidence was often uncorroborated and this led to a number of Northern Ireland Court of Appeal decisions which quashed confessions based on such uncorroborated testimony. After 1986 it seems unlikely that any prosecutions would be taken using supergrass informants. In terms of judicial independence, cases such as *R. v Gibney*[72], *R*   **21–181**

---

[70] T. Hadden (1990) 41 N.I.L.Q. 391.
[71] Lord MacDermott, "The Decline in the Rule of Law" [1972] N.I.L.Q. 475; and MacDermott "Law and Order. Times of Emergency" (1972) 17 Jur.Rev. 1–21.
[72] *R. v Graham* [1983] 7 N.I.J.B.

v Crumley[73] and *R. v Graham*[74] on supergrass trials illustrate how judicial discretion becomes important in setting the dividing line between acceptable and unacceptable police behaviour. Critics of judicial supervision of emergency powers in Northern Ireland have argued that a more interventionist perspective is required and that a written Bill of Rights might strengthen judicial willingness to protect civil liberties.

21–182   There is an added and more incipient problem raised by the use of emergency powers in Northern Ireland. Both emergency powers legislation and legislation for the prevention of terrorism, have blurred the lines between the specific and temporary powers required to meet an existing emergency and the need for permanent powers to meet any perceived threat for the future. There is also a concern that the effect of such wide powers has also blurred the distinction between the ordinary law and emergency powers. The full extent of the effect of the emergency in Northern Ireland has still to be measured in how ordinary legal powers and police practices may become conditioned by exceptional measures.

FUTURE DEVELOPMENTS

21–183   Northern Ireland's constitutional and political difficulties are accompanied by severe economic depression. Long-term unemployment remains endemic. Within the European Communities, Northern Ireland is an Objective 1 region eligible for a variety of funding. Northern Ireland's future seems linked to major economic and financial assistance both from the United Kingdom and from the European Community. It is a small region of 14,000 sq kms in area with a population of approximately 1.5 million. It shares similar traditions with the Irish Republic but it has no direct land link to any other Member States of the European Union and therefore remoteness and distance pose important issues in the future policy agenda for Northern Ireland.

21–184   The United Kingdom provides a block budget which is planned for three years ahead and is subject to annual review in the United Kingdom's Public Expenditure Survey. The peace process is expected to result in a reduction in funding to support security measures against terrorism.

21–185   Although Northern Ireland is linked to the economic aid provided by both the EC and the United Kingdom, generally Northern Ireland's economic policy has followed the United Kingdom's and has one of the largest public sectors within the United Kingdom. Northern Ireland has the highest rate of unemployment of all United Kingdom regions, a higher proportion of male unemployment is long-term, and there are relatively high numbers of low income families reflecting the combination of lower earnings, family size and dependence on social security. Northern Ireland's future is shaped by the implementation of government policy such as privatisation. Electricity and some transport industries are privatised. It is expected that further developments in North–South relations will help develop the tourist industry.

21–186   These economic factors will affect Northern Ireland's future constitutional and political development especially in a period of recession in the world economy. Northern Ireland is still dependent on agriculture which accounts for 89 per cent of

[73] *R. v Gibney* [1986] 4 N.I.J.B; and *R. v O'Halloran* [1979] N.I. 45.
[74] *R. v Crumley* [1987] 3 B.N.I.L.

total employment compared to the rest of the United Kingdom's average of 2.3 per cent. Diversification is limited because of climate, topography and distance from larger markets. European Community funding has therefore been widely applied and has the potential to have an important impact on regional development in Northern Ireland. Considerable attempts have been made to improve the infrastructure, industrial development and physical planning in Northern Ireland as a basis to provide the potential for long-term rather than short-term change. Also evident is the mixture of public funding and private enterprise seen in the policies adopted by the Government to encourage small businesses in Northern Ireland. Northern Ireland has unique experience of public funds mixed with private funds in an attempt to create jobs and improve the economic standing of the community.

SUMMARY AND CONCLUSIONS

Some tentative conclusions may be drawn from the Northern Ireland experience. The **21–187** question of the effectiveness of constitutional innovation and attempts to respond to violence in Northern Ireland have raised important issues about the role of legal and constitutional devices in solving complex political, social and economic problems. The need to resolve the Northern Ireland problem by constitutional means is linked to the need to find a political consensus. Northern Ireland has tested the British constitutional tradition of majority rule. Northern Ireland is likely to remain an important case study for constitutional innovation and change for some time to come. The experiences gained in attempting to create a stable, peaceful society may provide many lessons for the world's democracies.

FURTHER READING

P. Bew and G. Gillespie, *The Northern Ireland Peace Process 1993-96 A Chronology* (Serif, 1996).

G. Mitchell, *Making Peace* (Heinemann, London, 1999).

M. Mowlam, *Momentum The Struggle for Peace, Politics and the People* (Hodder and Stoughton, 2002).

Chapter 22

PUBLIC LAW AND MODERNISATION

INTRODUCTION

The election of a new Labour Government in 1997 has brought to the fore major **22–001**
constitutional change and unprecedented reforms in the area of public law. The final
chapter in the book draws together the analysis offered in the previous chapters of
major constitutional change and the future directions for the study of public law. The
coming into force of the Human Rights Act 1998 brings to the fore the question of
further constitutional reform notably a new Supreme Court for the United Kingdom to
act as a constitutional court covering the range of issues including Human Rights and
devolution. The case for and against a written constitution is also summarised.

The Common Law Inheritance

Continuity and change remain as enduring characteristics of constitutional arrange- **22–002**
ments within the United Kingdom. Each century may be seen to have contributed to
changes in public administration and in the constitution. The seventeenth century
curtailed growth in the Royal Prerogative and developed an administrative system
separate from the judiciary and episcopal influence. The eighteenth century reduced
corruption among office holders and sought greater efficiency in the system of public
administration. The nineteenth century, under the influence of the Northcote-
Trevelyan reforms, introduced into the civil service greater professionalism and
selection on merit. It also began a system of financial control for the accounting and
authorisation of expenditure by Parliament that has endured.

The legacy of the last century may be divided into two phases.[1] The first phase **22–003**
consists of broadening the electoral franchise, expanding the role of local government
and providing State intervention in the delivery of a range of new services, through the
growth in the Welfare State. The growth in legislation, containing comprehensive and
detailed drafting often with assorted codes of practice and circulars, is also a hallmark
of the present century. The second phase is distinguished by membership of the
European Community in 1972 and the development of privatisation strategies as well
as tighter constraints upon public spending. The question of the role of government in
the delivery of public services defined the relationship between the citizen and the

---

[1] See E.L. Normanton, *The Accountability and Audit of Government* (1966), pp.424–426; D.L. Keir, *The
Constitutional History of Modern Britain 1485–1937* (London, 1938).

State. In the 1970s and 1980s privatisation of many nationalised industries has marked a significant shift in the role of the State. Legislation has continued to grow in size and extent. Newly created regulatory agencies and reliance on contracts and licences set new challenges for public lawyers in developing legal analysis and techniques. Since the mid-1960s the development of judicial review has marked a significant development in the role of the judiciary in the supervision of many public bodies, agencies, government departments and local authorities. Since the 1970s the development of a new public management provides a fundamental change to relationships in the system of public management and administration.[2] The new public management has replaced the traditional approach to public life, based on stewardship and public duty, with a market-orientated approach to the delivery of public goods and services. This provides new terminology and a new way of describing the relationship between service provider and client: the principal, namely the purchaser or consumer of services, is distinguished from the provider, the public body or agency that provides the service. The latter may be part of the pre-existing public service or form a new competitive element whereby private and voluntary sectors may bid to provide goods and services. The provider is then engaged in the award of the contract, including negotiation of various conditions for performance. Set against this background of fundamental change in the way the public sector behaves is the development of standards and ethics in public life.

22–004   The Committee on Standards in Public Life (formerly known as the Nolan Commission, then the Neill Committee, and recently under a new chair, Sir Nigel Wicks) was set up in 1994 to recommend codes and principles to apply to the behaviour of M.P.s, ministers and others in public life. Broadly, the Committee has adopted a non-statutory approach to the setting of standards. Compliance is based on voluntary conformity and self-regulation. However, in certain areas, notably as part of its anti-corruption approach, the Commission advocated the setting-up of a new offence of misuse of public office.

22–005   The development of a strategy to tackle sleaze and corrupt practices in public life resulted from the cash-for-questions scandal, when it was proved that a number of M.P.s received cash for asking questions in the House arising out of the activities of a number of professional lobbyists. Evaluating the period from the end of the last century to the present-day requires an analysis of the process of major constitutional reform undertaken by the Labour Government since 1997.

Modernisation and Constitutional Reform

22–006   The current age of constitutional reform and the policy underlying much of the Government's thinking are summed up in the phrase "modernisation". It is a recurrent theme of many White Papers[3] and government documents. We have seen how all-embracing the phrase is in terms of setting a strategy for change. It covers central government and the civil service, the development of new regulation for privatised utilities, it underpins many changes in the way local government operates, including planning and environmental decision-making, and the organisation of the courts and legal services. Examples include shifting the role of local government to a more

---

[2] D. Oliver and G. Drewry, *Public Service Reforms*, 1996.
[3] *Modernizing Government*, Cm 4310 (1999).

community-based focus and the creation of a best value concept under the Local Government Act 1999.

Devolution to Scotland, Wales, Northern Ireland, London and some of the English regions has created an asymmetrical form to the Constitution. The sovereignty of Parliament is retained, while local administration is empowered through directly elected assemblies. At the same time an analysis of the legal powers of government reveals that many centralising powers are retained. One example of this is in terms of utility regulation in the Utilities Act 2000. The relevant Secretary of State retains regulatory controls over the industry, consistent with the privatisation experience as a whole. These changes reflect a continuation in the centralising control of government, and are commensurate with a marked reduction in the efficacy of parliamentary scrutiny, as parliamentary sovereignty has come increasingly to mean government sovereignty. At the same time, Parliament has tacitly accepted an accretion of judicial power—much of it judge-led, as well as judge-designed. An increase in judicial power has been accomplished through innovative ideas and thinking about the development of judicial review and its application to the ordinary citizen. The transformation of judicial power has also involved assimilation of many European elements into United Kingdom law, including the enactment of the Human Rights Act 1998, incorporating most of the European Convention on Human Rights. In matters concerning the European Union, the judiciary and not the United Kingdom Parliament has the final say.

Aside from the political policies and influences that underpin the Government's policies, it is argued in the preceding chapters that modernisation has brought about profound changes to the traditional constitutional checks and balances of government. The machinery of government and the parliamentary system of scrutiny is said to be too antiquated to fulfil the functions required of modern government. An increasingly critical analysis of existing laws and institutions and weaknesses in the present constitutional arrangements has highlighted a number of specific areas of concern.

There is concern that parliamentary control over government has been considerably weakened with the growth in, and the strength of, party government. Modern government, if endowed with a large majority, is said to have become insensitive to constitutional proprieties and resilient to criticism that is not weighted in parliamentary votes. Questions about the meaning and effectiveness of accountability over government have become an important theme in recent constitutional writing. One concern is that the "Next Steps" reforms in the civil service have moved institutions under democratic accountability to services commercially accountable to managers. It is questioned whether public services can be made commercially accountable. Is this form of accountability adequate? In theory, it is one that localises agency responsibility but in practice may weaken ministerial accountability because of its isolation from responsibility for any particular agency. There is also the broader issue of whether government should be treated as a business? This tendency to emphasise the corporate image of government may enhance management accountability but may lessen the importance of parliamentary scrutiny and political decision-making.

There is a predisposition in every political party once in government to begin tinkering with existing constitutional arrangements. Often this is ad hoc but in the current climate of fundamental change and re-alignment, it is important that time is spent in evaluating the consequences of change and their effect on the traditional

22–007

22–008

22–009

22–010

systems of checks and balances. Public law must meet that challenge and consider future directions.

A WRITTEN CONSTITUTION?

22–011   Historically the introduction of a written constitution has usually arisen out of crisis— some form of political upheaval or an attempt by newly independent countries to establish independence through international recognition of the government and institutions. Any apparent crisis in the United Kingdom's Constitution would appear to fall short of the criteria offered by any historical examples. Few countries appear to reform existing constitutional arrangements through a thoughtful reflection on its shortcomings and a peaceful introduction of reforms to placate any discontent.

22–012   Demands for a written constitution have come from the Liberal Democrats,[4] the Institute of Public Policy Research and from Charter 88. Prominent constitutional lawyers have called for a written constitution and an increasing body of intellectual opinion has favoured constitutional reform from political thinkers on both the left and the right in politics. However, contemporary writing of the 1980s and 90s is reminiscent of writing in the 1970s and even past diagnosis of the post-war period. Oliver[5] has identified a number of factors which may have created pressure for reform and may be summarised as follows.

22–013   The post-war consensus over the range of activities carried out by the public sector has come under strain. Polarisation of the two major political parties has contributed to marked differences in attitudes to the public sector. The election of Mrs Thatcher's Government in 1979 and four successive Conservative Party election victories thereafter have allowed many fundamental changes to be introduced into the delivery of public services. Privatisation is also relevant in the trend away from State ownership in favour of Public Company Act companies for the delivery of public services. Market forces and the consumer are perceived as satisfactory regulators of public services with the minimum of direct State intervention.

22–014   Changes in policy perceptions in the early 1980s about the role of local government have created tensions in the relationship between central and local government. The trend in favour of more centralised power has encouraged stronger central government as preferable to weak local authorities. Centralisation has a number of motives behind it. A desire to change existing institutions and cultures in line with a greater reliance on market enterprise is more readily accommodated with central control. Strong political ideologies in the 1980s facilitated more central control. Popular causes such as privatisations and council house sales to tenants are seen as attainable only from a strong executive government, and carry favour with those who see strong government as a virtue of the United Kingdom's political system. At the same time discontent over the United Kingdom's constitutional arrangements argues for reform, and some go as far as to include a written constitution.

---

[4] *"We the people . . ."—Towards a Written Constitution* (1990); F. Mount, *The British Constitution Now* (1992). Institute of Public Policy Research, The Constitution of the United Kingdom, (1991). Also see R. Blackburn (ed.), Constitutional Studies (1992).
[5] D. Oliver, *Government in the United Kingdom* (1991), pp.3–40.

Supporters of constitutional reform highlight the weaknesses in parliamentary   **22–015**
control over the Executive as evidenced by the accretion of centralised governmental
power. In the aftermath of a period of strong government with large overall majorities,
electoral reform is favoured, linked to the need for a fairer balance in the composition
of the House of Commons.

The arguments against adopting a written constitution emphasise the flexibility   **22–016**
inherent in existing arrangements. The tradition of an unwritten constitution has
reinforced the supremacy of Parliament in both the narrow legal sense, and in the
broader sense of political majoritarian government. Change may be accomplished
without any general rethink of the constitutional arrangements. Adaptation may be
seen as part of an organic growth unhindered by the restraint of a constitutional
requirement to give the judiciary a final say in any change. The virtues of the present
system must not be overlooked even if it is desirable to consider reforms. It is often
conceded that many of the reforms mentioned above may be enacted without a written
constitution. The strengths of a flexible unwritten constitution may be found in the
primacy given to the political process. This may be weakened by entrenching in a
written constitution those matters currently governed by convention or political
choices. A written constitution might mark a shift from political decision-making to
judicial scrutiny which may be too narrow and restrictive of the political choices on
offer to the electorate.

Enacting a written constitution may not be a panacea for all constitutional law   **22–017**
problems. The debate over whether a written constitution might be adopted or not
provides an opportunity for students of the Constitution to analyse and critically
examine existing arrangements which will undoubtedly contribute to a deeper understanding of the working of the United Kingdom's Constitution. Finally connected with
the development of new structures is the question of a new Supreme Court to act as a
Supreme Constitutional Court for the United Kingdom. As outlined in the discussion
on the separation of powers in Pt I of the book, the role of the Lord Chancellor as
head of the judiciary sits uncomfortably with the role of a judge as legislator and
politician. The significance of the Human Rights Act is that it reflects a shift towards
judicial decision-making. It may be concluded that, at the apex of constitutional power,
judges now command the heights controlling how power, generally defined, is
allocated, reviewed and assessed. Equally it is tempting to see the judicial role
increasing further to fill the void left by the weakening of parliamentary authority.

The Lord Chancellor's department is the centre of the administration of justice, a   **22–018**
department of government that in practical terms functions as an equivalent in this
country to a continental Ministry of Justice. The need for independence, underlined in
the *Pinochet Case*[6] and the legal difficulty of the Lord Chancellor sitting in the
Appellate Committee of the House of Lords commensurate with his role as a
government Minister and politician, suggests the need for a change. There are no
current plans for the creation of a new Supreme Court, an oversight in the policy of
"modernisation" and one which may help shape the future judicial role for the coming
years.

---

[6] *R. v Bow Street Metropolitan Stipendiary Magistrate Ex p. Pinochet Ugarte (No.2)* [2000] A.C. 119.

PUBLIC LAW SCHOLARSHIP[7]

22–019 What are the aims of public law? The question is asked of subjects such as tort, contract, criminal law or environmental law, yet this fundamental question as to the role and function of public law has been hardly considered. The answer is to be found in the assortment of aims and objectives associated with defining how government is accountable and representative. Controls exercised by Parliament and the courts are intended to provide citizens with assurances about the way government makes decisions, and transparency is a key element in public confidence. Public law is required to provide that transparency through systems of accountability, both *a priori* and *ex post*, and is intended to ensure that citizens' rights are protected and good administration supported. Internal systems of accountability need to be distinguished from external systems. The former are concerned with internal systems of audit, rules and conventions that apply to the exercise of ministerial discretion.[8] The latter take the form of external controls through Parliament, the courts, the media, and public opinion.

22–020 There is also an enormous dependency on Executive self-restraint. This is largely due to the overwhelming presumption in English law, at least until relatively recently, that if an action or decision is not categorically prohibited, it is legal. Government authority and power are assumed on the basis that the Executive may do anything unless prohibited by statute. An equally familiar presumption was that rights are intended to protect minorities, while the protection of the majority is afforded by Parliament. Majoritarian democracy assumes that the casting of even one more vote for, rather than against, a particular proposition commands the respect of the losing side. Abuse of power is prevented by the spirit of compromise that government will act with self-restraint and find a way to accommodate minority interests. In the eighteenth and nineteenth centuries, cohesion was provided by deference to authority, including government and the monarchy. In an age where deference has diminished, institutions have had to depend on persuasion rather than their status.

22–021 The liberty of the nation also depended on assuming good stewardship by the holder of public office. Today that assumption cannot be taken for granted, and in most cases the public interest requires that the holder of public office exercises power in an accountable way. News media intrude into the private and public lives of public figures. Increasing demands for transparency and verifiable outputs such as league tables arise out of public disquiet and mistrust.

22–022 Remedies available to the individual might take care of the exceptional case where there is a lapse of judgment or an error. The general presumption is that the ordinary law and self-restraint are sufficient to control arbitrariness. High dependency on Executive self-restraint is part of the history of the nation and the culture of the people. It is clear that the pre-eminent concern in Britain is political convenience, to allow the party in power to govern—a reflection of how the balance between the different elements of the constitution is expected to be struck.

---

[7] The ideas expressed here are adapted from my public lectures delivered in the summer of 2001 *Modernizing Britain: Public Law and Challenges* (P. Havemann and J. Mackinnon ed., University of Waikato, New Zealand, 2002).
[8] John F. McEldowney, "The Control of Public Expenditure" in *The Changing Constitution* (J. Jowell and D. Oliver ed., 4th ed., 2001), pp.190—228.

Gearty notes:

22–023

"Apart from this plethora of laws that makes up Britain's constitution, important clues to the nation's system of government are also to be found in the constitutional penumbra that lies between, on the one hand, the judicially enforceable requirements of the law, and on the other, the wholly unenforceable and merely transient dictates of political convenience. While it is true to say that no written constitution can remove entirely this penumbra, in which the constitution is guided more by the political majority of its principal actors than by law, it is equally clear that such non-legally enforceable rules of political obligation are far more likely to thrive in the empty spaces around an unwritten framework of government that they are when the whole system is laid out in a fresh and ambitiously comprehensive manner, for all to see and for future generations diligently to follow."[9]

Another dimension of public law is the setting of limits on economic power. Extensive economic powers, through instruments such as the system of budgeting and the borrowing of money, are in the hands of the executive. As Page and Daintith explain, economic powers are effectively under government control:

22–024

"The executive can do this because basic principles of our constitution recognize it as an autonomous body which can manage its own resources save where Parliament ordains otherwise, and give it co-ordinate power with Parliament in the all-important area of public expenditure."[10]

A striking feature of the United Kingdom's present-day constitutional arrangements is the growth in complex and all-inclusive legislation. It is remarkable that a "non-codified" common law system has developed in practice such comprehensive legislation. Some examples are the Utilities Act 2000, and the Terrorism Act 2000, but it is equally true of the Immigration and Asylum Act 1999 and the detailed regulation of elections under the Political Parties, Elections and Referendums Act 2000. The legislation is highly technical and detailed containing a vast array of supporting codes of practice, rules, regulations and guidance. Skills in interpreting and reading statutes have not been given sufficient attention in the design of many courses and in the way public law is taught. Public law has developed beyond the accretion of political power and defining its limits. Having developed a system of remedies from medieval times and ensured the economic liberty of commerce and contractual relationships in the eighteenth and nineteenth centuries, legislation has pushed the frontiers of public law to develop individual rights.

22–025

The Human Rights Act 1998 defines public law in terms of individual rights and their protection through law. Giving legal priority to rights in this way marks a profound shift to the judicial element of the Constitution. This triumph of judicial

22–026

---

[9] Conor Gearty, "The United Kingdom" in *European Civil Liberties and the European Convention on Human Rights* (C. Gearty ed., 1997), p.53.
[10] T. Daintith and A. Page, *The Executive in the Constitution* (1999), p.398. See T. Daintith, "Law as a Policy Instrument: Comparative Perspectives" in *Law as an Instrument of Economic Policy: Comparative and Critical Approaches* (T. Daintith ed., 1988), pp.3–55.

power over the other parts of the Constitution vests legal rules with a higher authority than the political process. In securing the promotion of legal rules, the question facing judges is how is judicial power in the hands of appointed judges to be made compatible with the democratic process?

22–027   Public law has also found its way into the study of what had been assumed to be discrete areas of private law, separate from administrative law or the European Community. Setting the boundaries of public law is going to be difficult as the human rights implications of legal powers spill over into private law cases. One example is in the law of contract and the impact of cases such as *Osman*.[11]

22–028   Public law scholarship has reflected the range and diversity of many recent developments in the changing shape of constitutional and administrative law. It is impossible to provide an exhaustive analysis of the formidable literature relevant to the subject and the student of the Constitution is referred to the bibliography for further references and additional reading. Many specialisms, often outside the traditional confines of law, are now required reading to understand some of the basics of public law. The question arises as to the future direction of change and the development of public law in the context of two apparently irrevocable trends. The first is the increasing influence of globalisation, with the pressure of the market economy and competition for scarce resources. This creates a tension between the national domestic interest and Britain's future role in the world. The second is the increasing influence and dependency on the part of the Member States on the economic and political power of the European Union. The rise of the Euro as a common currency has seen the demise of symbols of national economic sovereignty in each of the Member States that have joined the Euro zone. Planned expansion of the European Union is on the agenda, as is the creation of a common system of taxation. The latter is perhaps the greatest challenge, because the power of taxation is at the heart of economic and political sovereignty of the nation state. Defining the limits of the State's taxation policy will cause people to examine more closely the idea of the nation state. What is Britain's role? What impact will changes in the composition of the European Union have on our future constitutional relations with the European Union? These are key issues for the future. The response of the European Union to these changes is to consider a renewal of its Constitution, and a working group under the ex-French President Giscard d'Estaing[12] is working towards that objective. In that context, and in considering the broader question of the future of the unwritten checks and balances in the United Kingdom's Constitution, it may be timely to consider a number of questions. What are the aims of public law? How effective is public law in achieving those aims? How may the future of public law be best delineated? Is it time for the United Kingdom to adopt a written Constitution? There appear to be many lessons to be gained for the future development of public law from studying how the United Kingdom has adapted to change thus far.

22–029   Diversity in public law scholarship is partly a reflection of the unwritten constitution and the difficulties posed by the subject matter. The way forward is not easy to locate. The introduction of the Human Rights Act incorporating the bulk of the European Convention will alter profoundly the legal and political culture of the United Kingdom

---

[11] (1989) 29 E.H.R.R. 245. See C. Gearty, "Unravelling Osman" (2001) MLR 159.
[12] Third President of the Fifth Republic of France, 1974–81. I am grateful to Emma McEldowney for this information.

and thus the role of constitutional law. The reports of the Nolan Committee into the standards in public life are likely to propose the use of criminal offences for corruption in public office. This proposal will apply to both local and central government. A growing body of public law literature moves from the traditional and often historical concerns of constitutional law to question the theoretical development of the subject and seek explanations rooted in legal theory. There is little convergence as to how best to achieve this ambitious task. Craig has considered some of the approaches which are open to the future study of public law and favours an approach which allows the lawyer to[13]:

> "identify and assess the relevant background theory, consider the public law implications of it, and the political and social and economic background conditions within which it subsists."

While this methodology might not always find favour it represents a growing interest   **22–030** among public lawyers of the wider social and political ramifications of how laws work, how they might be applied and whether the legal arrangements are relevant when other factors may be relevant to how decisions are taken. There is some caution in considering whether lawyers do in fact have much, if anything, to offer. Writing on the area of discretion and law, Lacey[14] points out limitations in legal methodology and the potential for turning a broadening and enlightening development "into a piece of intellectual and practical imperialism in which lawyers merely incorporate ever more inappropriate areas of activity into their own analytic and political framework". The dangers of what Lacey calls "the legal paradigm" is that legal methodology may tend to operate using generalisation; it tends to "pigeonhole" solutions, operates dichotomies or opposites with either/or decisions, and may tend to assume that there are "right" answers found in some form of objectivity or truth. Furthermore, legal method may assume belief in its own self-importance and overestimate the value of the courts and the temptation to bring disputes within "a legal umbrella." Lacey's analysis calls for a pluralistic approach of pooling resources to problems. In the example of her study of discretion this means[15]:

> "The need to integrate empirical, interpretative and normative questions in an attempt to understand discretion and ultimately, to ensure the legitimacy and effectiveness of the exercise of social powers in particular contexts. Discretion must be taken, then primarily as a political question, and one whose centrality in contemporary society calls for the concerted attention of a number of related and interdependent disciplines."

Having established some form of methodology or approach, public lawyers are often   **22–031** uncertain as to how to establish principles rooted in constitutional law or theory. This problem is particularly acute when legislation is considered as to its policy and philosophy.

---

[13] Craig, "What Should Public Lawyers Do? A Reply" (1992) 12 (No.4) *Oxford Journal of Legal Studies* 565–577 at 565.

[14] N. Lacey, "The Jurisprudence of Discretion" in *The Uses of Discretion* (K. Hawkins ed., 1992), 361–388 at 362–363.

[15] Lacey, *op.cit.*, p.388.

22-032   Assessing how to evaluate legislation may require consideration of the political issues underlying the law. In the last decade or so this has given rise to much public law literature concerning some of the changes introduced by both Conservative and Labour governments. The division between legal and non-legal opinion becomes difficult to draw as public lawyers examine the writings of political scientists and related disciplines. The burgeoning literature that reflects interest in the political as well as theoretical issues underlying constitutional change is also the result of political scientists finding legal analysis helpful.

22-033   Daintith has pointed out that public lawyers may have difficulty in finding a suitably clear constitutional principle or criteria to judge whether political changes have a constitutional impact. This difficulty is compounded by a[16] "prevailing descriptive and eclectic mode of writing about the United Kingdom Constitution and public law". Further difficulties arise because[17]:

> "we have not formulated the twentieth- as opposed to nineteenth-century principles with which the recent legislation comes into conflict or which it purports to displace or modify."

22-034   Responses to the problems identified by Daintith have varied. Some have taken a critical view of the Constitution and sought to find expression through the value of "critique", and the need for reforms through the testing of the adequacy of existing arrangements. The political policies and ideology underlying law have also come under scrutiny, sometimes quite openly and directed at the ideology itself which is at the centre of government policy.

22-035   There has also been a notable growth in various specialist studies designed to highlight particular areas or problems traditionally not within the confines of public law. Innovative work in the area of discretion, regulation and on administration more generally sets new boundaries between the work of public lawyers and other related disciplines.

22-036   There appears to be common ground that the lawyer's task is to understand not merely legal doctrine but the wider context of its use, including the ideologies that underpin it and the variety of social forces that exert pressure for legal change.

22-037   An example of how this task might be taken forward is in the formulation of the principles of good administration, or the building up of principles containing the working practices of the Parliamentary Commissioner for Administration. The recurrent themes of accountability, control and scrutiny found in much public law literature require evaluation of different styles and techniques beyond a purely legal and court-orientated approach. For example, this may include scrutiny of the work of the National Audit Office and the Audit Commission.

22-038   This may suggest an agenda for further research into public law, such as that outlined by the Canadian Law Reform Commission, *Towards a Modern Federal Administrative Law*. This may include consideration of the control and regulatory functions of government, investigating the dispute-resolving functions of government, and an examination of the legal implications and limitations of the delegation of

---

[16] Daintith, "Political Programmes and the Constitution" in *Edinburgh Essays in Public Law* (Finnie, Himsworth and Walker ed., 1991), p.43.
[17] *ibid.*, p.46. T. Prosser, "Towards a Critical Public Law" (1982) 9 *Journal of Law and Society* 19.

government functions to private sector actors. Studying the work of tribunals and the effectiveness of informal grievance mechanisms are important in understanding the limits of legal rules and the potential for different methods of dispute resolution.

The future development of public law will benefit from the continuation of empirical **22–039** studies into judicial review. From this model further research might be undertaken on the effects of judicial review on public bodies, and the potential impact of a code of guidance on good administration examined. In devising future strategies it is essential that the problem-orientated and analytical tools of the common law tradition are continuously refreshed. The common law is inherently problem focused and the national legal culture reflects that pragmatic approach. A research register on public law is a good starting point, representing the diversity of interest in public law. Integrating empirical, interpretive and normative questions will set the future challenge for public law.

It is clear that the Human Rights Act provides a new and critical foundation for the **22–040** future of public law. This should not divert attention from the study of the many qualities and weaknesses of the parliamentary system and the diverse ways that government exercises power and is held to account. Public law is equally concerned with changes to our electoral system, Lords reform, the evolution of different approaches to regulation, the continued development of a comprehensive system of tribunals, the efficiency of the courts, the system for the appointment of judges, the evolving nature of devolution and local government and last, but most importantly, the changing nature of Parliamentary sovereignty to take account of Europe and a changing role of the judiciary.

The future development of public law is likely to reflect its inherent pragmatic **22–041** qualities: continuous change and steady growth with unpredictable results.

BIBLIOGRAPHY

RESEARCHING PUBLIC LAW

Students of public law face a bewildering array of writing, both legal and non-legal. The literature relevant to their studies includes primary and secondary sources. A broader view of the subject, resulting from the abandonment of an exclusively court orientated approach to the study of constitutional and administrative law, has led to public law scholarship expanding rapidly. The focus in many textbooks of a mainly descriptive approach setting out the legal rules has given way to a more critical and analytical style. It is clear that general treatises are more difficult to write as the specialist nature of the subject matter of public law demands specialist works and in-depth examination. The coming into force of the Human Rights Act 1998 has resulted in a marked increase in the literature on human rights. There is a temptation to see human rights issues infiltrating every element of public law. There is a proliferation of modules specialising in human rights and civil liberties. It is likely that the development of modules on human rights and an increase in the general discourse on rights may come to dominate public law with the result that it may become unfashionable to consider the various constitutional institutions and alternatives to the courts. This would be unfortunate as much of the distinctive building blocks of public law are about public institutions and decision-making. Government accountability, the exercise and control of executive power and the organisation of tribunals and administrative agencies deserve attention as part of the living constitution.

In law schools the content of courses in public law have widened. For example, courses on planning, housing, immigration, civil liberties or environmental law cover materials that provide important knowledge for lawyers interested in constitutional law and public administration. The study of public law includes consideration of the work of constitutional historians, political scientists, economists and philosophers. Students face a daunting task of how to evaluate such widely drawn sources and materials.

Any selection of the literature cannot be exhaustive. It is intended to provide a guide to offer students suggestions for further reading as an aid to understanding the subject. There is not available in published form any specialist bibliography dedicated to constitutional and administrative law. There are a number of general reference works which are helpful: *Index to Legal Periodicals*, Vol.1 (New York, 1960–61)–; *Index to Foreign Legal Periodicals*, Vol.1 (General Editor: W.A. Steiner, 1960)–; *International Political Science Abstracts*, Vol.1 (Paris, 1951)–; *Harvard Law School: Annual Legal Bibliography*, Vol.1 (Boston, Mass., 1961)–. *Halsbury's Laws of England* (1986)– provides useful references to cases and statutes relevant to both constitutional and administrative law. Catalogues available in the Squire Law Library, University of Cambridge and the Bodleian Law Library, University of Oxford are also useful for public lawyers.

The Bristol Centre for the Study of Administrative Justice has published in 1996 *Administrative Justice: A Working Bibliography, Working Paper Series No.1*, available from Professor Martin Partington, Department of Law, University of Bristol BS8 1RJ. There is also a vast amount of literature available from the Cabinet Office; and under the White Paper on Open Government Cm.2290, there is a *Code of Practice on Access to Government Information*. Information about government is available from: Open Government, Room 417b, Office of Public Service and Science, 70 Whitehall, London SW1A 2AS. The internet allows access to a wide variety of materials about the Government, the Royal Family, the Treasury and government departments. There is a separate Appendix containing useful references to the internet.

Sources and Materials

A wide range of primary sources may provide useful material for an understanding of the development of constitutional and administrative law.

In the Public Records Office, Kew Gardens, London, there are the minutes and reports of the Poor Law Commissioners (1830s); the General Board of Health (1840s); the Railway Commission and the Railway Department of the Board of Trade; the Opinion of Law Officers (1840s); and the Cabinet Papers.

Parliamentary Papers and *Hansard* Parliamentary Debates from the nineteenth century to the present time provide useful information. Access the following: *www.parliament.the-stationery-office.co.uk/pa/cm/cmhansrd.htm*.

Government-published reports are also relevant and the following are particularly useful:

The Northcote-Trevelyan Report on the Civil Service (1984 Parl. Pap. XXVII 1); *Report of the Royal Commission on the Rebellion in Ireland*, Cd.8279 (1916); *The Report of the War Cabinet*, Cd.9005 (1917); *The Report of The Committee on the Machinery of Government*, Cd.9230 (1918); *The Royal Commission on Police Powers and Procedures*, Cmd.3927 (1929); *The Report of the Committee on Ministers' Powers*, Cmd.4060 (1932); *Royal Commission on Justices of the Peace*, Cmd.7463 (1948); *Report of the Committee on the Political Activities of Civil Servants*, Cmd.7718 (1949); *Report of the Public Inquiry into the Disposal of Land at Crichel Down*, Cmd.9176 (1954); *Report of the Royal Commission on the Civil Service*, Cmd.9613 (1953–55); *Report of the Committee on Administrative Tribunals and Inquiries*, Cmnd.218 (1957); *Report of the Committee into the Working of the Monetary System*, Cmnd.827 (1959); *The Control of Public Expenditure*, Cmnd.1432 (1961); *Report of the Committee on Security Procedures in the Public Service*, Cmnd.1681 (1962); *Report by Lord Denning into the Profumo Affair*, Cmnd.2152 (1963); *Report of the Royal Commission on Tribunals of Inquiry*, Cmnd.3121 (1966); *Report of the Committee on Management in Local Government* HMSO (1967); *Report of the Committee on the Civil Service 1966–68*, Cmnd.3638; *Report of the Committee on Participation and Planning*, Cmnd.7468 (1969); *Report of the Royal Commission on Local Government in England 1966–69*, Cmnd.4040 (1969); *Local Government Reform in England*, Cmnd.4276 (1970); *Report of the Royal Commission on Local Government in Scotland 1966–1969 (the Wheatley Report)*, Cmnd.4150 (1969);

Report of the Tribunal appointed to inquire into Certain Issues Related to the Circumstances Leading up to the Cessation of Trading by the Vehicle and General Insurance Co. Ltd. (1971) (HL 80; HC 133); *Report of the Committee on Legal Procedures to Deal with Terrorist Activities in Northern Ireland*, Cmnd.5185 (1973); *Royal Commission on the Constitution 1969–73*, Cmnd.5460 (1973); *The Red Lion Square Disorders of 15 June 1974; Report of Inquiry by the Rt Hon. Lord Scarman OBE*, Cmnd.5919 (1975); *Report of a Committee to Consider, in the Context of Civil Liberties and Human Rights, Measures to Deal with Terrorism in Northern Ireland*, Cmnd.5487 (1975); *Report of the Committee on the Preparation of Legislation*, Cmnd.6053 (1975); *Local Government Finance: Report of the Committee of Enquiry*, Cmnd.6453 (1976); *Local Government Finance*, Cmnd.6823 (1977); *Observations on the Fourth Report of the Select Committee on the Parliamentary Commissioner for Administration*, Cmnd.7057 (1979); *Spending Public Money: Governance and Audit Issues*, Cmnd.7845 (1979–80); *Report of Council on Tribunals; The Functions of the Council in Tribunal*, Cmnd.7846 (1980); *The Royal Commission on Criminal Procedure*, Cmnd.8092 (1981); *Efficiency in the Civil Service*, Cmnd.8293 (1981); *Falkland Islands Review*, Cmnd.8787 (1983); *Financial Management in Government Departments*, Cmnd.9058 (1983); *The Review of Public Order Law*, Cmnd.8510 (1985); *The Conduct of Local Authority Business*, Cm.9797 (1986); *Report of the Review Body on Civil Justice*, Cm.394 (1988); *The Financing and Accountability of Next Step Agencies*, Cm.914 (1989); *The Work and Organisation of the Legal Profession*, Cm.570 (1989); *Contingency Fees*, Cm.571 (1989); *Report of the Committee on Privacy and Related Matters*, Cm.1102 (1990); *Competition and Choice; Telecommunications Policy for the 1990s*, Cm.1461 (1991); *The Working of the Select Committee System*, Cm.1532 (1991); *The Citizen's Charter*, Cm.1599 (1991); *Budgetary Reform*, Cm.1867 (1992); *Review of Press Self-Regulation*, Cm.2135 (1993); *Scotland in the Union*, Cm.2225 (1993); *Inquiry into Police Responsibilities and Rewards Report*, Cm.2280 (1993); *Royal Commission on Criminal Justice Report*, Cm.2263 (1993); *Better Accounting for the Taxpayer's Money: Resource Accounting and Budgeting in Government*, Cm.2626 (1994); *European Community Finances*, Cm.2824 (1995); *The Civil Service: Taking Forward Continuity and Change*, Cm.2748 (1995); *Legal Aid; Targeting Need*, Cm.2854 (1995); *The Citizen's Charter The Facts and Figures September 1995*, Cm.2970 (1995); *The First Report of the Committee on Standards in Public Life*, Cm.2850 (1995); *The Government's Response to The First Report from the Committee on Standards in Public Life*, Cm.2931 (1995); *Resource Accounting and Budgeting in Government*, Cm.2929 (1995); *The Second Report of the Committee on Standards in Public Life: Local Public Spending Bodies, Cm.3270 (1996); Striking the Balance: The Future of Legal Aid in England and Wales*, Cm.3305 (1996); *Inquiry into Legislation Against Terrorism*, Cm.3420 (1996); *Spending Public Money: Governance and Audit Issues*, Cm.3179 (1996); *Next Steps Agencies in Government: Review 1995*, Cm.3164 (1996); *Return to and Address of the Honourable House of Commons dated 15th February 1996. Report of the Inquiry into the Export of Defence Equipment and Dual-use Goods to Iraq and Related Prosecutions* The Rt Hon. Sir Richard Scott, The Vice-Chancellor (1996 HC 115) (HMSO, London); *The Citizen's Charter—Five Years On*, Cm.3370 (1996); *The Council on Tribunals, Tribunals: their organisation and Independence*, Cm.3744 (1997); *The Third Report of the Committee on Standards in Public Life: Standards of Conduct in Local Government in England*, Cm.3702 (1997); *Audit of Assumptions for the July 1997 Budget Projections*, Cm.3693 (1997); *The Governance of Public Bodies: A*

Progress Report, Cm.3557 (1997); *Rights Brought Home*, Cm.3782 (1997); *Modern Local Government: In Touch with the People*, Cm.4014 (1998); *Local Voices: Modernising Local Government in Wales*, Cm.4028 (1998); *Modern Public Services in Britain: Investing for reform. Comprehensive Spending Review: New Public Spending Plans 1999–2002*, Cm.4011 (1998); *Local Leadership, Local Choice*, Cm.4298 (1999); *Modernising Parliament—Reforming the House of Lords*, Cm.4183 (1999); *Modernising Government*, Cm.4310 (1999); *Report of the Royal Commission on the Reform of the House of Lords: A House for the Future*, Cm.4534 (2000).

The publications of the various departmental select committees have since 1979 led to greater information and transparency in the working of government. Departmental publications which are not normally published through HMSO should not be overlooked, particularly publications from the Cabinet Office, the Treasury, the Home Office; for example, *Legislation on Human Rights* (Home Office, 1976) and the Department of Environment. Listings of both departmental publications and HMSO publications may be found in the *Monthly List* published by HMSO.

The Treasury has prepared a useful guide on accounting and financial procedures for the use of government departments, in the form of a looseleaf: *Government Accounting* (2002–) and its sister publication *Resource Accounting* (2002–) available from the Stationery Office. The guide is regularly updated and covers important matters of constitutional propriety such as the 1932 Concordat between the Public Accounts Committee and the Treasury. In addition, the various internal treasury rules for the use within departments in the discharge of their responsibilities to Parliament in the conduct of financial matters, are contained in *Supply and other Financial Procedure of the House of Commons* (1977) available in the Treasury. This is a handbook for official use within departments. The Cabinet Office may be the source of important information, for example: *Select Committees: Memorandum of Guidance for Officials* (the Osmotherly Rules) (HMSO, 1980).

Various specialist Select Committees deserve mention such as the House of Lords Select Committee on the European Communities; the Public Accounts Committee; and the Select Committee on Procedure. Some House of Commons Papers that are particularly relevant to constitutional and administrative law are: *First Report of the Parliamentary Commissioner* (1967–68 HC 6); *Report from the Select Committee on Members' Interests (Declaration)* 1969–70 HC 57); *Liaison Committee: The Select Committee System*, (1982–83 HC 92); *Seventh Report from the Treasury and Civil Service Committee: Ministers and Civil Servants: Duties and Responsibilities* (1985–86 HC 92); *Eighth Report from the Treasury and Civil Service Committee: Civil Service Management Reform: The Next Steps* (1987–88 HC 494); *Third Report from the Select Committee on Members' Interests* (1989–90 HC 561).

An account of the procedures of *Parliament* is usefully provided by J. Griffith and M. Ryle, *Parliament* (1989); T. Erskine May, *Parliamentary Practice* (22nd ed., Butterworths, London, 1997). An account of British election results are collated by D. Butler, D. Kavanagh, *The British General Election of 1979, 1983, 1987, 1992, 1996, 2000)* (published in 1980, 1984, 1988, 1993, 1997 and 2001).

The various regulatory agencies such as the National Audit Office, the Audit Commission, and the Office of Fair Trading are useful sources of information on the working of government departments. The reports of the Parliamentary Commissioner for Administration, the Select Committee on European Community Legislation are also helpful. Students of regulation will find the annual reports of each of the Directors-General of telecommunications, gas, water, electricity useful in their role of reviewing the utilities. There is also useful information to be gained from the various annual reports, for example, the Crown Prosecution Service, or the Criminal Injuries Compensation Board. The Judicial Statistics for 1975 onwards are also useful.

In administrative law the various reports of the Law Commission are important, such as: "Report on Remedies in Administrative Law", Law Com. No.73, 1976; "Criminal Law: Offences Relating to Public Order", Law Com. No.123, 1983; "Administrative Law: Judicial Review and Statutory Appeals", Law Com. No.126, 1993. There is also the "Justice/All Souls Report, Administrative Justice: Some Necessary Reforms" (1988).

Various reports from pressure groups or specialist societies such as the Hansard Society; their *Report of the Commission on Electoral Reform* (1976), *Making the Law: The Report of the Hansard Society Commission on the Legislative Process* (Chair Lord Rippon) in 1993; and a recent report by the Hansard Society *Report on the Regulated Industries* (1996) are very useful. There is also *Report of the Hansard Society Commission on Parliamentary Scrutiny: The Challenge for Parliament: Making Government Accountable.*

The Constitution Unit, which has undertaken an independent inquiry into the implementation of Constitutional Reform at the Faculty of Laws, University College, London, provides some important research papers and briefing reports on a whole range of public law issues (email: constitution@ucl.ac.uk). The Institute For Fiscal Studies provides important research on a broad range of fiscal matters including public spending (email: mailbox@ifs.org.uk). The Public Law Project continues to collect data and information on judicial statistics with particular reference to judicial review. The Centre for the Study of Regulated Industries (CRI), established in 1991, is an independent research centre of the Chartered Institute of Public Finance and Accountancy. It provides interdisciplinary research into how companies and regulation are working. The European Commission, 8 Storey's Gate, London SW1P 3A is also an important source of information. European Union information is now available on the internet: *www.cec.org.uk.*

Many public law issues involve related specialist subject areas. For example in the case of the environment see: ENDS, Directory of Information on Environmental Information, Finsbury Business Centre, 40 Bowling Green Lane, London EC1R 0NE. The National Institute of Economic and Social Research, 2 Dean Trench Street, Smith Square, London SW1P 3HE provides useful analysis on a whole range of public sector economic and European issues. Many newspapers provide information on the internet. For example the *Guardian* operated an election network during May 1997 (see *http:// election.guardian.co.uk*). There are a number of helpful documents available from government departments. For example The Lord Chancellor and His Department (September, 1995) provides a useful up-date on how the Lord Chancellor's office fits within the constitutional framework of the administration of justice. Also useful is the *Strategic Plan 1996/97 and 1998/99 A Programme for the Future* (Lord Chancellor's Office, 1996).

Diaries of cabinet ministers, or ex-civil servants may be of historical and contemporary importance and are also a useful source for students of the constitution such as: R. Crossman, *The Diaries of a Cabinet Minister*, Vol.1 (1975); Vol.2 (1976); Vol.3

(1977); B. Castle, *The Castle Diaries 1964–70* (1984) and *1974–76* (1989); Nigel Lawson, *The View from No. 11* (1992); M. Thatcher, *The Downing Street Years* (1993); Alan Clark, *Diaries* (1993); Geoffrey Howe, *Conflict of Loyalty* (Macmillan, 1994); Peter Walker, *Staying Power* (Bloomsbury, 1995); Jim Prior, *A Balance of Power* (Hamish Hamilton, 1995); Margaret Thatcher, *The Collected Speeches of Margaret Thatcher* (Harper Collins, 1997). Biographies of major judges may also illuminate judicial attitudes and issues of policy; see for example: R.F.V. Heuston, *The Lives of the Lord Chancellors* (1964), or J.L. Jowell and J.P. McAuslan (eds.), *Lord Denning: The Judge and the Law* (1984). Also useful are the various writings partly anecdotal and partly biographical of judges, for example: Lord Hailsham, *Elective Dictatorship* (1976); *On the Constitution* (1992). Also useful are the biographies of major legal figures, for example: Richard Cosgrove, *The Rule of Law: Albert Venn Dicey, Victorian Jurist* (1985); Cecil Fifoot, *Judge and Jurist in the Reign of Victoria*; (1959); and Cecil Fifoot, *Frederic William Maitland: A Life* (1971); Roy Jenkins, *Gladstone* (Macmillan, 1995); Roy Jenkins, *Churchill* (Macmillan, 2001).

The private papers of Prime Ministers, Ministers and senior civil servants provide an important historical source, for example the Gladstone Papers or the Peel Papers in the British Library. Gladstone, in particular, is easily accessible in *The Prime Minister's Papers: W.E. Gladstone* (J. Brooke and M. Sorensen ed., 1971). Law journals and the main journals of political science, legal history, economics and social administration all provide useful sources of materials. Newspapers and periodicals also provide sources for the study of the constitution set against the background of the day-to-day life of the political parties.

SELECT BIBLIOGRAPHY

Ackerman, B., *Social Justice in the Liberal State* (Yale University Press, New Haven, 1980).

Adonis, A., *Parliament Today* (Manchester University Press, Manchester, 1994).

Alder, J., *Constitutional and Administrative Law* (3rd ed., Macmillan, London, 1999).

Allan, T.R.S., "Legislative Supremacy and the Rule of Law: Democracy and Constitutionalism" (1985) 44 Camb. L.J. 111.

——, "Dicey and Dworkin: the Rule of Law as Integrity" (1988) 8 *Oxford Journal of Legal Studies* 266.

——, "Pragmatism and Theory in Public Law" (1988) 104 *Law Quarterly Review* 422.

——, "Constitutional Rights and Common Law" (1991) 11 *Oxford Journal of Legal Studies* 453.

——, *Law, Liberty and Justice* (Oxford University Press, Oxford, 1993).

——, "Equality and Moral independence: public law and private morality" in *A Special Relationship* (I. Loveland ed., Clarendon Press, Oxford, 1995).

——, *Constitutional Justice: A Liberal Theory of the Rule of Law* (Oxford University Press, Oxford, 2001).

Allen, C.K., *Law in the Making* (Penguin, London, 1927).

——, *Democracy and the Individual* (London, 1943).

——, "Administrative Jurisdiction" [1956] *Public Law* 13.

Allen, M., Thompson, B. and Walsh, B., *Cases and Materials on Constitutional and Administrative Law* (6th ed., Blackstone, London, 2000).

Allison, J.W.F., *A Continental Distinction in the Common Law* (Oxford University Press, Oxford, 1999).

——, "Theoretical and Institutional Underpinnings of a Separate Administrative Law" in *The Province of Administrative Law* (M. Taggart ed., Oxford University Press, Oxford, 1997), pp.71-89.

Alston, P., *et al.*, *The EU and Human Rights* (Oxford University Press, Oxford, 1999).

Amery, L.S., *Thoughts on the Constitution* (Oxford University Press, Oxford, 1947; 2nd ed., 1953).

Amos, M., *The Science of Law* (University Press, London, 1870).

Andrews, J.A. (ed.), *Welsh Studies in Public Law* (London, 1970).

Anson, W.R., *The Law and Custom of the Constitution* (Oxford University Press, Oxford, 1886; 4th ed., 1909).

Armstrong, W. (ed.), *Budgetary Reform in the United Kingdom* (London, 1980).

Arndt, H.W., "The Origins of Dicey's Concept of the Rule of Law" (1957) 31 *Australian Law Journal* 117.

Arthurs, H., *"Without the Law": Administrative Justice and Legal Pluralism in Nineteenth Century England* (University of Toronto Press, Toronto, 1985).

Atiyah, P.S., *The Rise and Fall of Freedom of Contract* (Oxford University Press, Oxford, 1979).

——, *From Principles to Pragmatism: Changes in the Function of the Judicial Process and the Law* (Oxford University Press, 1978).

Attfield, R., *The Ethics of the Global Environment*, Edinburgh Studies in World Ethics, (Edinburgh University Press, Edinburgh, 1999).

Austin, J., *The Province of Jurisprudence Determined* (1832) (H.L.A. Hart ed., London, 1954).

Bagehot, W., *The English Constitution* (Introduction by R.H.S. Crossman) (1963).

Bailey, S.H., Harris, D.J., and Jones, B.L., *Civil Liberties Cases and Materials* 5th ed., London: Butterworths, 2001.

Baines, P., "Financial Accountability : Agencies and Audit" in *Parliamentary Accountability: A Study of Parliament and Executive Agencies* (P. Giddings ed., Macmillan, London, 1995).

Bamforth, N., "The application of the Human Rights Act to public authorities and private bodies" (1999) *Cambridge LJ* 159–170.

Barberis, P. (ed.), *The Civil Service in an Era of Change* (Dartmouth, London 1997).

Barendt, E., *Freedom of Speech* (Oxford University Press, Oxford, 1985).

——, *An Introduction to Constitutional Law* (Oxford University Press, Oxford, 1998).

Barendt, E. and Hitchens, L., *Media law: Cases and Materials* (Longman, London, 2000).

Barnett, H., *Constitutional and Administrative Law* (3rd ed., Cavendish, London 2001).

Barron, A., and Scott, C., "The Citizen's Charter Programme" [1992] 55 *Modern Law Review* 526.

Beck, U., *Risk Society* (Sage, London, 1992).

Beer, S.H., *Treasury Control: The Co-ordination of Financial and Economic Policy in Great Britain* (2nd ed., Clarendon Press, Oxford, 1957).

Bell, S. and McGillivray, D., *Ball and Bell on Environmental Law* (5th ed., Blackstone Press, London, 2000).

Bennion, F., *Bennion on Statute Law* (2nd ed., Longman, London, 1990).

Benn, T., and Hood, A., *Common Sense: A New Constitution for Britain* (Hutchinson, London, 1993).

Bentham, J., *The Works of Jeremy Bentham* Vol. III, (J.L. Bowring ed., 1843).

——, *A Fragment on Government and An Introduction to the Principles of Morals and Legislation* (W. Harrison ed., Oxford, 1948).

Bew, P., *Conflict and Conciliation in Ireland 1890–1910* Oxford University Press, Oxford, 1982).

Bew, P., Gibbon, P., Patterson, H., *Northern Ireland, 1921–1944: Political Forces and Social Classes* (Serif, London, 1995).

Binney, J.E.D., *British Public Finance and Administration 1774-92* (Clarendon Press, Oxford, 1958.

Birkinshaw, P., *Freedom of Information: The Law, the Practice and the Ideal* (Butterworths, London, 1988; 2nd ed., 1996; 3rd ed., 2001).

——, *Reforming the Secret State* (Open University, Milton, Keynes, 1990).

Bishop, M., Kay, J., and Mayer C., (eds.), *The Regulatory Challenge* (Oxford University Press, Oxford, 1995).

——, *Privatization and Economic Performance* (Oxford University Press, Oxford, 1994).

Blackstone, W., *Commentaries on the Laws of England (1765–9),* 4 vols. (15th ed., Strahan, Cadell and Prince, London, 1809).

Blackburn, R., *The Electoral System in Britain* (Macmillan, London, 1995).

Blackburn, R., and Plant, R. (eds.), *Constitutional Reform: The Labour Government's Constitutional Reform Agenda* (Longman, London, 1999).

Blackburn, R., and Polakiewicz, J., *Fundamental Rights in Europe* (Oxford University Press, Oxford, 2001).

Blom-Cooper, L., and Drewry, G., *Final Appeal: A Study of the House of Lords in its Judicial Capacity* (Oxford University Press, Oxford, 1972).

Bogdanor, V., *Devolution* (Oxford University Press, Oxford, 1979).

——, *Devolution in the United Kingdom* (Oxford University Press, Oxford, 1999).

——, *The People and the Party System. The Referendum and Electoral Reform in British Politics* (Cambridge University Press, Cambridge, 1981).

——, "Constitutional Law and Politics" (1987) 7 O.J.L.S. 454.

——, *The Monarchy and the Constitution* (Clarendon Press, Oxford, 1995).

——, *Power and the People: A Guide to Constitutional Reform* (Victor Gollancz, London, 1999).

Bogdanor, V., and Summers, R., *The Law, Politics and the Constitution* (Clarendon Press, Oxford, 1999).

Bradley, A.W., "Applications for Judicial Review—the Scottish Model" [1987] *Public Law* 313.

——, "The Sovereignty of Parliament—In Perpetuity?", in *The Changing Constitution,* (J. Jowell and B. Oliver ed., 2nd ed., Oxford University Press, Oxford, 1989), pp.25-52.

——, "Justice, Good Government and Public Interest Immunity" [1992] *Public Law* 514.

——, and Ewing, K.D., *Constitutional and Administrative Law* (12th ed., Longman, London, 1997).

Brazier, R., *Constitutional Practice* (Oxford University Press, Oxford, 1988, 3rd ed. 1999).

——, *Constitutional Texts* (Clarendon Press, Oxford, 1990).

——, *Constitutional Reform* (2nd ed., Oxford University Press, Oxford, 1998).

Bridges, L., Meszaros, G., and Sunkin, M., *Judicial Review in Perspective* (2nd ed., 1995).

Bridges, Lord, *The Treasury* (Allen and Unwin, London, 1966).

Browning, P., *The Treasury and Economic Policy 1964-1985* (Longmans, London, 1986).

Browne-Wilkinson, N., "The Infiltration of a Bill of Rights" (1992) *Public Law* 397.

——, "The Independence of the Judiciary in the 1980s" [1988] *Public Law* 44–57.

Buckland, R., and Davis, R., "Privatisation Techniques and the PSBR", (1984) 5 *Fiscal Studies*, 47–60.

Budge, I., Crewe, I., McKay, D., and Newton, K., *The New British Politics* (2nd ed., Longman, Harlow, 2001).

Burrows, N., *Devolution* (Sweet & Maxwell, London, 2000).

Butler, R., "The Evolution of the Civil Service—A Progress Report" (1993) 71 *Public Administration* 395–406.

Butler, D., Adonis A., Travers, T., *Failure in British Government: The Politics of the Poll Tax* (Oxford University Press, Oxford, 1994).

Byrne, Tony, *Local Government in Britain* (7th ed., Penguin, London, 2000).

Cabinet Office, *Public Bodies* (Stationery Office, London, 2001–).

——, *The Civil Service Yearbook 2001* (Stationery Office, London, 2001–).

Calvert, H., *Constitutional Law in Northern Ireland* (Stevens, Belfast, 1968).

Campbell, C., *Emergency Law in Ireland 1918–25* (Clarendon Press, Oxford, 1994).

Campbell, T., Ewing K.D., and Tomkins, A., (eds.) *Sceptical Essays on Human Rights* (Oxford University Press, Oxford, 2001).

Campion, *An Introduction to the Procedure of the House of Commons* (London, 1958).

Cane, P., *An Introduction to Administrative Law* (3rd ed., Clarendon Press, Oxford, 1998).

Cappelletti, M., *The Judicial Process in Comparative Perspective* (Oxford University Press, Oxford, 1989).

Carr, C.T., *Delegated Legislation. Three Lectures* (Cambridge University Press, Cambridge, 1921).

Chrimes, S.B., *English Constitutional Ideas in the 15th Century* (Macmillan, London, 1966).

Cocks, R.C.J., *Sir Henry Maine: A Study in Victorian Jurisprudence* (Cambridge University Press, Cambridge, 1988).

Cohen, R, *Global Diasporas* (University College Press, London, 1999).

Cooke, Lord, *Turning Points of the Common Law The 47th Hamlyn Lectures*, (Sweet & Maxwell, London, 1997).

Cornish, W.R., and Clarke, de N., *Law and Society in England and Wales 1750–1950* (Sweet & Maxwell, London, 1989).

Cosgrove, R., *The Rule of Law: Albert Venn Dicey Victorian Jurist* (Macmillan, London, 1985).

Craig, P.P., *Administrative Law* (4th ed., Sweet & Maxwell, London, 1999).

——, *Public Law and Democracy in the United Kingdom and the United States of America* (Oxford University Press, Oxford, 1990).

Craig, P.P, "Public Law, Political Theory and Legal Theory" [2000] *Public Law* 211.

Craig, P.P. and De Burca, G., *EU LAW: Text, Cases and Materials* (2nd ed., Oxford University Press, Oxford, 1998).

Crick, B., *The Reform of Parliament Revised* (2nd ed., Weidenfeld and Nicholson, London, 1970).

Crick, M., *Michael Heseltine: A Biography* (Hamish Hamilton, London, 1997).

Crossman, R.H.S., *Inside View* (Jonathan Cape, London, 1972).

——, *Diaries of a Cabinet Minister*, Vol.2 (Hamish Hamilton and Jonathan Cape, London, 1977).

Cullen, M., *The Statistical Movement in Early Victorian Britain* (Hassocks, London, 1975).

Cullingworth, J., *Essays in Housing Policy* (Allen and Unwin, London, 1979).

Dahrendorf, R., "Citizenship and the Modern Social Conflict" in *1688–1988: Time for a New Constitution* (R. Holme and M. Elliott ed., London, 1988), chap.7.

Daintith, T., "Public Law and Economic Policy" [1974] J.B.L. 9.

——, "The Functions of Law in the Field of Short-term Economic Policy" (1976) 92 L.Q.R. 62.

——, "Regulation by Contract: The New Prerogative" in *Current Legal Problems* (Lord Lloyd, R. Rideout and S. Guest ed., UCL, London, 1979).

——, (ed.), *Law as an Instrument of Economic Policy: Comparative and Critical Approaches* (W. de Gruyter, Berlin, 1988).

——, "Political Programmes and the Content of the Constitution" in *Edinburgh Essays in Public Law* (W. Finnie, C. Himsworth and N. Walker ed., Edinburgh University Press, Edinburgh, 1991).

——, "Between Domestic Democracy and an Alien Rule of Law? Some Thoughts on the Independence of the Bank of England" [1995] *Public Law* 118.

Daintith, T., and Page, A., *The Executive in the Constitution* (Oxford University Press, Oxford, 1999).

Dale, Sir William, *Legislative Drafting: A New Approach* (Butterworths, London, 1977).

De Burca, G., "The principle of proportionality and its application in EC law" (1993) *YEL* 105–130.

de Smith, S.A., *The Lawyers and the Constitution* (Inaugural Lecture, London School of Economics, May 10, 1960).

——, and Brazier, *Constitutional and Administrative Law* (8th ed., Penguin, London, 1998).

——, "The Boundaries between Parliament and the Courts" (1955) 18 M.L.R. 281.

de Smith, Woolf and Jowell's, *Principles of Judicial Review* (Sweet & Maxwell, London, 1999).

Davidson, Scott, *Human Rights* (Open University Press, Buckingham, 1993).

Dawson, J.P., *A History of Lay Judges* (Harvard University Press, Cambridge, Mass., 1960).

Denning, A., *Freedom Under Law* (Butterworths, London, 1949).

Devlin, P., "The Common Law, Public Policy and the Executive" (1956) *Current Legal Problems* 1.

Devine, T.M., *The Scottish Nation 1700-2000* (Penguin, London, 1999).

Dicey, A.V., *Introduction to the Study of the Law of the Constitution* (Macmillan, London, 1885; 8th ed., 1915; 10th ed., 1959 with intro. by E.C.S. Wade).

——, "Droit Administratif in Modern French Law" (1901) 17 L.Q.R. 302.

——, *Lectures on the Relation between Law and Public Opinion in England During the Nineteenth Century* (Macmillan, London, 1905).

——, "The Development of Administrative Law in England" (1915) 31 L.Q.R. 148.

Dickson, B., and Carmichael, P., *The House of Lords: Its Parliamentary and Judicial Roles* (Hart, Oxford, 1999).

Diplock, Lord, "Administrative Law: Judicial Review Reviewed" (1975) *Cambridge Law Journal* 233.

Drewry, G., and Butcher, T., *The Civil Service Today* (Blackwells, Oxford, 1988).

Drewry, G., "Lawyers in the UK Civil Service" (1981) 59 *Public Administration* 15–46.

——, *The New Select Committees* (2nd ed., Oxford University Press, Oxford, 1989).

——, "The New Public Management" in *The Changing Constitution* (J. Jowell and D. Oliver ed., 4th ed., Oxford University Press, Oxford, 2001).

Dworkin, R., *Taking Rights Seriously* (Cambridge, Mass., 1977).

——, *A Matter of Principle* (Cambridge, Mass., and London, 1985).

——, *Law's Empire* (London, 1986).

——, *A Bill of Rights for Britain* (London, 1990).

——, *Freedom's Law: The Moral Reading of the American Constitution* (Clarendon Press, Oxford, 1996).

——, *Sovereign Virtue* (Harvard University Press, Cambridge, Mass., 2000).

Efficiency Unit, *Improving Management in Government: The Next Steps* (Stationery Office, London, 1988).

——, *Making the Most of Next Steps: The Management of Ministers' Departments and their Executive Agencies* (Stationery Office, London, 1991).

Elliott, M., "The Human Rights Act 1998 and the Standard of Substantive Review" [2001] *Cambridge Law Journal* 301.

——, *The Constitutional Foundations of Judicial Review* (Hart, Oxford, 2001).

Ellis, E., (ed.), *The Principle of Proportionality in the Laws of Europe* (Hart, Oxford, 1999).

Erskine May, T., *Parliamentary Practice* (22nd ed., Butterworths, London, 1997).

Evans, A., *The EU Structural Funds* (Oxford University Press, Oxford, 1999).

Evans, P., *Handbook of House of Commons Procedures* (2nd ed., Vacher Dod Publishing, London, 1999).

Ewing, K., *The Funding of Political Parties* (Cambridge University Press, Cambridge, 1987).

——, *A Bill of Rights for Britain?* (Institute of Employment Rights, London, 1990).

——, "The Human Rights Act and Parliamentary Democracy" (1999) 62 *Modern Law Review* 79.

——, "A Theory of Democratic Adjudication: Towards a Representative, Accountable and Independent Judiciary" (2000) 38 *Alberta Law Review* 708.

Ewing, K., and Gearty, C.A., *Freedom under Thatcher: Civil Liberties in Modern Britain* (Clarendon Press, Oxford, 1990).

——, *Democracy or a Bill of Rights* (Society of Labour Lawyers, London, 1991).

——, *The Struggle for Civil Liberties* (Oxford University Press, Oxford, 2000).

Faundez, J., (ed.), *Good Government and Law* (Macmillan in conjunction with the British Council, London, 1997).

Feldman, D., *Civil Liberties and Human Rights in England and Wales* (Oxford University Press, Oxford, 2002).

Fenwick, H., *Civil Rights: New Labour, Freedom and the Human Rights Act* (Longman, Harlow, Essex, 2000).

Finer, S.E., "The Individual Responsibility of Ministers" (1956) 34 *Public Administration* 377.

Flegman, V., "The Public Accounts Committee: A Successful Select Committee?" (1980) *Parliamentary Affairs* 166.

Flynn, N., *Public Sector Management* (3rd ed., Prentice Hall, London, 1997), pp.117–119.

Foley, M., *The Politics of the British Constitution* (Manchester University Press, Manchester, 1999).

Fordham, M., *Judicial Review Handbook* (3rd ed., Hart, Oxford, 2001).

Forsyth, C.F., "Beyond O'Reilly v. Mackman: the Foundations and Nature of Procedural Exclusivity" (1985) 44 *Cambridge Law Journal* 415.

——, "The Provenance and Protection of Legitimate Expectations", (1988) 47 *Cambridge Law Journal* 238.

Forsyth, C.F., and Hare, I., *The Golden Metwand and the Crooked Cord* (Oxford University Press, Oxford, 1998).

Foster, C., *Privatisation, Public Ownership and the Regulation of Natural Monopoly* (Blackwell, Oxford, 1992).

Foster, R.F., *Modern Ireland 1600–1972* (Allen Lane, London, 1988).

Francis, M., "The Nineteenth Century Theory of Sovereignty and Thomas Hobbes" (1980) 1 *History of Political Thought* 517.

Freedland, M., "Privatising Carltona: Part II of the Deregulation and Contracting Out Act 1994" (1995) *Public Law* 21–26.

Freedman, S., *Discrimination and Human Rights: The Case of Racism* (Oxford University Press, Oxford, 2001).

——, and Morris, G., "Civil Servants: A Contract of Employment" (1988) *Public Law* 58–77.

Gallagher, M., and Vincenzo Uleri, P., *The Referendum Experience in Europe* (Macmillan, London, 1996).

Galligan, D.J., *Discretionary Powers* (Clarendon Press, Oxford, 1986).

——, "Judicial Review and the Textbook Writers" (1982) 2 *Oxford Journal of Legal Studies* 257.

Ganz, G., *Administrative Procedures* (Sweet & Maxwell, London, 1974).

——, *Quasi-Legislation* (Sweet & Maxwell, London, 1987).

——, *Understanding Public Law* (3rd ed., Sweet & Maxwell, London, 2001).

Gearty, C., *Terror* (Faber and Faber, London, 1991).

——, ed., *European Civil Liberties and the European Convention on Human Rights* (Martinus Nijhoff Publishers, London, 1997).

Ghai, Y., *Hong Kong's New Constitutional Order* (University Press, Hong Kong, 1997).

Glynn, John, J., *Public Sector Financial Control and Accounting* (Blackwell, Oxford, 1987).

Gordley, G., *The Philosophical Origins of Modern Contract Doctrine* (Oxford University Press, Oxford, 1991).

Graham, C., and Prosser, T., "Privatising Nationalised Industries: Constitutional Issues and New Legal Techniques" (1987) 50 *Modern Law Review* 16–51.

——, *Privatising Public Enterprises: Constitutions, the State and Regulation in Comparative Perspective* (Oxford University Press, Oxford, 1999).

Graham, C., *Regulating Public Utilities: A Constitutional Approach* (Hart, Oxford, 2000).

Grant, Wyn, *Pressure Groups Politics and Democracy in Britain* (Philip Allan, London, 1989).

Green, T.H., *Lectures on the Principles of Political Obligation* (London, 1907).

Griffith, J.A.G., *Central Departments and Local Authorities* (London, 1966).

——, *Parliamentary Scrutiny of Government Bills* (London, 1974).

——, *The Politics of the Judiciary* (5th ed., London, 1997).

——, "Administrative discretion and the courts—the better part of valour?" (1955) 18 M.L.R. 159.

——, "Judges in Politics: England" (1968) 3 *Govt. and Oppos.* 485.

——, "Whose Bill of Rights?" *New Statesman* (November 14, 1975).

——, "Standing Committees in the House of Commons" in *The Commons in the Seventies* (S.A. Walkland and M. Ryle ed., London, 1977).

——, "The Political Constitution" (1979) 42 *Modern Law Review* 1.

——, Administrative Law and the Judges (D.N. Pritt Memorial Lecture, London, 1978).

——, "Justice and Administrative Law Revisited" in *From Policy to Administration: Essays in Honour of William A. Robson* (J.A.G. Griffith ed., London, 1976).

——, "Constitutional and Administrative Law" in *More Law Reform Now* (P. Archer and A. Martin ed., Chichester, 1983).

——, "Judicial Decision-Making in Public Law" [1985] *Public Law* 564.

Griffith, J.A.G., and Ryle, M., *Parliament* (Sweet & Maxwell, London, 1989).

Hadfield, B., *The Constitution of Northern Ireland* (SLS, Belfast, 1989).

Hadfield B. (ed.), *Northern Ireland: Politics and the Constitution* (1992).

——, *Judicial Review: A Thematic Approach* (Gill and Macmillan, Dublin, 1995).

Hailsham, *The Dilemma of Democracy* (London, 1977).

——, "Elective Dictatorship" (The Richard Dimbleby Lecture, 1976), *Listener,* (October 21, 1976), p.496.

Hamson, C.J., *Executive Discretion and Judicial Control* (London, 1954).

——, "The real lesson of Crichel Down" (1954) *Public Administration* 383–400.

Hansard Society, *Report of the Commission on Electoral Reform* (Hansard Society, London, 1976).

——, *Politics and Industry—The Great Mismatch* (Hansard Society, London, 1979).

——, *Paying for Politics: Report of the Hansard Society Commission upon the Financing of Political Parties* (Hansard Society, London, 1981).

——, *Report of the Hansard Society Commission on Parliamentary Scrutiny: The Challenge for Parliament: Making Government Accountable* (Hansard Society, Vacher Dod Publishing Ltd., London, 2001).

Harden, I., "Corporatism without Labour: The British Version" in *Waiving the Rules: The Constitution under Thatcherism* (C. Graham and T. Prosser ed., Open University Press, Milton Keynes, 1988).

Harden, I., Hollingsworth, K., and White, F., "Value for Money and Administrative Law" [1996] *Public Law* 661.

Harlow, C.R. and Rawlings, R.W., *Law and Administration* (2nd ed., Butterworths, London, 1997).

——, *Pressure Through Law* (Sweet & Maxwell, London, 1992).

Harris, D.J., O'Boyle, M., and Warbrick, C., *Law of the European Convention on Human Rights* (Butterworths, London, 1995).

Hart, H.L.A., *The Concept of Law* (Oxford University Press, Oxford, 1961).

——, "Definition and Theory in Jurisprudence" (1954) 70 *Law Quarterly Review* 37.

——, "Positivism and the Separation of Law and Morals" (1958) 71 *Harv.Law Rev.* 593.

Hay, D., and Snyder, F., (eds.), *Policing and Prosecution in Britain 1750–1850* (Oxford University Press, Oxford, 1989).

Heald, D., "The Political Implications of Redefining Public Expenditure in the United Kingdom" (1991) 39 *Political Studies* 75–99.

——, and Steel, D., "Privatizing Public Enterprises: An Analysis of the Government's Case" (1982) 53 *Political Quarterly* 333–49.

——, and Georgiou, G., "Resource Accounting: Consolidation and Accounting Regulation" 73 (1995) *Public Administration* 571.

Heclo, H., and Wildavsky, A., *The Private Government of Public Money* (Macmillan, London, 1981).

Held, D., *Democracy and the Global Order* (Blackwell, Oxford, 1995).

Helm, D., 'A Regulatory Rule: RPI Minus X', in *Reshaping the Nationalised Industries* (C. Whitehead ed., Oxford University Press, Oxford, 1988).

——, (ed.), *The Economic Borders of the State* (Clarendon Press, Oxford, 1990).

Henley, D., *et al.*, *Public Sector Accounting and Financial Control* (4th ed., Chapman and Hall, London, 1992).

Henderson, R., *European Finance* (McGraw-Hill, London, 1993).

Hennessy, P., *Whitehall* (Fontana Press, London, 1989; rev. ed., 1990).

——, *Hidden Wiring* (London, 1995).

——, *The Blair Centre: A Question of Command and Control?* (Public Management Foundation, London, 1999).

——, *The Secret State: Whitehall and the Cold War* (Allen Lane, London, 2002).

Hepple, B., Cousley, M. and Choudhury, T., *Equality: A New Framework. Report of the Independent Review of the Enforcement of UK Anti-Discrimination Law* (Hart Publishing, Oxford, 2000).

Heuston, R.F.V., *Essays in Constitutional Law* (Stephens, London, 1964).

——, *Lives of the Lord Chancellors* (Oxford University, Oxford, 1989).

Hewart, G., *The New Despotism* (London, 1929).

Hix, S., *The Political System of the European Union* (Macmillan Press, London, 1999).

Hogan, G., and Walker, C., *Political Violence and the Law in Ireland* (1989).

Holdsworth, W.S., *History of English Law* (A.C. Goodhart and H.S. Hanbury ed., London, 1956), Vol.5.

——, "The conventions of the Eighteenth Century Constitution" (1932) 17 *Iowa Law Review* 161.

Hoppen, T., *Ireland Since 1800* (Longman, London, 1992).

Horwitz, M.J., *The Transformation of American Law 1780–1860* (Harvard University Press, Harvard, 1977) and *1870–1960* (Oxford University Press, Oxford, 1992).

House of Lords, Select Committee on the European Communities, *The Court of Auditors* (1986–87 HL 102).

——, *Financial Control and Fraud in the Community* (1993–94 HL 75).

——, Select Committee on the Constitution, *Reviewing the Constitution: terms of reference and methods of working,* First Report (2001–02 HL 11).

——, Select Committee on the Constitution, *Changing the Constitution: The Process of Constitutional Change*, (2001–02 HL 69).

Howe, Sir Geoffrey, *Conflict of Loyalty* (Macmillan, London, 1994).

Hughes, O.E., *Public Management and Administration* (2nd ed., MacMillan Press, London, 1998).

Ilbert, Sir Courtenay, *Legislative Methods and Forms* (Clarendon Press, Oxford, 1901).

Ingman, T., *The English Legal Process* (5th ed., Blackstone, London, 2000).

Institute for Public Policy Research, *A British Bill of Rights* (IPPR, London, 1990).

——, *The Constitution of the United Kingdom* (IPPR, London, 1991).

Irvine, Lord of Lairg, Q.C., "Judges and Decision-Makers: The Theory and Practice of Wednesbury Review" (1996) *Public Law* 59–78.

Jackson, R.M., *The Machinery of Justice in England* (E.J.R. Spencer ed., 8th ed., Cambridge University Press, Cambridge, 1990).

Jackson, P., and Leopold, P., O. *Hood Phillips and Jackson Constitutional and Administrative Law* (8th ed. London: Sweet & Maxwell, London, 2001).

Jaffe, L., and Henderson, E.G., "Judicial review and the Rule of Law: Historical Origins" (1956) 72 *Law Quarterly Review* 393.

Janis, M., Kay, R., and Bradley, A., *European Human Rights Law: Text and Materials* (2nd ed., Oxford University Press, Oxford, 2000).

Jenkins, R., *The Chancellors* (Macmillan, London, 1998).

——, *Churchill* (Macmillan, London, 2001).

Jennings, W.I., *The Law and the Constitution* (University of London, London, 1933).

——, *Parliament* (2nd ed., Cambridge University Press, Cambridge, 1957).

——, *Cabinet Government* (3rd ed., Cambridge University Press, Cambridge, 1959).

Johnson, N., *In Search of the Constitution: Reflections on State and Society in Britain* (Pergamon Press, Oxford, 1977).

Jones, B., Kavanagh, D., Moran, M., Norton, P., *Politics UK* (4th ed., Longman, Harlow, 2001).

Jones, Reginald, *Local Government Audit Law* (2nd ed., HMSO, London, 1985) with supplement, 1992.

Jowell, J., and Lester, A., "Beyond Wednesbury: Substantive Principles of Administrative Law" [1987] *Public Law* 368.

Jowell, J., "Proportionality: Neither Novel Nor Dangerous" in *New Directions in Judicial Review* (J. Jowell and D. Oliver ed., Sweet & Maxwell, London, 1988).

——, "Courts and Administration in Britain: Standards, Principles and Rights" (1988) Israel L.R. 409.

——, and Oliver, D. (eds.), *The Changing Constitution* (4th ed., Oxford University Press, Oxford, 2000).

——, and Woolf, *de Smith's Judicial Review & Administrative Action* (5th ed., Sweet & Maxwell, London, 1995).

Judson, M.A., *The Crisis of the Constitution: An Essay in constitutional and political thought in England 1603–1645*. (Rutgers University Press, New Brunswick, N.J., 1949).

Justice, *The Citizen and the Administration* (London, 1977).

——, *The Local Ombudsman: A Review of the First Five Years* (London, 1980).

——, *The Administration of the Courts* (London, 1986).

——, *All Souls, Review of Administrative Law in the United Kingdom* (London, 1988).

Kapetyn, P.J.G., and Verloren Van Themaat, *Introduction to the Law of the European Communities* (3rd ed., with Lawrence Gormley) (Kluwer Law International, The Hague, 1998).

Kay, J., and Thompson, D., "Privatisation: A Policy in Search of a Rationale", (1986) 96 *Economic Journal* 18–32.

Kay, J., Mayer, C., and Thompson, D., Privatisation and Regulation—the UK Experience (2nd ed., Oxford University Press, Oxford, 1986).

Keir, D., and Lawson, F.H., *Cases in Constitutional Law* (5th ed., Oxford University Press, Oxford, 1967).

Keir, D.L., *The Constitutional History of Modern Britain 1585–1937* (3rd ed. Adam and Charles Black, London, 1948).

Kelly, J.M., *A Short History of Western Legal Theory* (Oxford University Press, Oxford, 1992).

Kelsey, J., *The New Zealand Experiment* (Auckland University Press, Auckland, 1995).

King, A., *Does the United Kingdom Still have a Constitution?* Sweet & Maxwell, London, 2001).

Kiss, A., and Shelton, D., *Manual of European Environmental Law* (Cambridge University Press, Cambridge, 1993).

Kittichaisaree, K., *International Criminal Law* (Oxford University Press, Oxford, 2001).

Klug, F., Starmer, K., and Weir, S., *The Three Pillars of Liberty: Political Rights and Freedoms in the United Kingdom* (Routledge, London, 1996).

——, *Values for a Godless Age* (Penguin, London, 2000).

Laffan, B., *Finances of the European Union* (MacMillan, London, 1997).

Landes, D., *The Wealth and Poverty of Nations* (Abacus, London, 1998)

Lasok, K.P.E., *Law and Institutions of the European Union* (Butterworths, London, 2001).

Laski, H.J., *Studies in the Problem of Sovereignty* (London, 1917).

Law Commission, *Administrative Law: Judicial Review and Statutory Appeals*, Consultation Paper No.126 (HMSO, 1993).

Law Reform Commission of Canada, *Towards a Modern Federal Administrative Law Consultation Paper* (Ottawa, 1987).

——, *Policy Implementation, Compliance and Administrative Law, Working Paper No.51* (Ottawa, 1986).

Lawson, Nigel, *The View from No. 11* (1992).

Leigh, D., *Betrayed, The Real Story of the Matrix Churchill Trial* (Macmillan, London, 1993).

Leigh, D., and Vulliamy, (ed.), *Sleaze* (Fourth Estate, London, 1997).

Leigh, I., and Lustgarten, L., "The Security Service Act 1989" (1989) 52 *Modern Law Review* 801–40.

——, *In From the Cold: The Intelligence Services and National Security* (Oxford University Press, Oxford, 1994).

Lenaerts, K., *Constitutional Law of the European Union* (Sweet & Maxwell, London, 1999).

Leopold, P., "The Application of the Civil and Criminal Law to Members of Parliament and Parliamentary Proceedings," Chap. 5 in *Law and Parliament* (G. Drewry and D. Oliver ed.), Butterworths, London, 1998) pp.71–87.

Leyland, P., Woods, T., and Harden, J., *Textbook on Administrative Law* (3rd ed., Blackstone, London, 1999).

Lieberman, D., *The Province of Legislation Determined* (Cambridge University Press, Cambridge, 1989).

Likierman, A., *Public Expenditure* (Penguin Books, London, 1988).

——, " Resource Accounting and Budgeting: Rationale and Background" 73 (1995) *Public Administration* 562.

Lobban, M., *The Common Law and English Jurisprudence 1760–1850* (Clarendon Press, Oxford, 1991).

Locke, J., *Two Treatises of Government* (1690), (P. Laslett ed., Cambridge University Press, Cambridge, 1960).

Loughlin, M., *Local Government in the Modern State* (Sweet & Maxwell, London, 1986).

——, "Law, Ideologies and the Political–Administrative System" (1989) 16 *Journal of Law & Society* 21.

——, "Innovative Financing in Local Government: The Limits of Legal Instrumentalism" [1990] *Public Law* 372 (Pt. I); [1991] *Public Law* 568 (Pt. II).

——, *Public Law and Political Theory* (Oxford, 1992).

——, "The Pathways of Public Law Scholarship" in G.P. Wilson, (ed.), *Frontiers of Legal Scholarship* (G.P. Wilson ed., John Wiley, London, 1996) pp. 163–188.

——, *Legality and Locality: The Role of Law in Central–Local Government Relations,* (Oxford University Press, Oxford, 1996).

——, *Sword and Scales* (Hart, Oxford, 2000).

Loveland, I., *Constitutional Law: A Critical Introduction* (Butterworths, London, 1996; 2nd ed. 1999).

——, (ed.), *A Special Relationship? American Influences on Public Law in the UK* (Clarendon Press, Oxford, 1995).

Lustgarten, L., *Legal Control of Racial Discrimination* (Macmillan, London, 1980).

Macpherson, C.B., *The Life and Times of Liberal Democracy* (Oxford University Press, Oxford, 1977).

McAuslan, P., "Administrative Law, Collective Consumption and Judicial Policy" (1983) 46 *Modern Law Review* 1.

——, "Dicey and his influence on public law" [1985] *Public Law* 721.

——, "Public Law and Public Choice" (1988) 51 *Modern Law Review* 681.

——, and McEldowney, J.F. (ed.), *Law, Legitimacy and the Constitution* (Sweet & Maxwell, London, 1985).

——, "Legitimacy and the Constitution: the Dissonance between Theory and Practice" in *Law, Legitimacy and the Constitution* (McAuslan and McEldowney ed., Sweet & Maxwell, London, 1985).

McEldowney, J.F., "The Contingencies Fund and the Parliamentary Scrutiny of Public Finance" [1988] *Public Law* 232–245.

—, "The National Audit Office and Privatisation" (1991) *Modern Law Review* 933–955.

—, "The Nationalisation Legislation of the 1940s and the Privatisation Legislation of the 1980s: A Constitutional Perspective", in *Constitutional Studies* (R. Blackburn ed., Mansell, London, 1992), pp. 42–64.

—, "Administrative Justice" in *Rights of Citizenship* (R. Blackburn ed., Mansell, London, 1993), Chap.8, pp.156–78.

—, "The Control of Public Expenditure" in Jowell and Oliver ed., *The Changing Constitution* (3rd ed., 1994), pp.175–207; (4th ed., Oxford University Press, Oxford, 2000), pp.190–228).

—, "Criminal Law and the development of Labour relations in Nineteenth-Century Ireland" in *Festschrift in honour of Paul O'Higgins* (Hepple, Ewing and Gearty ed., Mansell, London, 1994), Chap.12, pp.267–93.

—, "Public utilities: Is the British experience a model for developing countries?" in *Good Government and Law* (Julio Faundez ed., Macmillan in association with the British Council, London, 1997), pp.147–62.

—, (ed.), *National and International Perspectives on Law and Privatisation* (British Institute of International and Comparative Law, London, 1999).

—, *Modernizing Britain: Public Law and Challenges to Parliament* (University of Waikato Press, New Zealand, 2002) edited: J. Mackinnon and Paul Havermann.

McEldowney, J., and McEldowney, S., *Environment and the Law* (Longman, London, 1996).

—, *Environmental Law and Regulation* (Blackstone and Oxford University Press, London and Oxford, 2001).

McCrudden, C. (ed.), *Anti-Discrimination Law* (Dartmouth, Aldershot, 1991).

McCrudden, C., "Northern Ireland and the British Constitution" in *The Changing Constitution* (J. Jowell and D. Oliver ed., 2nd ed., Oxford University Press, Oxford, 1989), pp.297–344.

McQuade, D., Fagon, J., *The Governance of Northern Ireland* (Belfast, Northern Whig, 2002).

Maitland, F.W., *The Constitutional History of England* (Cambridge University Press, Cambridge, 1908).

Marshall, G., *Constitutional Conventions. The Rules and Forms of Political Account-ability* (Oxford University Press, Oxford, 1984).

—, (ed.), *Ministerial Responsibility* (Oxford University Press, Oxford, 1989).

—, and Moodie, G.C., *Some Problems of the Constitution* (5th ed., Hutchinson University Library, London, 1971).

Mayer, C., and Meadowcraft, S., "Selling Public Assets: Techniques and Financial Implications" in *Privatisation and Regulation: The UK Experience* (J. Kay, C. Mayer and D. Thompson, ed., Oxford University Press, Oxford, 1986).

Mayer, C., "Public Ownership: Concepts and Applications" (1987) *Centre for Economic Policy Research Working Paper,* Vol.182.

Menski, W., *Comparative Law in a global context* Platinium, London, 2000).

Metcalfe, Les and Richards, S., *Improving Public Management* (Sage, London, 2nd ed., 1990).

Miers, D., and Page, A., *Legislation* (2nd ed., 1990).

Milhaupt, C.J., Mark Ramseyer, J., and Young, M.K., *Japanese Law in Context* (Harvard University Press, Cambridge, Mass., 2001).

Mill, J.S., *On Liberty* (1859) (G. Himmelfarb ed., Harmondsworth, London, 1974).

——, *Auguste Comte and Positivism* (1865): (Ann Arbor: Mich., 1961).

——, "Chapters on Socialism" (1879) 25 *Fortnightly Review* 226.

Miller, R., ed. *New Zealand Politics in Transition* (Oxford University Press, Auckland, 1998).

Milsom, S.F.C., *Historical Foundations of the Common Law* (2nd ed., Butterworths, London, 1980).

Mitchell, J.D., *Constitutional Law* (2nd ed., Edinburgh University Press, Edinburgh, 1968).

——, "The state of public law in the United Kingdom" [1966] 15 I.C.L.Q. 133.

——, "The constitutional implications of judicial control of the administration in the United Kingdom" (1967) *Cambridge Law Journal* 46.

Moore, J., "Why Privatise?" *Privatisation and Regulation: The UK Experience* (J. Kay, C. Mayer, and D. Thompson ed., Oxford University Press, Oxford, 1983).

Moore, V., *A Practical Approach to Planning Law* (7th ed., Blackstone, London, 2000).

Morrison, Lord, *Government and Parliament: A Survey from the Inside* (3rd ed. Oxford University Press, Oxford, 1964).

Munro, C., *Studies in Constitutional Law* (2nd ed., Butterworths, London, 1999).

National Audit Office, *Pergau Hydro Electric Project* (1992–93 HC 908).

——, *Resource Accounting and Budgeting in Government* (1994–95 HC 123).

——, *The Work of the Directors of Telecommunications, Gas Supply, Water Service and Electricity Supply* (1995–96 HC 645).

——, *State Audit in the European Union* (London, 1996).

——, *Audit of Assumptions for the Pre-Budget Report* (1997–98 HC 361).

Nicolson, I.F., *The Mystery of Crichel Down* (1986).

Nolan, Lord, *First Report of the Committee on Standards in Public Life*, Cm.2850; *Second Report of the Committee on Standards in Public Life*, Cm.3270–1.

Nolan, Lord, and Sedley, Stephen, *The Making and Remaking of the British Constitution* (Blackstone Press, London, 1997).

Normanton, E.L., *The Accountability and Audit of Governments* (Manchester University Press, Manchester, 1966).

Norton, P., *The Constitution in Flux* (Blackwell, Oxford, 1982).

O'Higgins, P., *Cases and Materials on Civil Liberties* (Sweet & Maxwell, London, 1988).

O'Keffe, D., "The court of Auditors" in *Institutional Dynamics of European Integration* (D. Curtin and T. Heukels ed., Kluwer, London, 1984).

O'Leary, B., "What should Public Lawyers Do?" (1992) 12 O.J.L.S. No.3, pp.304–18.

O'Riordan, T., Kemp, R., and Purdue, M., *Sizewell B: An Anatomy of an Inquiry* (1988).

Oliver, D., *Government in the United Kingdom* (Open University Press, Milton Keynes, 1991).

——, and Austin, R., "Political and Constitutional Aspects of the Westland Affair" (1987) 40 *Parliamentary Affairs* 20–40.

——, "Common Values in Public and Private Law and the Public/Private Divide" [1997] *Public Law* 21.

Oliver, D., and Drewry, G., *Public Service Reform: issues of Accountability and Public Law* (Pinter, London, 1996).

——, (ed.), *Law and Parliament* (Butterworths, London, 1998).

Olowofoyeku, A., *Suing Judges* (Oxford University Press, Oxford, 1993).

Palley, C., *The Constitutional History and Law of Southern Rhodesia 1888–1965* (Oxford University Press, Oxford, 1979).

——, *The Evolution, Disintegration and Possible Reconstruction of the Northern Ireland Constitution* (Barry Rose Publishers, Chichester, 1972). Also see (1972) 1 *Anglo-American L.Rev.* 368.

——, *The United Kingdom and Human Rights* (Sweet & Maxwell, London, 1991).

Pallot, J., and Ball, I., "Resource Accounting and Budgeting : The New Zealand Experience" 74 (1996) *Public Administration* 527.

Palmer, G., *Unbridled Power?* (Oxford University Press, Auckland, 1979).

Palmer, G., and Palmer, M., Bridled Power: New Zealand Government under MMP (Oxford University Press, Auckland, 1999).

Parris, H., *Constitutional Bureaucracy: The Development of British Central Administration since the Eighteenth Century* (Allen and Unwin, London, 1969).

Peacock, A.T., and Wiseman, J., *The Growth of Public Expenditure in the United Kingdom* (1961).

Plant, R., *The Plant Report* (IPPR, London, 1990).

Pliatzky, L., *The Treasury under Mrs Thatcher* (Blackwell, Oxford, 1989).

——, *Getting and Spending* (rev ed., Blackwell, Oxford, 1984).

Pocock, J.G.A., *The Machiavellian Movement: Florentine Political Thought and the Atlantic Republican Tradition* (Princeton University Press, Princeton, 1975).

Pogany, Istvan, "Privatisation and Regulatory Change in Hungary" in *Privatization and Regulatory Change in Europe* (M. Moran and T. Prosser ed., Open University Press, Milton Keynes, 1994).

Pollack, A., *A Citizen's Inquiry: The Opsahl Report on Northern Ireland* (Dublin, 1993).

Pollard, D., and Hughes, D., *Constitutional and Administrative Law* (3rd ed., Butterworths, London, 2001).

Porter, Theodore, *The Rise of Statistical Thinking 1820–1900* (Princeton University Press, Princeton, 1986).

Poulter, S., *Ethnicity and Human Rights* (Clarendon Press, Oxford, 1998).

Pound, R., "Liberty of Contract" (1908–9) 18 *Yale L.J.* 454.

——, "Law in Books and Law in Action" (1910) 44 *American Law Rev.* 12.

——, "The Scope and Purpose of Sociological Jurisprudence" (1911) 24 Harv.L.Rev. 591; (1911) 25 Harv.L.Rev. 140; (1912) 25 Harv.L.Rev. 489.

——, "The Call for a Realist Jurisprudence" (1931) 44 Harv.L.Rev. 697.

Power, M., *The Audit Explosion* (Demos, London, 1995).

Priest, G.L., "The Common Law Process and the Selection of Efficient Rules" (1977) 6 *Journal of Legal Studies* 65.

Prime Minister's Efficiency Unit, Improving Management in Government: the Next Steps (London, 1988) (Ibbs Report).

Prosser, T., "Towards a Critical Public Law" (1982) *Journal of Law and Society* 9: 1-19.

——, *Nationalised Industries and Public Control* (Oxford University Press, Oxford, 1986).

Rawls, J., *A Theory of Justice* (Oxford University Press, Oxford, 1972).
——, "Justice as Fairness: Political not Metaphysical" (1985) 14 *Philosophy and Public Affairs* 223.
——, "The Idea of an Overlapping Consensus" (1987) 7 O.J.L.S. 1.
Redlich, J. and Hirst, F. *A History of Local Government in England* (B. Keith-Lucas ed., Macmillan, London, 1970).
Reports., *Report of the Committee on Ministers' Powers*, Cmd.4060 (1932) (Donoughmore Report).
——, *Report of the Committee on Tribunals and Enquiries* (1957) (Franks Report).
——, *Report of the Royal Commission on Legal Services* Cmnd.7448 (1980).
Ridley, F.F., "There is no British Constitution: A Dangerous case of the Emperor's Clothes" (1988) 41 *Parliamentary Affairs* 340–61.
Robertson, G., *Freedom, the Individual and the Law* (7th ed., Penguin, London, 1993).
——, *The Justice Game* (Chatto and Windus, London, 1998).
Robinson, O.F., Fergus, T.D., Gordon, W.M., *European Legal History* 2nd ed., Butterworths, London, 1994).
Robson, W.A., *Justice and Administrative Law* (Unversity of London, London, 1928; 2nd ed., 1947; 3rd ed., 1951).
——, *Public Administration Today* (London, 1948).
——, "The Report of the Committee on Ministers' Powers" (1932) 3 *Political Quarterly* 346.
——, "Administrative Law in England 1919–1948" in *British Government Since 1918* (G. Campion ed., London, 1950).
——, "Administrative Justice and Injustice: A Commentary on the Franks Report" [1958] P.L. 12.
——, "Administrative Law" in *Law and Opinion in England in the Twentieth Century* (M. Ginsberg ed., London, 1959).
——, "Justice and Administrative Law reconsidered" (1979) 32 *Current Legal Problems* 107.
Rose-Ackerman, S., *Corruption and Government* (Cambridge University Press, Cambridge, 1999).
Roseveare, H., *The Treasury 1660–1870* (Allen and Unwin, London, 1973).
Russell, M., *Reforming the House of Lords: Lessons from Overseas* (Clarendon Press, Oxford, 2000).
Rudden, B., and Wyatt, D. (eds.), *Basic Community Laws* (6th ed., Oxford, 1996).

Sas, B., "Regulation of the Privatised Electricity Supply Industry" (1990) 53 *Modern Law Review* 485.
Scott Report: *Return to an Address of the Honourable House of Commons dated 15th February 1996. Report of the Inquiry into the Export of Defence Equipment and Dual-use Goods to Iraq and Related Prosecutions*, The Rt Hon. Sir Richard Scott, The Vice-Chancellor (1996 HC 115) (HMSO, London, 1996).
Schwartz, B., and Wade, H.W.R., *Legal Control of Government: Administrative Law in Britain and the United States* (Clarendon Press, Oxford, 1972).

Sedley, Stephen, "The Sound of Silence: Constitutional Law without a Constitution" (1994) 110 *Law Quarterly Review* 270–91.

Sedley, Lord Justice, *Freedom, Law and Justice* (50th Hamlyn Lectures, Sweet & Maxwell, London, 1999).

——, and Nolan, Lord, *The Making and Remaking of the British Constitution* (Blackstone, London, 1997).

Shell, D., *The House of Lords* (2nd ed., Oxford University Press, Oxford, 1992).

Shell, D., and Beamish, D., *The House of Lords at Work* (Oxford University Press, Oxford, 1993).

Silk, P., and Walters, R., *How Parliament Works* (4th ed., Longman, London, 1999).

Shortt, G, *Informations, Mandamus and Prohibitions* (Macmillan, London, 1887).

Simpson, B., *Human Rights and the End of Empire: Britain and the Genesis of the European Convention* (Oxford University Press, Oxford, 2001).

Skidelsky, R., *Politicians and the Slump: the Labour Government of 1929-31* (London, 1967).

——, *John Maynard Keynes* (Macmillan, London, 1983; Vol.3 Macmillan, London, 2000).

Skinner, Q., *The Foundation of Modern Political Thought*, 2 Vols., (Cambridge University Press, Cambridge, 1982).

Slapper, G. and Kelly, D., *The English Legal System* (4th ed., Cavendish, London, 1999).

Smith, L.B., "Accountability and Independence in the Contract State" in *The Dilemma of Accountability in Modern Government* (B. Smith and D. Hague ed., London, 1971).

Snyder, F., (ed.) *The Europeanisation of Law* (Hart Publishing, Oxford, 2000).

Stein, P., and Shand, J., *Legal Values in Western Society* (Edinburgh University Press, Edinburgh, 1974).

Steiner, H.J. and Alston, P., *International Human Rights in Context* (2nd ed., Oxford University Press, Oxford, 2000).

Sterett, S., *Creating Constitutionalism? The Politics of Legal Expertise and Administrative Law in England and Wales* (University of Michigan Press, Ann Arbor, 1997).

Stevens, R., *The Independence of the Judiciary: The View from the Lord Chancellor's Office* (Clarendon Press, Oxford, 1993).

——, *Law and Politics. The House of Lords as a Judicial Body 1800–1976* (Weidenfeld and Nicolson, London, 1979).

Stone Sweet, A., *Governing with Judges* (Oxford University Press, Oxford, 2000).

Sugarman, D., "Legal Theory, the Common Law Mind and the Making of the Textbook Tradition" in *Legal Theory and Common Law* (W. Twining ed., Oxford University Press, Oxford, 1986), Chap.3.

——, "The Legal Boundaries of Liberty: Dicey, Liberalism and Legal Science" (1983) *Modern Law Review* 102.

Sunkin, M., Bridges, Lee, and Meszaros, G., *Judicial Review* (The Public Law Project, London, 1993).

——, and Le Sueur, A.P., "Can Government Control Judicial Review?" (1991) *Current Legal Problems* 161–83.

——, and Payne, S., *The Nature of the Crown* (Oxford University Press, Oxford, 1999).

Taggart, M., "Tugging on Superman's Cape: Lessons from the Experience with the New Zealand Bill of Rights Act 1990" [1998] *Public Law* 266.

Thain, C., "The Education of the Treasury: The Medium Term Financial Strategy, 1980–84", (1985) 63 *Public Administration* 261–85.

——, and Wright, M., "Planning and Controlling Public Expenditure in the United Kingdom (Part 1). The Treasury's Public Expenditure Survey" (1992) 70 *Public Administration* 3–24; Part II, (1992) 70 *Public Administration* 193–224.

——, *The Treasury and Whitehall: The Planning and Control of Public Expenditure 1976–1993* (Clarendon Press, Oxford, 1995).

Thompson, B., *Textbook on Constitutional and Administrative Law* (3rd ed., Blackstone Press, London, 1997).

Thring, H., *Practical Legislation* (John Murray, London, 1902).

Tomkins, A., "Public Interest Immunity after Matrix Churchill" [1993] *Public Law* 650.

Tomlinson, J., *Public Policy and the Economy Since 1900* (Oxford University Press, Oxford, 1900).

Townshend, C., *Political Violence in Ireland* (Oxford University Press, 1985).

Treasury and Civil Service Committee, *Eighth Report, Session 1987–88, Civil Service Management Reform: The Next Steps* (1987–88 HC 494).

Turpin, C., *British Government and the Constitution* (4th ed., Butterworths, London, 1999).

Van Caenegem, R.C., *An Historical Introduction to Western Constitutional Law* (Cambridge University Press, Cambridge, 1995).

Von Meheren, and Gordley, J., *The Civil Law System: An Introduction to the Comparative Study of Law* (2nd ed., University Press, Boston, 1977).

Vogel, D., *National Styles of Regulation* (Cornell University Press, Ithaca and London, 1986).

Vickers, J., and Yarrow, G., *Privatisation and the Natural Monopolies* (London, 1985).

——, *Privatisation: An Economic Analysis* (Boston, 1988).

Vile, M.J.C., *Constitutionalism and the Separation of Power* (Oxford, 1967).

Wade, E.C.S. and Phillips, G.G., *Constitutional and Administrative Law* (London, 1931; 11th ed., 1993 by A.W. Bradley and K. Ewing).

Wade, H.W.R., *Administrative Law* (6th ed., Oxford, 1988).

——, Constitutional Fundamentals (London, 1980).

——, "The Concept of Legal Certainty. A Preliminary Sketch" (1940–1) 4 M.L.R. 183.

——, "Quasi-judicial and its background" (1949) 10 Camb. L.J. 216.

——, "The Twilight of Natural Justice" (1951) 67 L.Q.R. 103.

——, "The Basis of Legal Sovereignty" (1955) Camb. L.J. 172.

——, "Law, Opinion and Administration" (1962) 78 L.Q.R. 188.

——, "Unlawful administrative action—void or voidable" (1967) 83 L.Q.R. 499 (Pt I); (1968) 84 L.Q.R. 95 (Pt II).

——, "Sovereignty and the European Communities" (1972) 88 L.Q.R. 1.

——, "Procedure and Prerogative in Public Law" (1985) 101 L.Q.R. 180.

——, "What has happened to the Sovereignty of Parliament?" (1991) 107 L.Q.R. 1.

Wadham, J., and Mountfield, H., *Blackstone's Guide to the Human Rights Act 1998* (Blackstone, London, 1999; 2nd ed., 2001).

Waldron, J., *The Law, Theory and Practices in British Politics* (Routledge, London, 1990).

Walker, C., *The Prevention of Terrorism in British Law* (2nd ed., Manchester University Press, Manchester, 1992).

Waller, R., "The 1983 Boundary Commission: Policies and Effects" (1983) 4 *Electoral Studies* 195.

Waters, M., *Globalization* (Routledge, London, 1995).

Weatherill, S., and Beaumont, P., *EU Law* (Penguin, London, 1999).

Wheare, K.C., *Modern Constitutions* (2nd ed., 1966).

White, F., and Hollingsworth, K., "Resource Accounting and Budgeting: Constitutional Implications" [1997] *Public Law* 437.

——, *Audit, Accountability and Government* (Clarendon Press, Oxford, 1999).

Whittaker, E., *A History of Economic Ideas* (Longmans, London, 1940).

Wildavsky, A., and Zapico-Goni, E., (ed.) *National Budgeting for Economic and Monetary Union* (Institute of Public Administration, London, 1994).

Williams, D.G.T.,"Public local inquiries—formal administrative adjudication" (1980) 29 *International and Comparative Law Quarterly* 701.

——, "The Donoughmore Report in Retrospect" (1982) 60 *Public Administration* 273.

——, "The Council on Tribunals: the first twenty five years" [1984] *Public Law* 79.

Winch, D., and Burrow, J., *That Noble Science of Politics: A Study in Nineteenth Century Intellectural History* (Cambridge University Press, Cambridge, 1983).

Wistrich, E., "Restructuring Government New Zealand style" (1992) 70 *Public Administration* 119–35.

Woodhouse, D., "Ministerial Responsibility: Something Old, Something New [1997] *Public Law* 262.

——, *The Office of Lord Chancellor* (Hart, Oxford, 2001).

——, *In Pursuit of Good Administration; Ministers, Civil Servants and Judges* (Clarendon Press, Oxford, 1997).

Woolf, H., "Public law—private law: Why the divide?" [1986] *Public Law* 220.

——, *Protection of the Public: A New Challenge?* (Stevens, London, 1990).

Wraith, R.E., and Lamb, G.B., *Public Inquiries as an Instrument of Government* (1971).

Wright, M., *Treasury Control of the Civil Service 1854–1974* (Oxford University Press, Oxford, 1969).

Wyatt, D., and Dashwood, A., *Substantive European Community Law* (4th ed. Sweet & Maxwell, London, 2000).

Young, H., *This Blessed Plot: Britain and Europe from Churchill to Blair* (Macmillan, London, 1998).

Zellick, G., *Final Report of the Task Force on Student Disciplinary Procedures chaired by Professor Graham Zellick*, (CVCP, December 1994).

Zweigert, K., and Kotz, H., *An Introduction to Comparative Law* (2nd ed. Clarendon Press, Oxford, 1994).

APPENDIX: WEBSITE REFERENCES

There are a number of important websites that provide public lawyers with up-to-date literature on public law. There is no single directory. Reference to Matt Innis and Justin Johnson, *Directory of Think Tanks* (Politico's Publishing, London, 2001) provides an important resource.

WWW References

General Access to Government information, Parliament and local government
www.open.gov.uk

Cabinet Secretariat
www.cabinet-office.gov.uk/constitution/index.htm

Civil Service
www.civil-service.co.uk

Electoral Commission
www.electoral-commission.gov.uk

European Law
www.europa.eu.int

Human Rights. European Court of Human Rights
www.echr.coe.int

Lord Chancellor's website
www.lcd.gov.uk/
www.lcd.gov.uk/constitution/holref/index.htm

Judicial review:
www.lcd.gov.uk/

The Law Commission
www.lawcom.gov.uk/homepage.htm

Devolution:

Wales
www.wales.gov.uk/subiassemblybusiness/procedures/assemblyreview.htm

Wales Legislation Online
www.wales-legislation.org.uk

Northern Ireland
www.ni-assembly.gov.uk

Scotland
www.scottish.parliament.uk

Office of Fair Trading
www.oft.gov.uk

Equal Opportunites Commission
www.eoc.org.uk

The Commission for Racial Equality
www.cre.gov.uk

The Disability Rights Commission
www.drc-gb.org

The UK Parliament
www.parliament.uk

The Monarchy
www.royal.gov.uk

HMSO
www.tso.co.uk
www.hmso.gov.uk
www.official-documents.co.uk

Institutions and think-tanks

Amnesty International
www.amnesty.org.uk
www.liberty-human-rights.org.uk

The Adam Smith Institute
www.adamsmith.org

The Centre for Economic Policy Research
www.cepr.org

Centre for European Reform
www.cer.org.uk

Centre for Policy Studies
www.cps.org.uk

Centre for Reform
www.cfr.org.uk

Central Office of Information
www.coi.gov.uk

Charter 88
www.charter.org.uk

The Constitution Unit
www.ucl.ac.uk/constitution-unit

Democratic UK
www.democratic.org.uk

Demos
www.demos.co.uk

European Policy Forum
No website but see: *epftld@compuserve.com*

Fabian Society
www.fabian-society.org.uk

Institute for Public Policy Research
www.ippr.org.uk

The Hansard Society
www.hansardsociety.org.uk

Institute of Economic Affairs
www.iea.org.uk

John Stuart Mill Institute

www.jsmillinstitute.org.uk

Local Government

www.local.gov.uk

New Europe

www.new-europe.co.uk

New Policy Institute

www.npi.org.uk

Public Appointments Unit

www.cabinet-office.gov.uk

Social Affairs Unit

www.socialaffairsunit.org.uk

Environmental Data Services

www.ends.co.uk

Additional references (software packages, CD-Rom, film, video, audio-tape)
IOLIS software (University of Warwick)
Public Law Newsletter (Society of Public Teachers of Law)

Legal information

www.westlaw.co.uk
www.lawtel.co.uk
www.legal.com
www.lsrc.org.uk

Index